International Handbook of
Labour Market Policy and Evaluation

International Handbook of Labour Market Policy and Evaluation

Edited by Günther Schmid,
Jacqueline O'Reilly and Klaus Schömann

Edward Elgar
Cheltenham, UK • Brookfield, US

Published by

Edward Elgar Publishing Limited
8 Lansdown Place
Cheltenham
Glos GL50 2HU
UK

Edward Elgar Publishing Company
Old Post Road
Brookfield
Vermont 05036
US

A catalogue record for this book
is available from the British Library

Library of Congress Cataloguing in Publication Data
International handbook of labour market policy and evaluation / edited
    by Günther Schmid, Jacqueline O'Reilly, and Klaus Schömann.
        Includes bibliographical references and index.
        1. Full employment policies—Evaluation. 2. Labor policy–
    –Evaluation. 3. Labor market. I. Schmid, Günther, 1942–
    II. O'Reilly, Jacqueline, 1964– . III. Schömann, Klaus, 1961–
    HD5706.I6117   1996   96–21809
    331.12'042—dc20   CIP

ISBN 1 85898 344 4

Layout: Wissenschaftlicher Text-Dienst (WTD)—A. Zierer-Kuhnle, Berlin / pinkuin, Berlin

Printed in Great Britain at the University Press, Cambridge

Contents

Preface

This handbook provides a systematic overview of the state of the art in labour market policy evaluation at three levels. First, it outlines and evaluates the various methodological approaches adopted in previous evaluation research. Second, it focusses on particular target areas and evaluates the results of previous evaluation research on the impacts of different policy instruments and policy regimes in contrasting settings. Third, it offers an evaluation of institutional frameworks and existing labour market monitoring and information systems, pointing out where such systems are underdeveloped and where new approaches could be used effectively for intelligent policy design and empirical policy evaluation.

A unique feature of this edited collection is the presentation of a target-oriented approach to evaluating labour market policy. Instead of only attempting to measure the impacts of specific policy programmes along the dimensions of their specified programme goals, researchers following the target-oriented approach ask which combination of policies, under which economic and institutional conditions, contribute most to achieving broadly defined policy goals or targets. Unlike programme-oriented evaluation, the target-oriented approach to evaluation reviews the results of labour market policy evaluation from the aspect of the cumulative impact that interacting policies and policy regimes have on labour market performance and outcomes in selected target areas.

A second unique element of this handbook is its international approach. It presents the insights of renowned European and North American researchers who have first-hand experience in designing and conducting evaluation research. In all the chapters the authors apply an international comparative framework or contribute to the development of an international comparative research methodology as they assess contemporary developments in the field. Lastly, all chapters, except those in the methodological part, are organized around policy targets, with evaluation approaches and results being empirically compared across the whole range of areas that have been at the heart of current labour market policy concerns in OECD countries.

This handbook is intended for policy- and decision-makers, professional programme evaluators and academic scholars interested in labour market policy and policy evaluation. Practitioners may also gain valuable insights into ways to assess the appropriateness of different policy tools and policy approaches and into the requirements for systematic impact evaluation. This volume is designed not as a manual for programme implementors but as a compendium that draws on the wealth of experience from previous evaluation. It points out the advantages and pitfalls encountered when one must choose specific evaluation methodologies or introduce and implement particular policies. We hope these reflections will help push evaluation research forward towards providing support for more effective policy-making and implementation.

It is, finally, a pleasure to acknowledge the personal assistance and financial support provided to us over the three years of this book's production. Many people have invested an incredible amount of effort in moving this project from the early stages of conception to the final stages of publication. We are unable to mention all of them but feel deeply obligated to make a few exceptions.

First, we cordially thank our secretary, Karin Reinsch, who managed the intricacies of the entire project, including two large workshops in which all contributors discussed preliminary versions of their chapters. She did a splendid job and never lost her cheerful disposition in keeping the network of academics, editors, translators, word processors and publishers to a tight time schedule. She must have gained many valuable psychological insights into the complexity of minds working under continuous and increasing pressure, and we hope that this experience is at least some compensation for the frustration and exhaustion that her task inevitably entailed. We thank Bettina Recktor from WTD (Wissenschaftlicher Text-Dienst), who attentively managed the operative network of the text production. We quickly came to value her endurance and skill in surmounting virtually every difficulty and complication she encountered in this vast project. We thank the compositors of Pinkuin for their marvellous work in transforming the manuscript into its final format. We also thank the language editors David Antal, Niamh Warde and Andy Watt, who greatly improved the style of the contributions, painstakingly checked references and spelling, and saw to all the other chores that academics tend to delegate. We are much indebted to Holger Schütz, who prepared the index of the handbook. His gift of combining creative imagination and reliability is fully appreciated. We are also indebted to Christoph Albrecht, who managed the network of scholars, editors, translators and institutional supporters to which this volume partially owes its existence. We are sincerely grateful to the Directorate-General V of the European Commission in Brussels which provided generous financial support. We especially thank Armindo Silva and Sergio Piccolo for their promotion of this handbook and for the understanding they showed for academic time delays. Lastly, we wish to express our thanks to Edward Elgar and Julie Leppard for shepherding this project so enthusiastically through their publishing company.

As individuals, we have learned together, at first hand, about the difficulties encountered in coordinating such a large project but also about the rewards to be gained through cooperation. We are deeply grateful to our colleagues who joined us in this multidisciplinary enterprise. We want to thank at this occasion our advisory group, whose members provided valuable comments throughout the handbook's development: Anske Bouman (Netherlands), Christine Bruniaux (France), Karsten Jensen (Denmark), Jaap de Koning (Netherlands), Guy Standing (International Labour Office, Geneva) and John Temple (United Kingdom). We hope that the experience was a rewarding one for all, and particularly, that readers involved in labour market policy evaluation will find this handbook to be a rich and stimulating source of material and analysis.

Günther Schmid, Jacqueline O'Reilly, Klaus Schömann
Wissenschaftszentrum Berlin für Sozialforschung (WZB)
Social Science Research Center Berlin
May 1996

List of Contributors

Eileen Appelbaum is professor of economics and director at the Economic Policy Institute, Washington, DC. Her main research areas are labour economics and economics of institutions.

Peter Auer is a senior research fellow at the Wissenschaftszentrum Berlin für Sozialforschung (Social Science Research Centre, Berlin; WZB) and acting as programme manager for the Mutual Information System on Employment Policies (MISEP) for the European Commission. He has conducted studies in the field of labour economics and industrial sociology.

Lutz Bellmann is a senior researcher at the Institute for Employment Research (IAB), Nuremberg. His research interests include labour economics, especially wage structure and labour market policy, and panel analysis of firms.

Gudrun Biffl is a senior economic researcher in the Austrian Institute of Economic Research, Vienna. She also lectures in labour economics and business cycle analysis at the University of Economics and Business Administration, Vienna, and at the University of Innsbruck. She is consultant to the OECD on migration matters.

Anders Björklund is professor of economics at the Swedish Institute for Social Research at Stockholm University. His main fields of research are unemployment, evaluation of labour market policy, economics of education and income distribution. He is a member of the Economic Council of Sweden.

Christoph F. Büchtemann is a senior economist at the RAND Corporation in California and director of the Center for Research on Innovation and Society (CRIS). His principal research areas are international comparative research in labour economics, corporate adjustment and the economics of regulation.

Bernard Casey is a senior fellow and head of staff training at the Policy Studies Institute (PSI), London. He has been a frequent consultant to the OECD, especially on issues related to the transition from work to retirement. He continues to work in the area of the interaction of social insurance and employment policies.

Lennart Delander is a senior lecturer at Växjö University, Sweden. His principal research interests are in methodological issues related to the evaluation of labour market policy.

Lei Delsen is an assistant professor in the Department of Applied Economics at the University of Nijmegen, the Netherlands. He has published several books and articles on atypical employment and gradual retirement in the OECD countries.

Volker Eichener is manager of the Institute for Housing, Real Estate, Urban and Regional Development at the Ruhr University, Bochum. His research interests are European integration and regulatory and social policy.

Christine Erhel is a teaching assistant at the University of Aix-Marseille and a research fellow at the Laboratoire d'Economie et de Sociologie du Travail (LEST) in Aix-en-Provence, France. She has specialized in comparative research on European labour market policies.

Colette Fagan is a lecturer in sociology at the University of Liverpool, United Kingdom. Her research focusses upon European labour markets, gender relations and house-hold organization. Her recent research includes several reports coauthored with Professor Jill Rubery for the Equal Opportunities of the European Commission.

Jérôme Gautié is a teaching assistant at the University of Paris I–Panthéon Sorbonne, and a research fellow at the Séminaire d'Economie et du Travail–Mutations, Espace et Environnement, Travail et Emploi, Industrie et Services, Stratégies (SET–METIS), Paris. He has specialized in youth unemployment, minimum wage and labour market policies.

Bernard Gazier is a professor at the University of Paris I–Panthéon Sorbonne and director of METIS at the Centre National de la Recherche Scientifique (CNRS) Paris. He has specialized in labour economics (employment policies) and episte-mology (ethical aspects of economics).

Siv Gustafsson is professor of economics of the University of Amsterdam, director of the research group on 'Comparative Population and Gender Economics', chairper-son of the Belle van Zuylen Institute and a member of the board of The European Society for Population Economics, Local Tinbergen Institute.

James J. Heckman is Henry Schultz Professor in the Department of Economics, Uni-versity of Chicago, director of the Center for Social Program Evaluation at the Harris School and an affiliate of the American Bar Foundation.

Richard Jackman is a reader in economics at the London School of Economics and programme director for Human Resources at the Centre of Economic Performance. He has been a consultant to the World Bank and the International Labour Office.

Thomas Janoski is an assistant professor at Duke University in Durham, North Caro-lina. He has specialized in comparative methodology and political integration through naturalization.

Thomas Kruppe is a researcher at the Wissenschaftszentrum Berlin für Sozialfor-schung (Social Science Research Centre, Berlin; WZB) and at the Institute of Applied Socioeconomics (IAS) in Berlin. He is a sociologist working on compara-tive labour market analysis.

Robert M. Lindley is a professor in the Faculty of Social Studies and founding director of the Institute for Employment Research at the University of Warwick. His main research interests are the political economy of labour market policy and related questions of modelling and evaluation.

Friederike Maier is professor of macroeconomics and economic policy at the Fach-hochschule für Wirtschaft in Berlin (Polytechnic University, Berlin). She is in the network of Experts on the Situation of Women in the Labour Market of the Euro-pean Commission. She specializes in labour economics on women and employ-ment.

Nigel Meager is associate director of the Institute for Employment Studies at the University of Sussex, United Kingdom. He is a labour economist, and his research interests and publications have covered the functioning of national, regional and local labour markets; skill shortages; labour market flexibility and changing pat-terns of work.

Sylvie Morel has worked as a labour economist at Labour Canada (women's bureau), confédération des syndicats nationaux and the Human Rights Commission of Que-bec. She teaches at Université Laval, Quebec, specializing in comparative research on workfare and insertion policies.

Hugh Mosley is a senior research fellow in the labour market and employment research unit at the Wissenschaftszentrum Berlin für Sozialforschung (Social Science Research Centre, Berlin; WZB). He is a political scientist specializing in comparative research on labour market policies, especially working time issues and labour market regulation.

Harald Niklasson is an associate professor at Växjö University, Sweden. He specializes in methods of labour market policy evaluation and has written about management by objectives in labour market policies.

Jacqueline O'Reilly is a senior research fellow in the labour market and employment research unit at the Wissenschaftszentrum Berlin für Sozialforschung (Social Science Research Centre, Berlin; WZB). Drawing on firm case studies and longitudinal data, her research has focussed on working time flexibility in Britain, France and Germany.

Håkan Regnér is working on his doctoral dissertation at the Swedish Institute for Social Research at the Stockholm University. The topics of the work are evaluation of training programmes and the impact of on-the-job training.

Bernd Reissert is professor of political science at the Berlin Polytechnic University (FHTW). His research focusses on the financing of labour market policy and on local and regional labour market policy.

Ralf Rogowski is senior lecturer in law at the University of Warwick, United Kingdom. His main areas of research and teaching are comparative labour law, European law and sociology of law.

Jill Rubery is professor of comparative employment systems at the Manchester School of Management, University of Manchester Institute of Science and Technology (UMIST). She is also the coordinator of the European Commission's Network of Experts on the Situation of Women in the Labour Market.

Paul Ryan is a lecturer in the Faculty of Economics and Politics and a Fellow of King's College at the University of Cambridge. His research areas are the economics of training, higher education, labour markets and youth unemployment.

Ronald Schettkat is senior research fellow in the economic change and employment unit at the Wissenschaftszentrum Berlin für Sozialforschung (Social Science Research Centre, Berlin; WZB). His main research is on labour economics, economic growth theory and the economics of institutions.

Günther Schmid is director of the research unit on labour market policy and employment at the Wissenschaftszentrum Berlin für Sozialforschung (Social Science Research Centre, Berlin; WZB). He is also professor of political economics at the Free University of Berlin. His main research is on equity and efficiency in labour market policy.

Klaus Schömann is a senior research fellow in the labour market and employment research unit at the Wissenschaftszentrum Berlin für Sozialforschung (Social Science Research Centre, Berlin; WZB). His research focusses on transitions in the labour market, employment contracts, training and evaluation methodology.

Jeffrey A. Smith is assistant professor of economics at the University of Western Ontario and an affiliated faculty member of the Center for Social Program Evaluation. His research interests are in labour economics, the economics of education and programme evaluation.

Albert C. Tuijnman is Principal of the Education and Training Division at the OECD in Paris. His main research fields are on life-long learning, adult education, comparative education and the economics of education.

Ulrich Walwei is a senior researcher at the Institute for Employment Research (IAB), Nuremberg. His research focusses on institutional economics, international labour markets, nonstandard forms of employment and labour market policy.

J68 , J24

H43

I- 33

1. Theory and Methodology of Labour Market Policy and Evaluation: An Introduction

Günther Schmid, Jacqueline O'Reilly and Klaus Schömann

Over the past two decades, all major industrial societies have been plagued with high levels of structural unemployment. The Member States of the European Union (EU) have been particularly hit by this phenomenon. The average unemployment rate in the OECD rose from 3.4 per cent in 1965 to 7.8 per cent in 1994 and rocketed in Europe from 2.0 to 11.2 per cent in the same period. *The OECD Jobs Study* (OECD, 1994), the White Paper on *Growth, Competitiveness, Employment* (European Commission, 1994) and the Essen Summit Meeting of the European Council on 9 and 10 December 1994 identified five main causes for this disaster (European Commission, 1995): insufficient investment in vocational training, low employment intensity of economic growth, high nonwage labour costs, low effectiveness of labour market policy and long-term unemployment. Reemployment strategies for the European Union were formulated. These included improving employment opportunities for the labour force by promoting investment in vocational training; increasing the employment intensity of growth, in particular by encouraging a more flexible organization of work; reducing nonwage labour costs, in particular for unqualified employees; increasing the effectiveness of employment policy, in particular by moving from passive to active labour market policies; and implementing selective measures necessary to help the heterogeneous group of the long-term unemployed.

These issues lie at the heart of this handbook, with which we aim to contribute to the solution to structural unemployment by deepening the analysis of it and by enriching policy guidelines. Our ambition is to take stock by reviewing contemporary knowledge of evaluation research on labour market policy and to provide fresh insights by developing and applying new approaches. Section 1 of this introductory chapter outlines the need for and the rationale behind the new concept of labour market policy and evaluation advocated in this handbook. Section 2 addresses market failures and policy failures as a theoretical starting point for target-oriented evaluation research. Section 3 specifies these

1

failures for modern labour markets. Section 4 differentiates policies and policy types common in labour market policy. Section 5 reviews the methodological issues related to target-oriented evaluation research. Section 6 provides an overview of the handbook. Section 7 presents concluding remarks.

1   TARGET VERSUS PROGRAMME-ORIENTED POLICY EVALUATION

In common language use, the term *policy evaluation* has come to cover a broad spectrum of research activities. It has included different disciplinary viewpoints as well as heterogeneous, although often complementary, fields of inquiry such as policy formation, implementation and impact-assessment studies. Among these branches, the last-mentioned component, impact analysis, can be justly regarded as the core of policy evaluation. This simply reflects the fact that in modern societies public policy interventions tend to be justified primarily through their intended and actual impacts in their respective target areas. Policy evaluation, in the sense of assessing policy impacts by means of scientific investigation, is at the centre of the present handbook. In this context, policy formation and implementation analyses play a role in as far as they contribute to explaining the differential impacts of different policy set-ups and policy programmes.

Traditionally, labour market policy evaluation has been characterized by a strong focus on individual policy instruments and programmes. The impacts of these single-purpose programmes have been assessed in a top-down approach by contrasting explicit programme goals with measurable programme outcomes.[1] In these conventional approaches, policy formation and implementation processes have been treated largely as a black box. Intended effects are measured in monetary terms, for example, by means of an increase in earnings or revenue, which is then compared to the measured costs. In this model, the underlying rules for decision-making are simple. If the cost–benefit ratio is

---

1 For an overview of the state of the art, see Berk and Rossi (1990) and Wholey, Hatry and Newcomer (1994). For a metaevaluation of evaluations in technology policy in Germany, see Kuhlmann and Holland (1995). Bouder, Cadet and Demazière (1994), de Koning (1991), Haveman and Saks (1985), Jensen and Madsen (1993), Manski and Garfinkel (1991) and the OECD (1991, 1993) have provided very useful overviews and examples related to labour market policy. Haveman and Saks pointed to an important difference between the evaluation tradition in the United States and that in Europe: in the United States, evaluation is technically fairly advanced (especially in terms of experimental research) and professionalized, whereas evaluation is less professionalized but more strongly institutionalized in Europe. A good overview of the state of the art of institutionalized evaluation (auditing as a regular part of the process of governing) is found in the volume edited by Mayne, Bemelmans-Videc, Hudson and Conner (1992).

below 1, or when the balance is negative, the programme is judged not to be worthwhile. If the cost–benefit ratio for programme *A* is greater than that for alternative programmes *B* and *C*, preference will be given to *A* (see Figure 1.1).

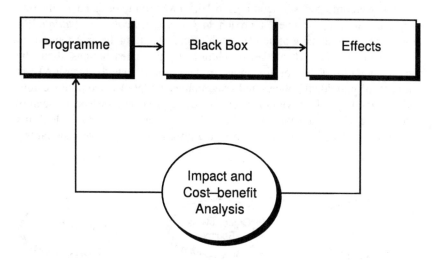

Figure 1.1   Traditional Programme Evaluation

In this way, programme evaluations have tended to neglect the incentives created by the interaction of different policy interventions and the cumulative impact of policy regimes on the disposition and observable behaviour of the relevant actors in the target area.[2] This omission may, indeed, explain why most programme-oriented evaluation studies have produced relatively disappointing results with regard to discernible genuine policy impacts on labour market behaviour and outcomes (Teitz, 1978; Wilensky, 1985).

By neglecting the links and interactions between particular policies and the embeddedness of institutional regimes governing a particular target area, conventional evaluation approaches have failed to develop notions about the complementary, mutual neutralization and functional equivalence or substitutability of different policies and programmes (Schmid and Schömann, 1994). The need to conceptualize and analyse the links, interrelationships and cumulative

---

2 In chap. 2, Heckman and Smith introduce the term 'substitution bias' for this interaction between different policy interventions.

impacts of different labour market policies appears to be all the more urgent in an era of intensified transnational policy coordination. Increasingly, policy-makers are becoming interested in cross-country comparative evaluation research in order to learn which policies are the most effective in reaching specified policy targets (European Commission, 1994 and 1995).

To overcome the shortcomings of the programme-oriented evaluation approach, we propose a new approach: *target-oriented policy evaluation*. It is the common organizing principle or 'philosophy' uniting the contributions in this handbook. Though guided by empirically grounded notions about the immediate observable or the more or less sophisticatedly measured net impacts of individual policies and programmes, target-oriented policy evaluation goes beyond conventional evaluation approaches. Instead of merely attempting to measure the impacts of a certain policy programme along the dimensions of its immediate prespecified programme objectives, the target-

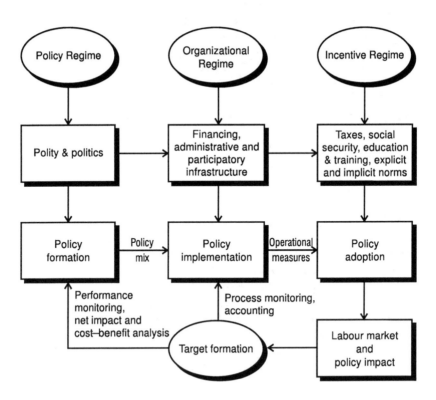

Figure 1.2 Target-oriented Policy Evaluation in Labour Market Research

oriented approach takes as its point of departure broadly defined policy goals or targets. Examples of such policy targets are increasing individual options for labour market participation, facilitating the school-to-work transition and increasing employment opportunities for the hard-to-place. With target-oriented evaluation research, then, one analyses which policies and policy combinations may be best suited for achieving these targets under different socioeconomic conditions as well as within different policy regimes.

The evaluation process itself comprises at least four steps: (a) defining the target on the basis of an analysis of policy and market failures; (b) monitoring the implementation process on the basis of financial and physical indicators; (c) monitoring performance and assessing the net impact by means of experimental and nonexperimental research techniques; and (d) estimating the net costs and benefits (taking into account opportunity costs). This four-step process can be illustrated by a simple model (see Figure 1.2).

In contrast to conventional, programme-oriented approaches, target-oriented evaluation research adopts a bottom-up perspective, which entails viewing policy impacts from the angle of the relevant agents. These agents include the people to whom the policy is addressed and their receptiveness to or rejection of a particular policy (policy adoption); the agents involved in, and responsible for, *policy implementation*; and the decision-makers in the political arena, who are core actors in the process of *policy formation*.

From this perspective, individual policies become visible as components of a wider institutional framework consisting of three elements: policy regimes, organizational regimes and incentive regimes. Policy regimes reflect the constitutional framework, or polity, which shapes politics as the struggle between groups representing different interests or between parties sponsoring different policy options. The outcome of these political struggles ultimately determines the substance and scope of labour market policy, that is, the policy mix. Organizational regimes set the financial conditions and the administrative infrastructure for the implementation of policies. Incentive regimes consist of a range of specific factors including taxes, social security arrangements, educational and training systems and explicit and implicit social norms, all of which create incentives or disincentives influencing the adoption of policies in the target area.

In total, this institutional framework defines the parameters for individual behaviour, thereby creating or supporting certain behavioural options while foreclosing or discouraging others. This broad perspective recognizes that both labour markets and policies designed to influence labour market behaviour do not exist in isolation and that systematic evaluations, therefore, need to develop an integrated approach. This approach also shows how the effective functioning of labour market policies depends on the interactions of different policy areas, such as the links between active labour market policies and labour law, and the interests and behavioural capacities of labour market agents within a given labour market structure.

Target-oriented evaluation thus draws attention to three core aspects of successful policy design and implementation: coordination, cooperation and adjustment. In the policy formation process coordination between goals and programmes is essential. In the implementation phase the interaction and cooperation of different actors will affect the policy's success. Lastly, the adjustment made by particular agents and target groups to previous policy interventions will shape the future range of policies to be adopted. In this manner, target-oriented evaluation research is a theory-driven approach (Chen, 1990) that rests on a set of general theoretical notions about the functioning of labour markets and the role of policy formation, policy implementation and policy adjustment in modifying market processes and market outcomes. At the core of these notions is the conviction that neither markets nor public policy can by themselves ensure optimal solutions to societal concerns. Rather, both markets and policies should be regarded as 'imperfect alternatives' (Kaufmann, Majone and Ostrom, 1986, p. 799; Wolf, 1987). If properly combined, coordinated and enriched with self-organized forms of cooperation, they have the potential to provide solutions superior to those achieved by market or policy regulation alone.

2   MARKET AND POLICY FAILURES

It is widely recognized (and has been once again demonstrated by the ongoing transformation of former socialist economies) that the existence of commodity, capital and labour markets rests on a complex set of institutional prerequisites. Such prerequisites are the assignment of clearly defined property rights, the creation and guarantee of a commonly recognized currency and the establishment and enforcement of certain behavioural rules and standards that, for example, exclude theft, robbery or slavery from the repertoire of admitted behaviours for maximizing individual utility. Markets and public policies that set the legal framework for private market transactions, therefore, are by no means alternatives but highly complementary forms of social organization. Moreover, although modern market economies have proved better at producing societal wealth for the vast majority of the population than their historical precursors or their former socialist rivals had, history also shows that pure markets are far from perfect mechanisms for coordinating socially desirable behaviour. Instead, markets are characterized by numerous imperfections that—without institutional corrections, checks and balances—are likely to result in undesired or suboptimal societal outcomes, or market failures. The main types of market failures are known in the literature as *external effects*, *incomplete information* and *power asymmetries* in the form of monopolies and monopsonies (Bator, 1958; Ledyard, 1987; Musgrave and Musgrave, 1980; Simon, 1982; Spulber, 1989; Stern and Ritzen, 1991; Wolf, 1987). In such instances, public policy interventions may effectively correct market imperfections and thereby enhance societal welfare in various ways: through establishing inalienable, nonnegotiable individual rights, by spreading risks for which the market would not provide adequate insurance or by producing and supplying public goods that, because of externalities, would not be sufficiently provided through the market.[3]

But despite the best of intentions on the side of policy-makers, public policies, too, are prone to failure. The literature refers to four main sources of policy failure: the state's monopoly as a producer of services, the lack of effective budget constraints, insufficient information-processing capacities of public agencies and self-interested bureaucracies (Le Grand, 1991; Musgrave and Musgrave, 1980; Niskanen, 1971; Simon, 1982; Wolf, 1987).[4] Thus, policies may be ineffective or even impair, instead of improve, the functioning of markets. Policy failures may have their origins and occur at various stages of the policy process. During policy formation, for example, where agreement on policy goals has to be moulded into viable programmes and translated into the given legal system, it is essential that sufficient political consensus exists. At the policy implementation stage legally codified policy programmes have to be merged into the behavioural repertoire of intermediary agencies in charge of enforcing, administering and selling a political programme to its specific target group. Lastly, at the adoption stage it should become evident whether the programme will be successfully linked into the behavioural dispositions and repertoires of those at whom it is targeted, so as to induce the desired behaviours and intended outcomes.[5]

The success or failure of policies at achieving their intended objectives thus essentially depends on three factors: (a) the choice of policy design and its implementation, (b) the coordination of a policy programme with other existing policies that influence the behaviour of agents in the target area and (c) the structure and dynamics prevailing in the target area itself. For the policy-maker, therefore, the relevant question is which policy design (i.e. which programme and programme mix, including their mode of financing and implementation, given the specific policy goals, policy constraints and the prevailing incentive structures in the target area) will be best suited to inducing those

---

3 For a discussion of market failures, see also chaps 13 (Walwei), 22 (Büchtemann and Walwei) and 25 (Schmid) in this volume.

4 For a discussion of policy failures, see also chaps 22 and 25.

5 Referring to these three critical stages in the launching of a policy programme, Teubner (1985, p. 309) spoke of the 'regulatory trilemma' facing policy-makers in modern market economies.

behavioural changes among target actors that are expected to lead most effectively to the intended outcomes, without producing undesired effects.

3   THE NATURE OF MODERN LABOUR MARKETS

The focus of the present handbook is on labour market policy as the ensemble of all those policy interventions that are intended to directly improve the functioning of labour markets in achieving socially desired outcomes. Because of certain peculiarities, labour markets are particularly prone to market failures and, therefore, pose particular challenges for policy-makers. This is reflected in the fact that, despite considerable cross-country variations in the mode of policy interventions, modern labour markets generally tend to be more regulated and subject to more direct policy interventions than other markets, such as commodity or capital markets.

First and foremost, the object of exchange in labour market transactions is inseparably connected with its seller, the worker. Moreover, negotiations, market transactions and actual exchange (i.e. the productive employment of labour in the production process) are distinct events in labour markets. Unlike spot market transactions, labour market contracts initiate continuous exchanges over time in the context of ongoing employment relationships, where each side has to ensure the other's compliance with the terms of the initial agreement. Furthermore, during the employment relationship the returns to relation-specific investments can be captured only if the relationship continues in the future. Finally, agents in the labour market have different resources, capacities and behavioural alternatives, which means that free or unconstrained negotiations between equal parties as a precondition of efficient market transactions cannot be taken for granted.

Both the temporal nature of the exchange between workers and firms and the fact that this exchange involves mutual sunk investments by both sides imply that labour market transactions are characterized by a high degree of uncertainty. Incomplete information on both sides involves the existence of informational asymmetries that, in turn, imply the risk of opportunistic behaviour and, therefore, may lead to market failure because neither party knows what the future holds. Efficient labour market contracting would presume that both parties succeed in devising institutions, that is, a set of mutually agreed, formal or informal, rules that (a) effectively deter opportunistic behaviour, (b) enable them to reap the full returns from mutual sunk investments and (c) ensure a sufficient degree of flexibility to cope with unknown future events.

For several reasons, the establishment of such institutions for employment relationships through mere private contracting, if it were feasible at all, would most likely involve high transaction costs. Moreover, private contracts between labour market parties, regardless of how carefully they are designed, may fail to rule out potential externalities. Negative or positive externalities occur when market transactions involve costs that are not part of the initial bargain, such as costs arising for communities or social security systems from major lay-offs. Additionally, free-rider problems may occur when benefits that accrue to third parties from private investments cannot be fully captured by the investors, as in the case with investments in human capital. Both high transaction costs and the existence of externalities may result in suboptimal outcomes from private market transactions or market failures. The latter call for policy interventions to create an effective supporting structure for private labour market transactions. Thus, reducing transaction costs (e.g. through providing information available to all market participants) and mitigating externalities from private optimizing behaviour (e.g. by forcing parties to consider the full costs of their transactions or by publicly subsidizing certain activities that produce social returns) may improve the functioning of labour markets and thereby enhance overall societal welfare. These factors imply that target-oriented evaluation research rests not only on detailed notions about the behavioural impacts of different labour market policies but also on empirically grounded assumptions about how labour markets would perform in the absence of self-organized collective action or public policy interventions.

Aside from preventing market failures, policy interventions may be motivated by social equity considerations and redistribution goals. Thus guaranteeing an adequate minimum income, creating equal employment opportunities, or compensating certain groups for social hardships produced by the market may become a matter for labour market policy. Equity as an objective of labour market policy may even result from efficiency considerations in as far as fairness and equality are productivity factors that, because of market failures, would not be ensured by private market transactions (Schmid, 1993).

From a theoretically guided, target-oriented perspective, the ultimate yardstick for evaluating labour market policies is whether they contribute to bringing about better solutions to societal problems than those achieved by the market alone. Key starting questions of target-oriented evaluation research are therefore which types of market failures may occur in different target areas and which types of policy interventions are best suited to compensate for and/or correct these failures.

In addition, the traditional dichotomy of markets and public policies needs to be complemented by other, intermediate forms of collective social organization. Such intermediaries have evolved in response to failures of pure market or policy coordination; they include firms (hierarchies), reciprocity-based networks (e.g. between producers and suppliers) and voluntary associations (labour unions, employers associations or chambers of trade and commerce). Furthermore, implicit norms, customs and social values, such as notions of fairness, have also to be taken into consideration (Lindberg, Campbell and Hollingsworth, 1991). So far, the role of these intermediate and informal kinds of socioeconomic coordination has been largely neglected in policy evaluation research.

4   POLICIES AND POLICY TYPES

Public policy analysis commonly distinguishes between types of policy. Although in reality they tend to occur in varying combinations, each of them has specific implications not only for its implementation but also for the evaluation of its respective impacts in the target area.

A classic distinction of market failure addresses four key policy areas: competition policies, structural policies, income policies and the public provision of goods or services. Competition policies address the issue of parity between market parties, are aimed at defining and assigning property rights, establishing and enforcing basic rules for market transactions and preventing monopolies or monopsonies. This scope includes civil law, antitrust regulations, guarantees of the right to form collective organizations, the prohibition of closed shops in labour relations, and the like. Structural policies aim to modify resource allocation in markets by influencing the relative prices of alternative economic activities. Examples are public subsidies, or selective tax exemptions for certain activities such as newly established businesses, emerging new industries facing high market entry thresholds or investments in R & D. Income policies modify the distribution of the returns to market transactions if the outcomes of private market exchange conflict with politically desired distributive goals. This aim includes social security policies providing compensation for various social risks such as illness, job loss and unemployment, invalidity and old age. Lastly, the state itself may act as a producer of public goods or services that would not otherwise be sufficiently provided through the market; this role includes, for instance, the public provision of basic education and public infrastructure as well as the public provision or support of merit goods, such as sheltered workplaces for severely disabled persons (Musgrave and Musgrave, 1980).

The above classic typology focusses on the different stages in the market process where public policy interventions occur and thereby reflects the different roles public policy has assumed since the early days of industrialization. Other typologies are based on a more instrumental notion and distinguish between different means, or tools, that public policy employs to achieve different objectives. Relevant distinctions of this kind include regulatory policies, procedural regulation, financial incentive programmes, information campaigns and infrastructural policies. Regulatory policies of the classic coercive type employ legal prescriptions and prohibitions as well as binding standards, licensing and permit requirements that directly prescribe certain behaviours while prohibiting and, in the case of noncompliance, penalizing others. Procedural regulation establishes binding procedural rules or mandatory negotiation arenas for the coordination of behaviour between different agents, without anticipating or prescribing the concrete outcomes of such coordination efforts. The intention behind financial incentive programmes is to influence or redirect behaviour by modifying the relative costs or rewards of behavioural alternatives faced by agents in the target area through direct subsidies, levies, taxes and tax exemptions, but without directly coercing agents to adopt a certain behaviour. The intention behind information campaigns, or persuasive policy programmes, is to induce certain behaviours by providing free information not directly available to market agents or by attaching positive or negative values to certain behavioural options as opposed to others. Lastly, infrastructural policies, by directly producing and supplying public goods, create additional options, leaving it to agents themselves to decide whether they want to make use of these options. It is clear that this list describes policy tools or elements on a scale of decreasing prescriptiveness and that in real life policy programmes tend to incorporate more than one of the elements outlined above (see, among others, Scharpf, 1991).

Further distinctions have been made in terms of the time horizons underlying public-policy interventions, the nature of agents involved in policy implementation and the kind of policy measures. Thus, one can distinguish between indefinite-duration programmes and temporary or experimental programmes of limited duration (also referred to as *sunset legislation*). Another classification focusses on the type of regulatory agencies in charge of administering the policy programme. For instance, regulation can be carried out by the state or the judiciary or can be delegated to quasi-governmental or nongovernmental intermediary organizations, such as trade associations, chambers of commerce or professional associations. A common distinction is the one between passive and active policies: passive policies are based on legal rights and entitlements that do not permit discretionary resource allocations by policy-makers or policy implementation agencies. By contrast, active, also known as proactive, policies do involve such discretionary powers to allow a greater degree of flexibility in adapting policy interventions to changing conditions in the target area and shifting political priorities.

5   ASSESSING POLICY IMPACTS

Once the sources of market failures and failures of alternative 'self-coordinated collective action' have been identified, the task of policy evaluation consists in defining criteria and providing supporting empirical evidence about which policy types and which policy mix promise superior solutions to societal coordination problems and thus contribute towards enhancing overall welfare. Conventional evaluation research has been based largely on an intrinsic approach in which programme outcomes are measured by the degree of achievement or nonachievement of implicit or explicit programme goals. Several basic underlying questions are examined: Did the programme reach its predefined target groups? Which direct policy effects can be observed in the target area? Did the programme *ceteris paribus* raise the earnings of the beneficiaries above those of the control group? Which indirect effects (including unintended side effects) can be observed? Were other programme goals accomplished? The question of whether programme implementation and administration have been conducted in an efficient manner, thus affecting programme impacts, is seldom addressed in conventional evaluation research.

In the conventional approach, accordingly, the success or failure of, for instance public job creation programmes, are empirically measured solely in terms of the number of participants or the relative shares of participants and nonparticipants who subsequently find regular employment. In the case of dismissal protection legislation, effectiveness has been frequently assessed on the basis of the number of dismissal cases or the number and outcomes of unfair dismissal suits filed by workers. With respect to intrinsic performance indicators, an interesting difference between American- and European-style evaluations may be noted in this context. Whereas European policy research tends to concentrate on take-up measures and distribution effects in terms of programme participation, American scholars tend to focus more on straightforward monetary measures, such as earnings effects (de Koning, 1991; Manski and Garfinkel, 1991).

However, such intrinsic programme performance indicators fail to provide answers to the more fundamental question of the wider policy impacts on the functioning of labour markets at large. For example, the chances of finding regular employment may not be significantly higher for programme participants than for nonparticipants, if selection effects (e.g. *creaming effects*) are adequately taken into account or if employers hired subsidized programme participants that they would have hired in the absence of employment subsidies (i.e. *deadweight effects* or *windfall profits*). Even worse, the policy may have only improved the employment opportunities of programme participants at the cost of a decline in job opportunities for nonparticipants (i.e. *displacement effects*). In such a case the programme itself would have merely effected a redistribution or reshuffling of, rather than an overall increase in, employment opportunities. Moreover, a programme may have unintended side effects that lie beyond the intended target area. Such side effects may be caused by the programme's financing, for instance, through *crowding out* resources from the private sector (via taxes) that would otherwise have been put to more productive use. Alternatively, *substitution effects* can create market distortions, the result being, for example, that firms employing subsidized programme participants are given a competitive advantage (e.g. in prices) over those firms not benefiting from programme subsidies. Lastly, opportunity costs must be taken into account if a programme has had a positive net effect on employment, it still is not clear whether alternative policies (including the discontinuation of existing policies or deregulation) would—*ceteris paribus*—not have achieved the same, or a greater, employment impact at the same, or a lower, cost.

The above makes clear that a target-oriented evaluation approach relies on more complex research designs involving an array of different evaluation methodologies that go far beyond the techniques commonly employed for simple programme accounting and policy monitoring of the conventional type. Among these methodologies, comparative approaches play an important role. Microlevel comparisons of the structure, behaviour and performance of programme participants versus nonparticipants through experimental and nonexperimental research designs allow systematic controls for selection effects. Micro- or macrolevel comparisons on the basis of *time-series or longitudinal data* covering periods before and after the introduction of certain policies as well as before and after programme participation permit systematic impact assessments and controls for unobserved programme outcomes. Systematic cross-regional or cross-country comparisons provide a means for assessing the relative success of contrasting policy approaches and policy regimes in achieving identical or similar policy objectives.

Moreover, for measuring the overall, intended and unintended, effects of policy interventions, target-oriented evaluation research cannot narrowly focus on immediate target variables such as net employment-creation, net earnings-effects, or the employment careers of programme participants versus nonparticipants. It is necessary to adopt a broader perspective that includes a whole array of micro- and macrolevel variables that may provide evidence of unintended side effects accruing in areas beyond the immediate target area— crowding-out effects, for instance. Such an approach requires detailed information about the total range of behavioural options of agents in the target area, which can be collected through special survey research complementing process-generated data on programme performance. Given that labour market policies do not operate in isolation, one also needs to understand the ways in which observable labour market behaviour and performance may be affected by the interaction of different policies in the target area. Such policy interaction may have a reinforcing or neutralizing effect. In these cases, aggregate impact analysis provides a methodology for assessing the respective contributions that different policies make to observable aggregate policy outcomes. Further, systematic cost–benefit analysis attempts to weigh the total costs of policy programmes (including their opportunity costs, costs for programme implementation and administration and costs due to unintended side effects) against their measurable (direct and indirect) benefits in terms of monetary equivalents. With such cost–benefit approaches, research must ask not only for the magnitudes of measurable costs and benefits but also where these costs and benefits accrue, that is, to which agents. Cooperation of various agents or coordination of policies may be seriously impaired if costs and benefits accrue to different parties or agents that can generate *institutional incongruence*. Finally, systematic policy evaluation must involve in-depth analyses of the policy formation and implementation process for linking measured programme outcomes to specific attributes of the programme structure and programme implementation. For example, the adequacy of chosen policy tools and the underlying assumptions about the administrative rationality of implementation agents or the adequacy of programme financing and of the governance structure in programme administration need to be taken into consideration by systematic evaluation research.

At the same time, the above list of evaluation methodologies and techniques makes clear that different types of policies require different methodological approaches. This fact can be illustrated by contrasting targeted active labour market policy with universalistic regulatory policies. Active labour market programmes commonly involve clearly identifiable target groups, programme participants and implementation agencies. In contrast, universalistic *programmes* establish binding rules and standards for all market participants, such as antidiscrimination norms and protection against unfair dismissal. They tend to preclude, therefore, certain evaluation techniques, such as experimental designs, *post-hoc* constructed control group analyses, or implementation studies, and they require more sophisticated evaluation approaches. For instance, even if one manages to arrive at an approximation of the magnitude and distribution of the direct costs of individual or collective dismissals imposed by dismissal legislation, information on actual dismissal cases does not provide enough basis to say very much about the overall behavioural responses to and other impacts of such legislation. The latter may essentially consist in preventing certain types of behaviour, such as large-scale dismissals, by rendering them more costly than alternative behavioural options (i.e. labour hoarding). Direct observable costs imposed by regulatory constraints may be quite different from the overall economic costs caused by policy interventions. Moreover, economic agents may try to evade regulatory constraints, such as dismissal protection or antidiscrimination legislation, by modifying their behaviour in other areas, say, hiring practices or decisions affecting firm location.

For evaluation, these policy differences have two important implications. First, as indicated above, the effects of policies may be manifested in areas other than the one targeted by the policy programme. Evaluation research, therefore, needs relatively detailed notions about the behavioural dispositions and repertoires of agents in order to identify those areas in which regulatory inputs may produce intended or unintended behavioural outcomes. Second, the impact of regulatory policies may be quite different in the introductory phase, when agents have not yet adjusted their behaviour to the new parameters set by a policy (adjustment itself being costly). After the policy has been in place for some time, agents may have been able to adjust their behaviour to the new situation.

Another important distinction in methodological approaches used by target-oriented research is the one between *ex-ante*, in-process and *ex-post* evaluations that each have different implications with regard to the choice of evaluation methodology. Most conventional evaluation research belongs to the *ex-post* category. Programme implementation, impacts, costs and benefits are assessed retrospectively. This research can take the form of either an overall assessment, after a temporary policy programme has ended, or an evaluation of an ongoing indefinite-duration programme (e.g. a new piece of labour legislation) that has been in place for a sufficient length of time to allow an assessment of its direct and indirect effects. *Ex-post* evaluations may provide hints for the design of subsequent programmes directed at similar policy targets. In-process evaluations, however, have the advantage of being able to directly analyse the implementation process of a policy programme and thus may produce valuable information supporting the administrative process and induce in-process improvements of programme design and administration. If tied into the policy programme itself, in-process policy monitoring and evaluation may be an important component of intelligent policy designs allowing modifications as the result of a built-in learning mechanism that allow modification through the process of implementation.

Ex-ante or formative evaluations, lastly, differ from both in-process and *ex-post* evaluations in their assessment of the likely range and potential impacts of alternative programmes and programme designs in the target area. Although *ex-ante* evaluations may substantially enhance the degree of rationality in programme design and formulation, examples of *ex-ante* evaluations are still very rare, partly because of the specific methodological problems they entail. Methodological approaches of *ex-ante* evaluations include systematic information-gathering about the size and structure of potential target groups and the likely number of programme beneficiaries. Established techniques employed in social and economic forecasting include micro- and macrosimulations, Delphi procedures and participatory procedures directly involving potential target groups in the policy-formation process. Formative evaluation may be used to examine the extent to which the policy of one country could be successfully adopted by another country; further, it can help one to identify which circumstances or conditions would be required to make such an adoption successful (Rose, 1990).

6   OBJECTIVES, STRUCTURE AND CONTENT OF THE HANDBOOK

The present handbook sets out to provide a systematic overview of the state of the art in labour market policy evaluation. In this sense it is an evaluation of evaluations at three levels. First, it outlines and evaluates the various methodological approaches adopted in previous evaluation research. Second, it focusses on particular target areas and evaluates the substantive results of previous evaluation research on the impacts of different policy instruments and policy regimes in contrasting settings. Third, it provides an evaluation of institutional frameworks and existing labour market monitoring and information systems, pointing out where such systems are underdeveloped and where new approaches could be used effectively for both intelligent policy design and empirical policy evaluation in the future.

A unique feature of this edited collection is the presentation of a target-oriented approach to evaluating labour market policy. Instead of only attempting to measure the impacts of specific policy programmes along the dimensions of their prespecified programme goals, researchers using the target-oriented approach ask which combination of policies, under which economic and institutional conditions, contribute most to the realization of broadly defined policy goals or targets. The target-oriented approach emphasizes the ways in which successful policy design and implementation depend on the coordination between policy goals and programmes on the one hand and agents' behavioural dispositions (interests) and repertoires (capacities) on the other. Unlike programme-oriented evaluation, the target-oriented approach to evaluation provides a basis on which to review the results of labour market policy evaluation research for the cumulative impact that interacting policies and policy regimes have on labour market performance and outcomes in selected target areas.

A further unique aspect of this handbook is its international approach in a threefold sense. First, the task of editing this collection of essays has given us the opportunity to assemble a group of renowned international researchers from western Europe and the United States who have first-hand experience in designing and conducting evaluation research. While drawing on their own expertise in the field, they have produced new and original insights and over-views of their respective specialist areas in evaluation research. Second, in assessing contemporary developments in the field, all the authors apply an international comparative framework or contribute to the development of an international comparative research methodology. Third, all but the methodo-logical chapters (part 2) are organized around policy targets and empirically compare evaluation approaches and results for target areas that have been at the heart of current labour market policy concerns in OECD countries.

This handbook is, therefore, intended to accomplish three objectives: (a) to improve our understanding of the contextual determination of labour market policy impacts and labour market outcomes, (b) to show the gaps in our current knowledge and research methodologies and to name and define those issues that need to be addressed in future evaluation research and (c) to assist policy-makers and statistical agencies in developing the informational prerequisites for systematic policy evaluation.

The intended audience of this handbook are policy decision-makers, pro-fessional programme evaluators and academic scholars interested in labour market policy and policy evaluation. Practitioners may also gain valuable insights from the handbook about how to assess the appropriateness of differ-ent policy tools and policy approaches and about the requirements for system-atic impact evaluations. The present handbook is not designed as a manual for programme implementors but as a compendium that draws on the wealth of experience from previous evaluation and points out the advantages and pitfalls encountered when one must choose specific evaluation methodologies or introduce and implement particular policies. We hope these experiences and reflections will help push evaluation research forward towards providing sup-port for more effective policy-making and implementation.

The handbook is divided into four parts. The six chapters of part I offer a critical look at the methodological approach of traditional evaluation research and at the tools available to evaluation researchers. They draw on a broad spectrum of cases where these different methodologies have been applied in past evaluation research. Part II contains fifteen chapters, each of which focusses on a particular target area defined around broader labour market policy goals common to most OECD countries and provides a critical review of the methodologies used in past evaluation research and of the results and evidence produced. The first set of chapters in the section deals with critical labour market transitions from the perspective of individuals and the effects of policy aimed at facilitating these transitions. The second set of chapters deals with specific policy approaches designed to address market failures and to correct undesired distributional outcomes of the labour market. The five chap-ters in part III of the handbook examine, from various angles, the effects that contrasting macroinstitutional frameworks and policy regimes have on labour market policy and labour market performance. Part IV provides an overview of labour market policy monitoring and future requirements both at the national and European level.

PART I: METHODOLOGY OF LABOUR MARKET POLICY EVALUATION

Traditional approaches to evaluation research have tended to be dominated by methodological techniques borrowed from the natural sciences. These approaches are discussed in chaps 2 through 7, which aim at showing the strengths and weaknesses of these various methods and their underlying theories. Estimation of the effects of policy changes is often comparable to the way scientists test new drugs: the impact of a particular policy is measured in terms of the different response patterns between the treated group and the control group. For methodological, ethical and practical reasons, however, such a perspective has its limitations. Therefore, a variety of other techniques, corresponding data sources and quantitative and qualitative methods also need to be applied, as the following chapters show.

The basic methodological questions of evaluation research are formulated by Heckman and Smith in chap. 2. The question usually asked in policy evaluation is: what are the effects of a policy on a specific target group? In more analytical terms: how does labour market performance change relative to the situation without this policy? To answer this question, the authors develop a rigorous framework introducing the basic distinction between experimental and nonexperimental evaluation. They attack the methodological difficulties involved in establishing an adequate counterfactual basis against which to compare net programme outcomes. Selection bias concerning participants, difficulties in using randomized selection procedures and possibilities of applying another programme as a substitute complicate the precise definition and operationalization of the counterfactual in experimental set-ups. A group of nonexperimental methods is then presented: instrumental variable estimators, fixed-effect estimators and specific sampling plans. The authors end the chapter with considerations on how to choose between various nonexperimental approaches.

The role of classical experiments in which prospective programme participants are randomly assigned to experimental and control groups in evaluation research is examined in chap. 3 by Björklund and Regnér. The main objections to this approach are discussed in the light of recent US experiments and three European ones. The authors conclude that the experimental approach is not a panacea but that it may provide useful insights into programme impacts. In particular, experimental studies of new programmes and of major changes in existing ones can be quite helpful, whereas studies of ongoing programmes encounter more difficulties. The authors recommend that European policy-makers consider this methodology more seriously, and they provide detailed suggestions on how to conduct experiments in three policy fields: mobility grants, training programmes under demand or supply constraints, and job clubs as an alternative mode of ongoing job search activities.

The use of longitudinal data in designing evaluation research where it can improve the estimations of programme effects is presented by Schömann in chap. 4. The author urges the widespread use of longitudinal designs in data collection. Four basic types of longitudinal information are discussed in terms of their advantages and drawbacks of each form. Besides the four 'pure' forms—panel data, retrospective data, administrative records and time-series data—the major unexploited potential of longitudinal designs lies in the mul-tiple combinations of these data sources. To illustrate the advantage of longitu-dinal designs in evaluations, the author chooses two subject areas: earnings after participation in training programmes and programmes facilitating exit from unemployment. He concludes that many evaluation questions can be answered and reliable estimates of programme effects can be obtained only if the time structure of events and policy interventions is precisely documented in the available data collection.

Aggregate impact analysis aimed at measuring the effects of labour market policy on macroeconomic performance variables such as aggregate employ-ment, unemployment and wages is discussed in chap. 5 by Bellmann and Jackman. This approach usually starts from the notion of a general equilib-rium. The authors highlight potential distortions of this equilibrium, and they reflect theoretically on how, in principle, labour market policies can correct such disequilibria. They argue that the best way to test for aggregate employ-ment impacts is to analyse the outflow rates from unemployment, both the overall and disaggregated according to specific target groups. They show how this method takes account of deadweight, substitution and displacement effects; lastly, they review empirical studies of outflow rates and summarize the available evidence of the efficacy of policies.

Cost–benefit analysis (CBA) provides a further methodological tool con-tributing to the design and evaluation of labour market policy as discussed by Delander and Niklasson in chap. 6. They concentrate on CBA as a 'way of thinking' about alternatives, by illustrating the meaning and applicability of the principles to be considered in measuring costs and benefits. They also cite in detail three attempts to calculate the costs and benefits of individual labour market policy programmes: an evaluation of an increase in staff at the public employment offices in Sweden, an evaluation of the costs and benefits of the US Job Corps programme and an evaluation of wage subsidies for disabled persons in Sweden. The authors conclude that 'thinking in terms of alternatives' should be integrated from the very beginning of the decision-making and policy implementation process. They argue that it should also be the task of decision-makers to initiate more evaluation research using a CBA framework.

In the final chapter of part I to be devoted to evaluation methodology, Schmid develops a systematic framework for process evaluation. Policy failure can lead to vague or inconsistent goals and to programme designs that are not suitable for the problem to be addressed. Furthermore, variations in implementing policy decisions can reinforce or reduce intended policy effects. Policy formation and implementation, therefore, are essential elements of process evaluation. The author examines the genesis of process evaluation as illustrated by the methodology of a few earlier studies. In a cybernetic model of the policy cycle, four 'filtering stages' that determine the final outcomes of labour market policies are distinguished: programme choices, implementation, take-up and impacts. Performance indicators for each of the four filtering stages are proposed. The author concludes that the development of 'cooperative labour market policy' as an evolving new paradigm makes the explicit and systematic inclusion of process evaluation even more necessary than before.

PART II: EVALUATING LABOUR MARKET POLICIES IN SELECTED TARGET AREAS

In the chapters assembled in part II of the handbook, the authors look in more detail at specific target areas for labour market policy interventions and the various approaches that have been taken to evaluate the performance and impacts of policies in these target areas. The first set of chapters is focussed on policies designed to facilitate individual's labour market transitions. Analogous to the theory of life transitions in psychology (life-span development approaches or frameworks of critical life events), labour market transitions can be regarded as a result of critical events or sudden changes, such as job loss, exit from the education system, family formation, separations or retirement. Such transitions may result in negative or positive results, depending on how people are able to cope with change. Transitions usually create tensions because customary problem-solving techniques fail or produce unintended outcomes in altered circumstances. Labour market policies can act as institutional mechanisms assisting individuals in coping with such critical labour market transitions. In the following chapters, labour market policies and their respective evaluations are reviewed in order to see whether they support efficient and equitable transitions from unemployment to employment, school to work, between family formation and paid employment and from employment to retirement.

Addressing the impact of unemployment compensation systems on labour market transitions, Schmid and Reissert examine in chap. 8 the basic types of unemployment compensation schemes in OECD countries. Comprehensive empirical evidence is provided on how different systems affect beneficiary rates, income replacement and the overall costs to society. The literature evaluating the incentives of unemployment compensation is critically reviewed on the basis of a framework that distinguishes sixteen transitions between employment, unemployment, participation in special programmes and inactivity. Further consideration is given to the institutional incentives for transferring funds from passive income replacement towards active reemployment or training promotion. In conclusion, the authors emphasize the need for more longitudinal studies of labour market transitions and for studies addressing alternative or complementary measures of unemployment compensation.

Policies intended to facilitate the transition from long-term unemployment to employment are the central theme of the chapter by Erhel, Gautié, Gazier and Morel in chap. 9. The authors first discuss the concept of 'employability' and define the characteristics of the 'hard-to-place'. Special emphasis is given to the difference between American workfare and European 'insertion', or reemployment, policies. The chapter provides an overview of current policy schemes addressing the hard-to-place in OECD countries, followed by a survey of the main evaluation studies on temporary public job creation schemes, targeted employment subsidies, special training schemes, job search assistance and related programmes. The authors conclude with a critical assessment of existing evaluation studies, indicating ways and priorities for improving policy implementation and evaluation in the future.

Policies designed to facilitate the crucial transition from school to work are the topic taken up by Ryan and Büchtemann in chap. 10. The chapter addresses 'compensatory' labour market programmes such as remedial education, youth training and work experience programmes targeted at jobless youth, school dropouts and the like; policies aiming at wages and labour costs in the youth labour market; and policies aimed at improving secondary schooling and the links between schools and employment. Evaluations of all three policy approaches are classified by their degree of methodological rigour, specifically with regard to modelling the counterfactual, in this case, what transition patterns would look like in the absence of policy interventions, and their main findings are reviewed. The authors note an inverse relation between the amount of estimated benefits and the level of methodological sophistication of the chosen evaluation approach, but they also emphasize that research findings vary strongly from study to study, thus hardly lending support to any generalizable conclusions about the effectiveness of policies designed to smooth the school-to-work transition.

Fagan and Rubery move on to examine transitions between family forma-tion and paid employment in chap. 11. They review existing arrangements in the Member States of the European Union to see whether they weaken or reinforce the traditional male-breadwinner model of household organization. Evaluation studies reveal that some of these policies are more effective than others in increasing employment continuity for women with young children. In particular, they compare the effects of various parental leave entitlements, policies to reduce working time temporarily and the public provision or subsi-dization of nonparental childcare, including school opening hours. Contrary to the neoclassical view, the authors argue that female specialization in unpaid work is inefficient. Several methodological issues are raised for future com-parative research. Emphasis is put on the differences in the organization of work across countries and on behavioural flow data and attitudinal data to track labour market transitions over the child-rearing years.

A further common policy target is to facilitate exits from the labour market in the form of pension provision as well as retirement and redundancy schemes provided by the public sector, by firms and through social policy. In chap. 12, Casey observes that previous evaluation studies have concentrated on the effectiveness of these policies in reducing unemployment, job replacement rates and cost-effectiveness. Many of these early retirement schemes have been linked with moves to encourage work-sharing as well as the social man-agement of work force reductions. However, contradictory policies are also being encouraged in order to extend the period that older workers remain in the labour market. The author notes that the popularity of such measures has declined in recent years as governments have sought to reduce expenditure. Increasingly, firms or individuals have been expected to pick up the costs of such early exit transitions. Unfortunately, there is a paucity of primary data collection and evaluation, a gap that raises concern given the costs of these schemes and the positive employment effect they can generate.

One of the key problems surrounding the costs of public labour market policies and those related to human resources within firms is that of 'free-riding', as when firm *A* reaps the benefit from firm *B*'s investment without sharing any of the costs. A classic example of such behaviour can be seen in the area of training, where firm *A* may poach trained employees from firm *B* by offering them higher wages. Such behaviour can create a downward spiral in the overall level of training provided by firms, for it is less costly for each individual firm to poach trained workers rather than to invest in training. Such an uneven distribution of costs and benefits is likely to lead to market inefficiencies, societal welfare losses and undesired distributional outcomes. It therefore requires corrective policy interventions. Aside from such market failures due to externality problems, market inefficiencies can also arise from high transaction costs and informational asymmetries, mobility restraints and social discrimination. Another set of chapters in this part of the handbook, therefore, deals with public policies designed to improve the functioning of labour markets by directly addressing the sources of market failure and of undesired distributional outcomes of unconstrained market transactions. A special emphasis of these chapters is on recent policies intended to increase labour market flexibility through improving information in the labour market, promoting life-long learning and skills adjustment, reducing insider–outsider segmentation in the labour market, supporting working time variability and enlarging the range of contractual options open to market participants.

The issue of job-matching and the role of public and private placement services for the unemployed is addressed by Walwei in chap. 13. The author provides a typology of countries depending on their mix of public and private services and summarizes the results of previous evaluation research on the effects and outcomes of these different institutional arrangements. In some countries the private sector has 'creamed' the easier-to-place candidates, leaving the public sector with the hard-to-place. In other countries there has been less differentiation between the services offered. As the public sector in many OECD countries is currently undergoing fundamental reforms towards integrating more market elements in public service provision, the public–private mix of placement services will be a key area of evaluation research in the future.

Market failures are particularly apparent when it comes to the issue of sex discrimination in terms of access to job opportunities and pay. In chap. 14 Rubery, Fagan and Maier, therefore, assess labour market policies aimed at reducing the inequalities and inefficiencies created by occupational segregation and discrimination by gender. Policy initiatives can focus on reducing segregation itself, for example, through affirmative action policies, or on reducing the penalties of occupational segregation, for example, through policies to implement equal pay for work of comparable worth. Changes in occupational segregation are not necessarily the result of specific equality policies but can be partly due to the dynamics of industrial and occupational restructuring. This structural change, therefore, casts doubt on the validity of conventional evaluation approaches focussing exclusively on shifts in the gender composition of occupations. There is a need for more workplace-based evaluations that do not take the occupational hierarchy as a given and that recognize that the implementation of equal opportunity policies cannot be treated as independent from changes taking place in employment relationships.

A further manifestation of market failure can be seen in skill shortages and mismatches. In chap. 15 Tuijnman and Schömann examine the role of life-long learning as one component of a high-skill, high-wage job strategy favoured by most European governments. Originally, the concept of life-long learning was advanced as a means of reducing inequality by narrowing skill differentials produced by the education system, but nowadays discussions in this area focus more on labour market efficiency and productivity aspects. A review of the evidence suggests that individual careers in terms of occupational status, earnings growth, immobility and unemployment risks are influenced by life-long learning. The macrolevel evidence of the productivity effects of life-long learning, by contrast, is much less encouraging about the potential of rethinking education and further training within a unified concept of life-long learning. Evaluations in this area remain deficient unless more direct ways of measuring competence, skill acquisition and skill depreciation can be developed and linked to the institutional background in which they originated.

Expanding in chap. 16 on the topic of new and alternative matching mechanisms, Meager reviews and evaluates labour market policies designed to stimulate self-employment for the unemployed as an alternative to dependent wage employment. He describes the economic and institutional context of the growth in self-employment and the policies supporting that context. Theoretical and practical problems involved in evaluating such schemes and the diverse evaluation methodologies used in previous research are discussed and assessed. Drawing on research in several European countries and the United States, the author critically examines some of the empirical findings emerging from evaluation studies. Lastly, it highlights some of the deficiencies in the existing research, notably the lack of evidence on the long-term implications that certain policies have for economic welfare, income levels and social security, namely, policies designed to extend the concept of self-employment to parts of the work force that have traditionally not been engaged in entrepreneurial activities.

Policies to improve labour market adjustment have also focussed on targeted groups, as Delsen shows in chap. 17, where he examines evaluation studies of policies designed to help the disabled obtain access to paid employment. The great cross-country diversity in institutional arrangements for vocational rehabilitation and employment for people with disabilities presents an ideal demonstration case for the value of a target-oriented approach. The author reviews the target formation process resulting in different operational definitions of disability, then discusses the various policy approaches: equal opportunity legislation, quota systems, dismissal protection, conventional vocational counselling and guidance services, training, special education, sheltered employment, wage and hiring subsidies and technical assistance for employees. The author concludes by emphasizing the need for policy mixes that are variably differentiated according to the heterogeneity of the particular target group and by calling for evaluation studies with a broader design and a focus on the integration process.

Biffl, in chap. 18, further develops the subject of targeted groups by focussing on policies related to integrating immigrant labour. Immigration has become a pervasive feature of labour markets in the industrialized world. The main policy targets, however, differ across countries and affect the timing, direction, volume and composition of immigration flows. Levels of immigration are to a large extent determined by the policies of receiving countries. However, international political pressures to accept people from specific source countries can put a strain on national immigration policies. Countries with an elaborate support system for immigrant integration have been more successful in establishing a multicultural society than those with limited integration support which has led to the rise of an ethnic minority underclass. The author argues that evaluation research has not yet taken fully into account the general tendency for migration systems to become more complex and the need for improved coordination between economic and social policies related to migrant labour.

Debates on flexible working time have also been seen as a means to improve labour market matching. In chap. 19, O'Reilly examines the theoretical debates and coordination goals associated with the use of part-time work at three levels: aggregate labour market effects in reducing unemployment and creating jobs, providing individual employees with working time flexibility over their life cycle and finally improving productivity and efficiency at the firm level. The range of active labour market policies that affect the behaviour of agents in this target area includes those providing financial incentives to encourage part-time work, entry and exit measures for young and older workers and part-time parental leave. Passive labour market measures include those involving incentive structures that emanate from the tax system, the social security system and employment security regulations, which influence the demand for and supply of part-time workers. The author examines the methodological problems and the substantive results of respective evaluations. Conclusions are presented on policy instruments that can be used to improve the functioning and coordination of labour market measures along with recommendations for future evaluation research.

The topic of policies promoting flexible working time is also at the heart of the study in chap. 20, by Mosley and Kruppe, who examine the effectiveness of short-time work programmes in stabilizing employment for workers who would otherwise be made redundant. A key issue is whether short-time work is used in a genuine attempt to preserve human capital, share out work and stabilize employment, or whether it is merely a 'soft' means of delaying dismissals. The authors compare various national schemes and contrast patterns and trends in the uptake of short-time work. They argue that the utilization of short-time work is related not only to the relative generosity of these schemes but also to other institutional factors, such as the stringency of employment protection laws and the degree to which other flexibility options are available to firms. The interaction between these factors is crucial to understanding how employers adjust the size of their labour force. In concluding, the authors argue that temporary or cyclical use of short-time work represents an efficient coordination mechanism of labour market policy but that the use of short-time work in structural adjustment is more problematic.

Work force adjustment through variable working time can be regarded as a functional equivalent for hiring and firing labour. In chap. 21 Rogowski and Schömann present a comparative evaluation of legal regulations that have an impact on the flexibility of employment contracts. The principal policy target in this chapter is increased numerical flexibility in the labour market. The authors focus their review on recent European policies for deregulating employment protection by facilitating fixed-term employment. They propose a theory-driven evaluation of national and comparative evaluation studies, which rests on hypotheses derived from both legal and socioeconomic theories of the labour market. Most evaluations of legal reforms have taken a very country-specific perspective, reflecting the context dependency of recent legal reforms and the specific features of national legal systems. Each country's system of regulation has a specific set of functionally equivalent policies to warrant flexibility in the use of labour inputs. In the authors' view, only a detailed microlevel analysis can provide the depth needed for national and subsequent comparative evaluations in this area.

Opinions strongly diverge as to the effects, costs and benefits of employment security policies and dismissal protection regulations. Büchtemann and Walwei, in chap. 22, attribute the continuing controversial debate about employment security regimes to the lack of conclusive evaluation results. This controversy, in turn, reflects the insufficient theoretical foundation of most previous evaluation attempts as well as the complexity of the issues involved. The authors, therefore, first develop a theoretical framework that yields a set of analytical criteria by which the impacts of actual dismissal protection regimes can be assessed and evaluated. This is followed by a brief characterization of contrasting regulatory regimes as they exist in Europe (statutory approach) and North America (common-law approach). A systematic review of different evaluation approaches shows that high standards in dismissal protection do not necessarily conflict with employment policy objectives and considerations of economic efficiency. Given the unsatisfactory state of evidence, however, the authors conclude with a plea for more detailed, theoretically grounded, empirical cross-country comparisons of starkly contrasting legal regimes.

PART III: EVALUATING INSTITUTIONAL FRAME-
WORKS OF LABOUR MARKET POLICY

Whereas the chapters of parts I and II focus on policies directed at improving the functioning of labour markets and policies aimed at particular target groups facilitating labour market transitions, the chapters assembled in part III of the handbook deal with policy targets at the meso- or macrolevel. We thereby acknowledge the growing importance of policy interventions intended to modify broader institutional frameworks such as employment administrations, industrial relations and wage-bargaining systems. That is, the focus of the evaluation approaches and studies reviewed in this part is not on the impacts of individual policies and policy programmes on labour market outcomes in different target areas. The emphasis in the following chapters is on the effects of macroinstitutional conditions that favour or inhibit the formation and implementation of effective labour market policies and that have beneficial or adverse impacts on aggregate labour market performance.

Chap. 23, by Janoski, tackles the issue of evaluating labour market policy at the macrolevel. The author begins with the large variation in labour market policy expenditure across industrialized countries. He assumes that labour market institutions might have a greater influence on expenditure patterns than do economic, demographic or political variables, which are usually cited to explain such variations. His analysis indicates that the existence of powerful employment services and works councils, of a dense and varied public or semipublic infrastructure for training and education and of tripartite corporate wage-setting arrangements create favourable conditions for active labour market policy. Autonomy and adequate resources of employment services turn out to be the strongest institutional variable, followed by corporate self-administration. The analysis is based on a rich and innovative institutional data bank on 18 OECD countries from 1950 to 1989. The author concludes that the institutional variables need to be further refined and complemented by indicators for the transformation of labour market regimes to allow more dynamic and sophisticated analysis.

Whereas Janoski is interested in the explanation of different levels of expenditure between countries, Bellmann and Jackman seek in chap. 24 to examine how expenditure affects other aggregate labour market variables. Although empirical work on the macroeconomic effects of labour market policy has been rare for lack of an appropriate theoretical framework, this gap has been addressed by several studies during the last decade. Bellmann and Jackman apply the labour market model developed by Layard and Nickell and offer estimates of their own based on international cross-sectional comparisons. Their results indicate that measures to increase labour force participation, intensify competition for jobs from unemployed outsiders and test the availability and willingness of job seekers to work tend to reduce wage pressure on firms and to increase regular employment. The effect that improved matching has on restoration of labour market equilibrium, however, is ambiguous. Measures designed to combat long-term unemployment have a positive labour supply effect that causes employment to rise. However, all effects are small, indicating that active labour market policy alone cannot solve the problem of high levels of unemployment in Europe.

One important reason for the failure or low effectiveness of labour market policies is the lack of an appropriate policy-formation process and of an adequate infrastructure to implement policy decisions. Because growing budget deficits have also restricted the scope for spending and because increased spending does not necessarily produce better results, there has been a growing concern with organizational reforms in the spirit of new public management. In chap. 25 Schmid takes up these issues by applying the analytical framework for process evaluation to the case of further training. The corresponding policy and implementation regimes of Denmark, Germany, the Netherlands and the United Kingdom are compared and their changes assessed in terms of their responsiveness and organizational efficiency. The author then attempts to measure the effect that variations in incentive regimes have on the level and selectivity of programme participation and on employment, unemployment, productivity and cost-effectiveness. The results are discussed in terms of a specific theoretical framework, coordination failures. The author concludes that the management of labour market policies must apply a mix of coordination mechanisms, in which both competition and cooperation are essential and complementary elements.

This topic is further developed in the contribution by Appelbaum and Schettkat, who, in chap. 26, evaluate the impact of wage-bargaining institutions on labour market performance. Conventional studies deal only with the employment and unemployment impacts of aggregate real wages and tend to define corporatist bargaining systems quite narrowly. The authors, by contrast, apply a broader institutional definition that includes coordination with government policies and takes into account the fact that variations in wage-bargaining institutions affect the wage structure and, hence, the employment structure and the employment intensity of growth. In times when employment growth correlated strongly with productivity growth, wage-bargaining systems did not matter much; in the era of the postindustrial service society, wage-bargaining systems and the way they are coordinated with governments are an issue of great concern. In the 1980s overall employment growth was weakest in those countries that lacked both high interindustry wage dispersion and highly developed corporatist institutions.

Job growth is also linked to taxation, which affects the price of labour. Gustafsson, in chap. 27, therefore develops a framework to study the impact of taxation on labour market performance. Taxes introduce a wedge between the price of supply and demand, a wedge that changes market equilibrium. A comparison of tax regimes in major OECD countries allows the author to comment on tax harmonization efforts and employment effects in the European Union. Economic theory suggests that any income tax on labour supply entails specific effects on the incentive or disincentive to work. However, empirical evaluations of tax reforms show that the endogeneity of wages to working hours, demand restrictions on working hours and separate or joint income taxation make it difficult to arrive at a precise estimation of income and substitution effects. With respect to the target-oriented approach, Gustafsson argues that the effects that tax reforms are likely to have on target groups and other workers must be considered in tax-reform evaluations if such evaluations are to yield a complete picture.

PART IV: EVALUATING POLICY TARGETS AT THE EUROPEAN LEVEL

The final three chapters in this handbook extend the examination of macro-level factors to policy targets at the European level. These three chapters identify policy initiatives stimulated by European policy agencies, which, with varying degrees of success, have attempted to achieve both social and economic integration within European labour markets. All three chapters examine the extent to which such European institutions have been able to implement, monitor and evaluate these policies.

The European Social Fund (ESF) is one of the largest European programmes to sponsor employment projects for less favoured regions in Europe. In chap. 28 Lindley briefly reviews the development of the European structural funds with special reference to the ESF and summarizes the experience with policy evaluation in terms of its relevance for the evaluation of the ESF. He examines the particular strategic challenges one encounters when evaluating the range of such heterogeneous programmes covered by the ESF and proposes a generic evaluation, an approach in which the researcher seeks to organize the available research base more rigorously, to develop it further and to apply it more effectively when evaluating projects sponsored by the ESF.

Further attempts to develop labour market policies at the European level are examined in chap. 29, by O'Reilly, Reissert and Eichener, who assess the extent to which universal labour standards have been established in the process of European integration. The chapter does not attempt to provide an analysis of the economic impact of national standards, which has been conducted by the OECD, but instead attempts to address the question of why some standards have been successfully introduced at the European level whereas others have been consistently blocked by national governments. The aim of introducing such standards is to prevent the development of social dumping in European labour markets. The chapter focusses on four key areas: workplace participation, working time, health and safety, and social security. These four areas highlight the varying degrees of success at achieving agreement at the European level. The authors argue that the key factors for successful agreement are related to changes in the decision-making process, the shape of coalitions opposed to or in favour of such regulations and the extent to which such standards challenge the embeddedness of national systems. A key issue for the future will be the extent to which the EU Commission will be able to secure effective implementation of its directives and to monitor their effects.

In the final chapter of the handbook, Auer and Kruppe address the issue of monitoring labour market policy. The authors review the state of the art and develop criteria that could be applied for a more systematic monitoring, accounting and comparing across the Member States of the European Union. For various reasons (decentralization, financial constraints, stricter accountability rules on governments and administrations, and new information technologies), a pragmatic, quick and down-to-earth approach to collecting ongoing information on process performance and results becomes urgent. In contrast to sophisticated *ex-post* evaluations, modern monitoring systems involve the establishment of close feedback links to the policy formation and implementation process. The authors conclude that monitoring systems in most countries are not very advanced and that new problems arise with the establishment of such systems, namely, adverse incentive effects for programme managers and a recentralization of target formation and control. Therefore, the involvement of monitoring bodies in the setting of goals seems important for ensuring the efficiency of 'intelligent' monitoring systems.

7   CONCLUDING REMARKS

In this introductory chapter we have sought to highlight the key debates and concepts that are central to the evaluation of labour market policy.[6] We have argued that the target-oriented approach advocated in this volume can provide a more fruitful analysis towards helping tackle the growing problems of long-term and structural unemployment in the contemporary labour markets of industrialized societies. Market and policy failures in the past have increased

---

6 We want to thank Christoph Büchtemann who participated in the first phase of conceptualizing the handbook and who contributed substantively to the first drafts of sections 2 to 5.

the need for a more thorough approach to evaluating labour market policy in the future and for the development of a range of policies that can facilitate effective intervention. Despite the breadth and diversity of the topics covered in this volume, we have tried to indicate the key themes that the reader will come across in many of these chapters. The key issues that appear to us to be central to the future of labour market policy and evaluation are the extent to which policy interventions can effectively be coordinated to enhance the flexibility and the functioning of labour markets. Such policies need to increase the opportunities for mobility and transitions within existing labour markets if we are to avoid the prospect that society will become even more segmented and polarized between the socially excluded working poor and the overworked working rich.

One of the key aims of this handbook is to provide an opportunity for those involved in decision-making, implementation and evaluation of labour market policy to look beyond their present concerns with particular programmes. It should allow the reader to reflect and draw on the positive and negative experiences from previous initiatives. It is hoped that such reflection will deepen understanding of how future policy can achieve its targeted goals more successfully than in the past by improving the coordination and cooperation of the actors involved. If the present handbook achieves only half of these goals, it will be a considerable step forward. It is in this spirit that we offer the present volume as a catalyst for future policy formation and evaluation.

REFERENCES

Bator, F. M. (1958), 'The Anatomy of Market Failure', *Quarterly Journal of Economics*, 72, 351–79.

Berk, R. and P. H. Rossi (1990), *Thinking about Program Evaluation*, Newbury Park, CA: Sage.

Bouder, A., J.-P. Cadet and D. Demazière (1994), *Evaluer les effets des dispositifs d'insertion pour les jeunes et les chômeurs de longue durée. Un bilan méthodologique*, Document no. 98 (Série Synthèse), Marseille: Cereq.

Chen, H.-T. (1990), *Theory-driven Evaluations*, Newbury Park, CA: Sage.

de Koning, J. (1991, May), 'Evaluation and Manpower Policy: The State of the Art', paper presented at the MISEP (Mutual Information System on Employment Policies) Meeting, Ryswyk, The Netherlands.

European Commission (1994), *Growth, Competitiveness, Employment*, White Paper (suppl. 6/93 of the Bulletin of the European Communities), Luxembourg: Office of Official Publications of the European Communities.

European Commission (1995), *Employment in Europe 1995*, Luxembourg: Office of Official Publications of the European Communities.

Haveman, R. H. and D. H. Saks (1985), 'Transatlantic Lessons for Employment and Training Policy', *Industrial Relations*, 24, 20–36.

Jensen, K. and P. K. Madsen (eds) (1993), *Measuring Labour Market Measures: Evaluating the Effects of Active Labour Market Policy* (Proceedings from the Danish Presidency Conference), Kolding, Denmark: Ministry of Labour, Denmark.

Kaufmann, F.-X., G. Majone and V. Ostrom (eds) (1986), *Guidance, Control, and Evaluation in the Public Sector*, Berlin: de Gruyter.

Kuhlmann, S. and D. Holland (1995), *Evaluation von Technologiepolitik in Deutschland*, Heidelberg: Physica.

Le Grand, J. (1991), 'The Theory of Government Failure', *British Journal of Political Science*, 21, 423–42.

Ledyard, J. O. (1987), 'Market Failure', in J. Eatwell, M. Milgate and P. Newman (eds), *The New Palgrave: A Dictionary of Economics*, London: The Macmillan Press, Vol. 3, pp. 326–8.

Lindberg, L. N., J. L. Campbell and R. J. Hollingsworth (1991), 'Economic Governance and the Analysis of Structural Change in the American Economy', in J. L. Campbell, R. J. Hollingsworth and L. Lindberg (eds), *Governance of the American Economy*, Cambridge: Cambridge University Press, pp. 3–34.

Manski, C. F. and I. Garfinkel (eds) (1991), *Evaluating Welfare and Training Programs*, Harvard: Harvard University Press.

Mayne, J., M. L. Bemelmans-Videc, J. Hudson and R. Conner (eds) (1992), *Advancing Public Policy Evaluation: Learning from International Experiences*, Amsterdam: North-Holland.

Musgrave, R. A. and P. B. Musgrave (1980), *Public Finance in Theory and Practice*, 3rd ed., New York: McGraw-Hill.

Niskanen, W. W. (1971), *Bureaucracy and Representative Government*, Chicago: Aldinge Atherton.

OECD (1991), *Evaluating Labour Market and Social Programmes: The State of a Complex Art*, Paris: OECD Publications.

OECD (1993), 'Active Labour Market Policies: Assessing Macroeconomic and Microeconomic Effects', in *OECD Employment Outlook 1993*, Paris: OECD Publications, pp. 39–80.

OECD (1994), *The OECD Jobs Study: Evidence and Explanations. Part I: Labour Market Trends and Underlying Forces of Change; Part II: The Adjustment Potential of the Labour Market*, Paris: OECD Publications.

Rose, R. (1990), *Prospective Evaluation through Comparative Analysis: Youth Training in a Time-space Perspective*, Studies no. 182, Glasgow: Centre for the Study of Public Policy.

Scharpf, F. W. (1991), 'Political Institutions, Decision Styles, and Policy Choices', in R. M. Czada and A. Windhoff-Héritier (eds), *Political Choice: Institutions, Rules, and the Limits of Rationality*, Frankfurt on the Main/New York: Campus and Westview, pp. 53–86.

Schmid, G. (1993), 'Equality and Efficiency in the Labor Market: Towards a Socioeconomic Theory of Cooperation in the Globalizing Economy', *The Journal of Socio-Economics*, 22 (1), 31–67.

Schmid, G. and K. Schömann (1994), 'Institutional Choice and Flexible Coordination: A Socio-economic Evaluation of Labour Market Policy in Europe', in G. Schmid (ed.), *Labour Market Institutions in Europe: A Socio-economic Evaluation of Performance*, Armonk, NY: M. E. Sharpe, pp. 9–57.

Simon, H. A. (1982), *The Sciences of the Artificial*, Cambridge, MA: MIT Press.

Spulber, D. F. (1989), *Regulation and Markets*, Cambridge, MA: MIT Press.

Stern, D. and J. M. Ritzen (eds) (1991), *Market Failure in Training*, Berlin: Springer.

Teitz, M. B. (1978, April), 'Evaluating Program Evaluation', *AIP Journal*, 214–18.
Teubner, G. (1985), 'After Legal Instrumentalism? Strategic Models of Post-regulatory Law', in G. Teubner (ed.), *Dilemmas of Law in the Welfare State*, Berlin: de Gruyter, pp. 299–326.
Wholey, J., H. P. Hatry and K. E. Newcomer (eds) (1994), *Handbook of Practical Program Evaluation*, San Francisco: Jossey-Bass.
Wilensky, H. (1985), 'Nothing Fails Like Success: The Evaluation-research Industry and Labor Market Policy', *Industrial Relations*, 24 (1), 1–19.
Wolf, C., Jr. (1987), *Markets or Governments? Choosing between Imperfect Alternatives*, Cambridge, MA: MIT Press.

PART I

Methodology of Labour Market Policy Evaluation

2. Experimental and Nonexperimental Evaluation

James J. Heckman and Jeffrey A. Smith

In an era of tight government budgets, credible evaluations of active labour market policies are important. Yet, much controversy surrounds evaluation research. Two points of view dominate the literature. Some analysts view social experimentation as the only valid evaluation method. Others recognize both the value and the limitations of social experiments. They advocate a more balanced approach that builds on recent advances in nonexperimental evaluation methodology.

This chapter states the evaluation problem and discusses controversies in the literature. We describe how social experiments solve certain forms of the evaluation problem and note that social experiments cannot answer many evaluation questions of interest. We then discuss both parametric and nonparametric nonexperimental evaluation methods. These methods utilize existing theoretical and empirical knowledge about the determinants of programme participation decisions and of outcomes such as earnings and employment.

In the final sections of the chapter, we briefly address other important issues. First, we consider the problem of choosing among alternative nonexperimental methods in a given context. The multiplicity of nonexperimental evaluation techniques in the literature is sometimes cited as an argument in favour of social experiments. We review the evidence for the claim that it is difficult or impossible to choose among alternative methods. We find that the evidence is weaker than is commonly believed. Second, we briefly consider the difficulties of evaluating programmes which affect nonparticipants or whose effects on participants depend on the size or composition of the participant population. The chapter concludes with a summary of our main points.

1 STATEMENT OF THE EVALUATION PROBLEM

1.1 Context

To make our discussion more concrete, we use the Job Training Partnership Act (JTPA) in the United States as an example of a 'typical' training programme.[1] The JTPA programme is very similar to programmes in Canada and in Europe that offer employment and training services to unemployed or reentrant workers. Like these programmes, the JTPA programme offers a menu of employment and training services, including remedial training in basic skills, classroom training in vocational skills, job search assistance and wage subsidies combined with on-the-job training at private firms. Participation in JTPA is voluntary, and applicants are screened by programme bureaucrats.

1.2   The Questions of Interest in Evaluating a Social Programme

There are many interesting evaluation questions. In the context of a training programme, the question that receives the most attention is the effect of training on the trained:

Q-1:   'What is the effect of training on the trained?' That is, how do their labour market outcomes change relative to what would have occurred in the absence of training?

This is the bottom line stressed in many evaluations. When the costs of the programme are subtracted from the answer to *Q-1*, and returns are appropriately discounted, the net benefit of the programme is produced for a fixed group of trainees. A second question is:

Q-2:   'What is the effect of training on randomly selected members of the population?'

This question is frequently confused with the first. Answers to this question are of interest if participation in an existing voluntary programme were to be made mandatory (assuming no general equilibrium effects). Other questions of interest are:

Q-3:   'What are the effects of subsidies, advertising, local labour market conditions, family income, race and sex on application decisions?'

Q-4:   'What are the effects of centre performance standards and local labour market conditions on training centre decisions to accept particular applicants and to offer them particular employment and training services?'

---

1 The JTPA programme and its recent experimental evaluation are described in Doolittle and Traeger (1990) and Bloom, Orr, Cave, Bell and Doolittle (1993).

Q-5:   'What are the effects of family income, race, sex and local labour market conditions on individual decisions to drop out from the programme and on the length of time taken to complete the programme?'

Q-6:   'What are the effects of labour market conditions and so forth on trainee employment rates and average wage rates following completion of the programme?'

and

Q-7:   'What is the cost of training a worker in the various possible ways?'

To focus on the essential features of the evaluation problem, we concentrate on only a few of the questions just listed. In particular, we restrict our attention to questions *Q-1* and *Q-2* and a combination of questions *Q-3* and *Q-4*:

Q-3':   'What are the effects of the variables listed in Q-3 and Q-4 on the application and enrolment decisions of individuals and training centres?'

To simplify the analysis, we assume throughout this chapter that there is only one type of treatment administered by the programme so that determining assignment to treatment is not an issue. We assume that there is no attrition from the programme and that the length of participation in the programme is fixed. These assumptions would be true if, for example, the programme occurs at an instant in time and gives every participant the same training, although the response to the training may differ across persons.

1.3   The Structural Approach

Structural approaches to solving the evaluation problem define models of the programme participation and outcome processes which, in principle, predict responses to programmes which have never existed. The structural approach is well illustrated by the early work on estimating labour supply responses to negative income tax (NIT) programmes. Such programmes operate by changing the after-tax wage rate and income level of participants. Under the neoclassical theory of labour supply, if one can determine the response of labour supply to changes in after-tax wages and income levels—the 'substitution' and 'income' effects, respectively—one can determine who would participate in a programme. From a common set of behavioural parameters one can simulate the labour supply effects of all possible NIT programmes.[2]

Early advocates of social experiments sought to design experiments that would produce the maximum possible independent variation in after-tax wage

---

2 See Ashenfelter (1983).

rates and income levels across sample members so that precise estimates of wage and income effects could be obtained. Cain and Watts (1974) argued that in the cross-section data available to them, wages and income were sufficiently highly correlated, and the variability in incomes was sufficiently small, that it was difficult, if not impossible, to separately estimate wage and income effects on labour supply. The variation induced in the data through careful experimentation enables analysts to obtain precise estimates of wage and income effects.

The structural approach is very appealing. It focusses on developing interpretable models of responses to programmes. It describes diverse programmes in a common framework and provides a common language for the synthesis of social scientific knowledge. Use of the structural approach in evaluation research forces evaluators to consider the behavioural implications of the estimators used and enables them to draw on social scientific knowledge when defending estimates. The structural approach provides an evaluation framework within which knowledge can accumulate across successive evaluations.

Although we draw on economic models to motivate and justify identifying assumptions, we do not dwell at length on the specifics of structural estimation, because the standard structural approach is based on parameters which are often different from the ones used by evaluators to answer the questions posed above. We return to this point later in the chapter. The difference between standard structural parameters and commonly used evaluation parameters is a source of great confusion in the literature. Many of the commonly used evaluation parameters are not structural parameters in the conventional usage of that term. Cumulating knowledge across studies with these parameters is more difficult; a point we develop further below.

1.4   The Evaluation Problem and a Model of Programme Evaluation

The essence of the evaluation problem is that the same person cannot be in two or more different labour market states at the same time. In the training context, for each trainee, there is a hypothetical (or counterfactual) state that consists of what he or she would have done without training. For each nontrainee, there is the hypothetical state of being a trainee. Define a variable D that equals 1 if a person participates in a programme and equals 0 otherwise. If a person participates, he or she receives outcome Y_1; otherwise he or she receives Y_0. Thus,

$$Y = Y_1 \quad \text{if} \quad D = 1 \tag{2.1}$$

$$Y = Y_0 \quad \text{if} \quad D = 0 .$$

Let Y_1 and Y_0 be determined by X. One way to define this relationship is through the mathematical operation of taking conditional expectations, with

$E(Y_1 | X) = g_1(X)$ and $E(Y_0 | X) = g_0(X)$. Presumably, X includes relevant aspects of the training received by trainees as well as background and local labour market variables. Adopting a linear specification, we write

$$E(Y_1 | X) = g_1(X) = X\beta_1 \tag{2.2a}$$

$$E(Y_0 | X) = g_0(X) = X\beta_0. \tag{2.2b}$$

If X exhausts all of the causes of Y_1 and Y_0, then the conditional expectations equal the values of Y_1 and Y_0, so that $Y_1 = E(Y_1 \frac{1}{2} X)$ and $Y_0 = E(Y_0 \frac{1}{2} X)$.

There are other ways to define the relationship between X and Y, such as postulating a simultaneous equations model that defines a deterministic relationship between Y_j and X, $j = 0,1$. In this model, $Y_j = g_j(X) + U_j$ where U_j is a 'shock'. For most of this chapter we assume $E(U_j | X) = 0$, so that $E(Y_j | X) = g(X)$.

Let Z denote variables determining programme participation. These variables characterize individual, family or institutional factors which operate to determine programme participation. Formally,

$$Z \in \Psi, D = 1; \quad Z \notin \Psi, D = 0, \tag{2.3}$$

where Ψ is a subset of the possible Z values. That is, if persons have characteristics that lie in set Ψ, they participate in the programme; otherwise they do not. In order to economize on symbols, we represent the entire collection of explanatory variables by $C = (X, Z)$, where X and Z may share variables in common. If one could observe all of the components of C for each person in a sample, and if $U_1 \equiv 0$, and $U_0 \equiv 0$, so that $Y_1 = g_1(X)$ and $Y_0 = g_0(X)$, one might still not be able to determine g_1, g_0 and Ψ. The available samples might not contain sufficient variation in the components of these vectors to determine g_0, g_1 or to identify Ψ.

Assuming no unobserved variables, and assuming sufficient variability in the sample components of the explanatory variables, one can utilize data on participants to determine g_1, data on nonparticipants to determine g_0, and on the combined sample to determine Ψ. It would thus be possible to construct Y_1 and Y_0 for each person and to estimate the gross gain to participation for each person in the sample. With knowledge of g_0, g_1 and Ψ, one can fully answer evaluation questions Q-1, Q-2 and Q-3' for each person in the available samples.[3]

As a practical matter, analysts do not observe all of the components of C. We know this because we can never predict Y_1 or Y_0 perfectly, nor can we

---

3 It is assumed in this statement that the support of the X and Z variables in the sample covers the support of these variables in the target populations of interest.

perfectly predict the value of D. The unobserved components of these outcome and participation functions are a major source of evaluation problems. It is these missing components that motivate treating Y_1, Y_0 and D as random variables, conditional on the available information. This intrinsic randomness rules out a strategy of determining Y_1 and Y_0 for each person. Instead, a statistical approach is adopted that focusses on estimating the joint distribution of Y_1, Y_0 and D conditional on the available information or some features of it.

Let subscript 'a' denote available information. Thus, C_a contains the variables available to the analyst that determine Y_1, Y_0 and D. These variables may include components of C as well as proxies for the missing components. The joint distribution of Y_1, Y_0, D, given $C_a = c_a$, is

$$F(y_0, y_1, d \mid c_a) = Pr(Y_0 \le y_0, Y_1 \le y_1, D = d \mid C_a = c_a) \quad (2.4)$$

where we follow convention by denoting random variables by upper-case letters and their realizations by lower-case letters. If (2.4) can be determined, and the distribution of C_a is known, it is possible to answer questions Q-1, Q-2 and Q-$3'$ in the following sense: one can determine population distributions of Y_0, Y_1 and the population distribution of the gross gain from programme participation, $\Delta = Y_1 - Y_0$, and one can determine the probability of the event $D = 1$ given C_a. Determining the joint distribution (2.4) is a difficult problem even from ideal experimental data. This is so because even in an experiment one cannot observe both Y_1 and Y_0 for anyone.

1.5   The Parameters of Interest in Programme Evaluation

Question Q-1 can be answered for the population, but not for the individual, if the joint distribution of potential outcomes, $F(y_0, y_1 \mid D = 1, c_a)$, is known for participants. From this, one can determine the distribution of impacts, $\Delta = Y_1 - Y_0$, given by $F(\Delta \mid D = 1, c_a)$. One can answer Q-2 for the population using the distribution of potential outcomes for all persons, $F(y_0, y_1 \mid c_a)$, which can be produced from (2.4) and the distribution of the explanatory variables by elementary probability operations. In this sense one can determine the gains from randomly moving a person from one distribution, $F(y_0 \mid c_a)$, to another, $F(y_1 \mid c_a)$. The answer to Q-$3'$ can be achieved by computing the probability of participation, $Pr(D = 1 \mid c_a)$, from (2.4).

Much of the evaluation literature defines the answer to Q-1 in terms of means of the outcome variables as

$$E(\Delta \mid D = 1, c_a) = E(Y_1 - Y_0 \mid D = 1, c_a) \quad (2.5)$$

and the answer to Q-2 as

$$E\left(\Delta \mid c_a\right) = E\left(Y_1 - Y_0 \mid c_a\right). \tag{2.6}$$

Despite the attention given to mean impacts in the evaluation literature, medians or other quantiles of the impact distributions $F\left(\Delta \mid D = 1, c_a\right)$ and $F\left(\Delta \mid c_a\right)$ are often of greater interest. In addition to mean impacts, when evaluating a social programme, it is of interest to know

(a) the proportion of participants who benefit from the programme: $Pr\left(Y_1 > Y_0 \mid D = 1\right)$;
(b) selected quantiles of the impact distribution for participants $\inf_\Delta \{\Delta: F\left(\Delta \mid D = 1\right) \geq q\}$, where q is a quantile of the impact distribution;
(c) the distribution of impacts for participants at selected points in the non-participation outcome distribution, $F\left(\Delta \mid D = 1, Y_0 = y_0\right)$;
(d) the expected value of the maximum of the two outcomes: $E\left[\max\left(Y_1, Y_0\right)\right]$.

These parameters all require knowledge of the joint distribution of $\left(Y_1, Y_0\right)$. Object (a) is of interest if one seeks to know how widespread the benefits of programme participation are, and object (b) is of interest if one seeks to learn the impacts for those who benefit the most (and the least) from participation. Object (c) is of interest if one seeks to determine how the distribution of gains depends on outcomes in the base, nonparticipation state. Object (d) is of interest if agents can choose between offers of Y_1 and Y_0, as in the case of a programme offering job subsidies where trainees also have an unsubsidized option. In this case, $E\left[\max\left(Y_1, Y_0\right)\right] - E\left(Y_0\right)$ is one definition of the option value created by the programme. (See Clements, Heckman and Smith (in press), who define and estimate several option values for the JTPA programme.)

Even if the mean impacts in (2.5) or (2.6) are zero, it is of interest to know what fraction of participants or of the population benefits from a programme. Knowledge of $F\left(\Delta \mid D = 1, c_a\right)$ is required to compute the first probability, which equals $Pr\left(\Delta > 0 \mid D = 1, c_a\right)$. In order to ascertain the existence of 'cream skimming', defined as training centres selecting the best people into a programme (those with high values of Y_0 and Y_1), it is necessary to know the correlation or stochastic dependence between Y_1 and Y_0. This requires knowledge of features of the joint distributions $F\left(y_1, y_0 \mid D = 1, c_a\right)$ and $F\left(y_1, y_0 \mid c_a\right)$.[4]

---

4 See Clements et al. (in press).

1.6   Selection Bias

The problem that Y_0 is missing for persons for whom Y_1 is observed motivates using outcomes for nonparticipants to infer what outcomes would have been for participants if they had not participated. The data routinely produced from the administrative records of social programmes and from ordinary nonexperimental comparison groups enable analysts to determine $F(y_1 \mid D = 1, c_a)$, the distribution of participant outcomes, and $F(y_0 \mid D = 0, c_a)$, the distribution of nonparticipant outcomes. The data available from programme records are sometimes sufficiently rich to determine $Pr(D = 1 \mid c_a)$, the probability of participation. But unless further information is available, or behavioural assumptions are invoked, these pieces of information do not suffice to determine (2.4) or even (2.5).

In general, for the same values of $C_a = c_a$, the distribution of outcomes that programme participants would have experienced had they not participated is not the same as the distribution of outcomes for nonparticipants. Thus,

$$F(y_0 \mid D = 1, c_a) \neq F(y_0 \mid D = 0, c_a) \quad \text{and}$$
$$F(y_1 \mid D = 1, c_a) \neq F(y_1 \mid D = 0, c_a),$$

(2.7)

which gives rise to the problem of selection bias in the outcome distributions. The more conventional statement of the selection problem is in terms of means:

$$E(\Delta \mid D = 1, c_a) \neq E(Y_1 \mid D = 1, c_a) - E(Y_0 \mid D = 0, c_a). \quad (2.8)$$

Put simply, persons who participate in a programme are different from persons who do not participate in the sense that the mean outcomes of participants in the nonparticipation state would be different from those of nonparticipants even after adjusting for C_a. For example, participants may be more motivated than otherwise similar nonparticipants. If motivation increases earnings as well as affecting participation, then participants would earn more than otherwise similar nonparticipants, even if they did not participate. Failure to control for this difference in an evaluation would lead the higher incomes of those with greater motivation to be incorrectly attributed to their participation in the programme.

A host of alternative methods has been proposed for solving the selection problem either for means or for entire distributions. Heckman (1990a, 1990b), Heckman and Honoré (1990) and Heckman and Robb (1985, 1986a, 1986b) offer alternative comprehensive treatments of the various nonexperimental approaches to this problem in econometrics and statistics. Heckman (1992) and Heckman and Smith (1993, 1995a) summarize the experimental approach. Regardless of whether experimental or nonexperimental methods are used, some untestable a priori assumptions must be invoked to recover the missing components of the distributions. All solutions to the evaluation problem rely on assumptions. Constructing counterfactuals usually generates controversy, because analysts often do not agree about what constitutes satisfactory assumptions. In sections 2 and 3 we discuss alternative sets of assumptions that underlie the experimental and nonexperimental evaluation approaches.

2   EXPERIMENTAL EVALUATION METHODS

2.1   How Experiments Solve the Evaluation Problem

The case for randomized social experiments is almost always stated within the context of obtaining answers to questions *Q-1* and *Q-2*.[5] From this vantage point, the participation equation that answers *Q-3′* is a 'nuisance function' that may give rise to a selection problem. Randomization makes participation statistically independent of (Y_1, Y_0, C) conditional on participation status for the subpopulation of persons who participate in the programme in the presence of random assignment. To simplify the notation we drop the 'a' subscript on C for the remainder of the chapter, leaving it implicit.

To state the case for randomization most clearly, it is useful to introduce two new variables. The first, D^*, is an analogue to the variable D previously defined, but indicates application to and acceptance into the programme in the presence of random assignment. Let $D^* = 1$ if a person would seek to participate in the programme in the presence of randomization; $D^* = 0$ otherwise. The second new variable, R, indicates randomization into the experimental treatment group conditional on $D^* = 1$. Let $R = 1$ if a person is randomized into the treatment group and $R = 0$ otherwise, where we assume that everyone randomized into the experimental treatment group participates in the programme. The probability that $R = 1$ given $D^* = 1$ is denoted by p, where we set $p = 1$ when there is no randomization.

D and D^* need not be the same if randomization affects participation decisions. In the standard approach to social experiments, randomization is implemented at the stage where D^* is revealed. Given $D^* = 1$, R is constructed to be independent of (Y_0, Y_1, C). Randomization does not produce Y_1 and Y_0 for the same person, and so in this sense does not solve the evaluation problem.

---

5 An important exception is the small literature on using experiments to estimate the effect of marginal changes in the scale of a programme. See Björklund (1988), Björklund and Moffitt (1987), Heckman and Smith (1995b) and chap. 3 of this handbook.

Proponents of randomization implicitly invoke the assumption that

$$Pr(D = 1 \mid c) = Pr(D^* = 1 \mid c, p) \qquad \text{(AS-2.1)}$$

for some p, or assume that it is 'practically' true, so that randomization does not alter the probability that persons seek admission to the programme. If this assumption is not true, the characteristics of participants under randomization differ from the characteristics without randomization. There are many reasons to suspect the validity of assumption (AS-2.1). When it fails to hold, experimental data estimate $E(\Delta \mid D^* = 1, c)$ rather than $E(\Delta \mid D = 1, c)$. Only if randomization is a permanent feature of the programme being evaluated is the former parameter of policy interest. If randomization affects the participation process, then these two parameters may differ substantially.

In addition, defining the outcomes in the presence of randomization as (Y_0^*, Y_1^*), experiments require the assumption that the outcome distributions are the same in the randomized and nonrandomized regimes. That is, they require the assumption that, for $(y_1^*, y_0^*) = (y_1, y_0)$,

$$F(y_1^*, y_0^*, c \mid D^* = 1) = F(y_1, y_0, c \mid D = 1). \qquad \text{(AS-2.2)}$$

Failures of (AS-2.1) or (AS-2.2) lead to randomization bias in the parameter estimates. We discuss this issue in more detail below.

If (AS-2.1) and (AS-2.2) are true, so that there is no randomization bias, then

$$F(y_1, c \mid D^* = 1, R = 1) \qquad \text{(2.9a)}$$
$$= F(y_1, c \mid D^* = 1) = F(y_1, c \mid D = 1),$$

$$F(y_0, c \mid D^* = 1, R = 0) \qquad \text{(2.9b)}$$
$$= F(y_0, c \mid D^* = 1) = F(y_0, c \mid D = 1),$$

and

$$E(Y_1 \mid R = 1) - E(Y_0 \mid R = 0) = E(\Delta \mid D = 1). \qquad \text{(2.10)}$$

Social experiments 'solve' the evaluation problem by using random assignment of would-be participants to directly obtain the missing counterfactual distribution, $F(y_0, c \mid D = 1)$. Simple mean difference estimates constructed through the use of participants and randomized-out nonparticipants answer question *Q-1* stated in terms of means, because the distribution of explanatory variables C is the same for participants and nonparticipants in samples conditioned on R. In this sense, randomized data are ideal. People untrained in statistics, such as politicians and programme administrators, understand means, and no elaborate statistical adjustments or functional form assumptions are imposed on the data.

Furthermore, (2.10) may be true even if (AS-2.1) and (AS-2.2) are false. This case holds for the widely used dummy endogenous variable model of Heckman (1978). For that case

$$Y_1 \equiv \alpha + Y_0, \tag{2.11}$$

where α is a fixed constant assumed to be the same for everyone and unaffected by random assignment. This model is termed the 'fixed treatment effect for all units model' in the statistics literature. In terms of the linear regression model, we may write (2.11) as $X\beta_1 = \alpha + X\beta_0$. Even if (AS-2.1) and (AS-2.2) are false, (2.10) is true because the effect of participation is the same for everyone, so it does not matter if the set of persons participating in the programme is different in the presence of random assignment than it would be in its absence. The dummy endogenous variable model is widely used in applied work. It is also common to parameterize α as a function of X, for example, $\alpha(X) = \phi'X$. Questions *Q-1* and *Q-2* have the same answer in these models, and randomization provides convincing answers to it.

The requirement of treatment effect homogeneity (the same α for everyone) can be weakened, and (2.10) can still be justified even if assumptions (AS-2.1) and (AS-2.2) are false. Suppose that there is a random response model, sometimes called a random coefficient model, such that

$$Y_1 = Y_0 + (\alpha + \varphi), \tag{2.12a}$$

where φ is an individual's idiosyncratic response to treatment after taking out a common response α and

$$E(\varphi \mid D^* = 1) = 0. \tag{2.12b}$$

Then (2.10) remains true if potential trainees and training centres do not know φ prior to enrolment and so use α in place of $\alpha + \varphi$ in making programme participation decisions. In this special case, even if responses to treatments are heterogeneous, the simple mean-difference estimator that uses the experimental data still answers the mean-difference version of *Q-1*. If regressors are present in the model for potential outcomes, then 2.12b must be augmented to include them in the conditions set. We show in section 3.4 that this special case is also required to apply the method of instrumental variables in a nonexperimental evaluation context.

2.2   Limitations on Random Assignment

There are a number of important limitations to social experiments. Heckman and Smith (1993, 1995a) and Burtless (1993, 1995) provide general discussions of the value of social experiments. In the remainder of section 2 we focus in detail on three types of limitations: randomization bias, substitution bias and the failure of experimental data to identify parameters that depend on the joint distribution of outcomes conditional on $D = 1$.

A number of other limitations of social experiments are discussed elsewhere. Heckman and Smith (1993, 1995a) discuss the role of institutional limitations in preventing the optimal timing of random assignment within the programme participation process. Burtless and Orr (1986) discuss ethical objections to random assignment, and Torp, Rauum, Hernaes and Goldstein (1993) describe how hostile bureaucrats undermined an experimental evaluation in Norway. Bloom (1984) and Heckman, Smith and Taber (1994) consider the problem of experimental treatment group members who drop out of the programme being evaluated, and therefore receive no treatment or only partial treatment.

Finally, we note that in addition to questions *Q-1* and *Q-2*, policy-makers also care about the answers to questions like those in *Q-3* to *Q-7* defined earlier.[6] Some of these questions might in principle be evaluated through random assignment designs, but practical difficulties would make it impossible in most cases. For example, while subsidies for programme entry or completion could in principle be randomly assigned, family background variables and local labour market conditions cannot be. Since experiments can answer only a subset of the questions of interest to evaluators, it remains important to build up the stock of basic social science knowledge required to successfully utilize nonexperimental methods both by themselves and as a tool for more extensive analyses of experimental data.

2.3   Randomization Bias

Assumptions (AS-2.1) and (AS-2.2) are entirely natural in the context of agricultural and biological experimentation, for which the Fisher model of randomized experiments was originally developed. However, the Fisher model is a misleading paradigm for social science. Humans act purposively, and their behaviour is altered by introducing randomization into their choice environment.[7]

---

6 See Moffitt (1992) for a discussion of the limitations of experiments in estimating programme entry effects.

7 Kramer and Shapiro (1984) show that randomization also creates controversy in clinical trials in medicine, which is sometimes held up as a paragon for social science (Ashenfelter and Card, 1985).

If individuals who might have enrolled in a nonrandomized regime make plans anticipating enrolment in training, adding uncertainty at the acceptance stage may alter their decision to apply or to undertake activities complementary to training. Risk-averse persons will tend to be eliminated from the programme. If training centres must randomize after a screening process, they may have to screen more persons in order to reach their performance goals. This could result in lowered trainee quality.

A recent report written by the Manpower Demonstration Research Corporation (MDRC) (Doolittle and Traeger, 1990), based on the authors' experience in implementing the recent experimental evaluation of JTPA, provides suggestive evidence on the practical importance of randomization bias. The participation of individual JTPA job-training centres in the experiment was not compulsory. In attempting to enrol geographically dispersed sites, MDRC experienced a training centre refusal rate in excess of 90 per cent. Doolittle and Traeger (1990) report that centres expressed major fears that the need to fill a control group while holding constant the number of persons served would force them to set lower standards for acceptance into the programme. A lowering of the quality of programme participants could impede centre performance and thereby reduce the incentive payments they receive based on the labour market outcomes of their trainees under the JTPA performance standards system. These types of administrative changes in response to randomization are an important source of randomization bias. The MDRC analysts concluded that (Doolittle and Traeger, 1990):

> Implementing a complex random assignment research design in an ongoing program providing a variety of services does inevitably change its operation in some ways ...The most likely difference arising from a random assignment field study of program impacts ... is a change in the mix of clients served. Expanded recruitment efforts needed to generate the control group draw in additional applicants who are not identical to the people previously served (p. 121).

The evidence suggests that randomization bias is not just a theoretical issue. Instead, it is an empirically important problem that is often ignored by advocates of social experimentation.

2.4   Substitution Bias

Substitution bias arises when members of an experimental control group gain access to close substitutes for the experimental treatment, such as similar services offered by other providers or the same service offered under different funding arrangements. This situation often arises in clinical trials when human subjects recognize that they have been denied treatment and attempt to obtain it elsewhere. In the presence of substitution bias, control group outcomes no longer correspond to the untreated state.

To see this, consider the following simple example. Suppose that half of the participants in some programme would gain $10 000 from receiving training, while the other half would gain only $100. Participants learn their type after acceptance into the programme but prior to receipt of training. Suppose further that the programme consists of a subsidy that reduces the effective price of training from $200 to zero. In an experimental setting, everyone in the treatment group would take training, but in the control group only those who would gain $10 000 would take training. For the remainder of the control group, the $200 cost would exceed the $100 benefit. The experimental mean impact estimate (excluding costs) would be $50. In contrast, if no one in the control group took training, the unbiased experimental impact estimate would be $5050. The $5000 difference between the two estimates represents the substitution bias that arises because half of the control group receives the training being evaluated.

The potential empirical importance of substitution bias is demonstrated by the evidence from the JTPA evaluation presented in Heckman, Hohmann, Khoo and Smith (1995). Administrative records indicate that 65 per cent of those in the treatment group actually received treatment in the 18 months following random assignment. However, according to the self-reports of the treatment group members, only 48 per cent received treatment during this period. Meanwhile, 32 per cent of the control group members self-reported receiving training from other sources over the same interval. Among eligible persons not participating in JTPA surveyed at four of the experimental sites, 15 to 24 per cent reported receiving training over a similar time period. These figures indicate that a substantial fraction of the control group received training during the period of the experiment. With the eligible non-participants serving as a benchmark, controls received training at a level well in excess of that normally observed in the low-income population eligible for JTPA.

The problem of substitution bias is not unique to the JTPA experiment. Many previous evaluations have encountered the same problems. For example, MDRC's evaluation of the Career Beginnings programme noted the availability of many close substitutes (Cave and Quint, 1991, pp. 36–51). Abt's study of the Food Stamp Employment and Training Program also encountered serious problems with substitution bias (Puma, Burstein, Merrell and Silverstein, 1990). Persons randomized out of programmes can often find good substitutes for them. An informative experimental evaluation must account for choices among the substitutes and the content of the substitutes. That is, in the presence of substitution bias, it is necessary to perform a complementary non-experimental analysis.

2.5   Bounding the Parameters That Can Only Be Identified from the Joint Distribution of Outcomes

Ideal experiments produce the marginal outcome distributions, $F(y_1 \mid D = 1)$ and $F(y_0 \mid D = 1)$, but not the joint distribution of outcomes, $F(y_1, y_0 \mid D = 1)$. These marginal distributions are sufficient to identify a number of parameters of interest, including the mean impact of treatment. Identification of many other parameters of interest requires knowledge of the joint distribution.

The problem of bounding the joint distribution $F(y_1, y_0 \mid D = 1)$ from the marginal distributions $F(y_1 \mid D = 1)$ and $F(y_0 \mid D = 1)$ is a classic problem in mathematical statistics. Hoeffding (1940) and Frechet (1951) demonstrate that the joint distribution is bounded by two functions of the marginal distributions which can be determined from experimental data, so that

$$Max\ [F(y_1 \mid D = 1) + F(y_0 \mid D = 1) - 1,\ 0] \leq F(y_1, y_0 \mid D = 1) \quad (2.13)$$

$$F(y_1, y_0 \mid D = 1) \leq Min\ [F(y_1 \mid D = 1),\ F(y_0 \mid D = 1)].$$

These bounds are often very far apart in practical applications. For simplicity, consider the case in which the outcome variable is discrete, such as employment. Those who are randomized into a programme may be employed, E, or not employed, N, after completing it. Those who are randomized out of a programme may also be employed or not employed in the evaluation period. The latent distribution underlying this situation is a bivariate binomial. Let (Y_1, Y_0) denote the outcomes in the two states, where $Y_1, Y_0 \in \{E, N\}$. The probabilities associated with the four possible outcome pairs are denoted by P_{EE}, P_{EN}, P_{NE} and P_{NN}, respectively.

How wide are the ranges implied by the Frechet–Hoeffding bounds in the discrete case? Clements et al. (in press) calculate these ranges using data from the JTPA experiment and find them to be very wide. Even without taking sampling error into account, the experimental evidence for adult males is consistent with P_{EN} (the fraction employed with treatment but not employed without it), ranging from 0.01 to 0.29.[8] The range for P_{NE} (the fraction not employed if treated but employed without treatment) is equally large. As many as 28 per cent and as few as zero per cent may have had their employment prospects diminished by participating in the programme. The two probabilities are not independent. Because the mean impact T is known, and $T = P_{EN} - P_{NE}$, high values of P_{EN} are associated with high values of P_{NE}.

---

8 Employment is defined as positive self-reported earnings in the 16th, 17th or 18th month after random assignment.

From this evidence we cannot distinguish between two stories: that the JTPA programme benefits many people by facilitating their employment but also harms many people by making them less likely to work than if they had not participated, or that the programme benefits and harms only a small fraction of those it serves.

Similarly wide bounds emerge from an examination of the earnings data produced by the JTPA experiment. For adult men, the correlation between earnings (over the full 18 months after random assignment) in the treatment and control states is bounded between -0.79 and 1.00, and the standard deviation of the impact of the programme (defined as the difference in earnings between the treatment and control states) is bounded between \$821 and \$21 857. For all four demographic groups, this important parameter is bounded away from zero, indicating that the data are inconsistent with a model of equal programme impacts across persons. These findings reveal the extent to which experimental data, unaided by prior information or additional assumptions, fail to provide precise estimates of many evaluation parameters of interest. Only if the evaluation problem is defined exclusively in terms of means can it be said that experiments provide a precise answer. Clements et al. (in press) present methods for incorporating prior information into the analysis of experimental data to reduce the uncertainty inherent in them.

3   NONEXPERIMENTAL EVALUATION METHODS

3.1   How Nonexperimental Methods Solve the Evaluation Problem

For the reasons just discussed, social scientists rarely, if ever, have access to true experimental data of the type sometimes available to laboratory scientists. The inability to use laboratory methods to independently vary treatments and thereby to eliminate or isolate spurious channels of causation places a fundamental limitation on the possibility of objective knowledge in the social sciences. In place of laboratory experimental variation, social scientists often use subjective thought experiments, in which assumptions replace the missing data.

Because minimal identifying assumptions cannot be tested with data (all possible sets of minimal identifying assumptions for a model explain the observed data equally well, at least in large samples) and because empirical estimates of causal relationships are sensitive to these assumptions, there is inevitably scope for disagreement in the causal interpretation of social science data. Context, beliefs and a priori theory resolve differences in causal interpretation (see Simon, 1957, for an early statement of this view). The problem of selection bias in the analysis of social science data is a special case of the general problem of causal inference in the social sciences. This section considers alternative assumptions that have been invoked to solve the problem of causal inference created by selection bias. We consider the plausibility of these assumptions in the context of well-formulated models of the impact of training on earnings. We present assumptions required to use two types of widely available data to solve the problem of estimating the impact of training on earnings free of selection bias: (1) a single cross-section of post-training earnings and (2) longitudinal data in which the same individuals are followed over time.[9]

We find that different and not necessarily more plausible assumptions can be invoked in longitudinal analyses than in cross-section analyses. The fact that more types of minimal identifying assumptions can be invoked with longitudinal data (because longitudinal data also can be used as a cross-section or a repeated cross-section) does not increase the plausibility of those assumptions that uniquely exploit longitudinal data.

In analysing the assumptions required to use various data sources to consistently estimate the impact of training on earnings free of selection bias, we focus in particular on how much prior information must be assumed about the earnings function and about the decision rule governing participation. We demonstrate that unless explicit distributional assumptions are invoked, all cross-section estimators require the presence of at least one regressor variable in the decision rule that determines participation in training that does not directly appear in the outcome equation. This requirement may seem innocuous, but it rules out a completely nonparametric cross-section approach. Without prior information, it is not possible to cross-classify observations on the basis of values assumed by explanatory variables in the earnings function and to do 'regressor-free' estimation of the impact of training on earnings that is free of selection bias. In contrast, longitudinal and repeated cross-section estimators do not require exclusion restrictions because they postulate that the observable and unobservable factors influencing outcomes are additively separable, and they make assumptions about the time-series properties of the unobservables. The assumption of additive separability is intrinsic to longitudinal methods whereas it is not intrinsic to most cross-sectional methods.

We consider in detail only the basic approaches for eliminating selection bias in nonexperimental evaluations. The vast majority of the applied literature relies on these basic approaches. They provide a simple context within which to discuss the important concepts. We focus on identification because the current literature in social science and statistics is unclear on this issue. Our focus on identification and on the tradeoffs in assumptions that secure identifi-

---

9 Heckman and Robb (1985, 1986a) provide a thorough discussion of methods for repeated cross-section data.

cation should make clear that we do not believe that there is a nostrum for selection bias that 'works' in all cases. In our view, the literature on selection bias and programme evaluation methods has been marred by analysts who claim to offer context-free universal cures for the selection problem, which are usually based on strong implicit behavioural assumptions.

Previous work on selection bias has often imposed unnecessarily strong assumptions, such as normality (see e.g. Little and Rubin (1987), who 'solve' missing data problems by invoking arbitrary normality assumptions). These strong assumptions were frequent targets in the criticism directed against the early work on econometric selection models (see e.g. the commentary on Heckman and Robb (1986b) in the Wainer (1985) volume). Part of the great variability in estimates obtained in some analyses using selection-bias procedures may be due to the imposition of different types of extra conditions not required to identify the parameters of interest. Real progress has been made in relaxing the strong distributional and functional form assumptions maintained in the earlier literature on controlling for sample selection bias. Examples from the large recent theoretical literature on semiparametric and nonparametric estimation include Andrews (1991), Cosslett (1991), Heckman, Ichimura, Smith and Todd (1995a, 1995b), Heckman, Ichimura and Todd (1995a, b), Ichimura and Lee (1991), Powell (1989, 1995) and the overviews in Heckman (1990a, 1990b, 1993). Newey, Powell and Walker (1990) provide an example of the application of some of these methods. Separating out essential from inessential assumptions is a primary goal of this section.

3.2   Notation and a Model of Programme Participation

To focus on the essential aspects of the econometric approach to the evaluation problem, assume that individuals experience only one opportunity to participate in training. This opportunity occurs in period k. Training takes a single period for participants to complete. During training, participants have zero earnings. We assume that earnings constitute the outcome measure of interest.

Denote the latent earnings of individual i in period t by Y_{0t} where the i subscript is suppressed to avoid clutter. Latent earnings are the earnings of the individual in the absence of training and correspond to Y_0 in the notation of section 2. Latent earnings depend on a vector of observed characteristics X_t.

In each period $t > k$, a person has a pair of latent outcomes (Y_{0t}, Y_{1t}) corresponding to the treated and untreated states. Using the representations of equations (2.2a) and (2.2b),

$$Y_{0t} = g_0(X_t) + U_{0t} \tag{2.14a}$$

$$Y_{1t} = g_1(X_t) + U_{1t} \tag{2.14b}$$

for $t > k$, and $Y_{0t} = g_0(X_{0t}) + U_{0t}$ for $t < k$. One interpretation of (2.14a) and (2.14b) is that g_0 and g_1 are conditional expectations, so that $E(Y_{0t} \mid X_t) = g_0(X_t)$ and $E(Y_{1t} \mid X_t) = g_1(X_t)$. Another interpretation of equations (2.14a) and (2.14b) is that they are functional relationships combining observed variables X_t and unobserved (by the analyst) random variables (U_{0t}, U_{1t}) to produce measured outcomes. This is the classical interpretation as in, for example, Amemiya (1985) and Haavelmo (1944).

A linear equation representation for (2.14a) and (2.14b) writes

$$Y_{0t} = X_t \beta_{0t} + U_{0t} \tag{2.15a}$$

$$Y_{1t} = X_t \beta_{1t} + U_{1t}. \tag{2.15b}$$

The most commonly used special case of this model assumes that $U_{0t} = U_{1t} = U_t$ and that β_{0t} and β_{1t} are the same except for the intercepts. This is the dummy endogenous variables model of Heckman (1978). In this model, the observed value of Y_t can be written as

$$Y_t = (1 - D) Y_{0t} + DY_{1t} = D\alpha + X_t \beta_t + U_t$$

for $t > k$ and as $Y_t = X_t \beta_t + U_t$ for $t < k$. Thus, in this model, $Y_t = Y_{0t} + \alpha D$, $t > k$.

Another commonly used special case retains the assumption that $U_{1t} = U_{0t} = U_t$ but allows the response to X to vary in the treated and untreated states, so that β_{0t} need not equal β_{1t}. In this case, the observed Y_t is given by

$$Y_t = D(\beta_{1t} - \beta_{0t}) X_t + X_t \beta_{0t} + U_t = Y_{0t} + D(\beta_{1t} - \beta_{0t}) X_t.$$

A more general model relaxes both assumptions, with the result that Y_t is given by

$$Y_t = (1 - D) Y_{0t} + DY_{1t} = X_t \beta_{0t} + DX_t (\beta_{1t} - \beta_{0t}) + U_{0t} + D(U_{1t} - U_{0t})$$

for $t > k$. This model is analogous to the random coefficient model of econometrics (see Judge, Hill, Griffiths and Lee, 1985). The impact of treatment depends on both observed and unobserved characteristics. This model is also the switching-regression model of Quandt (1972, 1988). In the context of this model, the answer to evaluation question Q-2, the effect of treatment on a randomly selected person in the population at large, equals $E(Y_{1t} - Y_{0t} \mid X_t)$. Under the assumption that X_t is exogenous, so that $E(U_{1t} \mid X_t) = 0$ and $E(U_{0t} \mid X_t) = 0$, we have $E(Y_{1t} - Y_{0t} \mid X_t) = X_t (\beta_{1t} - \beta_{0t})$. In the more general simultaneous equations model we obtain

$$E\,(Y_{1\,t} - Y_{0\,t}\,|\,X_t)\;=\;X_t\,(\beta_{1\,t} - \beta_{0\,t}) + E\,(U_{1\,t} - U_{0\,t}\,|\,X_t)\,.$$

The parameter that answers evaluation question *Q-1* is $E\,(Y_{1\,t} - Y_{0\,t}\,|\,X_t,$ $D = 1)$, where

$$E\,(Y_{1\,t} - Y_{0\,t}\,|\,X_t,\ D\ =\ 1)\;=\;X_t\,(\beta_{1\,t} - \beta_{0\,t}) + E\,(U_{1\,t} - U_{0\,t}\,|\,D\ =\ 1,\ X_t)\,.$$

Observe that the mean gain in unobservables from moving from state '0' to state '1' is part of the definition of the parameter of interest.

This parameter is unusual from the standpoint of conventional econometric structural analysis, where the $U_{0\,t}$ and $U_{1\,t}$ are usually treated as nuisance terms and the $\beta_{1\,t}$ and $\beta_{0\,t}$ are the 'structural parameters of interest'. In fact, under conventional definitions of exogeneity, $E\,(U_{1\,t} - U_{0\,t}\,|\,D\ =\ 1,\ X_t)$ is required to be zero. The difference between the conventional structural approach and the approach adopted in evaluation analysis arises because in the evaluation context the response to treatment is allowed to vary across individuals and because the parameter of interest is defined as conditional on choices made by individuals. Note that within the evaluation framework, if the population of persons being examined varies across studies, so will the estimated parameters. This makes it difficult to cumulate knowledge of the parameters across studies. The structural approach emphasizes the estimation of 'deep' parameters that are invariant to alternative conditioning schemes.

The answers to questions *Q-1* and *Q-2* coincide if $E\,(U_{jt}\,|\,D\ =\ 1,\ X_t)\ =$ $E\,(U_{jt}\,|\,X_t)$, $j\ =\ 0,1$. This occurs if $U_{0\,t}\ =\ U_{1\,t}$. It can also occur if $U_{1\,t}$ and $U_{0\,t}$ are mean independent of D given X_t, which is just the definition of these conditions.

In the context of separable models, the condition for selection bias in mean outcomes is that

$$E\,(U_{0\,t}\,|\,D\ =\ 1,\ X_t) - E\,(U_{0\,t}\,|\,D\ =\ 0,\ X_t)\ \neq\ 0\,.$$

In the context of the dummy endogenous variables model, the condition is $E\,(U_t\tfrac{1}{2}D\ =\ 1,\ X_t)\,{}^1\,0$, which is the conventional definition of exogeneity.

3.3   Decision Rules

The structural approach to programme evaluation investigates the relationship between D and the unobservables $(U_{0\,t},\ U_{1\,t})$. The decision to participate in training may be determined by a prospective trainee, by a programme administrator or both. Whatever the specific content of the decision rule, the structural approach describes it in terms of an index function framework (Heckman and MaCurdy, 1986). Let *IN* be an index of the net benefits to the appropriate decision-makers from taking training. It includes the loss of income in period k if training is taken. It is a function of observed variables Z and unobserved variables V. The Z variables may be included among the X variables. However, we demonstrate that the existence of some Z variables that do not appear in X is essential to several solutions to the selection problem adopted in the literature.

We define the index IN as

$$IN = IN(Z, V). \tag{2.16}$$

In terms of this function, $D = 1$ if $IN \geq 0$ and $D = 0$ otherwise. This is a specialization of the participation rule defined in (2.3).

A familiar linear equation representation writes $IN = Z\gamma + V$. The distribution of V is denoted by $F(v) = Pr(V < v)$. V is often assumed to be independently and identically distributed across persons but this is not required. Let $p = E(D) = Pr(D = 1)$ and assume that $0 < p < 1$. If V is distributed independently of Z, a requirement not needed for most of the estimators we consider, we may write $Pr(D = 1 \mid Z) = F(-Z\gamma)$ and obtain a familiar model of discrete choice.

Behavioural models of participation motivate the choice of variables to include in Z as well as assumptions about the time-series structure in the outcome process. We first consider a model of trainee self-selection based on a comparison of the expected value of earnings with and without training. For simplicity, we assume that training programmes accept all applicants. All prospective trainees are assumed to discount earnings streams by a common factor of $1/(1 + r)$. Training raises earnings by α per period, where α may be the same for everyone or may vary across trainees. While in training, the trainee receives a subsidy S, which may be negative if there are direct costs of programme participation. Trainees receive no earnings in period k. To simplify the expressions, we assume that people live forever.

As of period k, the present value of earnings for a person who does not receive training is

$$PV(0) = E_{k-1}\left[\sum_{j=0}^{\infty}\left(\frac{1}{1+r}\right)^j Y_{0,\,k+j}\right],$$

where E_{k-1} means that the mathematical expectation is taken with respect to information available to the prospective trainee in period $k - 1$. The expected present value of earnings for a trainee is

$$PV(1) = E_{k-1}\left[\sum_{j=1}^{\infty}\left(\frac{1}{1+r}\right)^j Y_{0,\,k+j} + \sum_{j=1}^{\infty}\frac{\alpha}{(1+r)^j}\right].$$

For a person considering training, the risk-neutral wealth-maximizing decision rule is to enrol in the programme if $PV(1) > PV(0)$ or, letting IN denote the index function in the decision rule of equation (2.16),

$$IN = PV(1) - PV(0) = E_{k-1}(S - Y_k + \alpha/r) > 0 .$$

Thus, the decision to train is characterized by the rule

$$D = 1 \quad \text{if} \quad E_{k-1}(S - Y_k + \alpha/r) > 0 ;$$

$$D = 0 \quad \text{otherwise.}$$

Let W be the part of the subsidy the analyst observes and associate with it coefficient ϕ. Let τ be the part that the analyst does not observe, so that $S = W\phi + \tau$. A special case of this model arises when agents possess perfect foresight so that $E_{k-1}(S) = S$, $E_{k-1}(Y_k) = Y_k$, and $E_{k-1}(\alpha/r) = \alpha/r$. In that case,

$$D = 1 \quad \text{if} \quad S - Y_k = W\phi - X_k\beta + \alpha/r + \tau - U_k > 0 ; \quad (2.17)$$

$$D = 0 \quad \text{otherwise.}$$

Then $(t - U) = V$ in equation (2.16) and (W, X_k) corresponds to Z in equation (2.16).

Suppose decision rule (17) determines enrolment, and that α is the same for everyone. If the costs of programme participation are independent of U_t for all t (so that both W and τ are independent of U_t), then $E(U_t | D) = 0$ only if the mean of the unobservables in period t does not depend on the unobservables in period k; that is, $E(U_t | U_k) = 0$ for all $t > k$. Whether U_t and D are uncorrelated hinges on the serial dependence properties of U_t. If U_t is a moving average of order of m, so that

$$U_t = \sum_{j=1}^{m} \eta_j \, \varepsilon_{t-j} ,$$

where ε_{t-j} are independently and identically distributed, then for $t - k > m$, $E(U_t | D) = 0$. However, if U_t follows a first-order autoregressive scheme, then $E(U_t | U_k) \neq 0$ for all t and k, as we discuss below.

The participation decision rules presented in this subsection provide a context for the selection bias problem. The estimators discussed in this section differ greatly in their dependence on particular features of these rules. Some estimators do not require that these decision rules be specified at all, whereas other estimators require specification of these rules in varying amounts of detail. Given the inevitable controversy that surrounds specification of decision rules, there is always likely to be a preference by analysts for estimators that require little prior knowledge about the decision rule. But, as we shall see, suppressing the economics of the participation decision often leads to informal economic analyses that make strong implicit behavioural assumptions.

3.4 Cross-section Solutions to the Evaluation Problem

Heckman and Robb (1985, 1986a, 1986b) present a comprehensive discussion of a variety of cross-sectional estimators. They demonstrate that it is necessary to have one variable in Z that is not in X in order to answer the evaluation question without making assumptions about the conditional means or distributions of (U_{0t}, U_{1t}). The requirement that there be a variable in Z that is not in X is called an exclusion restriction. The instrumental variable method is a widely used cross-sectional estimator that exploits this principle. It can clearly be applied to longitudinal data as well. However, what are conventionally called longitudinal estimators exploit the time-series structure of the unobservables. Cross-section methods based on a single cross-section cannot exploit such information. We begin our discussion with the instrumental variables estimator and consider the behavioural and statistical assumptions that justify its application. We then consider other cross-sectional estimators that invoke less severe behavioural assumptions, but only at the cost of making additional assumptions about means or distributions of unobservables.

3.5 The Method of Instrumental Variables

The method of instrumental variables is now widely used in evaluation research. It has recently been promoted by Angrist, Imbens and Rubin (in press), but was first discussed in the context of evaluation research by Heckman and Robb (1985, 1986a, 1986b). To understand the method in the simplest setting, consider the following commonly used model for evaluating programmes. Let Y be an outcome such as earnings.[10] Let $D = 1$ if a person participates in a training programme, and let $D = 0$ otherwise. Using a standard regression model, we write $Y = \beta + \alpha D + U$, where U is an error term with mean zero, so that $E(U) = 0$, and where α is assumed to be the same for everyone.

In this model, correlation of D with U gives rise to selection problems. Persons who would have high values of U (or Y) in the absence of the programme may be the ones who go into it. Formally, the concern about selection

---

10　We drop the t subscript throughout sections 3.5, 3.6, 3.7 and 3.8 for notational simplicity.

problems is a concern that $E(U \mid D = 1) \neq 0$. For example, if more motivated persons have higher U's and are more likely to participate, then this term would be positive, and simple regression estimates of β would be biased upward.

An instrumental variable Z has two properties. It is uncorrelated with U, so that $E(U \mid Z) = 0$, and it is correlated with D, so that $E(D \mid Z) = Pr(D = 1 \mid Z)$ is a nontrivial function of Z taking on at least two distinct values for two distinct values of Z. Applying these properties to the outcome equation and taking expectations conditional on Z, we have

$$E(Y \mid Z) = \beta + \alpha Pr(D = 1 \mid Z).$$

Consider two distinct values of Z, say Z_1 and Z_2, such that $Pr(D = 1 \mid Z_1) \neq Pr(D = 1 \mid Z_2)$. Evaluating at $Z = Z_1$ and $Z = Z_2$ in turn, we have $E(Y \mid Z_1) = \beta + \alpha Pr(D = 1 \mid Z_1)$ and $E(Y \mid Z_2) = \beta + \alpha Pr(D = 1 \mid Z_2)$. Subtracting one of these equations from the other and solving for α yields

$$\alpha = \frac{E(Y \mid Z_1) - E(Y \mid Z_2)}{Pr(D = 1 \mid Z_1) - Pr(D = 1 \mid Z_2)}.$$

Using sample moments to replace population moments, we obtain the instrumental variables estimator.

The method requires an instrument Z. How credible are the instruments commonly available in social science data sets? Under what conditions does the method work? Can the method be generalized to cover the models introduced above, where α differs among people? This section addresses these questions. We establish that in cases in which the responses to the treatment vary the instrumental variable argument fails unless person-specific responses to treatment do not influence the decision to participate in the programme. This requires that individual gains from the programme that cannot be predicted from variables available to observing social scientists do not influence the decision of the persons being studied to participate in the programme. In the likely case in which individuals possess private information about gains from the programme that cannot be proxied by the available data, instrumental variables methods do not estimate behaviourally interesting evaluation parameters. Instrumental variable models are extremely sensitive to assumptions about how people process information.

For the remainder of this section, we consider the model introduced in section 3.2, where the conditional means with characteristics X are given by $E(Y_1 \mid X) = g_1(X)$ and $E(Y_0 \mid X) = g_0(X)$. Then,

$$Y_j = g_j(X) + U_j, \quad j = 0,1, \tag{2.18}$$

where $E(U_0 \mid X) = 0$ and $E(U_1 \mid X) = 0$. In the traditional regression setting, $g_0(X) = X\beta_0$ and $g_1(X) = X\beta_1$. The observed outcome Y can be written $Y = DY_1 + (1 - D) Y_0$. Taking (2.18) for j equal to 0 and 1 and inserting them into this expression yields

$$Y = g_0(X) + D(g_1(X) - g_0(X) + U_1 - U_0) + U_0. \tag{2.19}$$

This is the 'two-regime' or 'switching-regression' model discussed in section 3.2.

The term multiplying D is the gain, which has two components. The first is $g_1(X) - g_0(X)$, the gain for the average person with characteristics X. The second component is $U_1 - U_0$, the idiosyncratic gain for a particular person. In this notation, then, let $\Delta = Y_1 - Y_0$, so that the average gain, which answers evaluation question Q-2, is given by

$$E(\Delta \mid X) = g_1(X) - g_0(X).$$

The effect of treatment on the treated, which answers evaluation question Q-1, is given by

$$E(\Delta \mid X, D = 1) = g_1(X) - g_0(X) + E(U_1 - U_0 \mid X, D = 1).$$

The latter expression differs from the former by the additional term $E(U_1 - U_0 \mid X, D = 1)$. This term indicates how much the average gain among participants differs from the average gain that would be experienced in the entire population. This is the expected gain to the movers from going from state '0' to state '1'. Although the average gain in the population is $g_1(X) - g_0(X)$, the gain will be different for participants. We may rewrite equation (2.19) in terms of these parameters as

$$Y = g_0(X) + DE(\Delta \mid X) + [U_0 + D(U_1 - U_0)]$$

and

$$Y = g_0(X) + D[E(\Delta \mid X, D = 1)] +$$
$$\{U_0 + D[U_1 - U_0 - E(U_1 - U_0 \mid X, D = 1)]\}.$$

This notation is dense, but it can be simplified. Let $g_0(X) = \beta(X)$ and let $\alpha(X) = g_1(X) - g_0(X) + U_1 - U_0$. Let $\varepsilon = U_1 - U_0$ and let $U_0 = U$. For simplicity, we leave the dependence of β and α on X implicit, so $\beta(X) = \beta$ and $\alpha(X) = \alpha$. Then (2.19) can be written as a dummy-variable regression,

$$Y = \beta + D\alpha + U. \tag{19'}$$

Now, however, even after conditioning on X, a varies in the population due to individual heterogeneity in response to treatment.

Equation (2.20) can be written as

$$Y = \beta + D\bar{\alpha} + (U_0 + D\varepsilon),\qquad(2.20')$$

where $\bar{\alpha}$ is the effect of placing an average person in the population into the programme. (In general, is $\bar{\alpha}$ a function of X, $\bar{\alpha}(X)$. Once again, the conditioning is left implicit.) The effect of treatment on the treated is

$$E(\Delta \mid X, D = 1) = E(\alpha \mid D = 1, X) = \bar{\alpha} + E(\varepsilon \mid X, D = 1) = \alpha^*.$$

The X plays no important role here because it is assumed to be mean independent of U, $E(U\frac{1}{2}X) = 0$. The analogue to equation (2.21) is

$$Y = \beta + D\alpha^* + \{U + D(\varepsilon - E(\varepsilon \mid D = 1))\}.\qquad(2.21')$$

Can one run a regression of Y on D with an intercept to estimate $\bar{\alpha}$ and α^*? The regression coefficient of D can always be written as the difference between two means. Let $\tilde{\alpha}$ be the probability limit—the value of the regression coefficient in large samples—under conventional assumptions. There are three alternative representations of this limit:

$$\tilde{\alpha} = E(Y \mid X, D = 1) - E(Y \mid X, D = 0)\qquad(2.22a)$$

$$\tilde{\alpha} = \bar{\alpha} + E(\varepsilon \mid X, D = 1) + [E(U \mid X, D = 1) - E(U \mid X, D = 0)]\quad(2.22b)$$

$$\tilde{\alpha} = \alpha^* + E(U \mid X, D = 1) - E(U \mid X, D = 0).\qquad(2.22c)$$

From (2.22b), we see that $\tilde{\alpha}$ is biased for $\bar{\alpha}$ by the amount

$$E(\varepsilon \mid X, D = 1) + [E(U \mid X, D = 1) - E(U \mid X, D = 0)].$$

From (2.22c) we see that $\tilde{\alpha}$ is biased for α^* by an amount

$$E(U \mid X, D = 1) - E(U \mid X, D = 0).\qquad(2.23)$$

Term (2.<23) is sometimes called the selection bias term. It indicates how the outcome in the base state differs between programme participants and nonparticipants. Such differences cannot be attributed to the programme. In terms of the previous notation, and recalling that $U_0 = U$,

$$E\,(U\,|\,X,\;D\;=\;1)-E\,(U\,|\,X,\;D\;=\;0)$$
$$=\;E\,(U_0\,|\,X,\;D\;=\;1)-E\,(U_0\,|\,X,D=0)$$
$$=\;E\,(Y_0\,|\,X,\;D\;=\;1)-E\,(Y_0\,|\,X,\;D\;=\;0)\,.$$

The difference between $\bar{a}$ and α^* is the difference between the unobservable gain for an average person in the population (defined to be zero) and the unobservable gain for the average participant. This difference is given by

$$E\,(\varepsilon\,|\,X,\;D\;=\;1)\;=\;E\,(U_1-U_0\,|\,X,\;D\;=\;1)\,.$$

Thus, α^* differs from $\bar{a}$ by the amount of the gain in unobservables between the two groups defined by D. These unobservables may be observed by the person deciding to go into the programme. They are unobserved only by the social scientist trying to estimate the impact of the programme. They coincide when the mean gain in the unobservable conditional on D and X is zero, that is, when

$$E\,(\varepsilon\,|\,X,\;D\;=\;1)\;=\;0\;=\;E\,(U_1-U_0\,|\,X,\;D\;=\;1)\,.$$

We now present two important special cases in which $\bar{a}\;=\;\alpha^*$. The first special case occurs when $U_1\;=\;U_0$. In this case, there are no unobservable components of the gain. This is the widely used dummy endogenous variable or common coefficient model introduced in section 3.2. It assumes that, conditional on X, the effect of programme participation is the same for everyone.

The second special case is more subtle. In this case, $U_1\;\neq\;U_0$ but U_1-U_0, or information correlated with or dependent on it, does not determine who goes into the programme. Suppose, for example, that people do not know $\varepsilon\;=\;U_1-U_0$ at the time they go into the programme. Their best forecast of ε is zero or some other constant. Then, if their experience of ε is typical of that of the entire population, $E\,(\varepsilon\,|\,X,\;D\;=\;1)\;=\;0$, and $\bar{a}\;=\;\alpha^*$. This case shares many features in common with the random coefficients model of traditional econometrics.

Observe that in either the case where $U_1\;=\;U_0$ or the case where ε is not forecastable at the time participation decisions are made, the problem of estimating $\bar{a}$ or α^* using the difference in outcomes between participants and nonparticipants comes down to the problem arising from D being correlated with, or stochastically dependent on, U.

Also, note that for the estimation of the parameters of (2.21′), it follows from the definition of α^* that D is uncorrelated with $D\,[\varepsilon-E\,(\varepsilon\,|\,X,\;D\;=\;1)]$ by construction. Thus, whether or not $E\,(\varepsilon\,|\,X,\;D\;=\;1)\;=\;0$,

$$E\,(\varepsilon - E\,(\varepsilon\mid X,\ D\ =\ 1)\mid X,\ D\ =\ 1)$$
$$=\ E\,(\varepsilon\mid X,\ D\ =\ 1) - E\,(\varepsilon\mid X,\ D\ =\ 1)\ =\ 0\,.$$

Even in the case where participation in the programme is made at least in part on unobservable components of the gain, if the coefficient of interest is α^*, the effect of treatment on the treated, the only source of correlation between the 'error term' and D arises from U.

Instrumental variables must satisfy two basic conditions and a third derived condition. First, the instruments must be mean independent of the error terms of equations (2.20′) or (2.21′), depending on the parameter of interest. Identification of $\bar{\alpha}$ requires condition

$$E\,(U + D\varepsilon\mid X,\ Z)\ =\ 0\,. \tag{IV-2.1a}$$

Identification of a* requires the condition

$$E\,[U + D\,(\varepsilon - E\,(\varepsilon\mid D = 1))\mid X,\ Z]\ =\ 0\,. \tag{IV-2.1b}$$

A second condition is that D depends on Z in the following way: thus

$$E\,(D\mid X,\ Z)\ =\ Pr\,(D\ =\ 1\mid X,\ Z) \tag{IV-2.2}$$

is a function of Z. In other words, Z is not fully explained by X. The assumption that the probability is defined for two or more values of Z, so that the probability of participation depends on Z as well as on X, is implicit.

A third condition is that the dependence of Y on Z operates only through D. This condition is really a consequence of the first two conditions, but its role is so central that it is worth considering separately. Keeping in mind that β, $\bar{\alpha}$ and α^* may depend on X, for $\bar{\alpha}$ the derived third assumption is

$$E\,(Y\mid X,\ Z)\ =\ \beta + \bar{\alpha}\,E\,(D\mid X,\ Z) \tag{IV-2.3a}$$
$$=\ \beta + \bar{\alpha}\,Pr\,(D\ =\ 1\mid X,\ Z)\,.$$

For a* the required assumption is

$$E\,(Y\mid X,\ Z)\ =\ \beta + \alpha^*\,E\,(D\mid X,\ Z) \tag{IV-2.3b}$$
$$=\ \beta + \alpha^*\,Pr\,(D\ =\ 1\mid X,\ Z)\,.$$

For two distinct values of Z, say Z_1 and Z_2, such that $Pr\,(D\ =\ 1\mid X,\ Z_1) \neq Pr\,(D\ =\ 1\mid X,\ Z_2)$, we can identify $\bar{\alpha}$ or α^* by forming a simple mean difference. Thus, from (IV-2.1a), (IV-2.2) and (IV-2.3a),

$$E(Y \mid X, Z_1) - E(Y \mid X, Z_2)$$
$$= \bar{\alpha} [Pr(D = 1 \mid X, Z_1) - Pr(D = 1 \mid X, Z_2)],$$

so that we have

$$\bar{\alpha} = \frac{E(Y \mid X, Z_1) - E(Y \mid X, Z_2)}{Pr(D = 1 \mid X, Z_1) - Pr(D = 1 \mid X, Z_2)}.$$

Replacing population means with sample means produces the instrumental variable estimator which, under standard conditions, converges to $\bar{\alpha}(X)$. By similar reasoning, (IV-2.1b), (IV-2.2) and (IV-2.3b) imply

$$\alpha^* = \frac{E(Y \mid X, Z_1) - E(Y \mid X, Z_2)}{Pr(D = 1 \mid X, Z_1) - Pr(D = 1 \mid X, Z_2)}.$$

Loosely speaking, instruments are variables that 'do not belong in the population outcome equation' but do 'belong' in the equation predicting programme participation.

In the common effect model, where $\varepsilon = U_1 - U_0 = 0$, Heckman (1978) shows that conventional instrumental variables methods would identify $\alpha^* = \bar{\alpha}$. In the model, where ε is not a determinant of D, that is, where

$$Pr(D = 1 \mid X, Z, \varepsilon) = Pr(D = 1 \mid X, Z),$$

or

$$Pr(D = 1 \mid X, Z, Y_1 - Y_0) = Pr(D = 1 \mid X, Z),$$

the same conditions have to be satisfied for Z, that is, it must be uncorrelated with U and not in the outcome equation. We can ignore the component $D\varepsilon$ because

$$E(D\varepsilon \mid X, Z) = E(\varepsilon \mid X, Z, D = 1) Pr(D = 1 \mid X, Z) = 0$$

because $E(\varepsilon \mid X, Z, D = 1) = 0$.

Thus, the two special cases where $\bar{\alpha} = \alpha^*$ are cases where we can use conventional instrumental variable methods. (Heckman and Robb, 1985, 1986a, 1986b, develop both of these cases further.) What about more general cases? Consider equation (2.21') associated with α^*. Since the only source of dependence between the error term and D is through U and not through $D[\varepsilon - E(\varepsilon \mid X, D = 1)]$, the instrumental variable method looks promising. If assumptions (IV-2.1b), (IV-2.2) and (IV-2.3b) are satisfied, the method can be used to identify α^*. What is required is a variable that affects participation but does not enter the parameters in the equation of interest. This requires that

$$E(\bar{a} + \varepsilon \mid X, Z, D = 1) = g_1(X) - g_0(X) + E(\varepsilon \mid X, Z, D = 1)$$
$$= g_1(X) - g_0(X) + E(U_1 - U_0 \mid X, Z, D = 1)$$

does not depend on Z.

This is mechanically satisfied in the two special cases where $U_1 - U_0 = 0$, or $E(\varepsilon \mid X, Z, D = 1) = 0$. It is also satisfied in a third special case where ε cannot be forecast by Z, but can be forecast by X. Heckman and Robb (1985, 1986a, 1986b) demonstrate that this condition is very difficult to satisfy in models with clearly stated decision rules. If individuals select into the programme on the basis of the gain in unobservables or on the basis of variables that are (stochastically) dependent on the gain in unobservables, this condition will not be satisfied.

Any application of the method of instrumental variables for estimating the mean effect of treatment on the treated (the answer to evaluation question Q-1) in the case where the response to treatment varies among persons requires that a behavioural assumption be made about how persons make their decisions about programme participation. The issue cannot be settled by a statistical analysis.

Consider an example that is widely cited as a triumph of the method of instrumental variables. Draft lottery numbers are alleged to be ideal instrumental variables for identifying the effect of military service on earnings (Angrist, 1990). The 1969 draft lottery randomly assigned different priority numbers Z to persons of different birth dates. The higher the number, the less likely a person was to be drafted. Persons with high numbers were virtually certain to be able to escape the draft. Letting '1' denote military service and '0' denote civilian status, if persons partly anticipate the gain, $U_1 - U_0 = \varepsilon$, or base their decisions to go into the military on variables correlated with ε, then persons with high Z who choose to serve in the military, and so have $D = 1$, are likely to have high values of ε. This violates assumption (IV-2.3b) and makes the lottery number an invalid instrument. It is plausible that the persons who are deciding to go into the military have more information at their disposal than analysts using standard data sets. If this information is at all useful in predicting the gain from going into the military, the draft number is not a valid instrument.

The draft lottery number is a poor instrument for two other reasons. First, Z is likely to be an X, because persons with high Z, and, hence, a low chance of being drafted, are likely to be more attractive to employers who want to invest in their workers. A person unlikely to be drafted is likely to be a better investment because he is less likely to be removed from the firm to perform military service. This causes (IV-2.3b) to be violated because Z is really an X. Second, switching from a capricious draft to a draft lottery reduces uncertainty and is likely to change the investment behaviour of persons of all levels of Z. In this instance, the switch from an ordinary draft to a draft lottery affects both α^* and $\bar{\alpha}$ since it fundamentally alters schooling and job-training investment decisions. Thus, knowing how military service affects earnings during the period of a draft lottery would not be informative on how military service affects earnings during the period of an ordinary draft.

As a second example, it is sometimes suggested that cross-state variation in welfare benefits might be used as an instrument for estimating the effect of treatment on the treated for participants in training programmes. Let Y_0 denote earnings without training, and let Y_1 denote earnings with training. The determinants of welfare benefit levels, Z, do not plausibly enter $g_0(X)$ or $g_1(X)$. But they could enter

$$E(\varepsilon \mid X, Z, D = 1) = E(U_1 - U_0 \mid X, Z, D = 1),$$

because if the distribution of (U_0, U_1) is the same across states, and if more generous welfare schemes discourage participation in the training programme because they induce people to stay out of the market, then if programme participants enter the programme with at least partial knowledge of $U_1 - U_0$, higher values of $U_1 - U_0$ would tend to be found among programme participants in high benefit states. In this case, assumption (IV-2.3b) is violated, and cross-state variation in benefits does not identify α^* through the method of instrumental variables.

It might be thought that since

$$E[U_1 - U_0 - E(U_1 - U_0 \mid X, D = 1) \mid X, D = 1] = 0,$$

or, equivalently, that since

$$E[\varepsilon - E(\varepsilon \mid X, D = 1) \mid X, D = 1] = 0,$$

that it follows that $E[U_1 - U_0 - E(U_1 - U_0 \mid X, D = 1) \mid X, Z, D = 1] = 0$. This is not true. In general, $E(U_1 - U_0 \mid X, Z, D = 1) \neq E(U_1 - U_0 \mid X, D = 1)$. Conditioning more finely on X and Z does not produce the same result as conditioning on X. Thus, even if $E(U \mid X, Z) = 0$, it does not follow that (IV-2.1b) is satisfied. In this case, Z is not a good instrument for identifying α^*. For similar reasons, (IV-2.1a) is unlikely to be satisfied even if $E(U \mid X, Z) = 0$ because

$$E(D\varepsilon \mid X, Z) = E(U_1 - U_0 \mid X, Z, D = 1) Pr(D = 1 \mid X, Z)$$

does not equal zero. In this case, Z is not a valid instrument for identifying $\bar{\alpha}$ either.

3.6   Selection on Observables

An alternative approach to the evaluation problem invokes the assumption that, conditional on X and Z, the distributions or the means of Y_1 and Y_0 are the same, irrespective of whether or not $D = 1$. This idea underlies the matching literature (Heckman, Ichimura and Todd, 1995a, b; Rosenbaum and Rubin, 1983). The basic idea is that conditioning on observable Z in addition to X eliminates selective differences in unobservables between participants and nonparticipants that are present if we only condition on X. Using the notation of Dawid (1979),

$$(Y_1, \ Y_0) \perp\!\!\!\perp D \mid Z, \ X, \qquad \text{(AS-2.3)}$$

where '$\perp\!\!\!\perp$'means that conditional on Z and X, Y_1 and Y_0 are statistically independent of D. A weaker form of this condition is mean independence, indicated by

$$E\left(Y_1 \mid D = 1, \ Z, \ X\right) = E\left(Y_1 \mid Z, \ X\right) \qquad \text{(AS-2.4a)}$$

and

$$E\left(Y_0 \mid D = 1, \ Z, \ X\right) = E\left(Y_0 \mid Z, \ X\right). \qquad \text{(AS-2.4b)}$$

This is all that is required to use observables to solve the selection problem for mean outcomes.

The method works because it allows us to use nonparticipants to estimate the effect of nonparticipation for participants. Thus, we can use the mean of nonparticipants

$$E\left(Y_0 \mid D = 0, \ X, \ Z\right) = E\left(Y_0 \mid X, \ Z\right)$$

to estimate the mean of participants if they did not participate:

$$E\left(Y_0 \mid D = 1, \ X, \ Z\right) = E\left(Y_0 \mid X, \ Z\right) = E\left(Y_0 \mid D = 0, \ X, \ Z\right).$$

Assumption (AS-2.3) also implies that the same method can be used to estimate the distribution of outcomes for nonparticipants in the participation state.

In a linear common coefficient model, with $U_0 = U_1 = U$ and $\beta_1 = \beta_0$, Barnow, Cain and Goldberger (1980) write

$$E\left(Y \mid D = 1, X, Z\right) = \alpha + X\beta + E\left(U \mid D = 1, X, Z\right),$$

and invoke assumptions (AS-2.4a) and (AS-2.4b) so that Z satisfies

$$E\left(U \mid D = 1, X, Z\right) = E\left(U \mid X, Z\right).$$

They also make a linearity assumption, $E\left(U \mid X, Z\right) = (X, Z)'\varphi$, and an absence of multicollinearity assumption, which is that $D - E\left(D \mid X, Z\right)$ is a proper random variable, so that X and Z do not perfectly predict D. Under these assumptions, least squares consistently estimates α. Note that one does not need an exclusion restriction if the goal is to estimate α. Provided that the X do not perfectly predict D, one can identify α even if φ and β cannot be identified.

Neither linearity of the outcome equation or of the conditional mean nor the common effect assumption is required to apply the method of selection on observables to estimate the evaluation parameters of interest. In principle, one can match participants and nonparticipants using common (X, Z) characteristics. For each (X, Z) cell, one can construct the difference

$$E\left(Y_1 \mid D = 1, X, Z\right) - E\left(Y_0 \mid D = 0, X, Z\right) \qquad (2.24)$$
$$= E\left(Y_1 \mid X, Z\right) - E\left(Y_0 \mid X, Z\right).$$

This consistently estimates the effect of treatment on the treated for a person in the (X, Z) cell. Taking the weighted averages of the cell estimates yields an estimate of the effect of treatment on the treated that does not rely on any functional form assumptions about the outcome equations or the conditional mean of the unobservables. Note further that no exclusion restriction is required once (AS-2.3) or (AS-2.4a) and (AS-2.4b) are invoked. Heckman, Ichimura and Todd (1995a, b) present a behavioural model where the method of matching is justified, extend this method and present empirical evidence on the validity of the method.

3.7 Selection on Unobservables

A more general principle, based on the work of Heckman (1974, 1976, 1979), does not invoke the strong assumption that conditioning on observables eliminates selection problems. Focussing solely on mean outcomes, this approach does not require the assumption that the unobservables do not enter the decision rule for programme participation that is critical to the instrumental variables method.

For means, the method is based on the equations:

$$E(Y_1 \mid X, Z, D = 1) = g_1(X) + E(U_1 \mid X, Z, D = 1) \quad (2.25a)$$

and

$$E(Y_0 \mid X, Z, D = 0) = g_0(X) + E(U_0 \mid X, Z, D = 0). \quad (2.25b)$$

The terms $E(U_0 \mid X, Z, D = 0)$ and $E(U_1 \mid X, Z, D = 1)$ are termed 'control functions' or 'generalized residuals' in the literature. Heckman (1974, 1976, 1979) assumes that (U_1, U_0) are jointly normal and are stochastically independent of (X, Z). This method produces the control functions $E(U_0 \mid X, Z, D = 0)$ and $E(U_1 \mid X, Z, D = 1)$ up to a finite set of unknown parameters. The g_0 and g_1 and parameters of the control functions can be identified in the parametric case using conditions given in Heckman and Robb (1985). A variety of distributional assumptions have also been proposed in the literature. Heckman and MaCurdy (1986) present a comprehensive survey. Amemiya (1985) considers this class of models in detail. Heckman (1990a) considers the nonparametric identification of g_1 and g_0 and the joint distribution of (U_0, U_1) in a model in which an index function characterizes the programme participation rule. He establishes the nonparametric identifiability of g_1 and g_0 and the joint distributions of (V, U_0) and (V, U_1) when there is an exclusion restriction and when Z has sufficient variation in a sense made precise in that paper and in Heckman and Smith (1995b). Heckman and Honoré (1990) consider conditions for the identifiability of g_1 and g_0 when the decision rule is to select $D = 1$ if $Y_1 > Y_0$ and $D = 0$ otherwise. For this decision rule, this model is known in economics as the Roy (1951) model.

The essential idea in the method is that with sufficient variation in Z, it is possible to identify g_1 and g_0, and, hence, the conditional means $E(U_1 \mid X, Z, D = 1)$ and $E(U_0 \mid X, Z, D = 0)$. To understand the idea, let Z assume values in $\bar{Z}^1$, so that $Pr(D = 1 \mid Z, X) = 1$ for $Z \in \bar{Z}^1$. Then for such values of Z, $E(U_1 \mid X, Z, D = 1) = 0$ if $E(U_1 \mid X, Z) = 0$, because in this subpopulation everyone participates in the programme. Thus, we can identify $g_1(X)$ in this subset. Similarly, for $Z \in \bar{Z}^0$, let $Pr(D = 0 \mid Z, X) = 0$. For this subset of values, we can identify $g_0(X)$. Thus, we can answer evaluation questions *Q-1* and *Q-2* because we can estimate

$$E(Y_1 - Y_0 \mid X) = g_1(X) - g_0(X)$$

if we assume that $E(U_1 \mid X, Z) = 0$ and $E(U_0 \mid X, Z) = 0$, provided that the full support of X is available in $\bar{Z}^1$ and $\bar{Z}^0$. Similarly, we can estimate

$$E(Y_1 - Y_0 \mid X, D = 1) = E(Y_1 \mid X, D = 1) - E(Y_0 \mid X, D = 1).$$

To construct the first term on the right-hand side of this expression, average (2.25a) over the Z conditional on $D = 1$. Thus,

$$E(Y_1 \mid X, D = 1) = \int E(Y_1 \mid X, Z, D = 1) \, dF(Z \mid D = 1).$$

This can be consistently estimated in a sample by taking an average over those Z for which $D = 1$. To construct the second term, observe that we can identify $g_0(X)$. Hence, we can form

$$E(Y_0 \mid X, Z, D = 0) - g_0(X) = E(U_0 \mid X, Z, D = 0).$$

Since we assume that $E(U_0 \mid X, Z) = 0$, we can estimate $E(U_0 \mid X, Z, D = 1)$ by using the law of iterated expectations,

$$
\begin{aligned}
0 &= E(U_0 \mid X, Z) \\
&= E(U_0 \mid X, Z, D = 0) \quad Pr(D = 0 \mid X, Z) \\
&\quad + E(U_0 \mid X, Z, D = 1) \quad Pr(D = 1 \mid X, Z)
\end{aligned}
$$

and solving we obtain

$$E(U_0 \mid X, Z, D = 1) = -E(U_0 \mid X, Z, D = 0) \, \frac{Pr(D = 0 \mid X, Z)}{Pr(D = 1 \mid X, Z)}$$

since we know $Pr(D = 0 \mid X, Z)$ and $Pr(D = 1 \mid X, Z)$. In the absence of sufficient variation in the regressors, functional form assumptions about the control functions or the distributions of the unobservables have to be invoked to implement this method. With sufficiently strong functional form assumptions, no exclusion restriction is required.

This method does not require the strong behavioural assumption required for the instrumental variables method. Agents can anticipate the unobservable components of the gain in making their participation decisions, and the method still produces consistent estimators that answer evaluation questions *Q-1* and *Q-2*. In practice, strong distributional assumptions are imposed. Björklund and Moffitt (1987) present an application of this approach to the programme evaluation problem. However, these distributional assumptions are not intrinsic to the method (Heckman, 1990b). Heckman and Robb (1985, 1986a, 1986b) discuss a variety of alternative assumptions that exploit cross-section data by invoking various distributional or functional form assumptions. Making such assumptions, it is not necessary to assume that $E(U_0 \mid X, Z) = 0$ or $E(U_1 \mid X, Z) = 0$ to solve the evaluation problem.

3.8   The Propensity Score as a Solution to the Problem of Selection Bias

In a series of papers, Rosenbaum and Rubin (1983, 1985) have advocated the use of the propensity score, $Pr(D = 1 \mid Z)$, in a matching estimation method for controlling or reducing bias in nonexperimental studies. They suggest using the propensity score to define matches, or using it in place of (X, Z) in defining cells, as discussed above in section 3.6. Provided that the average over some or all of the cells is the parameter of interest, it is possible to reduce the dimension of the matching problem substantially by using the propensity score. The propensity score can also sometimes be used to construct control functions analogous to those discussed in section 3.7.

In considering propensity score methods, two distinct issues should be distinguished. The first is a statement of conditions under which there exists a control function that depends solely on the propensity score (and some parameters). The second is the validity of matching methods. We do not discuss the second topic in this chapter beyond what we have already said in section 3.6.[11] To focus on the main ideas, we consider the simplest cases and consider only cross-section models.

The propensity score methodology is based on assumption (AS-2.3). That is, if there is selection bias, its only source must be selection on the observables as defined in section 3.6. Selection on unobservables is ruled out. Focussing on the common coefficient case to simplify the exposition, and using Theorem 3 of Rosenbaum and Rubin (1983), if (AS-2.3) is true, then

$$E[Y \mid D, X, Pr(D = 1 \mid Z, X)]$$
$$= X\beta + D\alpha + E[U \mid Pr(D = 1 \mid Z, X)].$$

The term $E[U \mid Pr(D = 1 \mid Z, X)]$ may be used as a control function in the sense of Heckman and Robb (1985, 1986a), as discussed above. A key assumption underlying the use of this method for the estimation of β is the existence of one exclusion restriction in Z. In contrast, if interest centres only in estimating α, no exclusion restriction is required. The only requirement is

---

11   The published literature on matching offers no formal proofs of any desirable property of matching estimators in the case in which regressor variables are continuously distributed. (It is trivial to establish optimality properties for matching in the case in which all regressors are categorical with finite categories.) Recent claims about the robustness of matching methods in the case in which the functional form of a regression model is unknown are not yet supported by published systematic theoretical arguments or by compelling Monte Carlo or empirical evidence. Heckman, Ichimura and Todd (1995a, b) present general theorems on the consistency and asymptotic normality of matching methods with continuous regressors.

that D cannot be perfectly forecast by X and Z. Since Z is not required to be independent of U, elements of Z need not be valid instruments for D. Assuming linearity of the control function in terms of $Pr(D = 1 \mid X, Z)$, one can identify α by regression methods. Alternatively, one can collapse the cell matching described in (2.24) down to matches on one-dimensional cells based on $Pr(D = 1 \mid X, Z)$. This reduction in dimensionality is a great practical advantage of the method. The method can also be applied to more general cases where the heterogeneous response model is appropriate.

As previously noted, selection solely on observables is a very special case of the general problem of selection bias. However, recent evidence presented in Heckman et al. (1995a, 1995b) suggests that with sufficiently rich data on Z, semiparametric methods based on the propensity score may effectively control for selection bias in evaluating the impact of training on earnings.

The propensity score can also be used in an entirely different setting in which there is selection on unobservables. Suppose that X and Z are independent of U and V in (2.16). In this case, discussed in Heckman (1980) and in Heckman and Robb (1986a), the conditional means of the observables, $E(U \mid D = 1, X, Z)$ and $E(U \mid D = 0, X, Z)$, can be combined into a 'control function' or 'generalized residual' that is solely a function of the propensity score. For the model considered here, defing $F(u, r)$ as the point density of U, V

$$E(U \mid D = 1, X, Z) = \frac{\int_{-\infty}^{\infty} u \int_{F^{-1}[1 - Pr(D = 1 \mid X, Z)]}^{\infty} f(u, v)\, dv\, du}{Pr(D = 1 \mid X, Z)}$$

$$= K_1 [Pr(D = 1 \mid X, Z)]$$

$$E(U \mid D = 0, X, Z) = \frac{\int_{-\infty}^{\infty} u \int^{F^{-1}[1 - Pr(D = 1 \mid X, Z)]}_{-\infty} f(u, v)\, dv\, du}{Pr(D = 0 \mid X, Z)}$$

$$= K_0 [Pr(D = 0 \mid X, Z)]$$

where $K_1 [Pr(D = 1 \mid X, Z)]\, Pr(D = 1 \mid X, Z) + K_0 [Pr(D = 0 \mid X, Z)]\, Pr(D = 0 \mid X, Z) = 0$, and where $K = K_1 D + K_0 (1 - D)$ is a control function that is solely a function of the propensity score and the unknown parameters of K_0 and K_1.

We may enter the control function K as a regressor in the outcome equation and thereby control for selective differences in unobservables,

$$E(Y \mid D, X, Z) = X\beta + D\alpha + K[P(D = 1 \mid X, Z)]$$

$$= X\beta + D\alpha + DK_1 [P(D = 1 \mid X, Z)]$$

$$+ (1 - D) K_0 [P(D = 0 \mid X, Z)].$$

This is just the method of control functions discussed in section 3.7. Conditions for identification of the parameters in this equation are given in Heckman and Robb (1985). As noted in section 3.7, control function methods may be applied to much more general models with heterogeneous responses to treatment and with unobservables anticipated by potential participants (see Heckman and Robb, 1985, and Björklund and Moffitt, 1987).

Note, however, that very different assumptions are required to justify this control function than are required to justify the control function for selection on observables implicit in Rosenbaum and Rubin (1983). Under the assumption that Z is distributed independently of U (or at least that one element of Z is uncorrelated with U), the appropriate elements of Z may be used as instruments for D, whereas in general they are not valid instruments under the assumptions of Rosenbaum and Rubin (1983). The validity of Z as an instrument is an artefact of the common effect model.

3.9 Longitudinal Methods

Without invoking functional form assumptions, cross-sectional methods that allow for selection on unobservables require an exclusion restriction, that is, a variable in Z that is not in X that satisfies the identification conditions described above. Longitudinal methods do not require such assumptions. They rely on the additively separable form of the outcome equations given by

$$Y_{jt} = g_j(X_t) + U_{jt}, \ j = 0,1 ,$$

and exploit assumptions about the time-series properties of the unobservables.

In place of exclusions restrictions, or assumptions about rich conditioning information, or assumptions about the functional forms of the conditional means or distributions of unobservables, or variation in the regressors, longitudinal methods invoke special assumptions regarding the time-series structure of the unobservables. For example, the widely used fixed-effect method that we discuss in the following section is based on the strong assumption that $U_{1t} = U_{0t} = U_t$. For simplicity, we adopt the linear-in-the-parameters specification typically used in applied work in our discussion of longitudinal methods, though this is not strictly required. Thus, we assume that $g_0(X_t) = X_t\beta_0$ and $g_1(X_t) = X_t\beta_1$. We also assume access to data on each person in at least two periods.

3.10 The Fixed-effect Method

This fixed-effect method was developed by Mundlak (1961, 1978) and refined by Chamberlain (1982). Array the $X_t, t = 1, \ldots, T$ into a vector X.

Assume a common coefficient model, so that α is the same for everyone and $X_t\beta_1 = \alpha + X_t\beta_0$. The fixed-effect method is based on the following assumption:

$$E(U_t - U_{t'} \mid D, X) = 0 \quad \text{for all } t, t' \text{ such that } t > k > t'. \quad (2.26)$$

As a consequence of this assumption, we may write a difference regression as

$$E(Y_t - Y_{t'} \mid D, X) = (X_t - X_{t'})\beta + D\alpha \quad \text{for } t > k > t'.$$

Suppose that condition (2.26) holds and that the analyst has access to one year of preprogramme and one year of postprogramme earnings. Regressing the difference between earnings in any postprogramme year and earnings in any preprogramme year on the change in regressors between those years and a dummy variable for training status produces a consistent estimator of α.

Some decision rules and error processes for earnings justify condition (26). For example, consider a certainty environment in which the earnings residual has a permanent-transitory structure:

$$U_t = \phi + v_t, \quad (2.27)$$

where v_t is a mean zero random variable independent of $v_{t'}$ for $t \neq t'$ and distributed independently of ϕ, a mean zero person-specific time-invariant random variable. Assuming that S in the decision rule of equation (2.17) is distributed independently of all v_t, except possibly for v_k, then condition (2.26) will be satisfied. With two periods of data (in t and t', $t > k > t'$), α is just identified. With more periods of panel data, the model is overidentified, so that condition (2.26) can be tested.

Condition (2.26) may also be satisfied in an environment of uncertainty. Suppose equation (2.27) governs the error structure of the earnings equation, and that $E_{k-1}(v_k) = 0$ and $E_{k-1}(\phi) = \phi$, so that agents cannot forecast innovations in their earnings but know their own permanent component. If S is distributed independently of all v_t except possibly for v_k, this model also produces condition (2.26).

However, these models are very special. It is very easy to produce plausible models that do not satisfy condition (2.26). For example, even if equation (2.27) characterizes U_t, if S in equation (2.17) does not have the same joint (bivariate) distribution with respect to all v_t, except for v_k, condition (2.26) may be violated. Even if S in equation (2.17) is distributed independently of U_t for all t, it is still not the case that condition (2.26) is satisfied in a general model. For example, suppose X_t is distributed independently of all U_t, and let

$U_t = \rho U_{t-1} + v_t$, where v_t is mean zero, i.i.d. random variable and $|\rho| < 1$. If $\rho \neq 0$ and the perfect foresight decision rule governs participation, condition (2.26) is not satisfied for $t > k > t'$ because

$$E(U_t \mid D = 1) = E(U_t \mid U_k + X_k\beta - \alpha/r < S) = \rho^{t-k} E(U_k \mid D = 1)$$
$$\neq E(U_{t'} \mid D = 1) = E(U_{t'} \mid U_k + X_k\beta - \alpha/r < S),$$

unless the conditional expectations are linear (in U_k) for all t and $k - t' = t - k$. In that case, we have $E(U_t \mid D = 1) = \rho^{t-k} E(U_k \mid D = 1)$, so that $E(U_t - U_{t'} \mid D = 1) = 0$ only for (t, t') such that $k - t' = t - k$. Thus, condition (2.26) is not satisfied for all $t > k > t'$. For more general specifications of U_t and stochastic dependence between S and U_t, condition (2.26) will not be satisfied. Only certain, very special behavioural models justify the use of the fixed-effect estimator. Despite their widespread use in applied work, many plausible economic models do not justify application of the fixed-effect method. As a result, lessons drawn from these methods are misleading. Fixed-effect estimators have generally been shown to produce very misleading estimates of the impact of training on earnings (Heckman and Smith, 1995c; LaLonde, 1986).

Finally, we note some anomalous features of first-difference estimators. First, virtually all of the nonexperimental estimators presented in the literature require a control group, that is, a sample of nontrainees. The only exception is the fixed-effect estimator in a time-homogeneous environment. In this case, if condition (2.26) holds, if one lets $X_t\beta = \beta_t$ to simplify the exposition, and if the environment is time homogeneous, so that $\beta_t = \beta_{t'}$, then the sample analogue of $E(Y_t \mid D = 1) - E(Y_{t'} \mid D = 1)$ consistently estimates α. The claim that 'if the environment is stationary, you do not need a control group' (Bassi, 1983, 1984) is false except for the special conditions that justify the fixed-effect estimator.[12]

Second, while most of the procedures considered here can be implemented with only postprogramme data, first-difference methods constitute an exception to this rule. Third, fixed-effect estimators are also robust to departures from the random-sampling assumption. For instance, suppose condition (2.26) is satisfied but that the available data oversample or undersample trainees, so that the proportion of trainees in the sample does not converge to $p = E(D)$. Suppose further that the analyst does not know the true value of p. Nevertheless, a first-difference regression continues to identify α. Many other procedures, both cross-sectional and longitudinal, do not share this property.

---

12 This point is developed further in Heckman and Robb (1985).

We now relax the common coefficient assumption and consider the application of the fixed-effect estimator when the response to treatment varies across persons. For estimating the parameter that gives the expected effect of the programme on randomly selected persons in the population (the answer to evaluation question Q-2), the first-difference method is critically dependent on the assumption that $U_{1t} = U_{0t}$. This assumption rules out heterogeneity in response to treatment that is not a deterministic function of the observables. If $U_{1t} \neq U_{0t}$, then a stronger condition is required to justify application of the first-difference method:

$$E(U_t - U_{t'} \mid D = 1, X_t, X_{t'}) = 0 \text{ for all } t, t', \text{ such that } t > k > t', \quad (2.26')$$

where $U_t = DU_{1t} + (1 - D)U_{0t}$ for $t > k$ and $U_t = U_{0t}$ for $t < k$. Rewriting this condition yields

$$E(U_{0t} - U_{0t'} \mid D = 1, X_t, X_{t'}) + E(U_{1t} - U_{0t} \mid D = 1, X_t, X_{t'}) = 0.$$

Condition (2.26) applied to U_{0t} sets the first term to zero. Setting the second term to zero requires the same type of restrictive condition needed to apply the instrumental variables method. It requires that, conditioning in the observables, participation in the programme does not depend on the unobservable component of the difference in outcomes between the two states. This is the condition required to estimate $\bar{\alpha}$ using the instrumental variables method.

However, estimating the effect of treatment on the treated (the answer to evaluation question Q-1) using the fixed-effect method only requires the assumption that

$$E(U_{0t} - U_{0t'} \mid D = 1, X_t, X_{t'}) = 0, \quad (2.28)$$

because the effect of treatment on the treated is

$$\begin{aligned} &E(Y_{1t} - Y_{0t} \mid D = 1, X_t, X_{t'}) \\ &= X_t(\beta_{1t} - \beta_{0t}) + E(U_{1t} - U_{0t} \mid D = 1, X_t, X_{t'}), \end{aligned}$$

so that the second term on the right-hand side incorporates in the definition of the parameter of interest one term in the definition of the bias for α Thus, under assumption (2.28), the first-difference method can provide an estimate that answers evaluation question Q-1, provided the other assumptions required to justify the fixed-effect method are satisfied.

Crucial to this result is the assumption that prior to period k, only one option is available to the trainee, so that $U_t = U_{0t}$ for $t < k$. If a second option is available prior to period k, then

$$E (Y_{1t} - Y_{0t'} | D = 1, X_t, X_{t'}) = X_t (\beta_{1t} - \beta_{0t}) - X_{t'} (\beta_{1t'} - \beta_{0t'})$$
$$+ E [(U_{1t} - U_{0t})$$
$$- (U_{1t'} - U_{0t'}) | D = 1, X_t, X_{t'}].$$

The fixed-effect method identifies this parameter, which is not the answer to evaluation question *Q-1*. Instead, this parameter gives the change in the effect of treatment on the treated between time periods t and t', if the assumption in (2.28) is valid.

3.11 U_t Follows a First-order Autoregressive Process

Most of the evidence on error processes in earnings equations speaks against the permanent-transitory model (see e.g. the evidence in MaCurdy, 1982). Suppose instead that $U_{1t} = U_{0t} = U_t$ and that U_t follows a first-order autoregression, so that $U_t = \rho U_{t-1} + v_t$, where $E (v_t) = 0$ and the v_t are mutually independently (not necessarily identically) distributed random variables with $|\rho| < 1$. Assume initially that the common coefficient model holds, so that α is the same for everyone. Substitution using the common coefficient version of (2.15) and the fact that U_t follows a first-order autoregression to solve for U_t yields

$$Y_t = [X_t - (X_{t'} \rho^{t-t'})] \beta + (1 - \rho^{t-t'}) D\alpha + \rho^{t-t'} Y_{t'} + \sum_{j=0}^{t-(t'+1)} \rho^j v_{t-j} \qquad (2.29)$$
$$t > t' > k \quad \text{is a condition on the equation.}$$

Assume further that the perfect foresight rule of equation (217) determines participation and that the v_j are distributed independently of S and X_k in equation (2.17).[13] If X_j is independent of $v_{j'}$ for all j, j' (an overly strong condition), then least squares applied to equation (2.29) consistently estimates α as the number of observations becomes large. (Efficiency can be improved by imposing the appropriate cross-coefficient restrictions.) As in the case with the fixed-effect estimator, increasing the length of the panel makes the model overidentified and therefore testable.

This method breaks down, in general, when responses to treatment are heterogeneous. To see this, note that $Y_t = DY_{1t} + (1 - D) Y_{0t}$, so that one can write

$$Y_t = X_t \beta_{0t} + DX_t (\beta_{1t} - \beta_{0t}) + U_{0t} + D (U_{1t} - U_{0t}).$$

---

13 Heckman and Wolpin (1976) invoke similar assumptions in their analysis of affirmative action programmes.

Let $U_{1t} = \rho_1 U_{1,t-1} + v_{1t}$ and $U_{0t} = \rho_0 U_{0,t-1} + v_{0t}$, where v_{1t} and v_{0t} are serially independent, mean zero random variables. Substituting these expressions for U_{0t} and U_{1t} into the preceding equation, and solving back to t', one obtains

$$Y_t = X_t \beta_{0t} + DX_t (\beta_{1t} - \beta_{0t}) + \sum_{j=0}^{t-(t'+1)} \rho_0^j v_{0, t-j}$$

$$+ D \left[\sum_{j=0}^{t-(t'+1)} (\rho_1^j v_{1, t-j} - \rho_0^j v_{0, t-j}) \right]$$

$$+ D \left[\rho_1^{t-t'} (Y_{1t'} - X_{t'} \beta_{1t'}) - \rho_0^{t-t'} (Y_{0, t'} - X_{t'} \beta_{0t'}) \right]$$

$$+ \rho_0^{t-t'} (Y_{0t'} - X_{t'} \beta_{0t'}) \ .$$

In an environment of perfect foresight, $v_{1, t-j}$ and $v_{0, t-j}$ determine D, given decision rule (2.17), and do not difference out as in the single-regime model. Even if the $v_{1, t-j}$ and $v_{0, t-j}$ are unforecastable from the vantage point of period k, the substitution strategy does not eliminate $U_{0t'}$ or $U_{1t'}$. It does not produce an estimate that answers evaluation question *Q-1*, the effect of treatment on the treated, because U_{1t} and U_{0t} are substituted out. This analysis demonstrates the dependence of this procedure on the assumption of a common treatment effect. Heckman and Robb (1985) present a comprehensive analysis of other longitudinal estimators.

3.12 Nonrandom Sampling Plans

The data available for analysing the impact of training on earnings are often nonrandom samples. Frequently, they consist of pooled data from two sources: (a) a sample of trainees selected from programme records and (b) a sample of nontrainees selected from some national sample. Typically, such samples overrepresent trainees relative to their proportion in the population. This creates the problem of choice-based sampling analysed by Manski and Lerman (1977) and Manski and McFadden (1981). Choice-based sampling is a special case of the problem of weighted distributions (Patil, 1965, or Rao, 1965), for which the well-known solution is to weight sample distributions back to random-sample proportions. Another source of potential problems is contamination bias, which can occur when the training status of persons in the comparison group sample is not known. Nearly all methods can be adjusted to account for choice-based sampling or measurement error in training status. Some methods require no modification at all. For example, all methods that are based on control functions are robust to choice-based sampling.

Heckman and Robb (1985) provide a comprehensive discussion of the robustness of alternative econometric models to choice-based sampling and to contamination. In general, using robustness to contamination bias or choice-based sampling as a criterion for selecting estimators does not suggest a clear ordering of cross-section, repeated cross-section or longitudinal estimators.

3.13   Choosing among Alternative Nonexperimental Methods

The multiplicity of available nonexperimental evaluation strategies raises the problem of how best to select among them in particular evaluation contexts. The literature typically follows LaLonde (1986) and Fraker and Maynard (1987) in concluding that this problem is difficult or impossible to solve, and represents another argument in favour of social experiments. We argue that the LaLonde (1986) and Fraker and Maynard (1987) studies have important limitations that reduce the generality of their evidence. Furthermore, we argue that these analysts failed to fully apply the available specification tests and failed to make use of the potential of cumulative evidence on earnings and participation processes in sorting among the alternative nonexperimental evaluation strategies they examined.

LaLonde (1986) uses an experimental evaluation of the National Supported Work Demonstration (NSW) as a benchmark against which to compare nonexperimental estimates. He uses the NSW experimental treatment group in conjunction with comparison groups drawn from the Current Population Survey (CPS) and the Panel Study of Income Dynamics (PSID) to estimate the impact of training. He employs several commonly used nonexperimental estimators and obtains a wide variety of impact estimates, most of which differ substantially from the corresponding experimental estimates. A limited set of model selection tests fails to eliminate the models that produce this variability.[14]

LaLonde (1986) has had a strong influence in promoting the use of experiments to evaluate social programmes in general and employment and training programmes in particular (e.g. Hansen, 1994, p. 101). Despite its influence, his study has important limitations that serve to limit the generality of its methodological conclusions.

Selection bias arises because of missing data on the common factors affecting participation and outcomes. The most convincing way to solve the selection problem is to collect better data. The data used by LaLonde (1986) either lack sufficient information to determine eligibility for the NSW programme, or eligibility was not considered as a screening criterion in forming comparison groups. Furthermore, the sample sizes are too small, and the geographical information available in LaLonde's data is insufficient, to place comparison

---

14 Fraker and Maynard (1987) use a similar strategy to evaluate alternative comparison group designs. Their study has the same limitations as LaLonde (1986).

group members in the same labour markets as programme participants. In short, the problem of selection bias documented by LaLonde (1986) arises at least in part from the crudity of his data. Heckman, Ichimura and Todd (1995b) demonstrate that these factors are significant sources of what is measured as selection bias.

A second limitation of the data available on the NSW participants and on comparison group members from the CPS and PSID is that many of the non-experimental estimators developed in the literature cannot be applied to them. For example, the data on NSW participants contain only a single year of information on preprogramme earnings, effectively ruling out the use of many estimators based on the longitudinal structure of earnings discussed in Heckman and Robb (1985). In addition, the relative paucity of conditioning variables or regressors in the CPS and the PSID rules out effective strategies for controlling for unobservables by including a rich set of observables. LaLonde (1986) also fails to address the choice-based nature of his sample, which affects the properties of many of the estimators he examines (Heckman and Robb, 1985). Inappropriate application of certain econometric methods causes part of the variability he finds.

A third limiting factor is that LaLonde's study treats the choice of a comparison group and the choice of an estimator as statistical problems rather than economic problems. As a result he ignores the potential of cumulative social science knowledge to guide these choices. Recent years have witnessed the accumulation of substantial empirical knowledge on the dynamics of individual earnings and the process of selection into social programmes. This knowledge is sufficient to rule out in advance some commonly used estimators of programme impact such as the fixed-effect or difference-in-differences estimator described in section 3.10. This estimator is almost always rejected in applications of specification tests to nonexperimental data (see e.g. Heckman and Smith, 1995c). By ignoring the evidence available from cumulative social science knowledge, LaLonde (1986) ends up testing only a weak and incomplete version of nonexperimental methodology.

A fourth factor limiting the generalizability of the findings from this study is its failure to utilize a variety of model-selection strategies based on standard specification tests. Heckman and Hotz (1989) reanalyse the NSW data and find that a simple set of specification tests successfully eliminates all but the nonexperimental models that reproduce the inference obtained by experimental methods. They conclude that specification tests remain a promising tool for nonexperimental analysts. However, Heckman (1993) and Heckman and Roselius (1994) discuss the limitations of these tests, and note that certain kinds of selection bias cannot be detected by them.

4   GENERAL EQUILIBRIUM

In most current experimental and nonexperimental evaluations, it is assumed that a partial equilibrium framework suffices to answer the evaluation questions of interest. That is, it is assumed that the effects of a given programme on each participant are independent of the number and composition of the other participants and that the programme has no effects on the labour market outcomes of nonparticipants. Although these assumptions greatly simplify the evaluation problem, they are often seriously violated in practice. For example, some of the unemployed workers who find jobs as a result of the additional human capital they obtain by participating in a training programme may displace other workers with less human capital who did not take training. This displacement represents a general equilibrium effect of the training programme that is not accurately captured by the partial equilibrium evaluation methods considered in this chapter. These methods consider only the effects of programmes on their participants and ignore any negative (e.g. displacement) or positive (e.g. externalities associated with higher levels of human capital) effects on nonparticipants.

Detailed consideration of general equilibrium evaluation methods is beyond the scope of this chapter. Auerbach and Kotlikoff (1987), Kydland and Prescott (1991), Shoven and Whalley (1992) and Tinbergen (1956) consider full general equilibrium analysis of policy impacts, whereas Davidson and Woodbury (1993) examine displacement in the specific context of a reemployment bonus programme for recipients of unemployment insurance. Heckman and Smith (1995b) discuss general equilibrium issues and relate the impact parameters discussed in this chapter to the concerns of traditional cost–benefit analysis.

5   SUMMARY AND CONCLUSIONS

The evaluation problem is fundamentally a problem of missing data. The missing data are the counterfactual outcomes that would occur if persons were in the state other than that in which they are observed. Thus, for a trainee, the missing data is what would have happened had he or she not taken training. All evaluation methods solve this problem by invoking assumptions. In the case of social experiments, one obtains the counterfactual outcome distribution for participants directly by randomly denying access to treatment to persons who would otherwise have participated. The necessary assumptions include the absence of randomization bias and the absence of substitution bias. With nonexperimental methods, one estimates the counterfactual outcome distribution (or features of it) by combining data on nonparticipants with assumptions about the outcome (e.g. earnings) and programme participation processes. At this level of generality, it is not obvious that the assumptions required to justify experimental methods are any more plausible than those required to justify nonexperimental methods, or that the assumptions required to justify a particular nonexperimental method are more or less plausible than those required to justify another.

In the existing literature, the assumptions required to justify experiments are often ignored or downplayed, while those required to justify nonexperimental methods are often overstated. Although certain commonly used nonexperimental methods rely on strong distributional assumptions about the unobservable components of the outcome and participation equations, these assumptions are much stronger than are required. We show, for example, that the assumptions required to justify instrumental variables methods are much less stringent, although finding an instrument that satisfies the required restrictions on behaviour may be difficult in practice. In comparison to cross-section data, longitudinal data allow different, but not necessarily simpler or more plausible, assumptions to be invoked. We show the limitations of the propensity score methods popular in the statistics literature but note that recent evidence suggests that improved data collection may make these methods an effective empirical tool. We also argue that the evidence that it is difficult or impossible to choose among alternative nonexperimental estimators is weaker than commonly believed.

We end the chapter with two important general points. First, although this chapter focusses exclusively on partial equilibrium evaluation methods, general equilibrium effects remain an important, but largely underexplored, area for evaluation research and are often completely overlooked in evaluation practice. Second, there is no reason to expect that a single method will solve every, or almost every, evaluation problem. All evaluation methods require assumptions. Evaluating the plausibility of those assumptions in each particular evaluational context is the most important step in solving evaluation problems.

REFERENCES

Amemiya, T. (1985), *Advanced Econometrics*, Cambridge, MA: Harvard University Press.

Andrews, D. (1991), 'Asymptotic Normality of Series Estimators for Non-parametric and Semi-parametric Regression Models', *Econometrica*, 59, 307–45.

Angrist, J. (1990), 'Lifetime Earnings and the Vietnam Era Draft Lottery: Evidence from Social Security Administration Records', *American Economic Review*, 80, 313–35.

Angrist, J., G. Imbens and D. Rubin (in press), 'Identification of Causal Effects Using Instrumental Variables', *Journal of the American Statistical Association.*

Ashenfelter, O. (1983),'Determining Participation in Income-tested Social Programs', *Journal of the American Statistical Association*, 78, 517–25.

Ashenfelter, O. and D. Card (1985), 'Using the Longitudinal Structure of Earnings to Estimate the Effect of Training Programs', *Review of Economics and Statistics*, 67, 648–60.

Auerbach, A. and L. Kotlikoff (1987), *Dynamic Fiscal Policy,* New York: Cambridge University Press.

Barnow, B., G. Cain and A. Goldberger (1980), 'Issues in the Analysis of Selectivity Bias', in E. Stromsdorfer and G. Farkas (eds), *Evaluation Studies Review Annual,* Vol. 5, San Francisco: Sage, pp. 43–59.

Bassi, L. (1983), 'The Effect of CETA on the Post-program Earnings of Participants', *Journal of Human Resources*, 18, 539–56.

Bassi, L. (1984), 'Estimating the Effects of Training Programs with Non-random Selection', *Review of Economics and Statistics*, 66 (1), 36–43.

Björklund, A. (1988), 'What Experiments are Needed for Manpower Policy?', *Journal of Human Resources*, 23, 267–77.

Björklund, A. and R. Moffitt (1987), 'Estimation of Wage Gains and Welfare Gains in Self-selection Models', *Review of Economics and Statistics*, 69, 42–9.

Bloom, H. (1984), 'Accounting for No-shows in Experimental Evaluation Designs', *Evaluation Review*, 8 (2), 225–46.

Bloom, H., L. Orr, G. Cave, S. Bell and F. Doolittle (1993), *The National JTPA Study: Title IIA Impacts on Earnings and Employment at 18 Months*, Bethesda, MD: Abt Associates.

Burtless, G. (1993), 'The Case for Social Experiments', in K. Jensen and P. K. Madsen (eds), *Measuring Labour Market Measures: Evaluating the Effects of Active Labour Market Policies*, Copenhagen: Ministry of Labour, pp. 15–34.

Burtless, G. (1995), 'The Case for Randomized Field Trials in Economic and Policy Research', *Journal of Economic Perspectives*, 9 (2), 63–84.

Burtless, G. and L. Orr (1986), 'Are Classical Experiments Needed for Manpower Policy?', *Journal of Human Resources*, 21, 606–39.

Cain, G. and H. Watts (1974), 'Toward a Summary and Synthesis of the Evidence', in G. Cain and H. Watts (eds), *Income Maintenance and Labor Supply*, Chicago: Rand McNally, pp. 328–73.

Cave, G. and J. Quint (1991), *Career Beginnings Impact Evaluation: Findings from a Program for High School Students*, New York: Manpower Demonstration Research Corporation.

Chamberlain, G. (1982), 'Multivariate Regression Models for Panel Data', *Journal of Econometrics*, 18, 1–46.

Clements, N., J. Heckman and J. Smith (in press), 'Making the Most Out of Social Program Evaluations: Reducing the Intrinsic Uncertainty in Evidence from Randomized Trials with an Application to the National JTPA Experiment', *Review of Economic Studies.*

Cosslett, S. (1991), 'Semiparametric Estimation of a Regression Model with Sample Selectivity', in W. A. Barnett, J. Powell and G. Tauchen (eds), *Nonparametric and Semiparametric Estimation Methods in Econometrics and Statistics*, Cambridge, UK: Cambridge University Press, pp. 175–98.

Davidson, C. and S. Woodbury (1993), 'The Displacement Effect of Reemployment Bonus Programs', *Journal of Labor Economics*, 11(4), 575–605.

Dawid, A. P. (1979), 'Conditional Independence in Statistical Theory', *Journal of the Royal Statistical Society*, Series B, 41, 1–31.

Doolittle, F. and L. Traeger (1990), *Implementing the National JTPA Study*, New York: Manpower Demonstration Research Corporation.

Fraker, T. and R. Maynard (1987), 'The Adequacy of Comparison Group Designs for Evaluations of Employment-related Programs', *Journal of Human Resources*, 22, 194–227.

Frechet, M. (1951), 'Sur Les Tableux de Correlation Dont Les Marges Sont Données', *Annales de l'Université, Lyon* Sect. A, 14, 53–77.

Haavelmo, T. (1944), 'The Probability Approach to Econometrics', *Econometrica*, 12, S1–S118.

Hansen, J. (ed.) (1994), *Preparing for the Workplace: Charting a Course for Federal Post-secondary Policy*, Washington, DC: National Research Council.

Heckman, J. (1974), 'Shadow Prices, Market Wages and Labor Supply', *Econometrica*, 42, 679–94.

Heckman, J. (1976), 'Simultaneous Equations Models with Continuous and Discrete Endogenous Variables and Structural Shifts', in S. Goldfeld and R. Quandt (eds), *Studies in Nonlinear Estimation*, Cambridge, MA: Ballinger, pp. 235–72.

Heckman, J. (1978), 'Dummy Endogenous Variables in a Simultaneous Equations System', *Econometrica*, 46, 931–61.

Heckman, J. (1979), 'Sample Selection Bias as a Specification Error', *Econometrica*, 47, 153–61.

Heckman, J. (1980), 'Addendum to Sample Selection Bias as a Specification Error', in E. Stromsdorfer and G. Farkas (eds), *Evaluation Studies Review Annual*, Vol. 5, San Francisco: Sage, pp. 69–74.

Heckman, J. (1990a), 'Varieties of Selection Bias', *American Economic Review*, 80 (2), 313–18.

Heckman, J. (1990b), *Alternative Approaches to the Evaluation of Social Programs: Econometric and Experimental Methods*, Barcelona Lecture, World Congress of the Econometric Society, 1990.

Heckman, J. (1992), 'Randomization and Social Policy Evaluation', in C. Manski and I. Garfinkel (eds), *Evaluating Welfare and Training Programs*, Cambridge, MA: Harvard University Press, pp. 201–30.

Heckman, J. (1993), 'The Case for Simple Estimators: Experimental Evidence from the National JTPA Study', University of Chicago. (Unpublished manuscript)

Heckman, J., N. Hohmann, M. Khoo and J. Smith (1995), 'Analyzing Experimental Data in the Presence of Substitution Bias', University of Chicago. (Unpublished manuscript)

Heckman, J. and B. Honoré (1990), 'The Empirical Content of the Roy Model', *Econometrica*, 58, 1121–49.

Heckman, J. and V. J. Hotz (1989), 'Choosing among Alternative Nonexperimental Methods for Estimating the Impact of Social Programs: The Case of Manpower Training', *Journal of the American Statistical Association*, 84, 862–80.

Heckman, J., H. Ichimura, J. Smith and P. Todd (1995a), 'Nonparametric Characterization of Selection Bias Using Experimental Data, Part I: Definitions, Applications and Empirical Results', University of Chicago. (Unpublished manuscript)

Heckman, J., H. Ichimura, J. Smith and P. Todd (1995b), 'Nonparametric Characterization of Selection Bias Using Experimental Data, Part II: Econometric Theory and Monte Carlo Evidence', University of Chicago. (Unpublished manuscript)

Heckman, J., H. Ichimura and P. Todd (1995a), 'Matching as an Econometric Evaluation Estimator: Part I, theory and methods', University of Chicago. (Unpublished manuscript)

Heckman, J., H. Ichimura and P. Todd (1995b), 'Matching as an Econometric Evaluation Estimator: Part II, empirical results', University of Chicago. (Unpublished manuscript)

Heckman, J. and T. MaCurdy (1986), 'Labor Econometrics', in Z. Griliches and M. Intriligator (eds), *Handbook of Econometrics*, Vol. 3, Amsterdam: North-Holland.

Heckman, J. and R. Robb (1985), 'Alternative Methods for Evaluating the Impact of Interventions', in J. Heckman and B. Singer (eds), *Longitudinal Analysis of Labor Market Data*, New York: Cambridge University Press, pp. 156–245.

Heckman, J. and R. Robb (1986a), 'Alternative Methods for Evaluating the Impact of Interventions: An Overview', *Journal of Econometrics*, 30, 239–67.

Heckman, J. and R. Robb (1986b), 'Alternative Methods for Solving the Problem of Selection Bias in Evaluating the Impact of Treatment on Outcomes', in H. Wainer (ed.), *Drawing Inferences from Self-selected Samples*, Berlin: Springer, pp. 63–107.

Heckman, J. and R. Roselius (1994), 'Evaluating the Impact of Training on the Earnings and Labor Force Status of Young Women: Better Data Help a Lot', University of Chicago. (Unpublished manuscript)

Heckman, J. and J. Smith (1993), 'Assessing the Case for Randomized Evaluation of Social Programs', in K. Jensen and P. K. Madsen (eds), *Measuring Labour Market Measures: Evaluating the Effects of Active Labour Market Policies*, Copenhagen: Ministry of Labour, pp. 35–96.

Heckman, J. and J. Smith (1995a), 'Assessing the Case for Social Experiments', *Journal of Economic Perspectives*, 9 (2), 85–110.

Heckman, J. and J. Smith (1995b), 'Evaluating the Welfare State', University of Chicago. (Unpublished manuscript)

Heckman, J. and J. Smith (1995c), 'Ashenfelter's Dip and the Determinants of Participation in a Social Program: Implications for Simple Program Evaluation Strategies', University of Chicago. (Unpublished manuscript)

Heckman, J., J. Smith and C. Taber (1994), 'Accounting for Dropouts in Evaluations of Social Experiments', National Bureau of Economic Research, Technical Working Paper no. 166.

Heckman, J. and Wolpin, K. (1976), 'Does the Contract Compliance Program Work?: An Analysis of Chicago Data', *Industrial and Labor Relations Review*, 19, 415–33.

Hoeffding, W. (1940), 'Masstabinvariate Korrelationstheorie', Schriften des Mathematischen Instituts und des Instituts für Angewandte Mathematik der Freien Universität Berlin, 179–251.

Ichimura, H. and L. F. Lee (1991), 'Semiparametric Least Squares Estimation of Multiple Index Models: Single Equation Estimation', in W. A. Barnett, J. Powell and G. Tauchen (eds), *Nonparametric and Semiparametric Estimation Methods in Econometrics and Statistics*, Cambridge: Cambridge University Press, pp. 3–50.

Judge, G., C. Hill, W. Griffiths and T. Lee (1985), *The Theory and Practice of Econometrics,* New York: John Wiley.

Kramer, M. and S. Shapiro (1984), 'Scientific Challenges in the Application of Randomized Trials', *Journal of the American Medical Association*, 252, 2739–45.

Kydland, F. and E. Prescott (1991), 'The Econometrics of the General Equilibrium Approach to Business Cycles', *The Scandinavian Journal of Economics*, 93 (2), 161–78.

LaLonde, R. (1986), 'Evaluating the Econometric Evaluations of Training Programs with Experimental Data', *American Economic Review*, 76, 604–20.

Little, R. and D. Rubin (1987), *Statistical Analysis with Missing Data*, New York: John Wiley.

MaCurdy, T. (1982), 'The Use of Time Series Processes to Model the Error Structure of Earnings in a Longitudinal Data Analysis', *Journal of Econometrics*, 18 (1), 83–114.

Manski, C. and S. Lerman (1977), 'The Estimation of Choice Probabilities from Choice-based Samples', *Econometrica*, 45, 1977–88.

Manski, C. and D. McFadden (1981), 'Alternative Estimators and Sample Designs for Discrete Choice Analysis', in C. Manski and D. McFadden (eds), *Structural Analysis of Discrete Data with Econometric Applications*, Cambridge, MA: MIT Press, pp. 117–36.

Moffitt, R. (1992), 'Evaluation Methods for Program Entry Effects', in C. Manski and I. Garfinkel (eds), *Evaluating Welfare and Training Programs*, Cambridge, MA: Harvard University Press, pp. 231–52.

Mundlak, Y. (1961), 'Empirical Production Functions Free of Management Bias', *Journal of Farm Econometrics*, 43, 45–56.

Mundlak, Y. (1978), 'On the Pooling of Time Series and Cross Section Data', *Econometrica*, 46, 69–85.

Newey, W., J. Powell and J. Walker (1990), 'Semiparametric Estimation of Selection Models', *American Economic Review*, 80 (2), 324–8.

Patil, G. (1965), *Classical and Contagious Discrete Distributions*, New York: Pergamon Press.

Powell, J. (1989), 'Semiparametric Estimation of Censored Selection Models', University of Wisconsin at Madison. (Unpublished manuscript)

Powell, J. (1995), 'Estimation of Semiparametric Models', in R. Engle and D. McFadden (eds), *Handbook of Econometrics*, Vol. 4, New York: Elsevier Scientific B.V., pp. 2444–521.

Puma, M., N. Burstein, K. Merrell and G. Silverstein (1990), *Evaluation of the Food Stamp Employment and Training Program: Final Report*, Bethesda, MD: Abt Associates.

Quandt, R. (1972), 'A New Approach to Estimating Switching Regressions', *Journal of the American Statistical Association*, 67, 306–10.

Quandt, R. (1988), *The Econometrics of Disequilibrium*, New York: Basil Blackwell.

Rao, C. (1965), 'On Discrete Distributions Arising Out of Methods of Ascertainment', in G. Patil (ed.), *Classical and Contagious Discrete Distributions*, New York: Pergamon Press, pp. 320–32.

Rosenbaum, P. and D. Rubin (1983), 'The Central Role of the Propensity Score in Observational Studies for Causal Effects', *Biometrika*, 70, 41–55.

Rosenbaum, P. and D. Rubin (1985), 'Constructing a Control Group Using Multivariate Sampling Methods That Incorporate the Propensity Score', *American Statistician*, 39 (1), 33–8.

Roy, A. (1951), 'Some Thoughts on the Distribution of Earnings', *Oxford Economic Papers*, 3, 135–46.

Shoven, J. and J. Whalley (1992), *Applying General Equilibrium*, Cambridge. UK: Cambridge University Press.

Simon, H. (1957), 'Spurious Correlation: A Causal Interpretation', in H. Simon (ed.), *Models of Man*, New York: John Wiley, pp. 37–49.

Tinbergen, J. (1956), *Economic Policy: Principles and Design*, Amsterdam: North Holland.

Torp, H., O. Rauum, E. Hernaes and H. Goldstein (1993), 'The First Norwegian Experiment', in K. Jensen and P. K. Madsen (eds), *Measuring Labour Market Measures: Evaluating the Effects of Active Labour Market Policies*, Copenhagen: Ministry of Labour, pp. 97–140.

Wainer, H. (1985), *Drawing Inferences from Self-selected Samples*, Berlin: Springer.

3. Experimental Evaluation of European Labour Market Policy

Anders Björklund and Håkan Regnér

There seems to be a remarkable paradox in evaluation research on labour market policy. In the United States policy programmes tend to be rather small in magnitude, but classical experiments based on randomization have been used frequently to evaluate these small-scale programmes. In Europe, on the other hand, total expenditure on labour market policy (relative to the size of the economies) is much higher, but only a few experiments have been conducted. Does this state of affairs mean that Europe has a lot to learn from the United States, or is it differences in the institutional settings which make experiments useful in the United States and useless in Europe?

In this chapter we will argue that experiments are feasible and can provide useful information about the effects of labour market policy in Europe as well as in the United States. There are, however, marked limitations to the extent that experiments can be used successfully. They are particularly useful for the analysis of new programmes and for well-defined changes in existing ones. We have drawn this conclusion from our examination of previous randomized experiments on labour market policies in the United States and of the few that have been conducted in Europe. Some experiments might be considered as failures, but there are others which can be viewed as successes in the sense that they have provided valuable new insights about the impact of labour market policy.

The study of such experiments is a central part of this chapter. Starting in section 1 with a short statement of the evaluation problem and a brief description of how classical experiments in principle can solve this problem, we proceed in section 2 with a review of the main problems associated with experiments. In section 3 we present and examine previous experiments in the light of these problems. With these experiences in mind, we propose, in section 4, a couple of experiments that can be used to evaluate some important European labour market policy programmes. Section 5 contains our main conclusions.

1   THE EVALUATION PROBLEM AND EXPERIMENTS

The question that interests most evaluators of labour market policy programmes is how the effect of a programme on participants compares with
how they would have acted in the absence of the programme. Because it is
impossible to observe participants in two competing labour market states,
here we have the core problem in all evaluation research. By definition, there
is for each participant an opposite state, that is, the state without the programme, and for each nonparticipant there is a hypothetical state of being a
participant (see Heckman, 1993, and Heckman and Smith, 1993, for more
general and thorough discussion). A person participating in the programme
($D = 1$) attains the outcome Y_1; for nonparticipants ($D = 0$) the outcome is Y_0.
There is also a set of variables (X_1 and X_0), generally including individual
background variables and variables describing the local labour market, which
determines the outcomes. The relation between these variables and the outcome measures can more formally be described by the following two linear
equations:

$$Y = Y_1 = X_1 \beta_1 + u_1 \quad \text{if} \quad D = 1 \tag{3.1}$$

$$Y = Y_0 = X_0 \beta_0 + u_0 \quad \text{if} \quad D = 0 \tag{3.2}$$

where u_1 and u_0 are characteristics that are not observed by the evaluator.
Typical outcome measures are earnings and employment, and if the programme has been successful it will generate higher future earnings or employment probabilities for participants.

The basic evaluation problem also includes the problem of selection bias,
which arises when selection of programme participants concerns unobservables. Selection bias can be present if, for example, the decision to participate
is the result of decisions made by persons eligible for the programme, by the
administrator or both. In the literature on nonexperimental evaluation a variety
of statistical models to adjust for this bias has been developed, and the fundamental problem with this approach is the choice between alternative estimators; for an analysis of the problem see Heckman and Hotz (1989) (US data)
and a similar study by Regnér (1993) (Swedish data). However, a perfect
experiment solves the problem using the method of random assignment, which
means that eligible participants are randomly assigned either to the programme or to a control group (the counterfactual) that does not receive any
treatment. There will be no average differences in unobserved characteristics
between the two randomly chosen groups, and, therefore, postprogramme differences can be attributed solely to the programme. The advantage with a
perfect experiment is that the simple mean difference in outcome measures

between the two groups is a consistent estimator of the true average programme effect. Thus, the problem of choosing between alternative estimators is eliminated (cf. chap. 2, section 2).

2   DIFFICULTIES WITH RANDOMIZATION

A properly designed experiment can solve many of the basic problems related to nonexperimental evaluation design. Even so, experiments can present problems of their own. Some may be caused by the experiment itself, whereas others are also likely to be evident in nonexperimental studies.

An experiment can give rise to *randomization bias*. Such bias occurs when the randomization procedure itself affects the behaviour of potential programme participants. If they know that the experiment will be carried out they may choose not to apply for the programme, which may lead to a significant change in the pool of applicants. Therefore, the treatment group might not be representative of the group that usually participates in the programme. Because the underlying population of eligible persons has changed, the estimated effects cannot be generalized to the true population. However, this change should not constitute a problem when the experimental evaluation focusses on a completely new programme.

If participants know that they are being studied the experiment can also affect their behaviour during the programme. It is possible that they will then work harder than under normal conditions, which implies that the experiment directly affects the outcome of the programme. The potential change in behaviour is generally referred to as the *Hawthorne effect*.

The experiment can also have an impact on the programme administrators. If they control the process of assigning individuals to the eligible group they can deliberately change their selection criteria so that the group is composed of persons unusually suitable for the programme. Bureaucrats can also alter the content of the programme, for example, by supplying new and more competent instructors, new books, computers and so on, which means that participants are better serviced than they would be under normal circumstances. The above are special cases of *disruption bias*, which arises when randomization itself alters the programme being evaluated.

Programme administrators can also intentionally offer the control group some other service that is a close substitute for the service received by the treatment group (*substitution bias*). Evaluations of new programmes may not be affected by this problem because close substitutes may not be available. Administrators can, of course, also behave in the opposite way, that is, they invest more effort in their work than usual when they know that they are part of an experiment.

The problem of *bureaucratic behaviour* depends on the programme-specific environment, and it is difficult to predict how damaging certain kinds of behaviour might be. As a general rule, the programme evaluator should explain the goals and purposes of the experiment; such elaborations may lead administrators to behave more in accordance with their ordinary work routines.

Random assignment is often considered impossible for *ethical reasons.* The main problem is that it is unethical to deny members of the control group access to the programme. The problem varies from programme to programme, from country to country and from time to time. If, for example, participation is a right that has existed for a long time and has even been written into the law, then it is probably impossible to implement the experiment. This is a significant difficulty because, even if the experiment is finally carried out, ethical considerations may be the major factor behind the reluctance of the bureaucrats to go through with it. It is probably easier to motivate random assignment in cases where new policies are being introduced or where there are more applicants than programme slots, that is, there is excess demand for a particular programme. Experiments may also be accepted if there is considerable uncertainty about the net returns to expensive labour market programmes.

High costs have often been emphasized as a major disadvantage of experiments, as compared to the standard nonexperimental approach. One reason could be that a lot of time has to be spent on the design of the study and the provision of information to administrators and participants, and the fulfilment of these tasks sometimes creates a long time gap between implementation and the final analysis. A long duration can be a major drawback if the outcome of the experiment is supposed to serve as an input to the political decision-making procedure. However, this is not a problem related solely to experimental studies; it can equally be a hindrance in nonexperimental evaluations based on surveys.

An underlying assumption in both experimental and nonexperimental designs is that nonparticipants are unaffected by the programme. The supposition may be valid, but one cannot ignore the possibility that members of the experimental group acquire new employment as an effect of the treatment, whereas the control group suffers the opposite effect. This is the *displacement effect* of the programme, and the degree of the problem varies with the effectiveness of the programme and the state of the local labour market. One can easily imagine an extreme case where every new job goes to enrolees in a programme and none to the control group. Here the programme only has a distributional effect. Although the above case rarely emerges, on a small local labour market there may very well be large displacement effects.

3   EXPERIMENTS IN PRACTICE

Obviously, experimental evaluations of labour market policies entail potential problems, but the question is if it is possible to avoid them through clever design and efficient administration. One way to answer this question is to examine the randomized experimental studies that have actually been conducted in the field of labour market policy and to try to learn from the experience gained in these cases. In this section we will present and discuss some of the most important recent US experiments and the three European experiments that we know of; the reader may consult Björklund (1989) for a similar presentation of the main experiments carried out up until the late 1980s. We believe that these studies offer interesting lessons both from the methodological and policy points of view.

3.1   Recent US Experiments

3.1.1   *The Job Training Partnership Act (JTPA)*[1]

The JTPA Programme was introduced in 1982; its purpose is to provide classroom training in occupational skills, on-the-job training in private firms, job search assistance and other employment and training services to economically disadvantaged Americans. The JTPA is federally funded, and the administration of the programme at the local level is carried out by so-called service delivery areas (SDAs). There are approximately 600 SDAs across the United States, and they design the mix of the programmes that will be supplied; they do not normally provide the services, rather in most cases they commission other agencies to this end. The organization of the services does, however, vary across SDAs, and some contract out for the majority of the services, including determination of programme eligibility, whereas others use their own staff to provide all but vocational skills training.

The selection of participants for JTPA varied during the 1980s. Prior to 1985 other agencies recommended participants to the programme, but subsequently, when the economy had recovered, the SDAs had to perform much of the search for participants themselves. Most of the SDAs that participated in the experiment had problems filling their training slots during the period of the study.

The experiment was carried out by Abt Associates Inc. and the Manpower Demonstration Research Corporation (MDRC) on the initiative of the US Department of Labor; it covers a sample of 16 SDAs around the country. Data were gathered on persons eligible for the JTPA services, who were then ran-

---

1   This section is based mainly on Dolittle and Traeger (1990).

domly assigned to either a treatment group allowed access to the programme[2] or to a control group denied access for 18 months. The random assignment was performed after participants had been assigned to a certain type of services, that is, they were not randomly assigned among types of services. The random assignment covered the period from November 1987 to September 1989, and a total of 20 606 persons were randomly assigned, approximately one-third of these to a control group.

The general impression is that the programme has significant positive earnings effects only for adult females. For adult males the effects are slight, and for young people it seems as if the programme actually has negative effects on their future earnings.

The experiment was affected both by bureaucratic resistance and randomization bias. When SDAs were asked to participate in the study approximately 90 per cent of them refused to be part of the experiment. The MDRC had to spend considerable amounts of time and money on information. They developed special information packages (pamphlets and videos) explaining the meaning and goals of the experiment, which they used to inform both administrators and programme participants. Even so, it was difficult to persuade SDAs to participate in the study, and SDAs that finally decided to take part received increased compensation for their efforts. On average, the compensation level rose by four times the original amount. The unwillingness to participate resulted in a nonrepresentative selection of SDAs. Compared with the true population, there are too many SDAs from the midwest region of the United States and too few from the South.

Data presented by the MDRC suggest that the main reason for nonparticipation in the experiment was ethical, that is, that SDAs participating would have had to deny members of the control group access to the programme. But the SDAs were also concerned that the assignment of a control group would lead to lower future enrolment in the programme. Most SDAs had an excess supply of training slots when the experiment was implemented, and they thought that the experiment would create an even lower demand for their services. Another concern was that the experiment could affect performance measures, for example, lower the share in employment after completed training. Such performance measures are important in the US system.

The concerns raised by the SDAs also led to a lowering of the exclusion period for the control group, which was originally 30 months. The SDAs judged it to be too long on ethical and operational grounds (loss of potential enrolees), and, therefore, it was shortened to 18 months. This may not affect

---

2 Approximately 70 per cent of the experimental group received on-the-job training or classroom training in occupational skills. The other 30 per cent benefited from job search assistance or other types of services.

the evaluation of the results, but it shows that bureaucratic behaviour and concerns have a considerable impact on the outcome of the experiments.

3.1.2 Unemployment Insurance Experiments[3]

Another important class of experiments has been conducted to evaluate reforms of the US Unemployment Insurance (UI) system. The general goals of the reforms have been to increase reemployment probabilities for UI claimants and to reduce the costs of UI. These experiments can be divided into two subgroups on the basis of their design. The first group, the *cash bonuses experiments*, offer payments to UI recipients who find jobs quickly and keep them for a certain length of time. The second group, the *job search experiments*, provide a combination of services, including more detailed information on vacancies, more job placements and increased enforcement of the job search requirements for the receipt of UI. Because both groups have the same goal, although using different means, they will be treated under the same heading.

Four experiments that use bonus payments have been carried out.[4] The first experiment was sponsored locally by the state; the others were financed partly by the US Department of Labor. The basic design of the experiments was straightforward and simple: eligible UI claimants were randomly assigned to either a control group, which received existing services and benefits, or to a treatment group, which was offered the bonus. One of the experiments also provided some additional services to the treatment group.

There are differences across the experiments concerning the amount of the bonus payment, the period during which participants had to find a job to qualify for the bonus (the qualification period) and the period they had to remain in the new job to receive the bonus (the reemployment period). Eligibility rules and the point in time at which the treatment group was informed about the bonus also vary. Nevertheless, each treatment group was offered a bonus, this being the central element of the experiment design, and thus the four experiments are dealt with as a group.

The size of the bonus in the Illinois experiment was a constant $500, which was about four times the average weekly benefit. The New Jersey experiment offered, on average, $1644 or about nine times the weekly UI benefit, but the bonus declined by 10 per cent of the original amount each week. The Pennsylvania experiment offered the same amount as the Illinois experiment; the

---

3 This section is based mainly on Meyer (1995).

4 The experiments are in chronological order; Illinois UI Incentive Experiments (1984), New Jersey UI Re-employment Demonstration (1986–87), Washington Re-employ Bonus Experiments (1988–89) and Pennsylvania Re-employ Bonus Demonstration (1988–89).

amount offered in the last experiment varied between $110 and $1250, at an average of about $560.

All bonus experiments (see Decker, 1992, for a thorough analysis of the New Jersey and Illinois experiments) show that economic incentives do affect time spent in receipt of benefits. Table 3.1 presents the average mean differences of weeks of benefits and quarterly earnings after the treatment between participants and nonparticipants. The Illinois experiment, for example, shows that weeks of benefits fell by 1.15 weeks. Supportive evidence is also provided by the results of the other experiments. The earnings effects are small and insignificant in all experiments.

Table 3.1   Effects of the Bonus Experiments on Weeks of Benefits and Quarterly Earnings

	Illinois	New Jersey	Pennsylvania	Washington
Weeks of benefits in benefit year	− 1.15 (0.21)	− 0.90 (0.25)	− 0.92 (0.27)	− 0.73 (0.34)
Quarterly reemployment earnings ($)	8 (66)	79 (85)	120 (70)	− 22 (127)

Note
Standard errors are in parentheses.

Source
'Lessons from the U.S. Unemployment Insurance Experiments' by B. Meyer, 1995, *The Journal of Economic Literature*, 33 (1). Copyright 1995 by B. Meyer. Adapted by permission.

One of the main advantages of these experiments is that they do not interfere with or interrupt an ongoing programme, nor do they have to address the issue of denying nonparticipants services, which largely affected bureaucratic behaviour in the JTPA experiment. However, Meyer (1995) notes two caveats concerning the experiments, which cannot be ruled out.[5] First, there may be displacement effects, that is, those eligible for the bonus act in a way that reduces the number of vacancies available to the control group. Second, it is possible that the UI claimants may reduce their receipt of UI because they are part of the experiment and not because of the bonus, that is, a Hawthorne effect

---

5 Actually, he mentions four caveats, but two involve the effects of a permanent bonus system, which points to the general problem of most experiments, namely, that it is hard to generalize experimental findings.

may arise. Davidson and Woodbury (1993) present evidence indicating that displacement effects may be a serious problem in the bonus experiments.

The job search experiments have the same goals as the bonus experiments, but instead of monetary rewards these experiments provide extended or personally designed services to the treatment group. Six job search experiments have been conducted, and they differ in a few dimensions,[6] for example, the time when potential programme participants are contacted, eligibility rules and the amount and types of extended services. However, the basic design is identical for all experiments, that is, eligible individuals are assigned to either a treatment group, which receives the extended services, or a control group, which gets the ordinary service.

Table 3.2   Effects of the Job Search Experiments on Weeks of Benefits and Quarterly Earnings

	Nevada I	Charleston	New Jersey	Nevada II	Washington	Minnesota
Weeks of benefits in benefit year	−3.90 (0.41)	−0.70 (0.39)	−0.50 (0.22)	−1.60 (0.30)	—	−4.32 (0.16)
Quarterly reemployment earnings ($)	—	—	28 (77)	—	292 (211)	—

Note
Standard errors are in parentheses.
— = data not available.

Source
'Lessons from the U.S. Unemployment Insurance Experiments' by B. Meyer, 1995, *The Journal of Economic Literature*, 33 (1). Copyright 1995 by B. Meyer. Adapted by permission.

Table 3.2 has the same design as Table 3.1 and illustrates that all experiments show a reduction of weeks of UI (see Johnson and Klepinger, 1993, for an in-depth analysis of the Washington experiment). Looking at the Nevada I experiment, we can see that extended services lead to a shorter benefit period

---

6 The experiments are in chronological order; Nevada Claimant Placement Programme (1977–78), Charleston Claimant Placement and Work Test Demonstration (1983), New Jersey UI Re-employ Demonstration (1986–87), Washington Alternative Work Search Experiment (1986–87), Nevada Claimant Employment Programme (1988–89) and Re-employ Minnesota Project (1988–90).

of almost four weeks. These experiments resulted in somewhat greater effects on duration of benefit than the bonus experiments.

A notable feature of all ten experiments is that, conditional on their respective policy design, they all find a positive impact on the probability of leaving the unemployment insurance roll, but only minor or no effects on earnings. There are differences in the magnitude of the estimated impacts on weeks of received benefits both across job search experiments and between these experiments and the bonus studies. It is not unreasonable to believe that the combination of services in the job search experiments had an effect on the results. Some of the basic differences are summarized in Table 3.3.

Table 3.3   The Main Characteristics of the Job Search Experiments

	Nevada I	Charleston	New Jersey
Treatments	(1) More intensive services, weekly interviews and eligibility checks, all services from the same personnel	(1) Two enhanced placement interviews and a three-hour job search assistance session required (2) Two interviews (3) One interview	(1) Periodic contacts with Employment Service required, job search materials provided (2) Job search assistance plus offer of training and relocation assistance
	Nevada II	Washington	Minnesota
Treatments	(1) Higher-quality Employment and Unemployment Insurance services, all services from the same personnel	(1) No requirement to report employer contacts (2) Individual job search (3) Intensive job search assistance with two days' job search workshop	(1) Intensive personalized job search assistance with all services from the same personnel

Source
Policy Lessons from the U.S. Unemployment Insurance Experiments by B. Meyer, 1992, The National Bureau of Economic Research, working paper no. 4197.

The largest impact estimate is reported for the Minnesota experiment, and the lowest for New Jersey. The extended services provided to the experimental group in the former study consisted of one treatment of intensive personalized job search assistance (JSA) from the same personnel. The latter provided two treatments, the first incorporating periodic contacts with the employment service (ES), which provided job search materials. The second treatment involved JSA and offers of training and relocation assistance. The first Nevada experiment had similar results to the Minnesota study, and it also used similar services, that is, one treatment of more intensive services with weekly interviews and careful checks of the eligibility of claimants to UI. All services were supplied by the same personnel at both the ES and the offices administering the UI. Similar services were also provided in the second Nevada experiment, although it emphasized the quality (not defined) of the ES and UI services. But also in this case the experimental group received all services from the same staff.

The Charleston and Washington experiments provided the most extensive treatments of all the job search experiments, in both cases in three parts. The first treatment in the Charleston experiment consisted of two refined placement interviews and a three-hour JSA session. The second treatment consisted of two new interviews, and the third comprised only one interview. The last experiment also consisted of three treatments. First, in contrast to all the other experiments, the Washington experiment started by carrying out fewer checks of participants' job search activities (in the United States claimants are required to actively seek work). Instead, benefit cheques were sent to participants until they indicated that they were not eligible. Participants were also instructed to engage in active job search, but they did not have to report on their activities. In the second treatment they received JSA tailored to their individual needs. The third treatment consisted of intensive JSA with a two-day job search workshop.

Meyer (1995) suggests that the key differences between the two classes of experiments are that the search approach does not create an incentive to enter the pool of UI claimants and that, because job search improves matching of employers and employees, displacement is less important. However, the Hawthorne effect might be even stronger in the job search experiments than in the bonus experiments because, by design, these experiments involve repeated contact with the treatment group, which probably leads this group to behave in accordance with the experiment.

As for the bonus experiments, these do not interfere with or interrupt an ongoing programme, which could be an important factor underlying the relatively successful outcome of these experiments.

3.2   European Experiments

3.2.1   *The Study of Intensified Employment Services in Eskilstuna, Sweden*[7]

This study was carried out in 1975 at the local employment office in the small town of Eskilstuna, situated in the middle of Sweden. The sample evaluated consisted of about 400 unemployed job seekers who had been registered at this office for three months or longer. The office in Eskilstuna received a personnel reinforcement for the period of the experiment, 10 March to 6 June 1975. The experimental group used the services of the employment office for an average of 7.5 hours during the experiment, as compared to 1.5 hours, on average, for the control group. The latter received normal service, which is why the study aimed at measuring the effects of increased service. Further, the additional resources made it possible for the personnel at the employment office to work more intensively on the problems of single individuals rather than providing more general labour market information to job seekers and firms looking for workers.

The initiative to carry out the study was taken by an individual researcher, Lennart Delander, who managed to get strong support both from the Swedish National Labour Market Board (AMS) and from the head of the local employment office in Eskilstuna. The researcher and the representatives of the administration shared a great enthusiasm for acquiring an opportunity to test whether intensified employment services would produce favourable effects. We have

Table 3.4   Effects of the Experiments on Personnel Reinforcement in Eskilstuna

	Experimental group (*n* = 216)	Control group (*n* = 194)
Percentage with a job at the end of the experimental period	48	34
Weeks of unemployment from the start of the experiment until the follow-up nine months later	11	18
Average monthly earnings for the employed (SEK)	3588	3386
Percentage with a permanent job	92	68
Percentage with negative attitudes concerning the quality of the work	12	27

Source
'Studier kring den arbetsförmedlande verksamheten' by L. Delander, 1978, *Statens Offentliga Utredningar*, 60. Copyright 1978 by L. Delander. Adapted by permission.

---

7 This section is based on Delander (1978) and our personal communications with him.

been told that the personnel working in the employment office were also well motivated to participate in the project. The study was financed by the research board of the Ministry of Labour.

On the whole, considerably positive effects were produced by this experiment. An overview of the most important results is presented in Table 3.4. The first two rows depict different quantitative measures of effects such as employment and unemployment. All the measures indicate distinctly positive effects for the experimental group. It is interesting to note from rows 3 to 5 that even the quality of the placements was improved. For the most part the margins were reported to be significantly different from zero, that is, it is unlikely that they were caused by mere chance.

To what extent are these results distorted by the problems discussed above? First, it is clear that neither ethical nor cost objections were raised against the study. Another problem that can be ruled out in this case is substitution bias. However, randomization bias and displacement effects might very well have been present, and in that case the estimated effects cannot be used to infer how a permanent reinforcement of personnel would affect the labour market.

A potential source of randomization bias in this case is that the personnel were very enthusiastic about trying out a new way of providing services, and maybe they were also eager to show that the new approach would have favourable effects. In general, such behaviour would yield an upward bias for the potential long-term effects, but in our view a bias of this kind does not invalidate the study. After all, it was shown that more resources and enthusiastic personnel really helped the target group! This positive impact effectively rules out the possibility of negative stigma effects connected with receipt of assistance from the public employment service. In both the Swedish and the US discussions on labour market policy the possibility of such negative stigma effects has been mentioned.

It is also obvious that long-term unemployed who found jobs thanks to the extra service might have displaced those who belonged to the control group. (Other groups of unemployed might also have been displaced.) Hence, the net effect on aggregate unemployment or employment cannot be inferred from the study. However, the conclusion that the effects were beneficial for the target group is not altered.

Our general conclusion is, therefore, that the Swedish Eskilstuna study, despite potential randomization bias and displacement effects, provided valuable insights concerning the effects of the programme that was evaluated.

3.2.2   The Norwegian Training Experiment[8]

In the late 1980s unemployment in Norway rose dramatically from its previously very low level of about 2 per cent to over 5 per cent of the labour force. In order to counteract this development, the government decided to step up active labour market policies. A programme of training courses for those who were unemployed or who were threatened with unemployment was the most important of these active labour market measures. About 1 per cent of the labour force participated in the new training courses in the early 1990s.

It is quite clear that a programme of this dimension should be evaluated, and the responsible government ministry invited two research institutes to carry out an evaluation study. The officers of the ministry were interested in an ambitious evaluation and asked for a classical experiment in addition to a nonexperimental study (not to be discussed here). However, the experimental study was limited to courses with excess demand, that is, more applicants than training slots. In this way the training courses could be filled to absolute capacity, in spite of the fact that the control groups had to be denied access.

In all, 18 local employment offices from three counties were selected for the experiment, which covered courses starting in August and September 1991; the purpose was to estimate the impact of these courses on the probability of participants having a job in May and November 1992. The average duration of the courses was only 5.3 weeks. Randomization took place on a course-by-course basis, which was a major practical complication in the implementation of the study.

Despite the support for the project forthcoming from the central ministry, many local administrators were quite sceptical and unwilling to cooperate. Their main argument was that those who would benefit most from training might not be allowed to participate. Further, Raaum and Torp report that they encountered worries that the selection procedures ordinarily used would be evaluated and potentially criticized. A number of measures were taken in order to win the cooperation of the administrators. For example, those applicants to be assigned to the control group were promised ordinary service from the local employment offices. In their report Raaum and Torp emphasize that some unemployed in the control groups might, therefore, have received services which were close substitutes for the programme under study.

The application procedure for courses was as usual during the experiment; the local administrators were requested to make a first selection among the applicants and to 'inactivate' those who did not meet the eligibility requirements for the course. Randomization into an experimental and a control group

8 This section is based on Raaum and Torp (1993) and our personal communications with them.

was to be carried out among those who survived this first screening by the local officers. Because under normal conditions there was always excess demand for the courses, the expectation was that there would be more remaining applicants than training slots; thus, random assignment could take place among these remaining candidates. However, the local administrators were aware of the study and could therefore alter their approach to this first selection of trainees in comparison to normal operating conditions. Raaum and Torp (1993) provide convincing evidence that the screening procedure for many courses was modified; for one course with only 10 slots, 70 out of 80 applicants were 'inactivated'!

With these limitations in mind, Raaum and Torp (1993) present a number of different analyses of the data. The general impression is that the programme had insignificant or minor positive effects on the main outcome variable, that is, the probability of participants being in employment 12 months after the course. They also emphasize that the impacts vary widely from course to course.

In our view it is a matter of judgement to what extent the experiment was damaged by bureaucratic resistance at local level. There seems to be no doubt that the selection of participants differed somewhat from selection procedures when the programme is in normal operation. Thus, the study might at best have provided an estimate of the impact of the training programme when selection is (somewhat) different from what it is in practice. If the administrators are normally able to select those who would benefit most from the programme, and the experiment prevented them from doing so, then one would expect that the experiment revealed an underestimate of the impact of the programme in normal operation. The general methodological lesson from this Norwegian experiment is, however, that a successful experimental evaluation of an ongoing training programme requires cooperative administrators at both the central and the local level.

3.2.3   The Restart Programme in the United Kingdom[9]

The Restart Programme was introduced in the United Kingdom on a national scale in 1987, at a time when unemployment was close to its 1983 peak level. The official objectives of the programme were to foster job search activities, to deter claims for benefits in the absence of eligibility and to provide information about vacancies and other opportunities. The main component of Restart consisted of an interview between the unemployed person and an officer (the 'Restart counsellor') at the local employment office. The interview took place after six months of unemployment. Attendance was compulsory in

---

9   This section is based on White and Lakey (1992), White (1992) and our personal communications with him.

the sense that benefits could otherwise be withdrawn. Job seekers received invitations to an interview on a certain date; the interviews typically lasted 20 minutes, and the aim was to reach a clear outcome, such as referral to a job, to a training or job programme or something else. Restart became one of the points from which individuals were referred to other active labour market policy schemes. However, programmes were also accessible via routes other than Restart.

The evaluation study was commissioned by the Employment Service, initially a division of the Employment Department Group and subsequently a government agency. The Employment Service explicitly wanted the study to be carried out as a randomized experiment. The data were analysed by the Policy Studies Institute, an independent research organization. The period of the study was March to June 1989, that is, when Restart had already been in operation for a couple of years.

The problem of denying eligible persons access to the programme affected the design of the experiment in several ways. First, the control group was kept rather small, comprising about 500 individuals. Second, these individuals were regionally well spread over the country. Third, those who were assigned to the control group and asked for a Restart interview were given an interview, as well as all the other services provided at this point in the programme. These aspects of the design seemed to eliminate objections to the experiment from the local level.

The analysis of the data focussed mainly on unemployment duration and exit rates out of unemployment. Overall, the effects of the programme were positive and quite strong as against the low cost of the interviews. However, even though the other active programmes were also available for the control group, it is possible that some of the effects were caused by the programmes in which the unemployed persons were placed after the interviews rather than by the interviews *per se*.

To what extent are the results of this study distorted by the typical problems of classical experiments? According to our information, no ethical objections were raised in the process of this study, nor was the experiment prevented by cost factors. There is a problem of substitution bias in the sense that those in the control group who asked for it received the same service as the members of the experimental group. This problem will make the simple difference estimator underestimate the total effect, the reason being that the difference in treatment between the groups is less than it would have been had the nonparticipants not received any service at all. However, this problem does not invalidate the findings, and it is interesting to note that there are favourable effects nonetheless. Finally, one cannot rule out displacement effects. Thus, as with all microdata studies, the total effects might not have been elucidated by the study (see chap. 5, section 2.1).

The purpose of a programme like Restart is to improve the employment prospects of the long-term unemployed. The results of the study definitely suggest that Restart achieves this objective, even though it cannot be ruled out that some of the effects are obtained at the expense of other groups. Our overall judgement is that a randomized experiment like the above provides valuable insights about the direction of the effects, even though uncertainty remains about the total effects.

4 PROPOSALS FOR EUROPEAN LABOUR MARKET POLICY

4.1 Mobility Grants in Sweden and Other European Countries

Mobility grants for unemployed workers who move to another region for a new job were introduced in Sweden during the 1950s. In the 1960s and 1970s about 30 000 persons per year, that is just below 1 per cent of the labour force, received such grants. The employment offices provided information about mobility grants and administered the programme as part of their regular activities. The grants have never been a major component of Swedish labour market policy, neither in terms of expenditure nor in terms of persons involved. Nonetheless, these grants have often symbolized the emphasis on job and geographical mobility in Swedish labour market policy.

In the late 1980s, however, the political support for this measure disappeared and the parliament decided to abandon the grants, except for some special cases of 'key personnel' who move to certain areas in Sweden. In the discussion that preceded this decision several arguments were made. One concern put forward by opponents of the grants was that they did not to any significant extent affect the behaviour of the unemployed job seekers, but rather constituted windfall profits for those who would have moved anyway. Another argument often heard was that the grants were misused, in particular among young people who had finished their studies or military service.

We are convinced that in this situation a classical experiment could have been conducted in order to learn more about the impact of these grants. Both the US experiments on bonus payments to the unemployed and the UK Restart evaluation can serve as models for a study. The starting point for an experiment must be a definition of the population of unemployed job seekers who would be eligible for the grant when it is in normal operation. From this population an experimental group that is to be offered the mobility grant will be randomly selected. It would, however, also be possible to select a number of experimental groups that are offered grants of different sizes or with different eligibility rules.[10] An additional possibility would be to differentiate the rules in other ways. For example, the mobility grants in Sweden used to be available to unemployed persons for an unlimited duration, and not only during a limited period of the unemployment spell, as is the case for most of the bonus payments in the United States. If the experimental groups were also differentiated in such dimensions, additional insights would be gained from the study.

Those who have been selected for the experimental groups must be informed about their entitlement to a grant (or a bonus) in the event of them moving to another region for a new job. They must also be informed about the conditions required of the new job; how long it must last, how many working hours per week are stipulated and so on. It would also probably be necessary to explain that this offer is part of an evaluation study. The information can be delivered to the experimental group(s) in several ways. One possibility, as in the case of the Restart Programme, is to send a letter announcing the availability of the grant. Another would be to inform the candidates during any one of their regular visits to the employment exchange offices. Contact by telephone would also be possible.

Finally, data must be collected about the labour market outcome for both the experimental groups and for the control group. In order to study the impact on rather detailed variables like working conditions, wage rates and life satisfaction in general, a survey of the experimental as well as of the control group would be necessary. Unfortunately, surveys often suffer from rather high non-response rates. However, for a study of this kind a survey is not necessary. The register information that is automatically generated by the employment offices in Sweden provides data on all persons registered unemployed in Sweden. Therefore, an outcome variable defined as 'registered as unemployed or not' would be available from the employment offices, thus removing the necessity for a survey. Further, it would be possible to collect other register information on annual earnings from Statistics Sweden.[11] A simple comparison of the means of the outcome variables for the experimental groups and the control group would be sufficient to show the results of the study. If the sample sizes are large enough, the results for specific groups (e.g. age groups) can also be obtained.

Let us now consider the potential objections to, and problems with, such an experimental evaluation. The ethical objections are not strong. Given that the politicians wanted to abandon the policy instrument and, hence, deny this service to the prospective beneficiaries anyway, it is hardly unethical to tem-

---

10 Of course, this raises the issue of how large the samples must be to allow inference with a reasonable degree of precision. This is an important question that is too often neglected, but we also refrain from addressing it here.

11 This has been done in a nonexperimental evaluation study of training by Regnér (1993) and eliminated the need for a survey.

porarily offer it to an experimental group and deny a control group the services. In particular, there is little danger of unethical behaviour in this case in view of the fact that the experiment is likely to yield valuable knowledge about the effects of a policy instrument. Another objection might be that the study could not take potential displacement effects into account. This is a valid objection in the same way as it is for the bonus-payments and Restart experiments. There is no doubt that the experiment cannot tell whether (for example) a higher employment rate for the experimental group would represent a net effect on employment or whether it would only reveal that this group found jobs that would otherwise have gone to other people. However, the experiment can tell whether the grants have a behavioural impact or not. Such knowledge is, of course, of a more limited nature than knowledge about the net employment effects of the programme, but it is nonetheless valuable knowledge. Note, also, that the political controversy about mobility grants was about their impact on mobility behaviour.

4.2   Training Programmes with More Applicants Than Training Slots

In European training programmes there are commonly more eligible applicants than available training slots. In such cases one can say that there is excess demand for training, or that the programme is supply constrained. As described above, this was the case in many courses offered in the Norwegian training programme of the early 1990s. The experimental evaluation we described in section 3 was confined to such supply-constrained courses. We have also been involved in the planning of an evaluation of the Danish training programme, and excess demand seems to have been the rule rather than the exception in this country.[12] In such cases an evaluation that addresses the traditional issue of the *average effect* for those who normally participate is often of great interest. It is also quite obvious that this situation raises the policy issue as to whether it would be beneficial to increase the number of programme slots so that the queues can be eliminated and more applicants be allowed to participate. The latter effect can be called the *marginal effect* for those who would be able to participate if the programme were larger.

Our opinion is that such a situation offers some interesting opportunities for experimental studies, provided that cooperation from the local administrators who make the final selection of applicants can be guaranteed. Consider first, however, an experimental design that can disclose the average effect of the programme in normal operation. In this case local administrators must make the same selection of applicants for the programme as they would have

---

12   This is work in progress; K. Langager at the Danish Institute for Social Research is in charge of the project.

done if it were to operate normally. The researchers must be allowed to randomly assign some of the selected applicants to the experimental group and some to the control group. The latter will, of course, be denied access to the programme. A simple comparison between the outcomes for the two groups would—with the usual caveat for displacement effects—provide an estimate of the average effect of the programme. The problem, however, is that the size of the programme must be reduced for the duration of the experiment, which might create an organizational problem and be a source of objections from the local administrators.

Fortunately, experiments can be designed such that this organizational problem is avoided and more valuable results are achieved. One possibility would be to ask the local administrators to select a larger number of participants than usual and then randomly choose the control group from this larger group. In such a case it might be possible to use all the programme slots, so that the organizational problem can be circumvented. A simple comparison between the experimental and the control groups would provide an estimate of the average effect of a larger programme than usual. If there is a political interest in expanding the capacity of the programme, an experiment that illuminates this effect might be considered very valuable.

Another, even more valuable, study can be carried out if the programme administration can rank the applicants according to the priority they would be given for participation in the programme. Suppose that 100 persons are normally allowed to participate, but for the experiment 200 prospective participants are selected, of which 100 are allocated to an experimental group and another 100 to a control group. Suppose, further, that the programme authority can rank the 200 selected participants according to the priority they would be given for participation in the programme; a ranking into two groups would be sufficient, namely the 100 persons who would be allowed to participate under normal conditions and 100 additional persons who would be allowed to participate if the programme were twice as big. The researchers can then select experimental and control samples from both groups. There would then be an opportunity to estimate the average effect of the programme under normal operation (the difference in outcome between the participants and nonparticipants in the first group) and the average effect for those who would be allowed to participate if the capacity were doubled (the difference in outcome between participants and nonparticipants in the second group). The latter effect can actually be considered the marginal effect of enlarging the programme.

Experiments like these might, of course, involve the problems discussed above. In the introduction to this section it was mentioned that the local administrators must accept the study and be willing to carry out the selection of the applicants according to the rules of the experiment. The Norwegian study demonstrated that such cooperation might be difficult to obtain. Under other circumstances, and with greater effort from the central level of the labour market administration, we believe that it might be possible to achieve better cooperation. Further, in the case of the experiment that requires ranking of the applicants into a high- and a low-priority group the local administration might even have incentives to cooperate because a successful outcome for the low-priority group might motivate additional resources for the programme. One might object that the ranking would generate incentives that might damage the experiment in other ways. We believe, however, that the local administration has two strong incentives in this type of study. First, to show that the high-priority group does better than the low-priority group; if not, their ability to select applicants could come into question. Second, to show that the low-priority group also benefits from the programme. It seems reasonable to believe that these two incentives together minimize the risk of invalidating the study and at the same time make it 'incentive compatible'.

Substitution bias, that is, the nonparticipants receive other services instead of the programme under study, is another potential problem that might arise. Careful monitoring of the evaluation project by the research team and from the central level of the labour market authority might help avoid this problem.

4.3 Training Programmes with More Training Slots Than Applicants

Some training programmes are also characterized by more training slots than applicants, which means that there is an excess supply of training, or that the programme is demand constrained. In the 1980s the Swedish training programme often had this characteristic, even though the situation could differ across courses.

In such a situation it can be of great interest to know whether it would make sense to make the programme more attractive by raising the training allowances. Hardly surprisingly, the National Labour Market Board of Sweden asked for higher training allowances during the 1980s, when there was an excess supply of training slots. The effect for those who would be attracted to a scheme by higher allowances can be called the marginal effect of a demand-constrained programme.

An experimental study that can shed light on this issue would be based on at least three random samples of prospective participants, in this case unemployed job seekers who are eligible for training. One group is invited to participate under the conditions that are in effect when the programme is operating normally. Another group is invited to participate under the alternative conditions (e.g. higher training allowances), which are the object of political discussion. And, finally, a control group is not permitted to participate. By comparing the outcomes for the first group and the control group, one would obtain the average effect of the programme under normal operation. By comparing the outcomes for the two experimental groups, one learns whether the programme has decreasing returns to scale; if the experimental group with higher allowances than the normal participants has a worse outcome, one can say that there are decreasing returns. Finally, a comparison between the experimental group with higher allowances and the control group would tell whether there are positive effects for those who would be attracted to the programme by higher allowances. Such a comparison would reveal the marginal effect of increasing the size of the programme by raising the training allowances. It should be noted that all these comparisons are made between experimental groups that are offered access to the scheme and a control group that is not allowed to participate. Therefore, the effects will be interpreted as the effects of offering the programme. (See Björklund, 1988, for more technical details about the relation between the effect of offering a programme and the effect of participation.)

4.4 Alternative Modes of Organizing Job Search Activities—Job Search Clubs

Our final proposal concerns alternative ways of organizing job search activities. Indeed, we are convinced that this is the field where the benefits of classical experiments are the greatest and where the traditional problems can be handled most easily.

The environment of the employment offices changes constantly, both because of structural changes in the labour market and because communications technology is subject to rapid modification. Therefore, the offices must regularly reconsider their mode of operation and pursue new and more efficient ways of fulfilling their functions. Classical experiments are particularly useful for evaluating and testing new types of work organization. In our examination of the experiments above we found that the US experiments in this field and the Swedish study of 1975 were quite successful. The Restart evaluation in the United Kingdom involved an ongoing programme, but the specific problems that can arise in such cases seem to have been avoided to a large extent, and this study of the way employment offices work yielded valuable insights.

A typical example of a programme that has not received the attention it deserves in European evaluation research is the organization of job search activities in groups or clubs, so-called job search clubs. The idea originated in the United States, but more and more European countries have found it interesting. The United Kingdom and Sweden initiated such clubs in the 1980s, and France has recently introduced them, too. The clubs can be organized in a number of ways, and this is a primary reason why proper evaluations are important; alternative designs for the operation of the clubs can be compared. The general idea, though, is that participants form a group and together with an instructor discuss how to look for vacancies, approach prospective employers and behave during job interviews. The job search clubs can be either voluntary or compulsory for UI recipients.

The design of the experiment can be made very simple along the lines of the US job search experiments and the Swedish Eskilstuna study. When the idea to implement job search clubs comes up on the labour market policy agenda, the target group of the programme first has to be defined. A random sample (or several, if more than one type of club is to be investigated) from the target group is then chosen as the experimental group. In the case of a voluntary club this group is offered the opportunity to participate; in the case of a compulsory club the group is required to participate in order to maintain their benefits. If the outcome variables of interest, unemployment duration or a similar indicator of job search success can be directly obtained from the registers of the employment offices, the rest of the target group can be defined as the control group. If a survey is needed to obtain the outcome variables, cost considerations might force the study to use a control group of limited size.

What then are the potential problems with, and objections to, such experimental studies? The ethical objections are not very strong. This is especially the case when it comes to voluntary job search clubs because no job seeker is denied a service to which he or she would normally be entitled. There is a risk of substitution bias, unless it can be guaranteed that the control group is not compensated by means of other programmes. Such a guarantee is dependent on cooperation from the personnel at the employment offices. Some randomization bias might appear; if, for example, the instuctors know about the experiment, then they might work more efficiently than otherwise. Finally, there is risk of displacement effects in the sense that the experimental group might find employment at the expense of the control group members. The latter two problems call for caution when interpreting the results. In order to make further decisions about job search clubs, it might be valuable, however, to know whether those who participated really did better than the control group. It might also be useful to know if one experimental job search group performed better than any other group.

5   CONCLUSIONS

There is no doubt that there are many problems associated with running a successful classical experimental labour market policy programme. We have also seen that problems were encountered in some of the actual experiments, which, if they have not rendered them total failures, have at least made the experiments less useful than expected. However, a number of experiments have produced valuable new insights. Therefore, we conclude that there is a role for classical experiments in future evaluation research in the United States as well as in Europe. We would like to summarize our views about the role that experiments can play in five points:

1. A precondition of experiments is that the members of the control group are denied the services provided by the programme for the duration of the experiment. This requirement rules out experiments in many cases where it is considered unethical to deny eligible persons access to the services of the programme. However, eligible applicants are often rejected in programmes under normal operating conditions, and in such cases a temporary use of random assignment might be considered acceptable in order that more can be learned about the outcome of the programme. Further, in cases of new programmes and changes in existing ones ethical considerations need not rule out an experiment.
2. Because new and modified programmes are good candidates for experiments, the decision to conduct an experiment must sometimes be made more or less simultaneously with the political decision about change of policy. Therefore, close contact between the political and research communities is desirable, so that the opportunities offered by this type of evaluation research can be fully exploited. Research and evaluation councils that are affiliated to the responsible ministries might help establish and promote such connections.
3. One prerequisite for a successful experiment is cooperation from the administrators at both the local and central levels. Ideally, the administrators will behave as if the programme were in normal operation, although this might be a tall order. The Norwegian study described above, for example, demonstrated clearly that noncooperative administrators at the local level had an adverse impact on the evaluation. Overly enthusiastic local administrators might also create problems if they behave in a different— and more efficient—way for the duration of the experiment than they would under normal circumstances. In both these cases we would argue that the operation of the programme will be different during the experiment than otherwise. However, this difference does not render the study totally useless. It might be valuable to know how a programme works under slightly different conditions, especially if current knowledge about the programme is insubstantial.
4. A major shortcoming of all studies—experimental as well as non-experimental—that infer the effects of programmes by comparing the outcomes for participating and nonparticipating individuals is that indirect effects are not taken into account. For instance, it is possible that those who receive

the extra service provided by the programme find employment at the expense of the nonparticipants, that is, there are so-called displacement effects. Experiments generally do not take such effects into account. For example, the US experimental studies on bonus payments to unemployed job seekers show that the reemployment probabilities are higher (and the duration of unemployment is shorter) for those who are offered a bonus, as compared to a control group that is not offered a bonus. This result shows convincingly that 'something happens' when incentives are changed. However, the US studies do not say very much about the impact that a universal introduction of a bonus system would have on aggregate reemployment probabilities or durations of unemployment. In our view the insights provided by these experiments are useful, even though some important questions remain unanswered.

5. Another limitation that must be kept in mind is that the focus of experiments is generally on the impact of a specific policy programme or a change in such a programme, with the researchers relying on the assumption that 'everything else is equal'. Quite often, and in particular in European countries, the various labour market policies constitute an integrated system of measures that should not be examined in isolation. A typical example is when training and employment programmes are used to test UI recipients' 'willingness to work'. In such cases one can expect the nonparticipants to change their behaviour because of the programmes, even though they are not actively participating. Therefore, special care must be taken when interpreting results from a programme that constitutes a significant part of a larger system of labour market policy, as sometimes is the case in European countries. We would say that experiments can be used to 'fine-tune' the individual programmes. Other methodological approaches, perhaps international comparisons in particular, are needed to evaluate the systems as such.

Obviously there are many reasons for emphasizing the limits of experimental evaluation research and the care that must be taken in interpreting the results. Nonetheless, we advocate that European countries follow the US example to a much larger extent than previously, that is, that they evaluate changes in policy and test new policies by means of experiments based on random assignment. This recommendation is made in the light of the extremely limited knowledge that we have today about the impact of labour market policy in European countries; for example, each time Swedish active labour market policy has been examined by international experts, a central observation has been how little is known about the impact of the policies. In the absence of a methodology that provides clear-cut answers to all the questions we can raise about labour market policy, we cannot afford to disregard the insights we can, after all, gain from many experiments.

REFERENCES

Björklund, A. (1988), 'What Experiments Are Needed for Manpower Policy?', *The Journal of Human Resources*, 23 (2), 267–77.

Björklund, A. (1989), *Evaluations of Training Programmes—Experiences and Suggestions for Future Research*, WZB discussion paper 89–3, Wissenschaftszentrum Berlin für Sozialforschung.

Davidson, C. and S. Woodbury (1993), 'The Displacement Effect of Re-employment Bonus Programs', *Journal of Labor Economics*, 11 (4), 575–605.

Decker, P. (1992), 'The Impact of Re-employment Bonuses on Insured Unemployment in the New Jersey and Illinois Reemployment Bonus Experiments', *The Journal of Human Resources*, 29 (3), 718–41.

Delander, L. (1978), 'Studier kring den arbetsförmedlande verksamheten', *Statens Offentliga Utredningar*, 60, 183–248.

Dolittle, F. and L. Traeger (1990), *Implementing the National JTPA Study*, New York: Manpower Demonstration Research Corporation.

Heckman, J. (1993), 'Alternative Approaches to the Evaluation of Social Programs', Department of Economics, University of Chicago. (Unpublished manuscript)

Heckman, J. and J. Hotz (1989), 'Choosing among Alternative Non-experimental Methods for Estimating the Impact of Social Programs: The Case of Manpower Training', *Journal of American Statistical Association*, 84 (408), 862–74.

Heckman, J. and J. Smith (1993), 'Assessing the Case for Randomized Evaluation of Social Programs', in K. Jensen and P. Madsen (eds), *Measuring Labour Market Measures*, Copenhagen: Ministry of Labour, pp. 35–95.

Johnson, T. and D. Klepinger (1993), 'Experimental Evidence on Unemployment Insurance Work-search Policies', *The Journal of Human Resources*, 29 (3), 695–717.

Meyer, B. (1992), *Policy Lessons from the U.S. Unemployment Insurance Experiments*, working paper no. 4197, The National Bureau of Economic Research.

Meyer, B. (1995), 'Lessons from the U.S. Unemployment Insurance Experiments', *The Journal of Economic Literature*, 33 (1), 91–131.

Raaum, O. and H. Torp (1993), *Evaluering av AMO-kurs: Sysselsättningseffekter og seleksjon till kurs*, SNF Report 72/1993, SNF, Oslo.

Regnér, H. (1993), *Choosing among Alternative Non-experimental Methods for Estimating the Impact of Training: New Swedish Evidence*, working paper no. 8, Swedish Institute for Social Research, Stockholm University.

White, M. (1992), 'Evaluating the Effects of the UK's Restart Programme', Policy Studies Institute, London. (Unpublished manuscript)

White, M. and J. Lakey (1992), *The Restart Effect: Does Active Labour Market Policy Reduce Unemployment?*, London: Policy Studies Institute.

A43, J24, J68

115-42

4. Longitudinal Designs in Evaluation Studies

Klaus Schömann[1]

The quest for more theory-driven evaluation (Chen and Rossi, 1983, p. 284; Rossi, 1991, p. 384) has implications for the methodology and basic design of evaluation studies, including the way data are collected. Most labour market theories or other theories relevant to processes on the labour market state hypotheses concerning desirable or undesirable changes in labour market outcomes. In their simplest form these theories make predictions about the expected result of participation in a certain labour market programme. Such a hypothesis may state, for example, a likely reemployment probability after programme participation. This chapter deals with questions of how such hypotheses can best be tested. In order to avoid undue overlaps with the preceding chapters, we refrain from differentiating experimental and non-experimental designs (cf. chap. 2 by Heckman and Smith in this volume and chap. 3 by Björklund and Regnér in this volume) and their analytical methods; longitudinal designs are common in both types of analyses. Similarly, the other methodologies presented in this volume, such as process evaluation and cost–benefit analysis, may also make use of indicators derived from longitudinal observations and data structures.

Frequently, evaluators are called upon to carry out evaluations *ex post*. That is, their evaluations start after a programme has ended. In such cases they usually have to rely on existing process-produced data sources. Alternatively, retrospective data collection may allow programme effects to be measured. Methodological problems of estimation and ways to cope with them in such evaluations are dealt with in chap. 2. The present chapter will focus on four ideal-type designs of evaluation studies in order to raise the awareness of critical design features of evaluations. The argument in this chapter is that longitudinal information is, in most instances, necessary for truly analytical evaluation studies (Blossfeld and Rohwer, 1995).

---

1 I would like to thank Albert C. Tuijnman for discussions at a very early stage of how to structure this chapter. Anders Björklund, Ulrich Rendtel, Uli Pötter, Rolf Becker and Sylvia Zühlke made helpful suggestions in finalizing it.

More emphasis needs to be put on designs of evaluation studies that will allow adequate comparisons of information from at least two points in time: before and after an individual's participation in a programme. Basing judgement of a policy merely on the number of participants that a programme has placed some time after it ends—a practice that is still common—is likely to over- or underestimate the effects of the programme. This risk is most obvious in cases where decisions governing programme participation are omitted from the analyses, as happens when programme effects are estimated on the basis of a single 'one shot' cross-section evaluation. Suppose, for example, that administrators of a high-quality programme select for participation in it only those persons whom they consider to be the best qualified among the unemployed. Without controlling for this positive selection into the programme, evaluators are likely to overstate the effects of the labour market measure as compared to a situation in which no such selection of participants has occurred. *Ad-hoc* surveys after programme participation are likely to yield misleading results and policy recommendations.

In the methodological literature on evaluation, this problem is called selection bias (Heckman, 1979, p. 153). Results on the efficiency of a measure are only trustworthy if these prior conditions are respected. Estimates of programme effects have to adjust results taking account of selection bias. Only such estimates are sufficiently reliable to allow statements about whether a transfer of a labour market programme to another setting (possibly to another region) or a sizeable expansion of the programme can be expected to yield similar results. A related methodological problem with achieving uncontaminated programme effects has to do with the issue of uncontrolled heterogeneity in a sample serving as the basis for estimating programme effects (Chamberlain, 1985; Heckman and Borjas, 1980, p. 247). Unobserved heterogeneity that is not controlled for in the estimates might be indicative of a state dependency. This is the case, for example, if the probability of recurrent unemployment appears to be high once unemployment has been experienced for the first time. However, previous unemployment might only be a proxy for other unobserved characteristics that are correlated over time. If such underlying processes remain undiscovered, evaluation studies are very likely to report misleading results and any policy conclusions derived from those results will have an unclear empirical basis.

This chapter proposes to apply more care in the early stage of data collection and design of evaluation studies. Only a combination of various longitudinal designs allows one to tackle the methodological problems mentioned above in subsequent statistical analyses.

1   DEFINING THE LONGITUDINAL IN EVALUATION STUDIES

Longitudinal research in the social sciences is no longer a new phenomenon. However, the understanding of what constitutes a longitudinal study is still expanding, with new forms of data and types of analyses being added to the stock of existing studies. In this section we examine recent innovative extensions of longitudinal evaluation designs and discuss definitions of longitudinal studies that have been proposed in the literature.

Writing on the history and rationale of longitudinal research, Baltes and Nesselroade (1979, pp. 1–2) noted how differently the label *longitudinal* is understood from one discipline to the next within the social sciences. During most of the 1960s and 1970s sociologists thought of longitudinal studies as those with a panel design, that is, repeated interviewing of the same individuals. Among psychologists longitudinal designs were most common in cohort studies (age-related repeated measurement). Economists and political scientists favoured time-series analyses, which have discrete measurement of time in yearly, quarterly or even monthly intervals.

Therefore, it is not surprising that the longitudinal dimension in evaluation studies was defined as 'the repeated measurement of a given phenomenon over time' (Nesselroade and Baltes, 1979, p. xi) or, even more generally, as investigations over time. The reformulation of the longitudinal element in research, which has been broadly identified as 'the time-ordered study of processes' (Baltes and Nesselroade, 1979, p. 2), captures the analytical element in longitudinal studies—that of dealing with processes. However, this understanding does not include the entire range of longitudinal studies that are carried out nowadays. Our definition draws on a broader concept of what constitutes a longitudinal study. Based on the theory-driven aspect of longitudinal evaluations, our definition originates more in advances in longitudinal methods and analyses of causation applied to longitudinal data than in the survey technique perspective. We define longitudinal studies as theoretically grounded analytical studies using data that contain explicit references to the time structure of information.

The qualification of longitudinal studies as analytical studies refers to the theory-driven element in evaluation studies (Chen and Rossi, 1983). The purpose of longitudinal studies is not just to describe different situations at different points in time but also to explain why there has or has not been a change in situations. This purpose thus has to do with explaining the processes involved in such change. In the case of labour market interventions these processes are policy interventions embedded in more general processes of job mobility or wage attainment. Even though few labour market theories explicitly deal with policy interventions, hypotheses about the likely results of interventions can be inferred from most labour market theories (Heckman and Robb, 1985, p. 159).

The time structure of information is, in fact, the crucial difference between cross-sectional and longitudinal studies. The very fact that a temporal sequence of cross-sections taken from different samples of the same population sometimes allows one to estimate the same parameters as one could from longitudinal data stresses the importance of using different points in time in such an estimation procedure (Heckman and Robb, 1985). For purposes of generalization the time structure of information has been added to the definition of longitudinal studies because, for example, event-history analyses of labour market processes and labour market institutions make appropriate use of the time structure of events. That structure may consist of the time until a specific change in the labour market behaviour of programme participants occurs, or it may consist of the time-related change in labour market institutions. Event-history analysis allows one to include the information provided by all respondents who are part of the population at risk of experiencing an event, such as job duration before the event of unemployment. So-called right censoring of events may consist in establishing the date of interview as the point after which no changes can be considered. Left censoring is involved when, for example, the point at which data collection begins is taken as the moment at which a job is considered to have begun.

In the following sections a synopsis of the major types of longitudinal studies will be presented along with a few examples of each type.[2] The strengths, and weaknesses, of specific longitudinal designs are discussed with the aim of providing guidance in the process of deciding, for example, which type of study best suits a given kind of research interest in evaluation studies.

1.1   Panel Studies

Our broad definition of the longitudinal element in evaluation studies encompasses studies in which the same participants are interviewed, as a minimum, at two different points in time. In some instances the time lag between the first and second contact may be very short. Examples of such research are follow-up studies focussed on changes after a specific intervention or the occurrence of a certain transition (e.g. school to work, or exit from the labour force). Typically, the researchers conducting studies of this kind would interview

---

2 The European Science Foundation has published an inventory of longitudinal studies in the social sciences (Schneider and Edelstein, 1990). However, many longitudinal studies that have been launched since then have not yet been documented in the printed data base available to us. Many additional studies now exist, especially in the field of labour market research. Most of them are of particular importance for our concern with labour market policy evaluations.

participants in labour market programmes once before entry into the pro-gramme and a second time some months after completion of the programme. Alternatively, such 'minimal' two-wave panel studies can span a considerable length of time. Research related to education and training frequently takes long-run effects into account, with a second interview of, for example, a cohort of programme participants being undertaken five or more years after they leave school or some other training institute. Long-term panel studies with a design specialized on labour market policies are still rare. A European exam-ple of this type is the OSA Panel ('Organiatie voor Strategisch Arbeidsmarkt Onderzoek'/Organization for Strategic Labour Market Research) in the Neth-erlands, which involves 4020 individuals and a biannual interview structure (Vissers and Dirven, 1994).

In the United States the major data sources for longitudinal evaluations of labour market policies are the National Longitudinal Surveys (NLS) of Labor Market Experience and the Panel Study of Income Dynamics (PSID). The NLS data were collected in several sequences. First, a cohort of 5000 men aged 45–59 years were interviewed regularly. At the same time a cohort of young men aged 14–24 were contacted and reinterviewed until 1981. Subsequently, new cohorts of women and of both sexes were added and are being followed. The PSID follows a yearly data collection plan that started in 1967.

Some longitudinal panel studies have much longer intervals between the interviews of the original participants. The Malmö study (Tuijnman, 1989) follows members of a cohort over time as their careers evolve. This prospec-tive study was started in 1938 with an interview of people aged about ten years. The same people have been recontacted seven times, at ages 15, 30, 35, 40, 43, 52 and 56 years. At various stages of the survey the set of questions asked has been adapted to policy issues of later periods when sampling, so control groups have not changed since the sampling of 1938. The wide range of infor-mation like home background, cognitive ability at age 10 and 20, initial and continued education, occupational careers and earnings allow one to control for a number of background variables. The long period covered in this survey makes it possible to construct time-dependent covariates and to control even for effects that business cycles *might* have on participation in labour market programmes.

The same persons may be interviewed more than the two times as called for in the minimal design of panel studies. In the social sciences the most commonly used large panel studies apply annual repetition of interviewing (see Table 4.1). Examples of such studies are becoming more numerous. The Panel Study of Income Dynamics (PSID) in the United States (Duncan and Morgan, 1984; Hill, 1992) and the Socioeconomic Panel (Sozio-ökono-misches Panel, SOEP) in Germany (Hanefeld, 1987; Rendtel, 1995; Wagner, Burkhauser and Behringer, 1994) have generated many successors with a

Table 4.1   The Structure of Panel Data

Points of Observation	Dependent Variable	Independent Variable (Time Dependent or Independent[a])	Programme Participation[b]
t_1	Y_1	X_1	D_1
t_2	Y_2	X_2	D_2
.	.	.	.
.	.	.	.
t_n	Y_t	X_t	D_t

Notes

a An example of a time-dependent variable may be labour earnings that change depending on the point of observation; a time-independent variable is the date of birth which rests unchanged during the whole period of observation.

b Programme participation is recorded at discrete points in time. Usually, the variable named D takes values of either zero or one at each point in time, thus denoting programme participants (see also chaps 2 and 3).

similar structure based on a sample of households interviewed over many years.[3] The European household panel in the Member States of the European Union is the latest large-scale study warranting mention in this context (Bechtold and Blanke, 1994). The first wave of interviews, which encompassed 60 000 households, was carried out in 1994 throughout the 12 EU Member States of that time. Interviewing will be repeated at yearly intervals.

More scarce are panel designs that focus on change in qualitative information. They could be used by researchers trying to ascertain the longitudinal quality of and satisfaction with job-search information provided by public or private placement services or evaluations of public reintegration programmes that offer special psychological assistance for those in need. Another area of application for qualitative panel designs is the social learning and moral development of skilled workers (Hoff, Lempert and Lappe, 1991).

A change of perspective occurred in the 1990s, when many researchers perceived a need not only for panels focussing on the supply side of the labour market but also for longitudinal assessment of the demand side. In other words firms were seen as potential users of labour market policies (Projektgruppe Betriebspanel, 1994). Except for more numerous firm-level panels for evaluat-

---

3 Accessibility has made the British Household Panel Survey (Buck, Gershuny, Rose and Scott, 1994) one of the better known panel studies, but there are many others. Most of them can be accessed through the Luxembourg Income Study based in Walferdange, Luxembourg.

ing economic success and failure of private sector firms, use of such data for labour market policy evaluations has been rare so far.

Panel data do have a number of drawbacks, however.[4] Obviously, not all persons who participated in the first round of interviewing are also available for subsequent interviews. Statistically, this problem of drop-out from the panel population is called attrition (Rendtel, 1995). Long-running panel studies must cope with both the loss of cases as the research evolves and the problem of item nonresponse common to all survey techniques (Verbeek and Nijman, 1992).

The number of drop-outs from a panel study can be high in some cases. After ten years of annual interviews, participants may have migrated and can no longer be interviewed, and some may no longer want to participate in the study. Both groups may bias estimates of programme effects. In the Michigan PSID, approximately 50 per cent of the sample was lost through cumulative attrition from the study's inception in 1968 to 1989 (Fitzgerald, Gottschalk and Moffitt, 1994). A somewhat larger degree of panel attrition has been registered in the German SOEP. From 1984 through 1991 one out of three of the original participants left the study, and no further information has been collected on these individuals (Rendtel, 1995, p. 11). If panel attrition is correlated with programme participation, this source for selectivity bias has to be dealt with if one is to arrive at reliable estimates of programme effects on such labour market processes as wage attainment (cf. Heckman and Robb, 1985; Verbeek and Nijman, 1992).

Besides the fact that panel studies are generally more costly than a single interview, there is the need to devote resources to measure and control statistically for the loss of information incurred by panel attrition. The higher the number of waves of interviews, the more seriously this issue has to be tackled (Rendtel, 1995). Even yearly interviewing will involve some imprecision due to retrospective or recall error, although it is less serious than that in studies based exclusively on long intervals between an event and a person's reporting about it. A useful way to classify nonresponses related to panel data is reported by Verbeek and Nijman (1992, pp. 264–5). They differentiated five types of nonresponse: (a) initial nonresponse, when individuals contacted for the first time decide not to participate in the survey; (b) unit nonresponse, no data are available for one unit, such as a member of a household; (c) item nonresponse, a specific variable, such as earnings, is missing; (d) wave nonresponse, the person or household does not respond in one or more waves of the study; and

---

4 Some analysts count among the drawbacks of panel studies that in many instances no information on the time between panel waves is collected. This impedes the analysis of labour market processes which hinge on precise information of employment or unemployment durations. This drawback can be abridged by shortening the time between panel interviews.

(e) attrition, individuals who have participated many times eventually cease responding. The conditions under which such nonresponse can be ignored have been discussed in methodological literature, and tests for ignorable and nonignorable selection rules have been derived (Rendtel, 1995; Verbeek and Nijman, 1992).

1.2   Retrospective Studies

Still less common in labour market research is the use of retrospective designs (although more common in sociology and demography), which rely on the capability of interviewees to recall events with sufficient accuracy. Retrospective studies are a way of retrieving longitudinal data in a single interview session. Whereas a retrospective study focussing on qualitative information can use a biographical approach (Bourdieu and Balazs, 1993), retrospective studies focussing on quantitative information elicited from representative samples use standardized forms of questionnaires or interviewing (Brückner, 1993; Mayer and Brückner, 1989) with an event-oriented design (see Table 4.2). The durations until a specific event (e.g. job loss) occurred are a major component of data collection that facilitates the application of longitudinal research methods (for an overview of such methods, see Tuma and Hannan, 1984).

Retrospective studies are commonly applied in demography to analyse the impact of policies and specific programmes targeted on families as one example. In the realm of evaluations of labour market programmes, there are still

Table 4.2   Retrospective Data Collection

Employed	t_0-t_1			t_3-t_4	t_4- interview[a]
Unemployed		t_1-t_2	t_2-t_3		
Programme participation[b]			t_2-t_3		

Notes

a The information of right-censored durations, such as spells in employment that continue beyond the cutoff in observation caused by the interview, can still be used in most statistical analyses of duration data.

b The observation plan stresses the importance of durations in employment, unemployment, the duration of programme participation or the waiting time for a job after programme participation.

only a few examples. The retrospective German Life History Study (see Mayer, 1990, 1993; Schömann, 1994; Schömann and Becker, 1995) has also served as a useful source of data for evaluating labour market processes and programmes, especially training programmes.

In its original form the German Life History Study included three birth cohorts: 1929–31, 1939–41 and 1949–51. Older and younger cohorts have since been added to cover additional time periods of labour market entry and different time-dependent participation in labour market programmes. The most important feature is that the structure of the data is not organized by year but by 'event history', which facilitates the analysis of labour market events resulting from programme interventions. Events in such analysis are, for example, job changes, career advancements and the growth in a person's earnings on the same job.

As with other sample surveys, retrospective studies are subject to bias due to nonresponse. More specifically, however, retrospective surveys have to cope with recall errors, that is, cases in which participants in the survey do not precisely recall dates of events. One way to cope with this source of error is to allow sufficient time for respondents to check against their own records the information they are asked to provide. Alternatively, a form of correction for selectivity can be introduced if certain life events or programme participation is recalled with differing precision by different respondents. Van der Vaart, Van der Zouwen and Dijkstra (1995) have proposed using checklists to improve the response accuracy on retrospective questions about attitudes and behavioural items.[5] A kind of sensitivity analysis of estimated effects due to recall errors might be carried out additionally to gauge these error margins (see Courgeau, 1991, and Schömann, 1994).

One can envisage mixed forms of retrospective and prospective studies for evaluation that start with a detailed retrospective questionnaire and then continue like a panel study. Financing such projects is very expensive, so this type of study has not been frequently exploited in the social sciences. An example is the retrospective study of birth cohorts of the former German Democratic Republic, which have been reinterviewed since Germany's unification (Huinink and Mayer, 1993). Longitudinal designs of that kind allow to differentiate between age, period and cohort effects in the most adequate way (Schömann, 1994).

---

5 They actually used a data set from a Dutch national panel on the process of social integration of young people born in 1961, 1965 or 1969, with waves of interviewing in 1987 and 1991 in which the missing information between the years of interviews is retrieved retrospectively.

1.3   Studies Based on Administrative Records

In most countries access to administrative records of social security contributions or pension contributions, for example, is severely restricted to public
authorities dealing with these confidential data (Blien and Rudolph, 1989;
Fachinger, 1994) or private insurance companies. The need to review employees' level of coverage periodically for sources of fraud and to monitor the
in- and outflows of these funds has led to an accumulation of large bodies of
data. The few existing longitudinal studies based on such social security records
usually draw a sample of persons from these individual records at a given point
in time and follow the occupational career of individuals over a number of years
(see Table 4.3). Special sample techniques such as oversampling participants in
labour market programmes and subsequently calculating weighted indicators
allow one to analyse long-run labour market outcomes of specific programmes
for participants or, more generally, for unemployment insurance systems. In
Germany such data is being processed with an eye to ensuring that they cannot
be traced back to individuals. The information will then become available for
purposes of policy evaluation. For an example of a longitudinal evaluation of
regional differences between labour markets, particularly wage policies, in
Germany, see Blien (1994). For a Canadian example, see Belzil (1995).

As with studies based on other types of longitudinal data, those based on
administrative records have their drawbacks. Because the data frequently

Table 4.3   Data Based on Administrative Records

Points of Measurement	Dependent Variable	Independent Variable (Time Dependent or Independent)	Programme Participation[a]
Entry into register t_1	Y_0 left censored; Y_1	X_1	D_1
$t_1 - t_2$	Y_2	X_2	D_2
.	.	.	.
.	.	.	.
Exit from register t_n	Y_t right censored	X_t	D_t

Note

a Most administrative records are based on formalized procedures that start recording information at entry into a programme, when a person enters a firm or begins his or her job (in the case
of social security records). Basically, both data structures of Tables 4.1 and 4.2 are possible. In
addition to right-censored durations, left-censored spells (no information of starting time available) may occur when administrative records are started while a programme is already in
operation.

originate in official records, their use is very restricted. These records are produced within standard administrative routines (i.e. process-produced data), so they usually contain only very limited information on family backgrounds, job-search processes or reasons for change in behaviour. Important explanatory variables may be missing altogether. Such gaps in the data complicate the estimation of well-specified models from these data. Statistically speaking, estimated effects may be misspecified because an omission bias in the estimates equation arises since important variables have not been considered. Possible remedies for the problem of missing information include drawing appropriate data from other sources or testing for the magnitude of misspecification in order to gauge the size, or at least the direction, of the potential bias.

Another kind of administrative data suitable for longitudinal analysis is records of labour market institutions in the widest possible sense. Such data may consist in the founding, extension, reorganization or termination of activities pursued by those institutions.

Company personnel records of employment durations, internal mobility and wages (Brüderl, 1991) can also be used for policy evaluations whenever a company is the target of specific public policies. If these two types of administrative data are available in sufficient number and if they include precise references to time, they can be used in longitudinal analyses of institutions and internal processes. In the few existing examples of this type of study, event-history estimation techniques are frequently applied (Janoski and Hicks, 1994, pp. 19–20). In event-history analysis the time structure of events is examined, with particular attention being accorded to the waiting time until an event occurs. Although event-history techniques have only rarely been applied to the study of administrative reforms, public employment services and the founding and dissolution of such labour market institutions as trade unions thus far, they do have potential in this regard.

1.4   Time-series Studies

Labour market policy evaluations based on time-series data relate mainly to the aggregate level, although there is a rapidly emerging body of evaluation studies in which researchers use sector- or even firm-level data and time-series estimation techniques. Theoretical models and estimation are discussed in chap. 5 on aggregate impact analysis by Bellmann and Jackman. Therefore, we only briefly mention some of the advantages and disadvantages of choosing one or the other method of analysis. Evaluation of long-run trends needs one form or the other of time-series data on the aggregate level (see Table 4.4). Even microlevel studies dealing with long-run processes include such information to capture changes in economic or demographic context variables (Blien, 1994; Blossfeld, 1989).

Klaus Schömann

Table 4.4   Time-series Data Structure[a]

Points of Observation	Dependent Variable	Independent Variable	Programme Participation
t_1	Y_1	X_1	D_1
t_2	Y_2	X_2	D_2
.	.	.	.
.	.	.	.
t_n	Y_t	X_t	D_t

Note

a The data structure is very similar to that for the panel. The major difference is the unit of observation, which is usually aggregate measures. In analyses based on time series, information on the total number of programme participants or total costs of a programme per year may constitute the basis for evaluation studies.

A major difficulty with single-country time-series studies is the identification of what processes are endogenous or exogenous. This distinction is particularly hard to make in cases when both endogenous and exogenous variables move closely in the same direction and variation in the indicators around a common time trend is relatively small. Studies of expenditure on active and passive labour market policies often have to deal with this kind of problem (Kraft, 1994, p. 11). It can sometimes be circumvented through comparisons of country cases or use of cointegration estimation techniques in analyses of many countries (Engle and Granger, 1987).

In recent years another type of study has arisen: a combination of time-series studies and individual cross-section data. Some authors refer to this group of studies as 'pseudo panel data' (Verbeek, 1992), which in fact constitute estimation based on repeated cross-sections. Such studies are classified as time-series studies because it is common to use lagged endogenous variables in the estimation of programme effects—standard practice in time-series models of the labour market (Collado, 1991). It is true that such data make it difficult to arrive at consistent estimates on a number of dynamic processes, but they do have the advantage of not suffering from panel attrition, even for lengthy series of observations.

1.5   Explanation and Causation

A common feature of the various longitudinal designs of evaluation studies is that the study of labour market interventions and policy outcomes is oriented to explaining change in labour market outcomes. The underlying causal relationships can be disentangled only if changes in policy outcomes can be attributed to previous policy interventions. Hence, a major goal of longitudinal studies is the analysis of reasons underlying constancy and change in socio-economic outcomes (Plewis, 1985; Tuma and Hannan, 1984).

The analysis of causal relationships makes explicit references to the timing of processes, events and interventions. In 1986, Zvi Griliches wrote in the *Handbook of Econometrics*:

> It is only relatively recently ... that econometric professionals had actually become involved in the primary data collection process. Once attempted, the job turned out to be much more difficult than was thought originally, and taught us some humility. Even with relatively large budgets, it was not easy to figure out how to ask the right question and to collect relevant answers (p. 1467).

On top of this concern we may add the time dimension to the difficulty of how to ask the 'right questions'. A more thorough concern for the timing of interventions and the time-related structure of labour market processes is likely to increase awareness for the importance of time-related context variables and institutional constancy or change.

A still recent advance towards an integration of individual-level information and aggregate data has been made in a group of what is known as multi-level linear models. Originating in a generalization of random-coefficient models, these multilevel models usually have a dependent variable measured at the individual level and independent variables measured at both the individual and group levels. What is called the group level may be regional information calculated on the basis of the individuals working in a specific region (Blien, 1994; Kreft and DeLeeuw, 1988). Although empirical applications have focussed on two levels (individual and region), the methodology allows for interactions of multiple levels of analysis.

2   APPLICATIONS OF LONGITUDINAL DESIGNS IN EVALUATIONS

Applications of longitudinal designs in evaluation studies are quite common now. In order to explain the potential and actual advantages of longitudinal designs, we comment on existing longitudinal evaluations and try to make more explicit the kind of research questions that are typically asked using such a design. The broadest variety of combinations of various types of longitudinal designs are found in two areas: (a) earnings as a measure of the outcome of training programmes and (b) facilitation of exit from unemployment. The following selection of evaluations has been determined largely by the number of available studies and interesting 'best practice' applications of longitudinal methods. The major result of this exercise is that the theoretical distinction between four types of longitudinal design presented above allows for multiple combinations of these types, depending on the primary research interest.

2.1   Earnings as a Measure of the Outcome of Training Programmes

Microlevel evaluation of human-resource training programmes frequently centres on the increase in the programme participant's labour earnings relative to those who had not participated in the programme. Measuring this change makes it necessary to choose comparison groups in order to indicate the size of programme effects. There still is an intense debate about whether experimental or nonexperimental control groups should be used for such comparisons (see chaps 2 and 3 in this volume). Instead of commenting on this debate, we highlight the longitudinal elements in both approaches.

One of the largest attempts to evaluate training programmes was undertaken in the United States in 1973. The Comprehensive Employment and Training Act (CETA) spurred massive collection of data with which to evaluate the effects of the programme. The first difficulty for practical evaluation of labour market programmes is that it frequently must encompass such broad programmes containing multiple measures. In the CETA evaluation, the programmes ranged from direct work experience to public-service employment, on-the-job training and classroom training. Information was collected from 6700 programme participants in 1975 and 13 300 participants in 1976. Subsequently, this data set was merged with data from the Current Population Survey (CPS, which corresponds to population census data) and Social Security Administration records on incomes from 1951 through 1978 to cover pre- and postprogramme periods of incomes of participants and control groups.

After several reviews of the literature on the CETA evaluation (see Bassi and Ashenfelter, 1986; Björklund, 1989), the general conclusion was that the CETA programmes had a 'modest impact of several hundred dollars on earnings for men and a somewhat greater effect on women' (Barnow, 1987, p. 189). The CETA case is of particular interest, first, because experimental and nonexperimental techniques were used in the same evaluation to allow comparisons of methods. Second, the idea of linking information on programme participants, census data on socioeconomic status and background, and declared incomes from social security records was a rare attempt to pool data from different sources.[6]

---

6 Increased concern with data protection since the mid-1970s makes a repetition of a similar effort to pool data unlikely in most European countries.

Despite careful handling of econometric issues involved in control group selection, sources of selectivity bias and issues of model specification, the estimated programme effects are clouded by various sources of uncertainty. Björklund (1989) demonstrates the error margins associated with every point estimate of regression coefficients. At a 95 per cent confidence interval, an estimated effect needs to be complemented by plus or minus two standard deviations of the corresponding variable. Results taken from Bassi (1984) show a positive programme effect of $740 on postprogramme earnings for the first year for white women. Assuming a 95 per cent confidence interval, the effect ranges from $480 to $1000. For women from minority groups the point estimate is somewhat smaller, $426, and with a standard deviation of $235 the programme effect ranges from $896 to $-44. In other words the point estimates in this case do not allow a definite, positive conclusion about the programme's effect. The error margins increase further in the analysis of men from minority groups. A practical conclusion from this evaluation, therefore, underlines the necessity of selecting samples large enough to reduce the size of standard errors associated with programme effects (Westergard-Nielsen, 1993). Larger samples are quite costly, however.

A second major source of differences in estimated effects stems from differences in the explanatory variables available, or derived for, the estimation (specification of the model). Some studies have drawn on individual retrospective information on labour force participation, data that add another type of longitudinal dimension to the evaluations. Attachment to the labour force, or labour force experience in general, is an important indicator of attitudes to work and might allow a frequently unaccounted-for source of unobserved heterogeneity to be eliminated.

Barnow (1987) mentioned that results of the CETA evaluation were sensitive to control-group members' commitment to the labour force. With inclusion of individuals who were not members of the labour force immediately prior to the survey in the control group, the estimated impact of the programme increased. If administrators of the CETA programme had chosen only persons with confirmed labour force attachment, programme effects for these persons might have been found to be small. Widening the group of eligible persons to those with unstable attachment to the labour force increased the size of positive effects, in particular for women (Dickinson, Johnson and West, 1986).

In most evaluation studies education is assumed to have linear effects on earnings (in this case education is entered directly in the model). Some researchers additionally test for nonlinear relationships (usually, this is done by adding the square of the values for education to the model). Because of the specification of the model applied in the estimation, these differences in model specification will cause substantial variation in other effects of explanatory variables common in all analyses. Model specification itself depends on theoretical considerations of programme evaluation and labour market theories.[7]

A major problem shared by all nonexperimental microlevel evaluation approaches is the difficulty in assessing the various stages of selecting the control group and the programme participants. The selection of programme participants involves at least two kinds of selection: (a) a self-selection of persons who apply for participation in the programme and (b) selection of eligible participants by the programme staff. This fact has a bearing on a programme administrator's choice of target groups for possible future programme participation. It stresses the importance of having detailed knowledge of individual characteristics, labour force experience and a person's attachment to the labour force. On the basis of such knowledge, programmes can be designed to match the specific needs of possible programme participants more closely than it otherwise might. The more a person's specific labour force background is taken into account by programme designers, the more effective their programme might probably be.

The sensitivity of programme effects that are based on longitudinal data hinges to a large extent on the definition of who is eligible to participate in the programme. Another intervening process that is hard to access is the rigour with which these rules are applied by programme administrators. The use of experimental evaluation techniques opens the possibility of a trade-off between 'good' programme evaluation and 'good' programme implementation. For the purpose of programme evaluation it is desirable to have a highly detailed programme and narrow guidelines for selecting people eligible for participation. On the other hand, an increase in scope for flexible programme implementation can enhance programme effects.

Even within an experimental setting some effects might remain 'external' to the evaluation. Aiming at the target group of welfare recipients similar to that of the CETA programme, a two-week training course on how to seek employment was given to 916 programme participants in 1980 in the state of Ohio (Burtless, 1985). Three groups were randomly selected for this experiment. One group received a tax-credit voucher that enabled employers of programme participants to obtain a tax reduction. Another group was endowed with a direct cash subsidy for the employer. The third group, the control group, had no wage voucher. Results showed that subjects who used their wage vouchers when approaching prospective employers faired worse than subjects without wage vouchers.[8] In this experiment wage voucher apparently func-

---

7 A possible way out of the difficulty of optimal model specification can be found in econometric tests. However, the subject is too vast to be dealt with here.

8 Within an eight-week period after the training in job-search techniques, 20 per cent of the control group had found employment as opposed to only 13 per cent of the participants provided with a tax-credit voucher and 13 per cent of those provided with a direct cash subsidy.

tioned as a 'signal' to employers that the applicants had been welfare recipients for some time. If the status of being a welfare recipient had negative associations among employers, the wage vouchers stigmatized the job seekers, leaving them with less probability of finding a job than the members of the control group.

Groot, Hartog and Oosterbeck (1990) analysed the structure of the decision-making process leading to participation in training. The choice to participate in training consisted of three options: on-the-job training, off-the-job training and no training. They further distinguished whether the decision-making process was simultaneous, that is, whether both the decision to take training and the decision on what type of training to choose were made at the same time, or whether the decisions are made sequentially. The dependent variable in the first step of the estimation is the probability of taking one or the other form of training. Subsequently, these estimates are included in wage equations, with the dependent variable being the change in the hourly wage rate in 1985 and 1986. This variable thus requires the figures on two years of earnings as basic longitudinal information.

Results suggested that the number of years of general education increases the probability that an individual will participate in on-the-job training but does not increase the probability that the same person will participate in off-the-job training. Groot et al. (1990) interpreted this result as evidence that formal education and on-the-job training are complementary perhaps because most on-the-job training is employer-initiated while off-the-job training is more likely to be initiated by employees. Similar results were obtained for West Germany by Schömann and Becker (1995) in a study based on samples of three birth cohorts and a retrospective design. However, estimates for the United States (Lynch, 1990) show that participation in on-the-job training is not increased by a higher level of general education. Differences in the organization of education and training systems from one country to the next and employers' attitudes towards on-the-job training might explain these divergent cross-national findings. If cross-national comparisons are the aim, such systemic differences would need to be measured in some way.

Other longitudinal evaluation research related to training includes an attempt to evaluate the public and private organization of training. In the study by Lynch (1990), formal off-the-job training in educational institutions working for profit was distinguished from training given in public institutes. Much less effort has been devoted to the impact of direct government assistance to training programmes. Such programmes might take the form of on- or off-the-job training and might contain some form of financial incentives for either employers or employees, or a mixture of both. Most evaluations of training and subsequent estimates of earnings profiles so far do not contain very detailed information on scholarships or any other form of financial assistance.

This shortcoming might seriously bias results because different financial arrangements will influence motivation and other outcomes.

In a Swedish study (Regnér, 1993) on the effects that participation in training has on subsequent earnings, it was found that participants in 1989 even had to accept decreases in their postprogramme earnings in 1990. One year later, however, the negative effect that was estimated for training to have two years after participation was already much weaker, indicating that training had a positive long-run effect on earnings. Unfortunately, there are still very few studies that attempt to capture the effects that macrolevel labour demand has on individuals. Long-run individual-level studies need to be merged with time-series data on labour market policies and business cycles to control for effects of macroeconomic labour market conditions on individual chances to leave unemployment. Even effects of training programmes appear to be dependent on the probability of receiving job offers, that is, on whether the labour market is buoyant or not.

However, independent of the design of longitudinal evaluations based on individual-level data, there is considerable agreement in the literature on the increasing effects that training programmes have on earnings (cf. Tuijnman and Schöman's chapter on life-long learning and skill enhancement in this volume). A cross-sectional design is restricted to research questions about the effect on earnings at a single point in time or to estimates of quasi-longitudinal effects by making use of comparisons of rates of return to education using tenure-based wage profiles (Heckman and Robb, 1985). Typically, longitudinal research addresses questions of whether on-the-job training enhances wages in the current job but not in subsequent jobs, or whether off-the-job training has little effect on earnings in the current job but contributes to higher earnings in later jobs or only after job change or change of employer (Becker and Schömann, 1995; Groot et al., 1990; Lynch, 1990; Schömann, 1994; Tuijnman, 1989).

Another practical guideline for conducting evaluations of the effects that training has on wages is the fact that most studies have shown effects to vary greatly between men and women (Westergard-Nielsen, 1993). Either the sample size needs to be large enough to allow full interaction of the variables involved (i.e. a separate estimation for men and women) or a number of gender-specific interaction terms must be included to control for different forms of selection mechanisms, occupational segregation and training outcomes.

2.2   Facilitating Exit from Unemployment

Evaluation of studies that focus on reemployment probabilities after programme participation or unemployment usually have longitudinal research designs and methods so that pre- and postprogramme employment opportunities can be compared. The process of leaving unemployment has received the most attention in recent years, especially duration dependence or lagged duration dependence (Heckman and Borjas, 1980). Major sources in the study of this process have been panel data such as the PSID in the United States, the OSA panel in the Netherlands, the SOEP in Germany, the Danish Longitudinal Data Base (LDB) and an Austrian sample from unemployment registers. The longitudinal element in the data consists in the observation of unemployment durations, especially so-called completed spells of unemployment. A standard cross-sectional questionnaire can identify only the duration of unemployment at one point in time without following the length of time a person continues to be unemployed. Even longitudinal data have to deal with uncompleted spells of unemployment at the time of interview, but in each subsequent interview more of these spells will be terminated by some sort of exit from unemployment.[9]

One of the earliest longitudinal studies featuring an event-history type of analysis, which allows for the inclusion of right-censored spells of unemployment in the probability of leaving unemployment, was the study by Lancaster and Nickell (1980), who used the General Household Survey (GHS) for Great Britain. Moffitt (1985) used process-produced data from the administration of unemployment benefits, Hujer and Schneider (1987) used a special survey on labour market status merged with data from the social security administration. Not until the PSID, the SOEP and similar panel studies had provided a sufficiently large number of cases did it become possible, for example, for the unemployed's return to employment to be examined, say, on the basis of a separate estimation for men and women (Hunt, 1991; Katz and Meyer, 1990; Wurzel, 1993). In most instances it took five years to launch the panel study, acquire a sufficient number of waves containing enough completed spells of unemployment, analyse the data and report it. Only samples of such administrative data as social security records (Belzil, 1995, with Canadian data) and retrospective designs are able to deliver results earlier (Galler and Pötter, 1987, using the retrospective information in the SOEP for Germany).

As in the studies on training issues of self-selection, motivation and discouragement are relevant in analyses of reemployment probabilities and durations. Allen, McCormick and O'Brien (1991) investigated the training policy in the United Kingdom by focussing on reemployment opportunities of the unemployed. In particular they focussed on the question of who will seek to be

---

9 Because this process of leaving unemployment depends largely on the existence of an unemployment insurance system and the particular features of that labour market institution, we focus on studies that include some indicator of the existence of and eligibility for unemployment benefits or assistance (see chap. 8 by Schmid and Reissert).

retrained, the answer to which constitutes the demand for retraining programmes. Because they assumed that brief spells of unemployment might be efficient for some workers, their view was that not all unemployed persons need to be retrained. Findings on the structure of the demand for retraining ought then to yield insights into the need for future retraining opportunities. Data was collected from a random sample of persons leaving a job centre in Sunderland in summer 1985. All the subjects had been actively seeking employment for at least four weeks.

The results were based on a sample of 203 unemployed males, of whom 133 had been made redundant. Results indicate that the probability of applying for a retraining course declines significantly after about nine months of unemployment. By that time most of the unemployed either have sought retraining or are very unlikely to seek any training, a circumstance that, in turn, reduces reemployment probabilities still further. The study is an interesting application of a longitudinal design because it provides evidence that search efforts for retraining can be regarded as an indicator of an unemployed person's motivation and self-confidence to leave unemployment. Only a longitudinal design is able to evidence such a change in a 'latent variable' that, as most researchers would agree, is certain to have an impact on the overall probability of leaving unemployment.

Another attempt to evaluate the reemployment probabilities of the unemployed has been presented by Ting (1991), who applied a socioeconomic approach. He inquired into the impact that job-training programmes have on the reemployment probability of displaced workers after a number of plant closures in the United States in the early 1980s. Data for this study were taken from the 1984 CPS Displaced Workers' Survey, a supplement to the Current Population Survey. The sample in the analysis consisted of persons ranging from 20 through 65 years of age who had been displaced from nonagricultural jobs since 1979 because of plant closures or relocation. The remaining sample of people meeting these conditions had 2394 individuals. The estimation method was a two-stage procedure. The probability that workers will be selected for one of several labour market programmes was estimated first, then the probability of employment at the time of the survey in 1984. The results suggested that basic skill training, job-skill training and on-the-job training increase the probability of reemployment relative to those who received no training or only job search assistance.

In the latter evaluation of the Job Training and Partnership Act (JTPA), Ting (1991) mentions an intrinsic difficulty with the microlevel evaluation of training programmes. It is due to the selection criteria applied by programme administrators. Some of the unemployed who are most likely to succeed in a course might be preferred by administrators, increasing the likelihood of an effect called 'creaming' of participants. 'Creaming' suggests the presence of simultaneity in the choice of participants for courses by administrators and higher reemployment probabilities of participants. But placement success and a repeated measurement of the selection process can make sufficiently reliable estimates of such creaming effects (Schömann and Becker, 1995).

Longitudinal research questions have been addressed by two studies in which long-term labour market opportunities of the unemployed, such as employment stability, were analysed. Breen (1992) analysed data from a follow-up study of postprimary school leavers in the Republic of Ireland. A cohort of school leavers was interviewed in 1983 and reinterviewed in 1984 and 1988 for the purpose of collecting their employment histories. In a model of job loss, prior state variables such as 'in unemployment prior to the current job' were found to have significant effects. Individuals who entered a job directly from a state-run programme or from unemployment spent a shorter time in that job before becoming unemployed again than those who lost their jobs after having been in full-time education prior to the current job. This result indicates that previous unemployment as well as participation in a state-run training programme can have an effect of stigmatization. Breen (1992) concluded that prior state variables provide proxies for other unmeasured characteristics of jobs rather than characteristics of individuals.

Programmes targeted on youth unemployment in Sweden were the subject of Korpi's (1994) evaluation of labour market programmes. His data came from a longitudinal survey of 850 youth in Stockholm who were unemployed in 1981. The sample was followed from 1981 through 1985. The sample was constructed in such a way that its members were those who held a job at time t conditional on the fact that the previous job spell $(j - 1)$ was either a spell in unemployment or a spell in either a relief job or labour market training if the preceding spell $(j - 2)$ was a spell in unemployment. Jobs were defined as either fixed term or open ended. Results indicated that employment stability was enhanced by participation in active labour market programmes. In general terms programme participation increased the duration of employment by a factor of two. Additionally, in the evaluation of transition models of the probability of becoming unemployed, comparatively high local demand for labour reduces the individual risk of becoming unemployed.

In one of the rare examples of an experiment in the state of Illinois, some of the randomly selected unemployed were offered a bonus if they became employed after no more than ten weeks of receiving unemployment benefits. The effect that this pecuniary incentive had on the reduction of unemployment duration was statistically significant but very small. This result implies that the employment, job-search and training choice of unemployed workers, as far as they have choices, 'do not seem to be governed simply, or even predominantly, by any simple trade-off between income and the irksomeness of labour' (Solow, 1990, p. 12).

3 CONCLUSION

The purpose of this chapter has been to clarify why theory-driven evaluations call for longitudinal research designs. The authors of the studies cited have derived testable hypotheses about likely effects of labour market interventions based on labour market theories, such as those of human capital, labour market segmentation and efficiency wages to name but a few. Most of the questions posed in research of that kind necessitate long periods of observation if a valuable test of these hypotheses is to be provided. Based on a broad definition of what constitutes the longitudinal element in evaluation studies, four ideal-type longitudinal designs were presented. As we have tried to show with our practical examples of longitudinal perspectives on labour market policies and evaluations, the major, but still underexploited, potential of the different types of longitudinal designs lies in the combination of various kinds of longitudinal information.

Because longitudinal studies are fairly expensive to conduct, sample size tends to be no greater than is necessary for making valid statements representative of the chosen reference group (be it a country, a region or a specific socioeconomic target group). However, this minimalist strategy has reduced the precision of estimations of the effects that labour market interventions have (Björklund, 1989). One possible strategy to reduce error margins associated with estimated effects of labour market programmes is, of course, to collect larger sets of data by either increasing the original size of samples or allowing longer periods of observation. Such a change would also increase the number of observations of completed spells of unemployment, for example.

The body of evaluation research that covers the time aspects of labour market programmes more specifically and measures time more precisely than in the past is growing, but is still modest compared to the number of *ad-hoc* evaluations. This neglect is largely due to a lack of suitable data with which to carry out such evaluations. Additionally, there is mounting concern that most programme evaluations are focussed only on effects that are measurable shortly after a programme's termination. These outcome indicators emphasize immediate postprogramme placement ratios, job mobility or exits from unemployment, and immediate postprogramme earnings. However, there is a risk that these indicators of interventions are, in many instances, too 'short-sighted'. That is, effects due to programme participation might not appear until some time later (as happens with effects on the stability or flexibility of employment, or with wage profiles on the same job). Some policy interventions that only indirectly aim at individual labour market outcomes—institutional reforms, for instance—are known to work more gradually, so their measurable effects involve considerable time lags.

Whereas the modelling of time-lag structures is current practice in macro-economic aggregate studies of policy evaluations (see Bellmann and Jackman, chap. 5 in this volume; Kraft, 1994), it is of little issue in microlevel evaluations of labour market programmes. Very few long-run longitudinal studies have dealt thus far with such effects or combine individual-level information with aggregate, national-level indicators. In particular, evaluation of continued training initiatives (Korpi, 1994; Schömann and Becker, 1995; Tuijnman, 1989; Tuijnman and Schömann, chap. 15 in this volume) have shown that benefits still attributable to programme participation are measurable some years after completion of a course. Theories of social change and changing perceptions that individuals have of their own occupational mobility and career patterns make it necessary to follow one or more cohort over a number of years to allow conclusions on changing participation patterns.

To improve targeting of labour market programmes, evaluations have to be based on more detailed knowledge about a person's labour market experience and other parts of the life course. More careful treatment of effects of unobserved heterogeneity or self-selection have a direct link to the improvement of policies. Dealing with the problem of unobserved heterogeneity allows estimation of more reliable results of programme effects and can show how a programme might be enhanced through more explicit statements of who is eligible. Hence, whether through retrospective data collection or through prospective follow-up of samples of participants and control groups, the path dependency of events and interventions is a notable determinant of programme success and failure.

One of the major aims of evaluation studies is to learn from previous or ongoing experiences for future labour market programmes. Such experiences are useful to more than one country or region if they specify, to the extent possible, the institutional setting in which processes and policies are embedded. Similarly, the generalization of results can be improved if robust indicators of business cycles are derived. Birth cohorts and historical circumstances at labour market entry have an impact on measurements of outcome, at least as partially determining effects. These factors have been ignored in many policy evaluations, a serious omission that has led to bias. Hence, the transferability of results to later periods or a different institutional setting is unduly restricted. Sample selection bias (Heckman, 1979) can impair parameter estimates and, subsequently, the validity of statistical inference based on them.

In our view there still appears to be a lack of long-run longitudinal evaluations, either prospective as a panel study (Tuijnman, 1989) or retrospective as a cohort-based analysis (Schömann, 1994; Schömann and Becker, 1995). Only with long-term perspectives of this sort, is it possible to capture career outcomes still due to programme participation. As far as policy is concerned, the predilection for the short-run perspective is all too obvious and needs no further comment, but many labour market initiatives must last quite a long time if they are to produce the expected outcomes.

This chapter underlines how important it is to account for a number of institutional factors that determine large parts of the selection mechanism governing programme participation. The factors include membership of a specific birth cohort, cohort of school leavers and cohort of first-time participants in a new labour market programme. The process of implementing a *specific* programme is crucial, though it is frequently omitted from evaluations. Microlevel evaluation, too, involves the issue of the extent to which specific programme evaluation is transferable to work in the same way if they were extended with additional funds. This matter touches to some extent on the largely unresolved micro–macro problem of aggregation: how can microlevel evaluations of many programmes be compiled to arrive at valid conclusions about the overall performance of labour market policies (Schmid and Schömann, 1993).

Only the combination of both macro- and microlevel evaluations make it possible to capture the deadweight, replacement and substitution effects of public programmes. Even a favourable microlevel evaluation of a public training programme can yield an unfavourable macrolevel evaluation if public initiative is crowding out private initiatives in this area. Lastly, there remains the issue that programme participants are simply enabled to jump the queue for job vacancies. A change in the structure of the queue for vacancies need not have an impact on its overall length. Therefore, policy evaluation research on the labour market must integrate the frequently unconnected fields of micro- or macrolevel evaluations irrespective of the predilections of scientific disciplines. More use of longitudinal designs are an important step in resolving most of these issues of policy evaluation.

REFERENCES

Allen, H. L., B. McCormick and R. J. O'Brien (1991), 'Unemployment and the Demand for Retraining: An Econometric Analysis', *The Economic Journal*, 101 (1), 190–201.

Baltes, P. B. and J. R. Nesselroade (1979), 'History and Rationale of Longitudinal Research', in J. R. Nesselroade and P. B. Baltes (eds) (1979), *Longitudinal Research in the Study of Behavior and Development*, London: Academic Press, pp. 1–40.

Barnow, B. S. (1987), 'The Impact of CETA Programmes on Earnings—A Review of the Literature', *Journal of Human Resources*, 22 (2), 157–93.

Bassi, L. J. (1984, February), 'Estimating the Effect of Training Programs with Non-random Selection', *The Review of Economics and Statistics*, 4, 36–43.

Bassi, L. J. and O. Ashenfelter (1986), 'The Effect of Direct Job Creation and Training Programmes on Low-skilled Workers', in S. Danziger and D. Weinburg (eds), *Fighting Poverty*, Cambridge, MA: Harvard University Press, pp. 73–89.

Bechtold, S. and K. Blanke (1994), 'Piloterhebung zum Europäischen Haushaltspane—Erfahrungen aus der zweiten Befragungswelle', *Wirtschaft und Statistik*, 8, 617–21.

Becker, R. and K. Schömann (1995), 'Berufliche Weiterbildung und Einkommensdynamik: Eine Längsschnittstudie über den Einfluß von beruflicher Weiterbildung auf Einkommensverläufe', Lehrstuhl für Makrosoziologie Technische Universität Dresden. (Unpublished manuscript)

Belzil, C. (1995), 'Unemployment Insurance and Unemployment over Time: An Analysis with Event History Data', *The Review of Economics and Statistics*, 113–26.

Björklund, A. (1989), *Evaluations of Training Programmes: Experiences and Proposals for Future Research*, WZB discussion paper FS I 89–13, Wissenschaftszentrum Berlin für Sozialforschung.

Blien, U. (1994, April), 'Analysing Regional Wages with Multilevel Linear Models', paper presented at the Conference of the Applied Econometrics Association, Aix-en-Provence.

Blien, U. and H. Rudolph (1989), 'Einkommensentwicklung bei Betriebswechsel und Betriebsverbleib im Vergleich—Empirische Ergebnisse aus der Beschäftigtenstichprobe des IAB für die Gruppe der Arbeiter', *MittAB*, 4, 553–67.

Blossfeld, H. P. (1989), *Kohortendifferenzierung und Karriereprozeß. Eine Längsschnittstudie über die Veränderungen der Bildungs- und Berufschancen*, Frankfurt on the Main: Campus.

Blossfeld, H. P. and G. Rohwer (1995), *Techniques of Event History Modeling. New Approaches to Causal Analysis*, Mahwah, New Jersey: Lawrence Erlbaum Associates.

Bourdieu, P. and G. Balazs (eds) (1993), *La Misère du Monde*, Paris: Edition du Seuil.

Breen, R. (1992), 'Job Changing and Job Loss in the Irish Youth Labour Market: A Test of a General Model', *European Sociological Review*, 8 (2), 113–25.

Brückner, E. (1993), *Lebensverläufe und gesellschaftlicher Wandel—Konzeption, Design und Methodik der Erhebung von Lebensverläufen der Geburtsjahrgänge 1919–1921, Part 1–5*, Berlin: Max-Planck-Institute for Human Development and Education.

Brüderl, J. (1991), *Mobilitätsprozesse in Betrieben. Dynamische Modelle und empirische Befunde*, Frankfurt on the Main: Campus.

Buck, N., J. Gershuny, D. Rose and J. Scott (eds) (1994), *Changing Households: The BHPS 1990 to 1992*, Colchester: University of Essex.

Burtless, G. (1985), 'Are Targeted Wage Subsidies Harmful? Evidence from a Wage Voucher Experiment', *Industrial and Labor Relations Review*, 39, 606–39.

Chamberlain, G. (1985), 'Heterogeneity, Omitted Variable Bias, and Duration Dependence', in J. J. Heckman and B. Singer (eds), *Longitudinal Analysis of Labor Market Data*, Cambridge, UK: Cambridge University Press, pp. 3–38.

Chen, H. and P. H. Rossi (1983), 'Evaluating with Sense: The Theory-driven Approach', *Evaluation Review*, 7, 283–302.

Collado, M. D. (1991), 'Estimating Dynamic Models from Time Series of Cross-sections', London School of Economics. (Unpublished manuscript)

Courgeau, D. (1991), 'Analyse des Données Biographiques Erronées', *Population*, 46, 89–104.

Dickinson, K. P., T. R. Johnson and R. W. West (1986), 'An Analysis of the Impact of CETA Programmes on Participants' Earnings', *Journal of Human Resources*, 21 (1), 64–91.

Duncan, G. J. and J. N. Morgan (1984), 'Behavioral Research with the Panel Study of Income Dynamics in Retrospect and Prospect', *Vierteljahreshefte zur Wirtschaftsforschung*, 4, 415–27.

Engle, R. and C. Granger (1987), 'Co-integration and Error Correction: Representation, Estimation and Testing', *Econometrica*, 55, 251–76.

Fachinger, U. (1994), 'Lohnentwicklung im Lebensablauf: Empirische Analysen für die Bundesrepublik Deutschland', Frankfurt on the Main: Campus.

Fitzgerald, J., P. Gottschalk and R. Moffitt (1994, February), 'A Study of Sample Attrition in the Michigan Panel Study of Income Dynamics', paper presented at the Conference on Nonresponse in Panels, Washington, DC.

Galler, H. P. and U. Pötter (1987), 'Unobserved Herogeneity in Models of Unemployment Duration', in K. U. Mayer and N. B. Tuma (eds), *Applications of Event History Analysis in Life Course Research*, Berlin: Max-Planck-Institut für Bildungsforschung, pp. 628–50.

Griliches, Z. (1986), 'Economic Data Issues', in Z. Griliches and M. D. Intriligator (eds), *Handbook of Econometrics*, Amsterdam: Elsevier Science Publishers, 3, 1466–514.

Groot, W., J. Hartog and H. Oosterbeck (1990), 'Training Choice and Earnings', discussion paper no. 9027, Department of Economics, University of Amsterdam.

Hanefeld, U. (1987), *Das Sozio-ökonomische Panel: Grundlagen und Konzeption*, Frankfurt on the Main: Campus.

Heckman, J. J. (1979), 'Sample Selection Bias as a Specification Error', *Econometrica*, 47, 153–61.

Heckman, J. J. and G. J. Borjas (1980), 'Does Unemployment Cause Future Unemployment? Definitions, Questions and Answers from a Continuous Time Model of Heterogeneity and State Dependence', *Economica*, 47 (187), 247–83.

Heckman, J. J. and R. Robb (1985), 'Alternative Methods for Evaluating the Impact of Interventions', in J. J. Heckman and B. Singer (eds), *Longitudinal Analysis of Labor Market Data,* Cambridge, UK: Cambridge University Press, pp. 156–246.

Hill, M. (1992), *The Panel Study of Income Dynamics: A User's Guide*, Newbury Park: Sage.

Hoff, E., W. Lempert and L. Lappe (1991), 'Persönlichkeitsentwicklung in Facharbeiterbiographien. Eine Längsschnittstudie', *Schriften zur Arbeitspsychologie*, Vol. 50, Bern: Huber.

Huinink, J. and K. U. Mayer (1993), 'Lebensverläufe im Wandel der DDR', in H. Joas and M. Kohli (eds), *Der Zusammenbruch der DDR. Soziologische Analysen*, Frankfurt on the Main: Suhrkamp, pp. 151–71.

Hujer, R. and H. Schneider (1987), 'Unemployment Duration as a Function of Individual Characteristics and Economic Trends', in K. U. Mayer and N. B. Tuma (eds), *Applications of Event History Analysis in Life Course Research*, Berlin: Max-Planck-Institut für Bildungsforschung, pp. 301–26.

Hunt, J. (1991), 'The Effect of Unemployment Compensation on Unemployment Duration in Germany', discussion paper, Department of Economics, Harvard University.

Janoski, T. and A. M. Hicks (1994), 'Methodological Innovations in Comparative Political Economy: An Introduction', in T. Janoski and A. M. Hicks (eds), *The Comparative Political Economy of the Welfare State*, Cambridge, UK: Cambridge University Press, pp. 1–27.

Katz, L. F. and B. D. Meyer (1990), 'The Impact of the Potential Duration of Unemployment Benefits on the Duration of Unemployment', *Journal of Public Economics*, 3, 337–62.

Korpi, T. (1994), 'Escaping Unemployment: Studies in the Individual Consequences of Unemployment and Labor Market Policy', discussion paper no. 24, Swedish Institute for Social Research, Akademitryck AB, Edsbruk.

Kraft, K. (1994), *An Evaluation of Active and Passive Labour Market Policy*, WZB discussion paper FS I 94–208, Wissenschaftszentrum Berlin für Sozialforschung.

Kreft, G. G. and E. D. DeLeeuw (1988), 'The See-saw Effect: A Multilevel Problem?', *Quality & Quantity*, 22, 127–37.

Lancaster, T. and S. Nickell (1980), 'The Analysis of Reemployment Probabilities for the Unemployed', *Journal of the Royal Statistical Society*, 143, 141–65.

Lynch, L. M. (1990, June), 'Private Sector Training and the Earnings of Young Workers', working paper no. 2060–88, National Bureau of Economic Research, Washington, DC.

Mayer, K. U. (1990), 'Lebensverläufe und sozialer Wandel. Anmerkungen zu einem Forschungsprogramm', in K. U. Mayer (ed.), 'Lebensverläufe und sozialer Wandel', *Kölner Zeitschrift für Soziologie und Sozialpsychologie*, 31 (Special issue), Opladen: Westdeutscher Verlag, 7–21.

Mayer, K. U. (1993), 'The Case for Micro-analytic Longitudinal Studies from a Social Policy Perspective: The German Experience', paper presented at the meeting on Research and Policy: The Use of Longitudinal Cohort Studies in the Policy Process, London, 15 March.

Mayer, K. U. and E. Brückner (1989), 'Lebensverläufe und Wohlfahrtsentwicklung. Konzeption, Design und Methodik der Erhebung von Lebensverläufen', *Materialien aus der Bildungsforschung*, no. 35, Berlin: Max-Planck-Institut für Bildungsforschung.

Moffitt, R. (1985), 'Unemployment Insurance and the Distribution of Unemployment Spells', *Journal of Econometrics*, 28, 85–101.

Nesselroade, J. R. and P. B. Baltes (eds) (1979), *Longitudinal Research in the Study of Behavior and Development*, London: Academic Press.

Plewis, I. (1985), *Analysing Change—Measurement and Explanation Using Longitudinal Data*, Chichester, NY: John Wiley & Sons.

Projektgruppe Betriebspanel (1994), 'Das IAB-Betriebspanel: Ergebnisse der ersten Welle 1993', *Mitteilungen aus der Arbeitsmarkt- und Berufsforschung*, 1, 20–32.

Regnér, H. (1993), 'Choosing among Alternative Non-experimental Methods for Estimating the Impact of Training: New Swedish Evidence', discussion paper, Swedish Institute for Social Research, Stockholm.

Rendtel, U. (1995), *Die Analyse von Paneldaten unter Berücksichtigung der Panelmortalität: Theorie und Empirie am Beispiel des Sozio-ökonomischen Panels (SOEP)*, Frankfurt on the Main: Campus.

Rossi, P. H. (1991), 'Comprehensive, Tailored, Theory-driven Evaluations: A Smorgasbord of Options', in W. R. Shadish, T. D. Cook and L. C. Leviton (eds), *Foundations of Program Evaluation: Theories of Practice*, Newbury Park: Sage, pp. 377–440.

Schmid, G. and K. Schömann (1993), 'Institutional Choice and Flexible Coordination: A Socio-economic Evaluation of Labour Market Policy in Europe', in G. Schmid (ed.), *Labor Market Institutions in Europe*, New York: Sharpe.

Schneider, W. and W. Edelstein (eds) (1990), *Inventory of European Longitudinal Studies in the Behavioural and Medical Sciences*, Strasbourg: European Science Foundation.

Schömann, K. (1994), *The Dynamics of Labor Earnings over the Life Course: A Comparative and Longitudinal Analysis of Germany and Poland*, Berlin: edition sigma.

Schömann, K. and R. Becker (1995), 'Participation in Further Education over the Life Course: A Longitudinal Study of Three Birth Cohorts in the Federal Republic of Germany', *European Sociological Review*, 11 (2), 187–208.

Solow, R. M. (1990), *The Labor Market as a Social Institution*, Oxford: Basil Blackwell.

Ting, Y. (1991), 'The Impact of Job Training Programmes on the Reemployment Probability of Dislocated Workers', *Policy Studies Review*, 10 (2/3), 31–44.

Tuijnman, A. C. (1989), *Recurrent Education, Earnings, and Well-being. A Fifty-year Longitudinal Study of a Cohort of Swedish Men*, Stockholm: Almqvist & Wiksell International.

Tuma, N. B. and M. T. Hannan (1984), *Social Dynamics: Models and Methods*, New York: Academic Press.

Van der Vaart, W., J. Van der Zouwen and W. Dijkstra (1995), 'Retrospective Questions: Data Quality, Task Difficulty, and the Use of a Checklist', *Quality & Quantity*, 29, 299–315.

Verbeek, M. (1992), 'Pseudo Panel Data', in Lmátyás and P. Sevestre (eds), *The Econometrics of Panel Data*, Dordrecht: Kluwer, pp. 302–15.

Verbeek, M. and T. Nijman (1992), 'Incomplete Panels and Selection Bias', in Lmátyás and P. Sevestre (eds), *The Econometrics of Panel Data*, Dordrecht: Kluwer, pp. 262–302.

Vissers, A. and H.-J. Dirven (1994), *Fixed-term Contracts in the Netherlands: Some Evidence from Panel Data*, WZB discussion paper FS I 94–212, Wissenschaftszentrum Berlin für Sozialforschung.

Wagner, G., R. V. Burckhauser and F. Behringer (1994), 'The English Language Public Use File of the German Socio-economic Panel', *The Journal of Human Resources*, 28 (2), 429–31.

Westergard-Nielsen, N. (1993), 'Effects of Training: A Fixed-effect Model', in K. Jensen and P. K. Madsen (eds), *Measuring Labour Market Measures: Evaluating the Effects of Active Labour Market Policies*, Copenhagen: Ministry of Labour Denmark, pp. 35–96.

Wurzel, E. (1993), 'An Econometric Analysis of Individual Unemployment Duration in West Germany', Heidelberg: Physica.

H43, ~~E24~~, J68 ~~R~~
J64

5. Aggregate Impact Analysis

Lutz Bellmann and Richard Jackman

In this chapter we discuss the aggregate impact of active labour market policies (ALMPs), that is, the effects not on particular individuals but on aggregate economic variables—in particular, employment and unemployment. We start by considering the mechanisms through which these types of policy can have aggregate effects and argue that any such analysis must, implicitly or explicitly, be based on some general equilibrium or macroeconomic model of the labour market. The first section of the chapter then continues with an outline of several possible models and a review of the scope for policy within them. We then turn to the evaluation of the aggregate effects of policy intervention. The chapter appraises the scope and results of econometric work in this area.

Do better job prospects or higher earnings from those who have participated in training schemes or been employed in temporary jobs represent a net gain to the economy, or do schemes simply enable participants to 'jump the queue' and take jobs that would otherwise have gone to other unemployed people? If one holds the view that the total number of jobs (or amount of work) cannot be affected by spending on labour market policies, then evidently their effects can only be distributional. It may be a goal of policy to give work to the young rather than to the old or to those with dependent children or to share it out more evenly (e.g. by policies to assist the long-term unemployed), but with a given stock of jobs these policies are unlikely to produce any economic or fiscal benefits to set against their costs.

By contrast, if one takes the view that ALMPs can alter the overall number of jobs and, hence, affect both output and unemployment in the economy as a whole, there are not only aggregate economic benefits but also a fiscal payoff in terms of increased tax revenues and reduced unemployment benefit outlays to set against the costs of the programmes. Equally, from an economic standpoint, it is possible for ALMPs to increase output only if one starts from a position where there are market imperfections. It thus becomes important to identify the nature of these imperfections in order to assess whether intervention can counteract them.

Researchers accomplish much of the empirical work by estimating augmented matching functions, that is, by relating outflows from unemployment to jobs to the stocks of vacancies and unemployed persons and thereby controlling for the level of ALMP intervention. An advantage of applying a matching function approach to the evaluation of the impact of ALMPs is that, unlike approaches used in studies based on individual unemployment duration, it takes into account the net impact of these schemes. The matching function approach is therefore complementary to microlevel duration models, which can better control for the effects of individual characteristics on hazard rates.

Moreover, the OECD countries attacked the same problems quite differently with respect to the implementation of ALMPs and sometimes transformed the design of these policies radically over time. Hence, by comparing matching function estimates internationally as well as before and after policy changes, one can learn much about the effects of ALMPs.

1   METHODOLOGY AND MODELS

We start with the effects that ALMPs have on the overall levels of employment and unemployment. The idea that ALMPs may be a means of reducing aggregate unemployment clearly reflects a departure from the traditional Keynesian perspective, according to which the level of unemployment was simply a product of the level of aggregate demand in the economy. Repeated experience in many countries of demand expansion ultimately leading to increased inflation has led to a recognition that governments cannot tackle unemployment in a sustainable way through demand expansion alone. Rather, the search is for policies that will reduce labour market imbalances, rigidities and distortions, an outcome that will then allow an expansion of demand to reduce unemployment without creating inflation.

The starting point is therefore the concept of the 'equilibrium' rate of unemployment (or nonaccelerating inflation rate of unemployment (NAIRU)). What determines the NAIRU? And in what circumstances is there a case for reducing it? We consider three basic types of model, describing within each (a) the underlying cause of unemployment, (b) whether unemployment in the model is efficient or inefficient and (c) how ALMPs can affect the equilibrium:

-   market-clearing (search) models;
-   nonmarket-clearing (e.g. union bargaining or efficiency wage) models;
-   structural models, which may incorporate minimum wages, payroll taxes and other 'wedge' factors.

1.1 Search Models

Search models investigate the determinants of employment and unemployment in an economy in which wages and prices are perfectly flexible, and there are no government regulations or noncompetitive labour market institutions. Their objective is to pin down the fundamental market frictions that attend the process of job allocation and create an irreducible minimum of unemployment in even the most flexible of labour markets. The models focus on the heterogeneity of workers and jobs, with the implication that some job matches will be more productive than others and, hence, that it will pay both workers and firms to search around for a productive match rather than settle for the first job offer or job applicant available. This process is assumed to take time either because of imperfect information, so that time is required to establish the characteristics of jobs on offer, or because there is a thin market where appropriate jobs turn up only from time to time.

Within such models, unemployment is 'productive' in the sense of enabling people to end up in more suitable jobs than would be the case if they were obliged to take the first job available. But this is not to say that the level of unemployment in such models is optimal. Inefficiencies in the search process may derive from various sources, of which the most important are (a) externalities in the search process itself, (b) the characteristics of information as a public good and (c) capital market imperfections.

As to the first point, there are both positive and negative externalities associated with search (Diamond, 1981; Pissarides, 1990). An individual deciding to prolong his or her search for work may expect to derive a private benefit from a better job match but, by increasing the number of applicants for vacancies, reduces the job prospects of other unemployed job seekers (a congestion externality). At the same time a larger pool of applicants may encourage firms to increase recruitment, thus assisting other unemployed people (a thick-market externality). Similar considerations apply to firms' decisions about vacancies. It is hard to establish empirically whether any of these externalities matter, and there is a presumption that they do not if there are constant returns to scale in the hiring function, which generally appears to be the case. In general, arguments for intervention along these lines have not had much impact on the policy debate, in part because the externalities themselves seem rather esoteric, but perhaps more importantly because there is no evidence to suggest that these factors are large in practice. In any event they are both positive and negative and may therefore cancel each other out.

As to the second source of inefficiency in the search process, having a single agency serve as the repository of information about job vacancies makes job search less costly. In the absence of private provision, this economizing effect would be a strong argument for public employment agencies.

But efficiency gains from a single supplier do not in themselves preclude private provision. A specialist newspaper or journal carrying job advertisements can charge both advertisers and readers, and the more advertisements it carries the more it may be able to charge. This arrangement can provide the incentive for an efficient pooling of information on job opportunities. In practice, job seekers in many spheres appear to be bombarded with information, so it is not clear that the private market provides insufficient information in this respect.

Public employment agencies tend to have a role in the less skilled and less professionally specific areas of the market, particularly in vacancies for unskilled or casual work. In these sectors private advertising may be less effective to the extent that it relies on specialist publications. Even so there is some doubt whether public employment agencies do facilitate job search. The microeconomic evidence on this point is somewhat unfavourable. There is evidence from many countries that, other things being equal, workers using the public employment services tend to be out of work longer than workers using other methods of job search (Blau and Robins, 1990; Osberg, 1993; Wielgosz and Carpenter, 1987). It is not clear, however, whether this reflects lower efficiency or a tendency for less enterprising people to rely on the public employment services. It can be argued, for example, that public employment services are a search agency of last resort to which people turn when other methods have failed. There is evidence that employers regard those sent by public employment services as of lower quality than those recruited through other search methods (Bishop, 1993; van Ours, 1994). Such findings suggest that these agencies are dealing with unemployed persons who are more difficult to place than others.

But this microeconomic evidence does not address the question whether overall job-matching in the economy is improved by public employment services. For example, the public agencies may provide a floor below which no one need fall, but the more qualified or energetic of the unemployed can do better on their own initiative.

A third market imperfection affecting job search stems from the capital market. Capital market 'imperfections' are likely to prevent unemployed people from borrowing to finance consumption during job search and may thus oblige unemployed people to take jobs even when, using a market interest rate, further job search could be expected to be a productive investment. Thus, unemployment would be inefficiently low. This argument is often cited to advocate payment of unemployment benefits, which enable people to finance consumption while searching for jobs. But paying people an income while unemployed also has the effect of reducing the incentive to find work. Logically, it could be argued that, on insurance principles, unemployment benefits be paid as a lump sum to compensate for the costs of job loss rather than as a weekly income (or that benefits be paid in the form of loans rather than grants).

Search models have proved a very useful framework for the analysis of the effects that payment of unemployment benefits has on the unemployment rate. The standard argument is that payment of unemployment benefits unconditionally for as long as people are unemployed will tend to reduce search intensity and raise the reservation wage (i.e. make people choosier about the type of work they are prepared to accept). These effects reduce the rate at which unemployed people take jobs and thereby raise equilibrium unemployment. If benefits are at all significant relative to income from work, there is little doubt that they can lead to inefficiently high rates of unemployment.

Thus, in search models with benefits, there will generally be scope for efficiency gains from policies that reduce unemployment and thus counteract the inefficiency resulting from the payment of benefits. One such policy is to subsidize or otherwise assist job search. Public employment services can assist job search directly, say, through assistance in making job applications and in meeting some of the costs incurred (as with 'job clubs'). But although such assistance can be expected to increase search intensity, it will also tend to raise the reservation wage (by making it more worthwhile for unemployed people to go on searching). Thus, in theory, assistance with job search may not necessarily increase the outflow rate from unemployment.

An important function of public employment agencies is to monitor the job search behaviour of the unemployed. Payment of unemployment benefits can, for example, be made conditional on job search activity. In fact, the entitlement to unconditional unemployment benefits, which is assumed in many theoretical studies, is not at all consistent with the job search requirements laid down in most unemployment insurance systems. For example, most stipulate that an unemployed person turning down a job can lose the entitlement to unemployment benefits. In the extreme case—a regime in which turning down a job offer leads to automatic termination of benefits—the reservation wage is reduced to that which would obtain in the absence of benefits.

Why? Imagine that an unemployed person receives a job offer. The options now available are either to take the job or remain unemployed without an entitlement to unemployment benefits. In choosing between these options, the unemployed person adopts the reservation wage appropriate to a regime without benefits, for that wage is now the alternative to taking the job even though, prior to the receipt of the offer, benefits were being paid. An unemployed person might then have to accept a job that pays less than the benefits previously received, though in practice the benefit officers may allow benefits to continue if the job offer pays less.

At first sight, conditionality appears to solve the capital market imperfection by allowing payment of unemployment benefits without having the adverse effect of raising the reservation wage. But further consideration shows that conditionality may create more problems than it solves. In particular, it can have the effect of lowering job search intensity. Imagine that an individual hears of a vacancy but is unsure whether it is at all suitable. If the individual applies for the job and is offered it, he or she may have no alternative but to take it whether or not it is suitable, for rejecting the job would lead to loss of unemployment benefits. People will restrict job search to the types of jobs they are sure they would want to take. In general, with the intensity of job search endogenous, there can be no presumption that making the payment of unemployment benefits conditional on job search activity will raise the out-flow rate.

Considerations of this kind may well help explain the fact that many unemployed people seem to spend rather little time looking for work and seem to fill out few job applications. For example, the 1978 Cohort Study of unemployed men in the United Kingdom (Wood, 1982; see also Layard, Nickell and Jackman, 1991, chap. 5) found that the average unemployed person made only one job application per month and spent only five hours per week looking for work (including reading the newspapers). Clearly, the emphasis of policies in recent years has been to encourage the unemployed to look for work more actively.

One can, of course, impose job search requirements on the unemployed. An example would be a stipulation that a given number of job applications be made per unit period. But if it is not in the private interests of the unemployed to receive unsuitable offers, it may be difficult to enforce this requirement. It will be in the interests of the unemployed to apply for high-quality jobs even though their prospects of receiving an offer are low, rather than lower-level jobs where they risk receiving an offer less attractive than the unemployment benefits.

In this context there can be a role for ALMPs, where the employment service itself becomes involved in making job offers (or making offers of places on training schemes). People refusing such offers could generally expect their unemployment benefits to be terminated. A variant of this arrangement in countries where entitlement to unemployment benefits is strictly limited to a given period (e.g. 60 weeks in Sweden and 30 months in Denmark) is that the employment agency is obliged to offer unemployed people a job or place in a training scheme before their benefits expire. In either case the choice is between taking a place on a government scheme and continuing as unemployed but without benefits. In general, unemployed people will take places on the schemes provided the payoff exceeds that of unemployment without benefits—which will typically be the case unless the unemployed person has a job in the 'informal' sector, family support or private income.

Such policies can increase the 'true' outflow from unemployment in several ways. First, some of the unemployed may not be averse to living on unemployment benefits, but when this option is denied them they will search harder for work, in the hope of finding a regular job preferable to a government scheme. Evidence from Sweden (Carling, Edin, Harkman and Holmlund, 1994) showed the outflow from unemployment into regular jobs to be increasing as unemployment benefits expired, leaving people to face the prospect of moving into government schemes (though the rate at which the outflow rate increased was slower than that in the United States just before benefits expired).

Second, as discussed in Jackman (1994), some of the unemployed have jobs in the informal sector or are supported by their families or other people, and this income together with the unemployment benefits is more attractive than regular work. Such people are therefore not actively seeking work and thus not properly entitled to unemployment benefits, but job search requirements may be difficult to monitor effectively, particularly in depressed labour markets. If benefits are withdrawn, some people in this group will remain inactive or in casual work but will no longer be a burden on public finances. Others, however, will seek regular work because the termination of benefit payment removes the incentive not to work.

Thus, ALMPs can limit what has been termed the problem of moral hazard in unemployment insurance. In a sense, by obligating people to work as a condition for continuing to receive support from the state, it separates those in need who cannot find work from those who are idle and fraudulent.

In such models, to the extent that frictional unemployment can be reduced by interventionary policies, the number of jobs presents no separate problem. In 'market-clearing' models of frictional unemployment, it has sometimes been conjectured (Beveridge, 1942) that the number of job vacancies and the number of unemployed people should be equal. A reduction in unemployment can then be achieved through more rapid job-matching simply by filling up existing vacancies with no need to create any additional jobs. In general, though, there is no reason this requirement need hold. In particular, if the characteristics of jobs differ more than the productivity of workers, then it will pay workers to devote more time to job search than firms do, and the stock of unemployed will exceed the stock of vacancies at any point in time (Reder, 1969). In that case, a reduction in unemployment cannot generally be achieved by filling existing vacancies; additional jobs must also be created. That task is no problem in a market-clearing model, however. Wages will adjust (i.e. fall) to create jobs for all who want them, given the structure of incentives on the supply side.

The main limitation of this framework is that it seems very difficult to believe that the duration of unemployment spells experienced by so many unemployed people, particularly in European countries, can be attributed to a preference for remaining unemployed at existing levels of unemployment benefits. The high rates and persistence of unemployment suggest that many unemployed people cannot get the type of work they want and for which they are qualified. There appears to be job rationing in at least parts of the labour market. There may be a secondary sector, where jobs can be found, but job opportunities in it may be limited and, to at least some of the unemployed, demeaning. We turn to two-sector models in due course but first examine the role of labour market policies in models of job-rationing.

1.2 Job-rationing Models

In job-rationing models, wages are set according to the objectives of employers or unions, which need not always be in favour of the market-clearing wage. Employers may concede wages in excess of the supply price either because they face a powerful union or because they may thereby motivate their workers to increase productivity. But if all employers follow such practices, wages then exceed the market-clearing level, resulting in an overall shortage of jobs.

Can the number of jobs in models of this type be increased by ALMPs? Clearly, the answer to this question must hinge on how wages are set. Consider, for example, a standard union wage-bargaining model (e.g. Layard et al., 1991). Wages are set in the bargain as a markup on the outside opportunity. The markup depends on factors such as union bargaining power and product market competitiveness, whereas the outside opportunity depends on the state of the labour market as indicated by the unemployment rate (as a measure of the likely duration of unemployment for anyone becoming unemployed), wages in other sectors, and unemployment benefits and other factors affecting the well-being of the unemployed.

In such models ALMPs can in principle affect the number of jobs through several channels (see in particular Calmfors, 1994; Calmfors and Lang, 1995; Calmfors and Nymoen, 1990). For example, if they encourage the unemployed to search harder for work, those currently employed will become more averse to losing their jobs (because more effective competition from the unemployed will make it more difficult for them to find new ones). With the outside option made less attractive, wages in the firm will be reduced and the number of jobs thereby increased.

Against this argument it may be noted that employed people who lose their jobs can also expect to benefit from ALMPs. If workers are not particularly worried about losing their jobs because they believe the government will help them find new ones, they need be less restrained in their wage demands. Through this channel ALMPs may be expected to lead to higher wages and, hence, fewer jobs. If ALMPs provide interesting or worthwhile training opportunities or temporary jobs for unemployed people, the experience of unemployment is made less unpleasant. This again may be reflected in a lower degree of wage restraint.

Overall, the effect of ALMPs on wages will therefore depend on (a) whether they are primarily directed towards assisting workers who have lost their jobs rather than, say, providing training for new entrants (Calmfors and Lang, 1995) and (b) whether ALMPs improve or worsen the welfare of individuals while unemployed. On the first point, in most countries government schemes are directed primarily at specific target groups (youths, the long-term unemployed) rather than at those who have recently become unemployed, though placement and other employment agency services are, of course, generally available to all unemployed people.

To be specific, let us assume that wages in the union bargaining model are affected not by the unemployment rate but by the expected duration of unemployment of a worker who becomes unemployed. The inverse of this expected duration—the probability per unit period of finding a job (i.e. the hiring probability, h)—is given in simplified form (Layard et al., 1991, chap. 5, p. 218) by

$$h_i = c_i h \left(V/cU, 1 \right) \tag{5.1}$$

where the average search effectiveness of unemployed people is c, and the search effectiveness of the worker at risk of unemployment is c_i. In this form of the model, what matters is not so much the level of unemployment as the search effectiveness of the stock of unemployed job seekers relative to the search effectiveness of the worker whose job may be put at risk in the wage bargain.

Some types of ALMPs, such as those targeted at young people, may be successful in raising the average search effectiveness of the unemployed but may have no effect on the search effectiveness of any employed worker who loses his or her job. Then it follows from (5.1) that, for a given c_i, any increase in c will be associated with a reduction in h_i, an increase in the expected duration of unemployment and, hence, greater wage restraint and more jobs. On the other hand, specific help to those becoming unemployed (an increase in c_i) will of itself have the opposite effect. If ALMPs raise the search effectiveness of everybody equally, they will increase c_i by as much as they increase c, but this will again raise h_i (since the elasticity of h with respect to V/cU is less than one). If everyone searches more effectively, unemployment durations will fall, even when ALMPs do not affect the relative advantages of different groups.

The provision of ALMPs targeted at the long-term unemployed raises the most problems in this context. If those currently in work have perfect foresight, they will recognize that should they lose their current job they may have difficulty finding a new one and thus face a risk of a long spell of unemployment. They may then, at the same time, recognize that the problems they will face should they enter long-term unemployment will be significantly alleviated by the provision of ALMPs. Hence, ALMPs targeted at the long-term unemployed can in principle have an adverse effect on wage-setting by mitigating the fear of long-term unemployment.

One can, we think, argue against this conclusion on one of two grounds. First, it is well known that the outflow rates from unemployment of the long-term unemployed are lower than those of unemployed people with shorter durations (e.g. Jackman and Layard, 1991). If this difference results from state dependence, so that the individual outflow rates from unemployment decline with duration, and if individuals are myopic in that they do not perceive that their prospects of finding a job will decline the longer they remain unemployed, then workers may take as their point of reference in the wage bargain not the experience of unemployed people as a whole but only the experience of the short-term unemployed. An increase in the outflow rate from long-term unemployment can then raise c but will not affect c_i, for workers are myopic in the wage bargain and refer only to outflow rates from short-term unemployment that they deem relevant to themselves. Policies directed at the long-term unemployed can then have beneficial effects in reducing aggregate unemployment.

Although the question of whether declining unemployment outflow rates are the result of state dependence or of heterogeneity has been the subject of innumerable analyses, the analysis by Calmfors and Lang (1995) shows that state dependence is not a sufficient explanation. The assumption of myopia is equally critical. Some survey evidence may support this assumption. For example, Gregory (1986) has cited findings from opinion polls in Australia that suggest that those in work, when asked about the outlook for finding another job should they become unemployed, thought their own prospects to be undiminished over a period when aggregate unemployment had increased sharply.

Although the assumption of myopia might be appropriate for interpreting particular historical episodes, such as times when unemployment is rising very sharply, as in the first half of the 1980s in Australia, it seems less attractive an assumption when long-term unemployment has become a permanent feature of the economic environment. But at the opposite extreme, the assumption of perfect foresight seems less than plausible in practice. The economic environment, and governments and government policies, are always liable to change, and it would be rash for a currently employed worker to base wage claims on any particular assumptions about policies towards the long-term unemployed a year or so hence. It may be no coincidence that Sweden, with its much more consistent commitment to policies to assist the unemployed, may be the only country where concerns have surfaced about the potential impact of ALMPs on the wage bargain.

In answer to the first of the questions raised above, there must therefore be a presumption that workers currently employed will generally regard ALMPs targeted at various disadvantaged groups in the labour market—young people, the long-term unemployed, the unskilled—as primarily of benefit to others rather than themselves.

With regard to the second question, whether ALMPs improve or worsen the welfare of unemployed individuals, the form of policy provided is the crux of the issue. If ALMPs subsidize job search, provide more opportunities for unemployed people or more generally reduce the disutility of unemployment, it seems inescapable that they must make unemployment a less fearful prospect. Thus, they improve the outside option in the wage bargain and thereby add to wage pressure. On the other hand, if, as discussed above, ALMPs are used in conjunction with benefit conditionality as a means of putting pressure on unemployed people to search harder for work, then the option of becoming unemployed is made less pleasant. In these circumstances ALMPs can reduce wage pressure even if unemployment durations fall.

The general conclusion is that, in this type of model, ALMPs that target disadvantaged groups, put pressure on unemployed people to search harder for work or make it more difficult to turn down job offers are most likely to be associated with lower wage pressure and more jobs. By contrast, policies that serve only to make the experience of unemployment more pleasant seem likely to have the opposite effects.

1.3 Structural Models

Many who have studied the causes of the persistent unemployment that afflicted many countries in the 1980s (e.g. OECD, 1990) have concluded that unemployment is now basically structural in nature. Though the term structural can cover a variety of phenomena, in this context structural models are those that focus on a cross-sectorial imbalance between labour demand and labour supply. If unemployment in an economy is mainly concentrated in particular sectors, can ALMPs have a role in alleviating the problems of these sectors and thereby reduce overall unemployment?

The most conspicuous sectorial imbalance in recent years has had to do with skills. In many countries there has been a marked shift in demand towards more highly skilled occupations and away from, in particular, unskilled and semiskilled manual work. Though the skills of the labour force have been improving, this process appears to have lagged behind the growth in demand for skills. As a result, the relative labour market prospects (and, in some countries, the relative wages) of skilled workers have improved and those of the unskilled have deteriorated, meaning that the bulk of the unemployed in most countries are unskilled.

Clearly, the appropriate labour market response to increased structural imbalance is greater mobility across sectors. From this perspective, there is an obvious role for ALMPs to assist labour mobility, specifically by providing training for unemployed workers to qualify them for work in sectors where the demand for labour is growing.

From the perspective of economic welfare, one may again ask what the causes of market failure are in this context and how far they can justify government intervention. Whether or not one accepts the argument that there is likely to be underinvestment in employer-funded training (because trained workers may leave the firm that trained them), there is clearly a fiscal disincentive for the unemployed. The payment of unemployment benefits reduces the incentive for unemployed people to incur the costs and risks of attempting to acquire new skills or qualifications.

To formalize this issue in a simple analytical model, we may envisage an economy with two types of jobs, skilled (sector 1) and unskilled (sector 2). For technological and other reasons there is a shift in the pattern of demand for labour at an exogenous rate of x jobs per year. Workers acquire skills and move from sector 2 to sector 1 at a rate in part exogenous (y workers per year) but in part depending on the economic incentives represented by wage and unemployment rate differentials between the two sectors. Initially, with x greater than y, the unemployment rate falls in sector 1 and rises in sector 2. Even in the absence of wage differentials, workers start to migrate from sector 2 to sector 1 because job opportunities are better there. The rate of migration induced (m) might be expected to be an increasing function of the difference between the benefit from migration and the cost:

$$m = m \{(u_2 - u_1)(1 - b) - c\} \qquad (5.2)$$

where u_1 is the unemployment rate of skilled workers; u_2, the unemployment rate of unskilled workers; b, the replacement rate; and c, the cost of training (b and c being measured relative to the wage). The unemployment rates in each sector measure the expected duration of unemployment and the cost (in terms of forgone income) of being unemployed for longer, relative to the wage, is $(1-b)$.

In equilibrium, the rate of increase of skilled jobs will be equal to the rate of increase of skilled workers, or

$$x = y + m \qquad (5.3)$$

so that

$$u_2 - u_1 = (m^{-1}(x - y) + c) / (1 - b) . \qquad (5.4)$$

In this simple framework, payment of benefit will increase unemployment differentials (structural unemployment). And government intervention to facilitate labour mobility through reducing the cost of skill acquisition will reduce the unemployment differential. Where the payoff from training takes the form of lower unemployment prospects, unemployment benefits cause the private return to fall below the social benefit, thereby justifying policy intervention.

These types of models also offer scope for policy intervention on the demand side. Structural unemployment can be reduced if the relative growth in the demand for skilled labour, x, can be reduced. Policies to slow down sectorial change can in this framework lower unemployment, though obviously at the expense of slowing economic growth. Such policies can take the form of either promoting more unskilled-labour-intensive methods of production within firms (e.g. shifts in employment or social security taxes to reduce the burden on the low paid) or encouraging policies focussed on sectors in which unskilled workers are employed (e.g. subsidies to manufacturing industries). Where sectorial unemployment rates are high, policies such as work-sharing or early retirement can be justified in some circumstances to the extent that those affected cannot reasonably be expected to find work in the expanding sectors.

These arguments are summarized in Table 5.1. The various models suggest that there is scope for ALMPs to raise employment and lower unemployment in the aggregate. The next question to address is, therefore, whether they have in

Table 5.1   *Synopsis of Arguments from Search Models Concerning Labour Market Policies*

	Reason for LMP	Argument	Policy Implication ALMP, Yes or No
1.	Externalities – congestion too many searchers + thick market	+ and – cancel	ALMP no
2.	Information is public good	Information about jobs already abundant	ALMP no
3.	Improve matching speed-up search process	Employers find ALMP recruited workers to be of lower quality	ALMP yes
4.	Capital market failure	Borrow for consumption during search	ALMP yes
5.	Unemployment benefits make people choosy	Inefficiently long search if UB high	Lower UB or conditional UB
6.	ALMP makes job offers and UB expires	a) Increased search intensity for people a) who dislike ALMP jobs b) Informal sector jobs can turn formal	Make UB conditional on suitable job offer

Notes
ALMP = active labour market policy; UB = unemployment benefits.

fact done so. This question can be approached by means of testing the specific assumptions whereby aggregative effects are generated within particular models. It may also be addressed by rather broad-brush methods, such as 'black-box' econometric models in which some aggregate variable (employment, wages or unemployment) is the dependent variable and a variety of possible causal factors, including some measure of ALMPs, are independent variables.

2   ALMPs AND THE OUTFLOW RATE FROM UNEMPLOYMENT

The critical issue is whether ALMPs raise the overall outflow rate from unemployment by helping unemployed workers return to employment. To establish the aggregate effect of policies, one needs to examine the overall outflow rate from unemployment rather than the effects on particular individuals. A study of the effect of programmes on individuals can establish whether individual *A*, who has been on the programme, has a better chance of subsequently finding a job than an otherwise similar individual *B*, who has not. This may be because *A*'s job prospects have improved whereas *B*'s are unchanged, but it may be because the programme has allowed *A* to jump the queue at *B*'s expense and has had no effect on the total number of unemployed people finding work.

2.1   Deadweight Loss, Substitution and Displacement Effects

Analysis of policy effectiveness is typically discussed in terms of deadweight loss, substitution and displacement effects. These terms are defined as follows (see Haveman and Hollister, 1991; OECD, 1993):

- *Deadweight loss* arises if a programme pays for something that would have happened anyway. For example, a firm taking on an unemployed person finds itself eligible for a recruitment subsidy, or an unemployed person signing up for a training course finds himself or herself entitled to some government grant.
- *Substitution* means that subsidized or programme-supported workers (e.g. workers who have been on a training programme) replace unsubsidized workers with no net effect on employment in the firm. For example, if there is a recruitment subsidy for long-term unemployed people, firms may hire them instead of the short-term unemployed. Similarly, a local authority or government agency in the public sector may recruit fewer regular workers in order to take advantage of schemes financed by the labour market authorities. For this reason it is common to impose a condition of additionality on public works programmes (see, e.g., Grubb, 1993).

– *Displacement* means the reduction or crowding out of regular employment elsewhere in the economy through competition in the goods market. For example, a firm employing subsidized workers is able to undercut, and thus acquire market share from, a firm employing regular (unsubsidized) workers. Of course, competition need not be confined to firms within the industry; firms employing subsidized labour and cutting their prices can attract consumers from other products. It is thus virtually impossible to identify displacement effects from microeconomic studies. A further problem is that displacement may be associated with actual job loss (an increase in the inflow to unemployment) rather than a reduced rate of recruitment in the firms affected.

Deadweight loss will be revealed by microeconomic evaluations of programme effectiveness if, for example, it is found that a particular programme has no effect on the prospects of individual programme participants leaving unemployment. But studies of the effects of programmes on individuals will not reveal the extent of substitution or displacement effects, which imply an increase in the outflow rates of targeted groups at the expense of reduced outflow rates (or increased inflow rates) for other, nontargeted, groups. An aggregate study of the outflow rate from total unemployment would, however, show whether there was a net effect of the programme. And, more informatively, studies of outflow rates of particular groups of unemployed people (say, by age or duration) may be able to identify not only the effects of the policy on the target groups but also the groups (if any) affected by substitution or displacement, and the magnitude of such effects.

A finding of zero (or less than 100 per cent) substitution or displacement does not necessarily mean that the programmes or policies have created completely new jobs for the formerly long-term unemployed. More likely, people in the target groups will have taken existing jobs, but the regular workers displaced from these particular jobs will have been absorbed into the labour market, where the normal processes of wage adjustment and market-clearing will operate to increase the number of regular jobs through the processes described in section 1, above.

But reliance on the general processes of market adjustment raises problems of the time horizon. One may accept that the labour market eventually adjusts but that this process can take time, with the corollary that higher rates of, say, short-term unemployment may be required for the adjustment process in the short run. Policies may need to have high short-run substitution or displacement effects in order to bring about the necessary adjustment in the long term.

For example, assume that wages in the economy are set in a bargaining process which responds to the level of short-term unemployment rather than total unemployment (as discussed in section 1.2). Suppose, too, that the government now introduces a policy, such as a recruitment subsidy, targeted at the long-term unemployed. In the short run, employers may substitute long-term unemployed people for other recruits, leading to a fall in long-term unemployment but a rise in short-term unemployment of equal magnitude (100 per cent substitution effect). The increase in short-term unemployment will, by assumption, depress wage settlements and thus lead to more jobs. This process will continue until short-term unemployment has fallen back to its original level. At this point the outflow rate from short-term unemployment will also have returned to its original level, and there will appear to be zero substitution. Regrettably, in most empirical studies it is not possible to distinguish between impact and long-run substitution or displacement effects.

2.2   Analytical Framework

An increase in the overall outflow rate from unemployment will, other things equal, be associated with an equal proportionate fall in the steady-state stock of unemployment. In the steady state, with the rate of unemployment constant, the inflow to unemployment (I) must be equal to the outflow from unemployment (A). The outflow rate (A/U) is the outflow divided by the number of unemployed people (U). With a given inflow I, a rise in the outflow rate implies an equiproportionate fall in the stock of unemployment:

$$U = U\,(I/A) = I/(A/U) = \text{inflow/outflow rate.}$$

The outflow rate from unemployment depends primarily on the general state of the economy. We need to assess the *incremental* effects of the various policies over and above the effects on unemployment outflows of changes in the state of the labour market. This requires a full analysis of the factors affecting the outflow from unemployment. Here we adopt the approach of Haskel and Jackman (1988), Layard et al. (1991), Lehmann (1990) and Pissarides (1986). The key variables are the state of the labour market, measured by vacancies V, and the average search effectiveness of the unemployed in the absence of employment measures, c. We then allow ALMPs to enhance search effectiveness, so that, with a given set of employment measures, actual search effectiveness is given by

$$c^* = c\,(1 + kM)\,,$$

where M is a vector of employment policy actions, and k measures the net effect that each has on average search intensity.

The outflow from unemployment is given by the hiring relationship

$$A = f(V, c^*\,U)\,, \quad \text{with} \quad f_1, f_2 > 0\,. \tag{5.5}$$

The assumption that the function f exhibits constant returns to scale is reasonable and supported by empirical studies. Therefore, (5.5) can be rewritten:

$$A/U = c^* f(V/c^* U) . \tag{5.6}$$

Writing (5.6) in log-linear form gives

$$\ln (A/U) = \ln c^* + b \ln (V/c^* U)$$

$$= b \ln (V/U) + (1 - b) \ln c (1 + kM)$$

$$= b \ln (V/U) + (1 - b) \ln c + (1 - b) kM$$

(assuming the effectiveness of measures sufficiently small to employ the approximation $\ln (1 + z) = z$).

2.3   Empirical Implementation

Empirical studies based on this framework have been implemented in the United Kingdom, West Germany and a number of other countries. Although the bulk of our discussion of empirical studies of the aggregative effects of ALMPs are to be found in chap. 24 in this volume, we conclude this section with a brief review of empirical studies that make use of the flow framework described above.

In the United Kingdom Haskel and Jackman (1988) examined the effects of the Community Programme, which provided noncommercial work of value to the community mainly for young people who had been unemployed for over six months during the 1980s. They found that the programme raised the outflow rates of young people but had an adverse effect on the outflow rates of 55 to 60-year-old workers, possibly because employers might otherwise have hired elderly people for work that could instead be undertaken more cheaply through the Community Programme. The overall effect on outflows was positive. Lehmann (1990, 1993) looked at the effects of the Restart Programme, which introduced mandatory counselling for unemployed people after six months of unemployment. He found that the Restart Programme increased the outflow rate from long-term unemployment but had a negative effect on the outflow from short-duration unemployment. Again, however, the overall effect was positive.

Bellmann and Lehmann (1990) investigated the impact of job creation, wage subsidy and further training and retraining programmes in West Germany. They looked at effects on the inflow into unemployment and on outflow rates by age and duration, on a cross-section of local employment office areas.

They were, however, able to establish a positive effect only for job creation programmes, which were found to raise outflow rates from short-term unemployment, whereas the impact of training and wage-subsidy programmes was insignificant. Earlier studies of German wage subsidy and Labour Promotion Act schemes by Schmid (1979, 1980) found substantial deadweight effects for the wage subsidy (75 per cent in the case of the federal government programme). He also found that the Labour Promotion Act was unsuccessful in improving placements of its target group, the long-term unemployed, but that it was helpful in placements of young people.

These estimates are in line with studies of the effects of wage subsidies in other countries, such as the United States (Bishop and Haveman, 1979), France (Kopits, 1978), Australia (Department of Employment, Education and Training, 1989), Ireland (Breen and Halpin, 1989) and the Netherlands (de Koning, 1991). These studies suggest combined deadweight and substitution effects of the order of 70 to 90 per cent of the gross number of jobs created (see also Hübler, 1982, and OECD, 1993, for reviews of empirical studies). For Sweden, Vlachos (1985) found that the majority of firms receiving recruitment subsidies would have made new hirings anyway.

With regard to displacement, Forslund and Krueger (1994) attempted an estimate of displacement by looking at sectorial employment by region. They found that employment in construction and building rose by only about one-third of gross job creation, suggesting displacement on regular employment on the order of 60 to 70 per cent, but that displacement was much lower in health and welfare. The status of these results is not clear, however. More employment in one sector may be at the expense of jobs in other sectors, and it is equally possible that workers displaced from a sector may, by raising the available labour supply in other sectors, bring about an expansion of employment elsewhere in the economy.

3　　CONCLUSIONS

In this chapter we have analysed the question of whether ALMPs can affect the total number of jobs in the economy. It started from the proposition that a sustainable increase in employment can be achieved only if the efficiency of the labour market is improved through elimination or reduction of the impact that imbalances, rigidities or fiscal or other distortions have.

We suggested that there are a number of channels through which ALMPs might in principle improve the efficiency of the labour market. They include assistance with the provision of information and advice on job search, and counteracting the adverse effects of payment of unemployment benefits on the intensity of search and on job acceptance. They also encompass the reactivation of unemployed people who have particular difficulty in finding work, such as the unskilled or the long-term unemployed, in circumstances in which the labour market as a whole will adjust to create more employment for the work force as a whole.

We then argued that the best method of establishing the existence of aggregate effects is to analyse both the aggregate and specific-group determinants of the outflow rates from unemployment. We showed that this method takes account of deadweight loss and of substitution and displacement effects. Lastly we briefly reviewed empirical studies of outflow rates and of the efficacy of policies.

REFERENCES

Bellmann, L. and H. Lehmann (1990, September), 'Active Labour Market Policies in Britain and Germany and Long-term Unemployment: An Evaluation', paper presented to the conference of the European Association of Labour Economists, Lund, Sweden.

Beveridge, W. H. (1942), *Social Insurance and Allied Services*, Cmd 6404, London: HMSO.

Bishop, J. (1993), 'Improving Job Matches in the U.S. Labor Market', *Brookings Papers on Economic Activity*, 1, 335–400.

Bishop, J. and R. Haveman (1979), 'Selective Employment Subsidies: Can Okun's Law be Repealed?', *American Economic Review*, 69, 124–30.

Blau, D. M. and P. K. Robins (1990), 'Job Search Outcomes for the Employed and Unemployed', *Journal of Political Economy*, 98, 637–55.

Breen, R. and B. Halpin (1989), *Self-employment and the Unemployed*, Dublin: Economic and Social Research Institute.

Calmfors, L. (1994), 'Active Labour Market Policy and Unemployment–A Framework for the Analysis of Crucial Design Features', *OECD Economic Studies*, 22, 7–47.

Calmfors, L. and H. Lang (1995), 'Macroeconomic Effects of Active Labour Market Programmes in a Union Wage-setting Model', *Economic Journal*, 105.

Calmfors, L. and R. Nymoen (1990), 'Real Wage Adjustment and Employment Policies in the Nordic Countries', *Economic Policy*, 11, 397–448.

Carling, K., P.-A. Edin, A. Harkman and B. Holmlund (1994), *Unemployment Duration, Unemployment Benefits and Labour Market Programmes in Sweden*, working paper no. 12, Department of Economics, Uppsala University.

de Koning, J. (1991, September), 'Measuring the Placement Effects of Two Wage-subsidy Schemes for the Long-term Unemployed', paper presented to the conference of the European Association of Labour Economists, El Escorial.

Department of Employment, Education and Training (1989), *Jobstart Evaluation*, Canberra, Australia: Canberra.

Diamond, P. (1981), 'Mobility Costs, Frictional Unemployment and Efficiency', *Journal of Political Economy*, 89, 798–812.

Forslund, A. and A. Krueger (1994), *An Evaluation of Swedish Active Labour Market Policy: New and Received Wisdom*, NBER working paper no. 4802, National Bureau of Economic Research.

Gregory, R. G. (1986), 'Wages Policy and Unemployment in Australia', *Economica*, special issue, 53, S53–S74.

Grubb, D. (1993), 'Some Indirect Effects of Active Labour Market Policies in OECD Countries', Paris: OECD. (Unpublished manuscript)

Haskel, J. and R. Jackman (1988), 'Long-term Unemployment in Britain and the Effects of the Community Programme', *Oxford Bulletin of Economics and Statistics*, 50, 379–404.

Haveman, R. and R. Hollister (1991), 'Direct Job Creation: Economic Evaluation and Lessons for the United States and Western Europe', in A. Björklund, R. Haveman, R. Hollister and B. Holmlund (eds), *Labour Market Policy and Unemployment Insurance*, Swedish Trade Union Institute for Economic Research (FIEF), Studies in Labour Market and Economic Policy, Oxford, UK: Oxford University Press.

Hübler, O. (1982), *Arbeitsmarktpolitik und Beschäftigung: Ökonometrische Modelle und Methoden*, Frankfurt on the Main: Campus.

Jackman, R. (1994), 'What Can Active Labour Market Policy Do?', *Swedish Economic Policy Review*, 1, 221–57.

Jackman, R. and R. Layard (1991), 'Does Long-term Unemployment Reduce a Person's Chance of a Job? A Time Series Test', *Economica*, 58, 93–106.

Kopits, G. F. (1978), 'Wage Subsidies and Employment: An Analysis of the French Experience', *IMF Staff Papers*, 25, 494–527.

Layard, R., S. Nickell and R. Jackman (1991), *Unemployment: Macroeconomic Performance and the Labour Market*, Oxford, UK: Oxford University Press.

Lehmann, H. (1990), *Employment Measures in Britain: Their Effects on the Overall and Duration Specific Outflow Rates from Unemployment*, working paper no. 1173, London: Centre for Labour Economics, London School of Economics.

Lehmann, H. (1993), *The Effectiveness of the Restart Programme and the Enterprise Allowance Scheme*, discussion paper no. 139, London: Centre for Economic Performance, London School of Economics.

OECD (1990), *Labour Market Policies of the 1990s*, Paris: OECD.

OECD (1993), *Economic Outlook*, Paris: OECD.

Osberg, L. (1993), 'Fishing in Different Pools: Job Search Strategies and Job-finding Success in Canada in the Early 1980s', *Journal of Labour Economics*, 11, 348–86.

Pissarides, C. A. (1986), 'Unemployment and Vacancies in Britain', *Economic Policy*, 3, 499–559.

Pissarides, C. A. (1990), *Equilibrium Unemployment Theory*, Oxford: Basil Blackwell.

Reder, M. (1969), 'The Theory of Frictional Unemployment', *Economica*, 36, 1–28.

Schmid, G. (1979), 'The Impact of Selective Policy–The Case of a Wage-cost Subsidy Scheme in Germany 1974–75', *Journal of Industrial Economics*, 27, 339–58.

Schmid, G. (1980), *Strukturierte Arbeitslosigkeit und Arbeitsmarktpolitik*, Königstein (Taunus): Athenäum.

van Ours, J. C. (1994), 'Matching Unemployed and Vacancies at the Public Employment Office', *Empirical Economics*, 19, 37–54.

Vlachos, V. (1985), 'Temporära lönesubventioner–En studie av ett arbetsmarknadspolitiskt medel', *Lund Economic Studies*, 34, Department of Economics, Lund University.

Wielgosz, J. B. and S. Carpenter (1987), 'The Effectiveness of Alternative Methods of Searching for Jobs and Finding Them', *American Journal of Economics and Sociology*, 46, 151–64.

Wood, D. (1982), *Men Registering as Unemployed in 1978–A Longitudinal Study*, London: Department of Health and Social Security (DHSS).

H43, D61

J68
J28

Sweden
US

6. Cost–benefit Analysis

Lennart Delander and Harald Niklasson

The aim of cost–benefit analysis (CBA) is to evaluate or assess 'projects' (or 'measures' and so on), that is, to provide a basis for *choices between alternative courses of action*. Usually, CBA is associated with 'public projects' (or 'public policy measures' and so forth), that is, with choices made within organizations that are expected to act in the public interest.

The main purpose of this chapter is to discuss and assess the possibilities for CBA to make fruitful contributions to the evaluation and appraisal of labour market policy (LMP) measures.

We do not look too closely at the theoretical foundations of CBA. Instead, we concentrate on a discussion about 'the way of thinking' represented by CBA and about the use and usefulness of CBA in the appraisal and evaluation of LMP projects. We do not present very detailed instructions or directions for the practical application of CBA to specific problems of choice. However, in the final part of the chapter we try to illustrate the meaning and applicability of the principles previously discussed. We do so by citing a few examples of attempts to calculate costs and benefits of LMP projects that have actually been carried out.[1]

1   THE FRAMEWORK

For a project to target a specified problem, at least two alternative courses of action have to be clearly defined. The *project* should be conceptualized as the transition from one of these policies (alternative A) to the other (alternative B). The *impacts* (or the *effects*) of the project are the *differences* between the course of events associated with B and the course of events associated with A.

The impacts of the transition from A to B at time 0 should not be thought of as changes in the state of the world from before to after time 0. They should be

---

1 The fundamental conceptions and reasonings in this chapter are based mainly on Sugden and Williams (1978) and Williams and Giardina (1993). Other important sources are Gramlich (1981), Hanley and Spash (1993), Layard and Glaister (1994) and Zerbe and Dively (1994).

understood as differences between two alternative courses of events (or alternative states of the world at specified dates) after time 0. The state of the world, including the conditions of life for target groups, will change with time in both cases—in one way if A is chosen, and in another way if B is chosen. As a consequence, the meaning of the specification 'to go on as before' or 'to do nothing' may become rather obscure, and the policy alternative in question must be stated more precisely.

The decision-maker is assumed to regard some of the impacts of the project as advantageous and others as disadvantageous. Hence, CBA has a bearing on the problems of assessment and aggregation faced by a decision-maker who wants to act in the public interest. The meaning of the phrase 'in the public interest' will be discussed later in the chapter.

In the following pages we make an explicit distinction between 'the analyst' and 'the decision-maker' (for a detailed discussion, see Sugden and Williams, 1978, especially pp. 229–42). The role of the analyst is to make CBAs. The role of the decision-maker is to decide, that is, *to choose between alternative courses of action.* Usually, we see the decision-maker as a public agency, for instance, the government or a local employment exchange agency. However, for simplicity's sake we sometimes talk about the decision-maker and the analyst as individuals.

Usually, we think about a CBA as an *ex-ante* exercise aiming at the *appraisal* of a project under deliberation. However, it is, of course, quite possible to carry out CBAs *ex post*, that is, as studies aiming at the *evaluation* of decisions (choices) that were made in the past. Such CBAs *ex post* may contribute to the basis for related CBAs *ex ante*.

1.1   The Role of CBA in Policy Analysis

The impact assessments necessitated by any specific CBA will always entail a great deal of guesswork. Of course, the analyst wants to be able to justify his or her guesses, for example, by means of impact evaluations related to the project under consideration.

Certainly, CBA widens the perspective of impact evaluation. Nevertheless, CBA may be perceived as a very narrow way of looking at things. The reason is that each and every specific CBA presupposes the existence of two well-defined policy alternatives. CBA is not, in itself, very innovative. *Which* policy alternatives and *which* problems of choice are recognized and seriously considered (e.g. subjected to CBAs) will greatly depend on the *sociopolitical and institutional settings* in which different decision-makers exist and operate and on the nature of the corresponding *policy formation and implementation processes* (see Schmid, chap. 7 in this volume).

Perhaps these settings and processes are such that the potentially superb policy alternative B remains undiscovered or undeveloped, so that the hypothesis that policy B is better than policy A is never formulated. Furthermore, even if everybody is aware of the existence of such an alternative B, the settings and processes may be such that no decision-maker is ever prompted to consider B as an alternative to A. Thus, CBA should be looked at as being complementary to, or as being integrated in, other, more comprehensive, critically scrutinizing kinds of *policy formation and implementation analyses*, including *process evaluations*.

It is also possible that the institutional frameworks are such that they do not induce decision-makers to engage in very much of the explicit 'thinking in terms of alternatives' that is needed for the initiation and use of CBAs, but rather give rise to more of a 'reactive' kind of 'decision-making', which is governed by different kinds of 'signals' or 'rules of thumb'. If so, in practice the role of CBA will be very limited, and few CBAs will be initiated by decision-makers. Furthermore, the CBAs carried out by independent analysts will perhaps be left to 'live a life of their own' outside the world of policy-making.

1.2 CBA as a Target-oriented Approach

CBA can be directly related to the *target-oriented approach to policy evaluation* that is given prominence in this book and that aims, among other things, at the identification of the policies that are best suited to achieving specified targets. The assertion that an optimal policy alternative has been identified entails the assertion that the impacts of the transition to any other possible policy alternatives aiming at the same target have been estimated and weighted and that costs have been judged to outweigh benefits. (CBAs representing an attempt to show how specified targets can be achieved at minimum net costs are often spoken of as *cost-effectiveness analyses*, CEAs.)

The target may be, for example, 'to improve the conditions of life for disabled individuals of working age' (see Delsen, chap. 17 in this volume). Starting from policy alternative A, meaning—in some specified sense—to go on as before', one might identify three other policy alternatives: 'to increase cash benefits' (B), 'to increase the use of wage subsidies' (C) and 'to increase the number of job opportunities in sheltered employment' (D). If none of these four alternatives can be ruled out as being impossible or uninteresting, then three CBAs are needed.

All three projects ('A to B', 'A to C' and 'A to D') will probably result in a net gain for the target group. If all three policy means involved are already extensively used in policy A, then it is quite possible that all three projects will result in a net loss for the group 'other individuals'. The aim of the CBAs initiated should be to find out which one of the three projects considered will entail the smallest sacrifice for 'other individuals' per 'unit of improvement' for the target group. What then remains is the question as to whether the corresponding minimum sacrifice for 'other individuals' should be regarded as small enough to justify the implementation of the project thus singled out.

Suppose that the CBAs mentioned have led to the conclusion that the project 'A to B', that is, 'to increase cash benefits', is better—in the sense indicated—than the other two projects considered. Furthermore, suppose that the CBA of 'A to B' has demonstrated that, in this case, an improvement for the target group equivalent to an increase in disposable income by ECU 1 will require a sacrifice on the part of 'other individuals' equivalent to a decrease in disposable income by ECU 2. Should the project 'A to B' be carried out?

The decision-maker has to decide, but neither of the two alternatives would constitute a violation of the public interest. B is in the interest of 'the disabled'. A is in the interest of 'other individuals'. C or D, however, are not in the interest of any of the groups. Thus, these two policy alternatives would entail a violation of the public interest.

The presupposition that the decision-makers want to act in the public interest simply means that a policy alternative will be ruled out if another feasible alternative exists, the transition to which makes it possible for the decision-makers to achieve an improvement for somebody without making somebody else worse off. Of course, the fact that the decision-makers very often carry out projects yielding losses for some groups and gains for others is not necessarily evidence of frequent violation of this presupposition.

By ruling out two alternatives and illuminating the consequences of the remaining project, the analyst has helped the decision-maker act in the public interest. If the CBAs are carried out (*ex ante* or *ex post*) by an independent analyst, then they will contribute to charging the decision-maker with accountability to the general public for the policies implemented. This aspect is a very important part of CBA (see Sugden and Williams, 1978, pp. 229–42).

1.3   The Identification and Elimination of Inconsistencies

Let us briefly consider a very common complication: the existence of many decision-makers operating with the same kinds of policy means. If these decision-makers apply different valuations, then the outcome of their joint choices may be 'inefficient' in the sense that there exist policy alternatives that are in the interest of everybody but that nevertheless remain undiscovered and/or unexploited. This possibility is easily demonstrated if we extend the example discussed.

Suppose that there are two decision-makers who select policy means, and suppose that one of those individuals rejects projects that result in an ECU 1.5

loss for 'other individuals' per ECU 1 gain for 'the disabled', whereas the other accepts projects that yield an ECU 2.5 loss for 'other individuals' per ECU 1 gain for 'the disabled'. Hence, there is a clear case of inconsistency in public decision-making. Considering the consequent state of the world, one realizes that it is possible for the two decision-makers, if they cooperate, to achieve improvements for both groups by substituting projects of the former kind for projects of the latter kind. Thus, the transition to such an alternative is in accordance with the valuations of both decision-makers.

An agreement between the two decision-makers resulting in the elimination of the existing inefficiency in the way indicated does not have to include an agreement on 'distributional weights' of the kind used in the discussion above. If, however, the decision-makers are operating independently of each other, for example, within the framework of a decentralized 'management-by-objectives system', and do not cooperate, then superior policy alternatives may remain undiscovered and unexploited. Thus, it emerges that one of the very important tasks for the analyst is to reveal, and thereby help eliminate, the existence of *inconsistencies* in public decision-making.

When it comes to LMPs, the identification of a number of more or less clearly defined target groups is often significant. The corresponding target variables represent different aspects of the conditions of life for individuals belonging to such groups. Each target variable can be influenced by more than one of the LMP means being used (and by other policy means). More than one decision-maker is involved in the corresponding policy formation and implementation processes. These decision-makers may differ greatly in the valuations governing their choices, more specifically in the 'prices' (for example, the distributional weights) implicitly attached to the target variables. The consequence may be the existence of significant inefficiencies. CBAs can contribute to the elimination of such inefficiencies as a consequence of the required *explicitness*. That is, the policy alternatives should be clearly stated, and the corresponding thinking in terms of the mutual advantages and disadvantages of different alternatives should be made visible.

1.4 CBA and Policy Formation

As indicated above, there are two slightly different ways of looking at the role of the analyst carrying out CBAs and, thus, at the role of CBA. One alternative is to assume that the analyst is employed by the decision-maker, or that the analyst is a consultant engaged for a specific task. The other alternative is to regard the analyst as an actor working independently of the decision-maker. In the former case the analyst participates in decision-making processes by assisting the decision-maker. In the latter case the role of the analyst is that of a critic or an accountant who is trying to make the decision-maker accountable to the general public, including the individuals affected by the decisions under scrutiny (see Pignataro, 1993).

In both cases the analyst starts from the presupposition that the decision-maker should regard projects as desirable if they are in the interest of everybody and as undesirable if they are in the interest of nobody. In both cases the CBAs carried out should be explicit and consistent in terms of the alternatives considered and the valuations applied. The aggregations inherent in CBA should induce consistent application of statable valuations that are not contrary to the public interest.

It is interesting to compare the role of CBA in public agencies with the role of profitability calculations in commercial firms in a competitive situation. The many decision-makers in such firms are expected to act in the interest of the partners. When deciding—that is, choosing between alternatives—the decision-makers are therefore expected to select the alternative that is commercially most profitable. Their incentives to do so are very strong. Failure to choose that alternative will be reflected in the profit and loss account. If they fail too severely or too frequently, then the firm will be eliminated by the competition. The decision-makers know that they must be able, on request, to justify their decisions to their superiors and to the partners as being in accordance with the profitability criterion. Problems of choice regarded as especially fateful are carefully analysed, often by consultants called in to assist the decision-makers.

One can argue that the role of CBA in public decision-making should be similar to the role of profitability calculations in the commercial sector. One can also argue that, in practice, commercial appraisals are often interpreted or treated as CBAs. The fact that a project carried out by a private firm proves to be commercially profitable is frequently regarded as an indication that the project is in the public interest. This observation will be the point of departure in the following section.

2   THE VALUATION AND AGGREGATION OF IMPACTS

A prominent feature of CBA, besides the quest for explicitness and consistency, is the use of a *unit of account* in valuation and aggregation procedures. Mainly for convenience, the unit of account (numeraire) chosen is almost always money.

When it is said that the gain of the project for an individual is ECU x, it means that *this individual* regards the consequences of the project as equivalent to being given (if x is positive) or being deprived of (if x is negative) the corresponding amount of money. That amount can also be interpreted as representing the individual's 'willingness to pay' to profit (if x is positive) or to be spared (if x is negative) from the net consequences of the project.

In the following we talk about the '*net benefit*' of the project as a weighted sum of all the individual gains and losses as defined above (with losses counting as negative). Thus, the aggregations that are inherent to CBA may necessitate the use of distributional weights. Certainly, at any setting of these positive weights the net benefit of a project with some winners and no losers will be positive, and the net benefit of a project with some losers and no winners will be negative. Thus, the use of such a CBA as a decision-making criterion will not be contrary to the public interest. In practice, however, most projects will, *per se*, mean gains for some individuals and losses for others.

2.1 Uniform Distributional Weights?

There is a presupposition in most CBAs that all individual gains and losses are attributed the weight 1. Given such a weight setting, the CBA for a specific project will constitute a straightforward summation of all individual gains and—given negative signs—losses, as defined above. Which motivations can be found for such a simple, but very special, weight setting?

One possibility is that it truly reflects the valuations of the decision-maker according to whom the value of an individual ECU x gain or loss is independent of the identity (or the group membership) of the individual affected.

Another motivation is based on the following observation: if the net benefit is larger than zero, according to the summation considered, then the aggregated gain of the winners (what the winners, at most, are willing to pay for getting the project carried out) is larger than the aggregated loss of the losers (what the losers, at least, must be paid to be compensated for their losses). In other words, the size of the 'common cake' increases. Or, put yet another way, then it is possible for the winners to indemnify the losers and yet remain winners.

Of course, the winners should not be expected to compensate the losers voluntarily. We can conclude, however, that if it is possible for the decision-maker to achieve—without significant costs—the compensating redistributions required for the indemnification mentioned, then a positive net benefit, calculated in the way indicated, means that the project should be accepted; a negative net benefit, that it should be rejected.

However, these motivations for calculating the net benefit as the straightforward sum of propensities to pay are not very convincing. It is quite obvious that most public decision-makers do not consider the value of an ECU x gain or loss to be independent of the group affiliation of the individual affected. It is also obvious that public decision-makers usually do not have the possibility of carrying out cost-free compensating redistributions between individuals or groups.

2.2   Commercial Calculations as CBAs

Let us look at the role and nature of CBA from a somewhat different angle. When it comes to projects that are decided upon by firms exposed to competition, it is very often asserted, or implicitly assumed, to be in the public interest that commercially profitable projects are accepted and that loss-generating projects are rejected.

The basis for this standpoint is given by economic theory: by the interpretation of *prices as reflecting not only propensities to pay but also opportunity costs*. Given some assumptions, the profitability calculation can be looked at as representing a summation of individual propensities to pay for the impacts of the project. The advantageous impacts are the increases in available amounts of marketed goods as a result of the project (via increased outputs), which ultimately accrue to the individuals. The propensities to pay for these impacts are calculated by means of current (or prognosticated) prices and are represented as revenues in the profitability calculation. The disadvantageous impacts are the decreases in available amounts of other marketed goods, and perhaps the increases in delivered amounts of labour as a result of the project (via increased inputs), which will ultimately burden the individuals. The corresponding propensities to pay, calculated by means of prices (including factor prices), are represented as costs in the commercial calculation.

This is why profitability calculations so often—when some conditions are regarded as at least approximately fulfilled—are looked at, or treated, as representing acceptable CBAs. If the activities of commercial firms were taken over by public agencies, then these agencies would, according to the interpretation indicated, often ask for the same kind of information and make the same kind of calculations as the commercial firms.

The conditions hinted at above concern such factors as the absence of significant 'external effects' and the presence of such a degree of competition that, for example, significant inefficiencies caused by monopolistic pricing do not occur. Very often these conditions are far from fulfilled. If it is believed that commercial profitability calculations will systematically or excessively deviate from the corresponding CBAs, then different kinds of interventions will probably be considered and perhaps introduced. If so, the mutual advantages and disadvantages of alternative ways to intervene ('to do something') and to the alternative not to intervene ('to do nothing') have to be considered. The available policy means fall into three main categories: (a) regulation, (b) taxes and subsidies and (c) public direction, by means of public production or purchases, of what is to be produced (Layard and Glaister, 1994, p. 3).

When it comes to the necessary public decision-making, *consistency* is called for. The design and interpretation of the CBAs applied by public agencies should be consistent with the *motivations* for (i.e. the way of thinking behind) the interpretation and acceptance of, in many cases, commercial profitability calculations as CBAs. As a consequence, the following main principle should be applied: every impact for which there exists a propensity to pay (positive or negative) should be included and attributed a value representing the size of that propensity. Often such a CBA can be constructed by means of fairly straightforward adjustments and additions to the corresponding commercial profitability calculation.

2.3   An Example

When a commercial profitability calculation is interpreted as a CBA, the changes in labour costs included in the calculation are regarded as acceptable approximations of the corresponding costs or benefits. Because of, among other things, the existence of involuntary unemployment and tax wedges, such an acceptance is reasonable only if the impact of the project on total employment in the economy is judged to be negligible.[2] When it comes to many LMP measures, this requirement is not fulfilled. Often, the principal aims of LMP projects are to achieve decreases in the unemployment experienced by different target groups. In such a case a calculation corresponding to a commercial analysis can sometimes be used as the point of departure for subsequent adjustments and additions aiming at the construction of the CBA needed.

Suppose, for example, that a rather small 'employment-creating' LMP project will entail the following impacts on a specified target group of individuals: (a) a decrease in the unemployment experienced by that group and (b) an increase by ECU 100 000 of the group's disposable income. Suppose further that these two impacts are regarded by the group members as being *equivalent* to an increase in the group's disposable income by ECU 80 000 with no change in unemployment. The increase in the group's gross labour income (the labour costs as perceived by the employers) is calculated to be, say, ECU 500 000. Given these data, 'the commercial calculation' should, according to the principle established above, be supplemented by an additional benefit equal to ECU (500 000 – 20 000) = ECU 480 000. The employment impact thus considered will, *per se*, mean an increase in the production of marketed goods, the propensity to pay for which is ECU 500 000 and a sacrifice on the part of the individuals affected corresponding to an ECU 20 000 propensity to pay. Thus, the employment effect will, *per se*, mean an increase in the size of the common cake by ECU 480 000.

It may ensue that the commercial calculation turns out to be mainly a cost analysis indicating, say, an ECU 550 000 'net project cost'. If so, and if the

---

2   This is a consequence of the existence, in the economy considered, of 'involuntary unemployment' and 'tax wedges'.

employment impact for 'other individuals' is judged to be negligible, then the CBA arrived at indicates that the project will mean an ECU 70 000 decrease in the size of the common cake. Of course, if the project is expected to generate employment effects for 'other individuals', too, then these effects also have to be taken into consideration in a way consistent with the treatment of the employment effects for the target group.

2.4   The Treatment of Distributional Effects

What has been established so far is a way of looking at the meaning and role of CBA, which has proved to be consistent if it is presupposed that projects enlarging the common cake should be accepted and those diminishing it should be rejected. But what about the aspects of distribution and equity, which are still missing? This absence is sharply at variance with the observation that such aspects play a prominent role in policy formation processes, such as when it comes to many kinds of LMP measures related to target groups.

The absence of questions of distribution and equity in commercial calcula-tions is easily explained. Enterprises have no incentive to take such aspects into consideration. However, if commercial firms were offered incentives to consider distributional impacts (i.e. to apply distributional weights) when appraising projects, their inclusion would probably not make much difference in many cases. The distributional effects, if charted, would often prove to be relatively insignificant. More important, however, is another aspect. In most cases it would be much more difficult to verify and estimate, even very roughly, the distributional impacts of a project than to reach conclusions con-cerning the sign of the change in the common cake (the sign of the net sum of the propensities to pay for the project's impacts).

Our interpretation is that it is judged to be in the public interest if most decision-making concerning the production of commodities and services is based on the criterion that projects that enlarge the common cake are accepted and those that lessen it are rejected. We do not regard this viewpoint as incon-sistent with the assumption that public decision-makers want to influence the distribution of the cake.

Let us return for a moment to the simplified example presented above. Consider two alternative messages delivered by the analyst to the decision-maker. The first: my CBA indicates that the project under consideration will result in an ECU 70 000 decrease in the size of the common cake. The second message, made possible by the data included in the example: my analysis indicates that the project will result in an ECU 80 000 gain for the target group and an ECU 150 000 loss for 'other individuals'. Obviously, these two mes-sages are quite consistent. However, the decision-maker will probably regard the latter message as much more informative than the former. Suppose that he or she rejects the project if given only the former message and accepts the project if given the latter. This does not mean that the decision-maker has acted inconsistently or contrary to the public interest. However, if it is also observed that this person is rejecting other projects while knowing that these projects will mean a loss of less than ECU 1.875 for 'other individuals' per ECU 1 gain for the target group (150 000/80 000 = 1.875), then the decision-maker has been exposed as acting inconsistently and, thus, as violating the public interest.

The fact that in many cases it proves unwarranted or impossible (too costly) to consider distributional impacts does not imply that public decision-makers have to, or should, refrain from considering such impacts when it is both justified and possible. Once again, however, we stress the importance of the quest for consistency and explicitness.

3   DIFFICULTIES AND POSSIBILITIES

The simple ways of thinking presented so far, which are based on the perception of CBA as a normative tool of applied welfare economics, may appear to be potentially very powerful. If they are, then why is the role of CBA so very limited in practice, for example, when it comes to the appraisal and evaluation of LMP measures?

First of all, it is worth repeating that CBA is not, *per se*, very innovative and that the initiation and use of CBAs depend on the existing institutional settings and the corresponding structure of incentives on the part of the decision-makers. There are, however, other, complementary explanations for the modest role attributed, in practice, to CBA. One explanation often proposed is that real-world applications, related to existing, well-defined problems of choice, always will entail a number of severe difficulties. The analyst and the decision-maker will always have to deal with incomplete information about the direct and indirect impacts of the project under consideration, that is, with uncertainty about the corresponding alternative courses of events (see, for example, Hanley and Spash, 1993; Zerbe and Dively, 1994). Furthermore, the actors will always have to deal with the difficulty—disregarded in our discussion so far—that impacts do not all occur during the same period (see, for example, Arrow and Lind, 1994; Stiglitz, 1994; Zerbe and Dively, 1994).

The problems we have mentioned cannot be conjured away simply by using alternative methods of evaluation or appraisal. Furthermore, all the kinds of difficulties mentioned so far are dealt with every day by numerous analysts making commercial profitability analyses and calculations. Such calculations are often—rightly or not—seen or treated as acceptable CBAs. Of course, any study aimed at the identification of the pros and cons of a project will necessitate impact assessments comparing alternative courses of events. Thus, many of the difficulties often attributed to CBA concern impact evaluations.

The information available is often incomplete, difficult to interpret or not highly reliable. However, the decision-makers cannot avoid making decisions; they simply have to make choices between alternatives. This necessity must be the point of departure for the analyst given the task of carrying out CBAs.

One hopes that the analyst's efforts in carrying out CBAs—to face the problems of the decision-maker while striving for explicitness and consistency—will increase the probability that the ultimate decisions will be in the public interest. After all, the analyst's efforts may reduce the risk that those decisions are based on inconsistencies, misconceptions, omissions, double-counting and other kinds of 'muddled thinking'. Alternatively, the analyst will contribute to making the decision-maker accountable to other decision-makers, such as the government or, ultimately, the voters.

However, an analyst intending to present a CBA has to deal with two key questions relating to a number of 'CBA-specific' problems and difficulties:

1. Which impacts should be identified and estimated?
2. How should these impacts be valued and aggregated?

3.1   Production Impacts

According to the principles presented in section 2, the attempt to carry out a CBA will normally necessitate, first, an attempt to calculate the affected individuals' net propensity to pay for the project's impacts on the total production of marketed goods (commodities and services) ultimately available for consumption. These production impacts are usually valued by means of prices, which are supposed to reflect the relevant propensities to pay.[3] Very often it is appropriate and practical to start with what can be looked at as a commercial calculation and then to introduce the corrections or additions that prove to be necessary for the calculation of the 'net production impact' (in the sense indicated above). As regards LMP measures, the need for such 'corrections and additions' is often related to the existence of employment impacts.

In section 2 we looked at an example of a project cost calculation (ECU 550 000) that had to be supplemented by a calculation of the in-

---

3 When relative prices are assumed to change as a consequence of the project, the production impacts have to be valued by means of 'shadow prices' in between the prices that will prevail in the two cases, so that changes in consumers' and producers' surpluses caused by the project are taken into consideration.

crease in production caused by the employment impacts of the project (ECU 500 000). Thus, the project considered would lead to an ECU 50 000 net decrease in the amount of goods ultimately available for consumption.

Certainly, real-world cases are always much more complicated. However, it should not be regarded as impossible, in practice, to estimate the signs and the orders of magnitude of 'the net production impacts' caused by LMP projects. The main prerequisites for such estimations are evaluations indicating the size and composition of the projects' direct and indirect employment impacts.

3.2   Unmarketed Goods

So far we have disregarded the possible existence of impacts for which the relevant propensities to pay cannot be assessed by means of current or expected prices. The project may affect environmental conditions, the availability of public goods, travel times, the frequency of accidents and illnesses and so on. If such impacts exist, the analyst has to introduce further corrections or additions. Of course, some impacts of the kind listed will influence the total amount of marketed goods available for consumption. This effect has to be reflected in the calculation of the 'net production impact'. Looking beyond the consumption of marketed goods, however, one might find significant propensities to pay for 'better environmental conditions', *per se*, or 'a smaller risk of being injured or killed', *per se*, and so forth. In the following paragraphs we concentrate on some other aspects of employment impacts.

In our previous example, the employment impacts may mean that some individuals consider it necessary to sacrifice 'spare time' or 'convenience' to achieve the additional delivery of labour. For such individuals the net gain of the project will be smaller than the corresponding increase in their disposable income. The effect of such negative signs is that the net benefit of the project is smaller than the minus ECU 50 000 'net production impact'. On the other hand, given 'involuntary unemployment' (or other kinds of labour market distortions), some other individuals may regard their net gains as *larger* than their income gains. If so, the effect is that the net benefit of the project is larger than minus ECU 50 000. Consequently, if we regard the net change in the production of goods as the net benefit of the project, then we assume that the net gain of the individuals affected by the employment impacts is equal to their net income gain, and no further corrections or additions are needed.

In our example in section 2, we assumed that the net gain for the group considered was smaller than its income gain: ECU 80 000 versus ECU 100 000. If this assumption is true, then the net change in total production will mean an ECU 20 000 overestimation of the net benefit. A supplementary cost item, equal to ECU 20 000 and representing the individuals' sacrifice of 'spare time' or 'convenience', has to be introduced. The net benefit will be minus ECU 70 000.

It should not be regarded as impossible, in practice, to obtain information about the signs and the orders of magnitude of the net income gains that accrue to different target groups as a consequence of LMP projects (that is, about items corresponding to the ECU 100 000 net income gain for the target group in our example). However, it may prove to be extremely difficult to estimate, even very roughly, the net total gain for individuals whose conditions of life are changed in many respects, and perhaps very dramatically so. The employment impacts in cases of involuntary unemployment (or other labour market distortions) may entail manifold and dramatic changes for the individuals affected.

In our example the net total gain for the target group was simply assumed to be ECU 80 000, meaning an ECU 20 000 willingness to pay for the removal of some kinds of sacrifices, for instance, the loss of 'spare time' or 'convenience'. According to the principles of CBA, the amount ECU 20 000 should represent a summation of the individuals' honest answers to well-defined questions about their propensities to pay as regards the impacts considered. The answers may vary widely among individuals. It is even possible that some kinds of impacts are perceived as disadvantageous by some individuals and as advantageous by others. Consequently, it may be very difficult, in practice, to estimate the sign and order of magnitude of the relevant sum of propensities to pay. This assertion is valid for most impacts that are not, *per se*, represented on the market for goods.

A number of methods to handle such difficulties have been developed and applied in CBAs of, for example, transport projects, environmental policies and health-care policies (for a number of examples, see Hanley and Spash, 1993; Layard and Glaister, 1994). Some of these methods—*'revealed preferences methods'*—try to exploit existing possibilities to disclose the preferences (the relevant propensities to pay) of the individuals by observing their behaviour, that is, their way of choosing between existing alternatives. Other methods—*'stated preferences'* or *'contingent valuation methods'*—are based on the answers given by respondents, representing the individuals affected, to a battery of questions about how they would choose given carefully selected hypothetical alternatives or about how they would act on carefully constructed hypothetical markets.

When it comes to CBAs of LMP projects we do think that attempts should be made to apply the kinds of methods just mentioned. As noted above, the impacts of LMP projects on the conditions of life of target group individuals are often manifold and dramatic. The decision-maker wanting to act in the public interest should ask for information about the relative importance, according to the individuals affected, of such impacts as related to changes in disposable incomes.

3.3 Individual Preferences and Decision-makers' Valuations

One crucial difficulty, which has to do with the fundamental principles of CBA, should now be mentioned: the preferences of individuals are not stable and, more importantly, are not independent of public policies. Furthermore, one of the purposes of policy measures, including LMP projects, may be to change the preferences—the pattern of behaviour—of individuals.

Consider two individuals who are unemployed today, that is, at time 0. One of them, L, has been unemployed for a very long period of time, the other, S, for just a few weeks. Some years ago both individuals were employed; their conditions of life were about the same; their preferences were almost identical. Then, however, L became unemployed; his job disappeared. At time 0 their conditions of life have been quite different for some years. As a consequence, not only their capabilities but perhaps also their preferences and patterns of behaviour have become quite dissimilar. Perhaps their answers to hypothetical questions, or observations of their behaviour, will reveal that S is much more anxious than L to get a job fairly soon. Such a difference between the individuals, as expressed in terms of propensities to pay, may mean the existence of a corresponding benefit entry in the CBA of an LMP project that implies that the elimination of the unemployment for S is substituted for the elimination of the unemployment for L. (Of course, L and S can be considered as representing two target groups.) But the preferences and the patterns of behaviour of the individuals at future points of time may depend on which policy alternative is chosen today. Why should the CBA give priority to the preferences that the individuals coincidentally hold at time 0 as a consequence of experiences in the past?

We are not suggesting that the decision-makers should regard information about the individuals' present preferences regarding the impacts of LMP projects as uninteresting. We just want to point out that the analyst and the decision-makers, when given such information, have to face difficult and important problems of interpretation and valuation. The decision-makers may hold valuations that go beyond distributional weights.[4] It is, for example, possible that the decisions they make are evidence of their adherence to the valuation that people should be anxious to have jobs, that is, that people should regard the net gain from getting a job as being not much smaller than the corresponding net income gain. If so, then these valuations should be spelled out or revealed by the analyst.

---

4 This possibility is sometimes discussed in terms of 'merit goods'. See, for example, Sugden and Williams (1978, pp. 179–80).

3.4   Budget Constraints

Evidently, public decision-makers are often very interested in the impacts that projects have on public revenues and expenditures, that is, in the impacts on public budget balances. This observation may reflect the existence of decision-makers' valuations other than the acceptance of individuals' valuations and the application of distributional weights. In the present context we disregard that possibility. The other possible interpretation is that the budget balance impacts are judged to influence the size and/or the distribution of the project's net benefit, calculated as the sum of individual propensities to pay.

In the following passages, we choose, for the sake of simplicity, to talk about 'the public budget balance', denoted B, thus disregarding the existence of many public budgets. Consider a project expected to result in an ECU 100 000 decrease in B. According to a preliminary CBA, the project will yield an ECU 50 000 net benefit, representing 'the net production impact'; other contributions to the net benefit are assumed to be negligible. We assume that the analyst, so far, has disregarded possible impacts of the financing of the decrease in B on the production of goods. Thus, before the financing of the decrease in B, the purchasing power of private actors has increased by ECU 150 000.

Now, suppose that the decrease in B is financed by means of an increase in taxes. This may be shown to be simply a redistribution of purchasing power. The final change will be zero for public actors and plus ECU 50 000, equal to the net benefit of the project, for private actors. According to this way of thinking, the decision-maker should not bother about the impacts on B; what is interesting is only the sign of the net benefit.

However, the increase in taxes should be regarded as implying a real cost, that is, a reduction in net total production. The kinds of tax parameters that are used in practice will entail the existence of tax wedges between the wages and prices that are relevant for firms, and the corresponding wages and prices as seen by the individuals. These tax wedges will cause different kinds of inefficiencies in the economy. If taxes are already high, then a further increase in taxes may lead to significant efficiency losses, that is, to a decrease in the net total production of marketed goods. Suppose, for example, that this real cost is ECU 0.6 per ECU 1 increase in taxes. Then the net benefit of the project considered will be ECU $(50\,000 - 0.6 \times 100\,000)$ = minus ECU 10 000. Another way of looking at things is to say that an ECU 1 change in B should be assigned the shadow price ECU 1.6, as expressed in the unit of account 'an ECU 1 increase in the purchasing power of the individuals'. According to this calculation, the net benefit of the project will be ECU $150\,000 - 1.6 \times 100\,000$, again, of course, yielding the net benefit minus ECU 10 000.

When thinking in terms of revealed preferences, we can say that the value attributed—by the government—to a marginal ECU 1 increase in public expenditure is ECU 1.6, given the assumptions stated above. A larger (smaller) value is inconsistent with the observation that the government has refrained from increasing (decreasing) taxes and expenditures. Consequently, the net benefit of the project will also be minus ECU 10 000 if the decrease in B is financed by means of reducing public expenditures.

We conclude that the calculation of the impacts on public revenues and expenditures should be regarded as an important element of CBA. Of course, the existence, in practice, of many public budgets, rather than just one, has to be taken into consideration in order to identify and eliminate inconsistencies caused by fiscal incongruences (see Schmid, chap. 7 in this volume).

3.5 The Choice of a Discount Rate

The impacts of a project always have a time dimension. If there exists a specified, unequivocal 'CBA real discount rate', then it is not difficult, technically, to complement the preceding expositions so that the timing of events and impacts, and the corresponding time dimension of costs and benefits, are taken into consideration. What is difficult, however, is to deduce such an unequivocal, well-founded CBA real discount rate.

In many cases, such as training or rehabilitation projects or projects with mainly preventive purposes, the most important benefit impacts are expected to occur later, perhaps much later, than the most important cost impacts. In such cases a relatively small change in the discount rate chosen may generate a change in the sign of the net benefit of the project. We also know that the regular use in CBAs of a discount rate equal to zero would entail significant inconsistencies and inefficiencies.

It is not possible for us in this chapter to summarize the large amount of existing literature on the choice of CBA discount rates and on the treatment in CBAs of uncertainty and risk (see, for example, Stiglitz, 1994; Zerbe and Dively, 1994, chaps 13–16). However, we do think that the timing of events and impacts should always be explicitly stated by the analyst. More generally, we maintain that the CBA should be arranged and presented in such a way that it becomes possible and easy for critical examiners to substitute their own assumptions, estimations (guesses) and valuations, including discount rates, for the ones used by the analyst. Of course, such exercises will be facilitated if some sensitivity analyses (calculations based on alternative assumptions) are also carried out by the analyst.

In terms of the further research required for the deduction of appropriate CBA discount rates, we reemphasize the importance of the quest for consistency. The existence of large differences between different public decision-makers as regards the discount rates used for similar kinds of projects should be revealed and eliminated, and the use of different discount rates for different kinds of projects should be justified. Furthermore, the discount rates used by public decision-makers should be consistent with the widespread acceptance of commercial investment calculations as reflecting acceptable CBAs (see Sugden and Williams, 1978, pp. 211–28). Real CBA discount rates deduced in the ways indicated will normally be smaller and much more stable than the prevailing nominal interest rates on borrowing.

3.6   Summary

Evidently, it is necessary to abandon the conception of a specific CBA as being essentially the calculation of 'the net benefit' of the project being studied. Starting from the framework and principles presented in sections 1 and 2 of this chapter and then considering the different kinds of difficulties discussed, we conclude that the attempt to carry out a specific CBA of a specified LMP project should entail:

1. an attempt to estimate the sign, the order of magnitude and the timing of the project's production impacts, as valued by means of current and/or expected prices;
2. an analysis of the project's impacts on income distribution, including, if considered justified, an attempt to estimate the sign, the order of magnitude and the timing of income gains for identified target groups;
3. an analysis of the existence, and the relative importance for the individuals affected, of kinds of impacts other than those covered under points 1 and 2 above;
4. an attempt to estimate the sign, the order of magnitude and the timing of the project's impacts on public revenues and expenditures; and
5. calculations of present values (or the equivalent), based on explicitly stated real discount rates and specified expected values.

Any decision-maker who wants to act in the public interest should regard such efforts as interesting, that is, as contributions to the basis for his or her decision-making. After all, the main purpose of CBA is to improve the basis for decision-making.

Of course, there may remain very difficult problems of interpretation and aggregation. If, in such cases, the decisive deliberations of the decision-makers are not made visible, that is, if the decisions arrived at are not explicitly justified, then the risk of inconsistencies in public decision-making, and the occurrence of consequent inefficiencies, may become considerable.

To be of practical importance, the CBAs carried out should be related to policy formation and implementation processes within the framework of existing institutional settings (see Williams, 1993, p. 79, for a list of questions that should be considered by anyone embarking on a project appraisal or evaluation). However, these processes and settings may be such that they do not generate CBAs. Thus, very optimistic ideas about the potentially fruitful role of CBA may be based on an overly naive conception of the behaviour and way of thinking of the actors involved (see Rizzo, 1993, for a more general discussion about the role of CBA in public decision-making processes). Given a decentralized 'management by objectives system', such as the kind applied by the labour market authorities in the Nordic countries, we would perhaps expect each authority to initiate evaluations and appraisals related to its own decision-making. (The case for decentralization in public decision-making and the reasons for central government involvement are discussed in Mayston and Muraro, 1993.) However, in practice the fulfilment of these expectations is very limited (see Niklasson and Tomsmark, 1994).

4   EXAMPLES

What follows below is a condensed description of three evaluations that differ with respect to the objectives of the evaluated social programmes and to the methods used to obtain estimates of what differences would emerge between cases where intervention is present and cases where it is absent. The first evaluation to be described concerns a programme with the goal of influencing the *matching processes* on the labour market. It is a study of an increase in staff at the Swedish Public Employment Service. The programme in the second example, the provision of vocational skills training, basic education and so on for economically disadvantaged youths, represented an effort to influence the supply side of the labour market. The final example concerns the use of a wage subsidy for the disabled to exert influence on the *demand* for labour.

As a strategy for assessing impacts, the evaluation of an increase in employment office personnel was based on before-and-after comparisons of two groups of employment offices in different communities, one in which employment office staff had been increased and one in which it had not. The assessment of the impacts of the programme for economically disadvantaged youths was based only on after comparisons between a group of participants in the programme and a group of nonparticipants. In the third evaluation, that of a wage subsidy for the disabled, the evaluator was obliged to resort to making educated guesses regarding the labour market status of disabled persons in the absence of intervention.

We have to be a little speculative when it comes to utilizing the results of the evaluations. Nevertheless, the three studies lend themselves fairly well to an illustration of the conventional three-way classification of uses of evaluations (Rich, 1977). Because the granting of extra funds for an increase in public employment service staff was designated as an experiment by the decision-makers, there is reason to believe that they were prepared to make *instrumental* use of the evaluation findings. As regards the evaluation of the programme for economically disadvantaged youths, one could contend that its findings might have been of *conceptual* use, that is, as a way of thinking about the possibilities for improving the employability of youths in that particular category. Judging from the presentation by politicians and policy-makers of the results of the evaluation of a wage subsidy for disabled persons, their purpose can be said to have been *persuasive*, that is, to defend the programme.

4.1   Evaluation of an Increase in Personnel at the Swedish Public Employment Service

In 1987 the Swedish government decided to grant the National Labour Market Board extra funds to be used for increasing the number of personnel in the Public Employment Service by 250 placement officers and counsellors (an increase of about 5 per cent). The government made it clear that the impact of the expansion of staff on job seekers and employer clients should be assessed. It was, however, also emphasized that real resource effects as well as effects on public expenditure and revenue should be estimated.

Estimates of impacts that could reasonably be attributed to the increase in personnel (net effects) were based on before-and-after comparisons of three employment offices where the staff was increased by between 15 and 25 per cent (*programme offices*) and three offices where the number of staff was either unchanged or was increased only slightly (*comparison offices*) (Behrenz, 1993). The offices in the two groups, representing medium-sized communities, were not chosen at random but on the basis of negotiations between the National Labour Market Board, the Ministry of Labour and the evaluators. Each programme office was matched with a comparison office in another geographic area that served a labour market resembling that of the programme office. Schematically, the logic behind the estimates of net effects can be presented as in Table 6.1.

Table 6.1   Design for Assessing the Net Outcome of the Increase in Staff

	Outcome Measures Regarding Job Seekers and Vacancies		
	Before expansion of staff	After expansion of staff	Differences
Programme offices	P_1	P_2	$P = P_2 - P_1$
Comparison offices	C_1	C_2	$C = C_2 - C_1$
Net effects			$P - C$

   Although the basis for the effect estimates was not ideal (a small number of communities, which were not randomly allocated), the design is an example of an effort to capture macroeffects by making use of communities as units of the analysis (Garfinkel, Manski and Michalopoulus, 1992).

The evaluation covered:

1. all job seekers (unemployed job seekers as well as prospective job chang-ers) who registered at programme and comparison offices during the two periods November 1986 through October 1987 (before the increase in staff) and May 1989 through April 1990 (after the increase),
2. all vacancies for jobs of more than ten days' duration registered with these offices during the two periods, and
3. all long-term unemployed (those who had been unemployed for more than six months) who were listed in the registers of the programme and compar-ison offices for November 1986 and November 1988, respectively.

4.1.1 Impact on Job Seeker Clients

As regards *unemployed job seekers* and *long-term unemployed*, the purpose of the evaluation was to estimate the effects on the *duration of unemployment* for those job seekers who:

1. obtained jobs on the open market,
2. obtained jobs on the open market or were placed in either jobs with a wage subsidy or sheltered workshops or who were placed in training other than that arranged at Employment Training Centres.

   For the sake of brevity, outcome (1) will be termed 'regular employment' below, and outcome (2) will be referred to merely as 'employment'.
   The analyses of unemployment duration for completed spells of unemploy-ment were based on equations in which logs were taken of the dependent variable:

$$Ln\ T \quad = \beta_0 + \beta_1 X_1 + ... + \beta_{15} X_{15} + e \qquad (6.1)$$
$$T \quad = \text{length of unemployment period}$$
$$X_1 - X_{15} \quad = \text{background variables}[5]$$

---

5 The background variables are gender dummy; age dummy; unemployment insurance dum-my; cash labour market allowance dummy; secondary school education dummy; university education dummy; two dummy variables representing experience in occupation sought; two dummy variables representing disability; immigrant dummy; UV-ratio; geographical mobil-ity dummy; employment office (programme or comparison office) dummy and dummy repre-senting training in occupation sought.

The results of the regressions do not suggest a satisfactory outcome of the increase in staff as regards duration of unemployment. This finding applies both to those unemployed who were struck from the registers of employment offices because they obtained regular employment (2433 in the before-period and 1863 in the after-period) and to those who obtained employment in a wider sense (2894 and 2116 in the before- and after-periods, respectively).

There were, of course, unemployed job seekers whose spells of unemployment were not completed by the end of the two observation periods, a circumstance that resulted in censored observations. Therefore, a model for analysing data with censored observations containing only partial information about the random variable of interest was used (see, for example, Kiefer, 1988, on the use of so-called hazard models in the analysis of labour market processes). However, it was just as impossible to conclude on the basis of that model that the staff increase had had an impact on the average length of spells of unemployment.

4.1.2 Impact on Vacancies

As regards *vacancies* reported to programme and comparison offices during the two periods, the aim of the evaluation was to measure the effects, if any, of the increase in staff on *the speed of filling vacancies*. Therefore, only vacancies without any specified application period were included in the analysis. The following estimating equation was used:

$$Ln\ DV = \beta_0 + \beta_1 X_1 + \ldots + \beta_9 X_9 + e \qquad (6.2)$$

$Ln\ DV$ = the logarithm of duration of vacancies in days

$X_1 - X_9$ = background variables[6]

Estimates of the parameter for the variable that specifies whether a job seeker was registered at a programme office or at a comparison office were used as a basis for conclusions regarding the impact of the staff increase. A comparison between these estimates for the before- and after-periods, respectively, indicated a significant effect, corresponding to a reduction in the duration of vacancies of about one day on average.

---

6 The background variables are fixed monthly salary dummy; two dummy variables representing required education; required experience dummy; only part-time employment dummy; part-time or full-time employment dummy; night-shift dummy; UV-ratio; employment office (programme or comparison office) dummy.

4.1.3 Benefits and Costs

One of the objects of the study was to estimate whether the staff increase resulted in a net increase in the value of goods and services produced. Therefore, real resource costs associated with the increase in staff were calculated and compared with the value of the increment in output arising from accelerated vacancy filling. This latter value was measured by people's willingness to pay for the increased amount of goods and services, which was estimated on the basis of average wage costs, as is shown in equation (6.3).

$$MVO = N\,[W\,(1 + t_1)\,(1 + t_2)] \tag{6.3}$$

MVO = market value of increased output in one year
N = increase in the number of 'production days' in one year as a result of accelerated vacancy filling = 4118 days
W = average daily wage = SEK 362
t_1 = payroll tax rate (and other incidental wage costs) = 0.5
t_2 = indirect tax rate = 0.25

Insertion of the above numbers into (6.3) yields an estimate of about SEK 2.8 million for the value of one year's increase in production resulting from a reduction by one day of the average number of days until vacancies are filled.

Real resource costs for a period of one year associated with the increase in personnel at the three programme offices (salaries, training and computer costs, costs for premises, incidental material and so on) were estimated at about SEK 3.45 million. Thus, according to the result of the estimates, the costs exceeded the benefits by SEK 3.45 – 2.8 = SEK 0.65 million annually. For costs and benefits to have broken even, an increase in the number of 'production days' by

$$N = 3\,450\,000\,/\,(362 \times 1.50 \times 1.25) = 5083$$

would have been necessary. Given that 2059 vacancies without any specified application period were registered at the programme offices during the after-period, this increase corresponds to a reduction in the duration of vacancies as a result of the increase in staff by (5083/2059) ≈ 2.5 days on average.

4.1.4 Public Finance Effects

According to the estimates in Table 6.2 (Behrenz, 1993), the sum of reductions in dependence on public assistance and increases in tax payments from a person in employment as opposed to unemployment amounts to about SEK 540 on average per day in the after-period.

*Table 6.2   Reduction in Expenditure and Increase in Income for the Public
Sector from One Day's Work Compared to One Day's
Unemployment*

	Average Sums for a Person with:		
	Unemployment insurance	Cash labour market allowance	No unemployment benefit
Reduction in expenditure	SEK 326	SEK 123	SEK 82
Increase in income from:			
Income tax	SEK 11	SEK 72	SEK 109
Payroll tax	SEK 145	SEK 145	SEK 145
Value-added tax	SEK 136	SEK 136	SEK 136
Total per day	SEK 618	SEK 476	SEK 472
Percentage of the unemployed	45%	5%	50%

Weighted average	$618 \times 0.45 + 476 \times 0.05 + 472 \times 0.50 =$ SEK 537.90

Source
From *Effekt- och effektivitetsanalyser av 1987 års personalförstärkning till arbetsförmed-
lingen* (Effect and Efficiency Analyses of the Increase of Staff in 1987 at the Employment
Service) (p. 108) by L. Behrenz, 1993, Lund: Department of Economics, University of
Lund. Copyright 1993 by L. Behrenz. Reprinted by permission.

The operating expenditures ensuing for the government as a result of the
staff increase at the programme offices were put at the same amount as the real
resource costs, that is, SEK 3.45 million. Given that 3442 job seekers registered at the programme offices during the after-period, a reduction in unemployment duration of an average [3 450 000 / (537.90 × 3442)] = 1.9 days as a
result of the increase in personnel would have been needed for the public
sector to emerge from the transaction with neither gain nor loss.

4.1.5   Overall Findings

In the approach taken to evaluate the increase in staff at Swedish employment
offices, the evaluator recognized the uncertainty associated with measuring its
effects but, nevertheless, concluded that the impact on the speed of vacancy
filling seemed to be very modest and that there was no evidence of effects on
unemployment duration. In consequence, the quantitative analysis indicated
that the investment failed the benefit–cost test and did not cover its budget costs
for the government. An experiment is, however, a prisoner of its environment—
in this case a boom, that is, a phase in the business cycle in which the capability

of the employment service to exert influence on the matching processes of the labour market could be more limited than when there is equilibrium (see also Walwei, chap. 13 in this volume). The evaluator, therefore, cautioned against generalizing the results to other settings, as regards the level of business activity.

4.2 Evaluation of the Benefits and Costs of the Job Corps

The aim of this evaluation was to assess the diverse effects of a social programme for economically disadvantaged youths, the Job Corps, in terms of both economic efficiency and distributional implications. To those who enrolled in the programme, vocational skills training, basic education and health care were provided in residential centres with the object of improving their employability (Long, Mallar and Thornton, 1981).

Estimates of the programme's effects were based on a comparison between Corps members and a group of nonparticipants selected on the basis of critical correlations between these and the participants (not a randomized control group).[7] Data were collected in a baseline interview and two follow-ups, of which the last took place when the Corps members had been out of the programme for an average of 18 months. Multiple regression techniques were used with the interview data to estimate effects indicating how Corps members' behaviour and experiences during the periods covered by the interviews differed from how they would have been in the absence of the Job Corps.

Because there was considerable reason to believe that at least some benefits would persist after the period covered by the interviews (impacts on Corps members' earnings and output, for example), Long et al. (1981) estimated these benefits by extrapolating from the interview data under the hypothesis that their magnitudes would decline over time. Benefits and costs were valued at prices during the period when the sample of Corps members entered the programme. A discount rate of 5 per cent per year was used in evaluating time-distributed benefits and costs.

The benefits and their costs were included in an accounting framework (summarized in Table 6.3) that allowed the analyst to address the efficiency of the programme as well as its distributional effects. The issue of economic efficiency (that is, the impact on the net value of goods and services available to society) is addressed in the *social perspective*, which includes resources saved, produced or consumed as a result of the programme, and excludes transfers of resources among members of society. The *Corps member perspective* addresses the programme's influence on the opportunities of those

---

7 Econometric techniques were used to account for sample selection biases between the Job Corps member and comparison groups, including unobserved differences that are likely to be present when a comparison group must be used instead of a randomized control group.

Table 6.3   Estimated Net Present Value per Corps Member ($)

Component	Society	Perspective Corps members	Rest of society
Benefits			
A. *Output produced by Corps members*			
1. In-programme output	757	83	673
2. Increased postprogramme output	3896	3896	0
3. Increased tax payments on postprogramme income	0	– 582	582
4. Increased utility due to preferences for work over welfare[a]	+	+	+
B. *Reduced dependence on transfer programmes*			
1. Reduced transfer payments	0	– 1357	1357
2. Reduced administrative costs	158	0	158
C. *Reduced criminal activity*			
1. Reduced criminal justice system costs	1152	0	1152
2. Reduced personal injury and property damage	645	0	645
3. Reduced value of stolen property	315	– 169	484
4. Reduced psychological costs[a]	+	+	+
D. *Reduced drug/alcohol use*			
1. Reduced treatment costs	30	0	30
2. Increased utility from reduced drug/ alcohol dependence[a]	+	+	+
E. *Reduced utilization of alternative services*			
1. Reduced costs of Public Service Employment, training and educational programmes other than the Job Corps	390	0	390
2. Reduced training allowances	0	– 49	49
F. *Other benefits*			
1. Increased utility from redistribution[a]	+	+	+
2. Increased utility from improved well-being of Corps members[a]	+	+	+
Total Benefits	7343	1823	5520

who participated in it, while the *rest of society perspective* investigates its impact on non-Corps members. Transfers between Corps members and non-Corps members cancel each other out when the net present values of benefits and costs are added up and do not appear in the social net present value.

Table 6.3—continued

Costs

G. *Programme operating expenditures*			
1. Centre operating expenditures, excluding transfers to Corps members	2796	0	2796
2. Transfers to Corps members	0	− 1208[b]	1208
3. Central administrative costs	1347	0	1347
H. *Opportunity cost of Corps member labour during the programme*			
1. Forgone output	881	881	0
2. Forgone tax payments	0	− 153[b]	153
I. *Unbudgeted expenditures other than Corps member labour*			
1. Resource costs	46	0	46
2. Transfers to Corps members	0	− 185[b]	185
Total Costs	5070	− 665	5736
Net Present Value (total benefits less total costs)	2271	2485	− 214
Benefit–cost Ratio	1.45	1.82	0.96

Notes
Details may not sum to totals because of rounding.

a   This item, considered to be a net benefit (+), is not measured in the analysis.

b   Because Corps members benefit from this item, it is presented as negative costs.

4.2.1 Benefits

The benefits originate primarily from two factors. First, all the basic needs of Corps members were taken care of by the Job Corps, and they were closely supervised. As a result, the members made less use of other public programmes and committed fewer crimes. Second, the participants received vocational training, basic education and other services that improved their long-term employability, resulting in increased production of goods and services, reduced welfare dependence and reduced antisocial behaviour in later years. The effects of the programme were valued by multiplying changes in Corps members' behaviour and experience, appraised on the basis of comparisons with the members of the group of nonparticipants, by estimated dollar values obtained from published data sources, interview data, accounting records of the Job

Corps and special studies conducted at Job Corps centres. The two largest benefits were associated with increased output and reduced criminal activity.

As regards increased output, there is a distinction in the analysis between goods and services that Corps members produced while enrolled in the programme and those that they produced after having left the Job Corps. The value of the output Corps members produced in conjunction with their vocational training during the programme (item A.1 in Table 6.3) was estimated as the price that alternative suppliers would have charged to provide the same goods or services. These prices, as well as the division of the value between Corps members and non-Corps members, were estimated on the basis of a number of case studies of randomly chosen work projects at Job Corps centres. The other component of the increased output of Corps members is generated after they leave the programme (A.2). It was valued on the basis of earnings effects according to interview data. The effects were assumed to fade out at a rate equal to 50 per cent every five years. The time horizon is the length of time that the average Corps member was expected to remain in the labour force: approximately 43 years after enrolling in the Job Corps. Postprogramme earnings effects are associated with increased tax payments, which represent a transfer from Corps members to non-Corps members (A.3).

The next most important benefit generated by the programme was *decline in criminal activity,* which reduces (a) the burden on the criminal justice system, (b) the personal injury and property damage associated with crime and (c) the amount of stolen property. Crime-reduction benefits were estimated on the basis of changes in arrests attributable to participation in the Job Corps programme. The resource savings associated with (a) and (b) represent benefits to society at large (items C.1 and C.2 in Table 6.3), whereas the reduction in (c) (item C.3 in Table 6.3) is a benefit to non-Corps members. However, part of its value was viewed as cost to Corps members, a standpoint based on the estimation that thieves net about 35 per cent of the value of stolen goods (note, however, that the value of the property losses to the victims does not change). The effect on criminal activity was assumed to fade out completely five years after leaving the Job Corps.

The above assumption was also used for the estimates regarding *reduced drug/alcohol use* and *reduced utilization of alternative services,* whereas the effect on *dependence on transfer programmes* was assumed to decay at a rate of 50 per cent every five years. Changes in the use of education and training programmes other than Job Corps, drug or alcohol treatment programmes and changes in administrative costs associated with reduced use of transfer programmes were treated as real resource savings, that is, as benefits to society at large (B.2, D.1, E.1). Reductions of training allowances and transfer payments do not enter the social perspective, for they merely affect transfers between Corps members and non-Corps members (B.1, E.2).

4.2.2 Costs

Operating expenditures for the centres and central administration costs (items G.1 and G.3 in Table 6.3) are costs to non-Corps members and to society, whereas cash allowances and in-kind transfers, programme expenditures on food, clothing, medical care and housing (G.2) merely involve transfers of resources from non-Corps members to Corps members. The values of these three cost items were computed as the average length of a Corps member's stay in the programme times the expenditure per enrolment month estimated on the basis of data from the programme's financial accounting system.

There are, however, costs that do not appear in the financial accounts. Programme participants forgo employment opportunities they would otherwise have taken, which results not only in forgone earnings for Corps members and a corresponding reduction in goods and services available to society (H.1) but also in forgone tax payments (H.2) from Corps members to non-Corps members. In addition to the opportunity costs of Corps-member labour, there were other resources used by the programme that did not appear in the Job Corps financial accounts (medical supplies and services provided by state and local agencies, meal costs reimbursed by the national school programme). The use of some of these resources represents a cost to society (I.1), but many items correspond to transfers from non-Corps members to Corps members (I.2).

4.2.3 Overall Findings

The net present value per Corps member presented in Table 6.3 represents a 'benchmark' estimate that incorporates the assumptions with which the evaluators were most comfortable: (a) earnings, tax and transfer effects fade out at a rate equal to 50 per cent every five years, (b) all other effects fade out completely five years after the individual leaves the Job Corps, (c) estimates of avoided arrests incorporate an adjustment upwards to account for underreporting in the interview self-reports, (d) the discount rate is 5 per cent, and (e) Corps members have working lives of 43 years after leaving the Job Corps. The results suggest that the programme yielded net benefits to society and to Corps members under the benchmark assumptions. The rest of society, which had to bear the costs of Job Corps operations and the transfers to Corps members, experienced a slightly negative present value from the programme. Thus, under the benchmark assumptions, the programme was estimated to represent a socially efficient use of resources and to entail a redistribution of resources from non-Corps members to Corps members.

Aware that there might be disagreement about these assumptions, the evaluators presented a set of alternate net present value estimates, each illustrating the effect of changing one of the key assumptions used in the benchmark estimate. The results of these tests suggest that the programme is economically efficient as long as effects do not decay at a rate of more than 50 per cent per year after the postprogramme observation period. In two other sensitivity tests net present value estimates were made using real discount rates of 3 and 10 per cent; in both cases, the social net present value is positive. In one test the net present value was estimated simply by using the data on arrests reported in the interviews. Because non-Corps members received most of the benefits from reduced crime, this change has the greatest impact on the net present value for the rest of society; the social net present value falls by almost 40 per cent but remains positive.

4.3   Evaluation of a Wage Subsidy for Disabled Persons

In 1987 the Swedish government decided to grant funds for an evaluation of the wage subsidy for disabled persons that was introduced in 1980. The decision constituted a response to discussions in the *Riksdag* (the Swedish parliament) and among the social partners and organizations for the disabled regarding the effectiveness and efficiency of the programme. The background, design and results of the evaluation, which was conducted by an independent researcher, were presented in a report published by the Ministry of Labour (Arbetsmarknadsdepartementet, 1989: 19).

The purpose of the wage subsidy for disabled persons, which is financed through the general national budget, is to avoid disability or early retirement pensions and to keep disabled workers in the regular, not just the sheltered, labour market. The subsidy is differentiated, with a higher compensation rate for persons with severe handicaps. Employment with a wage subsidy must be approved and workers referred by employment offices. (An examination of this and other Swedish disability policy programmes are found in Wadensjö, 1984.)

It is a well-known fact that there are many circumstances that make it extremely difficult or even impossible to put the best possible impact designs into practice. The choice left in such cases is either to use some less-than-perfect design or to perform no evaluation at all. In assessing the wage subsidy for the disabled, the evaluator can be said to have used 'the good enough' rule (Rossi and Freeman, 1985, p. 190), taking into account constraints of time, resources, practicality and feasibility that, for instance, prevented the use of a control or comparison group. As a matter of fact, the basis for estimating the net social value of the programme can best be described as a connoisseurial or expert assessment, that is, an educated estimate regarding the labour market performance of the population of disabled persons employed with wage subsidies in the absence of the programme (a 'shadow' control). Information from counsellors and placement officers at employment offices and from medical experts on physical and mental incapacity were gathered, along with data concerning a sample of disabled persons, and judgements were made. According to this part of the evaluation, there were no indications that a substantial number of the disabled workers could have obtained unsubsidized employment. Disability or early retirement pensions were assumed to be the alternative to employment with a wage subsidy. Therefore, under the benchmark assumption, the estimate of the net benefits of the programme was based on the assumption that disabled workers who were employed with wage subsidies did not forgo employment opportunities they would otherwise have taken.

4.3.1 Cost–benefit calculations

In the year covered by the evaluation (the fiscal year 1986–87), the average income in the group of about 47 000 disabled persons who were then employed with wage subsidies amounted to SEK 86 000. These earnings, adjusted downwards to account for reduced working capacity, were used as a basis for valuing the output of goods and services generated by disabled workers. The assumption underlying this procedure is that employers pay compensation equal to the value of a disabled worker's marginal product and that this value approximately equals employers' wage costs reduced by the amount of the wage subsidy. The following benefits were excluded from the calculations because they could not be quantified and valued appropriately: reduced costs for social services compared to the alternative of a large number of persons drawing disability or early retirement pensions; increased utility for members of the target population due to preferences for work over pensions; improved well-being and reduced psychological costs; increased utility for the rest of society because it may prefer to provide employment opportunities rather than direct transfer payments in the form of disability or early retirement pensions.

The value of the increased amount of goods and services associated with jobs that are realized as a result of the wage subsidy is given by

$$MVO = [W \times Q (1 + t_1) (1 - s)] / (1 - t_2) \qquad (6.4)$$

MVO = market value of increased output
W = average income from work per year; SEK 86 000
Q = number of persons for whom wage subsidies were paid during the year considered in the evaluation recalculated into full-time jobs; 47 000
t_1 = payroll tax rate; 0.40
t_2 = indirect tax rate; 0.08[8]
s = wage subsidy rate; 0.50 (the compensation was on average 50 per cent of wage costs including payroll tax)

---

8 The indirect tax rate has been adjusted downwards in view of the fact that about 70 per cent of the disabled workers were engaged in the production of public services that are not sold on markets.

Insertion of the numbers specified gives $MVO = $ SEK 3.075 billion, which corresponds to SEK 65 400 per full-time job.

Subsidized employment of disabled persons can be expected to result in displacement of other low-capacity workers. For lack of information regarding the size of such an effect, the cost calculations in the evaluation were based on the assumption that the duration of unemployment among job seekers in that category was prolonged by one month on average (an extension of about 30 per cent of the average length of spells of unemployment for job seekers in the category in question at the time of the study). The number of job seekers affected was assumed to be the same as the number of full-time jobs in the above calculation of benefits, namely, 47 000.

The values of losses of individual welfare and of output due to the displacement effect are given by

$$VLW \quad = \quad Q (W - U) \tag{6.5}$$

$$MVLO \quad = \quad [W \times Q (1 + t_1)] / (1 - t_2) \tag{6.6}$$

VLW = value of loss of welfare
Q = number of job seekers affected by the displacement effect; 47 000
W = average income from work per month; SEK 7200
U = average unemployment compensation for 22 days (corresponding to one month's unemployment); SEK 6400
$MVLO$ = market value of loss of output
t_1 = payroll tax rate; 0.40
t_2 = indirect tax rate; 0.08

Insertion of the numbers specified gives estimated costs of $VLW + MVLO =$ SEK 552.6 million. Thus, when a possible displacement effect of the assumed magnitude is taken into consideration, the net benefit of the wage subsidy for disabled persons during the year covered by the study was estimated to be $MVO - (VLW + MVLO) =$ SEK 3.075 billion $-$ SEK 552.6 million $=$ SEK 2.522 billion.

For the costs, calculated in the same way as above, to total the same amount as the benefits, the size of the displacement effect would have to correspond to a lengthening of unemployment duration for other low-capacity workers by as much as about 5.5 months on average.

As was mentioned previously, the above calculations are based on the assumption that the alternative to employment with a wage subsidy is a disability or early retirement pension. However, in order to ascertain the sensitivity of the result of the estimates to an alternative to the benchmark assumption, a simple test was performed. Division of the net benefit during the year covered by the study by the market value of output per disabled worker gives (SEK 2.552 billion/SEK 65 400 =) about 38 500 persons. If this many disabled persons—about 80 per cent of the number of persons for whom subsidies were paid during the year—could have obtained employment even without the subsidy, the net social benefit would have been eliminated. Given the rules governing the use of the wage subsidy and in the light of studies performed within the framework of the evaluation, such an outcome was considered to be completely improbable. It was, therefore, concluded that the wage subsidy in all probability gives rise to substantial net benefits to society.

4.3.2 Public Finance Effects

Disregarding a possible displacement effect and assuming that the alternative to employment with a wage subsidy is a disability or early retirement pension, we find that the financial costs for the public sector are:

1. wage subsidies paid to employers, and
2. decreased tax payments on income from disability or retirement pensions.

The following items represent decreased costs and increased income for the government and local authorities, respectively:

1. reduced costs for disability or early retirement pensions;
2. reduced payments of transfers related to earnings (rent allowance, for example);
3. increased tax payment on income from work;
4. increased payments of payroll tax;
5. increased payments of indirect tax on output from disabled workers.

According to the evaluation, the wage subsidy for disabled persons gives an estimated financial surplus for the public sector in the year covered by the evaluation of SEK 1.941 billion, under the assumption that subsidized employment does not result in displacement of other workers.

The occurrence of a displacement effect of the character and magnitude described above would result in costs for the government because of increased payments, net of tax, of unemployment compensation for 47 000 unemployed for an average of one month. Thereby, the total financial net effect would be reduced to SEK 1.749 billion.

4.3.3 Overall Findings

It was carefully pointed out in the study that its estimates of the net benefits to society at large and of the financial surplus for the public sector had to be taken with a pinch of salt, mainly because the labour market performance of disabled persons employed with wage subsidies was compared to judgements by the evaluator and other experts as to what changes were 'normally' to be expected for the target population if the programme did not exist. Nonetheless, the evaluator concluded that the results of the study suggest that the wage subsidy for disabled workers might very well be one of the most cost-efficient Swedish labour market policy programmes.

5   CONCLUDING REMARKS

Our main conclusion is that the initiation of evaluations and appraisals related to important problems of choice should be integrated into decision-making and implementation processes.

This presupposes that the actors involved perceive decision-making as corresponding to choices between alternative courses of action, that is, explicit 'thinking in terms of alternatives'. For example, it must be recognized that the implementation of a specific activity plan means that alternative activity plans aiming at the same targets have been rejected, that is, judged to be inferior. Consequently, each decision-making authority should be called upon, or given the incentive, to explicitly identify important problems of choice it faced and to justify the decisions it reached.

There is no doubt that the justifications requested will reveal serious deficiencies in the basis of the authority's decision-making. Consequently, each authority should also be called upon to try to initiate the kinds of studies, including impact evaluations and appraisals, that can alleviate these deficiencies. Bearing in mind that the efforts to justify the decisions made will necessitate a discussion in terms of pros and cons of different alternatives, the step to the initiation of studie—which we can call CBAs—proves to be quite a short one. After all, the main prerequisites for the initiation of CBAs are the establishment of an explicit thinking in terms of alternatives and the recognition of the existence of valuation and aggregation problems.

REFERENCES

Arbetsmarknadsdepartementet (1989), *Lönebidrag för arbetshandikappade* (Ds 1989: 19), Stockholm: Arbetsmarknadsdepartementet.

Arrow, K. J. and R. C. Lind (1994), 'Risk and Uncertainty: Uncertainty and the Evaluation of Public Investment Decisions', in R. Layard and S. Glaister (eds), *Cost–benefit Analysis* (2nd ed.), Cambridge: Cambridge University Press, pp. 160–78.

Behrenz, L. (1993), *Effekt- och effektivitetsanalyser av 1987 års personalförstärkning till arbetsförmedlingen*, Lund: Department of Economics, University of Lund.

Garfinkel, I., C. F. Manski and C. Michalopoulos (1992), 'Micro Experiments and Macro Effects', in C. F. Manski and I. Garfinkel (eds), *Evaluating Welfare and Training Programs*, Cambridge: Harvard University Press, pp. 253–73.

Gramlich, E. M. (1981), *Benefit–cost Analysis of Government Programs*, Englewood Cliffs: Prentice Hall.

Hanley, N. and C. L. Spash (1993), *Cost–benefit Analysis and the Environment*, Aldershot: Edward Elgar.

Kiefer, N. M. (1988), 'Economic Duration Data and Hazard Functions', *Journal of Economic Literature*, 26, 646–79.

Layard, R. and S. Glaister (eds) (1994), *Cost–benefit Analysis* (2nd ed.), Cambridge: Cambridge University Press.

Long, D. A., C. D. Mallar and C. V. D. Thornton (1981), 'Evaluating the Benefits and Costs of the Jobs Corps', *Journal of Policy Analysis and Management*, 1 (1), 55–76.

Mayston, D. and G. Muraro (1993), 'Project Finance and Decentralization in Public Investment', in A. Williams and E. Giardina (eds), *Efficiency in the Public Sector*, Aldershot: Edward Elgar, pp. 129–45.

Niklasson, H. and L. Tomsmark (1994), *Att målstyra arbetsmarknadspolitik* (TemaNord 1994: 573), Copenhagen: The Nordic Council.

Pignataro, G. (1993), 'The Role of Analysts in the Public Investment Decision-making Process', in A. Williams and E. Giardina (eds), *Efficiency in the Public Sector*, Aldershot: Edward Elgar, pp. 146–57.

Rich, R. F. (1977), 'Uses of Social Science Information by Federal Bureaucrats', in C. H. Weiss (ed.), *Using Social Research for Public Policy Making*, Lexington, MA: D.C. Heath, pp. 199–211.

Rizzo, I. (1993), 'The Public Decision-making Process and Cost–benefit Analysis', in A. Williams and E. Giardina (eds), *Efficiency in the Public Sector*, Aldershot: Edward Elgar, pp. 158–70.

Rossi, P. H. and H. E. Freeman (1985), *Evaluation. A Systematic Approach*, Beverly Hills, CA: Sage.

Stiglitz, J. E. (1994), 'Discount Rates: The Rate of Discount for Benefit–cost Analysis and the Theory of the Second Best', in R. Layard and S. Glaister (eds), *Cost–benefit Analysis* (2nd ed.), Cambridge: Cambridge University Press, pp. 116–59.

Sugden, R. and A. Williams (1978), *The Principles of Practical Cost–benefit Analysis*, Oxford: Oxford University Press.

Wadensjö, E. (1984), 'Disability Policy in Sweden', in R. H. Haveman, V. Halberstadt and R. V. Burkhauser (eds), *Public Policy towards Disabled Workers. Crossnational Analyses of Economic Impacts*, London: Cornell University Press, pp. 444–516.

Williams, A. (1993), 'Cost–benefit Analysis: Applied Welfare Economics or General Decision Aid?', in A. Williams and E. Giardina (eds), *Efficiency in the Public Sector*, Aldershot: Edward Elgar, pp. 65–79.

Williams, A. and E. Giardina (eds.) (1993), *Efficiency in the Public Sector*, Aldershot: Edward Elgar.

Zerbe, R. O. and D. D. Dively (1994), *Benefit–cost Analysis in Theory and Practice*, New York: Harper Collins.

7. Process Evaluation: Policy Formation and Implementation

Günther Schmid

The object of process evaluation is to examine the formation and implementation of policies and to elicit the systematic relationships that exist between policies and their effects. Variations in the implementation process are assumed to be an important determinant for the success or failure of policies. The ultimate goal is to identify the optimal design of implementation procedures. Where there is little chance of changing actual processes, then process evaluation can at least provide information as to how programmes should be adjusted to make them function more efficiently.

Too often such issues are treated as a 'black box' in the sense that they do not require analysis; they are taken for granted and thus neglected. However, three approaches that have been developed to fill this gap can be identified. Hasan (1991) assigns two functions to process evaluation: monitoring and controlling. Monitoring reveals whether programme design and implementation correspond to policy goals; controlling evinces whether the implementation of policies is efficiently managed. In terms of methodology, process evaluation is thought of as 'qualitative', and impact evaluation as 'quantitative'. Nathan (1991) sees impact evaluation as having its emphasis at the individual level, and process evaluation as being significant at the institutional level. The institutional aspects include regulative and financial incentives for the various administrative levels to implement programmes effectively in the intended direction. Schellhaaß and Schubert (1992) see, in principle, no difference between process and impact analysis. They recommend the inclusion of process characteristics as additional independent variables that have hitherto not been incorporated in impact analysis.

All three approaches correctly refer to central elements of process evaluation. In a theory-driven and target-oriented approach, however, process evaluation needs to be embedded in a larger context, that is, individual and institutional aspects as well as quantitative and qualitative methods should be included. Process evaluation cannot be restricted to 'opening up the black box' and to using 'empirical data to assess the delivery of programs' (Scheirer, 1994, p. 40). Politics, that is, the processes of policy formation and target selection have to be observed, too. Programmes, understood as 'a set of resources and activities directed toward one or more common goals' (Scheirer, 1994, p. 41), cannot be seen in isolation. They function within the context of other programmes, which might interact and influence the outcome (Gautié, Gazier and Silvera, 1994, p. 21). Process evaluation should also be a means to explain why certain policy measures are systematically preferred and others disliked, and why variations in implementation exist. Finally, process evaluation also has to study how these variations affect delivery performance and the policies' ultimate impact.

The aim of this chapter, therefore, is to develop a broader analytical framework for the study and evaluation of policy formation and implementation. Section 1 provides a brief overview of the genesis of process evaluation, exemplified by the methodology of a few studies in the field of labour market policy. The essential purpose of this summary is not to review once again the disparate state of the art but to develop criteria for a consistent and comprehensive framework.[1] Section 2 presents a cybernetic model that distinguishes four 'filtering stages' to determine the effect of labour market policies: policy choices, policy implementation, policy take-up and policy impact. Sections 3 and 4 consist of a categorical framework for the comparative analysis of organizational regimes, exemplified by the case of further training, and a discussion of performance indicators for each of the four filtering stages. Conclusions are drawn in section 5, and recommendations are made for further research.[2]

1   IMPLEMENTATION RESEARCH: THE STATE OF THE ART

It is important to remember that implementation research was started as a discipline in the United States as a reaction to the chronic discrepancy between (interventionist) policy-making at the federal level (in the mood of Lyndon

---

1 For useful introductions into practical methods of process evaluation from a strict programme-oriented perspective, see Rossi, Freeman and Wright (1979, pp. 121–58) and Scheirer (1994); the examples in these studies, however, refer to health, social and educational policy (e.g. drug prevention programmes, development of training curricula) and not to labour market policy. The reader is also advised to consult chap. 28 on 'generic evaluation' by Lindley in this volume, who develops a practical framework for auditing, monitoring and evaluating projects related to the European Social Fund.

2 I have benefited from comments by Christine Bruniaux, Bernard Gazier, Birgitta Rabe and Ralf Rogowski; I am also grateful to Niamh Warde for her skilful help in translation. Special acknowledgement goes to Jacky O'Reilly, who considerably improved my writing, both in clarity and style. Remaining weaknesses, however, are my own responsibility.

Johnson's 'Great Society') and the policy outcomes at the local or state level.[3] Implementation, defined as the 'carrying out of a decision', was found to be the culprit. One of the early studies by Pressman and Wildavsky (1973), who analysed the abortive effort by the US Federal Government to create 3000 jobs in Oakland, had an enormous impact on the first generation of implementation research.

The reason why implementation research originated in the United States and not in Europe is probably related to the type of policy intervention prevalent in the former. In the United States policy intervention is dominated by regulation, often combined with financial incentives. This type of policy intervention is more prone to visible failure than the European type of public policy, where the state often carries out its own decisions and where failures—under ideal circumstances—are successfully litigated or—under the worst circumstances—successfully hidden by the bureaucracy. No wonder, therefore, that implementation research in Europe was focussed more on regulatory types of policies; this focus became most prominent in the fields of environmental and labour market research (Mayntz, 1983). It is no surprise that the renaissance of implementation research occurs at a time when the state is increasingly withdrawing from the direct production of goods and services in favour of more market-oriented types of intervention.

1.1   First Generation of Process Evaluation

The first generation of implementation studies was characterized by a top-down single-programme approach (Goggin, Bowman, Lester and O'Toole, 1990; Sabatier, 1986). The question posed by such research was whether decentralized implementation of policies met the goals of the central policy-makers, and, if not, why not? The methodology used was mainly case studies and verbal interpretation of legal documents at the descriptive level. The conclusion drawn in most studies was that programmes failed: the policy goals were too vague or conflicting, the underlying causal theory of programmes was wrong, and implementers or 'street-level bureaucrats' were following their own policies or interests.

Only a few studies of this generation attained a methodological level worth mentioning. One of them is the (above-mentioned) classical study by Press-

---

3 In fact, implementation research was never really anything new in political science; it was merely a reemphasizing of one of the discipline's original and fundamental questions, namely, how societal aspirations ('politics') are linked with their efficient and effective realization ('administration'); this question has been lost in the increasing segmentation and specialization of the discipline (Hjern and Hull, 1982, p. 105).

man and Wildavsky, who developed some imaginative (and largely forgotten) tools such as decision trees and the concept of decision points and clearance points.[4] They demonstrated, using simple calculations, how the likelihood of programme success declines exponentially with rising numbers of decision points and necessary clearances. Two implications follow from this observation: policy design has to be as simple as possible, and potential implementation difficulties have to be considered in initial policy formation (Pressman and Wildavsky, 1973, p. 143). In other words, 'formative evaluation' must become a part of programme development, especially when it comes to concrete operational measures.[5]

1.2 Second Generation of Process Evaluation

The most fundamental criticism against these first-generation studies came from a group of largely European scholars who labelled themselves as 'bottom-uppers' (Hanf, 1982; Hjern and Porter, 1981; Hjern and Hull, 1982). This perspective was taken up by most of the implementation researchers in the 1980s, including those in the United States. They rejected the strict separation of policy formation and implementation by stressing that implementation itself is a policy formation process and that the autonomy of 'street-level bureaucrats' should not be viewed as a defect but as a strength (Ferman, 1990; Héritier, 1993; Mayntz, 1983; Palumbo and Calista, 1990b).

Implementation analysis, according to this view, should start not with a policy decision but rather with the actors involved in addressing a policy problem. It was expected and shown in several studies that 'adaptive implementation' either compensated for misspecifications of policy programmes or even brought about a learning process in policy reformation. The methodology, however, was still descriptive, or at most classificatory, in that its aim was to detect patterns in the networks of horizontal and vertical interactions. The hope was to end up with some middle-range theory by comparing the implementation processes of various policy areas across various regions or countries. In his critical review Sabatier (1986, p. 315), however, came to the

---

4 'Each time an act of agreement has to be registered for the program to continue, we call a decision point. Each instance in which a separate participant is required to give his consent, we call a clearance. Adding the number of necessary clearances involved in decision points throughout the history of the program will give the reader an idea of the task involved securing implementation' (Pressman and Wildavsky, 1973, p. xvi).

5 'Formative evaluation focusses on data collected from pilot situations and recipients while developing an intervention to obtain feedback about the feasibility of proposed activities and their fit with the intended settings and recipients' (Scheirer, 1994, p. 48). Or, in other words, and in a nutshell: formative evaluation as a part of policy formation corresponds to the pretest of large-scale empirical surveys.

conclusion that while the 'bottom-uppers' developed some rather imaginative tools, they were largely unable to transform their network analyses into a viable causal model incorporating the often indirect effects that legal and socioeconomic factors can have on individual behaviour.

Only a few of the second-generation studies included a mix of qualitative and quantitative methods or rudimentary theory-building.[6] Peters and Schmid, for instance, evaluated a wage-subsidy programme for regions with special employment problems in Germany. Using multiple regression analysis, they found that the large regional variation in the take-up of the programme was explained to at least 50 per cent by differences in implementation strategies (Peters and Schmid, 1982a, 1982b; Schmid and Peters, 1982). They were, however, not able to explicitly specify these implementation variables in the model and suggested that an inductive procedure could be used, that is, selection (via the residuals of the model) of the most extreme performers of implementation. By systematic comparison of the 'best' and the 'worst' performers, holding constant socioeconomic factors in the regions (e.g. industrial structure, size and structure of unemployment), even a purely descriptive analysis might then provide generalizable clues about optimal policy networks and implementation strategies.

Indeed, a complementary study revealed some interesting patterns concerning successful performers. First, those employment offices that had continuous and close contacts with employers performed well; second, those employment offices that actively involved local key actors (trade unions, chambers of commerce, managers of municipalities and schools) in the implementation process produced good results; third, those employment offices that disposed over a public infrastructure of training and counselling institutions succeeded in favouring disadvantaged groups (Scharpf, 1983).

In the same study Scharpf used exchange theory to explain and predict the relationship between implementers and addressees of incentives schemes such as wage subsidies. He found three important and interrelated results. First, there must be a balance between economic incentives and (normative) social conditions in programme design. Too narrow and ambitious selection criteria in favour of disadvantaged persons may lead to low take-up by (disinterested) employers, whereas too liberal rules might lead to high take-up, which, how-

---

6 This does not mean that qualitative analysis is scientifically inferior to qualitative analysis; the contrary may be the case if quantitative research does not follow the logic of inference, the guidelines of good research design and the principles of reliability and validity of data. However, because process evaluation relies heavily on qualitative approaches, I strongly recommend the excellent book by King, Keohane and Verba (1994) to the reader interested in techniques of good qualitative research; for German readers the review article by Hucke and Wollmann (1980) is still a useful introduction.

ever, would be accompanied by large-scale deadweight effects or windfall profits. Second, hopes that (market-oriented) incentive schemes are cheap in terms of implementation costs are not justified because attainment of the proper balance (mentioned above) relies on 'bureaucratic-intensive' implementation performed by competent managers in close interaction with the local network. Third, to do their job properly, implementers need great autonomy in adjusting the rules to the specific needs of the local area (Scharpf, 1983).

A more recent study carried out in the Netherlands was able to quantify regional variations in implementation procedures and to measure directly the impact on the results (de Koning and van Nes, 1991). In this study all 64 regional labour exchange offices were asked via a combined questionnaire and telephone survey how they implemented a wage-subsidy scheme for the long-term unemployed. The answers were related to outcome results, especially to the placement rates of the target groups, by controlling for differences in the regional labour market through cross-section and multiple regression analysis. The equations resulting from this exercise were then used to simulate the effect of changing implementation towards the best model.

It emerged that by changing from a 'demand-oriented approach' to a more 'supply-oriented' one, labour exchanges can improve their placement results by 38 per cent. In the demand-oriented approach implementers concentrate on the filling of vacancies as they make their way through the regular channels and select suitable candidates for the target groups. A supply-oriented approach is based on the characteristics of the job seekers and implies actively trying to find vacancies corresponding to the capabilities of the target group, for instance, by means of visits to potential employers, project-related implementation (establishing a task force), regular interviews with long-term unemployed, cooperation with other agencies and allocation of more personnel resources to the target group. In other words, labour exchange offices that cooperate with other organizations and carry out specific vacancy-prospecting activities for the target group have 38 per cent higher placement results than labour exchanges that do not. If all labour exchanges were to adopt a more supply-oriented approach, the average placement percentage would increase by about 10 per cent. If, in addition, each labour exchange deployed one additional staff member to carry out the scheme, a 20 per cent increase in total placements would result.

1.3   Towards a Third Generation of Process Evaluation

The last example can be considered a real pioneer in quantitative process evaluation. It demonstrates once again, however, the limitations of single-programme process evaluation. First, as the authors themselves ultimately acknowledge, additional staff input either adds to labour costs or, by necessity, is achieved at the expense of other activities. Additional information would be necessary for an estimation of the opportunity costs (see Delander and Niklasson, chap. 6 in this volume). Second, when the results of the study were published, the programme had already been modified several times and finally been integrated in a larger programme; thus, there was no possibility of testing the results under the same basic conditions. Third, it is doubtful whether elasticities found in a cross-section analysis remain the same in the dynamic process. As we know from principal-agent theory or from game theory, agents—in this case the employers—start to 'play with the rules'. This means that they adjust their behaviour to the new incentive structure, here that induced by wage subsidies, in their own interest. Many additional indirect or unintended effects can arise during this process of adjustment, for example, the effect of rotation, which means the replacement of subsidized persons in period 1 by other (perhaps more productive) subsidized persons in period 2; the favourable short-term distributional effect would deteriorate in the long term as the process continues.[7]

We can now summarize the lessons learned from the short review about the genesis of process evaluation and try to develop criteria for the evolving third generation:

- First, 'top-down' and 'bottom-up' views have to be integrated. Central guidance and control is still a widespread phenomenon, and often more effective than 'bottom-uppers' presuppose; innovative impulses, on the other hand, often come from the 'bottom', and there is more and more scope for choice between programme implementation strategies at the decentral level (Héritier, 1993; Sabatier, 1986).
- Second, in assessing the effectiveness of various types of policy-making, one needs to take a reasonably long time span into account, that is, at least five to ten years in view of learning processes in policy formation and implementation (Sabatier, 1986).
- Third, the implementation structure (e.g. the financing and organization of labour market policy) is itself becoming more and more an objective of policy-making, often even the single objective, instead of new programmes; this trend requires the development of new and reflexive kinds of performance indicators related not only to individuals as final addressees of policy-making but also to aggregate systems such as policy regimes and implementation regimes (Héritier, 1993; Palumbo and Calista, 1990a).
- Fourth, rather than start with a policy decision and then examine its implication, it is preferable to begin with a policy problem or a policy target and

---

7 For a stimulating discussion of 40 possible effects of wage subsidies see Gautié et al. (1994), especially the section on dynamic and interactive analysis (pp. 233–41).

then investigate the variety of actors actually and potentially involved in addressing it (Héritier, 1993; Sabatier, 1986).

– Fifth, the complexity of implementation can best be tackled by multiple methods, with efforts to collect evidence from different angles and to construct an intelligible picture of the puzzle; thus, implementation analysis is an art supported by various aspects of scientific craft (Goggin et al., 1990).

– Sixth, the composition of the picture has to be improved by more explicit theory-building and theory-testing, although the current state of the art means the complexity of the subject requires some deliberate eclecticism and modesty in terms of general theory; rather than aiming at an axiomatic system of nomological statements (i.e. statements of universal laws), 'pattern recognition' and 'pattern prediction' is the realistic goal of present-day implementation research (Mayntz, 1983, p. 16; v. Hayek, 1972).

– Seventh, policy formation and implementation are interrelated processes and embedded in a historically specific socioeconomic context. Path dependency and the fact that programmes are embedded in a larger 'policy landscape' have to be acknowledged in process evaluation (Héritier, 1993, p. 13), which should also incorporate a quest for functional equivalents in cross-national comparisons (Schmid and Schömann, 1994).

The following analytical framework of process evaluation is based on these lessons and is intended as a guideline for international comparative research. The conceptual background is systems theory, organizational sociology and institutional economics. An application of the framework can be found in Schmid, chap. 25 in this volume (The New Public Management of Further Training).

2   A CYBERNETIC MODEL OF PROCESS EVALUATION

The relationship between political systems and labour markets can be modelled in a simple cybernetic feedback loop (Figure 7.1). To begin with, in simplified cybernetic terminology: the political system 'sends signals' to the labour market in the form of programmes (regulatives and incentives), 'registers the return signals' (feedback), compares these to the set objectives (targets) and keeps altering the rules and programmes until the feedback 'confirms' that an objective has been met.

While the real world is somewhat more complicated, the structure of the labour market policy feedback loop remains the same: the political system registers deviations from its goals (e.g. 'full employment') caused by exogen-

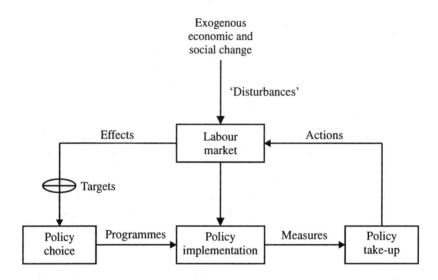

Figure 7.1 The Policy Cycle

ous 'disturbances' (economic and social change) that influence the labour market. These deviations are interpreted in more or less complex decision-making processes, and new policies are subsequently chosen (*policy choice*). The resulting programmes, which—in contrast to automatic feedback loops—may include setting new goals, pass into the existing structures for policy implementation; it may again be an objective of the political agenda to alter these structures. The resulting measures function either as positive or negative incentives for the behavioural disposition of the target groups, that is, the unemployed, the employed and enterprises (*policy take-up*). However, the *policy impact* of labour market measures is not identical with the sum of individual actions because exogenous changes ('disturbances') and the inter-dependency of individual actions can cause systematic failure of otherwise rational actors (Schelling, 1978). The changes on the labour market that ultimately ensue in turn have repercussions for the political decision-making processes; the system learns, or—given inadequate decision-making structures—does not.

So what makes the employment system work in the face of permanent changes in the economic and social environment? The next step is to identify the structural components, before I come to the institutional components that determine the coordination of the various actors in the labour market.

2.1   The Structural Components of Labour Market Policy Regimes

One can differentiate between an organizational regime's structural components in the narrower sense and its institutional components (Granovetter, 1979). Among the *structural components* are, first, the historical and, second, the relational dependencies. First, actors operate within a framework of organizations that have a history and thus a dynamism of their own. Second, they act within a framework of connections, so that bilateral relationships can produce additional effects. Actors should thus be perceived within the context of 'their' organizations, in this case private households, enterprises, labour market authorities or unemployment insurance systems, further training institutions, collective organizations and government at local, regional or national level.

The characteristic features of the labour market policy feedback loop and the effects it will have depend on how societies are coordinated. Modern societies can no longer be adequately described using traditional dichotomies such as 'market' versus 'state', 'public' versus 'private' or 'centralized' versus 'decentralized' (see, among others, Salamon, 1989). In postindustrial societies there are several decision-making centres, which vary in the way public and private resources are combined, and with respect to the constraints or opportunities open to actors to achieve their targets.

Individual actions are thus always shaped by social factors. The sum of the complex web of conditions under which individuals or actors operate is called an organizational regime. Actors who are involved in labour market policy include employment counsellors and placement officers in employment offices, directors and managers in enterprises, trade unionists and employer representatives, managers and instructors in training centres, politicians and party officials and, last but not least, the unemployed and the (future or formerly) employed themselves. The performance of employment systems depends on the way these actors are coordinated, which is a key concern for governing institutions.

2.2   The Institutional Components of Labour Market Policy Regimes

Among the *institutional components* are the written and unwritten laws, in other words the rules of society (North, 1990), to which one 'generally' adheres.

Four types of coordination mechanism can be distinguished: values and norms, which act as the precontractual conditions for action (i.e. rules on which *communities* are founded); contractual rules governing cooperation or competition (rules on which *associations* or 'societies' in the narrower sense are founded); prices and wages (rules on which *markets* are founded); and, finally, legislation (rules on which *states* are founded and on the basis of which legitimate power is exercised).[8]

Sanctions, that is, the means by which adherence is rewarded or nonadherence penalized, influence the extent to which these rules are effective. Incentives and disincentives to comply take different forms. There can be emotional or psychological forms of compliance or deviance towards the rules of the community; social integration or exclusion (even ostracism) for adherence or nonadherence to the rules of associations; economic gains or losses for adherence or nonadherence to the rules of the market; and political rights, that is, entitlement to benefits and rights to suit or imprisonment for adherence or nonadherence to the rules of the state.

In accordance with the four categories of coordination, we can classify institutional rules either as moral incentives (coordination by social norms, values or standards according to laws of cognitive dissonance, religious beliefs etc.); social incentives (coordination by cooperation or bargaining (negotiation) according to laws of social exchange or reciprocity); economic incentives (coordination by prices or wages according to market laws); political incentives (coordination by legal rules according to the principles of 'check and balances', majority or proportional rules of voting etc.). This framework has been developed in relation to influences drawn from the following authors: Deutsch (1966); Elster (1989, 1992); Etzioni (1968, 1988); Granovetter (1979); Le Grand and Bartlett (1993); Mayntz (1992); Okun (1975); Rawls (1990); Scharpf (1988, 1992); Williamson (1985).

All forms of coordination are effective in modern societies,[9] and organizational regimes can be distinguished according to the mix of coordination they incorporate. In liberal market economies, for example, competitive-individualistic guidelines for action, monetary incentives and competition between private organizations are dominant; the United States are close to this ideal type. In corporatist market economies decisions that are important for society, for example, wage determination, are agreed cooperatively in negotiations with the social partners, who are also very involved in the implementation of

---

8 Bessy, Eymard-Duvernay, Gomel and Simonin (1994) work with only three forms of coordination: regulation, incentives and cooperation (mostly in the form of networks). Regulation corresponds to my term of legislation, whereas the other two categories are organized differently in my framework. I find it useful to distinguish clearly between various types of incentives (moral, social, economic, political), and network coordination interpreted only as cooperative arrangements excludes the important form of coordination by bargaining and negotiating.

9 The terms community, association ('society'), market and state probably also refer—in this order—to historical stages of institutional evolution. The increasing interdependence of these coordination mechanisms and the expansion of their geographical validity are characteristic for modernization.

political programmes; Germany is an example. In welfare market economies concrete legal entitlements are a source of additional institutional support for solidaristic guidelines for action, for example, the right to paid parental leave, paid leave to care for an invalid or paid educational leave and the right of long-term unemployed to a job or training place; Sweden can be cited as an example.

As regards process evaluation, we must now ask whether differences in organizational regimes (policy, implementation and incentive regimes) make a significant difference with respect to the achievement of particular labour market objectives. In order to answer this question, we first need a categorical framework, so that we can determine relevant differences and dimensions of organizational regimes. Illustrative examples concerning further training will be provided so that the following deliberations have a central theme.

3   A CATEGORICAL FRAMEWORK FOR THE EVALUATION OF ORGANIZATIONAL REGIMES

The first step in process evaluation is to identify the relevant organizational regime. The three essential questions are: who decides on which policy and how, for instance, on a policy of further training? This question ascertains the type of policy regime. Who then implements, for example, the further training measures and how? This question concerns the type of implementation regime. How is the policy received by the target group? For instance, are the unemployed motivated to participate in the training courses offered, or do employers change their training policies if they receive recruitment subsidies combined with an obligation to provide training? Here, we are asking about the type of incentive regime. A categorical framework will be presented in the following, which can serve as a checklist for a full description of organizational regimes (Figure 7.2).

3.1   Policy Regimes

Policy regimes are the first 'filter' to determine policy choice and, thus, the type and the components of labour market policy. In addition, policy regimes also provide the institutional infrastructure on which effective implementation often relies.

Policy regimes can be characterized according to four modes of social coordination. Thus, labour market policy regimes have, *first, a value and attitude structure* that can be seen as a continuum between individualistic and communitarian action orientations. From the point of view of game theory, this duality can be classified further as orientations that are aggressive-

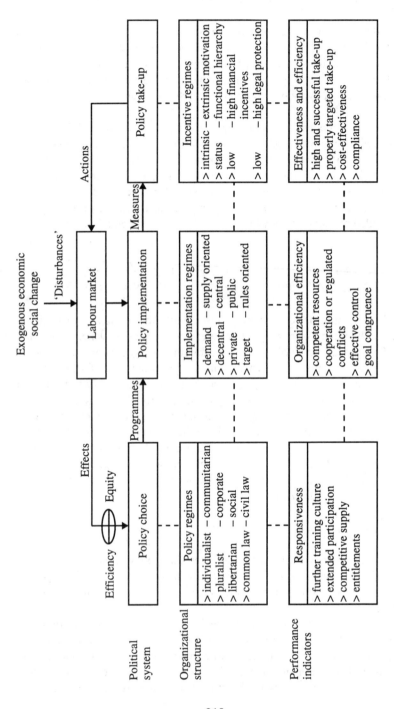

Figure 7.2 Analytic Framework for the Evaluation of Labour Market Policy Organization

individualistic (minimizing the benefit for others), competitive-individualistic (maximizing the benefit for oneself), solidaristic-cooperative (maximizing the benefit for oneself and others) and altruistic-communitarian (maximizing the benefit for others).[10] Labour market intervention in individualistic regimes will be more market oriented, as compared to regimes that are more communitarian and disposed towards promoting public infrastructure and legal claims, such as the entitlement to further training for the unemployed.

Second, the associative structure can be located between the two poles 'pluralist' and 'corporate'. Characteristic for corporate regimes are horizontal coordination through negotiations and ensuing contractual agreements between powerful interest groups (especially trade unions and employers' federations), where the state often participates as an equal partner in the negotiations. In pluralist regimes we typically find that varying pressure groups, which are usually not horizontally coordinated, influence decisions that remain the sole responsibility of central governments. Corporate regimes will display a more stable policy regime, including a favourable participatory infrastructure for policy implementation, whereas pluralist regimes are expected to be more volatile, in accordance with changing coalitions of interest groups. On the other hand, pluralist regimes may be more innovative than corporate regimes, where 'traditional interests' are often better organized than 'new interests'. See, among others, the paradigmatic literature by Olson on this point (1965, 1982) and the contribution by Appelbaum and Schettkat, chap. 26 in this volume.

Third, the social system of material exchange (the market) is characterized either as a more liberal or a more social market economy (if the basic orientation is capitalistic). Typical features of liberal market economy regimes are, for example, free labour markets on which wages are determined by marginal productivity and its market evaluation; in social market economies, by contrast, wage determination is subject either to collective negotiations or regulation by the state (incomes policy); in addition, the public sector is usually larger in social market economies, whereas it is inclined to be smaller in liberal market economies. Liberal market regime types will favour a training policy on the margin, which means concentrating on the least qualified because large wage differentials are a weak incentive for this target group to invest in human capital. Social market regimes, on the other hand, will emphasize universal training schemes (and may even tend to favour the better quali-

---

10 For game theory see, apart from the classic work by Neumann and Morgenstern (1947) and among many others, Rasmusen (1989). One of the essential deficits in social science theory is the question as to under which conditions which orientations for action evolve. Frank's (1988) stimulating work represents a remarkable step forward with regard to solidaristic and altruistic orientations.

fied) because low wage differentials are a weak economic incentive for the 'medium-trained person' to invest in human capital.[11]

Fourth, and finally, a state's basic *legal structure* can be founded either on the tradition of common law or civil law. The process of negotiation and the content of employment contracts in policy regimes based on a civil law tradition tend to be formally and universally regulated. Common law regimes, on the other hand, are more flexible and are based on case law and precedent, so that universally valid legal entitlements (e.g. the detailed regulation and uniform application of unemployment benefits or further training allowances) are less prevalent. Whereas common law regimes display a tendency towards continuous reregulation, constant refinements or minor reforms around a stable and comprehensive core of labour law are the characteristic feature of civil law regimes. Civil law regimes tend to provide a good legal infrastructure for the exclusion of opportunistic behaviour and for long-term planning because of their comprehensive coverage, whereas common law regimes may be more advantageous in terms of flexibility and innovation.[12]

3.2   Implementation Regimes

We can use much the same method to characterize implementation regimes as we did to define policy regimes. The first dimension, thus, concerns the *competence structure* (knowledge, attitudes) that *governs the behaviour* of the actors responsible for the implementation of, for example, further training programmes. The number of programme managers and their level of qualification and competence is of primary importance. As the study by de Koning

---

11 It is also interesting to see how policy regimes determine the function and, thus, the type of wage subsidies. As Gautié et al. (1994) have persuasively demonstrated, the United Kingdom (as a case approaching a liberal market regime in the 1980s), first, uses wage-subsidy schemes to a lesser extent than, for instance, Sweden (more of a social market regime) and, second, uses wages subsidies to induce lower wages, whereas social market regimes (again Sweden and also Germany) use wage subsidies for mainly anticyclical reasons and for compensating the low productivity of marginal workers. See Erhel, Gautié, Gazier and Morel, chap. 9 in this volume.

12 The comparative evaluation of legal systems is still in its infancy. In addition, common law regimes and civil law regimes are ideal types that in reality are extremely differentiated according to history and policy domains. Also, civil law is in a process of fundamental transformation. 'That transformation is symbolized in part by the decline of civil codes, in part by the rise of constitutions, and in part by the growth of European federalism (Merryman, 1985, p. 151). Due to the fact that the United Kingdom, the birthplace of the common law tradition, is a member of the European Union and the majority of the other Member States follow the civil law tradition, a *rapprochement* of the civil law and common law traditions could be expected. For a discussion of legal regimes from various points of view and in international comparison see the informative volume by Rogowski and Wilthagen (1994).

and van Nes has shown (see section 1.2), the general orientation of labour exchange officers towards demand (filling vacancies coming in from firms) or supply (actively searching for vacancies for the unemployed) can also make a difference, especially with respect to distributional effects.

The second dimension of implementation regimes is characterized by the *decision-making and responsibility structure*. The first question is whether decision-making on the use of resources and the transformation of the programmes into operative measures is autonomous-decentralized or hierarchical-centralized; cooperative decision-making structures would constitute an intermediate form.[13] A further question is whether the area of responsibility covers specific functions or is multifunctional. Accordingly, four subtypes of implementation structure can be distinguished in this dimension: structures that are fragmented and decentralized or integrative and decentralized, and those that are fragmented and centralized or integrative and centralized. Further training for the unemployed, for instance, could be decentralized to specialized public authorities or agencies (which can also be private enterprises). Alternatively, it could be managed by organizational units that are also charged with other functions, for example, management consulting or job placement. A third possibility might be specialized organizations, usually in the public sector, that operate hierarchically and centrally throughout the whole territory of the regime. A fourth option would be for these institutions to also have responsibility for other functions, for instance, implementing the unemployment insurance system and/or the system of job placement under the domain of the public sector.

The third dimension of implementation regimes is related to the *financial structure* and the *production structure* of the service provided. For instance, further training can be both financed and carried out either by private or public bodies. At one extreme, the unemployed finance their further training themselves, and the institutions providing the service operate on a commer-

---

13 At the implementation level, *incentives for cooperation* can govern actions independently of financial incentives, for example, when failure to cooperate results in loss of reputation in society; moreover, incentives to cooperate will depend to a large extent, as game theory suggests, on expectations as to whether further games with the same potential partners will be necessary or not in the future; distribution conflicts can be resolved more easily, too, if it is possible to repeat the game; thus, whether utility-maximizing behaviour is short term or long term depends to a large extent on incentives to cooperate. Note that there are at least five different reasons for cooperation: externalities, assistance, conventions, joint ventures and private ordering. Collective action theory deals with the first two types of cooperation, and bargaining theory with the last three. Collective action theory identifies the free-rider problem as the main obstacle to cooperation. Bargaining theory suggests that the main problem is failure to agree on the division of the benefits from cooperation. The interaction of both approaches is developed by Elster, who argues that collective action failures often occur because bargaining breaks down (Elster, 1989, p. 15).

cial basis. At another extreme, the tax-paying community provides the funding, and the further training is carried out in public training centres. Contributions to collective funds are an interesting intermediate form of financing whereby individuals acquire entitlement to benefits through payment of contributions; such equivalent relationships are explicitly prohibited if the training is financed from tax revenue (Schmid, Reissert and Bruche, 1992). Intermediate forms of production structure are public delivery of services against fees that cover a part of the costs, or private delivery of services with subsidized prices.

The fourth dimension of implementation concerns the *legal form and the content of the programmes*. Legally, the programmes can be designed for a specific purpose or they may have a conditional form. In the first case only the goals are predetermined, whereas the means to achieve these are left to organizations implementing the policy. In the second case the conditions under which certain legal entitlements must be satisfied are precisely formulated. Of course, I am referring here to ideal types that do not exist empirically in a pure form. Furthermore, target programmes and conditional programmes may be more or less complex (regulatory depth) and, accordingly, can allow room for manoeuvre when it comes to implementation.

An interesting, but not yet well understood, problem is the possible divergence between programme rationality and implementation rationality. In reviewing the genesis of process evaluation (see section 1.2), I made the argument that when implementation deviates from the rules (and even from the goals) of a programme, this should be regarded as a benefit rather than a deficit. Implementation rationality can overrule or compensate for programme irrationality, although this is not given. The missionary prodecentralization approach of the second generation of implementation research is called into question by the new rational choice theory (Elster, 1989, 1992). According to this criticism, implementers are local or regional agents and will therefore tend to maximize 'local utility' (individual rationality) instead of 'global utility' (system rationality), and, hence, they may come into conflict with each other.

An example of this problem can be seen in the case of the regional Saxonian government in south-east Germany. The background to this example is a general deficit of apprenticeship places in eastern Germany, where (in the summer of 1995) only 11 000 places were available for 55 000 applicants. The government offered a mobility incentive of DM 300 per month (about ECU 150) to school-leavers who found an apprenticeship place outside their home area. The neighbouring regional government in Mecklenburg-West Pommerania wrote a fiery protest letter, fearing that such a policy could lead to their scarce apprenticeship places being poached. This example shows how local rationales may generate irrational behaviour at the macrolevel when the consequences of individual actions are interdependent (Schelling, 1978). If all local governments were to offer such mobility incentives, these policies would have no effect.[14]

To generalize this point, the important distinction between act-utilitarianism and rule-utilitarianism made by Elster (1992, p. 222) will be recalled. The former enjoins us, on every single occasion, to perform the act that will maximize total utility on that occasion. The latter tells us to act according to the rule that, when followed invariably, will maximize total utility over time and space. In many circumstances the rule of acting according to act-utilitarianism will not maximize total utility over time and space.[15] Instead, utility will be maximized by following some other rule, even if in each individual case that rule yields results that are less than optimal. In local justice act-utilitarianism (or agent-restricted act-utilitarianism) is rampant. In process evaluation, therefore, care will have to be taken to distinguish between 'local effectiveness' and 'global effectiveness' in programme implementation.

As we have seen, the concrete measures that result from the implementation of the political programmes do not by any means guarantee global success. Another possible policy failure, to which I now turn, has its roots more in policy formation than in implementation. Even if programmes are effectively implemented from an administrative point of view, they may not correspond to the behavioural dispositions of those actors whose conduct is to be influenced. Thus, we come to the 'third filter', the incentive regimes, which determine whether and how political programmes and measures are accepted by the individuals they are designed for.

3.3   Incentive Regimes

At the first level, that is, the level of the *moral incentive structure*, motivations govern action. These may be sustained by internalized values (intrinsic motivation) or derive from external signals (extrinsic motivation). For the unemployed who previously had a highly skilled occupation we could assume that they will have a very strong, internalized motivation to catch up on the latest knowledge in their field so that they are better able to compete and to obtain future employment. If, in order to improve their prospects of reintegration, further training is only necessary in the sense of building on and expanding occupational or professional expertise ('advanced training'), then one can assume that there is a strong self-motivation, especially in countries where

---

14 The Saxonian government, however, defended the decision with the argument that in some regions, especially in western Germany, there is a shortage of apprentices to fill all the available places.

15 I have added the space dimension (to Elster's argument) because there is not only 'path dependency' but also 'space (or 'horizontal') interdependency'.

one's 'occupation' or 'profession' is an important indicator of social identity and status. For those who are unskilled or less skilled we could assume that they will derive their motivation for further training to a much greater extent from 'external' incentives, for example, from the real prospect of a job (which is not necessarily linked to better financial circumstances), a goal that can be achieved in the foreseeable future or a useful certificate. Both kinds of motivation demand a step-by-step or modular procedure. A strong identification with one's occupation can, however, be a hindrance if the situation on the labour market demands complete retraining. If the previous occupation or activity is in decline, for instance, shipbuilding or mining, internalized values can constitute extreme obstacles to further training. In this case external signals will be crucial if the motivational impetus for retraining is to be drawn out. Another prerequisite for willingness to retrain is the similarity between the new occupation and the essence of the old, in other words, the psychological distance between the previous and the required occupation must not be too great.

Second, the incentive, for example, to partake in further training can also have a social motivation if education significantly determines one's position in the social hierarchy. A further training policy founded on economic incentives, that is, higher earnings, will be less effective in an incentive regime dominated by status differentials than in a regime in which (performance-related) functional hierarchies are institutionalized. There will be a strong motivation to take part in further training, even without financial incentives, where education itself already generates status. Even when there is a strong correlation between economic and social status, intercultural differences concerning this relation are probably very important. This is illustrated, for example, by the varying significance afforded to income gains related to (further) training in the literature on evaluation: in continental Europe the goal of successful (occupational) reintegration—that is, status restoration—is considered more significant than the related increase in income, which is emphasized as a criterion for success in the Anglo-Saxon culture.[16]

The third structural characteristic of incentive regimes are the *economic incentives* already mentioned above, for example, financial rewards for investment in further training. Congruence between wage and educational structures is likely to create positive incentives for further training. By contrast, a wage structure that is practically inflexible with respect to skill differentials (in other words, efforts to attain better skills are not rewarded) will be an inauspicious environment for further training policies. On the other hand, wage or salary differentials can have a negative effect on motivation if the

---

16 The secret of success of the 'Protestant ethic' is thus probably rooted in the wide-reaching congruence between status assigned for economic reasons and status assigned for social reasons.

margins are too wide (for example, between an unskilled and a skilled worker, a nurse and a doctor). Economic incentives can also be rewards in nonmonetary form, for example, permission to use plant equipment for personal purposes.

Fourth, one must consider the *'political incentives'* derived from legal entitlements, laws and prohibitions, which may strengthen or weaken the other incentives. Legal entitlements that are linked to skills, such as access to certain occupations and according protection against (unfair) competition, can complement or compensate financial incentives.[17]

The aim of process evaluation is, of course, not only to describe the systems of policy formation and implementation. At the end of the day we want to come up with an assessment of performance and with concrete evidence of how the 'black box' should be improved to yield better results. In the next section, therefore, I go on to discuss possibilities for measuring process performance.

4   PERFORMANCE MEASURES OF PROCESS EVALUATION

Two different types of success or performance indicators must be taken into account in process evaluation. The first interesting question is whether the organizational differences in time and space lead to differences in the quality of processes, for example, better coordination of actors involved in implementing further training programmes (*process efficiency*). The second question is whether these differences also lead to an improvement in the allocative and distributional efficiency of labour market policy. The *effectiveness* of labour market policy also depends on the macrocontext, that is, on the economic structure of the problem and on the aggregate effect of many microdecisions (Figure 7.2). The ultimate goal of process evaluation is to trace labour market performance back to specific organizational structures and changes in them by holding constant the economic conditions.[18]

---

17 An example: within the framework of the structural reform of the German health-care system in 1992 (one reason was rising numbers and the expected oversupply of doctors) the insurance funds demanded that licences to practice as panel doctors should be restricted, among other things (and as a legal requirement), to those who partake in further training as a panel doctor.

18 If all three conditions have been fulfilled—high process efficiency, high allocative and distributional efficiency and high labour market effectiveness—then a favourable (if not optimal) cost–benefit relation can also be expected; see Delander and Niklasson, chap. 6 in this volume.

The dimensions of process efficiency are again classified according to the stages of a policy cycle (Figure 7.2): from policy choice to policy implementation, policy take-up and policy effects. The cycle incorporates consideration of cost–benefit relations of efficiency and equity through social justice leading to a new policy choice. The success indicators for the policy-choice process can be classified under the concept of *responsiveness*; those for policy implementation under the concept of *organizational efficiency*; and those for policy take-up under the concept of *policy acceptance*. The concepts are explained in the following paragraphs, and examples for the operationalization of such a process evaluation are provided.

4.1   Responsiveness

'Responsiveness' can be described, according to the tradition of systems theory, as the ability of an actor or a system to be open to the needs or desires of another actor or system (Deutsch, 1966, p. 230; Etzioni, 1968, p. 6; Le Grand and Bartlett, 1993, p. 15). Given that the basic goals of societies are not only different, but also usually vaguely formulated or in conflict with each other, it is difficult to define success indicators that can be clearly operationalized in policy regimes. It can be assumed for the members of industrially highly developed democracies, in which pluralism and participation are emphasized, that their values do not foster extreme (aggressive or altruistic) types of behaviour but follow a 'middle' (competitive and solidaristic) course. It could also be assumed that the majority favour an economy based on competition and productivity growth and that such regimes have institutionalized the selection of political leaders in competitive electoral procedures (party competition) plus many social entitlements (welfare state). Nevertheless, in the following definition of indicators for 'responsiveness' individual value judgements cannot be avoided.

In accordance with the typology of social coordination, the responsiveness of political systems can in turn be 'measured' at four levels. In connection with our chosen example of further training the respective key indicators are, first, a further training culture; second, participation in determining the training content; third, variety and flexibility of skills; and, fourth, entitlements to further training.

–   The existence of a *'further training culture'* reflects a common awareness regarding the significance of further training and a positive attitude towards further training. Because, as a rule, education is linked to positive external effects this criterion of process efficiency can be further qualified: in order to utilize positive external effects, that is, positive sum games, cooperation, which demands a certain amount of solidarity, is required. Thus, there can be no talk of a well-developed solidaristic further training culture until, in addition to its being held in high regard, there is equal opportunity to participate in further training.

- As regards the associative organizational structure, much speaks in favour of making use of *participative structures* to reduce uncertainty regarding the future need for further training. It is only through communication (Habermas, 1987) that 'actual knowledge' (Hayek, 1945), which is widely but not universally available, can be integrated, rapidly disseminated and strategically defined.[19] In particular, this would mean, for example, making collective actors (such as trade unions and professional associations) capable of acting strategically in the first place by legally sanctioning and guaranteeing them opportunities to participate.

- A third way to combat the uncertainty is to institutionalize *internal or external flexibility* in further training, that is, a variety of skills for one person, or in one production unit, or promotion of external mobility; on the supply side, moreover, the existence of many further training institutions guarantees the responsiveness of policy regimes. The justification for this last is based on the principle of 'requisite variety', whereby the internal complexity of a system must correspond to its external complexity (Ashby, 1970; Schmid and Schömann, 1994).

- *Legal entitlements* to training for low-skilled unemployed (or employed under immediate threat of unemployment) could be taken as a fourth indicator of responsiveness, as could the widening of options in the process of life-long learning through an institutionalized possibility of repeated further training phases.

The following are some proposals for operationalizing the responsiveness of labour market policy regimes. First, what is the *degree of activity* of labour

---

19 In the tradition of Thorstein Veblen, the Nobel prize winner Kenneth Arrow, for example, affords special significance to the emergence and dissemination of 'social knowledge' for evolution, economic growth and prosperity (Arrow, 1994, pp. 6–8). From this one can draw the useful conclusion that further training is attaining an increasingly strategic value. And, vice versa, the negative side of unemployment (especially long-term unemployment) becomes less an economic issue (especially when wage-compensation benefits are relatively generous) than an informational one, in the sense that the unemployed are excluded from the process of social knowledge exchange, especially the exchange and dissemination of 'technical knowledge'. Schellhaaß and Schubert (1992) rightly stress Hayek's important distinction between generalized knowledge, which can be centralized and distributed to all, and actual knowledge, which cannot be transferred to others without substantial loss of reliability or validity (Hayek, 1945). The effectiveness of policy formation and implementation processes depends to a large extent on proper organizational designs to solve this information problem. Schellhaaß' and Schubert's assumption, however, that decentralized implementation structures are *per se* more effective in tackling this problem than centralized structures is doubtful. One reason why this assumption must be critically tested is that nontransferable knowledge can be monopolized or used strategically.

market policy? This would measure the share of total expenditure on 'active' employment promotion in the labour market budget, amounting to 100 per cent if the budget includes no expenditure on 'passive' unemployment benefits or early retirement. The degree of activity shows to what extent the actors responsible for labour market policy are actually committed to full employment. Second, to what extent are governments *fiscally committed* to active labour market policy? The fiscal policy commitment can be measured by taking actual expenditure on labour market policy as a percentage of GDP, standardized to one percentage point unemployment. The indicator also measures the actual fiscal order of magnitude with respect to the degree of activity. If the fiscal policy commitment is weak, relative expenditure is low and decreases as unemployment rises; if the fiscal policy commitment is strong, expenditure is relatively high and remains constant as unemployment rises. The indicator for fiscal policy commitment can be specified for various policy instruments, for example, further training. In this case expenditure on further training for the employed should be included because it prevents unemployment and can relieve the burden on the labour market.[20] In the ideal case the vacancy rate should be taken as a basis for standardization because the extent to which the need for skills is unsatisfied can then be measured.

4.2   Organizational Efficiency

The conditions for the efficiency of organizations that are concerned with transforming programmes into concrete measures can again be described in four dimensions of societal coordination: competent resources for action, cooperation or regulated conflict (negotiation), effective control (or budget constraints) and goal congruence.

– The first condition for organizational efficiency is the availability of *competent resources for action*, that is, the personnel who are responsible for planning, implementing and executing, for example, the further training programmes must have the necessary capabilities and the required resources at their disposal. The number and the level of education of the personnel could be taken as indicators for this efficiency variable, likewise the existence of continuous training for the further training personnel, and professionally recognized quality standards against which the personnel's performance can again be assessed. Only in this way can some kind of professional further training ethics develop. In comparative research these indi-

---

20 Denmark and Sweden have programmes based on substitution of employees undergoing external training with unemployed for the duration of the training.

cators would have to be standardized by the 'problem load', for example, the number of unemployed.

- At the associative level, a high degree of participation in the form of *cooperation or negotiations within a framework of fair procedures for resolving conflicts* are cardinal success indicators for effective 'policy networks'. It is difficult to operationalize cooperation because one does not know in advance which actors should interact at which level in order to plan or implement further training. The conditions for cooperation may vary from country to country, but also from problem to problem. Different forms of cooperation are probably needed for the resolution of mismatch problems than for further training for difficult-to-place unemployed. Fair procedures for resolving disputes are the reverse side of cooperation; often conflicts of interest have to be battled out, for which established rules for negotiations and potential arbitration procedures are required.

  Here, too, it is difficult to measure success. The (low) amount of working time lost due to strikes is an expression of (good) industrial relations and can be seen as representing (good) cooperation between the social partners and the labour market authorities. Alternatively, little strife could indicate authoritarian management and fragmented, disorganized workers or social partners. In addition, the degree of organization in trade unions and employers' associations can be taken as another proxy for potential organizational efficiency; thus, for example, measures will be received more positively if the social partners are involved in the operationalization of the programmes and, given a high degree of organization, can also influence the personnel policy of the enterprises. Here, expert interviews and content analysis of documents and press commentaries can be a source of systematic information for process evaluation. One of the best overviews of and introductions to qualitative methods is provided by King et al. (1994).

- With respect to delivery structures, competition—on both the supplier and the buyer side—and performance control (monitoring) are two sides of the same coin, namely, organizational efficiency; together, the two requirements can be taken as a performance measure for *effective control*. In the first case the threat of being out-competed on the market exerts effective control (the systems theory term for 'feedback'); in the second case 'feedback' through performance-oriented monitoring implies sanctions, for example, in the form of lower budgetary allocations, no upward promotion or even dismissal (see Auer and Kruppe on monitoring, chap. 30 in this volume).

  Again, it is difficult to measure organizational efficiency at this level. It should be possible, however, to approximately determine actual competition on the supply and demand side using a case-study approach. Surveys of the target groups as to their satisfaction with the implementing bodies are another useful source of information, as are interviews with experts. Critical reviews of information systems that monitor performance (official statistics and documentation systems) can be informative. An analysis of organizational reforms with respect to changes in the content, form, frequency and distribution of documentation systems or statistics can provide further valuable data. The theorem of 'institutional incongruence'[21] has proved useful in evaluating financing structures; if there is a wide gap between the fiscal costs and returns of labour market policy, there may be an under- or overinvestment in, for example, further training.

– How do we identify 'good' or 'bad' formal (legal) rules for labour market programmes? One strategy is to assess *goal congruence*, that is, correspondence between targets and rules. A first prerequisite for proper targeting of programmes is a good theory as to why the labour market fails to meet the target (see chap. 1 in this volume). Thus, it is necessary to identify and to assess the theory underlying labour market programmes. The second prerequisite for proper targeting is goal congruence between the key actors in policy choice and policy implementation. If not even the implementers have the same explicit or implicit programme goals, organizational efficiency is very unlikely to be achieved. From a theoretical point of view, anticyclical expenditure on further training for the unemployed would be another indicator for inadequate programme regulation because it implies that active labour market policy is out-competed in phases of rising unemployment.

The time horizon of programmes is the subject of another approach. Continuity and explicitness of rules and targets are other factors that support organizational efficiency. Actors who constantly have to reckon with changes in laws or measures cannot develop stable behavioural expectations or behavioural routines; the probability of passive or opportunistic conduct increases. Stop–go policies are evidence of this type of organizational inefficiency, as is failure to sanction noncompliance with rules.

---

21 On fiscal incongruence see Bruche and Reissert (1985) and Schmid et al. (1992). In economic terms, 'institutional incongruence' means failure to internalize positive or negative external effects. There is a tendency towards cost explosion in implementation regimes in which programme administration is decentralized, but financial consequences are the responsibility of the central or collective level. One strategy that can be employed to curb cost explosion (i.e. inefficiency) is to set budget ceilings; strict conditional programming is another. The first grants decision-making scope to the decentral bodies when it comes to determining the content of the programmes; however, it is inflexible when the gravity of the problems varies from region to region; the second alternative leaves no scope for decision-making regarding content in the extreme case, but is flexible in the face of varying pressure across regions.

4.3 Acceptance

Acceptance is the generic term for successful policy take-up, which, as Figure 7.2 illustrates, is the outcome of the three preceding 'filters' (policy regimes, implementation regimes, incentive regimes). It is usually difficult to discern which filter was decisive for the quantity of participants actually achieved. In accordance with the four-dimensional classification introduced above, the following indicators for the ultimate performance (or success) of the whole process can be conceived: high utilization or take-up of the programme, social selectivity, cost-effectiveness and compliance.

- The first criterion, *high utilization of programmes or other policy measures*, is easy to measure for programmes by taking the number of participants in relation to the number of employed or unemployed. If there is a target number for the programme, the degree to which the target is met is the proxy for acceptance. If the number of participants falls far short of the target number, this is an indication of insufficient acceptance. Often two decisive pieces of information for determining the level of utilization are missing: the duration of the measure and information indicating whether the measure was successfully completed (drop-out rate). Thus, surveys of nonparticipants and drop-outs provide very important information concerning deficits either in the programme design or in the implementation (Rossi, Freeman and Wright, 1979, p. 131).
- *Social selection* or *social preference* is the performance measure in the social dimension. As regards further training, a particularly interesting question is whether the structure of the participants indicates preferential treatment or disadvantages for particular target groups on the labour market, and whether the incentives for the target groups in mind were adequate. A further training policy can be considered all the more successful the more it affects target groups that would have had no prospects without the policy. However, high utilization is often in conflict with high selectivity. One solution to this problem usually lies in the hands of the implementation managers, who react very sensitively to acceptance thresholds and tend, therefore, to favour groups that are highly motivated to avail of the programmes; there is thus a possibility that the most successful groups will be 'creamed off'.
- High *cost-effectiveness* is the main performance indicator in the economic dimension. Cost-effectiveness measures the degree to which a goal is met by expenditure of a certain amount of money, for instance, what percentage of a target group for further training (e.g. long-term unemployed) were encompassed by one unit of programme expenditure. For this indicator to be measured an explicit target must have been set initially. The use of cost-effectiveness measures may be useful in comparing programmes with the

same target (on cost–benefit analysis see Delander and Niklasson, chap. 6 in this volume). They may, however, yield false incentives if used as performance indicators in monitoring systems (on monitoring see Auer and Kruppe, chap. 30 in this volume).

– Finally, *compliance* with the law, that is, the lawful utilization of measures, is an indicator for successful policy take-up; not just utilization according to the letter of the law, but also in accordance with the spirit of the rules of the programme or measure. From the point of view of the 'political' incentive conditions (and as for all policy measures), a widespread belief in the legitimacy and equity of labour market policy is necessary. The following data can be taken to measure this indicator: for example, the relative number of return claims on public subsidies, the frequency of individual complaints, the relative number of applications turned down or the sanctions on refusal of a reasonable job or further training offer.

4.4   Labour Market Policy Success

The most important criteria for labour market success, again mainly taking further training policies for the unemployed as an example, can once again be classified in four dimensions: employment effect, distribution effect, productivity effect and efficiency.

– The *employment effect* indicates whether further training for the unemployed does ultimately lead to employment. If those threatened by unemployment undergo further training, success is reflected in avoided unemployment. The most important indicators for labour market success from this perspective are a shorter duration of unemployment and the reintegration rate immediately subsequent to the further training measure, or one to two years later (compared to a control group).

– The *distribution effect* indicates whether the measure has led to an improvement in social equity. The indicator works on the assumption that the requirement of fair competition on labour markets is often not given. Additionally, market processes can also generate new social inequalities. Indicators for positive distribution effects are reintegration of disadvantaged persons who have undergone further training, for instance, the low skilled, women reentering the labour market, the long-term unemployed, older workers and foreigners. The function of labour market policy as a social equalizer can also pertain to regions that are severely affected by unemployment. In this case a positive labour market effect would be reflected by a more rapid reduction of unemployment, which can be traced back to further training, or a lower risk of unemployment. Thus, in contrast to the acceptance indicator, the labour market effect is being measured here. High selectivity, in favour of women, for instance, is not an indicator for corresponding labour market success; high selectivity is a necessary but, in itself, an insufficient prerequisite for labour market success; direct or indirect discrimination in the recruiting process can nullify process success (i.e. responsiveness plus organizational efficiency plus acceptance).

- The *productivity effect* measures the rise in economic efficiency (input–ouptput relation) that has been achieved through general improvement of skills and the reduction of skills-related imbalances ('mismatching'). Although this criterion can be measured directly, it has only limited value in international comparisons. Productivity ratios in enterprises and in the wider economy depend on a multitude of factors, of which qualifications are only one. The following could be taken as more direct success ratios: reductions in the duration of vacancies, higher incomes or more rapid income increases for unemployed persons who have undergone further training and been reintegrated (compared to a control group) and reductions in occupational mismatch or regional unemployment differentials.

- *Efficiency* is an expression for the relationship between the net effects that have been realized and those that were intended (minus the unintentional effects) and the cost of achieving this effect (unassessed cost-effectiveness). A comparative standard is always presupposed in the assessment, either in the form of opportunity costs (what else could have been accomplished with the same money?), or in the form of an organizational comparison (what did agency A achieve compared to agency B?). If, for example, a six-month further training measure costs agency A less than agency B, and the reintegration success is the same, then agency A operates more efficiently. A wider concept of efficiency measures the relationship between cost and benefit (assessed in terms of cost-effectiveness). If, for example, the benefit of the measure carried out by agency A (e.g. the difference between the participants' earned incomes before and after the measure) exceeds the costs, and if no higher benefit could have been achieved elsewhere at the same cost (opportunity costs), then the measure is efficient.

In contrast to the acceptance indicators, which can be measured directly by number of participants and expenditure, in measuring labour market success we require additional analyses in order to assess the 'net impact', that is, gross impact minus deadweight effects (or windfall profits), displacement effects and substitution effects:

- *Deadweight effects* refer to the utilization of programmes or other policy measures for activities that would have taken place without the policy. For example, an enterprise hires an unemployed woman and receives a subsidy for on-the-job training; however, were it not for the programme the enterprise would have financed the training itself.

– One can distinguish two types of *displacement effect*: in the first case persons favoured by policies displace others, for example, a subsidized long-term unemployed person displaces a short-term unemployed person who would otherwise have got the job; a more grievous case would be an enterprise dismissing a worker with a view to receiving a wage subsidy on hiring another.[22] The second type of displacement effect refers to the situation in which subsidized enterprises achieve a position where they can offer lower market prices, so that enterprises in the same market segment that do not benefit from subsidies are disadvantaged. If, for example, textile firm A provides advanced training for its staff, which is financially supported by the employment office, while the competing enterprise B does the same at its own cost, A can then offer cheaper products and displace B from the market.

– There are also two types of *substitution effect*. The first case refers again to the product market, although this time—in contrast to displacement—different products are the issue. If grain farmers are subsidized, and therefore the product spaghetti as a consumption good is subsidized, potato farmers can suffer as a consequence because, assuming price elasticity for consumer behaviour, potato consumption may then fall off. The second form of substitution, which is given too little consideration in the literature, refers to competing policy programmes: the integration of an unemployed person through a newly introduced recruitment subsidy may simply substitute the participation of this person in a further training programme.

In all three cases, deadweight, displacement and substitution, there is no net effect or it is negligible. Whereas efficiency is always impaired by deadweight effects, displacement and substitution might be intentional; thus, they should not be considered negative in every case. For example, preferential treatment for one person at the cost of another (e.g. promoting women at the cost of men, disabled persons at the cost of abled persons, long-term unemployed at the cost of short-term unemployed) can be an explicit social policy goal (see Rubery, Fagan and Maier, chap. 14 in this volume; see also Delsen, chap. 17, and Erhel, Gautié, Gazier and Morel, chap. 9 in this volume). Further, substitution of capital-intensive employment by labour-intensive employment, by influencing factor prices through direct wage subsidies or tax exemptions, can be an explicit industrial or, again, social policy goal (see Erhel et al., chap. 9 in this volume).

---

22 In the literature the latter case is also labelled as substitution. The terms 'displacement' and 'substitution' are often interchanged because both refer to functional equivalent effects.

5   CONCLUSION

As shown in this chapter, the state of the art in process evaluation is fairly underdeveloped. Process evaluation has to be integrated into any comprehensive policy evaluation, but to date has been the big missing link in most evaluation studies. Without effective policy formation and implementation, policy choices, programmes and individual measures will remain suboptimal. Without process evaluation we will be unable to say if the results of a certain programme or mix of programmes can be expected to remain the same in the future or whether they can be transferred to other countries. We will also be unable to advise policy-makers on the design of better implementation, monitoring, controlling and learning processes.

The focus in this chapter has been on developing a consistent analytical framework for process evaluation. I identified four 'filtering stages' that affect the final impact of labour market policy and developed suggestions for the operationalization of performance indicators:

– The first stage of policy formation culminates in policy choices or programmes. The question at this stage of the process is whether decision-makers are responsive to the different needs of individuals and to the changing conditions of the economy, whereby sensitivity with respect to the implementation conditions is an essential element of high responsiveness. The 'black box' itself is becoming more and more an object as well as a subject of policy formation.
– The second stage of policy implementation concerns the transformation of policy choices or programmes into operational measures. At this stage, the issue is organizational efficiency, in other words programme implementation that is professionally competent, well coordinated with the key actors at the local level, cost-effective and legally stable, thus enabling the development of a long-term perspective (planning security), mutual trust relationships between implementers and targeted persons as well as cost-efficient routines.
– The third filtering stage, policy take-up, shows to what extent programmes and measures are appropriate to the motivations, interests and capacities of targeted people or groups. At this stage, the direct outcome performance of implementation can be measured, such as number of participants (gross employment impact), structural composition of participants (selectivity of programmes), quality indicators of measures (duration, drop-out rates etc.) and compliance with the rules.
– Fourth, and linking back to the first stage, in process evaluation we are interested in the feedback loop. Are policy regimes able to learn from the impact of their programmes or policy choices, including learning from

evaluation studies? Policy choices (programmes) may be conflicting, inconsistent or nontransparent. Recourse to systematic information on implementation (process analysis), outcomes (monitoring) and effects (impact analysis) may reduce the range of conflicts to the real issues, improve consistency and increase transparency. However, process evaluation is no guarantee for rational choices because there is always scope for different interpretations of results. Even the learning effect of real experiments is limited, for the impact of programmes may change drastically if they are implemented on a large scale (see Björklund and Regnér, chap. 3 in this volume).

The main conclusion resulting from this chapter is the advocacy of a new organizational paradigm for labour market policy, in which the analytical framework of process evaluation has to be taken into account. The implicit model behind the traditional frameworks has been the concept of a centralized and programme-oriented 'active labour market policy'. New frameworks have to be based on the assumption of a decentralized and target-oriented 'cooperative labour market policy'. In such a new paradigm the formation and implementation of programmes have to be taken as key determining variables and not just as constants or a 'black box'. Their embeddedness in the broader framework of employment policy and specific labour market regimes has to be acknowledged more so than has been the case in the past. Networks, public–private mixes and performance-oriented budget allocation will be essential ingredients of modern labour market policy. The emphasis of process evaluation, that is, the analysis of policy formation and implementation, has to be adjusted towards these new phenomena.

REFERENCES

Arrow, K. J. (1994, May), 'Methodological Individualism and Social Knowledge', *Papers and Proceedings of the American Economics Association*, 1–9.

Ashby, R. W. (1970), *An Introduction to Cybernetics* (2nd ed.), London: Chapman & Hall University Paperbacks.

Bessy, C., F. Eymard-Duvernay, B. Gomel and B. Simonin (1994), 'Les Politiques Publiques d'Emploi: Le Role des Agents Locaux', *La Lettre*, 33, 1–12, 34, 1–10, Centre d'Études de l'Emploi, 93 166, Noisy: Le-Grand.

Bouder, A., J.-P. Cadet and D. Demazière (1994), 'Evaluer les Effets des Dispositifs d'Insertion pour les Jeunes et les Chômeurs de Longue Durée. Un Bilan Méthodologique', *Cereq Document*, 98 (Série Synthèse), Marseille.

Bruche, G. and B. Reissert (1985), *Finanzierung der Arbeitsmarktpolitik*, Frankfurt: Campus Verlag.

de Koning, J. and P. J. van Nes (1991), 'A Quantitative Approach to Process Evaluation: The Case of the Vermeend–Moor Act', *Government and Policy*, 9, 111–18.

Deutsch, K. W. (1966), *The Nerves of Government. Models of Political Communication and Control* (2nd ed.), New York/London: The Free Press/Collier-Macmillan.

Elster, J. (1989), *The Cement of Society. A Study of Social Order*, Cambridge: Cambridge University Press.

Elster, J. (1992), *Local Justice. How Institutions Allocate Scarce Goods and Necessary Burdens*, New York: Russell Sage Foundation.

Etzioni, A. (1968), *The Active Society. A Theory of Societal and Political Processes*, New York/London: The Free Press/Collier-Macmillan.

Etzioni, A. (1988), *The Moral Dimension. Toward a New Economics*, New York/London: The Free Press/Collier-Macmillan.

Ferman, B. (1990), 'When Failure is Success: Implementation and Madisonian Government', in D. J. Palumbo and D. J. Calista (eds), *Implementation and the Policy Process. Opening Up the Black Box*, New York: Greenwood Press, pp. 39–50.

Frank, R. H. (1988), *Passions within Reason. The Strategic Role of the Emotions*, New York/London: W. W. Norton & Company.

Gautié, J., B. Gazier and R. Silvera (1994), *Les Subventions à l'Emploi: Analyses et Expériences Européennes*, Paris: La Documentation Française (Collection Document Travail et Emploi).

Goggin, M. L., A. O'M. Bowman, J. P. Lester and L. J. O'Toole (1990), 'Studying the Dynamics of Public Policy Implementation: A Third-generation Approach', in D. J. Palumbo and D. J. Calista (eds), *Implementation and the Policy Process. Opening Up the Black Box*, New York: Greenwood Press, pp. 181–98.

Granovetter, M. (1979), 'The Theory Gap in Social Network Analysis', in P. W. Holland and S. Leinhardt (eds), *Perspectives on Social Network Research*, New York: Academic Press, pp. 501–18.

Habermas, J. (1987), *Theorie des kommunikativen Handelns* (4th ed.), 2 Vols, Frankfurt: Suhrkamp.

Hanf, K. (1982), 'The Implementation of Regulatory Policy. Enforcement as Bargaining', *European Journal of Political Research*, 10, 159–72.

Hasan, A. (1991), 'Evaluation of Employment, Training and Social Programmes. An Overview of Issues', in OECD (ed.), *Evaluating Labour Market and Social Programmes—The State of a Complex Art*, Paris: OECD, pp. 7–18.

Hayek, F. A. von (1945), 'The Use of Knowledge in Society', *American Economic Review*, 35 (4).

Hayek, F. A. von (1972), *Die Theorie komplexer Phänomene*, Tübingen: Mohr.

Héritier, A. (1993), 'Policy Analyse. Elemente der Kritik und Perspektiven der Neuorientierung', in A. Héritier (ed.), *Policy-Analyse*, Opladen: Westdeutscher Verlag, pp. 9–39.

Hjern, B. and C. Hull (1982), 'Implementation Research as Empirical Constitutionalism', *European Journal of Political Research*, 10, 105–15.

Hjern, B. and D. Porter (1981), 'Implementation Structures: A New Unit of Administrative Analysis', *Organization Studies*, 2, 211–24.

Hucke, J. and H. Wollmann (1980), 'Methodenprobleme der Implementationsforschung', in R. Mayntz (ed.), *Implementation politischer Programme*, Königstein im Taunus: Anton Hain, pp. 216–35.

King, G., R. O. Keohane and S. Verba (1994), *Scientific Inference in Qualitative Research*, Princeton: Princeton University Press.

Le Grand, J. and W. Bartlett (eds) (1993), *Quasi-markets and Social Policy*, Houndmills/London: The Macmillan Press.

Mayntz, R. (ed.) (1983), *Implementation politischer Programme II. Ansätze zur Theoriebildung*, Opladen: Westdeutscher Verlag.

Mayntz, R. (1992), 'Modernisierung und die Logik von interorganisatorischen Netzwerken', *Journal für Sozialforschung*, 32 (1), 19–32.

Merryman, J. H. (1985), *The Civil Law Tradition. An Introduction to the Legal Systems of Western Europe and Latin America* (2nd ed.), Stanford, CA: Stanford University Press.

Nathan, R. (1991), 'Evaluation Strategies with Particular Emphasis on Demonstration Studies', in OECD (ed.), *Evaluating Labour Market and Social Programmes—The State of a Complex Art*, Paris: OECD, pp. 21–42.

Neumann, J. von and O. Morgenstern (1947), *The Theory of Games and Economic Behavior* (2nd ed.), Princeton: Princeton University Press.

North, D. C. (1990), *Institutions, Institutional Change and Economic Performance*, Cambridge: Cambridge University Press.

Okun, A. M. (1975), *Equality and Efficiency. The Big Trade-off*, Washington: The Brookings Institution.

Olson, M. (1965), *The Logic of Collective Action*, Cambridge, MA: Harvard University Press.

Olson, M. (1982), *The Rise and Decline of Nations*, New Haven, CON: Yale University Press.

Palumbo, D. J. and D. J. Calista (eds) (1990a), *Implementation and the Policy Process. Opening Up the Black Box*, New York: Greenwood Press.

Palumbo, D. J. and D. J. Calista (1990b), 'Opening the Black Box. Implementation and the Policy Process', in D. J. Palumbo and D. J. Calista (eds), *Implementation and the Policy Process. Opening Up the Black Box*, New York: Greenwood Press, pp. 3–17.

Peters, A. and G. Schmid (1982a), *Aggregierte Wirkungsanalyse des arbeitsmarktpolitischen Programms der Bundesregierung für Regionen mit besonderen Beschäftigungsproblemen, Zwischenbericht*, WZB discussion paper IIM/LMP 82–1, Wissenschaftszentrum Berlin für Sozialforschung.

Peters, A. and G. Schmid (1982b), *Aggregierte Wirkungsanalyse des arbeitsmarktpolitischen Programms der Bundesregierung für Regionen mit besonderen Beschäftigungsproblemen. Analyse der Beschäftigungswirkungen*, WZB discussion paper IIM/LMP 82–32, Wissenschaftszentrum Berlin für Sozialforschung.

Pressman, J. L. and A. B. Wildavsky (1973), *Implementation*, Berkeley/Los Angeles/London: University of California Press.

Rasmusen, E. (1989), *Games and Information. An Introduction to Game Theory*, Cambridge: Basil Blackwell.

Rawls, J. (1990), *A Theory of Justice* (10th ed.), Oxford: Oxford University Press.

Rogowski, R. and T. Wilthagen (eds) (1994), *Reflexive Labour Law. Studies in Industrial Relations and Employment Regulation*, Deventer/Boston: Kluwer Law and Taxation Publishers.

Rossi, P. H., H. E. Freeman and S. R. Wright (1979), *Evaluation. A Systematic Approach*, Beverly Hills/London: Sage Publications.

Sabatier, P. A. (1986), 'What Can We Learn from Implementation Research?', in F. X. Kaufmann, G. Majone and V. Ostrom (eds), *Guidance, Control, and Evaluation in the Public Sector*, Berlin/New York: de Gruyter, pp. 313–25.

Salamon, L. M. (ed.) (1989), *Beyond Privatization. The Tools of Government Action*, Washington, DC: The Urban Institute Press.

Scharpf, F. W. (1983), 'Interessenlagen der Adressaten und Spielräume der Implementation bei Anreizprogrammen', in R. Mayntz (ed.), *Implementation politischer Programme II*, Opladen: Westdeutscher Verlag, pp. 99–116.

Scharpf, F. W. (1988), 'Verhandlungssysteme, Verteilungskonflikte und Pathologien der politischen Steuerung', in M. G. Schmidt (ed.), 'Staatstätigkeit', special issue 19, *Politische Vierteljahresschrift*, 61–87.

Scharpf, F. W. (1992), 'Einführung: Zur Theorie von Verhandlungssystemen', in A. Benz, F. W. Scharpf and R. Zintl, *Horizontale Politikverflechtung. Zur Theorie von Verhandlungssystemen*, Frankfurt/New York: Campus, pp. 11–27.

Scheirer, M. A. (1994) 'Designing and Using Process Evaluation', in J. S. Wholey, H. P. Hatry and K. E. Newcomer (eds), *1994. Handbook of Practical Program Evaluation*, San Francisco: Jossey-Bass Publishers, pp. 40–68.

Schellhaaß, H.-M. and A. Schubert (1992), 'Internationale Entwicklungen der Evaluierungsmethoden für arbeitsmarktpolitische Programme', *Mitteilungen aus der Arbeitsmarkt- und Berufsforschung*, 3, 371–80.

Schelling, T. C. (1978), *Micromotives and Macrobehavior*, New York/London: W. W. Norton & Company.

Schmid, G. and A. Peters (1982), 'The German Federal Employment Program for Regions with Special Employment Problems. An Evaluation', *Regional Science and Urban Economics*, 12, 99–119.

Schmid, G., B. Reissert and G. Bruche (1992), *Unemployment Insurance and Active Labor Market Policy*, Detroit: Wayne State University Press.

Schmid, G. and K. Schömann (1994), 'Institutional Choice and Flexible Coordination: A Socioeconomic Evaluation of Labor Market Policy in Europe', in G. Schmid (ed.), *Labor Market Institutions in Europe. A Socioeconomic Evaluation of Performance*, Armonk/New York: Sharpe, pp. 9–58.

Wholey, J. S., H. P. Hatry and K. E. Newcomer (eds) (1994), *Handbook of Practical Program Evaluation*, San Francisco: Jossey-Bass Publishers.

Williamson, O. E. (1985), *The Economic Institutions of Capitalism. Firms, Markets, Relational Contracting*, New York/London: The Free Press-Collier/Macmillan.

PART II

Evaluating Labour Market Policies in Selected Target Areas

8. Unemployment Compensation and Labour Market Transitions

Günther Schmid and Bernd Reissert[1]

Unemployment compensation affects labour market transitions in many ways. In providing protection against the interruption of earnings due to unemployment, it also has an impact on incentives to work and to hire or to fire. In other words, the realization of its primary goal, that of protection or efficiency, can have negative secondary effects or side-effects on the functioning of labour markets because of adverse selection and moral hazard.

Adverse selection arises when those who are most likely to purchase unemployment insurance are those who are most at risk. In a private market arrangement this circumstance would lead to underinsurance because those most at risk could not afford the high premiums necessary to compensate their income loss. This market failure is the main reason for public unemployment insurance programmes that minimize adverse selection substantially by having compulsory coverage. Moral hazard arises when those who are insured alter their behaviour in a manner that makes it more likely that they will receive a benefit. Under an unemployment insurance regime, workers may voluntarily quit their jobs more often than without unemployment insurance, or they may stay longer in unemployment because unemployment insurance increases their 'reservation wage'. Employers may hire and fire more often because their 'social obligation' has been externalized to the unemployment insurance system.

With rising and persistent unemployment in the 1980s, the opinion became widespread that the negative side-effects of public unemployment compensation regimes became unbearable and even one of the main culprits for mass unemployment in Europe. On the surface, in fact, the 1994 share of long-term unemployed in the EU's 12 Member States was 48.1 per cent compared to only 12.2 per cent in the United States and 17.5 per cent in Japan (OECD, 1995). This alleged relation between long-term joblessness and unemployment compensation is highly contested. Evaluating the incentives of unemployment

---

1 The authors thank Holger Schütz and Sylvia Zühlke for computing assistance and information collection, and Eurostat in Luxembourg for providing the ELFS (European Labour Force Survey) data. Comments by Lutz Bellmann, Anders Björklund and Håkan Regnér on the first draft are gratefully acknowledged.

compensation schemes, therefore, needs careful scrutiny in order to guide the respective institutional reforms so hotly debated these days.

The aim of evaluating unemployment compensation systems is, then, to identify institutional arrangements that maximize the goal of protection—subject to the constraints of minimizing adverse selection and moral hazard and of bringing about more fluid 'transitional labour markets' (Schmid, 1995). Further evaluation criteria are equity objectives related to the distributional impact that unemployment compensation has on the income of individuals, firms and regions. Because adverse selection, moral hazard and equity concerns make the public provision of unemployment compensation costly to society, the question of institutional incentives to finance work instead of unemployment is another focus for targeted evaluation of unemployment compensation.

In this chapter we identify the basic types of unemployment compensation schemes currently operating in the European Union (EU), Japan and the United States (section 1). It provides evidence of the effects that unemployment compensation regulations have on beneficiary rates (section 2) and on income replacement according to various types of households and various durations of unemployment (section 3). The gross costs of unemployment compensation are measured (section 4), and the literature evaluating the incentive of unemployment compensation for employers, employees, unemployed and the inactive labour force is critically reviewed and summarized through a transition model (section 5). We then turn to the institutional incentives for transferring funds from 'passive' income replacement into payments for 'active' job or training promotion (section 6) and, lastly, address future tasks for evaluation research and prospects for reforms of unemployment compensation (section 7).[2]

1   INSURANCE SCHEMES VERSUS ASSISTANCE SCHEMES

There are two basic principles governing unemployment compensation: the insurance principle and the welfare principle. In the former, support is determined by insurance contributions paid prior to unemployment and by previous earnings (unemployment insurance). In the latter, the unemployed are provided with a guaranteed minimum level of income (unemployment assistance).

---

2 For a comprehensive review of literature covering the 1970s and 1980s, see Atkinson and Micklewright (1991) and Atkinson and Mogensen (1993). A very informative complement to this background is chap. 7 ('Unemployment Benefit Rules and Labour Market Policy') of OECD (1991) and chap. 8 ('Unemployment and Related Welfare Benefits') of the *OECD Jobs Study* (1994). For German readers the survey by Stobernack (1991) is useful. An excellent analysis of the Swedish system has been provided by Björklund and Holmlund (1991).

- Typically, the benefits offered by an unemployment insurance scheme are financed by wage-linked insurance contributions paid by employers and/or employees. They are available only to those who, during a previous period of paid employment, have paid insurance contributions. The duration of benefit entitlement is limited and depends on the length of previous employment. The benefit level is linked to previous earnings and, in some cases, to the duration of previous employment. Individual need criteria have no influence on benefit entitlement.
- Unemployment assistance benefits, on the other hand, are usually independent of previous earnings and contribution payments. They are means-tested and financed from general taxation. The level of benefit is oriented to need criteria and is lower than that provided by an unemployment insurance scheme. The duration of benefit is usually unlimited.

In most OECD countries, unemployment compensation systems consist of two layers of benefits. The first, paid during an initial period of unemployment, usually follows the principles of unemployment insurance. The second, paid if the spell of unemployment lasts longer, usually follows the welfare principles of unemployment assistance. In practice, however, the two types of schemes are not always clear-cut. The German unemployment assistance scheme (*Arbeitslosenhilfe*), for instance, is a needs-related benefit, but one whose level depends on previous earnings. The entitlement to British unemployment benefits, on the other hand, depends on payment of insurance contributions, but the benefit level is not linked to previous earnings. Countries also differ widely with respect to whether unemployment assistance is a separate benefit or is integrated into a scheme of guaranteed minimum income (social assistance, income support), which is available to all those in need, irrespective of whether, as registered unemployed, they are available for paid employment or not. On this basis three types of national support systems can be distinguished in the countries under consideration in this chapter:

1. unemployment insurance only: in Italy, Japan, the United States and Greece;
2. unemployment insurance and unemployment assistance: in Germany, Spain, France, Ireland, Sweden, Austria, Finland and Portugal;
3. unemployment insurance and guaranteed minimum income (social assistance): in Belgium, Denmark, Luxembourg, the Netherlands and the United Kingdom.[3]

---

3 A number of countries with an unemployment insurance and an unemployment assistance system also provide those not, or not adequately, covered by either of the two systems with a minimum income in the form of social assistance.

Unemployment insurance schemes operate in all the countries examined. The ideal-type characteristics mentioned above are, however, not always clearly visible in the national systems. As Table 8.1 shows, the regulation of unemployment insurance in the ten major EU countries, Japan and the United States is very complicated, diverse and often inconsistent.[4] As regards the mode of financing, the schemes in Germany, Spain, France, Japan and the United States appear to come closest to the ideal-type insurance principles. In these countries benefits are almost entirely financed from wage-related contributions. In the United States these contributions are even risk-related ('experience-rated'). The way in which the burden of contributions is divided between employers and employees varies greatly between these countries. The fact, however, that indirect wage costs can be shifted to prices or wages means that such differences are of relatively minor importance. In the other countries the financing of the unemployment insurance scheme deviates from the pure insurance principle in three ways.

1. Substantial and permanent subsidies are provided by the general government budget to the insurance fund (Belgium, Denmark, Italy, the Netherlands and Sweden).
2. A single contribution subsuming the funds destined for the unemployment insurance scheme is paid to the social-insurance system as a whole (Ireland and the United Kingdom).
3. Contributions are flat-rate rather than wage-related (Denmark and Sweden).

In all selected national systems, entitlement to benefits under the unemployment insurance scheme is conditional on a minimum period of insured employment. This period ranges from 6 months in France and the United States to 12 months in the majority of countries. Since the mid-1970s, countries with strong insurance principles (Germany, France, Spain and the United States, in particular) have reacted to the increase in long-term unemployment and the widening deficits in the unemployment insurance funds by raising the minimum period of employment and/or linking the duration of benefit entitlement more closely to the length of previous employment. In most countries the maximum duration of benefit entitlement now varies according to the length of previous employment (in some cases also with the age of the person affected); this duration can reach five years for older workers (e.g. in France) and is virtually unlimited in Belgium. In a number of countries (mostly those with

---

4 For data predating those in Table 8.1, see Reissert (1993, pp. 20–21) and Schmid (1994, pp. 86–91). For the regulation of unemployment compensation in some of the smaller EU Member States that are not represented here, see these sources.

Table 8.1   *The Regulation of Unemployment Insurance and Assistance in Europe, Japan and the United States, 1994*

	Belgium	Denmark	Germany	Spain
	Unemployment Insurance (UI)			
1. Title of benefit	'Allocation de chômage'	'Arbejdsløsheds-forsikring'	'Arbeitslosengeld' (Alg)	'Prestación por desempleo, nivel contributivo'
2. Financing	Contributions by employers (1.41%) and employees (0.87%); state subsidies cover a substantial part of expenditure	Fixed flat-rate membership contributions to recognized UI funds, employers' contributions, state subsidies cover about 80% of expenditure	Employers' (3.25%) and employees' (3.25%) contributions, state subsidies cover deficit	Employers' (6.2%) and employees' (1.6%) contributions
3. Qualifying conditions	Varies according to age from 12 months in insured employment during the past 18 months to 24 months during the past 36 months	Membership contributions of at least 12 months and employment of at least 26 weeks within the past 3 years	At least 12 months contributory employment during the past 3 years	12 months contributory employment in past 6 years
4. Waiting period	None	None	None, except if job voluntarily quit (12 weeks)	None, except if job voluntarily quit (6 months)
5. Rates of benefits (initial)	60% of gross wage (55% for cohabitants without dependants); taxable	90% of gross wage; ceiling of DKR 2545 per week; taxable	67% of net wage (60% for recipients without children); ceiling DM 7600 gross wage per month (West), DM 5900 (East)	70%; ceiling 170% of statutory minimum wage (220% for recipients with children); nontaxable
6. Duration and dynamics of benefits	Indefinite but degressive; benefit suspendable if duration doubles the regional average	2½ years	6 to 32 months depending on insured employment and age	4 to 24 months depending on insured employment; digressive (60% after 6 months)
7. Alternatives to regular unemployment compensation	Short-time working compensation; partial unemployment allowance	Compensation for involuntary part-time unemployment and layoff periods	Short-time allowance; promotion of winter production; bad weather allowance	Short-time working; early retirement
	Unemployment Assistance (UA) / Guaranteed Minimum Income (GMI)			
8. Title of benefit	No separate UA; GMI scheme: 'Minimex'	No separate UA; GMI scheme: 'Social Bistand'	UA: 'Arbeitslosenhilfe' (Alhi); 'Sozialhilfe' (GMI)	'Subsidio por desempleo' (UA); various regional social assistance schemes
9. Qualifying conditions for UA	—	—	Registered as unemployed but (a) not qualified for Alg or (b) has exhausted Alg; in case (a) at least 150 days insured employment in preceding year	Registered as unemployed but (a) not qualified for insurance benefits or (b) has exhausted those benefits; in case (a) at least 3 months insured employment
10. Size and duration of UA	—	—	57% of net earnings, 53% for recipients without children; means-tested; unlimited	75% of current minimum wage; means-tested; only for persons with dependants or over 45; 3 to 21 months (for unemployed > 52 until retirement age)

Table 8.1—continued The Regulation of Unemployment Insurance and Assistance in Europe, Japan and the United States, 1994

	France	Ireland	Italy	Japan
Unemployment Insurance (UI)				
1. Title of benefit	'Allocation de base' (AB); 'Allocation de fin de droits' (AFD)	'Unemployment Benefit' (UB) and 'Pay-related Benefit' (PRB)	'Trattamento ordinario di disoccupazione'	'Unemployment Benefit' (UB)
2. Financing	Employers' (4.18%) and employees' (2.42% to 2.97%) contributions	Employers' and employees' contributions included in overall social insurance contributions	Employers' contributions (4.41% industry, 1.61% commerce) and employees' contributions (0.30%); state subsidies	Employers' (0.55%) and employees' (0.55%) contributions; 25% of job seekers' benefit covered by state extra fund for 'employment stabilization' financed by employers' contributions only
3. Qualifying conditions	Depending on age; minimum for AB and AFD at least 6 months insured employment	At least 39 weeks contributions	Insured employment of at least 2 years, 1 year in 2 years preceding unemployment	At least 6 months contributions within a year preceding unemployment
4. Waiting period	Depends on the number of holidays not yet taken	UB: 3 days; PRB: 3 weeks; 6 weeks if unemployment voluntary or through misconduct	7 days; 30 days if unemployment voluntary or due to misconduct	None; 3 months if job voluntarily quit
5. Rates of benefits (initial)	AB: 40% + lump sum (FF 55.29/day); AFD: flat rate (FF 85.25/day); taxable	Flat rate (UB: IR£ 61/week) + 12% (PRB) of weekly earnings between IR£ 97.50 and IR£ 220; nontaxable	30% of last salary	60% of base wage (up to 80% for low wage earners); exclusion of bonus and overtime earnings
6. Duration and dynamics of benefits	4 to 60 months, depending on age and insured employment; digressive	UB: up to 390 days; PRB: up to 375 days (6 days per week)	180 days	Depending on age and length of contributions; min. 90 days; max. 300 days for elderly > 55
7. Alternatives to regular unemployment compensation	Short-time working; early retirement	—	Special unemployment benefit for redundant workers (80% up to 90 days); Wage Compensation Fund (CIG) for short-time work	Wage subsidies for employment stabilization and training in cyclical downturns
Unemployment Assistance (UA) / Guaranteed Minimum Income (GMI)				
8. Title of benefit	UA: 'Allocation de Solidarité Spécifique' (ASS); 'Allocation d'Insertion' (AI); 'Revenue Minimum d'Insertion' (RMI = GMI)	'Unemployment Assistance' (UA); GMI scheme: Supplementary Welfare Allowance	No general UA; 'Sussidio straordinario' (SS) in some regions; regional GMI schemes	No separate UA
9. Qualifying conditions for UA	ASS: unemployed but not qualified for or has exhausted AB/AFD; AI is for young people looking for first job, single mothers, ex-convicts etc.	Unemployed who do not qualify or have exhausted their right to UB	—	UB extendable in special cases (high regional unemployment, personal hardship)
10. Size and duration of UA	ASS: FF 74.01/day; AI: FF 43.70/day; means-tested; ASS unlimited; AI one year max.	Up to IR£ 61 per week depending on needs, durations of unemployment etc.; unlimited	—	—

Table 8.1—continued The Regulation of Unemployment Insurance and Assistance in Europe, Japan and the United States, 1994

	Netherlands	Sweden	United Kingdom	United States
	Unemployment Insurance (UI)			
1. Title of benefit	'Werkloosheids Uitkering' (WW)	'Arbetslöshetsersättning' (UB)	'Unemployment Benefit' (UB)	'Unemployment Benefit' (UB)
2. Financing	Employers' (2.3%) and employees' (0.9%) contributions; variation according to industry	Small lump-sum contributions to 45 trade union unemployment insurance funds; heavy state subsidies (>90%), 65% of which are refinanced from a special payroll tax	Progressive employers' and employees' contributions to National Insurance Fund	Employers' contributions; experience rated; varies from state to state; federal state contributions to cover administrative costs, employment services, and 50% of extended benefits
3. Qualifying conditions	At least 26 weeks employment during 12 months preceding unemployment	12 months of contributions, of which 5 months in the year previous to unemployment	Within the last 2 years contributions of at least 50 times the lower weekly earnings limit	Minimum earnings or 14 to 20 weeks employment in the year before; varies by state
4. Waiting period	None	5 days until 1988; abolished in 1989; reintroduced in 1994	3 days; up to 6 months if unemployment voluntary or due to misconduct	1 week in most states
5. Rates of benefits (initial)	70% of gross wage; taxable	80% (90% until 1992) of previous gross wage up to approx. medium-earnings level; taxable	Flat rate (UK£45.45 per week) and adult dependants' supplement; taxable	Varies by state; usually 50% of gross wage; low ceiling; taxable
6. Duration and dynamics of benefits	6 to 54 months depending on length of service and age; flat-rate extension for another year	Max. 60 weeks; persons over 55, 90 weeks	1 year	Max. 26 weeks in most states
7. Alternatives to regular unemployment compensation	Early retirement and disability pensions	Some form of short-time compensation ('permittering'); early retirement for labour market reasons	Redundancy payments; occupational pensions	Short-time compensation programmes present in 16 states; low take-up
	Unemployment Assistance (UA) / Guaranteed Minimum Income (GMI)			
8. Title of benefit	No separate UA; GMI scheme: 'Social Bijstand' ('Algemene Bijstandswet' (ABW), 'Rijksgroep-regeling Werkloze Werknemers' (RWW))	UA: 'Kontant Arbetsmarknadstöd' (KAS); GMI scheme: 'Socialbidrag'	No separate UA; GMI scheme: 'Income Support' (IS)	No separate UA; extended unemployment benefits (EB) under certain conditions
9. Qualifying conditions for UA	ABW, RWW: needy registered unemployed who do not qualify for or have exhausted their right to WW; scheme open to other persons in need	Paid to unemployed not eligible for UI; extension of UB for elderly	IS: registered unemployed who do not qualify for or have exhausted their right to UB; scheme open to other persons in need	EB: insured unemployment rate over 5% and 120% higher than the state rate for previous two years
10. Size and duration of UA	ABW, RWW: flat rates depending on age and status, e.g. HFL 1243 per month for singles living alone; means-tested; unlimited	Flat-rate benefit considerably lower than UB; max. 150 days (450 days for elderly); not means-tested	Flat rates depending on age and status, e.g. UK£198.03 per month for singles 25 years and over; means-tested; unlimited	EB an extension of UB for up to 13 weeks

Sources
Table 8.1 has been compiled from Hemmings, 1994; MISSOC, 1995; OECD, 1991, pp. 227–31, and national data.

low or short-term benefits, such as Italy, Ireland, the United Kingdom and the United States, but also in Sweden), benefit entitlement does not commence until after a waiting period of several days.

Where unemployment benefits are wage-related, the initial level of benefit (which is, however, often subject to ceilings) ranges from 30 to 50 per cent of the last gross wage (Italy, Ireland, Japan and the United States) and 70 to 90 per cent (the Netherlands, Sweden and Denmark). Only in Germany is the benefit rate related to net rather than gross earnings, and only in the United Kingdom are benefits flat-rate rather than related to wages. In some countries, including Belgium, Spain and France, the level of benefit is degressive, that is, benefit levels fall with increasing duration of unemployment, a response to the rise in long-term unemployment.

In a number of countries, there are important alternatives to unemployment compensation in operation. This is especially the case in Italy, where the general unemployment insurance system covers only a small share of the unemployed who have previously worked. In 1990, only an estimated 56 000 of the 468 000 unemployed with work experience received unemployment benefits, most of the remainder receiving payments from various special schemes. More importantly, the wage compensation fund (_Cassa Integrazione Guadagni_) guarantees a certain level of income to redundant workers who, however, remain formally employed. In Belgium and Germany (and to a lesser extent in France, Spain and in some US states), compensation for short-time working is a practical alternative to unemployment compensation. Without this scheme, the unemployment rate in Belgium during the 1980–82 recession would have been more than 2 percentage points higher than it was; in Germany, almost 1 percentage point higher (Vroman, 1992). Germany used this alternative most in the first phase of transforming the eastern German labour market after unification (see Mosley and Kruppe, chap. 20 in this volume). During cyclical downturns or in times of deep structural change, Japan enables employers to use wage subsidies for employment stabilization. Early retirement (especially in France and Germany), disability pensions (especially in the Netherlands) and redundancy payments (in the United Kingdom) are other alternatives to be mentioned (see Casey, chap. 12 in this volume).

Germany, France, Spain and Ireland have special unemployment assistance schemes, which provide, under certain conditions, needs-related support for unemployed persons who are not, or no longer, entitled to benefits from the unemployment insurance fund. In most other countries the only source of support for such unemployed persons is a general social assistance system, which guarantees a minimum level of income. In Sweden, unemployment assistance is not means-tested—in keeping with that country's tradition of universal income support. It is, however, quite low and has tended to exclude youth under 20 by instead providing a job guarantee (Björklund and Holmlund,

1991). With the exception of Spain and Sweden, unemployment assistance is paid for as long as the claimant has no other source of income and is available for employment. In Germany, Spain and Sweden, the unemployment assistance scheme is not open to all unemployed persons in need. It is restricted to those who were previously entitled to unemployment benefits or who had been employed for a short period of time. Unemployment assistance payments are usually flat-rate but are topped up according to age and family status. Germany is peculiar in her continued practice of relating unemployment assistance payments to previous or hypothetical wages or salaries, although at a lower level than is the case with unemployment benefits.

Taken together, the national systems of support for the unemployed (consisting of both unemployment insurance and unemployment or social assistance) are based to widely varying extents on the insurance or the welfare principle. Germany, France, Spain and, to a lesser extent, Japan and the United States seem to be the countries where unemployment compensation systems are most strictly governed by insurance principles, which establish a close link between previous employment, wages and paid contributions on the one hand and benefits on the other. The United Kingdom and, in part, Ireland and Sweden represent the opposite case, where this link is much weaker. Elements such as the financing of compensation payments from progressive (rather than proportional) contributions to a general social insurance fund or from the general state budget, the payment of flat-rate benefits and the differentiation of all benefits according to family status show that the British system is governed most by general welfare principles, which emphasize a minimum income guarantee, rather than insurance principles, which guarantee wage-related income (Clasen, 1994; Schmid, Reissert and Bruche, 1992, pp. 70–113).

The history of unemployment compensation regulations since the mid-1970s shows that there has been no convergence between systems governed by insurance principles and systems governed by welfare principles (Schmid et al., 1992, pp. 111–12). Under the pressure of rising unemployment and the increased financial burden on support schemes, the two types of systems have, indeed, further sharpened their respective profiles. Insurance systems of the sort in Germany, France and Spain have strengthened the link between insured employment and compensation payments, whereas the welfare-oriented British system weakened this link by abolishing an earnings-related supplement to the flat-rate benefit in 1981, introducing progressive insurance contributions in 1985, and gradually shifting the bulk of unemployment compensation payments from unemployment benefits to the general social assistance (income support) scheme.

2   BENEFICIARY RATES

The first goal for which unemployment compensation systems have to be evaluated is the extent to which employees receive a wage replacement if they become unemployed. An indicator for this primary efficiency goal is the beneficiary rate, that is, the share of the unemployed actually receiving benefits or assistance. Another indicator is the relative size of wage compensation—the replacement rate—which is the subject of the next paragraph. An interesting question is whether a tradeoff exists between these two goals. If unemployment insurance funds run a deficit, and if there are economic and political difficulties in increasing contributions or subsidies from the state budget, the policy response can either be to reduce benefits in relation to wages or to reduce the beneficiary rate through imposition of stricter qualifying conditions. Apart from changes in regulations, a reduction in the beneficiary rate can also result from changing labour market conditions, such as an increase in the number of long-term unemployed who have exhausted their benefit entitlement, or an increase of 'marginal labour' not meeting the qualifying criteria.

In practice, the total beneficiary rate varies markedly between the Member States of the European Union. According to the 1993 European Labour Force Survey (ELFS), the proportion of people claiming benefit among all those without at least one hour of paid employment per week but who are seeking work and are available for work ranges from 7 per cent in Greece to 87 per cent in Denmark (see Figure 8.1). These comparative data, however, need to be interpreted with caution because some of them deviate considerably from national data found in other publications, albeit publications partly based on other definitions.[5] Despite the methodological difficulties, differences in beneficiary rates between Member States remain substantial and require explanation.

At 47 per cent in 1993, France's beneficiary rate in particular is surprisingly low. This level may reflect the fact that the French unemployment insurance scheme is barely subsidized by the state budget and is thus more insurance-oriented than the schemes in Denmark and Belgium, for example, where the rates are approximately twice as high. Qualifying conditions for receiving benefits in those two countries are much less strict than in France,

---

5 For an excellent and detailed analysis of the great degree to which diverging definitions of unemployment can influence the beneficiary rate, see OECD (1994, Vol. 2, pp. 186–90). The ELFS applies the uniform ILO definition of unemployment—all those not in paid employment for at least one hour per week, but who are looking and available for work—which is very different from the definition used in a number of countries where registered unemployment is analysed. At the same time, it is possible that the ELFS underestimates the number of benefit recipients in some countries, say, because benefits are low or are so inadequately specified that survey respondents are not aware of receiving unemployment compensation.

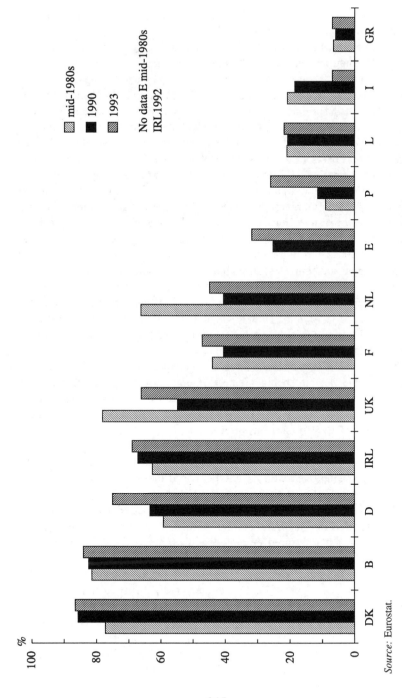

Source: Eurostat.

Figure 8.1 Share of Unemployed Receiving Unemployment Compensation in the EU (EU–12) in the Mid-1980s, 1990 and 1993

and the period for which benefits are payable is much longer (and even unlimited in the case of Belgium).

If changes in beneficiary rates since the mid-1980s are analysed, three groups of countries can be distinguished: countries with steadily increasing beneficiary rates (Denmark, Germany, Ireland, Spain and Portugal), countries with fluctuating beneficiary rates (the United Kingdom, France and the Netherlands) and countries with stable rates (Belgium, Luxembourg and Greece). Denmark is not only the country with the highest beneficiary rate but also the country in which the beneficiary rate rose most rapidly in the late 1980s. This reflects Denmark's success in reducing the relative number of long-term unemployed—who are likely to have exhausted their benefit entitlement—through active labour market measures. The large increase in the beneficiary rate in Germany is related to the reunification and the industrial restructuring of eastern Germany, which has led to a drastic increase of short-term unemployed core workers entitled to benefits. East German women in particular contributed to the increase in the beneficiary rate because of their much stronger attachment to the labour market compared to West German women.

In contrast, significant reductions in beneficiary rates occurred between the mid-1980s and 1990 in the United Kingdom (from 78 to 55 per cent) and the Netherlands (from 66 to 41 per cent), with a slight recovery in 1993. In the United Kingdom, the reduction was slightly stronger for women than for men. In the Netherlands, it was much larger for men than for women. In the United Kingdom, the decline, being greatest among short-term unemployed and young unemployed women, seems to have been caused by changes in the qualifying conditions. A major reform in 1987 reduced benefits to young unemployed if they refused an offer from the Youth Training Scheme or dropped out of the programme, and young people quitting jobs voluntarily had to wait longer before being eligible for benefits. Similarly, in the Netherlands, it is young unemployed who have experienced the biggest reduction in the beneficiary rate (from 69 to 42 per cent), also as a result of a major change in qualifying conditions. In 1987, the qualification period for continuing to receive benefits after the first six months of unemployment was extended to at least three years of insured employment within a period of five years, a requirement that rules out many young people.

Except for Belgium, women are less likely to receive unemployment benefits than men (see Figure 8.2). This circumstance is particularly the case in Ireland, the United Kingdom, the Netherlands and Spain, in which countries beneficiary rates for women are barely half those for men, but it is only slightly less true in Greece and Luxembourg. The first main reason for such a difference is that the relatively strict qualifying conditions of insurance schemes exclude more women, who are more likely to be only loosely attached to the labour market, than men. The second main reason is that means-tested unemployment assistance schemes tend, according to the traditional bread-winners model, to protect men better than women.

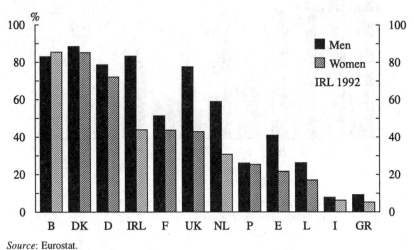

Source: Eurostat.

Figure 8.2 Share of Unemployed Men and Women Receiving
Unemployment Compensation in the EU, 1993

The strength of insurance principles in the unemployment compensation schemes of many Member States is also reflected in the age breakdown of beneficiaries (see Figure 8.3). In principle, the relation between unemployment protection and age is influenced by two offsetting factors. First, the older the person, the more likely he or she is to satisfy eligibility criteria. Second, the probability of being unemployed for a long period and thus exhausting entitlements to benefits tends also to increase with age. In some countries—Germany, France and Spain, where the insurance principle is especially pronounced—protection for older people was strengthened over the 1980s in response to persistent high unemployment by making the duration of benefits more dependent on age or on the duration of employment. In these countries, older people are now much better protected than younger people.

In other countries where the compensation scheme is based on insurance principles, though less strongly—Denmark, Portugal, the Netherlands, Italy and Greece—the same kind of relation between age and unemployment protection is apparent. In welfare-oriented systems, as in the United Kingdom and Ireland, where unemployment protection is largely designed to provide a min-

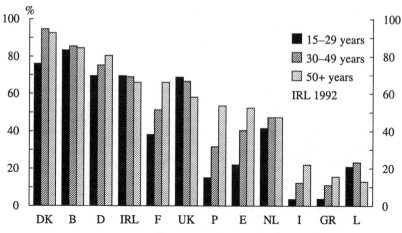

Source: Eurostat.

Figure 8.3   Share of Unemployed Receiving Unemployment Compensation by Age Group in the EU, 1993

imum level of income independent of previous earnings, there is no rationale for a policy of linking the duration of benefits to age or the length of previous employment. Beneficiary rates therefore do not increase with age in such systems. On the contrary, they even decrease slightly (see Figure 8.3). Just as older people tend to be better protected under insurance-based systems, the young are less well protected.[6] Insurance-based systems are, therefore, biased towards protecting core workers (mostly male and elderly) over marginal workers (mostly young, female and casual), whereas people tend to be more equally treated (with the exception of women who are not the main wage-earners) under welfare systems.

The degree to which beneficiary rates vary with the duration of unemployment reveals another interesting difference between insurance-based and welfare-oriented systems (see Figure 8.4). In Germany, France and Spain, where the systems are strongly insurance based, beneficiary rates of the long-term unemployed are lower than for those who have been out of work for 3 to 12 months. In the United Kingdom and Ireland, where the systems are largely welfare based, beneficiary rates tend to be equal or even higher for the

6 In France, for example, whereas 45 per cent of the unemployed were less than 30 years old in 1993, only 36 per cent of beneficiaries of unemployment compensation were also below that age. On the other hand, 10 per cent of the unemployed who were over 50 years of age accounted for 15 per cent of beneficiaries. In the United Kingdom (i.e. the welfare system), the corresponding figures are 45 to 47 per cent, and 18 to 16 per cent, respectively.

long-term unemployed than those unemployed for less than a year. This difference reflects the fact that insurance-based systems tend to exclude 'poor risks' (i.e. the long-term unemployed) from the receipt of benefits, whereas welfare systems tend to treat most of the unemployed equally, though only in the sense of guaranteeing a minimum level of income.[7] The absence of any particular exclusion of the long-term unemployed also characterizes other unemployment compensation systems that have only weak insurance principles and that are financed largely from the general government budget rather than from insurance contributions, as in Denmark, the Netherlands and Sweden.

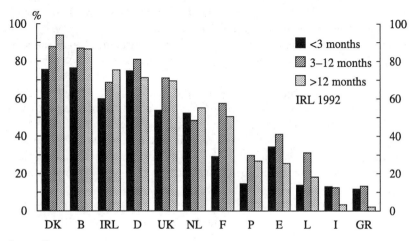

Source: Eurostat.

Figure 8.4 Share of Unemployed Receiving Unemployment Compensation by Duration of Unemployment in the EU, 1993

3   WAGE-REPLACEMENT RATES

The difference between insurance-based and welfare-based systems is also reflected in wage-replacement rates. In this section, we illustrate the variation in replacement rates by taking someone of prime age who becomes unemployed after holding a full-time job for the previous ten years, and comparing

---

7 This tendency of welfare systems, however, is distorted in the observed beneficiary rates because of early retirement or active labour market policy schemes. In these schemes, people who have exhausted their benefit entitlement are removed from the unemployment count, an arrangement that, *ceteris paribus*, thus increases the beneficiary rate.

cross-national differences in the percentage of the previous wage that a person receives.

It is assumed that the person concerned is 40 years old, either single or married, but without children, and was previously working at the average wage in the country concerned. Although such a hypothetical person is not necessarily representative of the unemployed, given their wide variety of personal characteristics, it is much more difficult to compile details for others, such as young people, older workers, those with no previous employment record, part-timers and so on. Gross wage-replacement rates—the ratio of pretax benefits to average gross wages—are calculated for the hypothetical person in each country on the assumption that (a) the person is single, (b) he or she is married with a spouse in full-time work and (c) the spouse is not in work but dependent on the unemployed person. In each case, benefits comprise all forms of compensation that apply (unemployment insurance benefits, unemployment assistance and guaranteed minimum income transfers) at the rates prevailing in 1991.[8]

In those countries most closely approximating to the welfare principle—the United Kingdom and Ireland—the *initial* level of benefit (compared with previous earned income) is among the lowest, and the level of benefit is dependent on family status from the onset of unemployment (see Table 8.2). This is in accordance with the welfare principle, which aims at providing a minimum level of income according to need rather than being related to previous earnings.

In most of the other countries the initial wage-replacement rate is significantly higher (ranging from 43 to 83 per cent) and is usually independent of family status. This reflects the fact that unemployment insurance in most countries ensures a wage-related income independent of family status and other criteria of need, at least for an initial phase of unemployment. It is interesting to note that the actual wage-replacement rate in a number of countries—Belgium, Denmark, Spain and Sweden—is significantly below the benefit rate set out in the unemployment insurance provisions (see Table 8.1). This fact is due to ceilings on the absolute level of benefits that can be claimed.

---

8 Our calculations are based on OECD data (Hemmings, 1994; OECD, 1994, pp. 171–223), with some adjustments being made where errors in these data were discovered. Italy and Luxembourg were excluded for the lack of comparable data. For Germany, where unemployment compensation payments are officially calculated in relation to net wages, the ratio of benefits (plus a fictitious income-tax payment) to gross wages was estimated so as to ensure comparability with the other countries. In order to assess the replacement of disposable income, net replacement rates measuring the ratio of aftertax benefits to net earnings would have been clearly preferable to gross replacement rates (Schmid et al., 1992, pp. 122–37). The necessary modelling of tax effects, however, proved to be too difficult. For a presentation of net replacement rates for OECD countries, though not differentiated according to personal characteristics of the unemployed, see OECD (1994, pp. 225–7).

Table 8.2   *Gross Wage-replacement Rates of Unemployment Compensation, 1991*

	Unemployment Compensation as a Percentage of Previous Earnings							
	At the beginning of unemployment spell				After 2 years in unemployment			
	All recipients	Single recipients	Married recipients with working spouse	Married recipients with dependent spouse	All recipients	Single recipients	Married recipients with working spouse	Married recipients with dependent spouse
S	83				22			
NL	70					34	34	39
E	66					0	0	25
P	65					30	0	34
DK	61				61			
GR		50	50	60	0			
SF	58					24	0	24
F	57				23			
J	49				0			
D	45					40	0	40
B		43	39	43		30	25	43
A	43					39	0	42
IRL		25	25	36		20	0	30
USA	34					4	0	8
UK		15	15	25		14	0	22

Sources
The OECD Jobs Study (Part 2, pp. 171–223) by OECD, 1994, Paris: OECD Publications; 'Benefit Entitlement and Replacement Ratio Data for the OECD Countries' by P. Hemmings, 1994, Paris: OECD (unpublished manuscript); national data; and own calculations.

As the individual spell of unemployment increases, the wage-replacement rate in most countries declines and becomes increasingly dependent on marital and family circumstances. The determining factor in this regard is that, after a given period, the unemployed exhaust their entitlement to benefits under the insurance scheme, meaning that claimants have to fall back on unemployment assistance or a guaranteed minimum income unless another source of income is at hand. After two years in unemployment, a married person whose spouse is employed is usually no longer entitled to any compensation at all, for their household income is above the minimum level. A single person or a married person with a dependent spouse, on the other hand, usually continues to be eligible for compensation for a long or even indefinite time, though at a lower level than at the beginning of the unemployment spell. In this case, rates also are usually lower for single than for married people with dependants.

Some countries, however, diverge from this general pattern as far as long-term unemployment is concerned. In Denmark, Belgium, France and the Netherlands, for example, a married person with a working spouse is still eligible for compensation after having been unemployed for two years. In Denmark, Belgium and Austria, the compensation level for married persons with a dependent spouse after two years of unemployment is still the same as at the beginning of the unemployment spell. In Japan and Greece, on the other hand, no compensation is available for the long-term unemployed. The same is true for the United States (with the exception of food stamps provided to persons in need) and for single persons in Spain.

Apart from the last four countries mentioned, the most obvious case of divergence from the general pattern of protection from long-term unemployment is the United Kingdom. Here, single and married people with dependants continue to receive compensation at the same low level as the initial insurance benefit, reflecting the emphasis that the welfare-based system places on providing a minimum level of income according to need irrespective of how long a person has been unemployed.

4   THE DIRECT COSTS OF BENEFIT SYSTEMS[9]

The intercountry differences in beneficiary and wage-replacement rates, described above, are reflected in the levels of public expenditure on unemployment compensation. Some countries spend significantly more than others on each unemployed person and vice versa. Denmark, the Netherlands and Belgium, for example, spend considerably more on unemployment protection than countries with similar unemployment rates like France and the United Kingdom, whereas Italy, Greece and the United States spend considerably less. Thus, the total amount spent on compensation in relation to GDP varies only weakly with the rate of unemployment (see Figure 8.5).

---

9 The overall fiscal costs of unemployment may, of course, be three to four times higher than the direct costs of benefits if one takes into consideration the costs related to forgone taxes, contributions lost and the indirect costs related to decreasing productivity, increase of the discouraged workers and so forth (see e.g. Bellemare and Poulin, 1994; Schmid et al., 1992, pp. 137–42).

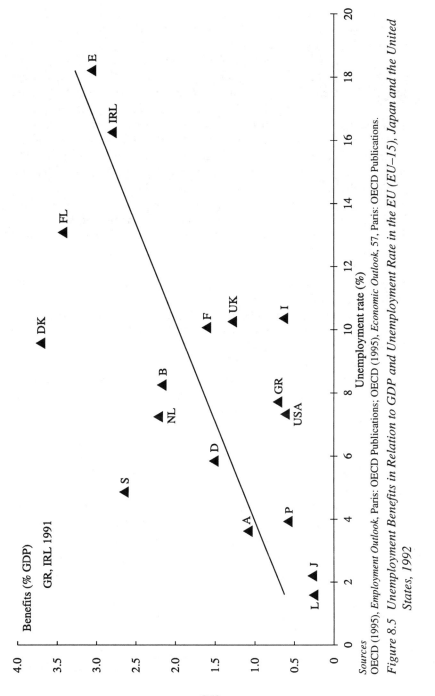

Sources
OECD (1995), *Employment Outlook*, Paris: OECD Publications; OECD (1995), *Economic Outlook*, 57, Paris: OECD Publications.

Figure 8.5 Unemployment Benefits in Relation to GDP and Unemployment Rate in the EU (EU–15), Japan and the United States, 1992

These differences are only to be expected in the light of the above description of system characteristics. Denmark and Sweden, for example, spend more than other OECD countries because of high beneficiary rates and generous wage-replacement rates.[10] Belgium pays unemployment benefits to an exceptionally high percentage of the unemployed for an indefinite period of time, and in the Netherlands wage-replacement rates are exceptionally high for the initial period of unemployment. In Greece and Italy, on the other hand, unemployment compensation schemes, as such, protect only a small share of the unemployed and, hence, their cost is low (though in Italy, at least, the burden of supporting the incomes of the unemployed falls on other items of the public budget). Lastly, the low spending by the United States is explained by both the short benefit period of 6 months and the low replacement rate compared to most European countries.

The level of expenditure on unemployment compensation does not appear to be related to whether systems are based on insurance principles or welfare principles. Expenditure per person unemployed in welfare-oriented systems like those in the United Kingdom and Ireland hardly differs from expenditure in insurance-based systems like those in France and Spain (see Figure 8.6). This finding reflects the main tradeoff between welfare-oriented and insurance-based systems: the former tend to provide low benefits for most claimants; the latter, high benefits for a limited number of core workers. Both can result in similar levels of public expenditure.

Another interesting difference between insurance-based and welfare-oriented systems emerges when one compares the changes that occurred in unemployment rates and expenditure on compensation between the mid-1980s and 1993. In most countries, expenditure related to GDP varied with the fall of unemployment in the late 1980s and the renewed increase in the early 1990s. In most cases, however, expenditure on each unemployed person increased relative to GDP (see Figure 8.6).[11] The significant exceptions are Ireland and the United Kingdom, where payments to the unemployed, adjusted for the dynamic of unemployment, declined significantly.

Because the United Kingdom and Ireland are the two countries where the compensation system is most strongly based on welfare principles, the evidence suggests that such systems are more prone than insurance-based systems are to reductions in unemployment compensation. This implication is

---

10 It is unclear how the OECD allocates unemployment benefits used for training or job creation measures in its statistical categories. The hunch, especially in Denmark, is that some expenditures allocated under unemployment compensation are in fact used to finance subsistence allowances for persons in active measures.

11 This increase was especially pronounced in Sweden and led the government to reduce the initial rate of benefit from 90 to 80 per cent (1993) and to 70 per cent (1994).

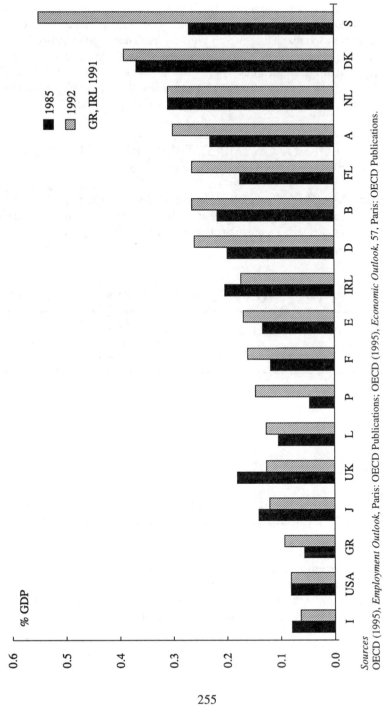

Sources
OECD (1995), *Employment Outlook*, Paris: OECD Publications; OECD (1995), *Economic Outlook*, 57, Paris: OECD Publications.

Figure 8.6 Unemployment Benefits per 1% Unemployment in the EU (EU–15), Japan and the United States, 1985 and 1992

not surprising because the strong link between contributions and benefits provides a sort of property right for insurance benefits that makes those benefits less prone to cuts than welfare payments are. Thus, welfare-related systems are less effective than insurance-oriented systems when it comes to the primary goal of insuring earnings during unemployment. But what about the possible secondary or side-effects? This question is the subject of the following section.

5   EFFECTS OF UNEMPLOYMENT BENEFITS ON LABOUR MARKET TRANSITIONS

The incentive effects of unemployment-compensation regimes (and, hence, their impact on the functioning of labour markets) can best be examined with a model of labour market transition. Flows in 16 possible directions can be distinguished (Table 8.3).

Table 8.3   Labour Market Flows Affected by Unemployment Compensation

From \ To	Employment	Unemployment	Labour market measure	Inactivity
Employment	1	2	3	4
Unemployment	5	6	7	8
Labour market measure	9	10	11	12
Inactivity	13	14	15	16

Unemployment insurance mainly affects flows 2 and 5, that is, flows of people moving from employment to unemployment and out of unemployment into a job. Of growing importance, but largely neglected so far, is the impact of unemployment insurance on the flows from unemployment to labour market measures (7) and from labour market measures to employment (9). Policy on compensation, however, may also indirectly affect the other possible flows, an eventuality considered below. These effects are stylized and will differ in detail according to the institutional arrangements in force in the selected countries.[12]

(1) Moves from one employment to another, or job mobility, may be encouraged by unemployment insurance in so far as they involve a greater risk of unemployment. This condition may apply, in particular, to moves from large to small firms, from permanent to fixed-term contracts of employment, or from the public sector to the private sector (the last-named move being relevant in recent proposals that civil servants contribute to funding unemployment insurance schemes). Unfortunately, there is no empirical evidence on how important these effects could be in practice. In theory, however, any support of functional mobility would indirectly prevent unemployment without entailing any serious negative side-effects. Aiming unemployment insurance at temporary part-time employment, which means supporting transitions from full-time to part-time employment and vice versa, would also increase options that endorse employment intensive growth and thus prevent unemployment. This approach would provide incentives for young parents raising children (for both men and women!) to stay in the labour market as well as for elderly employed persons to shift slowly instead of abruptly into the state of inactivity.

(2) Unemployment benefits may affect the flow from employment to unemployment in several ways. From the workers' point of view, unemployment insurance subsidizes the costs of searching for employment. It makes it easier for people to quit their jobs and spend time finding alternative, possibly more suitable work. Search theory in which an anticyclical rise and decline of voluntary quits is expected has not been confirmed by empirical research. On the contrary, voluntary quits increase at times of economic growth—when there are more jobs available—and decline during recession (Rothschild, 1988, p. 33). One reason for this fact is that voluntary quitting entails the risk of disqualification from unemployment benefits at least for a time (see Table 8.1).

Theory also suggests and empirical evidence shows that the probability of voluntarily leaving a job increases with the qualification for unemployment

---

12 The methodology has been adopted from Clark and Summers (1982) but has been extended by labour market measures and modified in terms of arguments. Four of these flows, the diagonals 1, 6, 11 and 16, have a special feature. Semantically, there are, of course, no self-referential flows. Unemployment insurance, however, can affect flows between different employment positions (e.g. between or within sectors and firms, flows known as mobility or labour or job turnover); flows from one labour market measure to another; and certain flows between various kinds of labour market inactivity (especially between housework and the informal economy). Flows from unemployment to unemployment are considered in the present context as factors that make unemployment self-perpetuating.

benefits, and it increases again with the qualification for the maximum duration of benefits if there is variability in this respect (Green and Riddell, 1994). This effect, however, seems to be very small for nonseasonal jobs, although little evidence is available. This possible effect raises the question of designing an optimal entrance requirement to unemployment insurance. Waiting periods (during which no benefits are paid) are one measure taken to solve this problem. There is, however, little evidence to suggest generally that a waiting period is an effective means of preventing abuse of the unemployment insurance system, that is, preventing voluntary unemployment. The argument has to be qualified in the case of elderly employed persons, who, as soon they have reached the maximum benefit qualification, may use (or abuse) unemployment insurance benefits for a long transition to inactivity. In this case, where the argument of mobility or job search productivity cannot be maintained, it seems justified to shift more of the burden of adjustment to the individuals. In general, then, a balance has to be kept between excessively high costs, which discourage voluntary mobility, and excessively low costs, which encourage ineffective job search or even abuse of the unemployment insurance system.[13]

Even more dubious is the explicit instrumentalization of unemployment insurance for early retirement. Several European countries have taken this method of tackling structural change. The strategy is to exchange elderly employed persons for young people by having the unemployment insurance scheme subsidize an intermittent period of unemployment for the former group (Casey, chap. 12 in this volume; Kohli, Rein and Guillemard, 1991). It is not only an expensive way to prevent long-term unemployment but also an inefficient one, for it excludes potential productive resources. Flexible retirement schemes (such as part-time retirement) subsidized by unemployment insurance, as mentioned above, would be much more preferable from both a social and economic point of view.

Turning to the employer's side, unemployment insurance makes it easier to dismiss workers because the people affected will tend to demand less compensation for losing jobs and because employers will tend to have less a feeling of responsibility for depriving them of their livelihood. Other things being equal, employers may, therefore, be more inclined to adopt methods of production that increase the risk of redundancy. This incentive is reduced when employers' contributions to unemployment insurance are risk-related, that is, if contributions increase with the number of layoffs or dismissals. There has been

---

13 In 1995 Germany introduced the rule that, in addition to the existing rule of suspending benefits for 12 weeks (*Sperrzeit*), the benefit duration is reduced by at least one-quarter of the entitlement period if employed persons older than 54 years (elderly workers) leave their jobs without good cause. Because these target groups have usually reached the maximum of 32 months of benefit entitlement, this new rule effectively reduces their benefit entitlement by 8 months.

a recommendation to introduce experience-rating for jobs highly sensitive to variable entrance requirements, which means low-wage seasonal jobs. The effectiveness of experience-rating for nonseasonal jobs is highly contested. A study, for instance, comparing firms under a regime of experience-rating (the United States) and firms under a regime of no experience-rating (Canada) found no evidence that the latter type of regime entailed increased layoffs or reduced training (Bechterman and Leckie, 1994).

Experience-rated unemployment insurance systems do not exist in the EU Member States, although such schemes have often been recommended. In fact, nonexperience-rated unemployment insurance systems heavily subsidize seasonal industries such as construction, hotels and catering.[14] Because any economy needs such types of jobs, it is a matter of political discretion to decide the extent to which this type of labour market flexibility should be indirectly subsidized in this manner. Abuse of such systems can easily be counteracted by administrative rules, such as a differentiated extension of the period to qualify for benefits. In summary, apart from temporary layoffs (which are fairly widespread in the United States and possibly Denmark), there is no evidence that unemployment benefits have a strong impact on flows from employment to unemployment (Atkinson and Micklewright, 1991, p. 1715).

(3) The case in which unemployment insurance provides incentives for transitions from employment into labour market measures is still rare, but it seems to be gaining importance. Its almost complete neglect in the literature is therefore not justified. A few countries (such as Belgium, Germany and Japan) have a long tradition of short-time work during recessions in which the unemployment insurance system pays prorated wage replacements. This programme is increasingly being adopted by other countries, or there are functional equivalents in the form of part-time unemployment benefits, as in France and the Netherlands (see Mosley and Kruppe, chap. 20 in this volume).

(4) In cases where elderly people out of work are no longer required to register as unemployed, they are no longer included in the unemployment count and no longer considered to be unemployed even though they might receive insurance benefits. In such cases, the flow from employment into inactivity will tend to be increased by unemployment insurance. On the other hand, the entitlement effect (Hamermesh, 1977)—the incentive for employees to remain in

---

14 An exceptional study in Canada found that experience-rating turns unemployment insurance contributions from a 'tax on jobs' into a 'tax on unemployment'. Under nonexperience-rated systems, there is a high redistribution in favour of primary and construction industry, but high intraindustry redistribution can be observed as well. Thus, industry-related experience-rating will also be resisted to some extent. Furthermore, only a small fraction of firms are net receivers (Corak and Pyper, 1994).

the labour force in order to become entitled to benefits—will tend to reduce the movement from employment to inactivity. Which of these two opposing effects is stronger remains an empirical question. In theory, long waiting periods in Germany (as for instance) will stabilize employment. Preventing unemployment in this way, however, has to be complemented by internal flexibility measures (training or short-time work compensation) in order to avoid negative side-effects.

(5) According to conventional economic theory, generous wage-replacement benefits reduce the probability that a person will move from unemployment into employment (Johnson and Layard, 1986). The longer the period over which the unemployed are entitled to claim benefit, the stronger the effect is. It becomes weaker, however, as the end of the benefit period approaches or as the rate of benefit declines. For people who are uninsured and out of work, the opposite effect is likely. That is, the existence of insurance schemes increases the incentive for them to find employment as quickly as possible in order to become eligible for benefits (Mortensen, 1977). To some degree, the insured and the uninsured may be in competition for jobs. Such competition tends to increase as vacancies become scarcer and as expected benefits become more generous. In addition, if active job search requires financial resources, then generous unemployment compensation would increase the resources devoted to systematic search and, hence, would increase the probability of return to work (Atkinson and Micklewright, 1991, p. 1700). This effect potentially offsets the negative effects of generous benefits on the incentive for the insured to look for work, and this tradeoff might explain why a great deal of empirical research into this issue has either produced contradictory results or found only a weak relation between unemployment insurance and the duration of individual spells of unemployment.[15]

The textbook relation between unemployment insurance benefits and moral hazard is upset by other factors as well, one example being the existence of labour market measures such as an effective placement service offering jobs and thereby testing the availability of work (see also the paragraph 7, below). And even where robust results are claimed, the effects are rather small. For instance, Meyer (1990, p. 780) reports that his results are towards the high end of the distribution of recent estimates: a 10 percentage-point rise in the replacement rate would be associated with an increase of about one and a half

---

15 For recent surveys, see Atkinson and Micklewright (1991, pp. 1710–15), Schmid et al. (1992, pp. 154–9) and Stobernack (1991). Layard, Nickell and Jackman (1991) come to the following conclusion: 'The basic result is that the elasticity of expected duration with respect to benefits is generally in the range 0.2–0.9, depending on the state of the labour market and the country concerned, although estimates as low as 0 ... and as high as 3.3 ... may be found' (p. 255).

weeks in duration. A study in Sweden found that the exit rate to employment had an elasticitiy of -0.06 with respect to the benefit level and that the mean duration of unemployment was only four weeks longer for recipients of unemployment insurance than for nonrecipients (Carling, Edin, Harkman and Holmlund, 1994, p. 19). Most studies do not specify the status of employment after a spell of unemployment. Evidence from a French study, however, suggests that a variable indicating receipt of unemployment benefits had a highly significant negative association with transitions to precarious employment but that the effect was less significant (men) or insignificant (women) for regular jobs (Atkinson and Micklewright, 1991, p. 1714).

In theory, at least, much speaks for generous unemployment insurance benefits in the short run and for degressive benefits in the long run to stimulate the movement from unemployment (or inactivity) into employment. Even stronger incentives, such as premiums in the form of capitalized benefit entitlements for finding jobs faster than the average jobless person, might be considered. Such incentives, however, should favour disadvantaged people or regions in order to avoid windfall profits for the advantaged. They could also be applied for specific aims, such as inducing transitions from unemployment into self-employment (see Meager, chap. 16 in this volume).

Japan has an especially interesting built-in incentive to foster moves from unemployment to employment. A 'reemployment bonus' is paid when beneficiaries start a new job within the first half of their benefit entitlement period. Depending on the original benefit entitlement and the timing of the start in the new job, the bonus is equivalent to a sum ranging from one-third to two-thirds of the capitalized value of the remaining benefit entitlement. For example, if the original entitlement to benefit is 90 days, a job seeker who enters employment can receive a lump sum, a bonus equivalent to 30 days of benefit, provided that fewer than 45 days of unemployment benefit have actually been paid. Because only jobs found through the public employment service qualify, one side-effect of the reemployment bonus may be to create an indirect incentive for employers to register their vacancies.

In countries where regular benefits have long or indefinite duration, a bonus that pays an unemployed person his or her remaining benefit entitlement is impractical or too expensive. A fixed bonus may make sense but is perhaps less likely to be a major element in the employment decision. The Japanese reemployment bonus, so enthusiastically praised by the OECD (1992, p. 143), constitutes only 7 per cent of all unemployment compensation expenditure. A thorough evaluation of this scheme is not available. It is not known, for example, if bonus receivers displace nonreceivers whose unemployment spells might be prolonged.

Several evaluation studies related to experiments in the United States are available. The Illinois experiment conducted in 1984 provided strong support for the reemployment bonus concept. For every dollar spent on bonuses, unemployment insurance benefit payments were reduced by more than two dollars, and the average duration of unemployment insurance benefits was reduced by 1.2 weeks (Woodbury and Spiegelman, 1987). The Pennsylvania and Washington experiments detected much lower impacts even of the more generous bonuses (O'Leary, Spiegelman and Kline, 1993), and they came finally to the conclusion that 'the bonuses are not cost-effective from the perspective of the [unemployment insurance] system' if one includes the costs of administering the schemes (Decker and O'Leary, 1994, p. 20). If one looks at the cost–benefit relation from a societal point of view, however, the last quoted study yields a positive result of $347 per claimant for the best designed type of reemployment bonus (high bonus, long qualification period).

Unfortunately, the results of the US evaluation studies are inconclusive, although they represent the best available evaluation methodology (see Björklund and Regnér, chap. 3 in this volume). This inconclusiveness stems not only from contradictory or quite divergent results but also from methodological problems. Even experimental studies cannot tell how the results would change if the experiments were transformed into regular and large-scale programmes, say, through learning effects of the actors involved. In addition, it has not been possible thus far to take the possibility of displacement into account. In an excellent and thorough assessment of evaluations of unemployment insurance experiments in the United States, Meyer (1995) adds two other unintended behavioural effects that very likely offset the small positive impact that financial incentives have on shortening unemployment. First, with a permanent programme, a higher fraction of eligible claimants might apply for the bonus, causing an increase in the costs of the bonus offer. The typical takeup rate of eligible claimants was only between 55 and 65 per cent in the experiments (participation effect). Second, by increasing the financial reward for short spells of unemployment insurance, a permanent bonus would probably increase the number of people unemployed between job changes and increase the number of unemployment insurance filers (entry effect). Meyer's conclusion, based on the review of job search experiments (as opposed to financial incentive experiments), supports the view that increasing the intensity of checks on eligibility for unemployment insurance, and combining that strategy with intensive placement services, is more cost-effective than financial incentives when it comes to ensuring the transition from unemployment to employment. However, more experimental studies are warranted to detect the right mix of control and services (Meyer, 1995, pp. 126–8).

(6) The probability that someone out of work will remain unemployed will clearly tend to increase if unemployment insurance benefits are available. Most empirical studies have found that the duration of benefits is more impor-

tant than their level (Atkinson and Micklewright, 1991, pp. 1716–17; Florens, Fougère and Werguin, 1990, pp. 455–63). Increasing the amount of time spent looking for a job, however, is not necessarily detrimental to allocative efficiency (Rothschild, 1988, p. 31). Indeed, an extended period of job search is probably necessary in specialized occupations. In these cases at least, making it easier for people to remain unemployed for longer is a desirable effect of unemployment insurance (Franz, 1982, p. 47). Moreover, improved matching of people to jobs might also reduce the likelihood of future spells of unemployment and, hence, the scale of movement out of employment into unemployment over the long term (Burtless, 1987).

(7) Comparatively little is known about the determinants of the transition from unemployment to labour market measures and the impact of differentials between unemployment benefits and allowances for the participation of various labour market measures. Remarkable exceptions are three excellent Swedish studies that modelled transitions from unemployment to labour market measures as well as the impact that the existence of job guarantees[16] had on the transition from unemployment to employment. The results of these studies differ slightly, however.

According to the one study (Korpi, 1994, p. 4), it seems likely that the slow decrease in the employment probability (against the evidence of almost all other countries) is due to the fact that labour market measures pick up the unemployed with the worst employment prospects. The study did not find any evidence suggesting that an increased availability of labour market programmes makes unemployed workers less inclined to search for and accept regular employment. The second study (Carling et al., 1994, p. 23) provides evidence that the escape rate to employment increases around the time benefits run out, an indication that the job guarantee has not completely eliminated the incentives to avoid benefit exhaustion through more aggressive searching at the end of the benefit period. Two other positive effects of labour market measures were mentioned. In the first study there was a clear negative effect of current unemployment on psychological well-being, participation in labour market measures improved it. There was also evidence that programme participation increased the stability of subsequent employment, thereby affecting the rate of inflow into unemployment (Korpi, 1994, p. 6).

---

16 The Swedish case is interesting for its unique combination of strictly limited benefits (no longer than 60 weeks for people younger than 55 years) and (since 1987) a job guarantee in the form of a right to a temporary public job ('relief job') or (as of 1993) a training programme, both providing the opportunity to reestablish the entitlement to unemployment insurance benefits for another 60 weeks after 5 months of programme participation.

The third study (Ackum Agell, Björklund and Harkman, 1995) came to more critical results. The combination of unemployment benefits, the entitlement to participate in labour market programmes and the requalification for unemployment benefits after just five months seemed to lead to recurrent spells of unemployment with intermediate phases of programme activity, seasonal work or replacement of those on leave from their permanent position in the public sector. The authors estimated that this group was at least 1 per cent of the labour force and recommended stricter work requirements. However, they acknowledged a tradeoff between equity and efficiency pointing out that a majority of the group with recurrent spells of unemployment consisted of the low-income workers.

The willingness to participate in labour market measures to improve skills and competencies is likely to increase if unemployment benefits fall relative to payments made to trainees on government schemes (Atkinson and Micklewright, 1991, p. 1714). In practice, however, most countries do not draw major distinctions, if any, between training allowance and unemployment benefits. Germany, for example, has successively reduced substantial differences established in the Employment Promotion Act (AFG) of 1969 and has even abolished such differences completely since 1994. In the United Kingdom, the government has paid a premium of at least £10 over weekly unemployment benefits since 1988. (However, the sum barely seems to compensate for the additional costs that training entails and does not stimulate additional training; see also Schmid, chap. 25 in this volume.)

The rationale for not providing clear incentives to participate in training measures seems to be the tradeoff between job search and training. On the one hand, during training people do not seek employment actively, although an active search might in many cases be more efficient than training for skills that may be not needed. From this perspective, training allowances higher than unemployment benefits might send wrong signals. On the other hand, as the British scheme acknowledges, there are clearly additional costs related to training measures, costs that should at least be compensated for. It may also make sense to create differential incentives by providing higher training allowances for low-skilled than for high-skilled unemployed.

(8) Unemployment insurance reduces the probability that an unemployed person will move into inactivity, even if he or she is effectively no longer available for work. There is no clear evidence available to what extent this 'abuse' significantly contributes to persistent high unemployment. Active labour market programmes, coupled with the need for the unemployed to prove periodically that they are actually available for work, would tend to limit the scale of abuse, as do early retirement schemes that enable someone out of work to become legitimately inactive.

(9) The flow from participation in labour market measures into employment may be affected by unemployment insurance indirectly through the entitlement effect. In most countries, some measures, such as those for full-time training, do not requalify a person for unemployment insurance benefits, whereas other measures, such as temporary public work or subsidized work in the private sector, do. All labour market measures involving requalification for unemployment insurance benefits thus reduce the probability that a person will reenter regular employment (see also the Swedish case in number 7, above). This speaks for the priority of training measures, which usually imply, apart from the positive impact on individual productivity, a positive incentive to enter regular employment. Unfortunately, no systematic evaluation is known about these relations.

(10) It follows from the previous paragraph that requalifying for unemployment benefits by participating in labour market measures increases the likelihood of entering unemployment again. Some schemes even intend this effect, especially in times of a deep recession. For example, one of the intentions behind Germany's scheme for temporary public work (ABM) is to redistribute public job opportunities in order to requalify long-term unemployed persons for unemployment insurance benefits during times when employment has to be rationed, such as in a recession. Apart from the equity objective, there is also a macroeconomic rationale behind this approach: the redistribution of income will stabilize effective demand. The danger of such a policy is that it may establish labour promotion careers and cement what is called a secondary labour market.

(11) This line of reasoning leads us to the next transition, the flow from labour market measures to other labour market measures. Again, the entitlement effect may bring participants in training measures to enter another labour market measure to requalify for unemployment insurance benefits. Another reason for getting stuck in a series of labour market measures may be that unemployment insurance schemes have given the wrong incentive, inducing a person to acquire, say, low-quality training instead of searching actively for or accepting a stable but initially low-paying job. On the other hand, 'promotion chains' may be very useful for many unemployed who otherwise would be very difficult to place in the regular labour market. Little is known or has been done in evaluation research to provide clear guidelines for dealing with these traps or tradeoffs.

(12) A corollary to the previous paragraphs is the potential indirect effect of unemployment insurance on the outflow from labour market measures into the status of inactivity. Any flow in this direction seems to be a waste in terms of a

cost–benefit balance. However, from the point of view of transitional labour markets, there is one case to be made in favour of such a transition. For elderly or handicapped people, labour market measures in the form of subsidized employment (e.g. payment of part-time unemployment benefits or wage subsidies for the last years before retirement) may make sense and seem to be applied to an increasing extent. Evidently, the establishment of such measures would increase the flow from labour market measures to partial inactivity. Again, little is known about such useful labour market bridges so far.

(13) The often mentioned entitlement effect of unemployment insurance likewise increases the probability that those who are not part of the labour force will join it. Moreover, when one household member becomes unemployed and is not insured, or is underinsured, other members not in the labour force may be impelled to seek employment in order to supplement household income. On the other hand, because unemployment insurance has to be financed, the wage-related contributions that employees are required to pay reduce their take-home pay and their incentive to seek employment. Employers' incentive to hire may decline to the extent that they find it difficult to pass on the contributions that they are required to pay, reducing the scale of movement from inactivity (or unemployment) into employment. Which of these effects predominates is an empirical question to which evaluation research does not yet provide clear answers.

(14) The entitlement effect of unemployment insurance may also induce inactive people to register as unemployed even if they receive no cash benefit. There are often nonmonetary benefits attached to registration, such as participation in special employment measures, use of placement and counselling services, reduced charges of a private or public nature (e.g. admission to the theatre, cinema, opera, or ticket prices for public transport) and credits for periods of unemployment with respect to other social benefits, such as health care and pensions.

(15) If labour market measures involve the qualification for unemployment insurance benefits, clearly then unemployment insurance also increases the probability of moving from inactivity into labour market measures.

(16) As a corollary of the previous paragraphs, the entitlement effects tend also to reduce the probability that someone will remain inactive. Unemployment insurance, in effect, subsidizes formal labour force participation and may, therefore, reduce the incidence of people working in the informal, or 'black', economy. In this regard, too, much remains to be done by professional researchers before firm conclusions can be drawn.

In summary, the incentive effects that unemployment insurance has on workers and employers are by no means clear-cut. Compensation schemes that guarantee a relatively high level of income, at least in the short term, almost certainly tend to increase the probability that someone will move from employment into unemployment and the time that he or she is likely to spend out of work, but the magnitude of this effect and its relevance for the functioning of the labour market are highly debatable or small. Moreover, other important effects, such as those on labour force participation and participation in labour market measures, must also be taken into account. For politicians who often think only in short-term voting cycles, this view, especially, helps avoid temptations to extend passive income transfers *ad ultimo*. In the following section, therefore, we consider more thoroughly the incentives to spend on active rather than passive labour market policy.

6   UNEMPLOYMENT INSURANCE AND ACTIVE LABOUR MARKET POLICY

There are obvious reasons for directing resources to job creation or skill promotion (active measures) instead of to pure income maintenance for the unemployed (passive measures). Not the least important are persistent mismatches between supply and demand for particular skills and apparently increasing deficiencies in public infrastructure. Another important reason is that net costs of active labour market policy (its actual costs to public budgets) are considerably smaller than the gross costs (public expenditures on active measures). Estimates of the fiscal costs of unemployment and evaluations of policy programmes in most countries emphasize that public expenditures on active employment measures lead to a reduction in the costs of unemployment because the unemployment benefits or assistance, that would otherwise be necessary, are replaced by the increased tax revenue and/or social security contributions that eventually come from the people reemployed as a result of those measures. Net costs of active labour market policy are thus relatively small, amounting to only a fraction of the gross costs (Schmid et al., 1992, pp. 137–41).[17]

In most OECD countries, however, public expenditure on unemployment compensation continues to be considerably larger than expenditure on active policies (see Figures 8.7 and 8.8). In 22 of the 24 OECD countries, 1992

---

17 Comparing the budgetary impacts of unemployment in 1982 to those of various labour market policies, Bruche and Reissert (1985, pp. 81–144) calculated for Germany that the public cost of full-time training came to 147 per cent of that of unemployment; the public cost of temporary public job creation ranged from 98 per cent (1981) to 110 per cent (1986); and the public cost of short-time work was only 92 per cent.

spending on active measures averaged less than half (0.94 per cent of GDP) that on unemployment compensation and early retirement (1.90 per cent of GDP). Thus, the average activity rate—the share of spending on active measures instead of only on income maintenance—was only about 33 per cent. The activity rate, however, ranged from 16 per cent (Spain) to 59 per cent (Portugal), with the Netherlands and France having almost exactly the mean value and Sweden (53 per cent) and Germany (46 per cent) being consistently above the mean (Figure 8.9).

Why, then, do most countries spend more on idle capacities than on productive work? One reason is institutional incongruence. Even if direct and indirect public costs for active labour market policy may be smaller than for direct and indirect costs of unemployment, the decreased burden on public budgets resulting from programmes that reduce unemployment does not in all countries accrue to those institutions responsible for funding active programmes. Frequently, the benefits are reaped to a considerable extent by institutions that have no part in active labour market policy (Schmid et al., 1992, pp. 205–9). Fiscal fragmentation, thus, is a severe institutional disincentive to prevent unemployment.[18]

Whereas spending on active measures is positively, albeit weakly, related to unemployment, the activity rate varies inversely with unemployment: the higher the rate of unemployment, the lower the relative expenditure on active policy (see Figure 8.10). This relation can be explained by the fact that spending on income maintenance tends to have priority over spending on active policy. As unemployment increases, therefore, expenditure on passive measures tends to crowd out that on active ones. Moreover, the higher the level of unemployment, the less effective active measures are likely to be in alleviating the problem and the more relevant macroeconomic policy is. A third interpretation is that a high activity rate supports the fight against unemployment. The possible existence of a 'causal chain' is corroborated by the fact that those countries with the largest increase in the activity rate also had the largest decrease in the unemployment rate between 1985 and 1992.

The scale of public expenditure is, of course, neither a sufficient nor an ideal measure with which to compare the effectiveness and efficiency of labour market policies. It neglects fiscal policies outside the range of selective labour market programmes and fails to take nonfinancial measures and private initiatives into consideration. Thus, a high activity rate connected with relatively high spending is in itself no guarantee that unemployment will be effectively prevented or reduced. Broad institutional evaluations and in-depth analyses of individual programmes are necessary before any final conclusions can be drawn.

---

18 For other political and institutional determinants of expenditure differences in active labour market policy, see Janoski, chap. 23 in this volume.

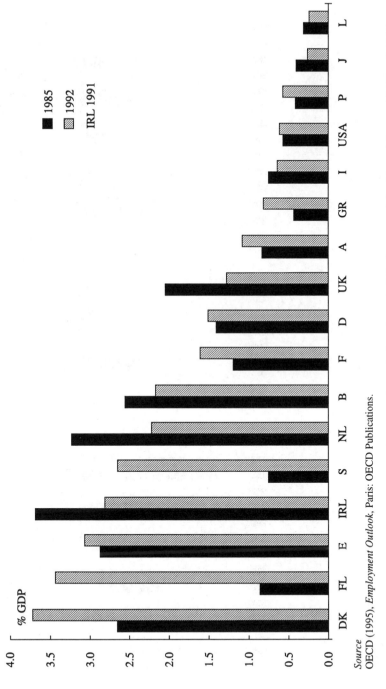

Source
OECD (1995), *Employment Outlook*, Paris: OECD Publications.

Figure 8.7 Unemployment Benefits in Relation to GDP in the EU (EU–15), Japan and the United States, 1985 and 1992

269

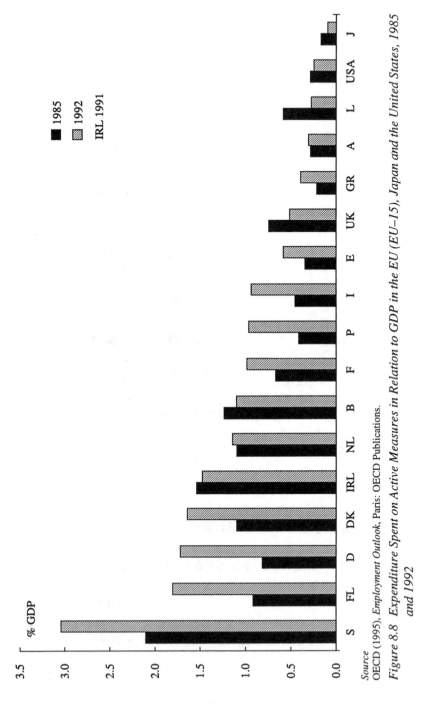

Source
OECD (1995), *Employment Outlook*, Paris: OECD Publications.

Figure 8.8 Expenditure Spent on Active Measures in Relation to GDP in the EU (EU–15), Japan and the United States, 1985 and 1992

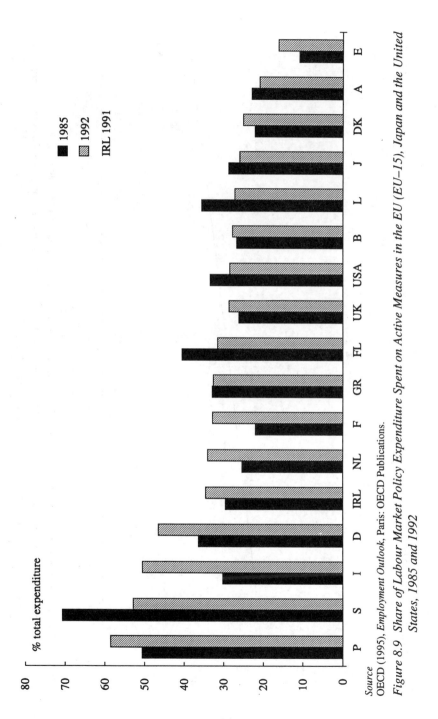

Source
OECD (1995), *Employment Outlook*, Paris: OECD Publications.

Figure 8.9 Share of Labour Market Policy Expenditure Spent on Active Measures in the EU (EU–15), Japan and the United States, 1985 and 1992

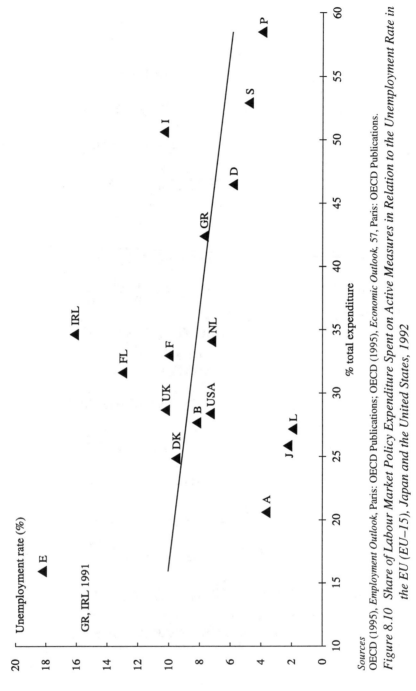

Sources
OECD (1995), *Employment Outlook*, Paris: OECD Publications; OECD (1995), *Economic Outlook, 57*, Paris: OECD Publications.

Figure 8.10 Share of Labour Market Policy Expenditure Spent on Active Measures in Relation to the Unemployment Rate in the EU (EU–15), Japan and the United States, 1992

7   CONCLUSIONS

In this chapter we have pointed to a tremendous variation in the regulatory regimes of unemployment insurance. Out of the many details there have emerged a few basic principles that ultimately determine the institutional arrangements and their adjustment to structural change. Welfare-oriented unemployment insurance systems (the United Kingdom being a model) are less effective at providing income protection but more effective at being equitable and, possibly, at restricting moral hazard than insurance-oriented systems are. Insurance-oriented unemployment insurance systems (Germany being a model) are effective at protecting income but tend to exclude marginal groups when there is persistent mass unemployment. Such systems are also more prone to moral hazard, especially if they provide practically indeterminate income protection. No convergence of these principles was observed.

The impact of unemployment insurance on labour market behaviour is by no means clear-cut. A few generalizations, however, can be made about the three different levels of analysis. From a macroeconomic perspective, an effective system of income protection for the unemployed stabilizes purchasing power. From a mesoeconomic perspective, a universal system of unemployment insurance has the advantage of redistributing purchasing power regionally, thus avoiding a vicious circle of depressed areas and declining purchasing power. A well-functioning compensation scheme is also crucial to maintaining good industrial relations. If trade unions know that their members are adequately protected if they lose their jobs, they may be more cooperative in adjusting to structural change. At the microlevel, a well-designed unemployment insurance system reduces divisions in society and provides some form of justice to those who lose their jobs through no fault of their own. The willingness of workers to be mobile and flexible in the labour market, to retrain and accept new jobs, which may involve higher risk of unemployment, is likely to be greater if generous unemployment benefits are available in the short term. In the long term, however, moral-hazard effects become more intricate and call for regulation differentiated by target groups and for coordination with active labour market policy.

Evaluation research is still challenged by the task of finding the right balance between efficiency and equity functions and controlling the moral hazard of unemployment insurance. This review has made it clear what type of information is needed if the decisions of urgent institutional reforms are to be enlightened further. First, modelling of the impact that unemployment insurance has on individual behaviour and on the functioning of the labour market has to be dynamic and must include various transitional flows between different positions of labour market activity or inactivity. Second, from a methodological point of view, more longitudinal studies are needed to measure long-term impacts and possible side-effects or unintended effects. Third, of special importance is the evaluation of alternative measures to support job search either by financial incentives (reemployment bonus, wage subsidies), control measures (stricter work requirements and tests) or services (intensive counselling, training, temporary public jobs). Fourth, the high costs of unemployment insurance and the increasing constraints on public budgets should lead to the detection of ingenious ways to use funds allocated to passive expenditure on active measures.

REFERENCES

Ackum Agell, S., A. Björklund and A. Harkman (1995), 'Unemployment Insurance, Labour Market Programmes and Repeated Unemployment in Sweden', *Swedish Economic Policy Review*, 2 (1), 101–28.

Atkinson, A. B. and J. Micklewright (1991), 'Unemployment Compensation and Labour Market Transitions: A Critical Review', *Journal of Economic Literature*, 29, 1679–727.

Atkinson, A. B. and G. V. Mogensen (eds) (1993), *Welfare and Work Incentives: A North European Perspective*, New York: Clarendon Press.

Bechterman, G. and N. Leckie (1994), *Employer Responses to UI Experience Rating: Evidence from Canadian and American Establishments*, Ottawa: Human Resources Development Canada.

Bellemare, D. and L. Poulin (1994), 'Les coûts économiques du chômage: plus de 30 milliards volatilisés au Québec en 1993' (Edition Speciale), *Forum Express*, 2, Montréal.

Björklund, A. and B. Holmlund (1991), 'The Economics of Unemployment Insurance: The Case of Sweden', in A. Björklund, R. Haveman, R. Hollister and B. Holmlund, *Labour Market Policy and Unemployment Insurance*, Oxford: Clarendon Press, pp. 101–78.

Bruche, G. and B. Reissert (1985), *Finanzierung der Arbeitsmarktpolitik*, Frankfurt on the Main: Campus.

Burtless, G. (1987), 'Jobless Pay and High European Unemployment', in R. Z. Lawrence and C. L. Schultze (eds), *Barriers to European Growth: A Transatlantic View*, Washington, DC: The Brookings Institution, pp. 105–62.

Carling, K. and P.-A. Edin, A. Harkman and B. Holmlund (1994), 'Unemployment Duration, Unemployment Benefits, and Labour Market Programs in Sweden', Working Paper series 12, Uppsala University, Department of Economics.

Clark, K. B. and L. H. Summers (1982), 'Unemployment Insurance and Labour Market Transitions', in M. N. Baily (ed.), *Workers, Jobs and Inflation*, Washington, DC: Brookings, pp. 279–323.

Clasen, J. (1994), *Paying the Jobless. A Comparison of Unemployment Benefit Policies in Great Britain and Germany*, Aldershot: Avebury.

Corak, M. and W. Pyper (1994), *Firms, Industries, and Cross Subsidies: Patterns in the Distribution of UI Benefits and Taxes*, Ottawa: Human Resources Development Canada.

Decker, P. T. and C. J. O'Leary (1994), 'Evaluating Pooled Evidence from the Reemployment Bonus Experiments', Staff Working Papers 94–28, Kalamazoo, MI: Upjohn Institute.

Florens, J.-P., D. Fougère and P. Werguin (1990), 'Durées de chômage et transitions sur le marché du travail', *Sociologie Du Travail*, 4, 439–68.

Franz, W. (1982), 'The Reservation Wage of Unemployed Persons in the Federal Republic of Germany: Theory and Empirical Tests', *Zeitschrift für Wirtschafts- und Sozialwissenschaften*, 1, 29–51.

Green, D. and C. Riddell (1994), *Qualifying for Unemployment Insurance*, Ottawa: Human Resources Development Canada.

Hamermesh, D. S. (1977), *Jobless Pay and the Economy,* Baltimore, MD: Johns Hopkins University Press.

Hemmings, P. (1994), 'Benefit Entitlement and Replacement Ratio Data for the OECD Countries', Paris: OECD. (Unpublished manuscript)

Johnson, G. and R. Layard (1986), 'The Natural Rate of Unemployment: Explanation and Policy', in O. Ashenfelter and R. Layard (eds), *The Handbook of Labour Economics*, Amsterdam: North-Holland, Vol. 2, pp. 921–99.

Kohli, M., M. Rein and A.-M. Guillemard (eds) (1991), *Time for Retirement: Comparative Studies of Early Exit from the Labour Force*, Cambridge, UK: Cambridge University Press.

Korpi, T. (1994), *Escaping Unemployment: Studies in the Individual Consequences of Unemployment and Labour Market Policy*, Swedish Institute for Social Research, Dissertation Series no. 24, Edsbruck: Akademitryck.

Layard, R., S. Nickell and R. Jackman (1991), *Unemployment—Macroeconomic Performance and the Labour Market*, Oxford, UK: Oxford University Press.

Meyer, B. D. (1990), 'Unemployment Insurance and Unemployment Spells', *Econometrica*, 58, 757–82.

Meyer, B. D. (1995), 'Lessons from the U. S. Unemployment Insurance Experiments', *Journal of Economic Literature*, 33, 91–131.

MISSOC (Mutual Information on Social Protection) (1995), *Social Protection in the Member States of the European Union. Situation on July 1st 1994 and Evolution*, Luxembourg: Office for Official Publications of the European Communities.

Mortensen, D. T. (1977), 'Unemployment Insurance and Job Search Decisions', *Industrial Labour Relations Review*, 30, 505–17.

OECD (1991), *Employment Outlook*, Paris: OECD Publications.

OECD (1992), *Employment Outlook*, Paris: OECD Publications.

OECD (1994), *The OECD Jobs Study: Evidence and Explanations; Part 1: Labour Market Trends and Underlying Forces of Change; Part 2: The Adjustment Potential of the Labour Market*, Paris: OECD Publications.

OECD (1995), *Employment Outlook*, Paris: OECD Publications.

O'Leary, C. J., R. G. Spiegelman and K. J. Kline (1993), 'Reemployment Incentives for Unemployment Insurance Beneficiaries: Results from the Washington Reemployment Bonus Experiment', Staff Working Papers 93–22, Kalamazoo, MI: Upjohn Institute.

Reissert, B. (1993), 'National Unemployment Support Schemes in the EC', *infor-MISEP* (Employment Observatory), 43, 19–27.

Rothschild, K. W. (1988), *Theorien der Arbeitslosigkeit. Einführung*, Munich: R. Oldenbourg.

Schmid, G. (ed.) (1994), *Labor Market Institutions in Europe: A Socioeconomic Evaluation of Performance*, Armonk, NY: M. E. Sharpe.

Schmid, G. (1995), 'Is Full Employment Still Possible? Transitional Labour Markets as a New Strategy of Labour Market Policy', *Economic and Industrial Democracy*, 16, 429–56.

Schmid, G., B. Reissert and G. Bruche (1992), *Unemployment Insurance and Active Labor Market Policy: An International Comparison of Financing Systems*, Detroit: Wayne State University Press.

Stobernack, M. (1991), 'Der Zusammenhang von Arbeitslosenversicherung und Arbeitslosigkeit im Lichte der Empirie: Ein Literatursurvey', *Zeitschrift für Wirtschafts- und Sozialwissenschaften*, 2, 251–71.

Vroman, W. (1992), 'Short-time Compensation in the U.S., Germany and Belgium', Washington, DC: The Urban Institute. (Unpublished manuscript)

Woodbury, S. A. and R. G. Spiegelman (1987), 'Bonuses to Workers and Employers to Reduce Unemployment: Randomized Trials in Illinois', *The American Economic Review*, 77, 513–30.

OECD 277-307

J68 J64

9. Job Opportunities for the Hard-to-place

Christine Erhel, Jérôme Gautié, Bernard Gazier and Sylvie Morel

The problem of the hard-to-place is an old one. Since World War II the integration of such groups has been conceived as a complementary challenge to the commitment to full employment. As Reubens (1970) noted: 'The concept of the hard-to-employ or the hard-to-place is optimistic and policy-oriented. In particular, it opens the possibility of gainful work for groups who previously have been neglected entirely or aided chiefly through financial assistance' (p. 6).

Two trends have affected the perception and development of specific policies towards disadvantaged groups since the 1960s and 1970s. First, there has been a broad trend towards specialization. Some groups, such as the disabled, were isolated and dealt with separately. Second, and more recently, mass unemployment, especially in Europe, has made more and more people 'hard to employ', generating new target groups and increasing their size. Accordingly, the employment policies addressed to the disabled are treated in chap. 17 of this volume. It is the long-term unemployed that are the central, although not exclusive, target of the policies studied here.

1 THE HARD-TO-PLACE

1.1 The Nature of the Problem

It is neither possible nor pertinent to present here a general discussion of the causes of persistent disadvantage on the labour market. Briefly, two main processes seem to be involved. The first is the permanent or temporary nonavailability or nonacceptability of jobs for some, more or less precisely defined groups. This condition is either absolute (general job rationing) or relative ('structural' imbalance between job characteristics and employers' requirements on the demand side, and workers' skills, expectations and behaviour on the supply side). Such a situation could result from a wide variety of labour market dysfunctions, including sluggish overall demand, employer and/or employee prejudice, social norms, institutional interventions aimed at other goals, lack of information, constraints on wage adjustments and so on.

The second process is a self-reinforcing mechanism. The probability of leaving unemployment generally declines as the duration of unemployment increases. There is a complex debate about the rationale underlying this process, and it seems that two complementary causes interact.

1. Heterogeneity: As discussed later, the hard-to-place population is heterogeneous, and individuals whose characteristics, skills and experience make them relatively attractive to employers have a higher probability of being recruited. Consequently, the remaining group becomes more and more difficult to place.
2. Skill deterioration and discouragement: Unless corrective measures are taken, the skills and motivation of unsuccessful job seekers will tend to deteriorate over time; the longer the duration of unemployment, the less intensive their search effort is likely to become. Partly because of this, employers prefer the short-term unemployed.

We briefly focus our attention on the aspects that are most relevant for the situations leading to the risk of exclusion from gainful employment. These consist of a mix of market failures and institutional failures.

Wage rigidities and low geographical mobility are classical deficiencies of labour markets in industrialized countries and have often been discussed. For the hard-to-place, the main problem is the discrepancy between their supposed productivity level and the wage generally considered adequate to cover minimum needs. But this problem can only be part of the problem because a number of studies have shown that the overwhelming majority of the long-term unemployed would be prepared to accept 'any wage offer' rather than staying unemployed. Unskilled people with little education and older workers in depressed areas are often reluctant to move towards more dynamic regions. Leaving home, relatives and friends is a decision taken only with great reluctance, if at all. Hard-to-place groups are thus frequently considered as 'noncompeting groups', to use the term coined by John Stuart Mill more than a century ago.

Information problems probably constitute the bulk of labour market deficiencies in this area. Consider statistical discrimination. According to a well-known analysis proposed by Phelps (1972), in order to assess the productivity and motivation of a job applicant, an employer may simply rely on the mean productivity of the group to which the applicant belongs. Such an attitude constitutes a cheap screening device, maybe the cheapest, especially in bad times. Depending on the nature of group productivity ascriptions, such 'rational' behaviour can lead to genuine discrimination. Stigma is a common feature on the labour market, and although helping job seekers to send the 'right' productivity signals can go some way to improving the situation, the problem seems to be more deeply rooted.

Problems inherent in the employment policies under review here, such as creaming, are discussed later. Here we mention only those effects that are due to other institutions. The scholarly debate and the related studies have focussed on the disincentives allegedly stemming from benefits systems. Unemployment insurance, welfare payments and minimum income allowances could undermine job seekers' efforts by providing financial support and at the same time usually taxing additional earned income. The evidence on this question is somewhat mixed and is discussed in chaps 8 and 27 of this volume. It is at least possible that disadvantaged groups could be affected by these disincentives and that individuals near the poverty line face a severe risk of demotivation.

Three main policy responses are possible. The first is to provide directly an employment-related service that is otherwise unavailable. Training or placement services for the poor are examples. The second main policy response, often bitterly discussed, is to remove directly or offset some of the constraints observed on the labour market which are considered to be a cause of slow employment adjustments. For example, the debate is still flourishing on suppression of the minimum wage in both the United States and Europe. A more sophisticated choice is the twofold treatment of the disincentives stemming from unemployment benefits. Payments are set to decline as the unemployment duration increases, and simultaneously incentives and remotivation programmes are provided. This practice leads to the third response, which is clearly a 'second-best' one: to attack the consequences of long-term unemployment and to affect, as far as possible, behaviour on the demand and/or the supply side of the market. Most of the policies developed by the OECD countries belong to this final category, which can be merged with the first and combined with the second, radical option.

1.2   The Concept of Employability

At first glance the concept of employability appears to be a natural approach to identifying and curing labour market disadvantages (Gazier, 1990). It measures individual performance according to a set of criteria thought to be relevant for recruitment and relies on the distinction between three types of personal characteristics:

1. objective, not susceptible to influence (e.g. age, gender, ethnicity, criminal record and past career);

2. objective, at least partially susceptible to influence (e.g. skills, geographical area, appearance);
3. subjective (e.g. motivation, behaviour).

Some authors have developed 'employability scales', combining sets of items for each type and attributing scores to these items. Such a procedure enables profiles of employability strengths and deficiencies to be identified and employability gaps to be bridged.

It seems natural to focus on characteristics susceptible to influence, to modify them and to try to compensate for the disadvantages over which no influence can be exerted. For example, an unskilled, unemployed, elderly worker could be offered retraining and helped to move out of a depressed area. This person might benefit from a targeted employment subsidy.

The problem here is that little attention is usually paid to changing personal and labour market contexts. A person who is considered hard-to-employ in one place or at one time might be quite 'employable' in another place or time as a result of changes either in the person's characteristics or in the number or requirements of available jobs. Leaving aside for a moment such disadvantages as physical and/or mental disabilities, one is left with characteristics that employers find more or less undesirable. Social norms and prejudice interact here with wage expectations and the relative market position of workers belonging to various groups. Such groups can be integrated or crowded out, depending on the looseness or tightness of the labour market. An essential observation is that firms' requirements vary according to the business cycle, and some supposed social 'disadvantages' are in actual fact merely criteria by means of which firms can rank and eliminate less desirable job seekers in times of job shortage. When the labour market is tight, such criteria become irrelevant.

This kind of individualistic approach based on the concept of employability is proactive, but entails the risk of overemphasizing the personal characteristics and behaviour of the job seeker and leaves open the question of collective action on the norms and the functioning of the labour market. As a consequence, in some countries (e.g. France) the concept of employability is used in a different sense, one restricted to a collective *ex-post* statistical variable for specified groups of unemployed persons: the rate at which they leave unemployment, that is, the opposite of the average unemployment duration. Under this approach slowing down in the business cycle leads to a decline in employability. The drawbacks of such an approach are the reverse of the problems encountered with the individualistic concept. It is objective and uncontroversial, but it neglects individual responsibility and room for improvement and puts an unduly strong accent on the impersonal demand side of the market.

In order to define and evaluate policies towards the hard-to-place, one should therefore be cautious in applying the concept of employability and ensure that it is always embedded in some well-defined social and economic context.

Another outcome of the debate on exclusion is that, strictly speaking, three levels of evaluation need to be distinguished in the assessment of the employment effects that such policies have: (a) direct effects (within a particular phase of the business cycle), (b) effects over the cycle (e.g. the capacity of hard-to-place to obtain or keep a job across the cycle, including declining phases) and (c) long-term effects (e.g. keeping the hard-to-place permanently in the regular labour market). In practice, this last effect is seldom achieved.

1.3   Definitions and Characteristics of Hard-to-place Groups

Given the large number of different features and situations that are conducive to labour market disadvantages, one can expect very different groups to be concerned at a given time and place. Thus, the mix of these various groups will evolve according to changing national and local contexts. This evolution is what lies behind the heterogeneity of the hard-to-place population. One can distinguish three main components:

1. The main group is well-defined: the long-term unemployed. The definition is subject to conventions, however, two aspects of which should be underlined.
   - How long is long-term? At the onset of mass unemployment, the threshold duration was six months; it is now most commonly one year. Some countries publish statistics on the number of unemployed for two or even three years and shape policies accordingly.
   - It is often possible to treat the long-term unemployed as 'socially disabled' persons, and in some countries (e.g. Sweden) some programmes are addressed simultaneously to both populations even though a clear distinction is drawn between the disabled and the 'socially disabled'. The long-term unemployed are very much in danger of becoming 'discouraged' as their growing motivational and psychological deficiencies increase their labour market disadvantages in such a way that they stop actively looking for jobs.
2. A less well-defined set of specifically disadvantaged groups looking for work is mainly characterized by a poor employment record and one or more specific problems: persons with a criminal record or very low educational attainment, young people experiencing recurring unemployment and short employment spells, and so on.

3. This group is composed of welfare recipients not in the active labour force, whether coming from long-term unemployment or not (e.g. mothers on welfare in the United States and minimum income recipients in most European countries). As a 'dependency problem' arises, reflecting the political and social value put on autonomy and financial self-support, welfare institutions frequently apply more or less mandatory provisions pushing them towards paid employment.

In addition to the heterogeneity of these three groups and the problems they face, it is also important to underline the *internal* heterogeneity of each sub-group of the 'excluded' population. For example, when analysing group 1 (the long-term unemployed), one expects to find a disproportionate number of elderly, low-skilled, poorly educated people. Although this is in fact the case, a significant number of the long-term unemployed are young, skilled and educated. Some, indeed, have a college degree. As was reported by the OECD (1992) for the Dutch case: 'In the Netherlands a significant minority (almost 10 per cent) of the long-term unemployed are highly qualified' (p. 11), and similar conditions apply in other countries. Similarly, ethnic minorities and women may sometimes be overrepresented, and the proportions differ widely.

As regards the scale of the problem posed by the hard-to-place, at the beginning of the 1990s, seven million people in the OECD, more than six million of them in Europe, had been unemployed for more than one year. Lack of comparative data, and sometimes of any data at all, precludes global evaluations of groups 2 and 3. In the United States more than four million mothers benefited from Aid to Families with Dependent Children (AFDC) at the beginning of the 1990s. And only 15 per cent of adult recipients participated in an employment programme (US Congress, 1993). Among disadvantaged youth, recurring unemployment is commonly observed.

2   A TYPOLOGY OF MEASURES

From the wide range of employment policies targeted at the hard-to-place, we have extracted five basic types of programmes.

2.1   Temporary Employment in the Nonprofit Sector

The goal of direct job creation programmes is to increase the available number of jobs while satisfying needs that are not met by the private sector. Such job creation schemes are generally characterized by restrictions on the type of employer (belonging to the public or nonprofit sector) and, usually, the type of employment, which must be of wider social benefit (e.g. benefit achieved through social, cultural or environmental projects. The employment must also usually be 'additional', which means that it would not have existed without public intervention).[1] Labour costs are usually directly financed, in part or in full, by national or local authorities. The programme may also contain a training component.

Such programmes exist in most OECD and EU countries. Examples include the United States (Community Work Experience Program, CWEP), Sweden (Buedskapsarbete, Ungdomslog for Youth), Germany ('Arbeitsbeschaffungsmaßnahmen', ABM), the United Kingdom (Job Creation Programme in the 1970s, which was replaced in 1981 by Community Enterprise Programme, translated into the better-known Community Programme and, in turn, replaced by Employment Action in 1991), France ('Travaux d'Utilité Collective', TUC, then 'Contrats Emploi Solidarité', CES) and Belgium (Third Work Network). All these measures have employed a significant number of hard-to-place persons: up to 260 000 in 1987 by the Community Programme and over 100 000 in the mid-1980s for ABM (Disney, 1992, pp. 90 and 164). These figures have since declined, however. Employment Action currently offers 60 000 places a year, and the ABM has been stabilized at about 80 000 a year since 1990. France is a special case in that it has maintained an upward trend (334 600 CES were signed in 1991) (MISEP, Basic Information Report on France, 1992). Although most of these recruitments are made in the public and nonprofit sector, some measures, such as the ABM and the more recent Projects for Employment in Denmark, do not exclude private sector employers.

Such employment tends to be short-term in nature. More durable jobs are sometimes provided by specific firms operating in the private sector, such as the French 'Associations Intermédiaires' and 'Entreprises d'Insertion'. Nevertheless, they are at the frontier between temporary and sheltered jobs.

2.2 Employment Subsidies

Subsidies to firms employing hard-to-place people. In order to offset the relative unattractiveness of the hard-to-place, subsidies are often provided as encouragement to employers (in the private sector) to recruit such persons and as a kind of compensation for the excess costs incurred by their recruitment (in terms of work familiarization and training). This type of programme consists basically of subsidies paid either as a lump sum on recruitment or as a continuing payment (ideally for a period corresponding to the extended time required to

---

1 This restriction is intended to avoid displacement effects; see below (section 4.1) for a discussion of the fiscal substitution effects.

familiarize the employee) and/or of a partial or complete exemption of the employer from social security contributions.

Many variants on this basic model are possible, but it appears to be one of the most widely used techniques for encouraging employers to recruit from particular target groups in many OECD countries. In the United States, subsidies consist of tax credits granted to the employers. Since 1978 the main programme specifically for the hard-to-place (defined as young people from economically disadvantaged families, ex-offenders living in low-income households, welfare recipients, disabled individuals) has been the Targeted Job Tax Credit, a tax credit amounting to 40 per cent of the first $6000 paid as wages during the initial year of employment (Levitan, Gallo and Shapiro, 1993, p. 88). The extent of the wage-cost subsidy varies considerably from one country to another. Germany, for instance, offered very high subsidy rates in 1982, when the *Eingliederungsbeihilfen*, whose purpose was to promote the hiring of the hard-to-place (long-term unemployed, older people, young people without professional skills), provided the employer with a wage-cost subsidy of up to 80 per cent during the initial period of employment (Schmid, 1982). France ('Contrat de Retour à l'Emploi', CRE), the Netherlands and Italy (Reintegration Contracts) grant an exemption from employer social security contributions[2] instead (see the relevant national Basic Information Reports by MISEP).[3]

Encouragement of self-employment and the creation of new enterprises. These schemes (discussed fully in chap. 16 in this volume) aim at promoting self-employment in general and are not specifically targeted at the hard-to-place. Nevertheless, a small percentage of the hard-to-place may benefit from such programmes (the highly motivated and skilled among them, which inevitably constitute but a small minority).

The Business Start Up Programme in Great Britain (which replaced the Enterprise Allowance Scheme) is particularly interesting in our context because it includes specific services for the hard-to-place (although the programme is targeted at all unemployed). 'Business centres' have been designed in order to help disadvantaged women and ethnic minority members to create their own businesses. The centres offer specific training, credits and commercial counselling. The weekly allowance varies between £20 and £90 and is available for between 26 and 66 weeks.

---

2 In the CRE scheme, a lump sum of FF 10 000 (20 000 in 1993) was also granted until 1994 for the hardest-to-place. Since June 1995, CRE has been replaced by the 'Contrat Initiative Emploi', which offers higher financial incentives.

3 Apart from these subsidy schemes, the OECD gives examples of nonmonetary attempts to 'increase employers awareness' (OECD, 1992, p. 41), such as publicity campaigns encouraging them to examine and, if necessary, modify their recruitment practices. Examples exist in the United States and in Australia.

2.3   Training Schemes

'Training schemes', as understood here, can range from classroom learning and other institutional training to on-the-job training. The general purpose of these programmes is to provide the hard-to-place with various forms of human capital, which will make them more attractive to potential employers.

Classroom training. Classroom training is the classical (and more or less academic) way of raising the skills of the hard-to-place and is usually contrasted with 'on-the-job training', which is an institutional arrangement by which private employers provide disadvantaged people work experience with practical training. Those two dimensions can be combined, either successively within comprehensive programmes (see section 2.5 on Comprehensive Schemes) or run simultaneously (in dual or alternating schemes).

Within classroom training, it appears that different types of content are required, given the diversity of the needs that hard-to-place persons have. The OECD (1992, p. 2) has distinguished between two major orientations: (a) remedial education for those who lack basic prerequisites (in this case specialized teaching staff is required, with new training methods) and (b) professional training for skilled or semiskilled jobs (training that should be relevant to actual needs on the labour market and therefore requires the involvement of employers).

Work experience. Work experience[4] has the purpose of imparting to hard-to-place persons the minimum behavioural skills needed for paid employment (respect for authority, punctuality and so forth). In the United States such measures were applied to disadvantaged youth (e.g. in the Summer Youth Employment Program) and to other hard-to-place subgroups (in the National Supported Work Experiment, targeted at women receiving AFDC, ex-addicts, ex-offenders and young drop-outs). In the Netherlands a specific placement network (the 'Job Pools') has been designed in order to offer a degree of work experience to the most difficult persons to place. Apart from these schemes oriented exclusively to work experience, temporary employment in the public (or nonprofit) sector can also be interpreted as a way of providing work experience to the hard-to-place (see section 2.1).

Efforts to adapt all these types of training to the skill demand on the labour market. The American JTPA (Job Training and Partnership Act, 1983) differed from the previous CETA (Comprehensive Employment and Training Act) in that it was based on cooperation between employers and public employment services in order to provide training suited to the employers' needs. The 1988 Employment Training Programme in the United Kingdom

---

4 Work experience can also stand separately from education and training activities, as shown by the CWEP for welfare recipients in the United States.

was designed to 'train the workers without jobs for jobs without workers', that is, to respond to skill demands on the local labour market. This type of interactive training programme has also been developed in Belgium (see the relevant MISEP Basic Information Report).

2.4   Widening and Improving Job Search

In ways similar to the training schemes, some programmes use the practice of systematic job-hunting techniques to provide hard-to-place persons with the basic skills required by the job search process and thereby raise their self-confidence and increase their probability of success. Such programmes generally take the form of one- to two-week training sessions and tend to be incorporated within more general job search schemes, such as job clubs or orientation/ motivation programmes.

The Restart Programme in the United Kingdom provides such skills in what are called restart courses. These one-week sessions, during which an individual plan for job search is drawn up, are targeted at the long-term unemployed and, indeed, are compulsory for those who have been without work for over two years and have refused or neglected to participate in employment or training programmes. From 1991 through 1992 120 000 places were offered (MISEP Basic Information Report, UK, 1992).

Motivation programmes are designed to help the hard-to-place formulate their own needs and aims and synthesize them in a reintegration plan. They also enable the employment services to play a more active role among the disadvantaged.

Personal interview is the instrument most frequently used in order to assess personal experience and draw up a reintegration plan, including orientation towards one or several employment or training schemes. Many examples could be given, such as the compulsory interview in the 13th month of unemployment in France, the *'Weer-Werk'* action in Belgium or the Restart Programme in the United Kingdom (personal interview every six months).

Another innovative option is to encourage self-help by promoting job-club schemes. Job-club members receive coaching and expert advice on job search techniques and have free use of facilities such as stationery, stamps, telephones and typewriters to enable them to undertake an effective search. Such programmes are not specifically targeted at the hard-to-place, except in the United Kingdom and Belgium, where the eligible population is restricted to the long-term unemployed. Some job-club schemes are compulsory. In the United Kingdom, for example, members must attend until a job has been found.

The idea behind this scheme originated in Canada ('job-search clubs'), subsequently expanding to the United States and New Zealand before being introduced in Europe in 1984. In the United Kingdom 940 job clubs now exist, and the model is also used in Sweden, the Netherlands and Belgium.

Financial incentives are offered in order to activate job search (and to put an end to it more rapidly by making low-wage employment more attractive). Many different forms of financial incentives may be consistent with this definition; one example is given below.[5]

The British Jobstart Allowance can be defined as a wage subsidy paid to the former unemployed. The amount of the subsidy is £20 a week for 6 months and is offered to any long-term unemployed person who takes a job paying £90 or less a week. In operation since 1986, this scheme appears to be a unique case of a subsidy paid directly to the former long-term unemployed recruit.

2.5   Comprehensive Schemes

Most countries have recently tried to develop comprehensive schemes. A good example of these programmes is the American Job Corps (created as early as 1964), which relies on a combination of basic and technical classroom training with individual assessment plans and personal counselling designed to help disadvantaged youths. We may also cite the Job Opportunities and Basic Skills (JOBS) programmes for welfare recipients, such as the Greater Avenues on Independence (GAIN) programme in California, which aims to increase the employment of AFDC recipients by providing comprehensive services including appraisal interviews, orientation in one of the two primary service tracks (basic education or job search activities), case-management services, childcare support and reimbursement of transportation and work-related expenses.

In Europe, the British Employment Training Programme, the French ('Actions d'Insertion et de Formation' (Integration and Training Actions, AIF)) and the Spanish Training Programme for the Long-term Unemployed also mix training (classroom training as well as on-the-job training) and individual counselling services.

The above description of the existing schemes, as partial and brief as it is, makes it clear that a wide range of measures are used to improve employment options for the hard-to-place. It also shows that the boundaries between the different categories are floating rather than hermetic.

---

5 Incentive systems can also be used to encourage the hard-to-place to complete a training programme. In Belgium, every long-term unemployed person completing a training programme (at least six months long) receives a subsidy of BF 10 000 in the last month of his or her programme (MISEP, Basic Information Report, Belgium, 1992, p. 119).

3   SOME OBSERVATIONS ABOUT NATIONAL EXPERIENCES

Among the measures to assist the long-term unemployed in the OECD countries, activities related to job search have gained in importance in recent years. Training is also widely seen as a necessary component of the set of policies designed to help the hard-to-place reenter the labour market. Conversely, there has been a relative decline of subsidized employment creation and public sector employment (OECD, 1992). Beyond these general trends, certain differences between the OECD countries need to be stressed.

In Europe, attention is paid to the long-term unemployed rather than to the 'economically disadvantaged' referred to in US terminology. European countries use direct job creation programmes for a large number of hard-to-place unemployed. Recruitment subsidies are also well developed.[6] In the United States, the emphasis is on supply-side programmes, that is, education and training measures.[7] Many of the job creation schemes previously in operation were dismantled during the Reagan administration.

Measures to assist the long-term unemployed in European countries have been implemented within a general framework of highly developed employment policies. Sweden, with its emphasis on active labour market policy, is the extreme case in this regard. By contrast, ambiguity and discontinuity is a main feature of employment policies in the United States: 'American employment policy was always an unsettled area, characterized by false starts, poorly implemented programmes, and a vacillating national commitment' (Weir, 1992, p. 8). Programmes for the hard-to-place tend to equate with American employment policy in its entirety. Understood as 'social welfare' policies, these programmes have proved politically unstable. They are unable to gain broad support from the population because only the poor benefit from them. The fact that labour market policies for the economically disadvantaged are financed through general federal revenues can also explain their sensitivity to changes in political priorities (Schmid, Reissert and Bruche, 1992).

American 'workfare' and French 'integration' policies are presented below in comparative form, because the two models stress societal differences in the organization of the transitions between the welfare system and the labour market. Both can, in fact, be seen as exemplifying the broader orientations of American and European employment policies. Workfare is typical of the

---

6 The United Kingdom is an exception; see 2.1.

7 For a full discussion of the US experience, see Bane, Ellwood and David (1994); Gueron and Pauly (1991); Manski and Garfinkel (1992); Mead (1986, 1992); Moffit (1992); Morel (1994); Murray (1984); and Nathan (1993).

American approach in dealing with the hard-to-place, whereas integration is more representative of the way European countries deal with this problem.

3.1 Welfare and Employment: A Comparison of American 'Workfare' and French 'Integration' (*Insertion*) Policies

'Workfare' and 'insertion' are two notions that reveal important national differences in welfare and employment policies. Both terms refer to employment programmes for welfare recipients, that is, recipients of AFDC in the United States and 'Revenu Minimum d'Insertion' (RMI) recipients in France.

Workfare and integration exhibit a number of similarities. Both terms appeared at the beginning of the 1970s and relate to programmes that can be labelled as 'active labour market policies'. The aim in both cases is to replace pure income maintenance programmes by a mix of financial support and employment activities. Thus, workfare and integration policies include a variety of job search, education, training, wage-subsidy and work-experience programmes, some of which are connected to national manpower policies. In both cases welfare receipt is linked to new obligations. Instead of promoting employment by strengthening work incentives, workfare and integration rely on mandatory requirements. In both countries welfare recipients can be sanctioned for noncompliance. Workfare and integration can be seen as 'contractual' approaches. Their underlying philosophy is one of 'mutual obligations' between the state and the welfare recipients. This can take the form of an agreement that specifies the two sides' obligations; in France, the law mandates such an agreement ('contrat d'insertion'). A final similarity is that workfare and integration face various implementation constraints, which lead to a wide gap between the goals and the programme outcomes.

Workfare and integration also reflect divergent orientations in welfare policies, however. Workfare's role is to combat 'welfare dependency', which is seen as synonymous with AFDC receipt, and to push families in the direction of 'self-sufficiency'. Integration aims to counter 'social exclusion', that is, to ensure that poverty is addressed not only in monetary terms but as a multidimensional problem, one requiring the deployment of a broad array of support services. Workfare is seen as a more 'punitive' approach to welfare reform because of its emphasis on the idea that the right to welfare engenders responsibilities to society. Integration, instead of focussing on the able-bodied recipient's obligation to try to become self-sufficient, stresses the obligation of society towards 'the excluded', that is, people unable to reach the mainstream of society. With what is called 'social integration' (social services in such domains as housing, health and education), integration policies are also conceived more broadly than workfare programmes, which are exclusively related to employment activities. Finally, integration is less entrenched in family issues than workfare is, a fact reflecting the different welfare-state structures. Unlike AFDC, which is a programme specifically for single-parent families, RMI is a minimum income scheme that does not discriminate on the basis of family status.

Workfare and integration can be seen as illustrating the passage from an 'income strategy' to a 'service strategy' (Nathan, 1993). However, embedded in their own institutional context and grounded in different conceptions of poverty and citizenship, they represent two distinctive societal approaches.

Societal differences between the United States and Europe can be seen in the way job quality is taken into account on the labour market. In the American case the problem is the growing number of the 'working poor', whereas in Europe high unemployment, especially long-term unemployment, is the central labour market dysfunction. Two different kinds of poverty emerge from these constellations, one based on unemployment, the other on low wages (OFCE, 1994). Different employment policies have been devised to address these problems, which also reflect divergent social norms concerning the performance of labour market institutions.

According to Levitan et al. (1993), the working poor remain America's glaring contradiction: 'The concurrence of work and poverty is contrary to the American ethos that a willingness to work leads to material advancement, and it negates the prevalent view that the cause of poverty among adults capable of work is deviant behavior, particularly a lack of commitment to work' (p. 3). In the United States the number of impoverished workers is substantial. In 1991 two million people working full-time year-round had earnings below the official poverty line (59 per cent more than in 1978), and 7.2 million poor individuals worked either in full-time jobs for part of the year or in part-time jobs (Levitan et al., 1993, p. 3). The position of the full-time working poor is very disturbing. As remarked by Ellwood (1988), these people end up the least secure of all: 'Full-time working-poor families are actually the poorest of the poor after transfers' (p. 103).

This situation has many causes. One of them is the general reluctance to set meaningful minimum wage standards. For example, the purchasing power of the federal minimum wage declined dramatically in the 1980s. The structure of the low-wage labour market has also changed tremendously since the 1970s. The number of well-paid manufacturing jobs has decreased, while service sector employment, which in most cases is poorly paid, has expanded. The growing wage inequality between less skilled and skilled workers is another cause of the problem represented by the working poor. Although widening income inequalities were characteristic of all OECD countries in the 1980s, this trend was less severe in European countries. In Europe minimum wages and wages in general have also held their value in real terms better than in the United States. Unemployment, however, has steadily increased. In 1993 the unemployment rate was 10.4 per cent in the European Community, compared to 6.7 per cent in the United States (OFCE, 1994).

To 'make work pay' was one of the main themes guiding the Clinton administration's welfare reform. This was a recognition of the fact that the welfare poor and the working poor shared common problems. To cover the range of employment policies towards disadvantaged groups in a comprehensive way, one must go beyond employment programmes and look at fiscal policies. In the United States, this perspective is especially relevant. The American federal government is increasingly relying on the Earned Income Tax Credit (EITC) to address the problems of the working poor and serve as an antipoverty programme in general. The EITC is a refundable subsidy on top of earned income directed primarily towards low-income workers with children.[8] In 1993 this credit was considerably expanded, and it is expected to become the largest cash or near-cash programme directed towards low-income families with children: in fiscal year 1998 the EITC is expected to cost the federal government 24.5 billion dollars, compared with the federal share of the AFDC programme, which is projected to be 16 billion (Scholz, 1994).

The EITC is a popular antipoverty programme because its aim is to encourage people to work. This aim is due to the fact that benefits increase with earned income (up to a maximum level). In 1994 (under the new law) the credit equalled 26.3 per cent of earned income (wages, salaries, self-employed and farm income) for taxpayers with one child[9] up to an earned income of $7750; hence, the maximum benefit was $2038 (Scholz, 1994).[10] The tying of benefits to work is widely seen as consistent with a 'pro-work' welfare policy. The expansion of EITC is also seen as an option that does not discourage hiring, for it raises earnings while maintaining constant the direct cost of labour to employers. As the costs are covered out of general tax revenue, that is, a loss in federal treasury revenue, EITC is a way to 'socialize' wage costs. In that sense, it is a substitute for the minimum wage. On the other hand, in becoming the corner-stone of public policies to support the working poor, EITC is serving to ease the pressures for wage increases and is thus contributing to the persistence of poor pay and working conditions. Like workfare then, its emphasis is on the value of employment *per se*, whatever the quality of jobs and the wage level.

In Europe in general, a deliberate choice has been made to ensure a high degree of social security and high incomes in terms of both wages and

---

8 A refundable credit means that if the amount of the credit exceeds what the taxpayer owes, he or she receives a payment for the difference.

9 Taxpayers with two or more children are entitled to a credit of 30 per cent of earned income.

10 Taxpayers whose incomes were above $7750 but below $11 000 received the maximum benefit. Beyond this income level, taxpayers were in the phase-out range of the credit. Their $2038 credit was reduced by 15.9 cents for every dollar of income earned above $11 000. The credit was completely exhausted at an income of $23 760.

substitute income such as unemployment insurance or minimum social benefits. A good example of this kind of policy orientation is the case of the Netherlands. In that country the legal minimum wage was set at a very high level, that is, HFL 2102.10 per month (for wage earners aged 23 and older) in 1991, and minimum social benefits were equivalent to 70 per cent and 90 per cent of this minimum wage for single people (aged at least 23) and single-parent families, respectively (MISEP, 1991, p. 20). Since then, this level of protection has been subjected to vociferous criticism. In other countries some employment policies have parallels to the American EITC. This is the case in France, with the growing use of exemptions from social security payroll taxes (or wage subsidies), and, above all, in Great Britain, where employment subsidies were redirected in the 1980s according to a strategy of wage-cutting incentives (Gautié, Gazier and Silvera, 1994, p. 142). Yet, such exceptions merely serve to confirm the general rule that European policy-makers are more concerned with the quality of labour market integration.

4   EVALUATION

Following Nicaise et al. (1994), one can distinguish between three categories of possible effects that such measures have:

1. Distributional effects (how the measure covers the target groups and how employment of the different categories is affected, including the estimation of possible side-effects for nontarget groups).
2. Labour market outcomes for the participants (employment opportunities, earnings, quality of jobs and so forth).
3. Macroeconomic effects (effects on the overall level of employment and unemployment, on wages and prices, on the government budget and so on).

We deal here only with distributional effects and outcomes for participants.[11] Very few studies try to estimate all these effects within a single framework, although a cost–benefit analysis has been tried in some.

It would, of course, be impossible to review here all the existing studies on our topic in the OECD countries.[12] We therefore opt to discuss the most representative evaluations for each category of programme (temporary employment

---

11 Consequently, no attempt will be made to compare the national performances in terms of rate of long-term unemployed in the labour force or among the unemployed.

12 As for other topics, there is an important quantitative and qualitative gap between evaluation studies in the United States and those in Europe. The US Department of Labor Report (1995) has provided a comprehensive survey of the evaluation research of the American programmes.

in the nonprofit sector, targeted employment subsidies, training, development of job search ability and comprehensive schemes).

4.1 Temporary Public Employment

The evaluation of temporary employment in the nonprofit sector and public service for the hard-to-place reveals mixed results. Although the direct effect on employment seems significant, labour market outcomes for participants are not always positive.

The coverage of the hard-to-place is generally better for temporary employment than for the other schemes, but in countries where unemployment is high even fully 'employable' persons sometimes enter this kind of scheme just to receive an income. There is a risk in this case of a substitution effect to the disadvantage of the hard-to-place. In France's CES at the beginning of the 1990s, for example, more than 50 per cent of the participants had a technical certificate or other diploma. The ABM programme in eastern Germany has had similar characteristics since unification.

The net employment generated by a public employment programme decreases in proportion to the incidence of fiscal substitution, such as when a local administration takes advantage of a federal subsidy to create a job that administration would have created otherwise. Unlike American studies, European studies have paid very little attention to this problem. But, as Haveman and Hollister (1991) have noted, 'programmes targeted on the disadvantaged will be less vulnerable to fiscal substitution because the skill mix of target group workers hired does not conform closely to the mix of regular public employees' (p. 39). For the US Public Employment Service (part of the CETA programme), for example, net new employment was estimated at between 40 and 60 per cent of the jobs created. The additionality principle—as it applies to the German ABM programme, for example—may be not enough to avoid fiscal substitution.

There is a risk of widening the gap between the hard-to-place and the regular labour market by putting them in 'side tracks' that sometimes turn out to be dead ends (Nicaise et al., 1994) and block the way back to regular employment. A 'lock-in' effect can arise, for example, alternating periods of temporary employment and unemployment.

Considerable research has been conducted into the German ABM programme. Outcomes in terms of employment probability are difficult to analyse because of the lack of an appropriate control group in all the studies. Spitznagel (1989) has established that immediately after leaving ABM only 22.4 per cent of the participants were in employment; this employment rate increased to 41.2 per cent 32 months later. An earlier study (Spitznagel, 1979) had observed 'ABM careers'—the vicious circle of unemployment–ABM–

unemployment—for the elderly unemployed and women. Cost–benefit analysis has been attempted (Spitznagel, 1985), but without the output value of the project being taken into account.

In a good evaluation, Bonnal, Fougère and Sérandon (1994, 1995) analysed the French TUC programme, which was very important in France during the 1980s. The analysis was based on a structural model of both duration and job search. Heterogeneity bias (at least in the first study) was properly controlled. Unfortunately, they looked only at young people, and it is unclear whether the results obtained can be generalized to all the hard-to-place. For young people without any qualification, the probability of finding a job was increased after a TUC, but the average duration of the job was shorter than that of jobs obtained after a training measure. Yet for those young people who had already earned a technical certificate, the outcomes seemed to be negative compared to the employment probability of those who had not participated in any measures. Estimates of pay levels on the first job obtained confirmed these results. After a TUC, there was no evidence of a comparative gain for the unskilled, and there seemed to be a negative effect for skilled women. The explanation may be that highly skilled persons who participate in temporary public employment are more vulnerable to stigmatization or loss of human capital than unskilled persons.

4.2   Targeted Employment Subsidies

If judgements about temporary public employment are circumspect, those about employment subsidies are generally pessimistic. Subsidies are usually insufficient to overcome the strong reluctance of the employers to recruit the least employable. On the other hand, wide targeting only results in large dead-weight effects. Financial incentives may be provided for youth lacking work experience (although high placement rates may result in this case from dead-weight effects), but they prove to be inefficient for the hard-to-place in the strict sense. One may conclude that conventional employment subsidies are generally unsatisfactory in dealing with long-term problems of that population (Schmid, 1982).

Evaluation of the Targeted Job Tax Credit (the United States) revealed that very few enterprises applied for the measure and, indeed, that employers appeared to be passing up opportunities to collect tax credits for decisions they were making anyway (Burtless, 1984). This resulted partly from an information problem (Bishop and Hollenbeck, in press) but might also have been the consequence of the fear of increased government control on the enterprise's books and operations. Creaming turned out to be significant. Two-thirds of the clients were under 25, and the proportion of welfare recipients was only 12 per cent. According to Bishop and Hollenbeck (in press), windfall and displacement effects were huge (between 75 per cent and 90 per cent). The following experiment highlighted the stigmatization effect (Burtless, 1985). In Dayton, Ohio, a manpower agency randomly divided clients into three groups. People in the two first groups were given a subsidy voucher (in the form of a tax credit or a cash subsidy), whereas those in the third group were given no voucher and did not know about the subsidy programme. In all, 21 per cent of the unvouchered clients, but only 13 per cent of those who had received a voucher, found a job by the end of the five- to eight-week search period.

A German employment subsidy programme (*Eingliederungsbeihilfen*) was evaluated by Schmid (1982). First, he pointed out that three target groups (old people, women and the long-term unemployed) were not reached by the programme as much as they should have been. Qualitative interviews in the employment agencies highlighted the very strong reluctance of employers to hire people with unstable occupational biographies and those lacking skills and work experience: 'For people with unstable job records or long unemployment histories, even a subsidy of more than 100 per cent would not help to place them' (Schmid, 1982, p. 192). The same study pointed out that workers were often reluctant to help integrate such 'outsiders'. It also provided estimates of net effects on unemployment from four multiple regressions. Deadweight seemed to be very significant for young people. The elderly and long-term unemployed were hard to place even with a large subsidy. Nevertheless, once placed they were more likely to remain in employment.

In the United Kingdom and France, interviews with employers have confirmed their strong reluctance to accept the hard-to-place, especially the long-term unemployed (Gazier and Silvera, 1993). Interviews with employers who had applied for the French CRE revealed that more than 50 per cent of the jobs created resulted from deadweight compared to the average of 80 per cent in the case of subsidies for youth (Gautié et al., 1994). This study also highlighted the fact that large firms seem to be more choosy. But this point was not confirmed by the Belgian survey presented by Van der Linden (1995). In that study almost 60 per cent of the firms reported that they would have hired the same disadvantaged person[13] even without a wage subsidy (36 per cent another person, and the remaining 12 per cent no person at all), and the deadweight effect did not appear to be higher in large firms.

Studies on the effects of subsidies paid to the job seeker rather than to the employer are very rare. We mention here only the cash-bonus experiment conducted in five US states.[14] To receive the bonus, the unemployment insur-

---

13 The disadvantaged persons were unskilled youth, long-term unemployed, welfare recipients, the disabled and women who had not been working for five years or more.

14 For more details on methodological aspects and results, see chap. 3 on 'Experimental Evaluation of European Labour Market Policy' by Björklund and Regnér in this volume.

ance recipients had to find a job within a certain period and had to remain in that job for a given time. The unemployment spell of the experimental group members seemed to be significantly affected. As there was no significant effect on their earnings, one may conclude that the reduction of the unemployment spell resulted more from a more intensive job search than from a lowering of the reservation wage, that is, the minimum wage considered acceptable by the job seeker.

4.3   Training

The first point to highlight is that training schemes must be carefully tailored to the abilities and requirements of the hard-to-place. Classroom training may be unsuited to people who experienced failure at school and have problems with their self-confidence and motivation. An additional difficulty is the potential mismatch between the provision of the training schemes and the needs of the employers. Programme designers face a dilemma here. Favouring the needs of the employers may lead to increased creaming, but a bias in favour of the hard-to-place may limit the employment-creating effects of the programme. Thus, an appropriate balance must be found between the interests of the hard-to-place and those of employers.

For many training schemes the drop-out rate is rather high, especially among the most disadvantaged. In Germany, for example, the study of the effectiveness of training for adults has focussed on the targeting of the training schemes (Disney, 1992). The least qualified had a high drop-out rate in classical training schemes, which has prompted the 'Bundesanstalt für Arbeit' to initiate measures to prepare them for training (Hofbauer and Dadzio, 1984). The drop-out rate was higher for retraining and refresher training than for the wage-subsidy scheme designed to aid vocational adjustment, that is, on-the-job training. Only 15 per cent of the participants receiving the 'familiarization allowance' (*Einarbeitungszuschuß*) of the German on-the-job training programme in 1989 had been unemployed for more than a year, only 12 per cent were more than 45 years old, and less than 10 per cent had no school-leaving certificate. One may therefore conclude that the scheme fails to reach the hard-to-place.

The Employment Training Programme in the United Kingdom aimed at responding to skill demand on the local labour market. But in 1989, for example, 60 to 70 per cent of the people who had been referred to the scheme failed to embark on training, and of those who did begin training only 43 per cent completed courses (Atkinson and Meager, 1989; Disney, 1992). Only 5 per cent of the trainees were older than 50, and more than 20 per cent had been unemployed for less than six months before entering the scheme (Finn, 1989).

Like Employment Training, the American JTPA is based on cooperation between employers and the public employment service and is aimed at providing training suited to employers' needs. The performance benchmark for the manpower policy agents is the placement ratio, which, according to Donahue (1989), gives officials and contractors powerful incentives to select from those eligible the trainees most likely to succeed, with or without any real increment in human capital.

On the basis of the available evidence it is not possible to conclude that any one type of training scheme (e.g. on-the-job training) always gives better results than another (e.g. classroom training). Success depends not least on the targeted population, as the evaluations of the CETA and JTPA programmes show.

The CETA programme has given rise to a great number of evaluations, many of them based on the data provided by the Continuous Longitudinal Manpower Survey (CLMS), which documents demographic characteristics and the changing labour force status of the participants, and by the Social Security Administration, which tracks earnings. For a survey of eleven of these studies, see Barnow (1987). The results were quite puzzling. The estimates of the effects on earnings varied widely for any given programme and population subgroup. The estimates were very sensitive to the model specification. Because of the nonexperimental nature of the data and the inability to adequately test the validity of the selection process assumptions, it appears impossible to compare the value of the different studies (Barnow, 1987). Nevertheless, three general conclusions seem to emerge from these studies (Haveman and Hollister, 1991). The CETA programme was most effective for those who had previously the least labour market experience. It was also more effective for women than for men. Among the different programmes, on-the-job training seemed to generate better results than simple work experience and classroom training.

According to Bishop (1989), however, the fact that studies have found that the most intensive form of CETA training, classroom training, had only modest effects on postprogramme earnings, whereas less intensive intervention, such as public service employment and on-the-job training contracts, had much more positive effects may be explained by stigma. From a methodological point of view, a longer follow-up would be necessary before drawing conclusions. Recent American studies indicate that it may take six years for the effects of improved academic skills to show up in the workplace (US Department of Labor, 1995).

An extensive evaluation of the JTPA has also been carried out on the basis of experiments with applicants randomly assigned to the control group or the treatment group (Orr, 1992). Some of the results differ from those found for the CETA. The effects of the programme varied with the degree of labour market disadvantage, as defined by three 'barriers' to unemployment: welfare receipt, limited education and limited work experience. The estimated impacts were better for those not facing these barriers. Results tended to be more significant for adult women than for adult men. The more striking finding is that the programme had a negative impact on the earnings of male school leavers.

In their study of the work experience programme 'Supported Work', Hollister, Kemper and Maynard (1984) also found that the results were positive for women on welfare but that the programme did not seem to work at all for low-income youth and ex-offenders (although it had some positive effects on former drug addicts).

In Germany, the outcomes of the training schemes in terms of employment seemed better for the on-the-job training schemes. But this result is due to the fact that the target groups (older workers, long-term unemployed, individuals with health restrictions and women) were underrepresented (Disney, 1992). The employment probability after training decreased with age. More generally, though, there was no suitable control group against which to evaluate the success of such programmes in reemploying participants. Comparing job status before training and two years after training, Hofbauer and Dadzio (1987) found that occupational mobility was higher for women.[15] But the net cost of these adult training schemes appears to be relatively high (Bach, Kohler and Spitznagel, 1986; Spitznagel, 1985). Moreover, econometric evaluation shows that further training and retraining are less successful than direct job creation measures when deadweight and substitution effects are controlled for (Disney, 1992).

4.4   Development of Job Search Ability

Provision of advice and counselling to improve job search ability seems to have proved its worth; at least this has been suggested by a number of experiments. In a series of random assignment experiments carried out in five American states (Minnesota, Nevada, New Jersey, South Carolina and Washington),[16] the effectiveness of a two-stage combination of profiling and job search assistance was studied. The profiling stage used demographic information and occupational biographies in an attempt to identify the unemployment insurance claimants who were the most likely to become long-term unemployed. Once identified, they received intensive job search assistance. The result was that the recipients found a job more rapidly than members of the control group.

---

15   The methodology of this study was severely criticized by Kasparek and Koop (1991).

16   See Meyer (1992). For more details on the methodological aspects and results, see Björklund and Regnér, chap. 3 in this volume.

Moreover, recipients did not end up in less well-paying jobs. (In fact they were better paid during the first year of employment than the members of the control group.) Once the decrease in unemployment (and thus the savings on unemployment insurance) and the increase in tax receipts were taken into account, the programme turned out to be macroeconomically cost-effective (about two dollars saved for each dollar spent on the programme).

An earlier Swedish experiment (Delander, 1978) conducted in the town of Eskilstuna in 1975 had led to similarly positive results[17] for the members of the group who had been provided more intensive job assistance. In this case, too, the quality of the jobs obtained by the experimental group members was higher than that for the control group.

The main problem with these experiments is that they were carried out at local level. At the macrolevel displacement effects may arise, leading to an overestimate of what can be achieved by job search assistance. Good results may sometimes also be due to statistical artifacts. For example, the Restart Programme introduced in the United Kingdom in 1986 has often been presented as an important factor behind the decline in unemployment in the United Kingdom in the late 1980s. According to official figures, approximately 20 per cent of the unemployed who were called for the interview subsequently left the unemployment register. But empirical study has revealed that only 5 per cent got a regular job or were placed in a community programme. In the great majority of cases, the problem of hard-to-place people is not primarily one of simple motivation or information deficiency. And, at the macrolevel, their unemployment does not simply result from frictional mismatch on the labour market.

4.5   Comprehensive Schemes

Comprehensive schemes include a mix of services ranging from job search assistance to different sorts of training and work experience. As a consequence this subsection partly overlaps with the two previous ones. We focus here on the American programmes targeted at the hardest-to-place, in other words, socially disadvantaged delinquent youths, welfare recipients and so forth.

The Job Corps programme gave the opportunity to carry out a high-quality evaluation (control for selection bias with the best econometric methods available at the time and careful cost–benefit analysis; see Long, Mallar and Thornton, 1981). The studies concluded that the estimated benefits in terms of earnings and lower crime outweigh programme cost. As Burtless (1984) put

---

17 For more details on the methodological aspects and results, see Björklund and Regnér, chap. 3 in this volume.

it: 'The comparative success of the Job Corps implies that expensive effort may be required to offset the effects of a life-time disadvantage' (p. 20).

Conclusions are less optimistic regarding the effects of the welfare-to-work programmes (US Department of Labor, 1995). Many of them have been rigorously evaluated using random assignment experiments. The GAIN programme implemented in California and Florida produced modest, but significant, gains in earnings and employment for the participants (Riccio, Friedlander and Freedman, 1994). But long-term studies have found that these gains tend to disappear after about five years. Moreover, unemployment and poverty remain high despite participation in these programmes. For example, 80 per cent of those who had participated to California's GAIN programme three years before had incomes below the poverty line at the time of the evaluation. Another conclusion of these evaluations is that, as noted in the context of the training schemes, programmes oriented to rapid job placement were more successful than those focussing on classroom training.

5   A CRITICAL ASSESSMENT OF EVALUATION STUDIES

What has been learned from the experience of western countries? What are the priorities for research, and what new studies need to be carried out in order to improve current knowledge about the problems involved?

5.1   Equity and Efficiency Considerations

When choosing the target groups and designing the programmes, one must strike a careful balance between equity and efficiency considerations. For example, there is always a temptation to adopt expedients to remove people considered as 'unemployable' from the unemployment register by transferring them to early retirement (if they are old) or other forms of income support, without taking into account their desire to work. On the other hand, social pressures can sometimes lead to persons on welfare being obliged to work, without attention being paid to the concomitant private and social costs (e.g. to some welfare mothers). As a consequence, according to Nicaise et al. (1994), equity should imply equal treatment for all and, as a rule, avoidance of a mandatory approach. But the debates about these issues are still very controversial. To workfare supporters, in whose opinion the labour market's major limitation is that job seekers often consider the pay or conditions of jobs unacceptable rather than that there is a lack of jobs *per se*, the compulsion to work can serve the goal of integration from an efficiency point of view (Mead, 1988).

5.2 Coverage and Targeting

An important issue is how to define a target appropriately. The duration of unemployment is not always a sound criterion. When poor 'employability' is due to personal characteristics (rather than to dependence on the state), it would be more efficient to identify such individuals at the beginning of the unemployment period. Moreover, duration criteria further handicap the recurrent unemployed, who might also need help to improve their 'employability'. A growing number of programmes take this point into account, defining the unemployment duration as the sum total of the recurrent spells of unemployment during a certain period.

Programmes often do not reach the hard-to-place as much as they should. This failure results from the attitudes of all the actors. The hardest-to-place, because of their lack of motivation and self-confidence, are reluctant to embark on schemes oriented to regular employment. Labour market policy agents are often tempted to cream, especially when they are themselves evaluated on the basis of simple performance standards like the placement ratio.[18] Employers, as we have noted, try to use the different measures while selecting people they would have hired anyway. As a consequence, programme designers face a crucial dilemma. If measures are too widely targeted, the underrepresentation of hard-to-place and huge deadweight effects may result. On the other hand, a programme more narrowly targeted will face two important obstacles: the strong reluctance of the employers and the danger that participants will become yet more highly stigmatized. Consequently, the challenge is to define client groups narrowly enough to prevent creaming and to overcome screening devices, but not so narrowly that employers have to accept unsuitable candidates or, in an effort to avoid doing so, refuse to accept any participants in the programme. In order to deal with this problem, employment office staff must perform positive screening and propose schemes suited to the needs of the hardest-to-place. Two dangers must be avoided. The first is trying to place people who are not 'employable' at all on the regular labour market: the inevitable failure will only worsen their problems. Yet, at the same time such people must not be placed in what turns out to be dead-end schemes outside the regular market, as happens with some forms of temporary public employment.

Another important point is that heterogeneity of the hard-to-place implies the need to provide various types of training and employment services. As the US Department of Labor Report (1995) notes, 'the findings argue against a "one-size-fits-all" model' (p. 63).

---

18 See, for example, the case of JTPA cited above.

5.3   Internal Consistency of the Labour Market Policy for the Hard-to-place

Internal consistency refers to the relations between the different labour market programmes.[19] For example, it is inconsistent to encourage early retirement—with the attendant risk of suggesting that all elderly workers are 'second-best' workers—while developing measures to encourage the recruitment of the elderly, as was the case in France, for example. Labour market policy must also avoid the multiplication of target groups and programmes that may lead to substitution effects between those different groups (Nicaise et al., 1994).

5.4   Pitfalls to Avoid and Dilemmas to Resolve

In countries with high unemployment there is a great temptation to favour distributional effects in the short run by launching large temporary employment programmes in order to rotate participants as much as possible and thereby increase the distribution of income,[20] and lower the unemployment statistics. But this goal may be achieved at the expense of the labour market outcomes of the hard-to-place participants—in terms of human capital accumulation and long-term employment prospects. Moreover, the impacts of these projects are often of limited economic value. An alternative would be to encourage the emergence of a 'second labour market' in social services activities where latent demand is great. This would, however, entail the risk of the displacement of private output in these activities. The challenge would then be to prevent this 'second market' from becoming a 'secondary market', where the disadvantaged are trapped without any prospect of mobility.

Employment subsidies have to be narrowly targeted in order to limit deadweight effects. The financial incentive must be proportional to the extent of the employers' reluctance that needs to be overcome but also high enough to offset fixed employment costs.[21] Given that for some groups even massive subsidies will not overcome employers' reluctance, suitable training seems to be the only solution. However, for the hardest-to-place, comprehensive training may be necessary. Nevertheless, the comparative success of the Job Corps implies that considerable investment will be required to overcome entrenched social disadvantage.

---

19 External consistency refers to the relations between labour market programmes and other forms of public intervention, such as welfare or unemployment benefits.

20 In countries where income support is weak or nonexistent, local labour force agents may choose to use labour market policy schemes as a means of maintaining the income of the unemployed in the short run rather than a means of solving employment problems.

21 From this point of view, simple exemptions from social security contributions may be not enough.

5.5   Priorities for Action and Scientific Progress

The lack of high-quality evaluation studies, especially in the European countries, has been remarked upon many times in this handbook. Even in the cases where many studies have been carried out, the results obtained often differ, leading to serious interpretational problems. In many cases, we could modestly conclude, as Björklund (1991) has for Swedish training schemes, that 'the results obtained are too uncertain to allow firm policy conclusions' (p. 90). Moreover, international comparisons are very difficult, because programmes vary widely between countries and macroeconomic and institutional contexts are specific to the various countries. Nevertheless, some general remarks can be made here.

A large number of studies focus on the effects on the earnings of the participants in labour market measures. But, as Bishop (1989) argues, there is evidence that participants in government measures are stigmatized on the regular labour market and consequently are often underpaid when hired, thereby causing evaluators to underestimate the actual productivity improvement due to the measures. One also must take into account the fact that the majority of jobs available for the hard-to-place are on the secondary market, where the remuneration of human capital is weaker. From a more general point of view, the long-run effects (and not only one to two years after) have to be more systematically studied, for they may be different from the short-run ones.

Even if the outcomes of the measures are well estimated, it is often difficult to attribute them to a well-identified cause. This is particularly the case for mixed measures, which associate subsidies, training and often nonstandard forms of employment contract (in terms of social security treatment and so forth). As Grubb (1994) has pointed out, in this case the impact of the subsidy is difficult to distinguish from the impact of deregulation and/or training.

Another problem is that it takes time for programmes to begin to work. As noted in the US Department of Labor Report (1995): 'Many of the success stories in training for the disadvantaged have come from programmes which were operating for five years or more before they were evaluated ... This indicates that the knowledge and experience built up through years of practice can be an important factor in determining a programme's success' (p. 63).

When considering the results of the studies on microdata which control for individual characteristics and correlate earnings and employment probability with measures, one must keep in mind the global economic and institutional context in which these studies have been carried out. First, the global shortage of employment, especially in Europe, must be taken into account when assessing the efficiency of the programmes for the hard-to-place. Training (or improving job search ability) is valued because instead of 'giving a fish' (like income support measures and temporary public employment) it 'teaches how to fish'. But, as Burtless (1984) put it, 'The alert trainee might reasonably ask: where is the fish?' (p. 19).

Second, even if jobs are available for the hard-to-place, they are often of poor quality in terms of stability and earnings. As Lange and Shackleton (1994) pointed out, little attention has been paid to the important issue of evaluating whether the jobs gained are stable or merely offer a temporary reprieve from unemployment. Consequently, the problem of the hard-to-place may be translated into a problem of the 'hard-to-maintain', or a problem of the 'working poor', as in the United States.

Finally, one must adopt a systemic approach to understanding and appreciating labour market policy for the disadvantaged. The vocational training system, the unemployment insurance and welfare system and firms' human-resource strategies all have to be taken into account to try to understand the situation of hard-to-place people. From this point of view, a general lesson is that everything must be done to promote a preventive approach.

All these remarks lead to a rather pessimistic conclusion: labour market policy measures for the hard-to-place are necessary, and will remain so in the future, but are far from sufficient to cope with the problem. In a persistent context of weak growth (compared to the postwar period) and the scepticism about ever returning to traditional 'full employment', western countries—especially European countries—will have to develop more ambitious solutions than simple temporary schemes or financial incentives, for reasons of both equity and efficiency.[22]

REFERENCES

Atkinson, J. and N. Meager (1989), 'Employer Involvement in Adult Training Initiatives', Institute of Manpower Studies, report no. 158, University of Sussex, Brighton.

Bach, H.-U., H. Kohler and E. Spitznagel (1986), 'Arbeitsmarktpolitische Maßnahmen: Entlastungswirkung und Kostenvergleiche', *Mitteilungen aus der Arbeitsmarkt- und Berufsforschung*, 19 (3), 370–75.

Bane, M., J. Ellwood and T. David (1994), *Welfare Realities: From Rhetoric to Reform*, Cambridge, MA: Harvard University Press.

Barnow, B. S. (1987), 'The Impact of CETA Programs on Earnings: A Review of the Literature', *Journal of Human Resources*, 22, 157–93.

Bishop, J. (1989), 'Towards More Valid Evaluations of Training Programs Serving the Disadvantaged', *Journal of Policy Analysis and Management*, 8 (2), 209–28.

---

22 See, for example, Schmid (1995).

Bishop, J. and K. Hollenbeck (eds) (in press), *The Effects of TJTC on Employers*, National Center of Research in Vocational Education, Columbus, OH: Ohio State University.

Björklund, A. (1991), 'Labour Market Training: The Lessons from Swedish Evaluations', in A. Björklund, R. Haveman, R. Hollister and B. Holmlund (eds), *Labour Market Policy and Unemployment Insurance*, Oxford: Clarendon Press, pp. 87–91.

Bonnal, L., D. Fougère and A. Sérandon (1994), 'L'impact des dispositifs d'emploi sur le devenir des jeunes chômeurs: une évaluation économétrique sur données longitudinales', *Economie et Prévisions*, 115 (4), 1–28.

Bonnal, L., D. Fougère and A. Sérandon (1995, May), 'Une modélisation du processus de recherche d'emploi en présence de mesures publiques pour les jeunes', *Revue économique*, 46, 1–11.

Burtless, G. (1984), 'Manpower Policy for the Disadvantaged: What Works?', *The Brookings Review*, 3 (1), 18–22.

Burtless, G. (1985), 'Are Targeted Wage Subsidies Harmful? Evidence of a Wage Voucher Experiment', *Industrial and Labour Relations Review*, 39, 105–14.

Delander, L. (1978), 'Studier kring den arbetsförmedlande verksamheten', *Statens Offentliga Utredningar (SOU)*, 60, 183–248.

Disney, R. (ed.) (1992), *Helping the Unemployed. Active Labour Market Policy in Britain and Germany*, London: Anglo-German Foundation.

Donahue, J. D. (1989), *Shortchanging the Workforce: The JTPA and the Overselling of Privatized Training*, Washington: Economic Public Institute.

Ellwood, D. T. (1988), *Poor Support, Poverty in the American Family*, New York: Basic Books.

Finn, D. (1989, Autumn), 'Employment Training: Success or Failure?, *Unemployment Bulletin*, Unemployment Unit.

Gautié, J., B. Gazier and R. Silvera (eds) (1994), *Les subventions à l'emploi: Analyse et expériences européennes*, Paris: La Documentation Française.

Gazier, B. (1990), 'L'employabilité: brève radiographie d'un concept en mutation', *Sociologie du travail*, 4, 575–84.

Gazier, B. and R. Silvera (1993), 'L'allègement du coût salarial a-t-il un effet sur l'embauche?', *Travail et Emploi*, 55, 60–70.

Grubb, D. (1994), 'Direct and Indirect Effects of Active Labour Market Policies in OECD Countries', in R. Barrel (ed.), *The UK Labour Market: Comparative Aspects and Institutional Developments*, Cambridge, UK: Cambridge University Press, pp. 183–213.

Gueron, J. and E. Pauly (1991), 'From Welfare to Work', Russell Sage Foundation. (Unpublished manuscript)

Haveman, R. and R. Hollister (1991), 'Direct Job Creation: Economic Evaluation and Lessons for the U.S.A. and Western Europe', in A. Björklund, R. Haveman, R. Hollister and B. Holmlund (1991), *Labour Market Policy and Unemployment Insurance*, Oxford: Clarendon Press, pp. 5–100.

Hofbauer, H. and W. Dadzio (1984), 'Berufliche Weiterbildung für Arbeitslose', *Mitteilungen aus der Arbeitsmarkt- und Berufsforschung*, 17 (2), 183–200.

Hofbauer, H. and W. Dadzio (1987), 'Mittelfristige Wirkungen beruflicher Weiterbildung', *Mitteilungen aus der Arbeitsmarkt- und Berufsforschung*, 20 (2), 129–41.

Hollister, R., P. Kemper and R. Maynard (eds) (1984), *The National Supported Work Demonstration*, Madison: University of Wisconsin Press.

Kasparek, P. and W. Koop (1991), 'Zur Wirksamkeit von Fortbildungs- und Umschulungsmaßnahmen', *Mitteilungen aus der Arbeitsmarkt- und Berufsforschung*, 20 (2), 129–41.

Lange, T. and J. Shackleton (1994, September), 'A Critical Assessment of Active Labour Market Policies', paper presented at the European Association of Labour Economists Annual Conference, Warsaw.

Levitan, S., F. Gallo and I. Shapiro (1993), *Working But Poor, America's Contradiction*, Baltimore, MD: Johns Hopkins University Press.

Long, D. A., C. D. Mallar and C. Thornton (1981), 'Evaluating the Benefits and Cost of the Job Corps', *Journal of Policy Analysis and Management*, 1 (1), 55–76.

Manski, C. and I. Garfinkel (1992), *Evaluating Welfare and Training Programs*, Cambridge, MA: Harvard University Press.

Mead, L. M. (1986), *Beyond Entitlement: The Obligations of Citizenship*, New York: Free Press.

Mead, L. M. (1988), 'The Potential of Work Enforcement: Study of WIN', *Journal of Policy Analysis and Management*, 7 (2), 264–88.

Mead, L. M. (1992), *New Politics of Poverty: The Nonworking Poor in America*, New York: Basic Books.

Meyer, B. (1992), 'Policy Lessons from the US Unemployment Insurance Experiments', National Bureau of Economic Research (NBER), working paper no. 4197, Cambridge, MA.

MISEP (1991), *Pays-Bas, Institutions, Procédures et Mesures*, Commission des Communautés Européennes.

MISEP, *Basic Information Reports on Employment Policies in Europe* (Belgium 1992, France 1992, Germany 1992, Italy 1992, Netherlands 1991, United Kingdom 1992), Brussels, European Community Publication.

Moffitt, R. (1992), 'Incentive Effects of the US Welfare System: A Review', *Journal of Economic Literature*, 30, 1–61.

Morel, S. (1994), 'Les programmes d'intégration à l'emploi pour les allocataires de l'assistance sociale. L'approche américaine du "workfare"', *Revue française des Affaires sociales*, 3, 125–45.

Murray, C. (1984), *Losing Ground: American Social Policy 1950–1980*, New York: Basic Books.

Nathan, R. (1993), *Turning Promises into Performances: The Management Challenge of Implementing Workfare*, New York: Columbia University Press.

Nicaise, I., J. Bollens, L. Dawes, S. Laghaei, I. Thaulow, N. Verdier and A. Wagner (1994, September), 'Pitfalls and Dilemmas in Labour Market Policies for Disadvantaged Groups', paper prepared for the European Association of Labour Economists Annual Conference, Warsaw.

OECD (1992), 'The Long-term Unemployed and Measures to Assist Them', *Labour Market and Social Policy*, Occasional Papers, 7, 94.

OFCE (Observatoire Français des Conjonctures Economiques) (1994), 'Groupe international de politique économique de l'OFCE', *Pour l'emploi et la cohésion sociale*, Paris: Presses de la Fondation nationale des sciences politiques.

Orr, L. L. (1992), *The National JTPA Study, Title II A: Impacts on Earnings and Employment at 18 Months*, Bethesda, MD: Abt. Associates Inc.

Phelps, E. S. (ed.) (1972), *Microeconomic Foundations of Employment and Inflation Theory*, New York: Norton.

Reubens, B. G. (1970), *The Hard to Employ. European Programs*, New York: Columbia University Press.

Riccio, J., D. Friedlander and S. Freedman (1994), *GAIN: Benefits, Costs, and Three-year Impacts of a Welfare-to-work Program*, New York: Manpower Demonstration Research Corporation.

Schmid, G. (1982), 'Public Finance Measures to Generate Employment for Hard-to-place People: Employer Wage Subsidies or Public Employment Programs?', in R. Haveman (ed.), *Public Finance and Public Employment*, Detroit: Wayne State University Press, pp. 189–209.

Schmid, G. (1995), 'Is Full Employment Still Possible? Transitional Labour Markets as a New Strategy of Labour Market Policy', *Economic and Industrial Democracy*, 16, 429–56.

Schmid, G., B. Reissert and G. Bruche (1992), *Unemployment Insurance and Active Labor Market Policy: An International Comparison of Financing Systems*, Detroit: Wayne State University Press.

Scholz, J. K. (1994), 'Tax Policy and the Working Poor: The Earned Income Tax Credit', *Focus*, 15 (3), 1–12.

Spitznagel, E. (1979), 'Arbeitsmarktwirkungen, Beschäftigungsstrukturen und Zielgruppenorientierung von allgemeinen Maßnahmen zur Arbeitsbeschaffung (ABM)', *Mitteilungen aus der Arbeitsmarkt- und Berufsforschung*, 12 (2), 198–216.

Spitznagel, E. (1985), 'Arbeitsmarktpolitische Maßnahmen: Entlastungswirkung und Kostenvergleiche', *Mitteilungen aus der Arbeitsmarkt- und Berufsforschung*, 18 (1), 0–23.

Spitznagel, E. (1989), 'Zielgruppenorientierung und Eingliederungserfolg bei allgemeinen Maßnahmen zur ABM', *Mitteilungen aus der Arbeitsmarkt- und Berufsforschung*, 22 (4), 523–39.

US Congress, House Committee on Ways and Means (1993), *Green Book 1993*, Washington, DC: US Government Printing Office.

US Department of Labor Report (1995, January), *What's Working (and What's Not)? A Summary of Research on the Economic Impacts of Employment and Training Programs*, Washington, DC: Office of Chief Economist.

Van der Linden, B. (1995), 'Effets de perte sèche et de substitution des formations professionnelles et des aides à l'embauche: une évaluation par enquête auprès des employeurs', *Bulletin de l'IRES*, 180, Université Catholique de Louvain-la-Neuve.

Weir, M. (1992), *Politics and Jobs: The Boundaries of Employment Policy in the United States*, Princeton: Princeton University Press.

10. The School-to-Work Transition

Paul Ryan and Christoph F. Büchtemann

The school-to-work transition concerns the institutional links between education and work as they affect young people moving between schooling and employment. It involves the worlds of both school and work. Policy typically straddles government departments responsible for education and labour, research, the disciplines of labour economics and educational studies.

Interest is confined in this chapter to advanced economies, to young people who leave formal education before receiving their first degree and to an age group that always consists primarily of teenagers but that extends to at least 25 years of age in the United States, France and Italy.

School-to-work issues are both qualitative and quantitative. That is, they are about labour quality and unemployment (Garonna and Ryan, 1991a). The quality issue is nowadays seen as acute in the United States, where many observers judge the skills of the 'lower half' of the work force to be inadequate for effective international competition, particularly in comparison with Germany and Japan, given the achievements of the educational and training systems of those national success stories. Skills deficiencies are widely attributed in both the United States and the United Kingdom to inadequate learning in schools and workplaces (Grant Foundation, 1988; National Commission on Education (NCE), 1993; US DE, 1993). A second quality issue concerns youth employment, particularly in the United States, where institutionalists view high job turnover as wasteful, whereas competitive theorists see it as productive (Osterman, 1980; Topel and Ward, 1992).

On the quantitative side, youth unemployment has risen sharply since the mid-1970s in most advanced economies, both absolutely and relative to adult unemployment (Garonna and Ryan, 1991a). The deterioration has been attributed variously to a declining availability of less-skilled, entry-level jobs as a result of technical change and increased competition from adult females and to declining quality of the teenage labour supply as more young people stay longer in full-time schooling (Ashton and Lowe, 1991). In addition, high youth unemployment has long been a structural feature in the United States, particularly among racial minorities and urban residents, where teenage joblessness rates rose during the 1970s to about one-half (Freeman and Holzer, 1986; Freeman and Wise, 1982; Rees, 1986).

There are three types of policy that address school-to-work issues. Schooling content policy focusses on study incentives, curriculum content, the links between education and work, and career counselling. A goal of payroll cost policy is to cut employers' costs of youth activity at the workplace in order to increase youth employment and training. Labour market programmes offer young workers various mixtures of remedial education, training, work experience and support services as antidotes to low skills and joblessness.

The policy mix varies from country to country. US policy emphasizes selective labour market programmes for the most disadvantaged young workers, supplemented recently by links between learning in school and at work. Intervention has ranged wider in Europe, where some subsidized activity to all unemployed youth is typically offered. France has rapidly increased the rates of both general and vocational qualification in secondary education and has instituted special contracts and subsidies to encourage employers to take on young workers. The United Kingdom favours work-based training for unemployed school leavers, supplemented by expansion of full-time vocational upper secondary studies. Swedish policy combines job creation in the public sector with employer-based training and work experience.

Questions arise immediately. Which policies work best? Indeed, which work at all? When particular policies do not work, is institutional change desirable? Can appropriate policies be developed within national political systems? In the United States, controversy has been endemic in all three policy areas. School-based and work-based approaches to youth vocational preparation have been variously recommended for the United Kingdom (Marsden and Ryan, 1990; Soskice, 1993). The merits of foreign school-to-work arrangements have been widely debated in France (Campinos-Dubernet and Grando, 1988; Verdier, 1994).

In this chapter answers are sought to such questions through a review of research findings. The objectives and the means of intervention are discussed in section 1, followed by evaluation methodologies in section 2. Evaluation results are discussed in section 3, followed in section 4 by the conclusions. Attention is confined to leading recent research, particularly that bearing on the United States, France and the United Kingdom. More comprehensive surveys of US labour market and school-based programme evaluations can be found in W. N. Grubb (in press) and Stern, Finkelstein, Stone, Latting and Dornsife (1995).

This survey aims at distinctiveness in two respects. First, consistent with a target orientation in policy evaluation (see chap. 1 in this volume), institutions such as apprenticeship, wage-for-age scales and school–employer linkages are considered, not just specific programmes such as the Job Corps.

Second, a wide range of evaluative methods, from social experiments to international comparisons, is considered with an eye to the contributions of the various options. All methodologies are seen as imperfect, but all can contribute to knowledge in one area or another.

1   POLICY GOALS AND OPTIONS

School-to-work discussions suggest a variety of potential policy goals. Those commonly encountered nowadays include:

1. widespread completion of upper secondary general education, along with appropriate achievement and certification, as well as access to continuing education thereafter;
2. high-quality vocational preparation for all, including vocationally oriented education, work-related training and preparation for life-long further training;
3. rapid transition to stable, career-oriented and well-paid employment;
4. low rates of youth unemployment, particularly long-term unemployment;
5. effective matching of young workers and jobs; and
6. equal opportunity among young people, with options both for changes of career track and for second chances at particular tracks.

Particular programmes often pursue single goals from such a list, such as increased educational attainment and higher pay. Others range still wider, pursuing lower criminality, drug use, pregnancy and so on.

Some ordering and reduction in the set of eligible goals is desirable. Welfare economics treats the above goals as at most intermediate ones, justifiable—if at all—only in terms of the ultimate criteria: efficiency and equity. Efficiency denotes maximum output value for a given set of inputs; equity, a fairer distribution of economic well-being. The status of some intermediate objectives is straightforward. Thus, long-term youth unemployment is doubly disfavoured, for it both lowers efficiency by wasting resources and damages egalitarian goals by disproportionately affecting the most disadvantaged young people.

The status of other intermediate goals is less clear. Some can be criticized on efficiency grounds for failing to consider costs as well as benefits. Universal youth qualification at upper secondary level and universal youth training have become policy goals in France and Britain, but they would be expensive to achieve and they might contribute little to productivity as long as skill requirements remain low in many jobs. The case for such measures must depend on equity rather than efficiency (Heckman, Roselius and Smith, 1994; Ryan, 1984).

Moreover, it is opportunity costs that matter for efficiency. On the assumption that resources for intervention are limited, the attributes of youth relative to other needy groups, such as the adult unemployed, are crucial. In education and training, efficiency favours slanting provision towards younger rather than older workers, given the faster learning and longer payback periods for youth. Losses of both efficiency and equity may, however, be lower for youth than for adult unemployment, given the shorter spells, lower state dependence and lesser responsibilities typical of youth unemployment (Ellwood, 1982; Garonna and Ryan, 1991a).

A different problem applies to goals 3 through 5, above. Even if they have priority, the policies appropriate to their pursuit depend on how the economy works. High rates of youth turnover and frictional unemployment in the United States are interpreted by institutionalists as evidence of a wasteful exclusion of young people from careers and training in segmented labour markets, particularly in contrast to the rapid incorporation of young Germans into career employment (Büchtemann, Schupp and Soloff, 1993; DeFreitas, Marsden and Ryan, 1991). Others infer a time-consuming, but productive, matching of heterogeneous workers and jobs under imperfect information (Klerman and Karoly, 1995; Topel and Ward, 1992), with German apprenticeship viewed as a wasteful delay in the matching process (Heckman et al., 1994). The desirability of policies lowering youth turnover differs radically according to which view is valid, yet evidence on the latter, though suggestive, cannot fundamentally resolve the issue (McNabb and Ryan, 1990).

Lastly, not all goals are reducible to efficiency and equity. Personal development, social cohesion, political unrest and child welfare have all motivated policies and justified institutions, from New Chance for disadvantaged teenage mothers in the United States to mass apprenticeship in Germany.

The upshot for this survey is that single-outcome evaluations are of limited value. By contrast, evaluations that include many outcomes, assign economic values, deduct resource costs and determine distributional effects—that is, cost–benefit analyses—are of particular interest. At the same time, comprehensive evaluation remains an elusive goal in the presence of exceptionally wide-ranging and diffuse public goals.

2   EVALUATION METHODS

Evaluation methods vary greatly in three primary respects: the range of benefits and costs covered, approximation to experimental conditions and assumptions about the labour market. The first aspect, discussed above, leads to a three-way distinction between studies that attempt cost–benefit analysis; those that assess impacts on at most a few outcomes, without valuing benefits;

and, least ambitious of all, those that aim only at qualitative assessment. In this section we consider only the latter two aspects: experimental status and labour market assumptions.

2.1   Experimental Status

Natural scientists commonly rely on experimental procedures to study cause and effect, using laboratory conditions to hold constant other influences on the outcome. Economists can rarely use laboratory experiments, relying instead primarily on the economy's statistical evidence for the variability of key influences across time and place.

In disentangling a particular cause and effect within the welter of interactive processes at work in the economy, two features are centrally important: the implementation of the counterfactual and the variability of the prospective causal variable. Let us examine each feature in turn.

2.1.1   Implementation of Counterfactual

The counterfactual asks 'what would have happened to the participants (or the labour force, economy and so forth) had the programme not been implemented, other things being equal?'. It is usually implemented by selecting agents who are unaffected by, say, a particular programme and who use their experiences as evidence of what would have happened to participants in the absence of the programme. The difference between their outcomes and those of participants, corrected as necessary for relevant differences between the two groups in other respects, indicates the effects of the programme.

Ways of implementing the counterfactual begin with social experiments or *highly experimental* methods in the terminology adopted here (method 1, Table 10.1). Eligible applicants are assigned randomly either to a treatment group or to a control group. In large samples, any differences between the underlying attributes of participants and controls are thus trivial at most, and the unadjusted difference in mean outcomes between the two groups is an unbiased estimator of programme effects.

The second set of methods is often termed *quasi-experimental*. One selects a comparison group of nonparticipants that is as similar as possible to the participant group. Regression analysis is used to adjust the raw difference in group outcomes for intergroup differences in other factors, such as labour quality. The simplest approach is method 3, which adjusts outcomes for all relevant observable attributes. Method 2 goes further, recognizing that most data sets do not include measures of all attributes, such as motivation and ability, upon which participation decisions are made. Method 3 is therefore potentially distorted by selection bias. Method 2 is therefore an attempt to

Table 10.1   Evaluation Methods, by Means of Implementing the Counterfactual

	Experimental status	Choice of control/ comparison	Adjustment to mean difference in outcomes
1.	High	Individual control group, randomly assigned	None
2.	Quasi	Individual comparison group, structural model	Adjusted for observables and unobservables
3.			Adjusted for observables only
4.	Weak	Grouped comparisons a. Other programmes	None
5.		b. Other age groups/sex	None
6.		c. Own history (before/after)	None
7.		d. Other countries	None
8.		e. Agents' speculations	Speculative
9.		f. Expert interpretation	n.a.
10.	Zero	Gross outcomes	n.a.

correct for unobservable differences between the two groups. It incorporates information on other outcomes presumably affected by the same unobservables, notably the participation decision itself.

Other ways of implementing the counterfactual might then be termed *weakly experimental*, for they do not hold all relevant influences constant. Outcomes for participants may be compared to those of participants in other programmes or to those of persons in nearby nonparticipant age groups (Table 10.1, lines 4 and 5), to the prior experiences of the participants themselves (line 6) or to comparable groups in other countries (line 7). Also included in Table 10.1 are speculative methods designed to indicate the counterfactual on the basis of informed opinion. Participants themselves may be asked to estimate what would have happened had the programme not been available (line 8). A judgement like that may be based on expert opinion, such as that of the analyst drawing on some mix of economic theory and operational evidence (line 9). Lastly, there are what can be called *nonexperimental* 'evaluations' that lack explicit counterfactual components, simply reporting outcomes for participants (e.g. job-placement rates (line 10)).

Theoretical sophistication and data requirements decline across the rows in

Table 10.1, from the exacting data requirements and econometric modelling of the first two methods, respectively, to the limited controls and even low awareness of the counterfactual of weakly experimental methods. Speculative methods are particularly susceptible to perceptual and political biases among agents or experts. Nonexperimental methods prove nearly worthless in practice (Gay and Borus, 1980).[1]

2.1.2   Identifying Variation

Implementing the counterfactual requires adequate variability in the causal variable of interest. If interest does not vary at all, its effects cannot be isolated. Data must be generated or selected so as to provide adequate identifying variation.

The closer the approximation to experimental conditions, the less the prospective difficulty, for an experiment ideally alters the key variable (e.g. programme participation, minimum wage coverage) and holds other influences constant. In practice, things prove more complicated. Social experiments generally lack the purity of the laboratory ideal. They suffer from crossover bias in particular because nonparticipants gain access to the same services as participants, thereby reducing identifying variation (Heckman and Smith, 1993). Quasi-experimental evaluations require reliable measures of relevant differences between participant and comparison groups in order to isolate the true variation in the key factor. In practice, their findings are sensitive to assumptions about selection processes and to the choice of a comparison group (Fraker and Maynard, 1987; LaLonde, 1986).[2]

Weakly experimental methods may compensate for their generally inadequate control variables with a greater ability to identify variation in those participant groups to be evaluated. Comparative and historical evidence is sometimes richer than microdata drawn from a single period and place, partic-

---

1 The evaluation methods outlined in Table 10.1 comprise varying mixes of individual and group data. In keeping with general practice in each area, the more experimental methods have been discussed here as applying to individual data; the less experimental ones, to grouped data. Such patterns are, however, far from binding, as illustrated by the use of grouped data with experimental attributes in research on minimum wages and individual data in international comparisons (Blanchflower and Lynch, 1994; Card and Krueger, 1995).

2 The appropriate correction for selection bias depends on the nature of both the programme's effects and time- and person-specific unobservables. Assumptions have to be made concerning both. Specification tests and comparison groups comprising eligible local nonparticipants appear to improve results (Heckman, 1993; Heckman and Hotz, 1989), but the ratio of assumptions to evidence remains uncomfortably high. Unobservables are potentially important but can only be proxied passively (through the unexplained variation in participation equations). Identifying variation is reduced still further when a programme is inadequately implemented in the first place, a possibility studied through process evaluation (e.g. Lee, Marsden, Rickman and Duncombe, 1990).

ularly when it is institutions rather than particular policies that are to be assessed (Ryan, 1991). Moreover, the limitations of weakly experimental methods can sometimes be reduced by combining approaches, as when changes over time are used in international comparisons in order to control for invariant national characteristics (Marsden and Ryan, 1991a).

We conclude that (a) no single method offers conclusive evidence, though social experiments often come closest to doing so; (b) multiple methods and sources of evidence are preferable to single ones; and (c) weakly experimental methods are often appropriate for research into institutional issues.

2.2   Labour Market Assumptions

The third methodological issue concerns assumptions about the labour market. The leading one is displacement: effects on nonparticipants that drive a wedge between effects on participants and those on the wider economy. When jobs are scarce, any gains in participant earnings may come at the expense of displaced nonparticipants. Moreover, time that participants spend in the programme may not impose an output cost on the economy if otherwise idle nonparticipants fill the jobs that participants would otherwise have occupied.

Evaluations in which displacement is ignored are prone to bias. Cost–benefit analyses in which it is ignored during participation underestimate net benefits, for the opportunity cost of participant time is overestimated. Evaluations in which displacement after participation is ignored overestimate net benefits, for increases in aggregate output attributed to ex-participants are overestimated. The two biases work in opposite directions.

The importance of displacement thus depends on labour market conditions and programme type. In competitive markets without involuntary unemployment, displacement is a second-order phenomenon comprising changes in marginal products as employment adjusts in the markets from which participants are drawn and to which they are sent. If there is involuntary unemployment, however, displacement becomes a first-order matter. Consider two types of programme. First, a programme may simply recycle participants within the same market segment. Displacement is then high on both counts, with indeterminate effects on net benefits. Second, a programme may move participants from surplus to deficit markets. Other employed persons are displaced in that case only while participating, as ex-participants fill long-term job vacancies without displacing other workers. Net benefits are underestimated if displacement is ignored. Work experience programmes for unskilled workers typically fall in the former category; occupational training programmes in scarce skills, in the latter (Johnson, 1979).

Although displacement is often taken a priori to be widespread (Haveman and Saks, 1985; Solow, 1990), appropriate information is rarely available, and it is seldom estimated in practice, even in the cost–benefit evaluations to which it is particularly relevant.

Assumptions about wage determination are important in other respects as well. Under competitive wage determination, pay equals the value of marginal products and leisure at the margin, providing evaluators with measures of both productivity and opportunity costs. With labour market segmentation and wage rigidity, access to good jobs is rationed and pay may indicate neither labour quality nor opportunity costs (Katz and Summers, 1988; Lindbeck and Snower, 1988; McNabb and Ryan, 1990).

The implicit assumption in most programme evaluation concerning wage determination and displacement is that the former is largely competitive and the latter therefore unimportant. The restrictiveness of the assumption creates doubt about the accuracy of many of the estimates considered below.

3   EVALUATION FINDINGS

In this section we review three categories of school-to-work issues: labour market programmes, reductions in payroll costs and changes in schooling itself. In each category, the methods used in practice are outlined before evaluation findings are examined. Leading recent studies are summarized in one or more tables for each category.

3.1   Labour Market Programmes

The programmes in question are those intended to improve participants' labour quality by means of services ranging from remedial education through occupational and job training, work experience and assisted job search to counselling and personal support services. A further goal may be gainful activity for otherwise unemployed participants, irrespective of long-term benefits. These programmes have also been called manpower policies and active labour market policies.

3.1.1   Evaluation Methods

In terms of scope, most evaluations in all countries have been single-outcome studies. They have been complemented in the past decade by a handful of cost–benefit assessments, primarily in the United States. In terms of method, the use of social experiments is confined largely to officially sponsored research in the United States, beginning with National Supported Work (NSW) in the 1970s and spreading to all major programmes for out-of-school youth. Similarly, the Job Corps is subjected to highly experimental evaluation. The

United States also dominates in the quasi-experimental categories, where numerous studies since the 1970s have evaluated all youth programmes while developing quasi-experimental methodology. Weakly experimental methods, now rare in the United States, were previously common (Levitan and Johnston, 1975).

British and French evaluations have recently started to appear in the quasi-experimental category, primarily for Britain's Youth Training Scheme (YTS) and the short-term contracts and subsidies offered in France to unemployed youth. Otherwise, only a handful of studies of Swedish and Irish programmes have been published, and econometric evaluation remains rare in Germany in particular (Björklund, 1991; Schellhaass, 1991). The burgeoning European academic research literature remains confined to the single-outcome format that dominated US research until recently.

Weakly experimental methods are also widely used in Europe, particularly by public authorities and at the least quantitative and analytical levels.

3.1.2 Evaluation Results

Evaluation findings tend to become less favourable to programmes as research methods rise in the hierarchy shown in Table 10.1. Simpler methods, such as gross-outcome reporting and before–after comparisons, often conclude that programmes have worked. More sophisticated methods, notably highly experimental ones, rarely find significant gains in particular outcomes and typically infer net social losses when cost–benefit analysis is used.

Thus, at the lower end of the evaluation scale, official evaluations of work-based youth training under Britain's Youth Training Scheme (YTS) typically report the proportions of participants who achieved a 'positive outcome' after leaving the programme and who were satisfied with the training it offered. No counterfactual is stated, but an implicit one may be inferred, namely, that few, if any, participants would have achieved positive outcomes had the scheme not existed (Breen, 1991; UK ED, 1991b). Similarly, the UK Treasury currently assesses programmes according to whether they deal with a market failure, such as an externality, identified by economic theory (UK ED, 1991a). Such a criterion can be easily satisfied by youth programmes, whatever their operational attributes.[3] Lastly, a European Commission evaluation of a programme for industry–university cooperation in training confined itself largely to implementation issues but nevertheless reached a favourable

---

3 The weakness of the Treasury criterion (Marquand, 1994) is illustrated by two recent byproducts: (a) interdepartmental conflicts in which the spending department (e.g. employment) uses economic expertise to emphasize the relevant externalities, whereas Treasury economists attempt to explode them; and (b) academic efforts to leave no stone unturned in the search for training-related externalities (Booth and Snower, 1995).

assessment of 'the impact of the COMETT programme' (CEC, 1993).[4]

At the other extreme, experimental evaluations of youth programmes in the United States have found few or no lasting benefits to participants (Table 10.2). The standard criterion of benefit is the gain that is generated in labour earnings by increased hourly pay and/or longer hours of work. Measuring outcomes at intervals varying between 1.5 and 9 years after disadvantaged American youths entered a programme designed for them, researchers found that none of the four programmes involved significantly affected the subsequent earnings of participants.[5]

The picture remains unfavourable to youth programmes when the scope of the evaluation is widened to cost–benefit analysis, as has by now been done for four major US programmes (Table 10.3). Positive social net benefits have indeed been estimated for the long-running, intensive Job Corps: $2300 per participant in the late 1970s, arising from increased earnings and reduced juvenile criminality. Another bright spot is the gains in educational achievement generated under projects like JTPA, Jobstart and the New Chance programme for low-income young mothers.

The same GED test scores that suggest increased achievement show, however, low educational validity or influence on subsequent employment (W. N. Grubb, in press). The gains associated with the Job Corps are also suspect, for they were generated by quasi-experimental rather than highly experimental methods, and negative net benefits were found by all three of the highly experimental evaluations. Supported Work, Jobstart and JTPA Title II-A show at most small gains in postprogramme earnings (as well as in programme income losses in some cases), limited and even perverse effects on crime rates, drug use and teenage pregnancy and significant resource costs of the programme itself.

Considerable uncertainty accompanies the best estimate of net benefits for each programme, and none of the research has paid serious attention to displacement effects. However, displacement biases could go either way for programmes such as these, and the results for Supported Work and JTPA do at least prove robust with respect to alternative assumptions. Apart from the question mark attached to the Job Corps, programmes for young American workers—unlike those for some other clienteles, notably adult welfare recipients—appear to have failed (W. N. Grubb, in press; Heckman et al., 1994).

---

4 The COMETT evaluation involved reports from seven independent experts, all national governments and a European-wide consortium of national consultancy firms but still produced no hard evidence concerning the effects of the programme. Whatever the limitations of officially sponsored evaluation research in the United States, its EU equivalent has yet to scratch the surface.

5 Sample sizes ranged from 861 (NSW) to 4361 (JTPA), but attrition typically reduced sample sizes over time, so even moderately large differences between the subsequent earnings of participants and controls can lack statistical significance.

Table 10.2 Evaluations of US Youth Labour Market Programmes Based on Social Experiments

| Programme | Operational Attributes | | | | | Estimated Effects | | |
	Period in place	Constituency	Services (treatment)	Length of period (yrs)	Earnings during programme[a] %	Total earnings %	Hourly wage in last period %
(1)	(2)	(3)	(4)	(5)	(6)	(7)	(8)
Supported Work	1975–81	Disadvantaged school dropouts, 17–20 yrs	wex, supp, js	3.0	A: + 170.0* (9 mos)	A: + 25.1	A: − 17.5
				9.0		A: 0	A: n.a.
Jobstart	1985–88	Disadvantaged high school dropouts, 17–21 yrs	ed, oct, js, supp	4.0	A: − 19.2* M: − 21.7* F: − 14.6	A: + 1.3 M: − 1.2 F: + 6.1	A: + 5.4 M: + 1.2 F: + 8.6
Job Training and Partnership Act (JTPA) Title II-A	1987–89	Disadvantaged, out of school, 16–21 yrs	ed, oct, ojt, wex, js	2.5	A: + 0.8 M: + 2.4 F: − 0.3	A: − 0.7 M: − 3.6 F: + 1.3	A: − 4.3 M: − 3.5 F: − 4.8
New Chance	1989–92	Mothers on welfare, dropouts, 16–22 yrs	ed, oct, wex, js, supp	1.5	F: − 26.1* (1 yr)	F: − 20.0*	F: − 6.3

Notes

* Significantly different from zero at $p = 0.05$.

a During first period(s) of evaluation (here, 0.5 to 1.0 years).

Col. (4): ed = general/remedial education; oct = occupational training; ojt = on-the-job training; wex = work experience; js = job search/placement; supp = support services (e.g. transportation, childcare, counselling); – Col. (5): Time elapsed between participation and measured outcome. – Cols (6–8): A, M, F denote all, male and female, respectively.

Sources: See p. 321.

319

Table 10.3 *Cost–benefit Analyses of US Youth Labour Market Programmes: Net Benefits by Category, Size and Distribution*

Programme	Evaluation Attributes		Net Benefits ($ Current) Per Capita			Benefit Categories				
	Period covered	Method	Partici- pants	Non- partici- pants	All (4) + (5)	Earnings	Educa- tional achieve- ment	Crime and drugs	Welfare receipt	Teen preg- nancy
(1)	(2)	(3)	(4)	(5)	(6)	(7)	(8)	(9)	(10)	(11)
Job Corps	1977–79	Q-E	+ 2485	– 214	+ 2271	+	n.a.	+	+	n.a.
Supported Work	1975–79	HE	+ 891	– 2355	– 1464	0	n.a.	0	n.a.	n.a.
Jobstart	1985–88	HE	+ 254	– 4540	– 4286	0	+	0	0	n.a.
Job Training and Partnership Act (JTPA)	1987–89	HE	– 620 (M)	– 2824	– 2904	0	+	–	0	
Title II-A			– 83 (F)	– 1087	– 1170	0	+	0	0	n.a.
New Chance	1989–92	HE	n.a.	n.a.	n.a.	–	+	n.a.	0	–

Notes

Col. (1): Programme contents in Table 2; Job Corps is residential programme for most disadvantaged 16–20-year olds, involving primarily general and vocational education and counselling. – Col. (3): HE and Q-E denote highly experimental and quasi-experimental research design, respectively. – Cols (7–11): +, 0, – indicate presence of benefit, no effect and loss, respectively, at $p = 0.05$.

Sources: See p. 321.

320

Sources to Table 10.2
From *The National JTPA Study: Overview, Impacts, Benefits and Costs of Title II-A* by H. S. Bloom, L. L. Orr, G. Cave, S. H. Bell, F. Doolittle and W. Lin, 1994, Bethesda, MD: Abt Associates, Exhibits 5, 6; *JOBSTART: Final Report on a Programme for School Dropouts* by G. Cave, H. Bos, F. Doolittle and C. Touissant, 1993, New York: Manpower Demonstration Research Corporation (MDRC), Tables 3, 5.2, 5.8, with estimates for females as unweighted means of those for those who do and do not live with their own children; 'New Evidence on the Long-term Effects of Employment Training Programs' by K. A. Couch, 1992, *Journal of Labor Economics*, 10, 380–88, Table 1; 'The Impacts of Supported Work on Youth' by R. A. Maynard, 1984, in R. G. Hollister, P. Kemper and R. A. Maynard (eds), *The National Supported Work Demonstration*, Madison: University of Wisconsin Press, pp. 205–38, Table 7.4; *The National JTPA Study: Overview, Impacts, Benefits and Costs of Title II-A* by L. L. Orr, H. S. Bloom, S. H. Bell, W. Lin, G. Cave and F. Doolittle, 1994, Bethesda, MD: Abt Associates, Exhibit 5.18, excluding males previously arrested; *New Chance: Interim Findings on a Comprehensive Programme for Disadvantaged Young Mothers and Their Children* by J. C. Quint, D. F. Polit, H. Bos and G. Cave, 1994, San Francisco: MDRC, Tables 6, 8.2, 8.3.

Sources to Table 10.3
From *The National JTPA Study: Overview, Impacts, Benefits and Costs of Title II-A* by H. S. Bloom, L. L. Orr, G. Cave, S. H. Bell, F. Doolittle and W. Lin, 1994, Bethesda, MD: Abt Associates; *JOBSTART: Final Report on a Programme for School Dropouts* by G. Cave, H. Bos, F. Doolittle and C. Touissant, 1993, New York: Manpower Demonstration Research Corporation (MDRC), Tables 2, 6, 7 and 7.9; 'A Benefit–cost Analysis of the Supported Work Experiment' by P. Kemper, D. A. Long and C. Thornton, 1984, in R. G. Hollister, P. Kemper and R. A. Maynard (eds), *The National Supported Work Demonstration*, Madison: University of Wisconsin Press; 'Evaluating the Costs and Benefits of the Job Corps' by D. A. Long, C. D. Mallar and C. V. D. Thornton, 1981, *Journal of Policy Analysis and Management*, 1, 55–76, Table 6; *New Chance: Interim Findings on a Comprehensive Programme for Disadvantaged Young Mothers and Their Children* by J. C. Quint, D. F. Polit, H. Bos and G. Cave, 1994, San Francisco: MDRC, Tables 3–6.

The inverse association which has been noted to exist between estimated net benefits and methodological sophistication has two potential causes. First, experimental kinds of methods implement the counterfactual more effectively, whereas cost–benefit analysis captures a wider range of variables, particularly programme costs. Second, evaluation methods and criteria often vary together. The criterion embodied in the more sophisticated studies is efficiency. Its counterpart in less sophisticated ones is often equity, in the form of short-term benefits to participants. Work experience programmes such as Supported Work satisfy the latter but not the former criterion: incomes of the participants increased (relative to those of controls) while they were on the programme, but net benefits to the economy as a whole were negative (Tables 10.2 and 10.3). Supported Work might have been evaluated favourably in Europe, given trans-Atlantic differences in goals as well as methods.

3.1.3 Quasi-experimental Studies

The findings of quasi-experimental evaluations of particular programmes vary according to how comparison groups were chosen and outcome effects modelled. Thus, the estimated effects of Supported Work on youth earnings rose three years after participation, were negligible in highly experimental evaluation and varied between minus $300 and minus $1900 in quasi-experimental studies (Table 10.4). Confidence in simple quasi-experimental methods has been further eroded by incoherent and unstable patterns of benefits across various sex/race categories (Barnow, 1987; Betsey, Hollister and Papageorgiou, 1985; Heckman and Hotz, 1989).

Such difficulties provide a warning about the contemporary reliance on simple quasi-experimental methods in European research, particularly because their results cannot be compared to those of social experiments. Evaluations of the most intensively studied youth programme in Europe, Britain's YTS, exhibit the variability from study to study typical of quasi-experimental US evaluations that used similar methods. Estimated wage effects for YTS vary between –8 per cent and more than +20 per cent (Table 10.5). Employment effects have mostly been inferred to be positive, but not all studies consider selection bias, and one study reports significantly negative employment effects. One simply cannot say from such evidence whether or not YTS raised the earning potential or employability of participants.

Some quasi-experimental evaluation has also been undertaken in other countries. Increases in subsequent employment have been inferred for publicly subsidized short-term training contracts in France ('Stages d'initiation à la vie professionnelle') and training and work experience in Ireland, but not for work experience contracts ('Travaux d'utilité collective') in France. Occupational training and job creation programmes do not appear to increase postparticipation earnings in Sweden, but they do prevent exit rates from unemployment from falling with spell duration by offering the least employable young workers a way out of unemployment (Ackum, 1991; Korpi, 1994).

Differences in evaluation findings for particular programmes, particularly YTS, may arise from differences in the periods involved, which create differences in market conditions and programme attributes between studies. In view of particular difficulty in choosing adequate comparison groups, the alternative explanation, suggested by US research experience, looks to differences in assumptions about earnings determination and programme selection.[6]

---

6 Differences between YTS evaluations should be curbed by reliance on just two longitudinal data sets in order to construct comparison groups. However, most participants lacked any prior earnings history from which to infer unobservable influences on YTS participation. Moreover, YTS was an entitlement programme, which guaranteed a place to all eligibles, so comparison groups of closely matched nonparticipants cannot be constructed. One must therefore resort to implicit comparison groups comprising the remainder of the age cohort. The results thus depend on accurate modelling and estimation of earnings and participation functions, but UK microdata lack the measures of ability and motivation required for such a task.

Table 10.4   Results of Experimental and Quasi-experimental Evaluations of
Supported Work (SW); Difference in Mean 1979 Earnings
between 17–20-year-old SW Participants during 1975–77 and
Members of Control or Comparison Groups (in 1979 Dollars)

Comparison group	Earnings Model			
	Basic	Unadjusted difference in earnings gains	Individual fixed effects	None
Basic	– 1179*	– 1154*	– 1547*	
Random sample	– 1937*			
Short cell match list	– 687*			
Statistical match	– 339			
Randomized controls				– 18

Notes
Average earnings male controls (all ages) were $5090 in 1978 (R. J. LaLonde, 1986, 'Evaluating the Econometric Evaluations of Training Programmes with Experimental Data', *American Economic Review*, 76, 604–20); all comparison groups taken from Current Population Survey.
* Difference significant at $p = 0.05$.

Source
From 'The Adequacy of Comparison Group Designs for Evaluations of Employment-related Programmes' by T. Fraker and R. Maynard, 1987, *Journal of Human Resources*, 22, 194–227.

3.1.4   Weakly Experimental Studies

Some evaluations rely on no more than moderately similar groups of nonparticipants in order to infer programme effects (Table 10.1). Participants in other programmes are widely used in French studies relating qualification types to employment outcomes (section 3.3, below). The opposite sex was used as a comparator in research on French 'mesures jeunes' (Chevalier and Silberman, 1988), an evaluation that highlighted poor outcomes for females. Young adults were used by Jonzon and Wise (1989) to suggest, from inverse associations between unemployment and activity on labour market programmes across different age groups, that youth unemployment was reduced by Swedish programmes, at least while they were in place. Similarly, D. Grubb (1994) attributed the dramatic decline of unemployment rates for 16–19-year olds relative to those of other ages in Britain during the 1980s to the large-scale implementation of YTS, given the absence of any equivalent scheme for adults.

The experience of groups in other countries can also provide weak comparators, albeit primarily for policies related to labour costs and apprenticeship

Table 10.5 Quasi-experimental Evaluations of Youth Labour Market Programmes Outside the United States: Attributes and Outcomes

Country and programme	Programme Attributes		Research Details				Mean Effects	
	Content	Eligibles	Author	Outcomes: date	Time lapse[a] yrs	Correction for selection bias	Hourly wages %	Employment % pts
(1)	(2)	(3)	(4)	(5)	(6)	(7)	(8)	(9)
UK: YTS	oct, wex	Unemployed 16–18-yr olds	Dolton et al. (1994a, 1994b)	1989	0–1	yes	M: – 8* F: – 14*	M: <0* F: 0
			O'Higgins (1994)	1986	0–2	yes	n.a.	+ 21*
			Whitfield and Bourlakis (1991)	1986	2–3	yes[b]	– 8*[c]	+ 4*
			Main (1991)	1987	1–3	no	n.a.	+ 14* +19*[d]
			Main and Shelley (1990)	1986	0–1	yes	+ 16	+ 11*
			Hutchinson and Church (1989)	1984	0–1	no	+ 39[d] – 8*	+ 17*[d] n.a.
France: a. SIVP b. TUC	a oct b wex	16–25 yrs, entrants, long-term unemployed	Bonnal et al. (1995)	1986–88	1–10	yes	n.a.	a. > 0* b. < 0
Sweden	oct; js	16–24 yrs unemployed	Ackum (1991)	1981–85	0–6.5	yes	–1 (oct)	n.a.
	oct; js	16–24yrs unemployed	Korpi (1994)	1981–85	0–6.5	no	n.a.	+*[e]
Ireland	a oct b wex	n.a.	Breen (1991)	1983–88	1 yr	yes	n.a.	a. + 7* b. + 10*

324

Notes
YTS = Youth Training Scheme; SIVP = 'Stages d'Insertion à la Vie Professionelle'; TUC = 'Travaux d'Utilité Collective'; oct = occupational training; wex = work experience; js = job search.
a Time elapsed between participation and measured effects.
b Wage equation only.
c For completers only.
d Range of estimates.
e Exit rates from unemployment.

Sources
From 'Youth Unemployment, Labour Market Programmes and Subsequent Earnings' by S. Ackum, 1991, *Scandinavian Journal of Economics*, 93, 531–43; 'L'impact des dispositifs d'emploi sur le devenir des jeunes chômeurs: une évaluation économetrique sur données longitudinales' by L. Bonnal, D. Fougère and A. Sérandon, 1995, *Economie et Prévision*, 115, 1–28; 'Assessing the Effectiveness of Training and Temporary Employment Schemes—Some Results from the Youth Labour Market' by R. Breen, 1991, *Economic and Social Review*, 22, 177–98; 'The Youth Training Scheme and the School-to-Work Transition' by P. J. Dolton, G. H. Makepeace and J. G. Treble, 1994a, *Oxford Economic Papers*, 46, 629–57; 'The Wage Effect of YTS: Evidence from the YCS' by P. J. Dolton, G. H. Makepeace and J. G. Treble, 1994b, *Scottish Journal of Political Economy*, 41, 444–53; 'Wages, Unions, the Youth Training Scheme and the Young Workers Scheme' by G. Hutchinson and A. Church, 1989, *Scottish Journal of Political Economy*, 36, 160–82; 'Escaping Unemployment: Studies in the Individual Consequences of Unemployment and Labour Market Policy' by T. Korpi, 1994, study no. 24, Swedish Institute for Social Research, Stockholm; 'The Effect of the Youth Training Scheme on Employment Probability' by B. G. M. Main, 1991, *Applied Economics*, 23, 367–72; 'The Effectiveness of the Youth Training Scheme as a Manpower Policy' by B. G. M. Main and M. A. Shelley, 1990, *Economica*, 57, 495–514; 'YTS, Employment and Sample Selection Bias' by N. O'Higgins, 1994, *Oxford Economic Papers*, 46 (4), 605–28; 'An Empirical Analysis of YTS, Employment and Earnings' by K. Whitfield and C. Bourlakis, 1991, *Journal of Economic Studies*, 18 (1), 42–56.

(see sections 3.2 and 3.3, below). For labour market programmes, the comparative content of studies at the national level is often weakened by considering countries in succession instead of in direct contrast (e.g. Greenaway, 1993). Truly comparative methods yield more leverage. Ryan (1994) used the unemployment rate of young adults as a comparator with which to assess the effects of youth programmes across advanced economies during the 1980s.

But the absence of statistical controls for other group characteristics threatens to distort such comparisons, just as lack of controls for individual attributes would distort comparisons in quasi-experimental microdata. For example, national institutions, cohort sizes and welfare regulations affect age-specific unemployment rates independently of labour market programmes. One possible response is to study changes over time in an attempt to remove group-specific fixed effects. Jonzon and Wise (1989) used the timing of policy changes and peaks in unemployment rates by age to 'identify' the effects of Swedish youth policies. Ryan (1994) related changes in relative youth unemployment to changes in relative spending on youth programmes and found moderately strong effects, with lags indicating causality.

Finally, researchers applying speculative methods ask participants (and, ideally, nonparticipants) what they would have done in the absence of a programme and use the findings to indicate the counterfactual against which programme effects are estimated. High rates of displacement under YTS have been inferred from employer responses, reducing considerably the prospective benefits of the programme (Begg, Blake and Deakin, 1991; Deakin, 1995). As estimates of displacement are few and far between, such estimates are highly valuable, even if widespread opposition to the substitution of YTS trainees for employees may lead employers to underestimate displacement (Ryan, 1995).

3.2   Reductions in Youth Payroll Costs

Youth payroll costs have constituted a major issue in contemporary school-to-work debates in the United States, Britain and France, among other countries. Deregulatory policies are intended to reduce those costs in order to increase youth employment and work-based training. Three policy categories can be distinguished. First, there is the direct alteration of wage structures, whether through lower wage-for-age scales in minimum wages and collective agreements, or, more radically, through the abolition of such scales in favour of competitive wage determination. Thus, the Dutch youth subminimum wage was reduced in the 1980s to between 30 and 100 per cent of the adult rate (for ages 15 to 23). Statutory minimum wages for young people were abolished in the United Kingdom in 1986. A teenage subminimum pitched at 85 per cent of the adult rate was inserted into the US federal minimum wage in 1990. Proposals to reduce youth minimum wages ('SMIC-jeunes') have been widely debated in France.

Second, youth payroll costs may be cut indirectly within a given wage structure by reducing nonwage employment and training costs, whether through lower payroll taxes, higher subsidies or restricted employment rights. All three methods have characterized special contracts for unemployed young workers in France, Italy and Britain.

Third, youth supply prices may be cut by reducing access to nonwage income, notably public benefits, either directly through youth access or indirectly through parental access. Thus, the young school-leaver's eligibility for public income support was eliminated during the 1980s in both Sweden and Britain.

The first two approaches aim to induce employers to increase their demand for youth labour and their supply of job-based training. The first one is also expected to reduce youth unemployment by reducing youth labour supply in favour of full-time schooling or leisure. The third approach is expected to increase youth labour supply and, as such, to increase unemployment and reduce school enrolments, but both Sweden and Britain have used it to steer young people into labour market programmes.[7]

Policies to price young people into jobs and training have proved controversial. Critics have denied that they provide significant benefits to youth, or they have asserted that any benefits are gained at the expense of other workers. The policies have also been attacked for promoting inequity in pay structures and conflict within the work force (Cette, Cuneo, Eyssartier and Gautié, 1995; Garonna and Ryan, 1991b).

3.2.1 Evaluation Methods

Evaluation research has concentrated primarily on minimum wages, which, given their low earnings potential and high training requirements, are widely expected to affect young workers with particular force. Until recently, research methods remained unsophisticated by the standards of labour market programmes.

US research on minimum wages was dominated by quasi-experimental methods subject to two limitations: (a) use of aggregate single-equation reduced forms, whose interpretation and whose stability over time are problematic and (b) use of time-series evidence in which both identifying variation in minimum wages and controls for other influences are relatively poor (Brown, Gilroy and Cohen, 1983). Similar problems characterized French research on youth employment subsidies.

Experimental evidence has been less readily generated for pay rates than for services to unemployed youth. The attempt by the US Income Maintenance Experiments of the 1970s to develop such data was marred by nonrandom assignment between control and treatment groups. Recent revisionist US research has, however, generated near-experimental evidence from increases in state and federal minimum wages—not by allocating agents randomly to treatment and control groups but by using similar employers in similar states, or in states with fewer low-wage workers, as near-experimental controls (Card and Krueger, 1995).

Lower down the scale in Table 10.1, weakly experimental methods have been used to study institutional pay structures, notably wage-for-age scales in collective agreements, which vary primarily over longer periods and between countries and thereby require historical and international compari-

---

7 Higher labour force participation rates among young people are welcome when they apply to young people who would not otherwise be in school, as is the case with many disadvantaged minority youth in the United States. Such rates are not welcome when they reduce educational participation, as was the case under YTS in the United Kingdom in the 1980s (Rees, 1986; Whitfield and Wilson, 1991).

sons (Marsden and Ryan, 1991a, 1991b). Finally, speculative counterfactuals have provided evidence on the displacement effects of youth employment subsidies (Begg et al., 1991). The range of evaluation methods in use has thus widened appreciably during the last decade.

3.2.2   Evaluation Findings

New research methods have caused an upheaval in the employment effects of US minimum wages, for youth as well as adults (Table 10.6). Previous consensus was that minimum wages had adverse, though moderate, effects on youth employment but none on unemployment, for higher youth pay was found perversely to reduce labour force participation (Wellington, 1991). Cross-sectional estimates based on individual microdata supported such conclusions, in contrast to the high estimates produced by state-level aggregates (Meyer and Wise, 1983; Welch and Cunningham, 1978).

Recent analysis of data with near-experimental status suggests instead that minimum-wage increases in the United States have had either no effect or mildly positive effects on youth employment. Thus, the 1988 rise in the California minimum wage is estimated to have *increased* teenage employment in California by 6 per cent, using the experience of five broadly similar states as a guide to the counterfactual. The labour force participation effect was again similar to the employment one, but a more plausible positive sign was found, leading to negligible effects on youth unemployment (Card, 1992).

Similar findings crop up in studies of fast-food restaurants in Texas and New Jersey, as well as of aggregate state-level employment (Card and Krueger, 1995). The generality of the results remains uncertain, but they can be interpreted as evidence of widespread employer monopsony power. The revisionists have defended their work effectively against critics of minimum wages, who have turned to such secondarily adverse effects as increased inducement of more able young people to leave school and enter the labour market, where they displace less-skilled employees but with little net effect on overall youth employment (Neumark and Wascher, 1995).

European research on minimum wages uses methods and data sets similar to those previously common in the United States and generally infers adverse effects on youth employment. Drawing mostly on aggregate time-series evidence, quasi-experimental studies of minimum wages in France and the Netherlands have found adverse effects on youth employment (Bazen and Martin, 1990; van Soest, 1989).

Weakly experimental evidence has also been used. One study of the French 'SMIC-jeunes' even imposes a priori values of key parameters in the relevant production functions in inferring moderately negative effects on youth employment (Cette et al., 1995). The reduction in the Dutch youth subminimum wage in 1981–83 was followed by a four-year cumulative reduction in the gap between the unemployment rates of school leavers and other workers, including a reversal of sign in 1986 (van Opstal and van de Pol, 1991). No study has yet used the high variability of youth relative minimum wages across countries.

Caution about these adverse European assessments of minimum wages might well be advised, however. The conclusions reached by US evaluations of labour market programmes have been revised as more sophisticated evidence and methods have come into use. That consideration suggests that European research may soon reach more favourable assessments of minimum wages as evidence and methods advance. Such a development may be under way in the United Kingdom (Machin and Manning, 1994). In any event, the effects of minimum wages on youth employment remain an open question. The US revisionists accept that minimum wages will reduce employment at some point as they rise relative to average earnings. As the minimum wage is a much higher proportion of average earnings in France than in the United States, negative employment effects may well predominate in the former country but not in the latter.

Minimum wages may also affect job-based training for young workers. If the ability of employers to pass along to trainees the costs of general training is constrained by wage minima, less training may be offered in the first place. Hashimoto (1982) found indirect evidence of such effects: lower subsequent wage growth for affected US young workers after increases in the federal minimum wage.

Wage-for-age scales in collective agreements instead of in minimum wages constitute an institutional feature rather than a policy variable. International variations in relative youth pay associated with such scales are marked in Europe, inviting use of international comparisons. The existence of wage-for-age scales has been judged a factor underlying higher youth employment shares in Germany, the Netherlands and the United Kingdom than in France, Belgium and Italy (Marsden and Ryan, 1991b). The postwar rise in scale rates for apprentices in the United Kingdom relative to those in Germany is interpreted as a primary cause of the decline in apprenticeship activity in the United Kingdom, with changes over time controlling for invariant national attributes (Marsden and Ryan, 1991a).

Such research suggests that the issue facing deregulatory policies is not just whether lower youth pay can increase youth activity at the workplace but also whether it is institutionally attainable in the first place. The German 'dual system' has long been characterized by multiyear apprentice rates pitched at less than half those of qualified adults in the same occupation. Yet, it took a protracted political struggle in the United States during the 1980s to institute a youth subminimum that involved only a 15 per cent discount lasting at most

Table 10.6 *Evaluations of Policies and Institutions Affecting Youth Payroll Costs*

			Research Attributes			Estimated Effect on Youth		
Policy area	Study	Data	Approach to counterfactual	Independent variable	Youth category yrs	Employment	Labour force	Unemployment
(1)	(2)	(3)	(4)	(5)	(6)	(7)	(8)	(9)
Statutory minimum wages	Wellington (1991)	US national time series 1954–86	Cyclical and other observables	Min. wage level and coverage	16–19	–0.06[a]	–0.08[a]	0
	Card (1992)	California 1987–89	Comparison area observables	Min. wage 27% rise, 1988	16–19	+ 6%*	+ 6%*	– 2%*
	Meyer and Wise (1983)	US workers 1973, 1978	Lognormal earnings distribution	Min. wage existence	16–19 20–24	– 7% – 2%	n.a. n.a.	n.a. n.a.
	van Soest (1989)	Dutch workers 1984	Ditto	Youth submin. 10% cut	15–22			– 28%
	Bazen and Martin (1990)	French aggregates 1963–85	Aggregate control variables	Min. wage 10% rise	16–19	– 5%	n.a.	n.a.
	Cette et al. (1995)	French employment structure	Indirect parametrization	Youth submin. 80% rate	18–26	0 to 4%	n.a.	n.a.
	Hashimoto (1982)	US cross section 1966–69	Human capital, observed and unobserved	Min. wage 1967–68 increases	14–24 males	– 15%*[b]	n.a.	n.a.
'Wage-for-age' scales	Marsden and Ryan (1989)	Sectoral, 6 nations 3 years	Adult pay	Youth relative pay	Male man <21	– 1.9%* to – 3.2*[a]	n.a.	n.a.
Employment subsidies	Marsden and Ryan (1991a)	Postwar FRG and UK app'ces	National changes over time	App. relative pay	Male apps	+	n.a.	n.a.
	Colin and Espinasse (1979)	1971–73 French macromodel	Macrostructural stability	1–2 years, no payroll taxes	School leavers	+ 7 to + 30%	n.a.	n.a.
	Begg et al. (1991)	1989 UK employer survey	Hypothetical scenario	No trainee payroll costs	16–17	+ 20%	n.a.	n.a.
Public income support	Venti (1984)	1971–75 US welfare households	Comparison group,[c] adjusted for observables	Income support and tax mixes	16–21, dependants	n.a.	– 30%*	0

330

Notes

Asterisks denote statistical significance at conventional levels.

a Elasticities.

b Effect on on-the-job training.

c Recipients of Aid to Families with Dependent Children.

Sources

From 'Incidence du salaire minimum sur les gains et l'emploi en France' by S. Bazen and J. Martin, 1990, *Revue Economique de l'OCDE*, 16, 199–221; 'YTS and the Labour Market' by I. G. Begg, A. P. Blake and B. M. Deakin, 1991, *British Journal of Industrial Relations*, 29, 223–36; 'Do Minimum Wages Reduce Employment? A Case Study of California, 1987–89' by D. Card, 1992, *Industrial and Labour Relations Review*, 46 (1), 38–54; 'Les effets sur l'emploi d'un abaissement du cout du travail des jeunes' by G. Cette, P. Cuneo, D. Eyssartier and J. Gautié, 1995, in G. Benhayoun and S. Bazen (eds), *Salaire Minimum et Bas Salaires*, Paris: L'Harmattan,; 'Les subventions à l'emploi' by J.-F. Colin and J.-M. Espinasse, 1979, *Travail et Emploi*, 1, 37–50; 'Minimum Wage Effects on Training on the Job' by M. Hashimoto, 1982, *American Economic Review*, 72, 1070–87; 'Statistical Tests for the Universality of Youth Employment Mechanisms in Segmented Labour Markets' by D. W. Marsden and P. Ryan, 1989, *International Review of Applied Economics*, 3, 148–69; 'Initial Training, Labour Market Structure and Public Policy: Intermediate Skills in British and German Industry' by D. W. Marsden and P. Ryan, 1991, in P. Ryan (ed.), *International Comparisons of Vocational Education and Training for Intermediate Skills*, Lewes: Falmer,; 'The Effects of the Minimum Wage on the Employment and Earnings of Youth' by R. H. Meyer and D. A. Wise, 1983, *Journal of Labour Economics*, 1, 66–100; 'Minimum Wage Rates and Unemployment in the Netherlands' by A. van Soest, 1989, *De Economist*, 137 (3); 'The Effects of Income Maintenance on Work, Schooling, and Non-market Activities of Youth' by S. F. Venti, 1984, *Review of Economics and Statistics*, 66 (1), 16–25; 'Effects of the Minimum Wage on the Employment Status of Youths: An Update' by A. J. Wellington, 1991, *Journal of Human Resources*, 26 (1), 27–46.

six months. Low wage-for-age scales must be legitimated by guaranteed training quality if they are to command widespread assent. The lack of suitable institutions helps explain why simple deregulatory proposals have made so little progress on this front in the United States in contrast to the situation in Germany, the more 'regulated' of the two economies (Heckman et al., 1994).

Research findings are scarcer for other policies in the labour cost area. Youth employment subsidies are implicit in labour market programmes such as YTS, whose effects were discussed above. Explicit employment subsidies are rarely offered to youth, though France did in the early 1970s temporarily suspend payroll taxes on up to two years of school leaver employment. Analysis of that policy, using a macroeconomic model to indicate the counterfactual, concluded that employment increased by between 7 and 30 per cent in the relevant age group (Colin and Espinasse, 1979).

Lastly, the effects that changes in nonwage income have on youth labour supply have been estimated from the US Income Maintenance Experiments of the 1970s (Venti, 1984). Because assignment to the programme was actually nonrandom, quasi-experimental methods had to be used, though without correction for selection bias. Increases in household welfare receipts and reductions in marginal income tax rates were estimated to have reduced youth labour force participation by 13 percentage points and increased educational participation by 9 points, with no significant effect on unemployment. Negative income taxes may thus encourage young people in low-income households to study rather than work.

3.3   Schooling: Curriculum and Links to Work

Other policies address the school-to-work transition from the schooling side, with a dominant interest in closer links between schooling and work. Lack of success on the part of labour market programmes, as noted above, encourages interest in policies aimed at earlier developmental stages, while young people are still in the system of formal education (W. N. Grubb, in press). These policies have implications for personal development, but they are typically judged primarily on standard efficiency criteria.

Five categories may be distinguished. First, attempts may be made to increase general educational attainment. The poor performance of US and UK secondary pupils in international tests, particularly relative to those of German and Japanese youth, has suggested inadequate learning in both national school systems, to the detriment of economic performance. Such concerns have prompted adoption in the United Kingdom of a National Curriculum and associated tests of achievement. In the United States they have sparked efforts to link employers' hiring decisions to student grades, so as to increase incentives to study (Bishop, 1992; Prais, 1993; Ryan, in press; US NCES, 1993).

Second, vocational curricula are advocated, for example, by the 'school for work' agenda in the United States and by public policy towards upper secondary qualifications in France (Green, 1995). Vocationalization may be conceived narrowly, say, in terms of traditional occupational training in US secondary schools, or broadly, in terms of—for want of a better term—a truly technical education that fuses abstract and applied elements to the benefit of each and that is capable of capturing the interest of most young people instead of acting as a bin for academic rejects. The latter ideal has long interested educationalists, particularly in Germany and the United States (Taylor, 1981). It has informed the development of vocationally oriented upper secondary studies in Britain during the 1980s, and since 1990 it has been a legal requirement for public funding of vocational education in the United States, where relevant initiatives include career academies, magnet schools and 'tech prep' programmes (Ryan, in press; Stern et al., 1995; Stern, Raby and Dayton, 1992).

Third, school-work integration juxtaposes schooling and work as potentially complementary activities. Secondary schools may offer external work experience placements to their pupils or insert work experience into the vocational curriculum, as is the case under 'coop education' and school-based enterprise, respectively, in the United States. More radically, apprenticeship combines part-time education with workplace-based occupational training. German apprentices enjoy a status intermediate between that of student and employee. Recently, both YTS in the United Kingdom and youth apprenticeship schemes in the United States have imitated aspects of German apprenticeship, though schools rather than employers have tended to organize courses in the United States.

Fourth, school–employer links have been developed by many US and UK local authorities following the example of the Boston Compact, under which an employer rewards selected local secondary students with summer work and permanent employment in return for meeting criteria related to grades and attendance in school. Japanese schools build links to particular employers, providing both routes to employment for their students and recruiting services for associated employers (Rosenbaum and Kariya, 1989).

Fifth, support services help young people make the transition from school to work, primarily through career guidance and job search assistance. In some US schools adults 'mentor' deprived pupils.

3.3.1 Evaluation Methods

These issues are so diverse and many of the policies have been so recently implemented that evaluations remain relatively scarce, except for traditional vocationalism. Moreover, highly experimental methods are not easily adopted, for entitlement norms and schooling requirements often rule out the withholding of services from randomly selected control groups. Rare exceptions include an optional summer programme for disadvantaged 14–15-year olds, admissions to career magnet schools in New York and, currently, integrated vocational and academic curricula in career academies (Crain, Heebner and Si, 1992; Sipe, Grossman and Milliner, 1988).

By contrast, quasi-experimental methods incorporating human capital earnings functions have long been used to study the links between pay and schooling (Mincer, 1974). Selection biases associated with ability and family background have been estimated (Willis and Rosen, 1979). Less sophisticated methods still dominate the school-to-work agenda, however. Single-outcome evaluations predominate, with only occasional use of even rudimentary cost–benefit analysis (Stern, Dayton, Paik, Weisberg and Evans, 1989). Regression analysis of individual histories has become the norm in US research on the effects of vocational studies on labour market outcomes, but because comparison groups often differ radically from participants and because correction for selection bias remains unusual, only limited confidence can be placed in its findings.[8] In such

---

8 Neglect of selection may well cause little bias, if educational selection is based on multiple, offsetting criteria, but there is no assurance that it does in general (Willis and Rosen, 1979).

a context, weakly experimental methods again have something to offer. International comparisons have been widely used to study both educational achievement and apprenticeship training.

3.3.2   Research Findings

Policies to raise the efficiency of general education in countries that find themselves lagging in comparative test scores are still being devised or implemented and have therefore yet to be evaluated.[9] Vocational programmes have, by contrast, been extensively evaluated in the United States, confirming the long-standing view that traditional occupational training in high schools has neither strong nor consistent effects on the earnings of its recipients (Table 10.7). Some studies find mildly positive effects on subsequent pay for either males or females (but not consistently for one or the other) and for the minority of participants who subsequently work in the occupation for which they were trained in school.

Low or zero personal gains from vocational studies in US high schools may reflect either selection bias or low educational value added. Vocational programmes tend to be taken by the less academically able, so studies that ignore selection by ability may underestimate benefits to participants. A study that corrected for selection bias found that only commercial courses raise pay, and then only moderately and for a predominantly female clientele (Altonji, 1992). Second, vocational courses may well teach little of use. The lack of national standards against which to judge attainments in the United States, unlike Germany, means that the informational and incentive structures needed to spur pupil achievement are both absent, encouraging low educational aspirations and skill outputs (Boesal and McFarland, 1994). The high resource costs of vocational curricula thus prospectively overwhelm any benefits to participants and society as a whole, although cost–benefit analysis has not been used to clinch the issue (Psacharopoulos, 1987).

Disappointing results do not necessarily generalize to the more ambitious variant of vocationalism, which seeks to integrate academic and vocational strands into a full technical education instead of simply providing prejob training. From evidence that specialization in vocational studies is associated with lower earnings prospects, Kang and Bishop (1989) inferred complementarity between vocational and academic secondary studies, though uncontrolled selection factors may have biased their finding. Two US initiatives that respond to the new vocational ideal, career academies in California and career magnet schools in New York, have been found to raise levels of educational

---

9 England's National Curriculum and associated tests will soon generate annual data with which educational net outputs can be estimated and related to educational inputs.

participation and achievement of group members relative to the corresponding levels of matched random controls (Crain et al., 1992; Stern et al., 1989). The goals of such programmes are comparably ambitious to the Humboldtian *Bildungsideal* in German education. Further research is needed to indicate whether their benefits prove durable and outweigh their costs.

The benefits of vocational programmes have also been evaluated at the postsecondary level in the United States. Vocational associate degrees offered by community colleges in the United States appear to confer only limited benefits on participants: medium-term gains in earnings disappear once controls are introduced for subsequent training and work experience (W. N. Grubb, 1993). Correction for selection bias does produce evidence of positive earnings effects, but for women only (Zilbert, Hearn and Lewis, 1992).

The links between educational credentials and access to employment have become a matter of interest in France, where the last two decades have seen the strengthening of such relationships. Research has moved beyond pure description to establish that qualification effects on employment survive the introduction of controls for some personal and social attributes, though selection bias has yet to be addressed (Affichard, 1981; Minni and Vergnies, 1994). International comparisons have contributed, too: the fact that occupational downgrading of newly qualified skilled workers in France is more extensive than that in the United Kingdom has been attributed to more widespread occupational markets and work-based training in the United Kingdom (Marsden and Germe, 1991).

Policies linking school and work simultaneously instead of only sequentially have also produced some evaluated successes. The leading research issue in the United States has been whether employment while in high school affects educational attainment and subsequent earnings. Even moderately high hours of employment during high school year appears not to damage educational achievement and may contribute to higher earnings after leaving school (Meyer and Wise, 1982). Subsequent research supports these findings for post-school earnings and employment, suggesting that moderate hours of employment actually raise educational achievement (Stern et al., 1995). The 1970s Youth Incentive Entitlement Pilot Projects in the United States, which offered paid employment to disadvantaged high school students, was found to have raised nonwhite employment rates, even allowing for displacement, largely by increasing enrolment rates (Farkas et al., 1983). Recent programmes to promote systematic work experience in US high schools through coop education have, however, created no consistent association between participation and subsequent labour market outcomes (Stern et al., 1995). The findings of most of these studies are, however, rendered tenuous by the absence or weakness of controls for selection bias.

Table 10.7 Evaluations of Work-related Attributes in Schooling

Attribute/ programme	Study	Evaluation method	Place and year of treatment	Time lapse (yrs)	Educational achievement	Effects on	
						Wages	Employment
(1)	(2)	(3)	(4)	(5)	(6)	(7)	(8)
Vocational courses: (a) secondary	Meyer and Wise (1983)	QE (3)	1969–72	1–4	–	0	0
	Rumberger and Daymont (1984)	QE (3)	1972–79	0–3	n.a.	M: 0 / F: +	M: + / F: +
	Kang and Bishop (1989)	QE (3)	1976–80	0–2	n.a.	M: + / F: 0	M: + / F: +
	Ziderman (1989)	QE (3)	Israel 1961–64	6–13	n.a.		0
(b) postsecondary	Altonji (1992)	QE (2, 3)	1969–72	12	n.a.	0, +[a]	n.a.
	Grubb (1993)	QE (3)	1972–	0–12	n.a.		M, F: 0[b]
	Zilbert et al. (1992)	QE (2)	1980–	0–3	n.a.		M: 0; F: +
Qualifications and employment	Affichard (1981)	WE (4)	1973 1979	0.75	n.a.	n.a.	0 +
	Minni and Vergnies (1994)	QE (3)	1989–92	0.75	n.a.	n.a.	+
Fusion of vocational and general curricula	Crain et al. (1992)	HE (1)	1988	0–3	+	n.a.	n.a.
	Stern et al. (1989)	QE (3)	1985–88	1–3	+	n.a.	n.a.

336

Table 10.7—continued Evaluations of Work-related Attributes in Schooling

Attribute/ programme	Study	Evaluation method	Place and year of treatment	Time lapse (yrs)	Effects on		
					Educational achievement	Wages	Employment
(1)	(2)	(3)	(4)	(5)	(6)	(7)	(8)
Work experience in school	Meyer and Wise (1983)	QE (3)	1968–72	1–4	0	+	+
	Farkas et al. (1983)	QE (3)	1978–80	0–2	+	n.a.	+
Apprenticeship	Sipe et al. (1988)	HE (1)	1987	0.3	+	n.a.	n.a.
	Tan et al. (1991)	QE (3) NE (7)	US, UK, Aus, 1970s	n.a.	n.a.	+	+
	Blanchflower and Lynch (1994)	QE (2) WE (7)	US: 1979–86 UK: 1964–81	11–19	n.a.	M: + F: 0	n.a.
	Bonnal et al. (1995)	QE (2)	Fr: 1986–88	1–10	n.a.	n.a.	+
	Marsden and Ryan (1990)	WE (7)	EC: 1966, 72, 78	0–3	n.a	n.a.	+
	Büchtemann et al. (1993)	WE (7)	US, FRG 1973–90	6–9	n.a.	n.a.	+
School–employer links	Rosenbaum et al. (1990)	WE (7, 9)	US, Japan	n.a.	n.a.	n.a.	+

337

Notes

a Industrial and commercial courses, respectively.

b Controls for subsequent job training and work experience.

Col. (3): HE, QE, WE indicate highly experimental, quasi-experimental and weakly experimental methods, respectively.

Col. (4): Place is the United States unless otherwise specified.

Cols (6)–(8): +, –, 0 indicate statistically significant increase, decrease and no significant effect, respectively, with conventional tests.

Sources

From 'Quels emplois après l'école: la valeur des titres scolaires depuis 1973' by J. Affichard, 1981, *Economie et Statistique*, 134, 7–26; 'The Effect of High School Curriculum on Education and Labour Market Outcomes' by J. G. Altonji, 1992, working paper no. 4142, National Bureau of Economic Research (NBER), Cambridge, MA; 'Training at Work: A Comparison of US and British Youths' by D. G. Blanchflower and L. M. Lynch, 1994, in L. M. Lynch (ed.), *Training and the Private Sector: International Comparisons*, Chicago: University of Chicago Press, pp. 223–60; 'L'impact des dispositifs d'emploi sur le devenir des jeunes chômeurs: une évaluation économetrique sur données longitudinales' by L. Bonnal, D. Fougère and A. Sérandon, 1995, *Economie et Prévision*, 115, 1–28; 'Roads to Work: School-to-Work Transition Patterns in Germany and the US' by C. F. Büchtemann, J. Schupp and D. Soloff, 1993, *Industrial Relations Journal*, 24, 97–111; *The Effectiveness of New York City's Career Magnet Schools: An Evaluation of Ninth Grade Performance Using an Experimental Design* by R. L. Crain, A. L. Heebner and Yin-Pong Si, 1992, Berkeley: National Center for Research in Vocational Education; 'The Youth Entitlement Demonstration: Subsidized Employment with a Schooling Requirement' by G. Farkas, D. A. Smith and E. W. Stromsdorfer, 1983, *Journal of Human Resources*, 18, 557–73; 'The Varied Returns to Postsecondary Education: New Evidence from the Class of 1972' by W. N. Grubb, 1993, *Journal of Human Resources*, 28, 365–82; 'Vocational and Academic Education in High School: Complements or Substitutes' by S. Kang and J. Bishop, 1989, *Economics of Education Review*, 8, 133–48; 'Institutional Aspects of Youth Employment and Training Policy in Britain' by D. W. Marsden and P. Ryan, 1990, *British Journal of Industrial Relations*, 28, 351–70; 'The Effects of the Minimum Wage on the Employment and Earnings of Youth' by R. H. Meyer and D. A. Wise, 1983, *Journal of Labor Economics*, 1, 66–100; 'La diversité des facteurs de l'insertion professionnelle' by C. Minni and J.-F. Vergnies, 1994, *Economie et Statistique*, 277, 45–61; 'Market and Network Theories of the Transition from High School to Work: Their Application to Industrialized Societies' by J. E. Rosenbaum, T. Kariya, R. Settersten and T. Maier, 1990, *Annual Review of Sociology*, 16, 263–99; 'Economic Value of Academic and Vocational Training Acquired in High School' by R. W. Rumberger and T. N. Daymont, 1984, in M. E. Borus (ed.), *Youth and the Labour Market: Analyses of the National Longitudinal Survey*, Kalamazoo, MI: W. E. Upjohn Institute for Employment Research; *Summer Training and Education Programme: Report on the 1987 Experience* by C. L. Sipe, J. Grossman and J. A. Milliner, 1988, Philadelphia, PA: Public/Private Ventures; 'Benefits and Costs of Dropout Prevention in a High School Programme Combining Academic and Vocational Education: Third-year Results from Replications of the California Peninsula Academics' by D. Stern, C. Dayton, I. Paik, A. Weisberg and J. Evans, 1989, *Educational Evaluation and Policy Analysis*, 10 (2), 161–70; *Youth Training in the United States, Britain, and Australia* by H. W. Tan, B. Chapman, C. E. Peterson and A. Booth, 1991, Santa Monica, CA: Rand; 'Training Alternatives for Youth: Results from Longitudinal Data' by A. Ziderman, 1989, *Comparative Education Review*, 33 (2), 243–55; 'Selection Bias and the Earnings Effects of Postsecondary Vocational Education' by E. E. Zilbert, J. C. Hearn and D. R. Lewis, 1992, *Journal of Vocational Education Research*, 17 (1), 11–34.

Evaluations of apprenticeship as a potentially systematic link between learning at school and work have been generally favourable. Highly experimental evidence has not been generated, but quasi-experimental research with attention to selection bias finds positive associations with subsequent earnings in the United States (Lynch, 1992). Similarities have been found between the earnings effects of apprenticeship in individual microdata for the United Kingdom, the United States and Australia, though thus far with little modelling of what are potentially crucial selection processes. Apprenticeship appears not to benefit female participants in the United Kingdom. For males, the contribution of apprenticeship to higher pay may reflect partly its function as a ticket of entry to submarkets offering high rents, but, because wage gains are no less in nonunion than in union employment, significant skill development may be inferred (Blanchflower and Lynch, 1994; Tan et al., 1991). Apprenticeship also appears to have a favourable effect on employment probabilities in French microdata (Bonnal et al., 1995).

Weakly experimental evidence, particularly international comparisons, also favours apprenticeship. The experiences of German youth, relative to those of American youth in twelve years of panel data, suggest that widespread apprentice training in Germany leads both to lower unemployment in the school-to-work transition and to a better match between skills supply and demand (Büchtemann et al., 1993). European countries with extensive apprenticeship training, as compared to those with less institutionalized youth induction and training, have enjoyed more favourable levels of youth employment and unemployment (Marsden and Ryan, 1990).

Comparative evidence is also important for school–employer links, which are close in Japan, but often remote or nonexistent in the United States. Japanese schools rank graduating students by academic performance, and associated employers usually hire according to the school's rankings, creating strong informational flows and incentives for pupils to study hard. High achievements in school and rapid transitions to career employment are fostered, helping Japan to avoid the high unemployment and high turnover of US youth labour markets. The contribution of school–employer links to the difference in youth outcomes cannot be isolated in the absence of controls for differences between aggregate unemployment rates and employment practices in the two countries. Moreover, the United States may gain from delayed selection, more second chances and better life-time matching of workers to occupations. The results do, however, suggest efficiency benefits from school–employer links in Japan and the desirability of closer links in the United States (Kariya and Rosenbaum, 1987; Rosenbaum and Kariya, 1989; Rosenbaum et al., 1990).

4   CONCLUSIONS

Evaluations of school-to-work issues have mushroomed in the past two decades. Their sophistication has grown rapidly. In the United States randomized selection and cost–benefit analysis have become the norm for labour market programmes, and near-experimental data have revolutionized research into minimum wages.

A variety of evaluative methods is still widely used. Single-issue evaluations using quasi-experimental methods are still common in academic evaluations in the United States, particularly for policies related to schooling. They have also become prominent in Europe, despite suffering from a low ratio of information to assumptions. Weakly experimental methods are also employed, notably for comparative and historical sources of identifying variation on institutional factors. In practice, the quasi-experimental and weakly experimental literatures have paid little attention to each other. We have juxtaposed them, seeing each as important and the two as complementary in school-to-work evaluation.

Evaluation findings prove mostly unfavourable to recent policy interventions. Negative conclusions are nearly unavoidable for most labour market programmes in the United States, which provide less benefit to youths than to adults, when they offer any at all, and which are mostly associated with efficiency losses in the aggregate. Similarly, standard vocational courses offer no consistent or durable benefits to young people, and cuts in minimum wages affect youth employment only weakly, and may well reduce it, under US conditions at least.

The conclusion is not, however, uniformly negative. The significant benefits found for the Job Corps may survive highly experimental evaluation. On the equity-related criterion of making participants better off during the programme, programmes such as Supported Work in the United States have merit even though they produce no lasting benefits, and that assessment has often been considered sufficient in Europe. Higher minimum wages would be widely welcomed were no job losses induced.

The problem with youth programmes lies partly in a disadvantaged clientele and partly in shallow measures (Wilensky, 1992). More benefit might be generated by more ambitious measures. Two contrasts between shallow and deep approaches are relevant here: first, between apprenticeship and labour market programmes; and second, between technical education and traditional vocational schooling. Considerable benefits have been attributed to apprenticeship by a variety of evaluative methods, and similar findings may emerge from current studies of career academies and other ways of fusing general and vocational studies. In each contrast, the more ambitious option is to aim for greater skill development, and it may succeed even though the less ambitious one is found to have failed. Both approaches are an attempt to train for inter-mediate skills, where genuine skill shortages are commonly encountered.

Any proposal for deeper policies must, however, address three issues. The first concerns institutional development. Apprenticeship and low youth pay-roll costs in particular can flourish only with sustained political commitment and institutional development, a scenario that involves the key interest groups of employers, employees, government and youth itself (Marsden and Ryan, 1991a; Soskice, 1990; Streeck, Hilbert, van Kevalaer, Mayer and Weber, 1987). The task is correspondingly great, particularly in countries that lack effective employer and employee representation.

Second, the most disadvantaged young people are unlikely to benefit directly from apprenticeship and technical education. Even in Germany, youth apprenticeships fail to reach about 10 per cent of school leavers, to whom standard labour market programmes are offered. But that reality does not mean that nothing useful can be done. The costly, intensive services provided to disadvantaged young people by the Job Corps in the United States have, thus far at least, been evaluated as long-term benefits to both participants and soci-ety. Even if those long-term gains were to disappear, a strong case could still be made in equity for providing gainful activity to the worst placed young people.

Lastly, deeper policies will also require evaluation, even though the task is more daunting than for standard programmes. The difficulty of evaluating institutions can be addressed with a variety of research methods, weakly experimental as well as quasi-experimental. If only the more accessible issues are considered in evaluation research, the bigger issues will be left to casual speculation and unduly pessimistic conclusions will be reached about the potential of public policy.

REFERENCES

Ackum, S. (1991), 'Youth Unemployment, Labour Market Programmes and Subse-quent Earnings', *Scandinavian Journal of Economics*, 93, 531–43.

Affichard, J. (1981), 'Quels emplois après l'école: la valeur des titres scolaires depuis 1973', *Economie et Statistique*, 134, 7–26.

Altonji, J. G. (1992), 'The Effect of High School Curriculum on Education and Labour Market Outcomes', working paper no. 4142, National Bureau of Economic Research (NBER), Cambridge, MA.

Ashton, D. and G. Lowe (1991), 'School-to-work Transitions in Britain and Canada: A Comparative Perspective', in D. Ashton and G. Lowe (eds), *Making Their Way: Education, Training and the Labour Market in Canada and Britain*, Milton Keynes: Open University Press, pp. 1–14.

Barnow, B. S. (1987), 'The Impact of CETA Programmes on Earnings: A Review of the Literature', *Journal of Human Resources*, 22, 157–93.

Bazen, S. and J. Martin (1990), 'Incidence du salaire minimum sur les gains et l'emploi en France', *Revue Economique de l'OCDE*, 16, 199–221.

Begg, I. G., A. P. Blake and B. M. Deakin (1991), 'YTS and the Labour Market', *British Journal of Industrial Relations*, 29, 223–36.

Betsey, C. L., R. Hollister and M. R. Papageorgiou (eds) (1985), *Youth Employment and Training Programs: The YEDPA Years, Committee on Youth Employment Programs*, Washington, DC: National Academy Press.

Bishop, J. (1992), 'Workforce Preparedness', in D. Lewin, O. S. Mitchell and P. D. Sherer (eds), *Research Frontiers in Industrial Relations and Human Resources*, Madison, WI: Industrial Relations Research Association.

Björklund, A. (1991), 'Evaluation of Labour Market Policy in Sweden', in *Evaluating Labour Market and Social Programmes: The State of a Complex Art*, Paris: OECD, pp. 73–86.

Blanchflower, D. G. and L. M. Lynch (1994), 'Training at Work: A Comparison of US and British Youths', in L. M. Lynch (ed.), *Training and the Private Sector: International Comparisons*, Chicago: University of Chicago Press, pp. 223–60.

Boesal, D. and L. McFarland (eds) (1994), *National Assessment of Vocational Education, Final Report to Congress*, Washington, DC: US Department of Education.

Bonnal, L., D. Fougère and A. Sérandon (1995), 'L'impact des dispositifs d'emploi sur le devenir des jeunes chômeurs: une évaluation économetrique sur données longitudinales', *Economie et Prévision*, 115, 1–28.

Booth, A. and D. J. Snower (eds) (1995), *Acquiring Skills: Market Failures, Their Symptoms and Policy Responses*, Cambridge: Cambridge University Press.

Breen, R. (1991), 'Assessing the Effectiveness of Training and Temporary Employment Schemes—Some Results from the Youth Labour Market', *Economic and Social Review*, 22, 177–98.

Brown, C., C. Gilroy and A. Cohen (1983), 'Time-series Evidence of the Effect of the Minimum Wage on Youth Employment and Unemployment', *Journal of Human Resources*, 18, 3–31.

Büchtemann, C. F., J. Schupp and D. Soloff (1993), 'Roads to Work: School-to-work Transition Patterns in Germany and the US', *Industrial Relations Journal*, 24, 97–111.

Campinos-Dubernet, M. and J.-M. Grando (1988), 'Formation professionnelle ouvrière: trois modèles Européennes', *Formation Emploi*, 22, 38–48.

Card, D. (1992), 'Do Minimum Wages Reduce Employment? A Case Study of California, 1987–89', *Industrial and Labour Relations Review*, 46 (1), 38–54.

Card, D. and A. B. Krueger (1995), *Myth and Measurement: The New Economics of the Minimum Wage*, Princeton: Princeton University Press.

CEC (Commission of the European Communities) (1993), *COMETT II: Evaluations*, Luxembourg: Office for Official Publications of the European Communities.

Cette, G., P. Cuneo, D. Eyssartier and J. Gautié (1995), 'Les effets sur l'emploi d'un abaissement du coût du travail des jeunes', in G. Benhayoun and S. Bazen (eds), *Salaire Minimum et Bas Salaires*, Paris: L'Harmattan.

Chevalier, L. and S. Silberman (1988), 'Peut-on encore parler d'insertion pour les jeunes sans formation?', *Formation Emploi*, 23, 74–8.

Colin, J.-F. and J.-M. Espinasse (1979), 'Les subventions à l'emploi', *Travail et Emploi*, 1, 37–50.

Crain, R. L., A. L. Heebner and Yin-Pong Si (1992), *The Effectiveness of New York City's Career Magnet Schools: An Evaluation of Ninth Grade Performance Using an Experimental Design*, Berkeley: National Center for Research in Vocational Education.

Deakin, B. M. (1995), *The Youth Labour Market in Britain: The Role of Intervention*, Cambridge: Cambridge University Press.

DeFreitas, G., D. W. Marsden and P. Ryan (1991), 'Patterns of Youth Employment in Segmented Labour Markets in the US and Europe', *Eastern Economic Journal*, 17 (2), 223–36.

Ellwood, D. (1982), 'Teenage Unemployment: Permanent Scars or Temporary Blemishes?', in R. Freeman and D. Wise (eds), *The Youth Labour Market Problem*, Chicago: National Bureau of Economic Research (NBER)/University of Chicago Press.

Farkas, G., D. A. Smith and E. W. Stromsdorfer (1983), 'The Youth Entitlement Demonstration: Subsidized Employment with a Schooling Requirement', *Journal of Human Resources*, 18, 557–73.

Fraker, T. and R. Maynard (1987), 'The Adequacy of Comparison Group Designs for Evaluations of Employment-related Programmes', *Journal of Human Resources*, 22, 194–227.

Freeman, R. B. and H. J. Holzer (1986), 'The Black Youth Employment Crisis', in R. B. Freeman and H. J. Holzer (eds), *The Black Youth Employment Crisis*, Chicago: National Bureau of Economic Research (NBER)/University of Chicago Press, pp. 3–20.

Freeman, R. B. and D. A. Wise (1982), 'The Youth Labour Market Problem: Its Nature, Causes and Consequences', in R. B. Freeman and D. A. Wise (eds), *The Youth Labour Market Problem*, Chicago: National Bureau of Economic Research (NBER)/University of Chicago Press, pp. 1–16.

Garonna, P. and P. Ryan (1991a), 'The Problems Facing Youth', in P. Ryan, P. Garonna and R. C. Edwards (eds), *The Problem of Youth: The Regulation of Youth Employment and Training in Advanced Economies*, London: Macmillan, pp. 1–31.

Garonna, P. and P. Ryan (1991b), 'The Regulation and Deregulation of Youth Economic Activity', in P. Ryan, P. Garonna and R. C. Edwards (eds), *The Problem of Youth: The Regulation of Youth Employment and Training in Advanced Economies*, London: Macmillan, pp. 35–81.

Gay, R. S. and M. E. Borus (1980), 'Validating Performance Indicators for Employment and Training Programmes', *Journal of Human Resources*, 15, 29–48.

Grant Foundation (1988), *The Forgotten Half: Non-College Youth in America*, Washington, DC: William T. Grant Foundation.

Green, A. (1995), 'Core Skills, Participation and Progression in Post-compulsory Education and Training in England and France', *Comparative Education*, 31 (1), 49–67.

Greenaway, D. (1993), 'Economic Aspects of Youth Training in Industrialised Countries', *Economic Journal*, 103, 1259–60.

Grubb, D. (1994), 'Direct and Indirect Effects of Active Labour Market Policies in OECD Countries', in R. Barrell (ed.), *The UK Labour Market*, Cambridge, UK: Cambridge University Press.

Grubb, W. N. (1993), 'The Varied Returns to Postsecondary Education: New Evidence from the Class of 1972', *Journal of Human Resources*, 28, 365–82.

Grubb, W. N. (in press), *Evaluating Job Training Programmes in the United States: Evidence and Explanations*, Training Policy Study, Geneva: International Labour Office.

Hashimoto, M. (1982), 'Minimum Wage Effects on Training on the Job', *American Economic Review*, 72, 1070–87.

Haveman, R. H. and D. H. Saks (1985), 'Transatlantic Lessons for Employment and Training Policy', *Industrial Relations*, 24, 20–36.

Heckman, J. J. (1993), 'The Case for Simple Estimators: Experimental Evidence from the National JTPA Study', technical report no. 5, Harris School Job Training and Partnership Act (JTPA) Project, University of Chicago.

Heckman, J. J. and V. J. Hotz (1989), 'Choosing among Alternative Nonexperimental Methods for Estimating the Impact of Social Programmes', *Journal of the American Statistical Association*, 84, 862–80.

Heckman, J. J., R. L. Roselius and J. A. Smith (1994), *US Education and Training Policy: A Re-evaluation of the Underlying Assumptions behind the 'New Consensus', Labour Markets, Employment Policy and Job Creation*, Boulder: Westview Press, pp. 83–121.

Heckman, J. J. and J. Smith (1993), 'Assessing the Case for Randomized Evaluation of Social Programmes', in K. Jensen and P. Madsen (eds) (1993), *Measuring Labour Market Measures: Evaluating the Effects of Active Labour Market Policy Initiatives*, Copenhagen: Ministry of Labour, pp. 35–96.

Johnson, G. E. (1979), 'The Labour Market Displacement Effect in the Analysis of Manpower Training Programmes', in F. E. Bloch (ed.), *Evaluating Manpower Training Programmes: Research in Labour Economics* (suppl. 1), Greenwich, CT: JAI Press, pp. 227–57.

Jonzon, B. and L. R. Wise (1989), 'Getting Young People to Work: An Evaluation of Swedish Youth Employment Policy', *International Labour Review*, 128, 337–56.

Kang, S. and J. Bishop (1989), 'Vocational and Academic Education in High School: Complements or Substitutes?', *Economics of Education Review*, 8, 133–48.

Kariya, T. and J. E. Rosenbaum (1987), 'Self-selection in Japanese Junior High Schools: A Longitudinal Study of Students' Educational Plans', *Sociology of Education*, 60, 168–80.

Katz, L. F. and L. H. Summers (1988), 'Industry Rents: Evidence and Implications', *Brookings Papers on Economic Activity*, 3, 209–75.

Klerman, J. A. and L. A. Karoly (1995), *The Transition to Stable Employment. The Experience of US Youth in Their Early Labour Market Career*, Santa Monica, CA: RAND Corporation.

Korpi, T. (1994), 'Escaping Unemployment: Studies in the Individual Consequences of Unemployment and Labour Market Policy', study no. 24, Swedish Institute for Social Research, Stockholm.

LaLonde, R. J. (1986), 'Evaluating the Econometric Evaluations of Training Programmes with Experimental Data', *American Economic Review*, 76, 604–20.

Lee, D., D. Marsden, P. Rickman and J. Duncombe (1990), *Scheming for Youth: A Study of YTS in the Enterprise Culture*, Milton Keynes: Open University Press.

Levitan, S. A. and B. H. Johnston (1975), *The Job Corps: A Social Experiment That Works*, Baltimore: Johns Hopkins University Press.

Lindbeck, A. and D. H. Snower (1988), 'Wage-setting, Unemployment and Insider–Outsider Relations', *The Insider–Outsider Theory of Employment and Unemployment*, Cambridge, MA: MIT Press, pp. 75–83.

Lynch, L. M. (1992), 'Private Sector Training and the Earnings of Young Workers', *American Economic Review*, 82, 299–312.

Machin, S. and A. Manning (1994), 'The Effects of Minimum Wages on Wage Dispersion and Employment: Evidence from the UK Wages Councils', *Industrial and Labour Relations Review*, 47, 319–29.

Marquand, J. (1994), 'Training Policy and Economic Theory: A Policy Maker's Perspective', in R. McNabb and K. Whitfield (eds), *The Market for Training*, Aldershot: Avebury.

Marsden, D. W. and J.-F. Germe (1991), 'Young People and Entry Paths to Longer-term Jobs in France and Great Britain', in P. Ryan, P. Garonna and R. C. Edwards (eds), *The Problem of Youth: The Regulation of Youth Employment and Training in Advanced Economies*, London: Macmillan, pp. 178–99.

Marsden, D. W. and P. Ryan (1990), 'Institutional Aspects of Youth Employment and Training Policy in Britain', *British Journal of Industrial Relations*, 28, 351–70.

Marsden, D. W. and P. Ryan (1991a), 'Initial Training, Labour Market Structure and Public Policy: Intermediate Skills in British and German Industry', in P. Ryan (ed.), *International Comparisons of Vocational Education and Training for Intermediate Skills*, Lewes: Falmer.

Marsden, D. W. and P. Ryan (1991b), 'The Structuring of Youth Pay and Employment in Six European Economies', in P. Ryan, P. Garonna and R. C. Edwards (eds) (1991), *The Problem of Youth: The Regulation of Youth Employment and Training in Advanced Economies*, London: Macmillan, pp. 82–112.

McNabb, R. and P. Ryan (1990), 'Segmented Labour Markets', in D. Sapsford and Z. Tzannatos (eds), *Current Issues in Labour Economics*, London: Macmillan, pp. 151–76.

Meyer, R. H. and D. A. Wise (1982), 'High School Preparation and Early Labour Force Experience', in R. B. Freeman and D. A. Wise (eds), *The Youth Labour Market Problem*, Chicago: University of Chicago Press, pp. 1–16.

Meyer, R. H. and D. A. Wise (1983), 'The Effects of the Minimum Wage on the Employment and Earnings of Youth, *Journal of Labor Economics*, 1, 66–100.

Mincer, J. (1974), *Schooling, Experience and Earnings*, New York: Columbia University Press.

Minni, C. and J.-F. Vergnies (1994), 'La diversité des facteurs de l'insertion professionnelle', *Economie et Statistique*, 277, 45–61.

National Commission on Education (NCE) (1993), *Learning to Succeed*, London: Heinemann.

Neumark, D. and W. Wascher (1995), 'The Effects of Minimum Wages on Teenage Employment and Enrollment', working paper no. 5092, National Bureau of Economic Research (NBER), Cambridge, MA.

Osterman, P. (1980), *Getting Started*, Cambridge, MA: MIT Press.

Prais, S. J. (1993), 'Economic Performance and Education: The Nature of Britain's Deficiencies', Keynes Lecture, Royal Academy, London.

Psacharopoulos, G. (1987), 'To Vocationalize or Not To Vocationalize? That Is the Curriculum Question', *International Review of Education*, 33 (2), 187–211.

Rees, A. (1986), 'An Essay on Youth Joblessness', *Journal of Economic Literature*, 24 (2), 613–28.

Rosenbaum, J. E. and T. Kariya (1989), 'From High School to Work: Market and Institutional Mechanisms in Japan', *American Journal of Sociology*, 94 (6), 1334–65.

Rosenbaum, J. E., T. Kariya, R. Settersten and T. Maier (1990), 'Market and Network Theories of the Transition from High School to Work: Their Application to Industrialized Societies', *Annual Review of Sociology*, 16, 263–99.

Ryan, P. (1984), 'The New Training Initiative after Two Years', *Lloyds Bank Review*, 152, 41–55.

Ryan, P. (1991), 'Comparative Research on Vocational Education and Training', in P. Ryan (ed.), *International Comparisons of Vocational Education and Training for Intermediate Skills*, Lewes: Falmer, pp. 1–20.

Ryan, P. (1994, May), 'Youth Unemployment: Public Intervention in International Perspective', paper presented to the Economic and Social Research Council (ESRC) seminar on unemployment, New University of Ulster.

Ryan, P. (1995), 'Trade Union Policies towards the Youth Training Scheme: Patterns and Causes, *British Journal of Industrial Relations*, 33 (1), 1–34.

Ryan, P. (in press), 'The Institutional Setting of Investment in Human Resources in the UK', in C. F. Büchtemann and D. Soloff (eds), *Human Capital Investment and Economic Performance*, New York: Russell Sage.

Schellhaass, H.-M. (1991), 'Evaluation Strategies and Methods with Regard to Labour Market Programmes: A German Perspective', in OECD (ed.), *Evaluating Labour Market and Social Programmes. The State of a Complex Art*, Paris: OECD, pp. 89–106.

Sipe, C. L., J. Grossman and J. A. Milliner (1988), *Summer Training and Education Programme: Report on the 1987 Experience*, Philadelphia, PA: Public/Private Ventures.

Solow, R. M. (1990), 'Government and the Labour Market', in K. G. Abraham and R. K. McKersie (eds), *New Developments in the Labour Market: Toward a New Institutional Paradigm*, Cambridge, MA: MIT Press, pp. 275–90.

Soskice, D. (1990), 'Reinventing Corporatism', in R. Brunetta and C. dell'Arringa (eds), *Labour Relations and Economic Performance*, London: Macmillan, pp. 170–211.

Soskice, D. (1993), 'Social Skills from Mass Higher Education: Rethinking the Company-based Paradigm', *Oxford Review of Economic Policy*, 9 (3), 101–13.

Stern, D., C. Dayton, I. Paik, A. Weisberg and J. Evans (1989), 'Benefits and Costs of Dropout Prevention in a High School Programme Combining Academic and Vocational Education: Third-year Results from Replications of the California Peninsula Academies', *Educational Evaluation and Policy Analysis*, 10 (2), 161–70.

Stern, D., N. Finkelstein, J. R. Stone, J. Latting and C. Dornsife (1995), *School to Work: Research on Programs in the United States*, Lewes: Falmer.

Stern, D., M. Raby and C. Dayton (1992), *Career Academies: Partnerships for Reconstructing American High Schools*, San Francisco: Jossey Bass.

Streeck, W., J. Hilbert, K.-H. van Kevalaer, F. Mayer and H. Weber (1987), *The Role of the Social Partners in Vocational Education and Training in the Federal Republic of Germany*, Berlin: European Centre for Vocational Education and Training (CEDEFOP).

Tan, H. W., B. Chapman, C. E. Peterson and A. Booth (1991), *Youth Training in the United States, Britain, and Australia*, Santa Monica, CA: Rand.

Taylor, M. E. (1981), *Education and Work in the Federal Republic of Germany*, London: Anglo-German Foundation.

Topel, R. H. and M. P. Ward (1992), 'Job Mobility and the Careers of Young Men', *Quarterly Journal of Economics*, 57 (2), 439–80.

UK ED (1991a), 'The Evaluation of Employment Policies and Programmes', in *Evaluating Labour Market and Social Programmes: The State of a Complex Art*, Paris: OECD, pp. 159–66.

UK ED (1991b), *YTS Progress Report, 1988/89*, Sheffield: Employment Department.

US DE (1993), *Goals 2000, Educate America: Building Bridges from School to Work*, Washington, DC: US Department of Education.

US NCES (1993), *Education in States and Nations*, Washington, DC: US Department of Education, National Center for Education Statistics.

van Opstal, R. and F. van de Pol (1991), *The Transition from School to Work in 1979–1987 in the Netherlands*, Onderzoeksmemorandum no. 82, 's-Gravenhage: Centraal Planbureau.

van Soest, A. (1989), 'Minimum Wage Rates and Unemployment in the Netherlands', *De Economist*, 137 (3).

Venti, S. F. (1984), 'The Effects of Income Maintenance on Work, Schooling, and Non-market Activities of Youth', *Review of Economics and Statistics*, 66 (1), 16–25.

Verdier, E. (1994, February), 'Vocational Training of Young People in France: A Resource Difficult to Exploit', *European Journal of Vocational Training*, 34–43.

Welch, F. R. and J. Cunningham (1978), 'Effects of Minimum Wages on the Level and Age Composition of Youth Employment', *Review of Economics and Statistics*, 6 (1), 140–45.

Wellington, A. J. (1991), 'Effects of the Minimum Wage on the Employment Status of Youths: An Update', *Journal of Human Resources*, 26 (1), 27–46.

Whitfield, K. and R. A. Wilson (1991), 'Staying on in Full-time Education: The Educational Participation Rate of 16-year olds', *Economica*, 58 (231), 391–404.

Wilensky, H. L. (1992), 'Active Labour Market Policy: Its Content, Effectiveness, and Odd Relation to Evaluation Research', in C. Crouch and A. Heath (eds), *Social Research and Social Reform*, Oxford: Clarendon Press, pp. 315–50.

Willis, R. J. and S. Rosen (1979), 'Education and Self-selection', *Journal of Political Economy*, 87 (5), S7–S36.

Zilbert, E. E., J. C. Hearn and D. R. Lewis (1992), 'Selection Bias and the Earnings Effects of Postsecondary Vocational Education', *Journal of Vocational Education Research*, 17 (1), 11–34.

11. Transitions between Family Formation and Paid Employment

Colette Fagan and Jill Rubery

The impact of motherhood on women's labour market participation has changed rapidly in recent decades. There is a common trend towards an increase in the proportion of women who remain in the labour market when they become mothers, but national differences still persist (Delacourt and Zighera, 1988; European Commission, 1994a; Meulders, Plasman and Vander Stricht 1993; Rubery, Fagan and Smith 1995; UN, 1994). A high and continuous rate of labour market participation over the life cycle has developed for women in France and the Nordic countries. In contrast, in other European countries the arrival of a young child frequently precipitates a labour market exit and subsequent reentry, in many cases on a part-time basis (e.g. the United Kingdom, western Germany). This long-term trend of increasing female activity rates is partly explained by demand-side factors, in particular the expansion of the service sector (Rubery and Fagan, 1994, pp. 153–6). However, interrelated supply-side factors have also contributed to the trend, either by raising women's employment prospects and aspirations, or by increasing the financial pressures on women's labour supply decisions. These factors include increased access to education, falling fertility rates, higher rates of divorce and lone parenthood, contemporary consumption patterns and periods of high inflation.

The increased integration of women into employment is one of the explicit objectives of the equal opportunities policy recommendations and programmes of both the OECD (1994a) and the Commission of the European Communities (1991). However, the integration of women into employment is not only an equality issue, but also has macroeconomic implications in terms of efficiency. This point is discussed in more detail in section 1, where we argue that institutional bridges that facilitate employment continuity over the early child-rearing years reduce labour market inefficiencies as well as promote sex equality. A comparative overview of the different types of policies to promote employment continuity for mothers is provided in section 2, focussing upon the Member States of the European Union. In section 3 we review several important studies that assess the impact of different national policy regimes upon maternal employment and raise several relevant issues

348

for evaluation research in this policy area. On the basis of this evidence, in the concluding section we identify the combination of policy instruments that appears to be most conducive to the reconciliation of employment and parental responsibilities and suggest pertinent questions and information requirements for future evaluation research.

1 WHY IS POLICY INTERVENTION NECESSARY TO RECONCILE EMPLOYMENT WITH PARENTAL RESPONSIBILITIES?

Women do most of the care work within the household. This responsibility constrains their labour supply and reduces the life-time earnings and occupational advancement of women compared to men. The need for policy intervention is easily justified on the grounds of promoting sex equality, but such intervention is often presented as a distortion of market efficiency. Indeed, some economists argue against policy intervention on the basis that the existing division of household labour is both efficient and reflects individual preferences and social norms (e.g. Main, 1993). The presumption of efficiency rests upon Becker's (1981) 'New Household Economics' model. Advocates of this approach assume that women anticipate spending a large portion of their life living with an employed man with whom they will have children, and that their maternal responsibilities will result in a reduced labour market involvement compared to men. This expectation leads women to make a smaller investment in education and makes them more likely to enter certain lower-paid jobs that are more compatible with household work than the higher-paid 'male breadwinner' jobs. At the point of setting up house together, the woman's lower wage provides an incentive for her to specialize in household labour, at the cost of a further reduction in human capital acquisition, while the higher-earning male continues to invest his labour in market work in order to maximize household income.

One criticism of the 'New Household Economics' theory is that it uses the existing sexual division of parental responsibilities to explain gender differences in labour market outcomes, such as women's lower earnings, but fails to address how these unequal outcomes restrict opportunities to change the division of labour, which reinforces the status quo (Berk and Fenstermaker-Berk, 1983; Humphries, 1995). This feedback from the demand side of the economy affects labour supply decisions. Individual preferences and expectations are embedded in the social environment and adapt in response to changing opportunities and experience over the life time and across generations (Dex, 1988; Rose, 1988). Hence, women's job preferences and their investments in education and training are at least partly influenced by the options that they perceive to be open to them. It is rational for women (and men) to expect that it is easier to enter traditional rather than nontraditional jobs when sex-segregated job patterns are clearly visible, when information on the associated wage differentials is largely unknown and when sex discrimination can be anticipated.

The organization of the household is, therefore, only relatively autonomous from the existing labour market conditions (Humphries and Rubery, 1984). The mutual conditioning between the two spheres of activity maintains the 'gender order' (Connell, 1987), for women's actual, or expected, domestic responsibilities contribute to the maintenance of sex-segregated employment patterns. The aggregate market failure that results is that women's skills are underused and underdeveloped in the labour market (see Rubery, Fagan and Maier, chap. 14 in this volume). Of course, women's labour supply is adapting to changing economic and social conditions, for younger generations are making fewer, and shorter, labour market interruptions over the early years of child-rearing. This trend might be interpreted as evidence that the market has not failed, but is changing slowly, and that efficiency will be achieved in the long run. However, if market failures persist in connection with maternal employment, then the economy may become locked into an enduring suboptimality that fails to make full use of women's skills (Bruegel and Perrons, 1995). Conversely, policy intervention might stimulate a long-term, cumulative 'upward spiral' through creating institutions that facilitate more continuous labour market involvement. Thus, intervention to promote sex equality may be a prerequisite for market efficiency instead of a cost (Humphries and Rubery, 1995; Schmid, 1994).

The 'bounded rationality' of labour supply decisions produces market failures at the household level. Individuals cannot obtain or digest full information about their future household circumstances or the implications of their current training and employment decisions. Women may remain childless or single despite their intentions, ending up with a more continuous labour market involvement than they perhaps expected when they entered the labour market. Those who marry or cohabit and interrupt their employment to have children may incur unexpected future costs if the man's wage is lost through unemployment, widowhood or marital breakdown. The market failure arising from marital breakdown is even acknowledged by economists who argue that the traditional household division of labour is efficient, for the gains from household specialization are disproportionately captured by the man, whereas the woman cannot recoup on her specialization in household labour (Main, 1993).

Households may not be behaving efficiently when the woman exits the labour market to raise children. Such interruptions frequently lead to a loss of occupational status upon labour market reentry, producing a negative impact on women's future earnings and pensions (Dex and Shaw, 1986; Dex, Walters and Alden, 1993; McRae, 1991). To maximize the household's income over the life time, it would be efficient for women to remain in employment when they have young children, even if childcare costs meant they worked for little immediate net financial gain. Furthermore, because employment discontinuities make women in couple households dependent upon their male partners for a large portion of their life-time income (Joshi and Davies, 1995), it may be efficient for men to meet some childcare costs rather than treating them as a female work-related cost. Alternatively, household efficiency might be maximized by both parents putting time into paid work and child-rearing, rather than one parent 'over-specializing' in unpaid work (Owen, 1987). This is because the sharp depreciation in the returns to employment associated with women quitting the labour market coexists with a diminishing rate of return to the amount of time invested in employment by a continuous worker. Few households are in a position to make this type of calculation of forgone household life-time income arising from employment interruptions. Indeed, evidence from the United Kingdom indicates that the usual financial consideration is to set childcare costs against the women's current wage and that the net return is an important influence on whether women return to employment at the end of maternity leave (Brannen and Moss, 1991; McRae, 1991).

Thus, where there is a lack of public policies to enable mothers to reconcile employment with childcare responsibilities, the private solutions that households find may be suboptimal in the long run due to unforeseen costs. Because it is plausible to presume that an immediate financial return to employment enhances women's work incentives, then efficiency gains might arise from the introduction of childcare subsidies, either via public provision or financial transfers to either parents or service providers. Furthermore, even if mothers prefer to remain at home to care for young children, the loss of occupational status upon labour market reentry may result from labour market barriers rather than skill depreciation. Barriers may include an overreliance by employers on employment experience as a proxy indicator for productivity, the limited age or occupational entry points to internal labour markets and seniority systems of job advancement. Longer parental leave entitlements or the option to return to work part time would reduce the underemployment of women's skills when they become mothers.

Policy intervention would not just produce efficiency gains for households, but would also address market failures arising from employers' behaviour and in turn produce aggregate gains for the economy. The immediate costs of women's employment interruptions for employers are the loss of experienced staff or the problems of mobilizing female labour in response to skill shortages. The longer-term global cost is the underdevelopment of women's contribution to the formal economy. Employers may, of course, introduce measures to retain or recruit mothers of young children, such as extended leave, flexible working or childcare subsidies. Indeed, some companies have introduced various 'family-friendly' policies in the United Kingdom after calculating that this approach was cheaper than the cost of replacing skilled workers who quit after maternity leave. However, reliance upon employer provision is vulnerable to the freerider problem. If only a minority of firms provide family policies, they may be subject to 'poaching' by competitors once the employee has less need for these policies, for example, when the child is older. Furthermore, if these initiatives are driven by short-term considerations, they may be curtailed in times of recession, which has already happened in many instances in the United Kingdom, thus undermining a long-term market-led expansion of family policies and contributing to future potential skill shortages when the economy picks up. In contrast, economy-wide policies to provide leave and childcare arrangements would spread the costs more evenly across employers and increase the overall female labour supply.

The loss of income resulting from employment interruptions to care for young children may create both wage and public expenditure pressures. Women's financial dependency in couple households creates a pressure for an implicit 'breadwinner supplement' to wages in male-dominated sectors. This pressure might be reduced by public funding of childcare to facilitate more continuous employment over the life cycle for women or paid parental leave to subsidize women's absence from employment. The loss of the women's wage may also increase public expenditure costs via benefits paid to low-income households, combined with the loss of income tax revenue. The tax gains and reduced benefit payments would to some extent offset the cost of funding of leave or childcare arrangements (Holtermann and Clarke, 1992). Furthermore, the growing polarization between dual-earner and nonearner households (OECD, 1995a, pp. 34–8), the increasing numbers of lone parents and other changes in the composition of households means that policies that remain locked into a traditional conception of the 'male breadwinner' model of household organization are becoming increasingly inappropriate. Policies such as parental leave and publicly funded childcare that are directed at parents and children rather than at particular types of households are likely to be a more efficient means of directing resources to people with family responsibilities.

Finally, there are wider social costs if households are unable to reconcile parenting with employment. The importance of ensuring that the future generation of workers is raised, educated and maintained is already recognized through the public funding of education, child-related transfer payments and various other family policies. Yet the difficulties that women face in combining employment with child-rearing in some countries may lead a growing proportion of women to limit their family size to one child, or even to remain childless. Such a family strategy has been suggested as part of the explanation for the dramatic recent falls in fertility rates in some countries, such as Italy and Germany (Bettio and Villa, 1993; Maier, Quack and Rapp, 1994), and these private solutions may create public costs in the future. This has long been recognized in French family policy, which is explicitly premised on the need to enable women to combine employment with motherhood, driven as much by natalism as by a concern to promote sex equality (Jensen, 1994). There is also a public interest in ensuring that there is adequate care for children. Lack of childcare provision will not necessarily reduce participation in the labour market, but may instead have a negative impact on children, leading to increased social problems such as juvenile crime.

We have argued that the 'breadwinner family' system—advocated as rational and efficient according to the New Home Economics approach—is in fact inefficient for households, employers and the economy. Policies that increase the integration of women into employment over the period of family formation and weaken the 'breadwinner family' model could therefore yield efficiency as well as equality gains. To achieve this aim a variety of policies will need to be coordinated, an issue we turn to in the next section.

2   COMPARATIVE OVERVIEW OF MATERNAL EMPLOYMENT POLICY REGIMES

The focus of this section is upon the two types of policy that are directly concerned with facilitating employment continuity over the family formation period: various entitlements to leave or reduced working time and the public provision or subsidy of nonparental childcare (including school hours). The particular combination of policies found in any country makes up the core of the 'maternal employment policy regime'. A complementary policy, which we do not address directly, is initiatives concerned with stimulating labour market reentry after an interruption. These reentry programmes differ from general active labour market policies for the unemployed because they are geared to the particular needs of women and often do not require women to be registered as unemployed to participate (see Rubery, Smith, Fagan and Grimshaw, 1996). The European Union's (EU) 'New Opportunities for Women' (NOW) programme has been set up to stimulate the development of these initiatives.

Policy intervention to support continuous employment for mothers with young children is strongest in what Lewis (1992) has conceptualized as 'weak breadwinner' states. These countries have an explicit policy commitment to facilitate employment continuity for women during the early child-rearing years through intervention to reconcile caring and earning responsibilities for male as well as female workers. The policy emphasis may either be upon flexible leave entitlements, as in Sweden, or subsidized childcare, as in Denmark (Leira, 1994). In contrast, the idea of promoting maternal employment is likely to meet most resistance in 'strong breadwinner' welfare states, where the state treats women primarily as wives and mothers rather than as labour market participants. Leave entitlements and public childcare provision is either limited, on the basis that child-rearing is mainly a private concern (e.g. United Kingdom, Ireland), or more extensive but implicitly organized to encourage mothers to spend the early child-rearing years at home and then to work part time (e.g. western Germany). France is a 'modified breadwinner' state, where the emphasis of family policy has been pulled in different directions over time according to the strength of different interest groups: equal opportunities advocates have sought to promote women's integration into employment, natalists have campaigned for policies to enable women to have more children while remaining in employment, and a more traditional 'familialist' lobby promotes large families, where the mother stays at home, as the best arrangement for society (Jensen, 1994). Recently 'familialist' policies have been deployed in debates about how to reduce unemployment in France (Gauvin, Granie and Silvera, 1994).

Table 11.1 reveals a broadly positive correlation between state provision for parental leave and childcare, and maternal employment rates for 12 Member States of the EU.[1] The employment rate is taken as the core indicator of integration. This is because the activity rate excludes some female unemployment hidden as nonemployment and may include some unemployed mothers who left their previous employment precisely because the job could not be reconciled with child-rearing responsibilities. The highest maternal employment rates are found in the Danish 'weak breadwinner' state, where a system of paid parental leave coexists with a comparatively high level of publicly funded childcare places. In contrast, the lowest employment rates for women with a child aged under three years are found in the 'strong' breadwinner states, where the policy environment is less supportive. However, the Portuguese maternal employment rate is high despite the limited childcare and leave entitlements, indicating that other societal features are also important. Furthermore, the incidence of part-time employment also varies: it is rare in the southern countries, it coexists with high full-time employment rates in Denmark, France and Belgium, while it is the dominant employment form for mothers in the United Kingdom, western Germany and the Netherlands, where it is associated with a 'women returner' pattern of labour market quits and reentry.

---

1 Comparable data on childcare funding and maternal employment rates were not available for the countries that only joined the EU in 1995 (Sweden, Finland and Austria).

Table 11.1 The Strength of the 'Male Breadwinner' Presumption in State Parental Leave and Childcare Funding Policies

Breadwinner presumption	Paid parental leave	% of publicly funded childcare places		% employment rate for mothers aged 20–39, 1991			
				Youngest child under 3 years		Youngest child aged 3–6	
		Under 3 years	3 years to school age	% employed (% of employed in part-time work)	% total activity rate	% employed (% of employed in part-time work)	% total activity rate
Weak							
Denmark	Yes	48	85	72 (31)	85	77 (39)	88
Modified							
Belgium	Lower payment	20	95+	59 (36)	68	62 (39)	71
France	Lower payment	20	95+	52 (27)	62	64 (27)	73
Strong							
Italy	Lower payment	< 10	85	42 (13)	50	42 (13)	51
Germany	Lower payment	< 10	65–70	38 (53)	41	48 (66)	52
Greece	Unpaid	< 10	65–70	39 (9)	45	40 (4)	46
Spain	Unpaid	< 10	65–70	32 (12)	43	35 (13)	48
Portugal	Unpaid	< 10	< 55	67 (9)	73	72 (7)	78
Netherlands	Unpaid: only part time	< 10	< 55	37 (87)	42	42 (89)	49
United Kingdom	Unpaid: only mothers	< 10	< 55	40 (65)	47	57 (71)	63
Ireland	Unpaid: only mothers	< 10	< 55	33 (22)	41	30 (34)	40
Luxembourg	Unpaid: only public sector	< 10	55–60	36 (29)	33	42 (37)	44

Sources: Childcare in the European Communities 1985–90. Women of Europe by EC Childcare Network, 1990, Brussels: Commission of the European Communities (DG X); *Changing Patterns of Work and Working-time in the European Union and the Impact on Gender Divisions* by J. Rubery, C. Fagan and M. Smith, 1995, Brussels: European Commission; Table 11.3 below.

Therefore, while we focus in this chapter on national leave and childcare policies, many other institutional arrangements also affect the way that families combine parental work with paid employment. On the supply side, family tax and benefit systems create incentive structures that may enhance or undermine the impact of policies designed to increase maternal employment. Although there is no simple relation between the level or form of aggregate female participation rates and either the taxation system (Schettkat, 1989; Vermeulen et al., 1995) or the level of child support (Bradshaw, Ditch, Holmes and Whiteford, 1993), targeted cuts in the marginal tax rates faced by married women would tend to increase their labour supply (OECD, 1994b). Policies that aim to facilitate maternal employment must also be coordinated with general family policy concerning children's rights and welfare, for these may embody contradictory presumptions as to whether mothers of young children should be encouraged to stay at home. Finally, to be effective, supply-side policies must also be coordinated with intervention on the demand side, for the type of jobs and wages that women have access to will affect their labour supply. Such intervention includes specific sex equality or 'gender' initiatives as well as the gender impact of general labour market policies concerned with the organization of education, training and recruitment systems, and regulations on wages and working time (see Rubery et al., chap. 14 in this volume).

2.1 Employment Continuity through Leave to Care for Young Children

The 1992 EU Directive for the Protection at Work of Pregnant Women has established the general right to a period of 14 weeks' paid maternity leave in all Member States. Statutory paid maternity leave already existed in most Member States, generally for between 14 and 18 weeks, combined with a payment that provides a high earnings replacement rate. The main impact of the Directive will be in the United Kingdom, where previously maternity leave was conditional on length of service and hours of work (EU Childcare Network, 1994). A complementary EU Directive to establish a statutory entitlement to Parental Leave and Leave for Family Reasons, such as to care for sick children, was proposed in 1983, but adoption of this Directive has been continually blocked, primarily by the United Kingdom.

Although a parental leave entitlement may be an encouragement for some women to reduce their labour supply when their children are young, a net increase in female labour supply can be expected for two reasons. First, women may be encouraged to enter employment and/or work full time up to the birth of the child in order to build up their entitlement (OECD, 1995a, p. 189). Second, the rewards from employment are largely protected from deterioration, in contrast to the situation faced by women who are forced to quit and then reenter the labour market when they want time off for child-rearing. However, while parental leave strengthens women's labour market attachment, it may also reinforce their 'second-earner' status in the 'breadwinner family' model, depending on the details of the scheme and how these interact with the societal and economic context. Four issues are particularly important: whether the leave is paid, the length and flexibility of the leave entitlement, whether it is complemented by public funding of childcare and whether men take leave as well as women.

Parental leave that is unpaid (e.g. Portugal, Greece) or supported by a low rate of benefit (e.g. Belgium, Germany) does little to transform gender relations because it presumes that the leave-taker has an employed partner or other means of financial support. This situation is exacerbated when the unpaid leave is explicitly restricted to women as an extension of maternity leave (e.g. United Kingdom, Ireland) or when parental leave is allocated per family rather than per individual, for then no specific incentive is provided to encourage men to take leave as well. Unless there is a high earnings replacement rate, there is a financial incentive for the leave to be taken by the women in couple households, given that average female earnings are lower. A low earnings replacement rate thus reinforces, or introduces, the pattern of women taking time off to care for young children. Furthermore, lone parents and low-income two-earner households will not be able to afford to take leave.

In countries where the dominant household arrangement is for women to quit and reenter the labour market it might be argued that it would be efficient to introduce leave with little or no financial replacement because the dead-weight costs of financing a labour market quit that might have happened anyway would then be avoided. However, the continued presumption of women's financial dependency on a spouse in the early years of childbirth legitimizes the 'family wage' premium in setting male wages in certain sectors of the economy, even if the requirement to be a sole breadwinner covers only a relatively short period of the life cycle. A more efficient alternative might be to concentrate resources on the early stages of family formation, that is, on the phase when household income needs are particularly pressing.

The length of leave extends from under one year in most countries to between two and five years in others (Austria, Finland, France, Germany, Belgium). A long leave period is not unambiguously beneficial. The experience of taking a long period of leave may reduce women's labour market attachment and be associated with an actual, or perceived, erosion of skills. In an attempt to redress this problem France and Spain have recently introduced legislation granting the right to reinsertion training at the end of the leave period (OECD, 1995a, p. 189). A more optimal arrangement may be to build some flexibility into the leave scheme. Of the 15 Member States, Sweden has the most advanced statutory leave provision, which combines a high level of payment with flexibility to take the leave on a full- or part-time basis in one or more instalments (see Table 11.2). Parents also have the right to work a reduced working day (75 per cent of normal hours) until their child reaches the age of eight, and the loss of earnings can be partly compensated through the flexibility of the parental allowance payment, which can be spread out to cover half-day or quarter-day leave (EU Childcare Network, 1994). The advantage of reduced hours rather than full-time leave is that parents are enabled to retain contact with employment and to maintain their knowledge and skill levels, to work part time without having to switch jobs and to increase household income if the leave payment is reduced on a pro-rata rather than earnings-related basis. The feasibility of working full-time or part-time hours will, however, depend upon the availability of part-time childcare. Employers may also benefit from retaining employees on reduced hours rather than through an extended absence, however, in some job areas it may be more difficult for employers to arrange part-time rather than full-time temporary cover for short periods of time. A flexible scheme is likely, therefore, to offer greater scope for a compromise between employee and employer requirements.

Unless parental leave is coordinated with the provision of childcare services, it may simply serve to postpone the point at which women exit the labour market. For example, the German statutory parental leave entitlement was extended from one year to three years in 1993, but in the context of limited, mainly part-time, childcare services in western Germany this extension makes it difficult for women to resume employment at the end of the leave period. Even where there is a relatively well-established system of childcare subsidies, the long-term effect of extending leave entitlements may be to shift resources away from childcare funding instead of expanding the options for reconciling earning and caring work. For example, the 1994 Act that extended statutory parental leave in Denmark also permits municipal authorities to supplement the national rate of parental leave benefit, which is due to fall in the coming years. One incentive for this local addition might be to reduce the demand for childcare services that are subsidized by municipal authorities (Boje, 1994, p. 80). If reduced demand leads to a gradual dismantling of service provision, then the result may be that the amount of leave taken by women is increased and the notion of women as 'second earners' is reinforced, unless extended parental leave also becomes a feature of male employment patterns.

There are general economic as well as equality objectives that require a high male take-up of parental leave where it is introduced or extended as part of a labour market policy of work-sharing, such as in the recently expanded Danish programme of leave and the Belgian 'career break' scheme (see Boje, 1994; MISEP, 1995; Rubery et al., 1995). If the leave is taken only by mothers, this imbalance may undermine the effective contribution that leave arrangements can make to work-sharing policies because the redistribution via leave may become concentrated in the female-dominated sectors, with very little impact on work-sharing between men or between the sexes.

Finally, leave arrangements are one aspect of more general working time policies that also affect the reconciliation of parental and employment responsibilities. The development of working time flexibility has mainly been driven by employers' needs, largely subordinating the needs and preferences of employees, particularly in the private sector (Bosch, Dawkins and Michon, 1993; Rubery et al., 1995). Where variable and nonstandard hours are increasing, then it may become more difficult to combine employment with the day-to-day organization of family lives. However, in some northern European countries the opportunity to switch to part-time work in the public sector has increased over the 1980s as a result of policies to promote sex equality and working time flexibility, and in some, such as France and Belgium, this opportunity coexists with a right to return to full-time work (Hewitt, 1993, Table 2.1). A bill that would give all employees the right to switch to part-time hours in their current jobs was recently proposed in the Netherlands (Plantenga and van Velzen, 1994). The right to work part time in a wider range of jobs would help to make part-time work less segregated and could complement more general work-sharing objectives. However, greater access to part-time employment may also increase gender division in working time unless steps are taken to encourage fathers to work part time as well.

2.2 Employment Continuity through Childcare Services and Subsidies

The availability of publicly funded childcare varies sharply between countries (Table 11.1). Of the countries presented, the highest provision is found in Denmark, France and Belgium, and provision in Sweden is of a similar order (Leira, 1994). There are few places for children under the age of three, regardless of the length or availability of parental leave (see Table 11.2). From the age of three years the number of places increases as children enter preprimary education, but there is still a shortfall until children reach the compulsory school age (OECD, 1995b). This deficit means that once leave entitlements are exhausted mothers are obliged to rely upon other family members to provide childcare or to make private market-based arrangements if they are to remain in or take up employment.

The opening hours of preschool and primary education must also be taken into account. The length of the school day, whether hours vary over the week or according to the age of the child, and the duration of school holidays are important considerations, for they are likely to influence the types of working

Table 11.2 Statutory Provisions for Parental Leave in the European Union Member States

A. Type of leave

	Individual or family right	Maximum duration	Leave period	Part-time option	Fractioning[a]
Paid					
Austria	Family	104 weeks	Until the child is 4 years old	Yes[c]	No
Belgium	Individual	260 weeks[b]	Throughout the whole career	Yes[c]	Yes
Denmark[d]	'F': family 'I': individual	'F':10 weeks 'I': 26 weeks[e]	'F': following maternity leave 'I': until the child's 9th birthday	'F' leave: no 'I' leave: no	'F' leave: no 'I' leave: yes
Finland[d]	Family	'B': 26 weeks 'E': until the child is 3 years old	'B': following maternity leave 'E': until the child is 3 years old.	'B': no 'E': yes	Yes
France	Family	Until the child is 3 years old[f]	Until the child is 3 years old	Yes	No
Germany	Family	Until the child is 3 years old[f]	Until the child is 3 years old	Yes[c]	Yes
Italy	Family	26 weeks	Following maternity leave	No	No
Sweden	Family	15 months	Until the child is 8 years old	Yes	Yes
Part time					
Netherlands	Individual	26 weeks	Until the child is 4 years old	Only part-time basis	No
Unpaid					
Spain[g]	Family	Until the child is 3 years old[f, h]	Until the child is 3 years old[h]	No	No
Portugal	Family	26 weeks[i]	Following maternity leave	No	No
Greece	Individual[j, k]	13 weeks	Until the child is 2½ years old	No	Yes
Unpaid and limited entitlement					
Luxembourg	Public Sector	52 weeks	Until the child is 4 years old	Yes[l]	No
United Kingdom	Mother	22 weeks	Extension of maternity leave	No	No
Ireland	Mother	4 weeks	Extension of maternity leave	No	No

Table 11.2—continued   Statutory Provisions for Parental Leave in the European Union Member States

B. Parental leave payment

	Coverage + employment conditions	Benefit type + level	Maximum duration
Austria	Economically active + employed for 52 weeks in previous 2 years	Flat rate. Basic: Sch 181 per day, enhanced: Sch 268 per day	2 years
Belgium	Employees with 12 months' service	Flat rate, conditional on recruiting replacement employee (20–25% average manual industrial wage)	260 weeks[b]
Denmark	Economically active. For 'F': worked 120 hours in 13 weeks before leave	Flat rate, related to unemployment benefit (UI = 65% average net manual industrial wage) 'F': 100% UI, 'T': 80% UI, falling to 60% in 1997	'F': 10 weeks 'T': 26 weeks[e]
France	From 2nd child + employed for 2 years in previous 5 years[m]	Flat rate (≈ 35–40% average net manual industrial wage)	Until the child is 3 years old
Finland	All parents	'B': 66% annual earnings 'E': flat rate, in range Mk 1908–3435 per month	'B': 26 weeks, 'E': until the child is 3 years old
Germany	All parents	Flat rate (22% average manual wage), income-tested from 7th month	104 weeks
Italy	Employees	30% of earnings	26 weeks
Sweden	All parents minimum earnings in 240 consecutive days before birth for earnings-related benefit	80% of earnings for 10 months, 90% for 2 months, flat rate for 3 months	65 weeks

Notes
a   Fractioning = the possibility of taking the leave in more than one portion over an extended period rather than taking it in one continuous period;
b   The duration of a 'career break' in Belgium is not directly comparable with parental leave in other countries because it refers to the whole career period and not to each child;
c   Only with employer's agreement;
d   Subscripts 'F' = shareable family leave, 'T' = individual leave, respectively, for Denmark, while 'B' and 'E' stand for basic and extended leave in Finland;
e   13 weeks if the child is over 1 year; the leave is expandable to 52 weeks with the agreement of the employer;
f   Including maternity leave period;
g   The last four weeks of paid maternity leave can be transferred to the father;
h   Since March 1995, job guarantee and security extends over the 3 full years;
i   Leave duration can be extended up to 2 years under special circumstances;
j   Employer may refuse leave if it has been claimed by more than 8% of the work force during the year;
k   The other parent should also be employed;
l   The entitlement to work part time may be extended until the child reaches 15 years;
m   Two years of work in the last ten years for the third child onwards.

Sources: *Employment Outlook* (Tables 5.1 and 5.2) by OECD, 1995a. Paris: OECD; *Changing Patterns of Work and Working-time in the European Union and the Impact on Gender Divisions* by J. Rubery, C. Fagan and M. Smith, 1995, Brussels: European Commission; *Social Welfare and Economic Activity of Women in Europe*, V/2184/94–EN by CERC, 1994, Brussels: European Commission.

Table 11.3   Weekly Opening Hours for Primary Schools

Countries	Compulsory entry age	Weekly hours of attendance
Long day		
Belgium	6	8.30–15.30. Closed Wednesday afternoon. One-hour lunch break unsupervised.
France	6	8.30–16.30. Closed Wednesday afternoon.
Long, interrupted day		
Spain	6	9.00–17.00 with three-hour lunch break. Lunch break is supervised in an increasing number of urban schools.
Netherlands	5, most start at 4 years	9.00–16.00. Closed Wednesday afternoon. Supervision available for two-hour lunch break. Increasing number of schools adopting shorter day (8.30–15.00 with one-hour break).
Shorter, continuous day		
Denmark	7	Hours set locally, usually within range 8.00–15.00, timing often varies day to day. Hours increase with age: 7 years = 15–22 hours/week, 10 years up = 20–27 hours/week.
United Kingdom	5, most start at 4 years	At 4 years usually attend for 2.5 hours per day (am or pm). 9.00–15.30 with supervised lunch break from 5 years.
Ireland	6, most start at 5 years	At 5 years usually attend on part-time basis. 09.00–15.00/ 15.30 with supervised lunch break from 6 years.
Half day		
Italy	6	8.30–12.30, Mondays–Saturdays. Some children attend for 8 hours per day.
Germany	6–7	4 hours daily, timing may vary. Children return home for lunch.
Greece	5.5	Hours increase with age: 5.5–8.5 years = 20 hours/week, 8.5–11.5 years = 24/26 hours/week. Many attend in morning (8.00–12.00) or afternoon shifts because of shortage of school buildings.
Portugal	6	9.15–16.00 with two-hour break. Lunch break is only supervised in some schools. Many attend in shifts due to shortage of school places: 8.15–13.00 or 13.00–18.00 (60% of schools operated shift system in mid-1980s).
Luxembourg	5, most start at 4 years	8.00–11.30/12.00 for 6 days plus 14.00–16.30 on 3 days. Lunch break is not supervised in all schools.

Source
Childcare in the European Communities 1985–90. Women of Europe, Supplement 31 by EC Childcare Network, 1990, Brussels: Commission of the European Communities (DG X).

hours arrangements that mothers want and/or the amount of out-of-school care that they need to arrange. For example, most kindergarten places in Germany are part-time places, and children return home at lunchtime (EC Childcare Network, 1990). This part-time attendance in Germany continues in primary school, compared to longer school days found in France and Belgium, for example (Table 11.3). Another important feature is whether lunch breaks and free periods are generally supervised at school (e.g. United Kingdom) or whether children are the parents' responsibility at this time (e.g. Germany). School attendance therefore needs to be coordinated with other childcare arrangements; either out-of-school childcare or by parents adjusting their working time. In France, for example, women commonly arrange their working time to accommodate schools closing on Wednesdays, while parents and employers organize after-school and school holiday cover (Dex et al., 1993; EC Childcare Network, 1990). The availability of publicly funded out-of-school childcare is negligible in most countries other than Denmark (EC Childcare Network, 1990).

The final issue is the organization of parents' working time itself. Not only are holiday entitlements longer in some countries than others (IRS, 1991), but daily and weekly working hours vary. Trends towards more flexible and non-standard working time arrangements may make it easier for some parents to negotiate arrangements that are compatible with school hours, but for others the organizational complexity of daily life will increase. Indeed, the funding of childcare may become a growing necessity to enable parents to respond to employers' demands for flexibility. Funding childcare may also have wider economic gains; indeed, the job creation potential of childcare services is identified in the White Paper on Employment (European Commission, 1994b).

An alternative to directly funded services is to provide tax relief for childcare costs. Tax relief is available in many EU countries, but it is generally less significant than the level of subsidies provided for childcare services (EC Childcare Network, 1990; Rubery et al., 1996). This situation is in contrast with the United States, where individual tax allowances are the main form of childcare subsidy and where parents rely on private nurseries and nannies. The reimbursements are typically small (estimated at less than 20 per cent of childcare costs in the mid-1980s), and not all women earn enough to receive them (Dex and Shaw, 1986). While tax relief may stimulate some market provision of childcare, there are certain limitations to the effectiveness of this approach. First, the market may not deliver quality care at an affordable price for those on low income, so a reliance upon the tax system may only facilitate employment continuity for women with high earnings. Second, in some countries the system and philosophy of the tax system may be incompatible with the introduction of this form of allowance. For example, the UK tax system has been simplified to minimize the number of deductible expenses over the past two decades, so that income tax is deducted at source for most employees and few complete an additional tax return. So, if only for administrative reasons, it would be more costly to introduce this allowance, in contrast to the situation in other countries where there is already a comprehensive system of tax allowances in place. Finally, if childcare provision is to meet educational goals as well as facilitate maternal employment, then subsidizing places and establishing quality standards may be more effective than coordinating the tax administration with the ministry that provides or monitors service delivery.

In the next section we review a selection of studies that represent attempts to evaluate the impact of different elements of these policy regimes on the labour market outcomes for women, as well as those that have provided some assessment of the potential costs and benefits to the state and to employers.

3   THE IMPACT OF DIFFERENT MATERNAL EMPLOYMENT POLICY REGIMES ON WOMEN'S LABOUR SUPPLY

Economists focus on the financial returns to employment when seeking to explain women's labour supply decisions. Econometric analyses typically seek to take into account a range of price variables: past 'human capital' investments in education, training and employment experience; current earnings potential; taxes and work-related costs, such as childcare; and alternative sources of income, such as state transfers or spouse earnings (for a review see Killingsworth, 1983). However, suitable information on factors such as childcare costs is rarely available, particularly for microlevel analyses. Furthermore, this approach rarely tests the influence of nonprice variables, for example, the degree of nonfinancial work commitment or different attitudes as to whether mothers should remain at home with young children, simply treating these variables as static and exogenous 'tastes'. The distribution of norms and preferences within the population is partially captured when qualifications or occupations are included in the model, because there is some correlation between aspirations and employment opportunities (Dex, 1988). However, a direct measurement of these characteristics is obviously preferable, particularly when one is seeking to generalize across countries, for national differences in attitudes to maternal employment are associated with different family policy arrangements (Alwin, Braun and Scott, 1992).

The 'institutional approach' emphasizes the influence of state policies on women's labour supply decisions, and researchers adopting this framework have used cross-national analyses to link differences in maternal employment patterns to the influence of childcare and other family policies in conjunction with the effect of demand-side differences. Partly due to data limitations many of these analyses have relied upon aggregate comparisons of broad employment indicators (e.g. Dale and Glover, 1990; OECD, 1994a; Rubery, 1988; Rubery et al., 1995), but some have sought to disentangle the effect of policies from other national variations by modelling labour supply functions using comparable national sources of microlevel household data (Dex and Shaw,

1986; Dex et al., 1993). A related approach has estimated the impact of national differences on the cost of motherhood, using typical female life-time employment profiles (Joshi and Davies, 1992).

A third approach is to monitor latent and actual demand and take-up of different policies, yet the available information on these aspects is generally incomplete (EU Childcare Network, 1994; Humblet, 1994) or difficult to compare cross-nationally because of different definitions, for example, in the area of childcare provision (EC Childcare Network, 1990).

3.1   National Maternal Employment Regimes and Policy Coordination

Dex et al. (1993) used the contrasting examples of France, where mothers have a high and continuous pattern of employment, and the United Kingdom, where a lower and more interrupted pattern is found, to explore whether the policy environment has an influence on maternal labour supply. Using comparable data sets, they conducted a regression analysis to isolate the impact of motherhood on participation from other national differences that might be expected to affect participation rates, such as education levels and wage differentials. Having a child under the age of three had the strongest negative effect on participation in both countries, while potential earnings had the strongest positive impact. However, these results coincided with two important differences: the negative effect of the young child was twice as strong in the United Kingdom, and the positive effect of individual earnings on participation rates was much stronger in France. Indeed, a French woman with a young child was twice as likely to participate when she had above-average earnings, whereas in the United Kingdom high potential wages did not counter the strong constraint exerted by the presence of a young child.

One interpretation is that women in the United Kingdom simply have a stronger preference for looking after their children. However, the authors refer to a previous multivariate analysis using the UK data (Dex, 1988) that showed the effect of attitudes was small compared with the constraint of arranging childcare. They therefore point to policy differences between the countries and conclude that in France the constraint exerted by a young child on women's labour supply has been 'dampened' by the system of subsidized childcare and long school days. They also suggest that the larger wage dispersion among French women, combined with differences in the tax system, means that there is a greater financial incentive for women with high earnings to participate in France.

This study demonstrates that the national policy environment has an impact on women's labour market participation. The benefits of such a policy are often calculated by reference to the cost of policies versus the gains in earnings for the women, with these gains taken as indicators of the productivity benefits of continuing participation. The differences in earnings dispersion between France and the United Kingdom, however, highlight an important methodological consideration for evaluation studies; namely, earnings depend not only on productivity levels but also on the institutional system of pay determination. Thus, if pay in female-dominated jobs—for example, nursing in the public sector—is kept at a low level, then a reliance on narrow price measures may constitute an underestimation of the productivity gains. Indeed, the total productivity gains in this case may be greater than the immediate private gains, if increased employment continuity were to reduce recruitment and training costs and to improve patient care.

One study that directly tested the impact of policy on women's employment continuity was a British survey of maternity rights conducted prior to the recent extension of these rights (McRae, 1991). Women who qualified for maternity leave were more likely to be in employment nine months after the birth than other mothers who had worked when they were pregnant, and they were also more likely to have returned to full-time employment with their previous employer. This positive influence of the maternity entitlement persisted when tested using logistic regression, but other variables were revealed to be more significant. Not surprisingly, women with high wages and qualifications were more likely to return, but the most significant effect was receipt of contractually enhanced maternity pay. This enhanced employment condition seemed to improve the effectiveness of the maternity leave arrangements, but an important caveat is that the receipt of such payments is frequently dependent upon returning to work for a period of three months (McRae, 1991, p. 137). It is thus possible that some of these women may have quit shortly after the survey was conducted, perhaps having returned with the intention of leaving after securing the benefits, or having found the stress of full-time work too great.

McRae's study (1991) demonstrates the importance of leave entitlements for promoting employment continuity in the initial period of family formation, but it also indicates the need for data that tracks movement over a longer period of time. Indeed, while education and earnings were important, a more significant relationship was that women who were taking maternity leave for their second child were more likely to return to employment than first-time mothers. A cross-national study using data covering a long time period in women's work histories also revealed that women who work continuously during the preschool years of their first child are more likely to go on to have continuous employment careers (Kempeneers and Lelievre, 1991, Tables 39–40). This trend is suggestive of a filter process over the period of family formation, whereby women who remain in employment after the birth of their first child have managed to make arrangements to reconcile employment with caring which equip them for combining employment with the birth of the second child. A common means of achieving such reconciliation in the United Kingdom and other northern European countries with only limited subsidies for childcare is likely to be through part-time work. In these national contexts the right to return to part-time work in the previous job might increase the retention rate for employers, indicated by McRae's (1991) finding that most of those mothers who returned but switched employers had done so to get part-time work. This supposition returns us to the childcare constraint highlighted by Dex et al.'s (1993) Anglo-French comparison and suggests that the effectiveness of one policy may be undermined by the lack of coordination with other institutional arrangements.

3.2   Take-up of Existing Policies, Latent Demand for Different Policies and Policy Coordination

Information on what policies women want, and how they will use them, is important for evaluating the effectiveness of intervention. Asking women about their preferred employment patterns and child-rearing arrangements provides some indication of the extent to which their existing labour supply is constrained, for example, by the lack of affordable childcare services. At the same time, an overreliance on attitudinal data will underestimate the potential use of services because preferences are shaped by the perceived opportunities and constraints. Similarly, information on eligibility and take-up gives some insight into whether the policy is reaching the target group, and as to the kind of features that contribute to the success or failure of a policy instrument, but it does not permit issues of additionality or deadweight to be assessed. However, the distinction between a policy effect and a deadweight effect is difficult to maintain when the policy intervention is influencing attitudes as well as behaviour.

Most women use their entitlement to paid maternity leave. This is because the leave protects the health of the mother and child while providing a high degree of employment security, and in most countries the high earnings replacement rate means that the immediate loss of income is minimal (EU Childcare Network, 1994). Nevertheless, some women may be forced to quit their employment before they are entitled to take leave if they do not have the right to move to alternative work when their current job endangers their health, for example, in Spain (Molto, 1994, p. 67). At the end of maternity leave maternal employment patterns diverge, both between countries and between different groups of women within countries, suggesting that there are coordination problems between the end of this entitlement and childcare or leave policies for the next stage of family formation.

The demand for childcare is monitored only in the minority of countries with comparatively well-established systems of childcare (e.g. France, Denmark, Belgium), and the lack of standardization in these national surveys, combined with the lack of information in most other countries, prevents cross-national comparisons (Humblet, 1994). Attitudinal data for Britain shows the importance of this information for evaluation purposes (McRae, 1991). The lack of childcare was the main reason why women who had intended to work after the birth were not employed at the end of their maternity leave. This reason was also given by 20 per cent of the women who did not plan to return to employment after childbirth, while two-thirds said that they wanted to care for their baby full time. These desires are influenced by the limited childcare services in Britain, but the data suggest that longer periods of leave would be popular for some women, whereas for others childcare problems delay their return to employment. These data reveal how the absence of childcare or extended leave makes it difficult for women with young children to return to employment and undermines the effectiveness of maternity leave provision.

Current survey sources and administrative records are not designed to provide adequate information on the take-up of parental leave (OECD, 1995a, p. 183). However, several clear findings emerge from a recent review of the evidence for the Member States of the European Union (EU Childcare Network, 1994). First, leave entitlements that are unpaid are rarely used. For example, less than 2 per cent of entitled parents took parental leave in France in 1992, and a disproportionate share of those taking leave were women with three or more children who thus received some financial support (Gauvin et al., 1994, p. 74). In contrast, a high female take-up is found in Sweden and Denmark, where the wage replacement rate is significantly higher. Furthermore, the number of parents using the new extended parental leave provision in Denmark has risen steadily, particularly since the legal entitlement has been in place (MISEP, 1995).

Other employment conditions also depress take-up. Employees are deterred from taking leave if their employment conditions on the return to work are not adequately protected, or where leave periods are excluded for seniority or promotion purposes. Another deterrent is employer reluctance, which is likely to be strongest in small businesses, where leave-taking may be more disruptive. A general lack of information on both sides also reduces take-up (EU Childcare Network, 1994, pp. 22–3). Low take-up may also reflect the availability of functional equivalents or superior alternatives in some countries. For example, in France the option of unpaid parental leave competes directly with the alternative of part-time work, particularly in the public sector, where the opportunity to work between 50 per cent and 90 per cent of normal working time constitutes a significant amount of flexibility for mothers (Gauvin et al., 1994, p. 16).

Take-up is also affected by sex and occupational status. Women with high levels of qualifications or earnings take fewer, or shorter, periods of leave. The influence of educational investment and earnings potential on labour supply provides some support for human capital theories (e.g. Becker, 1981), but high earnings also make it more feasible to pay for childcare. Another important influence is that women in these occupations are also likely to have stronger career orientations and more job satisfaction (Dex, 1988; Hakim, 1991). Conversely, longer periods of leave tend to be taken in the public rather than the private sector. This difference generally reflects enhanced financial support for leave in the public sector, combined with a workplace culture that is more supportive to leave-takers than that found in the private sector (Bettio and Villa, 1994, p. 44; EU Childcare Network, 1994). Men make extensive use of paid paternity leave and holiday entitlements to spend time with their children, but very few take parental leave, except in Sweden (EU Childcare Network, 1994). Like women, men are more likely to take leave if they are employed in the public sector, and they are also more likely to do so if they are employed in female-dominated jobs. Take-up is also highest for men who are highly educated and have well-educated partners with high incomes and a strong commitment to employment. In other words, male take-up seems to be higher in households where women take shorter periods of leave.

The main features of the Swedish leave scheme that encourage a comparatively high male take-up are its flexibility and the high level of payment: fathers make more use of the leave scheme as the children get older and tend to take short or part-time periods of leave (EU Childcare Network, 1994). Despite the steady increase in male take-up, the majority of leave in Sweden is still taken by women, who accounted for 93 per cent of all parental leave days taken in 1990. Information campaigns directed at fathers and employers have been undertaken in Sweden, but no evaluation research has been done on the effectiveness of these complementary measures. There is also no information available on the number of parents who take advantage of the right to work reduced hours in Sweden, but there is evidence that the lack of obligation on employers to organize work to support this entitlement means that parents who do make use of it are frequently squeezing the same amount of work into shorter periods of time, while others are reluctant to work reduced hours in case this creates additional work for colleagues (Widerberg, 1991).

The public cost of childcare subsidies and leave arrangements obviously depends on the generosity of the scheme and the degree of take-up, which will be related to each other (EU Childcare Network, 1994). Furthermore, simple estimates of the direct costs are inadequate. The net cost is significantly reduced by the second-round effects on tax gains plus reduced claims for income-related benefits, as shown in a recent UK estimate, for example (Holtermann and Clarke, 1992). Another reduction in net cost stems from the extent to which cover is provided by previously unemployed people, thus contributing to work-sharing. This seems to be the dominant pattern in Denmark, where 65 per cent of mothers taking maternity and parental leave were replaced by a substitute (EU Childcare Network, 1994). Shorter periods of leave, such as to care for sick children, are generally seen to be more disruptive and costly to employers, but where these formal leave entitlements do not exist the employer may be bearing costs anyway through parents claiming personal illness or being distracted at work. In general, there is a need for a more comprehensive approach to cost and benefits that would include more qualitative gains, such as increased employee satisfaction and loyalty (Holtermann, 1995).

3.3   The Impact of Different Maternal Employment Patterns on Life-time Occupational Mobility and Earnings

Studies using work-history data demonstrate that labour market interruption makes women vulnerable to a loss of occupational status upon reentry to employment, particularly if they return to part-time work (Dex and Shaw, 1986; Dex et al., 1993; McRae, 1991). Discontinuous employment patterns may therefore reduce life-time earnings through the lower hourly pay and shorter hours of work that follow an interruption, as well as through the more visible loss resulting from reduced years in employment (Joshi and Davies, 1992). Professional qualifications offer some protection from loss of occupational status, partly because well-qualified women tend to take shorter breaks and to return to full-time work. Indeed, there is some evidence from the United Kingdom that downward mobility for this group of women has fallen over time (McRae, 1991). It is women in the middle of the occupational hierarchy who are most vulnerable to loss of occupational status, particularly clerical workers, often because they have firm-specific skills, while there is little scope for women with low occupational status to move further down the hierarchy.

Work-history studies that emphasize the loss of human capital as the reason for the loss of occupational status or for reduced earnings following an employment interruption underplay the influence of the organization of the labour market. Important demand-side influences that contribute to the price women pay for an employment interruption include the exclusion of discontinuous workers from internal labour markets and the concentration of part-time jobs in more casualized and low-paid labour markets (Rubery, 1994, p. 34). These demand-side factors vary between countries. For example, there is very little emphasis on formal training or functional flexibility in the United Kingdom catering sector, and instead the industry uses part-time workers to provide numerical flexibility. Young workers and women returners fill the majority of these posts, and many of the women returners had previously held higher-paid and higher-status jobs (Rubery, Fagan and Humphries, 1992). In contrast, interruptions in Germany seem to be less likely to be associated with downward mobility than in the United Kingdom (Kempeneers and Lelievre, 1991), and in part this difference is probably due to the German labour market being more tightly organized around the formal qualifications acquired through the dual training system than is the case in the United Kingdom (Maier, 1995). Similarly, in countries where there are more opportunities to work part time in higher-level jobs women who want these hours of work have more scope to find a job that is similar to their previous employment (Rubery and Fagan, 1993).

It follows, therefore, that the financial loss associated with becoming a mother varies between countries, both because of different labour supply patterns and because discontinuity incurs different costs in different employment systems. Joshi and Davies (1992) estimated the amount of forgone earnings for a mother of two children who followed typical life-time employment patterns in the United Kingdom, western Germany, Sweden and France. This estimation was based on country-specific life-time earnings data and therefore incorporated national wage differences. For example, the rate of pay for continuously employed women in France rose sharply over the life cycle, showing that the pay penalty for interrupted employment is higher here than in the United Kingdom (Dex et al., 1993). In comparison, the number of years spent in employment had less of an impact on life-time earnings progression in Sweden. This result is largely explained by the narrower wage dispersion in the Swedish economy (Blau, 1992).

The lengthy periods of interruption and subsequent part-time employment that characterize maternal life-time employment patterns in the United Kingdom and western Germany was the most costly pattern, amounting to an estimated 57 per cent of forgone life-time earnings in the United Kingdom and a slightly smaller loss in western Germany (49 per cent). A significantly smaller loss was associated with the shorter interruptions and periods of part-time employment typical for Sweden (16 per cent). Continuous, full-time employment combined with short periods of maternity leave produced a minimal earnings loss for French mothers (1 per cent). Most of the earnings loss is attributed to the arrival of the first child in the United Kingdom and Germany, whereas in the other two countries the cost is more equally distributed between births (Joshi and Davies, 1992, pp. 573–4). Another study based on different data indicates that the cost of motherhood in Denmark is similar to the cost in Sweden: two children were found to reduce life-time earnings by approximately 20 per cent due to a combination of part-time employment and maternity leave absences (Bonke, 1992, pp. 311–15).

These studies of women's life-time earnings and employment trajectories demonstrate that it is the ability to follow a full-time continuous employment career, rather than the opportunity to participate in the female-dominated part-time labour market, that mitigates the impact of motherhood on women's pay careers and on their income in retirement. The impact of leave on the cost of motherhood falls in between, not just because of periods away from the job but because leave may also result in lower wage rates over the life cycle. Some evidence for this impact has been found in company records of leave use by men and women in Sweden. The study in question revealed that the cost was greater for men but that for both sexes there was some earnings recovery over time from absences taken in earlier stages in the work history. The reason for the higher cost for men was either that there was more scope for earnings growth in the jobs in which men were concentrated or that those who took leave were labelled as uncommitted, which might also explain why women who were better paid and more educated took shorter periods of leave than other mothers (Sundstrom and Stafford, 1994). To some extent the impact of extensive leave arrangements on gender differences in life-time earnings has been mediated by the comparatively low Swedish earnings dispersion, and the impact is likely to be greater in countries with greater earnings dispersion and, indeed, in Sweden in future as the wage system is decentralized.

The findings from these studies suggest that the analysis of work-history data as a means of understanding the impact of motherhood on women's life-time earnings and employment could be refined in two ways. First, if cross-national differences in the organization of the employment system are explicitly addressed, then it becomes clear that the cost of interruptions cannot be simply interpreted in terms of human capital and skill depreciation. Second, it may be important to build an explicit male comparison into the analysis as well, for the price of motherhood increases when it is expressed relative to male life-time earnings (Rubery, 1994, pp. 34–7). In other words, women's social role as mothers acts to depress the earnings of all women, even those without children.

4   CONCLUSIONS

Women's labour market interruptions connected with the period of family formation are becoming fewer and shorter (Rubery et al., 1995). Nevertheless, many women still quit the labour market when their children are young, resulting in a substantial loss of earnings from reduced years of earning plus lower future earnings stemming from downward occupational mobility at the point of labour market reentry. This loss is compounded in labour markets where motherhood is associated with a transition to part-time employment, for these jobs are concentrated in low-paid, low-level occupations.

The inefficiencies associated with labour market interruptions for households, employers and the aggregate economy become evident once a dynamic perspective is adopted. A more continuous labour market participation over the period of family formation would lead to a more optimal utilization of women's actual and potential skills in the economy. For the household more continuous participation would mean that life-time income would increase, and the unanticipated costs of labour market interruptions would be reduced.

Evaluation studies indicate that national policy environments have an important influence on the degree of employment continuity for women with young children. Entitlements to extended leave, either on a full-time or part-time basis, and subsidized childcare make the reconciliation of parental and employment responsibilities easier to achieve. At the same time, these studies also indicate how the effectiveness of one policy may be undermined by a lack of coordination with complementary policies. For example, full-time leave entitlements may simply delay the timing of labour market departure unless other leave or childcare arrangements exist.

The coordination of the different leave and childcare elements of parental employment policies is a necessary, but not sufficient, step to increase the effectiveness of these market interventions. The impact of these policy packages is likely to increase through coordination with, or at least consideration of, the organization of school and shop opening hours, the income tax and benefit system and 'gendering' labour market policies designed to promote work-sharing. Another important consideration is the organizational demands attached to different jobs within any economy. It might be easier to organize some jobs on a part-time basis than others, although what is seen as feasible by employers is likely to change through experience. Nevertheless, it may still remain more efficient for some to find a full-time substitute for an extended period of leave in certain occupations or workplaces, at least in the short term, when employers are learning how to integrate new leave entitlements into current organizational practices.

The Swedish model of flexible parental leave entitlements, where leave can be taken on a full-time or part-time basis at any time in the period prior to the child entering school, provides an effective bridge over the time-intensive period of child-rearing, as well as providing a variety of means of reconciling the needs of workers with those of employers. But the diversity of household and employer needs are unlikely to be fully reconciled through a system of leave entitlements, however flexibly organized. In some circumstances subsidized childcare may be a more optimal arrangement, suggesting that this is a complement rather than a substitute component of a coordinated parental employment policy regime.

Indeed, the effectiveness of any leave system will be undermined if it merely institutionalizes extended periods of maternal leave, reinforcing the sexual division of labour and so feeding back into the education, training and labour supply decisions of subsequent generations. Male take-up of parental leave is generally low, although increasing in Sweden, and thus motherhood still has a greater impact on life-time earnings and occupational progression compared to fatherhood. Until recently, this effect has been tempered in Sweden because of the narrow wage dispersion, but the current restructuring of the wage-determination system means that the cost of taking leave may increase in the future unless leave-taking becomes more widespread and less gender specific. Low male take-up of leave will also undermine the effectiveness of this tool for promoting work-sharing. Thus, while the recently extended Danish leave system is proving popular, further work-sharing gains could be achieved through stimulation of male take-up of parental leave.

While the available evidence points to the positive impact of extended leave and subsidized childcare on facilitating maternal employment, further research is needed to identify the optimal balance between different leave arrangements and childcare subsidies in different national and sectoral labour market conditions. In particular, given the importance of coordinating family policies with wider institutional arrangements for intervention to be effective, it is unlikely that a policy that works in one national context can simply be transferred to produce an identical outcome elsewhere. Three research questions seem particularly pertinent. First, what is the impact on women's employment and career trajectories of either one long period of leave, several short periods of leave, part-time work for a period of time or access to subsidized childcare? Second, what circumstances encourage male take-up of parental leave or reduced hours of work? Third, what are the costs and benefits of different arrangements to employers, and in which countries or sectors is more progress being made in the development and use of parental employment policies?

The information currently available for monitoring and evaluating current arrangements is perhaps less well developed than that available for many other labour market policy interventions. Flow information over the early years of parenting is needed to track the impact of these policies, as is more accessible and standardized information on take-up of leave and other working time reductions. Furthermore, improved attitudinal data on the reasons for quitting work and the constraints to taking up employment would enhance the value of the EU Labour Force Survey. However, workplace surveys are also required to explore how policies are implemented by employers. Finally, there is an important role for qualitative case-study research at the workplace that combines studies of both employees and employers. Such research could be focussed on identifying the barriers to the effective implementation of parental employment policies and on identifying innovation through research with 'leading-edge' companies.

REFERENCES

Alwin, D. F., M. Braun and J. Scott (1992), 'The Separation of Work and the Family: Attitudes towards Women's Labour Force Participation in Germany, Great Britain and the United States', *European Sociological Review*, 8 (1), 13–37.

Becker, G. (1981), *A Treatise on the Family*, Cambridge, MA: Harvard University Press.

Berk, R. A. and S. Fenstermaker-Berk (1983), 'Supply-side Sociology: The Challenge of the New Home Economics', *Annual Review of Sociology*, 9, 375–95.

Bettio, F. and P. Villa (1993), 'Strutture familiari e mercati del lavoro nei paesi sviluppati. L'emergere di un percorso mediterraneo per l'integrazione delle donne nel Mercato del lavoro', *Economica e Lavoro*, 2, 3–30.

Bettio, F. and P. Villa (1994), *Changing Patterns of Work and Working-time for Men and Women*, working paper for the European Commission, available from the Network of Experts on the Situation of Women in the Labour Market: Manchester School of Management, UK: UMIST.

Blau, F. (1992, September), 'Gender and Economic Outcomes: The Role of the Wage Structure', keynote speech, Fourth European Association of Labour Economists, University of Warwick.

Boje, T. (1994), *Changing Patterns of Work and Working-time for Men and Women: Towards the Integration or the Segmentation of the Labour Market*, working paper for the European Commission, available from the Network of Experts on the Situation of Women in the Labour Market: Manchester School of Management, UK: UMIST.

Bonke, J. (1992), 'Lifetime Income of Men and Women—The Case of Denmark', *Journal of Consumer Studies and Home Economics*, 16, 303–16.

Bosch, G., P. Dawkins and F. Michon (1993), *Times are Changing: Working Time in 14 Industrialised Countries*, Geneva: International Labour Organization.

Bradshaw, J., J. Ditch, H. Holmes and P. Whiteford (1993), *Support for Children: A Comparison of Arrangements in 15 Countries*, London: HMSO.

Brannen, J. and P. Moss (1991), *Managing Mothers: Dual Earner Households after Maternity Leave*, London: Unwin Hyman.

Bruegel, I. and D. Perrons (1995), 'Where Do the Costs of Unequal Treatment for Women Fall? An Analysis of the Incidence of the Costs of Unequal Pay and Sex Discrimination in the UK', in J. Humphries and J. Rubery (eds), *The Economics of Equal Opportunities*, Manchester: Equal Opportunities Commission, pp. 155–74.

CERC (1994), *Social Welfare and Economic Activity of Women in Europe*, V/2184/94–EN, Brussels: European Commission.

Commission of the European Communities (1991), *Equal Opportunities for Women and Men—Social Europe*, 3, Office for Official Publications of the European Communities, Luxembourg.

Connell, R. W. (1987), *Gender and Power*, Oxford: Polity.

Dale, A. and J. Glover (1990), *An Analysis of Women's Employment Patterns in the UK, France and the USA: The Value of Survey Based Comparisons*, research paper no. 75, London: Employment Department Group.

Delacourt, M.-L. and J. A. Zighera (1988), *Women's Work and Family Composition: A Comparison of the Countries of the European Economic Community*, DG V V/1795/88–EN, Brussels: Commission of the European Communities.

Dex, S. (1988), *Women's Attitudes towards Work*, London: Macmillan Press.

Dex, S. and L. Shaw (1986), *British and American Women at Work: Do Equal Opportunities Policies Matter?*, London: Macmillan.

Dex, S., P. Walters and D. Alden (1993), *French and British Mothers at Work*, London: Macmillan.

EC Childcare Network (1990), *Childcare in the European Communities 1985–90. Women of Europe* (suppl. 31), Brussels: Commission of the European Communities (DG X).

EU Childcare Network (1994), *Leave Arrangements for Workers with Children: A Review of Leave Arrangements in the Member States of the European Community and Austria, Finland, Norway and Sweden*, report prepared for the Equal Opportunities Unit, DG V, Brussels: European Commission.

European Commission (1994a), *Employment in Europe*, 381, Office for Official Publications of the European Communities, Luxembourg.

European Commission (1994b), *Growth, Competitiveness, Employment—the Challenges and Ways Forward into the 20th Century*, White Paper, Office for Official Publications of the European Communities, Luxembourg.

Gauvin, A., C. Granie and R. Silvera (1994), *The Evolution of Employment Forms and Working Time among Men and Women: Towards the Integration or the Segmentation of the Labour Market*, working paper for the European Commission, available from the Network of Experts on the Situation of Women in the Labour Market, Manchester School of Management, UK: UMIST.

Hakim, C. (1991), 'Grateful Slaves and Self-made Women: Fact and Fantasy in Women's Work Orientations', *European Sociological Review*, 7 (2), 101–21.

Hewitt, P. (1993), *About Time: The Revolution in Work and Family Life*, London: Institute for Public Policy Research/River Oram Press.

Holtermann, S. (1995), 'The Costs and Benefits to British Employers of Measures to Promote Equality of Opportunity', in J. Humphries and J. Rubery (eds), *The Economics of Equal Opportunities*, Manchester: Equal Opportunities Commission, pp.137–53.

Holtermann, S. and K. Clarke (1992), *Parents, Employment Rights and Childcare*, research discussion series no. 4, Manchester: Equal Opportunities Commission.

Humblet, P. (1994), *Monitoring Childcare Services for Young Children*, V/460/94–EN, Brussels: European Commission.

Humphries, J. (1995), 'Economics, Gender and Equal Opportunities', in J. Humphries and J. Rubery (eds), *The Economics of Equal Opportunities*, Manchester: Equal Opportunities Commission, pp. 55–86.

Humphries, J. and J. Rubery (1984), 'The Reconstitution of the Supply Side of the Labour Market: The Relative Autonomy of Social Reproduction', *Cambridge Journal of Economics*, 8 (4), 331–46.

Humphries, J. and J. Rubery (eds) (1995), *The Economics of Equal Opportunities*, Manchester: Equal Opportunities Commission.

IRS (1991), 'Working Time in Europe', *European Industrial Relations Review*, London: Industrial Relations Services.

Jensen, J. (1994, May), 'Family Policy and Women's Citizenship in Mitterrand's France', paper presented to the Crossing Borders conference, Centre for Women's Studies, Stockholm University.

Joshi, H. and H. Davies (1992), 'Day Care in Europe and Mothers' Forgone Earnings', *International Labour Review*, 132 (6), 561–79.

Joshi, H. and H. Davies (1995), 'Social and Family Security in the Redress of Une-quaOpportunities', in J. Humphries and J. Rubery (eds), *The Economics of Equal Opportunities*, Manchester: Equal Opportunities Commission, pp. 313–44.

Kempeneers, M. and E. Lelievre (1991), *Employment and Family within the Twelve. Eurobarometer 34*, V/383/92–EN, Brussels: Commission of the European Communities.

Killingsworth, M. (1983), *Labour Supply*, Cambridge: Cambridge University Press.

Leira, A. (1994), 'Combining Work and Family: Working Mothers in Scandinavia and the European Community', in P. Brown and R. Crompton (eds), *A New Europe? Economic Restructuring and Social Exclusion*, London: University College London, pp. 86–107.

Lewis, J. (1992), 'Gender and the Development of Welfare Regimes', *Journal of European Social Policy*, 2 (3), 159–73.

Maier, F. (1995), 'Skill Formation and Equal Opportunity—A Comparative Perspective', in J. Humphries and J. Rubery (eds), *The Economics of Equal Opportunities*, Manchester: Equal Opportunities Commission, pp. 203–18.

Maier, F., S. Quack and Z. Rapp (1994), *Changing Patterns of Work and Working-time for Men and Women: Towards the Integration or the Segmentation of the Labour Market*, working paper for the European Commission, available from the Network of Experts on the Situation of Women in the Labour Market: Manchester School of Management, UK: UMIST.

Main, B. (1993), 'Where "Equal" Equals Not Equal: Women in the Labour Market', *Sex Equality: Law and Economics. Hume Papers on Public Policy*, 1 (1), Edinburgh University Press.

McRae, S. (1991), *Maternity Rights in Britain*, London: Policy Studies Institute.

Meulders, D., R. Plasman and V. Vander Stricht (1993), *The Position of Women on the Labour Market in the European Community*, Aldershot: Dartmouth Publishing.

MISEP (1995), *Policies*, 49, 15–16.

Molto, M. L. (1994), *Changing Patterns of Work and Working Time: Towards the Integration or Segmentation of the Labour Market in Spain*, working paper for the European Commission, available from the Network of Experts on the Situation of Women in the Labour Market, Manchester School of Management, UK: UMIST.

OECD (1994a), *Women and Structural Change: New Perspectives*, Paris: OECD.

OECD (1994b), *The OECD Jobs Study: Taxation, Employment and Unemployment*, Paris: OECD.

OECD (1995a, July), *Employment Outlook*, Paris: OECD.

OECD (1995b), *Education at a Glance*, Paris: OECD.

Owen, S. (1987), 'Household Production and Economic Efficiency: Arguments for and against Domestic Specialisation', *Work, Employment and Society*, 1 (2), 157–78.

Plantenga, J. and S. van Velzen (1994), *Changing Patterns of Work and Working Time: Towards the Integration or Segmentation of the Labour Market in the NL*, working paper for the European Commission, available from the Network of Experts on the Situation of Women in the Labour Market, Manchester School of Management, UK: UMIST.

Rose, M. (1988), 'Attachment to Work and Social Values', in D. Gallic (ed.), *Employment in Britain*, Oxford: Basil Blackwell, pp. 128–56.

Rubery, J. (ed.) (1988), *Women and Recession*, London: Routledge & Kegan Paul.

Rubery, J. (1994), *Changing Patterns of Work and Working Time: Towards the Integration or Segmentation of the Labour Market in the UK*, working paper for the European Commission, available from the Network of Experts on the Situation of Women in the Labour Market, Manchester School of Management, UK: UMIST.

Rubery, J. and C. Fagan (1993), *Occupational Segregation in the European Community. Social Europe* (suppl. 3), Luxembourg: Office for Official Publications of the European Communities.

Rubery, J. and C. Fagan (1994), 'Does Feminization Mean a Flexible Labour Force?', in R. Hyman and A. Ferner (eds), *New Frontiers in European Industrial Relations*, Oxford: Blackwell, pp. 140–66.

Rubery, J., C. Fagan and J. Humphries (1992), *Occupational Segregation in the UK*, working paper for the Commission of the European Communities, available from the Network of Experts on the Situation of Women in the Labour Market, Manchester School of Management, UK: UMIST.

Rubery, J., C. Fagan and M. Smith (1995), *Changing Patterns of Work and Working-time in the European Union and the Impact on Gender Divisions*, report for the Equal Opportunities Unit, DG V, Brussels: European Commission.

Rubery, J., M. Smith, C. Fagan and D. Grimshaw (1996), *Women and the European Employment Rate*, report for the Equal Opportunities Unit, DG V, Brussels: European Commission.

Schettkat, R. (1989), 'The Impact of Taxes on Female Labour Supply', *International Review of Applied Economics*, 3 (1), 1–24.

Schmid, G. (1994), 'Equality and Efficiency in the Labor Market: Toward a Socio-economic Theory of Cooperation', in G. Schmid (ed.), *Labour Market Institutions in Europe*, New York: Sharpe, pp. 243–79.

Sundstrom, M. and F. Stafford (1994), *Time Out for Childcare and Career Wages of Men and Women*, Stockholm Research Reports in Demography, no. 85, University of Stockholm.

UN (1994), *Regional Platform for Action—Women in a Changing World—Call for Action from an ECE Perspective*, Preambular Declaration, UN E/ECE/RW/HLM/L.3/Rev.2. United Nations: Economic and Social Council, Economic Commission for Europe.

Vermeulen, H., S. Dex, T. Callan, B. Dankmeyer, S. Gustafsson, M. Lausten, N. Smith and J. D. Vlasblom (1995), *Tax Systems and Married Women's Labour Force Participation: A Seven Country Comparison*, working paper of the EC Human Capital and Mobility Female Labour Force Network, no. 95–8, ESRC Research Centre on Micro-social Change, University of Essex, United Kingdom.

Widerberg, K. (1991), 'Reforms for Women—on Male Terms—the Example of the Swedish Legislation on Parental Leave', *International Journal of the Sociology of Law*, 19, 27–44.

12. Exit Options from the Labour Force[1]

Bernard Casey

Exit from the labour force can take one of two forms. The first is temporary, such as is associated with participation in further education and training, with child birth and child-rearing, or with extended vacations or sabbaticals. The second is permanent, either intentionally or effectively so, and is associated with retirement or a substantial deterioration in health or loss of working capacity. Labour market policies with respect to the first form of exit are treated in other chapters of this handbook, namely, by Fagan and Rubery (see chap. 11 in this volume), Tuijnman and Schömann (chap. 15) and Schmid (chap. 25). This chapter considers the second form of exit and concentrates on labour market policies related to a specific target, namely, to relieve the labour market (and thus to reduce unemployment) by supporting 'early retirement'.[2]

1 THE EXTENT OF 'EARLY RETIREMENT'

One of the more remarkable developments on the labour market of western industrialized countries in the past two decades has been the fall in the proportion of older people in paid employment. This fall has affected those who are above the 'normal' retirement age (of 65) as well as those below it, but policy concern has so far been directed mainly at the increasing share of people five or ten years younger than this ceiling who are no longer working.

With respect to older men, the extent of their early exit from the labour market is immediately apparent from time series on participation and employment. These are summarized in the following table, which gives

---

1 The author would like to thank Günther Schmid and Holger Schütz for undertaking the final editing of this chapter, and Günther Schmid for helpful comments during its production.

2 For a critical appraisal of the appropriateness of the designation 'early retirement', see Casey and Laczko, 1989.

examples of countries where a larger and smaller fall in the employment rate[3] of men aged 55–64 occurred between 1975 and 1990.

Table 12.1 Change of Employment Rates of Older Men from 1975 to 1990 in Percentage Points in Selected Countries

Countries Where a Large Fall Occurred	age 55–59	age 60–64
Finland	– 16.8	– 27.1
France	– 17.1	– 36.0
Netherlands	– 16.2	– 41.5
United Kingdom	– 18.1	– 23.6

Countries Where a Small Fall Occurred	age 55–59	age 60–64
Japan	+ 2.4	– 6.2
Sweden	– 3.9	– 9.4
United States	– 5.4	– 9.6

Source
OECD, 1995.

With respect to older women, a straightforward examination of employment rates can be deceptive. The statistics for most western countries show a constant, or even rising, share in work, but what they depict is the situation of a succession of cohorts, each of which—as a result of increasing rates of female labour force participation—could be expected to display a higher share of its members in employment than its predecessor. A tendency for one cohort to leave the labour market earlier than its predecessor could coexist with a statistic showing a constant, or even increasing, employment rate if the initial employment rate of the later cohort were higher than that of the earlier cohort. Quasi-cohort analysis, based on comparing the employment rate of one five-year age group with that of the five-year age group five years its junior five years previously,[4] confirms that, in many western countries, the rate at which

---

3 The employment rate is the proportion of people of a given age group who are working measured in relation to all people of that age group. It differs from the participation rate in that it excludes unemployed people from the numerator.

4 For example, the employment rate in 1985 of women aged 50–54 was compared with the employment rate in 1990 of women aged 55–59. In effect, what was being done was to follow the former group over time, so that after five years it is described by the latter group (OECD 1995, pp. 95–9).

women left employment in the years before their 'normal' pension age was at least as high as the rate which men did, and that in a number of cases it was considerably higher (OECD, 1995, pp. 95–9).

The remainder of this chapter is divided into two broad sections. The first of these (section 2) is concerned with the various labour market and social policy provisions which have been used to facilitate early retirement. It looks at provisions that are the responsibility of the state and those that are the responsibility of firms. As well as describing labour market policy measures, it sketches a number of social policy measures which have had labour market consequences. The subsequent section (section 3) is concerned with the evaluation of some of the provisions which had very explicit unemployment reduction objectives. Referring to contemporary investigations, it looks at the impact of these schemes on unemployment rates and at their cost-effectiveness, before referring briefly to their possible wider consequences. A final section (section 4) provides a summary and draws some conclusions.

2   THE ROLE OF POLICY

Much of the trend towards early withdrawal from employment can be understood as a consequence of 'policy' if 'consequence' is interpreted to include unintended consequence, and if 'policy' is interpreted as the policy of the state as well as of the firm.[5]

As western industrialized countries grew richer over the postwar period, the generosity and coverage of state pension systems also increased. Similar developments occurred with respect to firm-based pension systems. In addition, individuals were able to build up their own savings, in the form of property, shares and bonds, and bank deposits. Some of the increase in wealth and income was used to finance earlier retirement rather than to improve living standards in retirement. Some was used to make more generous provision for those whose state of health rendered them unable to work, and some was used to permit early retirement by people who had experienced particularly arduous working lives (e.g. France), or who had spent a long period in employment and as a contributor to the pension system (e.g. Germany).

In the United States, an effort was made to make retirement more flexible by permitting benefits to be drawn early or late, subject to a reduction or appreciation in their value. While there is no evidence that the intention was to stimulate a change in the average age at which people ceased working, the extent of the reduction or appreciation of the pension was such that those who retired

---

5 Given the nature of this handbook, the emphasis here will be on the former.

early did not pay the full price for having contributed for a shorter period and having the prospect of drawing benefits for a longer period and that, correspondingly, those who retired late were not fully rewarded. Actuarial asymmetry of this sort, no doubt, encouraged early retirement.

The subject of this chapter is not, in the first instance, provisions with unintended consequences but provisions specifically directed towards promoting early exit from employment and from the labour market. The wide-scale application of early retirement schemes of this sort can be traced back to the start of the 1970s (see OECD, 1995), although smaller-scale examples predate this, and it can be seen as a clear consequence of the deterioration in labour markets and employment chances that occurred thereafter. The logic which motivated the various provisions was simple, almost simplistic. They were seen as a way of reducing open unemployment by recategorizing job losers as retirees, and of redistributing unemployment between those who valued leisure and those who did not. Many of the provisions in question were the direct responsibility of the labour market authorities and so were, in the strictest sense, 'labour market policies', but some were the responsibility of the social affairs authorities. In some countries they were promoted by firms, either individually or in combination, rather than the state, and in some of these countries firm provisions were as important as, or even surpassed in importance, state provisions. State provisions will be surveyed first, thereafter company schemes. A brief excursus will then be made to a number of provisions which primarily had social policy objectives but which can be seen, retrospectively, to have served labour market purposes.

2.1   Public Provisions with Labour Market Objectives

Four forms of policy measures can be identified in western industrialized countries.

2.1.1   *Early Retirement Pensions for the Unemployed*

Provisions permitting older unemployed people to draw an early retirement pension or an equivalent benefit are widespread. In some countries they have formed part of the old-age and retirement pension system (e.g. in Germany and Sweden); in others they have been set up alongside it and have been separately financed (e.g. in France and Denmark, where they were made part of the unemployment benefit system). Such provisions had their origins in the assumption that, even in relatively favourable overall labour market conditions, the chances of these older unemployed regaining employment are low. Benefit is either the same as an old-age pension, with no reduction for early liquidation, or higher.

In France, there have been two schemes of considerable size: the Income Guarantee in Case of Redundancy (which operated from 1972 to 1982), available to those aged 60–64, and the scheme run by the National Employment Fund (operating subsequently, but on a smaller scale in the 1970s, too), available to those aged 55–59. The number being supported by the first of these schemes reached a peak in 1983 (having entered in 1982), at the equivalent of nearly one in twelve of the relevant population; the number covered by the second peaked in 1988, at the equivalent of one in sixteen of the relevant population.

In Sweden, between 1974 and 1991, when the provision was abolished, receipt of an early old-age pension required that the claimant had received unemployment insurance benefits for 90 weeks. However, informal agreements about early retirement were often reached between the firm, the laid-off worker and the officers at the employment offices at the time of the redundancy. Subtracting 90 weeks from age 60 makes 58¼ the effective point at which early retirement can be initiated. Also, from 1972 to 1991, it was possible for those aged 62 and over who had exhausted their 450 days of unemployment benefits to be classified as fully disabled and to transfer directly to the receipt of an early old-age pension.

In addition to these countries, where changes have occurred since the 1970s, there has been a long-standing provision under pension law in Germany whereby people who have been out of work for at least 12 months can, subject to meeting contribution-related requirements, draw an unreduced age pension at 60. The 1989 German pension reform will abolish this provision in stages from 2001. The German early retirement pension for the long-term unemployed will be discussed further in the subsection on unemployment benefits.

2.1.2 Special Voluntary Early Retirement Schemes

In Denmark and in France, it has been possible for at least some workers to obtain benefits equal to, or in the latter case superior to, a full pension without having to have first been made unemployed. The declared objective of the Danish and the French schemes was to free up positions which might then be filled by unemployed people. The Danish Early Retirement Pay Scheme, which was introduced in 1979, has been taken up on a very wide scale. By the end of the 1980s, more than one in four of the population aged 60–64 was in receipt of an early pension under its terms. The French Guaranteed Income in Case of Retirement Scheme, which operated between 1977 and 1982, also allowed retirement at 60. In 1983 one in twelve of the population aged 60–64 was in receipt of a pension under its terms.

A number of countries introduced schemes for voluntary early retirement which included a specific obligation on the employer to replace the retiree with an unemployed person. The first schemes of this nature were introduced in Belgium (1976) and the United Kingdom (1977). Others were set up in France (1982) and Germany (1984).

The Solidarity Contracts in France (which were open for applications in 1982 and 1983) involved a significant number of older workers. For instance, in 1984 over one in twenty of the population aged 55–59 was in early retirement under the terms of the scheme. Unlike their counterparts under the Solidarity Contracts, who came from all occupations, those who took early retirement under the British Job Release Scheme were mainly low-paid workers in semiskilled or unskilled occupations. This partly reflected the flat-rate allowance paid under the British scheme, which, unlike the earnings-related allowance available in France, made early retirement under its provisions unattractive to those on average or above-average earnings.

In a number of countries, 'partial retirement' schemes have been designed to open up part-time jobs for the unemployed. A worker reducing weekly hours enables the employer to hire an unemployed person for the released hours. Relatively few people have taken up these schemes, however. In the case of the French scheme, there was little or no financial incentive to choose partial retirement rather than full early retirement under the Solidarity Contracts, and in the case of the British scheme, employees in firm-based pension schemes where benefits are calculated as a fraction of final salary would cut their pension entitlement if they were to participate and reduce their hours (see Laczko, 1988).

2.1.3 Disability Benefits Adapted to Labour Market Purposes

In a number of countries, mainly in the late 1960s and the 1970s, the likelihood that the applicant would be successful in obtaining a job was brought into consideration in the award of disability benefits. As a result, many awards were given for total disability in instances of partial incapacity where no suitable work was available. Disability pension schemes came to serve, in part at least, as compensation schemes for older workers who had difficulties in finding a job.

In Germany, as a result of a court ruling in 1969, people who were partially disabled (incapable of working more than on a part-time basis) were entitled to a full disability pension if no part-time job could be found on the local labour market. Prior to the ruling eligibility had been determined in 'abstract' terms—in terms of whether or not the person could work on a part-time basis. Henceforth, it was determined in 'concrete' terms—in terms of whether there was a part-time job available.

Until 1987 the Dutch disability benefit scheme recognized a loss of working capacity as low as 15 per cent and was relatively generous with regard to level and duration of benefits. In 1973 the bipartite council of the Joint Medical Service overseeing the system came to an agreement whereby partially disabled people unable to find suitable part-time work were eligible for a full disability pension. However, in 1987 the full disability pension was reduced from 80 to 70 per cent of prior income, and labour market conditions no longer influenced the evaluation of the degree of disability. Moreover, partial disability and partial unemployment were no longer to be treated as complete disability.

Analysis of the explanatory factors behind the growth of the rate of new disability awards in the Netherlands over the 1968–79 period (Van den Bosch and Petersen, 1983) has confirmed indications that disability pensions were indeed used as a form of unemployment compensation. The rate of entry into disability pension was highest in those branches of industry where the employment contraction has been greatest (Casey and Bruche, 1983). Many of the beneficiaries of disability benefits came from the older industrial sectors (textiles, clothing and construction), hard hit in the 1970s by industrial decline and downturns in demand.

In Sweden changes to disability benefits in 1970 and 1972 occurred as a response to increasing unemployment among older workers. In 1970, the Swedish social insurance authorities revised the relevant disability compensation legislation, requiring adjudicators making decisions about older workers 'to concern themselves mainly with the applicant's ability and possibility of obtaining a continued income through such work as has previously been done or through other suitable and available work' (see Casey and Bruche, 1983). Informal evidence is that disability requirements are enforced less strictly than usual for workers threatened by unemployment (Björklund and Holmlund, 1991). Equally, it has been quite common for employers, when reducing their work force, to top up the early, disability pensions during the period until normal retirement age is reached.

2.1.4 Continuous Payment of Unemployment Benefit and Relaxation of Registration Requirements

The unemployment compensation systems of a number of countries permit benefit to be paid to older unemployed people for longer than the standard period of entitlement and sometimes up to the normal pension age. Such provisions mean that the beneficiaries receive, in effect, an early pension. Labour force surveys may classify them as 'out of the labour force' rather than 'unemployed', since many are no longer actively seeking work.

In the Netherlands, those aged 57½ or older at the time they become unemployed retained the right to unemployment benefit until age 65. This provision gave some incentive to firms to dismiss workers who had reached the age of

57½, on the basis that the claimant is then on a relatively generous benefit until age 65. It also meant that, although recipients aged 57½ and older were counted as unemployed, they were effectively 'early retired'. Similarly, in Germany the fact that a pension is available to the long-term unemployed at 60 leads to redundancy agreements targeting workers aged 59 and over, as they can claim unemployment compensation for a year and then pass into receipt of an old-age pension. In the first half of the 1980s the duration of entitlement to unemployment benefit for older people was extended, and those aged 54 and over were eligible to receive compensation for as long as 32 months. The result was that redundancy practices popularly known as '59er actions' often became '57er actions'.

In addition to extending the duration of unemployment benefit, a number of countries have relaxed the requirement that the older unemployed register at employment offices. This means that the older unemployed are tantamount to being retired. In Great Britain, since 1981 long-term unemployed men aged 60 and over have no longer been required to register as job seekers in order to receive means-tested benefits. From 1983 the same dispensation was given to unemployed men aged 60 who had been registering only to build up their pension contributions record. These two steps have meant that older unemployed men are treated effectively as being old-age pensioners, and they are entitled to the same guaranteed minimum income. Between 1982 and 1985 registered unemployment among 60–64 year old men fell by two-thirds, and the number taken off the register was equivalent to one in eight of the male population in the relevant age range.

2.2   Company Schemes

With respect to provisions which are the responsibility of individual firms or groupings of firms, three types can be identified. Some are common to a number of countries, some are peculiar to a particular country.

2.2.1   Redundancy Arrangements

Firms faced with the need to reduce their work forces will often develop their own initiatives to smooth the process of reduction, and a frequent component of such initiatives is the offer of early retirement (see Casey, 1992a). As has been seen, in some countries—for example, Sweden or Germany—such provisions can be fashioned such that they complement those of the state social security system, whereas in others they can be fashioned to stand in their own right. Thus, in Great Britain older workers who accept redundancy are often awarded an enhancement to their occupational (or firm-based) pension entitlement, either in the form of a full or partial abatement of the reduction in benefits that follows early retirement, or in the form of the award of additional years of service. The costs of these enhancements are sometimes financed by the firm through a special, one-off payment to the pension fund or, as was often the case in the 1980s, out of pension fund surpluses. In 1986 about two-thirds of company pension schemes permitted an early pension to be paid with no, or only a partial, reduction when retirement was at the employer's request (Casey, 1992b). In addition, British law requires the payment of a lump sum to redundant workers, the level of which is determined by age and length of service, and larger firms often voluntarily increase the value of this lump sum, creating a benefits package for redundant older workers composed of an early pension and a one-off payment.

The 'Early Retirement Incentive Plans' (ERIPs) developed by large American firms seeking to reduce their labour forces either ease the conditions for eligibility for a company pension, or else pay supplements to the (often unreduced) pension for which the employee taking redundancy is eligible—for example, enhancing the benefit by the amount of the state pension which the employee will later be able to draw. Usually, such incentives are offered for a limited period of time only—hence the name 'window plan'.

In those countries where the social security system itself supplies a basic early retirement benefit, the role of the firm is limited to supplementing that provision. Thus, German employers making older workers redundant are often bound by a negotiated 'social plan' requiring that they top up unemployment compensation to the level of last net earnings for the period until those made redundant are eligible for an early public pension on the grounds of unemployment. Similar, collectively agreed top-ups exist in the Netherlands, with respect to both workers formally declared redundant and those who become eligible for invalidity benefits. The Swedish 'employment security funds' (for blue- and white-collar workers), which are financed by the collectivity of employers, make lump-sum, and sometimes continuing payments to older workers who lose their job through redundancy.

2.2.2 Measures to Encourage 'Timely' Retirement

A considerable number of American commentators have pointed to the actuarial unfairness of company pension schemes in that country (Ippolito, 1990). Company schemes are seen as encouraging early retirement even where their benefits are not supplemented or modified to deal with exceptional circumstances. Since employers pay the costs of these schemes, they can be presumed to be benefiting from them. Two ways in which they might do so are conventionally identified. First, the offer of the opportunity to take early retirement helps to enforce 'implicit' employment contracts whereby, in an effort to encourage loyalty to the firm, workers are paid less than their marginal product in the initial years of their career and more than it in the subsequent years. Incentives to 'early retirement' ensure that workers do not prolong this period of being paid in excess of marginal product beyond that necessary to ensure an equality of output and remuneration over the total stay with the firm. Second, the offer of an early retirement opportunity helps ensure that, despite the age discrimination legislation preventing employers operating a mandatory retirement age, employees retire at a time that the firm deems optimal.[6]

2.2.3 Voluntary Early Retirement Schemes

In response to high levels of youth unemployment, voluntary early retirement schemes, regulated by collective agreements at the level of the industrial sector and firm, were introduced in the Netherlands in the late 1970s. The coverage of these Early Exit Regulations (VUT schemes) grew rapidly; by the end of 1979 it had reached 80 per cent of private sector employment, and in the years which followed the minimum, retirement age was reduced from 63 or 64 to 60 or 61. The benefit paid to those taking early retirement bridged the period between the cessation of work and the date of entitlement to the state old-age pension, and since full social insurance contributions were maintained, future pension entitlements were unaffected. The gross replacement rate in terms of final pay varies between 70 per cent and 85 per cent. Although the government helped to promote some of the early experimental schemes and contributed towards their costs, VUT schemes were subsequently paid for in full as part of the collective bargaining process, so that effectively some of the costs were absorbed by forgone wage rises.

2.3   Relevant Social Policy Provisions

All of the provisions, state or firm, which have been discussed so far can be thought of as being labour market, or at least personnel management, policies. They were introduced in order to contribute to the better operation, or appearance, of the labour market, either within a country or within an individual firm. However, mention should also be made in a handbook such as this of a number of social policy provisions which have contributed to labour market policy objectives, even if this was not the intention of those who formulated them. Three examples are particularly relevant.

---

6 The reader should note that the implicit contracts referred to here are, by definition, unenforceable in law. A covert threat of demotion or transfer to less congenial work might be sufficient to influence a worker to accept retirement. Where representation structures are involved, workers might come under peer pressure to retire as the union might not wish the set of mutual understandings it has with management about how the work force is to be managed to be disrupted. Normally, it is hoped that the financial inducements offered by the pension scheme will suffice.

2.3.1 Early Retirement under the State Pension Scheme

As of 1973, Germany offered 'flexible retirement' at 63, subject to 35 years' contributions having been made. The reform was motivated largely by a wish to spread the benefits of postwar economic growth, but it also provided a convenient facility for enterprises trying to reduce their work force in the aftermath of the first oil price shock. Under the German pension reform of 1989, the 'flexible retirement' age is to be abolished, starting from 2001.

2.3.2 Partial Pensions

The Swedish partial pension scheme is well known as an instrument of social policy designed to adjust the transition from work to retirement and reduce the 'pension shock'. Under the scheme there exists no obligation on employers to accede to an employee's request to move to part-time working, or to recruit labour to fill the hours freed by the worker taking a partial pension. The costs of the scheme are met by a supplementary wage tax, payable by employers. Since they all have to pay, there exists an incentive for employers to utilize the scheme's provisions (Casey and Bruche, 1983). There are indications that some employers found the provision useful in helping to reduce their labour force (Laczko, 1988).

2.3.3 Invalidity Pensions without Special Labour Market Provisions

An investigation of the American invalidity pension system has suggested that the impact of changes in unemployment on the number of benefit recipients was asymmetrical: decreases in unemployment produced a fall in numbers only a third the size of the rise produced by similar sized increases in unemployment (Lando and Krate, 1976). A British study concluded that half the increase in inactivity as a consequence of disability among men aged 55–64 between the years 1970 and 1980 was due to increased unemployment (Piachaud, 1986), while a second, covering the years 1979 to 1984, suggested that the rise in unemployment over this period was the dominant explanation for the recorded growth in invalidity pensioning (Disney and Webb, 1991). In this respect it is notable that, in both the American and British schemes, eligibility is determined by reference to medical factors alone.

3   EVALUATION

The policies described in the previous section, whether state or firm, whether having intended or unintended consequences, were, in total, of some quantitative significance. No attempt has been made to assess how much they contributed to the fall in employment rates observed over the past two decades, although in some cases, for example France, that contribution appears large.[7] Nor, despite the considerable public expenditure which many of them have occasioned and which is illustrated in Table 12.2, have there been many

Table 12.2 *Expenditure on Provisions Promoting Early Retirement for*
         Labour Market Reasons in Selected Countries, Expressed as a
         Percentage of Gross Domestic Product

	1985	1986	1987	1988	1989	1990	1991	1992	1993	1994
Austria	0.13	0.14	0.17	0.16	0.13	0.11	0.09	0.08	0.10	0.13
Belgium	0.87	0.85	0.82	0.80	0.75	0.75	0.74	0.74	—	—
Denmark	—	1.26	1.24	1.24	1.26	1.22	1.25	1.29	1.40	1.41
Finland	0.47	0.57	0.62	0.59	0.55	0.51	0.52	0.49	0.48	0.46
France	1.21	1.05	0.90	0.77	0.65	0.56	0.47	0.40	0.38	—
Germany	0.01	0.02	0.02	0.02	0.02	0.02	0.30*	0.47*	0.59*	0.49*
Italy	0.29	0.30	0.33	0.33	0.34	0.29	0.27	0.26	—	—
Luxembourg	0.74	0.65	0.73	0.77	0.58	0.56	0.52	—	—	—
Spain	0.02	0.01	0.04	0.07	...	...	...	...	...	...
Sweden	0.12	0.11	0.11	0.10	0.09	0.08	0.08	0.06	0.05	0.02
Great Britain	0.05	0.03	0.02	0.01	...	...	...	...	...	...

Notes
* 1991 onwards includes the former GDR; — = data not available.

Source
OECD, *Employment Outlook,* various years.

---

7 Even in this case, a counterfactual would be necessary to determine the real impact. The decline in employment rates was no doubt facilitated by the early retirement schemes designed to reduce open unemployment and redistribute unemployment chances, but some or all of it might have occurred in their absence as a consequence of a combination of 'discouraged worker' effects, more extensive utilization of disability pension opportunities or the establishment of firm-specific early retirement opportunities.

attempts to evaluate how well the public policy goals proclaimed for them were being achieved.[8]

With respect to many of the provisions referred to, there exists little information other than that given in basic administrative data. This does no more than reveal how many people entered the scheme or were supported by it within the reference period (usually a year) and how much was spent on scheme management and on benefits. In some countries, information from administrative sources has been especially meagre—for example, that made available on the British Job Release Scheme—in others it has been much more detailed—for example that regularly released on the German Pre-Retirement Scheme (another scheme with a replacement requirement) which gives basic demographic and industrial characteristics of early retirees and of the people recruited to replace them. Where the policies are implemented by firms rather than by the state, any administrative data available remains at the level of the individual firm, and its aggregation is seldom, if ever, feasible.

The most extensive attempts to go further than monitoring and to assess the labour market impact of any of the early exit provisions discussed above relate, perhaps not surprisingly, to the special labour market schemes permitting early retirement, especially those where the early retirement is subject to a replacement condition.[9] Six schemes stand out in this respect, as Table 12.3 shows.

For each of these schemes, regularly produced administrative data, while a component of evaluation, was supplemented by data collected from employers and sometimes from people taking early retirement. In most cases the evaluation was a one-off process, although in the case of the Job Release Scheme, where administrative data was otherwise sparse, repeated, limited evaluation was undertaken over the measure's life.

Evaluation of the above schemes, since their object was to relieve the labour market, concentrated upon the extent to which they resulted in new jobs being opened up. A second line of inquiry, not pursued everywhere, was directed to the final costs of their achieving their end. These two issues will be addressed in turn. Thereafter, a number of wider issues will be raised.

---

8 Note that the table does not cover social policy provisions such as disability pensions (e.g. the Netherlands) or early pensions granted by the public pension system (e.g. Germany), nor does it cover provisions paid for by firms (e.g. the United States). Comparable earlier data do not exist, but expenditures in Great Britain were almost twice as high in 1983 as in 1985, and in France they had reached the equivalent of nearly 0.2 per cent of GDP by 1975.

9 Disability pension schemes usually generate a considerable quantity of administrative data but, as might be expected, these primarily refer to the conditions precipitating disability and the outcomes of rehabilitation measures.

*Table 12.3 Main Features of Selected Schemes Providing Early Retirement
for Labour Market Reasons*

Country and Programme	Maximum Duration of Early Retirement	Minimum Required Duration of Replacement	Financing
Belgium (1976–87)			
Legal Pre-Retirement	5 years, from 55 (w) or 60 (m)	6 months	state
Early Old-age Pension	5 years, from 60 (m)	12 months	state
Great Britain (1977–88)			
Job Release	5 years from 60 (disabled m) 3 years from 62 (other m) 1 year from 59 (w) until 65 (m), 60 (w)	unlimited contract of employment to be given	state
France (1982–83)			
Solidarity Contracts	5 years from 55 until 60 (pension age)	12 months	state
Germany (1984–88)			
Pre-Retirement	up to 7 years from 58 until pension age (normally 63 m and 60 w)	2 years or until entitlement to old-age pension, if less	employer, but state subsidy (35%) if replacement made
Netherlands (1977–79)			
Early Exit Regulations	from 63 or 64 later 60 or 61 until 65	no replacement condition	employer, but state subsidy in experimental phase
Denmark (1979 onwards)			
Early Retirement Pay	from 60 later 55 until 67	no replacement condition	state

3.1 Employment Effects

Schemes with a replacement condition require, by definition, that when a person takes early retirement a corresponding recruitment takes place. The German and British schemes were strictest in this respect, in that they laid down that the replacement either be made directly into the position vacated or, if it was made indirectly, that a clear link (in the form of a chain of transfers and/or promotions) be demonstrated. The Belgian and French schemes, by contrast, merely imposed an obligation to maintain total levels of employment in the enterprise as a whole not even restricting the effect to the particular establishment in which the person taking early retirement had worked.

Accordingly, the schemes could be used to facilitate quite significant restructuring of the labour force—on a spatial, occupational or operational dimension—rendering a judgement of the real replacement rate much more difficult to formulate. Moreover, although the early retirement could last up to five years in some countries, the minimum duration for which the replacement had to be maintained was often much shorter. For example, an early retirement under the Belgian Legal Pre-Retirement Scheme might last up to five years, but the replacement recruitment had to be maintained for only six months, and even under the much stricter German Pre-Retirement Scheme it had to be maintained for only two years.

None of the evaluations with which I am familiar sought to monitor participating firms over anything like the entire duration of an early retirement; most concentrated on, at most, the first year. In the case of the French Solidarity Contracts, one limited, and local, attempt was made to assess the extent to which replacements were direct rather than as a result of a chain of transfers and promotions. This estimated the direct effect at only 25 per cent—with such replacements more likely in small firms which had not developed strategic planning, and in firms which had actively embraced the social policy objectives of the scheme (Galland, Gaudin and Vrain, 1984).

For four of the above programmes efforts have been made to calculate *the effective replacement rate*, with the results being as follows: Belgium (Legal Pre-Retirement) 67 per cent; Great Britain (Job Release) 85–90 per cent; France (Solidarity Contracts) 95 per cent; Germany (Pre-Retirement) 50 or 80 per cent (50 per cent reflecting replacement recruitments, 80 per cent including redundancies avoided). These outcomes can be compared with those recorded for the two programmes which did not obligate replacement, namely, the Netherlands (Early Exit Regulations) with 66 per cent (including internal transfers as well as external recruitments) and Denmark (Early Retirement Pay) with 25 to 50 per cent.[10] In the case of the latter two schemes, and in part in the case of the German scheme, where the employer rather than the state paid the early pension but received a state subsidy if he or she made a replacement, the less than full replacement could have reflected the early retirements serving to avoid otherwise unavoidable redundancies. Adjusted estimates for the German scheme suggest a 'labour market effect', as opposed to a replacement rate, of some 80 per cent. In other words, in the absence of the scheme, the unemployment total would have been higher not by 50 per cent, but by 80 per cent of the number of scheme participants.

Calculating the *unemployment reduction coefficient* for the schemes—the amount by which registered unemployment was reduced relative to the

---

10   Sources for Belgium: André, 1985; for Great Britain: Bushell, 1984; for France: Magnier,
      Ricau and Jeancharles, 1984; for Germany: IAB, 1988.

number of people in early retirement—was the next step of some, but not all, of the evaluations. Results are available for four schemes. Great Britain (Job Release) 0.93 per cent; France (Solidarity Contracts) 0.5–0.65 per cent; Germany (Pre-Retirement) 0.60 per cent; the Netherlands (Early Exit) 0.25 per cent.[11]

The differences between the replacement rate and the unemployment reduction coefficient can be explained by recruitment from among the registered unemployed, recruitments which did not constitute genuine replacements, recruitments which would have occurred in any case and recruitments which were not sustained. The rather high coefficient for Great Britain can be explained by the Job Release Scheme's strictness in requiring that replacements be made from among the registered unemployed; the rather low coefficient for France by the Solidarity Contract's loose definition of replacement and the absence of a requirement to recruit from a particular source.

3.2   Scheme Costs

An interest in cost-effectiveness motivated much of the evaluation of the British Job Release Scheme. Such an interest was much less apparent in France, although there, too, estimations of cost-effectiveness were made. In Germany, the principal interest was in the distribution of scheme costs, both between different state institutions, such as the labour market authorities, the social insurance institutions and the exchequer, and between the state and firms.

Calculations on the basis of the unemployment reduction coefficient and representative values for the early retirement benefits paid out and the unemployment and other benefits saved, and taking account of increases in tax and social security revenue that might be consequent upon a scheme's operation, produced the following results: for Great Britain (Job Release), the net costs relative to the costs of unemployment benefits were 112 per cent, and the net costs relative to the average costs of all special employment measures were 90 per cent. In France (Solidarity Contracts), the corresponding figures were in the range of 115 to 175 per cent and 77 to 117 per cent.[12]

The German government provided estimates of the costs to the state of the Pre-Retirement Scheme when it was first proposed. Being estimates of gross

---

11 Sources for France: Lacroix and Guergoat, 1984, Frank and Tregoat, 1983; for Great Britain: Bushell, 1984; for Germany: Autorengemeinschaft 1991; and the Netherlands: SoZa, 1982, Autorengemeinschaft, 1991, and own calculations based upon social insurance statistics on scheme participants and estimates of the extent to which the scheme reduced unemployment.

12 Source: Casey 1985, based on Bushell, 1984, and Colin, Elbaum and Fontenau, 1984; in France, the more favourable outcomes refer to the 0.65 coefficient, less favourable to the 0.5 coefficient.

costs, they took account of the subsidies paid when replacement recruitments were made but not of the unemployment benefit savings consequent upon these recruitments (Bundestag, 1984). Subsequent 'model calculations', reacting to the government's proposition, sought to estimate these savings and went so far as to suggest that, while the scheme would bring costs to firms, the state as a whole would save money. Not only would expenditure on unemployment compensation payments be reduced, but some of the older workers taking early retirement under the new scheme would otherwise have taken early retirement under another, publicly financed provision—for example, the disability pension system (Helberger, 1985; Kirner, Meinhardt and Zwiener, 1984). On the other hand, some commentators pointed to the opportunities firms had to 'misuse' the Pre-Retirement Scheme and to claim subsidies for replacements which did in fact not satisfy its requirements (Schewe, 1984). If this were the case, firms would profit at the expense of the state. Once the scheme was actually up and running, interest in its costs declined, and no authoritative balance was made.

3.3   Wider Costs and Benefits

Benefits from an early retirement scheme can be accrued by other actors than the state, as Table 12.4 illustrates.

The costs and benefits described in the previous section relate almost exclusively to those given in the final row of Table 12.4. The gains to the employer, other than those resulting from the improper receipt of subsidies, have not been touched upon so far, nor have the gains to the people taking early retirement and those replacing them.

Although the net income position of those who take early retirement and of those who replace them can be calculated without great difficulty, most of the remaining costs and benefits referred to in the first three rows of Table 12.4 are, at best, difficult to quantify and, at worst, unquantifiable. The gains to an individual employer consequent upon work force rejuvenation are assumed to have been calculated when the viability of that action is assessed, although sometimes complaints are later heard of the loss of valuable skills or experience. The benefits and disbenefits of working and not working for older people are more the object of speculation than measurement, but in any case they are recognized to change over time, either as retirement becomes accepted, or as the first flush of enthusiasm for 'leisure, time for the family and hobbies' passes and the emptiness of retirement sets in. Since most commentators refer to the 'moral pressure' to which some contemplating early retirement are subjected—their being made to feel they have a duty to 'stand aside' and 'make way for a younger person'—there might, for some older people, be little benefit in giving up work.

Table 12.4 Benefits and Costs of Early Retirement Schemes for Different Actors

Actor	Benefits	Costs
Retiree	– increased leisure – early pension – no unemployment stigma[1]	– social status of working – social contacts of work – earnings from work forgone
Replacement	– social status of working – social contacts of work – earnings from work	– reduced leisure – unemployment compensation payment forgone
Employer	– better industrial relations and external image – younger, more productive work force – lower wage costs	– loss of experience – share of costs of early pension
Government	– lower unemployment total – higher tax and social security receipts[2] – lower expenditure on unemployment compensation	– expenditure on early pension – lower tax and social security receipts[3]

Notes

1 Assuming otherwise made unemployed.

2 Assuming early pension exceeds unemployment compensation or replacement occurs.

3 Assuming early pension lower than unemployment compensation or no replacement occurs.

Source
Adapted from Mirkin, 1987.

A further shortcoming of cost–benefit analyses of the type described in the previous section is its static nature. It fails to take account of the longer-term consequences of the pursuit of a policy. Three ways in which it falls short can be cited. First, in so far as early retirement schemes involve positive net costs to the state, they exert an upward pressure on taxes and/or an upward pressure on government borrowing. Both of these will ultimately have a dampening effect on employment and will increase unemployment. Second, in so far as their financing is the direct responsibility of employers, they push up labour costs and depress the demand for labour. Third, in so far as they reduce unemployment, they will have an impact on the rate of wage inflation. By increasing this, they will subsequently reduce the quantity of labour employed. Each of these outcomes illustrates what are conventionally termed 'second-round effects', and while they will not immediately, or even rapidly, negate any positive 'first-round effects', they need to be considered.

4   CONCLUSIONS

As explicit instruments of state policy to manage the labour market, measures to promote or facilitate the exit of older people from the labour market have experienced a strong decline in their popularity. It is notable that most of the strongly labour market-oriented, state early retirement provisions discussed in this chapter date from the late 1970s and the early to mid-1980s. Time series on public expenditure on labour market policy—see above—indicate a substantial retrenchment of such measures. Only Denmark and Belgium stand out as maintaining a commitment to such an approach. The retrenchment reflects, on the one hand, a rejection of the 'work-sharing'/'lump of labour' approach which the state schemes, at least implicitly, embraced, and, on the other, a distaste of paying people to do nothing, a criticism to which the state schemes were also open, rather than using the resources of active labour market policy to assist in the generation of jobs or the skilling and reskilling of the work force and those out of work.[13]

Nor were social policy provisions immune to the process of retrenchment, although they were less obviously touched by it. Some of the provisions granting early old-age pensions to older unemployed people have been, or are to be, abolished—for example, in Sweden and Germany. Some of the most generous provisions for extended payment of benefit to this group have also been withdrawn—for example, in Germany and the Netherlands. In a number of countries attempts have also been made to curb the growth of disability benefit systems by imposing considerably stricter eligibility criteria—for example, in Great Britain and the Netherlands.

By contrast, all the evidence, anecdotal and otherwise, suggests that company provisions have not only survived unscathed, but have often expanded. Clearly firms have an interest in managing work force reduction and restructuring in a socially acceptable fashion and in rejuvenating their work force. At least large and profitable firms appear willing to shoulder significant costs to pursue personnel policies which are directed to these ends. What is more, the retrenchment of state provisions on which they build their own schemes does not appear to discourage them. Rather, there is a tendency to plug the

---

13 Germany presents a possible counterexample to this thesis in that, in the wake of unification, the state engaged massively in the promotion of early retirement as a way to reduce the huge rise in unemployment in the former GDR.

deficits created by the state's full or partial retreat. Although their own provisions entail greater direct costs, they offer the opportunity for the employer to exercise greater selectivity, and to manage their work force according to their interests rather than the interests of their employees or the wider 'public interest'.

Whether there exists scope for future state involvement in exit promotion provisions is a difficult question. It is notable that, almost simultaneously with his introducing the Pre-Retirement Scheme and exhorting older workers to take advantage of it, the German Minister of Labour, who is also the Minister of Social Affairs, was warning employees that in future they would have to work longer in order that the financial integrity of the old-age pension system be maintained. In all western countries populations are aging, and the concern of governments and social policy-makers has been with looking for ways in which retirement can be deferred rather than brought forward. The United States led the way in raising the age of eligibility for an old-age pension, Sweden more recently followed suit; while Germany and France have taken steps to raise the *effective* pension age—by removing early pension opportunities or increasing the number of contribution years necessary to gain entitlement to full benefits. In Great Britain the planned equalization of pension ages involved an equalization upwards (women to 65) rather than downwards (men to 60).

If demographic pressures point in one direction, short- to medium-term labour market prospects still point to the need for policies that can reduce unemployment. This need suggests that 'work-sharing' and, as a specific form thereof, 'early retirement', might still be considered as providing a partial solution. However, if new provisions are to be developed, they will have to be developed along lines which ensure that the state is not paying for the benefits obtained by firms, and that the older people who leave the labour market early, and thereby enjoy extra leisure, make an appropriate contribution in exchange. There is scope in the state retirement systems of almost all western countries for greater flexibility regarding retirement ages, made possible by the offer of appropriate actuarial reduction and appreciation factors. There is also scope for adjusting state systems to permit partial as well as full liquidation of benefits, again subject to the necessary benefit adjustments. Moreover, as well as offering greater flexibility, partial retirement might offer the possibility for older people to stay longer in the labour force, thus going some way towards relieving the social security burdens of population aging.

Flexibility is often lacking in company pension systems as much as it is in state pension systems, although what is absent in this case is less the flexibility to retire early on a lower pension, but rather the flexibility to adjust working hours downward without prejudicing benefit entitlement. 'Money purchase', or 'defined contribution' schemes, the popularity of which is gradually spreading, offer considerably more opportunities in this direction than do many salary-related, or defined benefit schemes.[14]

Whereas a number of the early retirement schemes promoted by the state for labour market purposes have required replacement of the person leaving, this condition appears by no means necessary for achievement of the 'work-sharing' objective. As a number of the examples discussed in this chapter have shown, the most important contribution of an early retirement provision might well be the effecting of work force reductions in a socially acceptable manner. Moreover, the requirement of the employer to replace can severely restrict the opportunity of the older worker to exercise an early retirement option and may impose bureaucratic monitoring systems which undermine employer commitment.

With respect not to the substance of such early retirement provisions but their evaluation, only a few general observations can be made. Evaluations have been few and limited in scope, with many not proceeding beyond a basic monitoring of participants. The calculation of labour market effects followed little more than 'rule-of-thumb' procedures. What is more, there was no attempt to estimate the longer-term consequences of policies. All too often, these have merely been presumed, usually in retrospect, and often by potential detractors rather than proponents. Considering the sometimes substantial expenditure committed to such schemes by governments, both in absolute terms and in relation to expenditures on other labour market instruments, this finding must surely give cause for concern.

However, the paucity of evaluation material on specifically labour market-oriented provisions is dwarfed by the paucity of information on the various social policy provisions which have clearly contributed to the reduction in older people's employment rates. Some of these provisions—particularly disability pension schemes—have provoked concern for budgetary reasons. However, little is known about their employment impact and by which sort of firm or individual, and under which circumstances, they can be, or are, 'functionalized'. Equally, little is known about those provisions which are the preserve of firms themselves. Here the requirement for primary data collection is probably at its greatest, not least because it is here that some of the most interesting, and innovative, early retirement is taking place.

---

14 Money purchase schemes effectively provide a lump sum on retirement which can be used to buy an annuity or pension. The size of the lump sum depends upon the amount contributed into the scheme and the performance of the investments made with these contributions. Salary-related schemes pay a pension as a fraction of (usually final) salary, with the size of the fraction dependent on length of service. Clearly, switching to part-time work shortly before retirement is likely to reduce the pension paid under the latter type of scheme. However, under the former type of scheme it merely results in lower contributions and a slightly lower level of investment for a short period of time, so that the lump sum earned is only marginally smaller than it would otherwise have been.

REFERENCES

André, M. (1985), 'The Various Early Retirement Provisions in Belgium', in International Security Association (ed.), *Social Security, Unemployment and Premature Retirement*, Studies and Research, 22, Geneva, pp. 26–40.

Autorengemeinschaft (1991), 'Der Arbeitsmarkt 1991 und 1992 in der Bundesrepublik Deutschland', *MittAB*, 4, 621–34.

Björklund, A. and B. Holmlund (1991), 'The Economics of Unemployment Insurance: The Case of Sweden', in A. Björklund, R. Haveman, R. Hollister and B. Holmlund (1991), *Labour Market Policy and Unemployment Insurance*, Oxford: Clarendon Press, pp. 101–78.

Bundestag (1984, March), *Beschlußempfehlung und Bericht des Ausschusses für Arbeit und Sozialordnung zu dem von der Bundesregierung eingebrachten Entwurf eines Gesetzes zur Erleichterung des Übergangs vom Arbeitsleben in den Ruhestand*, BT–Drucksache 10/1175.

Bushell, R. (1984), 'Evaluation of Early Retirement Systems: Great Britain, the Job Release Scheme', Department of Employment, London. (Unpublished manuscript)

Casey, B. (1985), *Early Retirement Schemes with a Replacement Condition: Programmes and Experiences in Belgium, France, Great Britain and the Federal Republic of Germany*, WZB discussion paper IIM/LMP 85–6a, Wissenschaftszentrum Berlin für Sozialforschung.

Casey, B. (1992a), 'Redundancy and Early Retirement: The Interaction of Public and Private Policy in Britain, Germany and the USA', *British Journal of Industrial Relations*, 30 (2), 425–43.

Casey, B. (1992b), 'Paying for Early Retirement', *Journal of Social Policy*, 21, 303–23.

Casey, B. and G. Bruche (1983), *Work or Retirement? Labour Market and Social Policy for Older Workers in France, Great Britain, the Netherlands, Sweden and the USA*, Aldershot: Gower.

Casey, B. and F. Laczko (1989), 'Early Retired or Longterm-unemployed? The Situation of Non-working Men Aged 55–64 from 1979–1986', *Work, Employment and Society*, 4, 509–26.

Colin, J.-F., M. Elbaum and A. Fontenau (1984, April), 'Chômage et politique de l'emploi 1981–1983', *Observations et diagnostics économiques*, 7, 95–122.

Disney, R. and S. Webb (1991), 'Why Are There So Many Long-term-sick in Britain?', *Economic Journal*, 101 (405), 252–63.

Frank, D. and J.-J. Tregoat (1983), 'Une politique active en matière d'emploi et de lutte contre le chômage a marqué 1982', *Bulletin mensuel des statistiques du travail* (suppl. 104), 15–36.

Galland, O., J. Gaudin and P. Vrain (1984, December), 'Contrats de solidarité et stratégie des entreprises', *Travail et Emploi*, 22, 7–20.

Helberger, C. (1985), 'Die Kosten des Vorruhestands—Werden die öffentlichen Haushalte be- oder entlastet?', *Sozialer Fortschritt*, 34 (4), 73–80.

IAB-Kurzbericht (1988), *Aktualisierte Befunde zur Vorruhestandsregelung, Teil I: Globale und wirtschaftszweigspezifische Ergebnisse*, 21, Nuremberg: Institut für Arbeitsmarkt- und Berufsforschung.

Ippolito, D. S. (1990), 'Toward Explaining Early Retirement after 1970', *Industrial and Labor Relations Review*, 43 (5), 556–69.

Kirner, E., V. Meinhardt and R. Zwiener (1984), 'Mögliche Beschäftigungseffekte der Vorruhestandsregelung', *DIW–Wochenbericht*, 51 (18).

Lacroix, T. and J.-C. Guergoat (1984, June), 'Le succès des préretraites a permis de stabiliser le chômage', *Dossiers statistiques du travail et de l'emploi*, 3–4, 15–32.

Laczko, F. (1988), 'Partial Retirement as an Alternative to Early Retirement: A Comparison of Gradual Retirement Schemes in Britain, France and Scandinavia', *International Social Security Review*, 2, 172–96.

Lando, M. and A. Krate (1976), 'Disability Insurance: Programme Issues and Research', *Social Security Bulletin*, 39 (10), 3–17.

Magnier, G., G. Ricau and G. Jeancharles (1984, January), 'Application des contrats de solidarité. Résultats d'une enquête sur les conditions du respect de la clause du maintien des effectifs', *Dossiers statistiques du travail et de l'emploi*, 1, 17–32.

Mirkin, B. A. (1987, March), 'Early Retirement as a Labour Force Policy: An International Overview', *Monthly Labour Review*, 19–33.

OECD (1995), *The Transition from Work to Retirement*, OECD, *Social Policy Studies*, 16, Paris: OECD Publications.

Piachaud, D. (1986), 'Disability, Retirement and Unemployment of Older Men', *Journal of Social Policy*, 15 (2), 145–62.

Schewe, D. (1984), 'Die finanziellen Auswirkungen des Gesetzes zur Erleichterung des Übergangs vom Arbeitsleben in den Ruhestand für die Betriebe—Gutachten zum Vorruhestandsgesetz', IG Chemie-Papier-Keramik (Abt. Tarifpolitik), Hannover.

SoZa (1982), 'Rapportage Arbeidsmarkt 1982', Ministerie van Sociale Zaken en Werkgelegenheid, Den Haag.

Van den Bosch, F. and C. Petersen (1983), 'An Explanation for the Growth of Social Security Disability Transfers', *De Economist,* 131 (1), 65–79.

13. Improving Job-matching through Placement Services

Ulrich Walwei

The organization and the institutional regulation of job placement are currently undergoing comprehensive changes. New challenges and some criticism have led to efforts to reform public employment services, which are still the most important provider of placement services in most countries. The formerly bureaucratic establishments are developing more and more into customer-oriented service organizations. With the completion of the Single European Market, further progress has been made towards eliminating impediments such as an inadequate flow of information about available jobs and job seekers. The European Employment Services network (EURES) was established with the objective of facilitating cross-border mobility. Private agencies are also beginning to play a more important role in the area of job placement. The private sector experienced a boom, particularly in the 1970s and 1980s, and this trend seems to be continuing, also as a result of ongoing liberalization tendencies. But not very much is known about the possible effects of these changes on the side of the users of these services or on the labour market as a whole.

This chapter starts with some theoretical considerations about the role of placement services as intermediaries in the labour market and continues with an overview of alternative approaches regarding the institutional regulation and organization of job placement. In its main part the chapter examines different approaches taken by previous studies in evaluating the performance as well as the impacts of mediation activities provided by placement services. In the final section I summarize the empirical findings of these studies and conclude with some remarks on perspectives for future evaluation activities in this area.

1   LABOUR MARKETS AND INTERMEDIARIES: SOURCES OF MARKET AND POLICY FAILURE

Markets often lack transparency in many respects. Uncertainty abounds as to where one can obtain or offer something, what price must be paid or can be obtained, and as to the quality of the exchanged object. The lack of transparency can be reduced by efforts to acquire information; however, information is not usually provided free of charge. It costs time and money to collect information, and the price is usually the higher the more quickly the material is required. The fact that information has a price justifies the existence of certain mechanisms or institutions that are capable of providing an efficient exchange service. Examples of such channels of information are newspaper advertisements, informal contacts and intermediaries. There are two types of intermediary (middlemen), that is, market-makers and match-makers (Yavas, 1994). Market-makers set an asking price and a bidding price at which they sell or buy on their own account (e.g. specialists in the stock markets, used-car dealers). By contrast, match-makers do not trade; they simply match the buyer side with the seller side of the market (e.g. real-estate brokers, placement services). The services of match-makers may be enlisted if the net return of information for the exchange partners can thus be increased, notably by a higher gross return and/or lower transaction costs (compared with the cost and gross returns ensuing from the use of alternative channels of information).

Labour markets are a typical example of search markets. First, they are not in the least homogeneous; because jobs and skills differ greatly in terms of level and scope there is a wide variety of labour market segments. In addition, personal attitudes on both sides of the market play an important role. The heterogeneity causes problems when it comes to matching labour supply and demand. The matching process can be described by the matching function, which specifies the number of placements as a function of the number of job seekers and the number of vacancies (Blanchard and Diamond, 1989). But one has to bear in mind that the coexistence of vacancies and unemployed job seekers at any given point of time does not necessarily reflect mismatch because vacancy filling and job search will always lead to friction and will, therefore, take a minimum amount of time. One may only speak of mismatch if the number of vacancies and unemployed job seekers exceeds its frictional minimum. It should be pointed out that the frictional share of vacancies and unemployment may have risen over time due to higher skill requirements, which involve more intensive search.

The matching function generally incorporates many factors, including the geographical and skill distribution of jobs and workers, information flaws and search intensities. Therefore, mismatch may have several causes. The probability of a match depends on whether potential buyers or sellers get in touch with each other (contact probability), and whether a contract can be concluded (contract probability). Whereas geographical mismatch will mainly reduce the contact probability (because of an insufficient number of jobs or workers in a certain region), skill mismatch will predominantly reduce the contract probability (e.g. because job seekers do not meet employers' needs). Search intensity depends on the information available, the appropriate reservation wage and the level as well as the duration of unemployment benefits (see Franz, 1991;

Jackman, Pissarides and Savouri, 1990). Of course, the question as to whether and to what extent adjustment problems have contributed to the increase in unemployment in many OECD countries is empirical. Commonly used indicators for mismatch are the job vacancy rate associated with given unemployment (Beveridge curve), differences in unemployment rates across skill groups or regions, and the duration of unemployment and vacancies. Nevertheless, empirical studies suggest that efforts to measure trends in skill and geographical mismatch do not produce consistent evidence of worsening problems (Abraham, 1991). An explanation for these contradictory findings might be that an outward shift of the Beveridge curve (which would indicate increasing adjustment problems) may not only be interpreted as a permanent shift but also as a temporary shift for cyclical reasons (Hansen, 1970). However, the important issue is how the labour market responds to certain structural imbalances, regardless of whether they are of a permanent or temporary nature.

The role of employment services dealing with job placement can be regarded as that of an intermediary in the labour market. Employment services are matchmakers who narrow the set of buyers (firms) and sellers (workers). In doing so, they reduce uncertainty on both sides of the market and thus gain a surplus (Yavas, 1994). Uncertainty results from the fact that the search efforts of employers or job seekers may not lead to proper matches. One possible reason for this is, of course, the aforementioned heterogeneity of the labour market. Another reason is that the quality of jobs and the performance of workers are experience goods (Spence, 1973). Placement at its best relies on a good knowledge of companies' skill needs, on the one hand, and the suitability of workers, on the other. Only where placement services have expert knowledge of specific segments of the labour market can they expect to be involved in the search process as intermediaries. The use of intermediaries can be of financial benefit, especially whenever search can be expected to be very costly for the individual, whereas the opposite will ultimately be the case if search is effectively cost free (Yavas, 1994). Due to the labour market specifics mentioned above (quality uncertainties, experience goods), the market reputation of the placement service will be of considerable significance for its actual use. The placement service as such can be conceived of as an experience good (Buttler and Walwei, 1995).

Mediation by employment services may, therefore, constitute a means to correct certain market failures (e.g. those which result from flawed information). Jobs that are particularly difficult to fill and workers who are especially difficult to place may otherwise be lost to the market altogether. But increased market transparency through mediation alone is, of course, not a sufficient response to problems of geographical or skill mismatch. Policy measures that provide special incentives to unemployed job seekers (one example is financial support to promote geographical mobility) or that focus on skill enhancement (e.g. training programmes designed to improve the participants' employment prospects) should also be taken into account. The rationale behind the latter type of policies and their evaluation are dealt with in other chapters of this handbook (see chaps 9, 10 and 15 in this volume). I will concentrate here on the importance of the role of employment services as mediators between vacancies and job seekers.

Assuming that there is a need for mediation services in labour markets, the crucial question is how these services can and should be organized. On the one hand, market failures produce transaction costs, which may prevent market transactions. On the other hand, while these transaction costs can be reduced by policy interventions, the measures imposed might result in other transaction costs. In this case one would speak of 'policy failure'. There are three possible areas where policy failures may arise. The first concerns the efficiency and effectiveness of public employment services (PES). Efficient PES would need both adequate resources and to make full use of these resources in order to match both registered vacancies and registered job seekers in a proper manner. The second type of (potential) policy failure is related to the role of private employment services (PRES). The question in this context is whether more room on the market for PRES would lead to an increase or a decrease in the effectiveness of the matching process. The third possibility for policy failure concerns both public and private employment services. The activities of PES and PRES may result in mutual exclusion and/or the exclusion of third parties from access to information about job seekers and vacancies. Such exclusiveness of information may diminish the intended market transparency.

2   INSTITUTIONAL ORGANIZATION AND THE ROLE OF PLACEMENT SERVICES

2.1   Public and Private Agencies

Public employment services have existed in some countries since the beginning of this century and certainly from the 1950s onwards in all OECD countries. PES are generally a national body and are administered by government agencies or agencies under commission to the government. Exceptions to this rule are found only in Belgium, Switzerland and the United States, where the PES are run by regional authorities (Walwei, 1995). In most countries PES are financed out of general tax revenues. Some countries (e.g. Austria and Germany) finance their PES mostly from employer and/or employee contributions. With very few exceptions (large-scale mandates to fill appointments or to conduct expensive comparative tests on applicants are a case in point) PES do not charge fees.

Mediation services are normally an integral part of PES activities. In addition to job placement, PES are also responsible for other public-service tasks, such as ascertaining the availability of job seekers and producing quantitative and qualitative labour market information. They are additionally charged with promoting the reintegration of the unemployed into working life through active labour market policies (job creation schemes, wage-cost subsidies, training courses). The combination of these tasks has the advantage that comprehensive and active policies are provided from the same source. Specifically, PES are required to prevent structural unemployment and to improve the employability of the long-term unemployed and other difficult-to-place job seekers. In the case of these groups, active policies are often a prerequisite for successful placement. The most important organizational differences between OECD countries, however, are to be found in the area of unemployment benefit administration. In some countries the administration of benefits is undertaken by the PES, whereas in others the task is entrusted to another body. The advantages of such a division of functions lie in the promotion of a more service-oriented PES; however, the fact that separate bodies carry out partially overlapping activities has its disadvantages.

PES use different mediation procedures to fill registered vacancies. We distinguish between four types: self-selection, conditional self-selection, administrative matching and selective matching (Ours, 1994). In the cases of self-selection and conditional self-selection, PES play a rather passive role as mediators, that is, they concentrate their activities on the acquisition of vacancies and the compilation of files containing data on job seekers and available jobs. Self-selection is based on an open-file computer system, which provides clients with all the relevant information on screen. Both employers and job seekers have direct access to the system and have no further need to approach PES staff. Open self-service systems for job seekers have recently been established in many countries, though similar information systems for employers are still rare. Conditional self-selection mainly consists of the provision of basic information about vacancies to job seekers, either through online access or card registers. For further details the employer or job seeker must approach PES staff members. When job seekers are interested in a particular job, they are invited to consult a counsellor for an initial screening. Those considered suitable for the job receive the name and address of the prospective employer. Mediation procedures based on conditional self-selection are also called semi-open self-service systems. Both the open and the semi-open systems mainly provide information; placement staff spend no or only a little time on the selection of candidates.

By contrast, administrative matching means that registered vacancies are matched with registered job seekers. Potentially suitable job seekers are notified about appropriate vacancies, and, in the same way, employers may obtain the names of job seekers and contact these by themselves. Of course, administrative matching requires greater staff capacities than self-selection because the PES have to find suitable job seekers to match the vacancies. The most time-consuming procedure is selective matching. In addition to matching job seekers to vacancies, the PES invest time in screening candidates (e.g. with respect to ability, working experience, education and motivation).

The use of matching services offered by the PES is usually voluntary for job seekers but obligatory for recipients of unemployment benefit. Whereas in the case of self-service systems the unemployed are often not obliged to apply for vacancies, those matched by administrative or selective matching must apply for the proposed job. Firms seeking to fill vacancies have voluntary access to PES, with one important exception: mandatory notification of vacancies is the rule in some countries. But the practical significance of the regulation can be regarded as low because failure to register vacancies seems not to result in severe sanctions. This laxity might be accounted for by the fact that PES would probably not be able to fill all vacancies in an economy with suitable candidates. Moreover, considerable administrative effort would be required to enforce the regulation, and attempts to impose mandatory notification of vacancies might significantly impair the relationship between PES and firms who currently register vacancies on a voluntary basis.

There are several differences between PES and PRES. PES are set up by government or regional authorities, whereas PRES are established as a result of private initiative. PES normally provide their services free of charge, whereas PRES usually charge a fee. PRES can be operated with a view to profit or not. Because the sector covers a wide range of services, mediation can be a private agency's major or minor activity. Examples of PRES firms are headhunters (executive search firms), personnel consultants, outplacement firms, temporary employment and recruitment agencies and charitable self-help organizations (see International Labour Office, 1994, for details).

Headhunters and charitable self-help organizations specialize in services for particular groups of persons. Headhunters are mainly concerned with filling executive positions. In the case of self-help organizations, there is either a charitable institution involved that works for the socially disadvantaged (e.g. released prisoners), or an occupational or professional association, such as a trade union, that acts in the interests of its members. Recruitment agencies and personnel consultants specialize in candidate selection. The activities of temporary employment agencies and outplacement firms are only indirectly linked to actual matching. Temporary employment agencies do not place job seekers permanently, but hire out workers for a limited period of time. Should the workers be subsequently taken on by the user firm under permanent employment contracts, the temporary agencies are then actually performing a similar job to other PRES, for example, recruitment agencies. Outplacement firms primarily offer a very specialized type of consultancy service, which may include placement of employees who have been made redundant. Their services are aimed at facilitating the reemployment of such workers and are normally paid for by the previous employer.

2.2   Typology of Systems

There are three common models for the organization of matching services: monopoly, coexistence and market systems (see Figure 13.1). Monopoly systems can either consist of strict or moderate monopolies. The purpose of strict monopolies is to ensure that the PES are afforded a strong position through the prohibition of PRES of any kind and through the requirement of mandatory registration of vacancies. By contrast, in the case of moderate monopoly systems the use of PES is voluntary for both employers and job seekers (though not for the unemployed). In moderate monopoly systems PRES are allowed only in exceptional cases, that is, either for certain occupational groups (e.g. executives and entertainers) or certain activities (e.g. temporary employment). However, it must be noted that in monopoly systems where PRES are completely or partly banned there are legal and illegal ways to side-step such restrictions. Prohibition often primarily concerns recruitment activities by PRES and not personnel consulting (including selection) or temporary work. A survey commissioned by the International Social Security Association (ISSA) showed that at the end of 1994 only seven of twenty OECD countries were still adhering to the monopoly model (Walwei, 1995). Of these seven, one country (Turkey) had a relatively strict monopoly, whereas the other six operated with a more or less moderate monopoly.

In coexistence systems PES and PRES operate side by side. Even profit-making PRES are allowed, without any geographical restrictions and for all occupational groups. In regulated coexistence systems there are regulations for PRES with respect to licensing provisions and quality standards. Nine of the thirteen coexistence countries covered in the ISSA survey regulate PRES. In the other four countries the PRES can operate without special licences or regulations. Just like any other company, such agencies acquire their legitimacy by being entered in the commercial register and by declaring themselves to the tax authorities. The advantage of licensing provisions is that they create 'artificial' barriers to market entry in terms of staff and operating requirements. This impediment reduces the risk of harm to potential clients through irresponsible agencies that are interested only in short-term profit. Given the nature of the placement service itself, which entails quality uncertainties, 'black sheep' cannot be ruled out, even with limited market access. Quality standards and monitoring by state authorities may additionally provide some consumer protection. But regulations governing licensing and quality requirements should not impose standards that are so high that they may prevent market entry and thus reduce competition because—given placement services'

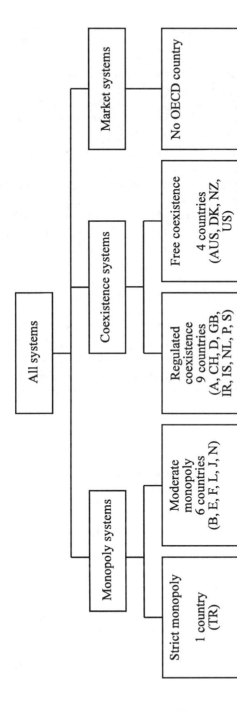

Source
Entwicklungen bei der Organisation der Arbeitsvermittlung by U. Walwei, 1995, ISSA working paper no. AC/28/2, International Social Security Association.

Figure 13.1   Typology of Job Placement Systems (1994)

dependence on reputation—healthy competition removes 'black sheep'. Often the long-term profit to be achieved may provide sufficient motivation for commercial PRES to act in a responsible manner.

In a pure market system (which does not exist in any OECD country) only PRES provide mediation services of any kind. Such a system does not necessarily imply the absence of any public intervention. For example, matching tasks may have been contracted out by PES to PRES. Nor must the absence of PES in countries where PRES are generally allowed (e.g. Uruguay) necessarily reflect a particularly liberal approach, but may also be accounted for by the stage of economic development reached by these countries.

Over time one can observe a vigorous trend towards liberalization in the PRES sector. According to the ISSA survey, in 1985 there were fourteen monopoly countries, compared to six coexistence countries. Since then the relationship has been reversed. At the end of 1994 there were thirteen coexistence countries and only seven monopoly countries. However, liberalization was introduced at different levels or only gradually. PRES have been conditionally admitted in Norway (1993), Spain (1993), Austria (1992) and Germany (1994). In Austria and Germany executive placement services were allowed to operate for the first time. In Norway special PRES dealing with artists and overseas placement were legalized. In Spain only nonprofit PRES were authorized to operate. PRES have been unconditionally admitted in seven other countries: Iceland (1985), Portugal (1989), Denmark (1990), the Netherlands (1991), Sweden (1993) and—following partial liberalization— Austria (1994) and Germany (1994). Further liberalization initiatives can be expected in the near future in the remaining monopoly countries. Even in regulated coexistence countries further liberalization steps have been taken or are imminent. For example, in New Zealand the licensing requirement for PRES was abolished in 1987. A similar step will probably be taken in the United Kingdom in 1995. Both reforms are aimed at reducing bureaucracy and increasing competition between agencies.

3   ASSESSMENT OF PLACEMENT SERVICE ACTIVITIES

3.1   Performance Measurement

Endeavours to evaluate the activities of placement services can have two different objectives: process measurement (performance evaluation) and outcome measurement (impact evaluation). In the case of placement services, performance evaluation measures what passes through the employment service; impact evaluation, on the other hand, is an attempt to assess what happens because of the existence of employment services. Whereas the use of PRES will, by and large, emerge from the free working of the market, the use of PES is heavily dependent on priorities set by legislators and financial authorities. In the case of PRES, additional resources, such as staff, will only be employed if additional profits can be expected. Therefore, profit itself can be seen as a quite obvious performance indicator for PRES. By contrast, in the case of (nonprofit-oriented) PES, the use of additional staff does not necessarily imply greater efficiency because the possible benefits of their activities are more difficult to measure. The main focus of most evaluation studies on the activities of employment services is on the role of PES. However, in some of these studies the performance of PRES or the outcome of PRES activities are used as points of reference.

Certain indicators are used to evaluate performance. Their purpose is to measure the relative market importance of employment services compared to other search channels (market share) and the satisfaction of their clients. Performance indicators are a source of quantitative information for managers of employment services, which they require to ensure efficient delivery of programmes and services; the indicators also provide timely notification when operational performance deviates from expected performance targets.

There are many possible indicators for the market share of employment services (see box below). One measures the proportion of job seekers or of vacancies registered with the employment service. This *registration or user rate* indicates how often employers or job seekers ask for placement assistance. The higher the rate, the more clients from either side of the market expect successful placement and the more often the employment service has the opportunity to assist employers or job seekers. The PES, in particular, might be interested in the proportion of unemployed job seekers registered with them. However, for two reasons a high registration rate of unemployed does not necessarily indicate PES effectiveness. First, in many countries unemployed job seekers are registered more or less by obligation with the PES. Second, many of those registered may not be actively seeking work and are thus not unemployed, according to the labour force survey definition (OECD, 1992).

Another indicator measures the *success rate of registrations or users*, that is, the proportion of vacancies filled or of users placed. The overall score depends on whether the employment service is able to offer vacancies to job seekers and candidates to employers (*attempt rate)* and whether—after an attempt—a contract between both sides can be achieved (*successful attempt rate*). A high score of successful attempts would indicate careful selection of candidates for vacant positions, and might be considered as a measure of quality and internal effectiveness. At the same time, a relatively high success rate might also imply a market approach that is too narrow. The success rate must, therefore, be viewed in relation to the registration (or user) rate.

Performance Indicators

A: *Vacancies*

$$\text{Registration Rate} = \frac{\text{inflow of registered vacancies}}{\text{inflow of total vacancies}} \quad (1)$$

$$\text{Attempt Rate of Registration} = \frac{\text{proposed placements}}{\text{inflow of registered vacancies}} \quad (2)$$

$$\text{Successful Attempt Rate} = \frac{\text{filled vacancies}}{\text{proposed placements}} \quad (3)$$

$$\text{Success Rate of Registration} = \frac{\text{filled vacancies}}{\text{inflow of registered vacancies}} \quad (4)$$

$$= \text{Attempt Rate} \times \text{Successful Attempt Rate}$$

$$\text{Penetration Rate of Registration} = \frac{\text{filled vacancies}}{\text{inflow of total vacancies}} \quad (5)$$

$$= \text{Registration Rate} \times \text{Attempt Rate} \times \text{Successful Attempt Rate}$$

$$= \text{Registration Rate} \times \text{Success Rate}$$

B: *Job seekers*

$$\text{User Rate} = \frac{\text{inflow of registered job seekers}}{\text{inflow of total job seekers}} \quad (1)$$

$$\text{Attempt Rate of Use} = \frac{\text{proposed placements}}{\text{inflow of registered job seekers}} \quad (2)$$

$$\text{Successful Attempt Rate of Use} = \frac{\text{placed job seekers}}{\text{proposed placements}} \quad (3)$$

$$\text{Success Rate of Use} = \frac{\text{placed job seekers}}{\text{inflow of registered job seekers}} \quad (4)$$

$$= \text{Attempt Rate} \times \text{Successful Attempt Rate}$$

$$\text{Penetration Rate of Use} = \frac{\text{placed job seekers}}{\text{inflow of total job seekers}} \quad (5)$$

$$= \text{User Rate} \times \text{Attempt Rate} \times \text{Successful Attempt Rate}$$

$$= \text{User Registration Rate} \times \text{Success Rate}$$

The arithmetical result of the registration rate or the user rate and the success rate is the *penetration rate*, that is, the proportion of all hirings that are made with the assistance of employment services. The penetration rate rises, *ceteris paribus*, the more employers or job seekers make use of the employment service and the more the employment service succeeds in matching clients and registered vacancies. Table 13.1 contains information about registration rates, success rates and penetration rates in OECD countries, based on vacancy fillings. The results will be discussed in section 4 of this chapter. The numerator of the penetration rate, that is, the number of placements, could also be related to other variables. The average operating cost per placement can be calculated on the basis of the total operating cost, and the number of placements per staff on the basis of the number of placement staff.

Table 13.1   PES Performance Indicators (OECD Countries: Data from the Early 1990s)

Countries	Monopoly (M) or Coexistence (C)	Total inflow of vacancies (1000)	Registered vacancies (1000)	Placements (1000)	Registration rate (%)	Success rate (%)	Penetration rate (%)
A[1]	M	1 000	267	120	27	45	12
AUS	C	2 300	607	397	26	65	17
B	M	562	142	95	25	67	17
CH	C	500	35	15	7	43	3
D[1,2]	M	6 364	2 157	1 532	34	71	24
DK	C	—	130	76	—	55	—
E	M	2 395	459	349	19	76	15
F	M	4 236	1 184	504	28	43	12
GB	C	6 000	1 987	1 459	33	73	24
IR	C	102	30	10	29	33	10
J	M	10 850	7 960	1 356	73	17	12
N	M	486	237	84	49	35	17
NL	C	1 100	243	130	22	53	12
P	C	—	53	28	—	53	—
S[1]	M	827	300	206	36	69	25
US	C	76 619	6 792	3 690	9	54	5

Notes
1   Austria, Germany and Sweden were monopoly countries until 1992.
2   The data refer only to western Germany.
— = data not available.

Source
Entwicklungen bei der Organisation der Arbeitsvermittlung by U. Walwei, 1995, ISSA working paper no. AC/28/2, International Social Security Association.

Another important performance indicator is the *response time*, which measures the time between vacancy registration and placement proposal. However, this indicator should be used with caution because a speedy response does not necessarily indicate good matching. Perfect matching takes time because the company's requirement profile and the candidate's qualification profile must be harmonized with one another as far as possible. The average response time may differ considerably across different jobs and, therefore, requires differentiated measurement. Finally, in recent years PES have regularly used *satisfaction surveys* in order to ascertain the needs of their clients and to improve and expand their range of services.

Market shares—as defined above—are being afforded an ever more important role as performance indicators. Nonetheless, several points of criticism can be made. The first problem concerns the definition of the relevant market for employment services. A commonly used measure for the total market is the total number of actual and potential hirings, that is, the change in desired employment, including replacement in cases of termination and retirement. However, 'desired employment' is difficult to define in empirical terms. In particular cases a vacancy might become available at the same time as a suitable person applies for a job. Another difficulty in measuring the relevant market results from the fact that many job seekers pursue employment through direct contact with employers. In such cases employers may not search actively but merely rely on the 'spontaneous' flow of job applicants. Taking this into consideration, an alternative concept might be 'desired hirings requiring active search'. But, again, search activities might still consist primarily of informal contacts, for example, with former employees or through present employees. A considerable portion of these vacancies may actually not be accessible for employment services. A third, more pragmatic, means to measure the relevant market might be all publicly announced vacancies, that is, vacancies registered with employment services plus vacancies published in newspaper advertisements.

The data used to calculate these market shares can be based either on particular survey data or on process-generated data. The results of both methods can vary considerably. On the one hand, the variations may be caused by problems related to statistical sampling and/or false indications by the parties concerned regarding the actual success of different search channels. On the other hand, process-generated data on placements and vacancy registrations might be distorted by over- or underestimations. Sometimes it is argued, especially with regard to PES, that operating statistics are manipulated because the number of vacancies filled is still an important measure for the success of local job centres. For example, the latter might make their figures look better by registering a vacancy when a job seeker (having successfully completed a training programme sponsored by the PES) finds a job elsewhere, and then recording this vacancy as having been filled by the PES. By contrast, many people may have found jobs with the help of the PES that do not show up in any statistics. The introduction of open self-service systems, especially, has created problems in this respect because self-service transactions are not easy to count. In countries where self-service is a significant means of job search or worker search, the registration rate is of greater importance as a performance indicator. Generally, not only the market share at a given point in time seems to be important but even more so its development over time. If the way the indicators are measured remains constant, the arising distortion may also be constant.

Another problem may arise because indicators that measure market shares (e.g. penetration rate, registration rate) not only reflect activity. They are also dependent on factors that cannot be influenced by employment services. First, a limited budget may mean that PES are denied the capacities they need to handle or to acquire vacancies successfully. Second, the number of vacancy registrations also seems to be related to the economic cycle. Whereas in a boom period the number of vacancies as well as the number of voluntary job seekers is high, and the corresponding market shares of the PES are comparatively low, the opposite is the case in recession. With respect to PRES, the situation seems to be quite the opposite.

Moreover, a high market share, especially in the case of PES, might be an unrewarding goal. In view of the incentive to achieve a high rate of placement, PES might specifically target those job seekers who are already in a strong position to find employment, that is, they might try to help job seekers with good prospects before they can help themselves. If this were the case, job seekers with unfavourable prospects would face the likelihood of being left to their own devices because efforts to assist them might result in poor figures in terms of market shares. Performance indicators like market shares only show how many vacancies have been filled by the employment services and how many people they have helped find employment. But what we know nothing about is the impact of these placements on the labour market. How many of the vacancies filled by employment services might have been filled with people with the same characteristics, and in the same time period, through the use of other channels. We also do not know how many people who find a job with any kind of help from employment services would have found comparable jobs in the same time without assistance. Impact evaluation studies may throw some light on these questions.

3.2   Microimpacts

The crucial question posed in evaluations of microimpacts is what would have happened to users had they not received services from an employment service.

Mediation services provided by PES or PRES do influence the costs and benefits of job search and hiring. The net benefits of employment services will emerge if, *ceteris paribus*, because of their activities, the gross benefits of search can be increased and/or the cost can be reduced. In the case of job seekers, several factors (always compared to other search channels) have to be taken into account: the cost of using agencies (which is zero in the case of PES and mostly in the case of PRES, too); the cost of acquiring and selecting job offers; the cost of being jobless or inadequately employed for a certain period of time; the characteristics of the job (e.g. initial or long-term earning prospects). Similar considerations can be made on the employer side. Relevant factors (again in comparison with other search channels) in this case are: the cost of using agencies (zero only in the case of PES); the cost of filling the vacancy independently (including newspaper advertisements and selection procedures); the cost of not filling or unsatisfactorily filling the vacancy; the productivity and the expected tenure of the worker.

Clear-cut results from evaluations of this kind can be derived from randomized experiments. Such analyses would need to compare the impact for individuals receiving a given service to the impact for persons who applied for, and were eligible for services, but were randomly assigned to a control group to which services were not provided. One can assume that the services provided by the PRES against a fee are cost-effective; otherwise, they would probably not be used. As already mentioned, the case of PES is different because their services are free of charge for users. But the services are not free with respect to society. PES are financed by taxpayers, who expect an efficient public body in return. Thus, randomized experiments would be particularly useful in the case of mediation services provided by PES. But, for obvious reasons, such experiments are highly unlikely. PES traditionally have been (and presumably will also be in the future) open to all clients. It would not be justifiable for PES services to be withheld from a designated group (however, see Björklund and Regnér, chap. 3 in this volume). Quasi-experimental design, by contrast, might be more feasible. For example, the PES could be asked to match a worker referred to a given vacancy with another similar job seeker who was not referred in a given period of time. In general, evaluation studies dealing with the microimpacts of employment services are still rare, though they have recently become more significant. The following examples are mainly taken from the United States. The studies examine the role of employment services with respect to job search outcomes, duration of vacancies, tenure and productivity of hired employees and the cost of hiring.

In several US studies the authors have asked whether the method of job search affects its outcome. Bortnick and Harrison Ports (1992) examine the job search methods applied by unemployed individuals. Data were taken from the Current Population Survey (CPS), which is a monthly household survey.

The approach taken in the study is to combine job search information from a given month with information from the following month, yielding a longitudinal perspective of the results of an individual's job search efforts. The job search method used by the unemployed individual in the first month was taken as the starting point, and its effect on his or her labour force status (employed, still unemployed, not in labour force) in the second month was then evaluated. Hence, the most common and the most successful methods of search can be calculated.

Other studies are based on a different approach. In a number of analyses PES-users are compared to similar nonusers on the basis of multiple regression models, whereby some observed factors that may affect job search outcomes (e. g. race, education and age) are held constant (see Jacobsen, 1994, for an overview). Typical questions asked in such studies are whether the use of the PES reduces the duration of joblessness or increases earnings. The type of data used in the studies varies. Some researchers rely on survey data, whereas others use process-generated data. As regards the validity of the studies, this will depend to a large extent on whether there are unobserved characteristics that effect both use of the PES and job search outcomes, and what kind of adjustments are made to account for the selectivity problem.

Job search outcomes have been dealt with from a different perspective in yet other studies, where the influence of various factors on the probability of the PES placing a given job seeker is analysed (e.g. Dercksen and de Koning, 1995; US General Accounting Office and Employment Service 1989, 1991). Differences in the cost-effectiveness of PES services are measured by controlling for external factors that influence the degree of difficulty in making a placement. If external factors, such as the labour market situation or worker characteristics, are held constant, the remaining variation in the likelihood of successful placement may be due to differences in management practices.

A very small number of studies have also been conducted on the effects of employment services on the filling of vacancies; for example, Ours (1994) studies the matching process by analysing the possible effects of different mediation methods on the duration of job vacancies. The author tries to explain hazard rates of vacancies using process-generated data. These hazard rates were calculated as the number of vacancies filled in a certain period by the PES or other recruitment channels divided by the number of vacancies still unfilled at the beginning of the period. Several possible determinants for the hazard rates were taken into account: required skills, characteristics of the employer and of the vacant job, local conditions and mediation methods. As already noted in section 2.1, mediation methods can differ with respect to intensity, that is, especially with regard to the use of the agencies' personnel capacities. In this respect Ours (1994) distinguishes between the effects of administrative matching and selective matching, that is, matching with or without careful screening of potential applicants.

The role of employment services with respect to the filling of vacancies is also the subject of the study by Bishop (1992), though the focus is on the quality and cost of job-matching. The quality aspect is captured by an analysis of the determinants of match profitability and productivity. Match profitability is considered to be high when there is a wide gap between a worker's productivity and his or her reservation wage. Productivity is measured by a comparison of expected productivity at the moment of hiring with realized productivity after the probationary period. Using employer survey data, Bishop (1992) examines the effects of different recruitment methods on the match profitability and productivity of the newly hired employee; several background characteristics (e.g. years of schooling, age, sex and race) are held constant within a multiple regression model. The other part of this extensive study is an assessment of direct hiring costs, that is, different costs resulting from the use of different recruitment methods. The costs are measured by the time that the firm devotes to recruiting, screening and interviewing job candidates.

3.3   Macroimpacts

At the microlevel, employment services can potentially facilitate the matching of labour and vacancies. An additional question is whether their activities lead to an increase in aggregate employment and a reduction in aggregate unemployment.

Employment services cannot, of course, correct serious imbalances on the labour market, such as high unemployment because, in general, they cannot create additional jobs for their clients. But the total number of vacancies has two components: the inflow and the average duration of vacancies.

Although the share of total vacancies made up of inflowing registrations might not be influenced by mediation activities, faster matching may, nevertheless, be achieved through more efficient employment services. Efficient employment services can reduce the duration of vacancies to a minimum, which is defined by an optimal matching of vacancies and job candidates. A shorter duration of vacancies at the microlevel (because of more efficient employment services) will not necessarily result in a corresponding increase in the number of employed persons. First, the effect might be weaker because firms are in competition with one another. The expansion in one firm as a consequence of (quicker) filling of vacancies could result in job losses and/or cancellation of vacancies in other firms. Second, should a vacancy be filled quickly because a worker is 'poached' from another firm, then a new vacancy would arise, which may be difficult to fill. Third, certain employment practices that have an impact on the total number of employed (e.g. temporary workers) might no longer be needed to the same extent were placement services more effective.

The potential impact of mediation activities on unemployment is another complex issue. The unemployment rate is the result of two different effects: the inflow of unemployed individuals and the average duration of unemployment spells. The UR curve in Figure 13.2 represents alternative combinations of inflow rates and duration figures, which lead to the same overall unemployment level, demonstrating that the level of unemployment can be reduced either by a decrease in the inflow rate and/or a decrease in the average duration of unemployment spells. In both cases a downward shift of the curve would be the result. We can also see that a movement leftwards along the curve would be equal to an improvement in the composition of unemployment, that is, higher inflow is accompanied by lower average duration. Job placement can influence the inflow rate, the average duration and the composition of unemployment.

Moreover, by supporting the matching process, efficient placement services contribute to a longer average duration of employment periods. They help place workers in the job in which they can be used most productively. As a consequence, mismatch will be less likely and the risk of becoming unemployed (due to a mismatch) will be reduced. If available jobs could be filled more rapidly and to a larger extent with unemployed job seekers, then the average duration of unemployment would decline. Although the possible effects of efficient employment services on employment and unemployment appear to be more or less positive, the effects on the composition of unemployment might be negative. Because efficient employment services would concentrate on the most promising job seekers when selecting applicants, there would be a progressive concentration of difficult-to-place persons among the remaining unemployed.

As for evaluation at the macrolevel, the main question in this context concerns the unknown effects of PES activities on employment and unemployment. The problem here is that vacancy-filling and placement of unemployed persons by the PES do not necessarily influence the labour market at all. Positive employment effects only result if jobs are filled by the PES that otherwise would not have been filled by other recruitment channels at all, or would have been filled at a slower pace. Positive effects on unemployment can only be achieved if the PES place unemployed job seekers who would otherwise not, or not that quickly, have found a job through other search channels. The existence and the extent of benefits for the labour market, therefore, depend on whether PES activities are accompanied by deadweight, substitution and displacement effects.

PES activities entail deadweight effects when employers and job seekers would have found similar workers or jobs by other means as quickly as they

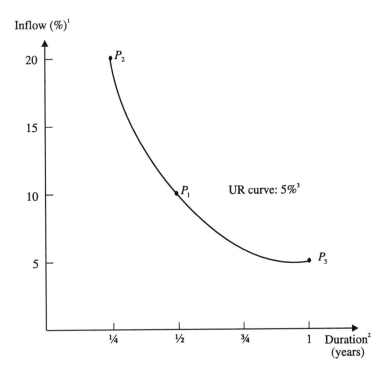

Notes

1 Inflow $= \dfrac{\text{newly registered persons during the year} \times 100}{\text{labour force}}$

2 Duration $= \dfrac{\text{average stock of unemployed}}{\text{newly registered persons during the year}}$

3 Unemployment Rate (UR) = Inflow × Duration

Figure 13.2   Breakdown of Unemployment

found them through the PES. Substitution effects are the adverse effects on the job search of workers who do not receive PES services and on firms that do not register with the PES. The resulting costs at the macrolevel may be: decreases in the short- and long-term earnings of and/or increases in transfer payments to non-PES-users; increases in the time it takes to fill vacancies and subsequent worker turnover among firms not registering with the PES. In the extreme case it could be that all user benefits are exactly offset by costs imposed on others. Finally, PES activities entail displacement effects when they drive out other suppliers of mediation services, such as private agencies.

As shown in the previous section, it is not easy to measure the micro-impacts of employment service activities, and it is even more difficult to assess empirically their impact on the labour market as a whole. In general, a detailed analysis of macroimpacts would require simulation models that use a set of interrelated variables and cover the global economy. As long as such models are neither available nor have been used for this purpose, one has to rely on more pragmatic approaches.

Clark (1988) attempts to explain the output qualities (measured as the number of individuals placed in permanent jobs) and production costs (output/staff ratio) of PES and PRES using multiple regression models. His data is taken both from the US Employment Service and a major PRES company, 'Snelling and Snelling'. Osberg (1993) deals with the job search methods of jobless workers, focussing on the determinants of their success in the early 1980s. The central question in the study is whether social benefits resulting from PES activities vary over the business cycle.

4   EFFICIENCY OF EMPLOYMENT SERVICES: FINDINGS OF EVALUATION RESEARCH

In empirical terms we know a great deal about the performance of employment services, but much less about the impacts of their activities. In Table 13.1 several PES performance indicators are compared across countries, and significant differences can be observed. But even in the countries with the highest PES penetration rates, no more than 25 per cent of all vacancies are filled through PES. In other words, the vast majority of vacancies are filled by other recruitment channels. Several national surveys on the recruitment behaviour of firms and on the search behaviour of job seekers indicate that newspaper advertisements and informal contacts are the most important channels for acquisition of information (OECD, 1992). The penetration rates of PRES are generally lower than those of PES (see Table 13.2). However, there are two countries where the opposite pattern holds: the United States and Switzerland.

There are indications that the penetration rates of PES have declined over the last 20 years. After a reduction in penetration rates had been recorded as early as the 1960s and 1970s in some countries (e.g. Germany, the Netherlands and the United States), the trend obviously continued during the 1980s. For instance, the following countries had higher PES penetration rates at the beginning of the 1980s (OECD, 1984): Austria (23 per cent), Belgium (20 per cent) and Switzerland (10 per cent). The reasons for the decline are manifold. First, the number of low-skilled jobs has declined in recent decades, especially in manufacturing. Many of these jobs were filled by PES serving their primary

*Table 13.2   PRES Performance Indicators (OECD Countries: Data from
              the Early 1990s)*

Countries	Number of PRES agencies (or licence holders)	Placements (1000)	Penetration rate (%)
CH	1 747	92	18
DK	340	9	—
GB	13 642	270	5
IR	250	—	—
NL	800	90	8
NZ	80	—	—
US	14 000	—	—

Note
— = data not available.

Source
Entwicklungen bei der Organisation der Arbeitsvermittlung by U. Walwei, 1995, ISSA working
paper no. AC/28/2, International Social Security Association.

clientele, that is, the unemployed, reentrants and new entrants into the labour
market. Second, during the period of high and increasing unemployment, the
welfare administration imposed new burdens on the PES and reduced capacities for mediation services. Third, self-service systems have been set up in
many countries, especially for job seekers, which, because of measurement
difficulties, potentially depress measured success and penetration rates (for
details, see section 3.1). Fourth, due to their emphasis on placing the long-term
unemployed, the reputation of PES may have suffered with employers. The
ISSA survey contains evidence that the main complaint of employers (in addition to insufficient screening of candidates) is the frequent inability of PES to
supply suitable workers (see Table 13.3). In other words, the stigma attached
to some candidates proposed by the PES seems to stigmatize the PES themselves (Walwei, 1995).

Moreover, PES are faced with other new challenges. With the completion
of the Single European Market, further moves must be made towards eliminating remaining impediments, such as an inadequate flow of information about
available jobs and job seekers. The establishment of EURES (Bosscher, 1994)
has been of special importance in facilitating cross-border mobility and transparency. EURES provides a European-wide exchange of vacancies and job
seekers, information about living and working conditions in the different
countries, and a better coordination of national employment policies. It can be

Table 13.3   Motives for Enterprises to Use PES

	Relative importance[1]
FOR (n = 27 countries)	
Need to use all recruitment methods	1.8
Low cost	1.7
Quality and speed of response	2.1
Social responsibility for unemployed persons	2.5
State subsidies	2.2
AGAINST (n = 25 countries)	
Unwillingness of unemployed to work	1.9
Applicants unsuitable	1.6
Services too bureaucratic	2.1

Note
1   There were three possible answers to both questions in the survey: (1) often cited, (2) cited in some cases and (3) none. Answers were weighed using the figures in parentheses and averages calculated. National experts in the area of employment services provided the answers.

Source
Entwicklungen bei der Organisation der Arbeitsvermittlung by U. Walwei, 1995, ISSA working paper no. AC/28/2, International Social Security Association.

seen as a network of the national PES. Especially with respect to internationally relevant vacancies and mobile job seekers, EURES requires high-quality inputs. At the moment, it is by no means clear how it can be ensured that— apart from the border regions—not only national 'nonsellers' are offered by national PES to feed the international system. The scepticism is founded on two facts. First, as already mentioned, the typical market segment served by PES generally does not include many jobs for mobile job seekers, such as 'Euro-executives' or university graduates. Second, because of severe national unemployment problems and the exclusiveness of information about vacancies at the national level, there seems to be no real incentive to pass on interesting job offers to the EURES system.

In contrast to PES activities, the number of PRES agencies and the placements achieved by them increased considerably in the 1980s and early 1990s (see Buttler and Walwei, 1995). The growth of the business is linked to the trend towards regulatory liberalization, the growing difficulties of firms in finding skilled labour, and their policy of externalizing certain functions of personnel departments (see Table 13.4). In order to meet the needs of their clients, PRES are highly specialized in terms of functions (e.g. selection and recruitment), regions and occupations. PRES are mainly active in large metropolitan regions;

their customers are more likely to be large enterprises and employed job seekers; they deal in vacancies requiring high or specialized skills. Because the placement spectrum ranges from executives to domestic staff, one can argue that wherever shortfalls in regional or occupational market niches occur for employers, attractive market segments are apparently available for PRES.

The comparison of PES and PRES market shares by segments of the labour market suggests that there is no or only little competition between the two. In countries where PES and PRES coexist, the situation can be described more or less as a complementary relationship. The PES give priority to placement of long-term unemployed. Primarily job seekers with relatively low skills and corresponding jobs are registered with the PES. In contrast, PRES deal mainly with jobs requiring high or special skills and, therefore, contact experienced job

*Table 13.4   Motives for Enterprises to Use PRES (*n = 13 Countries)

	Relative importance[1]
Contracting out of personnel department tasks	1.5
Provision of highly skilled workers and executives	1.5
Quick proposals	1.7

Note
1   See Note to Table 13.3.

Source
Entwicklungen bei der Organisation der Arbeitsvermittlung by U. Walwei, 1995, ISSA working paper no. AC/28/2, International Social Security Association.

seekers who are already employed. Table 13.1 above is further evidence that the performance of PES (as measured by the penetration rate) seems not only to depend on the given institutional model, whether PES monopoly or coexistence of PES and PRES. On the one hand, a monopoly does not, as such, guarantee a comparatively high penetration rate for the PES. On the other hand, coexistence does not necessarily yield a low penetration rate. Therefore, the extent to which these services are used by market participants appears to depend basically on the level of attractiveness of the market segment addressed by each service. For example, the main reason for the low penetration rate of PES in the United States as well as Switzerland is (apart from their relatively modest staffing and resource levels) to be seen in their focus on the difficult-to-place unemployed. This may result in a considerable loss of reputation among employers. In such a scenario the PES could eventually even lose their ability to serve the disadvantaged, as was the case in the United States (see Bishop, 1992).

Comparatively low PRES penetration rates may have other causes, as the case of Denmark shows. Even two years after liberalization, the PRES still had quite low penetration rates. A number of reasons for this phenomenon have been found (see Csonka, 1993, for details). First, liberalization took place during a period of economic stagnation and rising unemployment. Because there was a lack of vacancies to be filled, the potential markets for private agencies were also not available. Second, it obviously takes some time for PRES to establish their businesses and for firms and job seekers to involve them in their search efforts. Third, the lack of licensing and other quality standards, especially in the initial period, had—at least in certain sectors, for example, artists and overseas placement—a generally negative effect on the reputation of PRES because incidences of misuse were made public.

It is, of course, important and interesting to know how often and why PES as well as PRES are used. However, the benefits to the users and to the labour market can be reflected neither by absolute nor by relative figures. There are only a few evaluation studies that may provide answers to these questions. Their methodological design and the problems involved have been described above (see sections 3.2 and 3.3). The results should be interpreted with caution in view of the methods as well as the data used. Regarding job search outcomes for the unemployed, Bortnick and Harrison Ports (1992) found that 'checking with employers' was the search method most often used (approximately 72 per cent of those covered in the sample) followed by 'placed and answered advertisements' and the 'public employment agency'. Although PRES are obviously one of the least important search channels used by the unemployed, those who enlisted their services had the highest likelihood of finding employment in 1991. However, the results cannot be interpreted as suggesting that the use of PRES is the most efficient search method because the authors did or could not control for background variables, such as skills or qualifications of unemployed job seekers. Nevertheless, if job search through PRES is successful, even for unemployed job seekers, who may not use them very frequently, one could also think about establishing more possibilities for cooperation between PES and PRES. Although the complementarity of PES and PRES obviously restricts the scope for cooperation, limited areas of cooperation are not excluded, for example, bilateral recommendations in order to increase the matching possibilities for both types of agencies. In terms of the economy as a whole, cooperation between PRES and PES would also have the advantage that the exclusiveness of information in the private sector (which can be seen as a market failure) would be removed and the transparency of the labour market perhaps improved.

Quite similar conclusions have been drawn in several studies comparing PES-users to similar nonusers regarding their job search outcome (Jacobsen, 1994). Research of this kind suggests that placement services provided by PES substantially reduce the duration of joblessness. PES services also appear to have some positive effects on subsequent earnings. Because there are no direct user costs for PES services, the PES appear to be highly cost-effective. Further conclusions drawn in the studies are that the effectiveness of PES seems to be greater for women than for men, and greater after unemployment benefits have been exhausted than prior to exhaustion. Mediation services offered by PES also seem to play an important role in reducing unemployment insurance payments. The PES, therefore, can, in the view of Jacobson (1994), be seen 'as a "backstop" aiding job seekers who lack good information about the pay and location of jobs, or have failed to find jobs using other job search methods' (p. 31).

More mixed results regarding the effectiveness of employment services are presented in the very few impact studies that deal with the demand side. Ours (1994) found on the basis of process-generated data that, through intensive mediation (including screening), PES significantly reduce average vacancy duration, indicating that the PES might be able to improve the recruitment process. In contrast, Bishop (1992) found in his study based on an employer survey, in which several worker background variables were held constant, that referrals from PES (including other public agencies) were less profitable (by about 15 per cent of average productivity) than workers acquired from other recruitment channels. But his results also suggest that referrals from PRES were not significantly better (with respect to productivity) than new hires recruited through other channels (and even compared to the PES). Therefore, Bishop (1992) wonders how it can be explained, on the one hand, that employers request any referrals from PES and, on the other hand, that they pay substantial fees to PRES. One can expect lower hiring costs if these recruitment sources are used. But, comparing the time devoted to recruiting, screening and interviewing job candidates, it appears from Bishop's study that decision-making takes less time when informal channels are used and much more time when PES or PRES are involved. From this Bishop (1992) concludes that 'it would appear that employers either (a) are unaware of how poorly they fare with PES and PRES referrals, (b) are forced into using them by an absence of other applicants for a hard to fill job or (c) hire referrals from public agencies for altruistic reasons (e.g. they have been asked to give a disadvantaged or handicapped person a chance)' (p. 13).

I mentioned two studies above in which the overall efficiency of employment services at the macrolevel is investigated (Clark, 1988; Osberg, 1993). On the basis of a comparison of output qualities and production costs of PES and PRES, the notion of nonoptimal government output seems to be supported by the results presented in Clark (1988). However, the reliability of the results depends on the assumption that PES and PRES produce similar outputs. Clark (1988) measures output quality in terms of the number of individuals placed in permanent jobs, and on the basis of these results PES applicants appear to be harder to place because they are less skilled and to an extent less motivated. As a consequence, the data—not surprisingly—reveal higher costs for the public agencies. Osberg (1993) deals with benefits resulting from activities by Canadian PES and finds that social returns were substantial during the recession in 1983, but comparatively low during the boom periods 1981 and 1986. An explanation for the results might be that job search methods vary considerably over the business cycle.

5   CONCLUSIONS AND CONSEQUENCES FOR FUTURE EVALUATION

Summing up, one can conclude that the potential of mediation services provided by employment services of any kind consists primarily in being able to fill vacancies with suitable candidates and in finding suitable vacancies for job seekers as quickly as possible. At first glance, it seems to be of secondary importance whether this happens through public or private intermediaries. What is decisive is that institutional organization and regulation are designed such that maximum use can be made of the potential of mediation services. PRES are increasingly a part of labour market reality. Both current and planned liberalization measures will reinforce this trend. The advantage of PRES appears to be that they often address a different client group to that of their public counterparts. The creation of additional placement capacities and the opportunity to use PRES as an additional search or recruitment method would improve job-matching at least in certain market segments (e.g. vacancies with high or specialized requirements). At the moment, we do not have enough quantitative information about the services provided by PRES or their activities. In most OECD countries there is no requirement for private agencies to report any statistics. In order to fill the existing gaps in knowledge, surveys and analyses dealing with the use of PRES are required. This information may provide hints about what the market will be able to offer and in what areas public intervention will be necessary. Further evaluation researchers should also investigate whether the complementarity of PRES and PES exists *per se*, or only as a result of coexistence. Longitudinal analyses aimed at explaining shifts of the PES penetration rate (also in certain labour market segments) in countries where liberalization was recently introduced (e.g. Austria, Germany and Sweden) could constitute an approach to these questions.

But the current structural problems in the labour market (particularly the large numbers of long-term unemployed and existing skill bottlenecks) cannot, of course, be solved only by greater scope for the highly specialized

PRES. The main problem is to match the workers and the jobs that have been filtered out by growing competition on both sides of the market. In this respect the effectiveness of the PES still plays a key role because they have all the relevant information as well as the potential to combine placement with active labour market policies. PES also try to extend their full range of services to people in all localities, independently of the ups and downs of the economic cycle. However, PES placement activities have to be carefully evaluated in terms of cost and benefits. The mere number of placements reflects neither the effort invested nor the benefit of each placement. Such an evaluation is all the more important because there are indications that changes in the operation of job centres to counter increasing financial pressures may reduce their effectiveness in helping disadvantaged job seekers (OECD, 1984). For example, if a job seeker's own search in the labour market is made easier by the use of self-service systems, one also has to think about the size of placement staff. Greater emphasis on self-service must not necessarily lead to corresponding staff cuts but could also entail reallocation of personnel, for example, to tasks directly addressing the needs of the long-term unemployed. More studies on impact evaluation would be required for one to figure out to what extent the different types of services (e.g. self-service or intensive mediation) are needed, and it would be beneficial if more use were made of experiments in studies of this kind. For example, the effectiveness of different 'service packages' can be analysed if individuals (belonging to a certain target group) are randomly chosen. The advantage is that no individual is favoured or disfavoured according to *ex-ante* judgement. In addition, impact evaluation studies are a necessary precondition for performance measurement. They are needed to define reasonable performance standards, thus enabling cross-office comparisons of relative efficiency. Because of the complex interaction of factors, however, a great deal of additional work is required to determine which variables and estimation procedures should be used to measure performance as well as to define performance goals. In this context, too, one might think about using experiments more frequently. Comparative 'before-and-after' studies can be based on 'experiment regions' and control regions. Although the investigation of changes from 'before' to 'after' may be concerned with the development of performance indicators, a design of this kind would make it possible (e.g. by using mismatch indicators) to even analyse macroimpacts.

REFERENCES

Abraham, K. (1991), 'Mismatch and Labour Mobility: Some Final Remarks', in F. Padoa-Schioppa (ed.), *Mismatch and Labour Mobility*, Cambridge: Cambridge University Press, pp. 453–80.

Bishop, J. (1992), *Improving Job-worker Matching in the U.S. Labour Market*, working paper 92–40, Ithaca/NY: Cornell University, Center for Advanced Human Resource Studies.

Blanchard, O. J. and P. Diamond (1989), 'The Beveridge Curve', *Brookings Papers on Economic Activity*, 1, 1–60.

Bortnick, S. and M. Harrison Ports (1992), 'Job Search Methods of the Unemployed', *Monthly Labor Review*, 1991, 115, 29–35.

Bosscher, A. (1994), 'Introduction: Free Movement of Work and Migration', in Commission of the European Communities and Department of International Law of the Catholic University of Louvain UCL (eds), *The Future of the Social Policy*, Louvain-la-Neuve: Louvain University Press, pp. 199–206.

Buttler, F. and U. Walwei (1995), 'Different Institutional Arrangements for Job Placement', in F. Buttler, W. Franz, R. Schettkat and D. Soskice (eds), *Institutional Frameworks and Labor Market Performance. Comparative Views on the U.S. and German Economies*, London/New York: Routledge, pp. 248–59.

Clark, W. (1988), 'Production Costs and Output Qualities in Public and Private Agencies', *Journal of Labour Economics*, 11, 348–86.

Csonka, A. (1993), *Liberalization of Job-centre Services*, Copenhagen: The Danish National Institute of Social Research.

Dercksen, W. J. and J. de Koning (1995), 'The New Public Employment Service in the Netherlands (1991–1994)', in *EALE Proceedings*, Vol. 6, 7th Annual Conference, September 7–10, 1995.

Franz, W. (1991), 'Match and Mismatch on the German Labour Market', in F. Padoa-Schioppa (ed.), *Mismatch and Labour Mobility*, Cambridge: Cambridge University Press, pp. 105–39.

Hansen, B. (1970), 'Excess Demand, Unemployment, Vacancies, and Wages', *Quarterly Journal of Economics*, 84, 1–23.

International Labour Office (1994), 'The Role of Private Employment Agencies in the Functioning of Labour Markets', *Report VI*, International Labour Conference, 81st session, Geneva.

Jackman, R., C. Pissarides and S. Savouri (1990), 'Labour Market Policies and Unemployment in the OECD', *Economic Policy*, 11, 449–89.

Jacobsen, L. (1994), 'The Effectiveness of the US Employment Service', 2nd draft for the Advisory Commission on Unemployment Compensation. (Unpublished manuscript)

OECD (1984), *The Public Employment Service*, Paris: OECD.

OECD (1992), 'The Public Employment Service in Japan, Norway, Spain, and the United Kingdom', *OECD Employment Outlook*, 117–51.

Osberg, L. (1993), 'Fishing in Different Pools: Job Search Strategies and Job-finding Success in Canada in the Early 1980s', *Journal of Law and Economics*, 31, 379–93.

Ours, J. v. (1994), 'Matching Unemployed and Vacancies at the Public Employment Office', *Empirical Economics*, 19, 37–54.

Spence, M. (1973), 'Job Market Signaling', *Quarterly Journal of Economics*, 87, 355–76.

US General Accounting Office and Employment Service (1989), *Variation in Local Office Performance*, GAO/HRD, 89–116 BR, 3 August 1989.

US General Accounting Office and Employment Service (1991), *Improved Leadership Needed for Better Performance*, GAO/HRD, 91–88, 6 August 1991.

Walwei, U. (1995), *Entwicklungen bei der Organisation der Arbeitsvermittlung*, ISSA working paper no. AC/28/2, International Social Security Association.

Yavas, A. (1994), 'Middlemen in Bilateral Search Markets', *Journal of Labor Economics*, 12, 406–9.

J71
J78, J16

431-61

Europe

14. Occupational Segregation, Discrimination and Equal Opportunity

Jill Rubery, Colette Fagan and Friederike Maier

Gender segregation of employment is an important and persistent characteristic of western industrial societies. Policies to moderate or reduce segregation have significance for a variety of reasons. First, there is a commitment to equal treatment of men and women in the labour market in most western economies, including the United States and the European Union,[1] and gender segregation of employment may be a symptom and a cause of continuing gender inequality. Second, understanding the processes that result in the persistent gender segregation yields important insights into the overall operation of labour market systems, providing answers to otherwise perhaps mystifying phenomena—such as why most new jobs are taken by those outside the labour market and not by the registered unemployed, or why part-time work is adopted in some job areas and sectors and not in others. Third, gender segregation of employment raises questions about how efficiency and equity in labour markets is defined. From one perspective current patterns of gender segregation may be regarded as evidence of gender diversity. Even if women's potential skills are underutilized in the work force, welfare may still be maximized if it is assumed that women enjoy comparative advantage in domestic labour. Current preferences are taken to be independent of labour market systems and processes, and policy intervention is only justified in this case in areas where there is a mismatch between these current preferences and labour market opportunities.

An alternative perspective regards preferences as largely endogenous to the labour market system, such that the current household division of labour is in part a response to the gendered labour market in which women can expect a lower return to working than men (e.g. Humphries and Rubery, 1995). Therefore, women's decisions over training and jobs are influenced both by social expectations regarding the domestic division of labour and by their assessments of the realistic employment opportunities in specific labour market segments. The gender-segregated labour market imposes constraints on women's options, constraints that are reflected in women's expressed prefer-

---

1 The main focus of the chapter will be on European Union Member States, but with some reference to experience in the United States.

ences for particular types of jobs and employment careers. Options to make nontraditional choices are constrained by employers' use of gender as a useful indicator of potential behaviour and attitudes. This second perspective provides a much wider basis for policy intervention to change the nature of constraints on choices to be made by men and women and, hence, to improve the match between skills, aptitudes and jobs.

Gender segregation may be regarded not only as a symptom of gender inequality but also as a process that facilitates the production and reproduction of gender inequality. Male-dominated and female-dominated occupations provide a basis for continuing to differentiate the terms and conditions on which men and women are employed. Once the second perspective is recognized, the policy issue becomes not solely that of opening up job opportunities in nontraditional job areas but also of improving employment conditions in women's current employment areas. The target of policy is not the elimination of gender segregation but the elimination of the penalties attached to segregation, whether these be the constraints on women to exercise their full potential and skills in the labour market because of horizontal or vertical segregation or because the jobs in which women are clustered are undervalued. Segregation might even not be regarded as in itself a problem, given, for example, the high degree of gender equality achieved in the Nordic countries for pay levels despite highly sex segregated Nordic labour markets. However, income equality may be considered only one dimension to labour market equality, and the maintenance of gender segregation still leaves open the possibility that gender inequalities could increase in the future through widening occupational differentials.

However, changing the pattern of segregation is by no means a sufficient condition for gender equality. As we discuss below, the entry of women into nontraditional jobs may itself be associated with a transformation of the status and pay attached to those jobs, or it may lead to the development of occupational subdivisions that recreate a gendered division of labour. It may be more appropriate to regard the labour market as having interlocking gender and occupational hierarchies such that at each level of skill or qualification we find women in a lower-paid or lower-status position than men (Gottschall, 1995). These comments suggest that policy to reduce gender equality is more complex than the standard approaches of either positive or affirmative action or equal pay legislation and that, as a consequence, the evaluation of policy measures should involve a more holistic approach that identifies changes in the structure of jobs as well as changes in the gender composition of the work force. A broader and more qualitative approach to evaluation would also be supported by feminist writers who consider that gender equality does not solely or primarily involve the promotion of women within current labour market structures but involves, as the 'long agenda' (Cockburn, 1991), the transformation of the gendered and hierarchical structure of the labour market. Such transformational objectives are difficult to assess within policy evaluation analysis, but this wider perspective on the meaning of equality should be borne in mind.

This chapter is organized as follows. In the first section we review briefly the evidence of the extent and changes in gender segregation and inequality over recent years. In the second section we review the different theoretical explanations for the development and reproduction of gender segregation in the labour market in order to identify the nature of the problem and where the costs and benefits of the current system of gender segregation lie. In the third section we review the available evidence on the evaluation of the impact of gender equality policies. In the conclusions we propose a set of principles for policy development and evaluation in the future.

1   TRENDS IN GENDER SEGREGATION OF EMPLOYMENT

Gender segregation occurs across a range of employment dimensions. Women tend to be overrepresented relative to their share of the work force in a limited range of occupations; industries; types of firms; and particular forms of employment, such as part time or homeworking. These different forms of segregation are raised here primarily as a reminder that the labour market is not simply divided by occupations. Indeed as we have already argued, what matters in policy considerations are the penalties of segregation along a particular employment dimension. If the quality of employment offered between part-time and full-time jobs or between large and small firms differs significantly, then these dimensions to segregation will add significantly to the problem of gender inequality. However, we will concentrate for the most part on the more conventional measures of segregation, that is, those relating to segregation by occupation.

Gender segregation is traditionally measured by summary index measures (see Table 14.1 for data on Member States of the European Union and our discussion of measurement problems in section 3). The best way to measure and compare segregation across countries is to use a disaggregated occupational data set based on harmonized classifications. As these criteria are difficult to fulfil, Table 14.1 provides information only on the 12 European Member States from 1983 through 1990 (for details, see section 3 on Monitoring and Evaluation). These results revealed a persistently high level of segregation at the aggregate level of the labour market, with little change over the 1980s (Barbezat, 1993; Rubery and Fagan, 1993). This rather static picture of only small net changes in the level of segregation revealed by index measures

Table 14.1 Indices Measuring Trends in Occupational Segregation (All in Employment 1990)

Countries ranked by level of segregation	1983	1987	1990
Denmark			
Index of Segregation	—	—	0.59 (1)
Index of Dissimilarity	—	—	0.59 (= 1)
United Kingdom			
Index of Segregation	0.59 (2)	0.57 (1)	0.56 (2)
Index of Dissimilarity	0.62 (2)	0.59 (2)	0.57 (= 3)
Luxembourg			
Index of Segregation	0.61 (1)	0.56 (2)	0.54 (3)
Index of Dissimilarity	0.63 (1)	0.61 (1)	0.59 (= 1)
France			
Index of Segregation	0.53 (3)	0.53 (3)	0.53 (= 4)
Index of Dissimilarity	0.54 (5)	0.54 (= 6)	0.54 (= 6)
Ireland			
Index of Segregation	0.52 (4)	0.52 (= 4)	0.53 (= 4)
Index of Dissimilarity	0.57 (3)	0.56 (= 3)	0.56 (5)
Federal Republic of Germany			
Index of Segregation	—	0.52 (= 4)	0.51 (= 6)
Index of Dissimilarity	—	0.55 (5)	0.54 (= 6)
Netherlands			
Index of Segregation	—	0.50 (= 6)	0.51 (= 6)
Index of Dissimilarity	—	0.54 (= 6)	0.57 (= 3)
Belgium			
Index of Segregation	0.49 (6)	0.49 (8)	0.48 (= 8)
Index of Dissimilarity	0.55 (4)	0.56 (= 3)	0.47 (9)
Spain			
Index of Segregation	—	0.46 (9)	0.48 (= 8)
Index of Dissimilarity	—	0.51 (9)	0.53 (8)
Portugal			
Index of Segregation	—	0.43 (10)	0.43 (10)
Index of Dissimilarity	—	0.47 (10)	0.46 (10)
Greece			
Index of Segregation	0.50 (5)	0.50 (= 6)	0.35 (11)
Index of Dissimilarity	0.53 (6)	0.53 (8)	0.43 (11)
Number of countries ranked	6	10	11

Note
The fall in segregation in Greece between 1987 and 1990 is mainly due to the coding of agricultural employment.

Sources
Eurostat Labour Force Survey; International Standard Classification of Occupations (ISCO) (68) two-digit data. From 'Occupational Segregation of Women and Men in the European Community', by J. Rubery and C. Fagan, 1993, *Social Europe Supplement*, 3.

disguises divergent processes and trends of desegregation and resegregation within different parts of the employment structure. On the one hand, there has been a widespread increase in the share of high-level professional occupations held by women, not only in Europe but also in the United States. On the other hand, segregation in intermediate and low-level jobs has continued and even increased in some countries. Women have been increasing their share of clerical work, even in countries where this work was already highly feminized. Further down the occupational hierarchy the gendered division of labour has shown little sign of change, at least within the Member States of the European Union. Most manual production and transport jobs are still done by men, and most low-skill service jobs are done by women (Rubery and Fagan, 1993).

Even the entry of women into higher-level jobs and some male-dominated jobs has not necessarily resulted in an unambiguous reduction in segregation for two main reasons. First, women professionals remain disproportionately concentrated in traditionally female professions associated with care work. Much of this work is concentrated in the public sector, and in many instances women's share of male-dominated professions is also higher in the public than the private sector. This division between the public and private sector may become an increasingly important feature of gender segregation for this group of workers in the future, as may other employment dimensions such as employment contract or firm size. Second, where women have gained entry into nontraditional jobs, it has often been associated with a downgrading of the status of the occupation or the concentration of women in the less prestigious sections of the occupation or profession (Crompton and Sanderson, 1990; Reskin and Roos, 1990).

The increasing integration of women into the wage economy has so far not resulted in the development of a fully integrated and nonsegregated or nonsegmented employment system, but neither is the persistence of segregation associated with a stable and unchanging pattern of employment allocation by gender. While traditional gender roles may inhibit processes of labour market adjustment, gender differentiation may also provide an implicit or even explicit dimension to the process of employment restructuring. Moreover, where employment adjustment appears to be leading to changes in the traditional allocation of labour by gender, one needs to consider whether the longer-term outcome is likely to be greater gender integration or a process of resegregation around a new employment pattern.

The other traditional indicator of gender equality is the gender pay gap. Table 14.2 shows that progress towards gender pay equality, at least within European countries, also tended to slow down or even to falter in the 1980s. The United States are an exception to this trend, for the gender pay gap, having remained static during the 1970s when the European pay gap narrowed, fell significantly by 12 percentage points over the 1980s (with women's earnings increasing from 63 per cent to 75 per cent of men's from 1979 to 1989). However, this narrowing gap reflects the decreasing real wages of men as much as significant real wage gains for women (Mishel and Bernstein, 1993). On both pay and segregation indicators, therefore, gender equality remains an unfulfilled policy objective.

Table 14.2   Ratios of Female to Male Hourly Earnings in Industry (NACE 1 to 5): Manual Workers

	1980	1985	1991	1993
Belgium	70.3	74.3	75.6	75.7
Denmark	86.1	85.8	84.5	84.5
Federal Republic of Germany	72.4	72.8	73.8	74.4
Greece	67.5	78.8	79.2	77.1
Spain	—	—	72.2	77.1
France	78.3	80.8	80.3	80.8
Ireland	68.7	67.3	69.5	69.7
Italy	83.2	82.7	79.3[a]	—
Luxembourg	64.7	65.9	68.0	70.6
Netherlands	73.1	73.6	76.2	77.8
Portugal	—	—	70.8	72.7
United Kingdom	69.8	67.1	67.2	68.4

Note
a Calculated from national data (see 'Wage Determination and Sex Segregation in Employment in the European Community' by J. Rubery and C. Fagan, 1994, *Social Europe Supplement*, 4).

Source
Eurostat, *Earnings: Industry and Services*, various issues.

2   PROCESSES OF OCCUPATIONAL SEGREGATION AND THEIR IMPLICATIONS FOR POLICY

Contributions to theories of gender segregation have been made from a wide range of disciplines—economics, sociology, psychology, political science and organizational theory. However, for the purpose of this chapter we attempt to synthesize explanations of segregation from a primarily economic or labour market perspective, drawing upon other disciplinary perspectives to deepen the understanding of labour market processes.

2.1 The Dynamics of Segregation

Explanations of segregation need to be capable of providing both an understanding of current patterns of segregation and of how segregation patterns change over time from both a demand side and a supply side perspective. On the one hand, there may be a mutual conditioning between the supply and the demand side such that preferences and expectations of the gendered work force conform to the gender structure of labour demand, reinforcing the existing 'gender order' (Connell, 1987). On the other hand, pressures for change may come from either the demand side, that is, employer practices, or from the attitudes, expectations and actions of women themselves. A further requirement of any satisfactory theoretical framework is that it must be historically and institutionally rooted, such that it is capable of explaining both the similarities and the differences in segregation patterns over time and between countries.

Previous work on the dynamics of change in women's employment over the business cycle (Rubery, 1988), and more recent contributions to the analysis of changes in gender segregation by Reskin and Roos (1990), have provided the basis for identifying the key factors that underpin the system of gender segregation. Let us turn first to the factors that may lead to a gendered pattern of employment from the demand side. They can be categorized under four headings.

1. Diversity of skills: segregation may result from men and women offering different skills in the labour market, whether they be innate or learned skills and whether they reflect different socialization processes or different investments in human capital.
2. Gendered labour supply conditions and labour market segmentation: segregation may also result from differences in the terms and conditions—pay, working hours and job security, for example—on which men and women are available for work. These differences arise from a combination of supply-side constraints on women's employment, including the domestic division of labour and the unemployment and social security systems based on male breadwinner models of the family economy, and demand-side discrimination that results in crowding and the lowering of women's opportunity wage for the same productivity. Employers may exploit these differences in labour supply by segregating men and women into different jobs where different terms and conditions can be applied. Gender segregation may also be associated with divisions in the industrial structure based on productivity and capacity to pay. Firms with low capacity to pay may be particularly likely to recruit from disadvantaged groups such as women.
3. Statistical discrimination: employers may perceive men and women as offering different risks, with women more likely to quit, thereby leading

employers to reject women for jobs with high levels of firm-specific investment.

4. Taste discrimination: employers may exercise discrimination, in the sense of negative tastes, against the employment of either men or women in nontraditional jobs. Employers may be exercising their own tastes in circumstances where the market allows them discretion, or they may be responding to the views of customers or other workers, or they may simply be subconsciously reflecting the norms of the society in which they themselves have been socialized.

These four factors can provide insights into both the current patterns of discrimination and the dynamic development of segregation patterns resulting from changes in employer policies. As for the diversity of skills approach, the belief in fundamentally different gender attributes has been a major factor in explaining or at least legitimating gender segregation. Although these beliefs provide a basis for a segregation and ghettoization of women, they also provide a basis on which patterns of segregation may change over time. For example, the association of women with effective communication and social skills has recently increased the demand for female labour in certain nontraditional jobs, where there has been increased emphasis placed on customer care and other social skills (Reskin and Roos, 1990).

The second factor, differences in terms and conditions of employment, can provide both an explanation of, or may be interpreted as, a consequence of segregation. The latter approach is consistent with Bergmann's (1974) crowding model, in which the lower pay for women results from the crowding of women into a narrow range of jobs, leading to excess supply and lower earnings levels. However, Bergmann (1986) has herself suggested that the direction of causation is not always from segregation to lower pay, for where women do succeed in making entry into nontraditional jobs there may be an incentive for firms to establish subdivisions within these job categories to segregate male and female labour. This strategy enables firms to pay women wages that reflect their marginal opportunity wage in the external labour market. This brings the theory closer to the perspective that sees the different supply conditions for female labour as a causal factor in the creation of segregated labour markets. Employers divide their job structures into male and female segments to minimize the cost of meeting male expectations of high wages, job security, full-time employment and so forth (Beechey, 1977; Siltanen, 1994).

Differences in labour supply conditions may provide important clues to the dynamics of changing patterns of segregation. If an occupation becomes less attractive to men because it moves down the labour market hierarchy, as measured by pay, status, promotion prospects or perhaps security, employers may have to consider new sources of recruits. Employers may face the choice of either moving down the educational hierarchy or alternatively considering a change in the gender of the work force recruited. Thus, women may move into traditionally male job areas when firms find their traditional sources of male labour drying up while the female labour queue offers higher-quality and/or potentially more stable and committed labour at the given wage rate. In other circumstances firms may actively decide to change the gender composition of the work force when they seek to change the pay, status, skill level or other characteristics of the jobs to fit new market or technological conditions (Reskin and Roos, 1990).

The third factor, the perceived greater risk of employment interruption, provides an important antidote to the notion that individuals exercise free choice in their selection of occupations. Firm-specific skills are arguably more widespread than often assumed in the literature (Rubery, 1994), and where such skills are important, employers act as gatekeepers not only to the jobs but also to the training required to perform the work. Even if employers are correct that there are differences in average risks between men and women—a questionable perception—the use of gender categories to predict future behaviour clearly impedes the opportunity for individual women to exercise their own preferences and determine their own participation pattern and restricts the opportunity for individual households to adopt a domestic division of labour that is out of step with the dominant social norms. Changes in segregation may occur where employers 'learn' over time that the stereotypes do not hold. But such learning is likely to take place only when women have already entered the occupation in sufficient numbers for employers to be able to make realistic comparisons between men and women.

Although personal and societal norms and values normally sustain and reinforce patterns of gender segregation, these factors can also bring about a change in segregation patterns in particular circumstances as when legal regulations backed up by social opinion make it difficult for employers to maintain their reputation in the labour market as a good employer while actively discriminating in recruitment and selection decisions. An organization may adopt commitments to positive action programmes for a variety of reasons, including publicizing itself and establishing itself as a leading and innovative employer, but in the process of signing up to such schemes the organization may also have to reevaluate and change its perspective on gender roles.

On the supply side there is a matching set of factors that act to reinforce the processes of segregation but that at particular conjunctures may also lead to processes of change or to conflicts between employment aspirations and employment opportunities. On the one hand, women do make different choices in their selection of initial education and training and jobs, differences that cannot be fully explained by active employer selection processes. Women do seem to express a positive preference for certain forms of work, which may reflect a choice to utilize their comparative advantage (whether inherent or learned) in traditional female activities such as caring, and much feminist research over recent years has argued that the problem is not that women do low-skilled work but that the jobs women do are undervalued precisely because it is 'women's work' (Phillips and Taylor, 1980). These choices may also be influenced by expectations of career interruption due to domestic responsibilities (Polachek and Siebert, 1993), although recent increases in women's investment in education cast doubt on theories that explain segregation by women's unwillingness to invest.

Nevertheless, women's preferences and choices are also influenced by assessments of job opportunities. Changes in labour market opportunities feed back and influence women's educational and training choices, thereby undermining the idea that supply-side preferences are based solely upon biological or socially determined traits. For example, women have increased their representation in business and finance training over recent years in response to improved market opportunities in these once traditional male areas. Conversely, women's reluctance to train for certain nontraditional occupations may result from an expectation that the workplace culture might be unsupportive or even hostile and that unless the rewards are significant, the costs of being a pioneer in a man's world are simply not worth it (Bettio and Villa, 1992). In these circumstances the gendering of occupations and organizations can act as constraints on women's choices.

An actual, or presumed 'male breadwinner' system of household organization underlies a range of factors that lead to women's greater availability for work at low wages. Women often have more limited access than men do to unemployment benefits in welfare-state systems where entitlements are organized on the presumption of (male) full-time continuous employment and the financial dependency of (female) nonemployed spouses. They have access to some income transfers from spouses as well as to derived rights from their spouse's social security contributions. They may also have to find work that fits in with domestic responsibilities, forcing them to select part-time work regardless of whether the jobs match their skills and qualifications. Employers may exploit these different labour supply conditions to recruit women into low-paid, precarious and atypical jobs, both adding to the segregation of the sexes and making it difficult for women to break out of a household role as second-income earner with interrupted or contingent labour market participation.

Similar arguments can be made with respect to the third factor, employers' perceptions that women are more likely than men to quit or interrupt their employment careers. Women may be less likely to apply for jobs with strong internal labour markets if they fear high penalties if they quit the job for domestic and family reasons. Employers then find it less necessary to adapt their employment policies to meet the needs of those with domestic responsibilities. Thus, the supply side and the demand side may act to maintain traditional patterns of segregation. However, as we have already suggested, there are also tensions where women are no longer willing to adapt to this form of participation or where the labour market fails to deliver the form of employment necessary to maintain the male breadwinner model of household organization. Women's tendency to follow more continuous careers even in countries with traditions of discontinuous employment patterns could cause employers to reassess their gender stereotypes, at least with respect to highly educated women, among whom continuous careers are becoming more the norm in all countries (Rubery, Fagan and Smith, 1995).

The extent to which employment interruptions can provide a plausible explanation of segregation varies across countries because in some countries a high share of women do stay in the labour market and are as stable employees as men. In these cases the issue is whether women are forced into adopting a male life-cycle model because of the rigidities of the labour market that impose extremely high costs on those who quit. Another important issue for policy here may be the effect on fertility, for in the southern countries there is evidence that these labour market conditions may be forcing a choice between work and motherhood, with the consequence of a rapidly declining birth rate (Bettio and Villa, 1993).

Finally, where employers have the opportunity to exercise discrimination and discretion, the influence of the supply side on gender segregation is likely to be rather limited. In this regard the main influence of the supply side may occur through changes in the socialization of employers. An example would be changes in their own experiences of their mothers', wives' and daughters' involvement in the labour market.

Combining the demand side and the supply side, one can see that desegregation of occupations may come about from different processes. Jobs may change their position in the labour market queue, leading to a reassessment of the relative value of these jobs by men. Or employers may change their evaluation of women as potential employees, both for 'objective' reasons such as women's acquisition of qualifications and for more subjective reasons related to changes in societal norms.

2.2 Policy Implications

This analysis has suggested that evidence of apparent matching of employment patterns to supply-side preferences does not necessarily imply the absence of equity and efficiency problems. Individual women cannot exercise their individual choice to pursue particular careers if they are likely to encounter discriminatory employers or hostile and excessively masculine work environments. Moreover, even if women apparently freely exercise their preference for employment interruptions or part-time work, the implications of these choices do not necessarily represent an equitable or efficient outcome. In some labour markets the exercise of a choice to work part-time hours may force women into accepting low-grade and low-skilled work, from which there is little opportunity to regain their previous employment status. In principle, with appropriate policy interventions, greater opportunity for part-time work in all job areas could in fact result in decreasing segregation if women train for jobs and have continuous careers in job areas that they might previously have considered difficult to combine with domestic responsibilities. Policy intervention may be directed either at reducing the penalties associated with women exercising their preferences—through, for example, an improvement in the institutional environment for part-time workers—or at changing women's preferences to work part time by increasing the possibility of working full time (such as through provision of childcare facilities or the establishment of a shorter full-time week).

As we have already argued, the problem of segregation involves both the underutilization of women's skills and the undervaluation of the jobs that women do. The importance of these factors may differ between labour markets. In labour markets such as the United Kingdom and Germany, where women have interrupted careers, studies reveal that women face a strong likelihood of occupational downgrading on return to the labour market (Dex and Shaw, 1986; Dex, Walters and Alden, 1993; Engelbrech, 1989; Handl, 1988; McRae, 1991). In these circumstances there is likely to be a greater mismatch between women's potential (even measured by acquired training) and actual labour market position. Women also suffer from underemployment by being confined to a narrow range of skills and by facing greater barriers to upward promotion and acquisition of further training and skills over the life course. Where narrow pay differentials between job areas have reduced the problem of undervaluation of women's work, as, for example, in Nordic countries, concern may focus on vertical segregation and the exclusion of women from positions of power and authority. In many labour markets, however, the valuation attached to the jobs currently performed by women may be regarded as of primary concern, particularly as it is in these areas that employment has been expanding and that male-dominated areas have been contracting, reducing the possibility of large-scale transfers into male-dominated job areas (Rubery and Fagan, 1994). The concentration of women with different employers, such as small firms, or on different types of contracts, such as part-time work, may provide particularly great opportunities for undervaluation where labour market regulations allow differentiation of employment conditions.

Policies to reduce gender segregation do not necessarily only benefit women. The need for a more flexible gender division of labour may become a policy priority in view of the now well-publicized problems of unemployment for less-qualified men. A highly segregated labour market will reduce the scope for labour market adjustment. Segregated labour markets may be very rigid labour markets. In the United Kingdom, for example, many of the new jobs that in principle are available to the unemployed pay so little that only those in households that already have one earner can afford to take them, and this circumstance applies mainly to women. These trends are leading to divisions between work-rich and work-poor households (Gregg and Wadsworth, 1995). Policies to increase the attractiveness of these jobs to the unemployed, such as the establishment in the United Kingdom of a national minimum wage, could have the effect of increasing competition from men in female-dominated job areas.

The above analysis has made clear that supply-side action, such as training programmes, would be unlikely to be effective without action on the demand side to change both employer attitudes and male-dominated cultures. It is also clear that targeting the share of women within an occupation is in itself too narrow an objective. An alternative perspective is to consider the pay and promotion opportunities associated with women's work. However, even here there are problems because an improvement in pay or promotion opportunities may reopen the occupation to competition from men. These problems suggest, first, that it is necessary to develop a dynamic approach to policy evaluation in this area and, second, that gender segregation policies may need to be considered against a wider backdrop of interacting labour market and social institutions, including the pay structure, the level of unemployment and job creation, working time standards and childcare and welfare policy. Targeted policies to reduce segregation within specific job areas may have limited long-term effects on gender equality in societies where these broader institutions result in unfavourable or conflicting conditions for gender equality.

2.3 Policies that Address Segregation and Discrimination

Most of the policies specifically concerned with gender segregation and discrimination stem from a general commitment to equal treatment between men and women in European law and from Title VII of the 1964 Civil Rights Act in the United States. Also significant in the United States is the 1965 Executive Order requiring federal contractors to use affirmative action to ensure that discrimination is not practised in employment, an order that was extended in 1967 to include gender discrimination.

Within Europe the European Union has played a major role in stimulating the development of antidiscrimination policies at the national level. Article 119 of the Treaty of Rome (1957) established the responsibility for Member States to apply the principle that men and women should receive equal pay for equal work where the concept of 'equal work' has been expanded to 'work of equal value', so that segregated employment patterns in themselves cannot be used to justify different wage rewards for the sexes. The development of a legal framework has been central to the promotion of equal treatment in the European Union. The Council of Ministers has adopted several directives to promote equal treatment of the sexes, which the Member States have had to incorporate into national law, and several others are proposed to strengthen the legal framework (see Collins, 1991). The principle of equal pay for work of equal value was the subject of the first Directive on equality (1975), which was followed in 1976 by a Directive on equal treatment of men and women with regard to access to employment, vocational training and promotion, and working conditions. The 1976 Directive also clarified that the principle of equal treatment is not contravened by temporary positive action initiatives designed to correct an unequal situation in order to create equal opportunities. Other directives cover equal treatment in the field of social security and rights to maternity leave (see Fagan and Rubery on family policy, chap. 11 in this volume).

The Commission has also promoted labour market initiatives under three action programmes on equal opportunities (1982–85, 1986–90, 1991–95), with a fourth due to start in 1996. Initiatives stemming from these programmes include several recommendations, with codes of practice to guide policy implementation, to encourage Member States to take a range of initiatives to promote equal treatment. This includes a recommendation on positive action (1984), the protection of dignity of women at work (antisexual harassment) (1991), the extension of childcare and leave arrangements (1992) and a memorandum on job evaluation. Two initiatives have been set up within the framework of the structural funds: LEIs (local employment initiatives for women) started in 1984 provide grants to women starting up businesses in areas of high unemployment, and the NOW initiative (new opportunities for women) established in 1990 promoted opportunities for women in employment and vocational training (see Fina Sanglas, 1991).

The 1984 EU Recommendation on Positive Action was adopted to complement the equal treatment legislation influenced by the 'affirmative-action' policies developed in the United States (OECD, 1988; Reskin and Hartmann, 1986). This recommendation has been complemented by a positive action manual published in 1988. However, although it encourages Member States to formulate a policy on positive action, to set up positive action programmes in the public sector and to encourage similar initiatives in the private sector, there is no basis for its enforcement in law. European-level initiatives in the field of positive action thus stop well short of US policies towards affirmative action, which can be enforced by law, at least for federal contractors. Moreover, although the EU manual draws upon the guidelines developed by the equality enforcement agencies in the United States, there is no explicit reference to the use of numerical targets to achieve 'proportional representation' by job category throughout the workplace (de Jong and Bock, 1995).

The extent to which national policies have been implemented to further equal treatment varies from one European Member State to the next. All Member States have included in national legislation the principle of equal pay, but there are major differences between them in the extent to which this legal framework has included specific policies to facilitate implementation and, indeed, in the extent to which the legislation has led to litigation (Fitzpatrick, Gregory and Szyszczak, 1994). The extent and form of initiatives taken by governments, employers' organizations and unions to promote positive action vary between the Member States (Chalude, de Jong and Laufer, 1994; de Jong and Bock, 1995; Rubery and Fagan, 1993), although most have inserted clauses in their Equal Opportunities Acts to allow for preferential treatment of men and women with the aim of reducing existing inequalities (de Jong and Bock, 1995). Nearly every government has introduced positive action schemes in the public sector, although this ranges from comprehensive requirements to develop and monitor plans in some countries to rather piecemeal action in others. In Germany there is a federal law that the access of women to higher level positions should be promoted within the public sector once they have the equivalent qualifications of men, but this law is controversial and is being challenged by men in the country's Constitutional Court (Quack, Maier and Schuldt, 1992). Many of the initiatives in the public sector have emphasized the introduction of family-friendly employment practices alongside training initiatives and the adoption of equal opportunities policies for recruitment.

Activity in the private sector has been more uneven, although the legislation in most Member States of the European Union explicitly permits positive action. France has come the closest to requiring countries to implement positive action policies (de Jong and Bock, 1995). The 1983 Roudy Act established a legal requirement for private sector employers to produce a report on the position of women and men in the organization in order to stimulate the development of positive action initiatives. A similar legal requirement was adopted in Italy in 1991, but the practical effects are limited because the business community has so far refused to cooperate with the filing of reports. In Germany four *Länder* have regulations requiring firms that contract for public tenders to show they have effective equal opportunities policies, but these regulations have not been enforced, with some critics arguing that these regulations may contravene European law. In Belgium a decree passed in 1987 encouraging the private sector to take positive action, and legislation adopted in 1992 requires companies that have been permitted to restructure the employment of the work force to introduce positive action. In 1993 it became a requirement for companies to provide workers' representatives with an annual report on employment (Chalude et al., 1994). Legal requirements for positive action do not exist in the other Member States. Several governments—in the Netherlands and Belgium, for example—have run concerted information campaigns, established financial schemes and set up pilot projects to encourage private sector initiatives and monitor progress. Positive action has been a subject of collective bargaining in the Netherlands, Belgium and France, but the effects have been limited. For example, in the Netherlands only 8 per cent of agreements in 1990 included an obligation to draw up positive action plans (Chalude et al., 1994). The most significant initiatives taken by employers have developed in Denmark and the United Kingdom, and unions have been particularly active in pressing for positive action in Denmark and Italy (de Jong and Bock, 1995).

As is clear from the above discussion, the policies that may have most impact on gender equality are not by any means necessarily targeted gender equality policies, but instead also encompass a wide range of labour market policies and institutional features. Of particular importance may be features of the pay determination system, such as minimum wage protection, the size of interindustry and interoccupational wage differentials and the degree of centralized wage bargaining. Research suggests that these policies may be more important in reducing wage inequality than equal pay policies *per se* (Hunter and Rimmer, 1995; Rubery and Fagan, 1994; Whitehouse, 1992). Other policies that are relevant but that may not normally be considered within the focus of gender equality policies include the education and training systems (e.g. the extent or otherwise of internal labour market systems) (Maier, 1995), school provision and school timetables, tax and social security systems and working-time policy. In this chapter there is clearly only scope for assessing and evaluating targeted gender equality policies, but the potentially much greater importance of the whole spectrum of labour market and social institutions must be borne in mind.

3   MONITORING AND EVALUATION OF THE IMPACT OF POLICY ON SEGREGATION, DISCRIMINATION AND EQUAL OPPORTUNITY

3.1   Monitoring Change Using Labour Market Indicators

To evaluate policies it is first of all necessary to monitor and measure their effects. Monitoring problems arise both because of problems with internationally comparable data and because of conceptual problems relating to the most appropriate measures.

Summary index measures are the main indicators used to describe trends in occupational segregation across the employment structure, although these are sometimes supplemented by a disaggregated picture of changes in the shares that men and women have of occupational categories. There has been considerable debate concerning the appropriate method for constructing summary measures (see Blackburn, Jarman and Siltanen, 1993; Garnsey and Tarling 1982; Hakim, 1992, 1993a, 1993b; Jacobs, 1993; OECD, 1980; Siltanen, 1990a, 1990b; Siltanen, Jarman and Blackburn, 1993; Tzannatos 1990; Watts 1990, 1992, 1993). There are three types of problems with these measures. The first relates to how to construct the index. Different indices have been proposed, and the debate as to the most appropriate revolves around the issue of how to define a change in the degree of segregation when there are simultaneous changes taking place in the structure of employment and in the share of women in the work force. Using two different measures—the conventional index of dissimilarity and the newly proposed index of segregation, adopted recently by the ILO for its research into segregation (Siltanen et al., 1993)—Table 14.1 shows the degree of segregation in European Member States. Both measures indicate a high level of segregation with a high value of the index (between 0 and 1). In theory these two indices could give quite different results, but in practice they both show similar patterns for all Member States over this time period: similarly high levels of segregation and relatively slow rates of change in the 1980s.

The index of dissimilarity is based on the distribution of men and women across jobs in which women are under- or overrepresented in relation to their aggregate share of the work force. This index is thus sensitive to the share of women in the work force and the changes in the size of sectors in which women are under- or overrepresented. The index of segregation has been constructed so that the measure is independent of both these effects. On the basis of a technique known as marginal matching, jobs are ranked by the share of women employed, and a cut-off between female and male jobs is determined where the share of the total work force in female jobs equals the share of women in the total work force. The index measures the relative share of the female work force in 'female' and 'male' jobs.

The second type of problem relates to the choice of occupational classification schemes. The measured level of segregation is sensitive to the classification scheme adopted, so recorded differences in the level of segregation over time or place may simply be an artifact of a difference in the classification scheme. When national classification schemes are updated there are attempts to build in comparability, but even this is difficult to achieve (Marsh, 1986). Single-country time-series analyses have been conducted within the limitations of national data sets, but the lack of comparability between national occupational classification schemes and the difficulties of recoding has meant that very few cross-national studies have been able to directly compare the aggregate levels of segregation or men's and women's shares of occupations (Blackburn et al., 1993). Internationally harmonized data are mainly restricted to the seven major occupational groups (OECD, 1988) of the International Standard Classification of Occupations (ISCO), developed by the ILO (1968 version). The indices presented in Table 14.1 are based on European Labour Force Survey data at the two-digit level of the ISCO68 classification, allowing for about 80 occupations to be included. There are some doubts about the validity of this harmonized data, and the new ISCO88 classification may improve reliability and comparability, although problems still remain in its use within the European Labour Force Survey (see European Commission, 1995). However, even if the immediate data problems could be overcome, the existence of these harmonized data would reduce, but not eradicate, one of the main problems of international comparisons of occupations, namely, that societal differences in the way in which work is organized influences the different reward and status positions of apparently similar job titles (Marsh, 1986, pp. 124–7).

The third problem with overreliance upon index measures is that they hide divergent trends that are prevalent in patterns of segregation. Specifically, they obscure the fact that some parts of the employment structure are becoming desegregated while segregation is increasing elsewhere (Garnsey and Tarling, 1982; Rubery and Fagan, 1993). Others have argued that simpler indicators, such as the share of the work force employed in 'mixed' (sex integrated) occupations, may be a more useful tool than index measures are for monitoring change (Hakim, 1993a).

Another method of monitoring the impact of gender equality measures is to look instead at what might be considered a better measure of the gender equality target, namely, the gender pay gap. Even with this measure, however, there are both data and methodological problems. For international comparisons the main comparable data relate only to manual workers in industry or manufacturing (see Table 14.2), an employment sector accounting for an ever decreasing share of female employment. Average wage data including private and public services and part-time as well as full-time workers are rarely available, yet comparisons that include only a part of the labour market may be highly misleading, especially where countries differ in the share of the female and male work force captured by the data (Rubery, 1992). Even where such data exist, it is difficult to disentangle whether the changes in the gender pay gap are due to changes in the gender division of labour or to changes resulting from different trends in the valuation of 'male' and 'female' jobs. Women have recently improved their relative earnings in the United States, but disaggregation reveals that over 70 per cent of this change is attributable to declining wages for men (Mishel and Bernstein, 1993, p. 145). Ideally, there should be data sets that link occupations, earnings and gender, but such information is not readily available.

3.2 Monitoring Legislation and Positive Action and Equal Value Initiatives

An essential, if narrow, element of any evaluation of the impact of legislation is to monitor litigation. In the United States information on filed complaints and investigated complaints are collected by the relevant authorities. In addition, federal contractors with over 100 employees must provide information on the gender and race composition of their work forces. This information has been used by researchers (see below) to evaluate the enforcement and effectiveness of legislation.

The implementation and use of the equality directives within the Member States is monitored by the European Commission. This has revealed that litigation has been more widely used in some countries than in others, and it is mainly in the United Kingdom, Ireland and the Netherlands that strategic or targeted litigation is occurring. Country differences result from a number of factors, notably the ability of the industrial relations system to substitute for or to preempt legal conflict. Nevertheless, the volume of sex equality litigation is generally lower in every Member State than that of labour law at large (Fitzpatrick et al., 1994).

Monitoring of litigation can lead to evaluation of effectiveness, and within the European Commission areas have been identified for action to improve the effectiveness of the legislation. They include the establishment of legal procedures with effective sanctions and remedies, the further development and application of the concepts of 'equal pay for work of equal value' and 'indirect discrimination', the reversal of the burden of proof in all countries so that it rests with the employer rather than the complainant, and action to raise awareness of the extent and nature of rights and obligations under Community law among employers, unions, lawyers and individual men and women (Banks, 1991; Collins, 1991).

Being dependent on one-off surveys, monitoring of voluntary positive action initiatives is patchier. For example, a study was commissioned by the European Commission (ER Consultants, 1990) to identify the impact of its own Recommendation and Manual on Positive Action. This evaluation involved the distribution of questionnaires to 2700 companies, stratified according to Member State, sector and company size. The response rate was, however, very low (13 per cent). Such a response rate is likely to involve a bias, with those companies that had implemented some positive action being more likely to respond than those that had shown no such initiative. If so, the results were disappointing, for only 15 per cent of replies indicated that a positive action programme had been introduced.

3.3   Evaluating Equal Treatment Legislation and Affirmative and Positive Action Initiatives

3.3.1   Evaluating Equal Treatment Legislation

Assessing the impact of legislation on labour market trends is problematic. It is difficult to isolate the impact of legislation, given that its implementation frequently followed other societal changes, including the general increase in female work force. It is also impossible to identify control groups, given the nearly universal coverage of most legislation (OECD, 1988). The volume of litigation could be used as some measure of differences between countries, and in the United States some evaluation studies have concentrated on differences in complaints or investigated complaints between states (Beller, 1977, 1978, 1979, 1982; Freeman, 1973, 1981; Leonard, 1984a; Shulman, 1987) or in expenditure over time. Even in the United States these measures are problematic because litigation reflects both the extent of discrimination and measures to overcome it (Lee Badgett and Hartmann, 1995). Making comparisons between European countries on the basis of use of litigation would be much more problematic, for these countries differ in the availability of alternative remedies for the implementation of equal opportunities. In the absence of alternative indices, the length of time over which legislation has been in place was used in one European comparative study to identify differences between countries, the rationale being that it takes time to bring about the social and cultural changes that are essential for effective implementation (Dex and Sewell, 1995).

Further problems for evaluation arise from the difficulties inherent in dividing responsibilities between the impact of a policy initiative and the impact of general change in the economy. Thus, where there has been little apparent progress in narrowing the gender pay gap or reducing segregation, it may be, as Blau (1992) has argued, because equal opportunities policies for women are 'swimming against the tide'. When it comes to the disaggregation of policy from other effects, international comparative studies face even greater problems, if only because the form and direction of changes in economic trends and institutions may vary from one country to another.

It is partly for these reasons that there have been relatively few international evaluative studies on the impact of equal treatment legislation. Most individual countries are limited to a before-and-after evaluation, unless there is considerable variation over time in the implementation of legislation. In the United States there is greater scope for evaluation because of variations over time (with most activity on enforcement being concentrated in the 1970s and a marked reduction in enforcement from the Reagan administration onwards) and variations between states. In the United Kingdom, preliminary and follow-up studies revealed a significant impact of equal pay legislation on the gender pay gap even after controlling for the impact of incomes policies and other factors tending to narrow wage differentials over the same time period (Zabalza and Tzannatos, 1985); these results have been disputed by Borooah and Lee, 1988, and Chiplin and Sloane, 1988. Evidence from Australia and Sweden also suggests that legislation or collective agreements have been important in narrowing the gender pay gap (Hunter and Rimmer, 1995; Löfstrom and Gustafsson, 1991; OECD, 1988), but the results for the United States are more mixed, reflecting in part the failure of the gender pay gap to close until the 1980s.

The US evaluation studies have been reviewed by Lee Badgett and Hartmann (1995). These studies used multiple regression models to identify the impact of legislative enforcement on blacks and women (e.g. Goldstein and Smith, 1976; Heckman and Wolpin, 1976; Leonard, 1984b, 1984c, 1985a, 1985b, 1989, 1990). One major technical problem encountered was how to specify the enforcement variable, for activity revolving around complaints may indicate either strong enforcement or high discrimination. A second major technical problem in these studies was how to allow for possible divergent employment and wage effects for medium- to long-run adjustments over short-term adjustments. The results of these evaluation studies differed, and although most indicated that legislative enforcement has had a positive impact on both wages and employment for blacks, the results for white women are more mixed.

Moving beyond national evaluation, OECD (1988) reviewed the development of equal opportunities legislation in different countries and the available national studies that had attempted to evaluate the impact of legislation on labour market trends. It was concluded that equal opportunities and affirmative action policies in the European Union were less developed than those, for example, in North America, Australia and Nordic countries. It was also concluded that the mixed evidence from available studies was insufficient and too mixed for a full assessment of whether women's earnings have improved as a direct result of legislation rather than of other social and economic changes. Nevertheless, some attempts at international comparisons have been made. For example, Whitehouse (1992) used regression techniques to investigate the relative impact that equal pay legislation, unionization, public sector employment and centralization of wage bargaining had on the pay gap. In a sample of 13 OECD countries, she found public sector employment and centralization of pay bargaining to be more significant in reducing the pay gap than equal pay legislation or unionization. Similar results on the pay gap have been found from more qualitative evaluations of two or three countries (Hunter and Rimmer, 1995; Rubery, 1992).

A novel methodology was used by Dex and Sewell (1995) in their attempt to isolate the impact that equal treatment and equal pay legislation has on women from country differences in the structure of the economy, the tax and social security system, wage-setting institutions, the organization of childcare and   attitudes towards women's work force participation. The authors use Bayesian techniques to overcome problems of indicator measurement and missing data, specifically those problems that would require dropping countries or variables within a multiple regression analysis. The results may still be considered exploratory rather than confirmatory, but they did indicate that legislation (measured by length of time since implementation) has had a positive impact on the share of women employed in high-level occupations and on reductions in the female share of low-paid jobs, though not on the hourly earnings gap between women and men in manual jobs. Other rather general policies, too, have had an impact on women's employment. Government spending has influenced the percentage of women employed in high-level occupations, and low unionization and lack of childcare provision have both been associated with high ratios of women in low-paid work.

The investigation by Dex and Sewell (1995) highlights two important issues for evaluation studies. First, certain policies are likely to have more impact on some groups of women (e.g. the highly educated) than upon others, suggesting that, alongside aggregate measures, indicators need to disaggregate the analysis for different groups of women. Second, it is important to evaluate the impact of 'general' labour market policies, such as wage systems, as well as the narrower range of 'gendered' policy instruments.

3.3.2   *Evaluating Positive or Affirmative Action Initiatives*

Whereas equal treatment legislation tends to cover all organizations and all employment, positive action or affirmative action initiatives tend to be limited to a subset of organizations. Evaluations of positive action or affirmative action programmes can thus take a variety of forms. First, there is the monitoring and evaluation of the adoption of initiatives, particularly voluntary initiatives and the actual changes made at an organizational level. Second, evaluations, before and after, of women's positions within organizations adopting positive or affirmative action programmes. Third, there is the comparison between women's positions in firms using positive action or affirmative action programmes and women's positions in firms not implementing such programmes. European evaluations tend to be concentrated on the first approach and include some, often unsophisticated, attempts to assess the before-and-after effects. In the United States, however, there are now a wide range of studies that have adopted both the second and third approaches.

Within Europe, research on positive action schemes has thus generally been focussed upon assessing the extent of the spread of positive action initiatives and identifying 'best practice'. Most of these evaluations have found a relatively low incidence of take-up of positive action schemes.

As we have already noted, research has shown that the European Commission recommendation on positive action has been taken up by only 15 per cent of the firms that responded in a survey that had only a 13 per cent response rate. The most common initiatives reported by firms in that survey related to working time, leave arrangements and training. Generally, most of the initiatives developed in the private sector in the Member States have occurred in the banking and finance industry. The lack of development of positive action in the private sector is corroborated by the available national surveys on this subject (Chalude et al., 1994; de Jong and Bock, 1995). For example, even the comparatively strong legal incentives that have existed in France since 1983 have failed to stimulate significant progress, for only 30 firms have implemented positive action schemes.

The evidence on more recent initiatives is limited and mixed. The recent legislation in Italy has been actively resisted by employers, and as yet the government has taken few steps to enforce compliance. By contrast, the recent legislative reform in Belgium has encouraged the signing of collective agreements that encourage positive action (Chalude et al., 1994). The most widespread employer-led initiative seems to be the United Kingdom's 'Opportunity 2000' campaign, where both public and private sector affiliations have continued to grow since its inception in 1991. It now covers about 25 per cent of the work force (Hammond, 1994). Companies are encouraged to establish targets to monitor progress, and the share of companies that set targets has grown over time.

Where companies have introduced comprehensive positive action plans, evidence suggests that women's share of employment has tended to increase, although entry into higher-level occupations has tended to be slower.

Evaluation of the impact has tended to be based on the monitoring of changes in company practices in combination with changes in the female shares of different occupations. Additionally, the rate of change in the female share of employment at companies participating in 'Opportunity 2000' was compared to the rate of change in the female share of employment at nonparticipating organizations. This research has revealed that the rate of progress tends to be better in those companies that have developed positive action policies.

Control comparisons have also been used in the United States for companies that have been required to introduce positive action and to establish targets as a result of legal orders and contract compliance. These control comparisons are not without their problems, not least because noncontractors may change their policies and practices in line with the changes required of federal contractors. Moreover, although the studies tend to find consistent positive effects for blacks, the results for women are rather mixed (Lee Badgett and Hartmann, 1995). In a somewhat different study Osterman (1982) found that affirmative action programmes tend to reduce female quit rates, thereby providing an indirect indicator that women perceive themselves to have better opportunities in firms with affirmative action programmes. In terms of occupational advancement it seems that most of the impact has been in the women's share of professional and managerial jobs, whereas attempts to hire women in skilled blue-collar jobs have had less success (OECD, 1988; Reskin and Hartmann, 1986, p. 98). Some problems of using the women's share of occupational groups as an indicator of equality policies have been raised in a comparison of internal labour market systems in banks (Rubery, 1995). Increasing shares of women in higher-level jobs may be the result of new policies to recruit new management trainees or of internal promotion systems. If the former system is in operation, promotion opportunities for the predominantly female clerical work force may even have diminished. Thus, evaluations at the company level need to take account of differences in opportunities for different groups of women (Rubery, 1995).

Positive action programmes may be implemented not at the level of the organization but through training programmes. Such programmes aim to remove the first obstacle to women's employment in nontraditional areas, that is, women's lack of appropriate skills. Evaluations of programmes to improve women's representation within nontraditional areas in Germany have found that, although women have increased their share of nontraditional jobs, women still encounter more difficulties than men in obtaining employment (Wolf, 1992). Furthermore, research on eastern Germany has found that even if women succeed in finding employment in nontraditional areas they may not stay in that occupational area for long. For example, no more than 9 per cent of trained female mechanical fitters and 11 per cent of skilled female construction workers remained in the trade (Quack et al., 1992). This experience suggests that the male culture of the occupation may make it uncomfortable for women to work in these jobs even if they can find work.

These findings call for additional evaluation research at the organization and workplace level. Many statistical evaluations provide little information on the processes at work, how organizations respond and implement positive action plans and the conditions that may lead to resistance or compliance with changes in the sex composition of occupational areas. Where studies at the workplace level are carried out, the processes associated with change in the gender segregation of employment are revealed to be complex. Two types of qualitative evaluation studies can be identified. At the level of the organization, there are those studies that have followed attempts to implement positive action or equal pay policies (Acker, 1990; Cockburn, 1991). These studies reveal the political processes involved in implementing change at the level of the organization and identify the forms of resistance that may develop at different levels of the hierarchy or organization to policy implementation.

They also reveal that decisions to develop and implement a new policy, such as positive action or a new job evaluation scheme to implement equal value, may be tied into other managerial objectives, including, for example, changes to the wage-bargaining system or the occupational skill hierarchy. This type of evaluation is essential to identify the importance, say, of trade-union or workplace support for effective implementation.

An alternative qualitative approach is to take traditionally male-dominated occupations where women have in fact succeeded in making significant inroads and examine in depth the circumstances under which the change in segregation came about and the outcome that this change has had for gender equality. Reskin and Roos (1990) adopted this methodology, carrying out detailed case studies of occupations where women had made rapid entry in the United States in the 1980s. Changes in the sex composition of employment were found to be associated with changes in the occupation, changes having to do with technology, training, pay, status, customer requirements and so forth. Thus, whereas changes in women's labour supply characteristics, including changing qualification levels, contributed in several instances to changes in the gender mix, changes in the position of the occupation within the labour market hierarchy were often at least equally important.

These two types of qualitative studies cast doubt on the value of traditional evaluation techniques that take the occupational hierarchy as given and treat the implementation of equality policies as separable and independent from the production and reproduction of organizational politics and culture.

4   CONCLUSIONS

Segregation is a persistent phenomenon in labour markets and arises from a mutual conditioning of supply-side and demand-side forces. Individuals face structural constraints in the labour market as a result of employer practices. Furthermore, the preferences that women and men have for different jobs must be considered at least partly endogenous, arising out of current labour market and welfare-state institutions.

The main costs of segregation are borne by women, but the channelling of women into certain job areas is also a cost to society, for women's skills are frequently underused. Segregation also creates rigidities in the labour market, which may actually contribute to persistent unemployment among men. While segregation may be a cost to society as a whole, certain actors benefit from that fact, notably employers with access to cheap female labour, and some male workers who manage to retain a monopoly over better-paid job areas. These different interests and the dynamic processes of segregation mean that policies must be developed and coordinated to intervene at a range of 'pressure points'.

It is difficult to isolate the impact that specific equal opportunities initiatives have on changing levels of segregation from wider social and economic trends, including economic restructuring. Furthermore, changes in the shares that men and women have of different occupations may be accompanied by, or even triggered by, changes in the quality and nature of these jobs. Therefore, evaluations of change must consider changes in gender pay differentials alongside changes in the distribution of the sexes across the employment structure. At the same time, evaluations need to distinguish between different groups of women—between the more or the less qualified and between women with and without dependent children.

Different policy instruments and the associated indicators to evaluate progress need to be developed at the European, national and company level in order to monitor and evaluate change and continuity in the level and form of segregation. Most of the national policy initiatives in Europe have been stimulated by European-level intervention, a fact that indicates a continued need for the European Commission to act as a catalyst in this area. In addition to strengthening the legal tools available, it must promote the effective use of existing remedies by stimulating the cross-national exchange of information about developments in case law and successful policy initiatives. This action should be targeted at governments, employers' organizations and trade unions. At the same time it is important for equality issues to be integrated into the evaluation of wider labour market changes. Targets for progress could also be set for changes in the female share of occupational categories and gender wage differences in order to monitor progress in different countries. Such targets could be accompanied by a strong requirement for governments to develop positive action initiatives. To support this type of activity it is important to collect comprehensive occupational and earnings data that can facili-tate monitoring and evaluation.

Similar types of intervention are required at the national government level, but in a more detailed and tailored form, in order to be compatible with existing institutional frameworks and to address particular weaknesses in different aspects of particular national systems of equality legislation, education and training, childcare provision, industrial relations systems and so forth. For example, women's access to vocational training will be more important in countries where it has an important influence on labour market opportunities (Maier, 1995). In other countries improving the conditions of part-time work may be a higher priority than vocational training. More detailed monitoring of labour market trends and positive action initiatives is possible at the national level than the European level. This national monitoring needs to be supported by case-study evaluations to identify the reasons for both success and failure at the company level and to assess the qualitative changes in women's employment experience.

REFERENCES

Acker, J. (1990), *Doing Comparable Work: Gender, Class and Pay Equity*, Philadelphia: Temple University Press.

Banks, K. (1991), 'Equal Treatment in Community Law', *European Commission*, 62–76.

Barbezat, D. (1993), *Occupational Segmentation by Sex in the World*, Interdepartmental Project on Women (IDP), working paper no. 13, Geneva: International Labour Office.

Beechey, V. (1977), 'Some Notes on Female Wage Labour in Capitalist Production', *Capital and Class*, 3, 45–66.

Beller, A. (1977), *EEO Laws and the Earnings of Women*, Proceedings of the 29th Annual Winter Meeting, Madison, WI: Industrial Relations Research Association.

Beller, A. (1978), 'The Economics of Enforcement of an Antidiscrimination Law: Title VII of the Civil Rights Act of 1964', *Journal of Law and Economics*, 21 (2), 359–80.

Beller, A. (1979), 'The Impact of Equal Employment Opportunity Laws on the Male–Female Earnings Differential', in C. Lloyd, E. Andrews and C. Gilroy (eds), *Women in the Labor Market*, New York: Columbia University Press.

Beller, A. (1982), 'Occupational Segregation by Sex: Determinants and Changes', *Journal of Human Resources*, 17 (3), 371–2.

Bergmann, B. (1974), 'Occupational Segregation, Wages and Profits When Employers Discriminate by Race or Sex', *Eastern Economic Journal*, 1 (1–2), 103–10.

Bergmann, B. (1986), *The Economic Emergence of Women*, New York: Basic Books.

Bettio, F. and P. Villa (1992), *Occupational Segregation: The Case of Italy*, working paper for the EU Communities; available from the Network of Experts on the Situation of Women in the Labour Market: Manchester School of Management, University of Manchester, Institute of Science and Technology, UK.

Bettio, F. and Villa, P. (1993), 'Strutture familiari e mercati del lavoro nei paesi sviluppati. L'emergere di un percorso mediterraneo per l'integrazione delle donne nel mercato del lavoro', *Economica e Lavoro*, 2, 3–30.

Blackburn, R., J. Jarman and J. Siltanen (1993), 'The Analysis of Occupational Gender Segregation over Time and Place: Considerations of Measurement and Some New Evidence', *Work, Employment and Society*, 7 (3), 335–62.

Blau, F. (1992, September), 'Gender and Economic Outcomes: The Role of Wage Structure', keynote speech, Fourth European Association of Labour Economists, University of Warwick.

Borooah, V. and K. Lee (1988), 'The Effect of Changes in Britain's Industrial Structure on Female Relative Pay and Employment', *Economic Journal*, 98, 818–32.

Chalude, M., A. de Jong and J. Laufer (1994), 'Implementing Equal Opportunity and Affirmative Action Programmes in Belgium, France and The Netherlands', in M. Davidson and R. Burke (eds), *Women in Management: Current Research Issues*, London: Paul Chapman, pp. 289–303.

Chiplin, B. and P. Sloane (1988), 'The Effects of Britain's Anti-discrimination Legislation on Relative Pay and Employment: A Comment', *Economic Journal*, 98, 833–8.

Cockburn, C. (1991), *In the Way of Women: Men's Resistance to Sex Equality in Organizations*, London: Macmillan.

Collins, E. (1991), 'The Implementation and Development of Community Equality Law', *European Commission*, op. cit., 33–41.

Connell, R. (1987), *Gender and Power*, Oxford: Polity.

Crompton, R. and K. Sanderson (1990), *Gendered Jobs and Social Change*, London: Unwin Hyman.

de Jong, A. and B. Bock (1995), 'Positive Action within the European Union', in A. van Doorne-Huiskes, J. van Hoof and E. Roelofs (eds), *Women in the European Labour Market*, London: Paul Chapman, pp. 182–202.

Dex, S. and R. Sewell (1995), 'Equal Opportunities Policies and Women's Labour Market Status in Industrialised Countries', in J. Humphries and J. Rubery (eds), *The Economics of Equal Opportunities*, Manchester: Equal Opportunities Commission, pp. 367–92.

Dex, S. and L. Shaw (1986), *British and American Women at Work: Do Equal Opportunities Policies Matter?*, London: Macmillan.

Dex, S., P. Walters and D. Alden (1993), *French and British Mothers at Work*, London: Macmillan.

Engelbrecht, G. (1989), 'Erfahrungen von Frauen an der "dritten Schwelle": Schwierigkeiten bei der beruflichen Eingliederung aus der Sicht der Frauen', *Mitteilungen aus der Arbeitsmarkt- und Berufsforschung*, 1, 100–113.

ER Consultants (1990), *An Evaluation Study of Positive Action in Favour of Women*, Brussels: European Commission.

European Commission (1991), 'Equal Opportunities for Women and Men', *Social Europe*, 3, Luxembourg: Office for Official Publications of the European Communities.

European Commission (1995), *Employment in Europe*, Luxembourg: Office for Official Publications of the European Communities.

Fina Sanglas, L. (1991), 'The Third Action Programme and the Challenges of the Future', *European Commission*, op. cit., 13–22.

Fitzpatrick, B., J. Gregory and E. Szyszczak (1994), *Sex Equality Litigation in the Member States of the European Community*, V/407/94–EN, Brussels: European Commission (DG V).

Freeman, R. (1973), 'Changes in the Labor Market for Black Americans 1949–72', *Brookings Papers on Economic Activity*, 1, 67–131.

Freeman, R. (1981), 'Black Economic Progress after 1964: Who Has Gained and Why?', in S. Rosen (ed.), *Studies in Labor Markets*, Chicago: University of Chicago Press, pp. 247–94.

Garnsey, E. and R. Tarling (1982), *The Measurement of the Concentration of Female Employment*, working paper no. 6 on the Role of Women in the Economy, MAS/WP, 6 (82), Paris: OECD.

Goldstein, M. and R. Smith (1976), 'The Estimated Impact of the Antidiscrimination Program Aimed at Federal Contractors', *Industrial and Labor Relations Review*, 29 (4), 523–43.

Gottschall, K. (1995), 'Geschlechterverhältnis und Arbeitsmarktsegregation', in R. Becker-Schmidt and G.-A. Knapp (eds), *Das Geschlechterverhältnis als Gegenstand der Sozialwissenschaften*, Campus Verlag: Frankfurt on the Main/New York.

Gregg, P. and J. Wadsworth (1995), 'Gender, Households and Access to Employment', in J. Humphries and J. Rubery (eds), *The Economics of Equal Opportunities*, Manchester: Equal Opportunities Commission, pp. 345–64.

Hakim, C. (1992), 'Explaining Trends in Occupational Segregation: The Measurement, Causes and Consequences of the Sexual Division of Labour', *European Sociological Review*, 8 (2), 127–52.

Hakim, C. (1993a), 'Segregated and Integrated Occupations: A New Framework for Analyzing Social Change', *European Sociological Review*, 9 (3), 289–314.

Hakim, C. (1993b), 'Refocusing Research on Occupational Segregation: Reply to Watts', *European Sociological Review*, 9 (3), 321–4.

Hammond, V. (1994), 'Opportunity 2000: Good Practice in UK Organizations', in M. Davidson and R. Burke (eds), *Women in Management: Current Research Issues*, London: Paul Chapman, pp. 304–18.

Handl, J. (1988), *Berufschancen und Heiratsmuster von Frauen. Empirische Untersuchung zu den Prozessen sozialer Mobilität*, Frankfurt on the Main: Campus.

Heckman, J. and K. Wolpin (1976), 'Does the Contract Compliance Program Work? An Analysis of Chicago Data', *Industrial and Labor Relations Review*, 29, 544–64.

Humphries, J. and J. Rubery (eds) (1995), *The Economics of Equal Opportunities*, Manchester: Equal Opportunities Commission.

Hunter, L. and S. Rimmer (1995), 'An Economic Exploration of the UK and Australian Experiences', in J. Humphries and J. Rubery (eds) (1995), *The Economics of Equal Opportunities*, Manchester: Equal Opportunities Commission, pp. 245–73.

Jacobs, J. (1993), 'Theoretical and Measurement Issues in the Study of Sex Segregation in the Workplace: Research Note', *European Sociological Review*, 9 (3), 325–30.

Lee Badgett, M. and H. Hartmann (1995), 'The Effectiveness of Equal Employment Opportunity Policies', in M. Simms (ed.), *Economic Perspectives on Affirmative Action*, Washington, DC: Joint Center for Political and Economic Studies, pp. 57–97.

Leonard, J. (1984a), 'Anti-Discrimination or Reverse Discrimination: The Impact of Changing Demographics, Title VII and Affirmative Action on Productivity', *Journal of Human Resources*, 19 (2), 145–74.

Leonard, J. (1984b), 'Employment and Occupational Advance under Affirmative Action', *Review of Economics and Statistics*, 66 (3), 377–85.

Leonard, J. (1984c), 'The Impact of Affirmative Action on Employment', *Journal of Labor Economics*, 2 (4), 439–63.

Leonard, J. (1985a), 'Affirmative Action as Earnings Redistribution: The Targeting of Compliance Reviews', *Journal of Labor Economics*, 3 (3), 363–84.

Leonard, J. (1985b), 'What Promises Are Worth: The Impact of Affirmative Action Goals', *Journal of Human Resources*, 20 (1), 3–21.

Leonard, J. (1989), 'Women and Affirmative Action', *Journal of Economic Perspectives*, 3 (1), 61–75.

Leonard, J. (1990), 'The Impact of Affirmative Action Regulation and Equal Employment Law on Black Employment', *Journal of Economic Perspectives*, 4 (4), 47–63.

Löfstrom, Å. and S. Gustafsson (1991), 'Policy Changes and Women's Wages in Sweden', *International Review of Comparative Public Policy*, 3, 317–30.

Maier, F. (1995), 'Skill Formation and Equal Opportunity—A Comparative Perspective', in J. Humphries and J. Rubery (eds), *The Economics of Equal Opportunities*, Manchester: Equal Opportunities Commission, pp. 203–18.

Marsh, C. (1986), 'Social Class and Occupation', in R. Burgess (ed.), *Key Variables in Social Investigation*, London: Routledge & Kegan Paul, pp. 123–52.

McRae, S. (1991), *Maternity Rights in Britain*, London: Policy Studies Institute.

Mishel, L. and J. Bernstein (1993), *The State of Working America*, New York: M. E. Sharpe, Economic Policy Institute.

OECD (1980), *Women and Employment*, Paris: OECD.

OECD (1988), *Employment Outlook*, Paris: OECD.

Osterman, P. (1982), 'Affirmative Action and Opportunity: A Study of Female Quit Rates', *Review of Economics and Statistics*, 64 (4), 604–12.

Phillips, A. and B. Taylor (1980), 'Sex and Skill: Notes towards a Feminist Economics', *Feminist Review*, 6, 79–88.

Polachek, S. W. and W. Siebert (1993), *The Economics of Earnings*, Cambridge: Cambridge University Press.

Quack, S., F. Maier and K. Schuldt (1992), *Occupational Segregation in the Federal Republic of Germany and in the Former German Democratic Republic 1980–89*, Report for the European Commission, working paper, EC Network on the Situation of Women in the Labour Market, Manchester: UMIST.

Reskin, B. and H. Hartmann (eds) (1986), *Women's Work, Men's Work: Sex Segregation on the Job*, Washington, DC: National Academy Press.

Reskin, B. and P. Roos (1990), *Job Queues, Gender Queues*, Philadelphia: Temple University Press.

Rubery, J. (ed.) (1988), *Women and Recession*, London: Routledge & Kegan Paul.

Rubery, J. (1992), 'Pay, Gender and the Social Dimension to Europe', *British Journal of Industrial Relations*, 30 (4), 605–22.

Rubery, J. (1994), 'Internal and External Labour Markets: Towards an Integrated Analysis', in J. Rubery and F. Wilkinson (eds), *Employer Strategy and the Labour Market*, Oxford, UK: Oxford University Press.

Rubery, J. (1995), 'Internal Labour Markets and Equal Opportunities: Women's Position in Banks in European Countries', *European Journal of Industrial Relations*, 1 (2), 203–27.

Rubery, J. and C. Fagan (1993), 'Occupational Segregation of Women and Men in the European Community', *Social Europe Supplement*, 3, Luxembourg: Office for Official Publications of the European Communities.

Rubery, J. and C. Fagan (1994), 'Wage Determination and Sex Segregation in Employment in the European Community', *Social Europe Supplement*, 4, Luxembourg: Office for Official Publications of the European Communities.

Rubery, J., C. Fagan and M. Smith (1995), *Changing Patterns of Work and Working-time in the European Union and the Impact on Gender Divisions*, Report for the Equal Opportunities Unit, Directorate Generale V, Brussels, Commission of the European Communities.

Shulman, S. (1987), 'Discrimination, Human Capital, and Black–White Unemployment: Evidence from Cities', *Journal of Human Resources*, 22 (3), 361–76.

Siltanen, J. (1990a), 'Social Change and the Measurement of Occupational Sex Segregation by Sex: An Assessment of the Sex Ratio Index', *Work, Employment and Society*, 4 (1), 1–29.

Siltanen, J. (1990b), 'Further Comment on the Sex Ratio Index', *Work, Employment and Society*, 4 (4), 599–603.

Siltanen, J. (1994), *Locating Gender: Occupational Segregation, Wages and Domestic Responsibilities*, London: University College London Press.

Siltanen, J., J. Jarman and R. Blackburn (1993), *Gender Inequality in the Labour Market: Occupational Concentration and Segregation, a Manual on Methodology*, Geneva: ILO.

Tzannatos, Z. (1990), 'Employment Segregation: Can We Measure It and What Does It Mean?', *British Journal of Industrial Relations*, 28, 105–11.

Watts, M. (1990), 'The Sex Ratio Revisited', *Work, Employment and Society*, 4 (4), 595–98.

Watts, M. (1992), 'How Should Occupational Segregation Be Measured?', *Work, Employment and Society*, 6 (3), 475–87.

Watts, M. (1993), 'Explaining Trends in Occupational Segregation: Some Comments', *European Sociological Review*, 9 (3), 315–19.

Whitehouse, G. (1992), 'Legislation and Labour Market Gender Inequality: An Analysis of OECD Countries', *Work, Employment and Society*, 6 (1), 65–86.

Wolf, B. (1992), 'Frauen in "typischen Männerberufen"—ein hoffungsloses Unterfangen?', in S. Damm-Rüger (ed.), *Frauen—Ausbildung—Beruf, Realität und Perspektiven der Berufsausbildung von Frauen,* Vol. 14, Bundesinstitut für Berufsbildung, Tagungen und Expertengespräche zur beruflichen Bildung.

Zabalza, A. and Z. Tzannatos (1985), *Women and Equal Pay: The Effects of Legislation on Female Employment and Wages in Britain*, Cambridge, UK: Cambridge University Press.

15. Life-long Learning and Skill Formation

Albert C. Tuijnman[1] and Klaus Schömann

The Commission of the European Union (EU) and the Organization for Economic Co-operation and Development (OECD) recently published major studies of the causes of and possible solutions to the problem of high and persistent levels of unemployment in the advanced industrialized countries. Both the *White Paper on Growth, Competitiveness and Employment* (Commission, 1993) and *The OECD Jobs Study* (OECD, 1994a) have advanced life-long learning as an important component of a policy strategy aimed at overcoming structural barriers to job creation and economic growth. In the *White Paper*, life-long learning and continuing vocational training featured prominently among the policy options for action on jobs, where the EU countries are encouraged to implement efforts 'to create the basis in each Member country for a genuine right to ongoing training' (Commission, 1993, p. 17). Similarly, *The OECD Jobs Study* (1994a) stated: 'Extending and upgrading workers' skills and competences must be a life-long process if OECD economies are to foster the creation of high-skill, high-wage jobs' (p. 47). Among the choices open to government, two broad areas of concern were noted:

1. The need to improve the articulation of education, training, and employment policies in a framework of life-long learning, and to devise more effective implementation strategies as part of a coherent approach to a range of policy areas that include labour market and social insurance policies.
2. The need to achieve higher standards of learner attainment, and greater efficiency and effectiveness in the organization of educational production in a framework of life-long learning.

European societies are called upon to develop life-long learning because skill formation and updating is considered a prerequisite for enhancing economic and labour market performance leading to more growth in employment.

---

[1] The views expressed in this chapter are those of the author and do not necessarily reflect official views of the OECD or its Member countries.

Table 15.1 shows that it is in the latter area where the record of some European countries has trailed that of other societies both within and outside the region. Against this background, the labour market situation has become particularly worrying in Europe. Unemployment has tended to be persistent, ratcheting up in most countries with each recession. In some of these European countries at the same time there is a relatively low rate of labour market participation and employment growth (OECD, 1994b, p. 60).

Table 15.1   Economic Output and Employment Growth, 1960–1990 (Annual Percentage Change)

	GDP per head			Employment			Productivity		
	1960s	1970s	1980s	1960s	1970s	1980s	1960s	1970s	1980s
North America	3.0	1.8	1.6	2.0	2.3	1.7	2.3	0.5	0.8
Japan	9.3	3.9	3.4	1.4	0.8	1.1	8.9	4.3	2.8
EC	3.9	2.8	1.8	0.2	0.4	0.5	4.6	2.9	1.7
EFTA	3.6	2.6	2.1	0.6	0.7	0.9	3.9	2.2	1.5
Oceania	3.0	2.1	1.7	2.3	1.6	2.0	2.6	1.9	1.1
OECD total	3.9	2.4	1.9	1.0	1.2	1.1	4.0	2.1	1. 5

Source
From *The OECD Jobs Study: Evidence and Explanations, Part 1, Labour Market Trends and Underlying Forces of Change* by OECD, 1994b, Paris: OECD, p. 60. Copyright 1994 by OECD. Adapted by permission.

In the context of the European Union since the Maastricht treaty, the Member States have agreed to support a policy of enhancing professional education at the level of the European Union. Additionally, the signing of the social charter by 11 Member States has given new impetus to engage in life-long learning activities, not least because of equality considerations. Presumably, delayed periods of learning cannot compensate for lack of learning opportunities during earlier stages of the life course. The genuine right to receive a basic eduction, which is guaranteed in the industrialized countries, is more and more understood to include the right to some form of retraining if skills have become obsolete because of technological progress or a return to the labour market after a lengthy interruption. Similarly, rights to paid time off for training and education are referred to in both collective agreements and by statute in some industrialized countries, mainly in Europe.

At first glance it is not difficult to understand why life-long learning is being promoted as an element of a high-skills, high-wage jobs strategy. A highly skilled labour force is more flexible and adaptive to structural change than a low-skilled labour force. The corollary is that highly skilled workers are in a better position to take advantage of new opportunities than low-educated workers. Highly skilled people have a lower incidence of unemployment than low-skilled people, and if unemployment is encountered then people with the right skills will find their way into jobs more quickly and at lower cost to society than people who lack the skills in demand. Skill formation and adaptation should, therefore, be part of a jobs strategy. Moreover, because the skills of workers confer economies of scale to other factors of production, highly qualified workers tend to be more productive and achieve more value added for themselves (Schömann, 1994; Tuijnman, 1989), the workplace (Steedman and Wagner, 1989) and the economy as a whole (Barro, 1991; Lee and Lee, 1995; Lucas, 1993). Not only can a growing economy afford to pay higher wages than a slowly growing or recession-prone economy, it also creates new, high-paying jobs, frequently more than are lost as a consequence of restructuring. A highly skilled labour force is also an advantage in the competition for international capital investments. Accordingly, skill formation and skill adaptation should feature prominently among policy options in high-wage countries.

This analysis highlights a range of issues. First, skill formation is a matter of importance for the whole labour force, not only for youths and labour market entrants. Second, life-long learning implies a shift away from education and towards learning. Third, skill formation draws attention to the establishment and functioning of markets for learning and competence development. Finally, skill formation implies a need to improve the articulation of education, training, and employment policies in a framework of life-long learning. Based on such reasoning, high expectations surround the notion of life-long learning. But what is life-long learning, and how does it fit into a high-skill, high-wage job strategy? What are the implications of life-long learning for educational policy, labour market policy and social insurance policy?

In this chapter we address these questions by reviewing the concepts, principles and policy targets of life-long learning in the perspective of labour market policy and educational policy. In section 1 we consider the definition of life-long learning and describe in section 2 the policy targets associated with skill formation and life-long learning. In section 3 we then review economic and labour market theories and examine the assumptions that underlie the current advocacy of life-long learning as a crucial element in a high-skill, high-wage job strategy. In section 4 we present a summary of the research evidence on the efficiency and effectiveness of policies for life-long learning, including organizational elements. In section 5 we cite studies offering ample support for the validity of the accumulation hypothesis in life-long learning and the gendered pattern of participation. Finally, in section 6, we discuss implications for policy-makers and researchers involved in policy analysis and evaluation.

1   THE LIFE-LONG LEARNING CONCEPT

Generally, the philosophy of life-long learning is based on the idea that the organizing principle for all education and training should not be based on the traditional, 'front-loaded' approach, according to which learning is mainly confined to a sequence of compulsory schooling and formal education at the upper secondary and postsecondary stages of the educational system. Instead, it has been proposed that learning should be seen as a fundamental and life-long process of human development (Faure, 1972). Possibly as a consequence of a growing appreciation of its economic importance, this principle of life-long learning is now increasingly accepted, not least among policy-makers.

Life-long learning implies that learning takes place throughout life, that it is confined neither to any specific age group nor to education administered by educational institutions. The concept thus refers to all systematically organized learning activities associated with formal education as well as to learning that takes place in informal or nonformal settings (Colletta, in press; Coombs, 1973). Whereas formal education refers to any organized and systematic education provided by schools and other educational institutions, nonformal education may be defined as any organized and systematic educational activity that is carried on outside the formal system. In contrast, informal education refers to a life-long process of experiential and open learning—a process of informally acquiring certain values, attitudes, skills and knowledge from experience, from learning resources available in the environment and through independent, self-directed learning.

Life-long learning is a large, overarching concept with many adherents. Popular education, formal schooling, adult education, self-directed learning, continuing vocational training, on-the-job training, informal learning in the workplace and social education for senior citizens are examples of more specific elements (Sutton, in press). Life-long learning as a concept thus embraces all learning that takes place from infancy throughout adult life, in families, schools, vocational training institutions, universities, the workplace and in the community at large. Its merit lies in the challenge it brings to using institutional and age criteria as delimiting factors in educational policy. But in so doing it creates another problem. Because life-long learning denotes a philosophy and an ideal based on humanistic principles more than a concrete policy strategy, it so far has evaded precise definition. Because the concept cannot be defined in unambiguous, operational terms, it is not directly amenable to policy analysis and policy evaluation. This poses a serious problem, of course, in that it undermines the capacity of policy analysts and others to examine and understand the meaning of the proposals that are currently being advocated under its banner. Could it be that life-long learning is proposed as a panacea for solving all kinds of social ills and economic problems precisely because the term is not exact, not operationally definable, and therefore exceedingly difficult to measure and evaluate?

Only a broad view of learning and education as life-long learning allows meaningful comparisons of learning processes within societies, for different societies rely on very different institutional arrangements to work towards the same policy target. Conceptually, life-long learning activities can be classified in various ways. One way of thinking about life-long learning is in terms of the types of institutions that support learning. Formal, nonformal and informal education has already been mentioned as a useful classification. Another classification might be based on the degree to which the learning activities are supported by public spending or private initiative, whether for profit or not. However, life-long learning can hardly be described using dichotomous, two-category variables. For example, programmes are seldom funded on an entirely public or private basis. The use of continuous variables recognizes that many providers of life-long learning opportunities differ on classification criteria only in degree. Worthwhile criteria start from the premise that variables known to vary widely among the providers are relevant in principle. Institutions supporting life-long learning can thus be studied in terms of their size; recruitment strategy; certification practice; staff profile; modalities of teaching and learning; the distribution of costs, expenditures and income; and the degree of community involvement. Another group of relevant variables can be derived from characteristics of the learners, like initial educational attainment, age, sex, ethnicity, household composition, employment situation, occupational status, income situation, motivational orientations and leisure versus career orientation.

For the purpose of this chapter the latter distinction is especially relevant. Life-long learning activities can be classified in two ways, and specific policy targets are associated with each. The first category refers to the learning projects undertaken for personal development, consumption and the fulfilment of leisure. The second refers to the learning projects that relate to the current job or future employment. Whereas the former may be termed 'learning for consumption', the second can be described as 'learning for investment'. Although the distinction between learning for consumption and learning for investment is essential, the practical use of this dichotomy is limited. There are numerous examples where both the investment part and consumption component of learning activities cannot be separated. In fact, many countries dispose of legislation or collective agreements for paid or unpaid educational leave that acknowledge this difficulty. Additionally, problems arise because it is impossible to predict the uses to which knowledge and skills might be put in the future. Hence, all learning is largely an investment, albeit with uncertain returns.

Yet despite this difficulty, the distinction offers a theoretical means of conceptualizing the policy goals to which life-long learning is expected to contribute in the context of a high-skill, high-wage jobs strategy. For policy-makers it is usually the investment-related perspective—according to which life-long learning is considered an economically useful activity—that has made it an objective of education and labour market policy. The investment hypothesis holds that the costs of skill formation will be more than compensated by future private and social benefits measured, for example, in terms of increased individual productivity, increased economic growth or increased labour market flexibility. Flexibility is achieved when participants are better equipped to take up job opportunities in new forms of activities, including self-employment and new occupational fields. The concept of life-long learning involves a rethinking of the link between initial education and training and later learning activities. The concept underscores the complementary nature of further training and further education *vis-à-vis* the acquisition of a basic education and basic skills. Learning how to learn should be a focus during the initial years of schooling and training.

2   POLICY TARGETS OF LIFE-LONG LEARNING

Since the advent more than 30 years ago of human capital theory, which identified investment in human capital generally as an important policy target, the links between education and the economy have not only become more complex but, according to the OECD (1994a, 1994b, 1994c), also much more powerful than hitherto. Several factors have contributed to this potential rise in the economic value of education. The use of new technologies in production, communication and transportation has opened up new avenues for global trade and the flow of investment capital, and competition in national and international markets has intensified. Related factors, which may well be a consequence rather than an antecedent of the changed macroeconomic environment, are increases in product specialization, a tendency towards increasing earnings differentials and increased job instability.

These developments have brought to light structural problems in the labour markets and economies of certain European countries compared with their main competitors. Imbalance in public and private sector activity, high unemployment (especially among youth and young adults), a low level of job creation in the private sector, a low productivity and slow economic growth are among some of the problems portrayed in the analysis conducted for *The OECD Jobs Study* (OECD, 1994a). To this may be added the concern about increasing shares of long-term unemployment in most European countries, which indicates the higher risk of social exclusion as a consequence.

Persisting unemployment can be seen as one consequence of the limited capacity of countries to adapt and fully exploit opportunities offered by the newly emerging forms of global trade. Insufficient capacity to adapt to the changing environment is due in part to macroeconomic policies of the past, such as those promoting high budget deficits over many years and microlevel incentive effects of wage structures. Labour market policies have a supportive role to foster the capacity for adaptation. But rigidities in education and training systems, which stifle incentives for investment and high performance in learning, disturb market signals and perpetuate the gap between schools and workplaces. This has most likely contributed to ossifying the capacity of societies to adapt.

The best way to exploit the new economic evironment is to strengthen the capacity of firms and labour markets to adjust to change, improve their productivity and capitalize on innovation. This capacity depends first and foremost on competence: the competence of governments to organize a supportive macroeconomic environment; the competence of firms to organize production efficiently and make the right business choices; the competence of work teams to add value in a complex production process; and the competence of individual workers to perform their work tasks efficiently and effectively to reflect, innovate and learn. Clearly, competence is much more than knowledge; it is embedded not only in individual people, but also in teams, work organizations, governments and whole societies. Life-long learning has been implicated in this analysis because it is seen as representing a flexible strategy for skill formation that holds promise for alleviating the main shortcoming of conventional 'front-end' models of schooling (OECD, 1994c). Indeed, life-long learning calls into question the objectives, structure, content, and teaching methods of the formal education system at all levels.

Hence, a primary policy target of life-long learning is productivity increases, for they can be achieved at various levels by stressing a continued effort for productivity enhancement through learning processes. Closely related to productivity increases is wage growth or the strategy to keep wages at high levels and avoid the typically concave shape of age–earnings profiles. But before earnings from work are considered, the issue of occupational choice at labour market entry needs to be examined. Objectives for life-long learning are, therefore, occupation-specific and foster the role of occupational mobility and labour turnover in overcoming structural inertia in the labour market. Such structural inefficiency in labour markets may consist in rigid occupational segregation of men and women. Another factor in this inefficiency is that people who are not committed to or involved in life-long learning have different probabilities of becoming and staying unemployed. High on the agenda of policy targets for life-long learning are equity concerns such as opportunities for second-chance education or training for school drop-outs and reintegration into the labour market after career breaks or long-term unemployment. Similarly, it has been claimed that life-long learning policies could narrow wage or income inequality over the life course. These policy targets will be discussed on the basis of some necessarily selective evaluation studies in sections 3 and 4 of this chapter.

3   LABOUR MARKET THEORIES AND LIFE-LONG LEARNING

The new interest in life-long learning reflects changes in theory as much as changes in the policy environment, which were alluded to above. For example, current thinking about the economic role of life-long learning has been influenced by the so-called 'new growth' theories proposed by Romer (1986), Barro (1991), Levine and Renelt (1992), and Lee and Lee (1995). New growth theories present a partial reconceptualization of the neoclassical production function, but more prominence is now assigned to the role of 'intangible' factors. These factors, subsumed under the heading of 'knowledge', are entered as externalities in the production model. Hence, the knowledge factor is considered to confer economies of scale on the other factors in production. What is important, therefore, is not only the optimization of the primary production factors but especially their optimal allocation, given the strongly diminishing returns to investment in knowledge.

There is a substantial correlation between knowledge and competence, but they are not the same. Competence is a wider notion because it implies the capacity to organize knowledge and apply it to advantage in a concrete and demanding setting. The concept of competence draws attention to the three essential components of intangible capital: knowledge, organization and innovation in application. Competence thus refers not only to human capital but also to the social or cultural capital that exists primarily in the relations between people. Whereas knowledge is an important product of the educational system, competence is the sought-after criterion in skill formation. The shift in policy thinking from 'front-end' education to life-long learning reflects the desire of policy-makers to reorient educational systems towards producing competence rather than knowledge. Because competence derives its meaning in an applied setting, the term also calls attention to the screening and filtering mechanisms that provide the link between labour markets and the skill-formation process. This sense of the word is consistent with the emphasis on allocation in new growth theories (Eliasson, 1995).

From an economic perspective, skill formation involves the allocation of scarce resources to a learning process that is designed to produce competence. This process can be represented in an educational production function, which is a mathematical expression that relates inputs to outputs. Many factors can be included in such a function. For example, financial, human and physical capital items are usually included among the input factors, whereas educational attainment and different skills, values and attitudes are among the commonly measured outputs. The challenge of making the skill-formation process cost-effective thus refers to the search for efficient ways of converting or substituting resources. Life-long learning is advocated because it is believed to offer a flexible and efficient way of organizing the skill-formation process and so developing the human, cultural and social capital that is needed in pursuing a high-skill, high-wage jobs strategy. There are several problems, however, and an important one is that it usually takes a long time before the conversion of financial capital into human, cultural and social capital pays off in terms of increased productivity, economic growth and the creation of new, high-wage jobs.

As firms and labour markets change, some jobs will become obsolete, and others will be created. Employees who want to take an active role in this structural change may need to change jobs several times. Some large firms may develop a capacity to master such structural change in organizing internal reorientation of occupational careers. For most employees it will mean that job shifts between employers become more frequent. Hence, they need to acquire new competence to fill new vacancies. This circumstance implies a capacity and a willingness for life-long learning. Whereas the capacity to learn can be influenced only to a limited extent, this is not true either for the willingness of people to learn or for the creation of sufficient and appropriate learning opportunities (Smith, 1992). In both cases incentives play an important role. The efficiency of the labour market in assessing and pricing competence is at the heart of the incentive system that stimulates the development of competence. The market for competence thus provides a conceptual link between skill formation and the labour market (see Eliasson, 1995).

In view of the policy targets identified above, three theories are relevant: human capital theory; screening or filtering theory; and job-matching theory. Screening and job-matching theories are closely related. Both question the simple idea of a linear relation between an investment in skill formation and worker productivity, for such an investment may also lead to overschooling. Although the individual still tends to derive a positive return on overschooling, the costs may outweigh this return, especially for the society. Results suggest that overschooling in terms of an increasing percentage of a birth cohort achieving higher-level education will also lower returns to education for each individual. Comparing positive individual returns to education and the aggregate negative effect of many individuals pursuing higher education at the same time, one finds that there is still a considerable positive net effect for those investing in schooling (Schömann, 1994), suggesting a nonlinear relation between education and individual earnings.

The individual benefits of education are emphasized in the human-capital approach, using personal income as the criterion. The relationship between education and productivity is considered to be straightforward: more highly trained workers obtain a higher wage because their training confers competence which increases the capacity to perform efficiently on the job. Three relations are hypothesized: an effect of skill formation on competence development, an effect of competence on productivity, and an effect of productivity on earnings. Studies conducted in this perspective focus on the relation between education and personal income; the relevance that education has for productivity is usually taken for granted.

Compared with human-capital theory, the screening or filtering perspective assumes a different connection between competence and earnings. It holds that people invest in skill formation because the qualifications that are acquired can be used to inform potential employers that the incumbents possess certain scarce skills and other personality traits, such as motivation and perseverance, which are likely to make them more productive in a given job than competitors lacking these specific characteristics. Participation in life-long learning activities thus presents a means to identify and select workers with a high expected marginal productivity. In this perspective, it is not productivity itself but self-selection that forms the basis for the relation between skill formation and earnings. Hence, skill formation and its corollary, life-long learning, are not necessarily seen as representing a strategic investment in competence, for the purpose may also be to enhance signalling in information-poor and therefore imperfect labour markets.

Information is a central variable in both screening and job-matching theory. The two approaches are therefore closely related. In screening theory the emphasis is on the comparative advantage of the individual, who holds vital information, *vis-à-vis* the employer, who lacks such information. In job-matching theory it is held that both workers and employers can derive useful information from the fact that workers participate in life-long learning activities. This information can be used by both parties to improve the match between the skills possessed by workers and the competence demanded on the job. The central hypothesis is that life-long learning has a positive effect on productivity not only because it raises performance-relevant competence but also because it offers a signal for allocating the right people to the right jobs. Productivity increases are forthcoming only if the signals help improve the job match of an employee and if the new competence is actually used on the job. But if life-long learning widens the discrepancy between workers' competence and the skills demanded at work, then the effect on productivity may be nil or even negative.

The screening theory implies that life-long learning activities carried out in collaboration with employers or partially financed by employers are preceded by a selection process. In return for financial assistance employers want to participate in choosing from many potential participants among a firm's employees. A second screening process might be at work when it comes to sharing returns on investment in relevant skills acquired through learning. In some instances a training course could function as an 'assessment centre' of the productivity of employees, some of which might be selected for specific internal careers. In such instances the speed of learning in various situations could become the selection criterion for higher-level positions in the firm. This example only demonstrates that not all learning activities undertaken under the banner of investment in life-long learning will have positive outcomes for all individuals engaged in this process. On the other hand, life-long learning activities can be 'awarded' by an employer as a kind of fringe benefit that stresses the consumption aspect of some courses with uncertain future use.

4   RESEARCH STUDIES ON LIFE-LONG LEARNING

Theories abound, but what does the research evidence say about the efficiency, effectiveness and equitable outcomes of life-long learning in meeting multiple policy goals and satisfying high expectations? This section presents an overview of the research literature concerned with the measurement of the first- and second-order effects of life-long learning (see also Tuijnman, in press). Life-long learning features as both an independent and dependent variable in a few cases in these studies concerning the six primary policy targets identified above.

4.1   Life-long Learning and Occupational Status

There is much support for the hypothesis that life-long learning has significance for explanations of the differences in labour market status between workers with similar levels of schooling and work experience, even if other variables such as cognitive ability, achievement motivation and personal work histories are held constant. Findings from Swedish research indicate that the direct effect of initial education on occupational status reaches a maximum at about age 30 and then gradually decreases in strength. In contrast, the effect of further education and training increases cumulatively from early to late career (Tuijnman, 1989). As workers get older, the effect of schooling becomes increasingly mediated by further education and personal work histories. For workers older than 50 years the effect of further education on occupational status exceeds that of initial schooling. Bishop (1991) also found that job-relevant training of a formal type results in greater occupational mobility than on-the-job training and informal learning at the workplace. The explanation seems to be that the competence acquired in formal education is easier to certify and use in signalling than skills acquired informally on the job. This interpretation has implications for job mobility. More informal learning while on the job without a certificate is difficult to evaluate by other potential employers and is therefore more likely to increase a worker's attachment to a firm.

4.2   Life-long Learning and Labour Turnover

An important question is that of the relation between life-long learning, employment stability and occupational mobility in and across internal labour markets (Gehin and Méhaut, 1993). Life-long learning is often seen as an instrument for enhancing employment security and facilitating mobility. However, there is some evidence that these two goals are at odds. Theory predicts that firm-specific training improves employment security because the workers who have acquired skills that are central to the operations of the firm run less risk of being laid off at times of economic hardship than workers with general training. However, since trained workers are less likely to quit their jobs, customized skill formation in firms may also mean mobility between jobs (Mincer, 1987). In contrast, competence of a more general type facilitates mobility across internal labour markets. The pay-off of skill formation to the firm depends on how long workers remain in the service of the employer after having received the skill training. Firms are therefore likely to invest more in workers who are likely to stay. The best predictor of this probability to stay is in fact previous tenure with the same firm and participation in firm-based training. Longer job durations in a firm significantly increases men's probability of participation in further education and training (Schömann and Becker, 1995).

Trainees who receive firm-based education are, on average, less mobile prior to receiving the education than other workers, and their mobility is further reduced by that education (Mincer, 1989). Employment stability apparently promotes investment in skill formation, and such investment, in turn, promotes employment stability, since both employers and employees will try to maximize their returns. This is an important finding because it casts doubt on the oversimplifying arguments of 'Eurosclerosis' , that is, the low rate of job mobility and inflexible labour markets that stifle economic activities in Europe. Life-long learning when both employers and employees are committed to it is more likely to lead to longer-lasting periods of employment. Similarly, societies in which the wage and employment system is based on seniority wages and long-term employment relations implement larger life-long learning programmes so that the productivity of older workers remains continuously high.

4.3   Life-long Learning from a Gender Perspective

There is ample evidence that women's periods of employment are, on average, shorter than those of men, mainly because women move more frequently in and out of the labour force during their working life. This has consequences for their participation in life-long learning activities. If only employers perceive that women are more likely to quit a job after receiving further training, they are likely to bias selection into programmes towards a higher participation of men. A form of 'statistical discrimination' against women could be the outcome. Various studies have presented results supporting this hypothesis (Mahnkopf, 1991; Schömann and Becker, 1995). Employment duration within the same firm is a primary selection category for participation in training. Until the late 1970s and early 1980s differences in educational attainment used to be another gender-differentiating factor in life-long learning. However, levels and durations of education have since become much more equally distributed between men and women. Initial educational achievements will provide less basis for disadvantaging women in job-related life-long learning. More attention needs to be paid in evaluation studies to occupational choices that are still gendered and to sources of gender-biased teaching curricula.

Occupational segregation of women has contributed to lowering the number of women in life-long learning that contains strong components of investment in skills. In most countries women are underrepresented in high-technology, capital-intensive industrial sectors that have so far paid more attention to organizing continuous learning within their organization (Gehin and Méhaut, 1993). The public sector in general has granted more equitable access to internal training. However, public funds allocated to training centres or subsidies directly paid to individuals have not been spent with an eye to improving the distribution of such support between men and women (Schömann, 1993). More emphasis in evaluation of life-long learning efforts needs to be put on an equitable distribution of funds and training places. Although these results refer mainly to European countries, recent evidence for the United States shows that male recipients of training benefit from longer employment durations and higher intensity of training. Female recipients tend to compensate for their lack of company training possibilities by seeking training off the job (Veum, 1993).

4.4   Life-long Learning, Employment and Unemployment

The higher the level of initial education, the lower the incidence of unemployment generally is (OECD, 1994c). There is evidence that this applies also to further education and training (OECD, 1991a; OECD, 1991b). Compared with untrained workers, those who receive skill training show a lower incidence of unemployment. Mincer (1987) observes that workers with fewer than 12 years of schooling are 170 per cent more likely to suffer unemployment, and they experience periods of unemployment 30 per cent longer than workers with 16 or more years of schooling. Moreover, educated workers are likely to search for a new job while still employed, thus reducing search costs; educated workers acquire and process information more efficiently than less educated workers; and employers and educated workers both search more intensively to fill more skilled slots than is the case with less educated workers (Berryman, 1995). Because such education influences employment status independently of initial schooling, it also helps consolidate or strengthen the labour market attachment of workers. Life-long learning thus increases employability and decreases both the likelihood of becoming unemployed and the chance of remaining unemployed for a long time once laid off.

Various forms of training have proved effective at prolonging periods of employment and shortening durations of unemployment. In estimates of transition rate models of people in employment, it was found that on-the-job training generally increases the duration between events. In the study by Breen (1992) such events were either a job change to another employer or unemployment. This confirms that learning on the job reduces the risk of becoming unemployed and supports a preventive role of labour market policies. More common is the remedial role of further training policies, which offers the possibility of receiving training once a person is unemployed. In this case the policy target is to leave unemployment and to return to continuous employment. A longitudinal study of the effect of training programmes on the probability of leaving unemployment (Korpi, 1994) showed a positive effect of training on subsequent employment durations. These results imply that life-long learning can, at least potentially, be effective in reducing unemployment pressure in information-poor labour markets.

4.5   Life-long Learning and Productivity

Productivity can be measured in terms of the aggregate output of an economy, the output of an industry or a specific workplace and the output of an individual worker. Microlevel studies of the benefits of skill formation are focussed on the variables that carry meaning for individuals, for example, whether a qualification was obtained or whether improvements in life satisfaction, employment opportunities or earnings were recorded. By contrast, macrolevel studies are concerned with the effects of skill formation on labour supply and demand, the functioning of internal labour markets, productivity, and aggregate economic growth (see Dougherty, 1992).

Studies of the relation between educational attainment and aggregate economic growth often suffer from conceptual and methodological problems limiting the inferences that can be drawn from them. Nevertheless, the recent growth-accounting studies (Barro, 1991; Englander and Gurney, 1994; Jorgenson and Fraumeni, 1993; Levine and Renelt, 1992) have all reported statistically significant correlations between levels of educational attainment and the average growth rate of GDP per capita between 1960 and the mid- or late 1980s. The extension of these estimates by Lee and Lee (1995) included measures of human capital derived from students' scores on a science test administered in 1983–84 by the International Association for the Evaluation of Educational Achievement (IEA). The authors employed the science-test scores of secondary school students as an indirect measure of initial human-capital stock. Results based on 17 countries were consistent with these earlier studies but replaced the crude measure of school enrolment rates or years of schooling as a major component of economic growth by a measure of student achievement. These results have highlighted the importance of the organization and effectiveness of education systems, school curriculum, and teaching systems as well as student aptitudes for economic growth. However, it was still not possible in these studies to compare the aggregate growth effect of further education and training compared with schooling and initial tertiary education.

The effect of skill formation on the productivity of firms has been investigated in several studies. In these cases the possible indicators are the turnover of the firm multiplied by the average percentage share of value added in the turnover of the relevant branch; the annual growth of turnover by worker; the growth of production volume minus the growth of labour volume; profitability; and the change in market share over time. Research using matched firms in different countries by specific product and scale of operation compared the physical productivity of similar work teams, taking into account a number of environmental variables (Prais, 1989; Prais, Jarvis and Wagner, 1989; Steedman and Wagner, 1989). Differences in technology and worker qualifications obtained through training were consistently found to explain lower productivity in British compared to German firms and work teams.

Studies of the relation between further education and training and the productivity of firms have usually emphasized the role of firm-specific training. Blakemore and Hoffman (1989) and Bishop (1990), among others, reported a positive correlation between training effort and production output. Technological change is also a factor of importance because the pace of innovation and technological change is higher in high-productivity growth industries than in industries with lower-productivity growth. High-productivity, high-wage sectors recruit well-educated workers and invest more in training than low-growth sectors (Gill, 1989). Trainability of labour market entrants and job changers becomes the primary selection criterion among applicants for a job (Schömann, 1994). Employer-provided training, which contributes significantly to raising wages, is more extensive in large establishments with elaborate internal structures that operate in complex, competitive market environments (Knoke and Kalleberg, 1994). But studies unequivocally showing that this training investment has a direct impact on the output of firms are scarce. Exceptions are Barron, Black and Loewenstein (1989), Bishop (1987) and Mendes, Cohn and Kiker (1989), who found that training has a significant effect on labour productivity in firms. Barron et al. (1989) found that a 10 per cent increase in training investment led to a growth of 3 per cent in labour productivity. If training raises the productivity of workers, then it is also likely to have an effect on the aggregate output of firms.

4.6 Life-long Learning and Wage Growth

It is often assumed that the positive relation between education and personal earnings is indicative of differences in productivity between workers according to the acquired level of education. However, it has been found in micro-level studies that earnings, although predicted by the level of education, do not equal the real value of the marginal product (Bishop, 1991; Brown, 1989). The theory of implicit wage contracts explains this finding in terms of the distribution of risk-taking between workers and employers. Another explanation is that employers who carry most of the costs of specific training will offer incomes lower than the value of the marginal product. Since the value added of specific training is likely to fall in large measure to the employer, the return in terms of increased productivity is therefore likely to be greater than the return suggested by wage growth of employees.

Studies of average age–earnings profiles in industrialized countries have shown, according to Blaug (1976) and Psacharopoulos (1987), that the relation between formal education and earned income increases in strength up to a point between 40 and 45 years of age, and then levels off. The higher the level of initial education, the higher the age at which this peak is manifested tends to be. This can be interpreted as a reflection of decreasing marginal productivity, where depreciation sets in earlier for poorly educated than well-educated workers. The later in life the effects of formal education on earnings are estimated, the more likely it is that they are mediated by other variables, notably by the labour market positions previously held or through further education that leads to higher-level educational certificates. There is evidence that skill formation is also implicated in the strength of the relation between formal education and earned income: the turning point in earnings power arrives at a later age for workers with additional training compared with workers who lack such training (Mincer, 1991). The cumulative effects that further education and training have on earnings seem to increase with age (Brown, 1989; Tuijnman, 1989).

Estimates of the private rate of return on formal education show a great deal of cross-national consistency (Psacharopoulos, 1985). Most industrialized countries show returns on tertiary education similar to those in the United States, where the private return varied from 6 per cent in the 1970s to between 7 and 11 per cent in the mid-1980s (Cohn and Geske, 1990). Studies conducted in both developed and developing countries have found that the return on training provided to young workers is at least as high as that on tertiary education (Bishop, 1991; Brown, 1989; Lillard and Tan, 1986; Psacharopoulos and Velez, 1992).

Mincer (1991) reanalysed data collected in the United States in the 1970s and 1980s. Using an eight-year time span for depreciation, he found a return on one year with adult education and training of 23.5 per cent for all male workers, 26.5 per cent for new hires and 37.5 per cent for older cohorts. With the training investment written off over a 25-year period, the corresponding estimates were 12. 8 per cent for all workers, 16 per cent for new hires and 26 per cent for older cohorts. The private rate of return on adult education had thus been higher than the return on both schooling and tertiary education. Mincer (1991) concluded:

> The range of estimates of *worker* returns to training based on several data sets seems to exceed the magnitude of rates of return usually observed for schooling investments. Given the data on worker's firm tenure, it appears also that training remains profitable to *firms*, even in the face of average worker mobility. The rates of return here calculated may be large enough to suggest underinvestment in training relative to that in schooling (pp. 35–6).

Tuijnman (1989) finds that the direct effect of further education and training on individual earnings is not significant statistically once the job level is held constant in the equation. However, the indirect effect of further education on earnings mediated by job level is significant and positive. Job-matching theory offers a possible explanation for this finding. The theory holds that further education only increases earnings if it improves worker productivity. Hence, the pay-off to the individual depends on whether a qualification or other means of sending a signal to employers is obtained, whether the person can make effective use of the new skills on the job and whether the productivity gain is noticed and warrants higher pay.

One of the intervening processes, usually unobserved in studies that focus on the microlevel, is the existence of collective agreements that relate further training directly to career-track positions in a firm or an industry (Mahnkopf, 1991; OECD 1991a). If such agreements do exist, the link between learning and higher pay or upward job mobility is part of an agreement. In countries under socialist rule such certification of new skills has been directly related to job advancement and higher pay (Schömann, 1994), with the selection process of who has access to such training being restricted. In such an employment system it is no longer the level of educational attainment that determines wages, but changes in the level of education through further training both within firms and at job changes.

In recent estimates of the process of selection for further training (Schömann and Becker, 1995) and the effect of this selection process on earnings at job change and internal careers (Becker and Schömann, in press) a difference of this process between men and women has been found. Assessment of the selection mechanism and then of the impact that selection for training has on subsequent earnings shows that selection for training has a positive impact on men's internal career advancement and in-house job changes to better-paid positions. By contrast, women capitalize on selection for training while staying continuously in the same job.

Screening theory predicts that the private returns from education will exceed the social returns and that this imbalance will be more pronounced in further education and training than in secondary and tertiary education. The common assumption is that the larger the distance to compulsory education, the more the social rate of return diminishes relative to the private rate of return. Because workers usually sacrifice little or no pay to get further education or training, and because both firms and society subsidize a major part of the direct costs of this investment in skill formation, the individual return is likely to be higher than the social return. Unfortunately, there is little evidence to support or reject this hypothesis.

4.7 Summary of the Main Findings

Reviews of the main findings of the huge body of evaluations have also been attempted by other studies (Berryman, 1995; OECD, 1994c; Tuijnman, in press). First, educational attainment covaries with unemployment incidence.

The least qualified have a high unemployment risk compared to the well educated in the labour force. Life-long learning is implicated in this relation
because those who take part in further education, especially in employer-
sponsored training, experience fewer and briefer periods of unemployment.
Conversely, low-educated adults engage less in self-directed life-long learning
and receive less training from their employers than do the well-educated workers. Industries and firms in competitive, often technology-intensive sectors
where employment is growing require better-educated workers, invest more in
the provision of opportunities for life-long learning and pay higher wages than
employers in the less dynamic sectors of economic activity. Thus, although
many adults make use of the life-long learning opportunities that are available
to them, the opening up and stimulation of the markets for skill formation
brings a growing disadvantage for the least educated, least experienced, and
older workers in the labour force, who tend to have limited opportunities and
incentives to learn.

Finally, educational attainment and earnings are clearly related. The least
qualified in the labour force have low earnings compared to the well qualified.
The higher the level of initial educational attainment, the more the individual
and the employers will invest in subsequent education and training, which in
turn improve employability, raise productivity and increase earnings from
work. However, the above findings raise a number of critical questions about
the usefulness of a life-long learning strategy for raising the productivity and
wages of the least qualified in the labour force and those working temporary
jobs with unfavourable working conditions and probably coming from an
ethnic minority background. These questions are addressed in the next section.

5   RESEARCH ON COMPENSATION AND ACCUMULATION

This section presents the evidence of research on the compensation and accumulation hypotheses in life-long learning (Tuijnman, 1991). In a compensation perspective life-long learning is advocated because it offers the least-
skilled people in the labour force opportunities to update and enlarge their
skills and acquire new qualifications, which can be used to compensate and
off-set the disadvantages that have resulted from their initially low level of
educational attainment. While not denying the opportunity and second-chance
value of a life-long learning for all strategy, the accumulation perspective
takes a more pessimistic view. It holds that life-long learning cannot be
expected to contribute to an equal opportunity strategy, at least not without
'corrective' policy intervention, because the processes that influence the accu-

mulation of learning experiences over the life span are anchored in vastly unequal home and schooling backgrounds. Moreover, policy interventions in this field are in need of close monitoring and evaluation (Schömann, 1993) to assess the equitable implementation of a life-long learning policy. Unless programme objectives for public funds, like the inclusion of ethnic minorities, the long-term unemployed or women are carefully monitored, programmes might be devised to reinforce accumulation of skills rather than compensation of a lack of skills.

The accumulation hypothesis can be seen as an extension of the resource-conversion theory proposed by Coleman (1990). The conversion theory predicts that the cumulation of learning experiences over the life span is not accidental but rather is determined by the amount and quality of home resources and the level and quality of schooling initially received. The derived proposition is that the better the quality and the higher the level of initial educational attainment, the greater the prospect of accumulating additional learning experiences in adulthood and the higher the likelihood that these new learning experiences will have an impact on wage growth.

Although there are some exceptions (e.g., see van Leeuwen, Dronkers and Dronkers, 1992), the available research evidence overwhelmingly supports the accumulation hypothesis. The fears expressed by some theorists (e.g., Blaug and Mace, 1977; Stoikov, 1975), who in the 1970s examined the prospects that a recurrent education strategy might achieve a more equal distribution of both learning opportunities and the economic returns to education appear to have been confirmed. Longitudinal studies (Schömann and Becker, 1995; Tuijnman, 1989) found evidence in support of the accumulation hypothesis. Cross-sectional studies have also shown consistently that well-educated people benefit from life-long learning to a greater extent than poorly educated people (Dougherty, 1992; Lillard and Tan, 1986). Data collected by the OECD in the early 1990s showed, for 10 European countries, that participation in job-related or career-related further education and training was heavily biased in favour of those who have received a better education initially, those who are employed and those who have achieved good positions in the labour job market (Borkowsky, van der Heiden and Tuijnman, 1995). The relationship between initial education and job-related further education and training is illustrated in Table 15.2.

Rather than compensating for the low levels of educational attainment of many workers when they first enter the labour market, the observed patterns of opportunity to learn and actual participation in life-long learning tend to widen the skill gap among workers. There can be little doubt that life-long learning accentuates initial differences in educational attainment and achievement among employees and that the positive economic outcomes generated by such learning accentuate the positive economic outcomes associated with

*Table 15.2   Percentage of the Employed Population 25–64 Years of Age
Participating in Job- or Career-related Further Education and
Training during the Reference Period, by Level of Initial
Education*

	ISCED2[1]	ISCED3	ISCED5	ISCED6/7
Reference period 1 year				
Canada (1991)	19	25	38	44
Finland (1990)	28	47	73	74
France (1992)	20	31	58	39
Germany (1992)	11	23	38	44
Norway (1992)	16	33	53	62
Sweden (1992)	21	34	49	57
Switzerland (1992)	16	39	51	53
United States (1991)	10	30	49	56
Reference period 4 weeks				
Denmark (1991)	6	14	23	27
Ireland (1992)	2	4	8	9
Spain (1992)	1	6	5	8
United Kingdom (1992)	4	10	19	20

Note
1 ISCED stands for the International Standard Classification of Education. ISCED2 means completed lower secondary education; ISCED3, completed upper secondary education; ISCED5, completed nonuniversity tertiary education; and ISCED6/7, completed university education.

Source
National submissions of data to OECD, from 'Indicators of Continuing Education and Training' by A. Borkowsky, M. van der Heiden and A. C. Tuijnman, 1995, in B. Bucht (ed.), *Indicators of Education and Labour Market Destinations*, Paris: OECD, Centre for Educational Research and Innovation. Copyright 1995 by OECD. Adapted by permission.

those initial differences in educational attainment (Berryman, 1995). The labour market theories and the research evidence reviewed in previous sections suggest that there are two main explanations for this finding. First, it can be a result of self-selection in the labour market, meaning those who have invested most in their initial education continue to do so while in employment. Second, it may be that skill formation does not represent an alternative to initial education but rather complements it and renders it more efficient. Self-selection and complementarity are not necessarily in conflict, and both are supported by the evidence.

What are the implications for policy? If a concern with efficiency drives educational production, then policy will seek to control the costs of education while maintaining or increasing output. One way to go about this might be to deregulate and focus on the incentives for individuals to invest in their own learning; to remove barriers to learning; and to certify the value of produced competence. But such a policy might accentuate the gaps in both learning opportunities and outcomes. Whereas the explicit recognition of the social distribution of achieved competence is efficient from a labour market perspective, it runs counter to an ideal of promoting social equity (Eliasson, 1995). Hence, policy-makers seeking to optimize educational production in a framework of life-long learning need to balance the potential benefits against the risks. In this perspective it may be desirable from a social viewpoint for governments to retain some control over the markets for skill formation either by means of controlling the quality of learning, by playing the role of a coordinator between social partners or different regional levels of implementation, and, lastly, through initiating and financing programmes for specific disadvantaged target groups.

But interventions designed to limit the undesirable side-effects of a free market for skill formation may also limit the efficiency of that market. Policy interventions in life-long learning must therefore be considered against the background of other possible interventions, notably in the areas of labour market and social insurance policies. Insurance is needed to shield people and firms from the consequences of market failure and to prevent underinvestment in skill formation. Risk containment argues for developing a better system of human-capital accounting because lack of education and training is the single most distinguishing characteristic of the poor and excluded (Friedman, 1989).

The goal of improving the adaptive and innovative capacity of the labour force requires the implementation of supportive policies on at least three fronts (Hirsch and Tuijnman, in press). The first is unambiguous support for life-long learning, which requires ending the dependency of education and training systems on 'front-end' models of provision. The second element of policy is to transform skill formation from a process of selection and exclusion to one of comprehensiveness. The aims are to ensure that all young people leave the educational system with the minimum general and vocational qualifications needed for entering the world of work and that all adults, regardless of employment status, sex, age or ethnic background have access to sufficient opportunities for continued learning. The third policy priority is (a) to end reliance on detailed administrative planning as a way of deciding on the allocation of resources to skill formation and (b) instead to strengthen incentives for a market-like organization for learning and competence development.

6   IMPLICATIONS FOR LABOUR MARKET EVALUATION

The claim that worker skills are a major ingredient of productivity and economic competitiveness has found a large and receptive audience among policy-makers and researchers. It has put the issue of life-long learning back on to the list of priorities of labour market policies. The interest in life-long learning thus derives from an argument about the role of skills in influencing the adaptive and innovative capacity of the labour force. This argument is at the heart of a debate over whether and why the European economies have performed below expectation since the late 1960s (see Table 15.1).

Studies reviewed in this chapter indicate that misallocated and insufficient skills do indeed offer a partial explanation of why the cumulative input of capital, manpower and technology since the 1960s has produced lower-than-expected results in terms of labour market performance and job growth. This evidence, though albeit still partial, has focussed attention on the role of intangible variables such as the competence of workers, information and social and cultural capital in influencing the marginal productivity of other factors of production. In conclusion, skill formation has moved to the fore in the European debate on jobs because there is at least circumstantial evidence that competence does in fact confer economies of scale to the inputs of financial capital, labour and technology.

The attentive reader will have noted that there are still many lacunae in the knowledge about life-long learning and its role in a high-skills, high-wage jobs strategy. Indeed, the entire analysis stands or falls with the hypothesis that the investment in skills makes workers and firms more productive. In order to understand whether, how and to what extent workers' competence affects their productivity, studies of educational attainment and earnings will never suffice. Instead, it will be necessary to measure the independent and dependent variables directly. This view offers a strong argument for looking carefully at the dimensions of skills and competencies, how life-long learning helps workers to acquire them, and how they bear on production (Stern and Tuijnman, 1995). Additionally, life-long learning is highly dependent on the context in which such a policy is implemented. Factors like the cohort size of school leavers (Neuman and Weiss, 1995; Schömann, 1994) or the speed of technological developments are important intervening variables, albeit mostly neglected by evaluations in this field.

Labour market analysts usually rely on measures of formal educational attainment as a proxy for workers' knowledge and competence. This approach may be permissible in some instances, but not if the purpose of the analysis is to evaluate the processes and outcomes of skill formation in a framework of life-long learning. Direct measures of competence and related estimates of skill accumulation and depreciation are required for establishing a new concept of human-capital accounting, which many observers agree is needed if skill formation for all in a truly life-long perspective is to be a sound investment that yields the expected benefits (Vickery and Wurzburg, 1992). There is also a need to integrate findings from different levels of aggregation and to use different methodological approaches so that 'lessons' learned can be judged against the institutional background in which they have been implemented. Such information would also begin to create a more solid knowledge base for policy-making. Without a new approach in the form of human-capital accounting, policy discussion will continue to rest on assumptions about the contribution of skill formation to competitiveness and economic growth assumptions that are untestable because the required data are not available.

REFERENCES

Barro, R. (1991), 'Economic Growth in a Cross Section of Countries', *Quarterly Journal of Economics*, 56 (2), 404–43.

Barron, J. M., D. A. Black and M. A. Loewenstein (1989), 'Job Matching and On the Job Training', *Journal of Labor Economics*, 7 (1), 1–19.

Becker, R. and K. Schömann (in press), 'Berufliche Weiterbildung und Arbeitseinkommen—Eine Längsschnittstudie über den Einfluß beruflicher Weiterbildung auf Einkommensverläufe', Technical University of Dresden. (Unpublished manuscript)

Berryman, S. E. (1995), 'The Contribution of Literacy to the Wealth of Individuals and Nations', in A. C. Tuijnman, I. Kirsch and D. A. Wagner (eds), *Adult Basic Skills: Advances in Measurement and Policy Analysis*, New York: Hampton Press, pp. 18–32.

Bishop, J. H. (1987), 'The Recognition and Reward of Employee Performance', *Journal of Labor Economics*, 4 (4), Part 2, S36–S56.

Bishop, J. H. (1990), 'Job Performance, Turnover and Wage Growth', *Journal of Labor Economics*, 8 (3), 363–86.

Bishop, J. H. (1991), 'On the Job Training of New Hires', in D. Stern and J. M. M. Ritzen (eds), *Market Failure in Training? New Economic Analyses and Evidence on the Training of Adult Employees*, Berlin: Springer, pp. 61–98.

Blakemore, A. and D. Hoffman (1989), 'Seniority Rules and Productivity: An Empirical Test', *Econometrica*, 56, 359–71.

Blaug, M. (1976), *Introduction to the Economics of Education*, Harmondsworth: Penguin Books.

Blaug, M. and J. Mace (1977), 'Recurrent Education—The New Jerusalem?', *Higher Education*, 6, 277–300.

Borkowsky, A., M. van der Heiden and A. C. Tuijnman (1995), 'Indicators of Continuing Education and Training', in B. Bucht (ed.), *Indicators of Education and Labour Market Destinations*, Paris: OECD, Centre for Educational Research and Innovation, pp. 139–56.

Breen, R. (1992), 'Job Changing and Job Loss in the Irish Youth Labour Market: A Test of a General Model', *European Sociological Review*, 8 (2), 113–25.

Brown, J. (1989), 'Why Do Wages Increase with Tenure? On the Job Training and Life Cycle Wage Growth Observed within Firms', *American Economic Review*, 79 (4), 971–91.

Capelli, P. and N. Rogovsky (1995), 'Self-assessed Skill Needs and Job Performance', in A. C. Tuijnman, J. S. Kirsch and D. A. Wagner (eds), pp. 75–92.

Cohn, E. and T. G. Geske (1990), *The Economics of Education* (3rd ed.), Oxford: Pergamon.

Coleman, J. S. (1990), *Foundations of Social Theory*, Cambridge, MA: The Belknap Press of Harvard University Press.

Colletta, N. J. (in press), 'Formal, Informal and Nonformal Education', in A. C. Tuijnman (ed.), *The International Encyclopedia of Adult Education and Training*, Oxford: Elsevier Science.

Commission of the European Communities (1993), *Growth, Competitiveness, Employment: The Challenges and Ways Forward into the 21st Century*, White Paper, Bulletin of the European Communities (suppl. 6/93).

Coombs, P. H. (1973), *New Paths to Learning*, New York: International Council for Educational Development.

Dougherty, C. (1992), 'Evaluation of the Economic and Labour Market Effects of Continuing Education and Training: Practice and Policy Issues', in A. C. Tuijnman (guest ed.), *International Journal of Educational Research* (Effectiveness Research into Continuing Education), 17 (6), 549–64.

Eliasson, G. (1995), *The Markets for Competence and Educational Services: Microeconomic Explanations of Macroeconomic Growth*, Paris: OECD, Centre for Educational Research and Innovation.

Englander, S. and A. Gurney (1994, Spring), 'Productivity Growth: Medium-term Trends', *OECD Economic Studies*, 22, 49–109.

Faure, E. (1972), *Learning to Be. The World of Education Today and Tomorrow*, Paris: UNESCO.

Friedman, R. (1989), *The Safety Net as Ladder*, Washington, DC: Council of State Policy and Planning Agencies.

Gehin, J. P. and P. Méhaut (1993), *Apprentissage ou Formation Continue? Stratégies Éducatives des Entreprises en Allemagne et en France*, Paris: l'Harmattan.

Gill, I. (1989), 'Technological Change, Education, and the Obsolescence of Human Capital', PhD dissertation, Chicago: University of Chicago Press.

Hirsch, D. and A. C. Tuijnman (in press), 'The Demand and Supply of Learning Opportunities for Adults. Introduction to Section 5', in A. C. Tuijnman (ed.), *The International Encyclopedia of Adult Education and Training*, Oxford: Elsevier Science.

Jorgenson, D. W. and B. M. Fraumeni (1993), 'Education and Growth', Boston, MA: Harvard University. (Unpublished manuscript)

Knoke, D. and A. L. Kalleberg (1994, August), 'Job Training in U.S. Organizations', *American Sociological Review*, 59, 537–46.

Korpi, T. (1994), *Escaping Unemployment, Studies in the Individual Consequences of Unemployment and Labor Market Policy*, Swedish Institute for Social Research, no. 24, Akademitryck AB, Edsbruk.

Lee, D. W. and T. H. Lee (1995), 'Human Capital and Economic Growth: Tests Based on the International Evaluation of Educational Achievement', *Economic Letters*, 47, 219–25.

Levine, R. and D. Renelt (1992), 'A Sensitivity Analysis of Cross-country Growth Regressions', *American Economic Review*, 82 (4), 942–63.

Lillard, L. A. and H. W. Tan (1986), *Training: Who Gets It and What Are Its Effects?*, Santa Monica, CA: RAND Corporation.

Lucas, R. E. (1993), 'Making a Miracle', *Econometrica*, 61, 251–72.

Mahnkopf, B. (1991), *A Modernization Approach of German Trade Unions: Further Training through Collective Bargaining*, WZB discussion paper FS I 91–2, Wissenschaftszentrum Berlin für Sozialforschung.

Mendes de Oliviera, M. E., E. Cohn and B. Kiker (1989), 'Tenure, Earnings, and Productivity', *Oxford Bulletin of Economics and Statistics*, 51, 1–14.

Mincer, J. (1987), *Job Training, Wage Growth, and Labor Turnover*, National Bureau of Economic Research, working paper no. 2680, Department of Economics, Columbia University, New York.

Mincer, J. (1989), 'Human Capital and the Labor Market. A Review of Current Research', *Educational Researcher*, 18, 27–34.

Mincer, J. (1991), 'Job Training: Costs, Returns, and Wage Profiles', in D. Stern and J. M. M. Ritzen (eds), *Market Failure in Training? New Economic Analysis and Evidence on Training of Adult Employees*, Berlin: Springer, pp. 15–40.

Neuman, S. and A. Weiss (1995), 'On the Effects of Schooling Vintage on Experience-earnings Profiles: Theory and Evidence', *European Economic Review*, 39, 943–55.

OECD (1991a), *Further Education and Training of the Labour Force in OECD Countries: Evidence and Issues*, Paris: OECD, Directorate for Education, Employment, Labour and Social Affairs.

OECD (1991b), *Further Education and Training of the Labour Force: A Comparative Analysis of National Strategies for Industry Training in Australia, Sweden and the United States*, Paris: OECD, Directorate for Education, Employment, Labour and Social Affairs.

OECD (1994a), *The OECD Jobs Study: Facts, Analysis, Strategies*, Paris: OECD.

OECD (1994b), *The OECD Jobs Study: Evidence and Explanations, Part 1, Labour Market Trends and Underlying Forces of Change*, Paris: OECD.

OECD (1994c), *The OECD Jobs Study: Evidence and Explanations, Part 2, The Adjustment Potential of the Labour Market*, Paris: OECD.

Prais, S. J. (ed.) (1989), *Productivity, Education and Training: Britain and Other Countries Compared*, London: National Institute of Economic and Social Research.

Prais, S. J., V. Jarvis and K. Wagner (1989, May), 'Productivity and Vocational Skills in Services in Britain and Germany: Hotels', *National Institute Economic Review*, 4, 53–76.

Psacharopoulos, G. (1985), 'Returns to Education: A Further International Update and Implications', *Journal of Human Resources*, 20, 583–604.

Psacharopoulos, G. (1987), 'Earnings Functions', in G. Psacharopoulos (ed.), *Economics of Education: Research and Studies*, Oxford: Pergamon, pp. 218–23.

Psacharopoulos, G. and E. Velez (1992), 'Does Training Pay, Independent of Education? Some Evidence from Colombia', in A. C. Tuijnman (guest ed.), *International Journal of Educational Research* (Effectiveness Research into Continuing Education), 17 (6), 581–91.

Romer, P. (1986), 'Increasing Returns and Long-run Growth', *Journal of Political Economy*, 94, 1002–37.

Schömann, K. (1993), 'Focusing on the Micro-level', in K. Jensen and P. K. Madsen (eds), *Measuring Labour Market Measures*, Copenhagen: Ministry of Labour, pp. 141–66.

Schömann, K. (1994), *The Dynamics of Labor Earnings over the Life Course—A Comparative and Longitudinal Analysis of Germany and Poland*, Berlin: edition sigma.

Schömann, K. and R. Becker (1995), 'Participation in Further Education over the Life-course: A Longitudinal Study of Three Birth Cohorts in the Federal Republic of Germany', *European Sociological Review*, 11 (2), 1–22, 187–208.

Smith, R. M. (1992), 'Implementing the Learning to Learn Concept', in A. C. Tuijnman and M. van der Kamp (eds), *Learning across the Lifespan: Theories, Research, Policies*, Oxford: Pergamon, pp. 173–88.

Steedman, H. and K. Wagner (1989, May), 'Productivity, Machinery and Skills: Clothing Manufacture in Britain and Germany', *National Institute Economic Review*, 41–57.

Stern, D. and A. C. Tuijnman (1995), 'Adult Basic Skills: Policy Issues and a Research Agenda', in A. C. Tuijnman, I. Kirsch and D. A. Wagner (eds), *Adult Basic Skills: Advances in Measurement and Policy Analysis*, New York: Hampton, pp. 3–17.

Stoikov, V. (1975), *The Economics of Recurrent Education and Training*, Geneva: International Labour Office.

Sutton, P. (in press), 'Lifelong Learning and Continuing Education', in A. C. Tuijnman (ed.), *The International Encyclopedia of Adult Education and Training*, Oxford: Elsevier Science.

Tuijnman, A. C. (1989), *Recurrent Education, Earnings and Wellbeing: A 50-year Longitudinal Study of a Cohort of Swedish Men*, Acta Universitatis Stockholmiensis, Stockholm: Almqvist & Wiksell.

Tuijnman, A. C. (1991), 'Lifelong Learning: A Test of the Accumulation Hypothesis', *International Journal of Lifelong Education*, 10, 275–85.

Tuijnman, A. C. (in press), 'Economics of Adult Education and Training', in A. C. Tuijnman (ed.), *The International Encyclopedia of Adult Education and Training*, Oxford: Elsevier Science.

van Leeuwen, J. Dronkers and S. Dronkers (1992), 'Effects of Continuing Education: A Study on Adult Education, Social Inequality, and Labor Market Position', in A. C. Tuijnman (guest ed.), *International Journal of Educational Research* (Effectiveness Research into Continuing Education), 17 (6), 609–24.

Veum, J. R. (1993, August), 'Training among Young Adults: Who, What Kind, and for How Long?', *Monthly Labor Review*, 27–32.

Vickery, G. and G. Wurzburg (1992, October–November), 'Intangible Investment: Missing Pieces in the Productivity Puzzle', *OECD Observer*, 13–16.

16. From Unemployment to Self-employment: Labour Market Policies for Business Start-up

Nigel Meager

This chapter is focussed on labour market policies aimed at supporting self-employment, and their evaluation. In particular, I examine policies whose object is to stimulate self-employment as an alternative to dependent employment for the unemployed.

Traditional labour market policies concentrate on the creation and preservation of wage employment. An implicit assumption has been that self-employment was an archaic form of work, unsuited to a modern economy, and that outside certain sectors (such as agriculture, craft industries and small-scale retailing) and certain (mainly professional) occupations, the historical decline of self-employment would continue. This view has, until recently, been reflected in the relative lack of interest that academic researchers and labour market commentators have shown in self-employment (see Steinmetz and Wright, 1989).

Since the early 1980s, however, this decline has been arrested and, in some countries, reversed. Small business in general (Sengenberger, Loveman and Piore, 1989), and self-employment in particular, account for an increasing share of employment in industrialized countries. Indeed, in several countries, the 1980s saw an historically unparalleled growth in self-employment. This change applied particularly to the United Kingdom (Campbell and Daly, 1992), where self-employment almost doubled between 1979 and 1989. Recent years have seen renewed interest in self-employment among policymakers and academics, partly as a result of this empirical shift and partly because, as Birch (1977, 1979) stated, small business has been seen as a major engine of job growth, stimulating self-employment as an appropriate response to the unemployment crisis.[1]

When it comes to identifying the economic case for policies to subsidize self-employment among the unemployed (the subject of the present chapter),

---

1 This interest has also been strong in eastern Europe, where massive labour market dislocation has coincided with an ideological enthusiasm for free markets and 'entrepreneurism'.

the evidence from existing research is mixed (Storey, 1994, pp. 239–49). Implicitly at least, most such policies rest on the assumption of capital market imperfections or rationing, leading to a suboptimal rate of business start-up. A further common assumption is that capital markets discriminate against individuals with certain personal characteristics (relating to ethnicity, gender or current employment status) and that such individuals, as a result, enter self-employment at a less than optimal rate or tend to set up 'undercapitalized' businesses. As Storey (1994) noted, however, a common critique of such policies is that they subsidize self-employment among individuals poorly equipped (in terms of human capital) for business success and may create a market distortion (and displace existing businesses) rather than eliminate a market failure. Some of the evidence on these questions is considered further below (see section 4.4). Many such schemes, however, have broader objectives than a strictly economic concern with market failure (see section 2.1).

1   EXPLAINING RECENT SELF-EMPLOYMENT TRENDS

It is not my purpose to attempt to explain recent self-employment developments. Some understanding of these trends is, however, an important background to any discussion of self-employment policies and their evaluation, given that these policies were introduced in a period when the extent and nature of self-employment underwent considerable change in many countries.[2] A brief discussion of the nonpolicy factors affecting the volume and composition of self-employment and the roles played by those factors in different economic and institutional settings is therefore appropriate in order to set the subsequent discussion of labour market policies for self-employment into context.

1.1   Economic, Structural and Demographic Influences

Perhaps the only clear finding to emerge from recent research (Acs, Audretsch and Evans, 1992; Meager, Kaiser and Dietrich, 1992) is that no single factor can explain these developments. Rather, to explain differential trends in self-employment between countries, despite a convergent macroeconomic environment and a common policy stance supportive of self-employment growth,

---

2 There is a significant debate not only about the causes of these developments but also about the nature and definition of self-employment itself and the extent to which the 'new' self-employed really embody a stereotypical picture of the independent entrepreneur, or whether many of them should, rather, be seen as a form of 'disguised wage employees', dependent on large firms. Suffice it to note here that recent research confirms the extreme heterogeneity of the self-employed and the associated difficulty of treating them as a distinct analytical category.

one must take account of several interrelated influences on the level and composition of self-employment. Three such influences, in particular, are worth briefly summarizing here.

The economic cycle itself. It has been argued (Bögenhold and Staber, 1991) that growing unemployment and diminishing opportunities for wage employment 'push' people to enter self-employment. As others have pointed out, however (Meager, 1992a and 1992b), successful creation of and survival in a self-employed enterprise is more likely at times of economic growth. These two influences act in opposite directions, and the net response of self-employment to changes in the macroeconomy cannot be predicted a priori. At some times and in some countries, 'unemployment push' dominates; at other times and in other countries, the 'demand pull' effect dominates.

Structural change in the economy. The shift from manufacturing to services in most advanced economies tends to increase self-employment, given that the density of self-employment is traditionally higher in services than in manufacturing. In most countries, this effect more than outweighs the impact of declining agricultural employment (which tends, *ceteris paribus*, to reduce aggregate self-employment).

Changes in working patterns and contractual arrangements. There is evidence in many countries, that the 'contracting-out' of service functions by large employers, the growth of franchising and other shifts in the contractual organization of work have contributed to self-employment growth by generating a growing labour pool, 'self-employed' in name, but sharing many of the features of dependent wage employment (bar contractual security).

Two further influences identified in the literature are less plausible as major explanatory factors for recent self-employment trends. The first relates to changing demographic structures. Different parts of the work force have different propensities to enter self-employment. Hence, factors such as growing female economic activity rates, an aging work force and a growing ethnic minority share of the work force may contribute to a changing overall level of self-employment. In practice, however, these factors act in different directions (thus, growing female participation tends to reduce aggregate self-employment, while an aging work force increases it). Further, the scale and speed of these demographic changes are insufficient to have been a major contributor to the rapid growth in self-employment during the 1980s in those countries that saw such growth.

The second factor, it is argued, is that there may have been a recent change in popular attitudes towards self-employment. These arguments find most force in the United Kingdom, under the post-1979 influence of Thatcherism and the 'enterprise culture'. Such evidence as exists (see Blanchflower and Oswald, 1990; Hughes, 1992) does not, however, tend to support such a change.

1.2 Institutional Factors

Of the factors identified in the research discussed above, the three with the greatest purchase in explaining recent self-employment growth (the economic cycle, sectorial shifts and the influence of contracting-out) operated in most advanced economies over the 1980s and do not, therefore, help one distinguish countries where self-employment grew strongly (the United Kingdom) from those where it remained relatively stable (France and Germany) or declined (Denmark). To explain the United Kingdom's unusual performance in particular, one therefore needs to posit not only a historical conjunction of economic and structural factors favourable to self-employment during the 1980s (Meager, 1993). In addition, one needs to consider a range of influences in the legal and institutional environment, which may mediate the influence of these factors.

Thus, Meager et al.(1992) identified two such influences, in the specific case of an Anglo-German comparison. The first is the regulatory framework governing business start-up and entry to certain typical 'self-employed occupations'. The evidence suggests that this regulatory environment has been considerably looser in the United Kingdom than in countries such as Germany and that as a result, UK self-employment has been more responsive to short-term economic and structural influences. The second influence concerns the structure and regulation of the capital market facing the self-employed. It is clear that the UK capital market regime was both less strict than its counterpart in countries such as Germany and that it underwent considerable relaxation as a result of financial deregulation in the 1980s. This circumstance, coupled with factors such as growing home ownership and house-price appreciation (Keeble, Walker and Robson, 1993), generated an environment in which access to loan capital and provision of collateral was increasingly easy for potential self-employed people in the UK during the 1980s.[3]

These arguments have been developed more fully elsewhere (Meager, 1993), but the key point is that it is possible to develop a coherent explanation along these lines for different countries' self-employment experience. It is not possible, however, given a lack of comparable data and of an adequate theoretical framework for modelling aggregate self-employment levels,[4] to test in

---

3 Ironically, this suggests that the economic case for self-employment schemes (based on capital rationing) may have been weakest in the country which had one of the largest such schemes.

4 Given the heterogeneity of the self-employed, it may be inappropriate to model self-employment as a single aggregate. Different theoretical frameworks are necessary for the different components of self-employment. For those who are genuine 'entrepreneurs', an explanation rooted in the theory of the firm may be appropriate. For large groups, however, self-employment is largely a labour market phenomenon differing, at the extreme, from wage employment in name only. Given this diversity, it is unsurprising that no theoretical framework has adequate purchase on the development of all categories of the self-employed.

any rigorous statistical sense the relative contribution of the different influences to self-employment growth.

1.3   Impact of Other Aspects of (Labour Market) Policy

Labour market policies and institutions that are not targeted at self-employment may have an important impact on it, nonetheless. They are additional, related influences on aggregate self-employment and mediate the impact of any self-employment policy. It is, for example, particularly difficult to explain the continuing decline in Danish self-employment when the factors helping stem that decline in other countries (including a policy stance supportive of business start-ups) were equally present in Denmark (Meager, 1993). It has been argued, however, that the high wage replacement ratio of unemployment benefits in Denmark dampens any 'unemployment push' that might contribute to self-employment growth (OECD, 1992). Further, the relatively unregulated nature of the Danish labour market and the weakness of employment security measures may have been important (by reducing any presumed incentive for Danish employers to substitute subcontracting relations for employment relations). Such explanations are not, however, supported by the evidence for the United Kingdom, where self-employment grew faster than elsewhere during a period of rapid labour market deregulation. In any case, the general point remains that other policy and institutional influences need to be brought into the explanatory framework.

1.4   'Target-oriented' versus 'Measure-oriented' Evaluation

The discussion above is broadly consistent with one of the key underlying theses of the handbook, namely, that 'target-oriented evaluation' should encompass a wide range of independent variables that, in the light of existing theory, are likely to affect this target. These variables would not be limited to labour market policies, but would include other policies or institutional arrangements affecting the labour market.

This 'ideal' approach is rarely followed in practice, however, and most of the existing evaluations of self-employment schemes are of the traditional 'measure-oriented' type. Despite this fact, there is value in a comparative assessment of these studies. On the one hand, it is clear that if a key target is to increase the flow from unemployment to self-employment, it is necessary to know the full range of other (nonpolicy) factors affecting that flow, as well as the way in which the flow is affected (perhaps unintentionally) by other labour market policies (such as the role of employment protection legislation, as discussed above for Denmark). Within this institutional and policy environment, however, one also needs to know the full range of impacts of the measure being considered and the ways in which these impacts vary according to design features of the measure itself. In this context, therefore, effective measure-oriented evaluation retains considerable value necessitating a model that incorporates the best of both approaches and enables one to examine both the full range of factors (including the self-employment measure) affecting the unemployment–self-employment flow on the one hand (as discussed above) and the full range of effects (holding other factors constant) of the self-employment measure itself, on the other. In the remainder of this chapter, therefore, I consider the evidence for these effects.

2   PROBLEMS OF EVALUATING SCHEMES SUPPORTING SELF-EMPLOYMENT FOR THE UNEMPLOYED

In many OECD countries, including all the then-member states of the European Union, the 1980s saw, alongside increasing interest among policy-makers and academics in small business and self-employment, the introduction of labour market policies aimed at encouraging and subsidizing the unemployed to become self-employed (Barker, 1989). The scale of these schemes varied considerably in terms both of the number of participants and of their share of total labour market policy expenditure.[5]

These schemes, however, share a number of important characteristics. Although the eligibility criteria vary from one country to the next, a common feature is that such schemes offer unemployed people a regular allowance (or in some cases a lump-sum grant) in place of their unemployment benefit/allowance for a defined period corresponding to the 'start-up' phase of their self-employed activity. Indeed, one of the main attractions of such schemes to policy-makers is that under the strong assumption that the allowance recipients would otherwise have remained unemployed during this period,[6] the net exchequer costs of the scheme remain low (largely irrespective of the survival rate of the self-employed 'enterprises').

---

5 In Meager (1993) summary data for EU countries showed a general trend for such schemes to account for an increasing share of labour market policy expenditure. In some countries significant numbers of people have participated in these schemes. In the United Kingdom, for example, at its peak in the late 1980s, there were some 100 000 unemployed people entering self-employment each year through the Enterprise Allowance Scheme, constituting a significant proportion of the inflow to self-employment at a time when the stock of self-employment stood at about 2.5 million. The French scheme was of a similar scale, whereas in (West) Germany the scale was much smaller, with never more than about 20 000 people per year in receipt of bridging support (*Überbrückungsgeld*) under par. 55a of the Employment Promotion Act (*Arbeitsförderungsgesetz*) (IAB-Kurzbericht, 1991).

6 The important question of 'deadweight' in these schemes receives further consideration below.

In the remainder of this chapter, I first draw on the evaluation literature to examine the main conceptual and practical issues confronting any attempt to evaluate the impact of self-employment schemes for the unemployed. Second, I compare the different methodologies that exist for tackling such evaluations, and their relative advantages and disadvantages. Finally, I identify some of the main findings from existing evaluation studies of such self-employment schemes in a number of countries.

A number of problems must be confronted in evaluating these schemes, including (a) the identification of scheme objectives; (b) controlling for differences in the environment; (c) deadweight, displacement and substitution effects; and (d) issues of scheme design and implementation. I discuss each of them briefly below.

2.1   Identifying Scheme Objectives

It is important to note, in answering the question of why labour market policy should support the unemployed to enter self-employment, that the underlying objectives of such policies vary from country to country. Such variation needs to be taken into account in any internationally comparative evaluation of the schemes. Even at a national level, however, a clear articulation of objectives is a prerequisite of the evaluation process, particularly when such schemes may have multiple (and occasionally conflicting) objectives, which need to be taken into account in assessing impact.

At the most basic level, the immediate 'output' objectives of the schemes are similar: to increase the rate of outflow from unemployment (to self-employment). When it comes to wider impact, however, more variety of objectives can be discerned in official policy documents.

An objective common to most of the scheme designs is a direct reduction in unemployment through the movement off the unemployment register into self-employment of people who would otherwise have remained unemployed for an extended period. Many official evaluation studies interpret the gross effect of the scheme (in terms of the number of participants and the length of time they survive in self-employment) as equivalent to the direct unemployment effect. In practice, the net effect is highly sensitive to the extent of deadweight in the schemes (see section 2.3).

Many schemes also include the specific aim of some indirect reduction of unemployment through subsequent job creation in the enterprises set up by the self-employed participants. Again, to assess this effect, it is not sufficient to estimate (as many survey evaluations have done) the number of new jobs set up by the unemployed under the scheme. Rather, one must estimate what proportion of these jobs are genuinely 'additional', must take account of deadweight and displacement (see section 2.3).

Less explicit (except notably in the United Kingdom) is an objective that is essentially ideological, namely, the promotion and extension of an 'enterprise culture' among the labour force at large. The underlying argument appears to be that, through increasing the proportion of the work force that is experiencing periods of self-employment (particularly groups drawn from social classes that normally experience only wage employment), more 'positive' attitudes towards enterprise will be encouraged, a change that, in turn, will contribute to economic dynamism and adaptation to structural change. To an even greater extent than the other objectives, this kind of impact (being subjective and largely unmeasurable) is extremely difficult to assess. Nevertheless, there exist in some countries opinion polls and attitude surveys that include questions relevant for providing evidence of any such shifts.

In a minority of cases, notably Germany, an explicit objective has been the avoidance of low-quality, low-wage employment ('Vermeidung von unterwertiger Beschäftigung')[7] through the alternative of appropriate self-employment opportunities.[8] Whether or not it has been an explicit objective of the scheme, however, an important aspect of evaluation must include the effects of the scheme on income levels: how much do the new entrepreneurs and their employees earn? What effect does participation in self-employment have on their life-time earning prospects (including their access to social benefits and pensions, and their earnings in retirement)?

Finally, an objective that appears in official discussions of the schemes in some countries has to do with 'employability' as embodied in skills and 'human capital'. The argument is that even if the enterprises started under the scheme are unsuccessful, and even if the participants leave self-employment after (or during) the subsidy period, the skills and experience gained through business start-up will stand them in good stead in the labour market, improving their attractiveness to potential employers. This effect is difficult to measure directly, but in principle one can examine it by studying the subsequent employment histories of scheme participants to assess whether unemployed people leaving such schemes have an improved labour market position compared to unemployed people who have not entered the schemes.

2.2 Controlling for Differences/Changes in the Environment

Perhaps the most serious problem confronting any attempt to evaluate the impact of such self-employment policies is the need to allow for what would

---

7 For a description of the German scheme, see Kaiser and Otto (1990).

8 Interestingly, there is evidence in the UK scheme that policy-makers saw the low earnings of participants as an advantage of the scheme, through reduced wage pressure and inflationary expectations (Owens, 1989).

have happened anyway in their absence in a given country and to allow for intercountry differences in what would have happened without the policies (when policies are compared cross-nationally). The nature of and changes in the economic and institutional environment are clearly crucial for evaluation because they may constrain or support self-employment and the flow from unemployment to self-employment in the absence of the policy.

2.3   Deadweight, Displacement and Substitution Effects

Any methodology for the full evaluation of self-employment schemes for the unemployed must enable one to estimate the extent to which (a) those unemployed receiving a subsidy under the scheme would have entered self-employment in the absence of the subsidy (the 'deadweight' effect) and (b) the businesses or self-employed activities set up by scheme participants drive other existing unsubsidized businesses out of the market (the 'displacement' effect).

Substitution effects, the third type of 'compensating' effect that typically needs to be taken into account in policy evaluation, are less relevant in the case of self-employment schemes. In principle, they would become relevant only in the case of 'contracted-out' self-employment, or self-employment that falls under the category of 'disguised employment' (see section 1). If, for example, employers were encouraged by knowledge of the scheme's existence to change their contractual arrangements so that work that would otherwise have been undertaken by actual or potential employees is now undertaken by self-employed contractors (subsidized, as ex-unemployed, by the scheme in question), then clearly the gross scheme effect would be mitigated by this substitution. Given, however, that in most countries the regulations and implementation of the schemes exclude this option, this substitution is not a topic that has been examined in evaluation studies, and there are good reasons to anticipate that any such effect would be both small and somewhat exceptional.

2.4   Scheme Design and Implementation

Clearly, scheme impact can be significantly affected by the design parameters of the scheme itself as well as by the mechanics and process of its implementation (see Schmid, chap. 7 in this volume). Given that most evaluations of individual country schemes are both *ex post* and cross-sectional and that scheme design does not vary, this issue can be examined only through experimental methods (see Heckman and Smith, chap. 2 in this volume), through time-series analysis (when scheme design has changed over time), and (most importantly) through cross-national comparison of schemes that have different design parameters. The main exception is the interesting case of the United

Kingdom, where the implementation of the scheme has in recent years been devolved from the national labour ministry to local Training and Enterprise Councils (TECs),[9] which have some scope to vary the characteristics of the scheme away from the national model. This arrangement offers some potential for cross-sectional analysis of design impacts within one country.[10]

There are a number of design factors that are likely to be particularly relevant to scheme impact in the case of self-employment schemes for the unemployed. The main ones are considered below.

2.4.1 Eligibility Criteria

There are two relevant dimensions here. The first concerns the personal characteristics of scheme participants and the extent to which eligibility is drawn widely (e.g. to include all categories of unemployed) or is targeted on specific (usually disadvantaged) groups within the unemployed. The second dimension concerns the characteristics of the self-employed activity itself. Thus, to increase survival chances, some schemes require the proposed business to satisfy various financial criteria and show evidence of future viability.

All the national schemes introduced to date are designed to increase the flow from unemployment to self-employment, so eligibility has normally been confined to the unemployed. In most countries, eligibility is broad, covering all those entitled to unemployment compensation. Some countries (Germany, the United Kingdom and Ireland) have excluded the very short-term unemployed, whereas others (Portugal and Denmark) have confined eligibility to the long-term unemployed (although Denmark latterly reduced the required prior unemployment duration). Some schemes set additional eligibility criteria. (The Danish scheme, for example, has an age criterion, restricting eligibility to those over 25 years of age.) There are also, particularly if schemes with a local or regional coverage are considered, many examples where eligibility is targeted on specific groups: women, ethnic minorities and so forth.

Much of the research evidence suggests, however, that even when the schemes have wide eligibility, participants tend not to be representative of the eligible unemployed. As shown in Meager (1993), scheme participants are typically concentrated among certain segments of the unemployed (often the more 'advantaged' segments); thus, they are more likely than the average

---

9 See Bennett, Wicks and McCoshan (1994) for a comprehensive, critical account of the TEC initiative in the United Kingdom.

10 This potential has yet to be realized, however, because the only national evaluation of the scheme since its decentralization (Tremlett, 1993) did not include systematic assessment of the effects of local design variations.

unemployed person to be male, to have higher-level qualifications and to have been unemployed for a relatively short period of time.

A priori, it is not evident which kind of scheme design (wide or restricted eligibility) is likely to be the most effective in terms of policy impact. On the one hand, a scheme with wide eligibility and self-selected participants runs the risk of a high deadweight effect. On the other hand, a scheme focussing on disadvantaged groups or people who would not normally enter self-employment may exhibit lower deadweight, but it runs the risk of lower survival rates because these groups are less likely to possess the human and financial capital relevant to successful entrepreneurship.

As far as selection in terms of the kinds of businesses that can be subsidized is concerned, there are few examples of schemes targeted in this way, although the German scheme implicitly targets certain types of businesses and would rule out many of the low-income service-sector activities that are common in the British scheme.[11]

2.4.2 *Mode of Subsidy*

The two principal models of subsidization are the most common ones (payment of a regular allowance to the participants in lieu of unemployment benefit), and the French/Spanish model, which allows the option of having participants receive a lump-sum grant at the outset of the period of self-employment.[12] Normally, the sum involved is related to what the recipient would have received under the allowance model; that is, it is equivalent to a 'capitalization' of the recipient's unemployment benefit entitlement over the defined period.

The argument typically advanced in favour of the latter model is that it helps the self-employed overcome the capital constraints and barriers to entry associated with business start-up;[13] this assistance may, in turn, facilitate more securely-founded businesses, perhaps in sectors where survival chances are

---

11 The German scheme required that the proposed businesses be vetted by a 'competent' authority (such as a bank, chamber of commerce or professional association) and that it be shown that the businesses can generate a minimum level of income for the self-employed person. Recently, under the 1992 decentralization of the British scheme to local TECs, it has become clear that some TECs imposed restrictions on the kinds of business activities that could be subsidized (in terms of sector of activity, likely profitability and so on).

12 An experimental comparison of the two models has been made in the United States, where two pilot schemes were introduced. One was an 'allowance-based' model; the other included a 'lump-sum-based' model for the majority of participants (Wandner and Messenger, 1991); see section 4.9.

13 Assuming that unemployed potential entrepreneurs face markets for financial capital which are less than perfect (see the discussion at the outset of this chapter).

higher. Unless the survival rate is high, however, the disadvantage is that such an approach can considerably increase the exchequer cost of the scheme, depending on whether an 'unsuccessfully' self-employed person who returns to unemployment remains eligible for future unemployment benefits (with this exception, there is little difference between the two models from an exchequer cost perspective).

The mode of financing may, therefore, be expected to have at least two kinds of effect. First, it may influence the types of people entering the scheme. Thus, a lump-sum approach might be better at attracting participants from disadvantaged groups, who would be less likely to have significant amounts of their own capital; this effect, in turn, would reduce deadweight. Second, it may influence the types of business activity that the scheme participants enter and, hence, the survival rates of the subsidized businesses. A common criticism of the UK scheme (allowance based, with wide eligibility) has been that it encouraged a high rate of entry to markets with low entry barriers and low returns. In these crowded, mainly service-sector markets, survival rates are low and displacement relatively high (see section 4.4). A key question, therefore, is whether a lump-sum approach avoids this effect and achieves a 'better' sectorial distribution of scheme participants.

2.4.3 Training, Support and Advice

The different schemes vary in the extent of training and other support that is offered to scheme participants before or during the start-up phase of self-employment. Where such support is provided, it varies considerably in form. In some cases it is voluntary; in others, it is a requirement of participation. In some cases it links in with other small-business support and advisory mechanisms in the countries concerned; in others, it does not. In some cases it is provided only at the start of the self-employment period; in others, it is ongoing during (or after) the subsidy period.

Some of the literature suggests that effective support, while raising the running costs of the scheme, may weaken the trade-off between deadweight and survival identified above. Thus, although deadweight may be reduced through a concentration on disadvantaged groups, the necessary support input in the early months and years of self-employment is likely to be greater if a high survival rate is to be achieved.

2.4.4 Scale and Duration of Payments

A further dimension of design variation relates to the amount of subsidy involved and the duration for which it is received. Clearly, for a given gross policy cost, variation of the number of participants, the per-capita subsidy and the duration of payment, may influence the net employment effect and, therefore, the net cost per job created by the scheme itself.

In simple terms, to take two extremes, which alternative has the greater net effect? Under one extreme, a given budget may be spent on a small number of participants, receiving a relatively large payment for a long period of time. The Danish scheme, for example, rarely had more than 5000 participants per year, but paid them up to 50 per cent of their maximum unemployment benefit entitlement for a period of up to 3.5 years. Under the other extreme, similar expenditure may be spread more thinly with more participants, smaller payments and shorter payment durations. During most of the 1980s the UK scheme, for example, was a mass scheme with up to 100 000 participants per year, but the allowance was small (£40 per week) and payable for only one year. Other countries' schemes exhibit a range of payment variations between these two extremes (see Meager, 1993).

3   EVALUATION METHODOLOGIES

In order to assess the net effects of these schemes, a wide range of evaluation methodologies (for the most part, 'measure-oriented' in nature) has been deployed. In this section I consider the main categories of approach adopted, illustrating each with examples from the literature and discussing their relative advantages and disadvantages.

3.1   Experimental Evaluation

Experimental evaluation is, in many ways, the ideal model for evaluation, although for reasons of cost and political expediency, it is rarely followed. None of the European schemes has adopted such an approach, and the only significant example is to be found in the United States (Wandner and Messenger, 1991). In the US case, two pilot schemes (one with an 'allowance-based' approach, the other with a 'lump-sum grant-based' approach) were set up (in Massachusetts and Washington State). Early evaluation results from the two areas have recently become available (see section 4.9).

3.2   Administrative Data/Participant Surveys

These evaluation methods are the most common and have been adopted in most of the countries with schemes for subsidizing self-employment (the UK evaluation literature, in particular, includes a large number of studies of this type, some of which are reviewed in PA Cambridge Economic Consultants,

1990[14]). They involve use of administrative data to identify the characteristics of scheme participants together with surveys of those participants during and/ or after scheme participation to identify their perceptions, experiences, survival rates and so forth. The main drawback of this approach, apart from those of cost and time, is that conclusions about scheme effect *per se* are difficult to draw unless nonscheme participant entrants and their survival rates, among other dimensions, are compared to the corresponding dimensions of the scheme. Equally, reliance on scheme participants' perceptions or recollections to identify deadweight, and especially displacement, is fraught with difficulties (although the latter problem can be eased through collateral information from the competitors and customers of scheme participants; see Elias and Whitfield, 1987).

The international comparability of such data on their own is limited because they are inevitably collected with different research designs. As far as possible, however, I review these evaluation studies below (see section 4) and assess those comparative conclusions about scheme effectiveness that emerge from them.

3.3   Aggregate Impact Analysis

Using these approaches, one attempts to discern, usually through econometric methods, the effects of schemes as reflected in aggregate macrodata. Provided that an appropriate theoretical model exists, such methods have the strong advantage that they can, in principle, allow for deadweight and displacement in a way that microapproaches typically cannot and can enable one to identify a self-employment scheme's longer-term and 'second-round' impacts which may offset short-run gains (see also Bellmann and Jackman, chap. 5 in this volume). In the author's view, however, the utility of such approaches for evaluating self-employment schemes is constrained both by the lack of a robust theoretical model explaining self-employment flows and by the absence (in most countries) of adequate time-series flow data with which to estimate such a model statistically.

A few examples of such approaches exist, nevertheless, both on a time-series basis (Johnson, Lindley and Bourlakis, 1988; Meager, 1993) and on a cross-section (intercountry) basis (Meager, 1993). Some of the findings from these studies, too, are reviewed below. Most such studies do identify a statistically significant 'scheme effect', albeit often a relatively small one, suggesting

---

14 See also Allen (1987), Allen and Hunn (1985), Hunn (1984), Marston and Pattison (1989), Maung and Erens (1991), MSC (1983), Owens (1989), Owens and Demery (1988), Pattison and Demery (1988), RBL (1987), Simkin and Allen (1988), Smith and Tremlett (1990), Tremlett (1993) and Wood (1985).

that the gross impact of schemes for the subsidization of self-employment is not entirely negated by deadweight and displacement.

3.4 Other Approaches

Needless to say, a number of approaches contained in the literature on the evaluation of these schemes do not fall neatly into the above categories. Two examples are briefly described below.

3.4.1 Local Labour Market Studies

Given the theoretical and data deficiencies inhibiting aggregate macroanalysis of self-employment schemes, and given the a priori expectation of high displacement rates associated with such schemes, Elias and Whitfield (1987) have pointed out strong arguments in favour of intensive case-study analysis focussing on the local labour market and emphasizing the displacement question in particular. Such analysis, it is reasoned, would need to be concentrated on detailed interviews with scheme participants, their customers and competitors in the local market. The only evaluation study along these lines that I have uncovered was conducted in the United Kingdom and is briefly described below (see section 4.4).

3.4.2 Inferences from Representative Microlevel Flow Data

A new approach adopted in recent years (Meager, 1993) has involved the use of 'flow data' based on estimating transition rates between labour market states, using different countries' European Labour Force Survey data and, in particular, transition rates from unemployment to self-employment are estimated. The characteristics of people undertaking such transitions are compared with the characteristics of scheme participants, thereby enabling insights to be gained on scheme performance. With inflow data from these sources, for example, it is possible to examine the extent to which schemes are reaching population groups who do not 'normally' enter self-employment from unemployment. Similarly (in the light of the possible tradeoff between scheme targeting and survival rates discussed above), analysis of outflow data allows an examination of the survival rates of 'atypical' entrepreneurs (in the absence of policy) with which to compare survival rates among targeted scheme participants. Such data can, in principle, also be used to examine whether a given different policy design (e.g. a lump-sum grant-based approach or an allowance-based approach) is associated with entry into kinds of self-employment activity different from those found among 'normal' unemployment—self-employment inflows. Some findings from this approach are discussed below (see section 4.7).

4   EVALUATION RESULTS: SCHEME IMPACTS

Using the various methodologies described above, I now summarize some of
the conclusions emerging from the international research on the effectiveness
and impacts of the various schemes encouraging the unemployed to enter self-
employment (see Table 16.1). The following passages are based especially on
Meager (1993), in which I examined such schemes in EU countries, particularly the United Kingdom, France, Germany and Denmark. I also refer to work
on the experimental pilot schemes undertaken in the United States and to
recent UK research summarized in Storey (1994).

4.1   Deadweight

Given the importance of deadweight for overall scheme impact, it is unfortu-
nate that few of the existing evaluations of national schemes include an assessment of deadweight.

In the case of the German scheme, which originated in former West Germany, early evaluation studies (IAB-Kurzbericht 1991; Kaiser and Otto,
1990) have not included a full assessment of scheme deadweight. The surveys
included questions asking recipients how important the subsidy was to their
early months in self-employment, but there was no question asking recipients
whether they definitely would have set up in self-employment in the absence
of the subsidy.

In the absence of such data, Meager (1993) used flow data from the
'Arbeitskräfte-Gesamtrechnung' (a set of labour market accounting data) in an
attempt at an econometric estimation of the deadweight effect of the German
scheme ('Überbrückungsgeld') for initially subsidizing the transition from
unemployment to self-employment. The reader is referred to the original paper
for technical details, but essentially, these data were used to model the aggregate flow from unemployment to self-employment in West Germany from
1970 through 1985. The exercise was then repeated for the years 1970–89 to
allow for the introduction of 'Überbrückungsgeld' in 1985–86. The analysis
showed that 'Überbrückungsgeld' had a positive, statistically significant influence on the flow from unemployment to self-employment in the early years of
its operation (up to 1989). It suggested, furthermore, that the deadweight effect
of the scheme is small (no more than about 10 per cent). As pointed out in
Meager (1993), there are severe limitations to this kind of aggregate analysis
as well as problems with the data used (e.g. they included unpaid family
workers as well as the genuinely self-employed). However, the conclusion that
the level of deadweight is relatively low seems justified and is supported by
some of the limited survey data on the scheme, which show that for a majority
of participants (66 to 87 per cent) the financial support received through the

Table 16.1 Scheme Characteristics and Performance: Summary Indicators

	Germany (former West)	Denmark	France	United Kingdom
Scheme characteristics				
Eligibility (person)	Wide (unemployed more than 1 month)	Restricted (long-term unemployed and over-25s)	Wide (any unemployed)	Wide (originally, 8 weeks unemployed; now 6 weeks)
Eligibility (business)	Restricted (must gain approval from competent authority and meet minimum income requirements)	Wide (no restrictions or requirements)	Restricted (business plan must be vetted)	Medium (must have £1000 own capital, and some local areas vet business plan)
Payment form	Allowance	Allowance	Lump sum	Allowance
Payment levels	High (related to previous unemployment benefits)	High (up to DKr 5400 p.a.)	Medium (up to FF 43 000 in total)	Low (£40 per week; some local variation)
Duration	Low (initially, up to 3 months, increased to 6 months)	High (up to 3.5 years)	Not applicable	Medium (up to 1 year; some local variation)
Level of support or training provided	Low	High	Low	Medium
Number of participants	Small (up to 20 000 p.a.)	Small (about 5000 p.a.)	Medium (50 000– 70 000 p.a.)	High (100 000 p.a.; since fallen)
Characteristics of participants and activities				
Female participation	Low	High	Average	High
Youth participation	High	Low	High	High
Representation of service sectors	Low	High	Low	High
Representation of production/manufacturing	High	Low	High	Low
Scheme performance				
Deadweight	Low (<20%)	Average (41%)	Average (35%)	High (50–70%)
Survival rates (see Figure 16.1)	Unclear	Good	Average	Poor
Extra jobs per 100 participants	Unclear	Low (36 after 2 years)	High (97 after 5 years)	Low (35 after 5 years)
Displacement	(Likely to be low because of underrepresentation of service sectors)	(Likely to be high because of high level of subsidy and over-representation of service sectors)	(Likely to be low because of underrepresentation of service sectors)	High (>50%)
Employability impact	Unclear	Unclear	Unclear	Unclear
Income levels (average)	(Presumed high, because of eligibility criteria)	Low	Unclear	Low
Attitudinal impact	Unclear	Unclear	Unclear	Evidence suggests little or no impact

scheme was crucial in providing for the upkeep of the self-employed person and his or her family during the start-up phase of their new business. Allowing for data deficiencies, therefore, it is unlikely that deadweight in the German scheme exceeded 20 per cent in its early years.

Turning to evaluations of the Danish scheme ('Ivaeksaeterydelsen') (see Høgelund, Langager, Jakobsen and Jagd, 1992; Rosdahl and Maerkedahl, 1987), one finds evidence suggesting that deadweight rates are higher than in the German scheme. Of those persons who started on the scheme in 1985, only 17 per cent would definitely have set up in self-employment without the subsidy; a further 39 per cent said that they might have done so; and 44 per cent would not have. Assuming that half of those who were unsure would have entered self-employment without the subsidy, this implies an overall deadweight of about 35 per cent. A similar survey of starters on the scheme in 1989 suggests that deadweight had risen slightly (to about 41 per cent under similar assumptions).

Surveys of participants in the early years of the French scheme, 'Aide aux chômeurs créateurs d'entreprises' (European Commission, 1988), indicated rates of deadweight similar to those of the Danish scheme. In 1981, 21 per cent of the participants said they would have started in self-employment without the subsidy, and a further 51 per cent said that they would not have done so. Again if half of the remainder (who were unsure) are deadweight, this yields an overall deadweight estimate of 35 per cent.

Another scheme that has been subject to regular estimates of deadweight is the one in the United Kingdom. Estimates of deadweight have varied over time because the scheme was introduced in 1983, but in comparison with the deadweight in schemes of the other countries examined, deadweight in that of the United Kingdom appears high and has grown over time. Summarizing the results of earlier surveys, PA Cambridge Economic Consultants (1990) reported short-term deadweight estimates ranging from 30 to 40 per cent (long-term deadweight estimates are higher since 'deadweight' participants tend to have higher survival rates). For the calculation of scheme impact, deadweight of 50 per cent has conventionally been assumed in official estimates (NAO, 1988), but the most recent survey of participants—in 1992 (see Tremlett, 1993)—indicated that deadweight was as high as 73 per cent (although a proportion of the participants said that they would have started their businesses later had they not received the subsidy).

4.2 Survival Rates

Survival rates (the proportion of scheme participants still in business after a given period) also vary significantly from scheme to scheme, although direct comparisons are difficult because of the different periods over which survival rates are calculated in the different countries. For the German scheme, full survival data were not available, but limited data (IAB-Kurzbericht, 1991) have implied a relatively high survival rate, showing the proportion of 'Überbrückungsgeld' recipients from a given calendar year who had become unemployed again by 1 April of the following year,[15] that is, an average period of nine months after starting on the scheme. This proportion fell over time. For those starting in 1986 it was 11.5 per cent; in 1987, 7.8 per cent; in 1988, 5.9 per cent, and in 1989, 5.6 per cent (i.e. on average over the four years, a typical nine-month survival rate for the German scheme was about 92 per cent).

Evidence from the survey of starters on the Danish scheme in 1989 shows that the survival rate after 2 years of self-employment was 74 per cent; after 3.5 years (the period of eligibility of the scheme), the rate had fallen to 55 per cent.

Data from the French scheme have indicated survival rates of 85 per cent after one year, 75 per cent after two years and 53 per cent after five years.

Data from various surveys of participants in the UK scheme, summarized by Storey (1994), suggest the following survival profile: after one year, 87 per cent; after 18 months, 71 per cent; after two years, 59 per cent; after three years, 50 per cent; after four years, 44 per cent; and after five years, 40 per cent.

The survival data for the four countries are summarized in Figure 16.1 below. Care must be taken in interpreting the figure because the data do not all relate to the same period and do not take account of differences between overall small-firm survival rates in the different countries. (In particular, the short survival period covered by the German data limits the conclusions that can be drawn on that scheme.) In general terms, however, the data on the four countries suggest that the schemes had very similar survival rates during the first year, after which the patterns diverged somewhat (for the three schemes with longer-term data, at least), with the Danish scheme apparently outperforming the French scheme, which, in turn, appeared to perform better than the British scheme.

4.3 Indirect Job Creation

Most of the evaluation studies from individual country schemes provide data on the number of extra jobs (i.e. in addition to those of the subsidized self-employed beneficiaries themselves) created in the new businesses of the self-employed. As with the survival data, direct comparison of figures on indirect job creation is difficult because of the different periods over which these data are collected, but the main findings are summarized here, nonetheless.

---

15 This does not, of course, imply that all those who had not reregistered as unemployed remained self-employed.

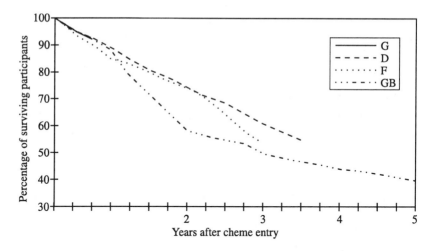

Figure 16.1　Estimates of Survival Rates of Self-employed Participants in the Four Schemes: Former West Germany, Denmark, France and Great Britain

Evaluations of the German scheme (IAB-Kurzbericht, 1991; Kaiser and Otto, 1990) concentrate on the characteristics and experiences of the subsidized self-employed themselves and do not, unfortunately, provide any information on extra jobs created in the supported enterprises. The most recent evaluation of the Danish scheme (Høgelund et al., 1992) estimates (on the basis of starters in 1989) that for every 100 starters on the scheme, there will be a net job creation effect (i.e. taking account of nonsurvivors) of some 36 jobs (excluding the jobs of the self-employed themselves) within two years after starting on the scheme. Drawing on calculations in Dossou (1988) and taking account of nonsurvival rates, one can estimate, for the French scheme, a net job creation effect of 97 extra jobs (excluding the subsidized self-employed themselves) per 100 participants after five years (a minimum estimate because the data are presented in ranges of employment size). For the United Kingdom, data from Maung and Erens (1991) (recalculated by Storey, 1994) suggest that after one allows for nonsurvival and excludes the subsidized self-employed themselves, some 35 (full-time equivalent) jobs per 100 starters were created after three years and a similar number after five years (i.e. the job loss effect due to nonsurvival is largely offset by job growth in surviving firms).

If it is true (and this may be a strong assumption) in the Danish case, like in the British, that the net job creation effect does not decline significantly over time, then for the three schemes for which I have data it is clear that the indirect job creation of the French scheme is significantly greater than that of its British and Danish counterparts.

4.4 Displacement

Displacement, or the extent to which the creation of new subsidized businesses run by the self-employed leads to job loss in existing competitor firms, is difficult to estimate, and there is little or no evidence of this effect of the schemes. As argued above, evaluation of displacement requires in-depth local labour market studies on a sector-by-sector basis, and the only example I have uncovered (Hasluck, 1990) is for the UK scheme. Hasluck (1990) looked at displacement in two sectors ('hairdressing and beauty' and 'business services') in a particular locality (the West Midlands of England) and found that in 'hairdressing and beauty' (a competitive market, with low profit margins) displacement was extremely high (close to 100 per cent), whereas in business services (a more capital- and skill-intensive market with higher entry barriers and specialized niches) it was as high as 50 per cent. In official evaluations of the UK scheme (NAO, 1988; Storey, 1994), the working assumption has been that displacement is 50 per cent for the scheme as a whole, but that estimate is likely to be conservative, in the light of the local labour market estimates. No similar estimates of displacement exist for the other national schemes investigated.

4.5 Income Levels

Internationally comparable data on the earnings of scheme participants are virtually impossible to come by. In this regard I therefore confine myself to noting that, with the exception of the German scheme, which required participants to show that their proposed business would generate a certain minimum level of gross income (in the late 1980s, this requirement was DM 3400 per month[16]), the available evidence suggests that average income levels among surviving participants are low in comparison with average earnings in employment. Thus, for the Danish scheme, the most recent evaluation (Høgelund et al., 1992) shows that two-thirds of starters in 1989 earned less than DKr 150 000 per year (gross). Many of the UK evaluations, too, contained income data showing a high proportion of participants to have been on very low incomes. The most recent evidence has suggested that income levels of survivors may have increased in comparison with earlier evaluations but remain low on

---

16 See Kaiser and Otto (1990). It is unclear from the available evidence how strictly this criterion has been enforced and how many subsidized businesses have achieved these earnings levels in practice.

average. Thus, Tremlett (1993) showed that 55 per cent of survivors were earning less than £200 per week after 18 months of self-employment.

4.6   Other Impacts: Employability and Work Force Attitudes

There is little research on the impact that schemes have on participants' subsequent employment histories. Such evaluations require longitudinal data (most evaluations are cross-sectional) and a control group of nonparticipant unemployed in order to isolate scheme effects on individual employment chances. The only study identified with such a control group methodology is the evaluation of the US pilot schemes, research that suggested a positive impact on employability (see section 4.9).

Evidence of the effects that schemes have on wider attitudes towards self-employment and entrepreneurship in the work force and of their contribution to the development of an 'enterprise culture' is even scarcer. However, attitude survey findings in the United Kingdom (Blanchflower and Oswald, 1990) suggest little or no growth in aspirations to self-employment in the population at large. Given that the United Kingdom has experienced the fastest growth in self-employment of any EU country since the early 1980s and is also the country in which political rhetoric stressing the virtues of 'enterprise' has been particularly strong, it seems unlikely that such self-employment schemes (of which the UK's was one of the largest) have had a major attitudinal impact.

4.7   Characteristics of Scheme Participants and Their Businesses

Finally, I summarize some of the evidence on the types of people who participate in these schemes and on the types of business they enter. The analysis is drawn from Meager (1993), in which I use Labour Force Survey data to compare in each country the characteristics of scheme participants and their businesses with the characteristics of the self-employed population as a whole in that country and with those of new entrants to self-employment in general.

Detailed results from the analysis of the data pertaining to four countries studied can also be found in Meager (1993). What they suggest is summarized in the following passage. In the German scheme, women are considerably underrepresented compared with the work force in general and the self-employed work force in particular, whereas young people (under 30 years of age) are slightly overrepresented compared with the self-employed work force in general. In sectorial terms, the scheme has a bias towards the production sector, with agriculture and the service sectors underrepresented among participants. The Danish scheme exhibits a strong overrepresentation of women compared with the self-employed work force as a whole, but young people are underrepresented, partly because of the age restriction on participation. There is also a strong bias towards the service sector. In France the gender composition of participants is similar to that of the self-employed work force as a whole, but young people (under 25 years) are strongly overrepresented. The French scheme has a strong bias towards the production and manufacturing sectors. Finally, in the UK scheme, women have in recent years been overrepresented compared with the self-employed work force as a whole (but the proportion of women on the scheme has grown strongly over time), and young people (under 25 years) are considerably overrepresented. There is also an overrepresentation of service-sector activities, but it is not as marked as in the Danish case.

4.8   Summary of Scheme Designs and Impacts

Table 16.1 provides very general indicative assessments summarizing the design and effectiveness of the schemes in the four countries studied in detail. They are expressed in relative terms, meaning that the description of a particular characteristic or impact as 'high', 'medium' or 'low' is relative to the corresponding characteristics or impacts recorded in the other countries. (The evidence refers, for the most part, to evaluations conducted in the late 1980s and early 1990s.)

4.9   The US Pilot Schemes

In this section I examine some interesting findings (Benus, Wood and Grover, 1994) from two pilot schemes set up in the United States to test the viability of self-employment schemes for the unemployed. Because of their experimental nature and the different US labour market context, it is true that these two pilot schemes are not directly comparable with the European schemes examined in this chapter. The pilot schemes are of particular interest, however, because, through use of a control group and the deployment of rigorous econometric impact evaluation, they provide useful additional evidence on scheme potential. The two schemes (in Washington State and Massachusetts) were evaluated from participant data collected in 1990 and 1991. In both schemes, unemployment insurance recipients were randomly assigned to two groups, only one of which received 'self-employment services'. In Massachusetts the services consisted of in-depth business counselling and training, and participants received a biweekly allowance equivalent to their unemployment insurance payments (analogously to the allowance-based European self-employment schemes). In Washington the model was closer to the lump-sum-based approach adopted in France. That is, participants also underwent training and received advice and business counselling while receiving an allowance equal to their unemployment benefits. After passing a number of 'milestones', however, such as completion of training, submission of a business plan and acquisition of external finance, these participants then received a lump-sum payment equivalent to their remaining benefit entitlement.

Given the random approach, participants were representative of the unemployed as a whole, and the scheme did not involve targeting. Several key, statistically significant findings emerged. First, in both pilot schemes, participants were more likely to enter self-employment than their counterparts, who were not eligible for the support. Second, compared with unemployed people who entered self-employment from the control group, participants were likely to remain self-employed for longer periods. (It is interesting to note that the effect was much greater in the Washington pilot scheme, where a lump-sum approach was adopted.) Third, in Massachusetts (but not in Washington) participants had higher earnings than nonparticipants during the observation period, mainly because of higher earnings in subsequent wage and salary employment rather than in the period of self-employment itself. This finding was consistent with the scheme's having increased participants' 'employability'. Further support for the 'employability' hypothesis is given by the fact that both pilot studies had a positive impact on participants' likelihood of subsequent employment and on the duration of that employment in the observation period. Finally, however, indirect job creation effects in both cases were negligible; neither pilot had a statistically significant effect on nonparticipants' employment.

The evidence supports the conclusion of the evaluators of the US pilot schemes:

> Given these results, we believe that self-employment programs like Washington State's SEED Demonstration and Massachusetts' Enterprise Project represent viable policy tools for promoting the rapid re-employment of Unemployment Insurance claimants. While the impacts of such self-employment programs on earnings remain ambiguous, their impact on employment outcomes appears robust (Benus et al., 1994, p. 61).

5   CONCLUSIONS AND POINTERS FOR FUTURE RESEARCH

I have briefly reviewed the research evidence on the design and effectiveness of self-employment schemes in five countries (Denmark, France, the former West Germany, the United Kingdom and the United States).

Unfortunately, the evidence available does not allow authoritative and comparable assessments of the overall effectiveness of all these schemes in terms of value for money as active labour market policies (e.g. net cost per job created). Storey (1994), however, has recently attempted such an exercise for the UK scheme. He used data similar to those presented above, taking into account, as I have done, survival rates, deadweight, displacement and indirect job creation. After combining the figures for these characteristics and for estimates of state expenditure on the schemes (net of benefits savings and administrative costs), he arrived at a total job-per-job gross of £2000. Given the fact that a proportion of the participants (excluding very low earners) also contribute tax and social insurance payments to the national exchequer, the net cost per job is likely to be even lower. Despite the many criticisms of the scheme, this result represents a very effective job creation policy, one with much lower costs per job created than many other active labour market policies.

As the analysis in this chapter has shown, the UK scheme for subsidizing the transition from unemployment to self-employment is in many ways outperformed by analogous schemes in other countries (in terms of deadweight, survival, displacement and indirect job creation). It is likely, therefore, that the schemes in those other countries also represent effective job creation policies.[17]

The evidence does, nevertheless, point to ways in which scheme design can influence scheme performance. First, provision of support as a lump sum rather than an allowance may help participants overcome capital barriers to entry and set up businesses in higher-margin, more protected markets (including production activities), where earnings and survival potential are higher and displacement lower. The US data support the notion that a lump-sum approach may improve survival probabilities. However, those data do not include characteristics of the businesses started, so it is not possible to explore the mechanisms involved here.

Second, similar benefits may be achieved by a high degree of selectivity in the businesses that can be supported (as in the German case, requiring a minimum income requirement and approval of the business plan). Although such selectivity is likely to improve survival (and possibly reduce displacement), it risks increasing deadweight (if the 'better' business proposals come from those who would enter self-employment anyway). It may also discriminate against women and other disadvantaged groups of the unemployed (including the long-term unemployed). Ideally, therefore, any process to select eligible businesses should be accompanied by a process to target particular disadvantaged groups for support, that is, those least likely to enter self-employment without the subsidy. Some combination of the German approach to vetting the businesses supported, and the Danish approach to targeting particular groups of unemployed may therefore be effective in this way.

---

17 As mentioned earlier, however, the cost per job created may rise exponentially if survival rates are poor where the scheme is administered through a lump-sum payment (as in France). The reason is that participants whose businesses fail return to unemployment and again become entitled to state benefits.

Third, if disadvantaged groups of the unemployed are targeted, it may be particularly important to provide appropriate support and training during the early years of self-employment. Compared with the schemes in the other countries studied, the Danish scheme appears to be particularly effective in this respect. It offers more extensive training and advice on business and management skills and more technical support in particular business areas. These characteristics contribute to the relatively high survival rate associated with the Danish scheme, despite its concentration on the long-term unemployed and its relatively high representation of female participants and service-sector businesses.

I conclude by drawing attention to some of the policy recommendations emerging from analysis of the UK schemes. As Storey (1994) argues, these schemes may be relatively effective as labour market policies, but they tend to be relatively ineffective as policies aimed at stimulating and supporting the small-business sector as a whole (compared to policies that support existing small businesses having clear growth and survival potential). It is clear, particularly where support is unselective, as in the United Kingdom, that the enterprises set up tend to be low-quality businesses with poor income prospects and poor prospects for growth.[18] A key characteristic of this part of the small-business sector in the United Kingdom is its high rate of turnover, with very high rates of small-firm creation and small-firm failure contrasting with the more stable patterns observed in countries such as Germany. As Storey (1994) concludes:

> The high risk associated with start-ups is a key element in support of the concept that local policy initiatives should be increasingly focused on established businesses with a trading record. . . . It remains open to serious question as to whether public policies designed to increase the rate of new firm formation are in the long-term interest of the UK economy (Storey, 1994, pp. 284–5).

Though this view may be extreme, there is little doubt that the international evidence suggests a strong case for a more targeted approach in labour market schemes designed to encourage self-employment among the unemployed. They should be targeted both in terms of the individuals who are subsidized

---

18 In the UK context Kitson (1995) has challenged the argument that enterprises started by the unemployed are likely to be less successful and have lower survival rates than those started by other groups. His analysis, however, which showed that small businesses started by the unemployed do not appear to have performance characteristics inferior to businesses started by other groups, was based on a sample survey of *existing small businesses* rather than on the inflow of business start-ups. Hence, newly self-employed whose businesses rapidly failed were, by definition, underrepresented, so the sample was biased towards those self-employed persons whose businesses had survived and grown.

(focussing on disadvantaged groups to reduce deadweight)[19] and the business activities that are supported (focussing on high-quality business plans with significant market and income potential in order to increase survival rates and reduce displacement).

There is little reported research on the longer-term implications of policies that encourage self-employment among groups (such as the unemployed) not traditionally the main source of 'entrepreneurs' and small-business proprietors. That this may, nevertheless, be an important dimension in assessing the longer-term impact of self-employment schemes, was suggested by Meager, Court and Moralee (1994, 1995). Through secondary analysis of a number of data sets, the authors examined the impact that the United Kingdom's rapidly growing rate of self-employment has on the levels and distribution of income. They looked, in particular, at earnings and wealth levels of groups of self-employed possessing the characteristics that were overrepresented among the 'new self-employed' of the 1980s and early 1990s. Such groups (women, people under 25 years, those with unemployment experience and those starting service-sector businesses).

The research showed, overall, a greater dispersion of incomes among the self-employed than among their employee counterparts. In particular, the distribution of incomes among the self-employed contains larger proportions of both very high earners and very low earners than does the income distribution of employees. The results suggest, *ceteris paribus*, that a growing share of self-employment contributes to overall income dispersion among the working population. Of particular interest, however, is the growing share of low-income self-employed during the 1980s (many of the personal and sectorial characteristics of whom were precisely those typically found among participants of the schemes discussed above). The research showed, through multivariate statistical analysis of household panel survey data, that a self-employed person in 1991 was more than three times as likely to fall into the bottom decile group of the labour income distribution as an employee with broadly similar characteristics (in terms of age, gender, qualifications, occupations and so forth). Of even more interest is that the study showed[20] that older people with self-employment experience during their work histories are especially

---

19 It is interesting that US and, to some extent, UK evidence suggest that self-employment can be an effective mechanism for the economic integration of some disadvantaged and socially excluded groups facing discrimination in wage and salary employment (such as ethnic and racial minorities and immigrants). There is a debate in the literature about the extent to which minority self-employment can also be a mechanism for further segmentation and 'ghettoization' of such groups (see Borjas, 1986; Erichsen and Sen, 1987; Jones and McEvoy, 1986; Light, 1979; Min, 1984; Waldinger, Aldrich and Ward, 1990).

20 Drawing on a unique survey-based data set of people in the age group of 55–69-year olds, which includes complete work history data, as well as very full data on the individuals' financial and personal circumstances in later life.

likely to be found in a growing group of people with very low incomes, savings and pension levels in old age. The evidence suggests that the breaks in social security and pensions contributions sometimes associated with periods of self-employment may have important implications for both the level of expected income in later life and the date of retirement. People with self-employment experience tend to retire later than their counterparts who have only wage-employment experience. This characteristic is associated not only with a desire to continue working beyond normal retirement age but also, in many cases, with a financial need to continue working.

An important empirical observation from earlier research on self-employment (see Burrows, 1991) is the extent to which the self-employed in general, and the 'successful' self-employed in particular, are disproportionately drawn from social backgrounds with traditions of self-employment and small-business ownership. In so far as this pattern is breaking down, with the new self-employed (including self-employment scheme participants) lacking this background, the question arises as to whether such new entrants have the attitudes and socialization relevant to success in self-employment to the same extent as their predecessors. Clearly, the answer to this question will affect both their earnings potential while self-employed and the likelihood of their making adequate provision for retirement. The UK results suggest a significant impact in this direction. Further research is required in order to look at the dynamics underlying the process by which self-employment experience can contribute to the generation of a group of individuals who have not only low incomes during their working lives but poor prospects for incomes in retirement and to identify appropriate policy responses. It is not yet clear how far similar results exist in other countries, but there is, I would argue, a strong case for further, internationally comparative research to examine these issues.

REFERENCES

Acs, Z., D. Audretsch and D. Evans (1992), *The Determinants of Variations in Self-employment Rates across Countries and over Time*, WZB discussion paper FS IV 92–3, Wissenschaftszentrum Berlin für Sozialforschung.

Allen, D. (1987), *Enterprise Allowance Scheme Evaluation: First Eighteen-month National Survey*, Sheffield: Manpower Services Commission.

Allen, D. and A. Hunn (1985, August), 'An Evaluation of the Enterprise Allowance Scheme', *Employment Gazette*, 313–17.

Barker, P. (1989), *Self-employment Schemes for the Unemployed*, no. 10, Paris: Organization for Economic Co-operation and Development, Local Initiatives for Employment Creation.

Bennett, R., P. Wicks and A. McCoshan (1994), *Local Empowerment and Business Services: Britain's Experiment with Training and Enterprise Councils*, London: UCL Press, University College London (UCL).

Benus, J., M. Wood and N. Grover (1994), *A Comparative Analysis of the Washington and Massachusetts UI Self-employment Demonstrations*, Bethesda: Abt.

Birch, D. (1977), *Job Creation in America*, New York: Free Press.

Birch, D. (1979), 'The Job Generation Process', final report to Economic Development Administration, Cambridge, MA: MIT Program on Neighborhood and Regional Change. (Unpublished manuscript)

Blanchflower, D. and A. Oswald (1990), 'Self-employment and the Enterprise Culture', in R. Jowell, S. Witherspoon and L. Brook (eds), *British Social Attitudes: The 1990 Report*, Aldershot: Gower.

Bögenhold, D. and U. Staber (1991), 'The Decline and Rise of Self-employment', *Work, Employment and Society*, 5, 223–39.

Borjas, G. (1986), 'The Self-employment of Immigrants', *Journal of Human Resources*, 21, 485–506.

Burrows, R. (1991), 'Who Are the Contemporary British Petit Bourgeoisie?', *International Small Business Journal*, 9 (2), 223–9.

Campbell, M. and M. Daly (1992, June), 'Self-employment: Into the 1990s', *Employment Gazette*, 269–92.

Dossou, F. (1988), 'L'impacte de l'aide aux chômeurs créateurs de l'entreprise', *Dossiers Statistiques du Travail et de l'Emploi*, 57–63.

Elias, P. and K. Whitfield (1987), *The Economic Impact of the Enterprise Allowance Scheme: Theory and Measurement of Displacement Effects*, report to the Manpower Services Commission, Coventry: University of Warwick, Institute for Employment Research.

Erichsen, R. and F. Sen (1987), *Hinwendung zur Selbständigkeit bei Gastarbeitern mit besonderer Berücksichtigung von Türken*, working paper on International Migration for Employment, Geneva: International Labour Organization.

European Commission (ed.) (1988), *Chômeurs Créateurs*, report, Brussels.

Hasluck, C. (1990), *The Displacement Effects of the Enterprise Allowance Scheme: A Local Labour Market Study*, project report, Department of Employment Programme, 1989/90, Coventry: University of Warwick, Institute for Employment Research.

Høgelund, J., K. Langager, L. Jakobsen and J. Jagd (1992), *Iværksætterydelsen*, Copenhagen: Socialforskningsinstituttet/Dansk Teknologisk Institut.

Hughes, A. (1992), 'Big Business, Small Business and the "Enterprise Culture"', in J. Michie (ed.), *The Economic Legacy, 1979–92*, London: Academic Press, pp. 296–311.

Hunn, A. (1984), *Enterprise Allowance Scheme*, Sheffield: Manpower Services Commission.

IAB-Kurzbericht (1991), *Wer hat in den Jahren 1986 bis 1989 Überbrückungsgeld nach 55a AFG bezogen?*, Nuremberg: Institut für Arbeitsmarkt- und Berufsforschung.

Johnson, S., R. Lindley and C. Bourlakis (1988), *Modelling Aggregate Self-employment: A Preliminary Analysis*, project report, Department of Employment Programme, 1988/89, Coventry: University of Warwick, Institute for Employment Research.

Jones, T. and D. McEvoy (1986), 'Ethnic Enterprise: The Popular Image', in J. Curran, J. Stanworth and D. Watkins (eds), *The Survival of the Small Firm*, Gower: Aldershot (Vol. 1).

Kaiser, M. and M. Otto (1990), 'Übergang von Arbeitslosigkeit in berufliche Selbständigkeit', *Mitteilungen aus der Arbeitsmarkt- und Berufsforschung*, 22 (2), 284–99.

Keeble, D., S. Walker and M. Robson (1993), *New Firm Foundation and Small Business Growth in the United Kingdom: Spatial and Temporal Variations and Determinants*, ED research paper no. 15, London: Employment Department.

Kitson, M. (1995), *Seedcorn or Chaff? Unemployment and Small Firm Performance*, working paper no. 2, Cambridge, UK: Economic and Social Research Council (ESRC), Centre for Business Research, University of Cambridge.

Light, I. (1979), 'Disadvantaged Minorities in Self-employment', *International Journal of Comparative Sociology*, 20, 31–45.

Marston, M. and K. Pattison (1989), *EAS Postal Survey: Quality and Impact of Monitoring*, ES Research and Evaluation Branch, report no. 37, Sheffield: The Employment Service.

Maung, N. and R. Erens (1991), *Enterprise Allowance Scheme: A Survey of Participants Two Years after Leaving*, London: Social and Community Planning Research.

Meager, N. (1992a), 'Does Unemployment Lead to Self-employment?', *Small Business Economics*, 4, 87–103.

Meager, N. (1992b), 'The Fall and Rise of Self-employment (Again): A Comment on Bögenhold and Staber', *Work Employment and Society*, 6 (1), 127–34.

Meager, N. (1993), *Self-employment and Labour Market Policy in the European Community*, WZB discussion paper FS I 93–201, Wissenschaftszentrum Berlin für Sozialforschung.

Meager, N., G. Court and J. Moralee (1994), *Self-employment and the Distribution of Income*, IMS report no. 270, Joseph Rowntree Foundation Programme of Work on Income and Wealth in the United Kingdom, Brighton: Institute of Manpower Studies.

Meager, N., G. Court and J. Moralee (1995), 'Self-employment and the Income Distribution', in J. Hills (ed.), *New Inequalities*, Cambridge: Cambridge University Press.

Meager, N., M. Kaiser and H. Dietrich (1992), *Self-employment in the United Kingdom and Germany*, London: Anglo-German Foundation for the Study of Industrial Society.

Min, P.-G. (1984, Summer), 'From White-collar Occupations to Small Business: Korean Immigrants' Occupational Adjustment', *Sociological Quarterly*, 333–52.

MSC (1983), *Enterprise Allowance: Some Early Results from the Questionnaire Survey*, Sheffield: Manpower Services Commission.

NAO (National Audit Office) (1988), *Department of Employment/Training Commission: Assistance to Small Firms*, report by the Comptroller and Auditor General, no. 655, London: HMSO.

OECD (1992, July), 'Recent Developments in Self-employment', *OECD Employment Outlook*, 155–94.

Owens, A. (1989), *Enterprise Allowance Scheme Evaluation; Sixth 6-month National Survey*, ES Research and Evaluation Branch, report, Sheffield: The Employment Service.

Owens, A. and S. Demery (1988), *Enterprise Allowance Scheme Evaluation; Fifth 6-month National Survey*, ES Research and Evaluation Branch, report no. 10, Sheffield: The Employment Service.

PA Cambridge Economic Consultants (1990), 'Evaluation of Jobclubs and the Enterprise Allowance Scheme in Great Britain', Cambridge, UK (Unpublished manuscript).

Pattison, K. and S. Demery (1988), *Enterprise Allowance Scheme: Third 18-month Postal Survey*, ES Research and Evaluation Branch, report no. 11, Sheffield: The Employment Service.

RBL (1987), *Enterprise Allowance Scheme Evaluation: Three-month National Survey*, London: RBL Research.

Rosdahl, A. and I. Maerkedahl (1987), *Uddannelses og iværksætterydelsen til langtiesledige*, Copenhagen: Socialforskningsinstituttet.

Sengenberger, W., G. Loveman and M. Piore (eds) (1989), *The Re-emergence of Small Enterprises: Industrial Restructuring in Industrialised Countries*, Geneva: International Institute for Labour Studies.

Simkin, C. and D. Allen (1988), *Enterprise Allowance Scheme Evaluation: Second Eighteen-month National Survey*, final report, Sheffield: Manpower Services Commission.

Smith, P. and N. Tremlett (1990), *Enterprise Allowance Scheme: 18 Month Interview Survey*, London: Social and Community Planning Research.

Steinmetz, G. and E. Wright (1989), 'The Fall and Rise of the Petty Bourgeoisie: Changing Patterns of Self-employment in the Post-war United States', *American Journal of Sociology*, 94 (5), 973–1018.

Storey, D. (1994), *Understanding the Small Business Sector*, London: Routledge.

Tremlett, N. (1993), *The Business Start-up Scheme: 18 Month Follow Up Survey*, London: Social and Community Planning Research.

Waldinger, R., H. Aldrich and R. Ward (1990), *Ethnic Entrepreneurs*, Newbury Park: Sage.

Wandner, S. and J. Messenger (1991), 'From Unemployed to Self-employed: Self-employment as a Re-employment Option in the United States', Washington, DC: US Department of Labor, Employment and Training Administration. (Unpublished manuscript)

Wood, D. (1985), *Two Years after the Enterprise Allowance*, London: Social and Community Planning Research.

17. Employment Opportunities for the Disabled

Lei Delsen[1]

The focus in this chapter is on vocational rehabilitation and employment promotion policies for disabled persons in the Member States of the European Union (EU) and in the United States. The diversity in institutional arrangements concerning vocational rehabilitation and employment for people with disabilities between these countries represents a potentially ideal area of application for the target-oriented approach of evaluation, that is, for an assessment of the optimal policy mix that will achieve certain targets under different socioeconomic conditions and sociopolitical and institutional settings. In section 1, I review the applied operational definitions of 'disability' and outline the size, the characteristics and the labour market position of the target group. In section 2 some major patterns and developments with respect to vocational rehabilitation and employment for people with disabilities in the institutional context are presented. Instruments that support the integration of disabled persons into open employment are reviewed in the sections 3–5, and the effectiveness of the various policy options is established on the basis of available evaluation studies. In section 3 legal intervention is discussed, that is, equal opportunity legislation, quota systems and protection against dismissal. In section 4 the following employment support services are investigated: mainstream vocational services, on-the-job training, special education and supported employment. Finally, in section 5, financial instruments to support open employment are reviewed, namely, wage subsidies, grants for workplace adaptation, technical aid and prevention and early intervention. Sheltered employment is the subject of section 6, while in section 7 the policies applied in the selected countries are summarized, conclusions regarding further research needs are drawn, and some policy recommendations are made.

---

1 The author would like to thank the participants in the workshops, particularly G. Biffl, G. Schmid and J. Smith, for their helpful comments on an earlier version of this chapter.

1 DEFINITION AND CHARACTERISTICS OF THE TARGET GROUP

1.1 Definition and Recognition

The definition of disability constitutes a basis for the classification of people into distinct (target) groups and is thus used to determine which individuals are eligible for different services. A wide array of definitions is applied in eligibility assessments, the choice depending on the purpose of the programme or the ministry, institution or body involved. The definitions incorporate the following dimensions: the severity or degree, the permanent nature, the types and the origin of disabilities (EC, 1988). Unclear definitions affect the efficiency of the measures adopted and constitute major barriers for evaluations of policies and programmes. Where the responsibility rests with the employer, for example, in France, the Netherlands, the United Kingdom and the United States, some external professional assessment is needed in order that the legislation is effective and invulnerable to manipulation. Moreover, questions of definition are crucial to an understanding of how goals and developments in this particular area interact with those of other policy areas, such as retirement policies and general labour market policies (OECD, 1992).

In almost all EU countries the definition of a handicap is related to work and income. Denmark, Italy and Luxembourg define a handicap as a reduction of work capacity. In Belgium, France, Germany, the Netherlands, Portugal, Spain and the United Kingdom a handicap is defined as reduced potential to find or retain a job. The definition in the United States is in line with the World Health Organisation's broad definition.[2] In Sweden disability is considered as a relationship between the individual and the environment (EC, 1988; Lunt and Thornton, 1993). Such a situational, noncategorical definition is an important element in effective transition and employment policies, for the labelling according to type of disability focusses attention on the individual's deficiencies and emphasizes the negative aspects of his or her situation. There is a move away from a static medical concept of disability to interpretations focussing on environmental aspects. This dynamic definition implies that the degree to which a disability is a handicap depends on the situation of the individual, the attitudes and expectations of others, and intervention strategies and environmental modifications (OECD, 1992, 1994a, 1994b). Within one country there may also be conflicts in the application of definitions of disabil-

---

2 An impairment is a psychological, anatomical or mental loss, or some other abnormality. A disability is any restriction on, or lack of, ability to perform an activity in the manner or within the range considered normal. A handicap is a disadvantage resulting from an impairment or a disability (WHO, 1980).

ity. For instance, in the United States the American with Disability Act (ADA) prohibits employers from discussing disability at interviews, while receipt of work-subsidy incentives is dependent on prospective employees declaring themselves as disabled (Lunt and Thornton, 1993).

1.2   Characteristics of the Population of Disabled People

Estimates of the size, composition and employment situation of people with disabilities are essential for the development of sound employment policies. The present statistics on the characteristics and the labour market situation of disabled persons are quite inadequate. Definitions vary widely across countries and across government departments within countries. In the OECD countries disabled persons make up about 10 per cent of the population of working age. Only about 30–40 per cent of persons with disabilities participate in the labour force, compared with two-thirds of the general population. In Europe and the United States the unemployment rate among disabled persons is two to three times as high as the general unemployment rate. Moreover, not only is the unemployment rate higher, but the duration of unemployment is longer. A considerable share of unemployed persons with disabilities are long-term unemployed (Grammenos, 1991; Haveman, Halberstadt and Burkhauser, 1984; Lunt and Thornton, 1993; McLaughlin, Florian, Neubert, Boyd-Kjellen and Frieden, 1992; OECD, 1992; Semlinger, 1984; Semlinger and Schmid, 1985). In Europe and the United States two-thirds or more of nonworking disabled people of working age have indicated that they would like a job and would be willing and able to accept a job, if a suitable job were available (Delsen and Klosse, 1992; Hardman, 1994; OECD, 1992). A paid job is preferred because it yields cash and satisfaction, is evidence of status and recovery and because work may be used as therapy (Wansbrough and Cooper, 1980). The increase in the value attached to paid employment is strengthened by the ensuing reduction of social security benefits.

The characteristics of the group of disabled people of working age are that they are mainly older male workers with a relatively low educational level and professional status. The number of disabled people increases with age. The majority of the working disabled are employed to carry out simple functions and in low-status and low-income occupations that correspond to their low level of education. They are frequently underemployed. The proportion of disability pensioners has increased in most countries and now exceeds the share of persons drawing unemployment benefits. The majority (50–80 per cent) of the disabled persons are physically disabled, mostly by motor impairment. About 5 to 15 per cent are mentally retarded or mentally ill.

The experience in Europe and the United States is that most reintegration takes place in larger enterprises. To a large extent this is reemployment and replacement of the enterprises' own old employees who are partially disabled. Recruitment from outside is negligible. Smaller firms employ relatively fewer disabled workers but recruit relatively more from outside. In general, enterprise policy towards disabled workers is limited to those who incur a disability while working in the company. A policy of taking on those who are outside the company and not participating in the labour market is very rare, especially in the industrial sector. The commercial service sector has the most favourable working conditions for employment of disabled workers (Delsen

Table 17.1   Public Expenditure and New Participants in Labour Market Measures for the Disabled in Selected OECD Countries, 1992/1993

	Vocational Rehabilitation		Work for the Disabled		Total	
	Public expenditure (% GDP)	New participants (% labour force)	Public expenditure (% GDP)	New participants (% labour force)	Public expenditure (% GDP)	New participants (% labour force)
Austria	0.03	0.4[a]	0.02	0.1[a]	0.05	0.5[a]
Belgium	0.05	—	0.10	—	0.15	—
Denmark	0.33	2.5	0.15	0.6	0.49	3.1
Finland	0.08	0.7	0.10	...	0.17	0.7
France	0.02	0.4	0.06	...	0.08	0.4
Germany	0.14	0.3[b]	0.11	—	0.25	0.3[b]
Ireland	0.14	...	...	...	0.14	...
Italy	...	...	...	...	...	...
Luxembourg	0.01	—	0.09	—	0.10	—
Netherlands	...	...	0.62	0.1	0.62	0.1
Portugal	0.05	0.1	...	...	0.05	0.2
Spain	...	...	0.01	0.1	0.01	0.1
Sweden	0.12	0.5	0.74	0.2	0.85	0.8
United Kingdom	...	0.1	0.02	0.1	0.03	0.1
United States	0.05	0.8	...	...	0.05	0.8

Notes
... = nil or less than half of the last digit used.
— = data not available.
a 1990.
b 1992.

Source
Employment Outlook (Table I.B.2, pp. 54–61) by OECD, 1994, Paris. Copyright 1994 by OECD. Adapted by permission.

and Bemelmans, 1987; Haveman et al., 1984; Lunt and Thornton, 1993; Mul, de Winter, Nijboer and de Haan, 1995; OECD, 1992; Sadowski and Rendenbach, 1989; Semlinger and Schmid, 1985; Seyfried, 1992).

As regards public policy towards the disabled, only data on special programmes are available (see Table 17.1). Vocational rehabilitation includes ability testing, work-adjustment measures and training other than ordinary labour market training. Work for the disabled includes sheltered employment and subsidies for regular employment. These measures do not cover the total policy effort in support of the disabled. In Sweden and the Netherlands, compared with other EU countries, very large public resources are devoted to work for the disabled (sheltered employment), while in Denmark expenditure on vocational rehabilitation is the highest. The number of new participants is also highest in Denmark. In the United States, despite the fact that expenditure on vocational rehabilitation is relatively low, the number of new participants is relatively high. With respect to work for the disabled, in Denmark the number of new participants is highest, although expenditure is moderate. High expenditures in Sweden and the Netherlands do not correlate with a high number of new participants.

Future employment prospects for people with disabilities may improve. The aging of the work force and the decrease in the growth rates of the labour force may compel employers to look beyond their traditional sources for entry-level workers, for instance to people with disabilities. The trend towards the service sector and white-collar work is increasing the range of employment opportunities for those with a physical impairment. Disabled people are also clearly benefiting from recent technological developments, especially those with a physical impairment; for example, there are now more possibilities for home work. However, workers with cognitive limitations or mental impairment are increasingly experiencing difficulty in finding work (Delsen and Bemelmans, 1987; McLaughlin et al., 1992; OECD, 1992; Sadowski and Rendenbach, 1989; Seyfried, 1992; Wadensjö, 1984).

2 INSTITUTIONAL CONTEXT

In each country a large number of independent institutions and services are involved in the rehabilitation of, the promotion of employment for and the schooling and training of disabled persons. They include ministries, social security bodies and (regional) organizations of (and for) people with disabilities with different objectives and cultural perspectives. Countries vary in their reliance on specialist or mainstream employment support services. In Sweden access to specialist services is limited to those who need special resources in order to search for, obtain and retain employment or for whom mainstream services are not sufficient. Specialist provisions are strong in countries with traditions of assessment of disability for the purposes of social security benefits or social welfare services (Austria, Belgium, France and the Netherlands). In a number of countries mainstream services are supplemented by specialized personnel, for instance, personal assistants in enterprises in Denmark (Lunt and Thornton, 1993; Seyfried, 1992).

In the United States and Denmark there is a change towards organizations of disabled people wishing to provide their own separate specialist services (Lunt and Thornton, 1993). Their involvement results in better services tailored to the special needs of disabled people (OECD, 1992). With the rise of disabled persons' organizations, in EU countries there has been an attempt to shift the responsibility for employment of disabled people away from the state towards the private sector (Lunt and Thornton, 1993; Seyfried, 1992). However, decentralization of decision-making means the central authorities are deprived of their power and responsibility to push forward a policy. Decentralization also leads to problems in monitoring and evaluating policy implementation because of the ensuing lack of communication and coordination in activities. Thus, decentralization has resulted in a fragmented and uncoordinated system of institutions, bodies, benefits and services, and in overlaps and conflict in policies (Delsen, 1989; Lunt and Thornton, 1993; OECD, 1992, 1994b; Seyfried, 1992).

In addition, institutional incongruence may retard the move towards integration.[3] For example, in France and Portugal the costs of integrated special education provisions are financed out of the state or local budgets, whereas those of segregated provisions are financed by the social security system. In these cases the education authorities are reluctant to promote integration if it is going to result in a transfer to their budget of considerable expenditure on separate education provisions hitherto borne by the social security system (OECD, 1994b). In Germany there is a slight financial disincentive for the public employment service (PES) to fund further training in preference to unemployment (see Schmid, chap. 25 in this volume).

At the microlevel institutional incongruence leads to moral hazard as a result of identification problems. Moral hazard is insignificant as regards the severely and the mentally disabled because these groups are relatively easy to identify. However, illness and occupational injury are relative concepts. Moral hazard could be mitigated if impaired persons were provided with funds or vouchers to purchase their own rehabilitation from a variety of sup-

---

3 Institutional incongruence means that the autonomy in decision-making and the financial responsibility for the consequences of the decision are unevenly balanced (see Schmid, chap. 7 in this volume for a discussion).

pliers in the private sector.[4] Moral hazard cannot be avoided in social security (Lindbeck, 1994). One can question the extent to which disabled persons themselves are able to choose the type, modality, method and direction of their own rehabilitation.

Unemployment, disability and early retirement benefits are communicating vessels. In the EU and the United States there is a considerable amount of hidden unemployment among disabled workers. All disability programmes are adversely affected by economic downturns: in times of recession applications for disability benefits increase. In assessing the degree of disability the unemployment rate is taken into account. Full disability benefits are used as a form of unemployment compensation (Burkhauser and Hirvonen, 1989; Casey, chap. 12 in this volume; Delsen and Reday-Mulvey, 1995; Haveman et al., 1984; Semlinger and Schmid, 1985; Zeitzer, 1994). Empirical evidence in the EU and the United States shows that gradual retirement prevents unemployment and reduces sickness absenteeism and full disability claims (Delsen, 1987, 1995; Delsen and Reday-Mulvey, 1995).

Means-tested social security may entail a risk of loss of income and free services for persons entering competitive employment (poverty and unemployment trap). Disability benefits (whether earnings-related or means-tested) are a disincentive for people to increase their economic independence. Disabled persons may be trapped in a part-time job.[5] These traps and financial losses should be avoided if employment for the disabled is to be promoted. Empirical evidence from North America (Harkness, 1993; Haveman et al., 1984) suggests that a disability pension is not necessarily a significant work deterrent. In part this is related to the replacement rates. Harkness (1993) concludes that disability pensions serve the socially useful purpose of discouraging the disabled from working in an unsuitable and/or undesirable job. Like unemployment benefit (see Schmid and Reissert, chap. 8 in this volume), disability benefits may actually increase labour market efficiency by supporting the disabled individual while he or she looks for a new, more suitable job.

---

4 Vouchers are to be preferred over deductibles and coinsurance. However, the introduction of vouchers for services may result in unacceptable segregation between social groups and problems with low-income groups.

5 For instance, in the United Kingdom the current welfare benefits system implies that disabled workers would be worse off and their housing situation prejudiced if they worked longer hours.

3   OPEN EMPLOYMENT AND LEGAL INTERVENTION

3.1   Equal Opportunity Legislation

Discrimination occurs when persons of equal productivity are offered different wages and unequal opportunities for employment. Discrimination may result, for example, from prejudice, differential information concerning the average productivity of majority and minority workers or from exploitation of workers. All EU countries apply (a right to) equal and fair treatment as regards access to mainstream vocational training programmes and employment as a reference instrument for disabled persons against discriminatory measures and practices. Federal disability discrimination legislation has recently also been adopted in Canada, the United States and Australia (Haveman et al., 1984; Lunt and Thornton, 1993). The ADA is the most far-reaching legislation. For the formulation of effective public policy it is essential to distinguish the employment and wage effects of health limitations from the limitations resulting from discrimination. The fact that health has a greater influence on employment than on wages implies that the ADA may be more important as a defence against wage discrimination than as a policy that increases the employment of persons with impairments. Wage discrimination deters disabled people from seeking employment. However, the disincentive effect accounts for only a small part of the differences in employment between nondisabled and disabled people (Baldwin and Johnson, 1994). Epstein (1992) opposes the ADA. He argues that it is simply not a sufficient justification for aid to the disabled to show that the benefits they (or some subgroup) derive from any social expenditure are positive. These benefits must also be larger than the associated costs, and the costs are ignored or systematically made light of under the ADA. The mismatch of cost and benefits is a fatal flaw of any antidiscrimination law for persons with disabilities. Antidiscrimination regulations are highly beneficial to some members of the target group, but not to all. In fact, they may lead to a reduction in job opportunities for certain expensive groups of disabled persons. Antidiscrimination legislation is always redistributive. Epstein concludes that the best solution is always to repeal all legislation that interferes with operation of the market. Bulow and Summers (1986) argue that affirmative action policies (quotas) and subsidies for desirable primary sector jobs for members of disadvantaged groups are likely to entail an increase in total welfare. Unequal treatment may result in an inefficient allocation of resources because prices do not accurately indicate social costs, and in a loss of valuable resources. Moreover, from the point of view of games theory excessive wage differentials may be considered as having an unfair effect on work incentives. Schotter and Weigelt (1992) show that the effects of affirmative action programmes on output depend on the degree of discrimination. This result can be explained by the fact that disadvantaged subjects tend to drop out and supply zero effort; a quota system enables promotion, that is, it becomes worthwhile to provide maximum performance, and this effect will be stronger the more severe the negative position of the workers. Moreover, more competition from the weakest group forces the privileged group to work harder. Hence, it is in the interest of a firm to prevent part of its labour force getting into a position with no prospects, for this will limit these employees' effort.

Employers who are averse to risks and who lack detailed knowledge about the consequences of various disabilities on work capacity may systematically refrain from hiring disabled people. Employers are prejudiced in the sense that they assume disabilities mean limited work capacity, potential trouble or higher costs. There is notable prejudice against disabled persons with psychiatric or cognitive limitations (Delsen and Bemelmans, 1987; Honey, Meager and Williams, 1993; Raskin, 1994; Semlinger and Schmid, 1985; Söder, 1994). Performance on the job depends on ability, and workers are heterogeneous in ability. The diversity may result in adverse selection because if ability and workers' reservation wages are positively correlated, firms with higher wages will attract more able job candidates (Akerlof and Yellen, 1986).[6] The efficiency priority can be countered by a wage subsidy, while the fear of problems can be reduced by the promise of support should trouble arise. An appropriate remedy for employer prejudice would be an improvement in available information and/or the regulation of hiring practices backed up by penalties for noncompliance. Once a person with a disability is hired, much of the destereotyping ensues as a natural result of daily interaction. The employer and fellow workers come to know the person with the disability instead of the 'disabled person' (Seyfried, 1992). There is a paradox here because the use of a stereotyped label may be necessary to destereotype attitudes towards persons with disabilities (Söder, 1994).

3.2   Quota Systems

Once the (re)integration of disabled people in open employment is accepted as a policy aim, two options are available: voluntary employment (United States, Sweden, Portugal and Denmark) and forced employment, that is, quota systems (other EU countries). The latter is related in part to the 1986 EC recommendation in favour of quota schemes (EC, 1988). The quota system is based on the principle of sharing open employment and on the need to provide a short-term answer to the problem of occupational integration for the disabled.

---

6 For the adverse selection model to yield a convincing account of involuntary unemployment, firms must be unable either to measure effort or to pay piece rates after workers are hired, or to fire workers whose output is too low (Akerlof and Yellen, 1986).

In practice most schemes are a form of affirmative action. The quota systems vary with respect to the degree of enforcement, the administrative arrangements, the sanction or the levy system and the actual quota percentage, and apply in the public and/or the private sector.

In Denmark and Sweden quotas have been rejected for reasons of ineffectiveness, execution problems and stigmatization. Quota jobs are procyclical. In the United Kingdom only a small (5 per cent) and decreasing number of employers fulfil the quota, while in Germany most firms fulfil or surpass their quota because of the operation of a fines/subsidy system. However, the German quota system, which is targeted at people who are severely disabled, has also been progressively less effective in securing the employment of disabled people because of the economic recession. Registration at the PES is encouraged by the belief in the efficacy of the quota scheme. Moreover, registration entails several advantages, for instance, special dismissal protection. Fines are collected in a special fund aiming at the vocational integration of the target group (Burkhauser and Hirvonen, 1989; Sadowski and Frick, 1992; Semlinger and Schmid, 1985; Seyfried, 1992). The British quota system failed because many disabled people see little point in registering at the PES, because they do not wish to identify or label themselves as 'handicapped' (stigma) and because the obligation on employers to seek a permit is not enforced (Lunt and Thornton, 1993; OECD, 1992; Wansbrough and Cooper, 1980). Also in other EU countries governments are unable or unwilling to enforce their statutory sanctions. In France many firms would rather pay the levy than employ disabled people (Seyfried, 1992). Although the ineffectiveness of quotas is a major issue in the discussion, research on their effectiveness in the various countries is limited. The control mechanism is inadequate, and one major conclusion is that the effectiveness of quota schemes depends on the form and the method of implementation (Schell, 1991). Because a quota scheme does not differentiate between various types of disability severely disabled people are disadvantaged. Quota schemes are most beneficial to the least disabled candidates for employment because companies tend to cream off, that is, hire, these in preference. Another problem with quotas is that the employer in some cases may exert influence as to who is to be classified as disabled (Lunt and Thornton, 1993; OECD, 1992; Raskin, 1994; Wadensjö, 1994).

Employers have a considerably more positive attitude towards the retention of existing employees who become disabled than towards the recruitment of disabled persons (Honey et al., 1993). Hence, a quota system may only safeguard or improve the position of the insiders, preventing a flow out of the labour market (retention), but not influence or perhaps even reduce the chances of disabled outsiders to be integrated into the labour process (recruitment) (Sadowski and Frick, 1992; Semlinger and Schmid, 1985; Seyfried, 1992; Seyfried and Lambert, 1989).

3.3   Protection against Dismissal

Evidence from the United Kingdom shows that the Employment Protection Act is designed to safeguard the position of existing workers, but that it hinders people with a psychiatric history in their search for employment (Wansbrough and Cooper, 1980). Experience in Germany shows that there is a lower risk of unemployment for severely handicapped persons with a job than for their nondisabled counterparts. Dismissal protection improves the competitiveness of socially disadvantaged persons, however, this group also faces a greater risk of remaining unemployed. These findings are in line with the insider–outsider argument. Dismissal protection discriminates against unemployed workers whose productivity is low, including severely handicapped persons, and may exacerbate their discrimination in the labour market. Employers can be expected to be, *ceteris paribus*, more reluctant to hire from this group the more their special rights entail additional dismissal costs (Lunt and Thornton, 1993; Sadowski and Frick, 1992; Semlinger and Schmid, 1985). Employment protection may lead to more stringent screening of applicants, making it harder for youths with disabilities to enter the job market (Wadensjö, 1994). The effects of dismissal protection on job distribution are therefore ambiguous. Assessment depends on whether persons are employed (insiders) or unemployed (outsiders) (Buttler and Walwei, 1993).

4   OPEN EMPLOYMENT AND SUPPORT SERVICES

4.1   Mainstream Vocational Training

Training activities have both medium- and long-term objectives. In all OECD countries measures to enhance the competitive power of individuals with disabilities are a corner-stone of policy. In order to encourage disabled people to participate in mainstream vocational training programmes, special support services, special financial arrangements and other provisions have been introduced, notably in Europe. Data on the integration of disabled people in mainstream vocational training are limited to placement rates, and the effectiveness of the measures cannot be established. In the field of education, decentralization of decision-making, budgetary restrictions and the 'hardening' of the school system will have negative effects on the development of integration (OECD, 1994b). There is a trend towards training that is more responsive to the needs of employers and the demands of the market and towards more competition among providers of services (Lunt and Thornton, 1993). These developments may lead to extensive creaming-off practices (at the expense of disabled people) (Burkhauser and Hirvonen, 1989) and/or high drop-out rates (see Erhel, Gautié, Gazier and Morel, chap. 9 in this volume).

Collaboration between schools, parents, state and local agencies, businesses and third-level educational institutions is essential for an effective transition from school to adult life. Moreover, in designing new approaches, the specific regional or local conditions have to be taken into account, and more flexibility is needed to adequately meet the training interests of certain groups of disabled persons. Policies, facilities and services for the transition from school to work of young people with disabilities and special needs should be an integral part of policies, facilities and services for all young people (OECD, 1994a; see Ryan and Büchtemann, chap. 10 in this volume). The United Kingdom and Sweden, in line with this new approach based on educational needs and addressing the problems related to the labelling and definition of handicaps, no longer classify as disabled those pupils who traditionally received special education (OECD, 1994b). However, even in ordinary education pupils may be labelled according to the way their needs are addressed. This is certainly the case for special classes within mainstream education. Barriers to integration may be the inconsistencies in diagnosis criteria used to identify students with special needs and the lack of an adequate data base that would enable appropriate planning.

4.2   On-the-job Training

There is another trend in Europe and the United States in the field of vocational training of disabled people towards more on-the-job training in ordinary work environments as a forerunner to placement. Some EU countries have maintained their apprenticeship models for disabled trainees. In the United States supported employment is used to encourage integrated employment–training (see below). On-the-job training is not only a guarantee for a high standard of training but also for a smooth transition into working life in most cases. The employer and the disabled person are also given an opportunity to get to know each other and to overcome prejudices. Most on-the-job training for disabled young people in Germany is provided by smaller firms, and one effect is that the trainees' prospects of permanent employment improve (see Seyfried, 1992 for evidence).

Experience with employment-cum-training for young people in France and Belgium shows that such contracts failed to promote on-the-job training. In the latter case employment probability as well as wages are negatively affected (Delsen, 1995; see Erhel et al., chap. 9 in this volume). Data on the effectiveness of training measures for disabled people are limited and many of the available statistics are related only to numbers of participants; no follow-up studies are available. Although there are examples of rehabilitation and training programmes with good results, a number of issues are deserving of further attention. First, general economic and labour market developments are leading to a growing demand for skilled workers, while changes in the composition (more mentally retarded and severely disabled persons and diversified disabilities) of the target group make rehabilitation and vocational training increasingly difficult; second, there is a bias towards persons with primary physical disabilities; third, there is an orientation towards industrial manufacturing work. For many disabled people the major barrier to the labour market may not be the lack of job-related skills but rather a lack of job-seeking skills. Disabled people have to learn how to sell themselves. Programmes for improving job search skills are becoming a valuable supplement to the traditional rehabilitation and training programmes (Lunt and Thornton, 1993; OECD, 1992; Seyfried, 1992).

4.3   Special Education

There is frequently controversy about legislation concerning special services for disabled people. Apart from providing services to selected groups, these laws have countervailing effects, for example labelling (OECD, 1992). The effectiveness of special education for youth is limited. Experiences in the United States show that 90 per cent of the students remain dependent after leaving school. In OECD Member countries employment departments and bodies focus on the reemployment of people who became disabled later in life, rather than on the employment of young persons with disabilities (McLaughlin et al., 1992). Again, this bias is in line with the insider–outsider argument (see sections 3.2 and 3.3). The lack of transition programmes for young people with disabilities often results in life-long dependence on income maintenance. Transition programmes from school to work should be based on a tripartite relationship between the young person, his or her family and professionals. Coordination and continuity are essential elements of successful transition (OECD, 1992).

Placement is made difficult by high unemployment rates, and cooperation with firms may be an alternative. Germany's special centres for the vocational rehabilitation of disabled people seem to be effective. The majority of their trainees are physically disabled, most having skeleton and motor impairment or internal disorders.[7] About 75 per cent of those who complete the courses at the centres are placed; only about 15 per cent are unemployed one year later. Dutch training centres are similarly effective. The success is partly due to the fact that participants are familiarized with modern technology and that the centres cooperate with firms regarding the provision of training places or practical sessions. Rehabilitation on the job is based on local labour market analysis. In some cases the special centres establish their own firm. The positive employment prospects

---

7 Also in the other EU countries training in specialized establishments is biased towards non-mental disabilities.

contribute to the motivation of the disabled and to better performance by the centres. Cooperation and the establishment of firms for the disabled imply a direct link between vocational rehabilitation and the creation of jobs. These trends can also be found in other EU countries, for example, Italy, Ireland, Denmark and Belgium (EC, 1988; Lunt and Thornton, 1993; Seyfried, 1992; Seyfried and Lambert, 1989).

4.4   Supported Employment

Supported employment is competitive employer-paid work combined with the provision of continuous on-the-job support where required to employers and to individual employees with (often severe) disabilities in order that the latter can perform a normal job in open employment. Individual work preferences are emphasized. The training–employment model is replaced by an employment–training model. The emphasis is on a guarantee that the job will be done, and job coaches employed by the placement body train, assist and support the worker in the work situation. The support may be quite intensive and is maintained at the level necessary for the person involved to stay in the job (OECD, 1992). Supported employment could replace wage subsidies and fill the gap between more conventional, fixed-term training programmes and long-term sheltered work (Lunt and Thornton, 1993; Schell, 1991). One significant advantage of supported employment might be reduced problems with transition to open employment. Supported employment focusses both on the supply and demand side of the labour market and comes in various forms (Hardman, 1994; Lunt and Thornton, 1993; Wansbrough and Cooper, 1980): individual placements, enclaves and mobile work crews.[8]

Given the relative infancy of most supported employment programmes, it would be premature to draw any conclusions regarding benefits and outcomes. However, ongoing evaluations indicate that severely disabled workers are able to succeed in jobs beside their nondisabled peers. Financial evaluations of the impact of supported employment are also still difficult. Research in the United States shows that these programmes are noticeably cheaper than traditional day centres, and especially sheltered employment. Continuous onsite training and assistance are more effective than vocational services in segregated settings. About 90 per cent of supported workers are mentally

---

8 Individual placement refers to intensive one-to-one training by a job coach for specific job tasks and nonwork behaviour. An enclave is a group of severely disabled people working under supervision in an ordinary and undifferentiated working environment, that is, employment for two to eight individuals with disabilities located in an industrial or business setting alongside nondisabled people and usually supervised by nondisabled people. Work crews consist of five or six individuals with disabilities and one crew supervisor and move from site to site. Work crews generally perform service jobs.

retarded (Hardman, 1994; Lunt and Thornton, 1993; OECD, 1992). For the United Kingdom, Pozner and Hammond (1993) found that supported-employment agencies are effective in achieving their aims and objectives and are helping large numbers of disabled people into ordinary paid employment, that is, real jobs with real wages in regular work settings, primarily entry-level posts within the service sector. The rate of job retention is excellent; only few difficulties in finding suitable jobs were reported, even in areas of very high unemployment. It appears that many clients are trapped in part-time jobs. The majority of agencies work with people with learning disabilities, but there are some indications that the model could also be used for people with other impairments. Clients with severe learning disabilities have been helped at a realistic and reasonable programme cost. Annual agency costs range widely between £1000 and £5000 per client assisted into and within employment. Other research indicates costs of between $5000 and $6000, the average for other employment provision methods. In the United States there are some indications of the long-term cost-effectiveness of the supported employment model as an alternative to other more traditional approaches, such as vocational preparation programmes, and of the effectiveness of the model in reducing people's usage of and dependence upon day services (Wehman, Sale and Parent, 1992). However, longitudinal studies are needed to examine more rigorously the efficacy of supported employment compared with other approaches. Cost–benefit analyses (see Delander and Niklasson, chap. 6 in this volume) are also needed to clarify the extent to which increased tax revenue and reduced benefits paid at exchequer level might offset or even outweigh programme costs.

5   OPEN EMPLOYMENT AND FINANCIAL SUPPORT

5.1   Wage Subsidies

Wage subsidies are in operation in all EU Member States and in the United States. A common feature of wage-subsidy schemes is the imposed time limitation, ranging from six months in Australia to three years in Norway. Although the amount of the subsidy varies between countries, in most cases it is 50 per cent or more. The aim of wage subsidies is to compensate for lower (initial) productivity and/or costs associated with special training and supervision. In the Nordic countries they are seen as a major strategy to assist disabled persons into the open labour market. Considering how widespread wage subsidies are, the lack of evaluation efforts is striking. There are indications that the proportion of people with disabilities entering open employment is not lower than the share of other disadvantaged groups in the labour market. However, wage subsidies may be a disincentive for employers to retain (nonsubsidized) employees with disabilities (Lunt and Thornton, 1993; OECD, 1992). Under Sweden's active labour market policy an extended scheme of temporary wage subsidies applies; supported employment for the disabled is an integral part of overall employment policy. The wage subsidies for disabled workers might very well be one of the most cost-efficient Swedish labour market policy programmes (see Wadensjö, 1994, and Delander and Niklasson, chap. 6 in this volume).

There are practically no impact evaluations regarding wage subsidies in Europe. Most examinations are not an attempt to estimate the effect of the programmes on the economic environment but to identify elements in programme design, control and administration that could be changed in order to increase the administrative effectiveness of the schemes. Most of these evaluations of wage subsidies are based on survey data from participating firms and regression analyses of macrodata. In the United States cost–benefit analyses are more often used. Definite conclusions on the effectiveness of wage-cost subsidies in Europe and the United States cannot be drawn due to the lack of data and information about appropriate control groups. The wage-subsidy policy has not resulted in an improvement of the labour market position of those affected. Moreover, the impact of subsidies on recruitment is disappointing, due to deadweight, displacement and substitution effects. The net effect is low and budget costs per net job created are high (Haveman et al., 1984; Haveman and Palmer, 1982). Experience in Europe and the United States shows that there may even be a negative impact on employability as a result of stigmatization. The modest earning gains are generally due to longer hours, not higher wages (see Delsen, 1995; Erhel et al., chap. 9 in this volume). Under the present conditions, wage-cost subsidies alone are an insufficient incentive for employers to recruit disabled workers because there is still a lack of accompanying specialized services. Follow-up support of both employee and employer by the PES are called for to achieve access to in-company training for persons with disabilities (OECD, 1992). Financial incentives are also an important supplement to quota systems. Only a combination of the two can be regarded as an effective means of achieving additional jobs for disabled people (Seyfried, 1992; Seyfried and Lambert, 1989).[9]

---

9 There is much less evidence of financial support payable to the disabled employee rather than to the employer. Exceptions are Belgium (cost of transport to work, work clothes and tools) and Ireland (support of the blind) (Lunt and Thornton, 1993). Provisions to encourage or sustain the self-employment of disabled people are also hardly developed, despite the wider international trend towards self-employment (Lunt and Thornton, 1993; Meager, chap. 16 in this volume). Like sheltered employment, self-employment also does not foster the integration of disabled people with other nondisabled workers, and yet may be seen as a highly suitable form of employment. The United Kingdom seems to be the country that has most systematically explored these possibilities. Rough estimates indicate that the success rate of self-employed disabled people is as high as that of their nondisabled peers (OECD, 1992).

5.2   Grants for Workplace Adaptation and Technical Aid

A central feature of disability legislation in the United States (ADA) is the requirement on employers to make reasonable accommodations (including modification of the physical layout or equipment used, job restructuring, part-time or modified work schedules, training materials or policy, and provision of aids or personal assistance) for the known limitations of disabled individuals, marking a move towards the concept of equality of opportunity (see section 3.1). Another feature is 'undue hardship' as 'an action requiring significant difficulty or expense'. Epstein (1992) opposes the universal access mandated in the ADA because it imposes losses in dollar terms on employers that are greater than the gains received by the workers concerned. Another shortfall of the ADA is institutional incongruence. Epstein is in favour of replacing it by federal grants to particular firms to spend in making their facilities accessible to certain classes of disabled persons. Federal grants would imply that the government concentrates its own resources by choice in the places where they are likely to do the greatest amount of good. In Europe the legal requirement of job and workplace adaptation is framed generally. The purpose of workplace adaptation and the development of technical aids is to eliminate physical barriers that prevent disabled persons from accepting jobs or training. The impact of their impairment on their productivity is minimized. Technical and organizational modifications to permit the integration of disabled workers may well benefit the firm itself (Seyfried, 1992). Practice shows that the level of take-up of public provisions for technical aids and workplace adaptations is low (Delsen and Bemelmans, 1987; Mul et al., 1995; OECD, 1992). Important reasons are the lack of expertise in the agencies involved, lack of coordination of effort and lack of information about the existence of these provisions.

5.3   Prevention and Early Intervention

Experiences with prevention and early intervention show that many people who develop a disabling condition and subsequently enter the income-support population could remain in the work force given adequate help and follow-up support while still in employment. Research also shows that early information—preferably while the person still has a work contract—is cost-effective and an efficient strategy for rehabilitating people back into working life. The economic benefits from prevention and early intervention could therefore be considerable. However, at present there is a general lack of data about the effectiveness of prevention at enterprise level (Delsen, 1987). Improvements in statistics and research are necessary. Attempts to promote retention in Europe and the United States by means of legislation show mixed results. The lack of an accompanying sanction and enforcement system is a problem. Also the nonclarity of the legislation and employers' interpretations of what is reasonable undermine these laws (OECD, 1992). In many countries there are no real incentives for employers to retain their marginalized workers. There are few comprehensive public programmes with the objective of encouraging employers and employees to improve the working environment and to initiate early rehabilitation measures, although the Netherlands and Sweden subsidize employers who initiate systematic routines for prevention and early rehabilitation. There is little information from Europe about services aimed at job retention and career promotion. This gap possibly reflects the overriding service and policy emphasis on recruitment rather than retention (Delsen, 1987; Lunt and Thornton, 1993; OECD, 1992).

For most disabled people part-time work is the only way to take part in the labour process. Moreover, part-time work allows those who have not had work experience or who have been out of work for a considerable length of time to become acquainted with working life and possibly move on to a full-time job. Thus, the promotion of part-time employment can contribute to the integration of disabled workers into open employment. Moreover, the introduction of part-time work is preventive; it reduces the risk of a worker becoming disabled. Experience in Europe and the United States shows that adapted work is of importance for limiting prolonged absenteeism and occupational disability (Delsen, 1989; 1995; Mul et al., 1995; O'Reilly, chap. 19 in this volume). As disability expenditure increases, increasing public awareness might stimulate the willingness to allocate larger sums to prevention. Labour market opportunities depend upon employer attitudes and the conditions under which disabled persons have access to work. Job redesign and accommodation can serve to prevent disability and reduce the social costs of disability just as much as advancement in medical science and technology can reduce impairments and help eliminate consequent disability.

6   SHELTERED EMPLOYMENT

Sheltered employment has been introduced in all EU Member States for those disabled persons who cannot (yet) be integrated into the open labour market. In most EU countries the mentally retarded are the largest group in sheltered employment. Exceptions are Austria, the Netherlands, Sweden and the United Kingdom. Workers with a severe handicap are finding it increasingly difficult to get access to sheltered jobs. A solution might be a quota system for severely disabled workers (Lunt and Thornton, 1993; Samoy and Waterplas, 1992). The long-term unemployed also have access to sheltered employment, making evaluation focussing on our target group more difficult.

The idea of sheltered workshops is to prepare disabled people for transition into jobs in the open labour market. Nevertheless, although a number of countries are now actively promoting transition, it is not the primary aim in any of them. However, higher exit rates may not be in the interest of the sheltered workplace. Organizations may not be willing to let go of the most productive workers (Delsen and Klosse, 1992; Lunt and Thornton, 1993; Samoy and Waterplas, 1992; Schell, 1991; Seyfried, 1992). In Austria the rate of transition into open employment is relatively high (5–7 per cent). The sheltered employment schemes in Belgium, France, Sweden, the Netherlands and the United Kingdom have low (<5 per cent) rates of transition into open employment. In France, the Netherlands and Sweden this is partly related to the fact that sheltered work wages are equal to labour market wages. Other sheltered employment schemes are criticized for not offering market-level wages, for poor working conditions, for causing segregation and for not encouraging integration with nondisabled workers. Hence, sheltered workshops fail to facilitate the entry of severely disabled individuals into open employment and are often a dead end. On the other hand, sheltered employment remains an important alternative for individuals whose disabilities prevent them from taking up other employment, even in a situation of shortage. Moreover, some groups simply cannot work under normal conditions (Lunt and Thornton, 1993; OECD, 1992).

German experience shows that a subsidy of 100 per cent for public service-sector jobs is cheaper than funding places in sheltered workshops (Seyfried, 1992). Cost–benefit analysis in Sweden indicates that wage subsidies are favourable investments and in Norway that sheltered employment is a lucrative investment for public authorities (OECD, 1992). Cost–benefit calculations of sheltered workshops (comparing real resources used and produced output) in the United Kingdom, the Netherlands and Sweden show that the unmeasured benefits to society (e.g. social and psychological well-being and less time spent on care by other family members) must be substantial to compensate for the measured net social costs attributed to the enterprise activities. However, the regular sheltered workshops in the United States generate substantial benefits (Haveman et al., 1984).

To bridge the gap between sheltered and open employment, new institutions have developed in the EU (Lunt and Thornton, 1993; Seyfried and Lambert, 1989): independent firms, cooperatives of disabled people and special departments for the employment of disabled people. These include, for instance, self-help and social firms in Germany, 'inside firms' in Sweden, *Grandfos* (nonsubsidized enclaves) in Denmark, enclaves (Fiat Turin) and cooperatives in Italy, enclaves (Daf Trucks) and external jobs in the Netherlands and contracts with sheltered workshops to fulfil the employment obligation in France. Semisheltered employment has a number of advantages over sheltered workshops (Seyfried, 1992; Seyfried and Lambert, 1989; Wans-brough and Cooper, 1980): it is cheaper for the exchequer; enclaves can be operated with a sheltered workshop as a base so that people may progress from the workshop to the more open conditions of the enclave and eventually open employment; employers are required only to pay for the value of work per-formed and are exempted from employment protection. These workers are hired out, relieving the financial burden on the firm. An advantage of enclaves relative to individual placement is that it is easier to create adapted work processes and organizational structures. Moreover, enclaves have been shown to be cost-effective. Another advantage of enclaves (where the workers are not employees of the firm) compared to sheltered employment is that disabled workers are more involved in the enterprise (see section 4.4). The semishel-tered jobs represent a springboard to open employment. Cooperation between disabled and nondisabled people is also beneficial; compensation of certain impairments is possible and social integration is established.

7   CONCLUSIONS, POLICY RECOMMENDATIONS AND RESEARCH AGENDA

Divergence across countries in institutional and policy mixes to create employment opportunities for disabled people can be explained by differences in economic conditions and in culture. Table 17.2 summarizes the main con-tents and results of the policies applied in the EU Member States and the United States.

Definitive conclusions concerning the effectiveness of the policies applied and the various instruments that support the integration of the disabled in the countries under review cannot be drawn (Lunt and Thornton, 1993; Mul et al., 1995; OECD, 1992). First, there is the problem of identifying policy objec-tives. It is only where legislation is recent that policy aims are clearly stated. Even in the latter case priorities shift with implementation. In certain countries policy is incremental, shifting marginally with the social and economic con-text. A second problem is the apparently low importance attached to ongoing evaluation. In part this problem relates to the absence of clear-cut policy goals. Evaluation studies with definite results are rare for all approaches and policies applied. Numerous factors that may have an influence on the effectiveness of the approaches are referred to in the relevant literature, although these state-ments are based mostly on impressions from practice and not on empirical quantitative research. There are no empirical, scientific evaluation studies con-cerning the exact course of reintegration processes and the way these processes are influenced by various factors. In general, there is insufficient information about the quality of the methods applied. Likewise information on cost and benefits is thinly spread, and not only quantitative data but also qualitative data on aspects of work participation (contents and conditions of work and labour relations) are lacking. That is why I cannot present conclusions about the effectiveness of present policy approaches in meeting the needs of persons with disabilities. Moreover, most research does not consider those disabled people who are eligible for programmes but not selected, and systematic exclusion is suspected. The least productive (least healthy) will not be selected (adverse selection; creaming in programmes and recruitment), and thus only those with relatively good prospects are covered by research. Information is not available either about these selection mechanisms or about the characteristics of the whole group that is eligible and accessed. Therefore, conclusions about the various measures and experiences with disabled people may be biased and incorrect.

The optimal policy mix is greatly affected by economic conditions in general and the degree of labour market demand in particular. I have shown in the previous sections that (special) training and schooling alone are insufficient to prepare participants for the regular labour market and that sheltered employment is a dead end. Integrated projects combining training and employment are more appropriate. Under present conditions quota systems and wage subsidies are no longer adequate to ensure a lasting improvement in the integration prospects of disabled people. There is need for a practical assistance within firms. Apart from the high unemployment rates, the changing structure of the population of disabled people also lends greater significance to semi-sheltered and supported employment in addition to the traditional instruments. These policies aim both at the supply and demand side of the labour market. Some disabled persons may prefer intensive support, whereas others do not need it; some may not want a regular job and prefer voluntary work or a meaningful way to spend their day. So supported employment is relevant for those who want a regular job and who need intensive support. Notably, psychiatric patients and persons with mental impairments need counselling and support. In view of the heterogeneity of the target group, the best option for improving employment opportunities for disabled people is a differentiated mix of policies and programmes for different groups, based on local labour market analysis. The policy mix should include vocational training and rehabilitation, job creation measures, support on the job, job search assistance, sheltered employment and part-time employment.

As regards future developments in the area of supply-side measures for people with disabilities, the emerging 'skill gap' in the labour market is of importance. An active labour market policy may be considered to be the overall framework and may also be of significance with respect to the retention of workers in the work force. Another major barrier to the integration of people with disabilities is the lack of coordination and collaboration. There is no coherent employment policy for disabled people, and this shortfall is further aggravated by decentralization. Solutions are to be found in the centralization of responsibilities in one body and in new patterns of cooperation to achieve an integrated range of necessary services. Coordination is needed to avoid opposition and duplication of effort, to establish concerted action and to assure (cost-)effectiveness.

The starting point for successful integration of disabled workers into the market sector ought to be the individual worker. Successful integration means matching the supply of labour by the disabled worker and the demand of labour by the firm. Information concerning the desires of the disabled worker, his or her capacity and preferences and the physical and mental requirements of the jobs on offer is thus needed. The lack of information at the level of disabled individuals, at enterprise level, and at the level of society as a whole is one of the major barriers to the integration of disabled workers into open employment. However, information alone is not enough for the realization of permanent jobs for disabled workers in the market sector. In all cultures attitudes towards people with disabilities are a major obstacle to integration and a change in these attitudes is vital to achieving the placement of a disabled worker within an enterprise (Delsen, 1989). Employers are not informed about the employability of people with impairments, and disabled people are considered to be a risk for the firm. There is no need for large numbers of disabled persons to be hired in an enterprise for attitudinal barriers to be overcome. The provision of information on best practices, on-the-job training, semisheltered and supported employment may clear the decks. A general lack of demonstrable results and economic benefits may be one of the main obstacles to the future expansion of employment promotion programmes for people with disabilities. More emphasis on evaluation and on public accountability for rehabilitation and employment programmes is therefore essential for future policy development (OECD, 1992). Because of the competition in the labour market people with impairments often find bad jobs with high labour turnover. Raskin (1994) proposes an occupation-oriented quota system designed to encourage the representation of disabled persons in the occupational groups where they are known to be generally underrepresented.

The available data on the labour market situation of people with disabilities are inadequate and do not provide a basis for policy development or evaluation of strategies and programmes. Areas that merit more research are (OECD, 1992) possibilities for adjusting national surveys in order to gather more comparable data on the labour market situation of people with disabilities and cross-national research projects focussing on the reasons for the differences in labour market participation to provide a better basis for further policy development. More priority must also be given to investigations into the relation-

Table 17.2 Occupational Segregation, Discrimination and Equal Opportunity

Country	Definition of disability	Legal intervention			Financial support		
		Equal opportunity legislation	Quota system	Dismissal protection	Wage subsidies	Grants for workplace adaptation and technical aid
Belgium	Any person whose effective employment capacity is reduced by at least 30% as a result of a physical disability or by at least 20% as a result of a mental disability.	Social Rehabilitation Act of 1963 establishes the principle of equal treatment in the area of vocational and social integration.	Act of 1963 states that private employers with a work force of ≥20 are obliged to employ disabled people. Quota not fixed. In public sector a number of posts are reserved for disabled people, e.g. 1200 in civil services and one for every 55 workers in local and regional authorities. Targets exceeded.	No explicit reference to disability in legislation.	Act of 1963. In private and public sector, wage-cost subsidies 1 year up to 100% while employee adapts to the job. Little use. Collective Agree- ment no. 26 of 1975. Private employers are compensated for diminished performance (1 year), 1989: 2553 employees subsidized.	Financial aid to recompense for the cost difference between standard equipment and an adapted model. Little use: in 1988 31 grants, involving BF 3 202 000.
Denmark	There is no official definition of disability.	No explicit reference in legislation.	No mandatory quota.	No explicit reference to disability in legislation.	Wage support to employers who take on elderly, slightly disabled persons. '60–40'-system: wage support up to 40% for those not entitled to early retirement pension. 'One-third'-system: for retired persons, support up to 1/3 of minimum wage. Results: 1937 employees in 1987.	Financial support for adaptation of work station and acquisition of tools and equipment. No data on use available.

	Definition	Legislation	Quota/levy system	Dismissal protection	Recruitment subsidy	Workplace adaptation
France	Any person whose possibility of obtaining or keeping employment is effectively reduced as a result of an impairment or reduction in his or her physical or mental capacities.	The Disability Act of 1975 states that the integration of disabled persons in the educational system and in professional and social life is a national obligation.	Act of 1987. 6% quota for firms ≥20 employees. Fines and subsidies. Employer may fulfil quota by subcontracting with sheltered workshop. Results: 1991 3%.	No explicit reference to disability in legislation. Measures to help the worker keep his or her job where he or she is threatened with dismissal.	Recruitment subsidy of FF 30 000 pro rata to every company; 50% of subsidy on recruitment in permanent job and 30% on fixed-term contract. Supplement only paid when converted into permanent job. No data.	Financial support for adapting work station and premises. Aid is limited to 80% of the costs. No data on use.
Germany	Severely Disabled Persons Act 1974: persons who are limited in their capacity for integration into society because of the effects of a physical, mental or psychological condition that is contrary to the norm, and where limitation of this capacity for integration is not merely of a temporary nature.	According to Social Code, any person who is physically, mentally or psychologically disabled has a 'social right' to assistance needed to establish equal treatment.	Severely Disabled Persons Act 1974: 6% quota for firms ≥16 employees; beneficiaries: severely disabled persons; levy per job not filled; one-off grant for meeting quota. Levies put in fund for employment promotion of target group. Results: 1982 5.6%; 1989 4.7%.	Severely disabled persons may be dismissed only after authorization from the competent institution, which examines the various possibilities of maintaining employment. Favours insiders.	Subsidy by PES to employer, up to 80% of wage paid to the severely disabled person and up to 100% of training allowance for up to 3 years on a sliding scale. Continued employment for at least 1 year. 1986–88 10 350 persons financed from levies.	Employers are required to provide severely disabled persons with the necessary technical aids, unless this would involve unreasonable demands or disproportionate expense. Levy revenues are used to assist employee and employer. In 1988 DM 4.5 million for technical aids.
Greece	People with special needs: people between the age of 15 and 65 who have limited capacity for occupational activity deriving from any permanent impairment or deficiency of a physical, mental or psychological nature.	The Constitution of 1975 lays down that people with special needs have a right to specific care from the state.	Law of 1986. 5% quota for firms ≥50 employees in public and private sector. There are no penalties or other type of enforcement. No data available.	Dismissals within the quota system are governed by special laws.	Subsidy of DR 2600 by Manpower Employment Organization (OAED) per day for 1 year per recruited disabled person. About 550 persons in 1988.	Financial support (max. DR 120 000) by OAED for workplace adaptation. In 1987 workplaces for 200 disabled persons.

Table 17.2—continued *Occupational Segregation, Discrimination and Equal Opportunity*

Country	Definition of disability	Legal intervention			Financial support	
		Equal opportunity legislation	Quota system	Dismissal protection	Wage subsidies	Grants for workplace adaptation and technical aid
Ireland	People who are at a disadvantage as a result of an impairment or disability that limits or prevents the accomplishment of a role that is normal for the individual concerned.	No explicit reference in legislation.	Since 1977 public sector 3% quota for registered severely disabled persons. Results: 2% in 1991.	No explicit reference to disability in legislation.	Employment Support Scheme: National Rehabilitation Board (NRB) supplements wages to increase employment opportunities for severely disabled people (80–50% work productivity). In 1991 95 employees.	Financial support by NRB (max £5000) to adapt workplaces and to provide special equipment. In 1993 £30 000 was spend on 16 jobs.
Italy	Act of 1992: those persons whose working capacity is permanently reduced as a result of physical, psychological or sensory impairment.	The Constitution of 1947 explicitly establishes that disabled persons are entitled to education and integration at work.	Law of 1968. 15% quota for firms ≥35 employees; beneficiaries: disabled people, widows, orphans and refugees. Fines used to train disabled. 1987: 98 743 disabled under quota.	Under quota system dismissal is only permitted if the disability endangers health or safety, or if there are no other possibilities of employment.	No measures at national level. Certain regions contribute to wage costs or social charges.	No measures at national level. Certain regions provide financial support for adapting work stations.
Luxem-bourg	Act of 1991: people disabled through accident or work or war and people with a physical, mental or sensory disability. Capacity for work reduction ≥30%.	No explicit reference in legislation.	Act of 1991: 5% quota for public bodies. 2% quota for private firms ≥50 employees; 4% ≥200 employees. Exemption from social security contributions if quota is exceeded. Penalty 50% of minimum wage per month.	No explicit reference to disability in legislation.	Wage-cost subsidy by Office for Recruitment and Vocational Retraining of Disabled Workers (OTH) depends on severity of disability: 40–60% of gross pay for 3 years.	Compensation by OTH for adaptation of workplace. In 1988 LFr 83 000. Provision is retained in the 1991 Act.

						Financial support for adapting work station and equipment.
Nether-lands	Those whose prospects of earning their living are substantially restricted by reason of infirmity, sickness or mental or physical differences. WAGW: those who receive an invalidity pension and those who benefit from special measures in order to carry out their work.	There is no specific legislation protecting disabled people from discrimination. The law (WAGW) imposes an obligation for employers and unions to encourage equal opportunities for everyone, as regards occupational (re)integration.	Act of 1 July 1986 (WAGW). 3–7% quota depending on industry. Beneficiaries: persons receiving invalidity allowance. Results: 2–3% in 1989.	Employment contract may not be broken during first 2 years of disability due to sickness. Lay-offs will not be authorized by the Regional Employment Offices even after 2 years of disability if the employer is still in a position to offer adapted employment.	All employers who take on a person who has been declared unfit to work can apply for a wage-cost subsidy of maximum 20% of salary for up to 4 years.	
Portugal	Any individual who, because of limited physical or mental capacity, encounters difficulty in obtaining or holding a job suited to his or her age, qualification or professional experience.	Under the Constitution of 1976 physically and mentally disabled persons enjoy full rights as all citizens. The State should act to ensure the transportation of these rights in practical terms.	No obligation.	Obligation to keep an employee who suffers an industrial accident for firms $\geq$10 employees and if the incapacity is temporary and <50%. In cases of collective dismissal disabled workers are given preference for job retention.	Lump-sum compensation during adaptation phase. Initial sum is gradually reduced to 25% after 9 months. Extension to 3 years. In 1991 425 people. Reduction (50%) of employers' social security contributions; 200 persons in 1991.	Subsidy for adapting work station and removing physical barriers up to a maximum of 12 x minimum wage.
Spain	Any person whose possibilities of participation in education, work or social activity are reduced as a result of physical, mental or sensory impairment, whether congenital or not, which is likely to be permanent.	Under the Constitution of 1978 the public authorities are obliged to implement a policy of rehabilitation and integration to guarantee disabled people the rights extended to all citizens (right to work, training and rehabilitation).	Law of 1983: 2% quota for firms with >50 employees. Decree of 1987: 3% in civil service. Beneficiaries: registered disabled persons with capacity for work reduction $\geq$33%. Financial sanction possible. Quota is not met.	Dismissal from a sheltered workshop must be confirmed by the National Social Services Office.	Recruitment subsidy for stable employment. Reduction of employers' social security contribution for disabled persons (70% for those aged under 45 and 90% for others). 3469 beneficiaries in 1987. Reduction of tax bill for each contract for disabled.	Subsidies for adapting work station and removing physical barriers up to PTA 15 000. No data available.

545

Table 17.2—continued   Occupational Segregation, Discrimination and Equal Opportunity

Country	Definition of disability	Legal intervention			Financial support	
		Equal opportunity legislation	Quota system	Dismissal protection	Wage subsidies	Grants for workplace adaptation and technical aid
Sweden	Disability is a relationship between the person and the environment.	No general law aimed at securing the rights of disabled people. Integration is secured by insertion of special paragraphs in provision.	No mandatory quota.	Disabled people are entitled to special protection under 1974 Security of Employment Act. Priority for further employment to be granted to disabled people.	Flexible wage subsidy for employer depending on work capacity of employee in relation to demands of the job. In 1991 44 500 employed with wage subsidy.	Grants for technical aids and services up to SEK 50 000. In 1989–90 4600 grants: 77% for established employees and 23% for newly recruited employees.
United Kingdom	The Disabled Person (Employment) Act 1944: a person who, on account of injury, disease or congenital deformity, is substantially disabled in obtaining or keeping employment, or in undertaking work on his or her own account of a kind that, apart from that injury, disease or deformity, would be suited to his or her age, experience and qualifications.	No explicit reference in legislation.	Act of 1944. 3% quota for firms ≥20 employees. Beneficiaries: registered disabled persons. Fines, but employers can obtain a permit. Results: 106 743 in 1987: 97 000 in 1988; about 1%.	The Act of 1994 provides that committees for the employment of the disabled can be required to report on any allegation of the dismissal of a registered disabled person without reasonable grounds. Favours insiders.	Weekly wage subsidies during the introductory phase. In 1986/87 1636 new participants.	Subsidy (max. £6000) for adapting equipment and premises. Loans for equipment and technical support services. In 1987–88 about 4200 disabled persons benefited from Special Aids to Employment Scheme.

United States	American with Disabilities Act 1990 (ADA): a disability is a physical or mental impairment that substantially limits one or more of the major life activities, a record of such impairments or being regarded as having an impairment.	Section 503 of the Rehabilitation Act 1973 requires every employer doing business with the federal government to take affirmative action. ADA extends section 504 of the 1973 Act to private firms with ≥15 employees: reasonable accommodation for the known limitation of the disabled individuals unless this imposes undue hardship. ADA also requires unbiased recruitment.	No obligation.	No explicit reference to disability in legislation (see equal opportunities).	Targeted Jobs Tax Credit up to 1 year to employer of 40% of the wage paid to an employee. 6.9% of total targeted people (39 448 in 1987) were disabled. Can be used for supported employment.	Tax credit and tax deductions for small (<30 full-time employees) businesses and tax deductions for big firms to change barriers to the disabled and elderly.

Sources

Report from the Commission on the Application of the Council Recommendation 86/379/EEC by EC, 1988, Brussels: Commission of the European Communities; 'Regulation or Deregulation of the Labour Market: Policy Regimes for the Recruitment and Dismissal of Employees in the Industrialised Countries' by M. Emerson, 1988, *European Economic Review*, 32 (4); *Disabled Persons: Statistical Data* (Vols 1–2) by S. Grammenos, 1991, Luxembourg: Eurostat; *Employment Policies for Disabled People. A Review of Legislation and Services in Fifteen Countries* (Research Series no. 16) by M. Lunt and P. Thornton, 1993, Sheffield: Employment Department, University of York; *Employment Policies for People with Disabilities: Report by an Evaluation Panel* (Labour Market and Social Policy Occasional Papers no. 8) by OECD, 1992, Paris: OECD.

ship between expenditure on cash transfers versus spending on active measures targeting greater involvement in the work force.

Most research on special education and handicaps has been too restricted, concentrating too heavily on studies of handicapped people and their characteristics and the different kinds of treatment given to these pupils. Most studies on integration have too short a time perspective; very little is said about the integration process as such. To counter this deficit we need studies with a broader design, including process-oriented effect studies on the whole group and educational settings (OECD, 1994b).

How can evaluation be improved? In the evaluation studies to date the focus has been on monitoring the costs and dimensions of the programmes rather than on programme performance and programme outcomes (OECD, 1992). Apart from more adequate data, it is important to distinguish between programme effects and nonprogramme effects, for instance by using control groups. One problem is the question how the changing economic climate of changing labour market conditions should be taken into account when analysing and interpreting evaluation results. Clear-cut goals are another prerequisite for meaningful evaluation of programme outcomes. Programmes often have multiple objectives and evaluation is thus more difficult. More emphasis on precise definitions of programme goals and more singleness of purpose is called for. Moreover, in view of the institutional complexity and the multiplicity of programmes, coordination of evaluation and research activities is essential.

REFERENCES

Akerlof, G. and J. L. Yellen (eds) (1986), *Efficiency Wage Models of the Labor Market*, Cambridge: Cambridge University Press.

Baldwin, M. and W. G. Johnson (1994), 'Labor Market Discrimination against Men with Disabilities', *The Journal of Human Resources*, 29, 1–19.

Bulow, J. I. and L. H. Summers (1986), 'A Theory of Dual Labor Markets with Application to Industrial Policy, Discrimination, and Keynesian Unemployment', *Journal of Labor Economics*, 4, (3), 376–414.

Burkhauser, R. V. and P. Hirvonen (1989), 'United States Disability Policy in a Time of Economic Crisis: A Comparison with Sweden and the Federal Republic of Germany', *The Milbank Quarterly*, 67, 1–29.

Buttler, F. and U. Walwei (1993), 'Employment Security and Efficiency: Assumptions in the Current Debate and Empirical Evidence for West Germany', in C. Büchtemann (ed.), *Employment Security and Labor Market Behaviour. Interdisciplinary Approaches and International Evidence*, Ithaca/NY: ILR Press, pp. 255–66.

Delsen, L. (1987), *Disability Prevention at Firm Level* (Research Memorandum 8705), Nijmegen: Institute of Economics, University of Nijmegen.

Delsen, L. (1989), 'Improving the Employability of the Disabled: A Practical Approach', *International Journal for the Advancement of Counselling*, 12, 125–35.

Delsen, L. (1995), *Atypical Employment: An International Perspective. Causes, Consequences and Policy*, Groningen: Wolters-Noordhoff.

Delsen, L. and Y. Bemelmans (1987), *Gehandicapten aan het Werk*, Maastricht: Presses Interuniversitaires Européennes.

Delsen L. and S. Klosse (1992), 'Integration of the Disabled in the Work Process: The Dutch Policy', *The Geneva Papers on Risk and Insurance*, 62 (17), 119–42.

Delsen, L. and G. Reday-Mulvey (eds) (1995), *Gradual Retirement in the OECD Countries. Macro and Micro Issues and Policies*, Aldershot: Dartmouth Publishing Company.

EC (1988), *Report from the Commission on the Application of the Council Recommendation 86/379/EEC of 24 July 1986 on the Employment of Disabled People in the Community*, Brussels: Commission of the European Communities.

Emerson, M. (1988), 'Regulation or Deregulation of the Labour Market: Policy Regimes for the Recruitment and Dismissal of Employees in the Industrialised Countries', *European Economic Review*, 32 (4), 775–817.

Epstein, R. A. (1992), *Forbidden Grounds: The Case against Employment Discrimination Laws*, Cambridge, MA: Harvard University Press.

Grammenos, S. (1991), *Disabled Persons: Statistical Data,* Vols 1–2, Luxembourg: Eurostat.

Hardman, M. L. (1994), 'Supported Employment: Quality Services for People with Severe Disabilities', in *Disabled Youth and Employment*, Paris: OECD, pp. 83–105.

Harkness, J. (1993), 'Labour Force Participation by Disabled Males in Canada', *Canadian Journal of Economics*, 26, 878-89.

Haveman, H., V. Halberstadt and R. Burkhauser (1984), *Public Policy towards Disabled Workers. Cross National Analysis of Economic Impact*, Ithaca/NY: Cornell University Press.

Haveman, R. H. and J. L. Palmer (eds) (1982), *Jobs for Disadvantaged Workers: The Economics of Employment Subsidies*, Washington: The Brookings Institution.

Honey, S., N. Meager and M. Williams (1993), *Employers' Attitudes towards People with Disabilities,* IMS report no. 245, Brighton: Institute of Manpower Studies.

Lindbeck, A. (1994), 'Overshooting, Reform and Retreat of the Welfare State', *De Economist*, 142 (1), 1–19.

Lunt, M. and P. Thornton (1993), *Employment Policies for Disabled People. A Review of Legislation and Services in Fifteen Countries,* Research Series no. 16, Sheffield: Employment Department, University of York.

McLaughlin, M. J., L. Florian, D. Neubert, G. Boyd-Kjellen and L. Frieden (eds) (1992), *Transition to Employment. Proceedings of the 1990 International Symposium on the Employment of Persons with Disabilities*, College Park: University of Maryland.

Mul, C. A. M., C. R. de Winter, I. D. Nijboer and H. F. de Haan (1995), *Methoden voor de (Re)Integratie van Gedeeltelijke Arbeidsongeschikten. Een Literatuurstudie*, Den Haag: Ministerie van Sociale Zaken en Werkgelegenheid.

OECD (1992), *Employment Policies for People with Disabilities: Report by an Evaluation Panel* (Labour Market and Social Policy occasional papers no. 8), Paris: OECD.

OECD (1994a), *Disabled Youth and Employment*, Paris: OECD.

OECD (1994b), *The Integration of Disabled Children into Mainstream Education: Ambitions, Theories and Practices*, Paris: OECD.

Pozner, A. and J. Hammond (1993), *An Evaluation of Supported Employment Initiatives for Disabled People*, Research Series no. 17, Sheffield: Employment Department, University of York.

Raskin, C. (1994), 'Employment Equity for the Disabled in Canada', *International Labour Review*, 133, 75–88.

Sadowski, D. and B. Frick (1992), *Die Beschäftigung Schwerbehinderter*, Idstein, Germany: Schulz-Kirchner Verlag.

Sadowski, D. and I. M. Rendenbach (eds) (1989), *Neue Zielgruppen in der Schwerbehindertenpolitik*, Frankfurt: Campus Verlag.

Samoy, E. and L. Waterplas (1992), *Sheltered Employment in the European Community: Final Report Submitted to the Commission of the European Community*, Brussels: Commission of the European Communities.

Schell, J. L. M. (1991), *Quotumregelingen in Verschillende Landen*, Den Haag: Ministerie van Sociale Zaken en Werkgelegenheid.

Schotter, A. and K. Weigelt (1992, May), 'Asymmetric Tournament, Equal Opportunity Laws, and Affirmative Action: Some Experimental Results', *The Quarterly Journal of Economics*, 511–39.

Semlinger, K. (1984), *The Employment and Occupational Promotion of the Handicapped in the Federal Republic of Germany*, WZB discussion paper IIM/LMP 84–4d, Wissenschaftszentrum Berlin für Sozialforschung.

Semlinger, K. and G. Schmid (1985), *Arbeitsmarktpolitik für Behinderte*, Basel: Birkhauser Verlag.

Seyfried, E. (1992), *Requirement for the Successful Integration of Disabled People into Working Life: Summary Report on a Study Conducted in Belgium, the Federal Republic of Germany, France, the Netherlands and the United Kingdom*, Luxembourg: CEDEFOP.

Seyfried, E. and T. Lambert (1989), *New Semi-sheltered Forms of Employment for Disabled Persons*, Luxembourg: Office for Official Publications of the European Communities.

Söder, M. (1994), 'Employers' Attitude and Handicap', in *Disabled Youth and Employment*, Paris: OECD, pp. 107–35.

Wadensjö, E. (1984), *Labour Market Policy towards the Disabled in Sweden*, WZB discussion paper IIM/LMP 84–4c, Wissenschaftszentrum Berlin für Sozialforschung.

Wadensjö, E. (1994), 'Trends in Labour Market Policies for Youth with Disabilities', in *Disabled Youth and Employment*, Paris: Organization for Economic Co-operation and Development, pp. 35–48.

Wansbrough, N. and P. Cooper (1980), *Open Employment after Mental Illness*, London: Tavistock Publications.

Wehman, P., P. Sale and W. S. Parent (1992), *Supported Employment: Strategies for Integration of Workers with Disabilities*, Boston: Andover Medical Publishers.

WHO (1980), *International Classification of Impairments, Disabilities and Handicaps. A Manual of Classification Relating to the Consequences of Diseases*, Geneva: World Health Organisation.

Zeitzer, I. R. (1994), 'Recent European Trends in Disability and Related Programs', *Social Security Bulletin*, 57, 21–6.

J61, J68
F22

551-65

18. Immigrant Labour Integration

Gudrun Biffl

Immigration has become a pervasive feature of economies not only in the traditional immigration countries but throughout the industrialized world. The United Nations estimates that over 60 million people, or 1.2 per cent of the world's population, reside in a country in which they were not born (United Nations, 1989). In the course of the 1980s and at the beginning of the 1990s inflows of migrants increased in almost all OECD countries. In Europe Germany emerges as the principal immigration country, with inflows of immigrants in the order of 1.2 million in 1992 and nearly 990 000 in 1993 (excluding ethnic Germans) (see Zimmermann, 1995). Since 1987 net migration represents the principal component (more than 60 per cent) of the increase of total population in western Europe. Net migration is less important in Australia and America, accounting for only a third and a quarter, respectively, of total population growth between 1982 and 1991.

Part of immigration is labour migration. In general, worker flows have tended to increase since the middle of the 1980s. And yet labour migration still represents only the smaller share of immigration flows—about 40 per cent in Switzerland, 30 per cent in Germany and France and a mere 20 per cent in the traditional immigration countries Canada and Australia. In fact, family reunification and refugees account for the major share of inflows of immigrants into OECD countries. Nevertheless, foreign labour is playing an increasingly significant role in the functioning of labour markets; it is subject to complex institutional regulations, which differ according to policy targets. Evaluation research is only starting to become important in this field as migration pressure mounts and policy-makers require sound impact analyses for policy guidance.

Policy targets in the field of migration differ according to national interests and may be classified into three broad areas. The first target is economic ends; migration is a source of labour in particular skill segments that ensures that labour does not become a limiting factor for economic growth. The second target concerns welfare; migration should not foster segmentation or limit the employment opportunities of nationals. The third target is a combination of business, military or diplomatic strategies that may be linked to migration;

immigration may be a domestic consequence of foreign policy and economic activities in sending countries.

Migration analysis must give consideration to the internationalization of production and the emergence of a new world order in industrial relations if it is to explain the upsurge in migration during the 1980s in spite of high and rising unemployment in the receiving countries. Migration surely has to be seen as an essential element of the way in which regional economies become integrated. The interplay of international and domestic markets and special labour demands in economies undergoing rapid economic growth and/or restructuring in the face of large income differentials between countries and regions go a long way in explaining the timing, direction, volume and composition of international migration. But one has to stress as well at the outset that the structure and trends of economic growth, of employment, of labour force participation and population growth are also of considerable importance for the size, structure and dynamics of migration flows. These factors vary widely internationally and account for many of the differences in migration developments across countries as well as the more general features of international relationships between countries.

Immigration, especially from eastern Europe and North Africa, will be an important factor in shaping European labour markets at the turn of the century, reflecting growing economic and demographic imbalances between western European countries, on the one hand, and North Africa, on the other, and intensifying economic ties between western, central and eastern European countries (see Appleyard, 1991; Biffl, 1991; Rudolph and Morokvasic, 1993; Salt, Singleton and Hogarth, 1994). Moreover, labour supply is augmented by immigration, which may enhance the flexibility and mobility of labour. Immigrants contribute to the diversification of the productive structure of an economy. Immigrants not only contribute to the supply side, the production potential of the economy, but also to the demand side. They exert pressure on infrastructure and may, thus, induce increased domestic investment. Hence, migrants have an effect on the labour market, either directly, via increasing labour supply, or indirectly, via increasing labour demand. Immigrants may influence prices and the profitability of production through the supply-side effect, that is, by affecting the scarcity and thus the price of labour, but also through the demand-side effect, particularly through their impact on infrastructure and housing.

The impact of migrants on the economy varies according to their legal status because different types of legal status, which are often linked to skills, mean migrants are afforded uneven access to the labour market, to public assistance, housing and so forth. A process of restructuring of labour by country of origin and migrant status is usually linked to the process of migration; such a process may lead to increased segmentation of labour markets and the society at large when avenues of labour and social mobility are closed. Tensions may arise if economic and social integration are not satisfactory. The challenge for labour market policy is obvious; careful evaluation, both of the size and dynamics of present and future migration processes and of the various national policy responses aimed at balancing social and economic efficiency and equity, is required.

This chapter starts out with a short overview of current migration regimes that follow one or the other of two avenues of migration policy orientation, the naturalization model or the foreign worker model. In spite of the wide variety of migration systems and policy goals of migration, a certain international convergence of policy responses is discernible, given the upsurge in migration in the 1980s and the desire in the countries receiving migrants to control migration flows and clamp down on illegal migration. Common criteria are being drawn up for the different migration categories, that is, labour migrants (work and training), family reunification, asylum seekers, refugees, students and immigration on humanitarian grounds. A review of results of impact studies on the effect of immigration on labour markets follows. Special attention is given to the recent increased effort by industrialized countries to control illegal migration.

1   MIGRATION SYSTEMS AND THEIR IMPACT

In order to demystify migration, the complexities of migration flows, the differing national interests and the asymmetry in the bargaining power of sending and receiving countries will be presented within the legal framework of a migration system. Two migration regimes will be highlighted:[1]

1. The 'naturalization' model, as developed by the United States, Canada and Australia, with the objective of settlement and integration of immigrants (population policy).
2. The 'guest worker' model, as developed by Switzerland, Germany and Austria, which was originally intended to satisfy short-term labour needs;

---

1   A third model resulted from colonial ties, as in the United Kingdom and to a degree in France and the Netherlands. This model is not going to shape massive migratory flows in the future, but it helps to explain why certain nationalities or ethnic groups are present in some countries and not in others. The model is still going to have some impact in the case of Hong Kong when it is reintegrated into the People's Republic of China in 1997. But no new waves of migration resulting from preexisting colonial ties can be envisaged so far. The modern migration flows of 'return' migration of ethnic Germans (*Aussiedler*) or Greeks from central and eastern European countries should not be seen in the context of this model but much rather as a consequence of extended European integration.

the prolonged employment of foreign workers led to the implementation of social and economic integration policies for the originally recruited foreign workers and their family members.

Migration policies in Japan and the rapidly industrializing countries of East Asia in the 1980s and in the Middle East are of the latter type, but there is no sign of these countries accepting temporary migrants on a permanent basis in connection with citizenship rights. The development of migration in Asia is well documented in Abella (1994); for migration to the Gulf States see Stalker (1994) and Shah (1994).

The main reasons for migration are different in each model and affect the timing, direction, volume and composition of immigration. In spite of the basic differences in recruitment or inflow strategies, similarities in the impact of migrants on the labour market and society at large can be discerned. Over time the migration systems have converged and become more complex. Traditional immigration countries have introduced instruments to allow and control short-term labour migration, whereas labour migration countries in Europe have reacted towards the tendency of migrants to settle with the introduction of integration measures.

The traditional distinctions between the two models of migration have become blurred since the 1970s, at least in the case of Europe *vis-à-vis* the model 1 countries. The migratory experience of the 1950s, 1960s and early 1970s in the traditional immigration countries (model 1) as well as the labour migration countries in Europe (model 2) was marked by growing labour demand, particularly in manufacturing industries in the period of rapid industrialization. Migration in these three decades is well documented, for example, by Collinson (1993) for Europe, Borjas (1994) for the United States, and Stalker (1994) and Freeman and Jupp (1992) for Canada and Australia. The migration flows of the 1980s and 1990s, on the other hand, bear the mark of increased internationalization and globalization of economies and of deindustrialization and tertiarization of advanced industrial economies.[2] The economic and social integration of the migrants of the 1950s, 1960s and 1970s was favoured by the general economic environment of the time, that is, the industrialization phase of economic development. The predominance of regular, steady, year-round employment of indigenous and often also migrant labour facilitated the integration of migrants during this period. By contrast, the transition from the Fordist model of production to flexible specialization and

---

2 The high and rising degree of internationalization of economies is accompanied by a sizeable and growing mobility of business persons, professionals, technicians and other highly skilled workers. The major part of this migration is temporary and tends to occur between industrialized countries.

decentralization, the rise of casual labour, the increasing importance of secondary labour and the shift away from industrial production towards services (with a limited degree of unionization) have to be seen as contributory factors to the increasing difficulties of migrants in achieving economic and social integration in the postindustrial societies of the 1980s and 1990s.

Migratory movements are to a large extent governed by the migration policies of the receiving countries, in other words, migration flows are mainly demand determined. But in the absence of push factors, that is, emigration pressure from source countries, mass migration would hardly exist. One has to see the rise of refugee movements in the 1980s in this context; they stemmed from the simultaneous presence of political and environmental push factors in the sending countries and economic pull factors in the receiving countries. The migration pressure from poor to rich countries is increasing, encompassing a larger number of countries (and nationalities and ethnicities) of emigration and a larger number of destination countries, including former emigration countries. Immigration has ceased to take place in countries and regions of low unemployment only and now also occurs in high unemployment areas. This change opens up questions about the driving forces behind the upsurge in immigration in the 1980s. Economic links and technology have created a transnational space for the mobility of capital and generated new conditions for the mobility of labour. Migration policies began to gain political weight during the 1980s and to encompass more than the traditional labour market orientation. Policies directed towards increased international cooperation became prevalent in the early 1990s as a result of the acceleration and globalization of migration flows. Immigration countries are striving to obtain better control over flows, including asylum seekers and illegal immigrants. At the same time, the more traditional concern of better integration of migrants in the host countries is a challenge to policy-makers.

2   SUMMARY OF THE MAIN POLICY RESPONSES TO IMMIGRATION

Migration systems react towards economic and social forces within the logic of the system, in other words, the original model mirrors a long-term vision. Immigration countries (the naturalization model) have a slow and limited reaction towards cyclical and labour market conditions, whereas countries with a labour migration base scenario (the guest worker model) react swiftly and markedly. The selection of immigrants and the management of immigration (regulation of work permits, points system, admission of family members etc.), integration into the work process (work incentives, education and training programmes), the provision of income security, immigration on humanitarian grounds and the like differ according to the basic model and adaptation as do the control mechanisms for migratory flows and work (border controls, control of illegal workers and/or residents, employer sanctions).

Because migration policies tend to change over time the impact of immigration varies over time even within a country. Borjas (1990) argues that the preference of the US immigration model of the post-1965 era[3] for family reunion without the introduction of special skill requirements for assisted family migration (in contrast to Canada[4]) had a negative impact on the skill composition of subsequent immigration flows into the United States and added to the segmentation of the labour market by ethnic minorities. The legislative change not only affected the skill composition but also led to an increase in the volume of immigration (see Bean and Fix, 1992). As a result of the US policy changes in 1965 and 1986,[5] the share of the foreign-born population rose from 4.7 per cent in 1970 to 7.9 per cent in 1990 (census data).

The immigration policy of the United States has hardly changed during the twentieth century and has included less administrative and financial support for the integration of immigrants than Australia or Canada.[6] Policy in Australia, by contrast, has been quite interventionist, with trade unions and the labour movement playing a vital role in the design of immigration policy, especially the rate, size and skill components of new entries; this approach has enabled Australia to better control the adverse consequences of increased labour supply. Of all immigration countries Australia has developed the most coherent immigration and settlement policy and the most elaborate inflow-control mechanisms; the latter have kept labour in short supply, compared to its relative abundance in the United States. Efficient external border controls and inflow regulations facilitated the integration of immigrants and favoured the acceptance rate of immigration by the indigenous population, as did expenditure on special integration support measures en route to a multicultural society with no immigrant (ethnic minority) underclass.

---

3 Abandonment of the national origin quota system in favour of admission of immigrants with family ties to US residents (see Reimers, 1985).

4 Between 1962 and 1967 the national origin restrictions for immigration to Canada were abandoned, but a points system for the admission of other than close relatives was introduced.

5 In 1986 the Immigration Reform and Control Act (IRCA) provided the legal framework for legalization of undocumented immigrants. Under the legalization programme financial aid was provided to states to cover increased costs resulting from integration of illegal immigrants. This move made immigration more costly and undermined support for sustained levels of admission of newcomers. Employer sanctions were introduced to curb new inflows of illegal immigrants.

6 Public expenditure for the integration of immigrants (legal as well as illegal) had increased substantially during the 1970s and 1980s; in particular, education, health and welfare budgets were affected by the increased inflow of migrants. The hope that this expenditure increase could be curbed was one of the reasons for the legislative change in 1986.

Western European countries had, by contrast, embarked upon the recruitment of temporary migrant workers in the late 1950s and early 1960s in order to satisfy a perceived temporary need for additional labour. As a large segment of the temporary migrants turned into permanent residents, the questions of economic and social integration became an issue. Integration efforts were necessary in order to avoid systematic marginalization and segregation of immigrants (Werner, 1994). The European Union and the individual Member States do not yet have a comprehensive law on integration that would encompass social protection, education and training, housing and cultural aspects. It has increasingly become accepted, however, that integration is a two-way process; the desire for integration on the part of immigrants depends upon the degree of certainty of the residence and employment status granted by the host country. The granting of permanent resident status is a necessary element of integration policies. It is conducive to investment in vocational training, language acquisition and improved housing on the part of the immigrant. Thus, special integration measures, which come into effect after a certain qualifying period of legal work and residence, were devised in Europe during the 1970s and 1980s. Acceptance of cultural pluralism (intercultural education, bridges between religions) is not universal, however. Specific support for migrants that goes beyond granting the maintenance of immigrants' cultural identity and is directed towards improving their economic and social position does not find universal acceptance either in model 1 or model 2 immigration countries (see Jayasuriya, 1990).

The most effective way to discourage immigration is to manipulate the immigrants' probability of obtaining and retaining a work permit. Work permits that are subject to cancellation or nonprolongation in the case of deteriorating economic conditions impose a greater risk on the migrant than policies directed towards settlement. However, because of supply-side self-selection mechanisms the price of a temporary work-permit system for migrants is a relatively unskilled migrant intake. Job insecurity in the host country is a greater discouragement to skilled potential migrants than to their unskilled counterparts because the opportunity costs for unskilled migrants are lower relative to their economic and social status at home.[7]

Borjas (1994) points out that the size and skill composition of the immigrant flow is jointly determined by supply-side considerations on the part of potential migrants and demand factors for immigrants. No systematic analysis of the factors that generate a demand function for immigrants has been undertaken to date. The lack of analyses is not surprising in view of the great variety of

---

7 Roy pointed out as early as 1951 (Roy, 1951) that the difference in income distribution by skills in the host and source countries is just as strong a determinant as absolute wage differences for the wish to migrate.

migration experiences among countries. There are winners and losers in any immigration policy that makes the demand function dependent on politico-economical decision-making processes (see Betts, 1988). Winners are those groups that gain from an overall increase in demand for goods and services in the domestic market, for example, land developers, builders, manufacturers and importers. Winners are also those occupational groups that profit from job creation because of population growth, for instance, teachers, social workers, professionals, administrators and workers in industries that expand with population growth. Consumers also profit from immigration through the availability of a wider gamut of goods and services as well as lower prices. Highly skilled labour is usually in a complementary position to unskilled labour, in other words, the majority of migrants; thus, the former group favours immigration. Marginal firms, too, reap some benefits from foreign workers. The losers are the disadvantaged groups on the labour market, who are in competition with migrants and fear for their jobs, wages and welfare benefits.

The supply-side decision to emigrate, given skill transferability on the part of the migrant, also depends upon a variety of factors. Emigration of highly skilled workers is more likely if the receiving country has a greater earnings dispersion by skill than the source country (i.e. high-ability workers are 'taxed' less, and less able workers are 'insured' less in the receiving country). Unskilled labour (whose skills are, by definition, highly transferable and whose earnings are below average in both the source and host country), on the other hand, will be attracted to those countries that have a limited dispersion of income by skill. Because there are migration costs linked with emigration the most highly skilled of the low-wage earners are likely to seek work abroad. The poorest stay in the source country because of liquidity constraints. Analogously, the probability of a return to the source country is also not independent of the skill structure of the immigrants. In the case of highly skilled workers the less able are prone to return because they have the greatest chance of improving their economic and social status by returning. Of the unskilled workers, on the other hand, the best of the group are more likely to return. Empirical research tends to support these theoretical notions (see, for example, Ramos, 1992).

3   REVIEW OF EVALUATION STUDIES ON THE SOCIAL AND ECONOMIC IMPACTS OF MIGRATION AND MIGRATION POLICIES

Institutions react to the micro- and macroeconomic impacts of immigration with policy measures. Policy targets are determined with the help of evaluation and impact studies. Specific targets are now being identified: effects on economic growth, on industrial restructuring (firm needs), on social and infra-structure policies (housing, education, health care, public transport), on tech-nology, on cultural integration and on the labour market. The political discus-sion on labour market effects is centred on the impact of migration on the employment opportunities of natives, in particular the degree of substitution and the wage impact. The other major issue is the degree of integration of immigrants into the labour market, in particular their economic progress and mobility.

There is an ongoing debate on the economic impact of immigration, and the results of most impact studies are inconclusive as to the net economic effect of immigration for the host society. The impact on the economies and the economies' labour markets has both a supply and a demand component.

3.1   Supply-side Effects: Migrants as Workers

(1) In the first phase of settlement immigrants are more mobile than locally born workers, which means factor resources can be allocated more efficiently. In the subsequent settlement phase this advantage is lost; migrants tend to settle in large cities and, thus, contribute to urbanization problems. This under-standing of the economic impact may result in policies directed towards allow-ing a continued flow of new arrivals (temporary work contracts, project-linked work) while restricting settlement and family reunion.

(2) Moreover, several studies on the supply-side effect of labour have focussed on the impact of immigrants on the employment opportunities and wages of natives (see Stromback et al., 1993; US Department of Labor, 1989). The general answer is that the higher the substitutability of immi-grants and natives the stronger the wage and/or unemployment effect of increased inflows. Empirical studies for the United States (Simon, 1989; Stark, 1991) suggest that direct competition between immigrants and natives is negligible because immigrants tend to be concentrated within certain labour market segments. Studies for Australia show (see Birrell, Hill and Nevill, 1984) that immigration has not increased segmentation because it is accompanied by integration support measures. Studies for Europe (De New and Zimmermann, 1994; Werner, 1994) show that small effects of immigra-tion on unemployment exist and that immigration has depressed the wages of blue-collar workers. The proliferation of the legal status of foreign workers has introduced a new social and economic stratification into European labour markets, as can be demonstrated by the stratifying effect of the work-permit system in Austria—it increased segmentation on the labour market and had a negative impact on equity developments in society (Biffl, 1993; Matuschek, 1985).

Employers welcome an increase in labour supply because of its dampening effect on wages. It is argued that lower wages lead to an increase in profits, which in turn allows a higher rate of investment, increased productivity and more economic growth. In view of the fact that many migrants are unskilled, however, the abundance of low-skilled workers appears to have encouraged employers to use labour-intensive rather than capital-intensive production methods, so that higher productivity did not ensue, although wages for unskilled workers were still depressed.[8]

If immigrants are kept in certain segments of the labour market either by institutional regulations (e.g. work permits for a restricted region, occupation, firm or season) or the absence of public financial and institutional support for integration into the wider economic and social community (leading to reliance on ethnic and family networks for economic and social support), immigrant and native labour are prone to become complements rather than substitutes. As a result, native workers may obtain a higher per-capita income because of economic rents resulting from segmentation of labour by legal status and/or ethnicity.

(3) A further aspect of immigration is highlighted in empirical research, that is, cost-saving on training and education in receiving countries through importing skilled foreign labour. This cost advantage should not imply that one can neglect local training and higher education, however, for that would entail long-term costs in lost opportunities for natives, particularly in times and areas of high unemployment (see Papademetriou, 1991).

3.2   Demand-side Effects: Migrants as Consumers

Immigration leads to increased demand for goods and services and thus contributes to economic growth. However, unless the consumption patterns of immigrants affect economies of scale, that is, induce greater productivity, immigration does not increase GDP per capita,[9] raising questions about the effect of immigration on productive investment. A growing population requires higher capital expenditure on social infrastructure (housing, roads and schools etc.). Investment in social infrastructure is linked with widening rather than deepening of capital, which means that productivity growth will hardly be boosted. Only if the employment of new (immigrant) workers is linked with the implementation of new technology with a view to facilitating econ-

---

8 Migration may have a significant impact on technological change. For a comparison between Sweden and Austria see Biffl (1994, pp. 180–201).

9 Only by assuming economies of scale can one predict positive effects on per-capita economic growth with econometric models.

omic restructuring and achieving more efficient modes of production (with an emphasis on the production of commodities for export markets) will immigration be linked with capital deepening and increased productivity. This relation has clear implications for migration policy, which, in order to achieve these objectives, has to be directed towards improving export performance.

3.3 The Effect of Immigration on Unemployment

Immigration has no clear-cut negative or positive effects on the level of unemployment, however, the structure is affected. There tend to be higher unemployment rates for foreign workers/immigrants than for natives. The difference is, to a large extent, a result of the concentration of migrant employment in manufacturing industries, which are experiencing employment declines. The restructuring and rationalization process currently under way in all sectors of the economy entails above-average job losses for unskilled workers, the group where migrants are more than proportionally represented (see Werner, 1994). Immigration may lead to increased competition for jobs. An oversupply of labour does not necessarily imply higher rates of unemployment in the receiving country—it may mean, however, an increasing number of cleaners, waiters, gardeners and home workers carrying out piece work, that is, an increase in marginal occupations and fringe employers outside the core economy. This rise in casual labour is observable in the labour markets of industrialized economies today, where peripheral workers drift in and out of employment while a core of highly skilled workers continues to retain stable jobs and high wages.

4   ILLEGALITY

Policies are often quite restrictive with regard to unskilled workers. The large surplus of this type of labour in sending countries and restrictive policies in receiving countries resulted in an increase in illegal immigration during the 1980s. In order to be able to assess the impact of this development on industrialized societies, the causal factors and structural elements of illegality have to be analysed in a country-specific context because countries tend to have different histories of black markets or informal economies. In the United States illegal immigration is a structural feature of immigration. The rise of illegal immigration in the late 1970s and early 1980s became a public concern and led to the passage of the Immigration Reform and Control Act in 1986 (IRCA), which was designed to curb illegal immigration by introducing employer sanctions for employment of illegal or 'unauthorized workers'. The IRCA did not address the more important pull and push factors that influence illegal immigration flows, in other words, it was not an attempt to reform the system for admitting legal immigrants (see Fraser, 1994). Japan introduced employer sanctions for the employment of illegal aliens in 1991.

Foreigners may enter a country legally, but the declared purpose of entry, for instance, tourism, might not be the genuine reason, which may in fact be clandestine labour. One has to differentiate between different forms of illegality on the labour market: (a) illegal residence and work, (b) legal residence and illegal or undeclared work (tax evasion) and (c) illegal employment and work practices. The latter two cases of illegality can also pertain to natives. Clandestine work tends to be concentrated in certain sectors of the economy in which individual employment contracts are permissible and atypical work is prevalent, for example, construction, tourism, agriculture, trade and production of clothing and leatherware, cleaning and domestic service. In order to combat the increase in the different types of illegality, a variety of measures is necessary. If the detection probability of illegal work practices or clandestine work is low and/or the penalties for firms are limited in relation to the savings in taxes and wages obtainable, then illegality is an attractive option for immigrants as well as natives. Experiences in Europe and the United States with legalization of illegals and the introduction of more severe border and work-permit controls in firms showed that these were short-term measures that did not tackle the real problem; illegal inflows returned to their former levels.

These results notwithstanding, controls of work practices and employment conditions are being stepped up in the industrialized countries. The access of illegal residents to social protection systems is being further restricted (see OECD, 1994). In France labour legislation was revised in 1991 to facilitate the struggle against the different types of illegality on the labour market. This reform was accompanied by the establishment of coordination mechanisms between different local administrative bodies and ministries.

5   CONCLUSIONS REGARDING FUTURE RESEARCH AND A COMMON EUROPEAN POLICY ON MIGRATION

The main parameters for future migration are the trend towards increased internationalization (overlaid by the formation of stronger regional economic blocs), the increased interlinkage of the central and eastern European countries with western Europe and the widening gap between socioeconomic differentials in North and South. Migration will expand as economic and demographic transitions proceed (see Pang Eng Fong, 1994; Teitelbaum, 1991). The structure of migration will reflect each country's stage and rate of economic development. A coordination of labour market strategies with economic and human resource development and integration is needed. The international consensus on the need for a global migration strategy is given. The specific route to be taken will depend on the outcome of sound impact analyses in both sending and receiving countries. The objective of this chapter was to provide an overview of the type of analyses available and the necessary ingredients of impact studies that could help define future policy directions. However, analysis will have to be extended to the relationship between trade and migration: it is vital for migration policy-makers to know to what extent movements of goods and factors of production are substitutes or complements. Ohlin (1933) pointed out that factor trade and commodity trade are substitutes: they act together towards equal factor endowments and commodity and factor prices. In the light of this theory, the elimination of barriers in the EU should have reduced the movement of labour and increased commodity trade. Commodity flows have increased, but factor mobility declined only in the case of unskilled workers. Migration of skilled workers increased during the 1980s because of unequal endowment of countries with technological capabilities. Skills that are complementary to certain technologies will move to those countries where they are used more efficiently in the production of export goods.

Wood (1994) argues that the change in trade[10] since the 1970s has had an influence on labour markets and contributed to the widening of wage differentials by skills in the industrialized countries. A better understanding of the relationship between trade and migration will be of particular importance for policy choice in the endeavour to achieve greater integration of central and eastern European countries into the western economies.

REFERENCES

Abella, M. J. (ed.) (1994), 'Turning Points in Labour Migration', *Asian and Pacific Migration Journal*, 3 (1), special issue, edited in cooperation with ILO, The United Nations University.

Appleyard, R. T. (1991), *International Migration: Challenge for the 90's*, Geneva: International Organization for Migration.

Bean, F. D. and M. Fix (1992), 'The Significance of Recent Immigration Policy Reforms in the United States', in G. P. Freeman and J. Jupp (eds), *Nations of Immigrants, Australia, the United States and International Migration*, Australia: Oxford University Press, pp. 41–55.

---

10 The old pattern of trade, whereby manufactured goods from the North were exchanged for primary products from the South, has been largely replaced by a two-way flow in manufactured goods; the North now specializes in the production of skill-intensive goods and services and the South in labour-intensive goods and services.

Betts, K. (1988), *Ideology and Immigration, Australia 1976 to 1987*, Melbourne: Melbourne University Press.

Biffl, G. (1991), *Migration in Europe in the 80's and the Prospects of Migration as a Consequence of the Transformation of Eastern European Countries*, WIFO–Vorträge, 49, International Conference on Migration, 17–21 June, Moscow.

Biffl, G. (1993), 'The Austrian Migration System', paper presented at the OECD/Canada/Spain Conference 'Migration and International Cooperation: Challenges for OECD Countries', 29–31 March, Madrid (Summary in OECD, 1994).

Biffl, G. (1994), *Theorie und Empirie des Arbeitsmarktes am Beispiel Österreich*, Wien/New York: Springer Verlag.

Birrell, R., D. Hill and J. Nevill (eds) (1984), *Populate and Perish? The Stresses of Population Growth in Australia*, Sydney: Fontana/Australian Conservation Foundation.

Borjas, G. J. (1990), *Friends or Strangers: The Impact of Immigrants on the U.S. Economy*, New York: Basic Books.

Borjas, G. J. (1994, December), 'The Economics of Immigration', *Journal of Economic Literature*, 32, 1667–717.

Collinson, S. (1993), *Europe and International Migration*, Royal Institute of International Affairs, London/New York: Pinter Publishers.

De New, J. P. and K. F. Zimmermann (1994), 'Native Wage Impacts of Foreign Labour: A Random Effects Panel Analysis', *Journal of Population Economics*, 7 (2), 177–92.

Fraser, J. R. (1994), 'Immigration in the United States and the Limits of Sanctions against Employers', in *Migration and Development: New Partnerships for Cooperation*, Paris: OECD, pp. 75–84.

Freeman, G. P. and J. Jupp (eds) (1992), *Nations of Immigrants, Australia, the United States and International Migration*, Australia: Oxford University Press.

Jayasuriya, L. (1990, Autumn), 'Rethinking Australian Multiculturalism: Towards a New Paradigm', *The Australian Quarterly*, 50–63.

Matuschek, H. (1985), 'Ausländerpolitik in Österreich 1962–1985 (Der Kampf um und gegen die ausländische Arbeitskraft)', *Journal für Sozialforschung*, 25 (2), 159–98.

OECD (1994), *Migration and Development, New Partnerships for Cooperation*, Paris: OECD.

Ohlin, B. (1933), *Interregional and International Trade*, Cambridge, MA: Harvard University Press.

Pang Eng Fong (1994), 'An Eclectic Approach to Turning Points in Migration', *Asian and Pacific Migration Journal*, 3 (1), 81–91.

Papademetriou, D. G. (1991), 'Migration and Development: The Unsettled Relationship', in D. G. Papademetriou and P. L. Martin (eds), *The Unsettled Relationship, Contributions to Labor Studies*, New York/London: Greenwood Press, pp. 213–20.

Ramos, F. A. (1992), 'Out-migration and Return Migration of Puerto Ricans', in G. J. Borjas and R. B. Freeman (eds), *Immigration and the Work Force: Economic Consequences for the United States and Source Areas*, Chicago: University of Chicago Press, pp. 49–66.

Reimers, C. W. (1985), *Still the Golden Door? The Third World Comes to America*, New York: Columbia University Press.

Roy, A. D. (1951, June), 'Some Thoughts on the Distribution of Earnings', *Oxford Economic Papers*, New Series, 3, 135–46.

Rudolph, H. and M. Morokvasic (eds) (1993), *Bridging States and Markets. International Migration in the Early 1990's*, Berlin: edition sigma.

Salt, J., A. Singleton and J. Hogarth (1994), *Europe's International Migrants, Data Sources, Patterns and Trends*, London: HMSO.

Shah, N. M. (1994), 'Arab Labour Migration: A Review of Trends and Issues', *International Migration*, 32 (1), 3–28.

Simon, J. L. (1989), *The Economic Consequences of Immigration*, Oxford: Basil Blackwell.

Stalker, P. (1994), *The Work of Strangers: A Survey of International Labour Migration*, Geneva: ILO.

Stark, O. (1991), *The Migration of Labor*, Oxford: Basil Blackwell.

Stromback, T., G. Biffl, S. Bushe-Jones, J. Clarke, P. Dawkins, S. Nicholls and A. Preston (1993), *Immigration, Skill Transfer and Industry Restructuring in Western Australia*, Canberra: Bureau of Immigration Research, AGPS.

Teitelbaum, M. S. (1991), *The Effects of Economic Development on Out-migration Pressures in Sending Countries, OECD/Italy*, International Conference on Migration, Rome, 13–15 March, OECD/GD, 91 (29).

United Nations (1989), *World Population at the Turn of the Century*, New York.

US Department of Labor (1989), *The Effects of Immigration on the U.S. Economy and Labour Market*, Washington, DC.

Werner, H. (1994), *Integration of Foreign Workers into the Labour Market—France, Germany, the Netherlands and Sweden*, ILO working paper MIG WP.74E, Geneva.

Wood, A. (1994), *North–south Trade, Employment and Inequality, Changing Fortunes in a Skill-driven World*, IDS Development Studies Series, Oxford: Clarendon Press.

Zimmermann, K. F. (1995), 'Tackling the European Migration Problem', *Journal of Economic Perspectives*, 9 (2), 45–62.

19. Labour Adjustments through Part-time Work

Jacqueline O'Reilly[1]

There has been a growing concern across advanced industrialized countries with improving working time flexibility since the economic crisis of the early 1970s. A variety of flexible working time schedules have been seen as a means to facilitate labour force adjustments. In some countries the use of part-time work has marked a significant change in employment patterns in recent years, whereas in other countries it has been negligible. Considerable debate has emerged over whether part-time work should, in general, be encouraged or whether its development as a form of labour market adjustment should be opposed.

What type of labour market adjustments does part-time work allow? What policy combinations have been developed to achieve these adjustment goals? And how has the use of part-time work been evaluated? In addressing these central questions in the following pages, I seek to identify the policy combinations that produce the most optimal form of labour market adjustment through the use of part-time work. I also outline areas for future evaluation research both in terms of themes to be researched and methodologies to be developed.

1 THEORETICAL DEBATES ON COORDINATION GOALS TO ENCOURAGE PART-TIME WORK

One of the problems in identifying the optimal outcomes to be achieved through the use of part-time work, like many of the facets of working time flexibility, is that such outcomes often cover a diverse and contradictory range of goals (Hinrichs, Roche and Sirianni, 1991). For example, part-time work (Delsen, 1995, p. 212) has been used to increase labour supply during slack periods, whereas it has been seen as a means to reduce unemployment during slack periods by encouraging work-sharing (Fines, Morrissey, Roche, Whelan and Williams, 1994; Meager, 1988; Mosley and Kruppe, chap. 20 in this

1 I would like to thank Ulrich Walwei, Günther Schmid and Lei Delsen for earlier comments on this paper, and David Antal for detailed comments during the copy-reading phase.

volume). Part-time work has also been seen as a transition mechanism, in particular for women wanting to reenter the labour market after a period of child-rearing. However, a significant debate exists as to whether part-time work offers access to the core labour market or whether it confines women to ghettoized employment. In fact, suboptimal outcomes have resulted from attempts to facilitate work force adjustments through the use of part-time work. Theoretical debate on the role that coordination failures of the market or policy could have in such cases have largely centred on three main issues: (a) the aggregate effect of part-time work on employment creation in the labour market in general, (b) attempts to increase working time flexibililty for individuals over the life cycle, or (c) increases that new working time arrangements bring about in productivity and efficiency at the firm level. In the following sections each of these coordination goals are examined in turn.

1.1 Labour Market Flexibility: Reducing Unemployment and Creating Jobs?

One of the goals behind increasing working time flexibility has been to encourage a wider distribution of employment. These arguments have often been at the core of policy to promote part-time work in countries like France, Germany and the Netherlands and have been voiced at the supranational level as well (see European Commission, 1994a). Certain forms of part-time, or half-time, employment have often been seen as a means of facilitating work-sharing or a reduction in working hours and thereby of potentially increasing the employment rate (Bäcker, Schäfer, Seifert and Scholz-Willig, 1994; Hegner, 1993; Walwei and Werner, 1995). According to McKinsey (1994), the extended use of part-time work in western Germany could lead to an increase of 1.9 million new part-time jobs, 1.4 million new full-time jobs and a 24 per cent increase in productivity. It could also reduce pressure on wages based on insider–outsider considerations. It has been argued that such a policy could help the long-term unemployed reenter the labour market, thereby contributing to a reduction in the costs of paying unemployment benefits, and preventing a further deterioration of individuals' human capital through inactivity. Schmid (1994b) has argued that a new concept of full employment could be developed through the use of such forms of work, with the aim of reducing structural unemployment by creating greater mobility in the labour market. Thus, part-time work could facilitate labour market adjustments by increasing working time flexibility and raising the employment rate.

However, the results of employment increases stemming from reduced working time or part-time work have often been disappointing, even to supporters of such programmes (de Neubourg, 1991, pp. 140–41; Hinrichs et al., 1991; OECD, 1994b, pp. 88–100). The lack of employment growth as a result of reduced working time can be due either to productivity growth in firms that relieves them of the need to take on extra labour to offset the reduction in hours, to previous overcapacity or to the organizational difficulty firms may have in introducing new working schedules. Failures to meet goals like reducing unemployment can also be linked to the fact that many of these new workers come from the ranks of the 'inactive' rather than the unemployed (Holst and Schupp, 1994; Rubery, Fagan and Smith, 1995; Sundström, 1991). This category of 'inactive' persons often comprises women who are not officially registered as unemployed or engaged in seeking work. Further, an unintended consequence of introducing shorter working time may lead to an increase in underemployment and an increase in the number of people looking for a second job or moonlighting (Pinheiro, 1995). Referring to the United States, Tilly (1992) argues that 'the forgone output and employment represented by five million people underemployed and involuntarily working part-time is equivalent to an additional 2.5 million people unemployed' (p. 36). A major issue surrounding the development of part-time work is related to the demand for this form of employment. Where working part time is involuntary, people may find other ways of filling their time or supplementing their income through paid informal activities.

By using a variety of active and passive measures governments have sought to encourage a greater use of part-time work (see section 2). These policies appear to have been less successful in some countries than in others. For instance, costs of such workers are relatively high in more regulated markets such as those in France (O'Reilly, 1994a). In the Netherlands, however, high levels of part-time work have not incurred disadvantaged forms of employment comparable to those in the United Kingdom, where labour markets have been more deregulated (Fagan, Platenga and Rubery, 1995). A key aspect of the development of part-time work is the relation between the quantity and quality of such jobs and the forms of labour adjustment they provide. Critics contend that the development of part-time work represents a growth in precarious employment with negative consequences for both equity and efficiency concerns (Schmid, 1994a), whereas others assert that better quality part-time jobs can be generated without entailing inferior employment conditions.

At both the market and policy level, work force adjustment through the use of part-time work has thus not always clearly increased aggregate levels of employment. In certain cases the approach can be seen to generate undesired consequences through double jobbing, moonlighting or creation of ghettos of disadvantaged forms of employment. Nevertheless, the goal of generating the quantity and quality of part-time jobs that will facilitate transitions from unemployment or inactivity to paid employment remains high on the agendas of policy-makers.

1.2   Employee Flexibility over the Life Cycle: A Question of Choice?

It is often argued that part-time work allows people to adjust their working time over the life cycle in relation to other demands on their time. For younger people part-time work can be a way of gaining access to the labour market and work experience. For older workers it can allow a gradual withdrawal from paid employment, or, with the advent of demographic trends indicating an aging of the work force, it could provide access to a previously untapped source of labour among retired workers who would like to continue in some form of paid employment, that is, on a part-time basis. However, part-time work is predominantly a female form of participation, a fact largely related to women's domestic responsibilities. Part-time work is often seen as a means to allow women to reenter or retain a foothold in the labour market while rearing children. Delsen (1993, p. 88) argues that part-time work reflects employers' accommodation of part-timers' wishes for flexible hours, although theorists of labour market segmentation place greater emphasis on the role that employers have in dividing up the labour market into advantaged and disadvantaged forms of employment (Rubery, 1993). Advocates of part-time work point to 'model' countries like Sweden when citing the advantages of part-time work. As Delsen (1995) states, for example, 'Swedish labour law and social security regulations give no incentive to create marginal part-time jobs. Also tax policy, partial pension, part-time parental leave and subsidised child care contributed to the high number' of secure part-time jobs' (p. 244). Sundström (1991) argues that, in Sweden, 'part-time work has not marginalized women but, on the contrary, has increased the continuity of their labor force attachment, strengthened their position in the labor market, and reduced their economic dependency' (p. 167). This argument is based on the facts that part-time workers in Sweden work relatively long hours, have job security, receive full social benefits and are highly unionized. Sundström (1991, p. 168) emphasizes the importance of the relation between working long hours and improving conditions for part-timers. For example, in 1985, only 19 per cent of Swedish part-timers worked fewer than 21 hours a week, compared to two-thirds of part-timers in Belgium, Britain, Germany and the Netherlands (see also Maier, 1991).

However, in most of the countries where part-time work has grown in recent years, it has been associated with the development of precarious employment rather than with the advantages identified in the Swedish model. In many countries part-timers receive inferior terms and conditions related not only to pay and fringe benefits but also to training opportunities and career development (Maier, 1994). Büchtemann and Quack (1989) have argued that it is not part-time work *per se* that determines precarious employment status and disadvantage. Instead, it is the disadvantages accruing to employees who work part time for extended periods.

Market and policy failures in this area have created disjunctures in the supply of and demand for part-time work. This reality can be seen through the effects of tax and social contribution systems where various thresholds distort both employers' and employees' choices concerning the number of hours worked. Either employers offer jobs with a low number of hours, or employees elect to constrain the number of hours they work in order to avoid paying contributions. The disadvantage to employees is that they may eventually have no entitlement to a range of social benefits, including pensions and unemployment insurance. For employers, curtailing hours in order to keep them within particular threshold bands acts as a disincentive to invest in training for these part-time workers and as an incentive to restrict part-time work to low-skill, low-pay jobs. Employees wishing to reduce their working hours may thereby be forced into downward occupational mobility. This is frequently the case for women, the result being a deterioration of their human capital. Alternatively, some employees may find that they are compelled to remain in full-time jobs. This situation represents an inefficient use of resources because it distorts the way employees' working time preferences are accommodated and the way jobs would be designed if these thresholds did not exist. The goal for the development of employee flexibility should be to make secure forms of part-time work an attractive choice and form of mobility for both men and women over different stages of the life cycle.

1.3   Firm-level Flexibility: Improving Productivity and Efficiency?

It has been argued that part-time work can increase firm-level flexibility in the organization of production and delivery of services (Atkinson and Meager, 1986; European Commission, 1994a). These issues have had considerable discussion in academic and policy circles in recent decades (see Delsen, 1995; O'Reilly, 1994a, chap. 2; Rosenberg, 1989). Much of this debate has been concerned with the extent to which firms have been able to develop different forms of flexibility successfully. Part-time workers can be employed to meet workload variations, provide alternative shift arrangements and extend operating hours or service availability. The use of such shifts can reduce labour costs because such staff members rarely receive wage premiums for unsociable hours or overtime. Using part-timers to lower wage costs has been a key advantage in countries where such workers are not covered by social contributions. Over the long term, firms can also offer part-time career breaks to retain skilled staff. They can also offer part-time jobs as a means of expanding the available pool of labour during periods of labour shortages by attracting people who are not able to work on a full-time basis. In the effort to reduce staffing levels in general, management in some firms encourages staff to use part-time work as a means of gradual exit from the company (O'Reilly, 1994a, p. 161). Advocates of part-time work also argue that such workers are more productive and have higher levels of commitment than to full-timers (McKinsey, 1994); they also have lower absenteeism rates (Marimbert, 1992, p. 94). Part-time work can thus make a significant contribution to overall economic efficiency within the firm.

However, not all firms appear to be willing to develop this type of flexibility. Part-time contracts are seen as problematic to manage in terms of providing continuity and quality; they can also cause resentment among full-timers who work with part-timers. Where team-working or polyvalence is being developed, it is sometimes more difficult to integrate part-timers (O'Reilly, 1994a). Although it is claimed that part-timers can be used to increase productivity levels, Tilly (1992) has suggested that employers may underestimate the productivity gains to be achieved, especially in more highly qualified jobs. In sectors where secondary forms of part-time work are comparatively popular, such as retailing, Tilly has argued that, in the United States, they have been accompanied by falling labour productivity.

> Thus when employers create secondary part-time jobs to cut labor costs, they may not be getting much of a bargain ... access to labor at low compensation levels makes productivity increases unnecessary for employers. Because many part-time service employers have chosen secondary part-time employment (the low-compensation, low-productivity option) as a means to reduce costs, they may have failed to search for or involve full-time work and higher compensation (p. 36).

This strategy leads to decreased organizational and economic efficiency over the long term.

A further problem with the development of part-time work in general has been its gendered imbalance. Given the attendant employment conditions in some countries, this imbalance suggests the perpetuation of sex discrimination in the labour market (Fagan et al., 1995). In contrast to policies of shortened working time, which are more commonly undertaken by men, part-time work is a female form of flexibility and work force adjustment. This circumstance indicates that there are certain rigidities preventing a broader take-up of part-time work by men or that employers use different forms of labour market adjustment depending on the gender composition of the work force (Beechey and Perkins, 1987).

Thus, in sum, part-time work provides labour market adjustments at the aggregate, individual and firm level. Developing positive, secure forms of part-time work is a normative goal. The aim should be to encourage high productivity and efficiency with a more equitable distribution of working time supported by the security provided by a system of social benefits so that these workers are not unduly exploited for the flexibility they provide. It is not obvious that these results will come about purely through market forces. In fact it is more likely that secondary, disadvantageous forms of part-time work will develop if the market is left to itself. Policy intervention is required in order to establish the collective rules under which companies compete in their use of labour (O'Reilly, 1994c). However, the nature of this intervention should be to facilitate an optimal form of part-time work that corresponds to both employee and employer requirements and has positive aggregate employment effects. I turn now to examine the range of different policies available to achieve these goals.

2   POLICIES AFFECTING THE BEHAVIOUR OF AGENTS IN THE TARGET AREAS

A distinction needs to be made between active labour market policies and passive policies (OECD, 1994b; Schömann, 1995). Active policies include financial incentives to either employers or employees and specific labour market programmes to encourage the use of part-time work. Programmes to facilitate youth entry into the labour market (see Ryan and Büchtemann, chap. 10 in this volume) or encourage part-time exit options for older workers (see Casey, chap. 12 in this volume) can also increase the overall rate of part-time work, as can parental leave agreements (see Fagan and Rubery, chap. 11 in this volume). Passive labour market policies include tax and social security systems (see Gustafsson, chap. 27 in this volume) and regulations on employment protection (see Büchtemann and Walwei, chap. 22 in this volume).

2.1   Active Labour Market Measures

2.1.1   Financial Incentives to Encourage Part-time Work

Active labour market policies designed to encourage the use of part-time work through reduction of marginal costs have tended to be focussed on either employers or employees (Maier, 1991, p. 53). An example of employer-oriented incentives was introduced in the Netherlands in 1980. However, by 1982 the subsidy arrangement provided to employers taking on part-timers was abolished because it was shown to have had no effect on employers' decisions (de Neubourg, 1991, p. 137). Where governments have experimented with such subsidies, as in Germany and the United Kingdom, employers have to see such payments as a short-term, one-off advantage. Delsen (1995) has argued that '[a] more effective way to create additional part-time jobs would be achieved by a structural reduction of marginal costs of the employer' (p. 121). However, that approach would imply changing the way pension premiums, employee insurances and taxes are levied. In France recent experiments to compensate employers who use part-timers can be seen from the 30 to 50 per cent reduction of employers' social security contributions introduced in 1993. This applies only to newly recruited part-time employees on open-ended contracts (from 19 to 30 hours per week) and to employees who requested to change from full- to part-time work (MISEP, 1993a, p. 13; 'New Law', 1993). Delsen (1995, p. 122) argues that this practice reduces 'the wedge between labour costs and net earnings', thereby benefiting both the employer and the employee.

Further measures at the firm level have been intended to encourage companies to make greater use of job-sharing (Fines et al., 1994; MISEP, 1994a, pp. 11–12; Mosley and Kruppe, chap. 20 in this volume). These programmes have increasingly focussed on particular target groups, such as the unemployed, or on job-training for the young (see also MISEP, 1994c, p. 25). In March 1994 the Belgian government sought to use job-sharing to widen the redistribution of work. Employers who introduced a job-sharing plan could reclaim a flat-rate deduction from their social insurance contributions (BF 25 000 per quarter), but only for a maximum of two years (SYSDEM, 1995, p. 4). Maier (1991) has asserted that labour market programmes in Belgium have had more effect than in other countries:

> [M]ore than 50% of all part-time employment in Belgium can be attributed to government labour market policies or is—in other words—subsidised part-time employment of otherwise unemployed or formerly full-time employed persons ... Bearing in mind that labour law and social security regulations in Belgium treat part-time and full-time workers equally so that the financial incentives are small, the government programmes seem to have had a massive influence on the growth of part-time employment (pp. 76–7).

A more employee-oriented approach was also developed in Belgium during the 1980s. Measures introduced in 1982 allowed partial entitlement to unemployment benefit to be retained by unemployed people who accepted to work part time. However, the gender take-up of this measure was very unequal: 80 per cent of these part-timers were women. As one effect of this policy, the levels of involuntary part-time work and dissatisfaction among these workers have been higher in Belgium than in other countries because of the pressure on the unemployed to accept part-time work (Maier, 1991; Walwei and Werner, 1995). At the same time, those working part-time and receiving unemployment benefit have had little incentive to move to full-time jobs, the reason being the effect of marginal tax rates when they lose their benefit entitlement. In an attempt to introduce budget cuts, the Belgian government has meanwhile sought to impose a levy on employers who used part-timers avoiding unemployment and further tried to encourage a greater move to full-time work (MISEP, 1993b, pp. 13–14). The government has since decided to diminish unemployment benefits gradually until 1 January 1996, after which time it will be abolished completely. More recently, the government of Flanders has sought to encourage a greater distribution of work by offering employees an allowance if they transfer from a full- to a part-time job: BF 3000 for those working from 51 per cent to 80 per cent of a full-time job, and BF 5000 for those working at a 50 per cent job. However, this plan does not appear to have had the success expected in creating 2000 to 3000 jobs for the region (SYSDEM, 1995, p. 4).

The Dutch government takes a very different view on promoting the use of part-time work through such measures (MISEP, 1994a, pp. 24–5). Subsidies to workers changing from full- to part-time work have an impact only on the area where part-time work is already growing, and it is argued that workers who want to change will do so without receiving a subsidy. In the Netherlands, employee incentives are organized through the unemployment benefit system. Workers who change to part-time work and subsequently become unemployed are entitled to receive unemployment benefit for three years on the basis of their previous full-time salary. However, this policy is not expected to have a major effect on employment. The Dutch government is currently examining how working time reductions can be used to avoid redundancies without creating barriers for firms that need to shed labour. Providing subsidies from the social insurance funds, as in France and Belgium, to promote working time reductions would require close scrutiny of company plans, which the Dutch government is reluctant to develop. It also argues that partial unemployment compensation for people taking a part-time job reduces incentives to look for a full-time job or take on additional part-time employment. There is fear that such a measure would be abused and that it would make spending difficult to control (MISEP, 1994b, p. 25). A less radical approach to the encouragement of part-time work can be seen in Germany. Rather than introduce substantial changes to the tax or social security systems, the German government has sought to convince companies of the advantages of part-time work ('Government Launches', 1994). According to Delsen (1995, p. 122), a similar approach has also been used very successfully in regions in the Netherlands.

2.1.2 *Part-time Work as an Entry or Exit Measure for Young and Older Workers*

In the United States it is common for young people to use part-time work as a means to finance their education (Tilly, 1992). In Europe the idea of using part-time work as a form of labour market entry has grown in popularity in recent years. In Germany the experiment with part-time modules of entry for trainees has been a key feature among the recent changes at Volkswagen (Seifert, 1994, pp. 29–30). In countries with particularly high rates of youth unemployment, such policies have been a central issue of debate, although in practice such policies have usually only had a marginal effect on overall levels of part-time work. In France, for example, the TUC ('Travaux d'Utilité Collective') is the largest part-time labour market measure targeted at the unemployed 16–25 age group. It provides a 3–12-month part-time training period. Maier (1991, pp. 77–8) argues that this programme is relatively insignificant because only 0.2 per cent of the labour force begins employment on it per year. In the Netherlands part-time work for young people accounts for less than 1 per cent of part-time employees in such labour market programmes.

In some countries employers have been encouraged to draw up 'solidarity agreements' by which the exit of older workers is offset by the entry of younger workers. Part-time work options have been seen as one way for this policy to be implemented. In the Netherlands collective agreements in the metal-working industry have allowed for early retirement in cases where employers agreed to take on younger workers for 32 hours a week, which counts as part time. De Neubourg (1991, p. 137) has estimated that this arrangement produced a 1 per cent increase in labour market activity by the end of 1984. The spectacular increase in the use of part-time work in the Netherlands is partly attributable to the fact that private and public sector employers have been taking on workers younger than 26 years on 32-hour-a-week contracts (de Neubourg, 1991, p. 138).

For older workers part-time work has been seen as a means of facilitating labour market exits. In Denmark demographic trends indicating an aging work force have encouraged firms to use part-time work as a way of attracting older workers to remain in the labour market (MISEP, 1995, p. 14). However, the way pension schemes are calculated can structure the attractiveness of part-time retirement: there is less incentive to change from full- to part-time work where the final year's pay is the basis for pension calculation, as in Greece. Where a longer reference period of earnings is taken into account it is more equitable and attractive for employees to consider part-time early retirement (MISEP, 1993c, pp. 13–14; see Delsen, 1995, p. 124, for more details on how pensions are calculated in different countries). 'In a number of OECD countries—Belgium, Canada, France, the United Kingdom, the United States—for the public pensions an earnings test applies. This is a disincentive to work for older workers, however, it may be an incentive for marginal part-time jobs' (Delsen, 1995, p. 124). Maier (1991, pp. 36–7 and 45–6) points out that part-timers, usually women, are often discriminated against in pension schemes. Delsen (1995, p. 124) suggests that the gendered segregation of part-time employment could be broken down by the introduction of a nationally mandated part-time gradual retirement scheme. The advantages of such a scheme would also reduce absenteeism, the costs of disability allowance and potentially, through the more equal distribution of workers, unemployment. Such relatively new measures have had the most success in Sweden (Delsen, 1995). In Denmark, Finland, France, Germany, Spain and the United Kingdom they have been less successful because of 'unfavourable labour markets; lack of financial incentives; rigid replacement conditions, and absence of social consensus' (Delsen, 1995, p. 125).

2.1.3 Part-time Parental Leave

The demand for part-time work is largely stimulated by the extent and quality of childcare that is provided. Where the extent and quality of childcare is limited, women are more likely to want short-hour part-time jobs. In countries like Sweden, where extensive childcare provision exists, part-timers work longer hours; in countries like France, where comprehensive provision is available, there is less demand for part-time work in general (Fagan and Rubery, chap. 11 in this volume; O'Reilly, 1994a; Delsen, 1995, p. 127; European Commission, 1994b).

Parental leave can be provided either through statutory entitlement or through individual company or collective agreements. The two need not be exclusive; company or collective agreements can supplement legal provisions. Unfortunately, there are no comprehensive sources of data on the extent and nature of such provisions. In general, statutory-leave arrangements have been more extensive in Denmark, Germany and Italy, and least well developed in Ireland, Luxembourg and the United Kingdom (European Commission, 1994b).

In some countries like Finland, France, Portugal and the Netherlands, parents with dependent children below a certain age are entitled to take a period of unpaid, part-time parental leave. By contrast, this period of parental leave is fully paid in Norway and Sweden, making part-time work there a comparatively common element in a broader range of jobs (European Commission, 1994b; Maier, 1994). A general right for part-time parental leave should in theory encourage the uptake of part-time work. Fathers in higher-income, higher-qualification jobs, particularly those in the public sector, are more likely to take up such leave arrangements if they exist, and paternity leave tends to have a higher take-up rate among men than parental-leave provision does. Unfortunately, there are no comprehensive, international comparative studies assessing the costs and benefits of leave arrangements.

2.2 Passive Labour Market Measures

2.2.1 Tax Systems

The structure of the tax system can shape the incentives and disincentives to use part-time work for both employers and employees. One can distinguish between systems based on a flat-rate contribution for each employee and systems based on ceilings and thresholds (see also Gustafsson, chap. 27 in this volume). Flat-rate contributions take no account of the time worked by employees and are a major disincentive to employers to use part-time work. Because the cost per employee is fixed, such systems are more likely to encourage the use of overtime, rather than of job-sharing or part-time work, as a form of flexible work force adjustment. Placing a ceiling on employers' contributions makes it more expensive to employ two part-timers than one full-timer, thereby discouraging the use of part-time work. Delsen (1995) argued that it also discourages the substitution of earnings of the wife for earnings of the husband. Ceilings have been abolished in Finland, Italy, Denmark, Norway, Sweden and Belgium, but they have been raised in France, Germany, Greece and the Netherlands (Euzéby, 1988). Delsen (1995) suggested that rather than removing the ceilings, taxation could be based on hourly rather than weekly, monthly or annual pay. 'This would be neutral, since it would make the contributions for each worker proportional to the time worked and independent of the number of people performing a given volume of work' (p. 127). He also suggested that employers replacing full-timers with part-timers could be reimbursed through the creation of special ceilings for the latter.

In the United Kingdom systems using thresholds as the basis for contributions have been a significant factor in accounting for the country's comparatively high levels of part-time work, even though that work is sometimes of an inferior status and the hours are so few that employers and employees do not qualify to make contributions (Delsen, 1995, p. 128; Euzéby, 1988, p. 556; Fagan et al., 1995, p. 7; Maier, 1991; O'Reilly, 1994b). These thresholds can act as a barrier preventing the transition from part-time to full-time work because the costs, both to employers and employees, are prohibitive in terms of marginal income returns. In Japan, for example, the tax threshold of ¥900 000 encourages both employers and employees to readjust their annual working hours so as to remain below this threshold (Delsen, 1995, p. 128.) Systems of joint taxation, such as the one in Germany, can encourage wives to earn up to the marginal rate of their husbands. A woman may make a trade-off between the income from hours spent in paid employment and payment for domestic services that she would otherwise provide unpaid. As a result she may curtail the hours she is available for paid employment, thus shaping the type of part-time work she wants.

2.2.2 Social Security

The methods of financing social security systems and calculating contributions, and the qualifying conditions for benefit entitlement, can discourage the use of part-time employment (Euzéby, 1988; Quack, 1992). In most European

countries, as well as in Japan, the United States and Canada, minimum requirements often exclude part-timers from entitlement to allowances for unemployment, sickness, disability, maternity leave and pensions. These minimum
requirements may stipulate minimum periods of employment, earnings' hours
worked and/or prior contributions (Delsen, 1995; Euzéby, 1988; Fagan et al.,
1995; ILO, 1989; Maier, 1994). In Spain, Greece and Italy part-timers all
receive social security and unemployment benefits proportionate to full-timers
(Delsen, 1995, pp. 116–21), although these countries have comparatively low
levels of part-time work.

Second, those receiving unemployment benefit may be unwilling to accept
part-time jobs if their earnings are not significantly more than their benefit
entitlement. They may also be dissuaded from accepting a part-time job where
benefit entitlement is calculated on the basis of their most recent job. If that
employment had been full time, they may be unwilling to accept a job that
would have the long-term consequence of reducing benefit entitlement. To
prevent moonlighting and facilitate the reentry of the unemployed into paid
employment, some governments (such as those of Denmark, Belgium, Finland,
France, Ireland, the Netherlands, Spain, Sweden and Switzerland, according to
Delsen, 1995, p. 121) have decided to maintain partial unemployment payments for those accepting a part-time job (Euzéby, 1988, pp. 554–5). However,
these payments can be very costly, and in Sweden and Belgium they have been
cut back (Delsen, 1995, p. 121). Differentiated treatment for part-timers under
these systems effectively encourages the use of marginalized part-time work
from both the employer and employee perspectives.

2.2.3 Employment Protection

The extent to which part-timers receive equal treatment with full-timers in
terms of legal protection and entitlement to fringe benefits varies significantly
from one country to the next (ILO, 1989). For example, in countries like
France the principle of equality is enshrined in labour law, whereas in the
United Kingdom there is no specific law mandating equality (Delsen, 1995,
pp. 112–13; O'Reilly, 1994a). Where formal legal equality between part-
timers and full-timers does exist, part-timers still often receive inferior terms
and conditions—in particular, short hours and low pay (Büchtemann and
Quack, 1989; Jallade, 1984; Maier, 1994). As stated by Delsen (1995),

> [e]vidence suggests that partial coverage by job security legislation, i.e. the exclu-
> sion from certain rights, encourages the growth of 'marginal' part-time work, and
> results in a more segmented labour market: rigid job security requirements cover-
> ing high-paid, senior full-time workers in large firms on the one side and more
> flexible, with part-time, low-paid, insecure workers in small business on the other
> (p. 115).

The importance of discrepancies in who is covered by employment protection is that they can shape the structure of advantaged and disadvantaged forms of part-time work, thus making them appear more or less attractive to employers and employees (see also Büchtemann and Walwei, chap. 22 in this volume).

In sum, the use of part-time work as a form of labour market adjustment can be significantly affected by a range of active and passive labour market policies. The optimal goal of achieving qualified, secure forms of part-time work that facilitate labour market mobility both at the aggregate, individual and firm level requires a careful coordination and combination of these policies. A key factor in their implementation is the relation between the quantity and quality of the part-time jobs they generate. Part-time jobs will not necessarily proliferate if working conditions and benefit entitlement deteriorate. In fact, the status of this type of employment will, in general, require upgrading if such labour force adjustments are to become more attractive to a broader audience than is currently the case. In the following sections I seek to identify research findings that can help improve the understanding of the role that policy-making plays in this target area.

3 EVALUATING THE IMPACT OF POLICY: METHODOLOGICAL AND SUBSTANTIVE RESULTS

An extensive range of research has been conducted on the issue of part-time work, although the studies involved have tended to be more like audits and monitoring than the strict evaluations implied by the methodologies laid out in the first part of this handbook. The reason is partly that the development of part-time work has tended to be associated more closely with passive labour market measures than with active programmes. Where more active measures have been used, as in Belgium, there has been a relative dearth of evaluation studies on how effective these measures have been. Significant interest in international comparisons of part-time work has grown in recent years as each country aims to evaluate how 'flexible' its own employment regime is relative to that in other countries. But before examining the results and methodologies used in prominent studies, I need to point out the problems in evaluating part-time work, both in general and from a cross-national perspective.

3.1 Comparing Part-time Work in Different Countries

Aggregate data on the levels and growth of part-time work reveal differences between a number of OECD countries (see Table 19.1). The Netherlands, Australia, Belgium and New Zealand have had the highest growth rates since

1973 (from 28 to 10 percentage points higher than all the other countries over this period). France, Canada, the United Kingdom, Japan, Sweden, Ireland, Denmark, Norway and Germany have had growth rates ranging from 8.0 to 5.0 percentage points, whereas Finland, Luxembourg and the United States have had growth ranging below 5 percentage points. In Italy the use of part-time work has declined.

Table 19.1   Part-time Work as a Proportion of Total Employment in OECD Countries

Country	1973	1983	1993	Change 1973–93 in percentage points
Australia	11.9	17.5	23.9	+ 12.0
Austria	6.4	8.4	—	—
Belgium	2.8	8.1	12.8	+ 10.0
Canada	9.7	15.4	17.3	7.6
Denmark	17.0	23.8	23.3	+ 6.3
Finland	3.9	8.3	8.6	+ 4.7
France	5.9	9.7	13.9	+ 8.0
Germany	10.1	12.6	15.1	+ 4.0
Greece	—	6.5	4.3	—
Ireland	4.0	6.6	10.8	+ 6.8
Italy	6.4	4.6	5.4	− 1.0
Japan	13.9	16.2	21.1	+ 7.2
Luxembourg	4.5	6.3	7.3	+ 2.8
Netherlands[a]	4.4	21.4	35.0	+ 30.6
New Zealand	11.2	15.3	21.1	+ 9.9
Norway[b]	20.8	29.0	27.1	+ 6.3
Portugal	—	—	7.4	—
Spain	—	—	6.6	—
Sweden[c]	18.0	24.8	24.9	+ 6.9
United Kingdom	16.0	19.4	23.4	+ 7.4
United States	15.6	18.4	17.5	+ 1.9

Notes
a Break in the series after 1985.
b Break in the series after 1987.
c Break in the series after 1986.

— = Data were not available at time of writing.

Sources
OECD Employment Outlook 1983, Paris: OECD; *OECD Employment Outlook 1994*, Paris: OECD. (These sources also provide a breakdown according to sex and sector of employment.)

Such data can provide an important source of longitudinal material, which gives approximate measures of the pattern of labour force participation. However, comparisons of aggregate data belie the fact that the study of part-time work from a cross-national perspective raises several methodological difficulties (Dale and Glover 1989; Dex, Walters and Alden, 1993). According to the ILO (1989),

> a valid conclusion on the evolution of part-time work within countries can be drawn from the study of national time series, but . . . international comparisons of levels of part-time work should be made with great caution. On the other hand, comparisons between countries of the distribution of part-time workers by industry, by sex or by age are less influenced by the concepts and methods of collection and are therefore reasonably reliable (p. 33).

One major problem in international comparative assessments of part-time work is the lack of a standard definition that could be applied to several countries. Among OECD countries there are essentially three types of classification system: (a) *self-definition*, where respondents define their own employment status; (b) a *cut-off based on normal working hours*, usually ranging from 30 to 35 hours a week; and (c) a *cut-off based on actual hours* worked during the reference week. The cut-off based on actual hours tends to yield a higher rate of part-time work than the classification based on normal hours (Delsen, 1995, pp. 18–19).

Another difficulty encountered when using national data sets for cross-national comparisons is the way categories have developed historically (Dale and Glover, 1989). These categories are not always directly transferable from one country to the next, an obstacle that complicates measurement of the same phenomenon. Substantive differences, such as the existence of conscription or the age of entering and leaving the labour force, affect employment and unemployment rates (see also Ryan and Büchtemann, chap. 10 in this volume). In addition, the way part-timers are counted shifts even within the same country. In the Netherlands, for example, changes introduced in the methods of data collection in 1987 led to an estimated increase of 4 per cent in the aggregate number of part-timers (see Fagan et al., 1995, Appendix A, for a more detailed explanation).

These criticisms indicate the importance of caution when using aggregate data, particularly in cross-national comparisons. To reject such data outright, however, would be to ignore an important source of longitudinal material. Researchers investigating developments in part-time work and the ways it is affected by a variety of active and passive labour market measures have dealt with the attendant methodological problems by using a range of approaches. One is aggregate secondary analysis based on data available from the OECD, Eurostat, or national labour force surveys. Another is the quantitative and qualitative examination of individual characteristics and preferences. A third consists of the case study focussed on the firm. The investigations cited below illustrate these approaches and some of the results obtained.

3.1.1   Aggregate Secondary Analysis of LFS and OECD Data

Studying part-time work in Sweden, Sundström (1991) used panel data compiled from the Swedish Labour Force Survey (LFS),[2] one of the advantages being that this information permits one to examine the stocks in and flows through employment categories on a longitudinal basis (see also Schömann, chap. 4 in this volume). Sundström (1991) maintained that the growth in Swedish part-time employment was largely due to the number of nonemployed women—predominantly married women and mothers with small children—entering the labour market from 1970 through 1982. In the late 1970s 'the propensity of full-time working women to reduce their hours of work became an additional source of part-time growth' (Sundström, 1991, p. 172). The categorization permitted by this data also allows examination of the stability of employment. Sundström (1991) found that 'the proportion of women changing several times between part-time employment and non-employment dropped, as did the proportion changing between full-time, part-time and non-employment' (pp. 170–71). Sundström was also able to identify changes in the flow to and from full- and part-time employment. From 1974 through 1981 there was a propensity for full-timers to move to part-time jobs but for part-timers to remain part time. From 1982 onwards this changed. Part-timers were more likely to move to full-time jobs, and full-timers were less likely to reduce their hours.

These results are extremely interesting when linked with institutional and regulatory changes occurring in Sweden at that time. Sundström (1991) stated that changes in the marginal tax rate for married women, together with opportunities for reduced working time, encouraged female labour market participation, particularly in part-time work: 'The credibility of this explanation is strengthened by trends in the 1980s; after marginal tax rates were reduced to a maximum of 50 per cent for most income earners, women's rate of full-time work increased at the expense of part-time work' (p. 173). According to Schettkat (1989), however, changes in marginal tax rates do not suffice to explain cross-national differences in women's labour supply. He suggested that account also needs to be taken of parental leave arrangements and child-

---

2 These data were prepared by the Institute for Forecasting Statistics in Sweden. The survey is carried out monthly by Statistics Sweden with a random sample of about 20 000 individuals representative of the Swedish population of ages 16–64 years. Each interviewee is interviewed eight times at three-month intervals.

care provision. In addition, O'Reilly (1994a) suggested that educational provision can have an effect on women's labour market orientation, with less well-qualified women having a more irregular career trajectory than women with higher qualifications (Rubery et al., 1995). In comparing West Germany and Finland, Pfau-Effinger (1993) raised the point that the process of industrialization and the integration of women into the economy can have a long-term effect on shaping labour market institutions. A similar point was made by Tilly and Scott (1987) in their comparison of France and Britain. All this research supports Schettkat's argument that institutions and work experience also need to be considered when examining utility curves. Although Sundström (1991) did say that childcare provision quadrupled in Sweden during the 1970s, she emphasized the importance of changes in the tax regime. Schettkat's (1989) argument is important given that the introduction of parental leave in 1974 effectively encouraged women to enter the labour market but also helped them reduce their hours.[3] This debate suggests that policy-makers need to be cautious about reducing explanations for changing labour market patterns to a single variable. Instead, one needs to understand the interrelation and effects created by the full range of policies affecting actors in the labour market.

Using OECD data, Delsen (1995) has conducted an analysis of the relationship between women's labour market participation and part-time work from a cross-national perspective. He argued that increased levels of female and male participation are related to high levels of part-time work (Delsen, 1993, p. 82). On the basis of an Ordinary Least Squares Estimate regression analysis between the share of part-time employment and the labour force participation rate for 21 OECD countries, he has argued that higher female participation rates was linked to high levels of part-time work. Second, a higher share of men working part-time encourages higher male participation rates. The higher coefficient for male workers suggests that the promotion of part-time work will have more effect on men than women. However, the problem with such aggregate analysis is that countries with higher rates of part-time work can distort explanations that could be applied to countries with high levels of female participation but lower levels of part-time work with different institutional arrangements. The affect of institutional peculiarities and their effects are ignored (see Pfau-Effinger, 1993; Rubery et al., 1995) which shows that high participation rates for women are not universally related to the use of part-time work, for example, in Portugal and Finland. Using such data, Delsen (1995, p. 39), nevertheless, also shows that, in countries like the Netherlands, there has been a relative increase in involuntary part-time work and that there

---

3 The initial arrangement provided for 6 months of parental leave at full pay for those who had worked at least 9 months prior to the childbirth. This leave was later extended to 15 months, with 12 months at full pay.

are varying levels of demand for this form of work, which is much less popular in southern European countries and among men.

3.1.2 Employee Attitude and Acceptance Surveys

More recently the issue of employee attitudes has been stressed in the debates on working time adjustment (OECD, 1994b). One of the reasons is that theoretical debates have increasingly focussed on the role of supply-side preferences as a causal factor in accounting for the growth and extent of part-time work within a particular country. Second, the issue of whether part-time work is voluntary or involuntary has emerged. Third, where governments have sought to promote part-time work, they have tried to identify untapped demand for it. Who wants to work part time: full-timers, the unemployed or those classified as inactive? Evaluations of this aspect of part-time work have been based on a variety of approaches, including both qualitative and quantitive ones.

A qualitative approach was taken by Watson and Fothergill (1993) to analyse attitudes of female part-timers in the United Kingdom and by Strümpel, Prenzel, Scholz and Hoff (1988) to analyse attitudes of male part-timers in Germany. In the UK study a series of 'focus-group' discussions was used. This sample was structured on the basis of characteristics identified in the Labour Force Survey. One of the advantages of this method is that it enables researchers to explore in more depth the motivation and constraints imposed on people taking up part-time employment. Watson and Fothergill (1993) found that most part-timers were unaware of the thresholds in employment protection surrounding the use of part-time work in Britain, although they were more aware of the tax and national insurance contribution thresholds. As shown by the debate between Sundström and Schettkat discussed earlier, this type of evidence is important when the purpose is to assess the impact of tax regimes on employee behaviour. Though most part-timers in Britain were satisfied with this form of work, finding convenient hours was the most important element in their job search. What had started for some women as a transition during the period of child-rearing had now become an end in itself, so that they no longer wanted to work full time. In the German study there was no attempt to obtain a representative sample, so the findings cannot be seen as typical of male part-timers. Nevertheless, Strümpel et al. (1988) identified households with unconventional working and childcare arrangements. They found that these male part-timers tended to be in their mid-30s, well qualified and employed in the public sector. Their main motivation for reduced working time was to take a more active and equal role in the upbringing of their children. They usually lived in a household with a well-qualified woman who had a secure income from full-time work in the public sector. However, men working part time are more commonly found among either young students or older semiretired males. Nevertheless, although the study by Strümpel et al. (1988) described exceptional cases of male part-timers, it is interesting not only because it was unique in focussing on male part-timers but also because it identified the importance of income *and* attitudes that are associated with flexible working time arrangements. As qualitative studies, both Watson and Fothergill (1993) and Strümpel et al. (1988) can provide significant information about transitions over a person's life time and about the importance of family values, although the limited sample size of such studies prevents them from being statistically representative. The use of focus groups, as in the UK study, complicates the effort to trace the effects of individual household circumstances to working time preferences, whereas individual interviews with both partners in the household, as in the German study, compensate for this deficiency. It is, therefore, important that such qualitative data be structured so as to link up with known quantitative evidence.

In cross-national case studies on firms, researchers have also sought to examine these questions by interviewing samples of full- and part-time employees about their work preferences and family situation (Gregory, 1987; O'Reilly, 1994a and 1994c). Among other things, this research has shown that women's preference for part-time work is significantly higher in Britain than in France. Explanations for such differences focus on the provision of childcare, which is more extensive in France than in the United Kingdom, thus allowing women in France greater opportunity to work on a full-time basis. Such research also suggests that higher levels of education in France increase women's motivation for full-time labour market participation. Thus, a number of policies interact and shape the environment in which women's preferences and women's willingness to accept part-time employment are formed.

A more quantitative cross-national approach has been taken by Alwin, Braun and Scott (1992), whose study drew on data from the 1988 International Social Survey Program (ISSP). Focussing on West Germany, the United Kingdom and the United States, they sought to examine the attitudes of men and women towards female labour force participation. The researchers were able to identify cross-national similarities, such as greater support among women than among men for female employment. They were able to document significant differences in the acceptablility of women working when there were preschool children in the family. Support for working women who have preschool children was greater in the United States than in West Germany. They argued that this was related not only to the levels of childcare, previous employment experience and age but also to the different normative patterns and institutional structures that regulate behaviour associated with the suitability of care for and nurture of young children in each country. Though such research is of interest in identifying cross-national differences, closer links need to be made between the nature of institutional arrangements and their effect on men and women's labour force participation within a given country.

Thus, employee-focussed researchers have examined attitudes and preferences and the link between policy regimes and their effect on these preferences. However, one problem in studying preferences in isolation is the need to link them to conditions in the household and the workplace and to individual's knowledge of how the tax and social security regimes actually impinge on them.

3.1.3   Employer Surveys and Company Case Studies

Attempts to overcome some of the weaknesses in aggregate and individual approaches have been made in evaluation research conducted at the firm level. Such studies have been based largely on employer surveys or company case studies (Atkinson and Meager, 1986; Blanchflower and Corry, 1986; Delsen, 1995; Gregory, 1987; Gregory and O'Reilly, in press; Hunter and MacInnes, 1992; Hunter, McGregor, MacInnes and Sproull, 1993; OECD, 1994b; O'Reilly, 1994a). The purpose has been to identify the type of flexibility that part-time contracts provide employers in the effort to facilitate work force adjustment. Researchers using quantitative approaches attempt to find the main reasons why employers are willing or unwilling to use this type of employment. In qualitative case-study research, by contrast, more attention is given to the process and dynamics of employment relations within firms, with the aim of understanding how changes in practices come about.

Such research has shown that the extent to which part-time work is located in low-skill jobs can depend on the sector (Gregory and O'Reilly, in press). Employers have a variety of reasons for using such labour contracts. In some circumstances they are a way of meeting particular workload demands (Atkinson and Meager, 1986). In others, as with career break schemes, they are a way of retaining skilled labour. In this way employers offer preferential part-time contracts to ensure that female staff will return to the company after a period of absence (usually associated with the period of family formation). In some countries such schemes are company specific, whereas in other countries they are more generally available. Such firm-level policies usually increase the overall level of part-time work (O'Reilly, 1994c).

New forms of technology can be used to complement existing labour force patterns or facilitate the implementation of new work schedules. However, technology *per se* does not determine the way labour is used. Instead, new technology is often integrated into existing working arrangements (Gregory and O'Reilly, in press). Constraints on the wider use of part-time employment can also be related to the attitudes towards it among managers and full-time employees (Delsen, 1995, p. 172; OECD, 1994a). O'Reilly (1994a), for instance, has shown that managers in France were more reluctant to use part-timers and that demand for this type of employment was less than in the United Kingdom.

The forms of labour adjustment that firms decide to develop—longer opening hours or quality of service provision, for example—can be related to changing business needs and forms of competition. The decision to compete on either quality or cost can have a significant effect on labour-use strategies. Reduced labour costs are an important consideration in the use of part-timers. In some countries firms can pay lower hourly wages, make lower national insurance contributions and provide fewer fringe benefits to part-timers. On the basis of a multivariate regression analysis of a managerial interview survey in eight European countries, Delsen (1995, p. 173) has argued that firms in Germany, Ireland and the United Kingdom were more likely than firms in other countries to cite hourly cost advantages in using part-timers. In Belgium, Denmark and the Netherlands firms were more likely to cite improved productivity through the use of part-timers. These differences suggest that regulatory thresholds on social contributions and employment protection play a significant role in encouraging the use and forms of part-time work. The extent to which part-time work is either marginalized and disadvantaged or integrated is clearly affected by the regulatory framework in which it develops. Appelbaum (1992) stated that 'improving parity between full-time permanent workers and those employed on a part-time or contingent basis reduces managerial incentives to sacrifice long-term productivity gains and reductions in unit labor costs in order to reap immediate but ephemeral reductions in payroll costs' (pp. 13–14). Fagan et al. (1995) have shown that part-timers in the Netherlands have better terms and conditions of employment than part-timers in the United Kingdom, although both countries have high levels of part-time work. This finding suggests that regulation of part-time work does not necessarily imply a reduction in the quantity of part-timers but can seriously affect the quality of part-time jobs.

Such studies can differentiate between the way part-time work is used in different firms and sectors, thereby enabling one to disaggregate trends identifiable from national data and specify the motivations and constraints that employers face when resorting to this form of employment. In this way policy-makers can learn about the differentiated effects of labour market policies related to forms of employment protection, tax and social security. Such data can also help policy-makers assess the effectiveness of active labour market measures that are already in force. However, some research of this type often tends to focus only on demand-side factors. Successful research conducted at this level needs to show the interaction between aggregate trends and the specificity of sectors, between employee preferences and a firm's needs as well as the effects of labour market regulation both on firms and employers.

As seen from the selection of empirical studies discussed in this section, the evaluation of part-time work as a form of labour market adjustment has identified a diverse range of policies and policy combinations that affect the optimal functioning of labour markets. These results highlight the complexity of coordinating effective policy intended to optimize aggregate labour market effects on job creation, employee flexibility for men and women over the life cycle and increases in firm-level efficiency and productivity.

4   POLICY INSTRUMENTS TO IMPROVE THE FUNCTIONING OF LABOUR MARKETS

As noted throughout this chapter, there is considerable controversy over the effectiveness of active financial policies or subsidies to firms or employees to encourage the use of part-time work. Where these policies have been linked to rather passive measures entailing a structural change in tax and social insurance systems, they appear to have had more effect than active measures. However, while not wanting to make part-time work prohibitively expensive for employers, governments need to ensure that employees are not financially penalized in the long term by accepting part-time work. A more concerted use of passive labour market measures would be required, although it would also imply the need to reform the system of employment protection so as to discourage employers from seeking marginal forms of part-time work. Tilly (1992, pp. 38–9) has maintained that policy goals could be achieved if part-timers received equal treatment in the areas of unemployment insurance, taxation and pro-rata access to benefits such as pension and health insurance. For the US case he has advocated the removal of social security caps where part-timers are, in effect, taxed at a higher rate than full-timers who exceed the earning caps. In the same context, he has favoured facilitating the portability of pensions and broadening access to universal health insurance coverage. Improving part-time jobs would involve boosting the minimum wage and indexing it to inflation. Part-time jobs would thereby become more attractive than dependency on social welfare or withdrawal from gainful employment, according to duRivage (1992, p. 91). By making a low-wage, low-productivity strategy less attractive, such an approach would also encourage employers to create more productive and skilled jobs. It could also be of particular benefit to the vast numbers of low-paid part-timers. By encouraging the provision of part-time work throughout company hierarchies, it would release better skilled workers, possibly including men, who wanted to take up part-time work.

Further, it is important for trade unions to increase their involvement in promoting and protecting the rights of part-time workers. Tilly (1992, p. 40) has added that the higher levels of unionization among part-timers in Canada explain why wage differentials between full- and part-timers are lower there than in the United States. This interpretation would appear to be supported by evidence from Sweden, where superior part-time jobs are also associated with higher levels of unionization among part-timers (Sundström, 1991). In terms of active policy measures, a broadened systematic and universal right to part-time entry and exit options, sabbaticals, parental leave and childcare could decisively improve the use and conditions of part-time employment in general.

5   FUTURE EVALUATION OF PART-TIME WORK

One of the results to emerge from evaluations of part-time work is that it covers a diverse range of developments. Despite the voluminous quantitative and qualitative research that already exists on the goals, forms, distribution, growth, use, attitudes and preferences for part-time work, critical gaps remain in the data and research themes. The sheer heterogeneity of part-time work complicates, for example, the examination of optimal goals. Clearly, certain types of part-time work are to be encouraged, whereas other types can be seen as a deterioration of working conditions. Referring to the United States, duRivage (1992) has pointed out that contingent work is varied and often hidden from statistical view, making it difficult to evaluate the extent to which new working patterns are a result of workers' demands or whether they 'belie deeper structural problems' (p. 120). In order to assess this viewpoint, one needs to break down the concept and category of part-time work into its constituent forms of employment. With increasing interest in cross-national comparisons, in particular within the European Union, the comparability of international data needs to be improved.

Further, there is a significant need for macrolevel studies of developments in the labour market to be integrated with microlevel studies within firms and households. Delsen (1995) has called for 'case studies of selected enterprises in an international comparative context—stressing the financial, technological and organizational context within which employment relations and occupational structures have evolved' (p. 274). If brought to bear on the use of part-time work as a form of labour adjustment, such studies could illuminate features that cannot be detected through macroanalysis. He has also recommended the use of longitudinal surveys of firms, such as the German firms panel survey, which could allow an examination of changing work patterns and tools applied to achieve work force adjustment. 'More research is required on the interaction and effect of economic institutions on economic performance' (Delsen, 1995, p. 275). Such research will need to be linked to the cost-effectiveness of labour market measures. Further, the choice to work part time is closely linked to household structures and how they change over time. Household panel data to be provided on a European level should provide a rich source of data to examine such relationships for the future.

Added to these requirements is the need to integrate developments in the public sphere of production with research on the domestic sphere of reproduction (Rubery, 1993). Such research would be extremely innovative given the tendency to analyse these two spheres independently. Such an approach would allow one to understand how working hours are linked to household constraints and incomes. It would also integrate the analysis of the effectiveness of passive and active labour market measures in relation to the effects of wage determination and to the impact of the social security system on the incentive to search for gainful employment.

In the future a number of facets need to be examined. For example, how can part-time work be used to facilitate work force adjustments? In seeking answers to that question, researchers will need to focus on many aspects, namely, the extension of job security for part-timers and other precarious forms of employment, the individualization of social security and the promotion of secure part-time jobs. The encouragement of job-sharing and part-time parental leave requires organizational support for firms. Further, reforms to develop separate income tax to replace joint taxation, abolition of thresholds in contributions and a high progressive tax rate together with the abolition of ceilings on social security contributions and flat-rate contributions need to be introduced. Added to these policies, gradual retirement schemes, a right to part-time employment, an agreement on target figures, quotas and feasibility studies would further stimulate the use of part-time employment in general. Clearly, the future of evaluation research on part-time employment will be a key issue in the forthcoming years for both firms, households and policy-makers at the national and international level.

REFERENCES

Alwin, D., M. Braun and J. Scott (1992), 'The Separation of Work and the Family: Attitudes towards Women's Labour-force Participation in Germany, Great Britain and the United States', *European Sociological Review*, 8 (1), 13–37.

Appelbaum, E. (1992), 'Structural Change and the Growth of Part-time and Temporary Employment', in V. duRivage (ed.), *New Policies for the Part-time and Contingent Workforce*, New York: Sharpe, pp. 1–14.

Atkinson, J. and N. Meager (1986), *Changing Working Patterns: How Companies Achieve Flexibility to Meet New Needs*, London: NEDO.

Bäcker, G., C. Schäfer, H. Seifert and B. Scholz-Willig (1994), *Kürzer Arbeiten— mehr Beschäftigung? Vorschläge zur Verkürzung der Arbeitszeit in Ostdeutschland*, Kleinmachnow, Germany, Landesagentur für Struktur und Arbeit GmbH Brandenburg (LASA).

Beechey, V. and T. Perkins (1987), *A Matter of Hours: Women, Part-time Work and Labour Markets*, Cambridge: Polity.

Blanchflower, D. and B. Corry (1986), *Part-time Employment in Great Britain: An Analysis Using Establishment Data*, Department of Employment, Research paper no. 57, London: HMSO.

Büchtemann, C. and S. Quack (1989), *'Bridges' or 'Traps': Non-standard Forms of Employment in the Federal Republic of Germany. The Case of Part-time and Temporary Work*, WZB discussion paper FS I 89–6, Wissenschaftszentrum Berlin für Sozialforschung.

Dale, A. and J. Glover (1989, June), 'Women and Work in Europe: The Potential and Pitfalls of Using Published Statistics', *Employment Gazette*, 99–107.

de Neubourg, C. (1991), 'Where Have All the Hours Gone? Working-time Reduction Policies in the Netherlands', in K. Hinrichs, W. Roche and C. Sirianni (eds), *Working Time in Transition: The Political Economy of Working Hours in Industrial Relations*, Philadelphia: Temple University Press, pp. 126–58.

Delsen, L. (1993), 'Part-time Employment and the Utilisation of Labour Resources', *Labour*, 7 (3), 73–91.

Delsen, L. (1995), *A Typical Employment: An International Perspective, Causes, Consequences and Policy*, Groningen, The Netherlands: Woltersgroep Groningen.

Dex, S., P. Walters and D. Alden (1993), *French and British Mothers at Work*, Basingstoke: Macmillan.

duRivage, V. (1992), *New Policies for the Part-time and Contingent Workforce*, New York: Sharpe.

European Commission (1994a), *Growth, Competitiveness, Employment: The Challenges and Ways Forward into the 21st Century*, White Paper, Luxembourg: Office for Official Publications of the European Communities.

European Commission (1994b), *Leave Arrangements for Workers with Children: A Review of Leave Arrangements in the Member States of the European Union and Austria, Finland, Norway and Sweden*, European Commission Network on Childcare and Other Measures to Reconcile Employment and Family Responsibilities, V/773/94–EN, Luxembourg: Office for Official Publications of the European Communities.

Euzéby, A. (1988), 'Social Security and Part-time Work', *International Labour Review*, 5, 545–57.

Fagan, C., J. Platenga and J. Rubery (1995), *Does Part-time Work Promote Sex Equality? A Comparative Analysis of the Netherlands and the UK*, WZB discussion paper FS I 95–203, Wissenschaftszentrum Berlin für Sozialforschung.

Fines, B., T. Morrissey, W. K. Roche, B. J. Whelan and J. Williams (1994), *Worksharing in Ireland*, Dublin: ESRI (Economic and Social Research Council of Ireland).

'Government Launches Part-time Work Initiative' (1994), *European Industrial Relations Review*, 247, 21–2.

Gregory, A. (1987), 'Le Travail à temps partiel en France et en Grande-Bretagne: temps imposé ou temps choisi?', *Revue Française des Affaires Sociales*, 3, 27–45.

Gregory, A. and J. O'Reilly (in press), 'Checking out and Cashing up: The Prospects and Paradoxes of Regulating Part-time Work in Europe', in R. Crompton, D. Gallie and K. Purcell (eds), *Changing Forms of Employment: Organisations, Skills and Gender*, London/New York: Routledge, pp. 207–34.

Hegner, F. (1993), *Teilzeit-Offensive: Weniger Arbeitslose durch Teilzeitarbeit*, LASA Study no. 12, Kleinmachnow: Landesagentur für Struktur und Arbeit GmbH Brandenburg (LASA).

Hinrichs, K., W. Roche and C. Sirianni (1991), *Working Time in Transition: The Political Economy of Working Hours in Industrial Relations*, Philadelphia: Temple University Press.

Holst, E. and J. Schupp (1994), 'Ist Teilzeitarbeit der richtige Weg? Arbeitszeitpräferenzen in West- und Ostdeutschland', Deutsches Institut für Wirtschaftsforschung, *Wochenbericht*, 35, 618–26.

Hunter, L. and J. MacInnes (1992, June), 'Employers and Labour Flexibility: The Evidence from Case Studies', *Employment Gazette*, 307–15.

Hunter, L., I. McGregor, J. MacInnes and A. Sproull (1993), 'The Flexible Firm: Strategy and Segmentation', *British Journal of Industrial Relations*, 31 (3), 383–407.

ILO (1989), *Conditions of Work Digest: Part-time Work*, 8 (1), Geneva: ILO.

Jallade, J.-P. (1984), *Towards a Policy for Part-time Employment*, Maastricht: European Centre for Work and Society.

Maier, F. (1991), *The Regulation of Part-time Work: A Comparative Study of Six EC-Countries*, WZB discussion paper FS I 91–9, Wissenschaftszentrum Berlin für Sozialforschung.

Maier, F. (1994), 'Institutional Regimes of Part-time Working', in G. Schmid (ed.), *Labor Market Institutions in Europe*, New York: Sharpe, pp. 151–82.

Marimbert, J. (1992), *Situation et perspectives du travail à temps partiel*, Paris: Rapport au Ministre du Travail, de l'Emploi et de la Formation Professionnelle.

McKinsey (1994), *Teilen und Gewinnen: Das Potential der flexiblen Arbeitszeitverkürzung*, Munich: McKinsey.

Meager, N. (1988, July), 'Job-sharing and Job-splitting: Employer Attitudes', *Employment Gazette*, 383–8.

MISEP (Mutual Information System Employment Policy), *Employment Observatory*, Policies, no. 42 (1993a), Wissenschaftszentrum Berlin für Sozialforschung.

MISEP, *Employment Observatory*, Policies, no. 43 (1993b), Wissenschaftszentrum Berlin für Sozialforschung.

MISEP, *Employment Observatory*, Policies, no. 44 (1993c), Wissenschaftszentrum Berlin für Sozialforschung.

MISEP, *Employment Observatory*, Policies, no. 46 (1994a), Wissenschaftszentrum Berlin für Sozialforschung.

MISEP, *Employment Observatory*, Policies, no. 47 (1994b), Wissenschaftszentrum Berlin für Sozialforschung.

MISEP, *Employment Observatory*, Policies, no. 48 (1994c), Wissenschaftszentrum Berlin für Sozialforschung.

MISEP, *Employment Observatory*, Policies, no. 49 (1995), Wissenschaftszentrum Berlin für Sozialforschung.

'New Law on Employment and Part-time Work' (1993), *European Industrial Relations Review*, 230, 26–8.

O'Reilly, J. (1994a), *Banking on Flexibility*, Aldershot: Avebury.

O'Reilly, J. (1994b), *Part-time Work and Employment Regulation: A Comparison of Britain and France in the Context of Europe*, WZB discussion paper FS I 209, Wissenschaftszentrum Berlin für Sozialforschung.

O'Reilly, J. (1994c), 'What Kind of Flexibility Do Women Offer? Comparing the Use of, and Attitudes to, Part-time Work in Britain and France', *Gender, Work and Organisation*, 1 (3), 138–49.

OECD (1994a), *Employment Outlook*, Paris: OECD.

OECD (1994b), *The OECD Jobs Study: Evidence and Explanation, Part II: The Adjustment Potential of the Labour Market*, Paris: OECD.

OECD (1994c), *Women and Structural Change: New Perspectives*, Paris: OECD.

Pfau-Effinger, B. (1993), 'Modernisation, Culture and Part-time Employment: The Example of Finland and West Germany', *Work, Employment and Society*, 7 (3), 383–410.

Pinheiro, J. (1995, May), 'Mesure du sous-emploi visible', paper presented at the Employment Observatory Annual Conference (Directorate General V and Eurostat), Lisbon.

Quack, S. (1992), *Dynamik der Teilzeitarbeit: Implikationen für die soziale Sicherung von Frauen*, Berlin: edition sigma.

Rosenberg, S. (1989), 'From Segmentation to Flexibility', *Labour and Society*, 14 (4), 1–24.

Rubery, J. (1993, July), 'The UK Production Regime in Comparative Perspective', paper presented at the International Conference on Production Regimes in an Integrating Europe, Wissenschaftszentrum Berlin für Sozialforschung.

Rubery, J., C. Fagan and M. Smith (1995, April), *Bulletin on Women and Employment in the EU*, for European Commission Directorate General V Manchester: University of Manchester Institute of Science and Technology (UMIST).

Schettkat, R. (1989), 'The Impact of Taxes on Female Labour Supply', *International Review of Applied Economics*, 3 (1), 1–24.

Schmid, G. (1994) (ed.), *Labor Market Institutions in Europe: A Socioeconomic Evaluation of Performance*, New York: Sharpe.

Schmid, G. (1994a), 'Equality and Efficiency in the Labour Market: Toward a Socioeconomic Theory of Cooperation', in G. Schmid (ed.) (1994), *Labour Market Institutions in Europe*, New York: Sharpe.

Schmid, G. (1994b), *Übergänge in die Vollbeschäftigung. Formen und Finanzierung einer zukunftsgerechten Arbeitsmarktpolitik*, WZB discussion paper FS I 93–208.

Schömann, K. (1995), *Active Labour Market Policy in the European Union*, WZB discussion paper FS I 95–201, Wissenschaftszentrum Berlin für Sozialforschung.

Seifert, H. (1994), 'Kürzer oder länger arbeiten?', *Aus Politik und Zeitgeschichte*, (Supplement to *Das Parlament*), B12–13, 24–34.

Statistisches Bundesamt mit Metzler-Poschel (eds) (1995, June), 'Die Arbeitskräfteerhebung der Europäischen Union', *Wirtschaft und Statistik*, 518–29.

Strümpel, B., W. Prenzel, J. Scholz and A. Hoff (1988), *Teilzeitarbeitende Männer und Hausmänner: Motive und Konsequenzen einer eingeschränkten Erwerbstätigkeit von Männern*, Berlin: edition sigma.

Sundström, M. (1991), 'Part-time Work in Sweden: Trends and Equality Effects', *Journal of Economic Issues*, 25 (1), 167–78.

SYSDEM (System of Documentation on Employment) (1995), *Labour Market Flexibility: Experiences from the 12 Member States*, draft report, European Commission, DG V, Brussels.

Tilly, C. (1992), 'Short Hours, Short Shift: The Causes and Consequences of Part-time Employment', in V. duRivage, *New Policies for the Part-time and Contingent Workforce*, New York: Sharpe, pp. 15–44.

Tilly, L. and J. Scott (1987), *Les femmes, le travail et la famille*, Marseilles: Editions Rivages.

Walwei, U. and H. Werner (1995), 'Mehr Teilzeitarbeit als Mittel gegen die Arbeitslosigkeit? Ein internationaler Vergleich der Teilzeitbeschäftigung und deren Einfluß auf den Arbeitsmarkt', Institut für Arbeits- und Berufsforschung (IAB) der Bundesanstalt für Arbeit, Nuremberg. (Unpublished manuscript)

Watson, G. and B. Fothergill (1993, May), 'Part-time Employment and Attitudes to Part-time Work', *Employment Gazette*, 213–20.

20. Employment Stabilization through Short-time Work

Hugh Mosley and Thomas Kruppe

Short-time work enables management to adjust labour inputs and costs quickly to changed business conditions by reducing working time for the existing work force rather than resorting to redundancies. It is a widespread internal mode of work force adjustment in coping with cyclical declines in labour demand. Short-time work also plays an important role in structural change by slowing the pace of redundancies, thereby facilitating the use of natural attrition and other 'soft' modes of adjustment.

Although enterprises may elect to pursue such a strategy even in the absence of a programme, public short-time work schemes provide a strong additional incentive for work-sharing in adjustment situations. Most European countries have explicit schemes to promote temporary reductions in working time as an alternative to layoffs. Normally, employees on short-time receive a wage-replacement benefit for hours not worked, usually paid through the unemployment insurance system. Within the European Union, Austria, Belgium, France, Germany, Italy, Portugal and Spain have special labour market programmes to promote temporary reductions in working time as an alternative to dismissals. In other countries more limited assistance is available in the form of compensation during temporary layoffs or for partial unemployment under unemployment insurance (Denmark, Ireland, Luxembourg, the Netherlands, Sweden and the United Kingdom). Canada adopted a work-sharing programme as an alternative to layoffs in the late 1970s, as have a number of US states (e.g. California).

1 GOALS OF SHORT-TIME WORK AND RATIONALE FOR PUBLIC INTERVENTION[1]

Like most public programmes, short-time work programmes have multiple targets or goals. These can be summarized in the form of three ideal-typical situations in which short-time work is used:

---

1 We thank Christoph Büchtemann for his helpful comments on an earlier draft of this chapter and Silke Bothfeld, Roberto Goldin, Stefan Speckesser and Robyn Wiesener for their assistance.

1. A short-term and temporary decline in output, especially for cyclical reasons. The goal of short-time work in this case is to stabilize employment temporarily and to assist the enterprise in retaining human capital.
2. A comparatively long, but temporary, decline in demand for labour. The same goals are applicable here, but with a longer time horizon. Upon completion of the restructuring, the work force of the rejuvenated enterprise is able to resume normal working time.
3. As an accompanying measure short-time work can be used to ameliorate the social consequences of mass redundancies. This application may involve either the termination of part of the work force in an enterprise undergoing restructuring or prolongation of the adjustment process in connection with the closure of an establishment. For the individual, 'structural' short-time work has merely a 'parachute function'—that of slowing the fall into unemployment. From a social perspective, it is used as a 'shock absorber' to buffer social tensions.

In each of these situations short-time work programmes are intended not only to stabilize employment but also to provide assistance to firms in economic difficulty. Moreover, structural short-time work does not even stabilize employment, it merely delays permanent layoffs. In its extreme form, usually at zero working hours, this use of short-time work is simply a 'soft' mode of external mobility in which employees remain for an extended period pro forma employees (Mosley and Kruppe, 1995). Because this chapter is primarily concerned with public policies to promote employment stabilization, we will treat this latter type of short-time work only peripherally.

Short-time work programmes represent an attempt to use public policy to intervene in the personnel strategies of firms by offering incentives for short-time work instead of layoffs in adjustment situations. Before turning to an examination of short-time work programmes and their evaluation, we discuss the rationale for this form of public intervention.

The classical rationale for short-time work, even in the absence of a public scheme, is based on the inherent advantages to the firm of preserving the employment relationship with its experienced workers even during an economic downturn. Short-time work enables the enterprise to avoid the costs of recruiting and training replacements in the following upswing and to avoid dismissal costs, including negative effects on employee morale. Moreover, short-time may enable the firm to reduce labour inputs more quickly in a downturn and increase production more quickly during the following upswing than would be possible with cumbersome redundancy procedures and external recruitment. For these reasons enterprises utilize short-time work even in the absence of a public programme. Huberman and Lacroix (1995) document the widespread use of this form of work-sharing in the

nineteenth and early twentieth centuries, even prior to the introduction of
public benefit schemes.

By regulating and subsidizing short-time work, public labour market
policy encourages the spread of short-time work in adjustment situations. The
overriding interest of public policy in promoting the use of short-time work
appears to be to substitute this form of work-sharing for open unemployment.
This policy preference for short-time work over unemployment can be ration-
alized in terms of the high external costs of unemployment (unemployment
benefits, individual and community impacts) that are not ordinarily reflected
in employers' decisions ('market failure'). Moreover, the direct costs to the
state or labour market authority of subsidizing short-time work are low in any
case because experienced workers would otherwise be entitled to unemployment compensation. Finally, in the absence of a short-time work programme,
unemployment insurance systems in effect subsidize the layoff option to the
detriment of work-sharing; the short-time work option in effect balances the
playing field by providing the same subsidy for both options.[2]

In more densely regulated European labour markets an important function
of short-time work programmes is to provide a flexibility option for employers. Typically, the existence of more stringent employment protection regulations makes the use of redundancies (i.e. layoffs) too expensive and too slow as
an instrument for short-term labour force adjustment. By restricting external
flexibility on the one hand and by providing a short-time work option on the
other, public policy promotes retention of employees by use of internal forms
of flexibility.[3]

Although there is in principle a persuasive case for a short-time work
option or even a subsidy (available evidence is discussed below), short-time
work programmes may in practice exhibit policy failure for a number of reasons having to do with the design features of the programme and their interaction with the national institutional framework. These implementation problems (e.g. low uptake, deadweight, allocative distortions), which occur in any
labour market programme, are discussed in sections 5–7, below.

2   SHORT-TIME WORK SCHEMES

There is considerable institutional variety in short-time work programmes,
a fact that has a significant impact on the performance of these schemes.

---

2 In fact, the relative costs of unemployment benefits for employers and employees differ from
country to country, and this is a way of fine-tuning schemes for policy purposes (see section 2,
below).

3 The short-time work option may reduce the reluctance to engage in new hires when economic
conditions are uncertain.

Table 20.1 summarizes basic features of short-time work programmes in four of the five major European labour markets: France, Germany, Italy and Spain (there is no short-time work programme in the United Kingdom). All four national short-time work programmes are applicable in principle to structural as well as temporary adjustment situations, although this development is very recent and weakest in France.

There are, however, major differences with regard to the level and duration of benefits provided and the share of costs borne by employers. Both the level and duration of short-time benefits are greatest in Italy, where workers on short-time receive 80 per cent of their previous gross earnings and where, in the case of structural benefits (CIG-S), short-time compensation may last up to four years.[4] Employees on short-time in Spain receive a degressive benefit for a maximum of two years. Employees receive 70 per cent of their previous earnings for the first 180 days and 60 per cent thereafter.[5] In Germany benefits are only slightly lower: 67 per cent (60 per cent for employees without children) of previous net earnings, normally for a maximum of two years. In France benefit payments are only 50 per cent of previous earnings, and the maximum duration is 700 hours (about nine months at 50 per cent of normal working time). Even under the new programme 'Temps réduit indemnisé de longue durée' (TRILD) the maximum duration is relatively short.

In situations of prolonged short-time work, especially when working hours are low, the relative attractiveness of unemployment benefits is an important consideration. In France unemployment benefits are considerably more generous (70 per cent) than short-time compensation, whereas in Italy regular unemployment benefits are extremely low (30 per cent), and special benefits for those who become unemployed because of collective redundancies were lower until 1991 and are still less attractive than short-time benefits (shorter duration, loss of employment status). Thus, the French worker is likely to prefer unemployment to extended structural short-time work, whereas Italian workers have a strong incentive to prefer short-time work. In Germany and Spain the wage-replacement rates are the same for short-time and unemployment benefits. An additional incentive for employees in France, Germany and Italy is that short-time work does not reduce their subsequent entitlement to unemployment benefits, whereas the duration of benefits is reduced in Spain.

From the point of view of employers' labour costs, the Italian programme is the most generous. Employers are, as a rule, required to bear only 8 per cent of

---

4 Such compensation is subject to a monthly ceiling currently equivalent to about two-thirds of average earnings in industry. Thus, even workers with average earnings may not receive an 80 per cent wage replacement rate if they are working zero hours.

5 Subject to a monthly ceiling equal to 220 per cent of national minimum wage.

Table 20.1 Short-time Schemes in France, Germany, Italy and Spain

Country	France		Germany	
	Regular programme	Structural intervention	Regular programme	Structural intervention
Programme name	Chômage partiel (Partial unemployment)	Temps réduit indemnisé de longue durée (TRILD) (Long-term short-time compensation)	Kurzarbeitergeld (Short-time compensation)	
Policy goals	To diminish the repercussions of temporary reductions in a company's activity on wage and salaries and to prevent redundancies	To assist firms undergoing prolonged restructuring	Maintaining employment in cases of temporary reductions in working time, avoiding dismissals	Special regulations allow use of short-time to avoid mass redundancies in industries undergoing structural change
Special conditions		None	The reduction of working time must be at least 10% of the normal working time and affect at least one-third of all employees with a duration of at least 4 weeks	
Employees	All employees[1]		All employees subject to unemployment insurance contributions[2]	
Benefits	50% of previous gross hourly wages. Moreover, there is a flat-rate minimum hourly benefit		Same as unemployment benefit: 67% (without child, 60%)	
Duration of benefits	700 hours a year	1200 hours over period of 12 to 18 months (TRILD)	6 (24) months[3]	24 months
Financing	State and employers using programme. Employer receives uniform payment from state for each hour and employee on short-time (1994 = FF 22). Employer pays difference between this amount and short-time benefit. Special state subsidies for up to 100% of employers' costs to avoid dismissals for economic reasons (CP-F.N.E.)	For hours in excess of 700, employer is reimbursed FF 25 per hour, FF 10 of which is now paid from the unemployment insurance funds (UNEDIC)	Same as unemployment insurance. Higher wage-replacement rates based on collective agreement are financed by the employer	
Social security	Employer pays no social security contribution for short-time		Employer pays employer's and employee's normal contribution for short-time (ca. 31% of gross earnings)	

Notes
1 Some part-time employees are excluded by law if their weekly earnings are less than 18 times the minimum hourly wage (SMIC). However, this provision appears to be unimportant in practice.
2 Only employees below threshold for unemployment insurance (<15 hours per week or < DM 580 per month earnings) and students are not covered.
3 Temporary extension to 24 months during the current recession. Benefits renewable after 3 months of normal working time for another period of 6 months.

Country	Italy		Spain	
	Regular programme	Structural intervention	Regular programme	Structural intervention
Programme name	Cassa Integrazione Guadagni Interventi Ordinari (Wage Compensation Fund; CIG-O)	Cassa Integrazione Guadagni Interventi Straordinari (Extraordinary intervention; CIG-S)		El expediente de regulación de empleo: suspensión temporal y disempleo parcial) (Application for employment regulation: temporary suspension and short-time work; ERE)
Policy goals	Compensation of earnings in cases of temporary interruption of a company's activity	Compensation of wages during prolonged economic difficulties in firms or sectors undergoing restructuring	Avoiding unemployment in cases of decrease in employment because of economic or technological reasons	
Special conditions	Firms with more than 15 employees (since 1991)[1]	Industrial companies with at least 15 employees and trade firms with at least 200 employees (since 1991)[2]	Working time must be reduced by at least one-third. Minimum of workers affected: 10% (in enterprises with less than 100 employees at least 10 workers)	
Employees	All employees with at least 90 days tenure[3]		All employees eligible for unemployment insurance benefits[4]	
Benefits	80% of gross earnings with a monthly maximum of L 1 248 021[5]		Same as unemployment benefits: 70% of previous earnings for the first 180 days and 60% thereafter[6]	
Duration of benefits	Maximum of 3 consecutive months[7]	a) In cases of restructuring a maximum of 2 years which can be extended twice for a maximum of 4 years; b) In case of crisis intervention maximum of 12 months[8]	Maximum duration of 2 years	
Financing	General contributions and user firms. All employers contribute to Wage Compensation Fund (CIG) administered by the Instituto Nazionale della Previdenza Soziale (INPS). Firms with less than 50 employees contribute 1.9% of wages, and larger firms pay 2.20%.	State, general contributions and user payments. Companies pay 0.6% and employees, 0.3% contributions; enterprises using CIG-S pay 4.50% of wage replacement benefits received by their employees (in firms with less than 50 employees, 3.0%). This user contribution doubles after 2 yrs of benefits. State finances any deficit	Financed through unemployment insurance (contributions of employers (5.2%) and the employees (1.1%))	
Social security	Employer pays no social security contribution for short-time		Employer pays no social security contribution for short-time	

Notes

1 Temporary extension to firms with 5 to 15 employees until end of 1995. – 2 Temporary extension to firms with 50 to 200 employees until end of 1995. – 3 Until 1991 white-collar workers were excluded from the CIG-O. – 4 Until 1993 the qualifying period was 6 months within the last 4 years; currently, one year in the last six. – 5 In 1993. This ceiling is equivalent to ca. 65% of average earnings in Italy. – 6 Unemployment insurance benefits subject to a maximum of 220% of the national minimum wage. Prior to 1993 benefits were 80% in first 6 months, 70% in second half year and 60% in second year. – 7 In exceptional cases benefit period can be extended up to 1 year. Firms which received benefits out of the CIG-fund for 12 months have a new claim after at least 52 days of normal activity. – 8 New intervention only possible after a period lasting two-thirds of the first intervention period and duration limited to 36 months within 5 years.

599

the costs of short-time work in the cyclical programme (CIG-O) and 4.5 per cent in the CIG-S (the latter rate doubles after two years). The employers pay no social security contributions for short-time. By contrast, the German scheme is surprisingly expensive for employers. Recent changes require German employers not only to bear their share of social contributions for short-time but also to pay contributions for employees on short-time. Moreover, collective agreements in many sectors frequently require that employers top up short-time benefits to a level ranging from 70 to 90 per cent of normal wages. Employers' costs are lowest in Spain, where all costs for short-time work are assumed by the unemployment insurance system and where there is no experience rating.[6]

3   FUNCTIONAL EQUIVALENTS

Firms also have a number of other potential alternative personnel strategies for combining flexibility in response to market contingencies with avoidance of excessive turnover costs. The availability and attractiveness of these options varies considerably across countries, depending on the institutional setting.

3.1   Temporary Layoffs

In some countries firms' responses to a decline in labour demand may take the form of temporary layoffs financed through the regular unemployment insurance system. This is particularly likely in countries with a low level of regulation of employment contracts, in which the costs of redundancies to employers are relatively low, but temporary layoffs occur to a certain extent in all employment systems.[7]

In the United States temporary layoffs are the most widespread pattern of short-term adjustment, with short-time work playing almost no role. The American economic literature on short-time work takes as its point of departure the unintended effects of the unemployment insurance system, which is said to favour temporary layoffs (Feldstein, 1978). For example, Burdett and Wright (1989) argue that 'the discontinuous benefit schedule [in the US unemployment

---

6 Supplements based on collective agreements appear to be rare or nonexistent.

7 Feldstein (1978) estimated that approximately 50 per cent of unemployment spells in the United States in the 1970s were temporary layoffs. In Canada in the 1980s, 60 to 80 per cent of layoffs were temporary (Corak, 1995). The corresponding estimate for Denmark was 40 per cent over the 1979–84 period (Jensen and Westergård-Nielson, 1990). Only 1 to 3 per cent of the unemployed were on temporary layoff in Sweden from the mid-1970s to the mid-1980s (Edebalk and Wadensjö, 1995). See also Fischer and Pichelmann (1991) and Mavromaras and Rudolf (1995) on this phenomenon in Austria and Germany.

insurance system] provides an incentive for the use of layoffs rather than work-sharing during economic downturns'.[8]

Partly as a result of this reasoning, short-time work is now available as an option in 20 US states (e.g. in California since 1978). However, these programmes have been little used, and they have had almost no impact on the adjustment behaviour of firms. Kerachsky, Nicholson, Cavin and Hershey (1986) estimated that less than 1 per cent of all employers in the participating states had ever used short-time work and that short-time accounted for less than 1 per cent of all unemployment insurance claims. Even among US employers using it, the number of hours reduced through layoffs was about eight times that reduced through short-time work (Kerachsky et al., 1986). Uptake of short-time work has remained at a low level (Vroman, 1992).

The low utilization of the short-time work programmes in the United States since its introduction clearly suggests that the existence of short-time work options alone is not a sufficient explanation for the US preference for temporary layoffs in comparison with the greater reliance on hours adjustment in Europe. Another important factor is Europe's much higher degree of legal regulation of employment contracts, especially employment protection regulations; temporary layoffs are simply not an option in short-run adjustment in most European countries.[9] Further possible explanations are the higher fixed costs of employment in the United States due to low tax ceilings in the social security system (FitzRoy and Hart, 1985) and the higher costs of employee benefits (Abraham and Houseman, 1993). Programme features also play a role: the wage-replacement rate in the United States is low, the maximum duration of benefits is relatively short, and the unemployment benefit entitlement is reduced by periods on short-time.[10]

---

8 A theoretical discussion leads the authors to conclude that short-time compensation also leads to inefficient hours per worker, or underemployment, unless there is experience rating of employer contributions and equal taxation of benefit income. In general, this literature argues that experience rating and equal taxation of income from benefits are most conducive to efficient levels of employment and hours.

9 An additional reason for low uptake of short-time work in the United States is the extent to which the pattern of reliance on layoffs is embedded in industrial relations practice and the preferences of employers, employees and unions. Only a small fraction of US collective agreements explicitly give employers the option of reducing working time. Collective agreements typically permit employers to reduce working time only temporarily as an initial response to fluctuations in demand. After a period stipulated in collective agreements (generally about four weeks), layoffs based on seniority begin (Medoff, 1979).

10 Forty-two per cent of Californian eligibles did not apply for short-time benefits apparently because they wished to 'save' their unemployment insurance entitlement, which, in the United States, is reduced by short-time (Kerachsky et al., 1986).

3.2   Flexibility in Working Time

Flexibility in working time regimes, especially the amount of variation permitted in individual working time in response to the firms' labour needs, is an important contextual variable in the utilization of short-time work. Short-time (like overtime) is defined in terms of standard contractual weekly working hours in an enterprise or industry. In most European labour markets, however, there is a strong trend towards increasing the flexibility of working time. This trend means not only greater use of weekend and shift work to increase utilization of plant and equipment but also greater flexibility in the definition of standard weekly working time for individuals. In more flexible working time regimes (such as those in much of German industry), contractual weekly working time is no longer a rigid standard that must be adhered to (e.g. 38.5 hours per week) but only an average that must be met over an extended balancing period (e.g. 6–12 months). Thus, enterprises can reach agreements with their work forces to work longer hours during peak periods of demand and shorter hours during slack periods on the condition that the contractual working time is worked on average over the applicable balancing period.

Clearly, such systems will reduce paid overtime and short-time to a certain extent. Whether they will have a major impact on utilization of short-time work programmes is less evident. They will reduce the need for compensated short-time work especially in coping with seasonal and other routine fluctuations in output, which in some countries are a major component in the use of short-time work. However, this type of increased flexibility in individual working time will probably have only a relatively limited impact on short-time work that is resorted to in order to cope with cyclical adjustment, which is still the major component of utilization. The reason is that flexibility over a balancing period requires (a) predictability and (b) fluctuations that fall within the balancing period. Neither of these conditions is met in the case of cyclical fluctuations. Moreover, in many countries threshold conditions governing the use of short-time compensation already preclude compensation for smaller fluctuations in working time: these costs normally have to be borne by the employer. For example, in Germany the reduction in working hours must amount to at least 10 per cent of normal working time and affect one-third of all employees for at least four weeks (see Table 20.1, above).

3.3   Temporary Employment

Firms may also achieve necessary flexibility through segmentation in an internal labour market in which a core labour force enjoys a high degree of employment security while the burden of economic contingencies is borne largely by fixed-term and other flexible forms of employment (e.g. agency temporaries and other contingent workers, subcontracting and so forth). However, fixed-term employment is a relatively small share of total employment in industry in most countries and is most frequently used as an extended probationary period for new hires, who subsequently receive permanent employment contracts (Schömann, Rogowski and Kruppe, 1995). Although the expiration of fixed-term contracts provides some additional room for manoeuvre in adjustment situations, it is not a real alternative to short-time work in quickly reducing the firms' labour costs in response to declines in demand while retaining experienced employees.

There is no systematic empirical evidence available from evaluation studies on the relationship between short-time work and working time flexibility or fixed-term employment. Mosley, Kruppe and Speckesser (1995) examined aggregate data at the sectoral level and found no evidence for a secular decline in the uptake of short-time work in France or Germany despite the increase in fixed-term employment and working time flexibility since the early 1980s. This issue needs to be addressed through the use of detailed industry-level data or firm-level surveys.

4   EVALUATING SHORT-TIME WORK SCHEMES

Short-time work programmes are a long-established instrument of labour market policy in Europe and have been introduced in the United States and Canada since the late 1970s. Nevertheless, there have been few systematic evaluations. Only in Canada and the United States have evaluations with a quasi-experimental design been commissioned by national labour market authorities. Since the US study (Kerachsky et al., 1986) was limited to only three states (short-time work is a state option in the United States),[11] the only full-scale national study is Graves and Dumas' (1993) evaluation of work-sharing in Canada. It was based on a relatively large sample of 620 user firms and a comparison group of 460 nonuser firms together with a linked survey of 2070 individual employees in these two groups of firms. In Europe only the use of short-time in eastern Germany has been researched with comparable intensity. Using data from the German Socioeconomic Panel, Büchel and Pannenberg (1992) and Schwarze, Rendtel and Büchel (1993) applied a quasi-experimental design in analysing the impact of short-time work on individual participants in the eastern German transformation process. Seifert, Ochs, Besselmann and Machalowski (1993) surveyed a large sample of over

---

11 A new evaluation study of short-time work has recently been commissioned by the US Department of Labor.

1000 eastern German enterprises using short-time.[12] However, the results of this research on the exceptional situation in eastern Germany cannot be generalized.

Other studies such as Lefèvre, Béraud and Sidhoum (1994), Tronti (1993) and Linke (1993) have been based largely on expert interviews, selective case studies and analysis of aggregate programme data. A few have been comparative (Abraham and Houseman, 1993; Mosley et al., 1995; Vroman, 1992).[13] Finally, Schenkel (1994) presents one of the few empirical analyses of participating firms identified in programme administrative records, including a survival analysis of the programme's impact.

Not only is there a relative lack of evaluation research, the monitoring data available in some countries is inadequate for assessing programme performance. In France, for example, data are collected at the national level only on authorized days of short-time work, but no programme data are available on actual uptake. In Italy, which has one of the largest short-time work programmes in Europe, no programme data are available on the duration of short-time work, although this has been a controversial issue. In no European country are there even data available on the extent to which short-time work is merely a prelude to permanent layoff rather than a bridge to continued employment.

In the following sections we organize our discussion of short-time work under five broad headings that represent the basic research questions for evaluation of short-time work in the light of programme goals: (a) levels, patterns and trends in programme uptake; (b) labour market impact; (c) impact on individual participants; (d) impact on enterprises; and (e) benefits and costs of short-time work.

5　PROGRAMME UPTAKE: LEVELS, PATTERNS, TRENDS

5.1　Short-time Programme Uptake and Its Determinants

The utilization of short-time work varies widely even among countries having programmes. Uptake is very high in Belgium, Italy and Spain, where it ranges from 6 to 8 per cent of dependent employment in industry in peak years,

---

12　A special panel survey of the labour market in eastern Germany also provides unique data on the labour market experience of participants in short-time work in that part of the country (Völkel, 1992).

13　Abraham and Houseman (1993) deal with short-time work only peripherally in the context of an econometric study of short-term adjustment in Belgium, France and Germany.

whereas short-time in Canada rises to intermediate levels of 2 to 3 per cent, even surpassing that in western Germany in peak years (see Figure 20.1). Short-time work in united Germany is consistently higher than in France, where short-time work never rises above 1 per cent of dependent employment in industry. In 1990–91 the level of use of short-time work in united Germany exceeded even that in Spain and Italy because of the heavy reliance on short-time work as an instrument of structural adjustment in the transformation of the eastern German economy. The introduction of a short-time work option in Canada has been very successful; the level of programme uptake, which has

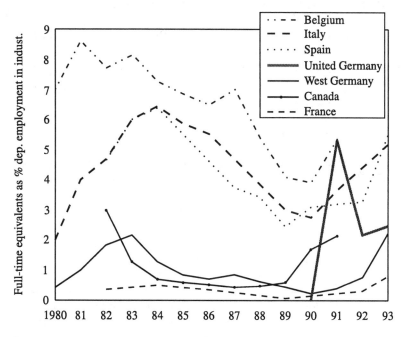

Source
Estimated on the basis of programme data and working-time data; from *Flexible Adjustment through Short-time Work: A Comparison of France, Germany, Italy, and Spain* by H. Mosley, T. Kruppe and S. Speckesser, 1995, WZB discussion paper FS I 95–206, Wissenschaftszentrum Berlin für Sozialforschung.

Figure 20.1   Short-time Work Utilization in Belgium, Canada, France, Germany, Italy and Spain, 1980–1993

reached approximately 200 000 participants in peak years, is comparable to that in many European countries.[14]

The principal determinants of utilization of short-time work in a given national setting can be summarized in a simple model (see Figure 20.2). They are (a) the type and magnitude of changes in the economic environment that give rise to the adjustment situation, (b) the characteristics of short-time work programmes themselves, (c) the labour market's regulatory framework, (d) the industrial relations environment and (e) firm characteristics. As the model suggests, the incentives for employers and employees to utilize short-time work are heavily dependent not only on economic conditions but on the characteristics of national short-time work schemes, the institutional context and the availability of functional equivalents.

The most important determinant of short-time working is fluctuations in economic output. In all countries, short-time work is also highly cyclical and highly seasonal (Vroman, 1992; Mosley et al., 1995). There are, nevertheless, marked cross-national differences in the level of utilization of short-time over the business cycle. They are strongly related to differences in national institutional frameworks. Economic factors alone cannot explain consistent national differences in uptake.

5.2   Incentives for Utilization of Short-time Work

The impact of the above elements of the national institutional framework can be interpreted as an incentive structure for employers to utilize (or not to utilize) short-time work. This incentive structure for employers can be summarized under five headings: (a) termination costs, (b) (re)hiring costs, (c) employee relations costs, (d) short-time subsidy and (e) availability of other flexibility options.

Whereas for employers short-time work is primarily important as a form of labour force flexibility, especially in the face of temporary declines in labour demand, for employees it is primarily an instrument for enhancing job security, albeit with a loss of income. The most fundamental effect of short-time work for employees as a group is that—for a given reduction in the volume of labour inputs—the burden of adjustment is shifted from a narrower to a wider group. For example, instead of making 10 per cent of the workers in a firm's work force redundant, the working time of all workers is reduced by 10 per cent. Since a strategy of work-sharing affects the interests of individual workers differently, it presupposes a significant degree of group solidarity.

Of the four major short-time work schemes we have examined in detail, the

---

14   A comparison of the US and Canadian experience with short-time work would be useful in clarifying the reasons for low uptake in the United States.

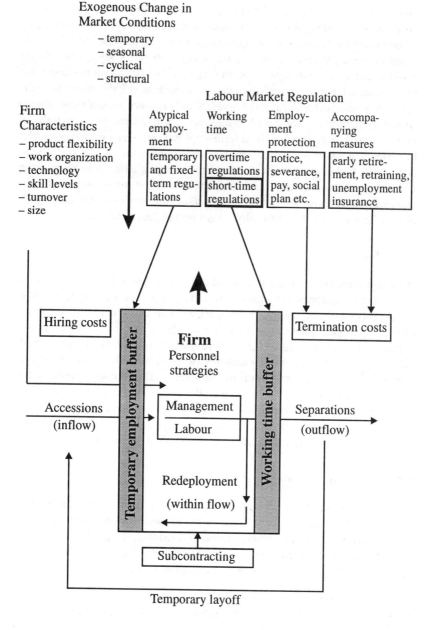

Figure 20.2 Short-time Work in Labour Force Adjustment

one in Italy clearly has a high level of use that can be explained by programme characteristics and regulatory and institutional factors, namely, the stringency of employment protection, the generosity of the short-time subsidy, trade union strength at the local level and the lack of other flexibility options. As for Spain's scheme of short-time work, the high level of utilization we found was to be expected, but it is surprising that it is as high as in Italy, where both the maximum permissible duration of benefits and the wage-replacement rate are somewhat higher (see Table 20.1). Moreover, Spain has, in contrast to Italy, an extraordinarily high level of fixed-term employment, which we would expect to serve as a functional equivalent for short-time work in adjustment situations. The higher level of use of short-time work in Germany in comparison with France appears to stem from Germany's more generous compensation to employees and, above all, to the fact that short-time work is potentially available in Germany for a significantly longer period than in France.

5.3 Sectors[15]

Although there are significant national differences in the level of short-time work in the countries we studied, the distribution of short-time work is remarkably similar across the four major European labour markets with short-time programmes. Short-time work is overwhelmingly concentrated in the industrial sector (see Figure 20.3). Whereas all sectors of industry have a high incidence of short-time work, short-time work is hardly used in the service sector.[16] One likely explanation is the strongly cyclical economic pattern, for adjustment situations regularly occur in the industrial sector, and short-time work for production workers is widely accepted as a routine response. Firms in the service sector are apparently able to rely to a greater extent on other adjustment strategies such as natural attrition and atypical employment.

5.4 Establishment Size

In all four countries large firms are much more likely to use short-time work as an adjustment strategy than are small firms, although the limitations of available data do not permit a precise comparison (Mosley et al., 1995). For both organizational and cultural reasons, small firms rely more heavily on external mobility than large firms. Moreover, they frequently face fewer restrictions in

---

15 See Mosley et al. (1995) for a more detailed discussion of cross-national patterns of uptake of short-time by sector and establishment size.

16 In the four countries examined in this chapter, a significant use of short-time work in the service sector is found only in 'transport and communication' (Spain) and in 'distributive trade, hotel and catering' (France and Spain).

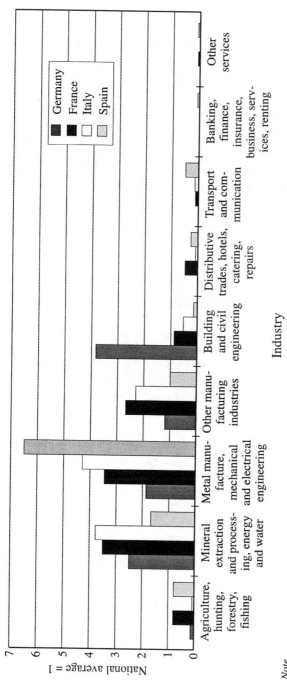

Note

The index of the relative incidence is computed simply by dividing the proportion of short-time work in a sector by that sector's share of dependent employment for each year; a value of 1 indicates that the percentage of all short-time work in a sector is identical with its share of employment. Figure 20.3 reports an average of these annual values for the 1983–91 period.

Source

Calculated on the basis of national programme data from *Flexible Adjustment through Short-time Work: A Comparison of France, Germany, Italy, and Spain* by M. Mosley, T. Kruppe and S. Speckesser, 1995, WZB discussion paper FS I 95–206, Wissenschaftszentrum Berlin für Sozialforschung.

Figure 20.3 Incidence of Short-time Work in France, Germany, Italy, and Spain by Industry, 1983–1991

doing so. For example, employment protection regulations are more stringent for large firms, and regulations concerning works councils (Germany, France), the requirements for social plans (France, Germany), special procedures for collective redundancies (France, Germany, Italy) and unfair dismissal legislation (Germany, Italy) have firm-size thresholds.

5.5   Structural Short-time Work

Maintenance of the employment relationship through short-time work or other forms of work-sharing may have negative effects on allocative processes in that necessary adjustment processes in the labour market and the economy are delayed. This is especially likely to be the case when the adjustment situation is structural rather than cyclical.

Since the mid-1970s, all major European labour markets except that in the United Kingdom have exhibited a trend towards use of short-time work in coping with structural change (Mosley and Kruppe, 1995). Italian labour market policy developed first and furthest in this direction (Tronti, 1993). By contrast, short-time work in France is a relatively small programme and, for cyclical reasons, the limited duration of benefits and low wage-replacement rates appear to offer suboptimal incentives even for short-time work (Lefèvre et al., 1994). Until 1993, when the new TRILD programme was introduced, France did not have a programme designed for structural intervention. In comparison with the existing scheme, the new programme provides for a higher level of support (1200 hours over a period of 12 to 18 months) for enterprises undergoing extended periods of restructuring (see Table 20.1, above).

In Germany it was the labour market crisis in the eastern German transformation process that led to the rapid expansion of structural short-time work as an alternative to mass dismissals. Until the crisis, structural short-time work had been common only in some industries (coal and steel). Short-time work—frequently in the form of layoffs—was used in practice as a social shock absorber in the aftermath of the miscalculated 'shock' transformation of the eastern German economy (Seifert et al., 1993). It was a quick response to an emergency, but it was also a distortion of the short-time work programme, for the exception became the rule. In 1990–91 Germany surpassed even Italy in the level of short-time work and, presumably, also in 'structural' use of short-time compensation.

6   LABOUR MARKET IMPACT

Because a primary goal of short-time work programmes is to maintain employment and avoid unemployment, their labour market impact is a principal concern in evaluation research. Moreover, estimates of the labour market effects of short-time work programmes are useful in assessing the cost-effectiveness of short-time work programmes in comparison with other labour market instruments. Given the limitations of the available data and the assumptions that have to be made, however, the estimates made by national labour market authorities are only approximations. This section illustrates the methodological problems of estimating the labour market impact of short-time work programmes. The example discussed is that of the estimating procedure used by the Institute for Employment Research (IAB) of the Federal Employment Service, the German labour market authority.

Because the actual reduction in weekly working time for workers on short-time may vary from a couple of hours to total layoff, the initial problem is to estimate the level of short-time work in terms of full-time equivalents. How this is done depends on the national programme data available. For example, German programme data report the number of participants and their reduction in normal working time only in four broad categories of percentage (10–25, 26–50, 51–75 and 76–100), and the total number of hours spent in the programme can be estimated only on the basis of a weighted average of these categories. Full-time equivalent participation in the programme is then calculated on the basis of statistics on annual working time adjusted to take into consideration absence from work due to sickness and annual leave. The German estimating procedure (Flechsenhar, 1979) understates programme impact by using average working time rather than by weighting working time by the incidence of short-time work, which is concentrated in industries in which working time is generally lower.

The resulting full-time equivalent figure is regarded as an estimate of the employment effect, that is, the number of positions saved through the programme. For example, the total number of participants in the programme during 1993 was 767 000 persons, and the estimated full-time equivalent employment effect was 228 000 persons. This procedure, however, overestimates the incremental employment effects of the programme because it fails to take windfall profits into consideration. Enterprises routinely hoard labour during cyclical downturns (Bosworth and Westaway, 1991), and short-time work programmes provide an additional incentive for a course of action that firms might pursue anyway. For example, in Canada it has been estimated that about 7 per cent of compensated short-time would not have resulted in layoffs even without the programme (Graves and Dumas, 1993).[17] We are not aware of

---

17 The principal reasons, based on the experience of the comparison group, are (a) resort to privately financed work-sharing, (b) labour hoarding in the firm's interest and (c) unexpected improvement in the economic situation.

other reliable estimates of windfall profits.[18] In order to minimize windfall profits, programmes may impose special threshold conditions. In Germany, for example, the reduction in hours must be at least 10 per cent of normal working time, must affect at least one-third of all employees and must last for at least four weeks.

Finally, in estimating the incremental impact that a short-time work programme has on unemployment, one must discount labour supply effects. In the official German estimates the reduction in the number of unemployed is considerably lower than the employment effect because the IAB assumes that, in the absence of short-time work, about one-third of the loss in employment would be absorbed by withdrawals from the labour force. Thus, in 1993 the estimated impact of short-time work on unemployment was only about 152 000 persons (Bach, Kohler and Spitznagel, 1986; Flechsenhar, 1979). Although it is necessary to estimate the percentage of workers who would otherwise withdraw from the labour force, the actual statistical assumption used in Germany (33 per cent) appears to be merely a rule of thumb. Interestingly, the IAB initially assumed that all persons on short-time in eastern Germany would have otherwise become unemployed. Clearly, the labour supply effect of this (and other) labour market programmes has to be estimated in each national labour market.

6.1   Impact on Individual Participants

The primary goal of short-time work programmes with regard to individuals is to stabilize employment (and income) by providing an alternative to layoffs. Second, by maintaining employment relationships, short-time work enables experienced workers to retain existing skills and avoid the devaluation of firm-specific skills, which may be of little value on the external labour market. Evaluation research should address these and related issues regarding the impact of the programme on individual careers.

The short-term employment impact of the programme is high because by definition work-sharing participants retain their jobs, albeit at reduced hours, instead of a corresponding percentage of the work force being laid off. The long-term incremental impact of participation in the programme on individual careers is, however, less clear cut for a number of reasons.

---

18 On the basis of a regression analysis of firm-level unemployment insurance claims Kerachsky et al. (1986) estimated 'lay-off conversion ratios' for three US states with short-time programmes. The results were, however, erratic varying from 0.01 to 0.95. In interviews, 20 per cent of user firms stated that they would not have resorted to layoffs even in the absence of the short-time programme. However, because of the small size of the short-time programme in the United States and the special features of the institutional setting, generalization from this experience seems unwarranted.

1. For many individuals, especially those in firms undergoing structural adjustment, short-time work may merely postpone dismissal rather than maintain employment ('parachute function'). This percentage is particularly high in Italy, eastern Germany and probably in Spain (Mosley and Kruppe, 1995; Seifert et al., 1993). Moreover, subsequent permanent layoffs may occur even where short-time work is not normally used for structural adjustment. For example, Graves and Dumas (1993) showed that 29 per cent of the participants in the Canadian short-time work programme were subsequently laid off, 21 per cent permanently.

2. A large percentage of employees who participate in short-time work subsequently leave their employer voluntarily in the course of natural fluctuation. Together these two factors mean that only a fraction of work-sharing participants continue to be employed by the same employer.[19]

3. On the other hand, in countries and enterprises utilizing layoffs, a high percentage of temporary and laid-off workers are able to return to their former employer after economic conditions improve (Feldstein, 1978). As noted above, this mode of adjustment is common in countries with less regulated employment contracts (e.g. the United States, Canada, Denmark) but also occurs elsewhere. Temporary layoffs are advantageous to employers and employees for the same reasons as short-time work: retention of firm-specific skills and avoidance of turnover costs. Graves and Dumas (1993) estimated that in Canada 35 per cent of persons laid off were again employed with the same employer at the time of the survey. In other words, medium-term employment continuity was only 24 per cent higher for workers who had been on short-time in comparison to those who had been laid off.

4. Many of those put on layoff find new employment (as do some of those on short-time).[20] Thus, in the medium term (18 to 30 months), the net difference in employment levels between participants and nonparticipants in short-time work in Canada was small. At the time of the interview 85 per cent of the former were employed, but so were 77 per cent of those persons who had been laid off. Nevertheless, the stress and psychological costs of economic uncertainty were certainly higher for those on layoff. This effect is indicated by the fact that those on layoff in the control group were almost three times as likely to express dissatisfaction with their financial status (41 per cent to 15 per cent), although the financial consequences were similar (i.e. those on layoff received comparable unemployment ben-

---

19 For example, Graves and Dumas (1993) estimate that only 59 per cent of Canadian participants in short-time work were still employed with the same employer 18 to 30 months later.

20 In the Canadian study 39 per cent of those put on layoff found new jobs (compared to 26 per cent for work-sharing participants) (Graves and Dumas, 1993).

efits).[21] These results may not be transferable to more highly structured European employment systems, for which there is, unfortunately, no comparable analysis. Furthermore, it is necessary to control not only for employment but also for earnings when assessing the impact of short-time work on individual careers.[22]

Another important question in the assessment of the impact that short-time work has on individual careers is whether individuals on short-time retain and develop skills. Clearly, employees on short-time are better able to retain existing skills because they continue to work, even though for reduced hours. Moreover, their firm-specific skills are less frequently devalued, because they experience less turnover. On the other hand, there is evidence that, although short-time work serves to maintain existing skills, it slows reskilling. Graves and Dumas (1993) found that employees on short-time have a lower rate of training to enhance existing or learn new skills (4 per cent of workers on short-time compared to 10 per cent in the control group).[23] Moreover, the higher percentage of those on layoff who move to new jobs (in the Canadian study 39 per cent to 26 per cent) means that those who do move to new jobs learn new skills at least on the job. While the available data are poor, efforts to combine training with short-time appear to have been generally unsuccessful. The reasons for this pattern are not clear. It may be due as much to the failure of employers to use the opportunity for training as to low motivation by individual workers.

Combining training with short-time work is an appealing strategy for using periods of slack work productively, especially prolonged periods of 'structural' short-time work. However, experience with public policy in this area has been disappointing. Participation in training has long been permissible in France and Italy for employees on short-time, whereas it was not possible in Germany until 1990 for structural short-time work and not until 1994 for those receiving regular benefits. This lag was apparently due to the greater concern in Germany about enterprises using short-time work to support their own training needs. This concern seems exaggerated because production workers on short-time are not usually priority recipients of company training. Moreover, there is in Italy and France no such reluctance about permitting training in the interest of the employer; the problem is rather the very low use of this possibility even where it is permitted (Mosley and Kruppe, 1995). In Canada employers are not only permitted but encouraged to use short-time for training

---

21 However, those on work-sharing usually retained job-related benefits, whereas 50 per cent of those on layoff lost them (Graves and Dumas, 1993).

22 See Schwarze et al. (1993) for an example of such an analysis.

23 At the firm level the ratio was even less favourable—3 per cent compared to 14 per cent.

purposes: the direct costs of training are reimbursed by the federal government (Graves and Dumas, 1993). Even so, the training rate remains low.

Linking training with structural short-time work, that is, short-time as an alternative to mass dismissals, is beset by special problems. Enterprises are primarily interested in training employees they want to keep. For older employees structural short-time work is frequently a form of pre-early retirement, and there is little interest in training. For less senior workers training (or other active measures) is indispensable, but it is difficult to see why it should take place on prolonged short-time work at zero hours. Although the incentive for employers to organize training is low in this situation, studies of the eastern German transformation process conclude that further training (Büchel and Pannenberg, 1992) and especially extended further training (longer than six months) (Schwarze et al., 1993) are important determinants of individual success in finding new employment or increasing earnings.

6.2   Impact on Enterprises

Assistance to firms in economic difficulty is also a major goal of short-time work programmes that has received little attention in evaluations. As discussed above, in densely regulated European employment systems short-time work provides an important flexibility reserve, which, in effect, suspends employment contracts during periods of slack work.

6.2.1   Labour Costs

Labour costs are reduced immediately, although the actual savings depend on the specific features of the national short-time work scheme (see Table 20.1, above). Mosley et al. (1995) estimate that Italian employers using short-time work bear only 3 to 5 per cent of total labour costs for short-time, that French employers must ordinarily bear 9 to 14 per cent[24] and that German employers must now bear 26 to 40 per cent of usual labour costs.[25] In the Spanish system, which has no experience rating, employers incur no ordinary labour costs

---

24   The lower figure refers to normal labour costs for an unskilled worker; the higher figure, to normal labour costs for a skilled worker, assuming that direct wages are 70 per cent of total compensation.

25   In Germany employers are required to bear the full costs of all social security contributions for pension insurance (19.2 per cent in 1994) and health insurance (about 12 to 15 per cent, depending on the insurance fund) or a total of about 26 per cent of normal labour costs (wages plus statutory charges). Although no systematic data are available, provisions in German collective agreements to top up short-time compensation have apparently become less frequent in the 1990s. The high estimate of 40 per cent of normal labour costs assumes that the employer must top up short-time benefits to 90 per cent of net wages for a worker without children with an average wage in the metal-working industry.

short-time. Moreover, termination costs are avoided, as are costs for rehiring and training workers during the following upswing.

Even in less regulated labour markets where short-term layoffs are possible, short-time work may offer cost advantages because, in contrast to layoffs, short-time work also includes higher-paid senior employees. Reduced costs for overtime may also be significant; Graves and Dumas (1993) estimated that firms in Canada saved Can$800 to Can$1800 per layoff avoided—the higher estimate including the overtime costs avoided (Graves and Dumas, 1993).

The benefits that the firm keeps from the retention of employees' firm-specific skills and its own avoidance of recruitment and training costs for replacements accrue only if the reduction in working time is actually tempo-rary and if the affected employees remain with the firm. Thus, any assessment of a firm's medium-term benefits from short-time work must take into consid-eration subsequent permanent layoffs or the impact of natural fluctuation (some employees may even leave because of short-time work). Firms antici-pating permanent layoffs have little incentive to use short-time.

Moreover, in countries where temporary layoffs are feasible, a significant percentage of laid-off workers may return under ordinary circumstances to their former employer even in the absence of a programme. For example, Graves and Dumas (1993) estimated that in Canada the job retention rate after about two years was only 24 per cent higher for employees who had been on short-time than for those who had been laid off. Estimates of savings in recruit-ment and retraining costs would have to be similarly discounted.

Because a firm's main rationale for short-time work is to retain firm-specific human capital and reduce turnover costs, use of work-sharing is likely to be more frequent in higher paid-and higher-skilled segments of the labour force. This is indirectly confirmed by Graves and Dumas (1993), who find a strong relationship between use of work-sharing and the average tenure of the work force.[26]

6.2.2   Employee Relations Impact

An important benefit of work-sharing ought to be improved industrial rela-tions. Only the Canadian study addresses this issue. Graves and Dumas (1993) found clear evidence of higher employee morale and positive attitudes towards the employer in firms that used work-sharing in comparison with firms that resorted to layoffs. Analysis of the unemployment insurance records of firms using short-time also showed that such firms had previously resorted less frequently to layoffs in the past.

---

26 Work-sharing participants had been employed an average of 52 months; the employees in the comparison group, an average of only 12 months (see Graves and Dumas, 1993).

6.2.3   Adjustment Speed

The employment response is quicker in adjustment situations in the United States than in Germany and many other European countries, where an hours response plays a larger role in short-run adjustment. Whereas FitzRoy and Hart (1985) argue that the volume of short-time work is too small to explain the cross-national differences in adjustment patterns, Abraham and Houseman (1993) conclude, on the basis of an econometric analysis of the speed of adjustment for production workers in France, Germany and Belgium, that these programmes make a significant contribution to the speed of hours adjustment in the manufacturing sector, in which short-time work is concentrated. Van Audenrode (1994) argues, in an implicit contract framework, that it is the interaction of the generosity of short-time work schemes with severance pay requirements that generates hours adjustment.

6.2.4   Economic Efficiency

A further question is the impact of short-time work on the short-term and long-term economic prospects of enterprises. Graves and Dumas (1993) found that Canadian enterprises on short-time did return more quickly to full production and were more profitable during the work-sharing agreement than firms that did not use short-time. However, they did not find any long-term effect on profitability or productivity. On the other hand, prolonged structural short-time work, in which most affected employees are not to be reinstated, may well retard adjustment at both the enterprise and individual levels. Schenkel (1994) found that the 10 per cent of the Italian firms whose application for assistance from the structural short-time work fund (CIG-S) was refused experienced a sudden decrease in their probability of survival. On the other hand, the same analysis showed no difference in the probability of survival either between firms that asked for an extension of assistance after the first intervention period (6 months)[27] and those that did not, or between those firms granted the extension and firms that were refused it. One possible interpretation is that initial assistance is more important for firms' survival than is prolonged short-time work.

7   BENEFITS AND COSTS OF SHORT-TIME WORK

Labour market programmes, like other public policies, have to be examined in terms of the benefits they produce in relation to the costs of the programme (see Delander and Niklasson, chap. 6 in this volume). Because short-

---

27   From 60 to 70 per cent of participating firms asked for an extension.

time work programmes have multiple goals (for individuals, enterprises and public policy), benefits are difficult to define as well as to measure. Where this issue has been addressed in the literature on short-time work, it has usually been practically formulated in terms of the relative cost to public budgets of short-time work in comparison with layoffs for an equivalent number of workers.

The comparison between the cost–benefit relation for short-time work and that for layoffs depends to a large extent on the particular features of national short-time work programmes and unemployment insurance systems (see Table 20.1, above). Whereas in some systems costs of short-time work are shifted heavily to employees (France) or employers (Germany), in others the public programme bears the bulk of the costs (e.g. Italy and Spain). Because recipients of short-time benefits would otherwise be eligible for unemployment insurance, the net costs of providing this option as an employment maintenance measure are in any case low, but they depend on specific features of the national system.

In Germany official estimates indicate that short-time work is markedly less costly to public budgets than is unemployment for an equivalent number of persons. Estimates based on a static input–output model with integrated multiplier effects are that 20 000 dismissals in 1994 in western Germany would impose a greater fiscal burden (DM 1.2 billion in lost revenues and increased expenditure) than the alternative of 60 000 short-time workers with a 33 per cent reduction in working time (DM 0.85 billion) (Bach and Spitznagel, 1992, 1994). In other words, the fiscal costs of the short-time work option are negative. The principal explanation for this difference in costs to public budgets is that employers pay pension and health insurance contributions for workers on short-time, whereas for the unemployed these costs are borne by the unemployment insurance fund. The model takes into consideration both direct and indirect taxes, social security contributions and the costs of unemployment and other social benefits incurred or avoided. Of course, the most favourable option from the point of view of fiscal costs is work-sharing without a short-time work subsidy.

By contrast, Graves and Dumas (1993) found short-time work to be more expensive than layoffs for the unemployment insurance fund in Canada, although there is no difference in funding or compensation for the two types of benefits. The three principal reasons are that (a) unlike unemployment insurance, there is no waiting period for short-time compensation, (b) 30 per cent of those on layoff never draw their benefits and, most importantly, (c) 29 per cent of those on short-time work are subsequently laid off and received unemployment benefits as well. Nevertheless, the authors concluded that additional costs to the public are more than offset by the social costs of employment that are avoided and the clear gains to employers.

8   CONCLUSIONS

The incentive structure for short-time work is strongly related not only to the generosity of short-time schemes but to other elements of the institutional framework, such as employment protection, flexibility options and labour representation. Based on turnover costs, the employer's own incentives to use short-time work are strongest in the classical case of short-time work as a response to temporary adjustment situations and very weak in the case of structural short-time work.

Analysis of estimated full-time equivalents shows the highest incidence of short-time work to be in Belgium, Italy and Spain. The level is lower in Germany, Canada and France. Uptake is lowest in the United States, where temporary layoffs are the usual response in short-term adjustment. This rank order of utilization results not only from the relative generosity of short-time schemes but from a variety of other institutional factors. In terms of employers' savings on labour costs during short-time, the German scheme for short-time work ranks surprisingly low.

In all the countries we studied, short-time work is highly concentrated in industry and disproportionately in larger enterprises. This fact is not a result of short-time programme characteristics and eligibility conditions; it is apparently rooted in differences in markets and adjustment style. An important policy question is whether short-time work is a form of work-sharing that can be extended, with appropriate programme changes, to white-collar workers and the service sector (or even the public sector) or whether other, new and different policy instruments are needed to spread work-sharing beyond its traditional boundaries.

If short-time takes place for reasons other than cyclical or other temporary declines in demand, the decisive question, in our opinion, is whether employees on short-time are likely to retain their jobs after a restructuring of the firm at which they work. Although a return to regular employment cannot always be foreseen with certainty, it should at least be envisaged as a clear goal if short-time work is to be used. If the only goal of short-time work is to delay dismissals for all or part of the work force, its use is problematic. In that case it merely slows the adjustment process in enterprises and sends false signals to individual workers. If, on the other hand, short-time work serves to preserve human capital and to stabilize employment, it fulfils an efficient coordination function of active labour market policy at low net cost.

REFERENCES

Abraham, K. G. and S. N. Houseman (1993), *Does Employment Protection Inhibit Labor Market Flexibility? Lessons from Germany, France and Belgium*, working paper 93–16, Kalamazoo: Upjohn Institute for Employment Research.

Auer, P., H. Gross, R. Kotulla and G. Rachel (eds) (1992), *Kurzarbeit und Qualifizierung in den neuen Ländern von der internen zur externen Anpassung: Erfahrungen aus Fallstudien und der Qualifizierungsberatung*, WZB discussion paper FS I 92–3, Wissenschaftszentrum Berlin für Sozialforschung.

Bach, H.-U., H. Kohler and E. Spitznagel (1986), 'Arbeitsmarktpolitische Maßnahmen: Entlastungswirkungen und Kostenvergleiche', *Mitteilungen aus der Arbeitsmarkt- und Berufsforschung*, 3, 370–84.

Bach, H.-U. and E. Spitznagel (1992), 'Arbeitsmarktpolitische Maßnahmen—Entlastungswirkungen und Budgeteffekte', *Beiträge zur Arbeitsmarkt- und Berufsforschung*, 163, 207–27.

Bach, H.-U. and E. Spitznagel (1994), 'Modellrechnungen zur Bewertung beschäftigungsorientierter Arbeitszeitverkürzungen', in *Beschäftigungsorientierte Arbeitszeitregelungen—Chance oder Illusion?*, workshop report no. 2, pp. 13–22, Nuremberg: Institute for Labor Market and Occupational Research of the Federal Institute for Labour (IAB).

Best, F. (1988), *Reducing Workweeks to Prevent Layoffs: The Economic and Social Impacts of Unemployment Insurance-supported Work Sharing*, Philadelphia: Temple University Press.

Bosworth, D. and T. Westaway (1991), 'Labour Hoarding and Recorded Unemployment in OECD Countries', in P. R. G. Layard, S. Nickell and R. Jackman, *Unemployment: Macroeconomic Performance and the Labour Market*, Oxford: Oxford University Press, pp. 150–64.

Büchel, F. and M. Pannenberg (1992), 'Erwerbsbiographische Folgerisiken von Kurzarbeit und Arbeitslosigkeit. Eine empirische Analyse für Ostdeutschland', *Mitteilungen aus der Arbeitsmarkt- und Berufsforschung*, 2, 158–67.

Burdett, K. and R. Wright (1989), 'Unemployment Insurance and Short-time Compensation: The Effects on Layoffs, Hours per Worker and Wages', *Journal of Political Economy*, 97 (6), 1479–96.

Corak, M. (1995), *Unemployment Insurance, Temporary Layoffs and Recall Expectations*, Ottawa: Human Resources Development Canada.

Dahms, V., M. Kaiser, M. Koller and H.-E. Plath (eds) (1993), 'Analyse der Arbeitslosigkeit und Kurzarbeit nach Berufsgruppen und Branchen in Ostdeutschland: Regionale Arbeitsmärkte und Arbeitsmarktpolitik in den neuen Bundesländern', *Beiträge zur Arbeitsmarkt- und Berufsforschung*, 168, 105–14.

Edebalk, G. and E. Wadensjö (1995, September), *Temporary Layoff Compensation and Unemployment: The Case of Sweden*, Proceedings of the European Association of Labour Economists (EALE) Conference, Lyon: EALE.

Feldstein, M. (1978), 'The Effect of Unemployment Insurance on Temporary Layoff Unemployment', *American Economic Review*, 68 (5), 834–46.

Fischer, G. and K. Pichelmann (1991), 'Temporary Layoff Unemployment in Austria: Empirical Evidence from Administrative Data', *Applied Economics*, 23 (9), 1447–52.

FitzRoy, F. R. and R. A. Hart (1985), 'Hours, Layoffs and Unemployment Insurance Funding: Theory and Practice in an International Perspective', *The Economic Journal*, 700–713.

Flechsenhar, H.-R. (1979), 'Kurzarbeit—Strukturen und Beschäftigungswirkung', *Mitteilungen zur Arbeitsmarkt- und Berufsforschung*, 3779, 362–72.

Grais, B. (1983), *Lay-offs and Short-time Working in Selected OECD Countries*, Paris: OECD.

Graves, F. and T. Dumas (1993), *Work Sharing Evaluation*, final report, Ottawa: Employment and Immigration Canada.

Huberman, M. and R. Lacroix (1995, September), *Work Sharing in Perspective: Implications for Current Policy*, Proceedings of the Seventh European Association of Labour Economists Conference, Lyon: EALE.

Institut für Arbeitsmarkt- und Berufsforschung (IAB) (1991), 'Kurzarbeit in den neuen Bundesländern', Parts 1–3, *Beiträge zur Arbeitsmarkt- und Berufsforschung*, 42 (13), 141–60.

Jensen, P. and N. Westergård-Nielsen (1990), 'Temporary Layoffs', in J. Hartog, G. Riddes and J. Theeuwes (eds), *Panel Data and Labor Market Studies*, Amsterdam: Elsvier, pp. 173–90.

Kerachsky, S., W. Nicholson, E. Cavin and A. Hershey (1986), *An Evaluation of Short-time Compensation Programs*, occasional paper 86–4, Unemployment Insurance Service, Washington, DC: Department of Labor.

Lefèvre, G., M. Béraud and N. Sidhoum (1994), *Le recours des entreprises au chômage partiel*, Paris: La Documentation Française.

Linke, L. (1993), *Kurzarbeit im Strukturwandel. Eine Analyse in der Bundesrepublik während der achtziger Jahre unter Einbeziehung erster Erfahrungen in den neuen Bundesländern*, WZB discussion paper FS I 93–206, Wissenschaftszentrum Berlin für Sozialforschung.

Macoy, R. and M. Morant (eds) (1984), *Short-time Compensation: A Formula for Work Sharing*, New York: Pergamon Press.

Mavromaras, K. and H. Rudolf (1995), '"Recalls"—Wiederbeschäftigung im alten Betrieb', *Mitteilungen aus der Arbeits- und Berufsforschung*, 2, 1–24.

Medoff, J. L. (1979), 'Layoffs and Alternatives under Trade Unions in U.S. Manufacturing', *American Economic Review*, 69 (3), 380–95.

Mosley, H. and T. Kruppe (1995), 'Kurzarbeit im Strukturwandel: Europäische Erfahrungen', *WSI Mitteilungen*, 7, 451–62.

Mosley, H., T. Kruppe and S. Speckesser (1995), *Flexible Adjustment through Short-time Work: A Comparison of France, Germany, Italy, and Spain*, WZB discussion paper FS I 95–206, Wissenschaftszentrum Berlin für Sozialforschung.

Pedersen, P. (1981), *Økonomiske effekter au arbejdsløshedsforsikring*, Copenhagen: Teknisk Forlag.

Richards, J. and A. Carruth (1986), 'Short-time Working and the Unemployment Benefit System in Great Britain', *Oxford Bulletin of Economics and Statistics*, 48 (1), 41–59.

Schenkel, M. (1994, December), 'The Cassa Integrazione Guadagni Straordinaria: Some Empirical Evidence from the Point of View of the Firm', paper presented at the WZB workshop 'Short-time Working and Structural Change', Wissenschaftszentrum Berlin für Sozialforschung.

Schenkel, J. and M. Zenesini (1993), 'Alcuni aspetti della Cassa integrazione guadagni: un'analisi empirica', *Rivista internazionale die Scienze sociali*, 94, 87–112.

Schömann, K., R. Rogowski and T. Kruppe (1995), *Fixed-term Contracts and Their Impact on Labour Market Efficiency and Individual Job Careers in the European Community*, report prepared for the Commission of the European Communities, Wisschenschaftszentrum Berlin für Sozialforschung.

Schwarze, J., U. Rendtel and F. Büchel (1993), *Income Effects of Unemployment and Short-time Work in the East German Transformation Process*, discussion paper no. 76, Deutsches Institut für Wirtschaftsforschung, Berlin.

Seifert, H., C. Ochs, K. Besselmann and G. Machalowski (1993), *Kurzarbeit und Qualifizierung. Bedingungen und Gestaltungsmöglichkeiten der Kurzarbeit zur Nutzung der beruflichen Qualifizierung*, research report no. 235, Bundesministerium für Arbeit und Sozialordnung, Bonn.

Tronti, L. (1993), 'Employment Protection and Labour Market Segmentation: Economic Implications of the Italian "Cassa integrazione guadagni"', in C. F. Büchtemann (ed.), *Employment Security and Labor Market Behavior: Interdisciplinary Approaches and International Evidence*, Ithaca: Industrial and Labor Relations Press (ILR).

Van Audenrode, M. (1994), 'Short-time Compensation, Job Security and Employment Contract: Evidence from Selected OECD Countries', *Journal of Political Economy*, 102, 76–102.

Völkel, B. (1992), *Kurzarbeit—eine Zwischenbilanz*, IAB workshop report no. 4, Nuremberg: Institute for Labour Market and Occupational Research of the Federal Institute for Labour (IAB).

Vroman, W. (1992), 'Short-time Compensation in the U.S., Germany and Belgium', Washington, DC: Urban Institute. (Unpublished manuscript)

21. Legal Regulation and Flexibility of Employment Contracts

Ralf Rogowski and Klaus Schömann

The subject of this chapter is the legal dimension of labour market policy. We analyse attempts to deregulate labour law systems that targeted increased labour market flexibility. The policy goals behind these labour law reforms were job creation, through the elimination of employment protection measures, increased transparency of labour law, through its simplification, and legal flexibility, with a view to facilitating personnel policies. These so-called deregulation policies were adopted in the 1980s in a number of European Union (EU) Member States and have been evaluated both theoretically and empirically in various national and international studies.

We discuss attempts to deregulate atypical employment in four major EU countries and report in particular on evaluations of legal policies concerning fixed-term contracts. We argue that a grasp of the specific legal dimension is indispensable for a comprehensive evaluation of labour market policies. In this context we distinguish between legal and nonlegal evaluations of law. However, our general opinion is that if researchers develop an understanding of the different perspectives of legal and economic evaluations, they will produce mutually reinforcing analyses. This understanding seems particularly relevant for future evaluations that adopt a comparative approach and methodology.

1   LEGAL AND SOCIOECONOMIC EVALUATION OF DEREGULATION

Evaluation of the legal regulation of labour markets and employment conditions varies according to academic disciplines. Nonlegal disciplines like sociology, political science and economics have developed different views of law as an explanatory as well as a dependent variable; these perceptions are rooted in conceptual paradigms adopted in the respective disciplines. Researchers from these fields treat law as one factor among others that can explain certain labour market developments. They proceed from the assumption that legal development rests on general social and economic developments.

Lawyers and legal academics, on the other hand, are not predominantly interested in the social impact of law. They are more concerned with legal factors and legal conditions that shape the development of law and usually view law as an autonomous force in society that can determine its own development.

The two approaches are characterized by distinct legal and nonlegal descriptions of law. In our view the approaches should be conceived of as complementary rather than mutually exclusive. The legal approach is relevant for a social or economic analysis and vice versa. We thus think it necessary within social science discourses on labour markets to adopt a conceptual framework that can appreciate the purely legal perspective. Traditional economic analyses of legal regulations, which treat law as an exogenous institutional context, will be augmented by approaches from this perspective.

1.1   Labour Law Theories of Atypical Employment

Labour law assessments of legal developments, such as the regulation of atypical employment, differ with respect to basic theoretical assumptions about functions and factors that influence the development of these regulations. The distinction can be demonstrated by a discussion of two labour law approaches that, on the surface, argue from different perspectives. The two approaches are the theory of the standard employment relationship and the reflexive labour law approach. They can be contrasted with a third approach, which treats law as an institutional context variable and is common in economic analyses of law.

1.1.1   *The Theory of the Standard Employment Relationship (SER)*

The theory of the SER distinguishes between the contract of employment and the relationship between employer and employee, which is defined as a status. The subject of statutory employment protection is the employment relationship, specifically, the establishment and protection of rights that are independent of the rights and obligations agreed upon in the actual written or unwritten contract of employment. Thus, the theory of the SER relies on the assumption that the status rather than the contract reflects the link between legal regulations and the factual relation between employee and employer. Employment protection measures must be understood as means to shape in legal terms the relationship as a status.

The concept of an SER further presupposes a certain 'normality' with respect to the conditions of such a relationship. A major assumption is that the relationship constitutes the economic basis for the employee. The legal protection of the SER is required in order to guarantee the livelihood of employees and their families. The SER is seen as a minimum condition for a satisfactory level of participation and integration in social life.

The theory of the SER views the employment relationship as typically characterized by full-time, permanent employment with one employer. Work is carried out in the company, which constitutes the most significant institution for the employee with respect to forming a social identity and participating in collective life (Fourcade, 1992; Gerritsen, 1995). Atypical forms of employment, including fixed-term contracts, are interpreted as forces that undermine the SER. Proponents of the theory of the SER argue that new forms of employment change important elements of the standard relationship and thus indicate a process of gradual 'erosion' of the SER (Mückenberger, 1985).

The SER theory was originally explicitly normative or prescriptive. Based on a so-called politicoeconomic assessment of social processes, new forms of employment, like part-time work, home work, agency work as well as temporary work and fixed-term contracts, were viewed as predominantly expressing employer demands. Therefore, one of the functions of labour law was to protect employees against these demands (Deakin and Mückenberger, 1989; Mückenberger, 1989).[1]

As of recently, a more positive attitude towards new forms of employment has been adopted in the theory of the SER. The previous rigid defence of an SER has been criticized for its reliance on an increasingly unrealistic model of a male wage-earner who is responsible for a family of non-wage-earners (Mückenberger, 1993). Furthermore, fixed-term contracts and other new forms of employment are no longer seen as being exclusively inspired by employer demands, but rather as an expression of general trends and cultural changes in life styles. Increased female participation in the labour market means that not only employers, but also employees are demanding new forms of employment, in particular part-time jobs. The task for labour law cannot be to prevent the flourishing of these new types of employment through unyielding negative appraisal of the erosion of a sacred SER. Instead, notions of social protection that are compatible with these new forms of employment must be developed in labour law (Keller and Seifert, 1993).

---

1   See also Däubler's proposal for a European Charter of Basic Rights (Europäische Grundrechts-akte), in particular Article 37: fixed-term contracts are only legal if they are concluded either on request of the employee or to replace another employee who is temporarily absent (Däubler, 1989).

1.1.2 The Theory of Reflexive Labour Law (RLL)

The theory of RLL proceeds from the assumption that legal development is only indirectly influenced by economic development. It postulates that, in modern labour law systems, legal innovations are most probably reactions to the social or legal consequences of previous legislation. Proponents of this approach are interested in the 'feedback loop from legal norm to social consequences to legal norm' (Teubner, 1986, p. 309). In particular, the theory of RLL focusses on the awareness of limits to legal regulation within labour law (Rogowski and Wilthagen, 1994).

The argument behind the theory, on the basis of a system-theoretical view of society, is that the legal system, like other social function systems, is constituted at the reflexive stage of its development by processes of self-reproduction. Norm creation is no longer an independent product of the political system. It is determined by internal factors, processes and structures of the legal system related to its autopoetic needs. According to this view, the development of the law is predominantly shaped by internal processes in the legal system.

The regulation of atypical employment is interpreted as a phenomenon of an increasingly complex labour law system. Thus, the regulation of fixed-term contracts is seen mainly as a reaction to problems created by the employment protection measures themselves. Accordingly, the legal regulation of labour markets and employment contracts is seen as a response to existing legal regulations concerning the labour market. Consequently, any evaluation of labour law has to start from the assumption that new legal regulations are shaped by, and are ultimately a product of, internal processes in the labour law system.

The RLL approach was applied in our analysis of legal regulation of fixed-term contracts in the EU (Schömann, Rogowski and Kruppe, 1995). We used it to show that regulation of fixed-term employment contracts and other forms of atypical employment is shaped by the respective employment protection systems and, in particular, by the dismissal norms in the countries studied. In countries with elaborate dismissal protection systems, for example, Germany and Spain, the regulation of atypical employment is to a large extent motivated by concerns related to 'protection' of the system of dismissal protection.

1.2 Law as an Institutional Context in Economic Analyses

In most economic and sociological studies on the labour market contractual aspects of the employment relationship between employers and employees are treated as a domain that is external to the main field of interest. Studies on the impact of legal regulations on labour market processes traditionally focus on wage or status attainment as outcome variables. Labour market regulations frequently fall under the *ceteris-paribus* assumptions, which basically do not change over longer periods of time. It is common in economic analyses to attribute a lack of labour mobility to inflexible institutional structures and labour regulations (OECD, 1993). However, this perspective has been challenged by the flexibility debate (Pollert, 1991) and by frequent attempts to use labour law reform as an instrument of labour market policy.

It is common practice in economic studies to rather crudely introduce institutional background variables into macroeconomic time-series models in order to explain the economic performance of countries. Legal institutions, systems of employment protection and fixed-term contract regulations are ranked on a single or multiple scale and frequently classified into simple dichotomies of 'flexible' or 'rigid' regulations. These static characteristics are then introduced as one of the explanatory variables into models of labour market behaviour. Such a use of labour market regulations in analyses of the labour market is, however, questionable in view of the high level of abstraction from independent developments of these legal regulations. Dynamic aspects of modifications introduced by collective agreements and labour-court decisions are not usually incorporated in the economic models (Schömann et al., 1995). In microlevel and macrolevel econometric models legal institutions are treated as exogenous factors. However, a change in perspective is required by the nature of institutional background variables. National systems of regulations do not pass from one discrete episode into another, they evolve over time. This is an indication that both law and changes in law over time display many features of an endogenous process, which needs to be treated accordingly in economic analyses.

There are few labour market theories that deal explicitly with durations of employment contracts. An attempt to use standard labour market theories and hypotheses about changes in the legal system to discuss these aspects of employment contracts can be found in Schömann and Kruppe (1993). Negotiations about wages and other employment conditions are treated in labour economics as transaction costs that only occur once, that is, during the hiring of an employee. The use of successive fixed-term contracts adds the dimensions of the expiry of each contract, of processes of renegotiation and of uncertainties as to whether a new contract will be concluded. The renegotiations induced by the expiry of the fixed-term contracts increase transaction costs for longer-lasting employment relationships.

Furthermore, incentives to invest in human capital are higher in long-term than in fixed-term employment relationships. In particular, retraining and other forms of education during employment are linked to returns to the previous employment. Due to the risk for the employer of nonrenewal of the fixed-term contract and the risk for the employee of unemployment after expiry of the fixed term, the incentive to invest in general, and particularly in firm-specific, human capital is reduced if the employment relationship is not a long-term affair. The reduced duration over which investment in human capital can be recouped might itself lead to a reduction of human-capital investment. In a comparative approach one hypothesis could be that countries with unstable employment patterns have lower initial investment compared to countries with low rates of fixed-term employment.

Theories of labour market segmentation consider primary segments as offering long-term, permanent employment and stable career prospects, whereas jobs in the secondary segment are characterized by lower wages, no further training possibilities, few career prospects and unstable employment patterns. Legal regulations of the employment relationship concentrate on employment conditions for employees in the primary segment and offer less protection for employees in the secondary segment of the labour market. From this perspective wage differentials between labour market segments are a result of the segmentation into different positions through the use of specific forms of employment contracts (Schömann and Kruppe, 1993).

Efficiency wage theories operate with an implicit assumption about labour law, that is, that shirking on the job cannot be controlled by labour law and cannot be sanctioned effectively by legal procedures. The legal facilitation of the use of fixed-term contracts figures in this model as a device to tighten 'worker discipline' in an employment system. However, the theory neglects implementation aspects such as how firms, employees or labour courts react to these changes in legal provisions.

2   ASSESSMENT OF POLICIES AND EVALUATIONS OF FIXED-TERM CONTRACTS

Most major Member States of the EU have experimented with a particular form of increased flexibility of labour market policies. These are attempts to 'deregulate' existing systems of employment protection and industrial relations and to shift legislative emphasis from employment protection to facilitated implementation of personnel policies and human resource management. In particular, regulation of atypical employment was discovered as a labour market policy instrument.

Deregulation led to a radical shift in emphasis in most labour law systems. In developed systems, legal regulation of the labour market tended to be a subsystem of labour law. This subsystem traditionally only consisted of regulations concerned with topics like labour administrations, vocational training and retraining, special programmes for transitory forms of employment and public and private labour exchanges. In contrast, norms concerned with the employment contract, dismissals or strikes constituted different parts of labour law, known as the law of employment protection and industrial relations. The new deregulation approach has blurred the traditional distinctions within labour law and has subsumed traditional fields of employment protection, such as the contract of employment and dismissal protection, under the heading of labour market regulations. In fact, it brought about a reappraisal of the legal view of employment protection and a substitution of the differentiated internal view of labour law by a simplistic, external concern with only one economic aspect, that is, the employment or unemployment rate. In the following (section 2.1) we shall describe policies and evaluations of deregulation in four Member States of the EU during the 1980s and 1990s which constituted challenges of varying degrees to traditional labour law concerns. The four countries are Spain, Germany, France and the United Kingdom; their regulation of fixed-term contracts is presented later in this section in Table 21.1.

Analyses of the impact of labour law on the development of atypical employment can benefit from a comparative perspective. However, most evaluation studies on fixed-term contracts or on government legislation that attempt to influence the use of this precarious (Michon and Ramaux, 1993) or flexible (OECD, 1993) type of work contract have been undertaken at the national level. Country-specific evaluations of fixed-term employment vary in size and design. The existing studies carried out in the four countries under comparison not only raise interesting aspects from a methodological point of view,[2] but implicitly pose challenging questions for comparative research. Ambitious future research should take up this challenge and engage in comparative analyses of the legal regulation of labour market policies and their impact on labour markets. Our attempt in this direction is discussed in section 2.2.

2.1   Country-specific Evaluations

Because labour law is a system of norms and rules that develops historically and that displays national traits of legislation, it is not surprising that most evaluation studies of deregulation and atypical employment have been single-country evaluations of proposed or actual changes to the legal system. The policies to reform existing employment protection systems vary between approaches that increase the flexibility of the system without reducing the

---

2 For further discussions of components of employment   protection systems, including the debate about the extent to which agency work or collective redundancies are functional equivalents of fixed-term contracts, we refer to Emmerson, 1988, Mosley, 1994, and Büchtemann and Walwei, chap. 22 in this volume.

level of protection and others that attempt to deregulate labour law by abandoning certain protective measures. The evaluation studies on these legal policies offer a broad range of perspectives through their use of individual-level data, firm-level data or national aggregate data. Some studies also include trade union or labour offices in their data design.

2.1.1 Spain

The Spanish law on atypical employment is a reaction to strict employment protection laws that date back to the Franco regime. Employers are enabled to enter fixed-term contracts in exchange for strict dismissal protection laws. Nevertheless, Spanish employers still need a valid reason for entering a fixed-term contract (see Table 21.1). Thus, the Spanish approach, in particular since the law of 1984, is strictly speaking not characterized by deregulation. Spanish employment policies, in particular the experiments with atypical forms of employment, 'reflect' the existing employment protection system and are meant as an amendment to, rather than a deregulation of, existing employment protection.

Spanish labour law is characterized by a wide range of atypical employment contracts. A number of these contractual forms were introduced for labour market purposes. Their purpose is to create incentives for employers to engage unemployed workers for a fixed period. Examples are the employment-creating contract for a minimum of one year and a maximum of three years or the practical-work contracts for young academics for a maximum of two years. If such a contract is concluded, it must be registered with the local labour office. Furthermore, the minimum wage law and working time regulations must be observed. In contrast to other countries, under Spanish labour law seasonal work is regarded as permanent employment that is only suspended at the end of each season.

Drastic changes have taken place in Spain with the creation of incentives to use fixed-term contracts and the rise in the number of employees in fixed-term employment (Schömann et al., 1995). The percentage share of fixed-term employees in comparison with the total number of employees rose from 10 per cent in 1984 to 30 per cent in 1991. At this stage the Spanish government realized that the number of fixed-term contracts in the Spanish economy indicated an overshooting of the amount of flexibility originally intended. It commissioned evaluations of the practice of fixed-term employment, and these were carried out by Alba-Ramírez (1991), Bentolila and Saint-Paul (1992), Jimeno and Toharia (1991) and by a group of experts (Segura, Durán, Toharia and Bentolila, 1991).

The report by Bentolila and Saint-Paul (1992) is based on a macroeconomic perspective of fixed-term employment. On the basis of a labour demand model of the Spanish economy, which is borrowed from Bertola (1990), they introduce labour endogeneity in the form of two types of worker who, it is assumed, differ in respect to productivity, wages and firing costs. A type one worker ('rigid' labour) is employed on a permanent work contract and entails considerable firing costs; a type two worker ('flexible' labour) employed on a fixed-term contract entails no dismissal costs. The wages and productivity of the two types of worker are assumed to be equal on the basis of efficiency-wage arguments, whereby fixed-term employees will be less costly in terms of wages but subject to higher monitoring costs due to shirking. Three policy regimes are distinguished: (a) fixed-term contracts are not permitted, (b) such contracts can readily be applied and (c) a transition from the employment system without fixed-term contracts to one that allows lower-cost dismissal. The application of this model to Spanish data has a short-term perspective because data from 1985 to 1988 are the basis for the estimates. A sample of 1214 manufacturing nonenergy private firms is the basis for the empirical analysis. Data on employment, balance sheets for capital stock and sales are applied using panel-data estimation techniques (Bentolila and Saint-Paul, 1992). Results confirm the hypotheses of the theoretical model that, in the employment regime with fixed-term contracts, both wage elasticity for fixed-term employees and the elasticity of flexible labour to an exogenous shock to the economy is higher for fixed-term employees than for permanent employees. In the case of Spain the introduction of fixed-term employment has resulted in a more procyclical reaction of labour demand, that is, rapid expansion in booms and faster discharge of employees by private firms during recessions. However, the effect of the introduction of fixed-term contracts was only 1.5 percentage point increase in the elasticity of labour demand during the observed period, which was mainly a booming period in Spain. During a recession a severe loss of jobs can be expected, accompanied by an additional drop in sales due to rapid job loss.

Jimeno and Toharia (1991) simultaneously carried out an evaluation of the evolution of fixed-term employment in Spain during the late 1980s. Their approach incorporates a more microlevel evaluation, starting with a description of personal characteristics of fixed-term and permanent employees during the recent past. The most important of the many legislative changes in 1984 was the abolition of the requirement of a specific reason for fixed-term employment and of the maximum term of three years. In making use of two sets of data, the Spanish Labour Force Survey and the Bank of Spain Survey on Firm's Balance Sheets, which contains information about firms' employees, the authors found that both sources suggest that the most intense use of fixed-term contracts was in small and newly created firms. Among the industrial sectors that employ more than 30 per cent of all employees on fixed-term contracts are agriculture, construction, shoe and leather production and hotels and restaurants. The age structure of fixed-term employees is skewed, that is, two-thirds of youngsters aged between 20 and 24 years are fixed-term employees.

In their multivariate assessment of the probability of having a permanent job after entering employment during the previous twelve months the authors estimate the probability for two points in time after unemployment one year previously. Results based on the Labour Force Survey confirm the age selectivity of fixed-term employment and the industrial sector selectivity. It also becomes apparent that most fixed-term employees entered the labour market from the status of nonparticipation in the labour force rather than from unemployment. Based on a theoretical model, Jimeno and Toharia (1991) present the hypotheses that the introduction of fixed-term employment gives rise to cooperation and efficiency effects due to the fact that distribution of permanent workers and fixed-term employees in a firm will have an impact on average productivity.

For the evaluation of legal systems and systems of employment protection in general Jimeno and Toharia (1991) attempt to estimate wage effects of fixed-term employment. There is no possibility, *de jure*, for different wages to be paid to two groups of employees: Spanish labour law actually prohibits collective bargaining agreements from specifying different wage rates for permanent and fixed-term employees, as is the case for male and female wage rates. Thus, any form of wage discrimination is apparently excluded *ex ante*. However, the evaluation of legal systems is dealing with just this kind of supposed functioning of the labour market. The multivariate empirical evidence for Spain regarding wage effects, based on a special survey by the Spanish Statistical Office in 1990, shows that hourly wage rates for fixed-term employees were, on average, 11 per cent lower than the wage rates for permanent employees with the same other characteristics, for example, age, sex, industrial sector or educational level.

In addition to the individual-level evidence of wage effects, Jimeno and Toharia (1991) also made cross-section estimates for various industrial sectors for a number of years, using as a dependent variable the growth in labour productivity computed from the industrial production index. With and without controlling for personal characteristics and the composition of the staff (percentage fixed/permanent employees) there appears to be a negative correlation between the share of fixed-term employment and labour productivity, although it decreases over time. At the industry level, Jimeno and Toharia (1991) find no evidence in support of a lower wage push effect of Spanish trade unions since the introduction of more fixed-term employees in most industries and firms, even allowing for the differential impact of firm-level wage bargaining. Another major outcome of the analysis was that wage rates and the percentage of fixed-term employees seem to be determined endogenously, which means

Table 21.1 Regulation of Fixed-term Contracts in Spain, Germany, France and the United Kingdom

	Spain	Germany	France	United Kingdom
Statutory sources	Workers' Statute of 1970; Law 32 of 2 August 1984; Law 18 of 3 December 1993	Sec. 620 of the Civil Code; Employment Promotion Act of 1985; Act on Fixed-term Employment in Universities and Research Institutes of 1985	L 122–1 (and the following provisions) of the Labour Code, as amended by the Law of 12 July 1990	Sec. 13 (2), 20 (2), 49 (4), 55 (2), 83 (2), 142 (1) (2) Employment Protection (Consolidation) Act of 1978
Requirement of reason	Eleven reasons, including specific purposes, but excluding seasonal work	Seven categories of reasons under case law, including seasonal work, replacement and temporary nature of work	Ten reasons, including seasonal work, replacement and temporary nature of work	No
Duration	Maximum fixed term 3 years	Statutory maximum for fixed-term contracts under the Employment Promotion Act is normally 18 months, in exceptional cases 24 months	Maximum duration varies between 9 months and 2 years, according to reasons for fixed term	No maximum or minimum
Renewal	Up to the maximum fixed term	In general only up to the maximum fixed term; four months' interruption before a new contract can be concluded under the Employment Promotion Act	Once, up to the maximum fixed term	Unlimited
Automatic conversion into permanent contract	Yes, in case of illegality of the fixed-term contract	Yes, if continued after the contractual or maximum fixed term and in case of illegality of the fixed-term contract	Yes, if continued after the contractual or maximum fixed term	Yes, if the fixed-term contract is concluded for less than a month and is continued beyond three months' employment
Compensation at the end of the fixed term	Yes, twelve days per year of service	No	Yes, 6% of gross salary, except in cases of seasonal work	No
National regulatory features	The use of fixed-term contracts is induced by strict dismissal protection regulations	The requirement of reasons for the use of fixed-term contracts was established by the Federal Labour Court	Close resemblance of regulation on fixed-term contracts and temporary or agency work	Common-law rules on contract apply in case of performance of a particular task

Source: K. Schömann, R. Rogowski and T. Kruppe, *Employment Observatory Policies*, 47, Autumn 1994, pp. 38–9. Copyright 1994 by Wissenschaftszentrum Berlin für Sozialforschung. Adapted by permission.

one operates largely independently of the other (Bentolila, 1991; Jimeno and Toharia, 1993, pp. 320–21; Segura et al., 1991).

Contemporaneous to the other studies, Alba-Ramírez (1991) provided additional evidence of the segmenting effects of the deregulation of fixed-term contracts in Spain. Similar to Jimeno and Toharia (1991), he finds increasing signs of segmentation as the effects of gender, household status, education and age become stronger in the late 1980s. In evaluations of firms' use of fixed-term contracts—also based on the Labour Force Survey—earnings equations are estimated in order to learn about a possible segmentation or discrimination effect to the disadvantage of fixed-term employees. The empirical tests estimate rates of return to tenure that are found to be positive and statistically significant for job duration of longer than 12 years, a form of wage increase due to seniority that fixed-term employees are unlikely to receive. The earnings differential between fixed-term employees and permanent employees, calculated on the basis of these data, is found to be about 12 per cent, controlling for industrial sector and other differences in job and personal characteristics.

Alba-Ramírez (1991) augments the individual-level analysis with estimates based on wage equations; he uses a sample of medium- and large-size firms taken from an annual survey carried out by the Ministry of Economics and Finance of collective agreements in firms employing more than 200 employees. Although the sample shows a lower overall level of fixed-term employees (probably because the sample was limited to larger firms), the results confirm firm-level estimates from other studies on Spain that firms with a higher percentage of fixed-term employees pay significantly lower average wages (about 3–4 per cent). In contrast to the study by Jimeno and Toharia (1991), Alba-Ramírez (1991) finds evidence that internal efficiency can be increased in firms as a consequence of reliance on more fixed-term employees. Because the size of the samples is small in both studies and the samples consist of selected firms, the results for Spain are inconclusive regarding the presumed productivity-enhancing effect of fixed-term employment when analysed at firm level.

2.1.2 Germany

The German version of labour law deregulation is based on a specific legal view. It is characterized by a reflexive approach that takes into consideration the basic principles as well as the judicial interpretations of existing employment protection laws. The German deregulation measures do not replace employment protection, but rather introduce the labour market perspective as an additional concern of labour law.

The main statute representing the liberal–conservative government's deregulation approach is the Employment Promotion Act of 1985. In this Act fixed-term contracts are treated as an instrument that can enhance flexibility in labour market conditions. Consequently, the judicial requirement (note: not a statutory requirement!) that a reason must be given for conclusion of a fixed-term contract was removed. Employers are free under this Act to engage new employees on fixed-term contracts. However, the fixed-term is limited to 18 months (two years in the case of a company established less than six months ago and employing less than 20 employees), and the contract cannot be renewed (unless there is a four-month time lapse between two fixed-term contracts).

Labour law in Germany is still dominated by the view that the use of atypical employment contracts must be the exception and permanent contracts of employment the norm. German labour law exhibits a distrust for fixed-term contracts and other atypical employment and stipulates that they are mainly instruments to circumvent dismissal protection. This view clashes with attempts to use labour law as an instrument of labour market policy, and the deregulation approach has thus led to tensions in the traditional doctrinal thinking about labour law in Germany.

In accordance with the restrictive legal view, evaluations carried out in the 1980s in West Germany focussed on the 'erosion' of employment security and the SER. Furthermore, legislators in Germany treated the Employment Promotion Act as an experiment by originally limiting its duration of applicability to only five years. The Federal Ministry of Labour commissioned large-scale evaluations of the Act, and its renewals at the end of the 1980s and in the middle of the 1990s were nominally linked to the outcome of these evaluations. So far the duration of the Act has been extended twice; it is currently in force until 2000.

The first evaluation of the 1985 Act was carried out by the trade unions. They commissioned a study to assess the social consequences of increased flexibility (Möller, 1988). The study was based on 20 case studies of firms in the service sector. It criticized efforts to increase labour market flexibility as creating a severe risk for workers in services, who might slide into poverty, and as enhancing segmentation of the work force within firms. In his overview of empirical evidence of the effects of deregulation Adamy (1988) collected and compared information from a number of national representative surveys like the Labour Force Survey and the Socioeconomic Panel. He reports a steep increase in fixed-term labour contracts between 1984 (before deregulation: 4.2 per cent in fixed-term employment) and 1986 (after deregulation: 8.0 per cent). He also presents evidence of the age selectivity of fixed-term employment, that is, young and new labour market entrants are more likely to be employed on fixed-term contracts.

Before the first renewal of the Employment Promotion Act two large-scale evaluation studies were initiated: Büchtemann and Höland (1989) for the government and Linne and Voswinkel (1989) for the trade unions. The latter study was based on a case-study approach and a series of qualitative interviews at firm, plant and shop-floor level. Segmentation into a core and a periphery work force and loss of solidarity and cooperative behaviour were found to be major negative 'side-effects' of the deregulation of the Employment Promotion Act. The study by Büchtemann and Höland (1989) was based on a secondary analysis of data from the Labour Force Survey and three special surveys: (a) a representative survey of 2392 private sector firms, (b) interviews with 1968 placement officers and representatives of the public employment service and (c) a survey of 6468 employed and unemployed persons, who were interviewed and then reinterviewed after six months to evaluate changes in employment status and the probability of transition from fixed-term to permanent employment contracts. Through this multilevel approach the study found that as many as 36 per cent of all new recruits in the private sector started jobs on the basis of a fixed-term contract (50 per cent in the public sector: Büchtemann and Höland, 1989, p. 42). Apart from the public sector, the new regulations were used intensively only by small firms that were exposed to seasonal fluctuations in their workload.

A major finding of the study by Büchtemann and Höland (1989) was that most of the additional hirings of fixed-term employees were not directly influenced by the deregulation of fixed-term contracts. Employers responded that only one out of five fixed-term contracts were concluded under the Employment Promotion Act, amounting to roughly 25 000 additional employees engaged on fixed-term contracts per year. The amount of substitution of permanent employment contracts by fixed-term contracts was estimated to total 75 000 annually. Hence, the evaluation of the extent of deregulation effects during the initial years showed it to be much smaller than feared by trade unionists, and also smaller than hoped for by the government.

Overall, the study by Büchtemann and Höland (1989) provides an innovative combination of data sets and different perspectives derived from employees, firms, managers and public placement officers. However, it lacks somewhat in multivariate estimation techniques. Their evaluation of the effects of the Employment Promotion Act remained preliminary, mainly due to the rather short observation period in which the transitions between fixed-term and permanent employment were assessed. The evaluation concluded that a relaxation of termination had only a marginal impact on the hiring practices of firms (Büchtemann, 1993, p. 293).

A multivariate evaluation of the effects of fixed-term employment on firm-level employment practices was carried out by Kraft (1993). His analysis of the speed of employment adjustment in West Germany from 1970 through 1987 was based on data from 21 West German manufacturing industries. The study used as a dependent variable the change in employment within the industry and a proxy for product demand and nominal wages. The author supplemented his analysis with information on the level of unionization. The presence of a particular union ('IG Metall') was used as a dummy variable that was supposed to capture the impact of the Employment Promotion Act in a spline function of the time-trend variable. However, contrary to findings in other studies by the same author (Kraft, 1994), the 1993 study reports a slow-down in employment adjustment since the introduction of deregulation in German manufacturing industries, particularly in industries dominated by col-lective bargaining by 'IG Metall'.

Based on a disaggregate analysis of monthly data from 202 industries during the period January 1977 to December 1992, Hunt (1993) estimated a model similar to the one used by Kraft (1993) and the Spanish evaluators. The information on employment adjustment, wages and sales is used in separate models of employment adjustments for blue-collar and white-collar employ-ees. The rather surprising finding by Kraft (1993) was confirmed, that is, that employment adjustment slowed down after the introduction of the Employ-ment Promotion Act in 1985.

Information provided by individual employees was analysed by Schömann and Kruppe (1993). Their data base was the eastern and western German Socio-Economic Panel (SOEP), and they asked two basic questions: (a) Who is most likely to be employed on a fixed-term basis? (b) Do employees with a fixed-term contract have lower earnings than employees on a permanent employment contract?

The results from four 'waves' of the SOEP data indicate that the introduc-tion of the Employment Promotion Act led to increased age selectivity of fixed-term employment, that is, more young employees were recruited into fixed-term employment than before, and increased the risk of blue-collar workers being engaged on fixed-term contracts. Patterns of industrial segmen-tation of fixed-term employees reveal that large-scale engineering firms and craft industries are unlikely to hire employees on fixed-term contracts. Fixed-term employees with similar education, labour force experience and skill lev-els and in the same industrial sector earn about 10 per cent less than permanent employees in western Germany.[3] However, no such wage effect was found until 1992 in eastern Germany, where wages were still substantially lower than in western Germany at that time. Unfortunately, the panel data do not allow a precise follow-up of employment spells over years. A longitudinal modelling of the transition process is limited by the fact that the question about fixed-term employment was asked only in the years 1985, 1988 and 1991, without sufficient precision concerning direct changes in between these points in time.

---

3 Very similar results were obtained for Spain and for the Netherlands by Vissers and Dirven (1994). They also used panel data and operated with a similar estimation technique.

A common weakness, at least in the German evaluations of fixed-term employment, is the focus of evaluations on a single change in legislation, notably the Employment Promotion Act. The problem arises because deregulation of fixed-term contracts by legal provisions was counteracted by collective agreements in some industries, mainly the manufacturing industries, which reduced the maximum length of fixed-term contracts to six instead of 18 months, as laid down by law. Most studies, particularly those focussing on the manufacturing industries, therefore have found counterintuitive results due to inadequate measurement of the various components of a country's employment protection and labour law in general.

2.1.3   France

There have been several attempts to introduce flexibility in the employment protection system in France since 1972. The Law of 3 January 1972 created for the first time a legal basis for the use of (a) fixed-term contracts and (b) temporary employment. From its beginnings the law tried to provide a comprehensive basis through establishing common legal rules for both temporary and agency work and fixed-term contracts.

Liberalization of atypical employment was introduced in 1979 and was partly repealed by the Auroux laws of 1982, which limited the use of fixed-term contracts and temporary employment. However, throughout the 1980s and 1990s both socialist and conservative governments have viewed these types of contract, and the use of labour law in general, as important instruments of labour market policies. This view was further supported by the industrial relations partners, who enforced the French approach to flexibilization through negotiation of regulations on atypical employment in collective agreements.

The restrictions introduced in 1982 were partly repealed in 1985, and the law has facilitated the use of atypical employment since then. Actual figures of employees in fixed-term contracts rose sharply until 1990 when new legislation again curbed the wider spread of fixed-term contracts (Michon and Ramaux, 1993). Evaluations of these changes have been carried out at various stages of the legal evolution, mainly with the focus on specific French experiences with this type of labour contract (Ministère du Travail et de la Formation Professionnelle, 1992).

As a consequence of the joint flexibilization of temporary employment under fixed-term contracts and agency or interim work in France, evaluations of deregulation policies have taken a comprehensive approach, which allows the analysis of changes in different legal domains, taking the view that these are still part of one single labour market. This perspective groups both fixed-term contracts and interim work in a category of nonstandard employment

(Michon and Ramaux, 1993), allowing researchers to highlight both similarities and differences to standard employment.

Such a combined view enables the evaluation, at least in broad terms, of the size of three possible effects (Michon and Ramaux, 1993): (a) A substitution effect constitutes the possibility of using one form of nonstandard employment instead of another after one specific form has been deregulated by legislators. (Indeed, for France during the 1980s Guergoat and Hocquaux (1991) have shown that such a substitution effect has occurred, but between different forms of fixed-term contracts: forms of subsidized fixed-term employment have been reduced compared to nonsubsidized fixed-term employment.) (b) A complementary effect is indicated when regulation of different aspects of the employment relationship jointly target an increase in their use. (c) An amplification effect occurs, when deregulation of one specific form of employment is a motivation for deregulation of another form and the two reinforce each other. Although there are difficulties finding empirical substantiation of these effects, the evaluation of the legal circumstances and joint deregulation and reregulation of agency work and fixed-term contracts in France shows the links between these forms of employment. Similarly, the legally permitted reasons for use of interim and fixed-term employment (see Table 21.1) are closely related in France, where they limit the effects of complementarity and amplification more so than in any other country.

However, no estimates of the wage-reducing effects of fixed-term contracts are available, although the results of a survey in 1984 suggested a 20 per cent lower wage cost for agency workers, mainly due to the fact that seniority status is not honoured for nonstandard employees (Henry and Guergoat, 1987). French analysts have focussed on research on what types of firms have extended their use of fixed-term or agency work. Based on surveys of firms and descriptive statistics over ten years, Guergoat and Hocquaux (1991) concluded that firm size is a differentiating category in the use of nonstandard employment. Fewer small firms use fixed-term contracts, but those that do tend to use them extensively. Generally it was found that between 1977 and 1987 the increase in nonstandard employment stemmed from the fact that more firms were using this form of employment contract rather than that firms had raised the share of nonstandard employees.

A sectoral difference in the use of fixed-term versus agency work can be identified. In France fixed-term contracts are mainly used for seasonal work and replacement of absent employees and primarily in the service sector, that is, hotels, restaurants, commerce and agricultural, including food industries (Michon and Ramaux, 1993, p. 107).

Although French analysts stress the difficulty in assessing the impact of legal changes on labour market outcomes (Michon and Ramaux, 1993, p. 96), the link or even correlation between the degree of flexibility introduced by legal reforms and the extent of recourse to nonstandard employment appears close in comparison to the German labour market, albeit less close than in Spain. Based on 24 case studies spread over two regions and covering the whole range of industries, Ramaux (1993) describes a prospective scenario in which both forms of temporary employment are likely to increase when the French economy is booming rather than in recession. In order to derive stronger comparative conclusions concerning recourse to fixed-term contracts, it is essential that the responsiveness of elasticities of use of fixed-term contracts be compared between countries; such comparisons are not available at present.

At the microlevel, there are a number of evaluation studies that deal with the topic of precarious employment as a socioeconomic category; the issue is mainly discussed in connection with studies on the socialization of youth (e.g. Join-Lambert and Viney, 1988; Nicole-Drancourt, 1992). Based on large school-leaver samples the analyses confirm for France the effect of extended probationary periods of fixed-term employment for young labour market entrants. In contrast to findings for Germany, the first access to the labour market does not significantly determine subsequent occupational careers in France. It is the quality of subsequent employment or the ensuing career dynamics that facilitate access to the labour market or lead to risks of social exclusion after recurrent spells of unemployment (Join-Lambert and Viney, 1988).

2.1.4   United Kingdom

The United Kingdom is a country in which the level of employment protection has been traditionally rather low. Nevertheless, under the heading of deregulation the conservative governments under Margaret Thatcher and John Major promised major reforms of existing employment protection laws throughout the 1980s and 1990s. These policies aimed explicitly at reducing employment protection and cooperation with unions in order to remove 'burdens on business' (Department of Trade and Industry, 1985).

During the 1980s protective legislation for women and young workers was repealed (Deakin, 1990), and certain categories of employees were excluded from employment protection. Probably the most important deregulation was procedural. The qualifying period of employment before a claim of unfair dismissal or redundancy payment can be brought to the Industrial Tribunal was raised from six months to one year in 1979 and to two years in 1985. However, despite radical rhetorical political gestures, deregulation has not touched the core of the employment protection system, which was introduced in the 1970s in the United Kingdom. This is mainly due to the fact that employment protection hardly intruded on personnel management decisions.

As Dickens (1994) comments: 'employers in Britain wishing to pursue flexibility strategies have not needed deregulation to do so' (p. 236).

It is necessary to interpret the British deregulation of employment rights in the wider context of the reform of the traditional system of voluntarist industrial relations. British labour law was characterized until the 1970s by abstentionism and recognition of autonomous regulation of wages and employment conditions through collective bargaining. The conservative governments of the 1980s and 1990s have deliberately undermined this traditional approach and the ability of the trade unions to provide employment protection through industrial action. Various Employment Acts in the 1980s as well as the Trade Union Act of 1984 and the Trade Union and Labour Relations (Consolidation) Act of 1992 aimed at curbing the trade unions by introducing election procedures and ballot requirements for internal trade-union affairs and in cases of industrial action.

Evaluations of labour market deregulation concerning fixed-term contracts are scarce in the United Kingdom. The flexibility debate was largely an issue of the 1980s (Pollert, 1991). Large-scale evaluations at the micro- or the macrolevel are not to be found. Nevertheless, descriptive evidence from the individual-level Labour Force Surveys and firm-level data from the Workplace Industrial Relations Survey (WIRS) indicate a rather stable level of fixed-term and temporary workers, who account for between 5 and 6 per cent of total employees between 1983 and 1987 (Casey, 1991, p. 182). However, the issue of whether overlapping forms of nonstandard employment create an accumulation of disadvantages or are an expression of individual preferences is still being debated. Researchers encountered the difficulty that a high share of respondents refused to provide a reason why they work on a fixed-term basis. Nonetheless, there is some evidence of a comparatively higher share of employees in the United Kingdom who themselves requested a fixed term and thus work voluntarily on fixed-term contracts. Only in regions with high levels of unemployment were an increased number of workers involuntary working on a fixed-term contract. A sectoral analysis revealed that the share of fixed-term employees has increased faster in the public sector than in the private sector during the 1980s in the United Kingdom (Casey, 1991).

It is quite common in the United Kingdom that fixed-term employment, agency work, part-time work and self-employment are grouped into one category of nonstandard employment. This broad notion of employment flexibility contrasts with the French perspective, where it only appears plausible to combine fixed-term contracts and agency work because they are regulated in the same manner. To some extent the British approach seems compatible with German attempts to view fixed-term contracts as functional equivalents of part-time work (Büchtemann and Höland, 1989; Delsen, 1995). However, the British approach seems to advocate going a step further and including the self-employed in the search for functional equivalents to fixed-term employment. In our view a proper comparison of atypical employees and self-employed requires an assessment of basic legal terms of self-employment and the underlying labour law model of a 'standard employment relationship'.

2.2   Comparative Evaluations

Comparative studies on the relationship between labour market regulation and labour market processes entail the difficulty of finding an adequate approach to both aspects, that is, to regulation and to processes embedded within institutional settings. There is a certain tendency for the study of processes to dominate research at the national level because it is assumed that the major elements of the institutional background are sufficiently well known, and there is no need to make them more explicit. Comparative evaluations of fixed-term employment focus on comparisons of specific features of regulation and recent changes thereof (Meulders, Plasman and Plasman, 1994; OECD, 1993; Walwei, 1991). Some studies almost exclusively deal with data-collection efforts (European Foundation for the Improvement of Living and Working Conditions, 1992) or try to assemble (Meulders et al., 1994; OECD, 1993) a lot of descriptive information on the distribution of fixed-term and permanent employees according to specific socioeconomic characteristics. The comparison at this level of abstraction of labour market processes frequently lacks depth of analysis as it can be achieved at the country level.

In comparative studies of many countries legal regulations are treated at some level of abstraction or generality, which is usually restricted to a by-country matrix of certain features of regulation. As regards the comparative evaluation of legal regulation of fixed-term contracts, column headings of elements of regulation are: (a) possible restrictions in the use of fixed-term contracts, (b) 'objective' justification or reason required, (c) options for renewal and (d) maximum duration of fixed-term contracts (cf. Emmerson, 1988, p. 796; Walwei, 1991, p. 26). The OECD matrix (1993, p. 19) is somewhat richer in features of fixed-term contracts in country regulations, including existence of termination benefits and dismissal protection and automatic conversion into open-ended employment, but, apart from a few exceptions, this matrix is crudely filled with yes and no answers. Any conclusions derived from such sets of regulatory details in connection with descriptive data analysis can only suggest lines of argument, without sufficient analytical rigour based on multivariate evaluation. An improved version of a comparison of country regulations is presented in the *Employment Outlook* (OECD, 1994, p. 144), where the focus is on the dynamics of regulation, notably the extent of recent changes in regulations governing fixed-term contracts. This extension is useful because some kind of path dependency of regulatory systems is acknowledged and some indication of the speed and extent of regulatory changes can be derived. A comparison of the differential adjustment patterns of dynamics of labour regulations with processes on the labour market would illustrate an interesting feature of employment systems that has received little attention so far.

In addition to studies that compare regulations and individual-level outcomes, there has been an evaluation attempt coordinated by the European Foundation for the Improvement of Living and Working Conditions (1992), which collected data at the establishment level (see also Delsen and Huijgen, 1994). The surveys asked about 'reasons behind the development of these forms of work; the advantages and disadvantages perceived by employers on the basis of their practical experience; and the degree to which a larger choice of forms of work meets the economic and social needs/wishes of employers and employees' (Delsen and Huijgen, 1994, p. 5). Managers from companies employing 45 per cent of the work force stated that in their enterprises fixed-term employees are always or mostly transferred to a status of permanent employment. Whereas this was generally not the case for seasonal work, a greater likelihood of renewal of fixed-term contracts was found if employers cited general uncertainty about the economic future of their enterprise as a reason for fixed-term employment (European Foundation for the Improvement of Living and Working Conditions, 1992).

However, the addition of another perspective and comparative assessment of fixed-term contracts, such as evaluation of the policy target, that is, the use of fixed-term contracts by employers, at one single point in time is unlikely to provide a reliable indicator for actual use of fixed-term contracts at the firm level or possible changes in use due to modifications of legislation. A similar survey at the establishment level carried out by the Directorate-General II of the Commission of the European Communities (1991) also led to the conclusion that a lack in flexibility in recruitment and dismissal was an 'important' or 'very important' impediment to recruitment of additional employees in industry. However, at least in some cases in Europe, employers in industry have agreed to collective contracts that limit the use and duration of fixed-term employment in their firms.

The study by Schömann et al. (1995) for the Directorate-General V of the Commission of the European Communities tries to do justice to both elements of the relationship, that is, the authors analyse the evolution of the legal system and match it with an empirical analysis of Community-wide data sources. However, only cross-section data and some limited retrospective information concerning the year prior to the survey are available. The size of the European Labour Force Survey (Eurostat, 1993), on the other hand, means that a large quantity of independent variables can be included in the analyses in order to capture most aspects of the industrial and occupational structure as well as family and labour force participation patterns in the Member States of the EU. For reasons of space we restrict our analysis here to the four countries discussed above because these are the countries with the largest institutional and regulatory variety concerning regulation of fixed-term contracts. Results for the twelve Member States of the EU in 1991 can be found in Schömann et al. (1995), as well as details on data description, variable definitions and estimation techniques.

The purpose of section 1.1, dealing with labour market and legal theories of employment contracts, was to identify theory-driven policy targets. Evaluations of fixed-term employment will have to address as a policy target the

Table 21.2   Factors Determining the Probability of Fixed-term Employment in 1991

	Spain	Western Germany	France	United Kingdom
Female	+	(–)	+	(+)
Single	+	+	+	+
Widowed, divorced, separated	+	+	+	(+)
Head of household	–	+	–	–
Spouse of head of hh.	(+)	+	(–)	(+)
	Spain	**Western Germany**	**France**	**United Kingdom**
Age (in five-year age groups, 15–19, ...)	+ 4	+ 4	+ 4	+ 1
EC national	(+)	(–)	(–)	+
Non-EC national	(+)	+	+	+
Compulsory education	+	–	–	–
A-levels/Bac/Abi/BUP/COU	(+)	–	–	–
Employment status one year ago				
	Spain	**Western Germany**	**France**	**United Kingdom**
Unemployed	+	+	+	+
In education	+	+	+	+
Inactive	+	+	(–)	+
Self-employed	+	(+)	(+)	+

Notes
The estimates are based on the full sample of the *Labour Force Survey* and include ten industrial sectors and six major occupation dummy variables. Full estimates are presented in Schömann et al. (1995). Abi = Abitur; Bac = Baccalauréat; BUP = Bachillirato Unificado Polivalente; COU = Curso de Orientacion Universitaria; — = data not available.

Source
Data from Labour Force Survey 1991 calculated by Eurostat, Luxembourg: Office des publications officielles des Communautés européennes on behalf of WZB.

sorting or selection mechanism that distinguishes fixed-term and standard employment contracts. A comparative evaluation of this sorting mechanism can capture the dynamic structure of employment systems and their consequences for recruitment under fixed-term contracts. Based on the European Labour Force Survey, Schömann et al. (1995) estimated multivariate logistic regression models of the probability of fixed-term employment, using the full sample size for 1991. Some selected results are presented in Table 21.2. The dependent variable measures whether the worker is employed on a fixed-term or a standard employment contract. A positive sign is to be interpreted as increasing the probability of fixed-term employment relative to the reference category. Signs in brackets are not statistically significant at the 5 per cent level of confidence.

In reading Table 21.2 across countries, we find that in Spain and France there is a significantly higher share of female employees on fixed-term contracts. Single, widowed, divorced and separated people are found especially to work fixed term more frequently than married people in the four countries. The most clear-cut pattern common to all Member States is the significantly higher probability of younger employees working on fixed-term contracts. For theoretical and historical reasons this pattern is hardly surprising because some Member States only began facilitating fixed-term employment in the mid-1980s. Therefore, persons in fixed-term employment are mostly new labour market entrants and, to a lesser extent, persons changing jobs. The strong age selectivity of fixed-term employment in the four European countries implies that young labour market entrants were predominantly affected by the adjustment of the legal framework to facilitate fixed-term contracts. Non-EC nationals were also more likely to be in fixed-term employment in Germany, France and the United Kingdom than natives of these countries. Relative to employees with third-level education (e.g. university diplomas), less qualified employees are actually less likely to be in fixed-term employment in the United Kingdom and western Germany in 1991. In Spain, however, less qualified employees have a higher risk of working fixed term.

The respondents provided information regarding their economic activity one year prior to the survey. This allows us to test in a rudimentary fashion the dynamics of recruitment in each of the four countries. We focus on sequences of unemployment and employment, time spent in education prior to employment and inactivity or self-employment in the previous year. For the four countries it is important to include this retrospective information in the analysis because the process of recruitment under specific forms of employment contracts is 'path dependent', meaning that previous periods spent in unemployment, participation in higher education or spells of inactivity reflect easily observable characteristics of employees or the unemployed. From a theoretical point of view, the segmentation theory of the labour market makes explicit reference to the importance of employment histories of workers. Employees with an unemployment record or interruptions due to inactivity seem to be considered as potentially unreliable. Recruitment under a fixed-term contract for reasons of an extended probationary period appears to be common practice in the four countries under consideration.

Comparing effects over years (see details in Schömann et al., 1995), we find a stagnating tendency to recruit fixed-term employees among the unemployed. A significant share of fixed-term employees was actually either economically inactive or still in full-time education one year prior to fixed-term employment. Relative to 1988, recruitment into fixed-term employment among the unemployed has decreased in both Germany and France. Whereas France has reintroduced some regulations governing fixed-term contracts, less regulation in Germany did not stimulate recruitment among the unemployed; the percentage of fixed-term employees remained the same in both countries. In France and western Germany the effect of age selectivity among the very young is also stronger than the recruitment of fixed-term employees from the unemployed. Nonstandard forms of labour contracts are, it seems, closely related to a more marginal attachment to the labour market.

3   CONCLUSIONS

We can conclude our overview of deregulation attempts and subsequent evaluation studies with some general remarks. The attempts to use employment protection reforms in order to increase labour market flexibility are largely limited by the existing labour laws, in particular dismissal protection. In fact, 'deregulation' often meant further regulation by adding a labour market policy perspective to the existing understanding of employment law. Furthermore, deregulation consisted only of limited exemption of certain categories of employees from regular employment protection. No Member State of the EU, with the exception of some procedural changes in the United Kingdom in which the qualifying period of employment was raised to two years, changed the dismissal protection system as such. The reform of labour law for labour market policy purposes was largely restricted by the existing legal principles and conditions of employment protection systems. The lesson of the deregulation attempts seems to be so far that regulation of fixed-term contracts is closely linked to dismissal protection. The reform of one part of the employment protection system has repercussions for other parts, which tends to invalidate incremental reforms to increase the flexibility of the institutional structures of the labour market. However, it is unclear whether a reduction of standards of employment protection, and in particular dismissal protection, is desirable. Some economists argue that a reduction of dismissal protection might in fact lead to an increase in transaction costs as a result of rapid labour turnover, which would have negative consequences for overall employment prospects (Franz, 1994).

The major evaluation studies of fixed-term contracts in France (Michon and Ramaux, 1993; Ministère du Travail et de la Formation Professionnelle, 1992), in Spain (Alba-Ramírez, 1991; Segura et al., 1991) and in Germany (Büchtemann and Höland, 1989; Infratest, 1994) have been single-country studies. They do not refer to experiences in other countries with similar labour market policy instruments, that is, they do not change the institutional context within which agents of the labour market act. This shortfall may be permissible given that changes in one country's legislation are the major subject of the evaluation reports, but it bears the risk that effective functional equivalents used in other countries will be undervalued. The advantage of single-country studies is that analyses of labour market processes can take for granted large parts of the institutional background of a country's employment system. However, an evaluation of parts of a legal system that treats law only as an external reference without its own dynamics adopts a static view of law and thereby overlooks the fact that legislation is itself not stable, but is continuously changed by amendments, collective agreements or judicial interpretations.

The evaluations carried out in the four countries under comparison demonstrate the advantages of country-specific evaluations. These are related to in-depth analysis of legal systems using a multilevel approach. In an evaluation from a country-by-country perspective each country's legal system is likely to be the source of some form of data on specific aspects of its regulation, for example, the impact of the wage-bargaining system on fixed-term employment or functional equivalents like agency work. The availability of individual- and firm-level longitudinal data concerning employment protection and cooperation with unions within countries should, eventually, enable the calculation of transition rates from fixed-term employment into permanent employment over longer periods. Even some of the national Labour Force Surveys could be analysed in this way, in view of the rotating participation system of segments of the respondents in these surveys.

However, despite the advantages of country studies we believe that future evaluation studies should include comparative analyses in order to contextualize national findings. For this purpose it is necessary to develop theoretically founded comparative dimensions. Examples of a promising comparative dimension could be the degree of formalization of employment relationships (see Schmid, chap. 7 in this volume), the extent of enforcement of rights through courts, compensation at the end of the fixed term or in cases of termination of the employment contract. From the socioeconomic perspective additional dimensions are transition rates from fixed-term into permanent employment, socioeconomic background or employment histories of fixed-term employees and the size of the wage differential for atypical employment. Comparative analyses of this kind might be of particular use in policy-making or legislative activities at the supranational level.

Comparative studies entail the difficulty that the depth of analysis of country studies must be maintained, while at the same time the multiple dimensions of the varying country employment systems should be made more explicit (Janoski and Hicks, 1994). Due to the historical evolution of systems of employment, some functional equivalents in one country may not be considered valid equivalents in another country, and hence detailed country studies will have little to offer for comparative evaluations. An extension of the 'many country cases and few differentiating variables' approach commonly practised seems to be required. We propose basing country comparisons of evaluations of legal aspects with labour market relevance on the study of theoretically founded labour market processes, using multivariate microlevel estimation techniques (see section 2.2). Ideally, such an analysis would be complemented by and combined with macroeconomic modelling to capture effects of full business cycles on these processes.

REFERENCES

Adamy, W. (1988), 'Deregulierung des Arbeitsmarktes—Zwischenbilanz des Beschäftigungsförderungsgesetzes', *WSI–Mitteilungen*, 8, 475–82.

Alba-Ramírez, A. (1991), *Fixed-term Employment Contracts in Spain: Labor Market Flexibility or Segmentation?*, working paper 91–29, Departamento de Economia Universidad Carlos III de Madrid.

Bentolila, S. and G. Saint-Paul (1992), 'The Macroeconomic Impact of Flexible Labor Contracts, with an Application to Spain', *European Economic Review*, 36, 1013–53.

Bertola, G. (1990), 'Job Security, Employment and Wages', *European Economic Review*, 34, 851–79.

Büchtemann, C. F. (1993), 'Employment Security and Deregulation: The West German Experience', in C. F. Büchtemann (ed.), *Employment Security and Labor Market Behaviour—Interdisciplinary Approaches and International Evidence*, Ithaca/New York: ILR Press, pp. 272–96.

Büchtemann, C. F and A. Höland (1989), *Befristete Arbeitsverträge nach dem Beschäftigungsförderungsgesetz*, research report no. 183, Bonn: Bundesminister für Arbeit und Sozialordnung.

Casey, B. (1991), 'Survey Evidence on Trends in Non-standard Employment', in A. Pollert (ed.), *Farewell to Flexibility*, Oxford: Basil Blackwell, pp.179–99.

Commission of the European Communities (1991), 'Arbeitsmarktentwicklungen in der Gemeinschaft—Ergebnisse einer Umfrage bei Unternehmern und Arbeitnehmern', *Europäische Wirtschaft*, 47, 7–164.

Däubler, W. (1989), *Sozialstaat EG? Die andere Dimension des Binnenmarktes (Strategien und Optionen für die Zukunft Europas)*, Gütersloh: Bertelsmann.

Deakin, S. (1990), 'Equality under a Market Order: The Employment Act 1989', *Industrial Law Journal*, 19, 1–19.

Deakin, S. and U. Mückenberger (1989), 'From Deregulation to a European Floor of Rights: Labour Law, Flexibilisation and the European Single Market', *Zeitschrift für internationales Arbeits- und Sozialrecht (ZIAS)*, 3, 153–207.

Delsen, L. (1995), *Atypical Employment: An International Perspective—Causes, Consequences and Policy*, Groningen: Wolters-Noordhoff.

Delsen, L. and F. Huijgen (1994), *Analysis of Part-time and Fixed-term Employment in Europe Using Establishment Data*, working paper no. WP/94/14/EN, Dublin: European Foundation for the Improvement of Living and Working Conditions.

Department of Trade and Industry (1985), *Burdens on Business*, London: HMSO.

Dickens, L. (1994), 'Deregulation and Employment Rights in Great Britain', in R. Rogowski and T. Wilthagen (eds), *Reflexive Labour Law, Studies in Industrial Relations and Employment Regulation*, Deventer: Kluwer, pp. 225–47.

Emmerson, M. (1988), 'Regulation or Deregulation of the Labour Market—Policy Regimes for the Recruitment and Dismissal of Employees in the Industrialised Countries', *European Economic Review*, 32, 775–817.

European Foundation for the Improvement of Living and Working Conditions (1992), *New Forms of Work and Activity, Survey of Experiences at Establishment Level in Eight European Countries,* Dublin.

Eurostat (1993), *Labour Force Survey 1983–1991,* Luxembourg: Office des publications officielles des Communautés européennes.

Fourcade, B. (1992), 'Evolution des situations d'emploi particulières de 1945 à 1990', *Travail et Emploi*, 52, 4–19.

Franz, W. (1994), 'Chancen und Risiken einer Flexibilisierung des Arbeitsrechts aus ökonomischer Sicht', *Zeitschrift für Arbeitsrecht (ZfA)*, 25, 439–62.

Gerritsen, D. (1995), 'Jenseits des "Normalarbeitsverhältnisses". Ansätze zu einer Sozialanthropologie der Beschäftigung', in S. Erbès-Seguin (ed.), *Beschäftigung und Arbeit. Eine Diskussion zwischen Ökonomie und Soziologie*, Berlin: edition sigma, pp. 101–21.

Guergoat, J.-C. and C. Hocquaux (1991), 'L'utilisation du CDD et de l'intérim par les entreprises', *Dossiers statistiques du travail et de l'emploi*, no. 75–76, Paris: SES–Ministère des Affaires Sociales et de l'Emploi.

Henry, R. and J.-C. Guergoat (1987), 'Le salaire des travailleurs intérimaires en octobre 1984', *Dossiers statistiques du travail et de l'emploi*, no. 33, Paris: SES–Ministère des Affaires Sociales et de l'Emploi.

Hunt, J. (1993), 'Firing Costs, Employment Fluctuations and Average Employment: An Examination of Germany', Department of Economics, Yale University. (Unpublished manuscript)

Infratest (1994), *Befristete Beschäftigung und Arbeitsmarkt. Empirische Untersuchung über befristete Arbeitsverträge nach dem Beschäftigungsförderungsgesetz (BeschFG 1985/1990)*, Munich.

Janoski, T. and A. M. Hicks (1994), 'Methodological Innovations in Comparative Political Economy: An Introduction', in T. Janoski and A. M. Hicks (eds), *The Comparative Political Economy of the Welfare State*, Cambridge, UK: Cambridge University Press, pp. 1–27.

Jimeno, J. F. and L. Toharia (1991), 'Productivity and Wage Effects of Fixed-term Employment: Evidence from Spain', Department of Economics, London School of Economics. (Unpublished manuscript)

Jimeno, J. F. and L. Toharia (1993), 'Spanish Labour Markets: Institutions and Outcomes', in J. Hartog and J. Theeuwes (eds), *Labour Market Contracts and Institutions—A Cross-national Comparison*, Amsterdam: Elsevier, pp. 299–322.

Join-Lambert, E. and X. Viney (1988), 'L'insertion des jeunes à la sortie de l'école entre 1983 et 1987', *Economie et Statistique*, 216.

Keller, B. and H. Seifert (1993), 'Regulierung atypischer Beschäftigungsverhältnisse', *WSI–Mitteilungen*, 9, 538–45.

Kraft, K. (1993), 'Eurosclerosis Reconsidered: Employment Protection and Work Force Adjustment in West Germany', in C. F. Büchtemann (ed.), *Employment Security and Labor Market Behaviour—Interdisciplinary Approaches and International Evidence*, Ithaca/New York: ILR Press, pp. 297–304.

Kraft, K. (1994), *A Comparison of Employment Adjustment Patterns in France, Germany, Great Britain and Italy*, WZB discussion paper FS I 94–207, Wissenschaftszentrum Berlin für Sozialforschung.

Linne, G. and S. Voswinkel (1989), *Vielleicht ist ja noch alles offen—Eine empirische Untersuchung über befristete Arbeitsverhältnisse*, Hamburg: Institut für sozialwissenschaftliche Forschung.

Meulders, D., O. Plasman and R. Plasman (eds) (1994), *Atypical Employment in the EC*, Dartmouth: Aldershot.

Michon, F. and F. Ramaux (1993), 'Temporary Employment in France: A Decade Statement', *Labour*, 7 (3), 93–116.

Ministère du Travail et de la Formation Professionnelle (1992), *Evolution récente du travail précaire*, Rapport au Parlement, Paris.

Möller, C. (1988), 'Flexibilisierung—Eine Talfahrt in die Armut. Prekäre Arbeitsverhältnisse im Dienstleistungssektor', *WSI–Mitteilungen*, 8, 466–75.

Mosley, H. G. (1994), 'Employment Protection and Labor Force Adjustment in EC Countries', in G. Schmid (ed.), *Labor Market Institutions in Europe: A Socioeconomic Evaluation of Performance*, Armonk/New York: M. E. Sharpe, pp. 59–82.

Mückenberger, U. (1985), 'Die Krise des Normalarbeitsverhältnisses', *Zeitschrift für Sozialreform*, 7, 415 ff., 8, 457 ff.

Mückenberger, U. (1989), 'Non-standard Forms of Employment in the Federal Republic of Germany: The Role and Effectiveness of the State', in G. Rodgers and J. Rodgers (eds), *Precarious Jobs in Labour Market Regulation. The Growth of Atypical Employment in Western Europe*, Geneva: International Institute for Labour Studies (ILO), pp. 267–85.

Mückenberger, U. (1993), 'Ist der "Sozialraum Europa" noch auf der historischen Agenda? Neue Beschäftigungsformen und deren europäische Regulierung', *WSI–Mitteilungen*, 9, 593–600.

Nicole-Drancourt, C. (1992), 'L'idée de précarité revisitée', *Travail et Emploi*, 52, 57–70.

OECD (1993), *Employment Outlook*, Paris: OECD.

OECD (1994), *Employment Outlook*, Paris OECD.

Pollert, A. (1991), 'Introduction', in A. Pollert (ed.), *Farewell to Flexibility?*, Oxford: Blackwell, pp. xvii–xxxv.

Ramaux, C. (1993), *Comment s'organise le recours aux CDD et à l'intérim*, working paper, Université de Paris I—Panthéon Sorbonne no. 919.

Rogowski, R. and T. Wilthagen (eds) (1994), *Reflexive Labour Law. Studies in Industrial Relations and Employment Regulation*, Deventer: Kluwer.

Schömann, K. and T. Kruppe (1993), *Fixed-term Employment and Labour Market Flexibility—Theory and Longitudinal Evidence for East and West Germany*, WZB discussion paper FS I 93–204, Wissenschaftszentrum Berlin für Sozialforschung.

Schömann, K., R. Rogowski and T. Kruppe (1994, Autumn), 'Fixed-term Contracts in the European Union', European Commission, *Employment Observatory Policies*, 47, 30–39.

Schömann, K., R. Rogowski and T. Kruppe (1995), *Fixed-term Contracts and Their Impact on Labour Market Efficiency and Individual Job Careers in the European Community*, WZB discussion paper FS I 95–207, Wissenschaftszentrum Berlin für Sozialforschung.

Segura, J., F. Durán, L. Toharia and S. Bentolila (1991), *Análisis de la contratación temporal en España*, Madrid: Ministerio de Trabajo y Seguridad Social.

Teubner, G. (1986), 'After Legal Instrumentalism: Strategic Models of Post-regulatory Law', in G. Teubner (ed.), *Dilemmas of Law in the Welfare State*, Berlin/New York: De Gruyter, pp. 299–325.

Vissers, A. and H. J. Dirven (1994), *Fixed-term Contracts in the Netherlands: Some Evidence from Panel Data*, WZB discussion paper FS I 94–212, Wissenschaftszentrum Berlin für Sozialforschung.

Walwei, U. (1991, January/February), 'Fixed-term Contracts in EC Countries', *Intereconomics*, 25–31.

22. Employment Security and Dismissal Protection

Christoph F. Büchtemann and Ulrich Walwei

Employment security and the impacts of legal restrictions on employment terminations by firms have been a regularly recurring controversy in the labour market policy debates of most western industrialized countries. Whereas proponents of employment-security regulations have maintained that restraints on employers' dismissal behaviour are necessary for establishing parity and fairness between the labour market parties and for stabilizing employment over the business cycle, critics have blamed such regulations for slowing down necessary work force adjustments, increasing fixed labour costs, reducing the allocative efficiency of labour markets and, thus, at least in part accounting for sluggish employment growth and persisting high levels of long-term unemployment in many European countries as compared to the United States. In the 1980s, such criticism, though frequently rooted in abstract notions rather than firm empirical evidence about the functioning of labour markets, spurred several European governments to introduce new legislation that selectively relaxes legal restraints on dismissal and layoffs and/or widens legal loopholes allowing statutory dismissal protection to be circumvented by, for instance, facilitating the use of temporary workers (see Rogowski and Schömann, chap. 21 in this handbook) or encouraging early retirement of older workers (see Casey, chap. 12 of this handbook). Despite these changes, which have left the basic systems of statutory dismissal protection largely intact, the debate about the allegedly adverse employment and labour market impacts of employment-security regulation has continued with undiminished intensity, as witnessed by the fact that both the *Employment Outlook* for 1993 (OECD, 1993, pp. 95–104) and the 1993 edition of *Employment in Europe* (Commission of the European Communities, 1993, pp. 173–85) each devote a whole chapter to the issue.

The debate on employment security has stimulated a great deal of research effort over the past two decades. However, most attempts to determine the actual labour market impacts of existing employment-security regimes (since the deregulation policies of the 1980s) have produced conflicting results, calling for improvements in evaluation methodology and design. In particular, most previous research has not been well grounded in theoretical terms, lacking a clear-cut notion of the specific nature of modern employment relationships and the potential sources of market failure inherent therein as well as of the differential impacts and implications of contrasting regulatory approaches. The unsatisfactory state of evidence also reflects the specific methodological difficulties involved in determining and measuring the complex and dispersed behavioural effects of universally applicable legal rules and standards. Unlike most 'active' policies that use 'tangible' incentive mechanisms (e.g. direct financial subsidies) to influence the behaviour of predefined target groups in a positively specified direction (e.g. participation in further training programmes), employment-security regulations do not prescribe any specific observable behaviour. They tend instead to be limited to defining minimum standards and procedural requirements for employment terminations and to providing a default setting that sanctions undesired behaviour (*unfair* or *unjustified* employment terminations) and specifies possible courses of action and/ or remedies for the direct victims of such behaviour. As a consequence, there are no discernible participants and nonparticipants. Behavioural changes induced by employment-security regulations are extremely difficult to observe, thus precluding most of the standard methodological approaches developed for and used in programme evaluation research.

When speaking of 'employment security and dismissal protection' in this chapter, we do not mean absolute security against job loss in the sense of guaranteed employment. In modern market economies, employment security can, for the vast majority of workers, only mean security from unfounded or arbitrary employment terminations.[1] That is, employment terminations are tied to certain standards, rules and procedures, the specification and 'strictness' of which tends to vary across different groups of workers, from situation to situation, and from country to country. As such, employment-security regimes must be viewed as a continuum rather than as a fixed point, ranging from legal prenotification requirements, seniority rules for layoffs and basic fairness criteria for disciplinary dismissals to comprehensive systems involving judicially enforced *just-cause* requirements, mandatory consultations with worker representatives and public authorization procedures. These regulations and their

---

1 An exception to this rule are *special* dismissal-protection regulations that apply to certain categories of workers, such as members of firm-level worker representation bodies (e.g. the German works councils), persons on military service, women during pregnancy and on maternity leave and severely disabled persons. However, in most of these cases, there is also the possibility of offering protected employees severance pay in order to induce them to quit. Such special protective regulations, which are not the focus of the present chapter, thus in effect merely raise the costs of employment terminations and do not provide any absolute protection against job loss.

cumulative impacts on workers, firms and aggregate labour market outcomes are at the very core of this chapter.

The remaining parts of this chapter are organized as follows. Section 1 discusses the basic characteristics of modern employment relationships and their implications for devising 'efficient' governance rules for employment terminations that mitigate the risks of both market and policy failures. This discussion yields a set of theoretically derived criteria for assessing the economic impacts of employment-security regimes and a list of questions that evaluations of dismissal-protection regimes ideally need to address. Section 2 presents a brief characterization of contrasting legal dismissal-protection regimes, particularly the European statutory approach versus the American common-law approach, and contains a critical discussion of attempts to classify countries by the 'relative restrictiveness' of dismissal-protection regulations. Section 3 provides an overview of the methodological approaches taken by previous performance assessment and impact evaluation studies and of different indicators used for measuring the effects of employment-security regulation on labour market outcomes. Section 4 summarizes the state of knowledge and outlines perspectives for future research.

1   THEORETICAL DISCUSSION

Any evaluation of employment security and dismissal-protection policies must start with setting out conditions for efficient[2] labour market transactions and their desired social and economic outcomes. Identifying these conditions provides a set of theoretically derived criteria by which existing dismissal-protection regimes and their impacts on economic behaviour and labour market outcomes can be evaluated. From an analytical perspective, the need for policy interventions in this area essentially hinges on two questions. First, from the viewpoint of maximizing individual and collective welfare, does the nature of modern labour markets and modern employment relations require special arrangements regarding the conditions and terms of employment terminations? Second, can the definition and enforcement of such terms and conditions be achieved more efficiently through public policy (legislation) than through mere private contracting by the individual labour market parties?

---

2 *Efficient* here simply denotes maximization of the output value derived from a given set and quantity of inputs.

1.1   Modern Labour Markets and the Nature of the Employment Relation

Theoretical labour market analysis since the mid-1970s has been strongly inspired by the empirical finding of prevailing long-term job attachments and delayed or incomplete employment adjustment to demand fluctuations. Several arguments have been proposed to explain why both firms and workers may, indeed, share an endogenous economic interest in open-ended, stable employment relationships over lengthy periods. Central to most of these arguments has been the notion of market imperfections due to *asset specificity* and *idiosyncratic exchange*. That is, exchanges between workers and firms (as opposed to transactions in classical commodity markets) involve specific irreversible investments in relationship-specific capital (*sunk costs*) that generate economic rents for both sides (dual monopoly) as long as the exchange between the two parties continues, thereby generating a mutual interest in long-term relations.[3] More specifically, most theoretical models in this tradition have focussed on fixed employment costs (*turnover costs*), which have to be incurred at the beginning of the employment relationship (costs for screening job candidates, hiring, specific training and matching workers to jobs). Other models have emphasized workers' higher risk aversion as compared to firms as a rationale for *implicit contracts* distributing income streams over longer periods. Still other theories, known as *efficiency wage* or *effort regulation* models, have focussed on information asymmetries and the costs involved in monitoring work effort in employment relationships. They have provided arguments why seniority-based pay and deferred compensation schemes may enhance efficiency. Lastly, *internal labour market theories* have combined several of the above explanations in order to account for the observed dualism of inertia in work force adjustment in some parts of the economy (primarily larger firms) and more rapid adjustments involving external labour turnover in others (e.g. occupational labour markets, as prevailing in the traditional crafts sector, or secondary labour markets primarily employing casual labour). In this view, internal labour markets 'develop as technological considerations require firm-specific investments and asymmetric information necessitates the monitoring of work effort: workers make sunk investments in training and monitoring by accepting deferred compensation. At the same time the firm makes sunk investments in shared training costs and in intangibles such as

---

3 Transactions between formally equal market participants and a clear definition and assignment of initial property rights are assumed in most of the models. Such property rights 'establish the initial distribution of rights, the exclusivity of the rights, and the mechanisms under which transfers of property rights are effected and recognized' (Spulber, 1989, p. 48). Without the assignment of clearly defined, exclusive property rights, market transactions cannot take place.

reputation in the labour market' (Cohen and Wachter, 1989, p. 245). Taken together, these theoretical approaches provide strong arguments why—even from a strictly microeconomic perspective—stable, long-term employment relationships are by no means incompatible with, but rather in many instances conducive to, economic efficiency and the maximization of societal welfare.

Moreover, theory also shows that long-term employment relationships between workers and firms necessarily involve a high degree of uncertainty for both sides. First, the existence of information asymmetries implies the risk of *opportunistic behaviour* by one party or the other. In order to reduce the risk of *shirking* by workers, firms will thus be inclined to design special compensation schemes rewarding work effort and at the same time will want to retain the right to dismiss workers whose work effort fails to match expected standards. Workers, on the other hand, in the absence of any binding rules or standards of fairness standards, cannot rely on their employers to refrain from dismissing them before they reach seniority and to compensate them for past work effort. This risk reduces workers' willingness to accept efficiency-enhancing deferred compensation schemes in the first place. Second, both parties share a lack of information and face uncertainty with regard to the future into which their relationship must continue if the returns to their initial shared investments are to be reaped. For example, the firm may be forced to reduce its work force and to abandon its promise of future compensation for past work effort in the event of an unforeseen major decline in the demand for its products. In the presence of information asymmetries and future uncertainty, the willingness of both parties to engage in long-term employment relationships involving sunk investments in relationship-specific capital, therefore, depends on whether they can devise and implement between them a governance structure that addresses the dual question of mutual trust and risk-sharing.

- *Mutual trust* requires safeguards against opportunistic behaviour by the other side. This means that firms cannot fire workers (or unilaterally alter contract terms) at will or arbitrarily, thereby depriving workers of their share in the rents from mutual sunk investments, and that workers cannot lower the firm's returns to such investments by withholding work effort (shirking) without facing dismissal.
- *Risk-sharing*, on the other hand, requires enforceable rules that both parties, each within their relative capacity, equally share the potential losses resulting from unpredictable future events. This arrangement implies that firms cannot be forced to maintain the employment relationship if, due to altered economic circumstances, their medium-term survival would otherwise be seriously jeopardized, but that they would have to compensate workers for unrewarded effort in the past.

Put differently, the feasibility of modern, open-ended employment relationships allowing the rents from mutual sunk investments to be reaped over a contingent future depends on whether both parties can agree on a contractual arrangement that, in addition to specifying hours and wages (as does the classical employment contract; see Hall and Lazear, 1984; Rosen, 1985), also spells out the exact conditions under which the relationship can be terminated by either side. The economic benefits inherent in the establishment and maintenance of standards, rules and procedures governing employment terminations thus seem to offer a powerful explanation for why implicit practices and/or explicit rules concerning probationary periods, disciplinary procedures, prenotification requirements, selection for layoffs and severance pay entitlements have been found to be quite common even in the absence (or prior to the introduction) of exogenously imposed legal constraints (for such evidence, see Büchtemann, 1993b). This would seem to have far-reaching implications for the evaluation of *unjust*-dismissal policies: if workers and firms have a genuine economic interest in establishing rules, standards and procedures for dealing with employment terminations, then the direct economic costs imposed by unjust-dismissal legislation may indeed be considerably less than predicted by models assuming perfectly competitive labour markets.

1.2   Sources of Market Failures and Rationales for Public Policy Interventions

From the above one could conclude that 'workers' rights in jobs do exist as a result of voluntary exchanges' (Addison, 1989, p. 136) and that, consequently, there is no need for legislation. This has, indeed, been the view taken by the proponents of a radical *laissez-faire* in labour relations, who have postulated that, given clearly defined and assigned property rights, unconstrained voluntary negotiations between private parties produce optimal results (see e.g. Epstein, 1984; Posner, 1984, pp. 990–95; Soltwedel et al., 1990). Conversely, any plea for (or defence of) employment-security legislation must provide evidence that mere private contracting in modern labour markets produces inefficiencies that can be avoided or minimized by third-party interventions.

Indeed, a large and growing body of research on labour law regulation (Leslie, 1989; Schwab, 1989) and regulation in other fields (see Cooter and Ulen, 1988; Shavell, 1984; Spulber, 1989) has pointed out various situations in which market failures are likely to occur and in which third-party regulation (legislation) may produce superior results. Such a situation is given whenever the negotiation and monitoring of private contracts would involve very high *transaction costs* that can be reduced by the establishment of general standards and rules by an external agency. With increasing sunk investments, increasing time horizons for reaping the rents thereof and an overall enhanced volatility in the economic environment, the transaction costs of privately negotiating individual contracts between firms and workers can be expected to rise. Another situation for efficiency gains through legislation is given when private parties (in our case: firms and workers) are likely to agree on terms that produce external costs for third parties not involved in the original bargain (*externalities*), pointing to the fact that real markets are frequently not fully competitive. In these cases, legal regulation forcing the parties to fully internalize the costs of their behaviour may be efficiency enhancing.

Binding legal standards may further increase overall efficiency if the enforcement of private contracts is very costly and legislation could provide enforcement at a lower cost. This is the case whenever contractual compliance is difficult to monitor, contract terms are vague and may give rise to conflicting interpretations, damages resulting from noncompliance are difficult to measure, and causation of damages or harms is difficult to establish. In such instances, conflicts over contract terms are more likely to arise and to entail costly information-gathering by external arbitrators in the course of lengthy case-by-case fact-finding investigations in which the actual terms of the contract and the behaviours of both parties during the employment relationship have to be retrospectively established. This process produces a high degree of legal uncertainty for both sides (see Kolstad, 1990). In fact, the aforementioned describes exactly those problems that have prompted several critics of the US common-law system to recommend the introduction of European-type unjust-dismissal legislation in the United States (see Gould, 1993, pp. 63–108; Krueger, 1991; Maltby, 1994). Given the growing complexity and contingencies involved in modern employment relationships,[4] the latter progressively cease to 'fit comfortably into the traditional common law scheme' (Leonard, 1988, p. 636; see also Fisher, 1994; Krueger, 1992).

Lastly, Levine (1991) has pointed out that private contracting may fail altogether to rule out the dual problem of adverse selection and moral hazard inherent in open-ended employment relationships involving sunk investments. As long as, say, the negotiation of just-cause requirements for employment terminations is left exclusively to the discretion of private parties, firms offering *just cause* are prone to attracting workers who in other firms following an at-will policy would face a higher risk of being dismissed. For the individual firm such adverse selection of job candidates and the ensuing higher risk of shirking once the workers are hired may create an incentive to discontinue offering just-cause standards for dismissals, thereby, of course, also affecting

---

4 In a unique historical analysis, Carter (1988) showed for the United States (California) that the duration of employment relationships and the importance of near life-time jobs have significantly increased between the late 19th and the late 20th centuries.

the lot of nonshirking workers. In such cases, legislation, by universalizing rules and standards for individual behaviour, may solve typical prisoner's-dilemma situations and thereby enhance overall efficiency.

The above reasoning implies that the direct economic costs imposed by dismissal legislation, which have been in the focus of the current debate on employment-security policies, need to be carefully weighed against the alternative costs of merely private contracting and—if the latter should fail—the socioeconomic welfare costs of forborne sunk investments. Moreover, as illustrated by the case of the United States, where legislation on the termination of employment relationships has been largely nonexistent, the absence of dismissal legislation means that conflicts arising out of the employment relationship (including contract terminations by the employer) are handled by *civil contract law*. The American experience, however, raises serious doubts as to whether civil contract law provides an adequate framework for dealing with the complexities of modern, long-term employment relationships (see Dertouzos and Karoly, 1993; Maltby, 1994; Troy, 1990). From the viewpoint of the economic theory of law, the costs and potential inefficiencies involved in relegating conflicts over employment terminations to the realm of civil contract law thus describe the opportunity costs of dismissal legislation.[5]

1.3   Elements of Efficient Dismissal-protection Regimes

The conclusion that legislation may, under certain conditions, be more efficient than mere private contracting does not yet answer the crucial evaluation question of which type of legislation is best suited to achieve these goals. The above theoretical discussion, however, can provide some general indications as to the basic attributes and elements of efficient employment-security policies.

First, in order to provide a supporting structure for investments in relationship-specific capital and the private returns resulting from them, efficient dismissal-protection legislation will have to be fashioned closely to the *sunk-cost rules* underlying private contracting in modern labour market settings. More specifically, this implies two things.

a) In order to mitigate the risk of *opportunistic behaviour*, efficient dismissal-protection regimes will contain clauses restraining employers' freedom to dismiss workers at will and tying individual employment terminations to the requirement of some objective and verifiable just cause, such as malper-

---

5 Along this line, Margolis (1987) has proposed a formal definition of an *efficient* legal regime as one 'in which property rights are assigned and liability rules are formulated so that the value of the things present in society, as measured by willingness to pay, is maximized over all alternative legal environments, given the costs of transacting' (pp. 473–4).

formance, shirking or misconduct on the side of the worker. Moreover, the risk of *adverse selection* of malperforming or shirking workers would seem to require the existence of a waiting or probationary period for newly hired workers, during which legal dismissal restrictions do not apply, thus allowing firms a careful on-the-job screening of novices without facing major termination restraints. Vice versa, given that investments in relationship-specific capital tend to increase with tenure, the strictness of the criteria and documentation requirements applied to individual employment terminations will increase with the worker's seniority.

b) *Risk-sharing* in the event of an economically induced decline in labour demand means that the firm retains the right to unilaterally terminate employees if a change in economic conditions requires it to do so, provided that the firm has ostensibly taken all 'reasonable'[6] efforts to prevent layoffs through alternative forms of work force and hours reduction, such as a hiring stop and/or work-sharing, for example. When layoffs become inevitable, the existence of deferred compensation schemes to elicit work effort and worker commitment would seem to require efficient dismissal-protection regimes to contain clauses demanding that junior workers will be laid off first (layoff by reverse seniority) and that layoffs of tenured senior workers involve severance payments as partial compensation for past work effort.

Second, in order to prevent *externalities* arising from private maximizing behaviour, efficient dismissal-protection regimes must include regulations forcing the private labour market parties to internalize the full costs of their rent-generating transactions. Generally, such externalities are given when the external costs caused by dismissals and layoffs exceed the costs that the labour market parties would have incurred by preventing dismissals or layoffs. In order to reduce external costs caused by layoffs, efficient dismissal-protection regimes will include *prenotification* requirements for nondisciplinary dismissals, enabling workers to search for new employment while still on the job, thereby reducing the burden to be carried by public unemployment insurance schemes due to frictional employment. Since the likelihood of finding new employment can be expected to differ across workers according to the specificity of their acquired human capital, prenotification periods will furthermore increase with age and/or tenure in the current job.

---

6 *Reasonable* in this context refers to all those measures that do not jeopardize the economic viability of the undertaking at large. In this sense, Cooter and Rubinfeld (1989) observed that 'the "reasonable man" of the law is not very different from the "rational man" of economics' (p. 1068). Most legal dismissal-protection regimes are based on the notion of a reasonable employer.

Moreover, major externalities tend to result from large-scale layoffs and mass dismissals that may produce a shock for local labour markets and impose various costs on local communities at large (e.g. in the form of declining local product demand or declining real estate prices). To minimize such externalities, efficient dismissal-protection regimes will include clauses requiring *advance notification* of intended major layoffs to local labour market authorities, with the latter in some instances being entitled to demand a stretching of layoffs to avert a local labour market shock.

Third, taking into account that the sunk-cost rules characterizing modern employment relationships (as well as the adverse external effects of layoffs) apply primarily to medium-sized and larger firms with internal labour markets, efficient dismissal-protection regimes will further include selective exemptions for small firms that lack the scope and organizational structures to take recourse to alternative modes of work force adjustment (e.g. attrition) and thus would face significantly higher costs due to dismissal protection than larger firms would.

Dismissal-protection legislation fashioned along these three core principles would seem not only to act as a safeguard against the risk of costly market failures but also, by providing a stable supporting structure for investments in relationship-specific capital, *encourage* such investments and thereby induce overall economic efficiency gains. Moreover, by assigning clearly defined property rights and setting *universal ex-ante* standards, rules and procedures for employment terminations, dismissal legislation, aside from reducing transaction costs involved in negotiating individual contract terms, also avoids the inadequacies of civil contract law for dealing with conflicts arising over the terms of employment contracts: in civil contract law, namely, conflicts over the terms of individual employment contracts, which are frequently vague, must be settled *ex post* through costly arbitration involving the establishment of *retroactive* liability rules for each individual case. As illustrated by the US experience, the enhanced legal uncertainty resulting from such *ex-post* determination of liability and the uncertain signals individual court decisions and precedents send to other market participants are likely to lead to undercompliance or overcompliance in that agents either do not adjust their behaviour at all or modify their behaviour beyond the point that would be socially optimal (see Craswell and Calfee, 1986; Spulber, 1989, p. 405). By establishing a general negligence rule applying to all employment relationships and imposing liability only on those who fail to comply (see Cooter, 1991, p. 13), legislation, by contrast, defines clear *ex-ante* guidelines for individual behaviour and, by specifying compensation formulas for unjustified job loss, enhances the predictability of damages due in the case of noncompliance.

1.4   Risks and Sources of Policy Failure

It is no coincidence that the above theoretically derived principles of efficient dismissal-protection regimes in modern labour market settings largely correspond to the basic structure and components of actual dismissal-protection regulations found in many European countries (as well as to explicit or implicit practices *voluntarily* adopted by many large firms in countries without dismissal legislation, such as Japan and the United States). Historically, the introduction of dismissal-protection legislation has been, as a common feature across many European countries, closely associated with the spread of internal labour markets and their typical concomitants of capital-intensive production, economies of scale, a high degree of division of labour, high costs of labour turnover and continuing firm-worker attachments. In fact, in those countries for which historical evidence is available, many of the rules and procedures required by dismissal legislation had already become common practice in large parts of the economy before such legislation was first introduced or extended in the 1960s and 1970s. In these cases, legislation appears to have taken the form of a mere codification of widespread de-facto practices that had evolved endogenously in dominant and advanced sectors of the economy (see Büchtemann, 1993a).

This view does not necessarily imply that dismissal-protection regimes as we encounter them today are efficient in the sense that the overall benefits emanating from them exceed their economic costs. Rather, just as we have been able to identify several sources of market failure that, in the absence of regulatory interventions, lead to suboptimal results, we can also identify several instances of policy failure causing inefficiencies and market distortions.

(a)   Design failures

Policy design failures are given when policy programmes interfere with the basic logic underlying efficient private contracting in labour markets with the result of discouraging mutual sunk investments in relationship-specific capital or preventing labour market transactions altogether. In the area of dismissal-protection legislation, such policy design failures are given, for instance, when dismissal-protection regimes are overburdened with distributional or social policy objectives that are not targeted at merely preventing externalities from private contracting. An example would be absolute employment protection regulations for certain groups of workers (e.g. severely handicapped or older workers). In the absence of supporting measures (e.g. targeted employment or training subsidies), such regulations force firms to bear the full costs for worker protection and thereby violate the risk-sharing principle underlying efficient employment contracts. Strict dismissal-protection regulations of this kind, therefore, tend to induce unintended behaviours, such as discrimination against protected groups in firms' hiring policies, thus creating typical insider–outsider problems.

Another instance of policy design failures is to be seen in vague standards and rules that fail to establish clearly defined property rights and/or to specify modes of recourse and penalties in the case of noncompliance and therefore give rise to conflicting interpretations and costly litigation, thus creating legal uncertainty.[7] Finally, inefficiencies can also result from legal thresholds, such as employment-based firm-size thresholds that determine whether the firm is subject to statutory dismissal-protection regulations or not. These thresholds produce inefficiencies (and frequently induce evasive behaviours by firms) in that hiring the one worker who raises the number of workers above the threshold causes the employment terms of all employed workers in the firm to change.

(b) Implementation failures

Another potential source of policy failures is the way in which public policy programmes, laws and regulations are implemented. In the case of dismissal-protection legislation, implementation rests primarily with the labour courts (or corresponding publicly mandated arbitration institutions or tribunals) and with special public authorization agencies (e.g. local labour offices for major collective layoffs or special boards responsible for deciding upon the justification of dismissals of special groups, such as disabled workers). Here, too, an important cause of inefficiencies may arise from judicial decisions made or precedents set by labour courts (or equivalent bodies). In concretizing uncertain legal norms, it may happen that they basically change the substance of laws (as compared to preceding judicial interpretations), thereby retroactively affecting existing definitions and assignments of property rights and, to the extent that such court decisions establish general precedents, altering the terms of all ongoing employment relationships within the specific jurisdiction (see Hamermesh, 1993). In fact, the now vast body of often inconsistent labour court decisions that redefine legal standards and the ensuing high legal information costs and legal uncertainty have been the focus of recent criticism of legal dismissal protection by German employers (see Deregulierungskommission, 1991, p. 135; Soltwedel et al., 1990, pp. 28–31). Likewise, in a recent European-wide survey of over 2000 firms (see UNICE, 1995, p. 33), the inconsistent implementation of legal norms by public agencies emerged as one of the core complaints about government regulation. Another type of imple-

---

7 An empirical indicator of such inefficiencies due to unclear standards would be the number of dismissals that are legally contested through litigation (see e.g. Barnard, Clark and Lewis, 1995, pp. 36–7).

mentation failure results from long authorization or arbitration procedures, which, aside from causing costly delays for the labour market parties, frequently preclude certain remedies (e.g. reinstatement of unjustly dismissed workers) because situations have changed when a decision or settlement is finally reached.

(c)   *Policy failures due to structural misalignment and institutional malcoordination*

One of the most frequent sources of policy failures is poor coordination between institutional incentives and legally required behaviours on the one hand and the changing opportunity structures as well as shifting behavioural dispositions and repertoires of economic agents (workers and firms) on the other. That is, regulatory interventions that may have enhanced efficiency in a particular historical situation and under specific economic conditions cease to do so when economic circumstances and prevailing forms of economic organization change. Moreover, the behavioural incentives and signals emanating from public policy interventions may be affected by changes in the wider regulatory and institutional environment in which they operate. For instance, enhanced market volatility and accelerated exogenous technological change may raise the employer's costs of employment security, thus reducing the firms' interest in continuing long-term employment relationships. In such an environment, in which adjustment speed becomes a core prerequisite for sustaining competitiveness (time competition), the institutionally stabilized logic of internal labour markets underlying most existing dismissal-protection regimes may indeed come into conflict with the requirement of a faster reallocation of labour and declining returns to investments in relationship-specific capital. The increasing misfit between dismissal-protection regimes and economic requirements and the ensuing inefficiencies are then to be seen as the result of a failure of public policy to adjust to changing economic conditions (institutional inertia).

A different situation is given when institutional or regulatory changes in other areas (e.g. rising legal minimum wages) discourage mutual sunk investments in relationship-specific capital or facilitate (and thereby encourage) the circumvention of dismissal-protection regulations (e.g. through fixed-term contracts). Given uncertainty and bounded rationality, employers may, for example, prefer hiring workers on fixed-term contracts, thereby, of course, not only reducing the potential cost of employment terminations but also forgoing the rents to be reaped from mutual sunk investments in the context of longer-term, open-ended employment relationships.

For evaluation research the above discussion of market and policy failures implies that assessing the impacts of dismissal-protection legislation on labour market efficiency and overall societal welfare requires not only a detailed analysis of existing dismissal-protection regimes and the characteristics of the various labour market settings in which they operate but also a careful balancing of their costs and benefits. From a theoretical point of view, the latter must also include the development of well-grounded notions of the *opportunity costs* of existing dismissal-protection regimes, that is, the likely costs and benefits of alternative approaches to managing the complexities of modern labour markets and modern employment relationships. It is clear that these criteria define ideal standards which, due to operationalization difficulties and data limitations, most actual evaluation research cannot possibly meet. However, they define a set of theoretically grounded criteria on the basis of which the designs, methodologies and results of previous evaluation studies can be judged with regard to their relative capacity to yield reliable policy recommendations.

2   CONTRASTING POLICY REGIMES

2.1   Institutional Diversity: Europe and the United States

Unlike the United States, most European countries have traditionally followed a legislative approach to regulating employment terminations. Nonetheless, European countries encompass a wide array of different dismissal-protection regimes, each of which has evolved more or less incrementally from different labour market conditions, sociopolitical environments, historical exigencies and policy motives rather than from a coherent and consistent policy concept. Depending on the circumstances and policy motives of their introduction, some of these policy regimes emphasize financial compensation for job loss and were originally designed as a mobility incentive rather than a guarantee of one's current job (e.g. United Kingdom). Others (e.g. Germany and Italy) focus more on job preservation and reinstatement in cases of unjustified dismissal. Still others were introduced primarily as special safeguards to prevent moral-hazard behaviour in the use of unemployment insurance benefits (e.g. France). Some are more legalistic, centralized and universal (e.g. France, Spain, Portugal and the Netherlands), whereas others (e.g. Italy and the United Kingdom) rely more heavily on contractual modes of regulation in the form of collectively negotiated procedures and remedies. Depending on the relative strength and importance of such collective elements in dismissal protection, the mere look at the existing body of statutory provisions may tell only part of the story.

Despite the variety of historical roots, underlying policy motives and institutional approaches, most European dismissal-protection regimes have many formal features in common, such as probationary periods, seniority-graded prenotification periods for separations by either party, mandatory consultation with workers' representatives, special administrative control or authorization procedures for major layoffs and plant closings, severance pay provisions to compensate for unjustified job loss and/or to cushion economic hardships resulting from work force reductions and worker reinstatement provisions as remedies in the case of noncompliance and procedural violations. Most important, and unlike the United States, all major European countries require dismissals to be grounded on *just cause* involving either personal shortcomings (such as malperformance, misconduct or frequent absenteeism) on the side of the employee or economic necessity (e.g. slack demand, abolition of position, plant closing) on the side of the firm. Whereas the exact definition of what is to be considered *just cause* and the procedural requirements for dismissals (e.g. prior warnings and documentation) tend to vary from country to country, most European dismissal-protection regimes concur in restricting employer penalties and worker remedies to arbitrary dismissals that deviate from an evolved majority rule of 'reasonable' or 'fair' employer behaviour (for detailed overviews of the regulations given in different European countries, see Barnardet al., 1995; Blanpain, 1990; Büchtemann, 1993a; CNEL, 1995; Kuechle, 1990; Mosley and Kruppe, 1992; Rodriguez-Pinero, 1992).

The picture would be incomplete without mention of the wide array of direct supporting institutions and accompanying programmes, such as unemployment benefits, work-sharing subsidies and early retirement schemes that can be assumed to have an immediate impact on the level and distribution of legally imposed dismissal costs. Such supporting institutions have played a major role in most European countries (less so in the United States) but show strong variations in objectives, mix, scope and implementation across countries (for details, see Schmid and Reissert, chap. 8; Casey, chap. 12; and Mosley and Kruppe, chap. 20 in this volume). Finally, countries differ in the extent to which labour law provisions offer loopholes for circumventing dismissal-protection regulations, such as through the use of fixed-term contracts or temporary workers hired from agencies (see chap. 21 in this handbook) or through subcontracting work to formally self-employed labour.

The United States, by contrast, has frequently been cited as the only highly industrialized country where legal dismissal restraints have been largely non-existent and, consequently, have acted as a 'reference' scenario in the European debate about labour market flexibility and deregulation. Until recently, the late 19th century doctrine of *employment at will*, according to which employment can be terminated without notice by either side at any time and for any reason, 'for good cause, for no cause, or even for cause morally wrong' (*Payne v. Western & Atlantic Railroad*, 1884), remained the law of

the land for the overwhelming majority of the US work force.[8] Legally binding and enforceable procedural rules for dismissals and layoffs have been
confined largely to public sector employees and to workers in the private
unionized sector, which, however, has experienced a continuous decline in the
past two decades (and now accounts for not more than 13 per cent of all
private sector employees).[9] Yet, coinciding with the decline in unionization,
the 1970s and 1980s witnessed a progressive erosion of the employment-at-
will doctrine as a growing number of state supreme courts, in recognition of
the increasing complexities of employment relationships, introduced far-
reaching exceptions to the doctrine. These exceptions have caused a surge in
wrongful discharge litigation through the civil courts, usually involving large
compensatory and punitive damage awards to plaintiffs who prevailed (see
Weiler, 1990, pp. 48–60; Youngblood and Bierman, 1994). The most consequential of these incursions upon employment at will had to do with (a)
breaches of *implied contract*, that is, dismissal of employees in a manner
contrary to company promises of employment security as laid down, for instance, in company brochures or employee manuals; and (b) breaches of the
covenant of good faith and fair dealing, that is, dismissal of employees
despite previous promotions and positive performance reviews that can be
understood as indicating an interest on the side of the employer to continue
the employment relationship.

Only very recently have state legislatures and the US federal government
both taken initial steps to enact statutory rules for worker displacements. The
late 1980s witnessed the introduction of a mandatory 60-days prenotification
requirement for plant closings and major layoffs in large enterprises and the
enactment of rudimentary (by European standards) just-cause standards for
employment terminations by the Montana state government (see Bierman,
Vinton and Youngblood, 1993). More legislation is likely to follow soon, for
the inefficiencies, mounting legal costs and high degree of legal uncertainty
caused by common-law incursions upon the employment-at-will doctrine (see
Krueger, 1991, 1992) have prompted a growing number of state legislatures to
introduce bills that, if passed into law, will initiate basic dismissal legislation
fashioned after the 1988 Montana law and the Model Employment Termina-

---

8 According to Stieber and Rodgers (1994), an estimated 73 million private sector US employees
   were employed at will in 1993.

9 An exception is to be seen in some provisions of the US unemployment insurance (UI) scheme,
   in which—unlike in its European counterparts—employer contributions are experience-rated
   (tied to the incidence of dismissals by the firm). This experience rating of unemployment
   insurance taxes and the restriction of UI-benefits eligibility to workers who have lost their jobs
   through no fault of their own involves an implicit just-cause principle inasmuch as the UI
   administration requires basic information about the reasons underlying discharges when it
   determines benefits eligibility (see Anderson and Meyer, 1993).

tion Act (META) drafted by the Uniform Law Commissioners.[10] Similar to many of its European counterparts, META includes a just-cause standard for all disciplinary and economic dismissals, one-year probationary periods, publicly subsidized arbitration and legal restrictions on individual contract waivers in exchange for a preemption of most common-law claims, a limitation on severance pay and the abolition of compensatory and punitive damages (for details, see St. Antoine, 1994).

2.2   'Relative Restrictiveness' of Dismissal Protection: Country Rankings

Despite the institutional complexities involved, several recent studies, each using different criteria and methodological approaches and covering different sets of countries, have attempted to classify different national dismissal-protection regimes according to their relative strictness or restrictiveness and their assumed costs for employer-initiated employment terminations (see Table 22.1).

The most comprehensive approach to classifying national dismissal-protection regimes was undertaken by Grubb and Wells (1993). Their 'strictness-of-regulation' index aggregates relatively detailed information on procedural requirements and delays, notice and severance pay due in cases of no-fault dismissals, and the definition and potential costs of unfair dismissals (including reinstatement provisions). Along these lines, Portugal, Spain, Italy, Austria and Greece have the strictest dismissal-protection regimes, followed by Germany, France, the Netherlands and Belgium, with Denmark and the United Kingdom exhibiting the least regulatory restraints on individual dismissals (see Table 22.2, column 4).

Altogether, the country rank orders resulting from these attempts at classification show a more or less uniform pattern, with the southern European countries (including France) heading the list in terms of restrictiveness or dismissal costs, and Denmark, the United Kingdom, Ireland and the United States being positioned at the other end of the spectrum. Germany fares somewhere in the middle. However, several shortcomings cast doubt on whether such broad classifications of national dismissal-protection regimes provide a useful starting point for evaluating their economic impacts.[11]

First, looking merely at statutory provisions of dismissal protection necessarily ignores the many subtleties of legal provisions and fails to take into

---

10 This quasi-governmental body is in charge of promoting nationally uniform statutes in areas where such uniformity seems desirable.

11 These shortcomings may also account for some of the differences in the ranking of individual countries across the studies surveyed, particularly for France, the Netherlands, Germany and Italy.

Table 22.1   Country Rankings According to the 'Restrictiveness' of Their Dismissal-protection Regimes

	IOE 1985	Kuechle 1990	Bertola 1990	Bentolila and Bertola 1990	Lazear 1990	Mosley and Kruppe 1992 (a)	(b)	Grubb and Wells 1993 (a)	(b)
Belgium	s	7	2	—	7	5	4	8	4
Denmark	m	—	9	—	6	10	7	10	7
France	f	5	3	2	5	4	6	6	9
Germany	f	6	5	3	8	6	8	5	6
Greece	—	7	—	—	4	8	3	4	1
Ireland	s	—	—	—	11	9	11	9	10
Italy	f	4	1	1	1	1	1	3	2
Netherlands	f	3	7	—	—	2	9	7	8
Portugal	f	2	—	—	3	7	10	2	5
Spain	f	1	—	—	2	3	2	1	3
Sweden	—	—	4	—	9	—	2	—	—
United Kingdom	i	8	6	4	10	11	5	11	11
United States	—	—	10	—	12	—	—	—	—

Notes

IOE (1985): based on subjective ratings by officials of national business associations; f = fundamental; s = serious; m = minor; i = insignificant obstacles to employment terminations. – Kuechle (1990): based on detailed information on statutory provisions. – Bertola (1990): based on IOE plus information about statutory provisions as reported by Emerson (1988). – Bentolila and Bertola (1990): based on computation of dismissal costs according to a formula incorporating information on statutory notice provisions, wages during notice periods, probability of appeal of dismissal by worker and average severance pay awarded. – Lazear (1990): based on information on statutory notice periods and average severance pay due for a worker dismissed after ten years of tenure. – Mosley and Kruppe (1992): (a) based on relative frequency of employers' assessment of 'insufficient flexibility in hiring and shedding labour' as a reason for 'not being able to employ more people'—very important/important/not so important; (b) based on information about statutory notice periods and weeks of severance pay for average worker. – Grubb and Wells (1993): (a) based on detailed legal information about procedural delays, notice periods, mandatory severance, litigation and settlement costs; (b) based on legal information on the conditions for hiring temporary workers and using fixed-term contracts.

Sources

S. Bentolila and G. Bertola (1990), 'Firing Costs and Labour Demand: How Bad is Eurosclerosis?', *Review of Economic Studies*, 57, 381–402; G. Bertola (1990), 'Job Security, Employment, and Wages', *European Economic Review*, 34, 851–86; M. Emerson (1988), 'Regulation or Deregulation of the Labour Market. Policy Regimes for the Recruitment and Dismissal of Employees in the Industrialised Countries', *European Economic Review*, 32 (4), 775–817; D. Grubb and W. Wells (1993), 'Employment Regulation and Patterns of Work in EC Countries', *OECD Economic Studies*, 21, 7–58; IOE (International Association of Employers) (1985), 'Adapting the Labour Markets', Geneva. (Unpublished manuscript); H. Kuechle (1990), 'Kündigungsvorschriften im internationalen Vergleich', *WSI Mitteilungen*, 43 (6), 392–400; E. P. Lazear (1990), 'Job Security Provisions and Employment', *Quarterly Journal of Economics*, 105, 699–726; H. Mosley and T. Kruppe (1992), *Employment Protection and Labour Force Adjustment*, WZB discussion paper FS I 92–9, Wissenschaftszentrum Berlin für Sozialforschung.

Table 22.2 *Indexes of 'Restrictiveness' of Dismissal-protection Regimes and of Temporary Work Regulation in Europe (Late 1980s/Early 1990s)*

	Procedural constraints (1)	Notice and severance pay for no-fault dismissals (2)	Difficulty of dismissal and legal recourses (3)	Aggregate ranking of strictness (4)	Fixed-term contracts (5)	Temporary workers (agency work) (5)
Austria	10.0[a]	10.0	11.0	13.0	5.0	—
Belgium	4.5	13.0	3.0	5.0	16.0	8.0
Denmark	1.0	11.0	5.0	4.0	2.5	4.0
Finland	14.0	9.0	4.0	9.5	11.5	—
France	9.0	7.0	6.5	6.0	13.0	3.0
Germany	13.0	2.0	12.0	9.5	14.5	6.0
Greece	8.0	12.0	10.0	12.0	10.0	10.0
Ireland	6.5	3.0	6.5	3.0	2.5	1.5
Italy	3.0	16.0	15.0	14.0	14.5	10.0
Netherlands	16.0	1.0	8.0	7.0	7.5	5.0
Norway	6.5	6.0	14.0	8.0	6.5	—
Portugal	12.0	15.0	16.0	16.0	9.0	7.0
Spain	15.0	14.0	13.0	15.0	7.5	10.0
Sweden	11.0	8.0	9.0	11.0	6.0	—
Switzerland	2.0	4.0	2.0	1.0	2.5	—
United Kingdom	4.5	5.0	1.0	2.0	2.5	1.5

Notes
(1) Consultation requirements and delays of notice. (2) Dismissals that are not contested as unfair and that entail arbitration. (3) Including definition of 'unfair dismissal' and possibilities of arranging trial periods. (4) Ranking that increases with the strictness of dismissal restraints. (5) Includes types of work for which such contracts are permitted, maximum allowable duration; restrictions on number of renewals.

a A high value on the indexes signifies a high degree of restrictiveness, a low value on the indexes a low degree of restrictiveness.

Sources
D. Grubb and W. Wells (1993), 'Employment Regulation and Patterns of Work in EC Countries', *OECD Economic Studies*, 21, 7–58; OECD (1994), *The OECD Jobs Study: Evidence and Explanations, Part 2: The Adjustment Potential of the Labour Market*, Paris: OECD.

account cross-country differences in their implementation and enforcement through labour courts and public-policy agencies, both of which can make a difference in terms of not only the direct dismissal costs they impose on employers but also their overall economic costs (e.g. by affecting the *predictability* of direct dismissal costs).

Second, such rankings ignore the varying importance of dismissal and lay-off restraints imposed by industry and/or firm-level collective agreements that complement statutory provisions and, in fact, frequently fill gaps deliberately left by legislation (e.g. in the case of Britain). Not considered in most rankings are also the role of supporting institutions, such as work-sharing subsidies and publicly funded or cofunded early retirement schemes, which in several countries (e.g. France and Germany) significantly reduce the potential cost of work force reductions for employers.

Third, whereas one could assume that some of the above shortcomings are avoided by rankings relying on 'wholesale' subjective assessments by employers and officials of business organizations, the validity of such assessments appears to be no less problematic, however; because they are based on national surveys, such assessments are usually not made from a cross-country comparative perspective. They lack an explicit *tertium comparationis,* so their reference yardstick (i.e. important compared to what?) remains unclear. Using them to construct a comparative index, therefore, seems to be highly questionable in methodological terms.

Lastly, rankings tend to be based on potentially untenable assumptions to the extent that direct costs imposed on employers by legislation are imputed from information on statutory requirements. For instance, procedural and notice costs are assumed to result from the difference between continued wage payments and the reduced value-added of the worker (due to the decline in demand for his/her services and/or adverse motivational effects) in the period between the firm's dismissal decision and the actual separation of the worker. In the event of economically motivated dismissals, however, one aspect ignored in this approach is that the magnitude of such legally imposed costs essentially depends on how far in advance the employer receives signals of an imminent decline in demand (e.g. in the form of a fall in the number of incoming orders).[12]

Given these shortcomings, the results of comparative evaluation studies using such country rankings as their independent variable should be interpreted with great caution. Such caution is also suggested by the fact that the statistical correlations between employers' subjective assessments (as documented in EU surveys) and country classifications based on information on legal provisions were found to be not very strong (see Grubb and Wells, 1993, p. 30).

---

12 For Germany, for example, it can be shown that the mean durations of prenotification periods for production workers in most cases remain well within the average time horizons of orders at hand (see Büchtemann, 1994, p. 94).

3   EVALUATION APPROACHES

The following sections give a brief and necessarily incomplete overview of the methodological approaches and results of previous evaluation research on dismissal protection. It should be noted that the now large body of research dealing with employment-security policies and dismissal legislation covers a broad spectrum of very heterogeneous studies by researchers pursuing varying objectives and using different methodological approaches, most of which cannot be categorized as evaluations in the strict sense of the word. Given the many actors involved, few studies have undertaken the ambitious task of analysing the actual workings and implementation of dismissal-protection regimes in their various facets and components. Such an analysis seems to be indispensable for assessing the actual *direct* costs imposed on employers, although the authors of the few studies that have done so mostly neglect the wider *economic* costs and impacts of dismissal protection. Likewise, there are very few studies whose authors have analysed the scope and cost effects of collectively bargained employment-security provisions, such as the *social plans* negotiated by German works councils in the event of major work force reductions.

Most studies, by contrast, have largely neglected the implementation aspect. Instead, they have focussed on the wider labour market impact of dismissal-protection regimes in terms of observable cross-country differences in aggregate labour market performance that can be related to differences in national (or state-level) dismissal-protection regimes, while controlling for a number of other factors affecting labour market outcomes. Other studies have tried to measure the impact that changes in dismissal-protection regulations over time have on labour market performance indicators, such as the speed with which aggregate employment (measured in terms of workers or hours) adjusts to changes in output or sales. Still other studies, primarily from the United States, have a microeconomic focus on selected components of dismissal-protection regimes, such as advance notice and probationary periods, and their impacts on job-search behaviour, postlayoff unemployment, wages and worker selection. Finally, in recognition of the methodological difficulties involved in identifying and isolating the genuine impacts that dismissal-protection regulations have on employer behaviour, the authors of some studies have taken a direct survey-based approach in collecting firm-level data about the perceived impacts that dismissal regulations have on firms' human resource management practices and work force adjustment policies.

In the light of the theoretical discussion above, a serious shortcoming of most studies (with the exception of those focussing on implementation aspects) is that they fail to distinguish between *disciplinary* dismissals and employment terminations for *economic* reasons, and implicitly focus instead on economically motivated worker displacements. The implication is that most empirical studies, aside from frequently resting on rather simplistic theoretical foundations, fail to address the issue of the difficult to measure economic *benefits* of dismissal-protection regulations, especially their impact on worker morale and firm–worker cooperation. Where studies have addressed this aspect, the evidence tends to be merely conjectural and not able to establish firm causal relations (see Brown, Reich and Stern, 1992; Levine and d'Andrea Tyson, 1990). Moreover, most studies suffer from a lack of direct observations on actual dismissal practice and incidence, reflecting the fact that corresponding data from either firm or population surveys are generally scarce and, if available, in most cases are not sufficiently compatible for cross-country comparative or time-series evaluation designs. As in other fields, therefore, one is confronted with a dilemma. Where theoretical models have become sophisticated enough to account for the complex effects of dismissal protection on workers, firm behaviour and overall labour market performance, nonavailability of appropriate empirical data prevents these models from being adequately tested. Vice versa, those data that are available in most cases do not permit a high degree of analytical sophistication, but rather necessitate gross simplifications, daring assumptions and aggregations in which the genuine impacts of dismissal protection tend to be difficult to identify.

In order to illustrate the different methodological approaches taken by previous evaluation studies and briefly summarize their core results, it is useful to distinguish performance assessments from impact evaluations. Studies in the former category take a direct look at various aspects of actual dismissal practice and incidence and the behaviour of the various actors involved in determining the process and outcomes of employer-initiated employment terminations. Studies of the latter type, by contrast, directly or indirectly address the *behavioural impacts* of dismissal protection and their measurable effects on firms' human resource management practices, employment adjustment patterns and overall labour market performance.

3.1   Performance Assessments

Studies subsumed under this heading include the few detailed effectiveness studies that have focussed on the entire implementation process of dismissal-protection regulations through its various stages, from the selection of dismissal candidates all the way to the settlements of disputed dismissal cases, as well as several studies that have looked at selected aspects in that process, such as the length-of-notice periods, litigation probability, the magnitude and distribution of severance pay and the incidence of remedies, such as compensatory damages or reinstatement. Studies under this heading, while focussing primarily on actual observable behaviour and thus necessarily neglecting behavioural changes induced by dismissal protection (the counterfactual), allow inferences about the *direct* costs of dismissals and thereby provide essential basic information for impact evaluations.

A core performance indicator is the actual *incidence* of dismissals under different dismissal-protection regimes and across workers representing different degrees of legal dismissal protection. In most countries, however, both individual and collective dismissals not exceeding certain thresholds need not be reported to public authorities, so information about dismissal incidence is not collected on a regular basis and, consequently, has been limited largely to one-time snapshots from special surveys that in most cases do not allow time-series observations and controls for business-cycle effects.

The little data available show that dismissal rates (i.e. as a percentage of the employed work force) tend to be quite low in most countries, even where statutory dismissal restraints do not exist. In the 1980s, annual dismissal rates (including both disciplinary and other terminations) amounted to not more than 4 per cent of the work force in West Germany (1984–87: 3.5 to 3.7 per cent), France (1984–87: 3.6 per cent), Italy (1984: 3.1 per cent) and the United Kingdom (1984–90: 3.5 to 4 per cent) (see Büchtemann, 1993b, p. 21). These findings are consistent with cross-country evidence from the European Labour Force Sample Surveys, which shows the proportion of workers dismissed from their jobs and subsequently unemployed to exceed hardly 1 per cent of all persons in dependent employment (see Mosley and Kruppe, 1992, pp. 139–42). Not counting temporary layoffs with subsequent recall (the percentage of which in all layoffs has been continuously declining over the past decade), one finds that the dismissal rates even in the United States tend to be relatively low compared to the common stereotype of uninhibited hiring and firing: according to different data sources, the US annual dismissal rate amounts to some 6 per cent of the employed work force (see Büchtemann, 1993b, p. 21; Stieber and Rodgers, 1994).

For Germany, a country with a complex system of statutory and collectively bargained dismissal restraints that cover the overwhelming majority of the employed work force (see Büchtemann, 1993c), time-series information on annual job separations and dismissal rates is available from the German Socio-Economic Panel, a nationally representative, longitudinal household survey (see Table 22.3). The data show only modest variations in overall annual job separation rates, but a markedly procyclical movement of annual dismissal rates from 1984 through 1994, which is contrasted by a markedly anticyclical movement of voluntary separations (quits). Thus, dismissal incidence declined noticeably during the long period of employment growth from 1984 through 1989, reaching a low of 1.2 per cent at the peak of the boom in the late 1980s. From 1990 through 1994, the period covering the

Table 22.3 Employment Separations from Dependent Employment (Excluding Apprenticeship) in West Germany by Type of Separation and Employment Status at the Time of the Survey (in Percentages)

	Total separation rate from dependent employment		Thereof			Share of workers with separation		Net Δ overall employ- ment	Net Δ total hours worked
			Dis- miss- als	Quits	Other sepa- rations	Employed time of survey	Not employed at time of survey		
1984–85	16.6	(n = 733)	3.5	4.4	8.7	57.2	42.8	+ 0.2	– 0.3
1985–86	17.2	(n = 869)	2.9	5.3	9.0	57.6	42.4	+ 0.7	– 0.6
1986–87	18.6	(n = 877)	2.5	7.2	8.9	62.9	37.1	+ 1.4	+ 0.7
1987–88	18.5	(n = 855)	2.6	7.2	8.7	56.8	43.2	+ 0.7	+ 0.0
1988–89	19.9	(n = 851)	2.0	7.6	10.3	59.3	40.7	+ 0.8	+ 1.0
1989–90	18.8	(n = 822)	1.2	7.2	10.5	65.6	34.4	+ 1.5	+ 0.2
1990–91	19.0	(n = 828)	3.0	8.4	7.6	65.8	34.2	+ 3.0	+ 0.8
1991–92	18.4	(n = 802)	3.9	7.6	6.9	58.7	41.3	+ 2.6	+ 1.6
1992–93	20.7	(n = 860)	4.9	8.0	7.8	57.5	42.5	+ 0.9	+ 1.7
1993–94	18.0	(n = 705)	6.3	5.3	6.4	45.0	55.0	– 1.7	– 3.1

Sources
German Employment Agency–Institute for Employment Research; Federal Socio-Economic Panel (SOEP), waves 1–10 (data kindly supplied by Dr. Jürgen Schupp, German Institute for Economic Research, DIW); calculations by the authors.

latest severe recession, annual dismissal rates increased to over 6 per cent, equalling over 1.4 million dismissal cases in 1993–94 (as compared to some 250 000 in 1989–90) and casting doubts on notions that dismissal restraints in Germany have rendered employment terminations prohibitively costly.

Regrettably, the above data on dismissal incidence do not allow a distinction between disciplinary dismissals and employment terminations for economic reasons. From other data sources, however, it is known that the former, depending on the point in the business cycle, tend to account for one-half to two-thirds of all employer-initiated job terminations (for Germany, see Falke et al., 1981, pp. 965–7; for the United States, Stieber and Rodgers, 1994). Disciplinary dismissals, though hardly ever addressed by systematic impact evaluations, thus play a major role in overall dismissal behaviour.

A more detailed picture of dismissal practices emerges from the few effectiveness studies conducted in the late 1970s and 1980s. The most comprehensive of these studies was conducted in Germany from 1978 through 1980 by a research group at the Max-Planck Institute for International Civil Law (see Falke et al., 1981) and included surveys of 612 private sector firms, 740 firm-level worker representatives, 880 dismissed workers and 243 labour court judges as well as thorough analyses of both court documents and collective master agreements. The results show that dismissals tended to be more frequent among small firms as well as among low-tenured workers. In only very few cases (8 per cent) did the works councils, which in Germany must be heard prior to all employment terminations, raise objections to dismissals intended by the employer. However, firms with a works council have been found *ceteris paribus* to have a lower dismissal incidence than firms without elected worker representatives (see Frick, 1995), indicating that employers with elected worker representatives more often pursue work force adjustment strategies emphasizing soft work force reductions (such as early retirement, worker buyouts and so on). Moreover, the study by Falke et al. (1981, pp. 965–7) found that in the late 1970s not more than 8 per cent of all dismissals entailed legal action by the dismissed employee, with the readiness to engage in litigation increasing with the length of service prior to being discharged, reflecting the commonly unspecified, vague terms of long-term employment relationships. The probability of unjust-dismissal litigation tended to be markedly higher (10 per cent) for disciplinary discharges than for economically motivated terminations (4 per cent), giving evidence of the more conflictual nature of the former. Altogether, almost one out of three disciplinary dismissals of workers with more than three years of tenure entailed legal action through a labour court.

Table 22.4 Annual Job Separations, Dismissals and Unfair Dismissal Suits Filed by Employees in West Germany 1984–1993

Year	Total number of job separations[a]	Thereof: dismissals[b]	Total dismissal suits filed[c]	Arbitration rate[d] (in percentages)
1984	5491	21.1	163.6	14.1
1986	5593	13.4	155.2	20.7
1988	5859	10.0	146.1	24.9
1990	6685	16.0	127.0	11.9
1992	6823	23.7	183.0	11.3
1993	6567	35.1	230.4	9.9

Notes

a Total number of job separations from employment subject to mandatory social insurance contributions (= 80 per cent of total employment); source: Federal Employment Agency.

b Calculated from various sources.

c Unjust dismissal cases completed by the labour courts; source: Federal Ministry of Employment and Social Affairs.

d Number of unfair dismissal suits filed divided by estimated number of dismissals.

Consistent with these findings, time-series data reveal a strongly cyclical pattern of dismissal litigation probability, with the likelihood of legal action by dismissed workers peaking in economic boom periods, when most terminations occur for disciplinary reasons (see Table 22.4).

The study by Falke et al. (1981, pp. 773–9) further showed that the majority of dismissal cases filed at a labour court actually are resolved in pretrial settlements, with only 15 per cent leading to court decisions (one-third of which were subsequently appealed through a superior court). In roughly half of all lower level and appellate court decisions, the worker prevailed. However, although German labour law views reinstatement as the prime remedy against unjust dismissals, actual reinstatement in the previous job was the rare exception, accounting for only 0.4 per cent of all unjust dismissal-litigation cases and 2 per cent of all successful lawsuits filed by workers. Instead, most prevailing plaintiffs in Germany obtained mere financial compensation for the job loss, which—as a rule—amounts to some 60 per cent of a month's gross wage per year of seniority.

Altogether, the available evidence for Germany seems to indicate that the *direct* costs of actual dismissals are usually lower than could be assumed by merely looking at the complex system of regulations covering employment terminations. Given the concentration of dismissals on low-tenure workers, actual notice periods tend to be quite short, not exceeding four weeks in half of all cases from 1984 through 1991 (see Frick, 1993, p. 9). Most of the few cases that end up in a labour court are resolved within a relatively short time, 64 per cent within not more than three months after filing (1993). According to data from the German Socio-Economic Panel, severance payments, including those originating from a collectively negotiated social plan, are involved in one out of five dismissals, and the median severance pay given amounts to roughly 45 days' gross earnings (see Büchtemann, 1994; Falke et al., 1981, pp. 101–15).

However, individual firms may face much higher severance pay expenditures than these data reveal, particularly if major work force reductions require a social plan to be negotiated between management and the works council and involve procedural delays by labour market authorities. An analysis of 163 social-plan agreements negotiated during the 1980s found that total severance pay expenditures under a social plan frequently exceeded DM 1 million, depending on the share and tenure profile of the work force affected, thus imposing quite a substantial burden, especially on smaller firms (Hemmer, 1988). Data from the European Union's Labour Cost Surveys, which are conducted at four-year intervals, show that total severance expenditures by manufacturing firms with 50 or more employees in West Germany have steadily risen over the past 20 years, reaching 1 per cent of total labour costs in the recession year 1992 (see Table 22.5). This large amount seems to give evi-

Table 22.5 Severance Pay Expenditures and Average Amount of Severance Pay per Person Employed in Manufacturing Establishments with 50 or More Employees: West Germany 1972–1992

	(1)		(2)		(3)		(4)	(5)
	Total severance pay expenditure –all firms– (DM 1000)	Percent-age change	Average severance pay per person employed –all firms– (DM)	Percent-age change	Average severance pay per person employed –large firms– (500+) - (DM)	Percent-age change	Share of severance pay in total labour costs per head (%)	Percentage change total labour costs per full-time worker
1972	157 703	—	21.1	—	30.3	—	0.1	—
1975	544 893	+ 245.5	74.0	+ 250.7	105.0	+ 246.9	0.2	+ 36.6
1978	567 267	+ 4.1	88.0	+ 18.9	122.3	+ 16.5	0.2	+ 23.8
1981	1174 464	+ 107.0	164.0	+ 86.4	226.2	+ 85.0	0.3	+ 27.3
1984	2514 080	+ 114.1	382.0	+ 132.9	538.9	+ 138.2	0.7	+ 22.3
1988	2650 313	+ 5.4	393.0	+ 2.9	526.2	− 2.4	0.6	+ 15.8
1992	6326 084	+ 138.7	758.0	+ 92.8	1223.5	+ 132.5	1.0	+ 21.7

Sources
Federal Statistical Office,*Personal- und Personalkostenerhebungen im produzierenden Gewerbe*, various vols; calculations by the authors.

dence that not only dismissals, but increasingly also other forms of job separations (e.g. induced quits, early retirement) involve severance pay by the employer. Projected on to *all* job separations that occurred in 1992, the average amount of severance pay, however, amounted to not more than DM 1400.

Another comprehensive effectiveness study was conducted by Dickens, Jones and Weekes (1985) for Britain, that is, a country where relatively restrictive qualification requirements mean that only some 65 per cent of all private sector employees are covered by statutory dismissal protection (Germany: 80 per cent). Unlike the German study, the British study focussed on disciplinary dismissals only, relying more heavily on the analysis of administrative accounts and other process-generated data accruing in the process of unfair dismissal litigation. The findings showed that in about one out of ten disciplinary dismissal cases the dismissed worker subsequently contested the fairness of the dismissal by filing a complaint through the Industrial Tribunals (ITs).

Two-thirds of all complaints filed are settled or withdrawn during prehearing conciliation by the neutral Advisory, Conciliation and Arbitration Service (ACAS). In only one-third of the remaining cases (or 10 per cent of all filings), the employer's dismissal decision was not upheld by the ITs, and reinstatement, though considered the primary remedy under British law, was eventually ordered for not more than 2 per cent of the prevailing plaintiffs. As in Germany, monetary compensation is the major remedy in practice, with the median award by ITs in 1992–93 not exceeding eight weeks' pay at a manual worker's pay rate and monetary settlements negotiated in prehearing conciliation procedures being even lower in most cases (see Dickens, 1994). Along the same lines, Root (1987) reported that only about half of the workers who had been made redundant actually received redundancy payments (reflecting the long qualification periods for eligibility under the 1989 Employment Act), which on average amount to not more than two months' gross wages. Thus, one can conclude from the available evidence that total direct dismissal costs faced by British firms are indeed low.

A third major effectiveness study refers to wrongful termination litigation under the US common-law system (see Dertouzos, Holland and Ebener, 1988). The study is based on a survey of legal cases filed in the Los Angeles Superior Court, a detailed analysis of public documents from 120 wrongful discharge jury trials in California from 1980 through 1986, as well as interviews with nearly 200 plaintiff and defence attorneys involved in at least one of the cases reported in the documents. The study yielded detailed data on personal characteristics and employment histories of plaintiffs, characteristics of the firms sued, information on the law firms representing plaintiffs and defendants, and the stakes involved in and outcomes of wrongful termination trials in California, that is, a state with one of the most sweeping common-law incursions upon the employment-at-will doctrine. Although the total number of annual wrongful-discharge civil court filings has been estimated not to exceed 15 000 for the entire United States (see Maltby, 1994), the study found California plaintiffs to represent a broad spectrum of employees from low-wage earners to corporate executives, and covering a wide range of tenure, extending from less than one year all the way to 15 or more years. The overwhelming majority (81 per cent) of the plaintiffs had been terminated for reasons of inadequate performance on the job, and 95 per cent of all cases filed were found to be settled by the parties before the beginning of jury hearings, reflecting the high transaction costs involved in court proceedings. In the remaining 5 per cent of the filings—those that did go to trial—plaintiffs prevailed in two-thirds of the cases, though mostly not until two years or longer after initial filing.

On average, juries awarded successful plaintiffs $650 000 in compensatory ($390 000) and punitive ($260 000) damages, with the median award amounting to $177 000. These large awards, the size of which was found to vary both with plaintiffs' age and previous earnings as well with the size of the defendant firm, however, tend to be reduced by roughly half in posttrial appeals and settlements; moreover, plaintiffs' legal fees amounted to on average from 35 to 40 per cent of total awards, and legal fees borne by defendants (firms) added up to some $80 000 for a typical wrongful termination suit, regardless of its outcome. After accounting for posttrial reductions and legal fees, the median prevailing plaintiff retained not more than $75 000 in net awards (i.e. 42 per cent of the initial award). Therefore, the authors conclude that 'most defendants would be better off paying the initial demands rather than going to trial' (Dertouzos et al., 1988, p. viii), while 'many terminated employees would have benefited from a system, like the one in Great Britain or the Federal Republic of Germany, that calls for modest, but automatic remedies when an employee is discharged' (Dertouzos et al., 1988, p. ix). Given the low incidence of wrongful termination suits, however, the aggregate direct costs of wrongful termination litigation in the United States are still relatively modest, amounting to an estimated $200 per dismissed-at-will employee during the 1980s.

Altogether, the studies cited above provide a varied picture of the performance of different dismissal-protection regimes and of the direct costs associated with actual employment terminations under different regulatory approaches. In particular, the US common-law system emerges as one involving comparatively high transaction costs without providing effective protection for the majority of at-will employees. However, studies focussing on dismissal incidence and the direct costs involved in actual dismissal cases fail to give evidence of, and may in fact grossly underestimate, the total economic costs (and benefits) of dismissal protection.[13] The latter are addressed by studies summarized under the category of impact evaluations.

3.2   Impact Evaluations

This category basically consists of two types of studies: (a) those which, using different methodological approaches ranging from mere descriptive statistics to sophisticated macromodelling, have inferred impacts of different national dismissal-protection regimes from observed cross-country (or cross-state) variations in labour market performance and outcomes; and (b) studies which have approached the issue from the other side, by directly collecting firm-

---

13 It should be remembered that the prime intention underlying most dismissal-protection regimes is to prevent unjust employment terminations rather than merely providing remedies for unjustly discharged workers.

level data about the behavioural changes and adjustments induced by dismiss-al legislation, thereby necessarily focussing on aspects of microeconomic efficiency and, in most cases, ignoring the wider labour market impacts of dismissal-protection regimes.

3.2.1 Macrolevel Evidence

At a fairly aggregate level, notions about the impact of employment-security regimes have been inferred from comparisons of the relative speed of work force adjustment to changes in industrial output across different countries (see Abraham and Houseman, 1993, 1994; Kraft, 1994; Maurau and Oudinet, 1988). Generally, these studies show large cross-country variations in employ-ment elasticities and employment adjustment speed, with Italy and France commonly exhibiting much more sluggish adjustment than Britain, the United States and the Federal Republic of Germany. For the period from 1970 through 1990, Abraham and Houseman (1994, p. 79) found the mean adjustment lag of manufacturing employment to variations in output to amount to more than 14 quarters in France and 5 quarters in Germany, but only 0.6 quarters in the United States. However, when looking at adjustments in hours worked (instead of in the number of workers), the adjustment patterns of the three countries are much more similar, indicating the greater use of working time reductions (short-time working) for short-term adjustment in Europe than in the United States. Yet, over time (i.e. within roughly one year), employment adjustment in Germany was found to catch up to US levels quickly (Abraham and Houseman, 1993, p. 73). This picture is supported by findings of a recent study by Kraft (1994), who compared the speed of manufacturing employment adjustment in four countries over the period from 1979 through 1990 in the framework of an equilibrium model. The results showed the fastest adjustment for Germany, followed by the United Kingdom, Italy, and finally France. To explain such cross-country variations in adjustment patterns, Abraham and Houseman (1993) emphasized not only the role of supporting measures, such as public work-sharing subsidies, but also differences in macroeconomic policy frameworks which, by influencing the amplitude of economic fluctu-ations, determine firms' need to adjust employment through major layoffs. The authors found that US–German differences in cyclical employment vari-ations partly reflect smaller fluctuations of shipments around the trend in Ger-man manufacturing industries than in their US counterparts, implying less pressure on German firms to reduce employment levels during economic downturns (see also Bertola, 1990).

Further evidence concerning the impact of employment-security policies on patterns of work force adjustment and external labour mobility has been inferred from international comparisons of employment stability and job retention rates based on tenure and job separation data (see Bellmann, Schasse, Wadsworth and Wolfs, 1992; OECD, 1993, pp. 119–49; 1994, pp. 64–7). Generally, it is found that both average employment tenure and retention rates in France, Germany and Japan significantly exceed those in Britain and the United States. However, much of the cross-country difference is accounted for by differences in the retention rates of low-tenured (i.e. recently hired) workers, for whom dismissal restraints tend to be rather weak in most countries. Particularly for Germany (and in contrast to Britain, Japan and the United States), the data reveal strong procyclical variations in the share of low-tenured workers in the work force, indicating that hiring stops during economic downturns play a major role in German (but not in British and US) firms' work force adjustment policies. Moreover, whereas for higher age groups the United States and Germany have quite similar tenure profiles and a high incidence of near life-time jobs, significant differences between both countries exist for younger workers (under 30 years), who show much more stable job attachments in Germany than in the United States. This finding may reflect the stabilizing effect of greater firm investments in early career training of workers in Germany.

A general shortcoming of both these approaches is that they fail to distinguish between those employment declines or job separations due to quits (which are voluntary by definition) and retirements and those due to dismissals or layoffs. They therefore do not allow reliable conclusions about the impact of dismissal restraints. Nonetheless, they cast doubt on the validity of country rankings in which, for instance, the United Kingdom is placed among the least restrictive countries and a significant difference in adjustment flexibility is assumed to exist between, say, Germany, a country with a highly elaborate system of legal dismissal regulations, and the United States, a country with very little statutory labour regulation.

A different approach to assessing the aggregate impacts of dismissal-protection regulations has used time-series analysis to determine changes in adjustment patterns after regulatory changes in national dismissal-protection regimes (see Abraham and Houseman, 1993, 1994; Burgess, 1988; Kraft, 1988, 1993). Taken together, these studies do not support the assumption that changes in the legal framework governing employment terminations in either direction (increases in protection and, vice versa, the deregulation efforts of the 1980s) have had a noticeable effect on observable employment adjustment patterns at the industry level. The absence of any such effects may be due to the fact that statutory changes frequently have been a mere legal codification of prevalent employment practice or, conversely in the case of deregulation, that they reflect stabilized patterns of firms' human resource practices that do not instantaneously respond to changes in the regulatory environment (behavioural inertia).

A major strand of research represents attempts to link cross-country differences in aggregate labour market performance and outcomes directly to the relative restrictiveness of national dismissal-protection regimes as operationalized in the form of the country rankings cited above (see section 1.2). Reflecting in part the shortcomings inherent in such country rankings and in part the many intermediary factors modulating the effects of dismissal-protection regulations, the results of these studies have been far from unequivocal and offer little support for firm conclusions about the impacts of different employment-security and dismissal-protection regimes.

In a widely cited cross-sectional, cross-country comparative study, Lazear (1990) found that the mean amount of severance pay for an average worker with ten years of tenure (as computed for 22 countries on the basis of information from legal textbooks) had a 'depressing effect on employment rates, labour force participation rates, and hours of work' (p. 717), though, probably because of discouragement effects, only a modest impact on unemployment levels. On the basis of the coefficients obtained, Lazear (1990) estimated that *ceteris paribus* 'a three months increase in severance pay would decrease the employment to population ratio by about 1.08 percent. In the U.S. that would cost just over a million jobs' (p. 719). Moreover, in countries that have experienced a marked rise in the amount of statutory severance pay over time, the ensuing increase in dismissal costs was found to explain a substantial share (in France e.g. as much as 59 per cent) of the overall increase in unemployment from 1956 through 1984, although the author sounds a note of caution with regard to the question of causality.

Against these straightforward conclusions by Lazear (1990), Bertola (1990) raised the objection that in high employment-security countries slower job growth in the economic upswing may be compensated for by smaller employment declines in the economic downturn, with both effects evening out in the medium term—an assumption that is supported by his analysis of manufacturing growth rates in 10 countries from 1960 through 1973 and from 1975 through 1986 (see also Bentolila and Bertola, 1990). Accordingly, Bertola (1990) found no correlation between the relative strictness of employment-security regimes and average unemployment levels, although high employment-security countries exhibited different unemployment dynamics, particularly a higher degree of unemployment persistence over time (hysteresis). Nor did the study find macroevidence of insider strategies in wage determination barring unemployed outsiders from access to employment in countries with stricter dismissal-protection regimes. Bertola (1990, p. 877) concludes that 'job security regulations should not be too quickly blamed for European countries' poor employment performance'.

The insider/outsider issue has been addressed by two other studies comparing selected aspects of labour market performance and work patterns across

European countries. Using a 'reputational ranking' of countries according to the relative strictness of employment-security regulation as reported in EU employer surveys, Mosley and Kruppe (1992) found a strong negative correlation between the degree of dismissal protection and the incidence of dismissals with subsequent unemployment. High employment-security and low dismissal rates were, in turn, associated with several measures of insider/outsider segmentation, such as high rates of long-term joblessness and low monthly outflows from unemployment, high youth unemployment (not so in Germany) as well as low relative unemployment rates of prime-age male workers. In contrast to Mosley and Kruppe (1992), the study by Grubb and Wells (1993), which is based on a more detailed country ranking approach, provides evidence that countries with strict dismissal-protection regimes for regular employees experienced a significant increase in fixed-term employment contracts and temporary work during the 1980s (except for Italy and Belgium, where these types of employment arrangements are also restrictively regulated). This evidence lends support to the notion that employers in countries with high levels of employment security have increasingly used such unprotected contractual forms for circumventing dismissal restraints applying to permanent employment.

The question of whether employment-security regulations slow down structural adjustment and the reallocation of labour from declining industries to innovative growth industries was addressed by Burgess (1994). Comparing cross-industry variations in employment growth for a sample of 10 countries (including France, Germany, Italy, Japan, the United Kingdom and the United States) for the period from 1971 through 1988 within a partial equilibrium framework, he found some weak indication that countries with more restrictive employment-security regimes have a somewhat slower speed of labour reallocation than Britain, Japan and the United States.

A final example of a macroapproach representing an attempt to assess the *economic* costs of legal dismissal restraints is the study of Dertouzos and Karoly (1993), who examined the impacts of civil court incursions upon the employment-at-will principle in the United States. The fact that only some states have recognized the furthest-going common-law doctrines of wrongful discharge provides a setting similar to a natural experiment, allowing for a methodology that explicitly models the endogeneity of these doctrines (whose adoption is modelled as a function of local factors such as prevailing political climate, legal environment and regional economic conditions) and controls for exogenous influences, such as industrial composition and aggregate demand. Based on industry-specific employment data for all 50 US states, analysis of the adoption of these doctrines by the state judiciaries revealed a significant negative impact on state-level aggregate employment performance and on the overall speed of work force adjustment in response to changes in economic conditions. Given the low *direct* costs of litigation over wrongful termination, these results may seem surprising. An explanation proposed by both legal experts and economists refers to the high degree of legal uncertainty created by *ex-post* court rulings, which vary from state to state, and the unpredictable, large damages awarded by juries under the common-law system, which has induced employers to take precautions against wrongful-discharge litigation by modifying their staffing practices, offering severance pay, and voluntarily adopting *due-process* rules for employment terminations (see Troy, 1990).

3.2.2 Microlevel Evidence

The aforementioned macroeconomic impact assessments all rest on more or less explicit assumptions about how both firms and workers (and their collective representatives) have modified their behaviour in response to the introduction of dismissal protection and/or how they would behave in the hypothetical absence of such regulations. Considering that in most European countries the introduction of dismissal-protection legislation dates back to the 1960s or even earlier and that such legislation tends to apply universally to all firms and workers sharing certain qualifying characteristics, thus precluding most experimental evaluation approaches, the empirical evidence on the microlevel behavioural changes induced by employment security regulations has been scarce. The few available studies can be classified into three categories: (a) quantitative and qualitative firm surveys in which corporate representatives were directly asked about the impacts of dismissal-protection regulations on their firms' human resource and work force adjustment practices, (b) studies in which researchers have tried to assess the impact that selected components of dismissal protection have had on workers' job stability and postdisplacement labour market experiences and (c) studies in which notions about the impacts of dismissal-protection regulations have been inferred from evidence about microlevel firm responses to recent labour law deregulation policies.

Studies belonging to the first category include some fairly general, business-climate firm surveys, such as two consecutive surveys on labour market flexibility that were conducted in 10 Member States of the European Community in 1985 and 1989 (see Hofmann, 1993). Although methodologically questionable (primarily because of their suggestive questionnaire wording), the results reveal major cross-country differences in firms' assessments of 'insufficient flexibility in hiring and firing' as an obstacle to increasing employment beyond current staffing levels: altogether, in 1985, far fewer British firms (7 per cent) and German firms (23 per cent) considered this factor 'very important' than their French (48 per cent) and Italian (52 per cent) counterparts. In the latter countries, according to these results, employment-security regulations seemed to have a major impact on firms' employment decisions and thereby on aggregate employment at large.

Somewhat contrary to these very general assessments, results of more detailed firm surveys undertaken in Britain and Germany showed that most firms attributed no major influence to employment-security legislation on their *firing* decisions (see the summary and references in Büchtemann, 1993b, pp. 34–6, and Dickens, 1994). This response applies particularly to dismissals for economic reasons and is consistent with evidence according to which dismissals tend to be strongly concentrated among a minority of 'hire-and-fire' firms (see Büchtemann, 1993c). Most employers have expressed a strong preference for alternative forms of soft work force adjustment, such as hiring stops and attrition, incitements to quit, worker buyouts involving voluntary severance pay and early retirement. If there has been an immediate impact on firms' human resource policies, it is rather in the area of disciplinary discharges, where dismissal protection, according to several employer surveys, has led to a more careful performance screening, especially of newly hired workers. These changes have been accompanied by increasingly widespread implementation of formalized firm-level disciplinary procedures, frequently combined with a centralization of dismissals, transferring such decisions from the level of immediate supervisors to that of the personnel department. Nor is there much evidence to support the view that dismissal-protection regulation has had a strong impact on firms' *hiring* behaviour. Again, if there has been an impact on firms' hiring behaviour, it has been primarily on the quality and selection of new hires rather than on their number. Notably, employers have been induced to conduct more careful productivity-oriented applicant screening so as to avoid mismatches and premature terminations. However, there is some anecdotal firm-level evidence that special protective regulations concerning employment terminations of certain groups of workers, especially disabled persons, have entailed discrimination against such groups in firms' hiring policies (see Büchtemann and Hoeland, 1989, pp. 292–4).

Research belonging to the second category includes the few, microlevel studies (primarily from the United States) that have focussed on the impact that dismissal-prenotification periods have on workers' job-search efforts and postdisplacement labour market experience (for the United States, see the summaries by Addison and Portugal, 1991; for Germany, see Frick, 1993). Based on longitudinal information from population surveys, all these studies have shown that prenotification of impending dismissals (be it formal or informal) and the length of the notice interval have a positive impact on workers' job-search intensity while still on the job and a negative impact on the probability of subsequently experiencing a spell of unemployment. By universalizing notice requirements, dismissal-protection legislation may thus have a mitigating effect on overall unemployment levels.

The third category of impact evaluation approach based on microdata consists of studies which have tried to infer the impact of dismissal-protection regulations from changes in corporate human resource policy induced by recent labour law deregulation policies (see chap. 21 in this volume). For the United Kingdom, Evans et al. (1985), based on a series of firm case studies, found that, although most British firms had welcomed the 1979 extension of the waiting periods for statutory unfair dismissal protection from 6 to 24 months by the Thatcher government, firms had not altered their hiring-and-firing behaviour in the following years, nor were they using the extended service qualification period for reverting to a hire-and-fire policy or prolonged probation periods for newly hired employees. A similar conclusion emerges from an evaluation study of the impact of legislation facilitating the use of fixed-term contracts in Germany (see Büchtemann, 1993c). During the first years after the enactment of this legislation, the overwhelming majority of private sector firms made no use of the new option to hire fixed-term employees not subject to dismissal protection. Where the new option was used (by not more than 4 per cent of all firms in the private sector), the prevailing motive for doing so was to prolong the probation of new hires, whereas the facilitation of external work force adjustment through hiring and firing or the substitution of additional workers for overtime work by the core work force played hardly any role at all. Likewise, studies conducted after the French government's 1986 abolition of the heavily criticized administrative authorization procedures for economically motivated dismissals found that this change had little notable impact on French firms' personnel policies. After a brief initial increase in the number of redundancies, the number of dismissals soon reverted to its previous trend and after 1987 declined to its lowest levels since the early 1980s (see Genthon and Maroni, 1989).

4   SUMMARY AND PERSPECTIVES FOR FUTURE RESEARCH

The preceding review of different evaluation approaches in the area of employment security and dismissal protection has shown that most evaluation research falls far short of adequately addressing the theoretically developed criteria for assessing the economic impact of dismissal-protection regimes. This inadequacy is due partly to the difficulties involved in operationalizing theoretical concepts for empirical research and to the fact that the data needed for this purpose are not available and would be very costly to generate, as illustrated by some of the more comprehensive effectiveness studies cited above. It is also partly accounted for by the fact that previous evaluation efforts in this area have often failed to address the complex issue in a systematic, theory-driven manner. Moreover, there remains a deep conceptual and methodological gap between detailed performance assessments and the mostly macrodata-based impact assessments that have been done. Whereas the former have focussed on the legal procedures and effectiveness of national dismissal-protection regimes, frequently neglecting their wider economic impacts, the latter have tended to ignore many relevant legal details, implementation aspects and supporting institutions of dismissal-protection regimes, which to a large extent determine the impacts that those regimes have on labour market outcomes. The many complexities involved, including the differential implications and effects of legal restrictions on disciplinary and economically motivated employment terminations, also appear to cast doubt upon the value of multicountry comparative methodologies for assessing the effectiveness and labour market impacts of dismissal-protection regimes. Such studies have to operate with gross generalizations and simplifications, particularly in the absence of matching data about their implementation and about the labour market setting in which they operate.

As a consequence of these difficulties and shortcomings, the results of most previous research have tended to be contradictory and inconclusive, hardly lending support to either of the controversial positions taken in the continuing debate on employment security policies. This circumstance is particularly apparent in the paucity of more than anecdotal evidence about the potential benefits and welfare-enhancing effects of standards and rules governing the termination of employment relationships that must be balanced against their economic costs. Circumstantial evidence that, for instance, the introduction of high-performance work and production systems in the United States has tended to go hand in hand with the voluntary firm-level introduction of fairness standards regarding worker discipline and risk-sharing in the event of economic adversity indicates that these benefits may indeed be substantial. From a theoretical perspective, such benefits, which accrue to firms, workers and the public at large, must be viewed against the costs and benefits of actual or conceivable alternative governance structures for employment relationships, for example, mere private contracting and the handling of conflictual cases through civil contract law, which define the opportunity costs of existing dismissal-protection regimes. Given that experimental evaluation designs appear hardly feasible in the area of dismissal protection, a promising path for future research, therefore, seems to lie in more detailed, empirically grounded cross-country comparisons of starkly contrasting regimes, such as the ones existing in Europe on the one hand and North America or Japan on the other.

REFERENCES

Abraham, K. H. and S. N. Houseman (1993), *Job Security in America. Lessons from Germany*, Washington, DC: Brookings.

Abraham, K. H. and S. N. Houseman (1994), 'Does Employment Protection Inhibit Labour Market Flexibility? Lessons from Germany, France, and Belgium', in R. M. Blank (ed.), *Social Protection versus Economic Flexibility. Is There a Trade-off?*, Chicago, IL: University of Chicago Press, pp. 59–94.

Addison, J. T. (1989), 'Job Rights and Economic Dislocation', in R. Drago and R. Perlman (eds), *Micro-economic Issues in Labor Economics: New Approaches*, New York: Harvester-Wheatsheaf, pp. 130–54.

Addison, J. T. and P. Portugal (1991), 'Advance Notice', in J. T. Addison (ed.), *Job Displacement: Consequences and Implications for Policy*, Detroit: Wayne State University Press, pp. 203–43.

Anderson, P. M. and B. D. Meyer (1993), 'Unemployment Insurance in the United States: Layoff Incentives and Cross Subsidies', *Journal of Labor Economics*, 11 (1), 70–95.

Barnard, C., J. Clark and R. Lewis (1995, April), *The Exercise of Individual Employment Rights in the Member States of the European Community*, London: Department of Employment.

Bellmann, L., U. Schasse, J. Wadsworth and G. Wolfs (1992), 'An International Comparison of Employment Tenure', Nuremberg: Federal Employment Agency 1992. (Unpublished manuscript)

Bentolila, S. and G. Bertola (1990), 'Firing Costs and Labour Demand: How Bad is Eurosclerosis?', *Review of Economic Studies*, 57, 381–402.

Bertola, G. (1990), 'Job Security, Employment, and Wages', *European Economic Review*, 34, 851–86.

Bierman, L., K. Vinton and S. A. Youngblood (1993), 'Montana's Wrongful Discharge from Employment Act: The Views of the Montana Bar', *Montana Law Review*, 54 (2), 367–84.

Blanpain, R. (ed.) (1990), *International Encyclopedia of Labour Law and Industrial Relations*, Vol. 1, Deventer: Kluwer.

Brown, C., M. Reich and D. Stern (1992), 'Innovative Labor-management Practices: The Role of Security, Employee Involvement, and Training: Final Report', Institute for Industrial Relations, UC Berkeley. (Unpublished manuscript)

Büchtemann, C. F. (ed.) (1993a), *Employment Security and Labor Market Behavior: Interdisciplinary Approaches and International Evidence*, Ithaca, NY: Cornell University Press (ILR).

Büchtemann, C. F. (1993b), 'Introduction: Employment Security and Labor Markets', in C. F. Büchtemann (ed.), *Employment Security and Labor Market Behavior: Interdisciplinary Approaches and International Evidence*, Ithaca, NY: Cornell University Press (ILR), pp. 3–68.

Büchtemann, C. F. (1993c), 'Employment Security and De-regulation: The West German Experience', in C. F. Büchtemann (ed.), *Employment Security and Labor Market Behavior. Interdisciplinary Approaches and International Evidence*, Ithaca, NY: Cornell University Press (ILR), pp. 272–96.

Büchtemann, C. F. (1994), *Employment Security in Germany: An Economic Analysis*, report prepared for the Italian Consiglio Nazionale dell Economia e del Lavoro, Santa Monica, CA. (Published in Italian in CNEL 1995).

Büchtemann, C. F. and A. Hoeland (1989), *Befristete Arbeitsverträge nach dem Beschäftigungsförderungsgesetz*, report on behalf of the Federal Minister for Employment and Social Affairs (BMA), Bonn: BMA.

Burgess, S. M. (1988), 'Employment Adjustment in UK Manufacturing', *The Economic Journal*, 98, 81–103.

Burgess, S. H. (1994), 'The Reallocation of Employment and the Role of Employment Protection Legislation', discussion paper no. 193, Centre for Economic Performance, London: London School of Economics and Political Science (LSE).

Carter, S. B. (1988), 'The Changing Importance of Life-time Jobs, 1892–1978', *Industrial Relations*, 27 (3), 287–300.

CNEL (Consiglio Nazionale dell Economia e del Lavoro) (ed.) (1995), *La Gestione Delle Eccedenze Di Personale In Europa. Gli studi-paese a confronto*, 2 Vols, Rome: Documenti CNEL.

Cohen, G. M. and M. L. Wachter (1989), 'An Internal Labor Market Approach to Labor Law: Does Labor Law Promote Efficient Contracting?', in B. D. Dennis (ed.), *Proceedings of the 41st Annual Meeting of the IRRA*, Industrial Relations Research Association (IRRA), Madison, WI: Industrial Relations Research Association, pp. 243–50.

Commission of the European Communities (1993), *Employment in Europe 1993*, DG V, Brussels, EU Commission, pp. 173–85.

Cooter, R. D. (1991), 'Economic Theories of Legal Liability', *Journal of Economic Perspectives*, 5, 11–30.

Cooter, R. D. and D. L. Rubinfeld (1989), 'Economic Analysis of Legal Disputes and Their Resolution', *Journal of Economic Literature*, 27, 1067–97.

Cooter, R. D. and T. Ulen (1988), *Law and Economics*, Glenview, IL: Scott, Foresman & Co.

Craswell, R. and J. E. Calfee (1986), 'Deterrence and Uncertain Legal Standards', *Journal of Law, Economics, and Organization*, 2, 279–303.

Deregulierungskommission (Unabhängige Expertenkommission zum Abbau marktwidriger Regulierungen) (1991), *Marktöffnung und Wettbewerb, Reports of 1990, 1991*, Stuttgart: Poeschel.

Dertouzos, J. N., E. Holland and P. Ebener (1988), *The Legal and Economic Consequences of Wrongful Termination*, report no. R–3602–ICJ, Santa Monica, CA: The RAND Corporation.

Dertouzos, J. N. and L. A. Karoly (1993), 'Employment Effects of Worker Protection: Evidence from the United States', in C. F. Büchtemann (ed.), *Employment Security and Labor Market Behavior: Interdisciplinary Approaches and International Evidence*, Ithaca, NY: Cornell University Press (ILR), pp. 215–27.

Dickens, L. (1994), 'Comparative Systems of Unjust Dismissal: The British Case', *Annals of the American Academy for Political and Social Science*, 536, 43–55.

Dickens, L., M. Jones and B. Weekes (1985), *Dismissed: A Study of Unfair Dismissal and the Industrial Tribunal System*, Oxford, UK: Basil Blackwell.

Emerson, M. (1988), 'Regulation or Deregulation of the Labour Market. Policy Regimes for the Recruitment and Dismissal of Employees in the Industrialised Countries', *European Economic Review*, 32 (4), 775–817.

Epstein, R. (1984), 'In Defense of the Contract at Will', *University of Chicago Law Review*, 51, 947–82.

Evans, S., J. Goodman and L. Hargreaves (1985), 'Unfair Dismissal Law and Employment Practice', research paper no. 53, London: Department of Employment.

Falke, J., A. Hoeland, B. Rohde, G. Zimmermann, F. Laaser, K. Lammers, M. Merz and D. Renter (1981), 'Kündigungspraxis und Kündigungsschutz in der Bundesrepublik Deutschland', *Forschungsberichte*, Vol. 47, ed. by the Federal Ministry of Labor and Social Affairs (BMA), Bonn: BMA, pp. 965–7.

Fisher, S. M. (1994), 'Legislative Enactment Process: The Model Employment Termination Act', *Annals of the American Academy for Political and Social Science*, 536, 79–92.

Frick, B. (1993), 'Employment Protection Regulations and Dismissals in Germany: Empirical Evidence from the Socio-economic Panel', University of Trier, Fachbereich für Betriebswirtschaft, Germany. (Unpublished manuscript)

Frick, B. (1995), 'Betriebsverfassung und Personalfluktuation', in K. Semlinger and B. Frick (eds), *Betriebliche Modernisierung in personeller Erneuerung*, Berlin: edition sigma, pp. 123–40.

Genthon, V. and P. Maroni (1989, August), 'Moins de licenciements économiques, davantage de préretraites et de conventions de conversion', *Dossiers statistiques du travail et de l'emploi*, 51, 41–5.

Gould, W. B. IV (1993), *Agenda for Reform: The Future of Employment Relationships and the Law*, Cambridge, MA: MIT Press, pp. 63–108.

Grubb, D. and W. Wells (1993), 'Employment Regulation and Patterns of Work in EC Countries', *OECD Economic Studies*, 21, 7–58.

Hall, R. and E. Lazear (1984), 'The Excess Sensitivity of Layoffs and Quits to Demand', *Journal of Labor Economics*, 2 (2), 233–57.

Hamermesh, D. S. (1993), 'Employment Protection: Theoretical Implications and Some U.S. Evidence', in C. F. Büchtemann (ed.), *Employment Security and Labor Market Behavior: Interdisciplinary Approaches and International Evidence*, Ithaca, NY: ILR Press, pp. 126–43.

Hemmer, E. (1988), *Sozialplanpraxis in der Bundesrepublik: Eine empirische Untersuchung*, Cologne: Deutscher Institutsverlag.

Hofmann, C. (1993), 'Institutional Barriers to Job Creation: Views and Expectations of Firms and Workers in the European Community', in C. F. Büchtemann (ed.), *Employment Security and Labor Market Behavior: Interdisciplinary Approaches and International Evidence*, Ithaca, NY: Cornell University Press (ILR), pp. 442–50.

IOE (International Association of Employers) (1985), 'Adapting the Labour Markets', Geneva. (Unpublished manuscript)

Kolstad, C. D. (1990), 'Ex-post Liability for Harm versus Ex-ante Safety Regulation: Substitutes or Complements?', *American Economic Review*, 80 (4), 888–901.

Kraft, K. (1988), 'Sind die Beschäftigungsverhältnisse in der Bundesrepublik über Zeit inflexibler geworden?', *Zeitschrift für Betriebswirtschaft (ZfB)*, (suppl. 2), 7–15.

Kraft, K. (1993), 'Eurosclerosis Reconsidered: Employment Protection and Employment Adjustment in West Germany', in C. F. Büchtemann (ed.), *Employment Security and Labor Market Behavior: Interdisciplinary Approaches and International Evidence*, Ithaca, NY: Cornell University Press (ILR), pp. 297–304.

Kraft, K. (1994), *A Comparison of Employment Adjustment Patterns in France, Germany, Great Britain and Italy*, WZB discussion paper FS I 94–207, Wissenschaftszentrum Berlin für Sozialforschung.

Krueger, A. B. (1991), 'The Evolution of Unjust Dismissal Legislation in the United States', *Industrial and Labor Relations Review*, 44 (4), 644–60.

Krueger, A. B. (1992), 'Reply to Jack Stieber and Richard N. Block', *Industrial and Labor Relations Review*, 45, 796–9.

Kuechle, H. (1990), 'Kündigungsvorschriften im internationalen Vergleich', *WSI Mitteilungen*, 43 (6), 392–400.

Lazear, E. P. (1990), 'Job Security Provisions and Employment', *Quarterly Journal of Economics*, 105, 699–726.

Leonard, A. S. (1988), 'A New Common Law of Employment Termination', *North Carolina Law Review*, 66, 631–86.

Leslie, D. L. (1989), 'Economic Analyses of Labor Law', in B. D. Dennis (ed.), *Proceedings of the 41st Annual Meeting of the Industrial Relations Research Association* (IRRA), Madison, WI: IRRA, pp. 227–35.

Levine, D. J. (1991), 'Just-cause Employment Policies in the Presence of Workers Adverse Selection', *Journal of Labor Economics*, 91, 294–305.

Levine, D. J. and L. d'Andrea Tyson (1990), 'Participation, Productivity, and the Firm's Environment', in A. S. Blinder (ed.), *Paying for Productivity: A Look at the Evidence*, Washington, DC: The Brookings Institution, pp. 183–243.

Maltby, L. L. (1994), 'The Projected Economic Impact of the Model Employment Termination Act', *Annals of the American Academy for Political and Social Science*, 536, 103–18.

Margolis, S. E. (1987), 'Two Definitions of Efficiency in Law and Economics', *Journal of Legal Studies*, 16, 471–82.

Maurau, G. and J. Oudinet (1988), 'Précarité et flexibilité: un essai de comparaison des industries européennes', *La note de l'IRES*, 18, 4–17.

Mosley, H. and T. Kruppe (1992), *Employment Protection and Labour Force Adjustment*, WZB discussion paper FS I 92–9, Wissenschaftszentrum Berlin für Sozialforschung.

OECD (1993), *Employment Outlook*, Paris: OECD, pp. 95–119.

OECD (1994), *The OECD Jobs Study: Evidence and Explanations, Part 2: The Adjustment Potential of the Labour Market*, Paris: OECD Publications.

Payne v. Western & Atlantic Railroad, 81 Tenn. 507, 518–9 (1884).

Posner, R. A. (1984), 'Some Economics of Labor Law', *The University of Chicago Law Review*, 51, 988–1011.

Rodriguez-Pinero, M. (1992), 'Individual Dismissals in the Member States of the European Community: The Advantages and Difficulties of Community Action', unpublished report on behalf of the Commission of the European Communities, DG V, Madrid.

Root, L. S. (1987), 'Britain's Redundancy Payments for Displaced Workers', *Monthly Labor Review*, 110, 18–23.

Rosen, S. (1985), 'Implicit Contracts: A Survey', *Journal of Economic Literature*, 23, 1144–75.

St. Antoine, T. (1994), 'The Model Employment Termination Act: A Fair Compromise', *Annals of the American Academy for Political and Social Science*, 536, 93–102.

Schwab, S. (1989), 'The Economics Invasion of Labor Law Scholarship', in B. D. Dennis (ed.), *Proceedings of the 41st Annual Meeting of the Industrial Relations Research Association* (IRRA), Madison, WI: IRRA, pp. 236–42.

Shavell, S. (1984), 'Liability for Harm versus Regulation for Safety', *Journal of Legal Studies*, 13, 357–74.

Soltwedel, R., A. Bothe, M. Hoffmeyer, C.-F. Laaser, K. Lammers, M. Merz and D. Renter (1990), 'Regulierungen auf dem Arbeitsmarkt der Bundesrepublik', *Kieler Studien*, Vol. 233, Tübingen: J. C. B. Mohr/Siebeck, pp. 28–31.

Spulber, D. F. (1989), *Regulation and Markets*, Cambridge, MA: MIT Press.

Stieber, J. and R. Rodgers (1994), 'Discharge for Cause: History and Development in the United States', *Annals of the American Academy for Political and Social Science*, 536, 70–78.

Troy, K. (1990), 'Rethinking Employment Security', *The Conference Board Research Bulletin* (New York), no. 244.

UNICE (1995, September), 'Releasing Europe's Potential through Targeted Regulatory Reform', UNICE. (Unpublished manuscript)

Weiler, P. C. (1990), *Governing the Workplace: The Future of Labor and Employment Law*, Cambridge, MA: Harvard University Press, pp. 48–60.

Youngblood, S. A. and L. Bierman (1994), 'Employment-at-Will: New Developments and Research Implications', *Research in Personnel and Human Resources Management*, 12, 303–24.

PART III

Evaluating Institutional Frameworks of Labour
Market Policy

J64 J68

23. Explaining State Intervention to Prevent Unemployment: The Impact of Institutions on Active Labour Market Policy Expenditures in 18 Countries

Thomas Janoski[1]

Explanations of labour market and other welfare-state expenditures have most often focussed on economic, demographic or political variables such as GNP per capita, unemployment rates, demographic shifts and left party power. Institutions, which plan, implement and often frame policies, are frequently ignored. This is because institutions are difficult to measure, especially because they seem to fluctuate little from year to year in their most important features. This chapter is focussed explicitly on institutional explanations of active labour market policy (ALMP) expenditures in 18 countries and compares their impact to political economy variables like unemployment rates and left party power. The intent is to identify the strength and efficacy of the institutional causes of active labour market interventions and, in so doing, to advance institutional theory to more dynamic analyses of institutions that foster cooperation and trust among the social partners and the state.

1 Please address correspondence to Thomas Janoski, Department of Sociology, 268 Sociology/ Psychology Building, Duke University, Durham, North Carolina 90088–0088.

    I am thankful for thoughtful comments from Anders Björklund, Lei Delsen, Jap de Koning, James Heckman, Bernd Reissert, Klaus Schömann and Günther Schmid. In the data collection phase of this project, I received important help from Günther Schmid, Bernd Reissert, Hugh Mosley, David Stambrook and Jan Johannssen. I also thank Elizabeth Glennie, Haven White, Christa McGill and Vanessa Tinsley for research assistance. This project was funded by NSF grant SES–92–11542, the Wissenschaftszentrum Berlin für Sozialforschung, the Swedish Bicentennial Fund, the Canadian Embassy Grant and the Center for International Studies at Duke University.

1 EXPLANATIONS OF ACTIVE LABOUR MARKET POLICY (ALMP)

Before World War II, many labour-exchange, job creation and even some job-training policies existed as part of overall policy measures, but ALMP was not used in name. Two Swedish economists, Gösta Rehn (1948) and Rudolph Meidner (1948), first wrote about ALMP as a social democratic strategy to keep inflation under control while pursuing full employment (see also Lewin, 1988, pp. 159–203 and 275). ALMP was recognized as a distinct type of policy when the OECD took up the Swedish policies and publicized them in the mid-1960s. Since then a number of studies have focussed on the impact of ALMP on economic growth and unemployment (Boreham and Compston, 1992; Calmfors, 1994; Esping-Andersen, 1987; Furåker and Johansson, 1990). In chap. 24 of this handbook, Bellmann and Jackman examine the impact of ALMP expenditures on unemployment, specifically the effects of job-placement, job-training and job creation policies.

The task of this chapter is to move to an earlier point in the policy evaluation process to focus on the determinants of ALMP. Among the studies pertaining explicitly to the creation of ALMP, some have explained the passage of particular ALMP laws (Blankenburg, Schmid and Treiber, 1976; Webber, 1982; Webber and Nass, 1984). Such studies often single out the important role played by social democratic parties, but they also note that whereas ALMP can be the result of high unemployment, important labour market laws are also passed when unemployment is low.

Only a few relatively large explanations of ALMP in advanced industrialized countries have been written. Therborn (1986) asked why some peoples are more unemployed than others. He bypassed unemployment, social democratic power and corporatism as explanations of commitment to full employment and stated that 'neither politics in general nor economics in general give us much help' (p. 22). Instead, he pointed to 'an institutionalized commitment to full employment' based on (a) an all-out effort to pursue full employment, (b) the use of Keynesian, or countercyclical, economic policies, (c) the full implementation of ALMP and (d) a conscious decision not to use high unemployment for other objectives (e.g. to lower inflation) (pp. 23 and 124–7).[2]

The members of the group led by Günther Schmid at the Wissenschaftszentrum Berlin für Sozialforschung have not only adopted the explanation of

---

2 Actually, the point on ALMP is sufficiently vague to encompass other policies—'specific mechanisms to adjust supply and demand in the labour market' (Therborn, 1986, p. 23). This allows Therborn to explain Austria, Switzerland and Japan, which have low ALMP, through a diverse set of policies he sees as being functionally equivalent to ALMP.

ALMP but also pursued an institutional explanation. Their approach can be seen in chap. 25 by Schmid and chap. 26 by Appelbaum and Schettkat in this handbook (see also Matzner, 1989; Schmid, 1989, 1990, 1993; and Schmid and Reissert, 1988). In examining six countries—Austria, Germany, France, the United Kingdom, Sweden and the United States—Schmid, Reissert and Bruche (1992) demonstrated that countries with financial institutions based on general revenues (e.g. Sweden) finance ALMP more liberally than countries with insurance-based revenues (e.g. Germany). Their explanation rested solidly on constraints imposed by revenue-producing institutions.

Two others have found evidence for left party power and economic variables causing ALMP. Muszynski (1985) argued that ideologies and 'the greater leverage enjoyed by an expanding labour movement in the 1960s' helped create ALMP in Canada (p. 299). In examining the United States and Germany with a time-series analysis of the past 30 years, Janoski (1990) presented an institutional explanation of expenditures that is based on left party power and unemployment in Germany and on demographic pressures and democratic politics in the United States. He also offered an institutional explanation showing that each time the United States passed a new law implementing ALMP, expenditures went down because of the organizational confusion caused by weak institutions, such as the US employment service. Janoski (1994) also extended the German model to Sweden.

However, cross-national studies explaining the rise and levels of ALMP expenditures in the 18 OECD countries have not been done, nor have studies using institutional variables. Much of the problem rests with the difficulties in finding and measuring the ALMP expenditure variable and the many different institutional variables. In this study, these barriers have been removed for ALMP and initially surmounted for institutions. Consequently, both institutional and macroeconomic variables are tested as competing explanations of ALMP in five time periods.

2   STRANDS OF INSTITUTIONAL THEORY

Recent works in sociology, political science and economics have all contributed to the burgeoning literature on institutional theory.[3] Institutional theory has traditionally looked at the formal and informal networks of agencies, constituencies and interest groups (Commons, 1934; Gouldner, 1954; Selznick, 1949; and Veblen, 1904). But this institutional approach tended to fall from

---

3 For more detailed reviews of institutional theory, see Dugger (1992), Eggertsson (1990), Hodgson (1989, 1993), Knight (1992), Powell and DiMaggio (1991) and Thelen and Steinmo (1992).

favour in the 1960s and 1970s more by failing to be developed with concepts and methods of its own than by being superseded or proved wrong. Since then a new institutionalism has developed in both sociology and political science (March and Olsen, 1984 and 1989; Steinmo, Thelen and Longstreth, 1992). In this approach, social institutions are patterned interactions set up and controlled by formal and informal norms, not structures of class, race, gender or other social categories (Steinmo et al., 1992, p. 11). These patterns refer to political institutions and voluntary associations with democratic or other forms of participation. The policy domain and organizational network literature form another facet of the organization of institutions (Burstein, 1991; Knoke, 1992; Knoke, Pappi, Broadbent, Kaufman and Tsujinaka, 1993). The structuring of policy domains refers to how organizations, groups and the public are tied together in specific networks, often with their own roles and ideologies.[4]

Economics is also marked by renewed interest in institutions. In historical institutionalism, attention to the ways in which norms evolve over time has greatly increased (North, 1993, pp. 12 and 17). In the regulation school, job control and policy regulations that have a major impact on economic growth and unemployment are stressed (Boyer, 1993). The transaction-cost approach centres less on norms and more on the rationality of choosing between markets and hierarchy, depending on the costs associated with the uncertainties of transacting in a market or maintaining hierarchical control over suppliers and producers (Williamson, 1975, 1985). Researchers using the social-choice approach look at the rational choosing of institutions that are based on largely market-oriented or rationality principles. These approaches range from the evolutionary and historical, which are the least reliant on individual rationality and markets, to the social-choice approach, which is the most rationalistic (Furubotn and Richter, 1993, p. 3).

Although this chapter cannot delve into the many controversies in institutional theory, it does follow two important leads offered by the 'regime-type' and 'governance-of-the-economy' approaches in the literature on new institutionalism. First, comparative social policy analysis was significantly advanced by Esping-Andersen's concept of 'welfare state regimes'. This approach provides generalizations about overall institutional structures that are specially geared to the welfare state in three groups of countries—those with social democratic, liberal or conservative regimes. Second, a most promising devel-

---

4 Organizational institutionalism represents another approach to institutions, but it is centred on how organizations develop norms and an ethos or culture not directly connected to rationality (DiMaggio, 1988; Fligstein, 1990; Powell and DiMaggio, 1991). Organizational theories differ somewhat from new institutionalism in that they are focussed on the impact of organizational environments on internal organizations and present a process-oriented theory that can apply to all organizations.

opment in institutional theory about the growth of markets, networks and hierarchies in the economy was achieved by Campbell, Hollingsworth and Lindberg (1991). They differentiated markets, networks and hierarchies into bilateral and multilateral interaction, which is translatable into restricted and generalized exchange (1991, pp. 14–28). But, the multilateral-interaction approach needs to be developed much further in the direction of generalized political exchange rather than simple multiparty interaction (Crouch, 1992; Janoski, in press; Marin, 1990a, 1990b). Using time as an important criterion, researchers seeking to create a more complete theory of labour market policy need to bring the creation, evolution and death of regimes to the forefront of institutional development. This effort will entail the development of long-run interests and cooperation, of which tripartism in social policy is an excellent example.[5]

A focus on comparative labour market policy presents new challenges and opportunities to the development of institutional theory. I begin this process by considering just a few of these issues. First, an institutional model is developed to explain ALMP. Second, institutional variables are constructed in a time series instead of national constants. These time-series variables are then aggregated into five-year periods from 1970 through 1989. Third, this institutional model explaining ALMP is tested with correlations and regression equations.

3   AN INSTITUTIONAL MODEL EXPLAINING ACTIVE LABOUR MARKET POLICY

The four types of institutions have an impact on ALMP expenditures: (a) the structure and powers of the employment service, (b) the presence of firm-level institutions such as works councils and codetermination mechanisms that interact with ALMP, (c) the more distant policies of national welfare-state institutions and educational systems and (d) the even longer-range policies of national institutions affecting wage and macroeconomic bargaining. These variables are put into a model, with each variable lagged and averaged for five years (see Figure 23.1).

---

5 One of the governance group's major contributions is the examination of changes or transformations of regimes as a primary point of research. Not only does this focus provide a more accurate picture of institutions, it also gives the underlying reasons or rationales for their existence. Welfare-state regimes and exchange perspectives have some commonality in that much of this research has been static and that attention to the structures and logics of the formation, transformation and replacement of institutions needs to be vastly increased in new research.

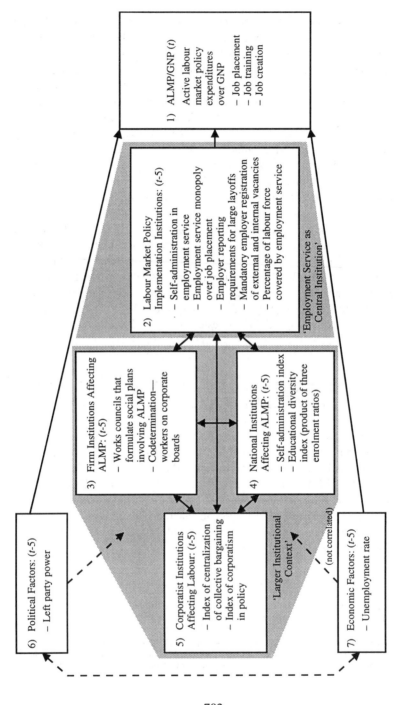

Figure 23.1 Cross-sectional Institutional Model of Active Labour Market Policy Expenditures as a Per Cent of GNP

702

In this chapter I contend that the more formal the cooperation is between labour, management and the state in tripartite arrangements at all levels of endeavour (national, state and local), the more likely it is that ALMP will be successful and that it will be funded at a high level. Let us look at the role of these institutional variables.

First, the employment service has the most direct impact on ALMP, for it plays a central role as a labour exchange and in many countries implements most ALMP policies (see chap. 13 by Walwei, on the employment service). With requirements that firms report all vacancies to the employment service, the service may have a monopoly on job placement. Furthermore, after the oil crisis, many states further required employers to notify the employment services well in advance of large layoffs and plant closings. A strong employment service will be better able to coordinate and/or implement a large number of active labour market policies more successfully when it has a strong presence in the labour market.

This existence of strong regulatory powers in the employment service will be reinforced by self-administration of the employment service by the social partners and various levels of the state. Tripartite policy-making brings labour, management and the appropriate level of government together on a regular basis to discuss the labour market and cooperatively plan policies. It tends to bind groups together under a common fate and thus promotes more generalized exchange. By the time policy is set, the social partners have already agreed on the programmes. This approach enhances the likelihood of successful implementation. Countries with weak employment services will create new agencies that get in each other's way and perform poorly in the labour market. The lack of self-administration means that labour and management observe state policies as outsiders and may decide to ignore, distrust or even fight government policies. And wary participants commit few resources and withdraw easily and early. A strong employment service with adequate power that includes the social partners in the policy-planning process will lead to a much more successful policy. In essence, the state can go a long way in shaping the labour market and the attitudes of the social partners through an agency with strong participation and powers of intervention.

Second, one step removed from direct policy planning, works councils and codetermination representatives on company boards of directors have an additional impact on ALMP. When a strong works council exists, corporations will work with the employment service and trade unions in formulating 'social plans' that most often include important aspects of ALMP. Both works councils and board representatives facilitate cooperation with the employment service in finding jobs for workers who will be laid off. Training may take place in the firm, or the firm may apply for short-time-work programmes that reduce the hours of work of each worker while they receive their regular pay. The result is greater time, planning and overall help for workers looking for new jobs.

Third, self-administration in other areas of the welfare state will produce results similar to self-administration in the employment service. Self-administration in pensions, health, disability, and unemployment insurance will further increase the context of generalized exchange among the social partners and the state. The role of self-administration is not direct; nonetheless, the unemployed need continued benefit protections while seeking work. Further, self-administration in the welfare state has a spill-over effect on labour market policy. It can prevent the endless bickering among employers and trade unions about whether workers are avoiding work through disability, health, and other programmes. Self-administration can have this effect because the social partners are administering these same programmes and are partly responsible for them.

The educational system, in structure and intensity, also has a major impact on the success of ALMP programmes. School systems that offer a wide variety of options and provide the basic occupational skills that can facilitate more advanced retraining will enhance the effectiveness of ALMP. School systems that offer homogeneous graduates with few occupational skills will make ALMP start from the beginning, a situation that will require extensive training of workers, who are not often familiar with the discipline or skills required for work. Having an effective apprenticeship system is particularly valuable in this regard.

Fourth, national institutions representing general cooperation throughout the economy will have a more distant, but still important, influence on ALMP. Corporatism with tripartite wage and policy bargaining between labour, management and the state will have beneficial impact on ALMP expenditures. If the tripartite logic and solidarity works with tripartite wage negotiations, it should have a similar effect at the level of employment service.

Finally, political economy variables, such as left party power, unemployment rates, labour force participation rates and other variables represent an approach that is not based on institutions. These variables may have a strong effect that should be controlled to measure the impact of institutional variables (Janoski, 1990, 1994).

This larger model differs greatly from those offered in most explanations of social policy because it combines macroeconomic and institutional approaches. The political economy is represented by unemployment and left party power, which usually are the centrepieces of the power-resources approach to the study of the political economy (see Korpi, 1983, 1991, and Shalev, 1983, among many others). The institutional variables—employment service, power-sharing within the firm, self-administration, educational diversity and corporatism—have theoretical connections to the state-centred approach of Katzenstein (1984, 1985), Skocpol (1992) and Skocpol and Orloff (1986), which has been renamed the polity approach. However, the complexities and conjunctural configurations of institutions in this research tradition have been handled primarily with qualitative research on no more than a few more case studies. As a result, these theories pass like two ships in the dark.

Often, the institutionalists mention 'institutional context' as being of tremendous importance, but this context is often vague. The complex of institutional variables in this chapter is presented as an attempt to specify this context by operationalizing many of the variables that would be used in the polity, or state-centred, approach to labour market policy. Some of these variables are highly correlated with each other, as one would expect with contextual effects, but even the more distant institutions are of some importance. Although the employment service undoubtedly has the strongest individual effects on ALMP, the other institutional variables provide a supportive environment. For example, a strong employment service without a legally mandated presence inside the firm (i.e. works councils and codetermination) or without legally mandated cooperation between management and labour in the rest of the welfare state (i.e. self-administration and corporatism) will have trouble implementing ALMP. This is where a context of social cooperation between the social partners has its effect.

4   MEASURING ACTIVE LABOUR MARKET POLICY AND INSTITUTIONS

Active labour market policy (ALMP) refers to direct government intervention in the labour market to prevent or alleviate unemployment. It generally consists of job-placement, job-training and job creation policies, which is the 'narrow' definition according to Calmfors (1994). ALMP does not consist of unemployment insurance, early retirement or other passive policies that do not move people into jobs. For most countries ALMP has not been as salient as pensions, health insurance and other measures of the welfare state. (Of course, Sweden, being the leader in this area, is the major exception.) In many countries, ALMP figures and reports are often scattered among many different ministries and reporting jurisdictions, which in some countries often change names and responsibilities. Consequently, it was quite a task to collect ALMP data in 18 countries.

The ALMP data in this chapter have been drawn from national sources. The countries where ALMP is salient, such as Sweden, Norway and Germany, report ALMP in one institutional source in or closely connected to the employment service. Other countries such as the United Kingdom, Finland and New Zealand disclose expenditures in reports by the ministry of labour or department of employment. Most of the remaining countries report ALMP in the details of national budgets and, in some cases, in combined national and regional reports on labour market policies. I used these national sources with adequate disaggregated figures in order to pick policy figures that fit the narrow definition of ALMP. Data were collected in a time-series format extending from 1960 through 1989. The exceptions to the national source rule were the Netherlands and Denmark, which began compiling such data in the 1980s, so I had to use secondary sources in the 1970s.

With one exception, these original data are comparable to OECD data reported for the 1986–90 period. They do not include funds for the early retirement of workers because these programmes do not create jobs for workers but rather remove workers from jobs by pensioning them out of the labour force. Such funds are clearly passive, not active, measures. OECD data are based on country reports, which sometimes come from quite excellent national analyses and other times from hurried compilations.[6] The ALMP data presented in this chapter are quite comparable to Schmid, Reissert and Bruche's (1992) data on five European countries and the USA from 1973 to 1988 and OECD data from 1986 to the present. Details on the calculation of ALMP are included in the Appendix of the chapter.

Italian ALMP data represent Cassa Integrazione Guadagni (CIG) figures supplied by Leon Tronti. The CIG is a mix of passive and active policies, but they are extremely difficult to separate (Ferrera, 1988, p. 492; Tronti, 1990). I have interpreted half the CIG expenditures as ALMP, but this assumption is probably an overestimation of Italian ALMP because most reports show that CIG is largely passive unemployment insurance policies. Nonetheless, Italy was clearly low on ALMP expenditures.

Finally, ALMP over GNP was averaged for ten years from 1950 through 1959 and then for five-year periods: 1960–64, 1965–69, 1970–74, 1975–79, 1980–84 and 1985–89. The final dependent variable for this study was the five periods from 1965 to 1989. All ALMP variables were divided by GNP at factor cost and are presented in Table 23.1 as five-year averages (see Table 23.1 for sources).

---

6 For example, Canadian officials informed me that their OECD figures were wrong and that they did not know what Canadian ALMP expenditures really were until they had completed a recent study.

Table 23.1 Active Labour Market Policy (ALMP) Expenditures Divided by
GNP at Factor Cost in 18 Countries, Averaged for Five-year
and Ten-year Periods[a] (in Percentages)

Country	1985–89	1980–84	1975–79	1970–74	1965–69	1960–64	1950–59
Australia	0.45	0.25	0.20	0.01	—	—	—
Austria	0.31	0.21	0.18	0.18	0.10	0.22	0.12
Belgium	0.50	0.49	0.29	0.10	0.10	0.11	0.15
Canada	0.44	0.53	0.50	0.57	0.50	0.37	0.03
Denmark	1.42	1.37	0.44	0.23	0.14	0.09	—
Finland	1.09	1.23	0.44	0.23	0.21	0.26	0.21
France	1.43	1.10	0.88	0.42	0.30	0.18	—
Germany	1.11	1.00	0.81	0.63	0.33	0.32	0.39
Ireland	0.95	0.67	0.37	0.22	0.19	—	—
Italy[b]	0.23	0.26	0.13	0.07	0.06	0.05	—
Japan	0.10	0.10	0.09	0.09	0.12	0.17	0.22
Netherlands	0.58	0.59	0.32	—	—	—	—
New Zealand	1.02	0.88	0.27	0.06	0.06	0.36	0.05
Norway	0.83	0.50	0.52	0.22	0.22	—	—
Sweden	1.81	1.94	1.75	1.40	0.95	0.75	0.27
Switzerland	0.23	0.01	0.02	0.001	0.002	0.007	0.02
United Kingdom	0.86	0.79	0.53	0.18	0.15	—	—
United States	0.21	0.23	0.38	0.18	0.15	0.04	0.02

Notes
a ALMP expenditures consist of policy expenditures on job placement and administration, job training and job creation. They include neither passive measures such as unemployment insurance nor early pensions to encourage workers to retire from the job market.
b Italian figures are based on the years 1986 through 1992 in OECD (1993) and CIG expenditures (*Cassa Integrazione Guadagni*). The CIG is a mix of passive and active policies that are impossible to separate. Half the CIG expenditures are interpreted in this table as ALMP, but as much as 90 per cent of them may be passive.

Sources
AUSTRALIA: Department of Employment and Industrial Relations (1980–90), *Annual Report*, Canberra: Australian Government Publishing Service; Department of Employment, Education and Training (1989–92), *Annual Report*, Canberra: Australian Government Publishing Service; S. Kesteven (1987–88), *Commonwealth Employment and Training Schemes since 1973–August 1987*, Current Issues Paper no. 1: Canberra: Legislative Research Service; Ministry of Finance (1962–90), *Budget Statements*, Canberra: Australian Government Publishing Service. AUSTRIA: Austria (1980–92), *Programmbudget der Arbeitsmarktverwaltung*, Vienna: Österreichische

Staatsdruckerei; Austrian Government (Budget) (1948–79), *Teilheft zum Bundesvoranschlag, Gruppe 1, Innenverwaltung, Kapital 15 und 16*, Vienna: Österreichische Staatsdruckerei. BELGIUM: ONEM (1950–92), *ONEM Rapport Annuel*, Brussels: Office National de l'Emploi. CANADA: Canada (1960–92), *Public Accounts of Canada*, Ottawa: Receiver General for Canada; Employment and Immigration Canada (1976–90), *Annual Report*, Hull: EIC; D. Papandreou, (1990), 'Historical Estimates of Selected EIC Program Expenditures', Strategic Policy and Planning Section, Policy and Program Analysis, Hull: EIC; Statistics Canada (1967–90), *Unemployment Insurance Statistics, Annual Supplement*, Ottawa: Statistics Canada. DENMARK: Nordic Council (1975–90), *Yearbook of Nordic Statistics*, Oslo: Norway; Danish Government, Labour Directorate (1974–92), *Arbejdsdirektoratets arsberetning*, Copenhagen: Arbejdsdirektoratet; OECD (1988–93), *Employment Outlook*, Paris: OECD. FINLAND: Ministry of Labour, Planning Division (1970–90), *Employment and Manpower Policy Measures in Finland*, Helsinki: Ministry of Labour; OECD (1988–93), *Employment Outlook*, Paris: OECD. FRANCE: Ministre de l'Emploi (1982, 1984), *Comptes de l'emploi: données physico-financières*, Paris: La Documentation Française; Ministère du Travail, de l'Emploi et de la Formation Professionnelle (1990, 1991), *Comptes de l'Emploi de la Formation Professionnelle—Dossier financier 1980–89*, Paris: La Documentation Française; *idem.* (1991), *Dépenses d'Insertion et de Réinsertion des Demandeurs d'Emploi: données financières 1975–89*, Paris: Division Emploi et Politiques d'emploi; *idem.* (1981), *Retrospective budgetaire du Ministère du Travail, 1960–80*, Paris: Service des Études et de la Statistique (internal document); Liaisons Sociales (1988), 'Tableaux Sociaux Statistiques Retrospective', *Liaisons Sociales*, 3 November 1988, no. 10329. GERMANY: Bundesanstalt für Arbeit (1952–92), *Amtliche Nachrichten der Bundesanstalt für Arbeit: Arbeitsstatistik, Jahreszahlen*, Nuremberg: BAA. IRELAND: Department of Labour (1967–90), 'Revised Estimates', in *The Department of Labour Annual Report*, Dublin: Stationery Office. ITALY: L. Tronti (1990), 'Employment Protection and Labor Market Segmentation: Economic Implications of the Italian "Cassa Integrazione Guadagni"', paper presented at the ILO, IILS, and WZB conference on Workers Protection and Labour Market Dynamics, 16–18 May; OECD (1988–93), *Employment Outlook*, Paris: OECD. JAPAN: Information calculated and supplied by the Japanese Ministry of Labour. NETHERLANDS: D. Moraal (1994, August), 'Evaluierung der Reorganisation der Arbeitsverwaltung in den Niederlanden', WZB discussion paper 94–204, Wissenschaftszentrum Berlin für Sozialforschung; OECD (1988–93), *Employment Outlook*, Paris: OECD. NEW ZEALAND: House of Representatives (1955–92), *Report of the Department of Labour*, Wellington: Government Printer; House of Representatives (1955–92), *Report of the Department of Social Welfare*, Wellington: Government Printer; House of Representatives (1955–92), *Estimates of the Expenditure of the Government of New Zealand*, Wellington: Government Printer; R. J. Gill (1989), *Inventory of Labour Market Measures, 1970–89*, Wellington: Department of Labour, Labour Market Analysis Unit. NORWAY: Arbeidsdirektoratet (1950–90), *Department of Labor Annual Report*, Oslo: Arbeidsdirektoratet. SWEDEN: Arbetsmarknadsverket (AMS) (1950–92), *Annual Report*, Solna: Arbetsmarknadsstyrelsen. SWITZERLAND: Switzerland (1970–90), *Öffentliche Finanzen der Schweiz*, Bern: Eidgenössisches Statistisches Amt; Switzerland (1950–90), *Statistisches Jahrbuch der Schweiz*, Basel: Verlag Birkhauser. UNITED STATES: US Department of Labor (1964–82), *Manpower Report of the President*, Washington, DC: Government Printing Office (GPO); US Department of Labor (1988–95), *The Labor Market Report of the Secretary of Labor*, Washington, DC: GPO; US President (1950–92), *Budget of the United States Government*, Washington, DC: GPO. UNITED KINGDOM: UK (1948–75), *Civil Appropriations*, London: HMSO; UK (various years), *Civil Estimates*, London: HMSO; UK (1976–92), *The Governments' Expenditure Plans*, London: HMSO; UK Manpower Services Commission (1977–84), *The Annual Report for the Manpower Services Commission*, London: HMSO.

5   MEASURING INSTITUTIONS OVER TIME

In the spirit of the 'governance of the economy' group, institutions were measured in a time-series fashion. Each variable was constructed from 1950 through 1989 (see Appendix for the actual coding). To begin with the employment service, five components are important. First, the style of administration of the employment service was measured according to the amount of tripartite self-administration of labour, management and the government. Second, the level of tripartite self-administration was measured according to whether it occurs at the federal, state or local levels. The third component represents the degree of employment service monopoly over job placement. Fourth, employer-reporting requirements ensure that a large number of vacancies are disclosed to the employment service and they were measured in two ways: internal vacancies meant those within the firm (i.e. promotions and lateral transfers); external vacancies meant those in the labour market. Countries scored higher when employers must report information on both internal and external vacancies (OECD, 1991, p. 218). With the layoff reporting requirement, employers are also required to inform the employment service of layoffs of 50 or more workers and of plant closings.

The scores pertaining to the style and levels of tripartite administration were added and divided by their maximum score (i.e. 3). The power that the employment services have over employers in the labour market consists of the remaining three components. They were added and divided by their maximum score. The sum of these two components was then multiplied by the percentage of the labour force served by the employment service. The result was an index that could vary from 0 to 2, but in practice it ranged from 0.13 in the United States to 1.09 in Germany (1980–84 figures). It captured a significant amount of the overall institutional strength of the employment service in these countries.

Neither the budget of the employment service nor its number of employees was included, for both are part of the outcome (i.e. the employment service budget is part of ALMP/GNP and employee wages come out of ALMP/GNP). To include the budget would have resulted in a partial tautology. Each component of the employment service index described above was an institutional feature of the employment service itself, and these components are based on legislation and regulation rather than funding. None of the measures required that the organization have a high or low budget. For example, France, Belgium and Austria scored high on the measure of employment service power; however, France spent a great deal on ALMP; Belgium, a moderate amount; and Austria, very little. A weak bureaucracy can spend a great deal of money trying to get around its weaknesses, especially during a crisis of high unemployment. Consequently, institutional characteristics of the employment service were clearly independent of ALMP expenditures.

The second group of institutions is based within firms. Works councils are measures of laws for different segments of the labour force, including state workers. Works councils in different sectors of the economy (categories change from country to country) were frequently legislated and then implemented. This variable uses the law (as a dummy variable), the percentage of the labour force that it covers, and parity and issue factors that measure the actual representation of true works council laws in each specific sector. The combined product of the law, the work force covered, and the parity and issue factors resulted in the final works council score in that sector. The same was done for the other sectors. The scores pertaining to the sectors were then added to produce an index that represents the percentage of the labour force effectively covered by works council laws.

The codetermination measure operates like the measure for the works councils. Because there are frequently different laws, a separate variable was computed for each sector (be it based on size, industry or the public–private divide). A variable was developed for passage of a law and for the segment of the labour force it covers. A parity factor measures the level of participation by labour representatives on corporate boards. The three measures were combined to provide the overall percentage of the work force covered by fully equal codetermination laws in each country.

Third, welfare-state institutions that involve self-administration provide a context for labour and management cooperation that encourages employer and labour cooperation in the labour market. In the self-administration index, scores for pensions, health, disability, and unemployment insurance, were added and then divided by four. The final measure shows how much labour, management and the state set policy in social welfare.

The educational variable includes a measure of the diversity of education systems. Diversity of school choice involves a measure of occupationally specific educational systems, especially those that encompass apprenticeship. This index was multiplied by the enrolment ratios for the compulsory secondary school system: (1) academic school systems (the *Gymnasium*, the high school and other schools leading to university or higher education), (2) vocational or semiprofessional schools (the *Realschule*, high schools that grant degrees in aircraft repair or other occupational licences) and (3) part-time continuation schools for apprenticeships (the *Berufsschule*, or high schools that require an apprenticeship and grant a licence upon graduation). In a manner analogous to a Gini coefficient, the three ratios were multiplied together: the more equal the ratios, the higher the index; the more unequal the ratios, the closer the index is to zero.

Fourth, corporatism variables express tripartism at a much higher level, measuring whether unions, employers and the state are involved in wage bargaining at the national and industrial levels. In this chapter an attempt is made to measure peak bargaining, not the causes of bargaining such as unionization or centralization. As a separate measure, I looked at how much employers, unions and the state are involved in policy bargaining. Although this activity was difficult to separate from wage bargaining when incomes policy is involved in wage bargaining, it was possible to separate other types of social policy from wage bargaining. This measure was computed at the national and industrial levels. These two types of corporatist bargaining were then combined into a larger corporatism variable.

Each set of independent variables and indexes was treated as interval-level variables because in most cases it was possible to characterize the individual components as dummy variables. When they included three categories, there was a clear sense that something of equal intervals is being added (i.e. one to three levels of government or one to three administering partners). Each set of independent variables and indexes was treated as interval-level variables also because many basic variables were combined into an additive index and often multiplied by a ratio representing the percentage of the labour force covered by the institutional feature involved. Since these variables were complex indices often representing different units of analysis, 'bang-for-the-buck' results (e.g. for each unit increase in x, there is a specific unit increase in y) were not particularly informative. Consequently, standardized beta (β) coefficients are used throughout the analysis.

In developing these institutional hypotheses, the analysis also includes left party power and unemployment. In many ways these variables will operate as controls by which to measure the impact of institutions. Left party power represents the percentage of seats controlled by parties of the left. Communist and other radical left parties were not included unless these parties traditionally participated in government (e.g. France and Italy).[7] Standardized unemployment rates are taken from OECD sources. The values for many of the institutional and macroeconomic variables for the first period of analysis can be seen in Table 23.2.

---

7 Election years are corrected according to partial year results (e.g. for an election in November the variable includes 11/12ths of the earlier period and 1/12th of the later period).

Table 23.2 Institutional and Political Economy, Macroeconomic Variables by High and Low Active Labour Market Policy (ALMP) Expenditures (in Percentages)

Country		Six Types of Institutional Variables: (1980–84)[a]						Macroeconomic Variables (1980–84)[b]	
(Ranked by 1985–89 ALMP/GNP)		(1) ES	(2) WC	(3) COD	(4) SELF	(5) ED	(6) COR	(7) Left	(8) UE
High									
Sweden	1.8	1.05	0.23	0.09	2.50	1.80	0.001	46	2.8
Denmark	1.4	0.56	0.07	0.12	2.00	1.29	0.85	48	9.6
France	1.4	0.79	0.13	0.08	1.80	1.14	0.40	59	8.0
Finland	1.1	0.41	0.00	0.09	1.00	1.00	0.002	27	5.1
New Zealand	1.0	0.17	0.00	0.00	1.00	0.67	0.35	49	4.1
Germany	1.0	1.09	0.84	0.30	2.30	0.97	1.04	42	6.0
Ireland	1.0	0.33	0.00	0.00	1.00	0.90	0.25	18	11.6
United Kingdom	0.9	0.45	0.00	0.00	1.00	0.56	0.24	38	9.5
Norway	0.8	1.00	0.40	0.04	2.30	1.46	0.09	46	2.5
Average	*1.16*	*0.65*	*0.19*	*0.08*	*1.66*	*1.09*	*0.36*	*41.4*	*6.58*
Low									
Netherlands	0.5	0.47	0.23	0.00	1.80	1.42	0.50	32	9.9
Belgium	0.4	0.84	0.28	0.01	1.60	1.24	0.10	30	11.3
Canada	0.4	0.17	0.00	0.00	1.00	0.33	0.05	11	9.8
Australia	0.3	0.13	0.00	0.00	1.00	0.89	0.16	48	7.3
Italy	0.2	0.27	0.00	0.00	1.70	0.89	0.87	42	8.6
Austria	0.2	0.61	0.85	0.32	2.30	1.87	1.09	50	3.2
Switzerland	0.2	0.17	0.00	0.00	1.40	0.79	0.73	25	0.6
United States	0.2	0.13	0.00	0.00	0.80	0.25	0.001	37	8.2
Japan	0.1	0.23	0.00	0.00	1.10	0.57	0.001	34	2.4
Average	*0.28*	*0.34*	*0.15*	*0.04*	*1.41*	*0.92*	*0.39*	*34.3*	*6.81*

Notes

a ES = Index of employment service power combining tripartite administration with employment service power over employers in the labour market; WC = Index of works councils; COD = Index of codetermination of corporate boards; SELF = Index of self-administration in four areas of the welfare state; COR = Corporatism index using direct bargaining measures covering wages and policy bargaining; ED = Educational enrolment index.

b Left party power using relative leftness (i.e. the United States has left party power because of democrats); UE = five-year average unemployment rate.

6   EXPLAINING ACTIVE LABOUR MARKET POLICY

ALMP expenditures divided by GNP differ considerably. It is no surprise that Sweden, the originator and proselytizer of ALMP, was the world's leader in six of seven periods. Sweden was the first country to pass the one per cent barrier of ALMP/GNP in the early 1970s, and it has continued to pass it.

Using Esping-Andersen's (1990) 'welfare state regime' theory, the countries were grouped according to ALMP into social democratic, conservative and liberal regimes (see Table 23.3).

Table 23.3   Active Labour Market Policy Divided by GNP at Factor Cost in 18 Countries by Type of Welfare-state Regime[a]

Regime Type and Country	1985–89	1980–84	1975–79	1970–74	1965–69
Social democratic					
Denmark	1.42	1.37	0.44	0.23	0.14
Finland	1.09	1.23	0.44	0.23	0.21
Netherlands	0.58	0.59	0.32	—	—
Norway	0.83	0.50	0.52	0.22	0.22
Sweden	1.81	1.94	1.75	1.40	0.95
Average	*1.146*	*1.126*	*0.694*	*0.520*	*0.380*
Conservative regime					
Austria	0.31	0.21	0.18	0.18	0.10
Belgium	0.50	0.49	0.29	0.10	0.10
France	1.43	1.10	0.88	0.42	0.30
Germany	1.11	1.00	0.81	0.63	0.33
Ireland	0.95	0.67	0.37	0.22	0.19
Italy	0.23	0.26	0.13	0.07	0.06
Average	*0.755*	*0.621*	*0.443*	*0.270*	*0.180*
Liberal regime					
Australia	0.45	0.25	0.20	0.01	—
Canada	0.44	0.53	0.50	0.57	0.50
Japan	0.10	0.10	0.09	0.09	0.12
New Zealand	1.02	0.88	0.27	0.06	0.06
Switzerland	0.23	0.01	0.02	0.001	0.002
United Kingdom	0.86	0.79	0.53	0.15	0.07
United States	0.21	0.23	0.38	0.18	0.15
Average	*0.416*	*0.400*	*0.284*	*0.152*	*0.150*

Note

a   For a complete explanation of regime types, see *The Three Worlds of Welfare Capitalism* by G. Esping-Andersen, 1990, Princeton: Princeton University Press.

The averages for the social democratic countries were always greater than those for the other two regimes, sometimes by factors of nearly two. The averages for the conservative regimes, while lower than the social democratic countries, were often 30 to 50 per cent greater than those for the liberal regimes (only in the 1965–69 period were they close). The correlations of Esping-Andersen's regime variables with ALMP were generally quite strong. The social democratic regime variables based on the universal distribution and equality of benefits were strongly correlated with ALMP for the two most recent of four periods ($r = 0.62, 0.61$) and moderately strong in the two earlier periods ($r = 0.38$ and 0.36). The liberal regime measure using indexes of means testing and the extent of private pension and health benefits had medium negative correlation also strongly correlated with ALMP for the two most recent periods, but in the opposite ($r = -0.54, -0.51$). The two earlier periods were weaker ($r = -0.27$ and -0.19). The measure for conservative regime type based on a strong civil service and diverse insurance systems for particular occupations is much more mixed and weaker, which is not surprising, given that Germany and Austria were in this group, with high and low ALMP, respectively ($r = -0.06$, -0.08, -0.06 and -0.10). This regime grouping provides some important evidence about the institutional structuring of ALMP expenditures according to welfare-state institutions (Esping-Andersen, 1990, p. 70).

The weaknesses of this 'welfare regime' approach for this chapter are twofold. First, there was considerable variation in each category. For instance, France and Germany from the conservative regime group had high ALMP. They could have easily fitted into the social democratic regime type, as New Zealand from the camp of liberal regimes could have. The averages for the groups wash out these outliers, but in statistical analysis the standard errors would be large. Second, Esping-Andersen's regime categorization is actually oriented to welfare-state variables, not labour market variables. Consequently, the theory is not exactly direct.

Institutional variables focussing on the labour market can explain much more. The most direct influence on ALMP was the power of the employment service, which was strongly and significantly correlated with ALMP in all five periods (see Table 23.4).

Whereas the variables for the codetermination and works councils were only weakly correlated with ALMP, the self-administration index was strong and significant in earlier periods (1970–74 and 1975–79) but not in the more recent ones. The two corporatism indexes had mixed results, but none was significant, and the education variable is even negative.

I simplified the indexes to create a firm index from works councils and codetermination variables and a corporatism index from wage- and policy-bargaining variables. The corporatism index was strongly correlated with ALMP for 1985–89, 1980–84, 1975–79 and 1970–74 ($r = 0.41, 0.50, 0.39$

Table 23.4 Zero-order Correlation Coefficients with Active Labour Market Policy (ALMP) and Institutional Variables in 18 Countries in Five Periods

Independent Variables (averaged and then lagged for five years)	1985–89	1980–84	1975–79	1970–74	1965–69
Employment service power, t-5[a]	0.57*	0.50*	0.65**	0.61**	0.52*
	(0.01)	(0.03)	(0.004)	(0.009)	(0.04)
Codetermination index, t-5	0.14	0.17	0.22	0.30	0.13
	(0.58)	(0.49)	(0.39)	(0.24)	(0.63)
Workers' council index, t-5	0.06	0.07	0.20	0.26	0.14
	(0.82)	(0.78)	(0.43)	(0.31)	(0.60)
Self-administration index, t-5	0.38	0.38	0.50*	0.56*	0.43
	(0.13)	(0.12)	(0.04)	(0.02)	(0.09)
Education diversity index, t-5	–0.13	–0.05	–0.19	–0.13	–0.31
	(0.61)	(0.84)	(0.45)	(0.61)	(0.24)
Corporatism in wages index, t-5	0.33	0.36	0.17	0.22	0.21
	(0.32)	(0.17)	(0.52)	(0.43)	(0.48)
Corporatism in policy index, t-5	0.18	0.39	0.26	0.37	0.31
	(0.49)	(0.13)	(0.35)	(0.17)	(0.28)
Left party power t-5	0.36	0.12	0.11	—	—
	(0.13)	(0.63)	(0.87)	—	—
Unemployment t-5	0.04	0.003	– 014	—	—
	(0.89)	(0.99)	(0.64)	—	—

Notes
a Each independent variable is lagged five years behind the dependent variable (i.e. employment service power from 1980 to 1984 predicts ALMP from 1985 to 1989).
* $p < 0.05$ level; ** $p < 0.01$ level.

and 0.45), but the firm index was rather weak ($r = 0.08, 0.10, 0.21$ and 0.28). On the whole, the strongest institutional variable was the employment service power, followed by self-administration. The other institutional variables are positive, except for the education index.

The employment service's strongest correlation was with ALMP, but the other variables were also strongly correlated with employment service power. This relation was to be expected, given the nature of institutional contexts. In the four most recent periods, the employment service was strongly correlated with the firm index ($r = 0.66$, 0.67, 0.63 and 0.64), the corporatism index ($r = 0.63$, 0.68, 0.69 and 0.77) and the self-administration index ($r = 0.83$, 0.82, 0.79 and 0.78), but not with the educational diversity index ($r = 0.14$, 0.14, 0.12 and 0.11). Despite the nature of contextual effects, these correlations make multicollinearity a problem and suggest that a regime-type variable might be appropriate.

In regression analyses, the employment service variables alone generally explained over 20 per cent of the variance in ALMP/GNP (adjusted R^2: 0.28, 0.20, 0.38, 0.33 and 0.22 going from the most recent to the least recent period). Because the employment service was so strongly correlated with ALMP/GNP, it should stand up well in multivariate analyses. When the employment service variable was put into the equation with left party power, unemployment rates and other variables, the results bore out this expectation (see Table 23.5).

Table 23.5 Regression Equations on Active Labour Market Policy over GNP (ALMP) in Five Periods (Standardized Betas with Levels of Significance Noted (in Parentheses))

	$t = 1985–89$	$t = 1980–84$	$t = 1975–79$	$t = 1970–74$	$t = 1965–70$
Employment service power t-5	0.50* (0.049)	0.55* (0.048)	0.82** (0.013)	0.6** (0.009)	0.52* (0.044)
Left party power t-5	0.25 (0.29)	–0.08 (0.79)	–0.09 (0.75)	— —	— —
Unemployment rate t-5	0.19 (0.39)	0.09 (0.74)	0.27 (0.41)	— —	— —
R^2 /	0.36	0.26	0.48	0.37	0.27
Adjusted R^2	023	0.11	0.33	0.33	0.22
n	18	18	18	17	16

Notes
* $p < 0.05$;   ** $p < 0.01$.

In the first three equations, the employment service variable was the strongest predictor of ALMP and is significant at the $p = 0.05$ level in all three periods. The standardized β was 0.50 in 1985–89, 0.55 in 1980–84 and 0.82 in 1975–79. Adjusted for small sample size, the variance explained was 23 per cent in 1985–89, 11 per cent in 1980–84 and 33 per cent in 1975–79. In bivariate regression equations, the employment service alone explained more variance (as reported above 28, 20 and 38 per cent) than the multivariate equations because the adjustment subtracts increments of variance with the addition of each variable.

In equations 4 and 5, the sample size dropped and the equations could not be computed. Table 23.5 shows the bivariate relationships with the employment service and ALMP/GNP. In each case the coefficients were significant, and 33 per cent of the variance in 1970–74 and 22 per cent of the variance in 1965–70 were explained.

In each of these five equations, Sweden was the country least well represented by the equation. This was because Swedish ALMP/GNP was underpredicted by the employment service, left party power and the unemployment rate. In many ways, Sweden was the leader and innovator in this area. Its level of expenditures was higher because it was a first mover, and to a large degree its social policy has been strongly 'imprinted' by ALMP.

These equations show the relative strength of the employment service as an institutional variable compared to the macroeconomic variables in a cross-sectional analysis at three different points in time. A comparison of bivariate results shows that the employment service was stronger than left party power and the unemployment rate in all five instances.[8] These results point to the need for a pooled cross-sectional and time-series analysis, where the institutional variables are made more dynamic than panel data. When this is done, institutional variables will have much more variation, but not enough to explain ALMP over time. Left party power and unemployment will be very strong in explaining variation over time, and institutions will not vary enough to be a factor. Across nations, however, the institutional variables will show their strength.

7   CONCLUSION

In this chapter I have taken the initial steps in measuring the impact of labour market institutions on active labour market policy. Finding the impact of institutions that constrain and cushion political and economic forces is a difficult task. Many of the past measures of institutions tended to be relative constants. Nonetheless, this chapter pushes labour market institutions towards operationalization in a dynamic panel format. I have also tried to measure the broader 'institutional context' within which labour market institutions operate. The tests show some strong and significant results in pursuit of the governance transformation concept.

---

8 The only institutional variable that clearly did not work was the educational diversity index.

Much remains to be done, however. Institutional variables can be further refined with a more complete analysis of changes from 1950 to the present. When these data are cleaned, a pooled analysis can be done. Second, labour market regimes should be constructed from the characteristic features of the labour markets in these 18 countries. Such work may include some of the variables in the literature on welfare-state regimes as well as unique aspects of labour market institutions. Third, the 'institutional contexts' of labour market policy can be more adequately assessed through LISREL or canonical correlation, both of which are based on factor analysis. This would overcome the multicollinearity problems caused by high correlations between institutional variables and would create an institutional index that would be maximized against ALMP. This more complex unobserved index would be a more effective assessment of 'institutional context'. Fourth, much more emphasis needs to be placed on transformations of labour market regimes. A number of transformations have clearly been present in the last forty years, with most countries going through diverse regime changes at different periods of time. Capturing these transformations of labour market regimes and developing their motivations and underlying logics will be a major challenge for institutionalists over the next decade.

APPENDIX—INSTITUTIONAL VARIABLES

Each set of independent variables were averaged for five-year periods: 1965–69, 1970–74, 1975–79 and 1980–84. The following sources were used: Bamber and Lansbury (1987); Crouch (1992); Ferner and Hyman (1992); Ferrera (1988); Flora (1988); Hartog and Theeuwes (1993); Kennedy (1980); National Center for Educational Statistics (1994); Olson (1988); OECD (1991, 1993, 1994; MISEP Reports (1987–94); Ricca (1988); Rogers and Streeck (1994); Rothstein (1992); Sisson (1987); UN (1991, 1993); Walwei (1991) and a variety of national and international statistical yearbooks. I also consulted T. Hubert (personal communication on employment services, n.d.).

1. Strength of the Employment Service (Column 1, Table 23.2):

1. Tripartite administration: 3 for tripartite policy administration (state, labour and employer representation; 2 for bipartite policy administration (state and employer representation); 1 for executive policy administration; and 0 for lack of any employment service;
2. Levels of administration: 3 for all three levels (federal, state or province, and local) of employment services; 2 for two of three levels; 1 for one of

three levels; and 0 for zero levels of self-administration in the employment service;

3. Employment service monopoly: 2 if both private and temporary agencies were banned; 1 if temporary agencies were approved but not private ones; and 0 if private and temporary agencies were permitted with minimal regulation;
4. Employer reporting requirements: 2 for required reporting of both internal and external vacancies; 1 for required reporting of external vacancies; and 0 for absence of vacancy reporting requirements;
5. Employers' reporting of layoffs to the employment service: 2 if report is required for more than 50 layoffs; 1 if report is required for more than 100; and 0 if no layoff report is required.

The first two and last two components listed above are added together and divided by their maximum scores. The sum is then multiplied by the percentage of the labour force covered by the employment service. This percentage removed government and self-employed persons from the numerator.

2. *Institutions within the Firm*

1. Works councils (Column 2, Table 23.2): Works council laws as a dummy variable were multiplied by the percentage of the labour force covered by each law (EC, 1990; OECD, 1970–93). The result was then summed for each sector that may have been covered. In countries where employer representatives were allowed on the works councils, a parity factor of labour representatives divided by total representatives was also applied. This reduced a country's score. An issue factor was also computed, with Germany as the standard. If works councils had no veto or codetermination powers, the issue factor would again reduce the score. These two adjustments account for the countries with works councils that scored low on this variable.
2. Codetermination or workers on company boards (Column 3, Table 23.2): Because there were frequently different laws, a separate variable was computed for each sector (be it based on firm size or industry). A dummy variable for the passage of a law was multiplied against the percentage of the labour force covered for each segment (EC, 1990; OECD, 1970–93). A parity factor measured whether there was equal representation with management on the corporate board. Where labour's representation was less than management's, the parity factor reduced the score proportionately.

3. Welfare-state Institutions

1. Self-administration (Column 4, Table 23.2): This measure averaged a self-administration score for the pension, health, disability and unemployment insurance sectors. The measure was scored as follows: 3 for tripartite self-administration; 2 for bipartite self-administration of management and labour; 1.5 for bipartite self-administration of management and the state; 1 for executive bureaucracy (the state manages the whole programme); and 0 for lack of any policy organization at all.

4. Education Systems

1. Educational diversity (Column 5, Table 23.2): Educational enrolment ratios came mainly from national statistical yearbooks and were checked by OECD (1986 and 1990) and UN (1991, 1993) sources. The three ratios were multiplied together and then multiplied by 30 to give the indexes a range of 0 to a little over 1.0.

5. Corporatism (Column 6, Table 23.2)

1. Peak wage bargaining measured whether unions, employers and the state are involved in wage bargaining at the national and industry-wide levels. Each of these six variables were scored as follows: 2 means that unions (employers or the state) were involved in the primary site of bargaining; 1 means that unions (employers or the state) were involved in a secondary site of bargaining; 0 means that unions (employers or the state) were not involved. The union, employer and state scores were then divided by their maximum scores and then added.
2. Peak policy bargaining: This component shows the extent to which employers, unions and the state were involved in policy bargaining. Although this is difficult to separate from wage bargaining when incomes policy was involved with wage bargaining, it was possible to separate other types of social policy from wage bargaining. This measure was computed only at the national level.

These two types of corporatist bargaining were then averaged into a corporatism variable.

REFERENCES

Bamber, G. and R. Lansbury (eds) (1987), *International and Comparative Industrial Relations*, London: Allen Unwin.

Blankenburg, E., G. Schmid and H. Treiber (1976), 'Legitimitäts- und Implementierungsprobleme "aktive Arbeitsmarktpolitik"', in R. Ebbinghausen (ed.), *Bürgerlicher Staat und politische Legitimation*, Frankfurt on the Main: Suhrkamp Verlag, pp. 247–80.

Boreham, P. and H. Compston (1992), 'Labour Movement Organization and Political Intervention', *European Journal of Political Research*, 22, 143–70.

Boyer, R. (1993), 'Labor Institutions and Economic Growth: A Survey and "Regulationist" Approach', *Labour*, 7 (1), 25–72.

Burstein, P. (1991), 'Policy Domains: Organization, Culture, and Policy Outcomes', *Annual Review of Sociology*, 17, 327–50.

Calmfors, L. (1994), 'Active Labor Market Policy and Unemployment: A Framework for the Analysis of Crucial Design Features', *OECD Economic Studies*, 22, 7–47.

Campbell, J. L., J. R. Hollingsworth and L. Lindberg (eds) (1991), *Governance of the American Economy*, Cambridge, MA: Cambridge University Press, pp. 14–28.

Commons, J. R. (1934), *Institutional Economics*, New York: Macmillan.

Crouch, C. (1992), *Industrial Relations and European State Traditions*, Oxford: Clarendon.

DiMaggio, P. (1988), 'Interest and Agency in Institutional Theory', in *Institutional Patterns and Organizations*, Cambridge, MA: Ballinger, pp. 3–22.

Dugger, W. M. (1992), *Underground Economics*, Armonk, NY: Sharpe.

EC (1990), *Enterprises in the European Community*, Brussels: Commission of the European Communities.

Eggertsson, T. (1990), *Economic Behavior and Institutions*, Cambridge: Cambridge University Press.

Ekeh, P. (1974), *Social Exchange Theory*, Cambridge, MA: Harvard University Press.

Esping-Andersen, G. (1987), 'Institutional Accommodation to Full Employment', in H. Keman, K. Paloheimo and P. Whiteley, *Coping with the Economic Crisis*, Beverly Hills: Sage, pp. 83–100.

Esping-Andersen, G. (1990), *The Three Worlds of Welfare Capitalism*, Princeton: Princeton University Press, p. 70.

Ferner, A. and R. Hyman (1992), *Industrial Relations in the New Europe*, Oxford: Blackwell.

Ferrera, M. (1988), 'Italy', in P. Flora (ed.), *Growth to Limits*, Berlin: de Gruyter, pp. 475–528.

Flanagan, R., J. Hartog and J. Theeuwes (1993), 'Institutions and the Labour Market', in J. Hartog and J. Theeuwes (eds), *Labour Market Contracts and Institutions*, Amsterdam: Elsevier, pp. 415–46.

Fligstein, N. (1990), *The Transformation of Corporate Control*, Cambridge, MA: Harvard University Press.

Flora, P. (ed.) (1988), *Growth to Limits*, Berlin: de Gruyter.

Furåker, B. and L. Johansson (1990), 'Unemployment and Labour Market Policies in the Scandinavian Countries', *Acta Sociologica*, 33 (21), 141–64.

Furubotn, E. and R. Richter (1993), 'The New Institutional Economics: Recent Progress; Expanding Frontiers', *Journal of Institutional and Theoretical Economics*, 149 (1), 1–10.

Gouldner, A. (1954), *Patterns of Industrial Bureaucracy*, New York: Free Press.

Hartog, J. and J. Theeuwes (eds) (1993), *Labour Market Contracts and Institutions*, Amsterdam: North-Holland.

Hodgson, G. (1989), *Economics and Institutions*, Cambridge: Polity.

Hodgson, G. (1993), *Economics and Evolution: Bringing Life Back into Economics*, Cambridge: Polity.

Hubert, T. (1993), 'Private Employment Services', Brussels. (Unpublished manuscript)

Janoski, T. (1990), *The Political Economy of Unemployment*, Berkeley: University of California Press.

Janoski, T. (1994), 'Direct State Intervention in the Labor Market', in T. Janoski and A. Hicks, *The Comparative Political Economy of the Welfare State*, New York: Cambridge University Press, pp. 54–92.

Janoski, T. (in press), 'Citizenship and Civil Society', Cambridge University Press. (Unpublished manuscript)

Katzenstein, P. (1984), *Corporatism and Change*, Ithaca, NY: Cornell University Press.

Katzenstein, P. (1985), *Small States in World Markets*, Ithaca, NY: Cornell University Press.

Kennedy, T. (1980), *European Labor Relations*, Lexington, MA: Lexington Books.

Knight, J. (1992), *Institutions and Social Conflict*, Cambridge: Cambridge University Press.

Knoke, D. (1992), 'Networks as Political Glue: Explaining Public Policy-making', in W. J. Wilson (ed.), *Sociology and the Public Agenda*, Newbury Park: Sage.

Knoke, D., F. Pappi, J. Broadbent and Y. Tsujinaka (1996), *Comparing Policy Networks: Labour Politics in the U.S., Germany and Japan*, Cambridge: Cambridge University Press.

Korpi, W. (1983), *The Democratic Class Struggle*, London: Routledge & Kegan Paul.

Korpi, W. (1991), 'Political and Economic Explanations for Unemployment: A Crossnational and Long-term Analysis', *British Journal of Political Science*, 21 (3), 315–48.

Lewin, L. (1988), *Ideology and Strategy*, Cambridge: Cambridge University Press, pp. 159–275.

March, J. and J. Olsen (1984), 'The New Institutionalism: Organizational Factors in Political Life', *American Political Science Review*, 78 (3), 734–49.

March, J. and J. Olsen (1989), *Rediscovering Institutions*, New York: Free Press.

Marin, B. (1990a), *Governance and Generalized Exchange*, Boulder, CO: Westview.

Marin, B. (1990b), *Generalized Political Exchange*, Boulder, CO: Westview.

Matzner, E. (1989), 'Policies, Institutions, and Employment', in E. Matzner and W. Streeck (eds), *Beyond Keynesianism*, Aldershot: Gower, pp. 231–60.

Meidner, R. (1948), 'Lönepolitikens dilemma vid full sysselsättning', *Tiden*, 9, 464–70.

MISEP (Mutual Information System on Employment Policy) (1987–94), *Employment Policies—Basis Information Report* for each individual EC country), Maastricht/Berlin: Commission of the European Communities.

Muszynski, L. (1985), 'The Politics of Labour Market Policy', in G. B. Doern (ed.), *The Politics of Economic Policy*, Toronto: University of Toronto Press, pp. 251–305.

National Center for Educational Statistics (1994), *Digest of Educational Statistics 1994*, Washington, DC: US Department of Education.

North, D. (1990), *Institutions, Institutional Change and Economic Performance*, Cambridge: Cambridge University Press.

North, D. (1991), 'Institutions', *Journal of Economic Perspectives*, 5 (1), 97–112.

North, D. (1993), 'Institutions and Credible Commitment', *Journal of Institutional and Theoretical Economics*, 149 (1), 11–23.

OECD (1970–93), *National Accounts Statistics*, Paris: OECD.

OECD (1986), *Educational Statistics in OECD Countries*, Paris: OECD.

OECD (1990), *Education in OECD Countries*, Paris: OECD.

OECD (1991), 'Unemployment Benefit Rules and Labour Market Policy', *Employment Outlook*, Paris: OECD, 199–231.

OECD (1993), 'Active Labour Market Policies', *Employment Outlook*, Paris: OECD, 39–80.

OECD (1994), 'The Public Employment Service in Japan, Norway, Spain and the U.K.', *Employment Outlook*, Paris: OECD, 227–54.

Olson, S. (1988), 'Sweden', in P. Flora (ed.), *Growth to Limits*, Berlin: de Gruyter, pp. 1–116.

Powell, W. and P. DiMaggio (eds) (1991), *The New Institutionalism in Organizational Analysis*, Chicago: University of Chicago Press.

Rehn, G. (1948), 'Ekonomisk politik vid full sysselsättning', *Tiden*, 3, 135–42.

Ricca, S. (1988), 'The Changing Role of Public Employment Services', *International Labour Review*, 127 (1), 19–34.

Rogers, J. and W. Streeck (1994), 'Workplace Representation Overseas: The Works Councils Story', in R. Freeman (ed.), *Working Under Different Rules*, New York: Russell Sage, pp. 97–156.

Rothstein, B. (1992), 'Labor-market Institutions and Working-class Strength', in S. Steinmo, K. Thelen and F. Longstreth (eds), *Structuring Politics*, Cambridge: Cambridge University Press, pp. 33–56.

Schmid, G. (1989), 'Die neue institutionelle Ökonomie: Königsweg oder Holzweg zu einer Institutionentheorie des Arbeitsmarktes?', *Leviathan*, 17 (3), 386–408.

Schmid, G. (1990), 'Institutions Regulating the Labor Market: Support or Impediments for Structural Change?', in E. Appelbaum and R. Schettkat (eds), *Labor Market Adjustments to Structural Change and Technological Progress*, New York: Praeger.

Schmid, G. (1993), 'Equality and Efficiency in the Labor Market: Towards a Socioeconomic Theory of Cooperation in the Globalizing Economy', *Journal of Socio-Economics*, 22 (1), 31–67.

Schmid, G. and B. Reissert (1988), 'Do Institutions Make a Difference?', *Journal of Public Policy*, 8 (2), 125–49.

Schmid, G., B. Reissert and G. Bruche (1992), *Unemployment Insurance and Active Labor Market Policy*, Detroit: Wayne State University Press.

Schmid, G. and K. Schömann (1994), 'Institutional Choice and Flexible Coordination', in G. Schmid (ed.), *Labor Market Institutions in Europe*, Armonk, NY: Sharpe, pp. 9–58.

Selznick, P. (1949), *The TVA and the Grassroots*, Berkeley: University of California Press.

Shalev, M. (1983), 'The Social Democratic Model and Beyond', *Comparative Social Research*, 6, 315–52.

Sisson, K. (1987), *The Management of Collective Bargaining*, Oxford: Blackwell.

Skocpol, T. (1992), *Protecting Soldiers and Mothers*, Cambridge, MA: Harvard University Press.

Skocpol, T. and A. Orloff (1986), 'Explaining the Origins of Welfare States', in S. Lindenberg, J. Coleman and S. Nowak (eds), *Approaches to Social Theory*, New York: Russell Sage Foundation, pp. 229–54.

Steinmo, S., K. Thelen and F. Longstreth (eds) (1992), *Structuring Politics*, Cambridge: Cambridge University Press.

Thelen, K. and S. Steinmo (1992), 'Historical Institutionalism in Comparative Politics', in S. Steinmo, K. Thelen and F. Longstreth (eds), *Structuring Politics*, Cambridge: Cambridge University Press, pp. 1–32.

Therborn, G. (1986), *Why Some Peoples are More Unemployed Than Others*, London: Verso, p. 23.

Tronti, L. (1990), 'Employment Protection and Labor Market Segmentation: Economic Implications of the Italian "Cassa Integrazione Guadagni"', WZB conference on Workers Protection and Labour Market Dynamics, 16–18 May.

United Nations (UN) (1991), *World Education Report*, Geneva: UN.

United Nations (UN) (1993), *World Education Report*, Geneva: UN.

Veblen, T. (1904), *The Theory of Business Enterprise*, New York: Scribner.

Walwei, U. (1991), 'Job Placement in Europe: An International Comparison', *Intereconomics*, 26, 248–54.

Webber, D. (1982), 'Combatting and Acquiescing in Unemployment', *West European Politics*, 5, 23–43.

Webber, D. and G. Nass (1984), 'Employment Policy in West Germany', in J. Richardson and R. Henning (eds), *Unemployment*, Beverly Hills: Sage, pp. 167–94.

Williamson, O. (1975), *Markets and Hierarchies*, New York: Free Press.

Williamson, O. (1985), *The Economic Institutions of Capitalism*, New York: Free Press.

24. The Impact of Labour Market Policy on Wages, Employment and Labour Market Mismatch

J41   J21

Lutz Bellmann and Richard Jackman

This chapter is primarily concerned with the empirical estimation of the effects of active labour market policies on various dimensions of the macroeconomic performance of the labour market. A number of theoretical and methodological issues have already been discussed by the authors in chap. 5 of this handbook.

Empirical work on the macroeconomic, as opposed to the microeconomic, effects of active labour market programmes (ALMPs) is rare. An immediate obstacle is the absence of an obvious theoretical framework within which to couch the analysis. One approach, formally developed by Baily and Tobin (1977), is that training programmes may change the skill composition of the labour force and thereby shift the Phillips curve and reduce the nonaccelerating inflation rate of unemployment. But this type of analysis, which relies on the standard expectations-augmented Phillips curve, can be criticized as being purely *ad hoc*, since the fundamental determinants of the equilibrium rate of unemployment are left unspecified.

Targeted employment subsidies were analysed within the framework of equilibrium models with market clearing by Jackman and Layard (1980), Johnson (1980) and Johnson and Layard (1986). A more general model, in which labour market equilibrium does not assume market clearing, is presented in Layard and Nickell (1986) and Layard, Nickell and Jackman (1991). This model can be used (e.g. Calmfors, 1994) to provide a basic framework for the analysis of the effects of ALMPs on a number of critical economic variables or processes that influence employment and unemployment rates: (a) the effects on the matching process, (b) the effects on the labour force, (c) productivity effects, (d) competition effects for insiders, (e) deadweight loss and substitution effects and (f) crowding-out effects.

We have discussed much of the empirical work on (e) and (f), and some of that on (d), in chap. 5 of this volume. In this chapter we are mainly concerned with (a), (b) and (c). The discussion will show that it is neither easy to infer the sign of these effects on, say, the level of real wages and regular employment nor, therefore, to infer the overall effect of ALMPs on total employment or unemployment from theory. Unfortunately, the empirical evidence is mixed, too.

We begin with an outline of the Layard–Nickell model as the basic analytical framework and indicate how the effects of ALMPs can be examined within this framework. In section 2 we then offer empirical estimates of our own, both of the aggregative effects of ALMPs on unemployment rates and of their effects on the structural factors listed above. These estimates are based largely on international cross-section comparisons. The implementation of ALMPs in OECD countries has often had something of the characteristics of a natural experiment. The different countries attacked the same problems quite differently and sometimes changed the design of these policies radically over time. Hence, by comparing estimates internationally as well as before and after policy changes, one can learn much about the effects of ALMPs.

1   THEORETICAL CONSIDERATIONS

1.1   The Layard–Nickell Model

The Layard and Nickell (1986) model has become a standard framework for labour market analysis. Drawing on Calmfors (1994), we show in this section how it can be developed to permit an analysis of the effects of ALMPs. The model assumes price-setting firms and noncompetitive wage determination. It can be formulated diagrammatically (see Figure 24.1) in terms of an employment schedule and a wage-setting schedule. The vertical axis in Figure 24.1 measures the real wage (the nominal contract wage deflated by the GDP deflator), with employment on the horizontal axis. The employment schedule *DD* is a downward-sloping curve, which shows the number of workers firms would want to employ in relation to the real wage. It depends on technology, the stock of capital, employers' (payroll) taxes and product market competitiveness. (Under perfect competition the *DD* curve is the demand for labour; more generally, firms set employment and the product price simultaneously.)

For the sake of simplicity, the labour force *L* is taken as given (independent of the real wage), and the curve *WW* shows the wage set in the wage bargain as a function of the employment rate (or, more precisely, the expected real wage corresponding to the money wage set in the wage bargain). In a union-bargaining model the position of this curve is determined by the 'outside options' of workers and the firm and by relative bargaining power. The wage struck in the bargain thus depends on the workers' legal rights, benefits or other income available during a strike, financial wealth, unemployment and product market competitiveness and the capital intensity of production (see e.g. Layard et al., 1991). Because both sides in the bargain take into account

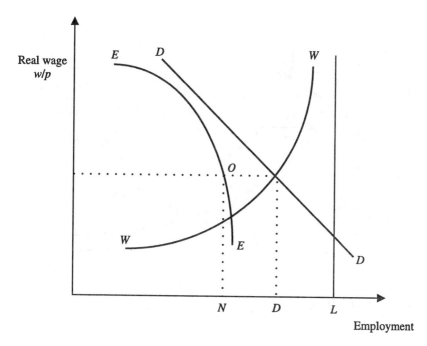

Figure 24.1   The Generalized Layard–Nickell Model

the expected consequences of wage outcomes for employment, the wage curve is in principle not independent of the employment schedule. For example, a 'neutral' increase in productivity can be expected to shift both the employment schedule and the wage-setting schedule upwards.

In Figure 24.1, the intersection of the employment and wage-setting schedules determines the wage and the planned, or expected, level of employment. In practice, however, not all jobs are filled all the time. The Beveridge curve (shown in Figure 24.2) describes the relation between vacancies and unemployment, along which hirings exactly match quits, so that employment stays constant. More vacancies will, in general, be consistent with lower unemployment, because the extra hirings due to more job vacancies need to be offset by fewer job matches due to a smaller number of job applicants if employment is to stay constant.

Superimposing the Beveridge curve on to Figure 24.1 gives the line *EE*, which shows the number actually employed, the difference between *DD* and *EE* being the number of vacancies at any point in time. The distance between *DD* and *EE* is determined by the efficiency of the job-matching process and thus depends on institutional arrangements affecting job search, the unem-

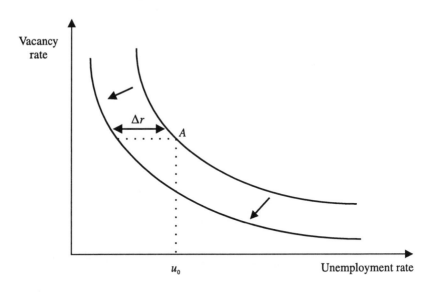

Figure 24.2   The Beveridge Curve

ployment benefit system and the provision of active labour market policies. Equilibrium in this system is represented by point O. At this point, N people are employed, the unemployment rate (Nonaccelerating Inflation Rate of Unemployment (NAIRU)) is $u = (L-N)/L$, and there are D jobs with a vacancy rate $v = (D-N)/N$. An increase in the NAIRU can thus be explained in terms of an upward shift in WW, a downward shift in DD or a shift leftwards of EE away from DD (though one should again recall that shifts in DD or EE will, in general, affect WW).

To analyse active labour market policy, Calmfors (1994) slightly modified this model. The reason is the need to distinguish between participation in labour market programmes and regular employment. For this purpose, the employment and wage-setting schedules are instead drawn with regular employment (excluding participation in programmes) on the horizontal axis in Figure 24.3. Participation is measured by the horizontal distance r_0 between the labour force L and the vertical line RR, which shows the remaining members of the labour force who are not participating in ALMPs. Because with these changes the intersection between the employment and wage-setting schedules at O determines regular employment, (open) unemployment is measured as the distance between the equilibrium point O and the RR curve.

The figure can be used to illustrate the various effects of ALMPs. Increased placement in training or job creation schemes can be depicted in Figure 24.3 as

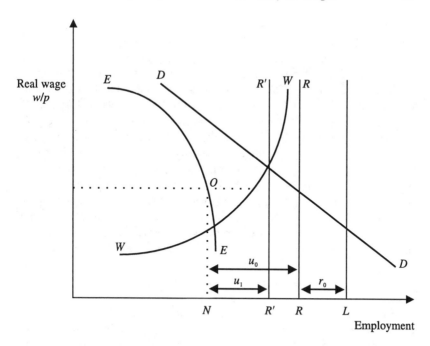

Figure 24.3   The Impact of ALMPs

a leftward shift of the *RR* line. If nothing else were to happen, the effect would simply be a reduction of open unemployment by a corresponding amount, so that the rate of unemployment decreases from u_0 to u_1. This will be referred to as the gross, or bookkeeping, effect of such an expansion of programmes. But if, as might normally be assumed, wage-setting were a function of the unemployment rate rather than of the proportion of the labour force in regular employment, the inward shift of *RR* would be associated with an equal inward shift of the wage-setting function *WW*. The expansion of programmes thus reduces regular employment and raises wages. To obtain the overall effect, one must therefore analyse how the determinants of wage-setting and of regular labour demand and labour force participation are affected.

1.2   Macroeconomic Analysis of ALMPs

1.2.1   Effects on the Matching Process

ALMPs are intended to improve the matching job openings offered by firm and job seekers in the labour market. Mismatch between different submarkets for labour may be eliminated to the extent that the qualifications of job seekers can be better adapted to the demand. The effectiveness of search can be improved by the placement service, and the results of participants on training courses can provide a signal to potential employers, reducing uncertainty about the employ- ability of job applicants. The Beveridge curve is modified then, first, to allow for more effective search of the open unemployed and, second, to include participants on schemes as well as the openly unemployed as job seekers, for regular job openings can be filled from the stock of openly unemployed or from the stock of programme participants (Calmfors, 1994, p. 11). The impact of improved efficiency of job search for the open unemployed is a rightward shift of the *EE* curve towards the *DD* curve in Figure 24.3. The outcome is a reduction both in unemployment and in vacancies. In a more complete model there could also be effects on the *DD* and *WW* curves, as discussed in chap. 5 of this volume. Assistance with job search might raise wage pressure by reducing the fear of unemployment. Or, because vacancies become filled more quickly, they become less costly to firms, and more vacancies are opened. This is equivalent to an increase of labour demand, shifting the employment schedule to the right.

An increase in participation in schemes might be expected to shift the *EE* curve leftwards to the extent that scheme participants search less actively than the openly unemployed. On the other hand, training and work experience can improve the employment prospects of participants, thus improving the match- ing process. However participants on training and job creation programmes may reduce their search efforts before the start of a potentially attractive course or in the knowledge that the employment services will find work for them.

1.2.2 *Effects on the Supply and Productivity of the Labour Force*

As seen by Budd, Levine and Smith (1988), Layard and Nickell (1986) and Layard et al. (1991), long-term unemployment is perceived as the main chan- nel of the persistence of unemployment. They argue that a prolonged adverse shock eventually causes an increased inflow into long-term unemployment, but that long durations of unemployment result in actual and perceived destruction of human capital. According to those authors, firms either perceive the long-term unemployed as less productive and discriminate against them or, given a degree of state dependence, the long-term unemployed in actual fact become less productive. Furthermore, discrimination or demoralization (or both) lead to a fall in the intensity with which the unemployed look for work. Whether the long-term unemployed are really less productive or are only per- ceived as such, whether their fall in search intensity is caused by discrimina- tion or demoralization, increased long-term unemployment means a reduction in the effective supply of labour at a given real wage.

Moreover, discouraged workers who do not find jobs will tend to leave the labour force. The risk of such negative supply effects appears greatest for elderly workers, especially where firms resort to early retirement as a method of reducing their labour forces, as has been the case, for example, in Belgium, France, Germany, the Netherlands and the Nordic countries. In addition, prospective entrants, in particular married women, may not enter the labour force in situations of high unemployment (Calmfors, 1994, p. 15).

Therefore, to the extent that ALMPs can combat long-term unemployment they can have a positive labour supply effect. For example, if the long-term unemployed can be enabled through job counselling to search more effectively, the *EE* curve will shift inwards and there will be more employment, for the labour market will operate with a smaller stock of vacancies. Perhaps more significantly, by creating more competition for vacancies, ALMPs can put downward pressure on wages, shifting the *WW* curve downwards. (For further discussion of the effects of ALMPs on wages, see chap. 5.)

The effects of training or temporary work for long-term unemployed people are more complex because one must also take account of the fact that people may well search less while on the schemes than when in open unemployment. The 'bookkeeping' reduction in open unemployment may, hence, lead to an upward shift in the *WW* curve at each level of employment. A new equilibrium would then be established with lower employment and higher wages. The labour market situation deteriorates in the sense that a lower proportion of the labour force is now regularly employed, and, hence, a larger proportion is either openly unemployed or participating in programmes. However, there is some evidence that wage pressure is much more sensitive to short-term than to long-term unemployment, so that placing the long-term unemployed on schemes may not have a significant adverse effect on wages.

Programmes targeting long-term unemployed and other marginal groups (young people, women, people not previously seeking work and immigrants) can also increase their competitiveness against the core groups of employees or the insiders. This may occur through several channels: by increasing their productivity, by substituting participation in labour market programmes for regular work experience when employers screen job applicants or by encouraging more active search behaviour. The analysis in these cases is just the same as for the long-term unemployed (see chap. 5 in this volume).

1.2.3 Incentive Effects

ALMPs generally offer higher compensation than unemployment benefits so as to give an incentive for the unemployed to attend training courses and to apply for a place on public programmes. In some countries, though, unemployed people who refuse offers of training courses or temporary work can be refused benefits, an arrangement that provides a financial incentive to take a place even in the absence of higher compensation. High compensation carries the same risks as generous unemployment benefits (Atkinson and Micklewright, 1991) in that the incentive to search for a regular job elsewhere in the economy is reduced.

There will always be a certain fraction of those receiving unemployment benefits who are not really searching for work. The higher the level of unemployment, the more difficult it is for the placement department of the public employment service to test the willingness to work of benefits claimants. However, the refusal of unemployed to take up a vacant job or a place on a training programme provides some proof of unwillingness to work (see Grubb, 1993; OECD, 1991). This so-called work-test effect of ALMPs was estimated by the OECD (1991), which found that more intensive counselling and testing of the unemployed may lead 5 to 10 per cent of the target group to leave the register.

2   EMPIRICAL RESULTS

2.1   ALMPs and Unemployment Rates

The fundamental question is whether ALMPs can affect aggregate economic variables such as the unemployment rate. It might thus be appropriate to start by looking at the aggregate data. Is there any evidence that more provision of active labour market programmes is associated with lower unemployment rates—either over time or across countries?

Evidence from cross-country comparisons on the impact of ALMPs has been contentious. The main features of the data have been described by Grubb (1994). Grubb has shown that in simple cross-country comparisons, spending on active policies tends to be higher in countries with higher unemployment rates, but much less than proportionately. Overall spending on ALMPs is thus positively correlated with unemployment, but there is a negative correlation between spending on ALMPs per unemployed person and unemployment.

The main problem in interpreting these results is that although the scale of provision of ALMPs can affect the unemployment rate, it is equally the case that the level of unemployment can affect spending on ALMPs. Observed correlations could be explained in terms of a 'policy-reaction function'—governments cutting spending per unemployed person when unemployment goes up—rather than in terms of lower ALMP spending leading to higher unemployment. (For further discussion of the political determinants of active labour market policy spending, see chap. 23 by Janoski in this handbook.)

One way of tackling this simultaneity problem has been based on the assumption that government policy on ALMP spending can be defined in terms of a country-specific level of spending per unemployed person, which is fixed, and a cyclical component. Over the cycle, ALMP expenditure may adjust a bit, but it does not adjust fully with unemployment, for it is difficult and costly to change the size of the programmes in the short run. With a given policy stance, this cyclical pattern will generate a positive correlation between unemployment and total ALMP spending but a negative correlation between unemployment and ALMP spending per unemployed person. The same pattern would be observed in cross-country comparisons where the different countries are at different stages in their business cycles.

If this were a correct representation of the policy-reaction function, the identification problem could be overcome by looking at average unemployment rates and average ALMP spending per unemployed person over the cycle. Average ALMP spending over the cycle would reflect the 'exogenous' stance of policy, and the relation between it and average unemployment would then measure the impact of ALMP spending. Layard et al. (1991) presented such an analysis, which showed a negative correlation between ALMP spending per unemployed person and unemployment during the 1980s.

It is, however, far from clear that this is the correct representation of the policy-reaction function. One could have argued, for example, as did the OECD (1993), that the policy-reaction function might take the form of the government committing, in the medium term, a given proportion of GDP to ALMPs rather than a given level of spending per unemployed person. This does not preclude cyclical variation, but, as before, such variation may be removed by looking at averages over a period of years. Thus, in carrying out a replication of the Layard et al. (1991) study, the OECD (1993) used total ALMP spending (as a proportion of GDP) rather than spending per unemployed person and found no significant effect of ALMPs on average unemployment over the cycle.

The difference between these approaches lies in the implicit assumption about the medium-term policy reaction to unemployment. The Layard et al. (1991) approach is that medium-term ALMP spending varies proportionately to the unemployment rate, whereas the OECD approach is that it does not vary at all.

To cast light on this issue, it may be useful to formulate the policy-reaction function explicitly. Here, we follow Jackman (1994). One may assume that in each country the government has a policy on active labour market expenditures. It may entail decisions on the type and standard of service to be provided to each 'client' and, thus, on outlay per potential client of some amount x^*. This may relate to the expected number of clients, which may be taken as a function of the expected unemployment rate u^e. It is not clear a priori whether one would expect x^* to be increasing or decreasing in u^e. On the one hand, the higher u^e is, the more costly it is to provide a high standard of service. On the other hand, the higher u^e is, the more serious the unemployment problem, the greater the incidence of long-term unemployment and so forth, and the greater the pressure to adopt active policies.

In the short term actual expenditure per potential client, x, falls if unemployment rises above its expected level, for provision cannot be adjusted perfectly flexibly in the short run and for budgetary reasons. Hence, actual expenditure per unemployed person is

$$x = x^* - b_1 (u - u^e) \dots \tag{24.1}$$

with

$$x^* = x^*_0 - b_2 u^e$$

so that

$$x = x^*_0 - b_1 (u - u^e) - b_2 u^e \dots , \tag{24.2}$$

where u is the unemployment rate, x^*_0 is a measure of the policy stance, $b_1 > 0$ and $b_2 = ?$

The relation we are interested in is the impact of policy on unemployment, that is, a relation of the form

$$u = u_0 - a_1 x + a_2 z$$

$$= u_0 - a_1 [x^*_0 - b_1 (u - u^e) - b_2 u^e] + a_2 z \dots \tag{24.3}$$

The objective is to identify a_1. Were it the case that $b_1 = b_2 = 0$, so that the variation in x arises from variation in x^*_0, then an estimate of equation (24.3) should identify the value of a_1. But if $b_1 > 0$ (with $b_2 = 0$), then the main variation in x may well arise from variation in u, as would typically be the case in a time-series regression, then, as the equation shows, one is essentially correlating unemployment with itself and will get a spurious result that says nothing about the efficacy of policy. A cross-section based on a period of years should, however, avoid this problem because $(u - u^e)$ should in principle be close to zero. And, as noted above, this is the approach adopted by both Layard et al. (1991) and the OECD (1993).

However, if b_2 is not zero, and the main variation arises from cross-country variations in u^e, we will again be correlating unemployment with itself, for over a period of years u will be close to u^e. But in this case the impact of u depends on the sign and magnitude of b_2, rather than of b_1, where there are, as already noted, several factors at work and the overall effect is ambiguous and might a priori be expected to be small. But a negative relation between u and x may now indicate not the efficacy of policy but a positive value of b_2 in the policy-reaction function (that is, a general tendency of governments to spend less on ALMPs per unemployed person when unemployment is persistently high).

It is, however, possible to estimate b_2 from equation (24.2) on the basis of time-series data for individual countries. A preliminary investigation (Jackman, 1995) suggested that, perhaps contrary to prior expectations, in most countries b_2 is positive and comparable in magnitude and significance to b_1. While this work is only at a preliminary stage, it does suggest that taking cyclical averages is not sufficient to remove the identification problem and that there is greater stability in ALMP expenditure as a proportion of GDP than in expenditure per unemployed person.

2.2 ALMPs and Key Labour Market Variables

In this chapter we extend the analysis of the macroeconomic effects of ALMPs in two ways. First, we make use of a panel (pooled time-series cross-section) data set to increase the number of observations and, hence, provide greater statistical power. Second, we examine not only the determinants of the unemployment rate but also the effects of policies on a number of the structural economic variables through which ALMPs may affect overall employment or unemployment. These include effects on labour force participation, effects on wages, changes in ratios of earnings deciles, improvements in the effectiveness of the matching process (shifts of the Beveridge curve) and the incidence of long-term unemployment (measured as a percentage of the long-term unemployed to total unemployed).

The argument that the effects of ALMPs on the job-matching process can best be assessed by reference to the Beveridge curve has been explored by Jackman, Pissarides and Savouri (1990). The argument is that fluctuations in demand and changes in wage-setting arrangements will affect an economy's positions on the curve but that ALMPs, in so far as they effect the efficiency of job-matching through the provision of advice and information and promote the search effectiveness of the unemployed, should shift the Beveridge curve.

In country studies on the Beveridge curve and ALMPs, neither Calmfors (1993) nor Jackman et al. (1990) were able to detect a relation between variations of the level of ALMP spending and shifts of the Beveridge curve. Bourdet and Persson (1995), comparing Sweden and France, found that the Beveridge curve moved inwards in France but not in Sweden.

Active labour market programmes may reduce wage pressure by increasing competition for jobs. But they may also add to wage pressure if employers are forced to pay higher wages to attract workers who could receive the same wages as programme participants. We will address the question of which effect is stronger by means of regression analysis on the cross-country panel data.

2.2.1 *Variables*

In principle, we make use of data for 17 OECD countries over a 19-year period, 1975–93, which yields 153 observations. However, data are not generally available for all countries for every year, so most of the regressions are based on a smaller data set with consequent loss of statistical power.

The dependent variables are the unemployment rate, the growth rate of employment, labour force participation rates for men and women separately, the increase of unit labour costs (in national currencies), the ratios of the ninth and fifth decile (D9/D5) and the ratios of the first and the fifth decile (D1/D5). (In these last two regressions, which are concerned with wage dispersion, the closer D9/D5 and D1/D5 are to one, the smaller the earnings inequality is.)

Our data for expenditure on ALMPs are based on work of the OECD. The categories follow the classification adopted by the OECD (1988).

1. Provision of public employment services (PES), that is, measures to facilitate contacts between employers and job seekers: the collection of information on job opportunities, the provision of an employment-exchange network to which employers are encouraged to notify vacancies, placement services, and so forth.
2. Training programmes for unemployed adults and those at risk (TRAIN): organization of training schemes by the government, payments to unemployed people attending courses, subsidies to employers who provide training to unemployed people, and so forth.
3. Subsidies for regular employment in the private sector (SUB): subsidies to employers for hiring unemployed people, assistance to unemployed people who set up their own business, and so forth.
4. Direct job creation in the public or nonprofit sector (DJC): temporary public employment programmes, government support to public works organized by local authorities or other agencies, provided that unemployed people are hired, and so forth.

For each category two variables are computed. The first refers to the ratio of government expenditure on ALMPs to gross domestic product. This computation may involve a problem because countries for which the same ratio is obtained spend strikingly different amounts per unemployed person. Following Heylen (1993), we therefore construct also a measure of real expenditure per unemployed person. For comparability across countries, expenditures are expressed in purchasing-power dollar values and are deflated by the gross domestic product-price index for the United States (1990 = 100). This variable, of course, suffers the endogeneity problem discussed above, because it is calculated by reference to the number of unemployed people.

Further, for both versions of the expenditure variable, we computed a measure of overall expenditure directed towards improving labour market efficiency. This measure, denoted by GALMP, is the sum of PES, TRAIN and SUB. Expenditures on direct job creation are not included, for they cannot be expected to serve this goal. As the OECD (1990, p. 51) admits, such policies have been introduced primarily for social objectives rather than as a means of improving labour market efficiency.

As a measure of the overall policy stance in relation to the labour market, the variable ACTIVE is defined as the proportion of expenditures on ALMPs to total expenditure of labour market policies (i.e. including unemployment benefits and early retirement schemes). ACTIVE is measured as the average of the years from 1988 to 1993 (Huckemann and van Suntum, 1994; results not shown in tables). However, there are a number of measures that are hard to classify under one or the other category of active or solely passive spending, and badly administered active programmes may degenerate into mere passive income maintenance irrespective of the size of the budget allocated (see Schömann, 1995, for a discussion). Proceeding to control variables, we took the definitions of two variables reflecting the generosity of the unemployment benefit system from Heylen (1993). RR stands for the wage replacement ratio (percentage) during the initial months of unemployment, and DUR for the maximum duration (in months) for which benefits continue at a reasonable level (both refer to 1985).

We also attempted to control for differences in institutional arrangements that can affect wage bargaining and macroeconomic performance. Calmfors and Driffill (1988) ranked countries according to the degree of centralization of wage bargaining (CI). Centralized bargaining systems (high-rank numbers) allow to internalize the favourable external effects of providing employment for a larger proportion of the labour force and moderating wages. This effect disappears in less centralized labour markets. This contrasts to wage bargaining at the firm level where wage responsiveness to unemployment is higher because the wage elasticity of labour demand is higher there. (These issues are further discussed by Appelbaum and Schettkat in chap. 26 of this handbook.) Again following Heylen (1993), we introduced a variable measuring institutional sclerosis (IS) from Choi (1983) which had been constructed to represent the ideas of Olson (1979) who analysed economic developments over time, especially the flexibility of wages and prices, as determined by the accumulation of organizations and common-interest groups (oligopolies, trade unions and so on) in modern industrial and democratic societies. Finally, we included union density (UNION) in order to control for insider power in wage bargaining.

Furthermore, we introduced a dummy variable to allow for temporary lay-off unemployment (TEMP) for four countries (Canada, Denmark, Italy and the

United States), which have temporary layoff rules. (Abraham and Houseman, 1993; Heylen 1993; Schmid and Semlinger, 1980, for discussion of short-time working allowances that might be a functional substitute for temporary layoff rules in Germany; see Mavromaras and Rudolph, 1994, for empirical evidence of recalls in Germany.) It is not only the number of people looking for jobs but also their effectiveness (i.e. the quality of their skills, their motivation) and search intensity that is relevant (see Layard et al., 1991). Since temporary layoff rules imply that workers who lose their jobs can be recalled, they tend to decrease the search effectiveness of the unemployed. That exerts a negative impact on the level of employment and labour market mismatch as well as on the wage-moderating effect of unemployment.

2.2.2 Estimation Results

The estimates for the effect that expenditures on ALMPs have on the unemployment rate are shown in Table 24.1. None of the four variables measuring expenditure on the different ALMP categories—the provision of public employment services (PES), training programmes (TRAIN), subsidies for regular employment in the private sector (SUB) and direct job creation (DJC)—are significant at a conventional level. Nor is GALMP, as the sum of PES, TRAIN and SUB, a measure of expenditures intended to increase efficiency, any better. The variable ACTIVE, the ratio of active to total expenditure on labour market policies, is significant at the 5 per cent level with a negative sign. Jackman et al. (1990) and Layard et al. (1991) reported a similar result (see also the discussion of the OECD, 1993, p. 70). The variable temporary layoffs exhibits a highly significant negative sign. That means that temporary layoffs reduce the unemployment rate. The insignificant results for the variables benefit duration and replacement rate are in contrast to the results obtained by Jackman et al. (1990) and Layard et al. (1991). The differences between the estimation results obtained by Jackman et al. (1990) and Layard et al. (1991) and the estimation results we arrived at may have methodological reasons and may be caused by the inclusion of different covariates. Jackman et al. (1990) introduced two dummy variables measuring the introduction of new programmes, together with allowing for the effects of corporatism and the vacancy rate, which they also interacted with the expenditure on ALMPs variable. By contrast, Layard et al. (1991) controlled for the change in inflation as well as for union and employer coordination. All these variables were significant at least at the 5 per cent level.

The estimates for the regressions with the incidence of long-term unemployment are quite different from those obtained for the unemployment rate regressions. Training measures and public employment service expenditures significantly decrease the proportion of long-term unemployed, whereas our

Table 24.1 *Estimates of the Effect That Expenditures on Active Programmes Have on the Unemployment Rate and the Incidence of Long-term Unemployment*[a]

| | Dependent Variables | | | |
| | Unemployment rate | | Incidence of long-term unemployment | |
Independent variables	A	B	A	B
UNION	− 0.012	− 0.017	0.385	0.015
IS	0.096**	0.106**	− 0.690**	− 0.278
CI	0.379*	0.325*	0.326	1.140
RR	− 0.065	− 0.028	0.920**	0.732**
DUR	0.066*	0.072*	1.552**	1.058**
TEMP	− 5.805**	− 4.271**	48.070**	10.451
DJC	0.003	0.001	0.037**	0.044**
SUB	− 0.020	—	0.098*	—
PES	− 0.008	—	− 0.112**	—
TRAIN	0.004	—	− 0.018**	—
GALMP/100	—	− 0.002	—	− 2.199**
Constant	1.945	− 1.602	− 48.471**	− 38.666*
R^2	0.763	0.721	0.949	0.938
$\bar{R}^2$	0.720	0.681	0.937	0.927
N	65	65	53	63

Notes
a Long-term unemployment as a percentage of total unemployment.
* Significant at the 5 per cent level.
** Significant at the 1 per cent level.

estimates suggest that direct job creation and subsidies to regular employment in the private sector significantly increase the proportion of long-term unemployment, in some cases perhaps because long-term unemployed persons will not be hired for these jobs if the subsidies are not restricted to the long-term unemployed. A longer duration of benefits and a higher replacement rate increase the proportion of long-term unemployed because of their negative impact on search efficiency. As expected from this line of reasoning, temporary layoff rules also significantly increase the incidence of long-term unemployment. Quite surprisingly, the more sclerotic the institutions, the lower the incidence of long-term unemployment.

The estimates of the effect that expenditures on active programmes have on the growth rate of employment are presented in Table 24.2. The variable ACTIVE, that is, the proportion of expenditures for ALMP to total expenditure of labour market policy, has a significant and positive effect on employment growth. Of the four variables measuring the impact of ALMP, the training variable was the only one with a significant sign. The variable GALMP, which included PES and SUB as well as TRAIN, was significant, too. How-

Table 24.2 Estimates of the Effect That Expenditures on Active Programmes Have on the Growth Rate of Employment

	Independent Variables Growth rate of employment	
Independent variables	A	B
UNION	-0.027	-0.024
IS	0.033	0.031
CI	-0.012	-0.039
RR	0.045	0.034
DUR	-0.015	-0.004
TEMP	-0.756	0.537
DJC/100	-0.115	-0.010
SUB	-0.006	—
PES	0.005	—
TRAIN	$-0.007*$	—
GALMP	—	$-0.005*$
Constant	-0.473	0.569
R^2	0.510	0.465
$\bar{R}^2$	0.419	0.388
N	65	65

Note

* Significant at the 1 per cent level.

ever, their influence was negative, a fact that sharply contrasts with the results expected from theory. The remaining variables were insignificant. Kraft (1994) conducted an empirical study on the effectiveness of labour market policy and applied a simultaneous equation model, with wages and employment being the endogenous variables. He found empirical evidence that passive labour market policy had a negative, and active labour market policies a positive, effect on the number of persons employed.

Table 24.3 reports the impact that expenditures on active programmes have on the labour force participation rate for men and women. For both, the vari-

Table 24.3 Estimates of the Effect That Expenditures on Active Programmes Have on Labour Force Participation

	Dependent Variables			
	Labour force participation rates of			
	men		women	
Independent variables	A	B	A	B
UNION	− 0.212**	− 0.207**	0.260**	0.268**
IS	0.150**	0.136**	0.029	0.047
CI	− 1.142**	− 1.069**	0.529	0.206
RR	− 0.248**	− 0.301**	− 0.240**	− 0.190**
DUR	− 0.306**	− 0.315**	− 0.418**	− 0.331**
TEMP	− 5.603*	− 7.700**	− 6.466*	− 0.308
DJC	− 0.006	− 0.003	− 0.015**	− 0.014**
SUB	0.029	—	− 0.058**	—
PES	0.013	—	0.053**	—
TRAIN	− 0.004	—	0.013**	—
GALMP	—	0.001	—	0.016**
Constant	114.754**	119.880**	67.909**	63.354**
R^2	0.781	0.744	0.943	0.919
$\bar{R}^2$	0.739	0.707	0.931	0.807
N	63	63	63	63

Notes
 * Significant at the 5 per cent level.
** Significant at the 1 per cent level.

able ACTIVE has a significant and positive effect. However, direct job creation and subsidies to private employers had significant negative effects on
female labour force participation. Whereas direct job creation had an insignificant impact on the male participation rate, subsidies to private employers had
a positive and significant effect. Similarly, training measures and improvements in public employment service tend to increase female participation, but
training measures decrease male participation significantly. As the sum of
TRAIN, PES and SUB, GALMP has a significant positive effect on the participation of women. High benefits and a long benefits entitlement exert a negative influence on the participation rate of both men and women. As expected,
temporary layoffs strengthen insiders' ties to the labour market and consequently decrease the participation rate for both men and women significantly.
Central bargaining systems and a high union density decrease the female participation rate. These differences could be explained by the fact that unions
represent a higher proportion of men and older workers. (Differences across
countries in the participation rates of men and women are largely due to differences in the retirement age. Where there is a big difference in the retirement
age, the female participation rate will be low and the proportion unionized
high.)

Table 24.4 shows the effect of expenditures on active programmes on
changes in ratios of earnings deciles. ALMPs tend to decrease the dispersion in
both the upper (D9/D5) and the lower (D1/D5) parts of the distribution significantly. Direct job creation and subsidies to private employers also seem to
decrease the dispersion at the upper tail, whereas resources spent for public
employment service and training programmes increase the dispersion at the
upper tail. Furthermore, direct job creation decreases dispersion in the lower
part of the distribution. As expected, the dispersion at the lower tail is also
reduced by institutional sclerosis. More surprisingly, however, high union
density and the existence of central bargaining systems tend to increase dispersion at the lower tail of the wage distribution. Temporary layoffs tend to
increase the dispersion at both ends of the distribution.

The regressions assessing the effect of expenditures on unit labour costs
reveal a significant and positive sign for the degree of activity on labour
market policies and a negative effect for direct job creation. This result can
perhaps be explained by the increased competition through public job creation
for the jobs within private firms. As expected union density and central bargaining lead to an increase in unit labour costs, as does a long duration of
benefit entitlement. This last result may be explained by the effects of benefit
duration on the proportion of long-term unemployed and labour force participation (cf. Tables 24.1 and 24.3), which tend to decrease the effective supply
of labour and increase unit labour costs.

Table 24.4 Estimates of the Effect That Expenditures on Active Programmes Have on the Dispersion of Wages

| Independent variables | Dependent Variables | | | |
| | D9/D5[a] | | D1/D5[b] | |
	A	B	A	B
UNION	0.008	0.010	− 0.003**	− 0.004**
IS	− 0.010**	− 0.011**	0.005**	0.005**
CI	0.074**	0.072**	− 0.009**	− 0.013**
RR	0.003	0.010	0.001	− 0.001*
DUR	0.006	0.011**	− 0.002**	− 0.003**
TEMP	0.329	0.767**	− 0.485**	− 0.485**
DJC/100	− 0.070**	− 0.083**	0.008**	0.014**
SUB/100	− 0.427**	—	0.001	—
PES/100	0.089	—	0.031**	—
TRAIN/100	0.031	—	− 0.002	—
GALMP	—	0.021	—	0.006**
Constant	1.000	0.322	0.712**	0.828**
R^2	0.917	0.831	0.991	0.983
$\bar{R}^2$	0.881	0.776	0.987	0.978
N	34	34	36	36

Notes
a D9 and D5 refer to the upper limits of the ninth and fifth decile.
b D1 and D5 refer to the upper limits of the first and fifth decile.
* Significant at the 5 per cent level.
** Significant at the 1 per cent level.

3   CONCLUSIONS

The labour market model developed by Layard and Nickell (1986) provides a convenient framework for studying the effects of ALMPs on the main macro-economic variables, in particular the level of real wages and 'regular' employment. The overall, or net, impact of ALMPs on employment is the number of programme participants less any fall in 'regular' employment resulting from the effects of labour market measures. The first section outlines the manner in which various types of ALMPs may be expected to influence aggregate labour market variables.

Among the various effects of ALMPs discussed here, the following can be expected to reduce wage pressure and increase regular employment: measures to increase labour force participation, measures to increase competition for jobs from outsiders, and the introduction of a work test. The effect of improved matching on the labour market equilibrium is ambiguous; employment is shifted to the right, but the wage-setting schedule may shift in either direction, depending on the nature of the policy. Measures designed to combat long-term unemployment have a positive labour supply effect, which causes employment to rise.

Table 24.5 Synopsis of the Empirical Results

	U	LTU/U	ΔL/L	LFP Men	LFP Women	D9/D5	D1/D5
UNION				−	+		−
IS	+	(−)		+		−	+
CI	+			−		+	−
RR		+		−	−		(−)
DUR	+	+		−	−	(+)	−
TEMP	−	(−)		−	(−)	(+)	−
DJC		+		−		−	+
SUB		+		−		−	
PES		−			+		+
TRAIN		−	−		+		
GALMP		−	−		+		+
Table	24.1	24.1	24.2	24.3	24.3	24.4	24.4

Notes
Only significant results are shown. Results significant in either model A or B are enclosed in parentheses.
U = unemployment rate; LTU/U = incidence of long-term unemployment; LFP = labour force participation rate; D9/D5 = relative upper decile; D1/D5 = relative lower decile; MM = ratio of unemployment rates of different occupational groups (mismatch).
UNION = union density; IS = institutional sclerosis; CI = central wage bargaining; RR = unemployment benefit replacement ratio; DUR = maximum duration of entitlement to benefits; TEMP = temporary layoffs (dummy: 1 = for Denmark, Canada, Italy, United States, 0 = other); DJC = direct job creation; SUB = subsidies for regular employment in the private sector; PES = public employment service; TRAIN = training measures; GALMP = sum of PES, SUB and TRAIN.

Problems of interpreting the results of empirical aggregate impact analyses could be overcome by means of surveys among persons placed (see de Koning, 1991) and interviews in local labour offices (see Schmid and Semlinger, 1980).

It may be concluded that microeconomic studies of ALMPs, which present evidence for an improvement in the situation of people who participate in such programmes, exaggerate their effect on total employment because they do not allow for displacement and substitution effects. But in any case, the means of active labour market policy are far too small to combat the persistently high level of unemployment in western Europe.

REFERENCES

Abraham, K. G. and S. N. Houseman (1993), *Job Security in America: Lessons from Germany*, Washington, DC: Brookings Institution.

Atkinson, A. and J. Micklewright (1991), 'Unemployment Compensation and Labour Market Transitions: A Critical Review', *Journal of Economic Literature*, 29, 1796–927.

Baily, M. N. and J. Tobin (1977), 'Macroeconomic Effects of Selective Public Employment and Wage Subsidies', *Brookings Papers on Economic Activity*, 1, 511–44.

Bourdet, Y. and I. Persson (1995), 'Does Labour Market Matter? Long-term Unemployment in France and Sweden', in J. Johannesson and E. Wadensjö (eds), *Labour Market Policy at the Crossroads*, Expert Group for Labour Market Evaluation Studies, Ministry of Labour, Stockholm, pp. 117–49.

Budd, A., P. Levine and P. Smith (1988), 'Long-term Unemployment and the Shifting U–V Curve: A Multi-country Study', *European Economic Review*, 31, 296–305.

Calmfors, L. (1993), 'Lessons from the Macroeconomic Experience of Sweden', *European Journal of Political Economy*, 9, 25–72.

Calmfors, L. (1994), 'Active Labour Market Policy and Unemployment: A Framework for the Analysis of Crucial Design Features', *OECD Economic Studies*, 22, 7–47.

Calmfors, L. and J. Driffill (1988), 'Bargaining Structure, Corporatism and Macroeconomic Performance', *Economic Policy*, 6, 13–61.

Choi, K. (1983), 'A Statistical Test of Olson's Model', in D. Mueller (ed.), *The Political Economy of Growth*, New Haven: Yale University Press, pp. 57–78.

de Koning, J. (1991), 'Measuring the Placement Effects of Two Wage Subsidy Schemes for the Long-term Unemployed', paper presented at the annual conference of the European Associations of Labour Economists (EALE), El Escorial, 26–29 September.

Grubb, D. (1993), 'Some Indirect Effects of Active Labour Market Policies in OECD Countries', Paris: OECD. (Unpublished manuscript)

Grubb, D. (1994), 'Direct and Indirect Effects of Active Labour Market Policies in OECD Countries', in R. Barrell (ed.), *The UK Labour Market*, Cambridge, UK: Cambridge University Press.

Heylen, F. (1993), 'Labour Market Structures, Labour Market Policy and Wage Formation in the OECD', *Labour*, 7 (2), 25–51.

Huckemann, S. and U. van Suntum (1994), *Beschäftigungspolitik im internationalen Vergleich: Länder-Ranking 1980–1993*, Gütersloh: Verlag Bertelsmann Stiftung.

Jackman, R. (1994), 'What Can Active Labour Market Policy Do?', *Swedish Economic Policy Review*, 1, 221–57.

Jackman, R. (1995, May), 'International Evidence on the Macroeconomic Effect of Labour Market Policies', paper presented at the Centre for Economic Performance Annual Conference, Stoke Rockford, UK.

Jackman, R. and R. Layard (1980), 'The Efficiency Case for Long-run Labour Market Policies', *Economica*, 47, 331–49.

Jackman, R., C. Pissarides and S. Savouri (1990), 'Labour Market Policies in the OECD Countries', *Economic Policy*, 5 (11), 450–90.

Johnson, G. E. (1980), 'The Theory of Labour Market Intervention', *Economica*, 47, 309–29.

Johnson, G. E. and R. Layard (1986), 'The Natural Rate of Unemployment Explanation and Policy', in G. E. O. Ashenfelter and R. Layard (eds), *Handbook of Labour Economics*, Vol. 2, Amsterdam: North-Holland, pp. 921–99.

Kraft, K. (1994), *An Evaluation of Active and Passive Labour Market Policy*, WZB discussion paper FS I 94–208 of the Research Area on 'Labour Market and Employment', Wissenschaftszentrum Berlin für Sozialforschung.

Layard, R. and S. J. Nickell (1986), 'Unemployment in Britain', *Economica* (suppl. 53), S121–S70.

Layard, R., S. J. Nickell and R. Jackman (1991), *Unemployment—Macroeconomic Performance and the Labour Market*, Oxford, UK: Oxford University Press.

Mavromaras, K. and H. Rudolph (1994, September), 'Recalls in the German Labour Market', paper presented at the annual conference of the European Association of Labour Economists (EALE), Warsaw.

OECD (1988), *Economic Outlook*, Paris: Publications Service of the OECD.

OECD (1990), *Labour Market Policies of the 1990*, Paris: Publications Service of the OECD.

OECD (1991), *Economic Outlook*, Paris: Publications Service of the OECD.

OECD (1993), *Economic Outlook*, Paris: Publications Service of the OECD.

Olson, M. (1979), 'An Evolutionary Approach to Inflation and Stagflation', in J. Gapinsky and C. Rockwood (eds), *Essays in Post-Keynesian Inflation*, Cambridge, MA: Ballinger, pp. 137–59.

Schmid, G. and K. Semlinger (1980), *Instrumente gezielter Arbeitsmarktpolitik: Kurzarbeit, Einarbeitungszuschüsse, Eingliederungsbeihilfen-Durchführung, Wirksamkeit und Reformvorschläge*, Königstein im Taunus: Anton Hain.

Schömann, K. (1995), *Active Labour Market Policy in the European Union*, WZB discussion paper FS I 95–201 of the Research Area on 'Labour Market and Employment', Wissenschaftszentrum Berlin für Sozialforschung.

25. New Public Management of Further Training

Günther Schmid

As unemployment increases and becomes more persistent, it also becomes increasingly 'structural', whereby 'structural' may have two meanings: either wages do not adjust to changing marginal productivity, or marginal productivity does not adjust to inflexible wages. In the first case one may speak of 'downward adjustment', in the second case of 'upward adjustment' to structural change. Since upward adjustment is more attractive for many reasons, attention is increasingly being directed towards further training or retraining in order to help the unemployed or workers under risk of redundancy to adjust to structural change. Defining the content of training, selecting the candidates, implementing programmes and monitoring the results can all be organized in different ways. Since growing budget deficits restrict the scope for spending increases, and since more spending does not necessarily mean better results, organizational reforms have been introduced to make policy formation and the implementation of further training more effective and efficient.

Most of these reforms are within the paradigm of 'new public management'. Although the various approaches differ, common features of this paradigm are the emphasis on management by objectives, performance-oriented budgeting, strengthening competition between suppliers, and the decentralization of decision-making and implementation (see, among others, Aucoin, 1990, and Hood, 1991). An evaluation of the effectiveness of these approaches must begin by looking at any available evidence that these institutional changes have contributed to a reduction in structural unemployment or to a facilitation of the adjustment processes to structural change. What differences exist within the emerging new paradigm, and do they matter? Another fundamental question relates to the classical trade-off between distributional and allocative objectives: should state-funded further training concentrate on the disadvantaged (the unskilled and the long-term unemployed) or on skill bottlenecks resulting from various market failures? How is the balance between equity and efficiency being altered by new public management? Are there organizational devices which could make these goals mutually supportive rather than mutually exclusive?

Systematic research to evaluate the different approaches to the organization of further training or retraining is practically nonexistent. Rather than reviewing the sparse and scattered literature available on the subject, I will apply the analytical framework developed in chap. 7 of this handbook and draw on empirical evidence from a large-scale explorative study undertaken at the *Wissenschaftszentrum Berlin*.[1] Other related studies or approaches will be included where appropriate in the course of the argument presented here.

The empirical evidence relates mainly to four EU Member States which were selected on the basis of significant differences in their employment regime and in the direction of recent organizational reforms of labour market policy. Germany (D) has always been regarded as an example of a strictly regulated labour market (an aspect viewed positively by some, negatively by others) and as an example (if not a model) of the integrated implementation of active and passive labour market policy. Denmark (DK) interested us as a country with a high level of further training activities, a liberal labour market regime (e.g. no statutory dismissal protection) and a distinctive tradition of corporatism at all levels of decision-making. We chose the United Kingdom (UK) as the 'deregulator's paradise'; the Thatcher government went furthest in Europe with its privatization reforms, thereby all but completely smothering the already weak spirit of corporatism. The Netherlands (NL) aroused interest world-wide when it radically decentralized and regionalized its labour market administration, granting the social partners (in addition to the regional authorities) far-reaching decision-making powers; however, unlike the United Kingdom, Dutch further training centres under the charge of the labour market authorities were not privatized.

In section 1, the policy regimes of these four countries are compared and their responsiveness to structural changes which affect skills and training needs are assessed. In section 2, the main differences in the implementation of further training policies are identified and related to indicators of organizational efficiency. An attempt is then made in section 3 to measure the effect of variations in incentive regimes on the level and selectivity of programme participation. In section 4, evidence of direct and indirect labour market effects is presented, and these results are evaluated in terms of cost-effectiveness. In section 5, the results are discussed on the basis of theoretical insights; guidelines are proposed for optimal public–private further training mixes. Conclusions are drawn in section 6.[2]

---

1 See Höcker, 1994; Linke, 1994; Moraal, 1994; Mosley and Degen, 1994; Schmid, 1994.

2 I have benefited from the comments I received when presenting the first draft of this chapter at the Handbook workshop in Berlin in June 1995; I am especially grateful for the comments by Karsten Jensen, who reminded me that Denmark's policy and implementation regimes are still in flux. Unfortunately, I was unable to include the most recent changes in 1995.

1 POLICY REGIMES AND RESPONSIVENESS

When societies are confronted with unprecedented problems they initially react along established lines, that is, in accordance with tried and tested behavioural patterns or models. 'Policy choice' is thus determined by rules of decision-making which have emerged in the course of a lengthy historical learning process and which change only very slowly. The ensemble of such institutional arrangements may be characterized as a 'policy regime' because it largely predetermines the political strategy whenever the environment is characterized by uncertainty.

The first step in assessing a policy regime consists of systematically describing the regime and any changes it has undergone. Such a description can be based on the four most important mechanisms of social coordination (see Schmid, chap. 7 in this volume): value structure, participation structure, market structure and legal structure (see the left side of Figure 25.1).

The *value structure* characterizes the dominant moral predisposition of the actors within a particular policy field. Such values, which are culturally determined and, at the individual level, are socialized in early childhood, channel individual behaviour. In other words, the question is: which principles can be identified as the general orientation for action? Is it maximization of one's own benefit (individualistic–competitive), or maximization of the damage to others (individualistic–aggressive), or maximization of collective benefit (communitarian–solidaristic) or maximization of the benefit to others (communitarian–altruistic)?

The *participation structure* characterizes the patterns according to which interests are articulated and defended in societies. Two ideal types exist in democratic societies: in 'pluralist regimes' common interests emerge *ad hoc* and battle for influence; in 'corporatist regimes' the interests of particular social groups are pooled on a long-term basis, and conflicts between these aggregated interests are resolved by means of regulated procedures between the parties concerned (e.g. negotiation on wages or training allowances). Pluralist regimes tend to neglect minority interests due to the importance of majority decision-making and the unequal power of pressure groups, whereas corporatist regimes tend towards proportional interest representation, but often at the cost of a slower pace of innovation and structural change.

The *market structure* reflects the dominant type of coordination prevailing in economic exchange processes. At the one extreme (market liberalism), prices are the sole determining factor, according to the law of supply and demand, whereas at the other extreme (social regime), exchange values are defined purely according to social criteria (e.g. needs or social status). Liberal market regimes tend to produce highly differentiated wage incomes in line with productivity differentials, whereas social regimes tend to reduce

Structure Variables	Policy Regimes		Responsiveness		Performance Indicators
(1) Value structure	individualist	communitarian	weak	strong	(1) Further training culture
(2) Participation structure	pluralist	corporate	low	high	(2) Participatory degree
(3) Market structure	libertarian	social	low	high	(3) Competitive supply
(4) Legal structure	common law	civil law	little	much	(4) Entitlements
(1)	→ D			→ D	(1)
(1)		DK		DK	(1)
(1)	→ UK		→ UK		(1)
(1)	NL			⌞→ NL	(1)
(2)		D ←	D		(2)
(2)		→ DK		→ DK	(2)
(2)	UK ←		UK		(2)
(2)		→ NL		→ NL	(2)
(3)	D ←			D ←	(3)
(3)		DK ←		→ DK	(3)
(3)	UK ←		→ UK		(3)
(3)		NL ←		→ NL	(3)
(4)		D ←	D ←		(4)
(4)		DK ←		→ DK	(4)
(4)	UK		UK ←		(4)
(4)		→ NL	→ NL		(4)

Note
→ *Change since the 1980s.*

Figure 25.1   Policy Regimes and Responsiveness

wage differentials through redistributive policies and minimum wage regulations.

The *legal structure*, finally, describes the rights and responsibilities provided for by law, both at a formal level (e.g. if societies are organized as federal or unitary states), and at a substantive level (e.g. whether the right to further training exists). In the one ideal case, common law 'rules', but can be rapidly modified if required (i.e. depending on shifting majority constellations); in the other legal tradition (civil law), rights are laid down constitutionally, are strictly formal, defined in detail and are thus difficult to change by political means.

The second step in assessing policy regimes involves evaluating the regimes and the changes which have taken place within them (see the right side of Figure 25.1). Here, measures relating to the four mechanisms of social coordination can be analysed in order to draw up possible performance indicators for a given policy field. For example, at the value-structure level, a well-developed further training culture reflects the adaptability (responsiveness) of policy regimes to structural changes on the labour market. A high degree of social participation (participation structure) in determining further training needs and in formulating further training policy is an indicator of success at the level of interest articulation. Effective market structures are characterized by a diversified supply of high-quality further training agencies and competitive structures which provide for choice between alternative further training provisions. Legal protection alongside de facto individual rights to further training and equity are features of a favourable legal structure with respect to further training.

There are two basic problems when it comes to evaluating policy regimes. How can we describe both the structural characteristics and the performance dimensions of policy regimes—their 'responsiveness'—coherently and plausibly? How can systematic links between structure and responsiveness be analytically determined and verified or falsified?

I have developed a two-dimensional grading system for both the structural analysis and the evaluation of policy regimes which combines qualitative description ('*Verstehen*') and quantitative assessment on one scale. The four structural and performance dimensions are defined as a quasi-dichotomy: between opposite extremes exists a continuum of positions. The countries are then positioned on this continuum on the basis of observation and evaluation; the positioning is subjective and can only be justified by reasoning.[3] However, it is conceivable that when this method of evaluation is at a more advanced stage—when the countries are positioned on the scale by experts using the

---

3 Due to the limited scope of this handbook, the following presentation of the results of Figure 25.1 must remain cursory; for more detailed discussion, see the literature cited.

Delphi[4] method, for example—reference numbers may be assigned to the ranking orders. Using this method, institutional changes can be indicated by an arrow, the length of which corresponds to the importance of the change; if there is no arrow, there was no significant change in the respective dimension of the policy regime during the period of observation. In addition to this system, I have also tried to develop quantitative indicators for the performance of policy regimes.

1.1   Changes in Policy Regimes over Time

The first result of the comparative international comparison (Figure 25.1) is a growing government commitment to further training on solidaristic–communitarian principles. With the exception of the United Kingdom, this also led to an actual increase in responsiveness—measured by expenditure on active labour market policy and on further training. Second, an intensification (in NL and DK) and a weakening (especially in UK, less so in D) of corporate structures is apparent. Moreover, there is evidence of increased decision-making powers at the local and regional levels in the regulation of specific issues (in NL, DK and to an extent in D), although in some cases increased powers for central authorities in setting framework regulations, for example, as regards standards of further training across sectors or regions (in UK and NL) can also be observed. Third, all countries made an effort to reinforce existing competitive structures, be it in the form of comprehensive privatization (in UK), deregulation (abolition of the labour market administration's monopoly on placement, first in UK, then in NL, DK and recently in D) or decentralization, regionalization and performance-oriented control of the public labour administration (in DK and especially in NL). There were also conflicting trends concerning the legal status of further training: whereas Denmark extended the legal right to further training to particular target groups and circumstances, such rights were abolished in Germany. In the Netherlands, the legal right was not reinforced, whereas de facto entitlement was.[5]

---

4 The Delphi method is a process of rank-order judgement by experts which continues until there is a consensus on the positioning or a stable distribution of rank order among the experts.

5 In the Netherlands, which has a constitution, but no constitutional court, the law is still strongly influenced by private and decentralized arbitration committees and those at the branch level whose rules and practices are de facto law. In no other country does policy implementation itself define the law so strongly as in the Netherlands. Although an immediate neighbour of Germany and France, countries with civil law traditions and legalistic practices (formalized procedures), the Netherlands has adopted a very pragmatic approach to the law, formalizing issues only when absolutely necessary and even then leaving many loopholes. 'By all indications Dutch legal culture uses less law than the surrounding countries' (Blankenburg and Bruinsma, 1994, p. 5). However, a tendency towards legalization is becoming apparent as a result of the process of European integration.

In distinguishing between these trends, a few specific details pertaining to Germany deserve mention. Even if no change took place in Germany at the formal, legal level during the observation period, the trend towards decentralization and regionalization has also made its effects felt at the operative level. The addition of five new federal states—the former GDR—led to a reinforcement of the federal principle in Germany. At a more practical level, the federal states (*Länder*) are increasingly assuming greater responsibility in matters of further training. Three reasons can be given for this: first, persistent mass unemployment is increasingly excluding the unemployed from schemes at federal level, so that the *Länder* or local authorities, who are the ultimate guardians of welfare (providing minimum social benefit etc.), are under increasing pressure to act; second, the planning and implementation of schemes increasingly require 'regionalized' insights and competence; third, the European Social Fund provides a stimulus in this regard because in order to be allocated funds, regions must present plans for their use and be willing to contribute financial resources of their own.

1.2   Performance Indicators of Policy Regimes

The activity rate, that is, the proportion of the total public labour market budget spent on active measures, can be taken as an indicator for responsiveness because it reflects a policy regime's actual commitment to full employment. However, because the level of employment is related not only to labour market policy, but also to social and economic policy, this indicator must be interpreted within a wider political context. As measured by this indicator, responsiveness has increased in all four countries since the mid-1980s, especially in the Netherlands (see Table 25.1). However, the data for recent developments show a greater degree of divergence.

The first surprise is the low activity rate in Denmark. Only just over a quarter of expenditure is on employment promotion, the rest is devoted to unemployment benefits or early retirement measures, the latter being particularly significant. While the activity rate in Denmark, and thus responsiveness as well, have increased in recent years, the overall picture painted by this quantitative analysis does not fit in with the preceding qualitative analysis, which would have led one to expect a high degree of commitment to full employment. The analysis of the implementation regime, especially its financing structure, will shed more light on this matter.

Germany exhibits a comparatively high activity rate: more than a third of expenditure is invested in 'active' measures. This result corresponds to the expectations which emerge from the analysis of the policy regime. As a result of reunification, this commitment shot upwards *nolens volens* for a few years in an attempt to cushion the shock of the drastic contraction of employment in the

Table 25.1 *Performance Indicators for Responsiveness (1) Activity Rate, (2) General Fiscal Commitment, (3) Further Training Commitment*

(1) Expenditure on Active Labour Market Policy as % of Total Expenditure

	1985	1990	1993	Δ (93–90)	Δ (93–85)
D	36.6	48.4	37.8	– 10.6	1.2
DK	24.2[a]	22.3	27.8	5.5	3.6
UK	26.0	39.0	29.5	– 9.5	3.5
NL	25.1	32.4	33.9[b]	1.5	8.8

(2) Expenditure on Active Labour Market Policy as % of GDP and One Percentage Point Unemployment

	1985	1990	1993	Δ (93–90)	Δ (93–85)
D	0.11	0.21	0.24	0.03	0.13
DK	0.16	0.15	0.18	0.03	0.02
UK	0.07	0.09	0.05	– 0.04	– 0.02
NL	0.10	0.14	0.14[p]	0.00	0.04

(3) Expenditure on Training for Unemployed as % of GDP and One Percentage Point Average Unemployment

	1985	1990	1993	Δ (93–90)	Δ (93–85)
D	0.04	0.07	0.10	0.03	0.06
DK	0.08	0.06	0.09	0.03	0.01
UK	0.01	0.02	0.01	– 0.01	0.00
NL	0.02	0.02	0.03[p]	0.01	0.01

Notes
a = 1986; b = 1992; p = estimated.

Source
OECD *Employment Outlooks*; OECD-datafile Expenditure on Labour Market Policy; author's calculation.

new *Länder*. However, to a great extent this increase in responsiveness can be correctly interpreted as an abuse of labour market policy by policy-makers in order to compensate for grievous errors in economic policy. The decline in responsiveness since the 1992–93 recession can be explained in part with respect to the rectification of this abuse, and also to the established mechanism with which active labour market policy is 'squeezed' by passive labour market policy in times of recession. This is a consequence of Germany's unique financing system: both active and passive policies are largely financed from the same purse, that is, from contributions (Schmid, Reissert and Bruche, 1992).

The activity rate in the United Kingdom also enjoyed a temporary boom, although it proved unable to survive the recession. One reason for the extreme decline in the commitment to full employment is the increasing restriction of the labour market policy programme to disadvantaged target groups. In contrast to Germany, the activity rate declined not so much because of rapidly increasing spending on unemployment compensation, but because of cutbacks in the budget for active measures; this is shown more clearly by other indicators (see below).

The activity rate in the Netherlands has risen steadily from a quarter to more than a third of expenditure; we can thus speak of a real improvement in labour market policy responsiveness. This corresponds to the results of, and the expectations which ensue from, the qualitative analysis. Nevertheless, the overall level is still moderate, particularly when it is taken into account that, in this case, expenditure on employment for the disabled was included in the activity rate and that such spending accounts for no less than half of total active expenditure.[6] If we disregard such expenditure motivated by social policy concerns, the reasons for the low commitment to full employment in the Netherlands are more difficult to determine than in the case of Denmark, where the financing structure provides a clue. An additional cause in the Dutch case is the strong emphasis placed on collectively agreed labour market policy, the financial consequences of which do not find expression in the labour market budget. However, one can expect that the large-scale labour market reform still under way will lead to a further increase in the activity rate. The dwindling willingness to introduce working time reduction (or work-sharing) without wage compensation will also force future governments to step up activity if they want to retain the cooperation of the trade unions.

The disadvantage of the activity rate, however, is that it tells us nothing about its relationship to the level of unemployment: the same activity rate can signify completely different levels of commitment in fiscal terms. The suggestion, therefore, is to use expenditure on active labour market policy as a percentage of GDP for each percentage point of unemployment as a standardized measure for the degree of fiscal commitment. Due to the significant positive correlation between expenditure on active labour market policy and the level

---

6 This is not taken into account in Moraal's (1994) paper, for example.

of unemployment the nonstandardized indicator so often used is not suitable as a comparative measure for the responsiveness of policy regimes.[7] The advantage of the standardized 'fiscal commitment' indicator is that it provides us with a quantitative conception of the degree of fiscal commitment to the goal of full employment.

As might be expected, Denmark comes off much better when observed from this perspective (see Table 25.1), even surpassing Germany in the mid-1980s. Indeed, the Danish policy regime was capable of improving responsiveness despite rising unemployment. The German regime was even more successful in this regard later in the period of reunification. The increase in responsiveness in the Netherlands, however, is probably more a consequence of the decline in unemployment (due to work-sharing), coupled with only a slight rise in real expenditure on active labour market policy. As indicated earlier, the United Kingdom is the only country in which responsiveness as measured by this indicator has declined notably.

Furthermore, the fiscal commitment of a policy regime to active labour market policy can also be analysed with respect to one single aspect, in this case further training. However, the standardization then needs to be applied to an indicator measuring further training needs. Since the vacancy rate is measured quite differently in individual countries and thus has varying validity, expenditure on further training for the unemployed and adult workers in employment as a percentage of GDP was standardized to the average rate of unemployment, in order to exclude cyclical fluctuations in unemployment from the equation (to which expenditure on further training should not correlate positively). Germany, with 0.1 per cent expenditure on further training per percentage point average unemployment (in 1993), is in first place for this indicator, too, although closely followed by Denmark. As expected, the figures for the Netherlands are lower on this indicator because a large part of the 'active' expenditure is on social policy measures. The responsiveness of the policy regime in the United Kingdom when seen from this perspective is not only low, but is also declining.

2   IMPLEMENTATION REGIMES AND ORGANIZATIONAL EFFICIENCY

Even if massive financial resources are made available, the best policy programme will fail if the organizational structure required for effective imple-

---

7 The indicator proposed here relies on the tacit assumption that the function of active labour market policy with respect to employment is the same for all levels of unemployment. The more a high level of unemployment is a demand problem (i.e. Keynesian unemployment), the less secure is this assumption.

mentation is missing or inadequate. Some of the questions which then arise are: who is to implement the further training policy? Is sufficient and adequately trained personnel available? Does the personnel have scope for flexibility in implementation, or are all matters centrally regulated according to rigid official rulings? Are the persons affected involved in the implementation process in any way? What economic incentives are offered to the programme managers? Are the schemes relatively stable so that long-term planning is possible, or can a 'stop-and-go' policy be expected? Do differences in implementation lead ultimately to differences in organizational efficiency?

In the following the national implementation regimes will be described and evaluated (section 2.1), again in accordance with the dichotomous grading system described above, followed by a preliminary attempt to introduce quantitative performance indicators for implementation regimes (section 2.2).

2.1   Changes in Implementation Regimes over Time

The normative orientation (at the level of the *value structure*) of those who plan, organize and carry out further training for the unemployed deserves particular consideration. In all four countries, the motive for organizational reform is identical, namely, to encourage those responsible for implementation to conform more closely to the needs of the (regional or sectoral) market. The idea is to steer the standard supply-side orientation of public labour market authorities more in the direction of a demand-side orientation, for example, through privatization. In the United Kingdom, however, an obvious institutional inconsistency was apparent: while the normative orientation of privatized programme managers clearly shifted towards demand (i.e. market needs), this shift has so far not been accomplished in practice due to the increasing restriction of further training schemes to problem groups. The normative orientation in the other three countries, in contrast, is still inclined more to supply, but a tendency towards a more even balance is clearly evident. A balanced normative orientation, one which takes both efficiency (best possible allocation of funds for *immediate* market needs) and equity (consideration for the disadvantaged position of the unemployed and their long-term market interests) into account, can only function within an organizational structure which provides a variety of implementation incentives. One possibility would be to give programme managers more room for manoeuvre in fixing maintenance allowances or fees for further training services. For instance, unskilled low-income earners (or the unemployed) may need a 100 per cent replacement of their (potential) earnings during off-the-job training, whereas skilled high-income earners may be satisfied with a replacement rate at the level of unemployment benefit (Figure 25.2).

Structure Variables	Implementation Regimes		Organizational Efficiency		Performance Indicators
(1) Competence and value structure	specialized demand oriented	generalized supply oriented	low	high	(1) Competent resources
(2) Decision and respons. structure	decentral fragmented	central integrated	little	much	(2) Cooperation and regulated conflict
(3) Financing and delivery structure	private private	public public	weak	strong	(3) Effective control
(4) Programme type and content	objectives firm specific	legal rules formal school	low	high	(4) Goal congruency
(1)		D / D ←		D ←	(1)
(1)	DK	DK ←		DK	(1)
(1)	UK ← / UK ←		→ UK		(1)
(1)		NL / NL ←		→ NL	(1)
(2)		D ← / D		D	(2)
(2)	DK	DK ←		DK	(2)
(2)	UK	UK ←	UK ←		(2)
(2)	NL ← / → NL			→ NL	(2)
(3)	D	D	D ←		(3)
(3)		DK ← / DK		→ DK	(3)
(3)	UK ←	UK		→ UK	(3)
(3)		NL ← / NL		→ NL	(3)
(4)		D ← / D		D ←	(4)
(4)	→ DK / DK		DK ←		(4)
(4)	UK ←	UK		UK	(4)
(4)	NL ←	NL ←		→ NL	(4)

Note
→ Change since the 1980s.

Figure 25.2   Implementation Regimes and Organizational Efficiency

As regards *interest articulation*, the United Kingdom has removed the last remnants of corporatism in its policy implementation structure, as elsewhere. However, in assessing whether this damages or benefits organizational efficiency, the character of the corporatism prevailing must be taken into consideration. It is possible that the damage resulting from a low degree of participation is actually limited in the United Kingdom because the trade unions are still largely organized by occupational group and are thus more of a hindrance than a help in achieving (the increasingly necessary) occupational mobility through more further training. The social partners in the Netherlands and in Denmark, by contrast, have been accorded greater responsibility, not only in policy choice, but also in policy implementation at regional level. While this is undoubtedly improving organizational efficiency in Denmark, since trade unions there are not only organized according to sector, but also according to region, it must be doubted whether the effect in the Netherlands is positive, in view of the extremely centralized organizational structure of the unions and declining union density.[8]

Only in Germany are both active and passive labour market policies implemented by the same institution. The dissociation of the two in the other countries does not lead *per se* to significantly better results; on the contrary, both spontaneous and legislative efforts to establish networks or to ordain collaborative interaction with a view to resolving the coordination problems which arise are evident in all these countries. A trend towards decentral 'one-stop service' agencies, consisting of easily accessible local offices offering a range of labour market services in one place, can be observed throughout Europe. But the integrated approach can be problematic, too, if there is no guarantee that the management of active measures is released from responsibility for the purely administrative aspects of the unemployment insurance system. If this is not the case, there is a danger—as in Germany—that implementation will be caught in a vicious circle: rising unemployment leads to a loss of operative resources for active programme implementation (as the cost of passive benefits rises), while the 'dole' image of the labour market administration tarnishes the 'customer-oriented' image of the active departments. It would appear that a clear-cut organizational segregation of responsibility for active and passive labour market policy, with provisions for coordination between the two, will ultimately be more conducive to a consistently service-oriented programme management than an integrated organizational structure which de facto is biased in favour of the administration of unemployment. The advantages deriving from professional specialization would appear to support this position, too.

---

8 In fact, Dercksen and de Koning (1995) report from a recent evaluation of the Dutch organizational reform that the hopes in tripartism at the regional level did not fulfil.

Germany is also an exception as regards the financing of active labour market policy. It is the only country which funds further training for the unemployed primarily from contributions to the unemployment insurance system. The advantage of such a financing structure is the stability of resources compared to the volatility of resources stemming from general tax revenues, which are subject to political discretion. This structure works fairly well under normal circumstances. However, integrated financing may lead to competition for scarce resources between 'active' and 'passive' labour market policy when unemployment is rising. In such a situation 'passive' expenditure tends to outcompete 'active' expenditure, and further training is implemented in procyclical rather than anticyclical fashion (see below). This is particularly problematic in view of the fact that retraining is most urgently needed during economic downturns.

Another problem with the German model of financing further training is the increasing burden of nonwage labour costs for employers and of social insurance contributions for dependent employees, whereas, for instance, the self-employed and civil servants (who profit at least indirectly from active labour market policy) are not called upon—as they do not pay contributions—to finance further training at all. Thus, both the scientific community and public opinion are increasingly calling for more financing from tax revenue. Denmark, on the other hand, which finances the bulk of further training from general tax revenues, appears to want to increase the share of funding from contributions. It seems that, in accordance with the character of training as a 'mixed good', a 'mixed financing' is one of the requirements of an efficient implementation structure for further training.

For policy implementation Germany relies on a diversified market comprising both public and private suppliers of further training. The problem with this implementation structure is the maintenance of quality standards; for instance, quality assurance temporarily ran out of control following the sudden boom of commercial training providers in eastern Germany, many of which offered qualifications of dubious value. Rigorous quality standards which are regularly monitored by independent institutions ('a TÜV for further training')[9] are now making inroads on this problem.

The Netherlands is an absolute exception with respect to the suppliers of further training; it basically relies on public further training institutions that are directly subordinate to the regional labour market authorities and are financed primarily from tax revenues. The most recent drastic budget cutbacks—and those on the medium-term agenda—are now forcing the regional

---

9 TÜV (Technischer Überwachungsverein) = Technical Monitoring Service—an organization both revered and feared in Germany—which monitors technical standards, for example, of cars, which are not allowed on the road without regular testing and corresponding certification.

authorities to reduce existing capacities and to buy services on the market; the likely end result of this process will be at least a partial privatization of the public further training centres, not least so that they can stand up to the competitive pressure coming from foreign (e.g. German) commercial further training establishments, or so that they will be in a position to enter strategic alliances or cooperative associations with them. In this case, the completion of the Single European Market seems to be leading to a convergence of implementation regimes.

There were three visible advantages of the public provision of further training services in the Netherlands: (a) flexibility in the range of courses, (b) concentration on disadvantaged persons in the labour market and (c) the systematic retention of excess capacities to meet unforeseeable emergencies or exceptional strain on the regional labour market (for example, due to large-scale closures or business start-ups). There are signs that these advantages are vanishing with the present trend towards privatization and that creaming, the selection of the most promising unemployed, is becoming increasingly prevalent.

Beyond the differences noted there are also a number of trends common to the four implementation regimes, and they are being reinforced, as mentioned above, through the completion of the Single European Market. Market orientation and competition are being intensified either through privatization, the purchase of external services or the sale of public institutions' own services. Performance-oriented budget allocations are another attempt at raising efficiency, and not only in the private sector; first steps in this direction have so far been restricted to the Netherlands and Denmark, however. While regional and local offices everywhere are gaining more autonomy in programme implementation, this regularly results in a precarious balance at central level between the ambition of qualitative control (greater efficiency and more regard for social needs) and the pressure to reduce spending. In other words, the central authorities are tempted to retrieve the loss of their autonomous control (ultimately a result of their loss of competence) by imposing budgetary fetters (see the case of the Netherlands) and through the regulation of the content of further training or through performance monitoring.

2.2   Performance Indicators of Organizational Efficiency

The multifarious nature of 'organizational efficiency' alone prohibits the use of simple measuring tools, and the lack of comparable data means that attempts to generate quantitative results are almost inevitably futile. Nevertheless, the following indicators, despite their shortcomings, will provide a few interesting results which complement the qualitative assessment of organizational efficiency discussed above.

We can take the number of persons involved in direct implementation as a measure for the commitment of effective resources. Working on the assumption that central control, administrative and monitoring utilities should claim the lowest possible share of resources, whereas operative utilities at the local level should be generously endowed, this measure can be further qualified by the extent to which resources are distributed decentrally. Two further qualifications are conceivable: since effective services are unthinkable nowadays without modern technology, a good infrastructure and, not least, high wages for personnel, overall expenditure on programme administration as a percentage of GDP and in relation to the number of implementation personnel can be enlisted as additional information.

Surprisingly, the United Kingdom in the 1980s shows the most positive figures for the number of implementation personnel in relation to the number unemployed, although there was a clear deterioration after privatization.[10] The opposite is the case in the Netherlands, where staff levels improved after the organizational reform, but are still lower than in both Denmark and Germany (Schmid, 1994, p. 49). However, if the qualifying indicators are included, the Netherlands has the best results for the decentralization indicator and for expenditure in relation to personnel. Only Germany beats the Netherlands with regard to overall expenditure on programme implementation; Denmark spends approximately half of that of the Netherlands, and Britain has the lowest budget of all for implementation personnel.

In order to measure the extent of cooperation within the infrastructure, we could count or evaluate the regulatory powers given to the social partners at the policy choice and implementation stages. A typology of network forms and an investigation into the number which exist could also be attempted. The degree of organization could be one indicator for 'cooperative capacity', that is, the ability of the social partners to get those they represent committed to joint action. The number of working days lost per 1000 workers due to strikes could be used as a qualifying characteristic for the nature of the relations between the social partners, which also tells us something about their ability to cooperate bilaterally.

The United Kingdom has the worst results for all three indicators (Schmid, 1994, p. 51). The low trade-union density[11] in the Netherlands is surprising and barely consistent with the transfer of large areas of responsibility for labour market policy to the social partners. Yet the Netherlands outshines the other

---

10 However, it is possible that this is a statistical artefact if privatized personnel were excluded from the calculation; I was unable to clear this point.

11 I know of no international comparative data concerning the degree of organization of employers; if the existence of this deficit should be confirmed, we have a disquieting shortfall in research into this field.

countries as regards all other indicators for cooperative structure; Denmark does slightly better overall than Germany.

To measure effective control we can take the ability of an implementation regime to place unemployed persons in a further training scheme at the earliest possible opportunity—provided the scheme is practical from the point of view of both supply and demand. The justification for this indicator should be immediately clear: most evaluation studies agree that the labour market impact of such schemes correlates negatively with the duration of the preceding period of unemployment (Schmid and Schömann, 1994).[12] However, rapid placement in a further training scheme relies on both a diverse and flexible further training infrastructure and a fiscal structure which provides positive institutional incentives wherever it is expedient to finance further training rather than unemployment.

Measured according to this criterion, the reform in Denmark was partially successful in that the duration of unemployment before participation in further training declined: in 1984, 49 per cent of unskilled participants (on AMU—adult vocational training—courses) had been unemployed for less than 100 days. The figure for 1991 was 67 per cent and in 1992 no less than 93 per cent. The corresponding figures for skilled participants are less impressive: 38 per cent in 1984 and 49 per cent in 1992.[13] Due to a lack of capacities, however, numerous unemployed persons evidently have to wait until they have acquired legal entitlement, that is, are classified as long-term unemployed.

Likewise in Germany the unemployed are usually placed on schemes at a relatively early stage, and here the trend is also improving. In 1983 only just over a quarter of all participants on further training schemes had been unemployed for less than 3 months, the figure rose to 40 per cent in 1991 and 39.1 per cent in 1992; only 18 per cent had been unemployed for more than one year (Linke, 1994, p. 71). The situation is less favourable in the United Kingdom. Though 30 per cent of participants in further training had been unemployed for less than 6 months in 1990–91, 42 per cent had been out of employment for over one year (Mosley and Degen, 1994, p. 45). However, this led the government to set stricter criteria regarding the duration of unemployment, so that the share of short-term unemployed is probably even lower today.

Finally, continuity, planning security and the right timing for the programmes are important features of organizational efficiency. The dynamics of

---

12 Mosley and Degen (1994, p. 46) also reported that in Great Britain the degree of successful reintegration of unemployed persons who have undergone further training falls as the duration of preceding unemployment rises; however, they rightly point out that it is difficult to detach the duration effect from the personal characteristics of the unemployed persons concerned and believe that the latter is the decisive factor in successful or unsuccessful reintegration.

13 The calculations are based on Höcker, 1994, Tables A 4b and A 4c.

Table 25.2 Growth of Expenditure for Further Training (FT) Compared to Growth of GDP and Unemployment

	Germany			Denmark			United Kingdom			Netherlands		
	Δ Exp. FT (real)	Δ GDP (real)	Δ Unempl.	Δ Exp. FT (real)	Δ GDP (real)	Δ Unempl.	Δ Exp. FT (real)	Δ GDP (real)	Δ Unempl.	Δ Exp. FT (real)	Δ GDP (real)	Δ Unempl.
	1	2	3	1	2	3	1	2	3	1	2	3
1984												
1985	25.9	2.0	1.7		4.3	−13.4	14.4	3.8	4.9	14.1	2.6	−7.4
1986	25.6	2.3	−3.3		3.6	−23.0	7.9	4.3	1.6	5.2	2.7	−4.6
1987	10.2	1.5	0	−0.6	0.3	1.3	53.4	4.8	−10.0	12.9	1.2	2.8
1988	6.1	3.7	0.6	−18.4	1.2	4.0	49.9	5.0	−19.4	2.3	2.6	−2.6
1989	17.3	3.6	−9.1	4.6	0.6	25.8	−8.8	2.2	−25.5	1.5	4.7	−8.4
1990	40.2	5.7	23.9	−4.7	1.4	3.4	−26.8	0.4	−10.2	−9.6	4.1	−7.5
1991	42.1	4.5	3.0	16.6	1.0	9.1	−13.7	−2.2	43.1	5.6	2.1	−5.0
1992	−14.1	2.1	14.5	15.4	1.2	7.5	−0.5	−0.6	19.5	3.3	1.4	−2.4
1993		−1.3	14.8	14.6	1.2	9.5		1.9	7.0		0.2	23.6
1994					4.0							
(1) Mean	19.16	2.68	5.12	3.93	1.88	2.69	9.48	2.18	1.22	4.41	2.40	−1.28
(2) Standard deviation	18.58	2.02	10.43	12.91	1.48	14.00	28.97	2.55	21.01	7.35	1.40	9.94
(3) Variation coefficient	97%	75%	204%	329%	79%	521%	306%	117%	1719%	167%	58%	−778%
(4) Regression coefficient 1/2 (standard error)	3.77 (3.20)			−0.63 (14.67)			7.93* (3.07)			−0.04 (2.01)		
(5) Regression coefficient 1/3 (standard error)	−0.06 (0.69)			0.49 (0.67)			−1.07* (0.30)			0.02 (0.29)		
(6) Regression coefficient 3/2 (standard error)	0.09 (1.96)			−8.44* (2.22)			−5.70* (2.25)			−5.52* (1.68)		

Note: * = Significant on the level of 1%.

Sources: OECD-datafile 1994, OECD Employment Outlook, 1994, and own calculations (Germany: since 1990 eastern and western Germany; therefore, time series for Germany are distorted).

public expenditure on further training provide an insight in this regard: the antithesis of continuity and planning security would be large-scale annual fluctuations in expenditure (fluctuations which exceed cyclical swings), while procyclical changes in expenditure would be at variance with the goal of anticyclical countermeasures. In other words, if expenditure on further training runs parallel to the economic trend or counter to changes in the unemployment rate (i.e. if expenditure drops when unemployment rises), then the timing must be assessed negatively.

Measured according to these criteria, the United Kingdom comes off worst once again. Not only is its fluctuation margin the highest (see row 2 in Table 25.2), but the dynamics of expenditure also exhibit a strong procyclical tendency (rows 4 and 5): expenditure rises as GDP does and falls as unemployment rises, and vice versa. Germany, too, suffers from extreme fluctuations, and expenditure is to an extent procyclical, although this is not apparent in the overall regression because at the beginning of a recession there is always an initial temporary anticyclical reaction which then becomes procyclical (see also Schmid et al., 1992). The dynamics of expenditure in Denmark and especially in the Netherlands are more uniform and also more goal congruent from the point of view of timing (although not to a statistically significant degree).

3   INCENTIVE REGIMES AND PROGRAMME ACCEPTANCE

An efficient implementation regime does not necessarily guarantee successful labour market policy. The programmes and schemes for implementation must also be accepted by those targeted by the policy. In our case we must therefore ask which incentives actually motivate the unemployed to undergo further training with a view to improving their prospects for reintegration.

The purpose of analysing incentive regimes is to try to discern whether labour market policy offers sufficient incentives to the unemployed to undertake further training.[14] Here we can distinguish between psychological, social, economic and political incentives—again in analogy to the four main social coordination mechanisms: is it the real—or supposed—improvement in employment prospects resulting from further training that is decisive, or is intrinsic motivation the underlying impetus? What incentives do social hierarchies offer individuals to improve their position through further training? Are there economic incentives, for example, a higher maintenance allowance than

---

14 Here we concentrate on the unemployed as the target group for policy implementation; if employers are the target of policies to induce a change of behaviour, analogous considerations have to be made.

unemployment benefit and/or the prospect of a job with better wages? Does further training perhaps offer the prospect of other 'rights', for instance, a job with good legal protection and accordingly high entry barriers for possible competitors?

All four dimensions play a part in the individual decision whether or not to accept a particular further training offer. In the following, attention will again be drawn to a few selected points from the reference study on the qualitative characterization of incentive regimes (Figure 25.3), and these structural characteristics will also be linked to quantitative performance indicators (Table 25.3).

A paradox emerges with respect to the psychological incentives: incentive regimes that are strongly marked by identification with a professional role—as in Germany—promote the intrinsic motivation to expand and develop abilities and knowledge connected with the specific 'occupational profile'. This is in principle favourable to further training, but can prove negative in cases where radical retraining is called for (e.g. retraining from a traditional industrial occupation to a modern service profession). Further training programmes consisting of long-term courses which are not directly job related can also have a demotivating effect on those with a low-skill level. The average duration of courses in Germany, for example, is considerably longer than in the other three countries (especially in comparison to Denmark), which explains the noticeable underrepresentation of the unskilled, whether in or out of employment, in further training. Modular and progressive training courses which are clearly job related are more suited to these target groups than lengthy courses in a school-like environment.

Extrinsic further training motives, that is, labour market signals and financial incentives, play a more decisive role in systems which lack a strong occupational identification. In this regard Denmark and the Netherlands are positioned between Germany and the United Kingdom, where occupational identification seems to be least significant. The primary function of further training in the United Kingdom is to compensate for the nonexistence or inadequacy of initial vocational training. However, because it is of such poor quality, the British further training programme for the unemployed offers extremely low incentives to participate. Consequently, the United Kingdom has the lowest figures for participation in and successful completion of further training (Table 25.3). The Netherlands and Denmark, in particular, provide flexible and more economically oriented modular systems which conform better to the motives of the less skilled unemployed than is the case in Germany. Denmark's further training diplomas, which are recognized nationally, also raise the propensity of employers to recruit certificated further trained workers. This fact is backed up by massive participation in Denmark, where programmes are generally of much shorter duration than in Germany. Moreover,

Structure Variables	Incentive Regimes		Policy Take-up		Performance Indicators
(1) Psychic incentive	intrinsic motivation	extrinsic motivation	low	high	(1) Take-up
(2) Social incentive	hierarchy of status	hierarchy of function	no	high selective	(2) Social selection
(3) Economic incentive	low wages	high wages	low	high	(3) Effectiveness of expenditure
(4) Political incentive	low legal protection	high legal protection	weak	strong	(4) Compliance with rules
(1)	← D			→ D	(1)
(1)		DK		→ DK	(1)
(1)		← UK	→ UK		(1)
(1)	→ NL			NL ←	(1)
(2)	D		D ←		(2)
(2)		DK		DK	(2)
(2)	UK		UK		(2)
(2)		NL	NL		(2)
(3)	D ←			D	(3)
(3)	→ DK			DK	(3)
(3)	UK		UK		(3)
(3)		NL		NL	(3)
(4)		D ←		D ←	(4)
(4)	→ DK			DK	(4)
(4)	UK		UK		(4)
(4)		NL		NL	(4)

Note
→ Change since the 1980s.

Figure 25.3   Incentive Regimes and Policy Take-up

Table 25.3 Indicators of Policy Take-up

	Germany 1987	Germany 1993	Denmark 1987	Denmark 1993	United Kingdom 1987	United Kingdom 1993	Netherlands 1987	Netherlands 1993
(1) Entries in further training								
(a) unemployed × 1000	355	764	67	114[a]	560	240	116	109
(b) employed × 1000	242	114	102	135[a]	106	13	4	–
(2) (1) as % of the labour force								
(a) unemployed	1.21	2.0	2.4	3.9[a]	2.04	0.89	1.79	1.47[a]
(b) employed	0.82	0.3	3.6	4.7[a]	0.39	–	0.06	–
(3) Unemployment rate	6.2	6.7	7.8	10.4	10.3	10.3	9.6	8.3
(4) (1) as % of unemployed	19.5	29.9	30.8	37.5	19.8	8.6	18.6	17.7
(5) Participants in year equivalence								
(a) unemployed × 1000	168	384	13	23	174[b]	130	27	37
(b) employed × 1000	178	81	5	5	?	–	–	–
(6) (5) as % of the labour force								
(a) unemployed	0.57	1.00	0.48	0.78[a]	0.63[b]	0.45	0.47[c]	0.53[c]
(b) employed	0.61	0.21	0.17	0.18[a]	?	–	–	–
(7) Selectivity of programme[f]								
> male short-term unemployed						0.63		
> female short-term unemployed						0.52		
> male long-term unemployed						0.87		
> female long-term unemployed						1.10		
> short-term unemployed	1.14[d]	1.02[d]	n.i.	n.i.	?	0.58	n.i.	n.i.
> long-term unemployed	0.66	0.64				0.93		
> male unemployed						1.08		
> female unemployed						0.87		
(8) Expenditure (million ECU)								
(a) for unemployed		8 325		357[c]		929		500
(b) for employed		446		96[c]		–		–
(9) Expenditure in year equivalence								
(a) for unemployed (ECU)		21 680		15 522		7 146		13 514
(b) for employed (ECU)		5 506		19 200		–		–

Notes: a) 1992; b) 1989; c) 1989; d) gross estimation; e) 1/3 of the expenditure for AMU is attributed to the unemployed; f) selectivity of programme = share of participants divided by share of unemployed; n.i. = no information.

Sources: OECD-datafile; Höcker, 1994: Tables A6, A7; Mosley and Degen, 1994: Tables 3 and 5; Linke, 1994: Tables 1 and 7, Figure A2; author's calculations.

while the financial incentives for further training for the unemployed have been gradually curtailed in Germany, Denmark is in the process of extending them. It is also noteworthy that hierarchically structured labour market segments (especially internal and public labour markets) offer additional social and political incentives for further training; there is evidence of this in all the countries investigated.

Figures on the flow of entrants into further training schemes show that Denmark has the highest level of activity and the highest level of acceptance for state-funded further training. Unemployed persons who participate in further training schemes account for some 4 per cent of the labour force; this is almost twice the figure for Germany (2 per cent), and much higher than the share in the Netherlands (1.5 per cent) and the United Kingdom (around 1 per cent). Due to the short average duration of Danish schemes, however, the ranking order of Denmark and Germany is reversed when participation is calculated in terms of full-time equivalents: on average, no less than 1 per cent of the labour force was participating in further training in Germany at any one time during 1993; the share in Denmark was about 0.8 per cent and in the Netherlands and the United Kingdom about 0.5 per cent (Table 25.3).

The 'creaming' phenomenon is apparent in all countries, that is, discrimination in favour of the most capable or the easiest to place within a target group, however, defined. Policy faces an efficiency–equity dilemma here: in terms of efficiency, unemployed persons requiring further training should embark on it at the earliest possible opportunity; in equity terms, however, such an approach might well serve to exacerbate the exclusion of the long-term unemployed. Thus, a twofold strategy is required, which Denmark comes closest to achieving: on the one hand, there are numerous further training courses on offer for young and capable unemployed persons which are organized separately from further training provisions for those in employment; on the other hand, those who have missed the boat and are facing chronic long-term unemployment have a legal right to carefully supervised further training or other schemes.

The success of labour market policy, however, ultimately depends on the contextual conditions of the labour market. Even for a given policy, implementation and incentive regimes, demographic developments (supply) or technological and economic structural change (demand) can influence the effectiveness of labour market policy. Thus, we turn now to an assessment of the actual success of further training policies on the labour market in the four countries selected.

4   THE LABOUR MARKET SUCCESS OF FURTHER TRAINING POLICY

Labour market policy success can also be described at the four levels corresponding to the dimensions of social coordination: (a) How quickly and permanently are the unemployed who have undergone further training placed in employment (employment effect)? (b) Are certain categories of the unemployed (e.g. the long-term unemployed) who have been further trained disadvantaged in the course of reintegration (distribution effect)? (c) How useful was the further training in the new job? Did it result in a higher income? Was the extent of skill mismatch reduced (productivity effect)? (d) How do the net effects of labour market policy or further training relate to the costs (cost–benefit ratio, efficiency)?[15]

Unfortunately, there are no satisfactory answers to these questions. There is a lack of systematic and longitudinal information, and where information is available it does not always meet minimum evaluation standards. It really is surprising how little systematic performance monitoring takes place, even of the most technically simple kind, despite rising expenditure on labour market policy; methodologically faultless impact assessments are very rare. An additional problem in assessing the success of the new public management approach is that the more fundamental reforms are too recent to have brought about sustainable changes, or they have not yet taken place at all, for example, in Germany. For these reasons it was only possible to put together a mosaic of scattered data of varying quality for the four case studies (Table 25.4). The following attempt to draw a comprehensive picture based on sound evaluation is therefore only a first step.

All the indicators suggest that further training usually fosters the reintegration of the unemployed into the labour market and shortens the duration of unemployment; even when the level of unemployment is high the reintegration rate is good. This success, however, depends very much on the quality of the further training, which has a temporal, a substantive and a formal dimension. The results of the comparison of the four countries indicate that the schemes should be initiated as soon after the onset of unemployment as possible, before a demotivation process sets in. The choice of the training content is important, too. For example, one of the few European studies using (quasi-experimental) control groups, a Dutch study, found excellent results for metal-working and building courses (reduction of the expected duration of unemployment by half), but no effect for clerical courses (de Koning, Koss and Verkaik, 1991).

---

15 In assessing the benefits of further training, its socio-psychological consequences (e.g. increase in self-confidence as a consequence of successfully completed further training) should also be taken into consideration, even if a quantitative measure is practically impossible.

Finally, implementation of the schemes must be both goal congruent and suited to the needs of the participants: for some participants, a particular goal (e.g. a new vocational qualification) can only be achieved in a long-term, full-time course, whereas for others a step-by-step procedure (modular organization) is more effective. Generally, job-related qualifications or fundamental retraining leading to certificates recognized on the labour market seem to be most effective in practice (OECD, 1993; Schmid and Schömann, 1994).

The evidence also clearly indicates the significance of the opportunity costs of further training, however. It seems that instead of 'parking' the unemployed in further training, from where the participants usually do not actively seek work, intensified job search and job placement can often make more sense; if existing qualifications are inadequate, they can then be augmented from the safe perspective of a job. This is an indication of the growing importance of coordination between structural policy and labour market policy, with the greatest stimulus for this trend probably coming from Denmark's flexible policy regime.

The finding that further training for the unemployed is the more successful the sooner it is implemented should not be allowed to obscure an equally categorical result, namely, that further training is also worthwhile for the long-term unemployed. Another target group for which most evaluations report favourable results are lone mothers receiving social assistance and women reentering the labour market (OECD, 1993; for Denmark: Rosholm, 1994). Careful preparatory guidance, constant supervision and intensive placement activities during the scheme, for example placement on work experience programmes, however, are the necessary ingredients to receive these positive results.

The individual productivity effects, as reflected in higher wages or salaries and better working conditions, correlate positively with the quality of the schemes; however, overall they appear to be moderate. Indeed, a study in Sweden has even reported negative results in terms of earnings (Regnér, 1993). One explanation for this unexpected observation, supported by sophisticated econometrics, was the adverse incentive effect of training schemes: an unemployed person without benefits or whose benefit period is approaching its end becomes eligible for another full period of benefits through participating in training for four months (see also Schmid and Reissert, chap. 8 in this volume). Thus, the prime motivation for participation in training may be the extension of unemployment benefits, and not the improvement of skills. These results suggest two conclusions: first, unemployment insurance should not encourage misuse of important policy instruments such as training; second, work organization as a whole, and the wage-structure and wage-determination processes in particular, should offer more incentives for further training of the unemployed or workers threatened by unemployment.

Table 25.4 *Labour Market Effects of Further Training*

	Germany	Denmark	United Kingdom	Netherlands
I. Employment Effect				
1. Reemployment effect of further training (as %)	half a year later (1991) – further training (FT): 72.6 – retraining (RT): 86.0 – in-firm training (IFT): 94.1	n.i.	Employment Training (ET): 33 (1990–91) Job Training Scheme (JTS): 70 (1985)	positive, but low net effect
2. Reemployment effect of further training after 1–2 years (as %)	9 months later (Hamburg Study): – FT: 75 compared to 47 (cg) – RT: 65 compared to 56 (cg)	n.i.	n.i.	after 2 years no significant differences
3. Reduction of unemployment	12 weeks less compared to nonparticipants	formal training shortened the total time in unemployment for prime-age women, but not for men	9% lower duration of unemployment compared to cg	50% lower duration of unemployment compared to cg
II. Distribution Effect				
1. Reemployment effect of further training (as %)	1991 M F FT 70.1 74.7 RT 84.1 87.9 IFT 93.7 95.0	AMU: lower risk to become unemployed only for men; no effect for long-term unemployed (ATB)	ET M F 28 41	highest net effect for the elderly; small number of unqualified people and ethnic minorities
2. Reemployment effect after 1–2 years by duration of unemployment (as %)	1986 >3 mon. 65.0 3–6 mon. 61.3 6–12 mon. 57.1 >12 mon. 43.4	UTB UDY >12 mon. 13 30	ET (1990/91) JTS (1985) 49 <6 mon. 6–12 mon. 29 47 >12 mon. ≈24	n.i.
3. Reintegration effect of further training after 1–2 years by duration of measure (as %)	1986 <3 mon. 54 4–6 mon. 56 7–12 mon. 57 13–18 mon. 69	<3 mon. 10 – 4–6 mon. 12 4 7–12 mon. 19 26 13–18 mon. – 41 Share of unemployed, who participate again in a measure 33–38 (1984–88)	n.i.	n.i.

Table 25.4—continued Labour Market Effects of Further Training

	Germany	Denmark	United Kingdom	Netherlands
III. Productivity				
1. Improvement of qualification	Hamburg Study: – 31% upward mobility compared to 15% cg – 74% qualified jobs compared to 55% cg	n.i.	ET reemployed participants: 26% improved, 56% unchanged; 17% changed for the worse	signal effect is probably stronger than the real growth of productivity
2. Improvement of income	– 28% lower wages compared to 38% cg – 72% higher wages compared to 53% cg	1% wage increase (i.e. men)	25% of participants have higher wages	n.i.
3. Reduction of mismatch	little improvement of the 'Beveridge Curve'	n.i.	probably no effect because of the small number and the concentration on problem groups	little improvement of the 'Beveridge Curve'
IV. Efficiency				
1. Cost-effectiveness	n.i.	n.i.	n.i.	n.i.
2. Cost–benefit	n.i.	n.i.	n.i.	n.i.

Notes
The 'Beveridge curve' expresses the relation of unemployment and vacancies; cg = control group; n.i. = no information.

Sources
Germany: Linke 1994, Kasparek and Koop 1991; Denmark: Höcker 1994, Westergård-Nielsen 1993, Rosholm 1994; United Kingdom: Mosley and Degen 1994; Netherlands: Morraal 1994, de Koning 1993.

The macroeconomic effects of further training, which the WZB team tried to measure using an econometric analysis of the Beveridge curve, remain indeterminate.[16] Due to the lack of information, we must also dispense with an overall evaluation as regards equity and efficiency, and thus also with qualified cost-effectiveness and cost–benefit comparisons.

5   DISCUSSION

I have identified various approaches to the 'new public management' of labour market policies related to further training and have tried to find evidence of their effectiveness and efficiency. Despite the diversity of approaches, recent developments point towards the emergence of a new paradigm of labour market policy: a trend away from an interventionistic 'active labour market policy' towards a more 'cooperative labour market policy', one which relies heavily on networks and networking at local and regional levels. However, networks require very special conditions to be effective as coordination mechanisms between markets and hierarchies. They cannot be designed in an ivory tower, and they cannot be regulated by law. They have to somehow evolve in an organic way and be properly complemented by markets and public infrastructure. Thus, it seems desirable to devote the final discussion to the typical coordination problems that arise in the process of implementing further training policies (see section 5.1), and to see which public management strategies might contribute to resolving these difficulties (see sections 5.2–5.4). On the basis of this discussion, it is possible to devise guidelines on how to formulate policy formation and implement further training policies more efficiently and equitably (see section 6).

5.1   Coordination Problems in Managing Further Training Policies

The first coordination problem stems from the fact that further training is a typical 'mixed good', featuring aspects of both 'private' and 'public' goods. Thus, further training generates positive external effects from which all benefit, so that free-riding can be expected. On the other hand, potential negative external effects should not be neglected either; these can emerge as a conse-

---

16 A slightly improved balance between vacancies and unemployment as a result of labour market policy was only observed in Germany. This unsatisfactory result can be put down in part to the poor quality of the data, but it is also to an extent due to the fact that the aggregated Beveridge curve is probably too inexact an instrument to reliably show the slight effects of state-funded further training, which are inevitably insignificant in comparison to the dimensions of unemployment (Schmid, 1994, p. 76).

quence of excessive specialization. A purely private sector response to this coordination problem will probably generate too little general, and too much specialized further training, while a purely public solution may yield a surplus of further training activities, unless problems of fiscal incongruity emerge as a result of institutional fragmentation. Since tight budget restrictions do not apply to publicly provided goods, because they are funded by the state, efficiency will suffer, too. In actual fact, mixed organizational structures are to be found in all four countries. However, since 'new public management' has shifted the emphasis towards privatization and decentralization, we must ask whether such an approach is the solution to this particular coordination problem.

The next problem concerns information. With respect to further training, there is, first, the uncertainty regarding future qualification needs and whether the unemployed are capable of acquiring these through further training. Second, one must reckon with a double asymmetry between the information held by those supplying and those demanding labour: the unemployed know little about their future job, and there is little that public placement services can do to change this, while the employers know little about the actual qualifications of the unemployed, and certification does little to improve this deficit.

Opportunism is another coordination problem which can appear in different guises. For example, do enterprises 'game with public programmes', such as utilize public further training schemes to save on training costs (deadweight or substitution)? Do programme managers exploit their scope for interpretation by selecting workers, whether employed or unemployed, who have good labour market prospects anyway (creaming)? Do the unemployed abuse further training provisions in order to extend their entitlement to wage-compensation benefits (moral hazard)?

Finally, equity is a coordination problem because individual opportunities for action are unevenly distributed and because the cards we are dealt are constantly being reshuffled. Since access to jobs and the selection of those to be laid off are increasingly determined by formal education and qualifications, much depends on finding a solution to this coordination problem, which is known as 'credentialism' or 'statistical discrimination'. In this area especially, as in chaos theory, small coincidences can have large-scale effects due to path dependency and self-reinforcing processes.

We will now discuss how the funding (section 5.2), organization (section 5.3) and regulation of further training (section 5.4) might contribute to aggravating or alleviating these coordination problems.

5.2   Financing Further Training

The question of financing has always been at the forefront of labour market policy reform. Fiscal incongruence is one possible element of coordination failure (section 5.2.1); socioeconomic inequality is a second (section 5.2.2) and false incentives a third (section 5.2.3).

5.2.1   Fiscal Incongruence

How can the institutional incentives to finance effective further training rather than financing unemployment be improved? What insights can be gained from our comparative study? Evidently, in purely financial terms, it makes little difference to the labour market authorities in the countries which primarily finance further training from tax revenues or universal social security funds (United Kingdom, Denmark and the Netherlands) whether they are financing unemployment or further training. Equally, this fiscal system fails to offer any explicit incentive to finance one rather than the other, unless further training leads to quicker reintegration and, thus, eases the fiscal burden, in which case the central funding body (usually central government) has an interest in encouraging the implementors to carry out more further training.

The United Kingdom had hoped to generate this incentive by privatizing planning and implementation. However, the desired effect failed to materialize because the implementation of the system of unemployment insurance (which now also includes placement) and active labour market policy programmes has remained under the charge of separate bodies, leading to coordination problems. One problem of this partition is that it hinders the placement of unemployed workers after further training. We have established, however, that the lack of political will to fund training programmes adequately was probably more to blame for the failure.

The surprising observation made earlier that Denmark lags behind all the other countries in its activity rate seems to be explained by its financing structure. The wage-compensation benefits granted by the unemployment insurance system in Denmark are relatively generous (see Schmid and Reissert, chap. 8 in this volume). Unemployment insurance is administered from trade-union funds, but is subsidized to a large degree from tax revenues. The trade unions thus have little incentive to press for active measures, especially since the average duration of unemployment is relatively low—in contrast to the other (European) countries—due to the guarantee of a place in a labour market policy scheme for the long-term unemployed, so that the burden of unemployment is more uniformly distributed. Since the qualifying conditions for receipt of unemployment benefit are also modest, some of the 'passive' expenditure probably has the function of compensating for temporary layoffs or short-time working; this function also comprises 'active' components in that it affords enterprises broad flexibility in human resource management. If this assumption is correct, then employers also have little incentive to change the system. The paradoxical result is: although the public and social infrastructure of further training in Denmark is much better developed than in the other countries, the financing structure is a hindrance to more dynamic further training for the unemployed. An example of this is the fact that the further training capacities for temporarily unemployed persons are insufficient, leading to long waiting lists.

In Germany the fiscal relief effects of further training for the Federal Labour Office are at least 20 per cent less than the cost of financing unemployment (Bruche and Reissert, 1985, p. 133). For those bodies directly involved in implementation there is thus a slight financial disincentive to fund further training rather than unemployment. This applies even when the central government, which bears ultimate financial responsibility, is included in the analysis. However, this institutional deficit was offset by a legal incentive in the form of a right to further training (until 1993), and the coordination of further training with the implementation of unemployment benefits and placement remains unproblematic. As in the other countries, the pressure on central government to act only rises when the duration of unemployment and the share of the national budget spent on financing it increases (in Germany unemployment assistance is financed from the state budget, i.e. by the taxpayer). The results of this comparative study would suggest that the financial disincentive for the German Employment Service be replaced, for example, by a conditional central government grant to the Federal Labour Office, and that the right to further training be restored.

5.2.2 Socioeconomic Inequality

Can financing systems compensate for the disadvantages suffered by the unemployed in the competition for good jobs? No country in the EU requires the unemployed to bear the total cost of further training, at least provided they would otherwise be entitled to unemployment benefit. In this respect, the financing systems do provide social compensation. However, in systems which are financed solely by contributions, such as in Germany, the compensatory function is—for reasons of equivalence under insurance law—largely restricted to those unemployed workers who have acquired sufficient entitlements to unemployment benefit during a relatively long period of prior employment. Thus, the prerequisite for financial compensation at the macro-level is that the 'average unemployed person' was previously in employment, a condition which is met increasingly rarely. In 1992, for example, only 56.5 per cent of German entrants into unemployment had previously been in employment, compared to only 78.6 per cent in 1982; 6.8 per cent of these came directly from school and the remainder (36.7 per cent) from the various forms of nonparticipation. In an increasing number of cases, therefore, the compensatory function has to be performed by local or state government, whose scope for active labour market policy is very limited.[17] The equivalence problem, which can curtail the socioeconomic compensatory function, does not arise in systems which are primarily funded from tax revenues (Schmid et al., 1992). Here, too, a conditional central government grant to the employment service could be one way towards improving the compensatory function of the financing system.

5.2.3 Inadequate Financial Incentives

There are practically no direct financial incentives[18] for the unemployed to undergo further training in preference to enduring the state of unemployment built into financing systems. Where they once existed,[19] they have now been abolished. As a rule, maintenance allowances during further training are equal to the unemployment benefits which would otherwise apply; at best a small supplement compensates for the higher cost of living (e.g. travel expenses to the further training centre, higher housekeeping costs).

Maintaining legal entitlement to unemployment benefit might be a further incentive, and there are grounds for this conjecture in Denmark. The opposite case is the United Kingdom, where potential participants are caught in a trap: due to uncertainty regarding their legal rights following further training, the unemployed were demotivated to take up potential offers; in addition, further training for the unemployed in British enterprises is primarily linked to productive work on the job, leading to claims of exploitation. The individual incentive to participate in further training must therefore derive from other sources.

Another means of increasing the direct individual incentive is to sanction failure to comply with a labour administration recommendation or requirement to participate[20] by revoking the right to unemployment benefit. We found

---

17 Moreover, the right to wage-compensation benefits expires as unemployment persists, as does entitlement to a maintenance allowance during further training. Freedom to participate repeatedly in further training was also restricted in 1994: training courses must now be separated by at least one year's employment.

18 In contrast to the stimuli under the 'incentive regimes', where 'rewards' after further training—such as higher earned incomes—are at issue, here we are talking about the incentives provided by unemployment benefit and maintenance allowance during further training.

19 Such as in Germany at the beginning of the 1970s, when maintenance allowances during further training amounted to 90 per cent of the previous net wage compared to 68 per cent for unemployment benefit.

20 For instance, following the obligatory restart counselling session in the United Kingdom (after 6 or 12 months).

little evidence that this instrument was actually used in any of the countries. On the other hand, even if sanctions are seldom enforced, the threat alone can suffice: if the unemployed are aware that their benefits may be at risk, they may well even accept inferior further training offers.

The practice of lowering further training allowances to the level of unemployment benefit appears questionable, especially in the case of training leading to a superior qualification, which requires high motivation and staying power. Here, financial concerns have a counterproductive effect. It is also questionable wherever alternatives are available to the unemployed which provide higher financial compensation than further training, even though their labour market impact may not necessarily be greater.[21] Such unjustified financial differentiation also impedes the implementation of combinations of such schemes or 'promotion chains', which means participation in dovetailed successive programmes.

5.3   Organizing Further Training

Decentralization, regionalization and privatization are the three main organizational elements of new public management. While decentralization primarily implies a spatial transfer of programme implementation to 'lower' levels (section 5.3.1), regionalization additionally implies that the scope for regional decision-making is enlarged (section 5.3.2). Privatization, however, constitutes the most radical type of organizational reform, in that all matters are entrusted to the forces of the market, market-oriented intervention with a view to addressing particular social or public concerns is permitted (section 5.3.3). The objective of all three elements of new public management is to combat four typical dimensions of government failure: information deficits, inflexible governmental control, a lack of tight budget restrictions and programme management lacking personal responsibility or performance incentives.

5.3.1   *Decentralization*

Our case studies show that flexibility in programme execution has increased considerably as a result of decentralization, but that new problems have arisen in its place. This applies above all to the United Kingdom, where the flexibility attained may have promoted operating efficiency in programme execution (accurate data were not available), but where labour market efficiency has certainly declined. The view that cost-effectiveness has improved is based on the introduction of price liberalization and tight budget restrictions. Anecdotal

---

21 For instance, the temporary public job creation measures (ABMs) in Germany which until
    1995 offered regular wages.

allusions in interviews to complicated methods of budget accounting and high transaction costs of monitoring, however, place question marks against this supposed increase in efficiency (Gay and Howells, 1994).

Alongside the debatable increase in cost-effectiveness, the fact that the selection of target groups is still determined at the central level is clearly only a partial and at that contradictory solution to the information and equity problem. The increasing restriction of target groups to include only the long-term unemployed has left programme managers little scope to concentrate on regional skill bottlenecks and, thus, to set in motion chain reactions which would ultimately also benefit the disadvantaged unemployed. It is also apparent that the employers' representatives on the Training and Enterprise Councils (TECs) are barely or at best selectively appraised of future information needs. Complementary information on general trends, collected at the central level, may be necessary, even if only to detect the comparative advantages at the regional or local level. On the other hand, the definition of quantity standards at the central level and their decentralized implementation leads to creaming, as has been shown especially in the Netherlands.

We can conclude from the above that *selective centralization* and *selective decentralization* seems to be the best strategy of improving organizational efficiency of further training (Aucoin, 1990, p. 129). Whenever policy decision-makers have specific strategic objectives to pursue, such as equal treatment or increasing the overall level of information, education and training, the mode of centralized public management makes sense. This requires a few and clearly defined priorities, corresponding operational indicators and effective monitoring of goal attainment (see Auer and Kruppe, chap. 30 in this volume). Whenever pressing political problems arise, such as skill mismatches or individual employment handicaps which are contingent in terms of space and time, a decentralized mode of public management is required both for effective policy formation and implementation. Performance-oriented budget allocation from the central to decentral levels may be a combination of both which leads to the next topic, the regionalization of labour market policy.

5.3.2 Regionalization

The most predominant form of regionalization is the devolution of central budgets to the regions in accordance with particular criteria concerning labour market conditions, granting them more or less free rein in implementation. The intention is to combat three coordination problems: the information problem (the regions know better what is good for them), budgetary discipline (tight budget restrictions are to be achieved through rigid budget ceilings) and equitable resource distribution (central allocation of funds according to objective criteria).

Let us first look at the issue of fair distribution. In Germany, because the unemployed enjoyed a legal right to further training (until 1993), there was no ceiling on regional further training funds. Research has shown that in practice this led to an underuse of funds in those regions which had the greatest need (in terms of the number of unemployed). Thus, in the 1980s the correlation between regional expenditure on further training and the regional rate of unemployment was actually negative (– 0.54), in contrast to the very positive correlation of 0.80 for regional expenditure on temporary public job creation measures—the only instrument with central fund allocation (Reissert 1989, p. 6). However, the negative correlation is not unconditional proof of coordination failure because of interference between the implementation of training measures and the implementation of unemployment insurance: in areas with high unemployment, operative resources are increasingly absorbed in the administration of unemployment; moreover, a diminishing number of the unemployed are entitled to a maintenance allowance during further training. The negative interference can be interpreted as coordination failure inasmuch as the correlation stems from these two factors. The other possible reason is that further training makes less sense the more unemployment rises, because the problem is then not so much one of inappropriate qualifications as of a shortage of jobs (insufficient demand); thus, it would be incorrect to deduce coordination failure merely from the negative correlation. The lack of highly differentiated data prohibits us from reaching a final verdict.

Central allocation of regional funds requires an objective allocation base. In the Netherlands the levels of employment and unemployment currently have weights of 0.25 and 0.75 in regional fund allocation.[22] However, it has become apparent that this kind of mechanical allocation does not reward particularly active employment offices. Therefore, proposals have been put forward for a more performance-related allocation base, for instance, by including as a weight the (absolute and relative) number of effective placements of the long-term unemployed. Yet here we come to the same conclusion as we did for decentralization: if more weight is to be given to successful implementation of labour market policy in decision-making, greater importance must also be attached to monitoring. The central labour market authorities in the Netherlands are complaining about a lack of monitoring, and there are still no convincing alternative systems in the other countries (see Auer and Kruppe, chap. 30 in this volume).

---

22 Denmark's allocation base (labour force 0.5, unemployed 0.25) also includes the number of enterprises with more than 2 employees—with a weight of 0.25—so that regions with a relatively large number of small and medium-sized firms are at an advantage; in other words, there is a financial incentive to design active labour market policy with this target group in mind. This is in complete contrast to the conditional programming observed in Germany until 1993, where legal entitlements and their decentral implementation determine expenditure.

As pointed out above, central allocation of regional funds is one way of counteracting the lack of tight budget constraints. The basic idea is that regional budget ceilings and their flexible implementation provide incentives for lean management and efficient resource allocation. Such budget ceilings are thought to replace the common principle of cost coverage in public agencies which makes no sense where opportunity costs have to be considered. Another desirable consequence of this measure is that it serves as a stimulus to mobilize local revenue, be it through charging fees for services (placement fees for the unemployed are still universally prohibited) or the active sale of services. The regional labour market authorities in Denmark and the Netherlands are now explicitly empowered to engage in this kind of additional fund mobilization, whereas this is not yet possible in Germany; the TECs in the United Kingdom are also permitted to employ this instrument. However, such market revenues do not as yet account for a significant share of total expenditure. The central authority in the Netherlands is applying a further market-oriented political instrument (albeit to a modest extent) in order to compensate for the negative consequences of mechanical fund allocation to the regions: a central experimental fund has been set up with a view to inducing competition between regional authorities to generate innovative projects. This allocative instrument could represent a way forward.

5.3.3 Privatization

Privatization is the most radical, but also the most controversial element of the new public management approach (Salamon, 1989). The primary motive behind privatizing the implementation of further training is the desire for more information concerning market needs and more effective performance monitoring through commercial budget restrictions, that is, the view that an inefficient organization will not survive market competition. Increased cost-effectiveness is only of secondary interest, as this—all else being equal—will be a direct consequence of the first outcome. Before we proceed, I should mention that the privatization of further training has so far only affected public service delivery, but not financial support. Even in the United Kingdom, where privatization has been pursued most consistently, further training for the unemployed is still funded by the state. This is an example of a 'quasi-market' (Le Grand and Bartlett, 1993).

The central structural prerequisite for achieving the objectives of privatization is competition between the privatized suppliers; otherwise monopsonistic public demand faces a private monopoly, with adverse results likely because the state forfeits direct control over both professional quality standards and price and wage determination when it privatizes the supply. Consequently, price competition has to take on the function of quality control. A second structural prerequisite for the efficiency of 'quasi-markets' is that competition also evolves on the buyer side, because if competitive suppliers remain dependent on only one buyer, the customer can dictate the conditions. In the extreme case this will lead to destructive competition between the suppliers.

The case study on the United Kingdom shows that, for various reasons, competition on the supplier side (consisting primarily of so-called 'training managers') is not yet well developed. First, they operate on local markets; second, they usually specialize in certain market segments; third, they frequently also perform an advisory function for the unemployed (in their own interests, of course); and, fourth, the entry requirements for competitors are very high. Due to limited competition the flow of information concerning vacancies or potential further training places is restricted because the training managers treat this knowledge as private property. Moreover, relationships based on mutual trust develop between the quasi-public placement bodies (TECs) and their subcontractors (the training managers), so that it is difficult for outsiders (potential new market entrants) to show that they are possibly offering better quality.

On the buyer side, the UK central government is still the monopoly purchaser of further training services for the unemployed. The further training infrastructure is as yet largely undeveloped in comparison to Denmark or Germany, for example, where the income of semistate and commercial providers also derives from further training for the employed, which is usually funded privately (by enterprises and/or workers). However, because the training managers are now (increasingly) providing other services, especially in the field of management consultancy, the monopoly on the buyer side has little impact. Since the TECs, as intermediary bodies, both implement other government schemes and (increasingly) offer purely commercial services on the market, the problem is more one of developing sufficient incentives for the implementation of the schemes.

In reaction to this problem, the British government has introduced a bonus system, so that in future mere participation in a scheme will not be rewarded as generously as actual success, that is, the reintegration of the unemployed. However, the problem with these kinds of bonus systems is that they reinforce the tendency towards creaming (i.e. selection of the most capable from the targeted group) which is already prevalent as a consequence of commercialization. This problem could be solved, in principle, if the bonuses were staggered according to social criteria, but this approach has not been practised as yet.

As already ascertained with regard to decentralization, privatization has so far done little to improve the amount and quality of the information generated. Indeed, the aforementioned tendency among competing suppliers to monopolize information indicates a deterioration in this respect. On the other hand, some TECs have begun to set up survey panels on the labour market situation in their regions which will improve the basis for decision-making. However, similar activities could also be introduced within a purely public framework, as shown by the systematic survey panels in the Netherlands. True to its centralized model, Germany has established a survey panel at federal level, which will probably not be very useful at the regional level due to the small sample size and data-protection difficulties. In the final analysis, both will be required: specific and problem-oriented surveys at regional or local level and centralized data systems to disclose general trends and provide bases for comparison.

Whether one week of further training (of the same quality) for one unemployed person is more cost-effective after privatization remains unclear. On the basis of the very limited information available, it seems to be a rather doubtful presumption. Since the privatized implementing bodies—in the United Kingdom, the TECs—now have to buy all training-related services externally, they incur substantial transaction costs which would not arise within a hierarchical organizational structure. The situation is further aggravated by the use of short-term contracts between the government and the private contractors, so that constant renegotiation is unavoidable. The negotiations between the TECs and the government alone are extremely time-consuming and result in tome-like contracts, which are barely up to date on publication. Because the suppliers are unable to develop a long-term perspective they refrain from investing in the costly infrastructure required for high-quality measures. This relates not only to machines and equipment whose acquisition cost will not be recouped years later but also to professional and thus expensive personnel. Economies of scale—which are necessary for high average efficiency—are thus not realized, and, at the same time, the advantages induced by a high level of competition on the supply side cannot develop.

The Netherlands are an interesting alternative model to the United Kingdom; here, further training for the unemployed is still primarily carried out in 35 regional training centres under the charge of the public labour market administration. These centres realize the necessary economies of scale without impinging on functional flexibility, that is, on the ability to adjust to changing needs. A functionally flexible supply relies on a broad performance profile, which small-scale private suppliers cannot provide. In addition, public agencies guarantee to some extent high-quality reserve capacities which can be used for unexpected challenges. And as there are solutions to 'market failure', there are solutions to 'state failure': in the Netherlands, corporate decision-making structures are one way in which the information problem and the problem of the institutional inertia of large public training capacities could be solved. A second possibility is the increasing pressure on public suppliers in the form of tight budget ceilings to sell their services on the external market. A third solution is the deregulation of any legislation involving a public monopoly, that is, the encouragement of private suppliers.

Due to the lack of data, we cannot ascertain here whether these control mechanisms are adequate. As mentioned above (see section 2.1), the Dutch model is increasingly being questioned in the Netherlands itself. Demands for privatization, or at least for greater competition in public further training centres, more performance-related budget allocation and greater networking with local actors are increasing. The most recent budget cutbacks touch the heart of the Dutch labour market administration and will enforce a 'slimming down' of the public further training centres.[23] The implementation structures in Denmark and Germany are positioned somewhere between the extremes of the United Kingdom and the Netherlands. In these countries, too, there are clear signs that networks are being formed at local or regional level.

5.4   Regulating Further Training

The regulation of further training through quality standards seems to represent a promising alternative. Irrespective of the policy regime involved, quality standards are capable of alleviating coordination failure, in particular the free-rider problem and the problem of information asymmetry. The rediscovery of the 'moral dimension' in economics (Etzioni, 1988), which points to the importance of unconditional communitarian values for effective social coordination, would appear to support this assumption. From this perspective there are a number of arguments in favour of viewing the British 'Investors in People' programme (IiP) as a prime example of the evolution of a 'moral' further training culture. First, this programme adopts a value-based standard as a lever to mobilize desired activities. In contrast to mere social conventions (such as traffic rules), standards such as 'quality' entail emotional values (Frank, 1988, p. 157), and are thus more effective incentives to cooperation than conventions or simple appeals. Second, compliance with these standards is rewarded with a certificate which can be used by firms as a sales or image-enhancing logo. Third, this type of quality certificate can serve as a selection criterion in decisions concerning further government subsidization. Finally, the British government underpins the impact of the programme by awarding financial subsidies, matching investment by firms participating in the programme pound for pound. Government funds totalling £39 million (about 50 million ECU) were earmarked for 1993–94 (Department of Employment, 1993, pp. 16 ff.).

In addition to incentive-oriented programmes of this type, voluntary and legal statutes designed to foster a communitarian further training culture will be essential. In countries with corporate policy regimes (Denmark, the Netherlands) moves to anchor further training as a collectively agreed right are now

---

23   The cutbacks for 1995 amount to HFL 100 million and for 1996–98 another HFL 400 million per annum; this money is to be given to the municipalities for job creation measures.

in sight. Denmark is in the process of extending legislation covering the entitlement of the long-term unemployed to further training to include extra provisions, for example, training or careers leaves, whereas the conservative-liberal government in Germany recently revoked this legal entitlement.

6   CONCLUSION

It is important to realize that the methodology of evaluating the (new) public management of labour market policy is still in its infancy. This chapter has outlined an approach, illustrated with reference to further training, which attempts to do justice to the complexity of the issue at hand, while still remaining practical, coherent and transparent. Although much remains to be done to improve the methodology, the application of this approach often founders on the lack of empirical data. This situation will only improve when effective monitoring systems (see Auer and Kruppe, chap. 30 in this volume) are established, enabling researchers to combine data on financing, organizational and regulatory structures with analyses of net employment effects.

For this reason conclusions regarding the characteristics of socially and economically efficient organizational structures must remain general and hypothetical in nature. One clear result, however, emerges *ex negativo*: simple solutions, as suggested by catch-phrases like 'networks', 'decentralization', 'deregulation', 'lean administration' or 'lean management' either do not exist, or merely confuse the issue. The message with which we end is, unfortunately, more complex: empirical evidence and theories of coordination failure indicate that the management of labour market policies has to apply a mix of coordination mechanisms, in which both competition and cooperation function as essential and complementary elements.

However, this mix is not arbitrary, but rather is determined by policy targets and the contextual conditions under which they operate. In the future there will cease to be a dominant paradigm of social control. Neither markets, centralized political control (hierarchies) nor the much-quoted networks point the way towards the labour market policy of the future. Labour market policy must undoubtedly serve to strengthen cooperative relations; competition between providers of further training must undoubtedly be stepped up; the effective control of labour administrations must certainly be improved through decentralization and performance-orientation; but a more active centralized control of quality standards and corresponding monitoring systems is unquestionably also necessary when clear and specific political priorities are at stake; and finally, the revitalization of an integrative code of communitarian further training ethics, embodying the right to further training if not *de jure* then at least de facto are wanted.

In the light of this, the following guidelines for the public management of further training as an essential element of labour market policy can be formulated:

- In order to address the inadequate budget constraints on public and semi-public bodies, effective information and control structures have to be implemented, for instance, by promoting competition between training suppliers and through monitoring systems and performance-oriented budget allocation (including pay) into public sector organizations. Non-carry-over annual budgets should be replaced by longer-term budgets and budget ceilings, thus encouraging greater economy in the expenditure of public funds.
- In order to tackle the problem of imperfect and unequally distributed information (in particular with regard to further training for the unemployed or for employees under threat of unemployment) more effectively, participative structures at local and regional level must be improved and regional autonomy in decision-making must be increased.
- In order to deal with the problem of further training as a public or semipublic good, in other words to discourage free-riders, both a comprehensive public infrastructure and incentives to internalize external effects are required. For instance, mobility potential declines with increasing length of employment in one and the same firm; the corresponding higher risk of (long-term) unemployment may be compensated for either by further training obligations or higher contributions to the unemployment insurance fund.
- In order to stimulate cooperative networks, support could be indirectly administered in the form of financial incentives (rewards for voluntary cooperation) or directly in the form of state mediation in coordination procedures. On the other hand, noncooperative behaviour may be punished by excluding defectors from public tenders or grants, or public disclosure by way of reporting obligations, for example, for large firms concerning issues of human resource management, with the danger of loss of reputation.
- In certain cases the networks will have to take the form of statutory redistribution systems (e.g. compulsory contributions to further training funds) in order to promote greater social justice and to prevent free-riding.
- Finally, every effort must be made to foster a further training culture based on the principles of solidarity through self-imposed communitarian values. We can only recognize and determine the general course of structural change; its pace and concrete local manifestation are, in principle, uncertain and uncontrollable. The potential for political intervention is limited, but nonetheless should be fully utilized. For example, information and motivation campaigns coupled with financial incentives for pioneer enterprises could serve to promote the creation of practical training opportuni-

ties for job-seekers engaged in further training as well as job rotation through the 'train and hire' system. Premiums for voluntary audits with respect to quality standards would be another possibility. The adoption of a universal entitlement to further training, implemented, however, on a decentralized, voluntary and self-organizing basis, is a further key element in the evolution of a civilized further training culture.

If these principles were put into practice, it could herald the institution of further training as a fourth pillar (besides elementary, secondary and university education) in the existing education system. The institutionalization of further training, in turn, could establish a self-regulated and continual cycle of work and training for the entire labour force and, at the same time, lend fresh impetus to the old notion of preventive labour market policy.

REFERENCES

Aucoin, P. (1990), 'Administrative Reform in Public Management: Paradigms, Principles, Paradoxes and Pendulums', *Governance*, 3 (2), 115–37.

Blankenburg, E. and F. Bruinsma (1994), *Dutch Legal Culture*, Deventer/Boston: Kluwer Law and Taxation Publishers (2nd revised and enlarged ed.).

Bruche, G. and B. Reissert (1985), *Finanzierung der Arbeitsmarktpolitik*, Frankfurt: Campus Verlag.

de Koning, J. (1993), 'A Method for Evaluating Training Policy for the Unemployed: The Dutch Experience', in K. Jensen and P. K. Madsen (eds), *Measuring Labour Market Measures*, Copenhagen: Ministry of Labour, pp. 265–93.

de Koning, J. (in press), 'A Method for Evaluating Training Policy for the Unemployed with Special Reference to the Frisian Situation', in C. H. A. Verhaar, P. M. de Klaver, M. P. M. de Goede, J. A. C. van Ophem and A. de Vries (eds), *On the Challenges of Unemployment in a Regional Europe*, Avebury: Aldershot, pp. 263–83.

de Koning, J., M. Koss and A. Verkaik (1991), 'A Quasi-experimental Evaluation of the Vocational Training Centre for Adults', *Environment and Planning C: Government and Policy*, 9, 143–53.

Department of Employment (1993), *The Government's Expenditure Plans 1993–94 to 1995–96*, London: HMSO.

Dercksen, W. and J. de Koning (1995), *The New Public Employment Service in the Netherlands (1991–94)*, WZB discussion paper FS I 95–207, Wissenschaftszentrum Berlin für Sozialforschung.

Etzioni, A. (1988), *The Moral Dimension. Toward a New Economics*, New York/London: The Free Press and Collier Macmillan Publishers.

Frank, R. H. (1988), *Passions within Reason. The Strategic Role of the Emotions*, New York/London: W. W. Norton & Company.

Guy, R. and D. Howells (1994), 'Training and Enterprise Councils: Are They Cost-effective?', *Policy Studies*, 15 (2), 19–36.

Hansen, L. (1991), 'Nonmarket Failure in Government Training Programs', in D. Stern and J. M. Ritzen (eds), *Market Failure in Training*, Berlin/Heidelberg/New York: Springer, pp. 215–33.

Höcker, H. (1994), *Reorganisation der Arbeitsmarktpolitik. Weiterbildung für Arbeitslose in Dänemark*, WZB discussion paper FS I 94–202, Wissenschaftszentrum Berlin für Sozialforschung.

Hofbauer, H. and W. Dadzio (1987), 'Mittelfristige Wirkungen beruflicher Weiterbildung', *Mitteilungen aus der Arbeitsmarkt- und Berufsforschung*, 2, 129–41.

Hood, C. (1991), 'A Public Management for All Seasons', *Public Administration*, 69 (1), 3–19.

Jensen, K. and P. K. Madsen (eds) (1993), *Measuring Labour Market Measures. Evaluating the Effects of Active Labour Market Policy Initiatives*, Copenhagen: Ministry of Labour.

Kasparek, P. and W. Koop (1991), 'Zur Wirksamkeit von Fortbildungs- und Umschulungsmaßnahmen. Eine kritische Auseinandersetzung mit den Untersuchungen des Instituts für Arbeitsmarkt- und Berufsforschung', *Mitteilungen des Instituts für Arbeitsmarkt- und Berufsforschung*, 2, 317–32.

Le Grand, J. and W. Bartlett (eds) (1993), *Quasi-markets and Social Policy*, Houndmills/London: The Macmillan Press.

Linke, L. (1994), *Reorganisation der Arbeitsmarktpolitik. Weiterbildung für Arbeitslose in Deutschland*, WZB discussion paper FS I 94–203, Wissenschaftszentrum Berlin für Sozialforschung.

Moraal, D. (1994), *Die Reorganisation der Arbeitsmarktpolitik. Weiterbildung für Arbeitslose in den Niederlanden*, WZB discussion paper FS I 94–204, Wissenschaftszentrum Berlin für Sozialforschung.

Mosley, H. and C. Degen (1994), *The Reorganisation of Labour Market Policy. Further Training for the Unemployed in the United Kingdom*, WZB discussion paper FS I 94–205, Wissenschaftszentrum Berlin für Sozialforschung.

OECD (1992), *High-quality Education and Training for All*, Paris: OECD Publications.

OECD (1993), 'Active Labour Market Policies: Assessing Macroeconomic and Microeconomic Effects', in *OECD Employment Outlook 1993*, Paris: OECD Publications, pp. 39–80.

Regnér, H. (1993), 'Choosing among Alternative Nonexperimental Methods for Estimating the Impact of Training: New Swedish Evidence', Meddelande, no. 8, Institutet för Social Forskning, Stockholm.

Reissert, B. (1989), 'Regionale Umverteilung der Arbeitsmarktpolitik: Hilfe für Problemregionen', *WZB–Mitteilungen*, 43, 5–8.

Rose, R. and E. C. Page (1990), 'Action in Adversity: Responses to Unemployment in Britain and Germany', *West European Politics*, 13 (4), 66–84.

Rosholm, M. (1994), 'Effektmaling af ATB m.v. Aarkus', Centre for Labour Market and Social Research. (Unpublished manuscript)

Salamon, L. M. (ed.) (1989), *Beyond Privatization. The Tools of Government Action*, Washington, DC: The Urban Institute Press.

Schmid, G. (1994), *Reorganisation der Arbeitsmarktpolitik—Märkte, politische Steuerung und Netzwerke der Weiterbildung für Arbeitslose in der Europäischen Union*, WZB discussion paper FS I 94–213, Wissenschaftszentrum Berlin für Sozialforschung.

Schmid, G., B. Reissert and G. Bruche (1992), *Unemployment Insurance and Active Labor Market Policy*, Detroit: Wayne State University Press.

Schmid, G. and K. Schömann (1994), 'Institutional Choice and Labor Market Performance', in G. Schmid (ed.), *Labor Market Institutions in Europe*, Armonk, NY: Sharpe, pp. 9–58.

Steedman, H. and K. Wagner (1987), 'A Second Look at Productivity, Machinery and Skills in Britain and Germany', *National Institute Economic Review*, 11, 84–95.

Streeck, W. and J. Hilbert, K.-H. Kevelaer, F. Maier and H. Weber (1987), *Steuerung und Regulierung der beruflichen Bildung*, Berlin: edition sigma.

Westergård-Nielsen, N. (1993), 'Effects of Training: A Fixed-effect Model', in K. Jensen and P. K. Madsen (eds), *Measuring Labour Market Measures. Evaluating the Effects of Active Labour Market Policy Initiatives*, Copenhagen: Ministry of Labour, pp. 167–99.

26. The Importance of Wage-bargaining Institutions for Employment Performance

Eileen Appelbaum and Ronald Schettkat[1]

The significance of institutions is not a matter of controversy in any of the social sciences, including economics, but there is disagreement as to which institutional arrangements best support the performance of the economy. In this chapter we discuss the likely impact of labour market institutions, in this case the wage-bargaining system, on employment in industrialized economies. Political scientists have discussed these issues under the label of 'corporatism' and, more recently, economists have taken up the discussion, often under the label of 'wage bargaining and economic performance'.

The general tenet of the literature is that institutions have a strong influence on labour market performance, but the specific relationship between wage-bargaining institutions and economic performance remains unclear. Some economists take the view that more organized wage determination means better compensation for external shocks and, thus, leads to a reduction in the nonaccelerating inflation rate of unemployment (NAIRU). This view of a negative linear relation between the centralization of wage bargaining and unemployment has been challenged in recent work, where it is argued that both centralized and decentralized wage-bargaining systems are able to produce favourable employment outcomes through wage restraint, albeit through completely different mechanisms. In a decentralized bargaining system wage restraint is achieved by market pressure, whereas in a centralized system the central wage negotiator internalizes the negative effects of overly high wage increases and, thus, acts as if the market coordinates wage determination. Countries with wage bargaining at an intermediate level, for example, with branch-level negotiations, are subject to the market power of organized labour, which does not internalize negative feedback effects. These countries, therefore, experience poorer employment performance.

1 We wish to thank Yan Yuan for extremely competent programming and Richard Jackman as well as Günther Schmid for their very thoughtful comments.

Usually, the literature deals with the employment and unemployment impacts of the aggregate real wage and not explicitly with the wage structure; nor is the employment structure of the economies with respect to industry discussed. However, the industrialized economies differ enormously as regards sectoral composition of employment and wage differentials. In the last two decades or so the industrial economies have exhibited a negative or at best zero correlation between productivity growth and employment growth by industry (Appelbaum and Schettkat, 1995). This fact is at variance with the positive correlations described by Salter (1960) as being characteristic of industrialized economies earlier this century, which provided the underlying rationale for the Swedish (Rehn–Meidner) model of wage and industrial policy. Under the new circumstances aggregate employment growth is dependent on a substantial expansion of employment in lower productivity-growth industries, mainly services.

The change in the relationship between productivity growth and employment growth coincided with rising unemployment; that is, with disequilibrium in the labour market. In this context labour market institutions achieved increasing importance. In conditions of near-full employment, and with nominal wages and employment rising most strongly in high productivity-growth industries, there was little scope for institutional differences between countries to have an effect on outcomes. As an inverse relationship began to develop between employment growth and productivity growth, however, the achievement of an overall increase in employment came to depend on an expansion of industries with lower productivity growth. The significance of institutional differences between countries then became apparent as different institutional settings proved to be more or less conducive to the promotion of employment growth in lower productivity-growth industries, usually services.

Here, we discuss theories of wage determination in industrialized economies as well as efforts to measure those institutional arrangements that affect it (see section 1). Most writers focus on the relationship between wage-bargaining institutions and aggregate wage restraint and, through this mechanism, on aggregate employment growth. But by the 1980s interindustry patterns of employment growth had emerged as an important influence on trends in aggregate employment, suggesting that a second effect of wage-bargaining institutions on wages, namely on interindustry wage dispersion, might also be important. The argument is that wage-bargaining institutions affect wage dispersion and, through this mechanism, affect employment growth in private services. In addition, we argue that a broader definition of corporatism (see section 2), which includes coordination with government, may affect employment growth in publicly provided or subsidized services. Our conclusion is that overall employment growth was weakest in the 1980s in those countries that lack both high interindustry wage dispersion and highly developed corporatist institutions.

1   WAGE BARGAINING AND ECONOMIC PERFORMANCE: THEORETICAL ISSUES

Some economists argue that the power of unions to fix wages increased over time because unemployment insurance and other welfare-state measures led to reduced wage pressure from the unemployed. Thus, a higher rate of unemployment is required if a noninflationary path of economic development is to be achieved. In other words, the NAIRU has increased over time. Although one finds cross-country evidence for the impact of welfare-state measures on unemployment (see, e.g. Layard, Nickell and Jackman, 1991), it is difficult to identify these relations in longitudinal analyses (see, e.g. Houseman and Abraham, 1995; Schettkat, 1995).

The effect of unemployment on the behaviour of unions as regards wage determination generally depends on the objective function of the union, which may be strongly influenced by the size and composition of the labour force share a union represents. Two effects of the extent of representation on collective bargaining have been identified: (a) with increasing comprehensiveness, unions gain market power that may be used to push up wages and working standards. At the same time, (b) as organizations encompass larger groups, the negative effects of wage bargaining become endogenous.[2] Mancur Olson's (1982) theory suggests that special interest groups are most damaging once they have gained a certain amount of power, but little responsibility.

For unions that organize only a fraction of the labour force (such as occupational or company unions) unemployment is only relevant if their membership is affected, because such a union will not have to give consideration to the financial costs of unemployment, the bulk of which are carried by people outside the organization. Most of these costs are external to the union's utility function. The situation is different, however, if the union's membership comprises the entire labour force, as in the case of centralized national unions. Now all external effects of the union's action enter directly into the union's utility function. If, for example, a wage increase generates unemployment, tax increases needed to finance the additional unemployment benefits will reduce the net wage increase for the union's membership. In other words, negative effects of its actions are endogenous to this union. The internaliza-

---

2 A comprehensive organization can exist at different levels, but a prerequisite is that the membership over which the organization has effective authority must be coterminous with the population that will bear any adverse consequences of action (Crouch, 1992).

tion of external effects is one way in which the degree to which a union encompasses the labour force can affect the wage-bargaining process. The other is the power of the unions to enforce wage increases. The latter can be assumed to be a positive function of the share of the labour force organized by the union.

If a union and an individual employer bargain over wages, the trade-off between a wage increase and employment greatly depends on the price elasticity of demand for the firm's product.[3] A monopolistic firm facing price-inelastic demand for its product can simply pass wage increases on to its customers without damaging demand. Monopolies are rare, and most firms are confronted with competitors who provide products that can serve as substitutes.[4] In the extreme case, that is, in an atomistic, perfectly competitive market, firms are facing a completely elastic demand, so that cost and subsequent price rises will reduce the demand for the product of a specific firm to zero.[5] Therefore, in perfectly competitive markets the trade-off between wage increases and employment at the firm level is quite clear and will be recognized by company unions in wage bargaining (for an excellent summary of the theoretical discussion on possible externalities of wage bargaining see Calmfors (1993)). In short, the power of unions at the company level is limited by competition in the product market.

The decisions of branch-level unions may be founded on a similar objective function to that of company unions. Again, a substantial proportion of the financing of unemployment can be externalized, but, at the same time, competitive forces may be less powerful because product market substitutes are less likely to be available and, therefore, branch-level unions will face lower demand elasticities (in absolute value) than company unions.[6] The power of a national union to fix wages will be even greater, but now the negative effects

---

3 Wolfgang Franz (1995) points out that, in the case of company bargaining, the wage conflict takes place in the firm, whereas branch-level negotiations shift the conflict away from the actual process and may, therefore, reduce frictions in production.

4 Price increases caused by wage increases can be expressed by: $d \log p = \alpha \, d \log w$, where p = price, w = wage, α = the share of labour costs that usually increases with the level of aggregation. The output effect then depends on the price elasticity of demand: $d \log Y = \eta \, d \log p$, where η = price elasticity of demand ($\eta < 0$). In competitive markets η would be equal to ∞; η will be lower for an industry than for a firm. Thus, the effects of α and of η work in different directions.

5 Synchronization of wage increases means that every firm in an industry is in the same position, and all firms may raise prices in accordance with cost increases at the same time.

6 The impact of increased world market competition, or, in other words, the growth of the exposed sector, should flatten the trade-off curve between centralization of the wage-bargaining system and likely negative effects. In the extreme case, when foreign products are perfect substitutes for domestic products, national institutions would become irrelevant. In effect, a national industry has no more power over price setting than a competitive firm in these circumstances.

of wage determination are entirely endogenous. If workers lose their jobs and become dependent on benefits, these benefits will be financed by members of the union; hence, overly high wage increases directly affect the members' net wages. Similarly, if wage increases induce inflation, the real wage of the union's members will be directly affected. Therefore, it is argued, centralized unions (and employers' associations) will take the macroeconomic effects of their actions into account because there is simply no outside world to which negative effects can be shifted.

Such considerations of Olson's theory have led economists (Calmfors and Driffill, 1988) to argue that wage bargaining at the company level (decentralized), but also at the national level (centralized), leads to favourable macroeconomic outcomes, such as low unemployment, low inflation and high employment rates. Economies with an intermediate level of wage bargaining, however, suffer from union power that does not internalize negative effects. These countries are, therefore, expected to experience less favourable macroeconomic outcomes.

However, it may be that the influence of wage restraint on company unions is substantially weaker in nonperfect markets. And, most importantly, the impact of wage changes in a company on product prices depends substantially on the amount of intermediate products this company uses. The share of wage costs in output is roughly 20 per cent at the firm level, whereas at the aggregate level it is about 70 per cent (Nickell, 1988). These figures suggest that the impact of the negative effects of wage determination declines monotonically with aggregation. In other words, the more encompassing the organizations are, the more they take the negative effects of their actions into account. The microhorizon widens to the macrohorizon as the degree of corporation increases. The relationship between the centralization of wage bargaining and wage restraint may, therefore, be negatively sloped from the beginning.

Depending on the assumed specific forms of the 'union wage-determination power function' (wage-restraint function) and the form of the 'externalization function', the resulting curve has different shapes and, consequently, quite different theoretical expectations as to the effects of wage bargaining on economic performance emerge. Figure 26.1 illustrates two possible relations. In the left panel the creation of negative external effects is above the internalization function and both are nonlinear, perhaps producing the hump-shaped curve for the net effect, as proposed in Calmfors and Driffill (1988). In the right panel, on the other hand, the internalization function of negative external effects is above the creation function, which may result in a negative linear function for the net effect. Authors who favour such a (linear) negative relation between the centralization of wage bargaining and wage restraint are Bruno and Sachs (1986), Layard, Nickell and Jackman (1991) and Soskice (1990).

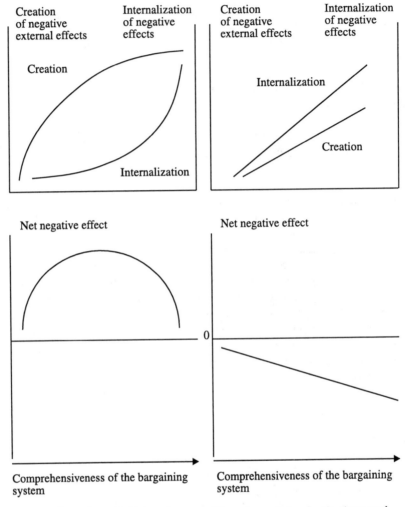

Figure 26.1   Some Relations between Wage-bargaining Institutions and
Negative External Effects

2   CORPORATISM AND WAGE BARGAINING: MEASUREMENT ISSUES

Broadly speaking, the literature on corporatism and wage-bargaining systems emphasizes the institutional capacity of societies to organize wage bargaining in accordance with macroeconomic needs. Lehmbruch (1984) gives three definitions of corporatism that are further developed in the literature: (a) the

Table 26.1   Ranking of Countries by Degree of 'Corporatism' in the 1970s

Countries	Rankings		
	min	max	median
United States	1	5	2
Japan	2	11	5
Canada	1	4	2
United Kingdom	1	6	4
Netherlands	5	11	8
France	1	6	4
Australia	3	9	6
Belgium	4	10	7
Germany	7	12	9
Austria	10	13	13
Norway	9	12	12
Sweden	9.5	13	11
Finland	6	13	9

Sources and brief characterization of original indices:
Calmfors and Driffill (1988): centralization of unions and employers' organizations;
Bruno and Sachs (1986): centralization of unions, shop-floor representation, employer coordination, existence of works councils;
Blyth (1979): level of bargaining, union and employer cooperation;
Cameron (1984): centralization of unions, control capacity of central organization, union membership;
Tarantelli (1986): degree of ideological and political consensus of unions and employers, centralization of bargaining, regulation of industrial conflict;
Lijphardt and Crepaz (1991): average of several other indices; Schettkat (in press): coverage and bargaining level based on OECD data.

development and strengthening of centralized organizations with an exclusive right of representation, (b) the privileged access of centralized organizations to government and (c) social partnership between labour and capital to regulate conflict between both groups and coordination with government.[7] The first definition is the one most in line with debates in economics about the effects of wage bargaining on economic performance. The third definition is

7 Crouch (1985) distinguishes between the Scandinavian countries, where social democratic parties represented labour's interests in governments for long periods, and government systems in which parties seldom gain an absolute majority and that are therefore based on consensus, as, for example, in the Netherlands, Germany and Belgium. He concludes that countries in which wage bargaining is coordinated are, at the same time, countries with a tradition of social democratic governments or are countries that are consociational. Other countries (United States, United Kingdom, Belgium, France, Canada, Ireland, Italy, Japan, Australia and New Zealand) are classified as liberal by Crouch. This classification roughly matches that of Lehmbruch (1984), who classifies Japan and France as 'concertation without labour', where, in the case of Japan, employers' associations dominate (see also Soskice, 1990). France, on the other hand, is characterized by the strong role of the state.

the most comprehensive and includes governments as well as workers and firms. It underlies the classification of some political scientists. However, even if one concentrates on the wage-bargaining process itself, corporatism is not a one-dimensional variable. Rather, the potential impacts of wage-bargaining systems depend, at a minimum, on the level at which bargaining takes place and on the share of workers covered by collective agreements.

No standard definition of 'corporatism' exists, institutional features are often difficult to quantify, and a combination of different variables in one indicator is always somewhat arbitrary. Not surprisingly, therefore, a substantial part of the literature deals with classification issues, and the same country may be labelled 'corporatist' in one study but 'noncorporatist' in another. Table 26.1 gives the minimum, maximum and median rankings of countries collected from such studies. Studies that cover all countries mentioned are included in the comparison. The variations are particularly high for Japan (nine points) but also substantial for other countries.

Some authors use union density as a means to capture the share of the work force affected by collective bargaining and to estimate the degree to which wage agreements are implemented and enforced. High union density leads, by definition, to high coverage, but, as the example of France shows (see Table 26.2, columns 1 to 4), high coverage can be achieved even with low union density. Collectively negotiated contracts extended by law to nonorganized employees and employers have similar effects to high union density (and/or the degree of employer organization) in spreading the coverage of the contracts (for an overview of extension rules see Hartog and Theeuwes, 1993).[8]

The level at which wage bargaining takes place is important as well. Layard et al. (1991, p. 138) argue, in line with Olson's (1982) analysis of the impact of specific interest groups, that the degree of union coverage can have very different effects, depending on whether the bargaining system is centralized or decentralized. When union density, and hence union power, is high but bargaining is decentralized, high inflation and high unemployment may result because the decentralized bargaining units do not take the macroeconomic effects of their actions into account. In a centralized bargaining system, however, the negative effects are internalized and, thus, unemployment and inflation will be low.

---

8 Legal extension may actually influence union density and the degree of employer organization. With legal extension workers will gain from collective agreements without being a member of a union and without carrying any costs; thus, the incentive to join a union may be reduced. Employers, on the other hand, may want to influence the results of negotiations if these apply to them and, thus, may have an incentive to join the employers' association. It is the actual coverage rate that is important, whether it is achieved by a high degree of union density or by extension.

Table 26.2 Indicators Characterizing Wage-bargaining Systems and Wage Differentials

	Union density		Coverage rate		Bargaining level		Comprehensiveness ranking[a]		Calmfors–Driffill index[a]		Wage differentials top decile/lowest decile		Variance of logarithms of industry earnings (%)[b]		Coefficient of var. industry earnings (%)[b]
	75	85	70s	80s	70s	80s	1970s	1980s	1970s	1980s	1980	1990	1975	1986	1985
United States	23	18	26	18	1	1	1	1	2	1	4.8	5.6	25.0	28.0	22.0
Japan	34	29	28	23	1	1	2	1	4	1	4.3	4.6	26.0	29.0	29.0
Canada	34	36	37	38	1	1	3	2	1	1	4.0	4.4	22.0	26.0	22.0
Switzerland	33	29	53	53	2	2	4	3	3	2	—	—	19.0	17.0	16.0
New Zealand	50	47	67	67	2	2	5	6	8	6	—	—	—	—	19.0
Portugal	52	52	70	79	2	2.5	6	7	5	7	—	2.6	—	—	—
United Kingdom	48	46	76	47	2	1	7	16	10	16	3.0	3.9	19.0	19.0	17.0
Netherlands	38	29	76	71	2.5	2	8	4	6	4	2.0	2.3	15.0	16.0	11.0
Spain	30	16	67	68	2	2	9	9	7	9	—	—	—	—	—
France	23	16	85	92	2	2	10	8	9	8	3.1	3.0	15.0	14.0	12.0
Australia	56	57	88	80	2	1	11	14	11	14	2.6	2.8	19.0	20.0	18.0
Belgium	55	54	90	90	2	2	12	5	15	5	2.5	2.3	17.0	19.0	15.0
Germany	37	37	91	90	2	2	13	12	14	12	2.6	2.5	21.0	25.0	12.0
Austria	56	49	98	98	3	2	14	13	13	13	3.4	3.5	21.0	25.0	21.0
Norway	53	56	75	75	3	3	15	15	12	15	2.1	2.0	9.0	10.0	13.0
Sweden	82	94	83	83	3	2	16	17	16	17	2.0	2.1	9.0	10.0	8.0
Finland	67	69	95	95	3	1.5	17	11	17	10	—	—	—	—	16.0

		Comprehensiveness ranking 1970s	Comprehensiveness 1980s	Calmfors–Driffill index	Wage differentials top decile/lowest decile		Variance of logarithms of industry earnings		Coeff. of var.
Wage differentials top decile/lowest decile	1980 [10]	−0.81	−0.65	−0.71	1.00				
	1990 [11]	−0.87	−0.76	−0.76	0.96	1.00			
Variance of logarithms of industry earnings	1975 [12]	−0.73	−0.55	−0.65	0.88	0.98	1.00		
	1986 [13]	−0.62	−0.61	−0.48	0.87	0.94	1.00	0.94	
Coefficient of variation of industry earnings	1985 [14]	−0.67	−0.63	−0.52	0.87	0.94	0.94		1.0

Notes

a low rankings = low degree of 'corporatism';

b hourly earnings weighted by employment; male and female earnings counted as distinct observations; manufacturing only;

— = data not available or not applicable.

Sources: See p. 800.

Sourcs to Table 26.2
Columns 7 and 8: *Behind the U-shape. Wage Bargaining Systems and Economic Performance* by R. Schettkat (in press).
Columns 10 and 11: 'Earning Inequality: Changes in the 1980s' by OECD, 1993, *Employment Outlook*, Paris: OECD, 157–84; values for UK, Japan and Australia estimates based on male–female deciles compared to averages wages from *Inter-country Comparison of Labor Force Trends and of Related Developments: An Overview*, NBER working paper, no. 1438, by J. Mincer, 1984. Values are not strictly comparable between countries.
Columns 12 and 13: 'Labor Market Institutions and Economic Performance' by R. Freeman, 1988, *Economic Policy*, 6, 63–80.
Column 14: *Measuring Employment Performance* by R. E. Rowthorn, 1994, background paper prepared for ILO, Geneva: ILO.

Rowthorn (1992) argues that coordination of wage bargaining does not necessarily depend on formal structures and that unions may coordinate wage bargaining outside these structures. This is the case with covert coordination, for example, in Germany, where the metal workers' union usually sets the benchmark for wage increases in other industries (see Meyer, 1990; OECD, 1994). According to Soskice (1990), not only can wage coordination take place outside formal structures, but it does not even require a centralized and highly organized labour movement. Japan is, in his view, an economy with coordinated wage determination, although it has a formally decentralized bargaining system.[9]

Thus, the theoretical debate suggests that an index that characterizes wage bargaining would need to capture the *coverage* and the *level* at which wage bargaining takes place. Even centralized wage bargaining will have little effect if only a small proportion of workers is covered. The *comprehensiveness index* displayed in columns 7 and 8 of Table 26.2 measures these two components of wage bargaining. It is not an attempt to measure corporatism according to the definition that includes government involvement. The advantages of this index are that it captures the components regarded as most relevant in the theoretical literature and that both components can be measured easily. Most importantly, data for the 1970s and the 1980s are available for both components for most countries. Hence, we are able to account for changes in the wage-bargaining systems.

The widely used index developed by Lars Calmfors and John Driffill (1988) is constructed by taking the sum of the level at which coordination of wage bargaining takes place (firm level; industry level; national level) and the number of central unions and employers' associations (no central union; more

---

9 This is the reason why Japan ranks high in the Tarantelli index. Low rankings for Japan (e.g. in the Calmfors–Driffill index) stem from company bargaining. Employer-coordinated bargaining may have different effects on the wage structure than bargaining coordinated by unions. Aggregate wage coordination can be achieved by the so-called *Shunto* offensive, but the Japanese economy is known to have substantial differences between small and big firms with respect to wages and working conditions, which may be the result of decentralized bargaining (Aoki, 1988; Deutschmann, 1989). Wage differentials are very high in Japan (see Table 26.2), but, according to Tarantelli (1986), these are based on distributional consensus and, consequently, Japan ranks high in his index.

than one central union and/or employers' association; one central union and one central employers' association). Therefore, this index cannot be used to measure how many workers are covered by collective bargaining. However, the Calmfors–Driffill index correlates highly with the comprehensiveness index ($r = 0.9$ for the 1970s, $r = 0.82$ for the 1980s).

Institutions are often regarded as being very stable, but most studies of corporatism and economic performance were published in the early and mid-1980s and refer mainly to the 1970s. Since then, however, substantial changes have taken place in some countries. In Sweden centralized bargaining disappeared in the early 1980s, in the United Kingdom the unions' influence diminished, and New Zealand switched from multiemployer bargaining to single-employer bargaining (see columns 5 and 6 in Table 26.2). However, there is no uniform trend towards more decentralized bargaining. In some countries wage bargaining became more centralized, and many countries did not change at all (for details see OECD, 1994).

3 BARGAINING INSTITUTIONS AND WAGE BEHAVIOUR

Calmfors and Driffill (1988) supported their proposed hump-shaped relation between real wage growth and the degree of centralization of the bargaining system with regressions of unemployment rates (employment rates) on their indicator for centralization (see section 3) in a hump-shaped (u-shaped) form.[10] This procedure has been criticized as being an overly reduced model because the effects should run through the wage-determination mechanism, which is better tested directly (Freeman, 1988). Most analysis deals with the impact of the wage-bargaining system on aggregate wage flexibility, which we will discuss only briefly before we turn to the wage structure. Testing for the responsiveness of wage determination to unemployment—the crucial variable—Layard et al. (1991), using the Calmfors–Driffill index, did not find the hump-shaped relation proposed by Calmfors and Driffill but, instead, a linear one. The more wage bargaining is centralized, the higher the responsiveness of wage determination to unemployment. Similar results, albeit on the basis of the comprehensiveness index (see Table 26.2), were achieved in another study of aggregate wage determination (Schettkat, in press).

Only a few studies of bargaining systems and economic performance take wage dispersion into account (Appelbaum and Schettkat, 1993; Freeman,

---

10 Countries at the low and the high end of the ranking (see Table 26.2) got a value of one. The adjacent countries were assigned the value two etc.

1988; Rowthorn, 1992). In general, wage-bargaining systems are associated with wage differentials in a linear way: low-ranking countries have high wage differentials and high-ranking countries have low wage differentials. Wage differentials are often calculated on the basis of national accounts data, which means that intraindustry wage differentials are disregarded. Recent work following the microdata study by Alan Krueger and Lawrence Summers (1988) has made more detailed information available (see Freeman and Katz, 1995; OECD, 1993). The general picture that emerges for wage differentials across countries from the different data sources displayed in Table 26.2 is very consistent (see lower panel in Table 26.2 for correlations). In cross-country comparison[11] wage differentials decline with increasing values of the ranking in Table 26.2 (columns 7 to 9).

Sweden, for example, is a country that ranked high prior to the early 1980s and was known for its solidaristic wage policy, which was intended to reduce wage differentials between industries and skill groups (Flanagan, 1987; Meidner and Hedborg, 1984). Sweden's wage differentials are still outstandingly low, although they increased throughout the 1980s when the Swedish bargaining system became more decentralized. However, compared to the institutional change in wage-determination institutions in Sweden, as indicated by the decline in the bargaining level (columns 5 and 6 in Table 26.2), wage differentials changed slowly. Austria, a country that ranks high on any measure of 'corporatism', has always had very high wage differentials (see Table 26.2).[12] The general picture is not affected by the measure of wage inequality used. The various measures for wage dispersion displayed in Table 26.2 correlate highly (see lower panel). This is empirical evidence that wage-bargaining systems not only affect aggregate wage flexibility (see above) but that they affect the wage structure as well. The latter may have been important in low-growth periods after the mid-1970s.

Relative wages play an important role in economic theory. Keynes (1936) regarded relative wages as the key variable for the explanation of workers' resistance to nominal wage reductions and acceptance of real wage reductions caused by price increases. Keynes' answer was that in the first case there is

---

11 Of course, wage differentials are difficult to compare between countries because gross and net wages may differ substantially, as may the services provided by the public sector.

12 Austria, however, seems to be an outlier because countries with a high comprehensiveness index tend to have low wage differentials. One explanation put forward for the Austrian–Swedish difference is the different historical development of the corporatist arrangements in the two countries (Therborn, 1992). In Sweden corporatist institutions—highlighted by the Saltjöbadan agreement (Meidner and Hedborg, 1984)—developed as a solution to industrial conflicts that damaged economic performance. In contrast, the Austrian labour movement was based more on consensus after World War II (Guger, 1992). Recently, Zweimüller and Bart (1994) argued that high values of wage dispersion in Austria are, to a large extent, caused by human capital differentials.

insecurity about the individual worker's position in the wage scale, whereas real wage reductions caused by price increases leave workers' relative positions unchanged (see also Tobin, 1972). Although this argument actually gives a rationale for nominal wage rigidity based on imperfect information, it became known as the irrational money illusion in the neoclassical synthesis. 'Equal pay for equal work'[13] is part of almost every union's programme, and more centralized unions are certainly better able to enforce such a concept.[14] However, some groups in the labour markets are in higher demand than others, and these groups constantly try to improve their relative position. Group-specific interests can be better controlled in a centralized bargaining setting,[15] and it may well be that a higher degree of centralization in the wage-bargaining system will result in lower wage differentials, as is confirmed by empirical analysis (Freeman, 1988; Schettkat, in press).

It has been argued that a greater wage dispersion was necessary in the 1980s because of changing skill requirements, and countries which could not provide the new type of labour because of inflexible educational systems experienced rises in wage inequality. Countries with a flexible response in the supply of skilled labour, on the other hand, were able to avoid increases in wage inequality (see Freeman and Katz, 1995). In addition, productivity nowadays may depend less on equipment than previously, while motivation, work organization and participation in decision-making may have gained in importance. Efficiency wage theory, for example, suggests that productivity is endogenous and that higher wages will improve productivity by various mechanisms (see Akerlof and Yellen, 1986, for an overview). Thus, it is efficient to pay higher wages. Gibbons and Freeman (1995) as well as Ramaswany and Rowthorn (1993) have used these mechanisms to explain the decline of centralized wage bargaining in Sweden.

---

13 Horst Albach (1995) shows that a standard wage leads to rationalization pressure in firms with below-average performance, but that it allows for innovative activity in firms with above-average performance.

14 One explanation is that low-paid members are overrepresented in unions and that this group pushes up wages at the lower end, thus reducing wage dispersion (Freeman, 1988). The Swedish 'solidaristic wage policy' (designed by Gösta Rehn and Rudolf Meidner; see Meidner and Hedborg, 1984) was intended to accelerate aggregate productivity growth compared to the market outcome (for arguments along similar lines see Bell and Freeman, 1985). This policy runs into problems, however, if employment in high productivity-growth industries ceases to expand, as seems to be case throughout the industrialized countries (see Appelbaum and Schettkat, 1993, for a theoretical argument).

15 This was a continuous problem for the Swedish LO (Meidner and Hedborg, 1984). Wage drift always existed in the Swedish economy; Flanagan (1990) reports that the wage drift measured between 20 per cent (white collar) and 45 per cent (blue collar) of wage increases in Sweden in the 1970s and 1980s. The wage drift varies, as expected, over the business cycle. It is high when unemployment is low, and it is low in recession (Edgren, Faxen and Odhner, 1973).

However, it may well be that wage dispersion itself influences the structure of economies as well. Behind the u-shaped (hump-shaped) relation between the employment (unemployment) rate and the bargaining system, as found by Calmfors and Driffill (1988), the wage structure and 'corporatism' in the wider sense may actually be hidden.

4   UNEMPLOYMENT AND EMPLOYMENT TRENDS

The nonlinear relations between wage-bargaining institutions and unemployment (hump-shaped) and employment (u-shaped) were discovered in the 1980s (Calmfors and Driffill, 1988; Freeman, 1988; Rowthorn, 1992). Calmfors and Driffill (1988) proposed a theoretical explanation for these non-linear relations in which extremes of the wage-bargaining institution scheme do well because they create aggregate wage restraint (see discussion above). However, Rowthorn (1992), using the Calmfors–Driffill index, discovered that the relations are valid for the 1980s but cannot be found for the early 1970s, when almost all industrialized countries were experiencing full employment.

In Table 26.3 we illustrate a regression analysis for unemployment rates and employment-to-population ratios (employment rates) on the Calmfors–Driffill index, which we use for comparisons with other studies. In line with Rowthorn's (1992) results (also based on the Calmfors–Driffill index), we do not find empirical evidence for a nonlinear relation between the comprehensiveness of the bargaining system and employment and unemployment rates for the early 1970s. If anything, there is a negative linear relation between the unemployment rate and the index. This relation changes in the 1980s, when the hump-shaped (u-shaped) relation for unemployment (employment) emerges. The difference is most apparent when changes in the rates rather than levels are used (lower panel in Table 26.3). In other words, the relationship between wage-bargaining systems and unemployment (employment) seems to have changed substantially between the early 1970s and the 1980s.[16]

Why is it, then, that the hump-shaped relation can be found in the 1980s, but is not apparent during the full-employment period of the early 1970s?[17]

---

16 It is not true, however, that countries with low increases in unemployment rates achieved them through reduced labour force participation. On the contrary, labour supply and employment performed better in countries at the extremes of the bargaining system than in the intermediate countries.

17 The sensitivity of the aggregate wage-determination process with respect to unemployment supports a positive linear relationship to the comprehensiveness of the wage-bargaining system (see Layard et al., 1991; Schettkat, in press).

Although institutions may have changed substantially, it is unlikely that the underlying structures in the economy created by these institutions have changed as rapidly.[18] In view of the facts that most employment growth has occurred in service industries and that some services are suffering from the 'cost disease' (Baumol, 1967), one explanation may be sought in differences between public and private sector growth. Employment in services with low productivity-growth rates may be traded in private markets if wages are sufficiently downwardly flexible, which may overcome the negative demand effect of rising relative prices in these services. Thus, in countries with less centralized wage-bargaining systems, which usually have lower wage dispersion, employment expansion may have taken place in privately provided consumer services.[19]

But economies with comprehensive bargaining systems and low wage differentials also experienced high employment growth, mainly in industries that provide services to consumers as well (Scharpf, 1990). However, in these cases employment and service provision is publicly organized (financed or directly provided). Public provision (demarketization: see Glyn, 1992) means the negative effect of rising relative prices for consumer services is overcome and, thus, employment expansion in these industries is enabled without high wage differentials. These considerations are supported by the positive linear relationship between the Calmfors–Driffill index and the ratio of public employment to population and the negative relationship to private service employment (see Figure 26.2).

These trends in household-oriented service provision seem to be the major differences in stylized employment development in countries with centralized and decentralized wage-bargaining systems. High wage dispersion allowed for an increase in private employment, even in jobs that do not have high productivity growth, but this means of employment creation was not available in the countries with centralized bargaining systems. Here, public employment expansion was the solution to the employment problem. That is, it was not the high level of integration of different interest groups in the bargaining system itself (corporatism in the narrow sense) but rather the interaction with government (corporatism in the broadest sense) that was behind the favourable employment trends.

---

18 Although wage-bargaining institutions changed over time, wage differentials did not change substantially when countries moved to less centralized bargaining. Decentralization seems to be connected to rising wage differentials, but this is a slow process, and the bargaining structure of the 1970s still explains international differences in wage differentials in the 1980s quite well (Schettkat, in press).

19 One has to keep in mind that, while international comparative analysis is able to account for institutional variety, at the same time, the number of available variables is very small, which limits the possibilities for analysis.

Table 26.3   Regression Analysis of the Labour Market Performance on Wage-bargaining Systems

Dependent variable		Independent variables		Summary statistics		
		Constant	CD-U	R^2	F	N
Levels						
Unemployment rate						
	70–73	3.32	−0.28	0.15	2.3	15
		(1.25)	(0.21)			
	85–89	3.13	0.74	0.23	3.78	15
		(1.81)	(0.38)			
Employment-to-population ratio						
	70–73	69.69	−0.54	0.04	0.55	15
		(5.35)	(0.73)			
	85–89	74.67	−1.84	0.22	3.67	15
		(4.60)	(0.96)			
Changes						
Unemployment rate						
	70/80s	−0.19	1.02	0.5	13.11	15
		(1.34)	(0.28)			
Employment-to-population ratio						
	70/80s	5	−1.3	0.25	4.3	15
		(3)	(0.63)			

Notes
CD-U = ranking of countries according to the Calmfors–Driffill index, in u-shaped form;
Level refers to average rates for the indicated period;
Changes are computed as follows: 70/80 = average for the period 1985–89 minus 1970–73;
The linear version of the indices was never significant.
In brackets: heteroscedastic consistent standard errors.

5   CONCLUDING SUMMARY

In this chapter we discussed the impact of wage-bargaining institutions on labour market performance, as measured by the employment-to-population ratio and the unemployment rate. We found a u-shaped (hump-shaped) relation between the degree of centralization of the wage-bargaining system and the employment-to-population ratio (unemployment rate) in the 1980s, but not in the early 1970s. The widely discussed nonlinear relation between centralization and labour market performance was mainly the result of developments that occurred during the 1970s and 1980s. Unemployment rose slightly— although from different levels—in economies at the decentralized, but also at the centralized, extreme, whereas economies in the middle experienced substantial increases in unemployment and low growth rates of employment.

Growth rates of employment-to-population ratios

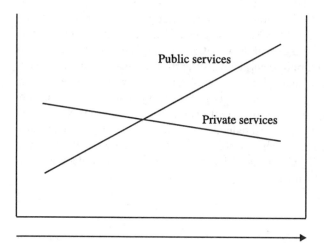

Centralization of the wage-bargaining system

Notes
Private services: community, social, personal, recreational;
Public services: government sector according to national accounts;
CD = ranking according to Calmfors and Driffill (1988).

Regressions:
Average growth rate private services = $R^2 = 0.37, F(1.8) = 4.8$
$1.5 - 0.08$ CD
$(0.19)\ (0.03)$

Average growth rate public services = $R^2 = 0.48, F(1.8) = 7.6$
$-0.25 + 0.23$ CD
$(0.42)\ (0.08)$
Heteroscedastic consistent standard errors in brackets.

Figure 26.2   Behind the U-shape: Stylized Relations between Private and Public Employment Growth and the Wage-bargaining System

Michael Brunos and Jeffrey Sachs' argument that inflationary pressure is reduced by aggregate wage restraint and that there is, thus, a linear decline in the NAIRU with the degree of corporatism may hold for the 1960s and early 1970s. But inflation was not a major problem in the 1980s; economic growth was much lower and unemployment was, in general, higher than in earlier periods. In the 1980s wage differentiation was probably more important for employment growth in the private sector than aggregate wage restraint, which is almost automatically achieved by high unemployment. The underlying employment trends are very different in countries with decentralized and those with centralized bargaining systems, although employment in services increased in both in the 1980s. It was private, market-oriented employment that expanded in countries with less centralized bargaining systems, whereas in countries with centralized bargaining systems it was mainly public employment that expanded and raised tax rates. Countries with an intermediate degree of centralization in the wage-bargaining system, however, did not experience the employment growth of the countries at the extremes but tried to hold unemployment down via a reduction of labour supply (e.g. through early retirement). But high transfers are costly as well and, consequently, tax rates rose here, too, albeit without the advantages of additional production, consumption and employment.

REFERENCES

Akerlof, G. and J. Yellen (1986), *Efficiency Wage Models of the Labor Market*, Cambridge: Cambridge University Press.

Albach, H. (1995), *Notwendige Innovationen in der Lohnpolitik*, WZB discussion paper FS IV 95–14, Wissenschaftszentrum Berlin für Sozialforschung.

Aoki, M. (1988), *Information, Incentives, and Bargaining in the Japanese Economy*, Cambridge: Cambridge University Press.

Appelbaum, E. and R. Schettkat (1993), *Employment Developments in Industrialized Economies*, WZB discussion paper FS I 101, Wissenschaftszentrum Berlin für Sozialforschung.

Appelbaum, E. and R. Schettkat (1995) (in press), 'The Employment Problem in Industrialized Economies', *International Labour Review*.

Baumol, W. (1967), 'Macroeconomics of Unbalanced Growth: The Anatomy of the Urban Crisis', *American Economic Review*, 57, 415–26.

Bell, L. A. and R. Freeman (1985), *Does a Flexible Wage Structure Increase Employment? The U.S. Experience*, NBER working paper, no. 1604, Cambridge, MA: National Bureau of Economic Research.

Blyth, C. A. (1979), *Interaction between Collective Bargaining and Government Policies in Selected Member Countries, Collective Bargaining and Government Policies*, Paris: OECD.

Bruno, M. and J. Sachs (1986), *Economics of Worldwide Stagflation*, Cambridge, MA: Harvard University Press.

Calmfors, L. (1993), 'Lessons from the Macroeconomic Experience of Sweden', *European Journal of Political Economy*, 9, 25–72.

Calmfors, L. and J. Driffill (1988), 'Bargaining Structure, Corporatism and Macroeconomic Performance, *Economic Policy*, 6, 14–61.

Cameron, D. R. (1984), 'Social Democracy, Corporatism, Labour Quiescence and the Representation of Economic Interest in Advanced Capitalist Society', in J. H. Goldthorpe (ed.), *Order and Conflict in Contemporary Capitalism*, Oxford:

Oxford University Press, pp. 143–78.

Crouch, C. (1985), 'Conditions for Trade Union Wage Restraint', in L. N. Lindberg and C. S. Maier (eds), *The Politics of Inflation and Economic Stagnation*, Washington, DC: Brookings Institution, pp. 105–39.

Crouch, C. (1992), 'Trade Unions in the Exposed Sector: Their Influences on Neo-corporatist Behaviour', in R. Brunetta and C. Dell'Aringa (eds), *Labor Relations and Economic Performance*, London: Macmillan, pp. 68–91.

Deutschmann, C. (1989), 'Labor Markets, Employment and Organization: Japan and West-Germany in Comparison', WZB conference paper, Wissenschaftszentrum Berlin für Sozialforschung.

Edgren, G., K.-O. Faxen and C.-E. Odhner (1973), *Wage Formation and the Economy*, London: Allen & Unwin.

Flanagan, R. (1987), 'Efficiency and Equality in Swedish Labor Markets', in B. Bosworth and A. Rivlin (eds), *The Swedish Economy*, Washington, DC: Brookings Institution, pp. 125–84.

Flanagan, R. (1990), 'Centralized and Decentralized Pay Determination in Nordic Countries', in L. Calmfors (ed.), *Wage Formation and Macroeconomic Policy in Nordic Countries*, Oxford: Oxford University Press, pp. 395–412.

Franz, W. (1995), *Die Lohnfindung in Deutschland in einer internationalen Perspektive: Ist das deutsche System ein Auslaufmodell?*, discussion paper, no. 24, Center for International Labor Economics, University Constance.

Freeman, R. (1988), 'Labor Market Institutions and Economic Performance', *Economic Policy*, 6, 63–80.

Freeman, R. and L. Katz (1995), 'Rising Wage Inequality: The United States vs Other Advanced Countries', in R. Freeman and L. Katz (eds), *Differences and Changes in Wage Structure*, Chicago: University of Chicago Press, pp. 29–62.

Glyn, A. (1992), 'Corporatism, Patterns of Employment, and Access to Consumption', in J. Pekkarinen, M. Pohjola and R. E. Rowthorn (eds), *Social Corporatism. A Superior Economic System*, Oxford: Clarendon Press, pp. 132–77.

Guger, A. (1992), 'Corporatism: Success or Failure? Austrian Experiences', in J. Pekkarinen, M. Pohjola and R. E. Rowthorn (eds), *Social Corporatism. A Superior Economic System*, Oxford: Clarendon Press, pp. 338–62.

Hartog, J. and J. Theeuwes (1993), *Labour Market Contracts and Institutions. A Cross-national Comparison*, Amsterdam: North-Holland.

Houseman, S. and K. Abraham (1995), 'Labor Adjustment under Different Institutional Structures', in F. Buttler, W. Franz, R. Schettkat and D. Soskice (eds), *Institutional Frameworks and Labor Market Performance; Comparative Views on the German and US Economies*, London/New York: Routledge, pp. 285–315.

Keynes, J. M. (1936), *The General Theory of Interest and Money*, London: Macmillan.

Krueger, A. B. and L. H. Summers (1988), 'Efficiency Wages and the Inter-industry Wage Structure', *Econometrica*, 56 (2), 259–93.

Layard, R., S. Nickell and R. Jackman (1991), *Unemployment. Macroeconomic Performance and the Labour Market*, Oxford: Oxford University Press.

Lehmbruch, G. (1984), 'Concertation and the Structure of Corporatist Networks', in J. H. Goldthorpe (ed.), *Order and Conflict in Contemporary Capitalism*, Oxford: Oxford University Press, pp. 60–80.

Lijphart, A. and M. L. Crepaz (1991), 'Corporatism and Consensus Democracy in Eighteen Countries: Conceptual and Empirical Linkages', *British Journal of Political Science*, 21, 235–56.

Meidner, R. and A. Hedborg (1984), *Modell Schweden. Erfahrungen einer Wohl-fahrtsgesellschaft*, Frankfurt on the Main/New York: Campus.

Meyer, W. (1990), *Bestimmungsfaktoren der Tariflohnbewegung. Eine empirische, mikroökonomische Untersuchung für die Bundesrepublik*, Frankfurt on the Main/New York: Campus.

Mincer, J. (1984), *Inter-country Comparison of Labor Force Trends and of Related Developments: An Overview*, NBER working paper no. 1438, Cambridge, MA: NBER.

Nickell, S. (1988), 'Discussion of Calmfors/Driffill', *Economic Policy*, 52.

OECD (1993, July), 'Earning Inequality: Changes in the 1980s', *Employment Outlook*, Paris: OECD, pp. 157–84.

OECD (1994), 'Collective Bargaining: Levels and Coverage', *Employment Outlook*, Paris: OECD.

Olson, M. (1982), *The Rise and Decline of Nations. Economic Growth, Stagflation, and Social Rigidities*, New Haven/London: Yale University Press.

Ramaswany, R. and R. E. Rowthorn (1993), *Centralized Bargaining, Efficiency Wages, and Flexibility*, IMF working paper no. 25, Washington, DC: IMF.

Rowthorn, R. E. (1992), 'Centralisation, Employment and Wage Dispersion', *The Economic Journal*, 102, 506–23.

Rowthorn, R. E. (1994), *Measuring Employment Performance*, background paper prepared for the ILO, Geneva: ILO.

Salter, W. (1960), *Productivity and Technical Change*, Cambridge: Cambridge University Press.

Scharpf, F. W. (1990), 'Structures of Post-industrial Society—or—Does Mass-unemployment Disappear in the Service and Information Economy?', in E. Appelbaum and R. Schettkat (eds), *Labor Market Adjustments to Structural Change and Technological Progress*, New York/Westport/London: Praeger Publishers, pp. 17–35.

Schettkat, R. (1995), 'The Macroperformance of the German Labor Market', in F. Buttler, W. Franz, R. Schettkat and D. Soskice (eds), *Institutional Frameworks and Labor Market Performance; Comparative Views on the German and US Economies*, London/New York: Routledge, pp. 316–42.

Schettkat, R. (in press), *Behind the U-Shape, Wage Bargaining Systems and Economic Performance*, paper prepared for OECD.

Soskice, D. (1990), 'Wage Determination: The Changing Role of Institutions in Advanced Industrialized Countries', *Oxford Review of Economic Policy*, 6 (4), 36–61.

Tarantelli, E. (1986), 'The Regulation of Inflation and Unemployment', *Industrial Relations*, 25 (1), 1–15.

Therborn, G. (1992), 'Lessons from Corporatist Theorization', in J. Pekkarinen, M. Pohjola and R. E. Rowthorn (eds), *Social Corporatism. A Superior Economic System*, Oxford: Clarendon Press, pp. 24–43.

Tobin, J. (1972), 'Inflation and Unemployment', *American Economic Review*, 62, 1–18.

Zweimüller, J. and E. Bart (1994), 'Bargaining Structure, Wage Determination, and Wage Dispersion in 6 OECD Countries', *Kyklos*, 47, 81–93.

27. Tax Regimes and Labour Market Performance

Siv Gustafsson

There is probably no single subject that has been the motivation for more research effort among academic economists than the effects of taxes on the functioning of the economy. The focus of this chapter is the labour market, which is the subject of three major fields of economic research: (a) theories of optimal taxation and the deadweight loss, (b) labour demand analysis and (c) labour supply analysis. I attempt to evaluate research results from these fields.

All tax instruments entail a wedge between supply price and demand price, but the impact of different tax instruments varies. A value-added tax (VAT) increases the price of goods and services and the price of consumption in comparison to savings. A wage-bill tax increases the demand price of labour but leaves labour supply price unaffected. It also increases the price of labour-intensive production more than it does the price of capital-intensive production. Income taxation affects labour supply through the introduction of a wedge that lowers the net wage to the worker. In the literature on optimal taxation attempts are made to ascertain which type of tax causes the least significant price distortions in the economy, contrasting actual tax devices with a lump-sum tax that has no effect on relative prices. However, actual tax systems also have income redistributive purposes, or at least must give consideration to ability to pay. Therefore, the second-best solution, that is, the one that causes the least deadweight loss, will be preferred to the best solution, the lump-sum tax. The deadweight loss is the additional cost of taxation, which is caused by consumers, producers or investors changing their behaviour because of relative price changes resulting from taxation (Auerbach, 1985; Musgrave and Musgrave, 1973; Slemrod, 1990).

The focus in the literature on labour demand is on substitutions between different factors of production: capital versus labour, educated workers versus less educated workers, men versus women, younger workers versus older workers. A tax on labour like the wage-bill tax would induce substitution of capital for labour; however, the extent of capital–labour substitution depends on the degree of elasticity for substitution. Much less effort has been devoted to labour demand analysis than to labour supply analysis. The most comprehensive recent contribution is that of Hamermesh (1993).

811

The effects of income taxes on labour supply is one of the most researched areas in microeconomics and microeconometrics. Mofitt (1990) is a collection of the most recent econometric solutions in the estimation of labour supply elasticities and the deadweight loss caused by progressive income taxation. These papers are methodological in character and give a good picture of the state of the art of the econometrical dispute. Atkinson and Morgensen (1993) is a compilation of papers that review tax systems and recent reforms as well as presenting research results on income taxation and work incentives for Sweden, the United Kingdom, Germany and Denmark. Aronsson and Walker (1995) summarize results pertaining to Sweden in particular and also provide valuable institutional information on recent policy changes in that country. A wage decrease such as income taxation introduces a substitution effect that implies that a worker now receives less per hour worked and is, therefore, more inclined to increase time spent on leisure, and an income effect that implies that he or she now has to work more hours in order to earn the same income. Which of the effects is greater is an empirical question. If the substitution effect is strong, it is likely that the tax system results in efficiency costs, or deadweight losses, because people then supply too little labour. An alternative tax system with less distortional effects, which would induce workers to supply more labour without pushing them on to a lower indifference curve, that is, without making them less happy with their situation, might be a worthwhile aim.

Price differentials in the European Union are caused by differences in the tax rates of Member States. This has been a worry in European Union politics since the beginning of the European Community (El-Agraa, 1990). In the face of European integration the different tax systems of Member States will affect resource allocation and potentially induce factor movements of labour and capital between countries. In this event countries will find their competitive situation altered, and efforts to harmonize taxes might be increased. There is, therefore, good reason to compare the tax systems of various countries and to try to evaluate their effects on equity and efficiency.

The outline of this chapter is as follows. In sections 1 and 2, I compare the regimes of different countries. Section 3 contains a brief discussion of the harmonizing efforts of the European Union. The definition and measurement of the deadweight loss are dealt with in section 4, followed by a review of the effects of taxes on work incentives and labour supply in section 5, which includes sections on the econometric controversy concerning solutions for the problem of endogeneity of net wages with working hours, work-hours packages as restrictions to free choice of working hours supplied and the effects of separate versus joint taxation of spouses' incomes. Finally, in section 6, I investigate the effects of taxes/subsidies on labour demand before providing some concluding comments. The emphasis in this chapter is on labour force participation and working hours, which also constitute the major part of studies on labour market impacts, although—as noted by Aronsson and Walker (1995)—sick leave, retirement decisions, decisions on whether to start an education, involvement in the underground economy and so on are also likely to be affected by tax regimes.

1 TAX REGIMES ACCORDING TO SOURCE OF INCOME

The structure of taxes in a country is developed on the basis of a number of considerations. Who is able to pay the tax? What is fair taxation? Which taxes and benefits will stimulate good behaviour and delimit unwanted behaviour? Is a tax regressive, that is, does it hit low-income earners harder, or is it progressive, that is, does it target high-income earners? Ideas about what is fair and what is desired behaviour, or which taxes will be more efficient in raising revenue while generating the least distortion, change over time in accordance with changes in the tax structure. Taxes and subsidies can also act as nontariff barriers to trade. Subsidies to whole industry branches, for example, shipbuilding, have been common in recent European history. A country that has a considerably lower VAT rate than other countries is at a competitive advantage when the tariff barriers have been removed and economic integration commences. Differences in personal income taxation may also result in different competitive advantages between countries, for example, in the competition for top executives. A country that has highly progressive income taxes may lose top executives. A country that discourages female labour force participation through a breadwinner ideology may in a future, more integrated Europe lose its two-earner couples and perhaps thereby also its top executives. The purpose of this section is to compare the tax regimes of various countries.

In Table 27.1 (adapted from Pechman and Engelhardt, 1990) we see the distribution of tax revenue according to source for a number of countries as of 1987. Five major categories are distinguished.

Taxes on personal income are often simply referred to as income taxes. Work effort is primarily affected by taxes due to the introduction of a wedge between the demand price, or gross wage, and the supply price, or net wage, of labour. Corporate income taxes are taxes on profits of firms; entrepreneurs often have the choice between showing a higher profit and earning a higher personal income before profit. The wage-bill tax is a percentage tax on the sum of wages that an employer must pay and, therefore, increases the demand price of labour. The motivation for a wage-bill tax has often been to cover nonwage costs of labour such as health, unemployment and pension insurance. Sometimes such social security contributions are split between the workers and the employers, one part being deducted from the workers' earnings like an income tax and the

Table 27.1   Tax Source as Per Cent of Total Tax Revenue in 1987

	Personal income	Corporate income	Wage bill	Goods and services	Property	Total
Australia	45.3	10.2	5.4	29.8	9.3	100.0
Canada	39.5	8.2	13.5	29.4	9.4	100.0
Denmark	50.8	4.6	4.4	35.0	5.2	100.0
France	13.2	5.3	46.4	30.3	4.8	100.0
Germany	29.0	5.1	37.2	25.5	3.2	100.0
Italy	26.1	10.4	34.6	26.4	2.5	100.0
Japan	24.6	22.8	28.5	12.8	11.3	100.0
Netherlands	19.8	7.7	42.7	26.0	3.8	100.0
Sweden	37.3	4.1	28.6	24.2	5.8	100.0
United Kingdom	26.6	10.6	18.1	31.4	13.3	100.0
United States	36.4	8.0	28.8	16.8	10.0	100.0

Source
'The Income Tax Treatment of the Family' by J. A. Pechman and G. V. Engelhardt, 1990, *National Tax Journal*, 43 (1), p. 4. Copyright 1990 by National Tax Journal. Adapted by permission. Original source: *Revenue Statistics of OECD Member Countries*, 1965–88, 1987, Paris: OECD.

other constituting a wage-bill tax, as in Germany and the Netherlands; in Sweden, on the other hand, social security contributions are entirely covered by a wage-bill tax, which is considerably higher than that of other countries. The most common form of taxes on goods and services are value-added taxes. Finally, property taxes are taxes on assets, such as taxes on the value of homes, which in many countries are lowered by deductions for mortgage interest rates.

Policy-makers have obviously chosen between different mixes of tax instruments, as illustrated by Table 27.1. Individual income taxes and taxes on goods and services, that is, VAT and wage-bill or payroll tax, tend to be more important as sources of tax revenue than corporate income taxes and property taxes, although there are major differences in the distribution between countries. Whereas Denmark obtains half of its tax revenue from personal income taxation, only 13.2 per cent comes from this source in France. The largest source of tax revenue is the wage-bill tax in Germany, France, Italy and the Netherlands. Property taxes and corporate income taxes are fairly insignificant sources of tax revenue in Denmark, France, Germany and Sweden, whereas they are a more important source of revenue in the Anglo-Saxon countries Australia, Canada, the United Kingdom and the United States. Compared to the other countries, Japan raises twice as large a share of tax revenue (23 per cent) in the form of a corporate income tax.

Table 27.2   Tax Regimes in OECD Countries

	Tax revenue as per cent of GNP	SWB	WBT	VAT standard
	(1)	(2)	(3)	(4)
Australia	30.1	8.3	9.0	—
Austria	41.0	18.5	22.7	—
Belgium	44.3	17.5	21.2	19.0
Canada	35.3	9.9	10.9	—
Denmark	38.1	—	—	25.0
Finland	43.8	18.8	23.2	—
France	37.8	28.2	39.3	18.6
Greece	—	—	—	18.0
Ireland	—	—	—	21.0
Italy	30.6	27.1	37.2	19.0
Japan	38.1	14.1	16.4	—
Germany	—	19.5	24.2	14.0
Luxembourg	—	—	—	12.0
Netherlands	46.0	22.6	29.2	18.5
Norway	45.5	15.1	17.8	—
Portugal	—	—	—	17.0
Spain	34.4	23.2	30.2	12.0
Sweden	56.1	27.2	37.4	25.0
Switzerland	31.8	13.0	14.9	—
United Kingdom	36.5	12.4	14.2	17.5
United States	30.1	16.3	19.5	—

Notes
SWB   = share wage-bill taxes in total earnings.
WBT   = wage-bill tax derived from (2): $t = S/(1-S)$ where t = WBT, S = SWB; figures for 1988.
—   = data not available.

Sources
The data in column (1) are from *OECD Revenue Statistics of OECD Member Countries*, 1990, Paris: OECD. Figures for 1989. The data in columns (2) and (3) are from *OECD Employment Outlook 1991*, Paris: OECD. The data in column (4) are from Swedish Taxation in an Integrated Europe by K. Andersson, 1992. Figures for 1 January 1992.

Choices between these major categories of tax sources will affect the labour market, but also details within each source of tax revenue. Further data about differences between countries is provided in Table 27.2. Column (1) shows total tax revenue as a percentage of GNP. Sweden collects by far the largest share of its GNP in taxes: 56.1 per cent in 1989. This is ten percentage points higher than other high-tax countries such as the Netherlands, Norway, Finland or Belgium, which all collect about 45 per cent of their GNP in taxes.

Column (3) shows the wage-bill tax derived from column (2). The highest wage-bill tax in 1989 was found in France, where employers had to deliver a sum equal to 39.3 per cent of employees' earnings to the tax authorities. France is closely followed by Sweden (37.4 per cent) and Italy (37.2 per cent). Such high wage-bill taxes make it very costly to employ workers, particularly if the personal income tax is also high. A personal income tax of 50 per cent and a wage-bill tax of 50 per cent would make the total wage cost three times as large as the sum of money the employed person receives, unless wage costs are deductible before income tax, as they are in companies, but not when a household employs domestic help.

The effect of VAT is an increase in the price of the goods and services on which it is levied. Column (4) of Table 27.2 gives the standard VAT rate in a number of countries. Two countries, Denmark and Sweden, had a VAT rate of 25 per cent in 1992.

In addition to the standard VAT rates, many countries levy extra high VAT on luxury goods such as cosmetics and perfumes, and extra low VAT on merit goods such as staple food and—in the Netherlands—flowers. In Sweden in 1993 the standard rate was 25 per cent, the rate for food and restaurants 21 per cent and the rate for hotels and personal transport 12 per cent (Fölster and Lindström, 1993). Recently (1995), the Swedish Social Democratic Government, in an agreement with the Centre Party (agrarian), decided to lower VAT on food to 12 per cent while keeping the standard rate of 25 per cent, illustrating that tax rates change constantly. Whether such a change is enough to transform a previously low-tax country into a high-tax country can only be analysed over a number of years. However, countries differ in their philosophy about the role of the welfare state, with some countries affording a minor, residual role to the state and others granting it a major institutional role. Esping-Andersen (1990) distinguishes between the Liberal Welfare State, taking the United States as a typical example, the Conservative Corporatist Welfare State, taking Germany as a typical example, and the Social Democratic Welfare State, exemplified by Sweden. These different philosophies on the role of the welfare state are determined by historical social processes and do not change very quickly. Consequently, one can observe some basic characteristics of the different tax regimes that remain fairly constant over time within a country.

2 INCOME TAX REGIMES

The most complicated tax is probably the personal income tax, because so many parameters vary. One country may appear to be a relatively low-tax country from the point of view of a high-income earner, but a relatively high-tax country from the perspective of a low-income earner. In order to compare income taxation between countries, Pechman and Engelhardt (1990) have computed deductions and effective tax rates for an average production worker

Table 27.3   Income Tax Regimes. Rates for Average Production Worker and High-income Earner

	Basic deduction		Basic deduction transferable from non-working spouse	Joint filing	Effective average tax rate		High-income single
	Single	Couple			Single	Family	
	(1)	(2)	(3)	(4)	(5)	(6)	(7)
Australia	18.8	37.6		no[d]	25.3	13.3	47.7
Canada	22.4	44.6		no[d]	19.3	6.3	43.1
Denmark	15.7	31.3	yes[a]	no[d]	43.2	28.7	66.1
France	18.2	36.4		yes[d]	8.1	− 7.2	46.2
Italy	8.1	12.5		no[d]	15.6	1.0	38.6
Japan	10.8	21.5		no[d]	7.8	0.8	53.1
Germany	18.2	23.5	yes[b]	yes[b]	20.1	5.7	53.3
Netherlands	27.2	35.2	yes[b]	no[b]	9.9	− 1.6	65.5
Sweden	7.9	15.8	no[b]	no[b]	36.1	20.3	69.8
United Kingdom	25.1	64.6		no[b]	18.7	1.8	38.1
United States	8.8	17.6	yes[c]	yes[c]	14.1	7.3	33.6

Sources

The data in columns (1) and (2) are from 'The Income Tax Treatment of the Family: An International Perspective' by J. A. Pechman and G. V. Engelhardt, 1990, *National Tax Journal*, 43 (1), p. 5. Copyright 1990 by *National Tax Journal*. Adapted by permission. Basic deduction as per cent of average production worker's earnings (APWE). Figures for 1989.

The data in columns (3) and (4) are from: a Pedersen (1993), pp. 241–88; b Gustafsson and Bruyn-Hundt (1991), pp. 34–8; c Nelson (1991), p. 17; d Pechman and Engelhardt (1990), p. 4.

The data in columns (5), (6) and (7) are from Pechman and Engelhardt (1990), p. 13. Column (5) single male production worker; column (6) married production worker with two children, husband earns 75 per cent of income; column (7) single maximum tax rate, earnings 20 times average production worker.

and a high-income earner for a large number of countries. Some of their results are presented in Table 27.3.

In columns (1) and (2) we see the amount of the basic deduction as a percentage of average production-worker earnings for a single person and for a couple. In 1989 Canada and the Netherlands had the most generous basic deductions for a single production worker; the United Kingdom had the most favourable rate (64.6 per cent) for couples.

According to these figures, only Sweden (under certain conditions) and the United States double the deduction for a couple in comparison to a single man. A Swedish production worker—if his wife does not earn an income of her own—only detracts his own basic deduction because Sweden has a completely individual tax system, according to which a nonearner has no right to transfer a basic deduction to his or her spouse. In comparing tax regimes, it is thus also important to know whether husband and wife are allowed to file jointly and use the basic deduction of a nonworking spouse or not. Columns (3) and (4) have been included in Table 27.3 for this reason. The Netherlands has separate filing but also the right for a nonworking spouse to transfer his or her basic deduction. Thus, the Netherlands has a mixture of joint and separate taxation with a larger share of couples de facto jointly taxed the higher the basic deduction (Gustafsson, 1995). In 1990 the basic deduction in the Netherlands was halved, which weakened the joint taxation element (Gustafsson and Bruyn-Hundt, 1991). In column (5) the effective tax rate for an average production worker if single is presented, and in column (6) the rate for an average production worker who is married, whose wife earns 25 per cent of the family income and who has two children.

Denmark taxes single production workers most heavily (43.2 per cent), and Sweden has the second-highest tax rate (36.1 per cent). However, the Swedish tax reform of 1991 resulted in a reduction of the average tax rate to 30 per cent for most workers and of the maximum marginal tax rate to 50 per cent (Gustafsson and Klevmarken, 1993). No reform of this kind had taken place in Denmark prior to 1993 (Pedersen, 1993), which indicates that income tax levied on lower incomes is now by far the most severe in Denmark. A production worker in France, the Netherlands or Japan pays very little tax, and those who have a family of two children even pay a negative tax (France and the Netherlands), because parents in these countries receive cash benefits for their children (Pechman and Engelhardt, 1990, p. 15). However, for the Netherlands the production worker pays social security contributions amounting to about 15 per cent of income which apparently are disregarded in the Pechman and Engelhardt (1990) figures. This is also the case in Sweden, explaining the reduction of the effective tax rate from 36.1 to 20.3 per cent if the production worker has two children, although married status has no influence whatsoever on Swedish tax rates.

Most countries have considerably lower tax rates for families with children than for single persons. Column (7) shows the effective tax rates in 1989 for a single person who earns 20 times more income than the average production worker. Sweden has the highest maximum tax rates, followed by Denmark and the Netherlands. The maximum tax rate is only half as large in the United States as it is in Denmark. Although, as mentioned above, Sweden lowered its maximum tax rate to 50 per cent in 1991 and also the Netherlands cut the high-income rate to 60 per cent in 1990, these rates are still far higher than those of Italy, the United Kingdom and the United States, the lowest-ranking countries with respect to tax rates for high-income earners.

3   TAX HARMONIZATION IN THE EUROPEAN UNION

Economists and politicians have worried that tax competition and inefficiencies will ensue as a result of differences in tax systems as the barriers between European countries are removed (Andersson, 1992; Fölster and Lindström, 1993; Sinn, 1990). When countries have different VAT rates, consumers can benefit by buying in low-tax countries. In order to counteract this possibility, VAT in Europe today is regulated by the destination principle, that is, exports are exempted from VAT, whereas imports are liable; in other words, VAT is paid in the country of destination rather than in the country of origin. Sinn (1990) points out that this principle will be difficult to sustain when there are no longer barriers in Europe, though not with respect to enterprises. They are subject to bookkeeping regulations and will have an interest in deducting VAT paid by them, because they are obliged to pay it on their sales. However, consumers have no such interest; they pay VAT on purchase but do not sell the commodity acquired to a third party, so they cannot claim a deduction. Harmonization of VAT rates has long been on the agenda of European Community officials, who recognize that the best way to avoid tax competition and allocation distortions would be to have equivalent tax rates across Member States. It has been difficult to arrive at an agreement because high-tax countries like Denmark and Ireland fear losses of tax revenue, whereas low-tax countries such as Germany fear political opposition to tax increases (Sinn, 1990, p. 492).

The European Union has been discussing harmonization of VAT between Member States for a long time. In 1987 it was suggested that there should be a standard VAT rate of between 14 and 20 per cent and a lower rate of between 4 and 9 per cent. In 1989 a minimum VAT rate of 14 per cent was proposed; in June 1991 this figure was raised to 15 per cent (Andersson, 1992). Under the terms of this regulation members of the European Union would be allowed to impose VAT rates of 25 per cent if they chose to. But demand for goods from countries with a high VAT rate might suffer. Andersson (1992) points to the difficulty facing a country like Sweden, with 25 per cent VAT, in attaining a private consumption level similar to that of Germany, which has a VAT rate of 15 per cent (figures for January 1993): Swedish consumers might buy directly in Germany after Sweden has joined the EU and barriers have been removed. Sinn (1990) vividly describes this possibility: 'Little imagination is necessary to visualize the growth of new types of firms that inform the consumers about foreign products and offer transportation services without being formally categorized as sellers' (p. 492). It has been argued that differences between countries' VAT rates could only function as an exchange rate if the VAT rate within the country were uniform. However, Sinn (1990) shows that this argument is wrong because investment goods are exempted from taxation, leading to different price ratios between low-tax and high-tax countries and consequential allocation distortions; the low-tax country will overspecialize in consumption goods. There is evidence, however, that some margin of difference between VAT rates is also sustainable where there are no barriers: in the United States, for example, VAT rates differ between states, cities and communities. Andersson (1992, pp. 73–6) presents the results of studies on sales and tax receipts. One conclusion is that, in spite of the fact that there are no borders, there is considerable diversity, from Michigan with 4 per cent VAT to Huntsville-Madison in Alabama with 9.5 per cent VAT (Andersson, 1992, p. 94). Another conclusion is that geographical distance is significant: if two cities with different VAT rates are geographically close, the city with the higher rate is likely to lose sales as well as employment.

The main focus of the discussion on tax harmonization has been value-added taxes, although the tax base, tax rates (including standard, minimum and maximum rates) and questions as to which goods should be subject to minimum rates have also been debated. In addition, there have been attempts to harmonize excise duties on alcoholic beverages, mineral oils and cigarettes (El-Agraa, 1990). Thus, the focus of interest has been on taxes on goods and services, whereas taxes on labour have been almost totally neglected in the tax harmonization debate, except in connection with social policy. The labour unions of the North have feared social dumping from southern Europe because of the less favourable working conditions prevailing there. Their strategy is to improve working conditions in the South, which would benefit workers as well as mitigating social dumping. However, such a policy must be implemented gradually because otherwise firms would go out of business, ultimately leaving the workers in the South in a worse position (Dølvik, 1993).

Although some discussion on harmonizing corporate tax rates has also been on the agenda of the EU, much more effort has been invested in the so far unsuccessful quest for European Monetary Union (EMU). Income tax regimes have not been on the agenda for tax harmonization, and the levels and ambitions of the welfare state are only incorporated into the discussion in connection with government budget deficits and government debts, which have been defined as admission criteria for EMU. Sinn (1990) is very pessimistic about the possibility of completing European integration without harmonized tax rates:

> Any country that tries to establish an insurance state would face emigration of the lucky who are supposed to pay and immigration of the unlucky who are supposed to receive! In an integrated Europe without tax harmonization consumers will win, the mobile part of the labour force will win and capital owners will win. Competition will exert a downward pressure on the VAT rates. The losers will be immobile workers, landowners, poor people and people dependent on large government sectors (p. 502).

4   THE DEADWEIGHT LOSS OR EXCESS BURDEN

A typical article in the field of public economics presents a general equilibrium model, solves it using the theoretically derived deadweight loss or excess burden and arrives at a total figure for the size of this loss by guessing parameter values or quoting them from available research. The empirical part of such a paper is more for illustration purposes, as is evident when one studies the collection of articles in the *Handbook of Public Economics* (Auerbach and Feldstein, 1985) and the short review of the field by Slemrod (1990). A typical article on labour economics starts by briefly presenting a theoretical model or simply referring to the standard economic model, then concentrates on specifying and assessing an econometric model using individual microdata, and lastly comments on the implied size of the deadweight loss (Aronsson and Walker, 1995; Ashenfelter and Layard, 1986; Mofitt, 1990). Whereas the focus in the previous section was on differences in the competitive situation between countries due to price distortion caused by taxes, the object of this section is to analyse which types of taxes cause the least efficiency loss. Because a per-capita tax or a lump-sum tax does not affect relative prices, in the comparison of actual taxes the lump-sum tax is therefore taken as the best solution, followed by the tax structure that has the least adverse effects on people's behaviour. Hence, the field is sometimes called optimal taxation research. 'The concept of excess burden measures the differences between the total loss of welfare (or the economic cost) of a tax as it is actually imposed and the loss which would result if the same tax revenue had been collected without distorting economic decisions in the private sector' (Musgrave and Musgrave, 1973, p. 444). The excess burden can also be identified from the Pareto efficient marginal conditions.[1]

1.   MRS of X for Z = MRT of X for Z = p_x/p_z

2.   MRS of L for Y = MRT of L for Y = w

3.   MRS of C_f for C_p = MRT of C_f for C_p = $1/(1+r)$

                MRS = marginal rate of substitution
                MRT = marginal rate of transformation

The three conditions highlight (a) the choice between consumption of good X and good Z, (b) the choice between labour and leisure and (c) the choice between present consumption and future consumption.

Condition 1 states that the consumer's willingness to substitute between good X and good Z (MRS) must equal the price ratio of the two goods, which is determined by the ratio of the marginal costs of producing them. The second condition states that a worker's marginal value of leisure for income must equal the wage earned, which is in turn determined by the worker's ability to transform working hours into production. The third condition states that the consumer's willingness on the margin to forgo present consumption for future consumption must equal the inverse of the interest rate. When taxes interfere with the above conditions we have a case of excess burden because the welfare of the consumer decreases as will be explained below.

The choices are illustrated in Figure 27.1. Starting with the choice between products, assume that VAT is levied on good X, whereas good Z is untaxed; or that good Z carries the minimum VAT rate, whereas good X is subject to the maximum rate. If the line BA is the relative price line or the marginal rate of transformation between X and Z in the absence of VAT, the line $B'A'$, with an unchanged price ratio, results if a general sales or value-added tax is introduced with the same rates for both goods. The result for the consumer is decreased utility as the optimum solution changes from E' to E''. If a higher value-added or sales tax is now imposed on X, the price line changes to BF and the optimum solution to E'''. The tax rate is $E''D$, which in the new situation equals $E'''H$. However, there is an excess burden in this situation because the consumer is now on a lower indifference curve i_3. A line drawn parallel to the previous budget line and at a tangent to the lower indifference

---

1 Pareto, Vilfedo 1848–1923. A Pareto optimal equilibrium means that it is not possible to increase the welfare of one agent by more than the loss thereby incurred by another agent. If the three conditions above are satisfied, this will be true.

curve i_3 will give an estimate of the excess burden, that is, the distance *RS* between the indifference curves i_2 and i_3. The distortions caused by taxes can now be analysed for single choices, assuming that other choices are kept constant. The interpretation is that the consumer would be better off at *E″* than at *E‴*, although the amount of tax paid remains the same (*E″D = E‴H*).

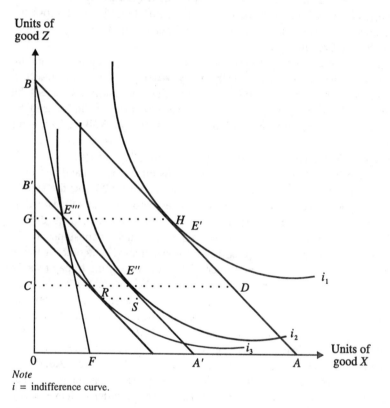

Note
i = indifference curve.

Figure 27.1   Adjustment to Selective and General Taxes

The same analysis can be applied to the choice between leisure (good *Z*) and work. If an income tax is introduced, market goods (good *X* in Figure 27.1) that are bought with earned income are taxed, whereas leisure is left untaxed. The situation *E″* results from a lump-sum tax, and the situation *E‴* from a proportional income tax. Comparing solution *E‴* to solution *E″*, the income tax causes a deadweight loss, because Condition 2 above is not met. The net wage to the worker differs from the wage the employer must pay, but the worker could have paid the same amount of tax while consuming less leisure (OC instead of OG) and would have had a higher utility at the same time.

If the axes of Figure 27.1 are relabelled so that good Z is present consumption and good X is future consumption, the same reasoning can be applied again. The pretax budget line is then $OB = (1 + i) \, OA$, where i = interest rate. A general consumption tax that taxes both present and future consumption would be neutral, whereas an income tax that taxes earnings and interest would violate Condition 3 above and result in a difference between gross and net interest rates. The distance between indifference curves i_2 and i_3 is a measure of the deadweight loss.

Utility is often difficult to measure, although indirect utility curves are estimated in the literature on labour supply. Attempts to measure indifference curves entail the additional difficulty that the estimates cannot be aggregated from an individual to society because they are influenced by taste differences and income distribution (Aronsson and Walker, 1995). An alternative much-used measure of the deadweight loss is the so-called Harberger (1964, cited by Musgrave and Musgrave, 1973) triangles. The triangles are estimated from the consumer surplus under the demand curve, as illustrated in Figure 27.2. The market demand curve is BA and the supply curve FS. OH units of the product are consumed before tax, and the consumer surplus is BFD because there is some consumer who would have been willing to pay the whole OB for a unit of the good. Another consumer would only be willing to pay some price a little lower than OB, another a lower price again, and so on to the consumer who would be willing to pay exactly OF. The last unit or marginal unit demanded is then evaluated by the consumer exactly at its price OF. If a sales tax of EF is introduced, then tax receipts will be EFKL; however, the consumer surplus is reduced by more than EFKL, namely, additionally by the triangle KLD. The triangle KLD is a measure of the deadweight loss caused by taxation and is also called the Marshallian measure of excess burden. Hicks (1942, cited by Auerbach, 1985) defined the *compensating variation* of a price change to be that amount of income that the consumer must receive in order to leave utility unaffected by the price change, and the *equivalent variation* as the amount of income the consumer would forgo to avoid the price change.

Hausman (1985) argues that it is incorrect to estimate the deadweight loss from the area under the uncompensated market demand curve because the compensated demand curves, which are defined to be pure substitution effects, are steeper. Another argument for the equivalent variation is presented in Van Soest, Woittiez and Kapteyn (1990):

> Contrary to the measure based on the compensating variation introduced by Diamond and McFadden (1974) this dead weight loss measure starts from the

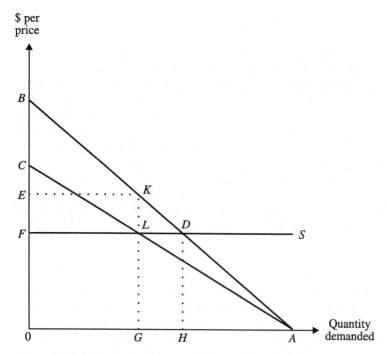

Figure 27.2   Excess Burden of a Selective Consumption Tax

maximum utility level that can be attained under the actual system and does not rely on the imaginary utility level which could be attained in a world without taxes (p. 529).

However, correct measurement of excess burden at the pretax or posttax utility levels can be seen as a pure index problem.

5   WORK INCENTIVES AND LABOUR SUPPLY

When an income tax is levied on a worker's earnings, there will always be two effects: an income effect (the worker finds his or her earnings decreased and will try to increase labour supply in order to maintain the previous income level) and a substitution effect (the worker finds that every hour of work now returns less income, and he or she will want to spend more time on other activities because it pays less to work). The decreased income is a loss of utility to the worker, which ideally is returned in the form of public goods and services. However, if the income level is held constant, we can study the substitution effect. If people's private calculus tells them it pays them to reduce their working hours in view of the net wage they receive, there may be a loss for society as a whole. This is the case if the worker reduces his or her working hours because progressive income taxation leads to a lower extra income for an additional working hour the higher the number of working hours in the initial situation. If the worker had opted for more working hours in view of an unchanged net wage for extra hours, then society as a whole would lose working hours. It is possible to think of a situation where the net hourly wage is the same for a ten-hour job as for a fortieth extra hour. This is the experiment that has to be carried out if one wants to calculate the deadweight loss. Researchers have attempted to quantify the size of the deadweight loss caused by the fact that progressive income taxation decreases the relative price of an additional hour of market work compared to leisure or household work, which are not taxed because time spent on nonmarket activities does not yield monetary gains.

What we want to know is the income-compensated elasticity of labour supply after tax. People base their decisions on net wages, and if workers are assumed to be indifferent, an estimate of the welfare loss will have to be based on income compensation. Several problems emerge in attempts to estimate this labour supply elasticity. One of them is the endogeneity of the net wage to the number of hours worked when income taxes are progressive. Another is the probability that workers are unable to choose their working hours, because jobs are typically offered in bundles of hours. There may be demand for a full-time or half-time worker, but employers are seldom looking for someone to work exactly 21 hours per week. These two problems will be discussed briefly in the following.

5.1   The Endogeneity of Net Wages to Working Hours

One of the most significant problems connected with progressive income taxation is depicted in Figure 27.3. Progressive taxation results in a nonuniformly linear after-tax budget constraint with three tax brackets and kinks at h_1 and h_2 working hours. The before-tax budget constraint, in contrast, is uniformly linear. A method to solve this problem has been proposed by Hausman (1981) and developed by Blomquist (1983); it is sometimes referred to as the Hausman–Blomquist model (Gustafsson and Klevmarken, 1993).

A person who is not participating in the labour market still has an income x_0, which is the worker's unearned income. The first tax bracket has a zero tax rate and the slope of the budget line coincides with the gross wage. The second tax bracket has a slighter slope because the tax is progressive. The extension of the budget line of the interval h_1 to h_2 to the vertical axis gives a new intercept x_1, which represents the virtual income of persons who have chosen to work any number of hours in the second tax bracket between hours h_1 and h_2. Similarly, persons working any number of hours from h_2 up to maximum working hours (h_3) are in the third tax bracket and are subject to an even higher marginal tax rate, resulting in a slighter slope again

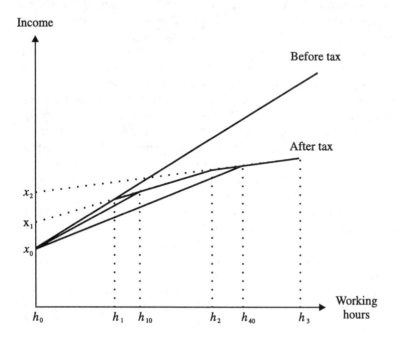

Figure 27.3   Budget Set with Virtual Incomes and Net Wages at 10 and 40 Hours: Progressive Taxation

and a higher virtual income of x_2. The distance between the before-tax budget line and the after-tax kinked budget set is a measure of taxes collected. The virtual incomes at the two kink points, h_1 and h_2 working hours, are undefined.

The model can be estimated by a maximum-likelihood estimation method with a search algorithm that the authors use to first ascertain the individual's tax bracket, then assign the corresponding virtual income and, finally, optimize working hours given the virtual income and the marginal wage rate. Using this method, Blomquist and Hansson-Brusewitz (1990) are able to show that there are substantial positive wage elasticities and negative income elasticities that result in positive compensated wage elasticities. This result is important because, according to economic theory income-compensated, own-price elasticity, that is, the quantity demanded of a good when its own price increases, has to be negative. If wages are increased, the income-compensated demand for leisure has to decrease and working hours have to increase, leading to a positive income-compensated wage elasticity of labour supply. In the literature (e.g. Aronsson and Walker, 1995; Atkinson and Mogensen, 1993; Mofitt, 1990) wage elasticities (E_w) and income elasticities (E_y) are estimated, and the compensated elasticity has to be positive ($E_w - E_y > 0$).

Blomquist and Hansson-Brusewitz (1990, p. 340) present results that imply that both men and women in Sweden would increase labour supply substantially at no utility loss if a lump-sum tax were introduced, that is, a tax that does not alter the relative price of work for leisure but that also has no income redistribution effects. Their estimated deadweight loss or excess burden for the Swedish tax system in 1980 is 15.7 per cent of taxes collected for men and 25.8 per cent of taxes collected for women. Aronsson (1993, cited by Aronsson and Walker, 1995) shows that for a married couple in Sweden the combined deadweight loss was 30 per cent of tax revenue in 1980; it decreased to 23 per cent in 1989 and to 8 per cent in 1990. This result is a powerful argument in favour of decreasing progressivity in the tax system and was one of many arguments for the Swedish tax reform of 1991, which reduced the marginal (and average) tax rate to 30 per cent for most workers and the maximum rate to 50 per cent (see Aronsson and Walker, 1995; Gustafsson and Klevmarken, 1993).

The Hausman–Blomquist method has been criticized for overestimating the wage effect and underestimating the income effect. Intuitively, a given variation in working hours has to be attributed both to effects from income variations and wage variations. If the income variable is inflated, as it is by the virtual income, and the wage variable is decreased by only considering changes within a given tax bracket, one would expect the estimated coefficient on income to be small and the wage effect to be large.

However, there are not many good alternative estimation methods. Attempts to directly regress labour supply responses from the marginal net wage rate will result in negative wage effects because one will observe that marginal net wage rates decrease as working hours increase, due to the progressivity of the tax system. This is the endogeneity problem. Whereas the tax system is exogenous to the labour supply decision, the net income and wage depend on it. MaCurdy, Green and Paarsch (1990) criticize the Hausman–Blomquist model because it imposes restrictions that force observations to comply with the Slutsky condition,[2] rather than estimating them from the data.

---

2 The Slutsky condition requires that the compensated own-price elasticity is negative. If the price of a good is increased, will people tend to buy less of the good, if the income loss incurred by the price increase is compensated for?

According to MaCurdy et al. (1990), this imposed restriction will definitely occur at interior kink points, that is, at points h_1 and h_2 in Figure 27.3, rather than letting the data determine the coefficients. Moreover, other points are also in danger of being contaminated by an a priori restriction (MaCurdy et al., 1990, p. 437). Gustafsson and Klevmarken (1993) conclude: 'Flood and MaCurdy drew the conclusion that wage rates and incomes are endogenous. If this is true, it might have far-reaching consequences for any analysis of labour supply' (p. 79). Zimmermann (1993) commented thus on the same controversy: 'The resulting very low income elasticity and the negative uncompensated wage elasticity in Flood and MaCurdy (1991) have, however, a high price: The estimated compensated wage elasticity is negative, which is inconsistent with economic theory. It is therefore not clear why the authors are so fully satisfied with their findings' (p. 218).

Although the solution proposed in Gustafsson (1992) is simple, it is robust and does not impose any restrictions. It shows positive wage effects and negative income effects for the labour supply of German and Swedish wives. Observed nonearned incomes at zero working hours are used rather than virtual incomes. Thus, in Figure 27.3 x_0 is always the income measure. The wage variable is calculated as the average net wage of, in this case, a married woman, if she were to work 10 hours or 40 hours, respectively. The net wage at 10 hours and the net nonearned income together with other variables are used to calculate the probability of the woman participating in the labour market at all; the net wage at 40 hours is used to calculate the probability of the woman working full time. In Figure 27.3 the net wage rate at 10 hours (w_{10}) is given by the line from x_0 to the after-tax budget constraint at h_{10}; the wage rate at 40 hours (w_{40}) is given by the line from the intercept x_0 to the before-tax budget constraint at h_{40}. Both w_{10} and w_{40} are exogenous because they only use information about the person's gross wage and the tax system. The method does not use a virtual income because this is a construct that makes nonearned income much larger than it would be in reality if the person did not work in the market. Gustafsson (1992) analyses these two points on the after-tax budget line separately; the model is only applied to analyse the different impacts of separate and joint taxation of spouses on work incentives for wives. There is no attempt to estimate the deadweight loss.

5.2 Demand Restrictions on Working Hours

The problem that workers may be unable to work the hours they prefer is addressed by Van Soest et al. (1990). They estimate the deadweight loss both in a model where the choice of hours is assumed to be free and in a model where workers can choose between work-hours packages. The deadweight loss in a situation with a nonuniformly linear tax system is depicted in

Figure 27.4. As in Figure 27.3, the first segment or tax bracket has a zero tax rate, that is, the gross wage rate is equal to the net wage rate in this segment.

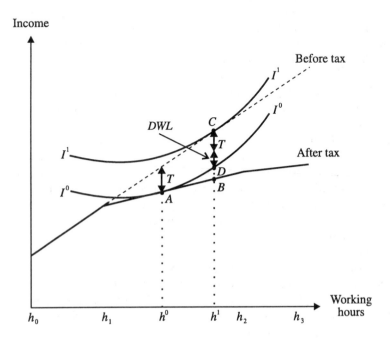

Notes
DWL=deadweight loss; *I*=indifference curve.

*Figure 27.4   Deadweight Loss in the Case of Progressive Taxation
          and Restrictions on Working Hours*

The individual chooses point *A* because this is the highest possible indifference curve the individual can obtain given the after-tax budget line. If *I* could receive the gross wage, he or she would have chosen point *C*, where indifference curve I^1I^1 is at a tangent to the before-tax budget line. The distance *CD* can be divided into the tax *T* and the deadweight loss *DWL*; the latter represents the extra taxes paid at h^1 hours if the individual had been compensated to remain at indifference curve I^0I^0, which he or she reaches at h^0 hours. However, at h^1 hours of work *BC* of taxes have to be paid, pushing the individual on to a lower indifference curve, which is not an optimal point because it cuts the budget line instead of being tangent to it (not drawn). The results presented in Van Soest et al. (1990) indicate that in the model with restrictions on working hours the deadweight loss is smaller than it is in the general model, where workers can choose their hours freely. This indicates that restrictions on working hours mean that workers are brought closer to points like *A*, where the deadweight losses are relatively small, than to points like *B*, where the deadweight losses are relatively large.

5.3   Separate versus Joint Income Taxation

One of the results presented in Van Soest et al. (1990, p. 538) is that if Dutch women were able to find jobs corresponding to their preferred hours of work, the female labour force participation rate would increase from 39.6 to 82.5 per cent. Most of these women, that is, almost three-quarters, would work less than 20 hours per week.[3] If restrictions on hours were removed, there could be more labour supply without any loss of utility to the individuals working longer hours, that is, welfare losses would decrease. Another aspect of the tax system is the discouraging effect of joint taxation on the labour supply of secondary wage-earners. Specifically married women who work at home and would consider taking a part-time job if subject to joint taxation, would be taxed at the high marginal tax rate applying to their husbands, most of whom work full time. Separate taxation has the exactly opposite effect: The small earnings of a part-time working wife are taxed at a low rate. This difference is illustrated in Figure 27.5.

At a given number of hours of work *h*, a working wife's net nonearned income is x_1^s and her wage rate is in the first interval with a zero tax rate. Her contribution to family income is the distance *ad*. If she were subject to joint taxation, she would have a higher nonearned income (x_1^g) because her husband would deduct two basic allowances, but her net wage would be taxed at a higher rate, depicted in Figure 27.5 as coinciding with the second interval of the separate taxation. The working wife's contribution to family income under the joint taxation system is the segment *bc*. These issues have been analysed by Gustafsson (1992) in a comparison of Sweden and Germany. Labour force participation was estimated for married women in each country. Then, for each couple the net wages were calculated at 10 and 40 hours, using both tax systems for both countries; husbands' net earnings under the assumption that their wives do not work were also computed for each country using both tax systems. In this way the following computations were made for Sweden (S):

---

3   In this study the variable preferred hours is formed according to a distribution assumption, whereas in a follow-up paper (Euwals and Van Soest, 1994) desired hours are directly measured. Euwals and Van Soest (1994) basically confirm the results of Van Soest et al. (1990).

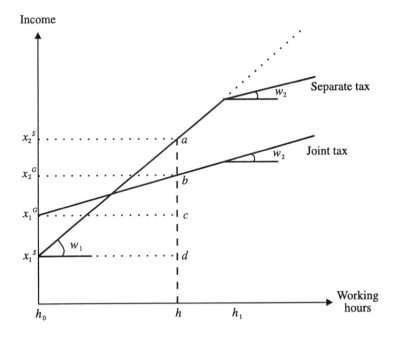

Notes
x = working wife's net nonearned income; w=net wages.

Figure 27.5   Budget Sets for Separate Versus Joint Taxation
of a Married Woman

$$p^S = a_1 x_1^S + a_2 w_{10}^S + \text{other variables} \qquad (27.1)$$

$$x^S = a_1 x_1^G + a_2 w_{10}^G + \text{other variables} \qquad (27.2)$$

and for Germany:

$$p^G = b_1 x_1^G + b_2 w_{10}^G + \text{other variables} \qquad (27.3)$$

$$x^G = b_1 x_1^S + b_2 w_{10}^S + \text{other variables} \qquad (27.4)$$

p = actual rate of labour force participation
x = predicted rate of labour force participation
a, b = estimated parameters
x = nonearned incomes, including husbands' incomes
w = net wages

The results of using income and wage variables computed for the other country to predict female labour force participation were that Swedish women, if subject to the German tax system, would decrease their labour force participation from 80 to 60 per cent, and that German women would increase their labour force participation from 50 to 60 per cent, if subject to the Swedish tax system. It is possible that the German tax system creates deadweight losses for married women in the same way that inflexibility in hours demanded by employers has been shown to do for Dutch women by Van Soest et al. (1990) and Euwals and Van Soest (1994). The most important reason for introducing the separate taxation system in Sweden in 1971 was a belief that the joint taxation system discouraged married women's labour supply. Using an aggregate time-series analysis, Schettkat (1987, 1989) fails to show a positive coefficient on Swedish women's labour force participation since the introduction of separate taxation—neither as a one-off shift nor as a change in the slope of the time series of female labour force participation. However, Löfström (1989) (also dealt with in Löfström and Gustafsson, 1991), using a more elaborate time-series model where other policy changes are allowed to influence the employment of women, presents evidence of a positive impact for Swedish industrial workers.

Besides the problem of estimating labour supply responses in the face of progressive taxation and the resulting endogeneity of net wages to working hours, there are numerous other problems to be solved in labour supply estimation. One aspect is a more accurate description of the budget set. Gustafsson and Klevmarken (1993) show the resulting marginal tax rates from income-dependent cash benefits and childcare subsidies, unemployment benefits, active labour market policies, the pension system and sickness cash benefits. Another is problems with estimating the simultaneous labour force participation decision of husband and wife and life-cycle aspects of the labour supply decision. Aronsson and Walker (1995) present some results concerning the simultaneous decision by husband and wife.

6   TAXES AND LABOUR DEMAND

Demand for labour is a derived demand, which is influenced by the demand for goods and services. In view of potential harmonization of taxes in Europe, two questions might be justified. First, are the tax rates of a specific European country detrimental to competitors offering goods and services in the European Union? Second, if the EU were to opt for harmonization, which standard should be chosen? Economic growth determines labour demand in an economy, and where a tax system is unnecessarily detrimental to economic growth it should be reformed. However, taxes may also alter the input mix into production if one factor of production is more heavily taxed than another. Therefore, it would be helpful to know the elasticities of factor demand for labour as against capital and of different kinds of labour as against each other. This is also an important part of labour demand. Hamermesh (1993) provides an excellent analysis and compilation of labour demand studies, arguing that policy evaluations often are too narrowly focussed in that they attempt to analyse labour market impacts for the specific group whose position a certain policy aims at improving rather than analysing the effects for the whole labour market. Evaluation studies should focus on the economic analysis of a measure's effects both on those workers targeted by the policy and on other workers. 'Put more bluntly, useful evaluation requires more of an economic focus, both in the questions asked and the methods used to answer them' (Hamermesh, 1993, p. 202). Hamermesh (1993, chap. 5) introduces a useful way of thinking about the effects of taxes and/or subsidies on labour demand. According to the Hamermesh classification, policies can be P-type or Q-type policies, depending on whether the policy changes the cost of employing all workers or some identifiable group of workers (P-policy), or whether it affects the supply of labour generally or a specific group (Q-policy). Policies are P-specific if only a specific group of labour is affected and P-general if all workers are equally affected, as is the case with, for example, a general wage-bill tax. An example of a P-specific policy would be a lower general wage-bill tax for a specific group of workers in a disadvantaged region, long-term unemployed or young unemployed, because this would reduce costs for employers of this type of worker.

Changes in migration laws, for example, the free movement of workers within the EU since January 1993, which allows European workers to migrate to where employment opportunities are better, constitute P-general policies.

Q-specific policies are most programs that increase the stock of trained workers. These latter include programs for developing skills through on-the-job training in the private sector, public-sector employment programs targeted to low-skilled workers and subsidies to higher education that increase the supply of highly trained workers, mandating labour–output ratios, such as requirement for minimum staffing of day care centres, are Q-specific policies (Hamermesh, 1993, p. 166).

Both P-policies and Q-policies, whether they are general or specific, can be classified according to the types of instruments they use into labour policies and nonlabour policies; the latter change the costs of substitutes for labour, for example, by subsidizing energy costs or investments. Further, policies can also have an impact on the cost of the working-hours mix, for example, in the form of a general premium for overtime work in excess of 40 hours per week, or by extending social rights to part-time workers that are more than proportional to their working hours. The effects of a change in payroll taxes or subsidies can then be analysed in terms of effects on wages and employment, according to the following two equations (Hamermesh, 1993, p. 168):

$$\frac{\delta \ln w^*}{\delta \tau} = \frac{\eta_{LL}}{\in - [1 + \tau] \, \eta_{LL}} \tag{27.5}$$

and

$$\frac{\delta \ln L^*}{\delta \tau} = \eta_{LL} \left[1 + \frac{\eta_{LL}}{\in [1 + \tau]^{-1} - \eta_{LL}} \right] \tag{27.6}$$

w^*	=	equilibrium wages
L^*	=	equilibrium employment
τ	=	wage-bill tax
η_{LL}	=	labour demand elasticity
$\in$	=	labour supply elasticity

If we start in a situation with a zero or near-zero wage-bill tax, the effects of the change can be interpreted for two polar cases. If the labour supply elasticity is close to zero, we will have only a wage effect and no employment effect. This can be seen in equations (27.5) and (27.6) and is illustrated in Figure 27.6, panel C. If, on the other hand, the labour supply elasticity is infinitely large, we will have only an employment effect and no wage effect, as can be seen in equations (27.5) and (27.6) and Figure 27.6, panel B. Figure 27.6 illustrates the effects of a decrease in the wage-bill tax.

A reduction of the wage-bill tax in panel A will have both wage and employment effects, whereas if labour supply is totally elastic, as in panel B, a reduced wage-bill tax will yield the intended increase in employment effect. However, if labour supply is totally inelastic, as in panel C, a lower wage-bill tax will only lead to increased net wages for the workers. For cases in between we would have both employment and wage effects, depending on the relative size of the labour supply and the labour demand elasticities. Hamermesh's conclusion, having studied numerous different estimations of labour supply and labour demand elasticities, is: 'There is only small scope in the long run for a payroll subsidy to increase employment or for a payroll tax to reduce it. Barring substantial improvement in empirical studies of tax incidence, we must tentatively infer that most of the burden of payroll taxes is on wages' (p. 172). Concerning subsidies for disadvantaged workers, Hamermesh (1993) concludes: 'The net employment effects of these policies depend on workers' choices among market work, household production and leisure – that is, on the supply elasticities of subsidized and other workers to the labour market' (p. 182).

This conclusion is not necessarily pessimistic; it only states that there is no simple answer to a difficult question. The specific situation in different coun-

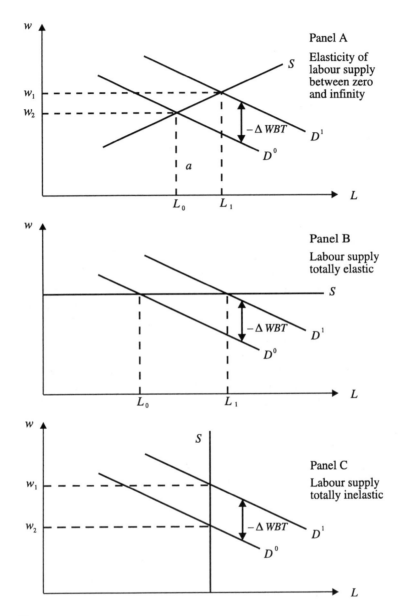

Notes
w = wages; L = employment; WBT = wage-bill tax;
S = labour supply; D = labour demand.

Figure 27.6   Wage and Employment Effects of a Decrease in Wage-bill Tax

tries as well as differences between countries should be studied. But there is certainly also a need to integrate and compile the fragmented research found in this area, that is, individual data and cross-section or panel studies on labour supply, time-series neoclassical growth models on labour demand and abstract theoretical analysis of optimal taxation.

7   CONCLUDING COMMENTS

Do we have any clear results concerning evaluations of the effects of tax regimes on labour market performance? One definite conclusion is that one needs to know labour demand elasticities as well as labour supply elasticities to be able to assess the impacts. This conclusion is a justification for the enormous research effort invested in evaluating the effects of the tax/subsidy system on work incentives and in estimating labour demand responses in economic growth models. It has been demonstrated in this chapter that it is extremely difficult to arrive at econometric estimates of labour supply elasticities. The complications have led to a controversy regarding methods, and also to disappointment because there seems to be no satisfactory solution in sight. It would be nice if one had a labour supply elasticity to plug into the Hamermesh equations because then we would be able to estimate the labour demand response and would know which policies would most enhance labour demand. However, I think that such a hope is in vain. I do not believe that there is one correct labour supply elasticity, but that it will differ across demographic groups and across countries with different institutional settings and different views on the proper roles of men and women. I think we will have to accept that, for example, the labour supply of mothers—although to a large extent determined by the net benefits to market work created by parental leave, day-care subsidies and individual versus separate taxation—is also influenced by the historically determined view among leading politicians and people in general on the proper role of women. Further obstacles, as noted above, are posed by the tendency in policy evaluation to disregard economic analysis rather than make use of it, and the very rudimentary economic reasoning behind the policy efforts towards harmonizing taxes within the European Union.

REFERENCES

Andersson, K. (1992), 'Svensk beskattning i ett integrerat Europa', *Medium Term Economic Survey 1992* (suppl. 2), Stockholm: Allmänna Förlaget.

Aronsson, T. and J. R. Walker (1995), *The Effect of Sweden's Welfare State on Labor Supply Incentives*, NBER/SNS project: Reforming the Welfare State, occasional paper, 64, SNS: Stockholm.

Ashenfelter, O. C. and R. Layard (eds) (1986), *Handbook of Labor Economics*, Vols 1 and 2, Amsterdam: North-Holland.

Atkinson, A. B. and G. V. Mogensen (eds) (1993), *Welfare and Work Incentives. A North European Perspective*, Oxford: Clarendon Press.

Auerbach, A. J. (1985), 'The Theory of Excess Burden and Optimal Taxation', in A. J. Auerbach and M. Feldstein (eds), *Handbook of Public Economics*, Amsterdam: North-Holland, pp. 61–127.

Auerbach, A. J. and M. Feldstein (eds) (1985), *Handbook of Public Economics*, Amsterdam: North-Holland.

Blomquist, N. S. (1983), 'The Effect of Income Taxation on the Labour Supply of Married Men in Sweden', *Journal of Public Economics*, 22, 169–97.

Blomquist, N. S. and U. Hansson-Brusewitz (1990), 'The Effect of Taxes on Male and Female Labour Supply in Sweden', *Journal of Human Resources*, 24 (3), 317–57.

Blundell, R. (1993), 'Taxation and Labour-supply Incentives in the UK', in A. B. Atkinson and G. V. Mogensen (eds), *Welfare and Work Incentives. A North European Perspective*, Oxford: Clarendon Press, pp. 135–91.

Dølvik, J. E. (1993), 'Economic Integration, the Nordic Model and Unemployment', in J. Fagerberg and L. Lundberg (eds), *European Integration: A Nordic Perspective*, Brookfield, VT/Aldershot: Avebury, pp. 353–79.

El-Agraa, A. M. (1990), *Economics of the European Community* (3rd ed.), New York: Philip Alan.

Esping-Andersen, G. (1990), *The Three Worlds of Welfare Capitalism*, Cambridge: Polity Press.

Euwals, R. and A. Van Soest (1994), 'Desired and Actual Labour Supply in the Netherlands', Department of Economics, University of Tilburg, The Netherlands. (Unpublished manuscript)

Flood, L. and T. MaCurdy (1991), 'Work Disincentive Effects of Taxes: An Empirical Analysis of Swedish Men', Department of Economics, University of Göteborg, Sweden. (Unpublished manuscript)

Fölster, S. and E. Lindström (1993), *Sveriges offentliga sektor i Europeisk konkurrens —konsekvenser av EES–avtalet och medlemsskap i EG/EU*, Consequence Investigation (suppl. 6), Stockholm: Allmänna Förlaget.

Gustafsson, B. and A. N. Klevmarken (1993), 'Taxes and Transfers in Sweden: Incentive Effects on Labour Supply', in A. B. Atkinson and G. V. Mogensen (eds), *Welfare and Work Incentives. A North European Perspective*, Oxford: Clarendon Press, pp. 50–134.

Gustafsson, S. (1992), 'Separate Taxation and Married Women's Labour Supply. A Comparison of West Germany and Sweden', *Journal of Population Economics*, 5, 61–85.

Gustafsson, S. (1995), 'Public Policies and Women's Labour Force Participation: A Comparison of Sweden, the Netherlands and Germany', in T. P. Schultz (ed.), *Investment in Women's Human Capital*, Chicago: University of Chicago Press, pp. 91–112.

Gustafsson, S. and M. Bruyn-Hundt (1991), 'Incentives for Women to Work. A Comparison between the Netherlands, Sweden and West Germany', *Journal of Economic Studies*, 18 (5/6), 30–65.

Hamermesh, D. S. (1993), *Labor Demand*, Princeton, New Jersey: Princeton University Press.

Hausman, J. (1981), 'Exact Consumer's Surplus and Deadweight Loss', *American Economic Review*, 71 (4), 626–76.

Hausman, J. (1985), 'Taxes and Labour Supply', in A. J. Auerbach and M. Feldstein (eds), *Handbook of Public Economics*, Amsterdam: North-Holland, pp. 213–64.

Löfström, Å. (1989), *Diskriminering på svensk arbetsmarknad. En analys av löneskillnader mellan kvinnor och män* (Umeå Economic Studies no. 196), Umeå: University of Umeå.

Löfström, Å. and S. Gustafsson (1991), 'Policy Changes and Women's Wages in Sweden', *International Review of Comparative Public Policy*, 3, 313–30.

MaCurdy, T., D. Green and H. Paarsch (1990), 'Assessing Empirical Approaches for Analyzing Taxes and Labour Supply', *Journal of Human Resources*, 23 (3), 415–90.

Mofitt, R. (ed.) (1990), *The Journal of Human Resources*, 25 (3), 314–558, special issue on Taxation and Labour Supply in Industrial Countries.

Musgrave, R. A. and P. B. Musgrave (1973), *Public Finance in Theory and Practice*, Tokyo: McGraw-Hill Ltd.

Nelson, J. A. (1991), 'Tax Reform and Feminist Theory in the United States: Incorporating Human Connection', *Journal of Economic Studies*, 18 (5/6), 11–29.

OECD (1991), *Employment Outlook*, Paris: OECD.

Pechman, J. A. and G. V. Engelhardt (1990), 'The Income Tax Treatment of the Family: An International Perspective', *National Tax Journal*, 43 (1), 1–77.

Pedersen, P. (1993), 'The Welfare State and Taxation in Denmark', in A. B. Atkinson and G. V. Mogensen (eds), *Welfare and Work Incentives. A North European Perspective*, Oxford: Clarendon Press, pp. 241–88.

Schettkat, R. (1987), *Erwerbsbeteiligung und Politik—Theoretische und empirische Analyse von Determinanten und Dynamik des Arbeitsangebots in Schweden und der Bundesrepublik Deutschland*, Berlin: edition sigma.

Schettkat, R. (1989), 'The Impact of Taxes on Female Labour Supply', *International Review of Applied Economics*, 3, 1–24.

Sinn, H. W. (1990), 'Tax Harmonization and Tax Competition in Europe', *European Economic Review*, 34 (2/3), 489–503.

Slemrod, J. (1990), 'Optimal Taxation and Optimal Tax Systems', *Journal of Economic Perspectives*, 4 (1), 157–78.

Van Soest, A., I. Woittiez and A. Kapteyn (1990), 'Labour Supply, Income Taxes and Hours Restrictions in the Netherlands', *Journal of Human Resources*, 25 (3), 517–58.

Zimmermann, K. F. (1993), 'Labour Responses to Taxes and Benefits in Germany', in A. B. Atkinson and G. V. Mogensen (eds), *Welfare and Work Incentives. A North European Perspective*, Oxford: Clarendon Press, pp. 192–240.

PART IV

Evaluating Policy Targets at the European Level

28. The European Social Fund: A Strategy for Generic Evaluation[1]

E60 H30

Robert M. Lindley

The European Social Fund (ESF) is the longest-standing of the European Community's fiscal policy instruments to deal specifically with labour market problems and to promote employment. It is now one of the three well-established Structural Funds; alongside it are the ERDF (European Regional Development Fund), the purpose of which is to reduce disparities between regions in their economic development, and the EAGGF, Guidance Section (European Agricultural Guidance and Guarantee Fund), which is used to co-finance national agricultural aid schemes and promote the development and diversification of rural areas. A fourth instrument has been added recently, namely, the FIFG (Financial Instrument for Fisheries Guidance), which is a source of assistance for restructuring the fisheries sector. Inevitably, there is some overlap between the funds in their involvement with labour market measures, although increasing attempts have been made by the Commission to integrate policy wherever possible.

The aims of this chapter are to (a) briefly review the development of the ESF (section 1); (b) consider the experience of labour market evaluation, broadly defined, and to sum up its relevance for the evaluation of the ESF (section 2); (c) examine the particular issues that arise in the context of promoting evaluation within the framework of the ESF, especially the problems stemming from heterogeneous programmes combined with widely different evaluation approaches (section 3); and (d) put forward an approach to ESF evaluation that seeks to organize more rigorously the available research base, develop it further and apply it more effectively (section 4). The principal conclusions are given in section 5.

---

1 This chapter draws substantially on a study prepared for DG V of the Commission of the European Communities as part of a project on 'Methods of Evaluation for the European Social Fund'. I am especially grateful to Aviana Bulgarelli, Jordi Planas and Claudine Romani for discussions in the course of the project. I should also like to thank John Temple, Jacqueline O'Reilly, Günther Schmid and other participants in the Berlin 'Handbook Workshops' for helpful comments on an earlier draft of the chapter. A more detailed treatment of the issues presented here is given in Lindley (1993).

Emphasis has been placed on the principles behind the development of the ESF and the current stage reached in its operation; administrative aspects are excluded, even though they are of considerable importance in practice. This applies especially to the choice of governmental level at which ESF programmes are controlled, the use of specialist agencies, the degree of disaggregation of the programmes into separate units and the relationships between the Member States and the European Commission in operating the procedures established at the European level (CEC, 1993a).

1 THE EVOLUTION OF THE EUROPEAN SOCIAL FUND

Several phases can be identified in the development of the ESF. The information in the earlier part of this section on the phases of reform and the corresponding statistics is drawn from the short introduction to the ESF in Nevin (1990); for the later phases see CEC (1989, 1991, 1992a, 1992b and 1993a). Each successive phase represents a move towards a higher level of expenditure and an attempt to clarify further the underlying rationale of the fund, to target the appropriate activities, to introduce a more substantial degree of monitoring and to provide for the eventual introduction of genuine evaluation.

Phase I: A Modest Beginning
The ESF was the only employment policy instrument established by the Treaty of Rome (Articles 123–7). During the 1960s the focus was on geographical and occupational mobility in a period of high economic growth, but few schemes were sponsored and the effect of the ESF was very marginal. As Nevin (1990, p. 212) points out, the average annual expenditure of about ECU 166 million (in 1986 prices) may be set against a European labour force of 75 million and further compared with an annual expenditure for the European Coal and Steel Community (ECSC) of ECU 62 million merely on redeployment of workers in the particular industries concerned.

The financing of the ESF under Article 200 left France and Germany providing 32 per cent each, and Italy 20 per cent of the total resources. These figures may be compared with the 28 per cent contributed by each of the three countries to the general EC budget of the period. Although the aim, primarily, was to help Italy, during the period 1960–71 44 per cent of payments under the fund went to Germany, compared with 36 per cent to Italy. The ESF contributed 50 per cent of the Member State's expenditure on projects, which could only be submitted by Member States. At this low level of spending, it is difficult to believe that the projects were crucially dependent for their implementation upon the provision of a Community contribution.

Phase II: Responding to Rising Unemployment
During the 1970s the ESF entered a second phase of development. In 1971 its financial treatment was absorbed into the general budget of the EC, and between the periods 1960–71 and 1972–77 the resources available were increased by a factor of five. Expenditure from the fund was split equally between (a) categories of workers (initially in agriculture and textiles, young people and the disabled) and (b) 'correction of unsatisfactory employment situations', which in practice meant depressed regions. There thus emerged the dilemma which was to face policy design in subsequent periods, that is, that of striking a balance between the treatment of particular groups of the labour force and the treatment of spatial economic areas.

In this phase of development of the ESF the labour market situation in Europe changed radically: between 1970 and 1978 unemployment trebled from two to six million (taking the EC9 figure—the original six Member States plus Denmark, Ireland and the United Kingdom) and unemployment among those aged under 25 years rose fivefold. By the end of 1978 a new category of ESF expenditure had been recognized: job creation schemes for young workers. A consequence was that the expenditure on young people, which had been 13 per cent of the total funds made available from 1972 to 1977, rose to 40 per cent during the period 1978–83. Given that total resources doubled between the two periods, the outcome was a sixfold increase in funding devoted to the situation of young people.

Phase III: Economic Depression and Spatial Targeting
The third phase of development occurred during a period when high levels of unemployment took hold in virtually all the Member States, with total unemployment doubling between 1977 and 1983. Increasing attention was given to the choice between targeting high-unemployment or low-income regions. The outcome was a decision to devote 40 per cent of the fund to the poorest regions, allocating the rest to areas of high unemployment, wherever they were located in the Community, with 75 per cent of the latter share devoted to young people. Attention was also paid to support for innovatory projects that might provide lessons of wider value to Member States. During the 1984–86 period the ESF moved much closer to achieving its broad objectives: the five richest countries together received only 10 per cent of the funding. Nonetheless, it is probably fair to say that the ESF was still more a 'source of encouragement' than a substantial instrument of policy. During this phase the maximum of 50 per cent contribution from the EC was maintained, but private as well as public bodies could apply. However, the EC would put into the latter schemes no more than was being contributed by the Member State. The overall outcome was that 6 per cent of the EC budget was spent via the ESF, largely on vocational training programmes, recruit-

ment and employment subsidies, resettlement programmes and the promotion of geographical mobility.

Phase IV: Major Reform—Promoting Cohesion and Accountability

The negotiations leading up to the Single European Act gave a significant boost to the status of the Structural Funds. While it is now commonly recognized that the purpose of the Structural Funds is to promote economic and social cohesion, this has not always been the case, especially in the period up to the watershed of 1988 when it was agreed to double both the ESF and ERDF by 1993, absorbing 25 per cent of the EC budget.

Four principles underlay the reform of the Structural Funds in preparation for the funding period 1989–93. First, the aim was to concentrate resources where they were most needed; second, the Commission was given the responsibility of promoting partnership between member governments, other agencies involved in socioeconomic development and the Commission itself; third, an emphasis was placed on a programmatic approach to the funding process, whereby a coherent set of projects would be put forward for support on the basis of a thorough assessment of the conditions of the economic areas concerned and targeted groups of the labour force; and, finally, a condition of granting the large increase in resources was that rigorous monitoring should become an integral part of the funding process.

Turning to the scale of Structural Funds expenditure, of the ECU 60 billion (1989 prices) devoted to the period 1989–93, almost two-thirds were allocated to Objective 1 regions—those which were lagging most behind the rest of the Community. These regions cover about one-fifth of the Community population. Note that Padoa-Schioppa (1987) estimated that investment of ECU 55–76 billion would be needed to raise the GDP of the least favoured regions by 1 per cent. Nonetheless, for these regions expenditure from the Funds was of some macroeconomic significance, amounting to between 2 and 2.5 per cent of GDP in Greece, Ireland and Portugal in 1989 and rising by about 1.5 percentage points by 1993.

The funds allocated to Objective 2 regions (those affected strongly by industrial decline) amounted to 12 per cent of the total; Objectives 3 (combating long-term unemployment) and 4 (occupational integration of those under 25 years of age) together received about 12 per cent; Objectives 5a (strengthening of agricultural structures) and 5b (rural development) were allocated about 5 per cent each; and approximately 2 per cent of the budget was set aside for transitional measures and Community initiatives with specific purposes (e.g. environmental schemes, cross-border cooperation, research and technological innovation, energy networks, equal opportunities).

As far as the distribution of the population is concerned, Objective 1 and 2 regions covered 22 and 17 per cent of the EU population, respectively; Objective 5b covered a further 5 per cent, whereas the other objectives and measures are 'horizontal' activities that do not relate to specific spatial areas of the population.

In terms of the balance between the different types of expenditure under the Community Support Frameworks (CSFs)[2] for the poorest regions, these regions varied quite significantly. For example, infrastructure absorbed about half of the support received by Italy and Spain, compared with only a quarter for Ireland. Labour market programmes accounted for 40 per cent of the funding for Ireland but only about 15 per cent for Greece and Italy.

Since, despite some overlaps, the separate Funds have different roles, we would expect their distribution across the different objectives to vary significantly. Over 80 per cent of the ERDF is associated with Objective 1, compared with about 64 per cent of the ESF and 55 per cent of the EAGGF. Most of the remainder of the ESF is devoted to Objectives 3 and 4 concerned with employment and training schemes. The balance of the EAGGF is spent on the development of rural areas.

Phase V: 'Reform of the Reform'

In preparing for the 1994–99 period of the Structural Funds, essentially the same principles enunciated under Phase IV were maintained (CEC, 1993a and 1994). However, an increasing effort is intended to be devoted to questions of evaluation. As regards the Fund itself, more discretion will be used in designating Objective 2 regions; Objectives 3 and 4 will be geared more to the need for adaptation to industrial change; Objective 5b, relating to rural diversification, will receive more emphasis, and Objective 6, dealing with fisheries, has been added. However, a further instrument of policy devoted to the four poorest countries has been introduced, namely, the Cohesion Fund. Taking the latter into account, contributions from the Structural Funds will reach about 3 per cent of GDP in the Objective 1 regions in 1999, the end of the current CSF planning period. The ERDF component will reach about 8 per cent of gross fixed capital formation.

The development of the Structural Funds has reached a stage where the evaluation of their impacts upon output, employment and income raises the full range of methodological difficulties. For the Objective 1 countries the scale of the Structural and Cohesion Funds taken together is of macroeconomic significance identifiable within macroeconomic models used for short-term as well as long-term forecasting and simulation. At the same time, other programmes or projects within, for example, the ESF have quite specific quantitative and/or qualitative aims working within the existing labour or training

---

2 Community Support Frameworks (CSFs) are the planning basis on which the Commission and the Member States agree in order to guide the allocation of the Structural Funds.

market structures or involving changes to those structures. More microlevel evaluation methods are then necessary. Between the macro- and microlevels there is a metalevel of regional/subregional or sectoral/subsectoral analysis that has produced a great number of studies, some of which border on the macro and others on the micro.

In the light of the above development of the Structural Funds, and with special reference to human resource issues, the following section outlines approaches to evaluation that are potentially most relevant for the ESF.

2   EVALUATION OF LABOUR MARKET PROGRAMMES

2.1   Different Areas of Evaluation Practice

Generally speaking, there have been five broad areas of policy that have given rise to different types of evaluation designed to establish their labour market effects:

1. Tax-subsidy policy bearing on employment, investment and, more recently, environmental objectives, taking full account of broader macroeconomic policy constraints.
2. Large-scale regional or subregional policy involving labour cost subsidies or capital investment subsidies.
3. State aid to specific industries (including public sector companies) motivated, in some cases, by concern for the regional consequences of decline.
4. Spatial development policy generating quite specific, often large-scale, economic events in an area.
5. 'Active labour market policies' involving employment and training measures, many of which have been spatially as well as functionally differentiated.

Whereas the evaluation practice found under each of these headings does vary a great deal, certain generalizations are possible on the reasons why the evaluation has taken distinctive directions.

After more than three decades of development of macroeconomic models, it is inconceivable that any evaluation of a major tax-subsidy initiative would proceed without the use of formal econometric models. But the quality of the data and the research base from which such models may be constructed varies widely across EU Member States.

Macroeconomic and multisectoral models for individual countries do exist in forms that capture substantial aspects of the behaviour of economic actors, and their results can form a quantitative basis for the sort of broader assessment required for decision-making. Integrated multicountry, multisectoral models have also been developed, notably, HERMES (CEC, 1993b) and E3ME (Barker and Gardiner, in press), for the European Union, though the treatment given to the labour sector is extremely crude in the former and still under development in the latter.

There does not seem to be an example of a purely multiregional model for an EU country capable of generating the standard macroeconomic variables at the regional level. There have been single-region models constructed in fairly *ad hoc* ways or for rather short periods, but few have any substantial track record in operational forecasting or policy evaluation. The development of *sub*regional models, as might be expected, has been very limited indeed.

The consequences of the above for the evaluation of policies designed to benefit particular spatial areas are quite significant. First, for large-scale fiscal intervention, such as regional employment and investment subsidies, operating via the market mechanism (i.e. by adjusting prices rather than directly manipulating quantities), there are very few working models with a structure that would automatically facilitate the relevant simulation analysis. Nor would existing models deal comfortably with the evaluation of the impact of a major investment project: at the regional level, for certain countries this would be more or less possible with some special manipulation of the model, but not at subregional level (see, however, Wilson, Assefa and Beard, 1995, for a recent modelling initiative).

Second, the *sub*regional models that exist are usually of *ad-hoc* construction and have very rudimentary behavioural content; they do not provide the basis for analysis of such frequently used policies as wage subsidies targeting particular groups of the labour force, subsidies for short-time work, recruitment subsidies, subsidies for the labour costs of trainers and the labour costs or allowances of trainees, subsidies towards the capital expenditure required for training, or creation of shared facilities for small enterprises to use. These are typical of ESF-style projects. There is, however, scope for using existing multiregional models or other *ad-hoc* single-region or subregional models to provide a 'background simulation/projection' that could capture the main features of the economic environment in the spatial area concerned. These features could then be fed into a more focussed evaluation of a project in the form of assumptions that need to be taken into account when interpreting such statistics as the proportion of trainees who obtain employment within a year of completing their courses or the proportion of jobs created that last for a year or more.

Turning to the third field of policy evaluation given above, that is, the effects of state aid to particular industries in difficulty, the methodologies used concentrate on assessments of corporate strategies and viability before and after rationalization and investment, with the emphasis placed more on the analysis of product market rather than labour market outcomes. The treatment of impacts on the different spatial areas where establishments are situated has not been tackled as such in the evaluation studies of industrial policy, though it has featured in the fourth evaluation group, often termed 'economic impact analysis'.

Economic impact analysis has had an extremely chequered history. The lack of adequate data both on the regional or local economic environment and on the specific impact 'event' being analysed has brought forth some analyses that show rather more ingenuity and guesswork than is perhaps appropriate. The context has usually related to one of the following: (a) major contraction of an industry; (b) major new industrial development involving a substantial construction phase; (c) service sector development requiring high-quality office-building and subsequent employment of well-qualified staff; (d) agricultural development; (e) promotion of tourism and leisure; (f) rural and urban infrastructure development; and (g) the impact of public sector institutional employment on local economies (government departments, educational establishments).

Some impact studies can benefit from the availability of existing regional or local economic models, but these are in a small minority. In the main the practice has been to aim for a judicious use of Keynesian multipliers estimated from survey data collected by the investigator or borrowed from other, more or less comparable studies (Lewis, 1988).

However, evaluators of labour market programmes are most unlikely to be provided with the resources to carry out impact studies. Moreover, even if they were, the scale of the typical programme/project in a selected spatial area will be small relative to the kinds of impact usually studied with the above approaches. Certainly, it would be inappropriate to propose that 'good-practice' evaluation should involve carrying out an impact analysis. However, the problem of constructing the 'counterfactual' is as troubling for the evaluation of small-scale policy interventions in small economies (i.e. the subregion) as it is for large-scale 'shocks' to those economies.

In some cases projects under the European Structural Funds may fall between the large, identifiable economic impact and the small, developmental intervention. Some recognition of this must be borne in mind when dealing with particularly disadvantaged regions where development assistance overall may amount to very substantial support, even if individual projects are relatively modest.

Finally, the 'active labour market policies' come closest in their nature and scale to the sort of projects supported under the ESF in a majority of European regions. There have been many examinations of such employment and training measures at different stages in their evolution. For example, Layard (1979), Lindley (1980, 1983, 1986) and Stern (1988) cover the build-up during the

United Kingdom's main period of policy experimentation, and Johannesson and Wadensjö (1995) present an up-to-date review of the lessons from mainly Swedish experience of labour market policies.

In the main, however, two different streams of research have contributed to the evaluation of specific schemes. The first is based on microdata relating to scheme participants and, sometimes, nonparticipants and seeks to assess the impact of participation in the scheme on the postscheme experience of the individual, notably the probability of being in employment, perhaps differentiated according to the relevance of the work to the type of training or work experience obtained on the scheme and the likely wage obtained. Techniques for both experimental and nonexperimental evaluation are reviewed by Heckman and Smith, and Björklund and Regnér (chaps 2 and 3, respectively, in this volume); related methodological issues and particular examples of evaluation are dealt with in other chapters (see also Jensen and Madsen, 1993, for a recent collection of studies on the effects of active labour market measures).

The second stream is concerned much more with the market situation to which a particular scheme might be introduced. It stems, in part, from early problems with ensuring adequate counterfactual/individual control group data in the microeconometric studies but also has its own rationale. This essentially recognizes that the scale of a number of schemes or their combined effect means that they cannot be handled adequately as marginal interventions requiring only a partial equilibrium treatment. Their wider ramifications need to be taken into account, as regards both the impacts on individuals and on nonparticipating organizations and the local, regional or even nationwide economic effects.

2.2   Labour Market Measures

The costs of recruiting, employing, training, 'maintaining', insuring and retiring workers can all be affected by state fiscal and regulatory policy, including special schemes to assist disadvantaged social groups and regions. But the boundaries between these different categories of subsidy and regulation are not always clear. Training and maintaining (the former devoted to enhancing the human capital available to the firm through promoting skill acquisition, and the latter to attending to the physical and psychological well-being of the work force) can be very closely associated with the costs of recruitment and initial orientation in the firm, as well as with the subsequent recurrent nonwage costs of employment. Employee insurance either through company-specific or statutory schemes can cover specific work-related risks in the fields of health, safety and redundancy as well as more general risks where the link with the employment situation in the firm is tenuous, if not nonexistent. The costs of retirement (including temporary withdrawal through sickness) borne by the employer or employee are influenced by the impact of such factors as work force size and age structure upon the viability of pension funds and the scope for supplementation of the basic pension. They can also be related to recruitment practices where the government seeks the displacement of older workers through voluntary early retirement in favour of certain groups of unemployed workers.

In evaluating the impact of different schemes, a number of basic concepts have been used, from which some simple performance indicators can be derived.

– *Deadweight effect*: The percentage of subsidized units (jobs or people) the status of which or whom has been unaffected by the subsidy.
– *Defensive (or 'domino') effect*: The percentage of subsidized units that would not have required the subsidy but for its payment to other units.
– *Substitution effect*: The percentage of subsidized units that substitute for nonsubsidized units in the same firm or, in the case of recruitment subsidies, nonsubsidized members of the labour force, whether inside or outside the firm.
– *Displacement effect*: The percentage of subsidized units that displace other units in nonsubsidized firms.

These concepts clearly embody the reactions of firms and their competitors to the subsidy regime in terms of potential changes in factor proportions, output, prices, profits and investment. Where the subsidy is quite large in relation to a particular industry's costs, the production and product market effects are likely to be significant and susceptible to direct measurement; there is then the possibility of conducting an impact study for that industry. In other cases the relatively modest scale of the impact upon individual firms or industries could, in any econometric analysis, easily be swamped by changes in other economic factors of wider significance. Under these circumstances in empirical evaluation great emphasis is likely to be placed on the use of sample surveys of subsidized and nonsubsidized firms.

Deadweight, defensive and substitution effects can, in principle, be derived from well-designed questions put to subsidized firms only. The measurement of displacement effects requires nonsubsidized firms to be included. The results, of course, are very rough and ready, but the approach does not compare unfavourably with those used in evaluating other forms of industrial incentive.

Not all those saved from unemployment by these schemes would have appeared on the unemployment count. If reductions in the latter are to be highlighted rather than increases in employment, some adjustment can be made to this end. A more compelling reason for making this adjustment is in order to take into account the savings of unemployment benefits and related transfer payments. By allowing for these savings plus redundancy payments avoided, together with the first-round effects of higher tax revenues and social security contributions, it is possible to give rough, rather short-run, estimates of net cost per net job created and net cost per person taken off the unemployment count. (See Delander and Niklasson, chap. 6 in this volume, for a broader discussion of cost–benefit analysis in this field.) Macrosimulation models (Layard and Nickell, 1980) or macroeconometric models (Turner, Wallis and Whitley, 1987; Whitley and Wilson, 1983) may be used to explore the longer-term dynamic properties, where the size of a programme makes its impact discernible at that level and where the mechanism of the programme can be represented within the model's structure by an appropriate manipulation of the parameters.

2.3   Evaluation in Context

The lessons from previous evaluation work also indicate that the context in which evaluation takes place is particularly significant in practice, quite apart from the limited scope for sophisticated technical analysis. Certain characteristics will affect the impact of a particular policy intervention or, indeed, the impact of any exogenous change that emanates from outside the spatial area concerned (country, region or subregion). Their effects often dwarf the significance of the precise design of a programme as to whether or not it is concerned with, for example, wage subsidies, recruitment subsidies, training, enterprise development or infrastructure support. Their importance in determining the kinds of monitoring scheme and the specific indicators chosen should not be underestimated.

Thus, programme impacts and, correspondingly, evaluation techniques will vary with the following programme attributes:

scale:
(a) the coverage of the programme relative to the size of the socioeconomic space for which the evaluation is being conducted and (b) the extent of the tax expenditure involved relative to the costs perceived by the actors whose behaviour is being influenced;

selective:
dealing only with a broad section of economic activity, whether distinguished by aggregate sector (e.g. agriculture or manufacturing), spatial area (e.g. poorer nations or regions) or major socioeconomic group (e.g. women);

targeted:
focussed more sharply on particular sectors (e.g. coal mining), subregions (e.g. level 2 of the Eurostat regional classification) or labour force groups (e.g. unemployed young people, women returning to the labour force);

transitory: where the policy is seen by the actors as being merely a
                         temporary measure, or one which may be used only recur-
                         rently from time to time;

countercyclical: where policy intervention is a reasonably predictable form
                         of countercyclical measure (rather than being considered to
                         be so *ex post*);

long term: where the policy intervention is seen to be a long-term
                         measure, even though aspects of it may be subject to vari-
                         ation according to socioeconomic conditions.

At one extreme, methodologies will be required to deal with small, targeted, transitory measures—at the other extreme, with large, nonselective,
long-term measures.[3] In the former case the technical problems of evaluation
may be dominated by the administrative problems of setting up and running
the project. Thus, it may take much longer to evaluate a project than the total
life time of the programme of which it is a part. Moreover, where policies and
their focus of implementation via programmes, or projects within programmes, are continually evolving, the nature of the relationship between
decision-making and evaluation needs to be spelt out.

The environment for evaluation of labour market and related regional,
industrial or social policies was an extremely dynamic and uncertain one during the 1980s and is turning out to be no less so in the 1990s. Several common
factors that impinge on the evaluation process are present in different areas of
policy-making and implementation:

1. The extent of policy experimentation and shifts in the rationale for policy.
2. The instability of delivery mechanisms.
3. The proliferation of schemes comprising different mixes of basic ingredients and delivery mechanisms.
4. Inadequate data for auditing, monitoring and evaluation.
5. Uncertain commitment of policy-makers to research and evaluation.

---

3 By way of illustration, all the UK employment subsidies during the 1980s were highly selective
in practice, even though not all were strongly targeted. For example, 90 per cent of the jobs
preserved under the Temporary Employment Subsidy (half of which were in textiles, leather
and clothing) and 95 per cent of the jobs supported by the temporary short-time work scheme
(with 60 per cent in metals and engineering) were in manufacturing. Approximately 75 per cent
of the small firms' subsidy, which began and ended by being limited to manufacturing, and
almost 50 per cent of the youth wage subsidy (Young Workers' Scheme), which had no industrial targeting as such, in effect also went to that sector. Equally important is the fact that all
these subsidies were transitory. *Ex post*, it is possible to see some of them in a countercyclical
light. However, this view would tend to exaggerate the degree of policy coherence, given the
way in which they evolved through occasional changes in eligibility criteria and value of
subsidy and through piecemeal extensions of the period allowed for applications.

In the light of the plethora of policy developments and implementation schemes from macro- through to microlevel, there is considerable need to look for continuity in the experience of previous policies and evaluations. This can be promoted, first, by recognizing the existence of life cycles of programme development and the influences that dynamic aspects can have upon both performance and the evaluation process designed to measure it. Second, where longitudinal evidence is very limited it is especially important to extract as much insight as possible from the available cross-sectional evidence (e.g. cross-occupational/industrial/regional/national). Third, a generic approach to the analysis of programmes or projects must be adopted in order to recognize the principal elements (e.g. subsidies to employment/recruitment/training), so that the analyses of particular initiatives can lead to as much insight as possible of relevance to other initiatives and, indeed, overall programmes.

Finally, given the wide range of, and changes in socioeconomic policies, greater emphasis should be given to the establishment of continuous monitoring systems rather than *ad-hoc* programme-specific surveys and administrative data bases. (See Auer and Kruppe, chap. 30 in this volume, for a review of the development of monitoring systems in EU Member States and the United States.) A number of improvements have been made in this respect in several EU countries, notably, the extension of national labour force surveys from annual to quarterly frequency, the introduction of an overlapping sample and additional questions to deal with precarious employment, occupation and so forth. Another promising development is the introduction of cohort surveys of young people.

3   IMPLICATIONS FOR MONITORING AND EVALUATION OF THE ESF

What can we conclude from this experience of evaluation of various forms of policy having direct effects on particular spatial areas and selected industries or socioeconomic groups within them, and which of these conclusions would be of relevance to the evaluation of the ESF?

Ultimately, the answer depends on the balance to be struck between 'basic' and 'progressive' evaluation. See Schmid, chap. 7 in this volume, however, for a much broader treatment of the evaluation process, together with the Introduction to this Handbook by Schmid et al. Clearly, a 'lowest common denominator' methodology could be adopted, based on the sort of evaluation that can be done currently by the Member countries that are least well equipped to carry out such analysis. Those with a poorly developed labour market information system and/or limited institutional competence to carry out the analysis would then dictate the nature of the evaluation. Alternatively, an approach may be adopted whereby an evaluation scheme is specified that incorporates agreement as to the path to be followed in progressively improving evaluation. The basic approach would, of course, be nested within the progressive approach.

In devising a progressive scheme, it would be worth treating auditing, monitoring and evaluation in a unified way, the first being a prerequisite for the second, and the second for the third. For example, financial control systems required for auditing should then have clear enough categories of expenditure and income as to be used directly in monitoring and evaluation. In these terms such 'evaluation' is, in fact, auditing or monitoring. If evaluation is to be given a higher priority it may be necessary to accept more explicitly that there will be a trade-off between the extensiveness of auditing, on the one hand, and monitoring and evaluation, on the other.

From the EU point of view, the division of labour between the Commission and national governments over the different elements of auditing, monitoring and evaluation will depend on the complexity of the tasks involved and concerns to promote common standards. However, it is clear from the sheer volume of projects involved that neither the Commission nor national governments will be able to conduct 100 per cent evaluation of projects. Indeed, it is doubtful whether all national governments will be able to monitor adequately all their ESF projects, and even arguable whether they will be able to audit them fully.

The Commission's evaluation strategy will, therefore, need to comprise four elements:

1. Proposals for the evaluation methodologies to be used at national level.
2. Rules for the selection of programmes/projects that will be evaluated.
3. Scrutiny of evaluation methods used and samples selected in the light of elements 1 and 2.
4. Proposals for progressive improvements in evaluation in the light of element 3.

Unless element 2 is included, the evaluation will degenerate into a game in which countries will have enormous scope to evaluate the most promising projects if they have the skill to select them a priori. Without elements 3 and 4 it will be difficult to raise the quality of evaluation. (Unless elements 2, 3 and 4 are included, countries will have an incentive to keep the evaluation at its most basic, that is, least costly, level because then they can evaluate a larger sample of projects than is required by the Commission and report those which give the most successful outcomes.)

Clearly, in practice administrative and diplomatic realities will have considerable influence, but if the evaluation of Structural Funds is to become more rigorous, as is intended, control will need to be exerted in the above manner.

The evaluation strategy will also need to take into account whether the aim is to evaluate the overall impact of the ESF or to use evaluation more directly as a management tool. The former would require the sampling of a reasonably representative selection of programmes/projects. The latter would deploy the evaluation budget in such a way as to sample more heavily at the margin dealing with countries/regions or types of programme/project where there were grounds for dissatisfaction with the standards of evaluation or prima-facie concern about the effectiveness of a certain type of programme.

In dealing with a group of countries and regions that vary greatly as to their levels of development, there must be some caution in using evaluation standards as a means of rationing the allocation of funds. It should be expected that richer countries will be able to meet higher standards because their statistical, evaluation and research systems will be more extensive. It would, therefore, compound the disparities that the Structural Funds are intended to remove if the distribution of funds depended on the evaluation standards.

However, one way to maintain standards and avoid the above problem is to adopt a generic approach to evaluation. This involves assuming that programmes/projects of particular types have 'similar' impacts in 'similar' labour markets and local economies across Europe. The concern of the Commission would then be to build up an evaluation data base in which studies are classified according to typologies of projects and local labour markets that are designed so as to identify the principal characteristics of projects and economic environments that bear upon the objectives of the ESF.

Hence, the Commission's evaluation strategy would be to compile a data base of good-practice, if not best-practice, evaluations and to require ESF programmes/projects to be classified according to the same typologies. The first phase of evaluation would be to compare proposals with previous experience with that kind of project. This would be a form of a priori evaluation that the Commission could itself perform, provided national governments produced suitably classified summary data.

Such a form of generic a priori evaluation would not disadvantage countries with less-developed statistical and evaluation systems, provided the economic conditions covered by projects in the evaluation data base are sufficiently representative. However, the supply of good-practice evaluations would be dominated by the more-developed regions and representativeness may not be sufficient. This imbalance would then offer a rationale for the Commission's evaluation research, namely, to sponsor good-practice evaluation in selected project–labour market combinations that would help to fill the gaps in the evaluation data base.

There would be a number of practical difficulties to contend with in developing the evaluation data base. Studies differ in their use of quantitative indicators by which to assess projects and in the degree to which qualitative information is taken into account. Considerable judgement would be required in rating the effectiveness of projects in relation to the promotion of equity, efficiency or other broad objectives such as communal cohesion. But these are no different from the judgements already being made by officials in the Commission and at national level or the judgements that will increasingly be required as the Structural Funds are subjected to more evaluation.

It is probably fair to say that there has been little *ex-post* evaluation of ESF projects but that auditing and monitoring are firmly established in several countries. No further reference will be made to the issue of auditing, except to say that it is imperative that the audit data should be classified in ways that relate to operational objectives and that allow for correspondence between the financial and nonfinancial audit data and the monitoring data. The latter should, essentially, develop out of the former.

The principal elements of the proposed approach are as follows:

1. Develop a classification of types of intervention by which the ESF objectives may be pursued.
2. Require all projects approved for funding to be allocated to one or more of these types of intervention.
3. Require key initial summary statistics on projects and their local economic environments that indicate the intended nature of the project and the degree to which the environment is likely to be conducive to success or failure.
4. Use the evaluation data base and elements 1–3 in order to provide a generic a priori evaluation.
5. Require monitoring information corresponding to the items covered in 3.
6. Use elements 4 and 5 to guide sampling of projects for evaluation.

In order to develop the sort of generic approach to evaluation indicated above, three principal ingredients need to be recognized in the overall evaluation process. The first relates to the type of project, the second to the type of spatial socioeconomic area and the third to the evaluation context (Table 28.1).

As regards projects, the principal points have already been made: human resources programmes achieve their effects through regulation, provision of a service and/or fiscal transfer to one or more groups of actors in the markets for education, training or labour. It is desirable to examine closely each programme and project within it in order to specify the principal mechanisms through which they operate to achieve not only the stated objectives but also other effects. The names given to programmes do not always capture their essential impacts; so programmes/projects need to be classified by mechanisms as well as stated objectives. The evaluation should proceed by seeking to reduce the presentational and operational complexity of a given project to its main components.

Table 28.1 Generic Evaluation: Principal Ingredients

1. Project type	
Project objectives:	short term/cyclical/long term
	demand-side orientation (direct job creation, indirect job creation)
	supply-side orientation (training, entrepreneurship, new business creation, infrastructure)
Project mechanism:	direct job creation, investment subsidy, wage subsidy, recruitment subsidy, training subsidy, enterprise development, infrastructure support (information, advice, shared facilities etc.)
2. Spatial area	reflecting type of locale in terms of its effects upon the relative difficulty with which projects might achieve objectives
3. Evaluation context	scale of project, selective, targeted, transitory, countercyclical, long term

The second ingredient required in developing a more generic form of evaluation is the classification of spatial areas. This needs to be done in such a way as to enable areas with similar underlying socioeconomic situations to be grouped together. If such a classification were possible, a link could be made between evaluation results obtained with a certain type of project in one area and potential results if the same type of project were to be carried out in another area belonging to the same spatial category. Thus, *ex-post* insights obtained in one area might be useful in *ex-ante* evaluation of similar projects not only in the same, but also in other areas.

The final ingredient relates to the evaluation context. Similar projects in similar areas may yield different results because one is more targeted than another, one is implemented during an economic recession and another at the peak of recovery and so on. The main factors that might distinguish otherwise almost identical projects and socioeconomic environments have already been discussed and are summarized in Table 28.1.

If care were taken to classify projects and spatial areas in this way, recognition of the different evaluation contexts would lead to an overall increase in the cost-effectiveness of evaluation studies. There would be scope for reducing costs of learning and exploiting economies of scale in the evaluation process. From the EU perspective, such a system would raise the rate of return from carrying out high-quality evaluation studies because positive externalities would be created by communication of the findings from one project context (type of project and type of locale) to others. The EU can promote more rigorous evaluation through both regulatory means and financial incentives. In the former the granting of support under the ESF would be conditional upon carrying out certain auditing, monitoring and evaluation procedures. In the latter contributions to the costs of evaluation might be made where it is particularly important to extend the range of evidence dealing with the effects of certain types of project in certain types of locale and evaluation context.

4   PROJECT INDICATORS—A GENERIC PERSPECTIVE

In the generic approach to evaluation an attempt is made to identify the essential characteristics of programmes or projects and of their effects. The aim is to extract the maximum insight obtainable from each evaluation, not only for the case in question but also for other related cases. In order to achieve this objective, generic evaluation needs to be planned in such a way as to produce 'transferable evidence'. First, the intention is to conduct rigorous evaluations of types of projects, covering different types of spatial socioeconomic environments. Second, a stock of evaluations is built up, the results of which are categorized so as to be applicable to other projects and environments that are 'similar'.

A number of aspects relating to the classification of projects are dealt with in this section, particularly from the point of view of the performance indicators generally required in evaluation.

The importance of the distinctions between auditing, monitoring and evaluation is now normally well recognized, though some blurring of the boundaries is inevitable in practice. For present purposes, it is enough to use the following definitions:

– *Auditing:* Establishing the basic facts regarding the levels of activity and expenditure contractually associated with them during each project.
– *Monitoring:* Following the progress of the project from approval through to completion, focussing on those aspects that are key to the project's levels of activity according to different dimensions of interest and to the internal effectiveness of the project.
– *Evaluation:* Judging the effects of the project on participating and nonparticipating individuals and organizations and evaluating the overall net benefits and costs at appropriate levels (e.g. subregion, region, nation, Community), covering financial and nonfinancial considerations.

As regards evaluation, we should also distinguish between comprehensive research into the socioeconomic effects of a project and an examination of whether or not it fulfilled the specific objectives set for it. In the latter case the exercise could be more limited than in the former, depending on how narrowly defined are the objectives.

The narrower concept of evaluation may actually involve no more than monitoring because the objectives may be set wholly in terms of project efficiency and short-term gross effects. Such a case would be a special training scheme to achieve lower costs per trainee without reducing their initial success in obtaining employment within, say, one month after course completion.

Clearly, it is possible to set objectives that remove any substantial element of evaluation (as opposed to monitoring) that seeks to assess the net impact of a programme. But such projects may not be approved in the first place because they are not sufficiently ambitious.

Indicators for use in auditing, monitoring and evaluation can be considered from several perspectives, but depend on recognition of certain basic types of information, as summarized in Table 28.2. Note that these indicators are concerned not only with the labour market processes affected but also with the policy management system. For example, items 1 and 5 can be combined to provide a picture of the 'project community' in relation to the local socioeconomic environment (item 6) and the 'nonproject community'. Some nonparticipating project managers, individuals and organizations may be significantly affected by the project: employment and training opportunities, incomes, local sales and output may be stimulated or displaced by the intervention of the project.

Two other forms of information are also relevant. The attitudes and opinions (item 7) of the actors in the project community provide potentially important qualitative information about the effectiveness of a project. In addition, similar projects may produce quite different results if they are conducted within very different regulatory and fiscal systems (item 8). For example, the social security rights of young entrants to the labour force will influence their participation rates in training and work experience programmes and their employment records on completion of the programmes.

In using these basic types of information, which are required for monitoring and evaluation, it is necessary to identify specific indicators. Some of the information summarized above may be collected systematically as part of the auditing and monitoring activities linked to specific projects, but that relating to the local economic environment (including potential 'control groups') can probably be more efficiently gathered separately. However, there are two broad groups of indicators that fall into the middle ground between these two areas: they correspond to the qualitative indicators dealing with aspects of the

*Table 28.2   Basic Information Relating to Monitoring and Evaluation
                  Indicators*

---

1. Characteristics of project:
   - project management
   - participating individual
   - participating organizations
   - the activity (e.g. types of training, jobs, new businesses)
2. Duration of project:
   - creation
   - selection of participants
   - the central activity
   - follow-up activity (where applicable)
   - monitoring period
   - evaluation period
3. Selection process:
   - populations from which participating individuals and organizations are selected
   - criteria for selection
   - applicants relative to population
   - selected relative to applicants
   - acceptances relative to selected
   - initial participants relative to those accepting
4. Project process:
   - attrition among participants during project by explanation for leaving
   - achievement rates at key stages (where applicable, e.g. in training with modular approach)
   - attendance rates
   - completion rates
   - certification rates
5. Postproject experience:
   - project management (other projects etc.)
   - participating individuals (work and training experience)
   - participating organizations (viability, continuing employment of individuals, involvement in further projects)
6. Local socioeconomic environment:
   - local economic prosperity and social welfare
   - threats and opportunities regarding local economic development
   - situations regarding certain target disadvantaged groups
   - nonparticipating project managers
   - nonparticipating individuals
   - nonparticipating organizations
7. Qualitative information:
   Opinion surveys of participating individuals during the project
   - financial arrangements
   - quality of organization
   - quality and relevance of training/work experience
   - reasons for joining
   - reasons for leaving
   Opinion surveys of participating organizations
   - financial arrangements
   - quality of organization
   - quality and relevance of training/work experience
   Opinion surveys of project managers
   - financial arrangements
   - quality of organization responsible for programmes at higher levels than the project
   - planning and strategic aspects.
   The key points to make about opinion surveys are that continuity in conducting them is required for reliable interpretation and that cross-national, even cross-regional, differences can be particularly difficult to assess.
8. Regulatory and fiscal framework:
   - conditions governing employment contracts
   - social security regulations and provisions
   - individual rights and equal opportunities regulations
   - collective agreements regarding all the above

---

within-project experience of participants and to the quantitative and qualitative postproject experience of participants. Both groups of indicators will rely on survey and case-study evidence rather than administrative information obtained during the project.

In practical terms, surveys and case studies will not be feasible for anything more than a minority of projects. In the light of this limitation a strategy for evaluation using an evaluation data base was advanced in section 3. The proposal is to focus the use of surveys and case studies upon generic types of projects that are already quantitatively important but are underevaluated in some contexts at least, or that are deliberately intended to be innovative and to shed new light on the effectiveness of certain new types of project.

In the middle ground between administrative monitoring data and survey sources of evaluation data there is a choice to be made as to how far to develop the former in areas that overlap with the latter (the follow-up survey as an extension of the administrative data system is a case in point). The choice will depend partly on the organizational structure for project management.

It may also be worth distinguishing the main indicators for evaluation from those that are indicators for explanation. For example, it is possible to conclude that a project has failed to increase the participation of disadvantaged groups in training programmes without knowing why it has failed to do so. Anticipation of possible influences upon such a participation rate might lead to the collection of relevant data, for instance, on the effort devoted to publicity and to making training available at particular times of the day or week to fit in with public transport and/or taking and collecting children to and from school. But these data may burden the basic monitoring/evaluation process without providing enough insight for conclusive analysis in the absence of a more specialized survey or case studies.

The aim of the surveys and case studies should be to shed light on one or more of the four 'quantitative summary effects' noted earlier (deadweight, defensive, substitution and displacement effects), on qualitative aspects of schemes and on the reliability of information collected for administrative auditing and monitoring purposes. In addition, there are macroeconomic and spill-over effects that can only be provided through rules of thumb derived from the operation of a fully specified macroeconomic model.

4.1 Classifications of Spatial Areas According to Economic Performance

Finally, let us turn to the significance of spatial classification in the evaluation process. Much evaluation of economy-wide programmes, such as youth training schemes, identifies spatial location as being an important factor in determining the employment experience of people and the impact of participation in a programme on that experience. Spatial location may be captured by spatial dummy variables in cross-sectional statistical analysis or by the actual values of indicators (such as regional or subregional unemployment rates) that are intended to represent the state of the local economy, especially the relative difficulty of finding employment.

However, Green and Champion (1991), using UK data, emphasize the difficulty of characterizing the local labour market in which a particular project is operating simply from the region or even subregion of which it is a part. By the same token, their results also point to the problem of establishing indicators that can be used to provide an adequate 'counterfactual assessment', if this is based at the regional level because of the availability of a regional economic and labour market model. The opportunities for more sophisticated evaluation apparently offered by the existence of such a model (see section 2) must be set against the manifest heterogeneity that the regional counterfactual would cover up.

If regions or subregions are poor classifications of socioeconomic areas because of their heterogeneity, is it possible to establish a better classification that might be more useful for policy implementation and evaluation? Cluster analysis techniques can be used to group members of a population with known sets of characteristics in such a way as to minimize the within-group variation and maximize the between-group variation. If the detailed data exist (e.g. for travel-to-work areas), it should be possible to do better than use administrative regions by exploiting information at the local level.

From the point of view of evaluation, the groups ultimately chosen should reflect the extent to which areas within these groups face similar current problems *and* share similar opportunities for solving them. Strictly speaking, the classification of areas would need to be redrawn to suit each labour market programme because the mix of policy objectives changes from one to another.[4]

In practice it would not be possible to differentiate the basic classification every time the programme being evaluated was changed. The classifications produced by Green, Owen and Hasluck (1991), for example, may be regarded as fairly general typologies. They provide a basis from which more tailor-

---

4 Areas that have one problem (e.g. long-term unemployment) may not have another (e.g. youth unemployment or lack of opportunities for women), at least to the same degree relative to other areas. More significant, however, in evaluating the overall effectiveness of a programme and the success of individual projects within it is the difficulty posed to the achievement of an objective by the underlying circumstances in different areas. Thus, one area with a high level of long-term unemployment may be about to benefit from the exploitation of a major oil field nearby or by the establishment of a power station, whereas another area with the same long-term unemployment situation may have no such prospect in view. The same project conducted in both areas could have quite different chances of 'success', as measured by the postproject employment records of participants.

made classifications might be produced, if this is really warranted. The variables used to construct the typologies were intended to capture (a) key structural characteristics of the local economy and labour market, (b) labour market outcomes relating to the interaction of supply and demand and (c) the extent of change during a chosen period.[5]

The classification, in effect, provides the potential for creating crude counterfactuals because most clusters are large and many members will not, in fact, have received development support; their economic experience over the period of a development programme, such as the ESF, may be used as a counterfactual against which to assess other areas' performances, where the latter have received funding. The scope for such cluster analysis consistently applied across European regions and subregions will, of course, be more limited than is the case for any single country. However, its application may be seen as an ultimate aim for developing the statistical system.

5   CONCLUSIONS

Given the growing scale and diversifying pattern of ESF activity, certain conclusions have been put forward in this chapter as to how the EU framework of evaluation might be organized. These are summarized briefly below:

1. Only a minority of projects will be the subject of 'good-practice' evaluation—resources available to support evaluation are unlikely to stretch beyond this limit.
2. The European Commission should require all projects to be classified a priori according to a generic typology embodied in an evaluation data base.
3. The evaluation data base should contain the results of existing 'good-practice' evaluation work in terms of key indicators that describe the characteristics of the programmes and the variety of their effects.
4. The strategy for evaluation should be twofold:
   (a) evaluate in order to fill important gaps in the evaluation data base;
   (b) evaluate projects that are most likely to fall near the boundary of acceptability rather than a fully representative sample of projects according to generic type and country/region.

---

5 The most frequently used spatial labour market indicators are those relating to unemployment, duration of unemployment and employment in certain sectors (e.g. in dynamic sectors such as business services), the buoyancy of the housing market and certain dynamic measures of labour market developments (e.g. recent changes in numbers unemployed, median duration of unemployment). Occasionally, it is also possible to add some measure of average income.

5. Spatial typologies should be developed so as to classify areas where projects have been evaluated, or are being implemented, in terms of factors likely to affect the success or failure of ESF projects (rather than use broad regional groupings): a project's spatial classification should be introduced into the evaluation data base.

6. The Commission should adopt a progressive rather than basic approach to evaluation so that evaluation standards can follow a path of improvement, according to the resources and experience of different European regions, and so as to avoid a tendency for the national evaluator to select a lower than is possible standard in particular instances.

Essentially, the above scheme is designed not only to promote more transparent evaluation but also to achieve more effective evaluation of evaluations across the socioeconomic policy space covered by the European Social Fund.

REFERENCES

Barker, T. and B. Gardiner (in press), 'Employment, Wage Formation and Pricing in the European Union: Empirical Modelling of Environmental Tax Reform', in C. Carrano and D. Siniscalco (eds), 'The Double Divided' (provisional title), Cambridge, MA: Kluwer Academic.

CEC (1989), *Guide to the Reform of the Community Structural Funds*, Luxembourg: Office for Publications of the European Communities.

CEC (1991), 'The European Social Fund', *Social Europe*, 2, Luxembourg: Office for Publications of the European Communities.

CEC (1992a), *Reform of the Structural Funds: A Tool to Promote Economic and Social Cohesion*, Luxembourg: Office for Official Publications of the European Communities.

CEC (1992b), *Fourth Annual Report on the Implementation of the Reform of the Structural Funds 1992*, Luxembourg: Office for Official Publications of the European Communities.

CEC (1993a), *Community Structural Funds, 1994–99*, Luxembourg: Office for Publications of the European Communities.

CEC (1993b), HERMES, *Harmonized Econometric Research for Modelling Economic Systems*, Amsterdam: North Holland.

CEC (1994), *Competitiveness and Cohesion: Trends in the Regions*, 5th periodic report on the social and economic situation and development of the regions in the Community, Brussels: CEC.

Green, A. E. and A. G. Champion (1991), 'The Booming Towns Studies: Methodological Issues', *Research Policy and Review*, 35, 'Environment and Planning A', 23, 1393–408.

Green, A., D. Owen and C. Hasluck (1991), 'The Development of Local Labour Market Typologies: Classifications of Travel-to-work Areas', Department of Employment research paper, London: Department of Employment.

Jensen, K. and P. K. Madsen (eds) (1993), *Measuring Labour Market Measures: Evaluating the Effects of Active Labour Market Policies*, Copenhagen: Ministry of Labour.

Johannesson, J. and E. Wadensjö (1995), *Labour Market Policy at the Crossroads*, Stockholm: EFA, Ministry of Labour.

Layard, P. R. G. (1979, July), 'The Costs and Benefits of Selective Employment Policies: The British Case', *British Journal of Industrial Relations*, 17, 187–204.

Layard, P. R. G. and S. J. Nickell (1980), 'The Case for Subsidizing Extra Jobs', *Economic Journal*, 90, 51–73.

Lewis, J. (1988), 'Economic Impact Analysis: A UK Literature Survey and Bibliography', in D. Diamond and J. B. McLoughlin (eds), *Progress in Planning*, 30 (3), 159–209, Oxford: Pergamon.

Lindley, R. M. (1980), 'Employment Policy in Transition', in R. M. Lindley (ed.), *Economic Change and Employment Policy*, London: Macmillan, pp. 330–82.

Lindley, R. M. (1983), 'Active Manpower Policy', in G. S. Bain (ed.), *Industrial Relations in Britain*, Oxford: Blackwell, pp. 339–60.

Lindley, R. M. (1986), 'Labour Demand: Microeconomic Aspects of State Intervention', in P. E. Hart (ed.), *Unemployment and Labour Market Policies*, Aldershot: Gower, pp. 154–75.

Lindley, R. M. (1993, September), 'Generic Evaluation in the Context of the European Social Fund', Colloque sur l'Evaluation des Politiques d'Emploi, Ministère de l'Enseignement Supérieur et de la Recherche, Paris.

Nevin, E. (1990), *The Economics of Europe*, London: Macmillan.

Padoa-Schioppa, T. (1987), *Efficiency, Stability and Equity: A Strategy for the Evolution of the Economic System of the European Community*, Brussels: Commission of the European Communities.

Stern, J. (1988, May), 'Methods of Analysis of Public Expenditure Programmes with Employment Objectives', Government Economic working paper no. 103, Treasury working paper no. 53, London: HM Treasury.

Turner, D. S., K. F. Wallis and J. D. Whitley (1987), 'Evaluating Special Employment Measures with Macroeconomic Models', *Oxford Review of Economic Policy*, 3 (3), 25–36.

Whitley, J. D. and R. A. Wilson (1983), 'The Macroeconomic Merits of a Marginal Employment Subsidy', *The Economic Journal*, 93 (372), 862–80.

Wilson, R. A., A. Assefa and J. Beard (1995), 'A Local Economy Forecasting Model (LEFM) for the UK Economy', paper presented at the European Symposium on Labour Market Developments, 18–19 May, University of Warwick.

29. European Regulation of Social Standards: Social Security, Working Time, Workplace Participation, Occupational Health and Safety

Jacqueline O'Reilly, Bernd Reissert and Volker Eichener

The European Commission has consistently argued that economic integration needs to be accompanied by social integration and cohesion if a unified market for the free movement of labour and capital, goods and services is to be created. However, attempts at such integration have met with several barriers and difficulties. The institutions and regulations which govern national labour markets still vary substantially. In some areas these differences have actually widened rather than narrowed. The fierce debates over the Social Chapter have led some to believe that the development of shared social standards will be neglected in the pursuit of economic goals. One fear is that this will lead to 'social dumping'. This means that governments will 'dump' their commitment to social regulation and labour standards in the face of increasing economic competition from both within and outside the Single European Market ('Hoover Affair', 1993), the aim being to achieve a competitive advantage over Member States with higher standards. This may, in turn, lead to a 'race' among the Member States to reduce social costs and, thus, to a general deterioration of social standards within the Union, out of a desire to maintain national employment levels.

Streeck (1994) argued that European integration is likely to lead to a frittering away of high-quality social standards, and recent reports from the OECD (1994) have suggested that European countries may need to remove high levels of labour protection in order to achieve economic growth. However, as McLaughlin (1994) pointed out, for both political and economic reasons Europe will not be able to reduce its labour costs to those in China or eastern Europe, for example. The desire of firms to move to less regulated European economies with lower social standards, and therefore encourage 'social dumping', is dependent on a number of factors. In particular, firms need to weigh up using low-wage, low-skill labour and the need to produce high-quality goods in high-productivity sectors. For example, Germany has one of the highest levels of wage costs in Europe, but it also has high levels of productivity and, therefore, low unit labour costs. Company decisions to transfer to low-productivity regions, both within and outside the boundaries of the EU, need to be seen in terms of the level of labour standards as well as other economic factors. Added to these considerations, recent research suggests that within certain European countries there is an increasing polarization between the rich and the poor and those in and out of work. There are also significant differences in unemployment rates between countries, with much higher levels of unemployment in southern and peripheral countries than in the core countries. These conditions raise major questions for the future of European cohesion, subsidiarity and harmonization. One of the major challenges facing the 'European project' is how to prevent social exclusion and encourage integration.

The aim of this chapter is to assess these developments and arguments by focussing on four key policy areas in which attempts to harmonize standards have occurred. These areas are: employee workplace participation, working time, occupational health and safety, and social security. The chapter does *not* attempt to provide an *economic* evaluation of labour standards in these areas, that is, an analysis of its impact on the behaviour of economic actors (firms, workers etc.) which has been attempted by the OECD (1994). Instead, it examines the impact of European regulation on *national* standards in the Member States of the European Union. More precisely, it asks whether European regulation has in fact influenced social standards in the Member States. The key issue is whether standards have been improved, or whether they amount to compromises at the lowest common level.

The main argument developed here is that the impact of European regulation on national standards varies widely among the four policy areas. Where European regulation has been most successful in influencing national standards, this seems to be largely due to three main factors. First, the nature of decision-making processes and the application of Qualified Majority Voting (QMV). In some policy areas this has removed the ability of one country to veto decisions, making it easier to arrive at an agreement on effective European standards. Second, where interest coalitions have been built up between the European Commission, national governments, employer and union organizations, it has been easier to secure the successful adoption of a particular measure. Third, where such regulation does not challenge established and embedded national practices, it is more likely to be adopted. The four cases discussed in this chapter illustrate this analysis and explain why regulation has been more successful in some areas than in others.

1   WORKPLACE PARTICIPATION

1.1   Debates on Regulation

Increasing industrial democracy by allowing workers to participate in firms' decision-making has been a long, drawn-out and bitter debate in the history of European social policy. The directive on information and consultation passed on 22 September 1994 marked a milestone achievement for the Commission. However, its impact on European labour markets is still being evaluated (Gold, 1994; Gold and Hall, 1994).

The Commission has been keen to develop European levels of communication and information since the 1970s, when a German model based on works councils was first proposed as part of the first draft of the European company statute (Blank, 1994, pp. 145–6). Although these initiatives floundered and failed, a European standard on workers' participation remained on the policy agenda, given greater or lesser priority, for several reasons. These were largely due to the growing number of company mergers and acquisitions within Europe (Marginson, Buitendam, Deutschmann and Perulli, 1993; Sisson, Waddington and Whitston, 1991). Where commercial decisions are increasingly being taken on the European level, the Commission argued, workers should have the right to be informed and comment on decisions which affect them. Moreover, the outcome of the restructuring initiated by the Single European Market project should be 'socially acceptable' and secure the backing of the European labour movement (Gold and Hall, 1994, p. 178). The general philosophy of the Commission was that economic integration should not be at the expense of the 'social dimension'. The legal vacuum that existed before the recent directive created the potential for social dumping, or what is known in the United States as the 'Delaware effect', where firms move from regions with a high level of codetermination to those with lower levels. The possibility of such firm behaviour was potentially damaging for the social cohesion of the integration project, either because it would result in job losses in countries with high levels of codetermination, or it would lead to a race to undercut such rights and thus to a deregulated 'downward' harmonization.

Criticism of these initiatives over the past twenty-five years came largely from employers' organizations, such as the Union of Industrial and Employers' Confederation of Europe (UNICE). They were opposed to a standardized form of worker consultation and information channels for Europe. They argued that a uniform system would be inflexible, given the diverse forms of company activities in the European Union. It would undermine existing national and company-specific solutions which had been developed to meet particular needs, as well as conflicting with the development of decentralized management structures. Further, it would incur considerable costs and would add to labour costs in general. More importantly, although this was not always stated explicitly, they were concerned that such a measure could eventually lead to European-level collective bargaining, thus encroaching on managerial prerogatives (Gold and Hall, 1994, p. 178).

1.2   The Current State of European Regulation

The Commission's directive on Works Councils is a slight misnomer in that it is essentially concerned with establishing employees' rights to information and consultation boards, rather than institutionalized forms of collective bargaining (Blank, 1994, p. 158; Streeck, 1994). The final directive replaces the original title 'works councils' with 'information and consultation' channels. The recent directive has been seen by some as a 'watered down' compromise, far removed from the Commission's original goals (Blank, 1994); however, Gold and Hall (1994, p. 181) argue that for the most recent draft directive 'the overall structure and policy of the draft have survived to a remarkable extent' through the process of ratification.

One of the key issues in evaluating the impact of this regulation is largely dependent on how strictly information and consultation channels are defined. In its weakest form this can be a bare minimum of information handed down to employees. Gold (1994) argued that such *direct* representation as a form of communication is, where workers only have the opportunity to communicate their opinions either as individuals or groups, for example, through quality circles ('Thriving on Diversity', 1993). A stronger definition entails a two-way exchange of information and consultation, where workers' opinions have some bearing on managerial decision-making. Gold (1994) defined this as *representational* participation, where works councils or trade unions adopt an overall perspective on the organization and its impact on employees as a whole. This latter definition is closer to the original goals of the Commission.

The initial proposal for a European company statute, including worker consultation, was largely based on the German model and driven by reforms to the German system in the mid-1970s.[1] Initial attempts to impose a universal two-tier board system were revised to 'make the various national structures compatible with each other on the road to convergence' (Blank, 1994, p. 148). However, this change was not implemented. In 1980 the 'Vredeling directive' on workers' participation attempted to ensure that employees of foreign subsidiaries enjoyed rights of consultation and information about their firm and its

---

1 For a more comprehensive overview of the history of employee participation initiative, see Cressey (1993) and Hall (1992).

operations: 'The parent company was to be obliged to provide employee representatives in subsidiary companies in different member states with certain information on the group's economic position and on any plans that might adversely affect employees' interests' (Blank, 1994, p. 155). However, this met with fierce hostility from employers' groups, as well as outright opposition from the UK government. Despite further revisions in 1983, limiting jurisdiction to firms with more than 1000 employees, and reducing the frequency and range of information to be accessed, the directive was opposed and eventually dropped. In 1983 a revised directive proposed two alternative models and raised the work force threshold for application of these provisions from 500 to 1000 employees (Streeck and Vitols, 1993, p. 8). The failure of this directive led to a revised draft in 1989 which offered a range of alternative options to the initial German model. In sum, the first proposed directive was intended to cover all firms; the Vredeling draft was largely focussed on multinationals; the recent draft is limited to the management of subsidiaries and transnational relations.

The Delors Commission revived interest in a 'Social Dimension' of the integration process. In 1990 a draft directive on European Works Councils was issued. These works councils were essentially concerned with providing consultation and information in a pan-European forum between worker representatives and group-level management: representation only took place at the headquarters of the company, and delegates were to be appointed to these councils from local plants. Compared to earlier directives, the requirements were comparatively flexible and limited. The breakthrough in getting the directive accepted was largely due to the reformed procedure for agreements on social policy related to the Maastricht treaty, which allowed QMV (Addison and Siebert, 1994, p. 20). Previously, unanimous voting had meant that the United Kingdom could successfully block all such measures. Under the reformed procedure, 44 out of 66 votes in the Council were enough to secure agreement ('New European Information', 1994). With the decision of the United Kingdom to 'opt out' of all social policy measures, the prospect of an agreement on works councils appeared imminent.

Although UNICE was adamantly opposed to such a measure, employer opinion was divided. This highlighted the fact that 'the directive itself was influenced by the prior existence in a number of companies of "prototype European Works Councils", albeit mainly in French-based, state-owned multinationals' (Gold and Hall, 1992; Gold and Hall, 1994, p. 179; 'Information and Consultation', 1993a, 1993b). UNICE changed its position of opposition in October 1991, faced with the revisions to policy-making resulting from Maastricht, and agreed to enter into negotiations with the European Trade Union Confederation (ETUC). This was essentially a defensive strategy: such negotiations would allow UNICE to fend off or delay EU legislation. After a breakdown of 'talks about talks', the Commission was determined to secure legislation.

Under the British and Portuguese presidencies the topic of works councils was not on the Council agenda; under the Belgium and Danish presidencies it was once again revived. The Belgium President issued a compromise statement, later taken up by the Danish President, in which the term 'works councils' was dropped in favour of the term 'information and consultation' procedures. Under the directive, if a company has more than 1000 workers, employed in two or more EU Member States, with at least 100 workers employed in the second state, it must establish a works committee to provide consultation and information annually on corporate strategies, such as closures and redundancies, new products and financial performance. Companies had until 22 September 1996 to negotiate and set up such a committee. After this date they were to adopt the structure stipulated in the directive. British employees do not qualify for inclusion, and British firms are not obliged to set up such procedures, due to the UK 'opt-out'. Nevertheless, since the directive was issued, a few leading firms in the United Kingdom have voluntarily entered into negotiations with trade unions; they include United Biscuits, Electrolux and Coats Viyella. A number of others are in the process of establishing negotiations.

1.3   Towards Upward Harmonization?

Estimates on the number of companies likely to be affected by this directive vary: UNICE suggests that 2000 groups will be affected, the ETUC have put forward a figure of 1200, and the Commission estimates that 1400 groups will be covered ('States Find', 1995) (see Table 29.1 for Commission estimates). The exclusion of the United Kingdom means that a number of British-based companies will not be included, as originally envisaged. Nevertheless, voluntary agreements within such companies suggest that they may be willing to set up information and consultation channels independently ('Information and Consultation', 1993a; 'Thriving on Diversity', 1993).

Voluntary committees have been established either to preempt the application of the directive, or because they are an economically efficient way for multinationals to manage a diversely distributed work force. The extent to which these develop, Streeck and Vitols (1993, pp. 6–7 and p. 18) argued, is dependent on the nature of national industrial relations systems; rather than generating convergence, they argued that the directive is likely to perpetuate national and sectoral diversity.

Marginson (1992) suggested that voluntary agreements on a European-wide approach are more likely to be adopted in companies with a common ownership structure at the European level, where there is enough common ground between operations in different countries, and where business opera-

Table 29.1 Number of Companies Likely to be Affected by the
Information and Consultation Directive

Base Country	Number of Companies (estimation)
Germany	290
France	180
Britain[a]	102
Netherlands	100
Belgium	50
Other EU members + 4[b]	278
Other countries[c]	200
Total	1200

Notes
a In respect of operations outside Britain.
b Denmark, Greece, Ireland, Italy, Luxembourg, Portugal and Spain, plus Austria, Finland, Norway and Sweden.
c Principally, the United States, Japan and Switzerland.

Source
European Commission, cited in 'Unions Will Campaign—All Out for Euro-council Deals Now', 1994, *Industrial Relations Europe*, 22 (262), 2.

tions are internationally integrated. They are also more likely to form in sectors where trade unions are already well established, in large firms which already have formal consultation procedures, rather than in smaller, nationally based, firms which are likely to remain untouched by the directive.

The Commission estimates that this directive will have a highly beneficial result on worker productivity and commitment, thus improving competitiveness. The costs associated with such meetings are estimated to be a maximum of 10 ECU per worker per year. But this figure is highly dependent on the number of workers, representatives and countries ('New European Information', 1994). As unit labour costs are more important than actual labour costs, the increased productivity resulting from this measure may well offset the costs involved.

Gold and Hall (1994) questioned whether these committees will be 'bolted on' or be integrated into management structures. They argued that:

The experience of existing, voluntary European-level bodies suggests that there may be a tendency for their role to develop over time, with informal arrangements becoming formalised, and information-only arrangements in some cases being extended to include a degree of consultation. On the other hand, plant and national self-interest on the part of employees may inhibit the achievement of common positions at European level. Such a factor may have constrained the role of the Volkswagen European Works Council—widely seen as the most developed of the current voluntary agreements—in respect of the plant closure of the Barcelona SEAT plant (pp. 183–4).

They also argue that the consultative role of the directive goes beyond the remit of the thirty-plus existing voluntary bodies, but that its impact on industrial relations is uncertain.

Clearly, companies will seek to introduce some form of collectively agreed information and consultation procedure before the final deadline of 1996, when they will have to adopt the standard directive format. The adoption of the directive means that the Commission will have the ability to enforce the provisions in all countries, except the United Kingdom (where some firms are setting up such committees voluntarily). In many senses the directive does mark a significant achievement (Goetschy, 1994; Ross, 1994), although Streeck (1994) has been more critical. The Commission seeks to introduce basic minimum rules to be achieved by the social partners rather than seeking to impose a common harmonized standard. In countries where works councils are well established this directive will have minimal impact, its potential strength lies more in countries which have no such legislation.

2 WORKING TIME

2.1 Debates on Regulation

The issue of working time has also raised considerable controversy, not only in recent debates on regulation within the EU, but also throughout the history of European industrialization. The outcome of these conflicts has produced different forms of working time regulation both between countries and between different sectors in individual countries. Since the mid-1970s, debate within the EU has been largely conflictual. The arguments in favour of regulating working time have largely focussed on two aspects: a reduction in working hours and increasing working time flexibility for employees and employers. Arguments that reductions in working time could lead to a more even distribution of employment has been the major thrust of trade union campaigns to encourage work-sharing (Meager and Buchan, 1988). However, Hinrichs, Roche and Sirianni (1991) argued that these goals have all but been eclipsed by employer demands for flexible working time arrangements. Within the EU, the White Paper on *Growth, Competitiveness and Employment* (Commission of the European Communities, 1994c) advocated increased working time flexibility, whereas the Social Charter (Commission of the European Communities, 1989) sought to remove the barriers to unfavourable working time arrangements. Employers have argued that these two documents are contradictory ('Officials Seek', 1994, p. 8). Goal displacement in several countries has resulted from a frustration with the limited effect of reduced working time on employment creation. Increasingly, greater concern has been given to introducing and encouraging flexible working hours. At the same time the Commission has sought to introduce agreed standards on working time to prevent 'social dumping', with companies preferring to produce in areas with limited regulation.

One of the problems with regulating working time in Europe is partly due to the variation currently existing between different countries. The concept of 'standard working time' is more popular in countries like France or Germany, than in Britain or Ireland, where there is a wider distribution of hours worked (Commission of the European Communities, 1994a). In particular, the United Kingdom stands out as a country with high dispersed patterns of working time. In other European countries employees tend to work within a narrow range of hours, and in some countries about half or more of the work force work within a single hour band. For example:

> In 1990, 9.7% of employees in the UK usually worked fewer than 16 hours per week in their main job compared to an EC average of 5.0%, and 16.0% of UK employees usually worked over 48 hours per week compared to an EC average of 6.8% (Watson, 1992, p. 540).

These differences have made it more difficult for the United Kingdom to agree to common standards and regulations on working time. The position of the UK government has been to challenge the legal basis of the decision-making on which such directives have been agreed. Employers, especially in the United Kingdom, have been opposed to regulation which would reduce their flexibility and operating/opening times—especially in countries like the United Kingdom where working time has in recent years been deregulated; for example, Sunday opening in selective sectors. Hinrichs et al. (1991) suggested that

> [t]he picture that emerges from recent developments in Western European nations, and over a longer period in the United States, suggests that we may be witnessing the demise of standardised working-time regulations and arrangements that were developed by unions and employers—and often underwritten by governments— over a period of more than a century (p. 4).

Demands for these changes have come about both because of employer interests as well as demands from employees for greater freedom and choice. However, it is not always clear that the benefits of more flexible working time arrangements are equally distributed. The growth of part-time work, short-time working and temporary or on-call arrangements have further undermined the pattern of a standard working week. The arguments for regulating working time have largely focussed on the potential to encourage job creation and employment flexibility while preventing the spread of unfavourable working conditions.

Resistance from employers is based on their perception that such regulation encroaches on their freedom to manage. This is particularly true for British employers who under national labour law enjoy the freedom of contract, whereas the employment practices of those in countries like France are regulated by a 'Code du Travail' (O'Reilly, 1994a, chap. 9). Employers have also been more fiercely opposed to reductions in working time than to increases in wages. This is because it is difficult to offset reductions in working time with increases in productivity, work organization needs to be rescheduled, and thus can entail a relative increase in labour costs.

Trade unions have been at the forefront of campaigns to reduce working time, although their members have often been in favour of giving greater priority to higher wages rather than more leisure time. Although unions have been in favour of reductions in standard working time, they have often been very hostile to the introduction of forms of flexible working time like part-time work. This is because such arrangements can potentially undermine negotiations on pay for standardized working hours. In countries like Britain, where part-time work is more common, trade unions have sought to improve the protection available to these workers, whereas in countries like France, where part-time work is less significant, trade unions have tended to be opposed to this development in principle.

A further problem with the regulation of working time lies in the diversity of employee preferences: male workers are more likely to prefer a block cut in hours on one day of the week (usually Fridays) or a nine-day fortnight, whereas female workers have shown greater preference for earlier finishing times, allowing them to combine domestic work and paid employment (Hinrichs et al., 1991; O'Reilly, 1994b). Early retirement tends to be seen more favourably by young than by older workers, who may have to leave employment with lower-level pension contributions. This diversity impinges on unions' ability to launch a strategic and unified campaign.

The problems of reducing working time and regulating diverse forms of flexible working hours continues to pose significant problems for the future of European integration and the prevention of unfavourable working conditions. However, the current directives appear to do little more than stipulate a basic minimum, which most states currently observe.

2.2   The Current State of European Regulation

The first draft directive on working time regulation was submitted to the Council of Ministers in August 1990. During discussions, disagreement focussed on the length of the maximum working week. Initially, Germany was opposed to a maximum limit of 48 hours a week, whereas France wanted this threshold to be lower. In June 1993 a common position was agreed upon by the Council ('Working Time Directive', 1993); the directive had to be implemented by Member States by 23 November 1996.

The directive specifies minimum health and safety requirements for the organization of working time. It establishes minimum periods of daily rest of 11 consecutive hours per 24-hour period; a weekly rest period of 24 hours (plus 11 hours daily rest) which 'in principle' includes Sunday; all workers are entitled to an annual leave of four weeks (most countries already guarantee this); breaks for workers exceeding six hours a day should be stipulated by collective agreement or national legislation; the maximum weekly hours should not exceed 48, although this may be averaged out over a four-month period (or six months through collective agreement). Protective measures are also applied to night work which cannot exceed more than eight hours in a 24-hour period; night workers are to receive free medical check-ups.

The directive does not apply to all workers, and a significant number of derogations are permitted. For example, those working in transport, at sea, and doctors in training are not covered by this directive. Workers who have 'unmeasured or autonomous decision-making powers' are also excluded, for example, managing executives, family workers or religious workers. Derogations can also be obtained for workers working away from home, in security and surveillance activities, activities requiring continual presence, for example, in hospitals, prisons, the media, emergency and utility services or agriculture; as well as industries subject to regular seasonal fluctuations, such as tourism, postal services and agriculture ('Working Time Directive', 1993, p. 17). Derogations can largely be made by means of collective agreements or national legislation.

Member States have to adopt laws which comply with the directive within three years of it being passed, or they must ensure that such measures are achieved through collective bargaining. Member States have the option of not including the 48-hour maximum week (Article 6) in the immediate implementation of the directive. Seven years after the directive they will be required to implement this, but before this time the Council and Commission will reappraise the relevance of this threshold. Nevertheless, employers cannot force workers to work more than 48 hours a week, and are required to keep records on workers working longer hours. Further, those states which decide not to implement the four-week minimum annual leave will be obliged to do so approximately six years after the initial introduction of the directive. In the meantime workers are to have a minimum of three weeks' annual leave.

The directive was passed by QMV on the basis that it was a health and safety measure according to Article 118 A of the EC treaty. However, the UK government, which abstained, has challenged the legal basis of the directive in the European Court of Justice, initiating proceedings on 7 March 1994.

2.3   Towards Upward Harmonization?

In most cases this directive fails to go beyond existing working time practices in a majority of Member States. It also makes extensive provision for agreements to be obtained through collective bargaining at the national and sectoral level. It allows considerable flexibility in implementation and future review, and from this point of view can be seen as providing only the minimum basis for common standards on working time.[2]

The figures in Table 29.2 seem to suggest that on average most countries currently comply to the 48-hour threshold. However, average figures do not tell us about the distribution of working time: in most countries the majority of workers work within a standard full-time band, except for the United Kingdom where there is the widest distribution of working time (Commission of the European Communities, 1994a). The UK opposition to the directive is largely based on the estimated costs of introducing such regulations in that country:

> 3.0% of hours worked in 1991 would have contravened the 48-hour maximum working week, and 0.4% would have contravened the minimum rest periods (11 hours a day and 24 hours a week). In addition it was estimated that in 1991 extension of the right to 20 days' paid vacation to all workers would have raised firms' labour costs by £1.4 billion, or about 0.5% of the wage bill (Addison and Siebert, 1994, p. 17).

Considerable controversy exists over evaluating the significance of this directive. Addison and Siebert (1994, p. 14) have taken a more optimistic perspective when they argue that 'now that the principle of a 48-hour week has been accepted, it is much easier to legislate further limitations on working hours'. However, the Commission has had to accept a 'watering down' of draft directives in the process of ratification. In the end employers can get around this regulation through collective agreements, and national governments are not obliged, in the initial period, to implement this clause. To a large extent future regulation will depend on the interest coalitions developed within European

---

2 Further disputes have arisen over regulations concerning nonstandard working time, most significantly the use of part-time and temporary work. (See also chap. 19 by O'Reilly and chap. 21 by Rogowski and Schömann in this volume.)

*Table 29.2 Actual Weekly Hours Worked in the European Community
(Average for Men and Women)*

Base Country	1983	1992
United Kingdom	42.3	43.4
Ireland	40.2	40.4
Portugal	—	41.3
Spain	—	40.6
Greece	41.0	40.5
Germany	40.9	39.7
Luxembourg	40.0	39.7
France	39.7	39.7
Netherlands	41.0	39.4
Denmark	40.5	38.8
Italy	39.2	38.5
Belgium	38.6	38.2
EU–12		40.3

Note
— = data for Spain and Portugal not available for 1983.

Source
Eurostat (Statistical Office of the European Communities), quoted in 'States Find Common Ground on National Euro-council Rules', 1995, *Industrial Relations Europe*, 23 (266), 1–2.

institutions as well as the power of trade unions to negotiate in collective bargaining.

3   OCCUPATIONAL HEALTH AND SAFETY

3.1   Debates on Regulation

The harmonization of regulations concerning health and safety at work is one of the core elements in the completion of the Single European Market, and one which has had the most success. Divergent *product* standards, such as safety requirements for machinery and equipment, are nontariff trade barriers in the sense that they exclude foreign-made products which do not meet national safety standards from domestic markets. Germany—both the largest producer and market for machinery in Europe—in particular has been suspected of protecting its domestic market by a sophisticated system of technical standards. The EC directive on machinery was a direct attempt to open up national markets for machinery by harmonizing safety standards. *Process* standards, rules on production process are also subject to different levels of regulation and protection. These affect the cost relations between the European countries: countries with a low level of health and safety at work will benefit from significant cost advantages over countries with higher standards.

Before European harmonization came into effect, both the level of regulation and the level of actual safety varied greatly in Europe. In 1991, the number of fatal accidents per 1000 workers in Spain (0.134) was nearly ten times that in the Netherlands (0.015) (ILO, 1993). In the Netherlands, 15.1 per cent of the workers think their health or safety is at risk because of their work, compared with 62.6 per cent in Spain, many of whom are afraid of occupational injuries (Paoli, 1992, p. 105). According to the results of the First European Survey on the Work Environment 1991–1992 (Paoli, 1992), Denmark and the Netherlands have the highest levels of safety, directly followed by western Germany; Belgium, the United Kingdom and Luxembourg are slightly above average; Ireland, Italy and eastern Germany are ranked in the middle; France is below average, followed at some distance by Spain, Portugal and Greece which have the most dangerous working conditions.

Regulatory systems and the intensity with which they are implemented vary considerably between Member States from 'mechanistic' to more 'innovative' approaches. Traditional 'mechanistic' approaches, found in the most highly industrialized societies, tend to focus on accidents and diseases, risk prevention and technical safety. More innovative approaches are found in countries with the best record for safety: Denmark and the Netherlands. These countries have adopted health concepts from Sweden which include both physical and mental health as well as psychological well-being. In these countries the scope of occupational safety has been extended to the whole working environment and linked to the technical and social development of society. By contrast, in the southern Member States neither approach has been rigorously introduced nor enforced; the existing legislation has been characterized as 'inadequate' or 'rhetorical', and is further weakened by serious implementation deficits (Baldwin and Daintith, 1992; Vogel, 1991). The harmonization of these national standards was motivated by economic considerations as well as concern for social cohesion in Europe.

3.2   The Current State of European Regulation

The heterogeneity of these national systems acts as an incentive for companies to practice social dumping. It had been assumed that low-standard countries would only be interested in the harmonization of product rather than process standards. This would allow them access to the European market with the advantage of producing cheaper products that did not entail the costs associated with process standards and the improvement of employees working conditions (Rehbinder and Stewart, 1985). Such a perspective predicted that countries with low standards would be able to form a significant bloc against Member States seeking to initiate a common upward harmonization. Thus, a slow process, based on the lowest common denominator, has been envisaged (Scharpf, 1994).

The events that occurred after 1985 consequently came as a surprise. The Commission of the European Communities recognized the danger that competition between the Member States could lead to a weakening of health and safety protection. As a result it initiated a comprehensive regulatory programme with the 'essential aim' of preserving or improving the level of protection attained by the Member States, as stated in the preamble of the Safety and Health at Work Directive (European Communities, 1989a). The Framework Directive resulted in a burgeoning range of specific directives on workplaces, work equipment, the use of personal protective equipment, display screen equipment, handling of heavy loads, temporary or mobile work sites, fisheries and agriculture, noise, hazardous substances and others. The European directives for process regulation, including the Framework Directive, are based on Article 118 A—the health and safety at work article—and provide a harmonized minimum standard that national regulations may exceed but must meet. The harmonization of product standards, which was pursued in parallel with process regulation, was based on Article 100 A of the Single European Act providing for a total harmonization of product requirements. The first, and most important, directive on safety requirements for products was the Directive on Machinery (European Communities, 1989b), followed by several specific directives on pressure vessels, personal protective equipment, gas-consuming devices and medical devices, among others.

Prior to 1985 it had taken on average ten years to pass technical harmonization directives because of the extremely difficult negotiations between the Member States. After the Single European Act came into effect, the 'New Approach to Technical Harmonisation and Standardisation' was introduced. This, together with the White Paper on the Completion of the Internal Market and a Council Resolution of 1985, sparked off the issuing of occupational health directives like fireworks. The key element of the 'New Approach' is that European legislation is restricted to setting the 'essential requirements'. The specific details of harmonized European standards are regulated by the private-law European standardization bodies: CEN (European Committee for Standardization), CENELEC (European Committee for Electrotechnical Standardization) and ETSI (European Telecommunications Standards Institute). The passing of the Machinery Directive symbolized the effects of the 'New Approach'. It triggered immense activity in standardization with nearly one hundred technical committees, several hundred working groups and thousands of technical experts involved. Although the work has not yet been completed (partly because technical standards are regularly updated), references to European Standards (EN) are stamped on most machines and equipment as well as private household goods, such as children's toys, sold in the European Union.

Despite this vigorous activity, the regulatory programme of the European Union in the field of health and safety at work is far from being completed. Some of the directives have already been amended. For example, the Machinery Directive, originally passed in 1989, was revised in 1991. Moreover, the Health and Safety at Work Directive provided the basis for more than the seven specific directives originally planned. Directives on radiation, carcinogenic substances, biological substances, safety signs, mining industry, pregnant women, physical agents, transport activities, temporary jobs, medical treatment on ships, transportation of handicapped persons, and working adolescents have either been passed or proposed by the Commission. Although the deadline set out in most of the directives was 31 December 1992, transposition into national law is, as ever, still far from complete. The delays reflect the difficulties of national governments in adapting to the new regulations from Brussels.

3.3   Towards Upward Harmonization?

Since 1989 European regulation on health and safety has produced some startling results (Eichener, 1993) in that the Council has decided to introduce a very broad and innovative concept of safety and health at work. European regulation goes beyond the traditional mechanistic approach and has adopted the innovative Scandinavian concept and extended it to include six key principles: universal coverage, employer responsibility, a broad concept of health, organizational aspects, a risk-assessment approach and the concept of absolute safety requirements regardless of technological restrictions.

(a) Protection of all employees in all sectors

With the transposition of the European directives into national law, for the first time in history, virtually all employees are covered by government protection at their workplaces in most Member States. Due to historical developments, most national regulations excluded large groups of workers. The enlarged scope of protection alone thus means a most significant improvement of national protection standards.

(b) *Employer obligation to safeguard and improve occupational health*

Employers are not only obliged to satisfy all regulations and to react to official inspection (as in most national regulations), but must *proactively* care for the safety of the employees according to the latest state of the art.

(c) *A comprehensive concept of health, including psychological aspects*

Traditionally, in most European countries safety at work regulation was restricted to avoiding hazards to physical health like mechanical injury, poisoning or radiation. The European directives adopted the innovative health concepts of the World Health Organization or the International Labour Office which include psychological—or 'soft'—aspects of health like psychological stress, fatigue and even discomfort.

The practical consequences of this comprehensive concept are that health and safety at work take account of ergonomics and the humanization of work. For example, monotonous work cycles are to be avoided. The revolutionary quality of this legislation can be appreciated if compared with health and safety at work regulation in Germany, where the humanization of work has been a political goal since the early 1970s, but has never been considered as an item for government regulation, only for government support.

(d) *Including the working environment*

The European regulatory concept goes beyond the mechanistic approach in another respect. Traditionally, health and safety at work regulation was restricted to technical components, to tools, machinery, equipment and workplaces. The European directives include the regulation of work organization and working time, the employers' obligations for risk analyses, information and training, considerable information and participation rights for workers and their representatives, medical examinations, training of the workers and other aspects of social relations, which have traditionally not been items of legislative regulation but of autonomous arrangements between the social partners at firm or collective level.

(e) *The risk-assessment approach*

This is central to the Machinery Directive (European Communities, 1989b). The risk-assessment approach is innovative, because it makes the effective prevention of hazards obligatory. Both manufacturers of machinery and employers have to anticipate risks, including those resulting from combination effects, and to take measures to avoid them by a multistep programme. Together with the obligation to take the latest state of the art into account, the preventive character of the risk-assessment approach may contribute to a new orientation towards higher levels of safety in most Member States (Pickert, 1992, p. 88).

(f) Absolute safety requirements

Traditional health and safety at work regulation relates to the state of the art in technology. The safety level which is usually provided by regulation is relative, because it depends on what technology allows. For example, highly developed sensor technology can automatically stop the parts of moving tools. Whereas technology is dynamic, regulation is basically static and lags behind technological development, thus frequently remaining below the technologically achievable level of safety. According to progressive lawyers, resolving this problem requires a 'dynamization of law' (Wolf, 1987, p. 387). This approach can be seen from the Machinery Directive, where absolute requirements are stipulated, regardless of the technological possibilities and restrictions. Although it may not be possible to achieve these at the time when the law is passed, the idea is that they should anticipate future technological progress.

European health and safety at work legislation has prevented social dumping and encouraged a comprehensive, consistent and innovative regulation process. Even the 'minimum standard' provided by the 118 A directives is higher than the existing protection levels in most Member States. The Framework Directive's general obligation to ensure the safety and health of the workers 'certainly cannot be viewed as a minimum, or graduated, standard. Rather, it appears to require the imposition on all employers of a duty to achieve a particular result: the health and safety of their workers' (Baldwin and Daintith, 1992, p. 12). The Display Screen Equipment Directive is an example of a particularly radical change to most national forms of regulation, with its special regard to software ergonomics and even to the protection of personal data (European Communities, 1990).

Transposing the European regulations into national law turned out to be more difficult than expected. When the directives were passed by the European Council, many national actors were not fully aware of the consequences. Even experts tended to underestimate the impact of the European regulation. Initially, it was expected that European directives would either fit into existing systems of national regulation or merely specify lower standards. Only the United Kingdom seemed to recognize from the beginning that the EC had replaced the national legislator as 'the principal engine of health and safety law' (Baldwin and Daintith, 1992). The full impact of these directives became visible when they had to be implemented within national systems. It was particularly difficult for Member States with traditional health and safety systems to adapt to the innovative regulatory philosophy. In particular, the broad scope of regulation introduced by the working environment concept (instead of the narrower workplace approach), the innovative health concept, including mental stress, and the participation of workers presented a formidable challenge. It became clear that the European Union was in the driving seat.

The acceptance of these innovative standards within the European Council was eased because of the expectation by almost all Member States that enforcement structures would be weak (see Baldwin, 1992, pp. 229–30, for the United Kingdom, the Netherlands, Italy, Spain, Germany and France). Initially, there was no administrative capacity for law enforcement until the establishment of the European Agency for Health and Safety at Work which has started to build up its own implementation structures and may sometime begin to check how far its regulations are actually observed within the workshops and offices of Europe. Not before then can we expect to see a change in the above-mentioned safety figures.

4   SOCIAL SECURITY

4.1   Debates on Regulation

As with other aspects of labour standards, social security systems in the Member States of the European Union have developed in very different ways. Organizational forms, modes of financing, conditions of entitlement to benefits and the extent and duration of benefits all vary significantly between Member States. Despite the fact that the European Union is steadily moving towards a single labour market and economic area, national differences in some subsystems, particularly in unemployment compensation systems, have actually widened rather than narrowed since the early 1970s. This has been due to the southern extension of the Community, but also to different national strategies attempting to cope with rising unemployment (Reissert, 1993; Schmid, Reissert and Bruche, 1992). National systems of social security tend to be based either on an insurance or a welfare principle. The social insurance system, or 'Bismarckian' model, where benefits are largely financed from wage-related contributions linked to previous employment and earnings can be found in Germany, France and Spain. Welfare systems, or the 'Beveridge' model, found in countries like the United Kingdom, Ireland and Denmark, are largely financed from general taxation rather than from contribution payments; such systems guarantee a minimum income or flat-rate benefit variable only according to marital status or the number of children.

Table 29.3 Social Security Expenditure and Financing, 1993

	Expenditure on Social Security as % of GDP	Wage-related Contributions as % of Total Spending on Social Security
Netherlands	33.6	54
Denmark	33.2	7
France	30.9	78
United Kingdom	27.8	41
Belgium	27.6	68
Germany	27.6	63
Italy	25.8	66
Luxembourg	24.9	51
Spain	24.0	65
Ireland	21.4	38
Portugal	18.3	54
Greece	16.3	—
EUR 12	27.8	61

Note
— = data not available.

Sources
Adapted from *Social Protection Expenditure and Receipts 1980–1993* by Eurostat (Statistical Office of the European Communities), 1995, Luxembourg: Office for Official Publications of the European Communities, pp. 16–25; and authors' own calculations.

National systems of social security also differ widely with respect to levels of spending and financing (see Table 29.3). Social security spending (as a percentage of GDP) is higher in northern than in southern Europe and is closely correlated to the national level of economic performance, that is, per-capita GDP (Chassard, 1992, p. 17; Commission of the European Communities, 1993b, pp. 41–2; Wilensky, 1975).

The coexistence of such diverse national social security systems within a single labour market and economic area may lead to at least three problems (see, among others, Chassard, 1992; Deakin and Wilkinson, 1992; Mosley, 1990; Walwei and Werner, 1991). First, it can create mobility barriers. Workers moving from one Member State to another, in which the level of benefits are lower or entitlement conditions tougher, face the risk of losing, partially or entirely, their acquired social protection. Such differences present a potential obstacle to the optimal allocation of labour within the European Union. Second, criticisms of 'benefit tourism' are based on the argument that people migrate to countries where benefits are particularly generous and entitlement conditions lax. Third, differences between social security regimes can distort labour costs and thereby encourage 'social dumping'. For example, if social security is financed out of wage-related social contributions it may not be possible to offset the resultant high level of indirect wage costs by a correspondingly high level of labour productivity. Increasing competitive pressure within the Single European Market may therefore induce individual Member States to reduce their level of social security, and thus the social costs borne by employers, in order to gain a competitive advantage over other Member States. This could lead to a 'race' between the Member States to reduce social costs, and thus to a general deterioration in social protection within the Union.

4.2   The Current State of European Regulation

With the aim of at least mitigating the first two problems—the obstacles to the mobility of labour and the danger of 'benefit tourism'—in 1971 the European Community passed a regulation, based on Article 51 of the EEC treaty, which sets out social security conditions for migrants within the Community (see Altmaier, 1992; European Communities, 1992; Reissert, 1993; van Raepenbusch, 1991; Wanka, 1991; Watson, 1992). By means of this regulation, the European Community enables workers to accumulate qualifying periods for social security benefits in various Member States and to transfer their claims to most social security cash benefits from one Member State to another. For unemployed migrants, however, the 'export' of unemployment compensation is only permitted for a short period of time and is subject to restrictive conditions. The European regulation for migrants can thus be seen as an attempt to find a balance between two conflicting aims: to increase the mobility of labour and to prevent 'benefit tourism' (Commission of the European Communities, 1993a, pp. 53–4).

However, these regulations are not sufficient to resolve these problems. Employed workers can transfer their qualifying periods of employment and contribution payments when moving to another Member State, and, should they become unemployed after moving, they receive unemployment compensation according to the conditions prevailing in the new country of residence. This may reduce mobility when benefit conditions are less favourable in the new country of residence (Simon, 1990, p. 30). On the other hand, even the tightly restricted opportunity given to unemployed people to 'export' their unemployment compensation (the aim of which is to enable the unemployed to seek work in another Member State) can be used, at least to some extent, by people migrating for purely personal reasons, who are not really seeking work in their new place of residence. Such individuals can rely, it is argued (Wanka, 1991, p. 99), on the fact that the employment office in the new country of residence (which after all does not have to bear the cost of the export of benefits) will not be in a position to verify, nor will have an interest in checking whether they are actually available for work. In view of such problems, at least in theory, the efforts made by the European Commission and the southern Member States to increase the scope for unemployment compensation export have so far been unsuccessful. They have met with stiff resistance from Member States with relatively generous benefit conditions and a relatively large proportion of foreign workers, on the basis that any extension of the right to export unemployment benefits would be to their disadvantage.

In order to cope with the problems of cost advantages and disadvantages and 'social dumping', the European Commission has sought to bring about minimum standards for social security systems in all Member States (Commission of the European Communities, 1993a, pp. 43–4, 60–61; Commission of the European Communities, 1994b, pp. 52–3). In the view of the Commission, such minimum standards would ideally bring about a convergence of social security systems (Chassard, 1992). Until the ratification of the Maastricht treaty in 1993, however, the European treaties did not provide any legal basis for the setting of such minimum standards. The Commission was therefore restricted to proposing nonbinding recommendations on the 'convergence of social protection objectives and policies', which, following a large number of modifications, were adopted by the Council in July 1992 (Council, 1992).

Since ratification of the Maastricht treaty, the legal situation has changed. The European Community does now have a legal basis for setting minimum standards in the area of social security, though only for 14 of the 15 Member States: the Protocol on Social Policy that was added to the Maastricht treaty and the consequent Agreement on Social Policy that was concluded between the Member States with the exception of the United Kingdom ('Agreement', 1993). In Article 2, par. 3, this agreement authorizes the Council, with the exception of the United Kingdom, to adopt, by means of directives, minimum requirements in the field of 'social security and social protection of workers'. By 1995 this authorization had still not been put into effect, though; unlike the decisions on workplace participation, this authorization requires unanimous voting in the Council. No directive setting minimum requirements for social security had been envisaged.

4.3 Towards Upward Harmonization?

Minimum standards for social security systems in the European Union do not seem to have gone beyond the lowest common denominator of existing national systems. In the area of unemployment compensation, for example, the 1992 Council recommendation on the 'convergence of social protection objectives and policies' stipulates that Member States should

> provide employed workers who have lost their jobs with either flat-rate benefits, or benefits calculated in relation to their earnings in their previous occupation, which will maintain their standard of living in a reasonable manner in accordance with their participation in appropriate social security schemes subject to their active availability for work or for vocational training with a view to obtaining employment (Council, 1992).

With this wording, the Council recommendation (which is not binding on Member States) does not express a preference for either flat-rate or earnings-related benefits and thus does not go beyond defining the lowest common denominator of existing unemployment compensation systems in the Member States. The original draft of the recommendation, drawn up by the Commission of the European Communities, had expressed a clear preference for protecting redundant workers through an insurance scheme by recommending that workers who have lost their jobs should receive 'an allowance representing a significant part of their previous earnings' (Commission of the European Communities, 1991, p. 12). The thinking behind this was to prevent social dumping motivated by wage-cost considerations by promoting a wider diffusion of insurance systems. However, the Commission's preference did not survive deliberations in the Council because the Council recommendation required the unanimous approval of all Member State governments. Similar modifications of the draft can be seen in other areas of social security. This experience seems to show that a convergence of national social security systems is unlikely to be achieved in a decision-making system that requires unanimous voting by the Member States.

However, the situation is different in the case of the European regulation on social security for migrant workers. This regulation has not encountered any considerable opposition by the Member States because it provides mainly an administrative framework for the coordination of social security claims that migrants would have had anyway *vis-à-vis* different national social security systems. In most cases, this regulation does not constitute any severe additional burden or disadvantage for individual Member States. In cases where this is less clear, however, as in the case of benefits for unemployed migrants, there has been strong opposition by those Member States that would have had to bear an additional burden.

5 EXPLANATIONS FOR THE DIFFERING SUCCESS IN CREATING LABOUR STANDARDS

The four key areas examined in this chapter indicate the varying levels of success achieved in harmonizing European social standards. We have seen that occupational health and safety regulations have had the most success, whereas social security regulation has had only minimal effect. In this chapter we have identified the goals of harmonization and the current state of European legislation. As evaluation of these standards is at present difficult, given that many have not yet been fully implemented and monitored, we have preferred to focus on the factors which account for the success or failure in reaching agreement on common rules at the European level.[3] We have argued that the changes in the decision-making procedures, the development of coalitions and the extent to which directives disrupt nationally embedded systems are the key factors accounting for the success or failure of agreement on these rules. In this conclusion we seek to elaborate this argument.

5.1 Decision-making Rules

The cases cited reflect the different legal basis for decision-making procedures. One of the most significant factors in breaking up the stalemate in issuing European directives was the introduction and extension of QMV. This effectively removed the ability of one country, notably the United Kingdom, to exercise a veto on agreements. The Protocol on Social Policy, that was added to the Maastricht treaty when the United Kingdom refused to accept a Social Chapter, authorized the remaining Member States to adopt an Agreement on Social Policy which was annexed to the Protocol ('Agreement', 1993). In Article 2, this Agreement authorized the Council, with the exception of the United Kingdom, to use directives to adopt minimum requirements for the gradual implementation of social policy in a number of areas, that is, in the field of 'information and consultation of workers' on the basis of QMV. Prior to this, agreement had required unanimous voting.

The effect of decision-making procedures can be seen in the 'successful' cases of occupational health and safety as well as workplace participation; agreement was reached by QMV, according to Article 118 A of the EC treaty and Article 2, paras 1 and 2, of the Agreement on Social Policy for these policy areas, respectively. One of the reasons for the limited success in the case of social security is that it requires unanimous voting from the 14 remaining Member States, which continues to present a substantial barrier to achieving

---

3 See OECD (1994) for an attempt to assess the economic impact of national labour standards.

consensus. Scharpf (1976, pp. 42–5) has argued that formal involvement in interorganizational or intergovernmental decisions is the key to achieving agreement. However, in the European case the existence of a two-tier legislative process has also created problems of legitimacy and consensus, as it is not always clear which voting procedure will be used. This problem is illustrated by the working time directive. This was passed by QMV on the basis that it was an occupational health and safety regulation according to Article 118 A of the EC treaty. However, the UK government has challenged the legal basis of this decision. This measure would not have been passed under unanimous voting procedures. Concern for this legitimacy issue will be raised at an intergovernmental conference in 1996.

The use of QMV is likely to bring about European standards that go beyond the national standards of some individual Member States. Where unanimous agreement in the Council is required, it is unlikely that standards will go beyond the lowest common denominator, if any such directive is passed at all.

5.2   Coalition Building

The second key factor accounting for the extent to which directives have been passed or not relies on the nature of the political coalitions that have been built up to support or oppose such measures. In the case of workplace participation, once decision-making procedures changed, it became easier for a coalition of interests to build up sufficient support to push the directive through. However, recognition also needs to be given to the fragmented nature of this coalition of interests. Employers were strictly opposed to such a uniform measure, which they saw not only as potentially expensive, but as a restriction on their managerial prerogatives. Nevertheless, within employer organizations there were significant interests, most notably from French and German firms, who were prepared to support a negotiated form of consultation committees. These firms saw such an initiative as offering the means of securing employee commitment for introducing organizational change more effectively. The trade union movement was largely in favour of improving their representation and access to corporate information, although differing national and ideological positions meant that the Commission proposals were sometimes viewed with suspicion as potentially undermining existing rights secured at the national level. Nevertheless, the ETUC was in favour of such committees and with the Commission pushed for regulation on this issue. With the support of the Parliament and a section of the employers they were able to reach agreement on a directive.

In the case of health and safety, the expected opposition from Member States with lower standards did not emerge. This was for several reasons. First, such states benefited from product standardization as it allowed them greater access to the richer northern markets. Second, the implementation of health and safety processes, even within national legislation, is very weak, so it did not seem to matter greatly whether these directives were passed, because it was unlikely that they would be stringently implemented. Third, significant redistribution of resources through the European Social Fund (see chap. 28 by Lindley in this volume) have given peripheral countries an incentive to accommodate demands for improved social standards. Addison and Siebert (1994, p. 18) argue that in the future 'enhanced subsidies for the lagging regions should tend to make them more willing to enforce higher standards'. There has been no lobby of political interests promoting harmonization on social security, and in the case of working time, derogations averted conflict between France and Germany. The 'successful' incidents indicate that where coalitions of interest can be built up, albeit with sometimes conflicting motives and interests, the existence of such a coalition can bring about agreement on standards at the European level. The result of conflicts between coalitions of pro-European and pronational groupings will determine the extent to which common standards are accepted and implemented.

5.3   The Embeddedness of National Regulations

The third key factor accounting for the success or failure on agreements at the European level is the extent to which such regulation requires a fundamental reorganization of nationally embedded regulations. The case of social security is a particularly good example of how fundamental reform would be disruptive to national systems. Where agreement has been reached with regard to foreign workers this is largely due to 'filling the gaps' in existing national legislation. National social security systems have long traditions and are closely embedded in the overall institutional systems, particularly in the industrial relations systems, of each country. The design and practice of each national social security system is closely linked to the system of wage determination, the system of employment protection, the role of unions and employers' associations and the role of private insurance. Any major change in national social security systems therefore has far-reaching implications for other policy areas and for the overall institutional system of each country. It is also for that reason that decisions aiming at a European convergence of social security systems seem to be particularly difficult to achieve.

The situation is different in the other policy fields. Occupational health and safety appears as a rather 'technical' policy field which is only loosely linked to the overall institutional and industrial relations system of each country and therefore less likely to resist major changes. In a similar way, the European regulation of workplace participation in multinational firms (which are the only firms affected by the European directive) does not seem to affect existing national styles of management and, thus, other policy issues. In these policy fields, European regulation could be achieved because it did not have major implications for other policy areas.

Rubery (1992) suggests that attempts at harmonization will occur at several levels, subject to various political and economic influences:

> the enthusiasm with which the European idea is embraced will depend on how it complements or contradicts agendas at a local level. The actual implementation of European policies is thus likely still to reflect specific cultures and political agenda, with countries implementing policies selectively to suit their internal requirements. Such a scenario does not suggest, however, stagnation in social and cultural systems, but evolution, through the interplay of transnational, pan-European and domestic influences (p. 254).

In conclusion, we can note that, as Addison and Siebert (1994) argue, some directives have been subject to 'dilution' in the process of enactment, but that the Commission has also pressed for increased capacity to secure enforcement. The European Court of Justice now has the power to fine countries which do not enforce directives. Given the fact that many of these directives have only recently reached the stage of ratification, even in the most successful cases of occupational health and safety and workplace participation, evaluation of the impact of these directives requires them to be fully implemented and monitored. This will be a key evaluation research issue for the future.

REFERENCES

Addison, J. T. and W. S. Siebert (1994), 'Recent Developments in Social Policy in the New European Union', *Industrial and Labour Relations Review*, 48 (1), 5–27.

'Agreement on Social Policy Concluded between the Member States of the European Community with the Exception of the United Kingdom of Great Britain and Northern Ireland' (1993), in M. Gold (ed.), *The Social Dimension: Employment Policy in the European Community*, London: Macmillan, pp. 232–5.

Altmaier, P. (1992), 'Unemployment Benefits', *Social Europe*, 3, pp. 38–45.

Baldwin, R. (1992), 'The Limits of Legislative Harmonization', in R. Baldwin and T. Daintith (eds), *Harmonization and Hazard: Regulating Workplace Health and Safety in the EC*, London: Graham & Trotman, pp. 223–51.

Baldwin, R. and T. Daintith (1992), *Harmonization and Hazard: Regulating Workplace Health and Safety in the EC*, London: Graham & Trotman.

Blank, M. (1994), 'The Prospects for Codetermination in the EC', in G. Bosch (ed.), *International Integration and the Regulation of Working Conditions*, SAMF working paper no. 1994–5, Gelsenkirchen: Arbeitskreis Sozialwissenschaftliche Arbeitsmarktforschung (SAMF), pp. 143–61.

Chassard, Y. (1992), 'The Convergence of Social Protection Objectives and Policies: A New Approach', *Social Europe* (suppl. 5), pp. 13–20.

Commission of the European Communities (CEC) (1989), *Communication from the Commission Concerning Its Action Programme Relating to the Implementation of the Community Charter of Basic Social Rights for Workers*, COM (89), 568 final, Brussels: CEC.

Commission of the European Communities (1991), *Proposal for a Council Recommendation on the Convergence of Social Protection Objectives and Policies*, COM (91), 228 final, Brussels: CEC.

Commission of the European Communities (1993a), *European Social Policy: Options for the Union*, Green Paper, Luxembourg: Office for Official Publications of the European Communities.

Commission of the European Communities (1993b), *Social Protection in Europe 1993*, Luxembourg: Office for Official Publications of the European Communities.

Commission of the European Communities (1994a), *Employment in Europe,* COM (94) 381, DG V, Brussels.

Commission of the European Communities (1994b), *European Social Policy*, White Paper, Luxembourg: Office for Official Publications of the European Communities.

Commission of the European Communities (1994c), *Growth, Competitiveness and Employment: The Challenges and Ways Forward into the 21st Century*, White Paper, Luxembourg: Office for Official Publications of the European Communities.

Council of the European Communities (1992), 'Council Recommendation of 27 July 1992 on the Convergence of Social Protection Objectives and Policies' (92/442/ EEC), *Official Journal of the European Communities*, L 245, p. 49.

Cressey, P. (1993), 'Employee Participation', in M. Gold (ed.), *The Social Dimension: Employment Policy in the European Community*, London: Macmillan, pp. 85–104.

Deakin, S. and F. Wilkinson (1992), 'European Integration: The Implications for UK Policies on Labour Supply and Demand', in E. McLaughlin (ed.), *Understanding Unemployment*, London: Routledge, pp. 196–214.

Eichener, V. (1993), 'Social Dumping or Innovative Regulation? Processes and Outcomes of European Decision-making in the Sector of Health and Safety at Work Regulation', EUI working paper no. SPS 92/28, Florence: European University Institute.

European Communities (1989a), Council Directive no. 89/391/EEC on Safety and Health at Work, *Official Journal of the European Communities*, L 183 (29 June), p. 1.

European Communities (1989b), Council Directive no. 89/392/EEC on the Safety of Machinery, *Official Journal of the European Communities*, L 183 (29 June), p. 9.

European Communities (1990), Council Directive no. 90/270/EEC on Display Screen Equipment, *Official Journal of the European Communities*, L 156 (21 June), p. 14.

European Communities (1992), Consolidated Version of Council Regulation (EEC) no. 1408/71 on the Application of Social Security Schemes to Employed Persons, to Self-employed Persons and to Members of Their Families Moving within the Community, *Official Journal of the European Communities*, C 325 (10 December), p. 1.

Eurostat (1995), *Social Protection Expenditure and Receipts 1980–1993*, Luxembourg: Office for Official Publications of the European Communities.

Goetschy, J. (1994), 'A Further Comment on Wolfgang Streek's "European Social Policy after Maastricht"', *Economic and Industrial Democracy*, 15 (3), 477–85.

Gold, M. (1994), *Direct Communications in European Multinationals: A Case Study Approach*, Dublin: European Foundation for the Improvement of Living and Working Conditions.

Gold, M. and M. Hall (1992), *European-level Information and Consultation in Multinational Companies: An Evaluation of Practice*, Dublin: Office for Official Publications of the European Communities.

Gold, M. and M. Hall (1994), 'Statutory European Works Councils: The Final Countdown?', *Industrial Relations Journal*, 25 (3), 177–86.

Hall, M. (1992), 'Behind the European Works Councils Directive: The European Commission's Legislative Strategy', *British Journal of Industrial Relations*, 30 (3), 547–66.

Hinrichs, K., W. Roche and C. Sirianni (eds) (1991), *Working Time in Transition: The Political Economy of Working Hours in Industrial Nations*, Philadelphia: Temple University Press.

'The Hoover Affair and Social Dumping' (1993), *European Industrial Relations Review*, 230, 14–20.

ILO (International Labour Office) (1993), *Yearbook of Labour Statistics 1993*, Geneva: ILO.

'Information and Consultation in European Multinationals, Part 1' (1993a), *European Industrial Relations Review*, 228, 13–19.

'Information and Consultation in European Multinationals, Part 2' (1993b), *European Industrial Relations Review*, 229, 14–20.

Marginson, P. (1992), 'European Integration and Transitional Management–Union Relations in the Enterprise', *British Journal of Industrial Relations*, 30 (4), 530–45.

Marginson, P., C. Buitendam, C. Deutschmann and P. Perulli (1993), 'The Emergence of the Euro-company: Towards a European Industrial Relations?', *Industrial Relations Journal*, 24 (2), 182–90.

McLaughlin, E. (1994), 'Flexibility or Polarisation?', in M. White (ed.), *Unemployment and Public Policy in a Changing Labour Market*, London: Policy Studies Institute (PSI), pp. 11–34.

Meager, N. and J. Buchan (1988), 'Job-sharing and Job-splitting: Employer Attitudes', *IMS Report*, 149, Brighton: Institute of Manpower (IMS).

Mosley, H. (1990), 'The Social Dimension of European Integration', *International Labour Review*, 129 (2), 147–64.

'New European Information and Consultation Draft' (1994), *European Industrial Relations Review*, 245, 18–23.

OECD (1994), *Employment Outlook*, Paris: OECD.

'Officials Seek Close Match in National Euro-council Rules', (1994), *Industrial Relations Europe*, 22 (263), 1–8.

O'Reilly, J. (1994a), *Banking on Flexibility: A Comparison of Flexible Employment Strategies in the Retail Banking Sector in Britain and France*, Aldershot: Gower.

O'Reilly, J. (1994b), 'What Flexibility Do Women Offer? Comparing the Use of, and Attitudes to, Part-time Work in Britain and France in Retail Banking', *Gender, Work and Organization*, 1, 138–50.

Paoli, P. (1992), *First European Survey on the Work Environment 1991–1992*, Luxembourg: European Foundation for the Improvement of Living and Working Conditions.

Pickert, K. (1992), 'Die europäischen Normungsarbeiten zur Maschinensicherheit und zur Gefahreneinschätzung', in TGB (Europäisches Technikbüro der Gewerkschaften für Gesundheit und Sicherheit) (ed.), *Die Mitwirkung der Gewerkschaften an den europäischen Normungsarbeiten*, Brussels, pp. 79–88.

Rehbinder, E. and R. Stewart (1985), 'Environmental Protection Policy', *Integration through Law 2*, Berlin: de Gruyter.

Reissert, B. (1993, Autumn), 'National Unemployment-support Schemes in the EC', in Commission of the European Communities (ed.), *Employment Observatory— Policies (informISEP)*, 43, 19–27.

Ross, G. (1994), 'On Half-full Glasses, Europe and the Left: Comments on Wolfgang Streeck's "European Social Policy after Maastricht"', *Economic and Industrial Democracy*, 15 (3), 486–96.

Rubery, J. (1992), 'Productive Systems, International Integration and the Single European Market', in A. Castro, P. Méhaut and J. Rubery (eds), *International Integration and Labour Market Organisation*, London: Academic Press, pp. 224–56.

Scharpf, F. W. (1976), 'Theorie der Politikverflechtung', in F. W. Scharpf, B. Reissert and F. Schnabel, *Politikverflechtung*, Kronberg: Scriptor, pp. 13–70.

Scharpf, F. W. (1994), 'Mehrebenenpolitik im vollendeten Binnenmarkt', discussion paper 94/4, Max-Planck-Institut für Gesellschaftsforschung, Cologne.

Schmid, G., B. Reissert and G. Bruche (1992), *Unemployment Insurance and Active Labour Market Policy: An International Comparison of Financing Systems*, Detroit, MA: Wayne State University Press.

Simon, G. (1990), 'Ein Standpunkt zur Mobilität der Bevölkerung in der EG: Tendenzen und Perspektiven im Vorfeld des Binnenmarktes', *Soziales Europa*, 90 (3), 22–36.

Sisson, K., J. Waddington and C. Whitston (1991), 'Company Size in the European Community', *Human Resource Management Journal*, 2 (1), pp. 40–64.

'States Find Common Ground on National Euro-council Rules' (1995), *Industrial Relations Europe*, 23 (266), 1–2.

Streeck, W. (1994), 'European Social Policy after Maastricht: The "Social Dialogue" and "Subsidiarity"', *Economic and Industrial Democracy*, 15 (2), 151–78.

Streeck, W. and S. Vitols (1993), *European Works Councils: Between Statutory Enactment and Voluntary Adoption*, WZB discussion paper FS I 93–312, Wissenschaftszentrum Berlin für Sozialforschung.

'Thriving on Diversity: Another View of MNC Information/Consultation' (1993), *European Industrial Relations Review*, 238, 19–23.

'Unions Will Campaign All out for Euro-council Deals Now' (1994), *Industrial Relations Europe*, 22 (262), 2.

van Raepenbusch, S. (1991), *La sécurité sociale des personnes qui circulent à l'intérieur de la Communauté économique européenne*, Brussels: Story-Scientia.

Vogel, L. (1991), *A Survey of Occupational Health and Safety Services in the Member States of the European Community and the European Free Trade Association. First Interim Report: The Existing Legal Frameworks in the Different States*, Brussels: European Trade Union Technical Bureau for Health and Safety.

Walwei, U. and H. Werner (1991), 'Soziale Sicherung bei Arbeitslosigkeit im Europäischen Binnenmarkt: Konsequenzen für die Bundesrepublik Deutschland?', *Beiträge aus der Arbeitsmarkt- und Berufsforschung*, 142, 72–88.

Wanka, R. (1991), 'Wechselwirkungen zwischen dem europäischen Recht und den Vorschriften über das Recht der Arbeitslosenversicherung der Bundesrepublik Deutschland', *Beiträge aus der Arbeitsmarkt- und Berufsforschung*, 142, 89–103.

Watson, G. (1992, November), 'Hours of Work in Great Britain and Europe: Evidence from the UK and European Labour Force Surveys', *Employment Gazette*, 100 (11), 539–57.

Wilensky, H. (1975), *The Welfare State and Equality*, Berkeley: University of California Press.

Wolf, R. (1987), 'Zur Antiquiertheit des Rechts in der Risikogesellschaft', *Leviathan*, 15 (3), 357–91.

'Working Time Directive–Common Position' (1993), *European Industrial Relations Review*, 235, 15–18.

30. Monitoring of Labour Market Policy in EU Member States[1]

Peter Auer and Thomas Kruppe

Unlike the subject of evaluating labour market policy (LMP), that of monitoring does not yet have a large body of literature. The topic of monitoring is all the more present in current debates on the performance of LMP. Scarce resources, uncertain results and the trend towards decentralization of delivery has led to an increasing need for an instrument permitting a more continuous and comprehensive follow-up on policies than selective *ex-post* evaluation can provide. As the monitoring of LMP is neither amply analysed in literature nor, at least in Europe, easily grasped empirically because of its relatively recent development, this chapter on the question of monitoring LMP is mainly exploratory. In section 1 we attempt to define monitoring both empirically (on the basis of expert interviews) and theoretically (on the basis of what little literature exists on the subject); in section 2 we discuss the reasons for the recent effort to introduce such systems in the Member States of the European Union (EU); in sections 3 and 4 we sketch the functions of monitoring systems, cite initial evidence on how partial monitoring systems are set up in some Member States and report about the difficulties that Member States' labour market authorities have encountered in doing so. In the final section 5 we discuss some of the implications and make recommendations for monitoring systems in the light of selected experiences in the EU and the United States.[2]

---

1 During this study a considerable amount of internal administrative, regulatory, statistical and other official material was received. Other valuable input consisted of interviews conducted with a range of programme administrators and researchers in many countries.

2 The present chapter is part of a larger ongoing study of monitoring systems in the EU. The study will later provide an overview of Member States' experiences with monitoring systems. It is based on some of the scarce literature on the topic (including that in the United States) and on several expert interviews conducted in France, Germany, Austria, Portugal and Sweden. Material collected through a questionnaire sent to experts in all EU Member States will be incorporated in a later version.

1 WHAT IS MONITORING?

There is presently no clear-cut concept of monitoring. This ambiguity in the definition of the term made it rather difficult to collect empirical information on the subject because it was not always clearly understood in the interviews what monitoring activities are. At the same time, there was a clear trend in all the countries visited to engage in rather performance-oriented evaluation and monitoring of financial and physical indicators (participants in measures) of active LMP which, in turn, may be used to change programme implementation. However, these activities usually come under the name of follow-up, reporting, controlling or evaluation. Only sometimes are they called monitoring.

What is said in the literature on monitoring? In the final report of a group evaluating employment policies in several EU Member States (MISEP, 1989), British evaluation specialists regarded monitoring as consisting in the control of quantifiable objectives set by the programme administration. However, they noted that attaining quantitative goals might hinder the realization of qualitative goals; hence, the importance of evaluation (MISEP, 1989, p. 14). In their report monitoring had no feedback loop, and only evaluation was said to lead to reappraisal of and change in programmes. In that narrow concept monitoring is basically a tool of the administration to control the 'face value' of programmes (spending and participation). Evaluation would then consist in looking behind this 'face value' through, say, calculation of the net cost of programmes, through cost–benefit analysis or assessment of medium- and long-term integration effects of measures via longitudinal studies. Based on sophisticated quantitative analysis, evaluation has, according to this study (MISEP, 1989), an important qualitative aspect that monitoring does not.

By contrast, Bellmann and Walwei (1994) note in a discussion on qualitative labour market information that one of the most widely used forms in the field of programme implementation is monitoring. 'At a more sophisticated level, *monitoring* yields target-related performance indicators for programme administrators. And through this type of *evaluation* it is possible to assess, for example, whether or not the size of a recruitment subsidy is sufficient to induce the targeted take-up by employers' (p. 9). Here the distinction between evaluation and monitoring as well as between qualitative and quantitative is blurred. Hasan (1991) sees monitoring as part of 'process analysis'. So does Schmid (chap. 7 in this volume). However, Melchior (1992) explained how the monitoring of the JTPA (Job Training Partnership Act, the largest and most important US training and employment programme) has evolved from process orientation towards result orientation. If one takes a narrow view, then this change corresponds to a shift from monitoring to evaluation. However, 'performance management systems' such as the one legally mandated in JTPA have much of the continuous monitoring system and effective feedback loop (and incentive and sanctions) that many European schemes do not have. For Schmid, too, feedback is an essential part of monitoring: 'Effective feedback through monitoring involves sanctions in [the] form of lower budget allowances, bans on promotion or even dismissal' (Schmid, 1994, p. 19).

Monitoring is, therefore, linked to the process of LMP delivery in many ways. In a broader perspective, however, *results* have to be monitored as well. In other words, difficulties in the distinction between evaluation and monitoring remain. The problems become evident if one begins by examining the basic elements of an evaluation concept which consist of five elements (see e.g. Kuhlmann and Holland, 1995, p. 17, and Meyer-Krahmer, 1990, p. 211): (1) Is the programme generally valid? Have the assumptions been right? (2) Has the target group been reached? (3) What direct and indirect effects have there been? (4) Have the goals been reached? (5) Have implementation and administration been efficient?

It appears that points 2 and 4 are at the core of monitoring systems but that all other aspects—with the exception of point 1, possibly the indirect effects of point 3 and the more analytical aspects of point 4—can at first sight be assessed by evaluation as well as by monitoring. However, monitoring is much more a tool to document performance or failures in reaching preset goals, not to explain them, which latter task falls to evaluation. Although the exact borderline between monitoring and evaluation is therefore hard to define, there seems to be a pragmatic understanding of what monitoring activities are: regularly conducted observation of statistical indicators of LMP input/output and performance (outcome) for the purpose of improving programme implementation and even programme design. Affholter (1994) defines monitoring, especially the monitoring of outcomes, as the 'regular (periodic, frequent) reporting of programme results in ways that stakeholders can use to understand and judge those results' (p. 97).

2   WHY THE MONITORING OF LMP IS BECOMING IMPORTANT TODAY

Active LMP as a standing instrument of national governments' economic and social policy intervention was introduced at different times. For example, Sweden introduced it in the late 1950s; Germany, in the late 1960s. France has had a full-fledged employment policy only since the mid-1970s and early 1980s. In any case, such policies have been implemented in most of the EU Member States for some time now. Spending on such policies has increased, and an ever greater number of people go, at some point in their working lives, through active LMP schemes, mainly vocational training and job creation.[3]

Despite the fact that LMP has found its place in economic policies, it has remained a subject of controversy, with not a few people thinking that it basically distorts the labour market and, instead of responding to market failure, induces nonmarket behaviour in firms and individuals by granting generous subsidies more often than not to people and firms not needing them. This kind of uneasiness with LMP is not mainly due to a lack of evaluation research (nor the lack of sophisticated evaluation methods) but rather perhaps to the complexity of evaluation research and its often contradictory results. Nobody has as yet counted the number of evaluation studies that were conducted to measure the impact of these policies in the EU. However, the evidence from all these studies is not conclusive and often prompts policy-makers to wish for 'one-armed economists'.[4] Although the effects of policies are certainly complex and although the methodological instruments for adequately illustrating those effects have become ever more sophisticated, the need of policy-makers for more down-to-earth knowledge of the effects has remained. Indeed, the need has lately been forcefully restated, such as when financing by the European Social Fund (ESF) was being arranged. Critics of evaluation research fault the complexity of the results (along with the sometimes 'esoteric' language used to present them). They also rebuke evaluation research for 'bad timing', that is, the fact that evaluation in general is an *ex-post* exercise and that results do not become available until months or years after the studies have been commissioned. Kuhlmann and Holland (1995) cited such a criticism in their metaevaluation of technology policy. After describing how a particular evaluation study is chosen, a contract signed and the work started, the authors contended that

> some substantial time later, in comes a report ... It is too voluminous to be read by anyone who would be in a position to make those decisions. It's too technically esoteric to be understood by them if it were on time and they were to read it. And there's a good chance it has become irrelevant, policy-wise, to the issues which triggered it at the outset. The results are that, first, it goes on the shelf where it is unused and uninfluential in policy, program and budget decisions. And second, even worse, when its existence is belatedly and critically recognised, it contributes negatively to the reputation of evaluation (Evans, cited in Kuhlmann and Holland, 1995, p. 247).

---

3 In the EU and EFTA (European Free Trade Association) countries, about 3.1 per cent of GDP was spent on LMP in 1993–94 (1.03 per cent on active and 2.06 per cent on passive measures). In 1991 about 8.0 per cent of the labour force entered active programmes in Ireland, almost 10 per cent in France, 5 per cent in Italy and 7 per cent in Sweden (OECD, 1994, p. 53).

4 Policy-makers are facetiously said to complain that economists usually give unclear council by stating 'on the one hand ..., but on the other hand ...'.

This censure, which was stated in the context of technology policy, might apply only to a particular kind of evaluation (selective, subcontracted evaluation). But the problems that are cited afflict many evaluation studies in the LMP field as well. Written from the point of view of those who use evaluation, these critical facts show the need for a more 'on-line', less complex, 'ready-to-use' instrument with which to compare outcomes with goals set and to provide enough information to enable administrators of LMP programmes to change certain targets, allocate additional money or allocate money differently.

There are also reasons for evaluation research itself to have a system of systematic information-gathering and observation of LMP indicators organized at a basic level, because useful first-hand information on some crucial indicators will relieve evaluators from the task of collecting such data themselves. As stated by Lindley (chap. 28 in this volume), a progressive evaluation scheme (for the ESF) involves treating auditing, monitoring and evaluation in a unified way, the first being a prerequisite for the second and the second being a prerequisite for the third. If one accepts this idea, then a monitoring system (as well as an auditing instrument—that is, basically a financial accounting system—for monitoring) is crucial for evaluation. One can add that these systems fulfil their functions on different levels and that, whereas an effective monitoring system might well reduce the need for certain types of evaluation, it will principally allow evaluators to address those questions that cannot be solved by the observation of quantitative indicators alone. For example, it is hard to imagine how a monitoring system might cope with deadweight, substitution or displacement, the drug effect (addiction to subsidies) or other issues unless very complex data systems permitting cross-references are developed.[5] We will return to these effects and the question of whether they can be addressed by a monitoring system.

There are still other and more immediate reasons that make the monitoring of LMP both necessary and possible.

1. Fiscal constraints, lean administration and the reform of the public sector. The ideas on the new public service, which involve a shift from bureaucratic and centralized rule-making towards decentralized and market-oriented responsibilities and assessment systems and a general awareness of public spending (which also involves increased auditing by comptrollers), have contributed to the pressure to set up monitoring systems. Together with decentralization (see below), the introduction of private sector management methods (e.g. management-by-objectives, 'profit centres' or

---

5 Gautié, Gazier and Silvera (1994, p. 205) have collected 40 different possible micro- and macroeconomic effects found by economists evaluating employment programmes.

'cost centres') in the public sector has also compounded the need for assessment of results. Partially related to that need there is increasingly a 'built-in' obligation to have the performance of labour market programmes monitored and evaluated. As mentioned before, this commitment is part of the JTPA. The French five-year employment law (a medium-term law on employment measures), too, has introduced an obligation to assess results. In Portugal such built-in monitoring (quarterly impact measurement) was provided for in a decree mandating training and job creation measures for the long-term unemployed in 1994, but it has since been discontinued.

2. The decentralization of LMP implementation. Handing down responsibilities for LMP programmes to lower administrative levels and thus decreasing the control possibilities inherent in centrally administered programmes could complicate LMP monitoring. But decentralization promotes the introduction of monitoring systems in two ways. First, it provides local agents with information. Second, it provides central bodies with information on their local branches. The latter effect leads to enhanced control possibilities for central bodies, for they can compare the results of their local agents. It also provides better targets for local agents, for they can see the results of similar agents. The trend towards expanding the discretionary power of decentralized levels (e.g. the latitude that local employment offices have for deciding which measure—say, job creation or job training —is suitable for their clients) also entails increased monitoring. After all, local agents must legitimate their allocation choices.

3. The increase of ESF financing for Member States' LMP[6] and provisions for follow-ups. The reform of the structural funds in 1989 led to multiannual programming and greater involvement of the Member countries in monitoring the implementation and effects of measures cofinanced by the ESF. A guide entitled *Monitoring Operational Programmes* was issued, and systems for monitoring had to be set up through partnership arrangements between the European Commission and the Member States. It was stated that the structural funds should be spent in 'accordance with the objectives established, the regulatory provision, and according to the principle of sound financial management' (DEE, 1994, p. 6). Article 25 of council regulation 4253/88 required the Commission and the Member States to ensure the 'effective monitoring of the implementation of assistance from the funds' (DEE, 1994, p. 7). The Member States were responsible for producing for each programme a series of physical and financial indicators that would make it possible to measure the progress and management of the

---

6 In 1991, about 13 per cent of EU spending on LMP was financed through the ESF. However, this figure varies considerably across the Member States, reaching, for example, about 25 per cent in Portugal.

programme and any associated problems. The difficulties that Member States encountered in implementing effective monitoring systems have led most of our interviewees so far to regard the influence of ESF regulations on monitoring as rather marginal. However, special monitoring units have been set up in several countries (e.g. the evaluation unit established in Ireland for the ESF programme there). And with ESF cofinancing of measures becoming more important, there are spill-overs from ESF monitoring to national monitoring activities and vice versa.

4. The European Commission's efforts to make EU GNP growth more employment intensive, not least by an activation of labour market policy (European Commission, 1994), lead to an enhanced need for monitoring. In the wake of subsequent European council meetings, and especially since the resolutions of the European council meeting in Essen (December 1994), employment and employment policies must be monitored by the Commission, which has to report on developments every year from late 1995 on. The Commission, with the help of the Member States, Eurostat and its employment observatories (MISEP, SYSDEM), intends to establish employment policy indicators, which should permit follow-up on national policies in financial and physical terms. These activities will also lead to an increase in national monitoring.[7]

5. The spread of computer technology. Technological advances have made monitoring possible at lower levels of the organization and can facilitate data transfer through data networks. These changes have paved the way for setting up monitoring systems. In this area, many sophisticated systems have been or soon will be developed. They include the French system STEF ('Serveur télématique emploi formation'), which transmits entry flows in selected measures from the local offices of the Ministry of Labour to DARES ('Direction de l'Animation de la Recherche, des Etudes et des Statistiques'), the ministry's body responsible for monitoring LMP programmes (for more detail, see below). The Employment Delegation ('Delegation à l'emploi') of the Ministry of Labour also runs a computer system called PALERME ('Programme d'analyse locale et d'évaluation rapide des mesures d'emploi') but there is currently an effort to set up a new and more integrated general management system for employment policy—

---

7 MISEP is the Commission's Mutual Information System on Employment Policies which regularly reports about employment measures taken by the countries and runs a basic, annually updated information series on each Member State. SYSDEM (System of Documentation on Employment) informs readers about general trends in employment and about studies in the field of employment. For political reasons (e.g. subsidiarity) and the fact that the Commission has no supranational employment policy other than ESF financing, these monitoring activities will in fact remain at best good information systems on employment policies of the Member States.

the GPI ('Gestion des procédures d'intervention'). Partial programmes (all of which are becoming more and more comprehensive) exist in many countries, but Sweden is about to launch a nationwide system of programme-monitoring called PRESTO and an overall computerized information and monitoring system called AIS (AMS Information System).

In summary, the physical and financial importance of LMP, the uncertain, selective and often outdated results of evaluation, the move towards the new public service and decentralization, increasing EU activities and funding, and the general pressure of tight budgets with the advent of 'lean administration' have all contributed to increasing the need for a more 'on-line', less complex and more transparent system for following up on LMP. In addition, the development of information technologies has provided the technical infrastructure for the establishment of monitoring systems.

Given increased spending and uncertain results, financial control institutions have, in general, tightened their grip on policy implementation bodies, a reality that also explains the efforts to introduce stricter monitoring. The relative importance of these two factors, which are common to all EU Member States, varies from country to country. For example, the obligation to monitor ESF cofinanced measures may have greater impact on monitoring in the 'southern rim' countries and Ireland than, say, in France, the United Kingdom or Germany, which already have a developed apparatus for evaluation. Improvement in the financial accountability of policy implementation bodies is also being compelled by country-specific obligations and circumstances. France, for instance, mandates that LMP programmes implemented through the five-year employment law are to be monitored. In Germany, there was the financial crisis that beset the country's job creation schemes (ABMs) in the first half of 1993, after which point admission to the programme had to cease for the rest of the year even in eastern Germany if political intervention would not have allocated additional funds. Portugal, too, has tightened financial control over LMP programmes because of similar deficits in the budget for active LMP measures.

Despite all these factors, progress towards the establishment of full-fledged monitoring systems remains slow. Before examining the obstacles further, we outline what could be an ideal-type LMP monitoring system and what its role and function could be in the assessment of LMP.

3　　FUNCTIONS OF A MONITORING SYSTEM

Ideally, the monitoring and evaluation of active LMP would encompass continuous information gathering, continuous financial and physical monitoring of specified indicators and regular evaluation of specific aspects of whole programmes or of the impacts of the programmes. The information thus provided to the agents implementing the programme would allow them to adjust budget flows, and policy-makers could then quickly amend or discontinue existing measures and design new ones. There would be clear hierarchies in the possibilities that different actors involved in programmes have to modify them. At the local level implementation agents with wide discretion over programme spending could—in view of their own monitoring results—change the focus in some programmes and reallocate funds to others (e.g. if a target group is underrepresented or if take-up is slow). At higher levels labour market authorities would have wide discretion in fine-tuning their programmes by means of operational indicators in order to reach carefully preestablished, clear goals. At the top levels of the policy formation process, decision-makers with the clear goal of enhancing labour market performance would evaluate the results of programmes on the basis of this information and discontinue inefficient programmes and stimulate and establish more efficient and promising ones.

Preconditions for monitoring are the determination of programme goals quantifiable in financial and physical terms (e.g. spending by local agents, take-up and share of target group), the establishment of physical and financial indicators (possibly also a combination of both, such as spending per participant) and the observation of these indicators at certain reasonable time intervals (e.g. monthly or quarterly) depending on the schedule of programme implementation and the resources devoted to monitoring. It would also be necessary to specify not only final but also intermediate objectives. For a programme lasting a year, for instance, both financial and physical take-up should be measured against preestablished goals at monthly or at least quarterly intervals so that timely corrective action can be taken.

In this ideal world, monitoring would thus consist of:

1. goals specified by the political and administrative authorities at the national, regional and local levels;
2. a definition of indicators that allow goals to be measured;
3. the actual monitoring process based on 1 and 2 and on information gathering (statistical information on financial and physical indicators in relation to 1 and 2); and
4. feedback loops to ensure that observed irregularities are addressed adequately.

Figure 30.1 illustrates that 'ideal-type' monitoring process. It starts at policy formation in which programmes and individual measures are chosen. Even at this early stage, however, clear goals for programmes must be defined, and indicators making it possible to measure progress towards those goals must be

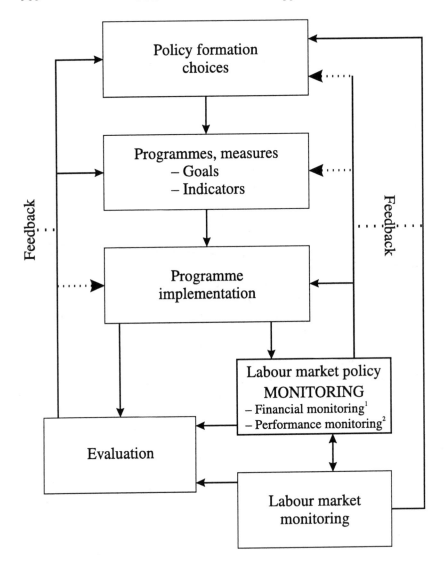

Notes

1 Controlling the outflow of budgets and the number of clients served in relation to the goals set.

2 Observation of selected result indicators (e.g. postparticipation employment).

Figure 30.1   Monitoring of Labour Market Policy

established if monitoring is to be effective. In other words effective monitoring must be written into laws and ordinances (as is the case with the JTPA in the United States and the French five-year employment law of 1994). After programmes have been implemented, a continuous process of observation should begin, the timing of which may vary from measure to measure. A quarterly observation period seems a reasonable compromise, but for short-time programmes shorter periods might be appropriate. The core function of monitoring is the detection of indicators turning 'red' and subsequent remedial action (feedback). Feedback between monitoring and programme implementation is stronger than between monitoring and policy formation. However, results of monitoring in which the standard performance of programmes is measured should also be fed back to policy formation. Evaluation, in which deadweight, substitution effects and other factors are also taken into consideration, offers a more profound assessment of programme impacts than monitoring does and affects programme implementation. For the same reason, evaluation affects policy formation more strongly than mere monitoring does.

However, monitoring will leave to evaluation only those indicators that cannot be observed directly and regularly. A relatively simple monitoring system will allow for a national and regional or local breakdown in order to facilitate comparisons between agencies. For any given programme it should at least be based on the regular (monthly, quarterly) observation of:

- the budget allocated and the budget used (breakdown by target groups and target sectors, if appropriate),
- planned participation and actual participation (breakdown by target group and target sectors, if appropriate),
- costs per head per hour (on the basis of 1 and 2) and breakdown by target group/sectors.

Thus, monitoring systems would provide useful information on financial and physical take-up and costs, and 'outliers' could be detected through the comparison of all local units that indicate variations in goal achievements and needs for changes and programme modifications.

The indicators listed above allow the close monitoring of fund outflows and participation in relation to preset goals and permit comparisons of per-capita costs between different measures. The indicators are therefore mostly of value to a programme administrator. They are basically input–output based and must, therefore, be supplemented by outcome–performance measures such as the employment status of the participants after participation or the skill levels achieved in training programmes (see Affholter, 1994). Regular monitoring could eventually even cope with some of the unintended effects of measures like deadweight. In an evaluation of a German wage-subsidy programme, Schmid (1980) found evidence for deadweight because the subsidy was disproportionately often used in the construction industry during spring, a period when activity in the construction industry usually increases. Thus, it seemed plausible that a large share of the hirings would have taken place even in the absence of the subsidy. A monthly monitoring of take-up by industry could have detected this very rapidly and could have induced a timely change of entitlement criteria.

If one links the monitoring of LMP to the monitoring of the labour market (a connection, however, that implies a more sophisticated system than most of those currently in place), then effects like the substitution of nonsubsidized workers by subsidized workers or even displacement (substitution of firms with nonsubsidized workers by firms that receive subsidies) can be detected early. These possibilities of monitoring, however, depend on the sophistication of statistics. They also have a legal dimension because those very effects, though clearly unintended, must not be illegal.

In general the linkage between LMP monitoring and labour market monitoring is crucial to further development of LMP monitoring. The links exist in two ways. On the one hand, the labour market situation (e.g. unemployment and employment) is an important criteria for the distribution of LMP funds across constituencies. On the other hand, the impact of LMP on, say, employment and unemployment is bound to show up in labour market monitoring indicators.

4   THE REALITY OF MONITORING

In general we have not yet found that 'full-fledged' monitoring systems exist in the countries reviewed. The exception is Sweden, which has such monitoring systems in several regional labour market offices and which is about to introduce nationwide systems. Even in Sweden, though, the process has been lengthy and is only now reaching completion. Henceforth, data about what was budgeted and what was actually spent will be available on-line for each labour market office or labour market institute (those taking care of handicapped persons) for all labour market measures. Analogous information about participants, too, will be accessible. During counselling sessions, individual placement officers or career counsellors are thus able, for example, to calculate the expenses for their customer on-line. Individual placement officers have great discretion over the allocation of most funds. Only for special cases or programmes do superiors have to be consulted. This far-reaching decentralization has also become possible because the monitoring system gives placement officers and superiors alike the possibility of quickly checking the most important variables. The check on conformity of the budgetary or participant goals set is supplemented monthly by figures on results, which also comprise labour market figures. Results are not yet displayed on-line, but they will be on-line in the AIS ('Arbetsmarknadsverketsinformationssystem'), which is to be installed by 1996. Continuous budget checks, monthly result follow-ups, annual customer surveys (on firms and individuals) and biennial staff surveys constitute the evaluation of the regional labour market administration. The regional office spends two days a year auditing each of its local branches, and the central office conducts a three-day check of each regional branch office every second year. Of course, the results of monitoring play an important role in the audits and leave more time for discussion about problem areas that can be detected through comparison of all local and regional offices.

Sweden, therefore, seems to be very close to having a comprehensive monitoring system. Other countries do have bits and pieces of monitoring activities in certain areas, such as the long-term unemployment programmes or the conversion training in France, and certain training activities in Germany. But overall, there is currently no comprehensive, systematic and continuous follow-up on physical and financial indicators of the different measures of employment policies. Obviously, this judgement depends on the definition that we apply to monitoring, but the experts interviewed in the Member countries generally share the view that monitoring is still mostly experimental.

Although there is a clear trend to install such monitoring systems in all the countries reviewed, it is difficult to measure the state of the art of the activities. In Germany, where the Federal Employment Service ('Bundesanstalt für Arbeit', BA) and its research branch, IAB ('Institut für Arbeitsmarkt- und Berufsforschung'), have the right and duty to evaluate the effectiveness of programmes, there is currently an attempt to develop a broad instrument that can be used for monitoring a variety of programmes. As expressed by one of our experts from within the administration, however, 'this system is still in a very early phase of development'. Other projects such as 'performance-oriented management', which aims at introducing management-by-objectives into labour market programmes, have also been started. These activities have to be seen in the context of the 'employment office 2000' in which efficient, result-oriented employment offices are to be set up throughout Germany by the year 2000.

Another technology facilitating at least partial monitoring is an electronic data system originally created to support the implementation of job creation in eastern Germany. It has now been refined and turned into a common software product for the whole of Germany. For example, the average costs per head for persons placed in job creation measures can be delivered through this system to all local employment offices, thereby permitting comparison of these figures. As far as result-oriented monitoring is concerned, there is a quarterly report on the employment status that former participants in labour market training measures have six months after their training. Some sort of monitoring exists for almost all measures, but not a comprehensive system enabling local agents to monitor spending and participation of all programmes regularly.

The same holds true in France, where several administrative units are in charge of monitoring. Recently, the necessity of monitoring LMP more closely has led to increasing collaboration between these units (see below). Although no general monitoring has been set up yet, different programmes (like the one for the integration of the long-term unemployed) are more closely tracked than others. In Austria and Portugal, too, partial monitoring of LMP exists. In both countries formal responsibility for monitoring lies with the Ministry of Labour, but the recently reorganized employment service (AMS) in Austria and the Institute for Employment and Vocational Training in Portugal sometimes have a very important role to play because they are directly responsible for implementing most programmes and providing data for monitoring.

The general impression gained from our first expert interviews is that all EU Member States are currently engaged in setting up monitoring activities. They are trying to follow the implementation of LMP more closely than used to be the case, but one cannot clearly place the different countries on a scale ranging from 'no system to fully implemented system'. The one exception is Sweden, which we would place at the top of the list. The analysis of trends in monitoring does not yet allow us to compare countries. However, countries do experience problems in setting up monitoring systems. Although there are problems common to all, some countries are also confronted by complications relating to their particular administrative structure and other specific factors. We therefore discuss particular findings from countries in terms of:

1. problems of coordination between different agencies in charge of monitoring,
2. the lack of clear goals in employment policy measures,
3. the lack of data with which to construct monitoring indicators,
4. the lack of resources in personnel and funds for effective monitoring,
5. problems of feedback between monitoring and policy implementation or design and
6. problems of acceptance and incentives.

4.1   Problems of Coordination and Cooperation between Agencies

A country's specific institutional network of employment policy delivery and the responsibilities for follow-ups has a bearing on problems that arise with the coordination and cooperation between different agencies. Problems are stronger where responsibilities are divided (e.g. between the Ministry of Labour and the employment service). For example, France can be seen as a case with many actors involved. The ministry is in principle responsible for following-up on LMP and has a special unit for that purpose: DARES (see above). However, monitoring also involves DAGEMO ('Direction de l'Administration générale et de la Modernisation', Directorate for Administration and Modernization), and the Employment Delegation ('Délégation à l'emploi', DE) has also its say. In addition, the employment service ANPE ('Agence nationale pour l'emploi') carries out follow-up activities, the 'progress contract', with the state having enhanced the monitoring obligation of the ANPE. On another level other public or parapublic agencies or institutions such as AFPA ('Association pour la formation professionnelle des adultes') (adult training centres) and UNEDIC/ ASSEDIC ('Union nationale d'emploi dans l'industrie et le commerce'/'Association pour l'emploi dans l'industrie et le commerce') (unemployment insurance) are also involved in following up on measures. As for labour market statistics in general, there is 'no single ... system on the subject' (Chastand, 1994, p. 27). Overall, the picture is thus one of considerable fragmentation and ensuing problems with communication and cooperation between these actors.

However, one should not overstate such problems, for there is an increasing trend towards much more cooperation between these actors. It has much to do with the renewed efforts to monitor employment policies, implying that actors with access to different data sources cooperate. For example, DARES uses data provided by ANPE. More importantly, the integrated general management system for employment policy (GPI), when in place, will involve DAGEMO, DARES and DE and, partly because financial data play an increasing role in monitoring, will be managed under the responsibility of DAGEMO. This new system will contain financial and physical data provided on-line in a common format through the departmental services of France's Ministry of Labour and should, therefore, greatly facilitate monitoring. In summary, many actors are involved in the follow-up on labour market policies in France, but the pressures to arrive at an effective monitoring system have led to more cooperation between those actors than there used to be. Of course a potential for communicational problems among them remains. And, with continuing decentralization, responsibility for some of the programmes (e.g. vocational training) will be shifted to other levels (e.g. to the regions). In the absence of a comprehensive system, such change will reduce central monitoring capacities.

In Portugal, the responsibility for the monitoring of LMP activities lies in principle with the central General Directorate (GD) of the Ministry of Labour, which was created in 1991. Monitoring cannot be done without the collaboration of the main implementation body, the Institute for Employment and Vocational Training (IEFP) and its regional and local offices. In principle the IEFP provides the General Directorate with data, but the experts we interviewed indicated that collaboration is not always easy. Communication problems (e.g. relating to data) also arise between the GD and the regional implementation bodies. One of the problems is the lack of financial data at the GD level.

Basically speaking, Germany does not face coordination problems, for responsibilities are more clearly divided and the BA has the duty to follow up measures. For that purpose the BA has its own research institute for employment research, the IAB. However, the central operating unit (*Zentrale Fachabteilung*) and the other operating units (*Fachabteilungen*) for specific programmes (job creation or training) monitor policies. In the present phase of setting up monitoring systems in Germany, there is an effort within the BA/IAB to collaborate. Several working parties (e.g. interdepartmental working groups on follow-up and evaluation—'Wirkungsforschung'—both in the BA and within the IAB) have been established.

So far, the monitoring that the Swedish Labour Administration (AMS) conducts on LMP activities, our example of 'best practice', faces few problems of coordination or cooperation. As in Germany, it is the task of the AMS to follow up on LMP measures. A rather high degree of decentralization has been achieved, but the tradition of establishing goals through dialogue between local and regional labour offices and between regional and central labour offices reduces possible interest divergence. The Ministry of Labour has had relatively minor influence in the day-to-day work of the AMS thus far. The relation between the two institutions seems to be changing, however, because the sharp deterioration in the employment situation is bringing the ministry back in as the central agent for LMP. This shift may have adverse effects on programme implementation (see the conclusion).

4.2   No Clear Programme Goals

It seems obvious that indicators measuring the attainment of goals are hard to establish if those goals are unclear. It is all the more difficult to establish such indicators when there is a multitude of sometimes conflicting goals that have to be reached simultaneously by one programme. The same is true for the interests of different actors. An example of conflicting goals in programmes is the target-group orientation of programmes promoting the self-employment of previously unemployed workers. Hard-to-place persons, in particular, often lack the high motivation and skills needed to set up their own business. A low take-up rate or high failure rate could be the consequence of a programme in which this fact is ignored.

As for the interests of actors, the short-term effect of reducing unemployment by any measure of active LMP is in general important for politicians, especially if elections are pending. The importance of the medium- and long-term integration effects and the skill enhancement potential that the labour market administration seeks in a measure is then often secondary. At the political level the criterion for a programme's success is in this case its short-term employment effect. Longer-term effects of enhancing the labour market structure might be neglected. But it has been demonstrated that short-term effects and long-term effects often counteract each other. Performance assessment of the JTPA, for instance, shows that

> performance standards and incentives that promote immediate employment entry do not necessarily result in the long-term labour market success of JTPA's participants. The department's response has been to deemphasize cost measures as an incentive and to focus on improving post-program performance measures of long-term employability, job retention and earnings for adults, and skill enhancement for youth (DOL, 1994, p. 2).

Another example is the volume target for Swedish employment policy measures in 1995, which was more or less arbitrarily increased a good deal by the Swedish Ministry of Labour in response to pressure from high unemployment rates, public opinion and opposition parties. This change can be seen as being directed against the former bottom-up dialogue procedure for establishing the goals of the AMS with the county employment service and has led to conflicts between the AMS (and the county labour administration) and the Ministry of Labour. The volume target that has been set also restricts the discretion of the county and local employment service, which are decentralized. While they are free in principle to use the funds allocated for different measures, the high volume target leads them to fund mostly inexpensive measures such as those for work life experience ('Arbetslivsutveckling', ALU) instead of more expensive ones such as those for training.

4.3   The Lack of Data

Lack of adequate data hinders the setting up of monitoring systems. This problem has different dimensions: the lack of physical or financial data itself, unequal data access by different actors (and poor communication between them), barriers owing to regulations for ensuring the protection of personal data, the important problems of data comparability[8] as well as accuracy of data and the problems of data collection (e.g. manually collected on administrative

---

8 For example, the Irish monitoring system for LMP measures cofinanced by the ESF had difficulties because the data provided by the different agencies involved were not comparable. The number of participants in training was said by one agency to be those assisted in the year to date in respect of whom claims have been made by companies, by another as participants as full-time equivalents, by yet another as the estimated number of participants (DEE, 1994, p. 29). Similar experiences with the noncomparability of monitoring data from the five regional employment offices in Portugal have been reported in our interviews.

forms rather than transposed into digital format). The latter obstacles still exist even in certains programmes in Germany.

In Portugal, there are relatively fine-tuned data on physical indicators, but financial indicators are not always available. One reason is that the agency having central responsibility for following up on employment policies (the General Directorate for Employment and Vocational Training) is distant from financial control management. Another problem lies in the time it takes to generate data. Even if there is an indicator conceptualized by programme managers, the time before figures are available tends to be lengthy. A different problem with a similar effect is that of abundant data that people do not know about and useful data that lie idle where they have been collected.

4.4   Scarce Resources

Tight budgets and lean administration reduce the possibilities of allocating financial and personnel resources to monitoring even as the administrative and political pressures to monitor increase. Moreover, high and rising unemployment means that local agents have to increase the time they allocate to their clients and decrease the time they spent on monitoring. The problems are more severe in some countries than in others. In Portugal, for instance, recruitment was halted in the early 1980s, so the problems of an aging work force now coincide with a closed labour market in the labour administration.

According to OECD data provided by Höcker (1994), however, the intensity of service rendered by one public employment service agent dealing with active LMP is (at least statistically) greater in Portugal, than in either Germany or France. In Germany such an agent serves an average of 60 unemployed people; in France, as many as 130; whereas in Portugal one public employment service agent has to deal only with about 50 unemployed persons. On the other hand, it is hard to collect figures on the number of people having to do with monitoring in the public employment services and ministries of labour, so such a figure can only be used as a crude proxy to measure personnel resources. As for other resources (e.g. financial), the only comparable figures existing are the expenses (in percentages of GDP) for administration and placement. According to one indicator based only on the personnel involved in programme implementation (see Schmid, 1994, p. 49), labour market authorities in Germany spend 0.16 per cent of GDP on mere programme implementation; in France, 0.9 per cent; and in Portugal, 0.11 per cent. We repeat, though, that these figures only vaguely hint at the relative strength of the services that may be engaged in monitoring the activities of LMP programmes.

4.5   Feedback Problems

Because empirical evidence of monitoring of LMP itself is scarce, evidence of feedback on monitoring is also rare. The problems with feedback between monitoring and programmes is multifaceted. Basically, more or less technical decisions on relatively minor changes in the allocation of money must be distinguished from major changes, in which political decisions are usually involved and in which feedback is mediated through a sometimes lengthy decision-making process with uncertain results. 'Technical' feedback also depends greatly on the discretionary latitude enjoyed by regional and local programme agents, freedom that has tended to increase everywhere. In principle this discretion in matters of allocating funds to programmes is 100 per cent in Sweden, but there are limits, such as those defined by the previous year's spending structure, by the goals set once the planning has been completed (see above) and, presently, by the volume target that is determined centrally. In France and Germany this discretion is still rather closely circumscribed. For certain French programmes, such as that consisting of three measures for the long-term unemployed,[9] local agents are authorized to decide on the allocation of funds in any of the three up to a limit of 30 per cent of total funds. Since 1993, local employment offices in Germany have been allowed to exercise discretion over 20 per cent of the money allocated to either job creation or training. In Germany this shift to more decentral responsibility for fund administration and programme choice is an outcome of the financial crisis in 1993, when funds for job creation programmes were depleted early in the year.

That is, local corrections in fund allocation are possible within certain limits. However, with the possible exception of Sweden, where standardized monitoring now permits continuous observation of basic financial and physical indicators, even these corrections at the local level have not been the outcome of systematic programme monitoring but rather of local experience, expertise and local decision-making involving local social partners. In more centralized environments, such as in Portugal, local implementation units do not enjoy this degree of discretion.[10]

---

9 Those measures are a lump-sum wage subsidy ('Contrat de retour à l'emploi', CRE), a short-term adaptation training course ('Stage d'adaptation à l'emploi', SAE) and work-training arrangements ('Stage d'insertion et de formation à l'emploi', SIFE).

10 An interesting example of feedback due to the availability of comparative data (although not directly in the area of labour market policy) has been reported from France. The monthly review of job search activities for 22 regions has shown that there was a large regional variation in the ratio of those excluded from benefits per control interview. Over time this variation has greatly diminished. This harmonization was said to be due to monitoring, as regional officials were able to compare the results with other offices.

In summary, only a routinized monitoring system that is part of the administrative process of programme implementation within a decentralized organization can quickly react to 'irregularities' in indicators (such as a deviation from planned goals), reallocate money or take other corrective action. An example is the nationwide system now being installed in Sweden, where some regional employment offices have a longer tradition of monitoring.

For the moment there is no systematic evidence of feedback between monitoring and the policy formation process. Monitoring and feedback seem to belong to different spheres (e.g. administrative and political), where it is often the case that different interests imply different goals (see above). The abolition or amendment of measures or the introduction of new measures have, therefore, rarely been a result of monitoring (or evaluation) but rather a consequence of political intervention.

4.6   Problems of Acceptance and Incentives

Agency theory (the neoclassical theory of the firm) suggests that supervisors are imperfectly informed about the work effort of employees and that monitoring (in addition to incentives or sanctions for observed good or bad performance) is the instrument that helps resolve this problem (Fama and Jensen, 1983). However, recent research pertaining to the 'social exchange contract'—where trust exists on the grounds of lasting exchanges, with principals giving trust, loyalty and recognition (and, one should add, employment security and pay) and workers giving effort in return—suggests that monitoring can even signal a breach of trust (Barkema, 1995). In that case workers could respond by breaking their part of the social exchange contract and even lower their effort levels. In that context monitoring will be ineffective, even detrimental, as far as performance is concerned.

Although the theory applies basically to private firms, the public employment service has adopted management methods of the private sector (such as management-by-objective and decentralization of decision-making), and such 'principal–agent' problems do exist when monitoring is introduced. In our interviews it was reported that the principals must make an effort to convince the agents that monitoring predominantly serves to improve the organization's performance and that it was not designed to control their personal work effort.

There is not much evidence on the effectiveness of incentives to stimulate programme performance. One way to stimulate effectiveness is to top up the salaries of the directors of local employment agencies that are efficiently managed. Linked to this approach are the possibilities for allocating money to alternative measures more freely than has been the case thus far. Combining these two incentives could improve the effectiveness of programme delivery, but the danger is that short-term performance might be preferred to long-term effectiveness. In the US's JTPA, good performers (efficient delivery areas) receive 'bonus' resources that can be used for innovative projects or for increased services to the neediest participants (DOL, 1994). This allocation of reserve money to good performers, combined with broadened delivery freedom at the local level, can also increase effectiveness without necessarily neglecting the target populations that are comparatively resource intensive. However, Courty and Marschke (1995) showed that individual JTPA programme managers can 'game' the performance award system and tend to maximize their incentive awards instead of serving their customers in the best possible way. Although these authors seem to attach too much importance to the incentive award as a basis for management's activities (it is on average only 3 per cent of a service delivery area's budget), they do point to an important general problem. If an incentive system that incorporates performance measures is not exactly aligned with the true goal of the organization, a moral hazard can arise. This problem has led also to the discontinuation of a cost–benefit indicator within JTPA because of creaming (preference for the 'easy' cases, i.e. those that are the least expensive to serve and, therefore, the most likely to increase the programme's measured outcome). The 1995 volume goals that were set by the Swedish Ministry of Labour will have a similar thrust, meaning that the most successful delivery areas (regional and local employment offices) will be those that can place the most people in the least expensive measures. (However, there are almost no overt incentives in the Swedish system, for no extra money is allocated to successful offices, and the salary bonus, if it exists at all, is very small.)

5   CONCLUSION

The present chapter has presented some of the problems in the current process of setting up LMP monitoring systems in the Member States of the EU, has outlined the reasons why the monitoring of LMP performance is becoming more important and has sketched the functions of a monitoring system. Far from having established monitoring systems, most Member States are still in the process of installing such systems for the observation of LMP indicators. Thus, the object of research still resembles a 'moving target' difficult to grasp empirically. However, some main trends have emerged. On the one hand, monitoring will be tied to the routine administrative process of programme implementation and will permit the combined observation of financial and physical indicators of LMP. On the other hand, monitoring will involve the continuous assessment of results. Ultimately, a combination of input (expenditure), output (participants) and outcome (performance) indicators will constitute such monitoring systems. The reasons for the present efforts to set up LMP monitoring systems are manifold but have much to do with decentralization of implementation in a period of financial constraints. The pressures to render the public sector more efficient than it has been have led to the introduction of management methods that used to be applied only in the private sector. Management-by-objectives or the idea of cost centres, ideas that have gone together with decentralization, have also introduced aspects of competition in the public sector. But the devolution of tasks hitherto executed centrally has made the measurement of results all the more necessary. During the era of centralization (which persists in certain countries, such as Portugal) working to rule was important and monitoring consisted mainly in controlling if rules were obeyed by programme implementation; in the period of decentralization, the important focus is more the monitoring of performance (which sometimes simply means the striving to achieve specified goals of spending and participation).

It is surprising that administrative monitoring was not introduced earlier, but it seems that the spending of public money did not used to be subject to such constraints. In two of the surveyed countries, it was precisely a lack of financial monitoring that led to problems with programme delivery. Consequently, one of the basic aims of monitoring systems is to allow a steady and controlled outflow of assigned budgets. Providing information on where public money goes and how the money can be allocated most efficiently for reaching predefined goals is, of course, a basic purpose of a monitoring system. The combined observation of money allocated/money spent and participation planned/actual participation by delivery area/sector and so forth is the core feature of any system for monitoring employment policies. These rather simple input/output data can be supplemented with results indicators to produce a comprehensive system of LMP observation that would allow agents on all levels to follow up employment measures.

The fact that aspects of financial constraint currently seem to be the main focus of attention creates some concern that the interest in efficient public spending will eventually mean that programmes will be evaluated primarily according to their immediate success (e.g. low per-capita spending) and that they will infringe on longer-term and qualitative goals. In the same vein, it seems that interest at the political level is no longer focussed on sophisticated and long-term evaluation research but rather on down-to-earth, timely and clear performance assessments.

At this stage of our research any recommendations must be preliminary, but some lessons can already be drawn. The Swedish experience (as evidenced by one county labour office that was admittedly rather advanced in its monitoring system) shows that monitoring of preset budgetary and participation goals does make it possible to improve the convergence of planning and actual outcomes. However, it seems that if goals are set 'democratically' from the bottom up and if local agencies have a say in their establishment, the chances of achieving them are enhanced. The new trend to set goals centrally at the ministerial level (with the help of parliament) and impose them on the labour market service makes goal fulfilment much harder and works against real decentralization. Although monitoring is in fact only a 'neutral' instrument, it seems, therefore, that the involvement of those who monitor in the setting of goals is important for the efficiency of the instrument. In the light of the experience with the JTPA in the United States, it seems that programme performance is enhanced if there is a built-in function to monitor it. As formulated by DOL (1994):

> Perhaps the most important lesson from our experience with using a performance driven management system is that local programs respond remarkably well to the required performance indicators. Once performance standards were implemented, employment rates and wage levels for individuals leaving the programme rose and continued to increase each year (p. 1).

Thus, building in performance indicators in programmes—as is the case in the French five-year employment law—is a step in the right direction.

Monitoring implies the availability of indicators pertaining to all regional and local delivery areas and, hence, implies comparisons between them. It could thus enhance effective programme delivery. There is, however, the problem of pressure to harmonize LMP programme performance in areas that differ in their points of departure (in terms of target-group shares or the situation of the local economy, for example). That is, local adjustment of performance indicators is essential (see also Barnow, 1995). Sensitive data, as, for example, per-capita cost, must be adjusted to take account of local variation.

In conclusion clear-cut goals, clear financial and physical indicators of performance, concise statistics, appropriate time intervals of observation, feedback to guide the lowest level of the delivery organization, feedback to amend programmes in case of nonperformance, incentives for good performers and increased local freedom to manage delivery would all form part of an optimal 'package deal' and would pave the way to the efficient monitoring of LMP. Finally, a very important aspect of monitoring, which has evident control aspects, is acceptance: only a dialogue between the observers and the observed, especially when it comes to defining the goals to be set and monitored, is likely to bring about satisfactory results.

REFERENCES

Affholter, D. P. (1994), 'Outcome Monitoring', in J. S. Wholey, H. P. Hatry and K. E. Newcomer (eds), *Handbook of Practical Program Evaluation*, San Francisco: Jossey-Bass-Publishers, pp. 96–118.

Barkema, H. G. (1995), 'Do Top Managers Work Harder When They Are Monitored?', *KYKLOS*, 48, 19–42.

Barnow, B. S. (1995), 'Performance Management and Programme Impact in the Job Training Partnership Act: Exploring the Relationship between Them', Interim Report, Johns Hopkins University, Baltimore, MD.

Bellmann, L. and U. Walwei (1994), *Public Employment Services and Labour Market Information*, Labour Administration Branch Document 40–3, Geneva: International Labour Organization (ILO).

Chastand, A. (1994), 'Statistiques et Politiques de l'Emploi', *Courrier des Statistiques*, 70.

Courty, P. and G. R. Marschke (1995, June), 'Moral Hazard under Incentive Systems: The Case of a Federal Bureaucracy', paper prepared for the 7th Karl Eller Center, 'Business/Academic Dialogue, Reinventing Government and the Problem of Bureaucracy: Implication for Regulation and Reform', University of Chicago.

DEE (Department of Enterprise and Employment) (1994), *Evaluation Report: Recording and Reporting Systems*, Dublin: ESF Evaluation Unit.

DOL (US Department of Labor) (1994), 'Performance Standards: Lessons Learned', Washington, DC. (Unpublished manuscript)

European Commission (ed.) (1994), *Growth, Competitiveness and Employment*, White Paper, Brussels and Luxembourg.

Fama, E. F. and M. C. Jensen (1983), 'Separation of Ownership and Control', *Journal of Law and Economics*, 26, 301–51.

Gautié J., B. Gazier and R. Silvera (1994), *Les Subventions à l'Emploi: Analyses et Expériences Européennes*, Paris: La Documentation Française.

Hasan, A. (1991), 'Evaluation of Employment Training and Social Programmes: An Overview of Issues', in OECD (ed.), *Evaluating Labour Market and Social Programmes: The State of a Complex Art*, Paris: OECD, pp. 21–42.

Höcker, H. (1994), 'The Organisation of Labour Market Policy Delivery in the European Union', *inforMISEP Policies*, 48, 26–35.

Kuhlmann, S. and D. Holland (1995), *Evaluation von Technologiepolitik in Deutschland*, Heidelberg: Physica.

Melchior, A. (1992), 'Performance Standards and Performance Management', in US Department of Labor (ed.), *Dilemmas in Youth Employment Programming. Findings from the Youth Research and Technical Assistance Project*, Vol. 2, Research and Evaluation Report Series 92c, Washington, DC: Department of Labor, pp. 77–142.

Meyer-Krahmer, F. (1990), 'Evaluation der Wirksamkeit von Instrumenten der Forschungs- und Technologiepolitik', in H. Krupp (ed.), *Technikpolitik angesichts der Umweltkatastrophe*, Heidelberg: Physica, pp. 210–14.

MISEP (Mutual Information System on Employment Policies) (1989), *Rapport Final du Groupe de Travail sur les Evaluations des Mesures de Politique d'Emploi*, European Centre for Work and Society, Maastricht, Netherlands: European Centre.

OECD (1994), *Employment Outlook*, Paris: OECD.

Schmid, G. (1980), *Strukturierte Arbeitslosigkeit und Arbeitsmarktpolitik*, Königstein: Athenäum.

Schmid, G. (1994), *Reorganisation der Arbeitsmarktpolitik. Märkte, politische Steuerung und Netzwerke der Weiterbildung für Arbeitslose in der Europäischen Union*, WZB discussion paper FS I 94–213, Wissenschaftszentrum Berlin für Sozialforschung.

List of Acronyms and Technical Terms

ABM	*Arbeitsbeschaffungsmaßnahme* (job creation measure; in the Federal Republic of Germany, a scheme for temporary public employment)
ADA	American with Disability Act (disability discrimination legislation; United States)
AFDC	Aid to Families with Dependent Children (welfare programme for single-parent families in the United States)
AFPA	*Association pour la Formation Professionnelle des Adultes* (Association for Adult Vocational Training; adult training centres in France)
AIF	*Actions d'Insertion et de Formation* (Integration and Training Actions; comprehensive labour market scheme in France)
AIS	AMS Information Service (an overall computerized information system for monitoring the performance of labour market policy programmes in Sweden)
ALMP	active labour market policy
AMS	(a) *Arbetsmarknadsstyrelsen* (the Swedish Labour Administration); (b) *Arbeitsmarktservice* (the recently reorganized employment service in Austria)
ANPE	*Agence National pour l'Emploi* (National Employment Agency, the French employment service)
ASSEDIC	*Association Pour L'Emploi dans l'Industrie et le Commerce* (unemployment insurance funds in France)
BA	*Bundesanstalt für Arbeit* (Federal Employment Service in the Federal Republic of Germany)
CBA	Cost–benefit Analysis
CES	*Contrats Emploi Solidarité* (Employment Solidarity Contract in France)
CETA	Comprehensive Employment and Training Act (United States)
CIG	*Cassa Integrazione Guadagni* (Wage Compensation Fund; Italy)
CIG-O	*Cassa Integrazione Guadagni Ordinari* (Wage Compensation Fund Ordinary Intervention; Italy)
CIG-S	*Cassa Integrazione Guadagni Straordinari* (Wage Compensation Fund Extraordinary Intervention; Italy)
CLMS	Continuous Longitudinal Manpower Survey (United States)
COMETT	Community Action Programme for Education and Training for Technology (EU programme for industry—university cooperation in training)
CPS	Current Population Survey (United States)
CRE	*Contrat de Retour à l'Emploi* (Back-to-work contract; a lump-sum wage subsidy for the long-term unemployed in France)
CWEP	Community Work Experience Programme (temporary employment measure in the United States)
DAGEMO	*Direction de l'Administration Générale et de la Modernisation* (Directorate for Administration and Modernization; France)

DARES	*Direction de l'Animation de la Recherche, des Etudes et des Statistiques* (Directorate for Research, Studies and Statistics, the French Labour Ministry's body responsible for monitoring labour market policy programmes)
DE	Delegation à l'Emploi (agency of the French Ministry of Labour)
DEE	Department of Enterprise and Employment in Ireland
DG	Directorate-General (Subdivisions of the European Commission)
EAGGF	European Agricultural Guidance and Guarantee Fund
EC	European Community
EEC	European Economic Community
EITC	Earned Income Tax Credit (in the United States, a refundable subsidy on top of earned income directed primarily towards low-income workers with children)
ELFS	European Labour Force Survey
ERDF	European Regional Development Fund
ESF	European Social Fund
ETUC	European Trade Union Confederation
EU	European Union
EURES	European Employment Services Network
EUROSTAT	Statistical Office of the European Union
GAIN	Greater Avenues for Independence (labour market programme in California)
GDP	Gross Domestic Product
GHS	General Household Survey (Great Britain)
GMI	Guaranteed Minimum Income
GNP	Gross National Product
GPI	*Gestion des Procédures d'Intervention* (a new, more integrated, computerized general management system being developed in France as a means of measuring performance of labour market policy programmes)
HERMES	Harmonized Econometric Research for Modelling Economic Systems (macroeconomic model for the EU)
IAB	*Institut für Arbeitsmarkt- und Berufsforschung der Bundesanstalt für Arbeit* (Institute for Employment Research, the research branch of the German Federal Employment Service)
ILO	International Labour Office
IRCA	Immigration Reform and Control Act (United States)
ISCO	International Standard Classification of Occupations
ISSA	International Social Security Association
JOBS	Job Opportunities and Basic Skills (labour market programmes for welfare recipients in the United States)
JTPA	Job Training Partnership Act (training scheme in the United States)
LDB	Longitudinal Data Base (panel data base in Denmark)
LISREL	Linear Structural Relationships (structural equation models with latent or unmeasured variables; the name also refers to a widely-used computer programme to estimate these models)
LMP	Labour Market Policy
LO	*Landsorganisationen* (Swedish Trade Union Confederation)

MDRC	Manpower Demonstration Research Corporation (United States)
MISEP	Mutual Information System on Employment Policies (employment observatory of the European Commission)
MISSOC	Mutual Information System on Social Protection in the European Community
NACE	Nomenclature of Economic Activities in the European Community
NAIRU	Nonaccelerating Inflation Rate of Unemployment, 'equilibrium' rate of unemployment
NLS	National Longitudinal Surveys of Labour Market Experience (United States)
NSW	National Supported Work (labour market programme in the United States)
OECD	Organization for Economic Co-Operation and Development
OSA	*Organiatie voor Strategisch Arbeidsmarkt Onderzoek* (Organization for Strategic Labour Market Research; Netherlands)
PES	Public Employment Service
PRES	Private Employment Services
PSID	Panel Study of Income Dynamics (United States)
QMV	Qualified Majority Voting (EU)
RMI	*Revenu Minimum d'Insertion* (guaranteed minimum income benefit in France)
SAE	*Stage d'adaptation à l'emploi* (a short-term adaptation training course for the long-term unemployed in France)
SER	Standard Employment Relationship
SIFE	*Stage d'insertion et de formation à l'emploi* (work-training arrangements for the long-term unemployed; France)
SMIC-jeunes	*Salaire Minimum de Croissance pour les Jeunes* (youth minimum wages in France)
SOEP	*Sozio-ökonomisches Panel* (Socio-Economic Panel; panel study in Germany)
TECs	Training and Enterprise Councils (quasi-public bodies responsible for the implementation of several ALMP measures in Britain)
TJTC	Targeted Job Tax Credit (United States)
TRILD	*Temps réduit indemnisé de longue durée* (long-term short-time compensation scheme in France
TUC	*Travaux d'Utilité Collective* (social utility work programme in France)
UB	Unemployment Benefit
UDY	*Uddanelsesydelse* (training allowance and programme for long-term unemployed)
UI	Unemployment insurance
UNEDIC	*Union Nationale d'Emploi Dans l'Industrie et le Commerce* (central body responsible in France for the unemployment insurance system)
UNICE	Union of Industrial and Employers' Confederation of Europe
UTB	*Uddannelsestilbud* (training programme for long-term unemployed)
VAT	value-added tax
WIRS	Workplace Industrial Relations Survey (United Kingdom)
YTS	Youth Training Scheme (Great Britain)

Index